ENGLISH DRAMA

1900–1930

THE BEGINNINGS OF THE MODERN PERIOD

ENGLISH DRAMA

1900–1930

THE BEGINNINGS OF THE MODERN PERIOD

BY

ALLARDYCE NICOLL

CAMBRIDGE
AT THE UNIVERSITY PRESS
1973

Published by the Syndics of the Cambridge University Press
Bentley House, 200 Euston Road, London NW1 2DB
American Branch: 32 East 57th Street, New York, N.Y.10022

Library of Congress Catalogue Card Number: 70–171679

ISBN: 0 521 08416 4

Printed in Great Britain
at the University Printing House, Cambridge
(Brooke Crutchley, University Printer)

CONTENTS

Chapter Four

POPULAR ENTERTAINMENT: MUSICALS, REVUES AND MELODRAMAS *page* 152

Chapter Five

THE MINORITY DRAMA 215

Chapter Six

THE "GENERAL" DRAMA 324

PREFACE

It would seem to be desirable, at the very start, to comment on the relationship between the present book and the previously-published six volumes of *A History of English Drama, 1660–1900*.

When, in 1946, the text and hand-list for the fifth volume of the *History* were finally completed, I certainly did not have the slightest intention of carrying on the survey into the twentieth century. The range of that 'history' had been firmly pre-determined: it began with the year when Charles II, happily restored to his throne, reopened the playhouse doors which had been barred-up by the Puritan authorities, and now it had come to its planned conclusion at the end of Queen Victoria's lengthy reign. This being so, it seemed eminently fitting, some time later, to complete the historical record by presenting, in a sixth volume, a comprehensive alphabetical index of plays produced and published during these two hundred and forty years.

Inadequate although the survey itself, the various hand-lists and the final index may have been, all had involved me in a great deal of laborious effort, so that the completion of the task was accompanied, not surprisingly, by a very real feeling of relief that the arduous task of gathering the relevant facts and figures had at last reached its appointed end.

As time passed by, however, I gradually found myself tormented by several thoughts which may here be briefly summarised. First of all, there came a fuller appreciation of what had, of course, previously been recognised – that the modern English theatre-world, although anticipated vaguely during the final years of the Victorian era, was essentially a creation of the twentieth century. To this was added the conviction that the thirty years from 1900 to 1930, besides establishing the foundation for all that was to follow later, had been possessed by a spirit characteristically its own. Still further, it became clear that this spirit derived its power from more than one source: certainly an age which witnessed the full growth of Shaw and Barrie and Galsworthy had greatness in the air, yet the sense of being in the presence of something new and fresh arose not merely from a contemplation of its more notable individual achievements: with almost equal force it arose from an appreciation of the way in which a vast congregation of almost innumerable play-producing societies, most of them inspired by novel aims, brought something entirely fresh into being. During the preceding years there had been several great playwrights, but never anything quite like this: even although few of the dramas sponsored by these enthusiastic associations have any considerable worth, the collective effort introduced to the stage a sense of endeavour and, more significantly, a confident hope such as barely can be discerned in earlier times.

Since the enthusiastic excitement out of which these associations were born had also quickened into existence a remarkable number of books – critical, historical, biographical and autobiographical – concerned with 'modern' theatrical affairs, it seemed at first as though this subject must have been thoroughly scrutinised, yet a general examination of these books effectively (and surprisingly) dissipated that over-confident assumption. Apparently the only attempt to survey the activities of the young enthusiasts is a not very lengthy but certainly very rare little volume, the appeal of which, since it is written in German, is strictly limited. Still more important is the fact that those who nowadays may wish to investigate in depth the over-all dramatic interests and achievements of this period have not been provided with any fairly comprehensive guidebook, however brief, or even with maps outlining the nature of the ground to be prospected.

The final outcome of all these reflections was the perhaps somewhat reluctant decision to start preparing a panoramic view of what was happening within the specific scope of the Edwardian and early Georgian era, and, in particular, to compile a concise statistical record of playwriting, play-production and play-publication which might, hopefully, prove of service to any interested travellers wishing to investigate this territory in greater detail.

The present book, then, both is and is not a continuation of the more extended 'history' concerned with the years 1660–1900. It is a separate volume: yet it could not have come into being if the theatrical activities of the preceding ages had not already been examined. Maybe a simple illustration of the combined kinship and contrast is to be found in two facts: first, that references back to the 'history' are so frequent as to demand use here of the abbreviation '*H. E. D.*', and, secondly, that the divergent nature of the material presented in this volume has demanded the provision of an entirely fresh series of abbreviations, deviating markedly from those which had conveniently served for the earlier hand-lists.

I welcome the opportunity given to me here to express sincerest thanks to those who in various ways have given me assistance during the course of my enquiries. The assemblage of material would have proved utterly impossible if the Lord Chamberlain and the Comptroller of his office at St James's Palace had not courteously permitted me to borrow, volume by volume, the massive Day-Books recording the titles and dates of the thousands of dramas submitted for licensing within the course of the first three decades of the century. I was thus enabled, at leisure, to prepare the basic entries for the hand-list; and, at a later stage, this task was very materially aided by the fact that the Cambridge University Press arranged, under the personal direction of R. J. L. Kingsford and Peter Burbidge, to have my original manuscript catalogue of authors and plays, theatres and dates, transformed into more manageable typescript. To many libraries and librarians I am indebted – to the British Museum, to the London Library, to Birmingham University Library (where Anthony Nicholls, its Deputy Librarian, has been unsparing of his time in answering my enquiries and in securing desired texts), to the library and librarian of the British Drama League, to the Pittsburgh University Library, to the Birmingham City Library, and, of course, to the Gabrielle Enthoven Collection and its curator, George Nash, at the Victoria and Albert Museum.

In the preparation of this book it was, obviously, most helpful to have on my own shelves as many printed plays of the period as I could possibly secure, and here I wish to express thanks to Antony Parish, former student and present friend, who, himself a keen collector of earlier dramatic literature, not only directed my attention to several booksellers possessed of relevant material but also purchased on my behalf many texts which he correctly thought might prove useful to me; to Noël Woolf, of Samuel French Ltd, who aided me in double manner – by kindly arranging to let me have on loan his firm's order-books (volumes accurately recording the precise dates when its numerous plays were printed) and by enabling me to acquire copies of a large number of titles which had become out-of-date; and to John and Barbara

Kavanagh, of Motley Books Ltd, who were responsible for directing my attention to the very interesting collection of typescript plays written by W. V. Garrod.

Both the Birmingham Repertory Theatre and the Liverpool Repertory Theatre kindly provided me with complete lists of their numerous productions, and Gerald Morice, from his store of knowledge, assisted me in solving some problems concerning out-of-the-way 'society' activities in London. James Arnott generously devoted time to giving me factual information relating to the work of the Scottish National Theatre Society; Arthur Fedel, expert in knowledge of the modern Irish theatre, drew my attention to several facts and sources of information which I easily might have missed; the Belfast City Librarian sent me information concerning some playwrights active in Northern Ireland during the early years of the century; and Mrs Elizabeth Lloyd Evans (Llwydferch) gave me an invaluable manuscript list of plays, both original compositions and translations, written in the Welsh language. To all I present my sincerest thanks.

July 1971 A.N.

CHAPTER I

THE ADVENT OF THE MODERN THEATRE: INTRODUCTION

IN 1952 St John Ervine categorically declared that "the revolutionary change in the character of the theatre, not only in Great Britain, but throughout the world", came into being "immediately after the death of Queen Victoria in 1901".[1]

At first glance, and even after second more careful scrutiny and consideration, this statement may seem to veer very far away from the mark. Interpreted strictly in accordance with its own specific terms, it appears to ignore the radical innovations, in content, in form and in sense of purpose, made by many notable nineteenth-century playwrights in divers European countries; and even if we limit the scope of the generalisation so as to make it apply solely to Queen Victoria's own dominions, it leaves out of account all those numerous dramatic developments which aroused such excitement in London during the century's final decade. It ignores the impact made by *The Second Mrs Tanqueray*, *The Notorious Mrs Ebbsmith* and *Trelawny of the "Wells"* between the years 1893 and 1896; it dismisses by implication the force exerted during the same years by *Lady Windermere's Fan*, *A Woman of No Importance* and, most significant of all, *The Importance of Being Earnest*; it disregards the power exhibited in *Michael and His Lost Angel*, *The Liars* and *Mrs Dane's Defence*.

Nevertheless, when we examine Ervine's declaration more closely still, we must be forced to agree, against our own first

[1] Foreword to Rex Pogson's *Miss Horniman and the Gaiety Theatre, Manchester* (1952), p. vi.

judgments, that he was absolutely right. Although there had indeed been a remarkable surging forwards during the last years of Victoria's reign, this movement, in which culmination and anticipation were combined, belonged almost entirely to the nineties. Wilde's meteoric stage career exploded into darkness in 1895, and, while Pinero and Jones continued to write for the theatre during the earlier years of the twentieth century, obviously their force after 1900 was slight compared with their impact in the past: what these two authors produced later was interesting and even at times admirable, but already it was coming to seem somewhat old-fashioned. After the turn of the century it is not of these men we think: our minds go rather to Bernard Shaw, to Sir James Barrie, to Somerset Maugham, to John Galsworthy, to Noël Coward. Certainly, since the middle nineties the first of this group of dramatists had been pleasantly and unpleasantly prophesying things to come in *Widowers' Houses*, *You Never Can Tell* and *Mrs Warren's Profession*, but it was not until after 1904 that the playhouse really discovered Shaw. Before 1900, it is true, Barrie had attracted the public with his *Walker, London*, *The Professor's Love Story* and *The Little Minister*, but the Barrie who captured the rapt attention both of the generality and of the élite did not come on stage until *The Admirable Crichton* was presented in 1902. As for Maugham, he who was to become, in the phrase of a contemporary, "the theatre's darling", his early dramatic efforts had remained in their own days completely unregarded, and his glittering star was not fully discerned until about 1908. Galsworthy's first drama, *The Silver Box*, did not appear until 1906, and, of course, the stage had to wait for many years before it was enlivened by Coward's jaunty footsteps.

Thus, even although there were several playwrights of consequence who straddled the centuries, and even although it is easy to see how older styles continued to persist amid new forms, in essence we are forced into full agreement with St John Ervine's belief that shortly after 1900 a fresh start was being made. And the more intimately we examine the general theatrical conditions amid which the dramatists brought their scenes into being, the more firmly we realise that here was a world possessed of an animating spirit the like of which the nineteenth century, even in its latest years, had never known.

If, however, this be accepted and we concur in regarding the year 1901 – or, for convenience, the year 1900 – as the beginning of a new period, it may reasonably be asked whether there is any valid justification for treating as an integral unit the following thirty years, when we must admit both that this course of time was split in two by a mightily powerful catastrophe, the First World War, and that we cannot cite any outstanding historical or theatrical event which might be taken as determining its appropriate close in 1930. How, it may be asked, can we possibly regard as an entity a period so shattered? What reason have we for pausing at the mere conclusion of thirty years? Surely, we may say, a more fitting procedure would be to accept the first fourteen years of the century as an independent epoch, and then to regard the twenty-odd years from about 1919 to 1939 as a second, separate, era possessed of its own special and characteristic features – until these, in turn, were rent asunder by the impact of another devastating conflict.

These queries and this argument demand careful consideration. It would be idle and utterly foolish to deny that for four years from 1914 to 1918 the London playhouses for the most part sank into becoming mere purveyors of the cheapest entertainment, that many of the stage activities which had given distinction to the Edwardian and Georgian days were either rudely terminated or seriously interrupted, that the dramatic movement which had been gathering force since 1900 was sharply arrested, and that the twenties introduced several fresh developments in dramatic subject-matter, in style, and in theatrical presentation. Yet, after all this has been freely admitted, a surprising fact remains – immediately after the Armistice and the re-establishment of peace-time conditions, the theatre as a whole proceeded to carry on from where it had left off, pursuing or stressing with greater emphasis the forms, concepts and aims which had found their origins during the century's earliest years. There is plentiful evidence to show how the repertory movement, temporarily thwarted, gained fresh momentum; there is equal evidence to demonstrate how largely the more interesting plays written after 1920 were, in substance, influenced by and dependent upon the plays which had appeared before 1914. The later dramas may sometimes appear different, yet close examination suggests that most of them were either bringing to completion the trends which had been established during the earlier years or else elaborating what had previously been tentatively essayed.

In saying this, however, it is necessary to introduce a qualification, and this qualification leads to a consideration of 1930 as a terminal date for the period. Again, at first sight the choice of this year may assuredly appear to lack any clear and valid justification. Certainly no single particular theatrical event at that time can be likened, let us say, to the high-astounding terms which startled and excited the audiences which had listened to Marlowe's *Tamburlaine* in 1589 or to John Osborne's angry flow of rhetoric in 1956. That must be freely conceded: yet this admission in no wise weakens the general impression that the passing of the twenties into the thirties marked a change in the theatre from one movement into another. This impression rests not upon one single outstanding event but on the concurrence of many things which, although individually and separately perhaps of no particular significance, unite in creating an image of a motivating force now nearing its conclusion and of a new spirit, consequent upon changing conditions, which is taking its place. In fact, contemplation of what was happening during the late twenties strangely tends to make us feel that we have been here before: just as the final years of the nineteenth century witnessed the culmination of what had been aimed at by Tom Robertson and others many years before, while at the same time it was tentatively hinting at something different, so we sense that these later years were reaching the termination of an old journey and suggesting the start of another. The evidence is varied, scattered and complex, but cumulatively it suggests that the theatrical change which occurred round about the year 1930 was, in fact, as great as any to be discovered in the stage's annals.

If we thus accept as an integral unit the first thirty years of the present century, one thing, one concept, one word must seize upon our attention. What, more than any other development of the period, may be taken as its distinguishing mark is the constant flow of books, accompanied by a spate of articles long and short, enthusiastically and anxiously devoted to scrutiny of the then current theatre and drama as well as to the ardent advocacy of novel experimental forms both in staging and in play-construction. It is true that during the earlier part of the nineteenth century various authors, most of them poets, had expressed dissatisfaction with the stage of their own time, but almost all of these had contented themselves with generalised denunciations of existing conditions and with vaguely sentimental contemplations of the past – usually a Shakespearian past. A foretaste of something different did not come until 1882, when William Archer published his *English Dramatists of To-Day* – a title difficult to parallel in any other earlier publication. This volume not only was concerned specifically with an attempt to determine which young English authors might show promise of making significant contributions to the drama but also indirectly anticipated its author's lifelong rejection of the Elizabethan tradition and gave expression to the critical approach which explained his devotion to the new Ibsenian model. At that time, however, and even onwards to the close of the century, this approach made its appeal only to a relatively small circle: Archer's enthusiasm was supported by several other writers, among whom Bernard Shaw was manifestly the most eminent, but the truly significant fact is that, during the final years of the Victorian age, the chief critical journal concerned with stage affairs, *The Theatre*, was edited and controlled by a man, Clement Scott, who, if Gallup polls had been invented in those days, would assuredly have been acclaimed the most popular and the most influential critic of his time and who was definitely an unflinching conservative, staunchly opposed to the Ibsen cult.

When we move into the present century we find everything changed. Between 1900 and 1930 the book titles which greet us are *Modern Dramatists*, *The Contemporary Drama of England*, *The New World of the Theatre*, *A Study of the Modern Drama*, *An Outline of Contemporary Drama*, *The Youngest Drama*, *The Modern Theatre in Revolt*, *Tendencies of Modern English Drama*, *The Twentieth-Century Theatre*, *Modern Dramatists* – and it does not matter that some of these were of American origin, some of English, since during these years the same mood was animating enthusiasts on both sides of the Atlantic and since almost always there was double, simultaneous publication of such volumes in London and in New York. "New", "Young", "Contemporary", "Modern" now became the familiar and up-to-date epithets, and of them all the last was the most characteristic – being used not only in critical studies but in many other ways as well. Plays a-plenty now were produced with titles exploiting "modern" adventuresses, crusaders, daughters, martyrs, miracles, slavery, ways and women. Eagerly the dramatists employed the same adjective in descriptions of their works: numerous plays were called "modern comedies", others were "modern fantasies", others still were "modern moralities". Such titles and descriptive labels – and they are to be found by the score – were clearly designed to advertise the fact that, besides dealing with contemporary scenes and characters, the plays to which they were attached were animated by a new spirit; and, consequently, this central and characteristic epithet demands particular and immediate examination. Needless to say, the word "modern" is itself an ancient one, long familiar alike in conversational parlance and in critical prose, but it is important to observe that before the beginning of the present century its application was generally temporal in significance: its common meaning was simply "that which belongs to the present time", without any implication of an evaluating judgment. As such it could be extended so as to suggest broadly a distinction between contemporary times and ages past, as in "modern writings" as opposed to "classical writings", or it could be narrowed down so as to refer to one particular moment – as when, for example, David Garrick's satirical comedy, *The Modern Fine Gentleman*, displayed a fop who dressed himself and behaved in the manner fashionable in one specific year, 1757. True, Jonathan Swift and others, when engaged in their battle of the books, could bring more into the significance of the term; but even when the critical argument was designed to plead for liberty to go beyond mere imitation of the Greeks and the Romans, there was comparatively little suggestion of an aggressive cultivation of the new in and for itself, or of an attempt to prove that the new, simply because it was new, must possess virtues superior to those in the old. As often as not, indeed, when an evaluatory concept was attached to the word, there was a tendency to make it more or less condemnatory, as in Shakespeare's use of "modern" to indicate the trite, the shallow and the commonplace – "to make modern and familiar things supernatural and causeless". It must be admitted that during the latter half of the nineteenth century the significance of the term was sometimes extended in the vocabulary of philosophy for the purpose of describing and estimating certain newly-formed ideas and trends: but, even so, such extended meanings hardly impinged upon the world of the theatre until after 1900, and it is with the theatre that we are here concerned.[1]

As we voyage into the Edwardian era we can easily see how the word not only suffers a great sea-change but also assumes a dominating importance such as it never had had in the past. Already in 1911 Ashley Dukes observed that, although frequently misused, the term "modern" had become "a convenient weapon for the younger generation, often hard pressed for an adjective broad enough to embrace

[1] Of course, Ruskin's strange (and quite inappropriate) title for his *Modern Painters* inevitably must come to mind, but even cursory consideration of its use for these volumes must show that there is nothing here which bears directly upon the twentieth-century's employment of the term.

all its vaguer aspirations, a bludgeon wherewith to belabour the out of date".[1] This statement, sounding so strangely familiar in a modern "mod" manner, is particularly significant because it firmly associates the early twentieth-century "modern" with the concept of youth. Frequently, on casting our minds back, we are inclined to think of this idea of youth as coming explosively, after the Armistice, in the twenties, but in order to appreciate the drama from 1900 onwards it is essential to note that the upsurge of the young, with their own aims and aspirations directly opposed to those of the middle-aged and the elderly, was a powerful force long before the coming of the war. Ample evidence of this comes from examination of the plays produced during the century's first decade and a half, and numerous comments might be quoted on the subject. Thus, for example, in 1930 Somerset Maugham, after having attended a few Chelsea parties and listened to "the conversation of the cultured young" at that time, enquired "if it ever occurs to them that in our day we were just as silly as they", and with this thought in mind he proceeded to cast a retrospective glance at himself as he was in 1904 – one of a group of "earnest" young would-be dramatists. "It was," he wrote,

> it was the middle class with its smug respectability and shameful secrets that offered us our best chance to be grim, ironical, sordid and tragic. We were not gay, life was too grave for that; we were not light, our admiration for Ibsen had taught us to leave that to the French. We went the whole hog.[2]

Maugham's comments remind us that the "younger generation" was in fact a movable object repeating itself, sometimes inspiringly but also at times rather boringly, during these thirty years and that from the beginning to the end it tended to be desperately serious – indeed, "solemn" might be a term more appropriate. Already in the first years of the century several commentators had stressed the prevalence of "all kinds of theories" which were being discussed in

[1] *Modern Dramatists* (1911), p. 13.
[2] Preface to *The Collected Plays* (1931, reprinted 1952), p. viii.

advanced theatrical circles with a fervour wellnigh devotional, and many years later, in 1922, when the first "International Theatre Exhibition", supplemented by a series of lectures, was opened,[1] one commentator pithily expressed what was a fairly widespread view in declaring that "perhaps the strongest impression made by the whole course of lectures, and the exhibition itself, is that the people of the theatre have become exceptionally self-conscious".[2]

When in 1913 Gilbert Cannan was enthusiastically proclaiming the virtues of the adolescent rebels –

> All over the world it is being discovered that what was good enough for the fathers is not good enough for the children, and a generation is springing into manhood which demands the right to examine its heritage and to discard everything that it finds to be worthless, useless and injurious. This generation is discovering that it is possible to rebel against the sins of its forebears and it is rebelling with all its might[3]

– he was not merely reflecting the sentiments of the younger generation in 1913, he was also speaking for those whom Maugham called "the cultured young" in 1900, in 1922 and in 1930.

Ashley Dukes had said that this perpetual younger generation was "often hard pressed for an adjective broad enough to embrace all its vaguer aspirations", and this means that any attempt to provide a formal definition of the term "modern", apart from a general sense of rebellion, is doomed to failure. On the other hand, while this is true, at least some of the main qualities implied in its employment may be determined without too much difficulty.

First of all, the term, as used by the earnest young drama-

[1] This was a joint venture of the Victoria and Albert Museum and of the British Drama League. The six lectures were delivered by Gordon Craig, Bernard Shaw, Harley Granville-Barker, Basil Dean, E. F. Strange and John Drinkwater.

[2] *The Curtain*, i, no. 8, Aug. 1922, 92. This not very well-known monthly "Review of the Drama" was edited by Charles Hope from the Twenty-One Gallery.

[3] *The Joy of the Theatre* (1913), p. 2.

tists, certainly was designed to indicate the current serious self-consciousness which is patent in all the comments referred to above, from those of Maugham to those of Cannan. It was, in fact, a label deliberately selected by the various groups of enthusiasts who were breaking away from the acceptance of the theatre as a place of entertainment, whether that entertainment was provided by a *Charley's Aunt* or a *Hamlet*, who sought rather to establish a theatre of ideas, artistic or social, and who, as Dukes elsewhere noted, were already tending to create a collection of "schools", and "cults".[1] Secondly, the word always implied the concept of a search for novelty – novelty in artistic form, in subject-matter, in moral views. "Modern", therefore, not only meant revolt, the casting aside of hitherto accepted standards, the general rejection of customarily received conventions, it also enclosed within itself the thought of ideas and achievements of hitherto untried kinds. And thus, thirdly, the term went beyond time present: in deserting the past, it set its gaze, or at least tried to set its gaze, on the future: if "the drama of to-day" came to be a common subject of discussion, equally common, and usually associated with it, was that of "the drama of tomorrow". Indeed, in his discussion of the significance of the word "modernity", Ashley Dukes had emphasised that the word applied specifically to the interests of those writers who were "in touch with, or in advance of the thought of their own time";[2] and manifestly the various publishers who at that time were issuing collections of new plays under such general headings as *Plays of Today and Tomorrow* and *Dramas for the Theatre of Tomorrow* were seeking to satisfy an active preoccupation on the part of their

[1] Dukes, of course, was by no means alone in observing this trend: it was referred to by numerous commentators from the very beginning of the century, and by 1907 the annual survey of stage affairs in *The Stage Year Book* felt justified in selecting the prevalence of "all kinds of theories" as the dominant and characteristic feature of the immediately preceding years. Although this trend certainly was stimulated largely by movements in France, Germany and other European countries, often through the intermediary of American intellectual groups, it must be admitted that, in essence, it sprang directly from native sources.

[2] *Modern Dramatists* (1911), p. 9.

public.[1] This was something novel in the dramatic world. During previous ages there had occasionally been a few individual authors – a Ben Jonson, for instance, or a Tom Robertson – who consciously sought to be timely innovators, but almost without exception these men had been intent chiefly upon their own individual efforts: they were not members of any "School", nor did the thought of the theatre's future agitate their minds so actively as it did the minds of those young intellectuals who applied themselves to the playhouse during the early years of this century. Thus was created the pattern still enduring among us: those books and articles published forty, fifty or sixty years ago on what was then the theatre of tomorrow provided the view-point and ultimately the inspiration for, let us say, a recent special issue of *The Tulane Drama Review* devoted to the theme of "What's Next in the Theatre?" and for the choice of "After the Theatre of the Absurd, What?" as a major topic for discussion by the delegates attending the 1967 congress of the International Theatre Institute.

Such connotations of the term "modern", however, do not by any means exhaust its comprehensive significance, and, in particular, they do not suggest an attitude which prevailed widely, even universally, in these intellectual self-conscious circles. There was a general tendency on the part of the earnest young men not merely to condemn in a negative manner the theatre of entertainment because of its appeal to the unenlightened, but positively to find peculiar virtue in dramatic productions which proved displeasing to the common run of playgoers. Sometimes this tendency was kept in reasonable check, yet there were many enthusiasts who seemed to believe that the more limited the appeal the greater was a new drama's inherent worth. And, connected with this, there was the inevitable corollary – a self-satisfied faith in what the modern movement was currently achieving. "The great period" was the phrase selected by Frank Vernon in

[1] C. W. Daniel, in publishing a series of *Plays for a People's Theatre*, characteristically declares that these dramas "will merit the attention of those whose eyes are turned towards the future".

1924 to describe the progress of this "modern" drama from the start of the century,[1] and most of those who belonged to the advanced circles would have automatically accepted this description as nothing save an obvious truth. In a preface to Laurence Housman's *Little Plays of St Francis* (1922) Harley Granville-Barker categorically expressed his conviction that "there is an art of the theatre and there is a theatrical industry, and it is absurd to expect that the interests of the two can be continuously identical; it is difficult, rather, to see why nowadays they should ever coincide".[2]

This argument readily leads in two further directions, with the conclusion that little or nothing which the "theatrical industry" produces can be of real worth and that plays which make small appeal are likely to be excellent. In this connection, eminently symbolic and thought-provoking is a record, presented by Robert H. Ross,[3] concerned with three poet-friends who were actively interested in the "modern" drama in the early decades of the century. As a preface to this record it must be emphasised that these three poets were, as persons, unaggressive: all, indeed, might have been described as gentle – Gordon Bottomley, who, despite the bushy black beard of which he was so proud, was a man of mild disposition, John Drinkwater, generally balanced and calm, Lascelles Abercrombie, politely retiring and shy. In 1915 Bottomley's short play, *King Lear's Wife*, was produced by Drinkwater at the Birmingham Repertory where it attracted meagre and largely antagonistic audiences, and Abercrombie, present in the theatre, described the event: he did not hesitate to designate the piece as "the high-water-mark of modern drama"; he observed that the few spectators "loathed the play", with the implication that this fact proved its virtue. When the newspapers appeared with harshly critical reviews Drinkwater took pleasure in reporting that the author simply laughed at them "out of his great

[1] *The Twentieth-Century Theatre* (1924), p. 37.
[2] *Little Plays of St Francis* (1922), preface, p. vii.
[3] *The Georgian Revolt: Rise and Fall of a Poetic Ideal, 1910–22* (1967), pp. 150–3.

beard" and that all the three friends remained "a contented party in the middle of it all". Ross is fully justified in his general conclusion that for all of them "commercial failure ...was virtually prima facie evidence of artistic success".

Even so, the picture is not so simple, since several of those who belonged to the high-brow circles, although rarely would they admit their back-sliding, dreamed at times of the glories of popular triumphs. Edward Percy, for example, interestingly introduces into his *Trespasses* (1923) a character-portrait of a contemporary young playwright, and since the portrait is sympathetic and presented without irony it deserves attention. The young man, Miles, is shown engaged in composing a play which he himself describes as "good" and which, he declares, could not possibly be a success precisely because of its goodness. His fiancée, Patience, anxious to become his bride, expresses the desire that he would "try and write a really bad play", so that he and she "could have something to marry on". Rejecting this plea, he tells her that he could never bring himself to descend to the deplorable levels of public taste, and proceeds to let her know that he wants to watch his scenes "acted in the most exquisite theatre you ever saw, built for one – with no critics and no leading ladies and no commercial managers". Yet, when one of his pieces is unexpectedly accepted for production by a commercial management (described as "the Strohmeyer people") he is immediately rapt into seventh heaven.

Quite clearly, there is genuine interest in exploring this territory, in trying to assess what of value was created by the élite intellectuals of the modern movement, in seeking to estimate what the despised stages of the actor–managers and the commercial entrepreneurs had to offer, and in endeavouring to determine the relationship between these two. This interest is, of course, very considerably increased by the fact that an examination of the English theatre from about 1900 onwards must, for us, have an immediate concern different in kind from that with which we contemplate the corresponding activities within any previous era.

We scrutinise, let us say, the mighty surge of the Elizabethan drama and stand amazed at the power and imaginative vigour which render valid the present-day concept of "Shakespeare Our Contemporary", and yet, in the end, we recognise that our minds are set here upon the creations of an age irrecoverably past. Certainly Shakespeare, possessed of the ability to delve down towards depths of basic and enduring truths about mankind, can still speak to us intimately, can continue to live in our midst; but the playhouse world and the social milieu amid which he pursued his career is strange to us – a realm of farthingales, of doublet and hose, the outward semblance of which bears no likeness to our own dress and whose commonly accepted ideas constantly puzzle us and occasionally startle in their strangeness. Equally alien appear the Whitehall gallants who pirouetted around Charles II; alien, too, appear their successors, the brocaded, bewigged, coffee-house-haunting gentlemen of the Augustan period. In Victorian days, it is true, the surface of life began to assume patterns more familiar: the industrial revolution was blackening the countryside; men's civil attire was manifestly shaping itself towards our present style. Notwithstanding all of this, however, the nineteenth century, even in its latest years, is still divided from us by a barrier; its general atmosphere is redolent of the past; Victoria's reign, like that of the first Elizabeth, has now been covered with the patina of history; its furnishings and its knick-knacks have been transferred from the junk-shop's second-hand into the connoisseur's antique.

Just as soon as we step over the threshold of the new century, the general environment suddenly is invested with recognisably familiar features. No doubt in Edwardian and later Georgian days the women's dresses and the men's suits have their oddities, yet these costumes are obviously close to our own, and when we watch films of the twenties the flappers' miniskirts look just as ridiculous and just as unbecoming to most women as the miniskirts of today (or is it already yesterday?) will seem in twenty years' time. During the reign of Edward VII automobiles start to oust horse-drawn landaus from the streets; the ubiquitous taxi-cab takes the old growler's place; at home – and in the first scenes of innumerable plays – telephones become irritatingly useful; great liners contract the Atlantic wastes; above, in the skies, aeroplanes, at first startling, gradually become so common as to occasion only fleeting glances; just as the old century moves into the present the film is invented and soon blows itself up into a potent force; from the cat's-whisker wireless comes the establishment of the British Broadcasting Company, followed, in 1926, by that of the British Broadcasting Corporation. Clearly, the thirty years from 1900 to 1930 are organically connected with, and are attached by firm bonds to, the world in which we now live.

Nor do these bonds depend simply upon closeness in time. Of course this closeness gives strength to the living links connecting the two periods – so that, for example, thousands of people for whom the words "Diaghileff Ballet" are now nothing more than an unfamiliar title and an obscure myth find themselves brought into contact with the reality when Karsavina steps onto the television screen to describe the early glories of the Ballets Russes – so that those for whom *Mrs Dot* and perhaps even *The Circle* remained merely the names of old plays could, a year or two ago, actually see the author of these comedies and from his own lips listen to reminiscences of his youthful days – so that the idol of youth in the twenties, Noël Coward, could not merely be heard thus reminiscing but could be popularly accepted as a dramatist of the sixties. This is all beyond question, and there still remains something else of greater significance.

In many respects, the most advanced trends in the theatre of the present era are, strangely, closer in spirit to those inspiring the first decades of the century than they are to those of the thirties, the forties or the early fifties. This need occasion no surprise. Fashion – whether theatrical or of the tailored kind – frequently displays a tendency to somersault backwards over an immediately preceding generation and to seize hold upon modes and manners in vogue some three or four decades earlier. The remote past tends to appear, if colourful, alien to us; the very recent past almost always seems old-fashioned, unworthy of esteem, indeed something against which it is proper and necessary to revolt; whereas the past which lies at one remove from the present may well be regarded both with nostalgic affection and even with an awareness of qualities deserving of appreciative attention. Quite frequently a boy or a girl may find themselves closer to Granny than to Mum. If we listen to a group of musicians playing lutes, viols and recorders, our appreciation of their melodies, while it may be vivid, has about it an element of the historical-antiquarian: whatever loveliness the madrigals bring to us is far-distanced. The favourite songs of just a few years ago may fail to appeal, may even, surprisingly, sound dull to us. But, on the other hand, if, on the same television screen, we watch and hear programmes such as "The Singing Years" or "Old-Time Music Hall", the impact made upon us is of an entirely different kind – a mingling of two impressions, a sense of things bygone (and perhaps in their going accompanied by regret) and a sense of kinship.

Thus, in our own age, while the theatrical revolution is on the billboards and while the cultural barricades are being set up, we encounter numerous things which, in divers ways, recall to mind the playhouses of the century's first decades. Here are dramatic experiments anticipating our own; here are theories, cults and fashions, here are aspirations, which are akin to what we now have in our midst. No doubt even the most advanced of the young generation in, say, 1910, would have been shocked by many things now freely accepted and familiar; no doubt, looking back, today's revolutionary experimenter may often be tempted to dismiss contemptuously what the youth of 1910 considered gloriously advanced; yet, when all has been said, being "with it" now is akin to being "with it" then. For that reason alone a survey of early twentieth-century theatrical movements and achievements, their qualities, their successes, their failures and their fate, must have an interest and a value peculiarly its own.

CHAPTER II

THE THEATRICAL WORLD

A consideration of the drama within any period cannot be effective and valid unless the plays written during that time are related to the theatrical conditions amid which they assumed their being. This is a general truth, almost universally accepted; but it may be said with assurance that its force is nowhere greater than it is for the thirty years between 1900 and 1930. This was the period when "the theatre" ceased to be one single thing, when "the other theatre" arose to take a place – a place ever more and more significant – alongside the familiar "commercial" stage, and, although no doubt everyone is aware of this simple dichotomy, perhaps comparatively few appreciate to the full what diverse forms were associated with "the other theatre" during that age or what powerful impulses, both from within and from without, caused the theatrical realm as a whole to translate itself from an old world into a modern.

The story is complex, involving amateurs as well as professionals, sometimes seeming to be hopelessly confused and confusing, and often tending to draw the theatre's traditional centre away from London. It is a story which cannot be told, as it were, in a single straight line, and at the very start there may be hesitation as to whether it may not be more profitable to examine a series of novel developments before proceeding to estimate what changes were being wrought in the previously established pattern. This hesitation, however, must be laid aside, with the realisation that an appreciation of the story's significance can best be gained by beginning with a glance at London's West End playhouses as they were in the first years of the Edwardian era.

1. *London's West End and Beyond*

In or about the year 1901 a theatre-loving Italian journalist, stationed in the metropolis, proceeded to look around him and, with a free indulgence in the use of ejaculatory exclamations, expressed wonder at what he saw.[1] "London is overrun with theatres!" he cried:

> The theatrical craze has become a very madness. In London, where every thing passes unobserved; where the continuous rush is so level and monotonous; where the life of the streets, with all its phases and episodes, melts, as it were, and merges into one single, immense, confused, tiresome roar; in London, where, more than in any other city on earth, the crowd is so characterless and inscrutable, one of the few things which make a striking impression on the spectator is the daily spectacle afforded by the masses of playgoers on their way to and from the theatre.

He described the daily sight at the great central railway stations when, each evening, the trains arrived bearing "hundreds and thousands of fair ladies elegantly attired, accompanied by their well-groomed male escorts", all flocking to their seats in stalls or boxes, and he found "no less interesting and noteworthy" the sight of those "interminable" files of humbler "patrons of the pit and galleries", patiently waiting for the opening of the playhouse doors.[2]

Needless to say, the eager interest displayed by so many members of the public in play productions meant that those concerned with the conduct of stage affairs lived in happy

[1] Mario Borsa, *The English Theatre Today* (1908), pp. 1–4. This volume had been translated by Selwyn Brinton from the original Italian *Il Teatro inglese contemporaneo*, published at Milan in 1906. Note may be taken of the fact that Brinton admits to having made several alterations in the text: "the theatre world", he states, "moves so quickly that since" the time when Borsa wrote his Italian volume "we have found it advisable in this new edition to entirely revise the work, adding new facts, fresh points of interest, and bringing it thoroughly up to date". However, the general picture of theatre-going in the West End must belong to the time when Borsa was first forming his impressions of London's playhouses – and this would seem to have been between 1902 and 1906.

[2] In *Carriages at Eleven* (1947) W. Macqueen-Pope gives a general picture of Edwardian and early Georgian playgoing.

times. Of course they had their ups and downs, of course they suffered some dismal failures, but in general this theatrical realm was a happy and prosperous one; and from the very beginning of the century the prosperity was reflected in the active building of new playhouses and in the extensive remodelling of earlier structures.[1] The very first few years of the century, for example, saw the old Novelty Theatre reconstructed as the Great Queen Street Theatre; the Haymarket was remodelled, as was the Criterion; and to the already ample number of London's playhouses were added the Apollo (1901), the new Gaiety (1903), the theatre which itself bore the name of New (1903), the Aldwych (1905), the Scala (1905), the Waldorf (1905) – soon to be freshly titled as the Strand – and Hicks' (1906), likewise destined to be changed in name when, less than three years later, it became the Globe. Obviously, there is no need here to list all their many successors, but one general observation deserves to be made. There was, of course, an almost complete cessation of these building activities during the war years,[2] but it is important to note that the last years of the period, even although theatrical conditions were entirely different from and assuredly far less prosperous than those prevailing in Edwardian times, witnessed a revival, or continuation, of energetic playhouse construction until suddenly it was brought to an abrupt halt in 1931 with the openings of the Westminster, the Saville and the reconstructed Sadler's Wells. After that date there was apparently nothing for nearly thirty years: not until 1959, when the Mermaid was opened and the Queen's restored after its war damage, did London see anything of the kind such as marked the first thirty years of the century.

[1] Excellent accounts of individual London playhouses are given by Raymond Mander and Joe Mitchenson in *The Theatres of London* (revised second edition, 1963) and *The Lost Theatres of London* (1968). Diana Howard, in *London Theatres and Music Halls, 1850–1950* (1970), presents a rich array of factual information concerning these buildings and their managers.

[2] The only new theatre opened during that period was the St Martin's, and this was, as it were, an oddity, since it had been planned as early as 1912, and in 1914 its structure was already well advanced.

Nothing, perhaps, could more potently demonstrate what may be called the integrity of the period at present under review. True, the openings of the Westminster and the Saville carry us on past the year 1930, but obviously these houses had been planned some considerable time before – and, in any event, if St John Ervine's opening date of 1901 be accepted, then the three decades might be thought to have reached their end just as the year 1931 was inaugurating a fresh epoch.

Among these West End theatres, old and new, three – perhaps even four – distinct groups may be distinguished. During the earlier years the most important of these groups was made up of the playhouses ruled over by the actor–managers, inheritors of the Irving–Lyceum tradition.[1] Herbert Beerbohm Tree, who became Sir Herbert in 1909, thus modified Irving's mantle to suit his own less eccentric figure. Although not gifted with his companion's magnetic genius, his romantically histrionic style, his skill in interpreting unconventional and grotesque rôles and his opulently spectacular productions at His Majesty's patently associated him with the master of *The Bells*. At his beloved theatre audiences could expect to see gorgeously-mounted Shakespearian revivals, agreeably sentimental shows such as Michael Morton's *Colonel Newcombe* (1906) or L. N. Parker's *David Copperfield* (1914), and a discreet variety of other plays, including some of the Stephen Phillips' poetic variety.[2]

[1] Hesketh Pearson excellently surveys this subject in *The Last Actor-Managers* (1950), and there are comments on it in his *Modern Men and Mummers* (1921). A. E. Wilson has an impressionistic picture of *Edwardian Theatre* (1951), and the theme is, of course, dealt with in several of the volumes written by W. Macqueen-Pope. Recently Frances Donaldson has re-examined the work of *The Actor-Managers* (1970) in a well-informed and well-balanced account of their activities. While it is in no respect historical, Leonard Merrick's novel *The Actor Manager* (1898) deserves mention: in itself it can hardly be deemed to merit the inflated praise given to it by William Dean Howells, but it has considerable interest for its sympathetically-drawn picture of such a manager intent on furthering the good of the stage. In *Theatrical Cavalcade* (1942) Ernest Short presents an entertaining survey of theatre and drama from the days of the early actor–managers on to the outbreak of war in 1939.

[2] Max Beerbohm was responsible for editing an interesting collection of essays on his brother (1920): Hesketh Pearson presents a detailed

The shaping and moulding of the repertoire at His Majesty's so as to accord with the actor–manager's abilities and interests may be taken as typical: in similar wise other members of this group gave to their houses qualities and styles fitted for the exploitation of their own histrionic powers. Like Tree, for instance, George Alexander, knighted in 1911, had established himself firmly by the close of the nineteenth century, but the tone of his St James's was completely different from that of Beerbohm's His Majesty's, even when at times some of their offerings were of the same sort. Shakespearian dramas were presented here, too; and if Tree selected *Herod* for production in 1900 and *Ulysses* two years later, it was Alexander who was responsible for introducing *Paolo and Francesca* in 1902. This handsome and distinguished actor, however, always impeccably attired and the very pineapple of politeness, found his true ideal not so much in dramas of the poetic kind as in the "high-class" social plays associated with the Pinero tradition or else in works of a stylistically romantic cast. In these his refined elegance and poised technique were permitted free scope: from the days of Oscar Wilde's polished refulgence and the adventuresome grace of Edward Rose's *The Prisoner of Zenda* on to the simmering emotionalism of J. B. Fagan's *Bella Donna* (1911) he gave to his theatre its own special dignified deportment.[1]

Somewhat akin to Alexander was Charles Wyndham (knighted in 1902), who from 1899 to 1903 ruled the theatre designated by his own name and, later, from 1903 to his death in 1919, the New Theatre – for the building of which he was responsible. All of these actors basked in the sunshine of public esteem and each had his own particular following. It is said that at one of the performances of Pinero's *His*

record of his stage career in *Beerbohm Tree, His Life and Laughter* (1956): Tree himself was responsible for two autobiographical volumes – *Thoughts and Afterthoughts* (1913) and *Nothing Matters* (1917).

[1] For an appreciative study of this actor's work see A. E. W. Mason, *Sir George Alexander and the St James's Theatre* (1935). Naturally, his management of this house is fully recorded by Barry Duncan in *The St James's Theatre: Its Strange and Complete History* (1964).

House in Order, presented at the St James's in 1906, two ladies started to discuss the tense scene in which the hero persuades the heroine to hand over to him some private letters. "I should have done that," declared one of the pair, "Would *you*?" – to which her companion replied thoughtfully, "No, not to George Alexander. But I would to Charles Wyndham". And there were scores of others who would not have hesitated to give to the actors of their choice anything that might be asked. The flamboyant Lewis Waller, a player more peripatetic in his management, had his own wide following; Arthur Bourchier drew crowds to the Garrick; even greater crowds went to the Haymarket when Cyril Maude was in control of its fortunes and were led by his piping when he moved to the Playhouse;[1] after having been associated with various stages, the politely polished Gerald Du Maurier (knighted in 1922) – a man who could suggest as many nuances from his expert manipulation of a cigarette as any early Georgian beau could from that of a snuff-box, attracted his own large company of admirers to Wyndham's.[2]

The actor in management was, indeed, the very symbol of those early years of the century, whether he leased a theatre or built one for himself. Seymour Hicks, knighted in 1935 and described by some as the theatrical "Admirable Crichton", was responsible for the construction of the Aldwych in 1905 and gave his own name to the Hicks' in 1906.[3] During the course of his busy life, Charles Hawtrey (knighted in 1922) at various times was in management at no fewer than eighteen playhouses; Johnston Forbes-Robertson (knighted in 1913), most intellectual and reflective of all Hamlets, similarly moved his company from stage to stage,[4] as did the romantically-inclined John Martin-Harvey (knighted in 1921), almost the last of the actors wholly unashamed of their own theatricality, master both of polite

[1] See his *Haymarket Theatre, Some Records and Reminiscences* (1903) and *Behind the Scenes with Cyril Maude* (1927).

[2] See Daphne Du Maurier, *Gerald: A Portrait* (1934).

[3] See his *Twenty-five Years of an Actor's Life* (1910), *Between Ourselves* (1930), *Me and My Missus* (1939) and *Vintage Years* (1943).

[4] See his *A Player under Three Reigns* (1925).

melodrama and of poetic Maeterlinck,[1] the handsome, charming and skilled Fred Terry, and the strange Oscar Asche who, after winning distinction in a number of Shakespearian rôles, revelled in the oriental spectacularism of Edward Knoblock's *Kismet* (1911) and of his own far less distinguished *Chu Chin Chow* (1916).[2] Nor was this merely the age of actor–managers: from time to time actress–manageresses also ventured to control theatres of their own. Thus, in 1901 the beautiful Lily Langtry not only leased the Imperial but in effect rebuilt that house;[3] in 1907 Lena Ashwell leased the Great Queen Street Theatre (later the Kingsway) and guided its fortunes until 1916, while, later, in 1924, she took over the Bijou and renamed it the Century; so, too, in 1910 Gertrude Kingston settled down at the Little Theatre, boldly starting her first season with a production of *Lysistrata*. With these actor–managers and actress–manageresses may be associated a second important group of West End producers, the various impresarios in command of theatres where, with serious intent, they promoted their own styles of production. Of these the American-born Charles Frohman may be taken as a characteristic example – a manager who gave spirit, vigour and distinction to the Duke of York's and other playhouses which came under his kindly and alert régime.[4] Such individuals, actively and seriously concerned not merely with their own stages but with the theatre as a whole, clearly stood in close association with the actor–managers.

Two other groups remain, both of which will demand further examination later, and both of which may be introduced here by reference to what is without doubt the

[1] See George Edgar, *Martin Harvey* (1912); *The Autobiography of Sir John Martin-Harvey* (1933); M. Willson Disher, *The Last Romantic* (1948).

[2] See *Oscar Asche, by Himself* (1929). *Chu Chin Chow* created a record with its 2,238 performances.

[3] Despite royal patronage, however, her management was not successful. Similarly without success Ellen Terry took over the same theatre a few years later.

[4] See Isaac F. Marcosson and Daniel Frohman, *Charles Frohman, Manager and Man* (1916).

most famous playhouse in the whole of the metropolis, Drury Lane. During the greater part of the nineteenth century this Theatre Royal had struggled against adversity and was rescued from complete disaster only after Augustus Harris, who had taken over its management in 1879, succeeded in capturing public support by specialising in the presentation of extraordinarily exciting spectacular melodramas.[1] Fundamentally his successor Arthur Collins pursued the same course: from the frenzied chariot race of *Ben Hur* in 1902 and the pair of races in *The Whip* of 1909 – one showing horses galloping on the stage and another presenting a contest in speed between a motor-car and a train – on to about 1920 he kept the theatre prosperous by such means, and when, shortly before his retirement in 1924, he saw that the taste for melodramas was beginning to decline, he astutely moved from them to the world of such expansive musicals as *Decameron Nights* (1922) and *Angelo* (1923): these proved attractive to the public, and similar pieces were presented by his successor, Sir Alfred Butt, whose *Rose Marie* (1925) and *The Desert Song* (1927) drew great crowds into Old Drury and were destined to be long remembered.

The extraordinarily large capacity of this old Theatre Royal and its elaborate stage machinery placed it in a unique position, but the appeal made by its productions was by no means similarly unique: indeed, both its melodramas and its musicals may serve to remind us that shows of these two kinds probably gathered together greater numbers of spectators in theatres large and in theatres small than did any others during those years. Under the aegis of George Edwardes the Gaiety, Daly's, the Apollo and the Prince of Wales's became for many playgoers synonymous with "theatre",[2] and there were many other producers, skilled

[1] The story of this theatre's fortunes is well traced by W. Macqueen Pope in his *Theatre Royal Drury Lane* (1945). Detailed information concerning its origins and present structure are presented in the recently published thirty-fifth volume of the *Survey of London* (1970), prepared by F. H. W. Sheppard.

[2] For further notes on the theatres which specialised in musical plays see below pp. 154–61.

and unskilled, who followed his lead. We are, of course, not likely to forget the significance of the musical comedies of that period: they are well established in the stage's memory. But perhaps we may be apt to ignore the fact that Drury Lane's melodramas did not by any means stand alone in London's West End. From 1907 onwards for many years Irving's old playhouse, the Lyceum, conducted on the principle of "popular drama at popular prices", specialised in melodramatic productions, and the success of these productions is amply indicated by the private fortunes thus amassed by its managers, Walter Melville and his brother Frederick. So prosperous, indeed, were they at the Lyceum that they found it profitable to build the new Prince's Theatre in Shaftesbury Avenue, to assume its management as well as that of the Lyceum, and to make its repertoire consist almost entirely of melodramas.

The fare thus presented at Drury Lane, the Lyceum and the Prince's provides an effective introduction to another group of playhouses – the ring of district and surburban theatres which were spread out in a wide-ranging sweep embracing the metropolis. Here melodrama freely flourished, although it must be observed that gradually, during the twenties, this kind of entertainment began to lose its hold on the public and that several of the stages which had previously depended almost entirely on such dramas were transformed into half-way houses between the "provinces", where try-outs of new plays were to become ever more and more frequent, and the central core. As the years advanced a marked increase can be seen in the number of plays which, having had their premières in Birmingham, Manchester and elsewhere, moved up some weeks later to surburbia and thence were transferred to more august quarters and graced with more fashionable audiences.[1]

The surburban ring, of course, faded imperceptibly on its

[1] Among a number of volumes which give accounts of some of these suburban playhouses particular mention may be made here of Albert Douglass' *Memories of Mummers and the Old Standard Theatre* (1924) and of A. E. Wilson's *East End Entertainment* (1954).

circumference into the "provincial" – a motley array of structures large and small, reasonably luxurious and drearily uncomfortable.[1] Theatres Royal of all shapes and sizes abounded, for by this time the once-esteemed and rather exclusive regal epithet had lost most of its distinction by reason of indiscriminate multiplication. The rapidly-expanding larger cities, moreover, now capable of providing audiences which numerically might vie with those in London, could support more than one playhouse apiece: Birmingham thus had five houses extending from the large Theatre Royal down to a humble Coutt's; Liverpool's needs were met by no less than seven, four of them with titles reminiscent of metropolitan establishments (the Court, Prince of Wales's, Lyric and Adelphi) as well as two rejoicing in the appellations of the Shakespeare Theatre and the Grand Opera House. Of special interest among these provincial playhouses are those which were beginning to proliferate at seaside resorts. The nineteenth century had been responsible for discovering the joys of the ocean beach and its blousy bathing-suits were preparing the way for present-day bikinis; decade by decade the number of visitors to the seaside increased, and early in the twentieth century it was discovered that at many of these centres the erection of theatres could be a well-paying proposition. With the development of the holiday trade, added to the development of residential areas round the coasts, numerous villages grew into small towns, numerous small towns into what were almost cities. An expanding Brighton thus became the proud possessor of four theatres,

[1] No attempt has yet been made to prepare a comprehensive record, even in summary form, of the playhouses beyond London's limits. Information concerning some of them is to be found collected in articles and booklets prepared by local historians: Alfred Loewenberg's *The Theatre of the British Isles, excluding London* (Society for Theatre Research, 1950) is an invaluable guide to studies of this kind. The first volumes of *The Stage Year Book* (those for 1908, 1909 and 1910) included a very useful "Stage Provincial Guide", but this was discontinued in later issues. The material presented in these sections was issued separately in 1912 as *The Stage Guide* and a later edition of that volume, revised by A. W. Tolmie, appeared in 1946. In 1928 James M. Glover issued a *Theatre Managers' Handbook* which endeavoured to list all the then still existing metropolitan and provincial theatres and music-halls.

Blackpool of two; Bournemouth had its Theatre Royal, Eastbourne both a Theatre Royal and a Devonshire Park. At these, during sunny or should-be sunny weather, numerous plays, especially farces and musical comedies, made their first bows before the public.

With these seaside houses the roster of English stages and managements at the beginning of the century almost reached its uttermost limit, but not quite. Travelling companies, possessed of no regular homes, still carried on the ancient traditions of the strolling players, and, although many of them were of no account, some few were of considerable significance. Fundamentally, for example, the troupe led by Edward Compton consisted of itinerants who only occasionally came to London – but their service in keeping alive knowledge of the old "legitimate comedy" deserves the highest praise: without the aid of the company organised by Frank Benson, who was knighted in 1916, Stratford-upon-Avon could not so soon or so firmly have made itself Shakespeare's theatrical home:[1] Ben Greet (who was knighted as Sir Philip Ben Greet in 1929) not only was producer at the Old Vic from 1915 to 1918 but was also the leader of a company which carried the plays of Shakespeare far and wide: nor should it be forgotten that Bernard Shaw's reputation outside the metropolis depended largely upon the tireless activities of Charles Macdona's touring actors, and that thousands of villagers from north to south owed virtually all their dramatic experiences to the Arts League of Service Travelling Theatre.[2]

Of all kinds were these itinerant companies, including even some groups which, as it were, had strayed into the twentieth century from early Victorian times and even earlier: the last of these, the tent-theatre which belonged to the Holloway family, struggling on in an alien world, characteristically was

[1] Naturally, his company's activities are discussed in the numerous books devoted to the "Memorial" theatre at Stratford-upon-Avon. Benson himself has an autobiographical *My Memoirs* (1930) and Lady Benson has another set of reminiscences in *Mainly Players* (1926).

[2] A full account of their activities appears in Eleanor Elder's *Travelling Players* (1939): see below p. 87.

forced to bring its work to an end around the year 1930. Although neither this nor any other kindred troupe had anything to offer to the drama, the presence of these itinerant actors and their vanishing at the termination of the present period should not be completely ignored: they are worthy of at least a tiny corner to themselves in the total picture.[1]

Here, then, we come at last to the uttermost reaches of the theatrical realm proper. But everyone knows that alongside this realm there extended another vast imperial domain – that of the music-halls with their variety programmes.[2] As

[1] In "Barnstorming Days" (*Studies in English Theatre History* (Society for Theatre Research, 1952), pp. 114–23) Sir Barry Jackson presents some entertaining reminiscences of such performances. The only production which I was able to see (at Holloway's tent-theatre, then stationed at Bromsgrove) has left a vivid memory of four things: (1) the tent itself, with its rather handsome early-nineteenth-century ceiling, composed of large square painted panels; (2) the conventional use of the limited stock of scenery (so that, for example, the opening scene of a melodrama supposed to take place outside a Canadian ranch had a backdrop vaguely reminding one of the palace of Versailles); (3) the lively local audience evidently in close communion with the strutting performers; and (4) the obvious employment of histrionic conventions familiarly accepted both by players and public. The clearest demonstration of these conventions came in what was the heroine's "big" scene: here she appeared in a cave (represented by two rocky side-wings), immured therein by the villain: alone on stage she indulged in a lengthy soliloquy in which tearfully she bemoaned her fate. Before this speech came to its conclusion, however, a little girl rose from the front bench of the auditorium and advanced towards the footlights, stretching out a small bunch of humble flowers. The actress, evidently expecting some gesture of this kind, immediately stopped speaking, moved forwards to the edge of the stage, took the bouquet, pressed it to her rather ample bosom, bowed twice to the applauding audience, stepped back and to the side, held out the flowers to a hand which obligingly was thrust out from behind one of the wings – and then, returning to her rôle, delivered the final words of her lamenting monologue.

[2] The music-hall has a fairly well-stocked library of its own. Factual information concerning the hundreds of houses, large and small, within the metropolitan area is presented by Diana Howard in her *London Theatres and Music Halls 1850–1950* (1970). The early development of *The Variety Stage* (1895) is traced by C. D. Stuart and A. J. Park, and there are numerous volumes, both anecdotal and historical, which are concerned with its fortunes during the present century. Among these may be mentioned Harold Scott's well-documented *The Early Doors: Origins of the Music Hall* (1946), *British Music Hall* (1965) by Raymond Mander and Joe Mitchenson, *The Story of the Music Hall* (1935) by

the century opened, even a summary list of the more important of the halls included some half a hundred houses; Liverpool had eight music-halls to its seven theatres; even a then small town, such as Leicester, could find audiences sufficient to fill its Empire, Floral Hall and Tivoli. At that time many of these were independently owned and managed, yet already there were signs of a movement towards the establishment of great combines with wide-ranging properties and interests. The music-halls were, very definitely, a flourishing industry.

In at least one sense these hundreds of variety houses may be regarded as forming part of the theatre world in general: both they and the playhouses were maintained by "live" performances, and at a certain level they inclined to draw close together. Even as early as 1900 some of the theatre's curtain-raisers and duologues might hardly be distinguished from similar pieces which occasionally were being included in variety bills; and both were inclined to abandon their familiar differences when they put on almost identical shows in the form of musical comedy and pantomime. They were kin to each other, and yet distinct, and there can assuredly be no doubt concerning the basic family rivalry between them. They competed for audiences, and many theatre-men, although they usually were diplomatically cautious in any direct remarks they made about their fellow-performers, could not escape looking with considerable misgivings at this popular type of entertainment which, having developed so mightily during the latter half of the nineteenth century, still showed no indication of having attained its full stature, still seemed capable of moving from strength to strength. Even in the midst of the prosperous conditions which Mario Borsa had described with such astonished wonder there were at least some playhouse managers who looked towards the future with some unease.

Archibald Haddon, *Music-Hall Nights* (1925) by D. C. Calthrop, *Idols of the 'Halls'* (1928) by H. Chance Newton, and *Winkles and Champagne* (1938) by M. W. Disher. To a few of the more important houses special studies have been devoted (as, for example, Felix Barker's *The House that Stoll Built* (1957): references to particular historical records of such a kind are provided in Diana Howard's volume cited above.

2. *Commercialism, the Music-Hall Empire and Trade-Unionism*

Throughout the first few years of the new century the main outlines of the pattern thus set continued to endure, but gradually, with the passage of time, the lines and colours began to change, and the established picture started to assume fresh forms.

Within this picture the most significant alteration was the increasing commercialisation and industrialisation of the stage. The first and salient development was the rapid decline and eventual extinction of the hitherto dominant actor–managers. While they flourished, controversy had raged concerning their worth, and many vehement theatrical enthusiasts never ceased from inveighing against the system they represented. P. P. Howe, for example, in castigating the "falsities" which he claimed to discern in the plays written by H. A. Jones, decided that these could all be traced back to the evil influence of the stars for whom that author composed his works.[1] "It is the Trail of the Actor–Manager that we have come upon," he categorically asserted:

The dramatist blazed this trail with *The Silver King*, and he has never ceased to follow it. We understand now what Mr. Jones meant by a due regard for the requirements of the modern stage. The "requirements of the modern stage" are the Actor–Manager's requirements. The Actor–Manager's requirements are, stated shortly, that he shall be "a bright, shrewd man of the world, about fifty" with a third act in which to decide the destinies of several persons, a fourth act in which to lay siege successfully to a younger heart that has long held out against him...and a free permission throughout all four acts to tell the story of his life, whenever it may seem to him to be apposite.

Some ten years later, Frank Vernon was engaged repetitively and retrospectively in plucking the same harsh strings.[2] While grudgingly prepared to admit that the system had been

[1] *Dramatic Portraits* (1913), pp. 74–7.
[2] *The Twentieth-century Theatre* (1924), p. 23.

responsible for introducing to the public several dramas which in his opinion were worthy of esteem,[1] he felt compelled to condemn outright all who were associated with this vicious circle.

As a matter of fact, however, Vernon's aggressive attack was already somewhat out of date. By the time he was thus putting on the judicial black cap, the accused had become a corpse: the deaths of Alexander and Wyndham in 1918 almost exactly coincided with the vanishing of the whole group of which they had been such prominent members. And, ironically, even as these men were disappearing from the scene, other critics, no less modernistic in their approach, were beginning to list, not their vices, but their virtues. They recalled that the Academy of Dramatic Art had secured its premises in Gower Street through the generosity of Beerbohm Tree; they ceased to smile superciliously at Frank Benson's athletics and turned instead to chronicle favourably all he had done for Shakespeare; they gave due praise to the manner in which Martin-Harvey had striven to encourage the poetically-inspired drama; and at least one or two among them were observing that such wild generalisations as those put forward by Howe simply did not correspond with the facts. While there assuredly were plays which offered to an actor–manager parts of the kind he had described, most of these outstanding performers had been willing to appear in many different rôles, even in rôles which could hardly be called sympathetic – as when, for example, Arthur Bourchier in 1906 suitably interpreted Arthur Sutro's central character in *The Fascinating Mr Vanderveldt*, a smarmy and deceptive would-be lady-killer who is most properly and most effectively exposed and shamed by the heroine. Within a year or two this recognition of what the actor–managers had done for the theatre was developing into a half-contrite regret at their disappearance, and by 1950 Hesketh Pearson, dispassionately

[1] His examples of such plays may now appear to be a trifle erratic in choice: Henry James' *Guy Domville* (1895), Oscar Wilde's *The Importance of Being Earnest* (1895), Stephen Phillips' *Paolo and Francesca* (1899), E. Rose's *The Prisoner of Zenda* (1896) and J. H. McCarthy's *If I Were King* (1902).

summing-up, could declare that "their merits outweighed their deficiencies, that even when their taste was bad it was more satisfactory than the later alternative of running a theatre with no taste at all".[1] Twenty years later it is important, not only historically but for the sake of the theatre in our own time, that we should fully appreciate how the wheel has moved round in a complete circle, how the sneering onslaughts made against these distinguished actors by the young rebels who imagined that they had things better to offer are now looked upon as impertinent and, in a strangely paradoxical way, reactionary, and how the latest recorder of the achievements of these actor–managers properly emphasises, not any vices they may have had, but their genuine virtues. In her unbiassed scrutiny of their achievements, Lady Donaldson[2] has not the slightest hesitation in declaring her opinion that these theatrical artists "were vital to the development of the English drama. By the strength of their personal characteristics they brought the middle and upper class back to the theatre and changed the condition and status of their profession. They introduced new standards of production and acting, and without state aid kept a repertory of classical plays in production." She takes due note, too, of the way in which they spread their interests beyond those of the particular stages of which they were managers. "They set up schools for dramatic art and established a benevolent fund for the members of their profession." And, above all other things should we take note of Lady Donaldson's observation that "they added colour to the social scene and invested the theatre with magic". They realised what so many later innovators have ignored, that without magic and wonder and mystery the playhouse must remain utterly lifeless.

The plain truth is that, whatever disadvantages may have been associated with the system, the theatres controlled by these men maintained a certain artistic stability in the West End. Of course their object was to appeal to the public,

[1] *The Last Actor–Managers* (1950), p. vi.
[2] Frances Donaldson, *The Actor–Managers* (1970).

and in order to achieve this end they had to select plays suited to their own histrionic styles; of course they could not afford to risk too much experimentation and they tended to rely on the works of authors with whom they had co-operated previously; and of course, too, when we consider their activities, we realise that they were, in their own way, "commercial", laying out their money in their productions and necessarily expecting to be rewarded with the profits. At the same time, they themselves were artists, intent to spare no pains in their attempt to arrive at perfection; risky as it might be, they showed themselves prepared at times to engage in experimental efforts, and, within their own limits, they were willing, indeed even eager, to encourage the dramatists of their age.

Their vanishing, therefore, left a serious gap, and this gap was further widened by the disappearance, almost at the same time, of the related group of West End managers which had been represented by such men as Daly and Frohman. It is true that the great Charles B. Cochran took over, in a somewhat more flamboyant manner, the activities of the latter,[1] that Basil Dean, after having spent several years as an actor and manager at Manchester, Liverpool and Birmingham, in 1919 became managing director of a large producing syndicate, Reandean Limited, and that for some time Barry Jackson played an important part in London's theatrical affairs. It is also true that the earlier group of actor–managers was succeeded by a notable new generation of players all of whom were distinguished by "style" and who collectively might well be described as "classical" in their approach to the stage. John Gielgud, himself the author of an essay on "Tradition, Style and the Theatre

[1] Several volumes, autobiographical and biographical, fully outline his varied efforts. In *Secrets of a Showman* (1925), *I Had Almost Forgotten* (1932), *Cock-a-Doodle-Do* (1941) and *A Showman Looks On* (1945) he has told his own story. In addition, the records of his work have been narrated by J. Cleugh in *Charles Blake Cochran* (1938), by C. Graves in *The Cochran Story* (1951) and by E. Short in *Sixty Years of Theatre* (1951). Noël Coward presents an intimate account of his asociation with him in *Present Indicative* (1937). For his services to the stage he was honoured with a baronetcy in 1948.

To-Day",[1] stands as their representative – the company to which Ralph Richardson, Laurence Olivier, Peggy Ashcroft, Sybil Thorndike, Flora Robson and Edith Evans each made their individual contributions. Rightly, all have been honoured as the earlier performers had been,[2] and the honours were deserved not only for their own personal achievements but also, collectively, for the stability they gave to the theatre at a time when the way was left wide open for speculators, often not at all interested in the playhouse as such, often less anxious to maintain high standards than to reap quick profits. Some of these newcomers were no more than gamblers who purchased theatres simply in order to let them at inflated rents; others leased theatres from owners or other lease-holders in the hope, reasonably assumed, that they could profitably sublet them to other tenants; on occasion, as many as four or five intermediaries, all trying to cash in on the vicious game, might intrude between the playhouse proprietor and the producer of plays.

Usually, this change in organisational method within the theatre world is dated after the year 1918 and is explained by reference to post-war conditions. Thus, for example, Daphne Du Maurier, in narrating her father's life-story, has no hesitation in dealing with the subject in such a manner. "The days of the great actor–managers", she writes when she comes to chronicle this period,

> The days of the great actor–managers had gone for ever, and a new financial spirit had come into being. The theatre was invulnerable no longer; outside influences bore down upon it, and the little sacred world of drama and comedy became a pit for profiteers and a juggling game for clumsy amateurs.
>
> To make money, more money, and yet more money, was the only goal in mind, and those who refused to be exploited, and to their sense degraded, must fall by the way. The American

[1] *Shakespeare Survey*, iv, 1951, 101–8.

[2] Gielgud was knighted in 1953, Richardson in 1947; Oliver became Sir Laurence in 1947 and in 1970 was created the first stage Lord; Peggy Ashcroft became Dame Peggy in 1956, Sybil Thorndike became Dame Sybil in 1931, Flora Robson became Dame Flora in 1960, and Edith Evans became Dame Edith in 1946.

invasion began, and the English stage was swamped with American plays and American actors and actresses. The managers and business men followed in the wake. American methods were introduced, and their influence was felt in every quarter; box-office returns were of sole importance in this trade that was no longer an art or a profession. If English plays lay dusty and unread in drawers, and English actors and actresses were out of work, it did not matter so long as there was a queue outside the pit and the non-acting manager could drive past in an enormous car with a cigar in his face and say to an admiring companion, "Seen my little show? It's the biggest thing in town. I'll get you a box for to-morrow night."[1]

For this picture of degradation there was certainly ample justification, except perhaps for the implied assumption that there existed numerous important plays which could not find a producer; yet we must remember that the change had already come into being several years before: the new conditions did not, in fact, have to wait until the arrival of post-war conditions and an American invasion; these had already begun before the outbreak of hostilities, and British managers were responsible for their development. Already in 1913 Gilbert Cannan was speaking of "the anarchy of the theatre",[2] and during the same year Laurence Housman, lecturing on "The Conditions of Modern Drama" at the City Temple, focussed his attack upon the "Man of the World" who had laid his graspingly controlling hands on the theatre of the age. This "Man of the World" did not, at the start, travel across the Atlantic from New York; he simply strolled over to the West End from the world of variety: Frank Vernon assessed the situation correctly when he remarked that "the telescoping of music-hall management with musical-comedy management and then with legitimate management" was cause of the confusion.[3]

The years before the war were the period when those who owned the music-halls were prospering mightily, so much so, indeed, that by 1909 rumours were rife concerning the

[1] Daphne du Maurier, *Gerald: A Portrait* (1934), pp. 205–6.
[2] *The Joy of the Theatre* (1913), p. 13.
[3] Frank Vernon, *The Twentieth-Century Theatre* (1924), p. 121.

possibility of a giant merger, involving the far-flung interests of Stoll and Moss Empires, reminding us of more recent rumours and realities of Cotton and Clore, ICI and Courtaulds, Banks Barclays, Martins and Lloyds. More new houses were being hastily erected in order to cope with increasing public demand: almost at random we may select a single year, say 1911, and see it as a symbolic date partly because during its twelve months no fewer than sixteen important variety houses were freshly built or completely refashioned in London and elsewhere, and partly because it was then that the King chose for a gala performance, not a "legitimate" theatre, but Edinburgh's Empire – an apt token of the prominent position which had now been attained by the music-hall world.

Since the music-hall, except in one limited area, has comparatively little to do with drama, it might well be thought that this vast development could have little interest for us save as a force magnetically drawing thousands of playgoers away from the standard stage; yet something more must be said about one resultant consequence of the development itself. Quite naturally, with the expansion of ever mightier and more powerful managerial combines, the variety performers soon began to think of means whereby they might protect their own interests. Nor must it be forgotten that these artists, belonging to a branch of the profession where tradition and decorum were less strong than in the playhouses whose history went back to the dim reaches of the sixteenth century, were prepared to take more direct action in this way than might seem proper to those associated with the regular stage: and such action came to them the more easily since of necessity they were all itinerants, without attachment to any individual managers – indeed, often having no personal contact at all with those who had engaged their services.

Already in the latter part of the nineteenth century societies for their mutual good had come into existence. The Music Hall Artists' Association was launched in 1885, and two friendly societies, the Grand Order of Water Rats and the

Terriers' Association, were organised between 1889 and 1890. Then, in 1897, something fresh occurred: the rather strangely-named Music Hall Artists' Railway Association provided a practical demonstration of what could be achieved by joint concerted action – it succeeded in negotiating three-quarter rail fares for parties of five or more, a very important matter for those who, in order to fulfil their engagements, were forced continually to move from town to town; and because of this triumph it became a powerful organisation with influence extending far beyond its own restricted confines. Soon, out of this background, the spirit of trade-unionism strode jauntily onto the boards.

In 1906 the Variety Artists' Federation was formally established, and almost at once it marshalled the first theatrical strike in England; and although the story of this innovation is directly concerned solely with variety entertainment, the results of what came to be known as "The Music-Hall War" later exerted so widely pervasive a force and the war in itself was so symptomatic of changing conditions that at least a brief outline of the main facts deserve notice. The whole story, fully chronicled in the pages of *The Stage* and *The Era* and sufficiently novel to occasion fairly full reports and comment in the ordinary newspapers, involved various issues, but basically it arose from an attempt on the part of the music-hall artists to break the strict controls imposed upon them by the managers. Trouble started when, in December 1906, an attempt was made at Brixton to move performers engaged at one house onto another stage. The now truculent Variety Artists' Federation immediately challenged this action; a strike was ordered and this was followed both by an ineffective settlement and by the drawing-up of a "Charter". The performers' declaration of independence, however, was rejected by several of the London managers, whereupon, at a mass meeting held in January 1907, a comprehensive National Alliance was formed embracing the Federation, the Amalgamated Musicians' Union and the National Association of Theatrical Employees. Various halls were blacklisted, and those Londoners who passed their doors were confronted by the unfamiliar sight of pickets standing on the pavements outside. In a desperate effort to defeat the threatening members of the National Alliance, a new managerial body called the London Entertainments Protective Association sought to gain support from the then wide ring of provincial managements, while the Alliance countered by securing the blessing of the General Federation of Trade Unions. During the period of struggle, the Scala was leased by the strikers, both for great mass meetings and for a reception–performance brilliantly illuminated by a glittering galaxy of stars. Eventually peace was restored, with victory gained by the Alliance through an award promulgated by a Conciliation Board.

More, however, was yet to come. The following year, 1908, produced a quarrel about the unpaid appearances of variety artists at charity matinées as well as an attack launched against music-hall agents; and similar rumblings continued to reverberate for some time thereafter. The particular issues do not concern us here, but the general moving force – the idea of trade-unionism – which had thus been introduced into the music-hall world could not fail to exert an influence upon the world of the dramatic stage: and this obviously is of considerable significance.

Certainly the actors moved more circumspectly than their variety colleagues, but soon the spirit animating the Alliance began to enter their sphere too. In 1908 those concerned with the control of the playhouses had formed two federations – the Theatrical Managers Association and the Society of West End Managers – an action which may be regarded as a protective precaution inspired by anxieties consequent upon the battlings within the music-hall realm and upon certain ominous movements among their own personnel. Only a few months before, a "Reform Party" had got busily to work within the hitherto decorous Actors' Association and succeeded in placing their representatives on the council: still further, elated with this success, they then demanded that the Association's stables should be cleansed and purified by the driving-out of the actor–managers – whereupon immediately Squire Bancroft, George Alexander, F. R. Benson, Arthur Bourchier, John Hare, H. B. Irving, Cyril Maude, Edward Terry, Beerbohm Tree and Charles Wyndham – a mighty roster – accompanied by several council members, tendered their resignations. And, as if this were not enough, the same months witnessed the establishment of another organisation, the Actors' Union, which – to the stupified horror of many – was actually registered as a trade-union.

There could be no doubt which way the wind was blowing: by the close of another decade the Association itself, with a membership which had soared from under a thousand to six thousand, was reconstituted according to trade-union principles, an event which prompted those who had become alarmed by the progress of theatrical socialism to set up, in June 1924, the Stage Guild as a rival body designed to bring all theatre-men (actors, managers, authors) into one single happy all-embracing society.[1] This last attempt, however, was doomed to failure: the Guild lasted for only five years, its demise being hastened by an unfortunate incident which occurred in 1929. In September of that year an insignificant musical comedy called *Open Your Eyes* collapsed on tour: the promoter–manager did a midnight flitting with the cash, leaving his wretched actors, penniless, stranded in a provincial town. At once, quite naturally, excited voices were raised urging the need for action, and on October 2, almost at the close of this period, the Association and the Guild held a joint meeting: at this, after expressing angry regret at the

[1] An excellent example of the troubles incurred by even the best-intentioned managers is suggested by a collection of letters and hastily-printed handbills relating to Sir John Martin-Harvey which are summarily described in Ifan Kyrle Fletcher's Catalogue no. 225, item 223. These show that in 1924 the Association attempted to force the actor–manager to agree to a form of contract dictated by them and to force his actors to belong to its own "closed shop". This collection includes a copy of a handbill boldly headed "Keep Away from Sir John Martin-Harvey's Company", copies of which were distributed at cities through which he was touring, together with opposition leaflets issued in his support by the Stage Guild. His own letters declare pathetically that he was being "driven to death" by the campaign, his artistic endeavours completely disrupted by politics.

inability of the law to proceed against bogus or fraudulent managers, the assembled members decided to combine their forces.[1] Thus the tentative endeavours of these three decades reached their inevitable conclusion: 1929 brought with it at once completion to the efforts of thirty years and the heralding of something new.

The events briefly chronicled above do not perhaps have in themselves direct pertinence to the drama of the age, yet they serve as concrete illustrations of the changes within the theatrical structure and as reflections of the mood animating those concerned with playhouse affairs. In particular, they must be borne in mind as we turn to consider the most characteristic development of the age, the rise of the repertory movement. Before this is examined, however, something more must be said about an unexpected and startling innovation which completely altered the balance of forces within the realm of entertainment.

3. "*My Lady Kinema*"

The music-hall war had broken out in 1906, at a time when the variety stage was in the full flush of triumphant success, but between that date and 1929 this success suffered a mighty shock.

In 1900 readers of *The Era* and other professional papers could have seen, among a diversity of advertisements designed to appeal to those interested in theatrical matters, an announcement set forth by L. Gaumont & Co. Describing themselves as "The Cinematograph Pioneers", those in control of this firm reproduced an illustration of their "Chromo Projector" – an "ordinary" model costing £8. 5*s*. and a "professional" model £25; and prospective purchasers were informed that they could also be supplied with "all the latest and, above all, *the best*, Comic, Topical, or Trick Films" on over 3,000 subjects.

[1] A particularly vivid picture of the menace of bogus managers is given by J. Graham in *An Old Stock-Actor's Memories* (1930), pp. 102–13.

It may be confidently assumed that only a very few who scanned this advertisement thought of the projector and its films as other than a mere curiosity. True, the Lumière Brothers had excited a little flutter of interest when, on March 3, 1896, they had demonstrated their similar machine at the Empire music-hall, but the interest was directed towards a scientific novelty rather than towards an object which might be regarded as possessing any practical and wide entertainment potentiality. One or two showmen, certainly, started to carry around their Gaumont or other professional projectors and, renting small halls for a day or two in some of the smaller towns, to display their comic, topical and, especially, trick films before meagre audiences. At the same time, various music-halls inaugurated the fashion of running off a film at the conclusion of their variety turns as a kind of freak attraction. And that was virtually all.

Then, about six or seven years after the beginning of the century, suddenly there came palpable premonitions of a boom to come. One perceptive journalist, writing in 1907 and looking into the future, was thus able to express his belief that, "when the history of the present century comes to be written, kinematography" would "figure largely in its records".[1] Before the close of the following year divers London "theatres" designed specifically for film displays were already in business – the Kinematograph Hall in Tottenham Court Road, the Bijou Picture Theatre in Dulwich, two Electric Palaces in Lewisham and Marylebone, the Bioscopic Tea Rooms in Leicester Square, and the Electric Pavilion in Great Windmill Street. So extensively had these multiplied within the next few months that at the beginning of 1910 a Kinematograph Act was passed, controlling the use of inflammable film; from then on the opening of new "palaces" and "pavilions" proceeded apace all over the country. Soon the music-halls realised that, in order to keep up their appeal to the public, this new form of entertainment had to be included in their bills, not simply as an occasional novelty presented while spectators were groping for their wraps and

[1] *The Stage Year Book, 1908*, p. 47.

cloaks, but as a standard feature: by April 1914 the Coliseum thus started to project Klein's serial of *Find the Woman*, promising its patrons that one act would be shown each week. And, if we look at the advertisements printed in the professional periodicals during that year we can see no fewer than thirty firms, established in or near Wardour Street, engaged in supplying equipment, in renting films, in considering scenarios for filming and in employing "artistes to take part in filming comic and domestic sketches, &c.".

The boom continued throughout the war years, and thence roared onwards. For an indication of what was happening we need only turn to compare *The Stage Year Book* of 1908 with that for 1920. In the former the prophecy concerning the coming importance of the cinema had been merely an oddity, just a short note, a mere guess: in the latter, fact took the place of prediction, with the issuing of a broad survey of "The Kinema Year" and with photographs of silent-picture stars reproduced alongside those of prominent stage actors and actresses.

In general, it may be said that until at least the middle twenties the majority of those whose chief interest lay in the prosperity of the playhouse tended to see in this development nothing but good. Almost everywhere there was comfortable acceptance of the view that "My Lady Kinema – The Eleventh Muse"[1] could do little to injure Thalia and Melpomene, that she was not concerned with the living theatre, and that the "drama can have no enemy but the one that comes from within". Even ten years later, in 1924, J. T. Grein was expressing precisely the same optimistic belief.[2]

Nor was it merely with indifference that most dramatists and theatre-men viewed what was happening in their midst: most of them secretly looked with doubly auspicious eyes upon "My Lady Kinema". First, they rejoiced to find that, as the film industry expanded, a new lucrative source of

[1] The phrase is the title of an article by Arthur Coles Armstrong in *The Stage Year Book, 1914*, pp. 33–8.

[2] *The New World of the Theatre* (1924), pp. 138–9.

income was being offered to them – and here, of course, it must be remembered that, whereas in the United States there was an early trend towards the establishment of the cinematographic studios in California, removed by thousands of miles from New York's theatrical centre, those in control of the English studios tended to select locations close to London – with the result that stage actors engaged in productions within the metropolitan ring could easily combine their appearances in the playhouses with appearances before the rolling cameras. And there was a second cause for rejoicing, even if the sense of exultation had perforce to be kept discreetly restrained. The plain fact was that the effects of the cinema's rise in popularity soon came by many to be considered with secret approval: it was discovered that the novel entertainment provided by the picture-houses did not materially lower attendance at the playhouses while at the same time it was shattering completely the empire of variety. About the end of the century's first decade the music-hall magnates – who had previously shown no deeply-felt regret concerning the inroads they had been making on the play-going public – were becoming seriously worried and were solemnly inviting sympathy for their sorry plight as the increasing success of this new filmic rival proceeded to draw away numbers of their erstwhile patrons. Desperate efforts were made to remedy the situation, and at least one of these had the paradoxical effect of bringing theatres and music-halls together, even while it exacerbated their basic competitiveness. By 1909 various critics were stressing "the growing popularity of sketches and scenes" in the halls, attributing this largely to the appearance there of prominent theatre stars who had been "tempted by the charm of variety and the large salaries" and who sought for suitable scripts by means of which they might display their talents.[1] It was in that year, on December 20, that H. A. Jones became the first well-known author to see the performance of a one-act play commissioned in this manner: on that day his *The Knife* was given at the Palace by Arthur Bourchier and

[1] *The Stage Year Book, 1910*, p. 36.

Violet Vanbrugh. In the same year Cyril Maude, during the run of a comedy at the Playhouse, agreed to appear also at the Coliseum, and his record of the event amply reflects the excitement of the occasion:

It was very hard work playing in that piece, but very paying! In those days at the Coliseum the management did not pay by cheque, they paid in coin, and, mind you, it was in the days of sovereigns. My salary, which was a huge one, frightened me. I sent quickly for Turner, my manager at the Playhouse, to take it safely away![1]

About the same time Joe Graham describes a conversation he had at Birmingham with Sir George Alexander:

"And now," said he, "I want to ask your advice on a different matter. Stoll has offered me £500 a week for a month at the Coliseum in our 'off' season. Why? I can't flatter myself for a moment that I should draw anything like that amount to his treasury, and I know he has offered the Kendals £700 on the same terms. Again, why?" "Well," said I, after a brief pause for reflection, "I can only give you my own opinion, for what it's worth. I know Mr. Stoll to be a very shrewd man. He never does anything he hasn't thought out. As you know, all seats at the Coliseum are bookable. Playgoers everywhere are clamouring for us to do likewise, which would, of course, speedily spell 'bankruptcy' for the lot of us. Now, I think that possibly Mr. Stoll would like to show you, and all the other West End 'stars' he can rope in, to his music-hall patrons at prices from 3*s*. 6*d*. to 1*s*., under circumstances which, on the enormous stage of the Coliseum, would certainly prevent you from appearing to anything like the same advantage as in your own theatres, and so undermine your market value in the eyes of general playgoers."

On this occasion Alexander, after walking up and down the room for a few moments, suddenly ejaculated, "I feel you're right, Graham, and I shall refuse the offer straight away"[2] – but even he could not long resist the hypnotising glitter of the sovereigns: at the beginning of 1913 he was appearing at the Palace in Max Beerbohm's *A Social Success*. So great

[1] Cyril Maude, *Behind the Scenes with Cyril Maude* (1927), pp. 203–4.
[2] Joe Graham, *An Old Stock-Actor's Memories* (1930), pp. 245–6.

was the rush of those who sought the genuine golden guineas, that by 1912 the Lord Chamberlain, albeit a trifle hesitantly, found himself compelled to extend his licensing system beyond the theatres so as to embrace the variety houses. And the traffic was not all in the one direction. These short plays performed in the halls obviously proved popular – so popular indeed that some of the playhouses, seeking to hold on to their audiences, were induced to present programmes consisting of triple and even quadruple bills. Some tinkling verses by Mostyn Pigott serve to illustrate what was happening:

The more the subject I survey
  The more I feel I'm getting nervy;
I feel my hair is growing grey
As I perceive to my dismay
  The advent of the topsy-turvy;
And I get plaintively perplexed
At thought of what's to happen next.

For instance, music-halls intent
  On finding anything that fetches
Show very clearly they are bent
On giving plays of sentiment
  And also Grand Guignolesque sketches,
And are not backward nowadays
In playing even Shakespeare's plays.

Their chief reliance now they place
  On turns that aim at the dramatic
And they can pretty clearly trace
Their patrons in nigh ev'ry case
  Exhibiting in style emphatic
That they undoubtedly incline
To stars like Sarah the Divine.

And on the other hand we find
  The theatres their methods changing
And framing programmes of a kind
That show they have it in their mind
  That matters call for rearranging:
Their triple bills, one can but feel,
Are very near to vaudeville.

And if front-pieces they require
  No more they give us one-act dramas
But "entertainers" they will hire
Who sing the songs that never tire
  Concerning flappers and pyjamas:
In their opinion, thus they show
Variety is all the go.

I gaze around as in a trance
  And, with my breath distinctly bated,
I see things to the pitch advance
When theatres to song and dance
  Are quite completely dedicated,
And when the halls the home will be
Of tragedy and comedy.[1]

A scrutiny of the new sketches presented at the music-halls during the year 1912 shows that this is not by any means a fanciful picture. The majority of the three hundred odd pieces of this kind were performed by playhouse actors and not by variety artists; among these are to be found Arthur Bourchier and Violet Vanbrugh in a "problem" called *The Man in the Case*, by V. H. Virens, Beerbohm Tree in an "episode of military life", *The Man Who Was*, by Kinsey Peile, Cyril Maude in an "incident in the life of Mrs Gamp", called *Sairey Gamp*, by J. C. Carr, George Grossmith and Ellaline Terriss in a "burlesque drama", *She Was No Lady*, contrived by Grossmith himself, Martin-Harvey in a one-act version of the final scenes in *A Tale of Two Cities*, Norman McKinnell in an "incident" entitled *The Diamond Coronet*, and Sarah Bernhardt in the third act of Victor Hugo's *Lucrèce Borgia*, in the fourth act of *La Reine Élisabeth* and in *Une Nuit de Noël sous la Terreur*. If, however, the greater part of Pigott's ironic prediction was destined to be fulfilled, one thing was not: for the music-halls the writing was plainly and ominously spelt out on the walls, and the variety Empires were slowly being destroyed by the Picture Palaces. By 1925 only an odd few of the larger London halls remained reasonably faithful to the old traditions, and, two years

[1] *The Stage Year Book, 1913*, pp. 14–15.

later, even the once-popular and distinguished Empire, where Lumière's invention had first been shown in London, had to give itself over to the films, and commentators were freely noting that variety artists were being saved from complete ruin and extinction only through the emergence of another novelty, the BBC.

It certainly did seem certain that the theatre had become rid of its only serious rival, and that its performances, if properly pursued, could easily outvie the attractions of the silent screen. Then suddenly, towards the very close of this period, those who went to see *The Jazz Singer* (1927) were startled by hearing the raucous recording of Al Jolson's voice. Without doubt, almost all who listened to those distressing sounds must have regarded them much as the spectators in the Empire of 1896 regarded the exhibition of the Cinématographe or as the readers of 1900 regarded the advertisement of Gaumont's projector. Very few could imagine then that shortly the silent film, seemingly so securely established, would be rendered silent indeed, or that the playhouses would be confronted by an unexpected and troublesome antagonist: but they were soon to learn. During the year 1928 the technical advance of the "speaking film" proceeded with surprising acceleration, and by 1929 it had become clear that these films had come to stay. The mood prevalent in the theatre during the closing months of the twenties has excellently been recorded by Daphne Du Maurier when, towards the end of her penetrating portrait of her father,[1] she traces the immediate effect of the talkies. They had taken over some of the largest variety houses; it was now "*démodé* to go to the theatre and it was fashionable to wander into the Empire or the Plaza" – where "three and sixpence bought a comfortable chair, the right to smoke, and a programme packed with incident", all of which

> weighed heavily in the balance with the twelve-and-sixpenny stall, the boiled shirt, and the long intervals that awaited the audience in the legitimate theatre. The screen could show both Africa and the North Pole within the space of a few minutes,

[1] *Gerald: A Portrait* (1934), pp. 279–86.

whereas the theatre could only offer false walls and a painted backcloth. The screen could skip generations and continents without losing conviction, which the stage, for all its revolving platforms and tricks of lighting, never quite succeeded in doing.

"This sudden overwhelming invasion of the talkies found the London theatre unprepared", and here, for an actor such as Gerald Du Maurier, was the end. In September of that fateful year 1929 he forced himself, with a heavy heart, to present a revival of *Dear Brutus* – but

it was a poor affair compared with the original play of twelve years before; everyone was miscast, and Gerald seemed to make no effort with the production. The magic had gone; the enchanted wood was nothing but a group of painted trees; the characters drifted on and off the stage as though it was an easy though rather boring way of passing the regulation two and a half hours, and Gerald himself was a lost and rather puzzled Harry Dearth who looked as though he might turn to the audience any moment and say, "It's no good. I don't feel it any more. I've forgotten what it was all about. Harry Dearth isn't here.... Go back to Wyndham's in the middle of the night, when the watchman's dozing in his chair and the boards are creaking; you'll find Dearth there with little Lob and the rest....But he's not here."

With the advent of the talkies in 1929 the entire theatrical picture proceeded to assume a new design entirely different from that which had been created during the century's first three decades.

4. *The "Modern" Movement: (a) the Repertories*

The older design, however, has by no means been fully described in the preceding brief summary of its lines and colours, extending from the decorous polish supplied by the actor–managers to the more garish pigments and bolder outlines provided by the music-halls and the picture-palaces. Indeed, it must be clearly evident that there has been left out what must be regarded as the most typical, the most denotative and perhaps the most important theatrical development within the years 1900 to 1930, and, moreover, a force which succeeded in laying a foundation for the theatre of the present.

In order properly to appreciate the nature of this development several things have to be kept in mind. First of all, it has to be observed that certain conditions operative in the Victorian playhouses had effected a complete revolution from what prevailed in earlier times. The way in which the Garrick theatre became transformed into the theatre of Irving is, of course, well-known, but, even although the general story needs no retelling, two or three of its chief features and consequences require to be emphasised here.

If we look through the pages of *The London Stage* which record performances in London between 1767 and 1776 we find a pattern which may be illustrated by the choice, at random, of a particular week – that from October 27, 1770, to November 3. At Drury Lane, spectators could have seen *Romeo and Juliet* on the Monday, *The Maid of the Mill* on Tuesday, *King Lear* on Wednesday, a repetition of *Romeo* on Thursday, *The Provok'd Husband* on Friday, and *The Stratagem* on Saturday: within the same six days Covent Garden presented *King Lear*, *Venice Preserved*, *The Brothers*, *Barbarossa* and *Love in a Village*. Obviously, the ability of the playhouses thus to vary their programmes depended upon two basic facts: each theatre had its own permanent company of players thoroughly familiar with a number of stock dramas, and in the production of these plays the audiences were entirely willing to accept the employment of stock scenery – the easily managed wings, borders and backdrops of almost infinite application. If, furthermore, we turn to consider conditions prevailing in the country as a whole, we observe that, while certainly many performances outside of London left a very great deal to be desired, there existed a fairly extensive ring of independent local companies either established in their own Theatres Royal or else touring among the humbler houses set within the confines of their particular circuits. Here, too, the players, the plays and the settings were all, in general, stock.

Within the second half of the nineteenth century, all this was changed, or at least in the process of changing. Even if actor–managers tended to engage their companies for seasons and not simply for particular productions, the stock-company system was disappearing in London, and outside of the metropolis many of the hitherto independent local companies gradually were being extinguished, their place being taken by touring groups engaged to carry London's latest successes to the provinces. At the same time, audiences in general were being trained to expect a different kind of theatrical setting – not a purely conventional background such as was provided by the old flat wings-and-backdrop, but stage-pictures heavy and often three-dimensional, above all specially designed and built for the particular plays to which they belonged. Needless to say, this meant that, quite apart from the continually rising costs of materials and workmanship, the theatres more and more found themselves unable to function unless selected plays were put on for extended runs. In 1821 the hundred nights of *Tom and Jerry* aroused a flutter of excitement: a century later this record seemed very tame when *Chu-Chin-Chow* proceeded on its non-stop career of over 2,000 presentations.

By about 1890 various persons, both from within and from without the theatre, were beginning to decry the troublesome and disadvantageous results of this newly-established system. Young stage aspirants, it was pointed out, were now finding it difficult to secure such effective training as had previously been provided by the provincial stock companies; even if good fortune or influence enabled them to find engagements in London, they frequently were prohibited from gaining variety of experience since, as often as not, they had to spend dreary months in repeating, night after night, the same few lines of their minor rôles. Attention, too, was drawn to the equally serious problems confronting the young playwrights. In the eighteenth century, if a playhouse manager thought he saw some possible interest in the script of a new play by a hitherto untried author, he was not risking much by introducing it into his season's programme: the scenes and costumes could easily be taken out of the store-rooms, the company of actors was there at command, and, if the spectators did not approve of the piece, it could without any trouble at all be dropped from the bills after one, two or three performances. Under the new conditions, on the contrary, a manager was compelled to consider his scripts with very great care, since a failure could involve him in serious loss; and thus there was a natural tendency on his part to give preference to dramas composed by playwrights of already proved ability, members of the so-called "Ring". Players and playwrights thus were handicapped, and other critics of the newly-established system proceeded further by pointing out that playgoers, too, were suffering; not only were they denied the chance of seeing possibly interesting experimental plays by young authors, they were being denied an opportunity of gaining an acquaintanceship either with representative plays culled from the national heritage or with the more important among the works of contemporary foreign dramatists.

These weaknesses and disadvantages inherent in the system were thus being catalogued, and during the second half of the nineteenth century at least a few individuals were starting to launch ventures designed to ameliorate the prevailing conditions. In 1871 John Hollingshead, as he himself tells us,[1] when he was manager of the Gaiety "invented the Experimental and Miscellaneous Morning Performance" designed "to invite trial trips of actors, actresses, authors, and pieces, without much regard for the old restrictive principles of management"; in 1881 Edward Compton formed his Comedy Company by means of which he kept the plays of Sheridan, Goldsmith and their fellows vital on the stage; two years later Frank Benson's Shakespeare company was established; in 1886 Ben Greet began his series of outdoor performances, and three years later still Janet Achurch, taking over the management of the Novelty, sought to offer at matinées some "plays not popular enough to meet the

[1] *Gaiety Chronicles* (1898), pp. 179–89. Several other efforts of a similar kind are noted in *H. E. D.* v, 54–67.

demands of audiences who went to the theatre in the evening";[1] immediately after this, Beerbohm Tree, then manager of the Haymarket, varied his runs with special performances of "plays that were generally regarded as above the average playgoer's intelligence" (among them the first Ibsen drama to be presented by a prominent West End manager) and, although this did not quite make him "the father of the repertory movement in England",[2] the importance of these experiments was considerable. At the same time a group of young professional actors founded an organisation called the Dramatic Students, designed both to offer them opportunities for improving their own skills and to allow at least a limited public the chance of seeing plays of a rarer sort.

Among these several ventures before 1900 three are of special significance. In 1891 J. T. Grein, inspired by his intimate knowledge of what was happening in various Continental centres, was responsible for instituting the Independent Theatre, an association which aimed at giving, on Sundays and at Monday matinées, "performances of plays which have a literary and artistic rather than a commercial value".[3] Although this venture received the support of a limited number of prominent literary figures such as George Meredith, Thomas Hardy, A. W. Pinero, H. A. Jones and Frank Harris, although it brought to public attention several important foreign plays, including Ibsen's

[1] F. Foxwell, *Censorship in England* (1913), p. 250, quoting Frank Charrington, Janet Achurch's husband.

[2] Hesketh Pearson, *Beerbohm Tree* (1956), p. 60.

[3] An intimate portrait of this innovator is drawn by his wife, "Michael Orme", in *J. T. Grein: The Story of a Pioneer* (1936). N. H. G. Schoonderwoerd has a more detailed, and a more important, study, *J. T. Grein, Ambassador of the Theatre, 1862–1935: A Study in Anglo-Continental Theatrical Relations* (1963). Grein himself, who was a dramatic critic, published several volumes of interest, among which perhaps the essays collected in *The World of the Theatre* (1921) and *The New World of the Theatre* (1924) are the most significant: he was also responsible for founding, in 1912, a journal called *The Independent Theatre Goer*. His use of the term "independent" was itself borrowed from the Continent: for this see Anna Irene Miller, *The Independent Theatre in Europe from 1887 to the Present* (1931).

Ghosts, and although through its sponsorship Shaw's *Widowers' Houses* first came upon the stage, it was greeted with a considerable amount of abuse and a very great deal of apathy: never having more than 175 members on its rolls, it struggled on amid constant financial difficulties through only twenty-two productions until it was disbanded in 1897. Three years after the establishment of the Independent Theatre, William Poel's Elizabethan Stage Society came into being. Already in 1881 a finger-post pointing to the future had appeared in an obscure performance of the first quarto version of *Hamlet*, directed by Poel at St George's Hall: he was then twenty-eight years old and at that time fanatically devoted both to the stage in general and to the Elizabethans in particular. After spending two years as manager of the Royal Victoria Coffee Hall (which soon was to become the Old Vic) and giving up most of his leisure to his self-appointed duties as "Instructor" to the Shakespeare Reading Society, he eventually created his own organisation partly for the purpose of reviving largely forgotten plays of the sixteenth and seventeenth centuries, and partly for that of restoring to the stage the conditions which had been operative in the Elizabethan period: continually he stressed the value of the open stage platform, and he never ceased his battle against the familiar contemporary proscenium-arch, picture-frame theatrical structure.[1] And finally, just as the Victorian period was reaching its close, the Stage Society started its distinguished career, destined to bear it onwards into the thirties of the present century. That it succeeded in carrying on for so long and in exerting such considerable influence was no doubt due largely to the wide support it received during its early days, but when we contrast it with the preceding Independent Theatre we may believe that in part it owed its good fortune to the fact that, whereas Grein's venture of 1891 belonged definitely to the nineteenth century, this Society's

[1] A detailed account of his various stage activities is provided by Robert Speaight in *William Poel and the Elizabethan Revival* (1954): this includes both a chronological list of his productions and a useful catalogue of articles on his stage activities.

establishment in 1899 really made it part of the new movement which belonged to the twentieth.[1]

This reflection requires some further thought. When we survey the diverse "advanced" endeavours up to the founding of the Stage Society, we realise that they had been characterised by certain common features: for the most part, they were what may be called "remedial", in the sense that they aimed principally to correct defects in the current theatrical régime rather than to inaugurate something new; except for Janet Achurch's short-lived management of the Novelty, the scope of each was restricted; all of them came into existence through the enthusiasm of single individuals; and not one of them gained any large body of support even among the more intellectual groups of playgoers. What they attempted to achieve, and what actually they did achieve, warrants full attention and praise, yet, if our object be to examine the theatre and drama of the twentieth century, they must be seen to belong to a pre-historical era.

What happened in the months just before and just after the year 1900 was something entirely different, so startlingly novel that, although its roots may be traced backwards and downwards throughout the concluding decades of the Victorian age, it must be kept strictly apart from that which had gone before. First of all, the twentieth-century movement as a whole, despite the fact that it did not always receive as much public support as might have been expected, can be described only as a vast upsurge in which professionals and amateurs alike were swept forwards by a kind of unseen power, and in which, precisely because they were not inspired merely by the enthusiasm of a few individual leaders, they exerted such a force as had never before been experienced by the theatre in England.

Two concrete illustrations will clearly demonstrate the

[1] Unfortunately there is no comprehensive account of this Society. A record of its earliest activities appears in a pamphlet issued in 1909, *The Incorporated Stage Society*, *Ten Years*, *1899–1909*, but no later accounts of a similar kind seem to have been published. Attention may here be drawn to the interesting reviews of its productions from 1914 to 1935 which are included in Sir Desmond MacCarthy's *Drama* (1940).

strength of the pervading influence which was at work. In 1904 a young man in Birmingham, Barry Jackson, began to amuse himself with private theatricals presented in his father's house; a little group gathered together, including among their number an insurance clerk, then in his early twenties, named John Drinkwater; soon this small company discovered an old, forgotten, sixteenth-century *Interlude of Youth* and this they felt impelled to perform at various localities in the surrounding countryside. The Pilgrim Players thus were born, and from the Pilgrim Players, of course, arose the Birmingham Repertory Theatre. Jackson became famous as its founder, and Drinkwater, after his extraordinarily successful *Abraham Lincoln* in 1918, joined the ranks of the most prominent dramatists of the period: and yet the entry of both into the world theatrical came almost by chance. Neither was there any sense of remedial purpose in their early efforts, nor were they hypnotised by any dazzling glow from the footlights. Looking back twenty-five years afterwards and trying to convey to others the feeling of excitement which animated the Pilgrim Players, Drinkwater stressed his surprise on realising, in retrospect, that all the enthusiasm they devoted to their humble presentations surged up, as it were, from within themselves and was not inspired by any outside influence: at that time they remained completely ignorant of what was happening elsewhere, in no wise conscious of the fact that their enterprise was merely one among many similar ventures scattered throughout the British Isles – all of them taking shape "independently of, and, for all practical purposes, unknown to each other".[1] Even more significant is a second, similar, record narrated by the man who was to become organiser of the far-flung work of the British Drama League. In 1907 – the very year when Jackson, Drinkwater and their friends were engaged on their first production of *The Interlude of Youth* – Geoffrey Whitworth came down from Oxford and, as he tells us, "was fortunate enough to secure employment on the staff of one of our leading publishers". Happily proud

[1] *Discovery* (1932), pp. 147–9.

of his position, with excellent prospects, he proceeded to apply himself wholeheartedly to the duties assigned to him. At that time he had hardly any interest in the stage: yet, just twelve months later, happening by chance to read a newspaper paragraph which announced the launching of a scheme for a Shakespeare Memorial Theatre, he was, quite inexplicably, seized by "a great restlessness", and, without the slightest hesitation or inner debate, sat down at his desk and wrote a letter to the planning committee, asking to be appointed its secretary.[1] Nothing could better demonstrate the compulsive drive which mysteriously animated so many individuals at this period; this was no stage-struck fancy: something electric seemed to be in the air; an invisible, intangible Zeitgeist was at work. Once more we must decide that here was no "remedial" effort, consequent upon an awareness of weaknesses in the current theatrical structure: it was instinctive, aiming not at improvement but at the creating of things new.

Unfortunately no detailed study of this novel and interesting development has yet been made, and here, of course, it would be improper to present more than a brief general survey. Perhaps, because the tangle is so complex, no such detailed investigation of the subject as a whole will ever be made, and even for a rapid conspectus it is difficult to decide how best to map out the material. Clearly, the new repertory movement demands our attention first, although even here we realise, almost immediately, the prevailing confusion which surrounds us. The word "repertory" meant one thing to one person, something quite different to another; one of the most notable and influential ventures of the kind deliberately refused to apply the term to its company; some enthusiasts preferred to speak of "Endowed Theatre", or "Artistic Theatre", or "Organised Theatre"; Ivor Brown declared that "repertory is a silly name – both dull and inaccurate", Harold Brighouse declared his belief that it was "a daft word", while Granville-Barker came to the conclusion that its use had "become almost a curse".

[1] *The Theatre of My Heart* (1930), pp. 1–5.

Perhaps, however, we can cope with this particular confusion: much harder is it to keep a steady path when we recognise, as we must, that the work of such playhouses cannot be treated as an independent unit, that their activities cannot fully be appreciated without considering the associated work of the scores upon scores of dramatic and theatrical societies established during those years. Nor may any sharp separation be made between amateurs and professionals: even although most of the repertories belonged to the latter category, some of them did not, while almost all owed their being to preceding amateur effort. Thus, while it seems convenient and proper – perhaps even essential – to separate the repertory playhouses and the play-producing societies, it is impossible to hold them rigorously apart: the two are, in fact, inextricably intertwined, and while the one group is being examined the thought of the other must firmly be kept in mind.[1]

[1] The best – indeed almost the only – general record of amateur and professional ventures during the earlier years is Harry Bergholz's little-known *Die Neugestaltung des modernen englischen Theaters, 1870–1930* (1933): this, although by no means comprehensive, effectively presents much factual information and also includes several interesting statements contributed to the author by individuals active in this sphere. Some of the information has been taken from the facts and opinions submitted in evidence to the Adult Education Committee of the Board of Education and printed in its valuable report, *The Drama in Adult Education* (1926). Norman Marshall's *The Other Theatre* (1947) deals selectively, and often summarily, with the more important efforts from the twenties to the mid-forties. It is to be regretted that, in general, intimate records of most of the societies and even of some among the repertories are scanty, and it is likely that many may now be irretrievably lost. The chief source of information concerning their more public activities is to be found in the pages of *The Stage* and *The Era*, as well as in those of *The Era Annual* and *The Stage Year Book*: however, the former series of volumes, inaugurated in 1868, ceased publication in 1919, while the latter, beginning not until 1908, broke off its serial issues in 1928 and did not resume publication until 1949. Local newspapers, of course, must contain much material on dramatic activities within their respective areas, but clearly a methodical search through their files would be a task so enormous as to be possible only for a co-ordinated band of enthusiastic researchers. Among books relating to the English repertory movement and on similar movements abroad may be noted: P. P. Howe, *The Repertory Theatre: A Record and a Criticism* (1910); Basil Dean, *The Repertory Theatre* (1911); Mario Borsa, *The English Stage of To-Day* (1908); St John Ervine, *The Organised Theatre* (1924); Geoffrey Whitworth, *The Theatre of My*

A consideration of the origins of the earliest of these theatres illustrates this in an emphatic manner, and it also serves to stress the way in which the new twentieth-century movement was being inspired by forces distinct from those which had led to the formation of the nineteenth century's Independent Theatre. Just as the one age was moving into the other, an almost completely political association, "Inginidheanna-h Eireann" ("The Daughters of Ireland"), founded by the revolutionary Maude Gonne, began to present a few tableaux and sketches in Dublin. Those participating were almost entirely intent upon the promotion of nationalistic sentiment; their humble attempts at dramatic performances were designed, not to encourage the theatre, but to carry their political objectives forward. Almost immediately after this came the publication of a letter signed by W. B. Yeats, Lady Gregory and Edward Martyn in which these three authors declared their intention of sponsoring the production "in the spring of each year" of "certain Celtic and Irish plays", with the ultimate aim of building up "a Celtic and Irish school of dramatic literature": this letter led to the formal establishment of the Irish Literary Theatre and to its first performances, in Dublin's Antient Concert Rooms, of Yeats' *The Countess Cathleen* and Martyn's *The Heather Field* (May 8 and 9, 1899).

If the stage ventures of "The Daughters of Ireland" must be styled frankly "nationalistic", the scheme outlined by the three signatories, although also animated by patriotic emotions, may best be categorised as "literary" and "self-interested", since the trio were mainly concerned with creating this "school" of Irish playwrights and with

Heart (1930); Harley Granville-Barker, *The Exemplary Theatre* (1922): relevant American books are P. W. Mackaye's *The Civic Theatre* (1912), Sheldon Cheyney's *The Art Theatre: A Discussion of its Ideals, its Organisation and its Promise as a Corrective for the Present Evils of the Commercial Theatre* (1917; revised edition, 1925), and Constance D. Mackay's *The Little Theatre in the United States* (1917); Anne I. Miller's survey of the independent theatre in Europe has been cited above. Cecil Chisholm has a useful survey and assessment of the repertories operative towards the conclusion of the 1900–1930 period in his *Repertory: An Outline of the Modern Theatre Movement* (1934).

providing for themselves an opportunity for getting their own writings onto the stage. And associated with these impulses soon came another. A Dublin electrician named W. G. Fay found himself caught up by the spirit of the time, spent much of his leisure in acting, discovered the joys of that characteristic development of the age, "play production", joined the three authors in founding "The Irish National Theatre Company", and became the first manager of the Abbey Theatre after Annie E. F. Horniman, charmed by the Irish players and their plays, provided the means for converting "the Hall of the Mechanics' Institute in Abbey Street" into a proper playhouse.[1]

This is not the place for any attempt at an account, however condensed, of the Abbey. It is sufficient to note that acrimonious debate attended the discussions as to whether Miss Horniman's offer should be accepted, that, when a decision was reached, several of the players seceded and were instrumental in forming a more strictly nationalistic group under the title of The Theatre of Ireland, that Miss Horni-

[1] There is an extensive library of books and booklets relating to the Irish theatre and particularly to the Abbey. Among these may be mentioned: Cornelius Weygandt, *Irish Plays and Players* (1913; reprinted 1966), Ernest Boyd, *Ireland's Literary Renaissance* (new edition 1923) and *The Contemporary Drama of Ireland* (1918), A. E. Malone, *The Irish Drama, 1898–1928* (1929), Stephen Gwynn, *Irish Literature and Drama in the English Language* (1936), Una Ellis-Fermor, *The Irish Dramatic Movement* (1939) and Gigi Lunari, *Il movimento drammatico irlandese, 1899–1922* (1960). A particularly vivid account of the start of the movement is to be found in *The Splendid Years: Recollections of Maire Nic Shiubhlaigh, as told to Edward Kenny* (1955). *The Story of Ireland's National Theatre* (1929) is recounted by Dawson Byrne, and there are several other similar studies such as Gerard Fay's *The Abbey Theatre* (1958) and Lennox Robinson's *Ireland's Abbey Theatre* (1951). Some of these include lists of productions, although it may be noted that the dates given in different lists do not always agree and that some of them are demonstrably wrong. A great deal of intimate material appears in various biographical and autobiographical works – for example, W. G. Fay and C. Carswell, *The Fays of the Abbey Theatre* (1935), Lady Gregory, *Our Irish Theatre* (1913) and her *Journal, 1916–1930* (1946), George Moore, *Hail and Farewell* (1925) and W. B. Yeats, *Autobiographies* (1926). Much relevant material culled from Joseph Holloway's voluminous diaries has now been made available by R. Hogan and Michael J. O'Neill in *Joseph Holloway's Irish Theatre* (3 vols. 1967–1970).

man herself was interested only in dramatic excellence, and that, although the Abbey's directorate tried their best to make theatrical quality their chief objective, the day had to come when the English sponsor was forced to sever her association with the playhouse she had been largely responsible for inaugurating. In this connection it is interesting to observe that one of the fieriest among the militants, Maire Nic Shiubhlaigh, later found herself forced in retrospect to admit that "if the Abbey had remained subordinate to nationalism, political as well as cultural, it might never have achieved the success it did. It had to stand outside the nationalistic movement in order to make its mark in the theatre of the world"[1] – words which deserve to be deeply pondered by all those who are inclined to subordinate theatrical endeavours to political aims.

Not deterred by her somewhat unfortunate experience in Dublin, Miss Horniman, now associated with and advised by Ben Iden Payne, decided to devote herself to the creation of a repertory playhouse in another centre. Choice was made of Manchester, where already there had been considerable stirring of interest in the possibility of stimulating a "regional" dramatic movement, largely concentrated in the work of the Manchester Playgoers' Society. A tentative trial run was launched on September 23, 1907, at the Midland Hotel Theatre, and this proved so encouragingly successful that the following year she took over the Gaiety, formed a company, presented a short season in the spring, reconstructed the playhouse and finally opened it as a repertory (although with a deliberate avoidance of that title) on September 7.[2]

[1] *The Splendid Years* (1955), p. 75. All the related Irish theatrical activities of this period remain outside the scope of the present survey, chiefly because of their nationalistic aims. Among them were the Leinster Stage Society, the Gaelic Repertory Theatre, and the National Players, as well as the play-producing group established at Cork, the home of J. B. MacCarthy and Daniel Corkery. Towards the beginning of the century the Ulster Literary Theatre Society was established on the model of the similarly-named Dublin venture, and ultimately, in 1929, this grew into the Belfast Repertory Theatre.

[2] A full record appears in Rex Pogson's *Miss Horniman and the Gaiety Theatre, Manchester* (1952). Harold Brighouse has an interesting personal

Throughout the course of its career up to 1917, the Gaiety succeeded in developing still another theatrical impulse: in its stress on the "regional" it may perhaps be associated with the Irish theatre's "national" motivation, but in addition it tended to place particular emphasis upon what may be called the "social" content of the new plays which it selected for production. Although the war compelled it to close its doors after only a few active seasons, memories of what it had achieved were a potent force in the establishment of the Rushholme Theatre, opened in 1923, where the repertory idea was pursued on more popular lines; and it should be remembered that from 1916 onwards the Unnamed Society, an active amateur association which soon managed to transform a disused carpet warehouse into its own Little Theatre, carried on the tradition set up by the Gaiety in giving support to young local playwrights: in this its director, F. Sladen-Smith, himself the author of several of the dramas it has presented, played an important rôle.

Ireland thus had had its theatrical renaissance, the stage enthusiasts of the English Midlands had begun to stimulate the dramatic exploitation of regional themes and characters, and it was only to be expected that the same spirit should penetrate into Wales and Scotland. Unfortunately in the former area the goal was not reached during this period: although numerous amateur associations were founded, although performances of plays were introduced into meetings of the Eisteddfod and although the year 1914 saw the adoption of a scheme for the setting-up of a Welsh National Drama Company, nothing even vaguely resembling the Abbey or Miss Horniman's Gaiety was brought into being during those years.[1] Scotland was more fortunate. Suddenly,

account of its early days in "The Manchester Drama", an essay reprinted as a pamphlet from *The Manchester Quarterly*, xxxvi, April 1917, 75–90. A journal designed to support the work of the theatre, *The Manchester Playgoer*, edited by Ben Ormerod, was launched in 1911.

[1] Despite this, there was a fairly active application to the drama by several authors. A general account of these plays appears in Olive E. Hart's *The Drama in Modern Wales: A Brief History of Welsh Playwriting from 1900 to the Present Day* (1928).

and rather unexpectedly, a Scottish Playgoers' Company (later to be known as the Scottish Repertory Theatre Company) took over the Glasgow Royalty Theatre in 1909 and there, for several years, a permanent company under the lively direction of Alfred Wareing did excellent work. Even although it was admittedly inspired by what had been achieved in Dublin and by what was being aimed at in Manchester, its inception and general objectives were different. No doubt George Calderon was correct in declaring that it had come into being "as a direct effort of Scotsmen in general, and Glasgow men in particular, to throw off an allegiance (which they had never given) to London's despotic sway in the Drama",[1] but his correctness was, so to say, restricted and confined: what he really meant was that this repertory's chief aim was to present to Glasgow audiences plays distinct from those popular London successes which were borne northwards by touring companies from the metropolis: essentially the theatre owed its creation, not to nationalistic sentiment or to any urgent wish on the part of young dramatists for a stage on which their writings might be shown, but to a desire on the part of at least a section of the public to have the opportunity of seeing a variety of good and interesting plays. Thus to the other diverse motivations already mentioned may be added that of the "playgoers". The repertory was founded by "some of Glasgow's leading citizens", acting in conjunction with two University professors, W. Macneile Dixon and J. S. Phillimore; while one or two original Scottish plays crept into its programmes, these programmes were comprehensive in their variety; the theatre's focus was set, not on regional scenes, but on scenes of dramatic quality.

At the start it received fair support, but soon it found itself in financial difficulties, was temporarily suspended in 1912, and finally closed its accounts in 1915. Meanwhile, something akin to the spirit animating certain perfervid Irish dramatic associations began to become apparent in other quarters. In 1913 D. Glen MacKemmie, who, in the

[1] Note at the end of his play, *The Fountain* (1911).

words of Gordon Bottomley,[1] "was secretary, inspiration, engine and boiler of a patriotic association in Glasgow, The St Andrew's Society,"

> struck by the Abbey Theatre's success, conceived that a drama branch of his Society might further his one devotion of Scottish Nationalism. He looked around, and was advised that a good amateur actor, one Ralph Purnell, an Englishman working in Glasgow, was the man to help him artistically. Between them they launched their branch; and it succeeded so well that eventually it outgrew the St. Andrew's Society, and took on a separate being of its own.

Although this account may require some modification and expansion, Bottomley's words well reflect the emotions which brought the new movement into being. The war interrupted immediate development of this more patriotic venture, but at the beginning of 1921 the offshoot from the St Andrew's Society, now called the Scottish National Players, presented three original Scottish plays at the Royal Institute in Glasgow, and in the following year it was reconstituted as the Scottish National Theatre Society.[2] In 1927 a new organisation came into being, with the support of Sir James Barrie, Neil Munro and Sir Johnston Forbes-Robertson, and during the year following Robert Fenemore established the Masque Theatre in Edinburgh as a professional touring group.

The Glasgow Repertory, meanwhile, had been largely responsible for the start of a kindred venture in Liverpool. At a meeting of the Liverpool Playgoers' Society in 1910 there came a happy conjunction of events: Alfred Wareing delivered an inspiring account of what was happening in Scotland; several members of the audience expressed a wish to contribute to a guarantee fund for a similar venture in their own city; W. W. Kelly, an enthusiastic theatre-man

[1] Private letter, dated July 12, 1933.

[2] See a pamphlet entitled *The Scottish National Theatre Venture* (1953). Like several other similar organisations, this play-producing society launched a magazine of its own, *The Scottish Playgoer*, but apparently it did not endure beyond the year of its birth, 1923.

who, after an active career in the United States, had settled down in England as manager-proprietor of Kelly's Theatre, offered to lend his playhouse for a trial season; and a bright young local author, Ronald Jeans, already dazzled by the stage, persuaded an actor-friend of his, Basil Dean,[1] to join with him in promoting the experiment. So successful was the trial season that a Limited Liability Company was formed on a broader basis than had been attempted elsewhere, drawing its finances, not from single generous donors or from a limited circle of supporters, but from the investments made by no fewer than 1,300 shareholders. The Star Theatre was purchased, and, after renovations, was opened, as the Playhouse, by the Liverpool Repertory Theatre on November 11, 1911. Here too, of course, the war brought dark times, and there was a danger that the Playhouse might have to close: what is particularly interesting is the fact that in 1914 the salaried members of the house immediately founded a "Theatre Artistes' and Staff's Commonwealth" and made themselves responsible for carrying on its performances, thus establishing the basis for its later distinguished career.[2]

By this time the development of repertory theatres had become such as to induce the Stage Society, at its meeting on December 11, 1911, to set up a Repertory Theatre Association, designed to assist the already existing organisations and to stimulate still further developments of a like kind.[3] The next important event, a most notable one, occurred with the opening, on February 13, 1913, of the Birmingham Repertory Theatre, the first company of its kind to possess

[1] The earliest part of Basil Dean's long and distinguished career is recorded in *Seven Ages: An Autobiography 1888–1927* (1970).

[2] Grace W. Goldie provides an excellent account of the Playhouse's accomplishments and vicissitudes in *The Liverpool Repertory Theatre, 1911–1935* (1935). The only regrettable feature of this volume is that she does not indicate the precise dates of the numerous plays which were first presented by this company – a particularly unfortunate omission since it would seem that even the theatre's archives do not possess a complete and detailed record.

[3] The term "repertory" had now become so potent that purely amateur groups seized upon it, as, for example, did the "Bushey Repertory Theatre" when it gave its first performance on November 29, 1913.

a home designed especially for its own use. The success, then and later, of this organisation depended largely upon a set of fortunate conditions determined in the main by one man.[1] In Barry Jackson, knighted in 1925, it found both a wealthy Maecenas and an inspiring director whose early training in architecture and music and whose experience with the Pilgrim Players had given him a keen awareness of the problems and aims of actors, producers and scenic-artists – without, however, leading him towards a desire to apply himself exclusively to any one of these theatrical arts – a man who set his gaze on the single objective of bringing to his audiences the best and most impressive plays, ancient and modern, native and foreign, which he could find. Throughout its long career, the Birmingham Repertory did not neglect local authors: John Drinkwater, indeed, was one of its original founders: but in the choice of plays no national, regional, social or ideological considerations influenced its management.

Naturally, the outbreak of war in 1914 curtailed, even terminated, further developments within the repertory sphere, and, when hostilities ceased, rapidly rising costs introduced a serious new problem. Yet just as soon as normal life resumed, the movement caught up at the point it had left, although it may be noted that, in general, the new impetus was related rather to that exemplified in the Glasgow and Birmingham repertories than to that which had been a powerful force in Dublin and Manchester. It should be noted, too, that during these later years the activities of some among the larger

[1] Bache Matthews, in *A History of the Birmingham Repertory Theatre* (1924), narrates the early activities of this playhouse, and the story is carried on in T. C. Kemp's *The Birmingham Repertory Theatre* (revised edition, 1948): a later, excellently appreciative, survey of its fortunes appears in J. C. Trewin's *The Birmingham Repertory Theatre, 1913–1963* (1963). Its influence outside its native home is dealt with by G. W. Bishop in *Barry Jackson and the London Theatre* (1933). The ultimate source of its being is, of course, to be sought in the amateur ventures of the Pilgrim Players (see above p. 55): interesting records of their aims and wanderings may be found in two volumes of *The Scallop Shell, being the Organ of the Pilgrim Players* (1911): later, in 1923, the theatre inaugurated another journal, *The Gong*, but this was short-lived.

amateur groups and of several professional managers began to play an ever larger part in this development. A few examples may be cited as illustrations. During the summer of 1914 a Little Theatre had been established by the Bristol Playgoers' Club: although the conditions then prevailing forced it to shut its doors almost immediately, the spirit which had inspired its creation remained, and in 1923 it was restarted, through the joint endeavours of the Playgoers' Club and the city's Rotary Club. A glance at the list of its productions from then on to 1930 indicates that its well-chosen programme of plays was deliberately designed to be "popular", in the best sense of that word.[1] As early as February 10, 1913, a group of amateurs ambitiously launched a Sheffield Repertory Theatre, giving their first performances at a local Temperance Hall; later, they engaged H. M. Prentice as a professional producer, took a further step by bringing in two professional players, a "leading man" and a "leading lady", and, finally, after converting a disused chapel into a playhouse, increased the number of professionals to four.[2] At the other extreme stand playhouses such as the Alexandra in Birmingham. This theatre, bought in 1911 by Leon Salberg, early welcomed extended visits from the Raynor Repertory Company – a group, run by Harold Raynor, which, despite its twentieth-century title, was what at an earlier date would have been called a "stock" circuit troupe. Later, in 1927, an Alexandra Repertory Company was formed, and, although at first its productions left much to be desired, the almost unbroken career of this organisation, together with its steadily rising standards, calls for due attention and praise.[3]

[1] See *A Short History of Bristol's Little Theatre: First and Second Seasons* (1925): this may be associated with M. E. Board's *The Story of the Bristol Stage, 1490–1925* (1926).

[2] In 1928 this organisation became a limited liability company: a statement of the organisation was printed in 1942, as a *Memorandum and Articles of Association of the Sheffield Repertory Company Ltd.* On its activities see T. A. Seed, *The Sheffield Repertory Theatre: A History* (1959).

[3] The way in which a commercial organisation such as this is bound up with later developments of a non-commercial kind is well illustrated in the

Thus, in various centres and under diverse organisational methods, the repertory concept was pursued. Adventuresomely, the Plymouth Repertory Theatre was set up by two professional theatre-men, G. S. King and H. D. Parry, in 1915; after continuing for many years, it gave way in 1929 to a new organisation, The Plymouth Repertory Players, under the inspiration of G. B. Copping. The Southend Repertory Theatre, performing under the direction of H. Hodgson-Bentley at the local Ambassadors', was established in 1923. During the early twenties, several citizens of Leeds suddenly became active in three quite separate directions. A forward-looking industrialist, W. B. Dow, started by organising lectures on drama for his employees and by taking groups of them to professional productions: interest thus being aroused, the next step was almost inevitable – the workers' desire to act their own pieces: Dow accordingly converted a hall into a playhouse, all the performers and spectators contributed one penny a-piece to cover expenses, and what was then known as the Industrial Theatre expanded by associating itself with amateur groups from other factories: in 1921, J. R. Gregson was appointed as Welfare Coach, and for three years a varied and exciting programme of plays was presented, the venture closing only because a trade depression restricted Dow's ability to continue his support and led to a decline in the paying membership.[1] Meanwhile, just about the time when the Industrial Theatre was nearing its close, Lascelles Abercrombie and Laurie Ramsden were responsible for setting up the Leeds Arts Theatre: this

activities of Leon Salberg's son, Derek. In 1936 he succeeded his father as general manager of the Alexandra, thereafter directing its fortunes, while concurrently he has played a prominent part in assisting the Arts Council (as a member of its Drama Panel) and the National Theatre (on the board of which he was an original member). M. F. K. Fraser has a detailed account of *The Alexandra Theatre* (1948).

[1] This was by no means an isolated experiment. Other industrialists are known to have engaged in similar activities: thus, for example, John Drinkwater's early "masques" were commissioned by George Cadbury "for performance by a large number – between two and three hundred –" of his employees at Bournville (*The Collected Plays of John Drinkwater* (1925), vol. i, preface, p. vii).

operated on a semi-amateur, semi-professional basis, aiming particularly at the encouragement of young authors, and towards the end of the present period plans were being made for its transformation into a wholly professional playhouse. The third movement was the establishment, largely due to the inspiration of Charles F. Smith, of the Leeds Civic Playhouse: here the actors were almost wholly amateur, presenting their productions under the guidance of such directors as J. R. Gregson, Nugent Monck and Edith Craig, and what particularly distinguished it was the fact that, instead of charging for tickets, it relied upon a silver collection from those attending its performances. As in a microcosm this one city thus provided an image of the larger whole. The Industrial Theatre might almost be regarded in its inception as "educational", linking up with the interest reflected in the report on *The Drama in Education* published in 1926: the Arts Theatre in its very name evokes thought of the whole tradition which stemmed from the Moscow Art Theatre: while the term "Civic", particularly when associated with the abolition of a box office, points forward to the idea that, as Alfred Wareing expressed it, "there is as definite a place in the civic life of our great cities for a free theatre as for the free library and art gallery".

Thus from divers sources the little theatres continued to spring forth. In 1923 J. B. Fagan assembled his young professional company of Oxford Players, with the announced intention of specialising in the performance of dramas rarely if ever seen on the stage. At Hull, the enthusiasm of the local Amateur Dramatic Society induced a visiting director, A. R. Whatmore, to gather together some professional actors for a trial repertory season in 1924 in a lecture hall; this was so well received that the town's Playgoers' Society successfully raised a guarantee fund; the lecture hall was refitted, and soon the enterprise had grown sufficiently strong to be formally transformed into the Hull Repertory Theatre. A similar venture in Newcastle likewise rose out of a lengthy amateur tradition, stretching back to the Clarion Dramatic Society of 1911: during the early twenties the relatively novel term, "People's Theatre",[1] was applied to some of the productions, and in 1928 a Repertory Playhouse, part-amateur and part-professional, was established. At Northampton the local Repertory Players, aided by the associated Playgoers' Society, succeeded in the hard task of giving regular seasons at the Opera House from 1927 onwards.[2] And theatres at two other centres, Cambridge and Norwich, deserve particular mention because, paradoxically, they stand contrasted in their inception and organisation, and because they both arose out of a common interest in "stage production". The Cambridge Festival Theatre was opened, in 1926, by Terence Gray in a playhouse constructed out of a religious meeting-hall which itself had originally been fashioned out of the old Barnwell Theatre Royal. Here "theatre" and not "drama" ruled, with concentration on directorial art and scenic novelty and with unceasing controversy arising from its brief but bizarrely tempestuous career.[3] Utterly different was the atmosphere at the Maddermarket Theatre at Norwich. Its origins are to be found in some performances which a group of amateurs, headed by Nugent Monck, presented in 1914 within the hall of an ancient inn. Hardly had they started their activities when war came, but the impulse which had stimulated their association remained unimpaired. The hall was re-opened in 1919, and the reception given to the company was such as to warrant further extension; an abandoned church was converted into an Elizabethan-style playhouse, opened in 1921, and soon the Norwich Players and their inspirer were acquiring a

[1] For further uses of this term see pp. 72 and 83. Its first appearance in England seems to have come in 1912 when a Yiddish People's Theatre was established in Shoreditch.

[2] See Aubrey Dyas, *Adventure in Repertory* (1948).

[3] Apart from its actual performances, this theatre tried to excite attention and interest by various means: the programmes were printed in such a manner that they might be read even when the house-lights were down; a lively *Festival Theatre Review* was published by the management; and, for those to whom drink as well as drama made appeal, the resources of an exquisite cellar were available for its patrons. See Terence Gray, *Dance Drama: Experiments in the Art of the Theatre* (1926).

reputation extending far beyond their native home. Although the programmes were by no means confined to Elizabethan dramas, obviously Nugent Monck's chief interest lay in open-stage presentations, and thus, despite the fact that Terence Gray looked forward towards expressionistic modernism while Monck looked back to what already had attracted Poel, Norwich and Cambridge strangely united in a common objective.[1]

In all these different yet related ways the vacuum caused by the demise of the old stock-companies was being filled up during these years, and the place of the Victorian Theatres Royal was being occupied by the Repertories. Meanwhile, it was but natural that in London many anxious voices were to be heard pleading for a theatre which might offer to an interested public plays different from those provided by the actor–managers and the commercial entrepreneurs; and, in a limited sense, it might almost be said that London was indeed first in the field. The Abbey was not opened until December 27, 1904: the famous Court seasons had started three months earlier, on October 24. The story of how these seasons came into being is well-known: J. E. Vedrenne, then manager of the Court, invited Harley Granville-Barker to take charge of a production of *The Two Gentlemen of Verona*; the latter agreed on condition that the theatre should sponsor six matinées of Shaw's *Candida*; the success of the matinées and the intimate rapport established between the two men led to the idea of trying a new experiment in "repertory"; and thus the Court, during its next three seasons, made

[1] See R. H. Mottram, *The Maddermarket Theatre* (1929). Attention may here be drawn to one other organisation which, although it can hardly be described as a repertory theatre, was closely related to what was happening in that area. At Bath, a Citizen House had been established in 1913, chiefly for the purpose of providing accommodation for classes for adults arranged by the Workers Educational Association. The following year an additional building, which included a Little Theatre, was opened as a Soldiers' Club; Christmas 1915 saw the start of theatrical performances with the presentation of a mystery play; and later the House inaugurated a kind of theatre school for amateurs, with instruction in all branches of stage work, and at the same time organised a travelling group which carried plays round the nearby countryside.

theatrical history.[1] Thirty-two plays in all were presented, and London's playgoers were offered dramatic variety of an entirely unaccustomed kind. Nevertheless, when we examine the programmes it becomes amply evident that in two very important respects the "repertory" system adopted here was far removed from that which was so eagerly desired by the *avant-garde*. First, out of 988 performances no fewer than 701 were of eleven plays by one single author, George Bernard Shaw. Those seasons were responsible for bringing this dramatist to public notice and for doing so they deserve warmest praise – yet this distinctly does not come within the true concept of "repertory". And secondly, without in any respect seeking to belittle the significance of the Court's work, it may reasonably be said that the Barker–Vedrenne partnership was, in fact, not an experiment in the setting-up of a new kind of playhouse, but rather an adaptation of the existing actor–manager theatre. Nor were Granville-Barker's later efforts different. In September 1907 he and Vedrenne ran a similar season at the Savoy, and during the early summer of the following year they organised a series of matinées at the Haymarket, while in 1909 the former persuaded Charles Frohman to launch a season at the Duke of York's – but, despite the public interest displayed in some of the offerings, this last venture resulted in a loss, closing after 128 performances of ten plays. Nor was Granville-Barker's later attempt, in conjunction with his wife Lillah MacCarthy, to create a London "repertory" playhouse at the St James's in 1913 any more profitable.

The spirit which gave life to these experiments can be traced in many quarters, some of them rather unexpected. On the same April day in 1909 when Frohman announced

[1] Desmond MacCarthy's *The Court Theatre 1904–1907* (1907) gives a full account of what was achieved during these years and usefully adds as an appendix reproductions of the programmes for the various plays. It should be observed that the sub-title to this volume is "A Commentary and a Criticism". Irving Zucker gives somewhat wider range to *Le Court Théâtre (1904–1914) et l'évolution du théâtre anglais contemporain* (1931). For later critical analysis of this venture see *Harley Granville Barker* (1955) by C. B. Purdom. Further discussion appears below, pp. 218–20.

his plans for the Duke of York's season, Herbert Trench advertised a proposed scheme at the Haymarket whereby half of each week was to be devoted to a long-run piece and the other half assigned to a variety of new plays of a less popular kind. Nothing came of this latter proposal, but even the voicing of such an idea has significance. When, too, Beerbohm Tree inaugurated his "Afternoon Theatre" in 1908 he was clearly under the influence of current theories, and he actually used the term "Repertory" for the 1910 "London Theatre Festival" which he organised at His Majesty's. In 1910 Gertrude Kingston started her experimental programme at the Little Theatre, and from 1919 to 1929 Lena Ashwell's Players were active at the Bijou (which she re-named the Century) and elsewhere: in 1923 the Reandean management followed the tradition set by Frohman and Tree by running "Playbox" matinées at the St Martin's. Of a more revolutionary character was J. T. Grein's attempt, also in the year 1923, to establish a People's Theatre at the Whitechapel Pavilion; this endeavour proved a complete failure, but that phrase, "People's Theatre", was fascinating numbers of enthusiasts during this time, so that, besides its employment at Newcastle,[1] it was adopted by Nancy Price when in 1930 she launched her People's National Theatre at the Fortune, while, as will be seen later, there were authors and publishers ready to write and print series of "Plays for a People's Theatre".

Although not inspired by any "repertory" concept, Nigel Playfair's management of the Hammersmith Lyric between 1918 and 1929 may be said to belong to the same milieu:[2] his skill in engaging and encouraging such artists as George Sheringham, Lovat Fraser, Doris Zinkeisen and Norman Wilkinson made it a colourful oasis for many weary playgoers. The Hampstead Everyman was opened in 1920, the "Q" in 1924, the Barnes in 1925, and these, added to the Queen's and the Regent under the direction of Barry Jackson,

[1] See above p. 69.

[2] See Sir Nigel Playfair, *Hammersmith Hoy* (1930) and his *Story of the Lyric Theatre, Hammersmith* (1925).

combined to offer London's public a fairly rich selection of plays both native and foreign, while the Arts Theatre Club, founded in 1927, provided still another playhouse for special experiments. About the same time Peter Godfrey and Molly Veness started work in restricted quarters at the top of a warehouse in Floral Street, Covent Garden, running their Gate Theatre Salon as a club,[1] which, because the productions gave to *avant-garde* spectators their first glimpses of German and Russian revolutionary expressionism, attracted sufficient attention to warrant its removal, under the revised name of Gate Theatre Studio, on October 22, 1927, to a roomier home in Villiers-street at what had once been Gatti's Restaurant and Music Hall.[2]

All of these undertakings were consciously and deliberately inspired by theatre enthusiasts, but meanwhile, somewhat like Topsy, there began to grow up almost unnoticed a completely unexpected development in a derelict music-hall across the Thames beyond Waterloo Bridge. Originally built in 1818 as the Coburg, and later called the Victoria, this house had specialised in melodrama until it was – unsuccessfully – transformed into a music-hall. This was the time when in many large cities groups of social reformers, realising the evils of drink, were acquiring or building public houses, restaurants and hotels designed to be run on a temperance plan; and perhaps it was not surprising that one of the most energetic among London's reformers, Emma Cons, should have had the happy thought of purchasing the vacant building which once had dispensed both liquor and variety, and of opening it, in 1880, as the Royal Victoria Hall and Coffee Tavern. At first, customers were enticed within by fitful song and instrumental music, but when the management passed into the hands of Miss Cons' niece, Lilian Baylis, films were introduced, then came performances of operas in English, and finally in 1914 the "Old Vic",

[1] Originally opened on October 30, 1925.

[2] A not dissimilar venture, although less successful, was Play Room Six, or Playroom 6, established by Reginald Price and Hilda Maude at 6 New Compton Street in 1927.

against the advice of almost every theatre expert in London but aided by a boldly generous gift from the musical comedy author and manager Sir George Dance, audaciously and almost impudently set itself up as Shakespeare's London home. During the war years Sir Philip Ben Greet conducted its presentations, while during the twenties a series of skilful directors (Robert Atkins, Andrew Leigh, Harcourt Williams) and a company of very great actors, including in their number Sir John Gielgud, Sir Ralph Richardson and Sir Laurence Olivier, advanced its reputation step by step so that those who first had scoffed – and maybe even shuddered – at its performances and its pretensions now richly lauded the theatre and the extraordinary lady whose pertinacity had brought it into being.[1]

Shakespeare thus found his London home, and appropriately the same years provided him with a permanent residence in his own native town. Here the initial impetus had come from a generous donation made by Sir Charles Flower for the inauguration of a summer festival in 1879 and for the building of a Memorial Theatre; but it was only when Sir Frank Benson took charge in 1886 that this centre slowly but with a certain sureness of step made steady advance. In 1925 it secured its Royal Charter, displayed the strength necessary to overcome the disaster which befell it when, during the following year, its theatre was destroyed by fire, and finally in 1932 settled down within its new Royal Shakespeare Theatre.[2]

[1] There are many accounts of this theatre's fortunes. Among these may be mentioned particularly: H. Chance Newton, *The Old Vic and Its Associations* (1923), E. J. Dent, *A Theatre for Everybody* (1945), Harcourt Williams, *Four Years at the Old Vic* (1935) and *Old Vic Saga* (1949), Cicely Hamilton and Lilian Baylis, *The Old Vic* (1926). In 1938 two volumes were devoted particularly to the theatre's foundress – *Lilian Baylis*, by Sybil and Russell Thorndike, and *Vic-Wells: The Work of Lilian Baylis*, a composite collection of essays under the editorship of Harcourt Williams.

[2] The history of this playhouse too is well documented: among the extensive literature attached to it may be cited: M. C. Day and J. C. Trewin, *The Shakespeare Memorial Theatre* (1932), A. K. Chesterton, *Brave Enterprise: A History of the Shakespeare Memorial Theatre, Stratford-upon-Avon* (1934), Ruth Ellis, *The Shakespeare Memorial Theatre* (1948) and T. C. Kemp and J. C. Trewin, *The Stratford Festival* (1953).

Many cultured precisians had, at the start, smiled contemptuously at Benson's muscularly athletic treatment of Shakespeare, just as they had dismissed the Old Vic's early productions as deplorably awful, fit fare for the rough popular audiences who crowded past its doors: nevertheless, what is particularly interesting in the story of these two endeavours is this – that although numerous intellectual idealists such as Granville-Barker and Archer worked hard for the establishment of a National Theatre, no such Theatre at this time came into being through their efforts, while a playhouse which had originated in a social reform concept has now expanded into the headquarters of the National Theatre Company; and that another playhouse, which began in a small town as an expression of civic pride, eventually developed into the Stratford–Aldwych Royal Shakespeare Company, and as such may properly be regarded as a second national theatre. In stage affairs, as in life generally, providence often works strangely its wonders to perform.

This impression of strangeness is further increased when we turn to consider the various impulses which during the first years of the century brought earlier vague talk about a national theatre from the sphere of ineffectual speculation fairly close to practical reality. It is, of course, quite right that we should give due praise to Archer and Granville-Barker for their *A National Theatre: Schemes and Estimates* which, issued privately in 1904, was made public three years later;[1] but it was not this which in May 1905 prompted the

[1] This was the first attempt to discuss the project in practical terms, although it should be noted that the idea had been in the minds of several men from the middle of the nineteenth century onwards. The bibliographical account of *English Theatrical Literature 1559–1900* (1970) prepared by J. F. Arnott and J. W. Robinson cites as the first plea for the establishment of such a playhouse a pamphlet by "Dramaticus" printed in 1847: this was followed in 1848 by William Wilson's demand for a theatre devoted to the production of Shakespeare's plays: in 1871 Tom Taylor advocated the institution of an English "Comédie Française", a proposal backed up shortly afterwards by a *Scheme for the Establishment of a National Theatre (somewhat similar to the "Comédie Française")*, written apparently by S. Stringer Bate; in 1878 George Godwin delivered

introduction into the musical comedy *The Spring Chicken* (produced at the Gaiety) of a song chanted by George Grossmith, clad in Shakespearian costume –

> The day of the National Theatre
> Enthusiasts tell us is near.

The "Schemes and Estimates" had, certainly, been endorsed by an imposing roster of men prominent in the theatre world – Irving, Bancroft, Barrie, d'Oyly Carte, Hare, Jones and Pinero; yet, looking back, perhaps we may come to decide that the true driving force came unexpectedly from a modest proposal made by an otherwise forgotten Mr Bishop for the erection of a statue to England's Bard. This suggestion led to the offer by a certain Mr Bridges of £1,000 (later increased to £2,500) for just such a purpose, and early in 1905 a Shakespeare Memorial Committee was formed to determine precisely what should be done with the money. No immediate action was taken, and three years later Sir John Hare sent a letter to *The Times* arguing that, while statues might be regarded as quite satisfactory in their own way, a bolder attempt to set up a Shakespeare playhouse would be much more worthy of respect and support. A second group, accordingly, was constituted under the imposing title of the National Theatre Shakespeare Memorial Committee: this body, after considerable consultation, estimated that such a theatre might involve expenditure of half a million pounds; an anonymous donor (Carl Meyer) sent in a cheque for £70,000; a petition was addressed to the London County Council asking for a site, and a public appeal was launched;

a plea for a national theatre at a Cheltenham Congress of the Social Science Association; and this seems to have inspired J. R. Planché, during the following year, to prepare his *Suggestions for Establishing an English Art Theatre* (a particularly interesting anticipation of the later use of this term). After 1900 the subject became more frequently discussed – and discussed at greater length. Thus, for example, Walter Stephens' *A Plea for a National Repertory Theatre* (1905), although issued a few months after Granville-Barker and Archer had completed their first *Schemes and Estimates*, was presented to the public a couple of years before the publication of their volume: this volume, it may be observed, was revised as *A National Theatre* in 1930.

the year 1916 was suggested as an auspicious date for the opening of the proposed theatre and for the holding of a Shakespeare Exhibition. However, in spite of the promulgation of an illustrated booklet containing such photographs of foreign national theatres as might be likely to shame the British public into creating a similar playhouse of their own, in spite of the publication of ardent supplications like Walter Stephens' *The Proposed World's Tribute to Shakespeare: A Plea for the Erection of a Memorial Statue and National Theatre* (1905) and H. A. Jones' *The Foundations of a National Drama* (1913), and in spite of fund-raising efforts like "The Masque of Shakespeare" (held in Regent's Park on July 30, 1910) and the "Shakespeare Ball" (at the Albert Hall, June 20, 1911),[1] the committee had not succeeded in gathering more than an additional £30,000 before its work was suspended in 1914. It is true that London's most distinguished actors enthusiastically supported the efforts of the Shakespeare Tercentenary Committee which organised a performance of *Julius Caesar* at Drury Lane on May 2, 1916, and which was responsible for the publication of a magnificently illustrated *Tribute to the Genius of William Shakespeare*, but obviously that year was not a propitious one for the further discussion of plans for the erection of a new theatre.

Thus the tercentenary arrived and went: and when the question came once more into debate, the committee found itself split in half. One group was all in favour of using the accumulated funds to support already-existing companies engaged in presenting Shakespearian plays, but this proposal was vigorously opposed by others, led by Sir Israel Gollancz: and deadlock resulted. Mainly through the activities of Geoffrey Whitworth, a conference was held at Stratford-upon-Avon in 1919; in 1924 William Archer unsuccessfully pleaded for the launching of a fresh public appeal; the British Drama League not only announced a competition for a national theatre plan but also was largely responsible

[1] See Mrs George Cornwallis-West, *Shakespeare Memorial: Souvenir of the Shakespeare Ball* (1911).

for encouraging the Board of Education to prepare its report on *The Drama in Adult Education* (1926);[1] and in 1929 new moves were being made when, after discussions with several interested members of Parliament, a panel was set up to "promote an agreed scheme for submission to the Prime Minister".[2]

In themselves, perhaps, these and other related facts may be thought to possess no more than slight historical interest, yet they have real, and deeper, significance for the way in which they indicate the forces operative at the time. In thinking of the development of the national theatre idea we are naturally inclined to consider its inception and growth in terms of the few notable volumes which presented the arguments in favour of its establishment, or in terms of the larger conferences which sought to encourage support for its aims, but a true appreciation of what was happening at this juncture in the theatrical world can be gained only from consideration of the lesser things as well as of the large, of what may seem at first to be unimportant on the periphery as well as of what appears immediately significant in the centre.

5. *The "Modern" Movement: (b) Societies, Pageants and Festivals*

Centrally placed and of paramount importance in the development of the new movement during the early years of the present century was, of course, the creation of the repertory theatres, associated with the concept of the subsidised playhouse as opposed to the commercial: here was something significantly novel and distinctive. Nevertheless, even the most cursory survey of this development must reveal at once that neither the philosophic concept nor the practical endeavours can be separated from the second characteristic development of this period – a development which, although

[1] See above pp. 57, 68 and 78.

[2] Most of the various moves were, naturally, recorded and given comment in *The Stage*, and the story is summarised in R. Findlater's *The Unholy Trade* (1952) and in Geoffrey Whitworth's *The Theatre of My Heart* (1930) and *The Making of a National Theatre* (1951).

of almost equal value, is often neglected or cavalierly dismissed. If the repertory theatres were a representative feature of the time, so too were the proliferating theatrical societies and clubs. Some of these were associations of professionals, and at least the more active, from the Stage Society to the Repertory Players, are not likely to be ignored. Already has been noted the way in which several of the repertories grew originally out of amateur enthusiasms: the Abbey assumed its being from a venture of this kind, and the Birmingham Repertory was metamorphosed out of the Pilgrim Players. These, too, cannot escape notice; and with them will be associated what was achieved at the Maddermarket in Norwich. In addition, some individual efforts may be borne in mind; the Stockport Garrick Society, for example, which was founded – as a break-away from a Unitarian Sunday School – in 1901 and which was still vigorously carrying on its performances at the close of this period, included among its productions a wide selection of the "advanced" drama of those years; or the related Altrincham Garrick Society, which has a record no less remarkable, with more than 150 plays, 22 of them original, given between 1913 and 1929.[1] The dramatist Herbert Swears has left us memorable testimony concerning the way in which some of these associations had developed the skills of numerous actors and actresses who later were to become well-known on the professional stage,[2] and, perhaps even more significantly, the prolific playwright Louis N. Parker has freely acknowledged his indebtedness to the amateurs who called themselves the Strolling Players, to the club organised by William Jackson Houlston at Erdington and even to the Stock Exchange Operatic and Dramatic Society through whose enthusiasm three of his works were brought before the public.[3]

Consideration of the achievements of individual groups, however, no matter how worthy these may be, is of less

[1] The importance of this association is well emphasised in Cecil Chisholm's *Repertory* (1934), pp. 180–6.

[2] *When All's Said And Done* (1937), pp. 65, 78–91.

[3] *Several of My Lives* (1928), pp. 270–1.

importance than a comprehensive appreciation of the force collectively exerted by the hundreds of dramatic clubs, both amateur and professional, which, as it were, suddenly exploded into being between the start of the century and 1930. Regarded separately, scores – perhaps hundreds – of these clubs call for no attention, yet when we take the area as a whole hardly anything can be put completely aside as devoid of interest. No profit could accrue from examining in particular the activities of, let us say, the Commercial Travellers Histrionic Society or of any other similar spouters' associations whose members rarely, if ever, raised their sights beyond the more antiquated titles in French's catalogues, or else the *Original Dramas, Farces, Operettas, &c. for Amateurs* published by Abel Heywood and Son, or the *Free Performing Original Plays* issued by Felix McGlennon. For these dreadful essays in the lesser drama no acting fees were demanded, and it must be assumed that the dozens of minor amateur societies seized upon them for their cheapness alone. Yet even so – even when we go further and recognise the truth inherent in Norman Marshall's assertion that the amateur is "seldom interested in the theatre as a whole"[1] – these groups cannot be summarily dismissed from notice: in their very numbers they testified to the manner in which the "idea" of the theatre had seized upon the imagination of the age.[2]

Another entirely different category of societies might likewise tend to be neglected, not because the attention of their members was directed towards trivial objectives but because they usually did not seek themselves to participate

[1] *The Other Theatre* (1947), p. 85. Several interesting comments on the contributions made by the non-professionals appear in an article, "Aspects of the Amateur Movement" in *The Stage Year Book 1921–1925*, pp. 19–25.

[2] Perhaps we might be justified in going still further by taking note of the increasing number of social, and particularly working-men's, clubs which at this time demonstrated an interest in having dramatic performances at their annual and other meetings. The scope of this development can be gauged by the facts that in 1907 no fewer than 2,177 were registered on the rolls of a central federation and that at least three professional acting companies existed almost entirely for the purpose of catering to their needs.

in stage activities; yet, when their objectives are examined with care and when, once more, the societies themselves are taken not separately in isolation but as a collective unit, they can be seen as a force which, although anticipated in the latter years of the nineteenth century, was thoroughly characteristic of the spirit at work within the period and which in various ways played a notable part in the advancement of the new movement. With the formation of a London Playgoers Club in 1884 a fresh trend was suggested,[1] and this was broadened by the establishment of the Gallery First-Nighters Club in 1896 and of the O. P. Club in 1900. After 1900 similar groups sprang up almost everywhere, not only in the larger cities but also, as for example with the Worcestershire Playgoers Association, in areas geographically larger and less densely populated; and of even greater significance than their numbers was the fact that in their several districts they began to take an active part in sponsoring and supporting better kinds of dramatic performance. It has already been observed that some of the repertory theatres arose out of the stimulus provided by such local associations, and it may be further noted that there was hardly one of these playhouses, whatever its origin, which was not materially assisted in the pursuing of its work by some sort of club representing the audience.

In proceeding from brief general comment regarding these groups as a whole to more particular examination of the play-producing and play-encouraging societies the problem of how best to deal with their diverse activities becomes much more acute. So numerous were these organisations that it would be tedious and unprofitable to record them all by name, and even if this were to be attempted the fact that for many of them no detailed information is available would render a *catalogue raisonée* ill-balanced and almost certainly misleading. Still further, even if only a selected few were taken to represent the movement as a whole, a false impression would assuredly be created, since a large part

[1] For an account of its activities see B. W. Findon, *The Playgoers Club, 1884–1905: Its History and Memoirs* (1906).

of their interest and value depends upon their variety. All that can be attempted here is a kind of impressionistic survey, with ample choice of diverse examples, and this, it would seem, may best be accomplished by examining the expansion of this "society" movement in terms of time.

During the very first years of the new century, it must be admitted, things seemed to move rather slowly. The Stockport Garrick Society was founded in 1901[1] and the Mermaid Society in 1903,[2] but the general rush did not arrive until about 1905. By that time the Mermaid Society had grown into a Mermaid Repertory Theatre Society, producing a number of plays at the Great Queen Street Theatre, and alongside it emerged a New Stage Club, an English Drama Society and an association called the Pioneers.[3] Of these, the last was of particular importance. Created and guided by Herbert Swears, with the friendly assistance of a committee which included among its members Arthur Bourchier, W. L. Courtney, H. B. Irving and Violet Vanbrugh, its stated aim was "to produce plays dealing with all kinds of movements of interest at the moment" and to assist "social, political, and other Societies" through "the organisation of performances by professional or amateur players". Both its prominent sponsors and its implied emphasis upon the "modern" call for particular attention, and undoubtedly, until its end in 1908, its productions (which included Masefield's *Nan*) proved a real stimulus to those interested in promoting the new drama.[4]

[1] See above p. 79.

[2] Under the direction of Philip Carr, this was responsible for presenting a number of out-of-the-way plays. No doubt it served as a model for the many similarly-titled groups which later sprang up in colleges and universities.

[3] The Mermaid Society can be traced on to 1908, but little information is available concerning the New Stage Club. There is some reason for believing that the English Drama Society of 1905 may have been reconstituted in 1909 as the English Play Society, but the exact relationship between these two groups is not absolutely certain.

[4] In *When All's Done and Said* (1937), pp. 108–38, Herbert Swears records its activities from its inception in a letter addressed to the editor of *The Referee* in April 1905 onwards until, in the summer of 1908, he was forced to abandon his labour of love.

The next five years showed the movement gathering strength. A Literary Theatre Club, established in 1906 (and, as its name suggests, clearly influenced by the Dublin venture) carried on its activities until 1913. The following year came a significant development within the Actors Association when several of its members banded together as the Play Actors; from that year until 1928 this organisation played an important rôle by bringing forward both interesting foreign plays and plays by English authors. The Play Actors, of course, were purely professional, but non-professionals as well joined them in their efforts: about the same time came the formation of the Cambridge Marlowe Society and of the Amateur Players Association – the latter an anticipation of the British Drama League to come.[1]

Throughout the country we catch glimpses of newly-formed small groups akin to Birmingham's Pilgrim Players, while London saw the creation of various organisations, some of them with novel aims. A New Productions Club (also known as the Dramatic Productions Club) was added to the other similar bodies already active, and it was companioned by a Playwrights Association founded with the specific purpose of bringing untried dramas before at least a limited public, and also by a Rehearsal Company animated with kindred objectives.[2] A considerable number of performances were given by such new groups as the Civic and Dramatic Guild, the Curtain Raisers, the Dramatic Debaters and the Argonauts.[3] The first of the distinctively "political" organisations, the Actresses' Franchise Club, was founded in 1908, and from this came the Woman's Theatre of 1913:

[1] A National Operatic and Dramatic Association had been established in 1899, but apparently it was concerned more with musical performances than with the promotion of dramatic productions. Concerning an Amateur Dramatic Union, which was in existence by 1909, there seems to be little information available.

[2] The activities of the Playwrights Association led eventually to the setting up of the Playwrights Theatre in the early twenties.

[3] Naturally, the nature and the practical efforts varied considerably: most of them were broad in their aims, but others were akin to the Civic and Dramatic Guild, which seems to have been founded mainly for the purpose of presenting Shaw's *Press Cuttings*.

only a couple of years later, in 1910, the Socialist Party Dramatic Club was established.

Then suddenly the stirring in the air became a great gusty gale which continued to blow strongly until the outbreak of war. Closely-set isobars now covered the entire map of the country. The lead of the Stockport Garrick Society was followed by similarly-named associations at Altrincham,[1] Marple and Bury, while at the same time other enthusiasts were busily, although in somewhat humbler manner, occupying themselves with the task of stimulating dramatic interest among rural communities. It is certainly true that as early as 1894 there is record of the formation in Grasmere, under the inspiration of a rector's daughter, Miss Fletcher, of a local acting group intent upon performing a native dialect play: but one swallow does not make a summer, and the development of the village drama movement had to wait until the twentieth century for its widely-spread activities. Nor were such activities merely widely-spread, their interest rests even more upon their variety. No doubt much of the dramatic fare promoted in these country districts was deplorably poor; no doubt in certain other districts the principal endeavours differed hardly at all from those which had animated the work of Miss Fletcher in 1894, so that, for example, the activities of the later Grasmere Players were simply an extension of her earlier efforts: yet we can hardly refrain from experiencing surprise at observing how diversified were the aims of many of these groups. The presentation of Shakespearian dramas occupied the attention of the amateurs at Mell in Somerset; the Stoneland Players of West Hoathly in Sussex, even more ambitiously, concentrated upon the production of Greek dramas; the Cotswold Players did their best to bring poetic plays of different kinds before their local audiences; various companies, such as the Village Players of Hildenborough in Kent and of Great Hucklow in Derbyshire, eagerly selected for performance original plays or playlets written by authors resident in their areas; while several

[1] See p. 79.

other groups materially aided in encouraging the vogue of the pageant.[1]

The same expanding enthusiasm was evident in London, where every year that passed saw the formation of fresh play-producing associations – the New Players Society, the Oncomers Society (guided largely by H. F. Maltby, and aiming not only to present original plays but also to bring before the public and the managers "players not known in London"), the Adelphi Play Society (established by Maurice Elvey chiefly for the purpose of producing translations of Strindberg's works), the Dickens Repertory Company, the Drama Society (apparently the same as the London Drama and Arts Society, founded in 1911 and directed by Rathmell Wilson), the Black Cat Club (designed to provide a meeting-place for all who were "interested in the higher aims of the drama" and to present "one-act plays of merit"),[2] the Twelfth Night Players, the Foreign Theatre Society (also called Cosmopolis, with headquarters at 201 High Holborn), the Connoisseurs, the Arts and Dramatic Club, the Play-

[1] Precise records concerning the activities of these village performances as a whole are difficult – sometimes, indeed, impossible – to secure. Mary Kelly's *Village Theatre* (1939) unfortunately deals more with philosophical considerations than with practical achievements, and, although we may be grateful for the relevant information included in *The Drama in Adult Education* (1927), we must recognise that within its limited scope only a few representative organisations could be dealt with. For an appreciation of the wide range of dramatic work presented by these amateurs *A List of Plays for Young Players and Others*, published under the auspices of the Village Drama Society in 1928, deserves special attention: among the nearly four hundred titles cited are scores of comedies, dramas, fantasies and idylls written by numerous well-known authors, from Austin Dobson to John Drinkwater and Lord Dunsany, from Edna St Vincent Millay to A. A. Milne and Allan Monkhouse, from Bernard Shaw to Alfred Sutro and J. M. Synge. In view of the fact that hardly any of the rural acting groups were fortunate enough to find historians of their efforts, particular interest attaches to the survey made by L. du Garde Peach of *The Village Players, Great Hucklow* (1952), in which the uninterrupted activities of this association throughout a period of twenty-five years are recorded.

[2] The Richelieu Hotel in Oxford Street was the social centre, while the performances were given in the "Arts Centre" at 92 Mortimer Street: in 1913 the latter was described as "a meeting place where persons interested in Art can freely mix with artists".

fellows, the strangely-named Theatre in Eyre,[1] the Sidelights Dramatic Club, the Stage Players, the Advance Players, the Play Producers, the Century Play Society, the Authors Producing Society, and so on almost *ad infinitum*. Several of these hopefully-established organisations, of course, had but brief careers, but at least a few carried on their work for many seasons and even surmounted the difficulties of the war years: thus, for example, the Pioneer Players, established in 1911, succeeded – largely through the inspiration of Edith Craig – in remaining active until 1921; another group which exerted a long-enduring influence was the Morality Play Society, inspired largely by Mrs Edith Lyttleton and Mrs Percy Dearmer, the object of which was "to produce original Moralities, Mysteries, and Miracle plays, and other modern plays of an ideal nature".[2]

The deep and enduring impulse behind this expansive movement as a whole is well demonstrated by the fact that, although necessarily there had to be a sharp halt after 1914, at least a few new associations, both general and specialised in aim, made their appearance even during the period of hostilities, while a further vigorous surge forward came just as soon as general conditions permitted. A London Repertory Theatre performed at the Court in 1917; some enthusiasts established an Indian Dramatic Society, which, both under that title and with the more cumbersome appellation of the

[1] It may be assumed that this body, founded by Mrs Edith Lyttleton in 1912, took its name from the Eyre Arms Assembly Room in Finchley Road.

[2] The roster of names of its committee-members was mightily impressive. Princess Marie Louise was president, and the list of other committee members extended from the Earls Beauchamp, Plymouth, Portsmouth and Lytton to prominent theatrical personalities such as Tree, Benson, Bourchier, Martin-Harvey, Poel, Ellen Terry, Gertrude Kingston and Lena Ashwell, in addition to a variety of others like Sidney Colvin, Oliver Lodge, Charles Stanford, Henry Wood, Acton Bond and Cecil Sharp. It should be noted here that the above record of play-producing clubs is selective merely: if a total register were to be attempted, it would have to include both a large number of what might be styled "ordinary" amateur groups without any specialised aims and of other bodies, such as the Poetic Drama Society and the French Play Society, concerned with the promotion of special kinds of dramatic work.

Union of East and West Indian Art and Dramatic Society, remained sporadically active from 1915 to 1924; during 1915 and 1916 a London Welsh Stage Society put on several plays. When the time came for the resumption of the earlier activities, the later pattern was essentially the same as that which had already been established, and the emotional drive, released after having been pent-up for nearly five years, not only made its colours richer but also gave it a fresh firmness of outline. So successfully had the "Village Players" pursued their efforts that in 1918 an all-embracing Village Drama League was founded, and the spread of theatrical work in the countryside was aided considerably by the formation of the National Federation of Women's Institutes (1917) and of the Arts League of Service (1919), the latter equipped with its own travelling theatre.[1] What strides forward were being made in this sphere is amply demonstrated by the facts that publishers now found it profitable to issue anthologies of "Plays for Villages" and that such an established author as Harold Brighouse could apply himself to the writing of his *Plays for the Meadow and Plays for the Lawn* (1921) and his *Open Air Plays* (1926).

In 1919 came the launching of the British Drama League, with its four-fold aim of binding together the numerous amateur associations, of setting higher standards for them all, of encouraging young dramatists and of stimulating interest in the national theatre concept. The same year, too, saw the arising of the Phoenix out of the Stage Society, with its objective of allowing London audiences to have an opportunity of seeing many Elizabethan and Restoration dramas, most of which were at that time completely unknown to the stage.

Thereafter, until about 1928, such endeavours continued without any abatement. The British and International Dramatic Association, the Poetic Players, the Curtain Group and People's Theatre Society all testified in their titles to expanding and sometimes novel interests. The Repertory Players joined the other existing bodies engaged in presenting

[1] *Travelling Players: The Story of the Arts League of Service* (1939), by Eleanor Elder, gives a full record of this notable venture.

Sunday productions of original plays;[1] the Interlude Players, otherwise known as the Interlude Theatre Guild, under the inspiration of Clive Currie pursued a kindred course; at Bedford Hall in Chelsea the Pax Robertson Salon offered a particularly interesting series of foreign plays in new English translations. Both the Forum Club and the Lyceum Club sponsored their own stage societies. Local groups multiplied apace from London's centre (The St Martin's-in-the-Fields Players), on through the suburbs (The Play and Pageant Union of Hampstead Garden Suburb) and into the surrounding countryside (The Rickmansworth Players). The important Fellowship of Players, devoted to the performance of Shakespeare's dramas,[2] and the equally important 300 Club, inspired by Mrs Geoffrey Whitworth in an attempt to assist young authors, were established at this time. Dozens of other units, such as the Pivot Club, the League of Arts, the Shakespeare Students Society, the Revival Players, the 1920 Players and the Lancelyn Players, added their motley tints to the general picture. The Renaissance Theatre and the International Theatre Society both belonged to 1925; in the following year, with strong professional and other support, the irate Lord Lathom organised the Venturers Society for the production of his own banned plays and of others which had similarly run foul of the censorship; 1927 witnessed the opening of the Arts Theatre Club, and about the same time the Sunday Players added still another to the already formidable array of such producing bodies.[3]

The whole of this teeming world of clubs, societies and

[1] This important association, founded in 1921, did not abandon its activities until 1968.

[2] Its president was Arthur Bourchier. For some comments on its work see J. T. Grein, *The New World in the Theatre* (1924), p. 52.

[3] Among the many other organisations which made their own distinctive contributions were the Dramatic Arts Centre Repertory Company, the Half-Circle Club, the Partnership Players, the Young Age Theatre, the Prentice Players, the Foundlings, the Trial Players, the New Pilgrims, the Playaday Players, the Playmates and the New Play Club. To these should be added a number of specialised groups such as the Greek Play Society and the Roswitha Society. And note should also be taken of the

guilds seemed to indicate that the force which had come into being at the very start of the century had now gained such strength as to warrant its continuance into the following decade: yet, strangely, when we examine this record with care, we realise that the years from 1925 to 1930, even while they displayed the increasing power of the original force, were manifesting signs of another kind. Those who banded themselves together in the formation of the Sunday Players were, in reality, now become old-fashioned: concurrently, numerous key members of the Stage Society – longest-enduring and most distinguished of all these bodies – were making open declaration of their belief that the aims with which their association had been founded no longer had any real value amid the changed conditions of the time: although their attempt to wind up its affairs was defeated in 1930, their assessment of the situation was fully justified when the thirties allowed this Society to sink quietly into oblivion. And, while we may take this as a symbol of the way in which earlier purposes, projects and designs were beginning to lose their force and value, two other noteworthy developments which came in the year 1927 may be taken as symbolic of things to come – the formal establishment of the St Pancras People's Theatre and of the Gate Theatre Studio in the Strand.[1] Up to this time civic sponsorship of dramatic

way in which some of the university dramatic societies began to search round for original writings which they might put upon the stage: thus, for example, the Birmingham University group in 1925 chose Alfred Hayes' version of Pushkin's *Boris Godunov* for production, and student actors in several universities were responsible for most of the performances of Laurence Housman's *Little Plays of St Francis*. A Catholic Play Society appeared at this time, differing from the (Roman) Catholic Stage Guild of 1911 in that its object was, not social, but directed towards the presentation of religious plays; although originally founded in 1917, the (Anglican) Catholic Stage Society did not become really active until the twenties; at this period, too, the British Jewish Literary Society began to show a marked interest in the drama; and there even came into being a Players Guild of the Theosophical Society. The aims of all these organisations were subsumed in the creation of the Religious Drama Society.

[1] For the first see *The End of One Story: A Souvenir of the Borough of St Pancras* (1964): Raymond Mander and Joe Mitchenson have an account of the second in *The Lost Theatres of London* (1968). See p. 73.

performances had been no more than a dream, and hardly any of the clubs had thought of planning, within the course of a single year, more than three or four productions. The action taken by the St Pancras Council, therefore, was a definite innovation, while the Gate Theatre Studio, instead of being, like the various "studios" occasionally used in previous years for club performances,[1] merely large rooms in which from time to time different groups sought to entertain their subscription audiences, was a formal venture on the part of Peter Godfrey and Velona Pilcher to set up a regular theatre which, because theoretically run as a "club", was free from interference either by the London County Council or by the Lord Chamberlain. Although ideologically the People's Theatre and the Gate stood miles apart from each other, they yet were closely associated in pointing forwards towards the thirties and the forties.[2]

[1] Among these may be mentioned the studio at 92 Victoria Street, home of the Amateur Players Association from 1905 to 1909, and in 1910 handed over to the Women's Institute; a rather obscure studio in Bedford Street, which may have been let out to different societies for their performances; a Studio Club in Regent Street; and a "Greek Studio" in Flood Street, Chelsea. In 1911 a "Boudoir" in Kensington was used for some performances, and this may be the "Studio Theatre" of 1928.

[2] It would have been inappropriate to provide space in the present volume for any comprehensive survey of the various halls used for play-performances by clubs and societies during the first three decades of the century: but two comments may be made here. The first is that the profusion of these small "play-places" was one of the most characteristic theatrical developments of the period; and the second is that so far no one has made even a tentative endeavour to explore their range. The working definition on which Diana Howard bases the contents of her *London Theatres and Music Halls 1850–1950* (1970) – "a hall that was used by its owner or lessee primarily for the purpose of providing dramatic or variety entertainment by paid performers, to a paying audience, with a view to making a financial profit" – excludes them entirely, although perhaps it ought to be observed that, strictly applied, it ought also to have excluded the Old Vic as well: Raymond Mander and Joe Mitchenson have some interesting notes on club theatres of the later "Gate" type, but they largely ignore the earlier halls and studios. In none of the several volumes devoted to providing a record of "theatres" operative during these years is there indication of the way in which various halls (many of them apparently unlicensed for stage performances) were so freely and frequently engaged by play-producing associations as to demand inclusion

With these is to be associated something else. What may be styled the present-day "festival concept" was suddenly brought to the notice of the public during the same month, August 1929, by two entirely different and unrelated experiments which independently drew their inspiration from the same source; and here we see the start of what was to become a prominent feature of the age to follow. It truly was the start, for the few odd premonitions which may be found in earlier years had virtually nothing to do with what spread so widely from the thirties on to our present days. It is true, of course, that the term "Festival" was often attached to the performances given at Stratford-upon-Avon by the Benson company,[1] that Beerbohm Tree used it for his Shakespearian performances presented between 1905 and 1913, that the Glastonbury Festival of Music and Drama was established in 1915,[2] and that in 1919 the Gaelic word "Oireachtas",

among the stages on which interested members of the public could see performances of numerous interesting and out-of-the-way dramas (particularly "modern" experimental works, native and foreign – such places as the Clavier Hall, the (small) Albert Hall, the Steinway Hall, the Queen's Gate Hall, the Rudolf Steiner Hall, Victoria Hall, King George's Hall, Caxton Hall, Ladbroke Hall, King's Hall (Covent Garden), St James's Hall, Bedford Hall (in Chelsea, home of the very active Pax Robertson Salon) as well as the various "halls" of the Etlinger School, the Margaret Morris School and the recently established Academy of Dramatic Art. Nor can one find in these volumes any references to the dramatic significance of such institutions as the Cripplegate Institute in Golden Lane (which in 1913 and 1914 was graced with the name of "Dramatic Centre"), the Passmore Edwards Settlement in Tavistock Place, and the Mary Ward Settlement (which in 1924 was also called the "Dramatic Art Centre"). Particulars concerning at least a few of the halls available for the use of play-producing groups are included in the various issues of L. Carson's *The Stage Guide* (a periodical volume first published in 1908).

[1] Even as early as 1864 Nicholas Michell published an ode called *The Shakespeare Festival; or The Birth of the World's Poet* in which he declared that "pilgrim-thousands pour their waves" into "Stratford town".

[2] The Glastonbury Players and their "Festival" had been doubly inspired. Of their two sponsor–creators, one, Reginald Buckley, sought to imitate what had been accomplished at the Wagner Festspielhaus at Bayreuth, while the other, Rutland Boughton, was chiefly animated by a desire to build up a colony of artists at Glastonbury and by a dream of founding there an "Arthurian" centre: both agreed in wishing to promote what the former called "Anglo-Celtic Folk Art". Buckley's *The Shake-*

accompanied occasionally by its English equivalent, "Festival", was applied to some summer performances. In none of these instances, however, was the term invested with the connotations so familiarly attached to it now.[1]

Certainly it must be admitted that one element essential to our own interpretation of the word was being developed during the early years of the century in the cult of the "pageant". For the inauguration of this cult one man, Louis Napoleon Parker, must be regarded as responsible, and fortunately he has left a vivid account both of the inception of the pageant and of the principles determining its form.[2] In so far as the first is concerned, a precise date can be adduced: on Thursday, June 9, 1904, Parker records that he received a "harmless-looking letter" addressed to him by the Rev. Arthur Field which "hurled" him "into a new orbit; snatched" him "out of the idyllic calm of the theatre, where" he "had to deal with tens and twenties", and set him "struggling with hundreds and thousands": in this letter Field had informed him that the following year would be the Twelfth Centenary of the founding of Sherborne abbey, school and town by St Ealdhelm, and had blandly asked "what was to be done about it". Parker, ever a tireless enthusiast, immediately found himself fired by the challenge, and one month later saw him addressing a Sherborne town meeting, with in his hands a logically-conceived scheme for the first show of its kind – a scheme which became the model for the dozens of similar spectacles demanded by other towns anxious to celebrate events in their civic histories: of these, Parker himself was responsible for five which followed his initial Sherborne effort – Warwick (1906), Bury St Edmunds (1907), Dover (1908), Colchester (1909) and York

speare Revival and the Stratford-upon-Avon Movement (1911), which also includes some chapters on "Folk-Art" written by Mary Neal, expounds the concepts which led, four years later, to the Glastonbury experiment: it also fully indicates how different was the "festival idea" at that time from the "festival idea" of today.

[1] Terence Gray, of course, used the term "Festival" for his Cambridge playhouse, but clearly this theatre was in no wise conducted according to "festival" principles.

[2] This account appears in his *Several of My Lives* (1928), pp. 277–98.

(1909). Without any doubt these pageants are to be accepted as ventures peculiarly characteristic of the years between 1904 and the middle twenties, but in spirit they are more closely akin to the aspirations of those intent upon cultivating "folk art" than to the objectives of those who later applied themselves to the organisation of theatrical summer festivals. Parker's massive displays certainly showed how visitors could profitably be attracted to the particular localities in which they were presented, but, even so, they too have to be dismissed as ancestors of the festivals of today.

What happened in August 1929 must be seen as definitely novel, unheralded, and unrelated to anything which had previously been attempted in England. The epoch-making Malvern Festival, dedicated to Bernard Shaw and owing its being to the initiative and support of Sir Barry Jackson, together with the Canterbury Festival, largely the creation of George Bell (then Dean of Canterbury and later Bishop of Chichester),[1] both acknowledged as their direct inspiration and model, not the Wagner Festspielhaus, but what had been achieved by Max Reinhardt at Salzburg. These two ventures, concurrent in time, are to be looked upon, not as a culmination of anything which had preceded them in England, but as a complete innovation and as the start of something new – the one leading on to the dozens of local dramatic festivals which have become so familiar in our own times, and the other pointing towards the work of T. S. Eliot and beyond.

6. *Shifting Scenes*

In 1913 appeared a volume entitled *The Future of the Theatre*, written by a perceptive and well-informed critic, John Palmer. Among many noteworthy comments on the stage of that time and expressions of hope for what the following years might bring, the author makes two assertions – one of them a basic truth, firmly set upon a foundation of incontrovertible matters of fact, and the second a prognostication disastrously wide of the mark. "Perhaps," he says, "the

[1] See Ronald C. D. Jasper, *George Bell, Bishop of Chichester* (1967).

most characteristic dramatic development of the last ten years is the gradual insinuation into a position of authority and importance of the producer. For producers are not a necessity in the production of plays. They are a fashionable luxury of the time. They are also a most important symbol of the present state of the drama." That is the first statement: and this is the prophecy:

> The producer will disappear. In twenty years' time people will wonder how the name of this mysterious functionary came into programmes and posters. They will speculate as to the nature of his office – wonder where precisely he fitted into the dramatic scheme. Plays, they will argue, are the natural fruit of an artistic collaboration of dramatic authors with players. The rest is machinery set in motion by a stage-manager. Who, they will vainly inquire, was the mysterious third person who was in the habit of "producing" plays? Who was this person who knew more about the theatre than the men who were writing for the theatre, and more about the conduct of a scene than the players whose art it was? They will be unable to picture the degradation of a dramatic day when producers were a necessary and wholesome corrective for the egotism, ignorance and artistic insensibility of players; and a necessary safeguard for dramatic authors ignorant of stagecraft and out of touch with the English theatre.[1]

Quite clearly this prophecy was completely in error: no passage of twenty years was to cause the director to vanish from the theatre: indeed, it may well be thought that this "functionary", no longer "mysterious", is now far more firmly established than he was when Palmer was writing. The obvious error in the prognostication, however, ought not to make us believe that the statement itself is incorrect: Palmer declares that (at least in England) the director did not come into being until the beginning of the present century – and, incredible though this assertion may seem, its truth is proved by numerous contemporary comments. Even as late as 1934, Cecil Chisholm, writing about the repertory movement,[2] could confirm Palmer's words by stating firmly that

[1] *The Future of the Theatre* (1913), pp. 43, 54–5.
[2] *Repertory* (1934), p. 32.

only "latterly" had "that new and disturbing element, the producer," come "into his own", while only a few years earlier, in 1930, Sir Arthur Pinero, casting his mind back over the course of the stage which he knew so well, could refer to this disturbing functionary as "that modern excrescence of the theatre".[1] The technical use of the term "producer" and the theatrical philosophy determining the nature of his function were indeed characteristic creations of the early twentieth century: of that there can be no doubt whatsoever.

During preceding years, when stock companies prevailed, many plays must have been brought before the public largely through the collective activities of actors and actresses trained according to a well-established tradition and all intimate with the qualities possessed by their fellows. There had, of course, to be a stage-manager to call them to rehearsals, to select the particular pieces of stock-scenery which might be appropriate for the selected comedies and tragedies, to supervise the work of the scene-shifters and the property-men; but essentially the stage-manager was not given any interpretative function, and many of those who fulfilled such duties were probably akin to the excitable and hidebound O'Dwyer whom Tom Wrench engaged as his factotum in *Trelawny of the "Wells"*. Nevertheless, Pinero's historical reconstruction of the early career of Tom Robertson reminds us that sometimes at least the stage-manager was instructed to work according to the wishes of someone higher than himself on the theatre's staff. It may be said that usually this happened on one of two occasions – when a star-actor took control or when an author was given the opportunity of interpreting his own play. We know, for instance, that David Garrick took pains in coaching the Drury Lane company before his 1751 revival of Ben Jonson's *Every Man in his Humour* – although characteristically he seems to have allowed the actor Henry Woodward to pursue

[1] *Two Plays* (1930) preface. It is interesting to observe that in one of the first books devoted to the new style of play direction, Frank Vernon's *Modern Stage Production* (1923), there is quoted a letter, written by Gordon Craig, with the title "Producer or Stage Manager?".

his own way in the part of Bobadill: and throughout the nineteenth century actor–managers such as Charles Macready, Samuel Phelps, Charles Kean and Henry Irving clearly had to take personal control of their more important productions. Throughout this century, too, we encounter instances of playwrights who for one reason or another were active participants at rehearsal: Tom Robertson, whom Pinero presented as Tom Wrench, had to undertake this task because he was trying to break away from traditional dramatic styles, and it is well known how much the success of the Savoy operas owed to the careful drilling imposed upon the performers by the martinet W. S. Gilbert.

The mention of Gilbert serves to call attention to the fact that, when the time came for John Palmer's "mysterious third person" to start his activities and to assume his title, this person arose out of the musical stage, even although his summoning-forth was due to the generally changing conditions in the theatre of the time. Almost every feature of these new conditions called for his presence. The innumerable amateur groups clamoured for instruction; the *ad hoc* companies assembled by the Sunday play-producing societies needed direction precisely because they often consisted of actors and actresses who had not previously had had opportunities of performing together; several among the later actor–managers were coming to realise that, if they were to give of their best in the star parts, there were advantages in transferring the general direction of their plays to someone else; other managers, such as Charles Frohman, obviously needed to engage experts for the handling of their shows; the many touring companies assembled to carry London successes throughout the country required guidance if their performances were to be effective; and even the new repertories, particularly those which utilised both professionals and amateurs and those which had rapidly changing programmes, demanded similar instruction. All combined, therefore, to lead towards the development of a kind of stage management different from that which had previously prevailed: one might even go further, and suggest that a double force was at work. The conditions at the beginning of the present century were such as to render necessary the participation of overall directors, while, at the same time, numerous individuals, both amateur and professional, suddenly discovering that there was now a novel and unexpected chance of exercising authority, helped to provide still further impulse in the founding of dramatic groups over whom they might exercise their control.

What is surprising about this new development is the suddenness with which it came into existence; it was, indeed, so sudden that the introduction of the term "producer" may be dated to within a year or two. It has been observed above that Gilbert supervised the rehearsals of his comic operas down to the smallest details, but he remained only an author–stage-manager enlarging the limits of his authority. Something slightly different emerged at the Gaiety when, under the inspiration of George Edwardes, that theatre came to specialise in musical comedies of varying kinds: it need hardly be said that these shows, whether of the romantic story type or of a more mixed quality, required painstaking and expert supervision, and, since the quality of the shows themselves depended upon the co-ordination of spectacle, music, dancing and choral performances, there was a natural tendency to speak of a "George Edwardes production" in the sense that he had been responsible for bringing such-and-such a play before the public. Gradually, however, Edwardes found it profitable to assign the actual stage-management to others, and some confusion began to arise when these men also were referred to by the same designation.

Meanwhile, in 1901, the already established movement within the sphere of musical comedy moved on to the dramatic stage: that year saw the appointment of Dion Boucicault as "producer of plays" for Charles Frohman and the start of Hubert Druce's activities in a similar sphere for Beerbohm Tree and Weedon Grossmith. How novel was the practice and how difficult it proved for the theatre to grow accustomed to it can be demonstrated in many ways. The theatrical application of the words "produce" and "producer" were unknown to the compilers of the *Oxford English Dictionary* when the relevant volume of that work appeared in 1910: for a number of years after 1901 even professional theatre journals were inclined to put both these words in inverted commas: and confusion was not averted when attempts were made to introduce still another new term, "director". Thus, for instance, a notice of *The Blue Moon* in 1905 described Robert Courtneidge as "the producer", because he was then the lessee of the Lyric theatre, and proceeded to speak of him as "one of our cleverest and most artistic stage producers", alluding to the excellence of his direction; during the same year photographs were published of Frank Curzon and Austen Hurgon, who were responsible for the staging of *The White Chrysanthemum*, the former being described as the man "who produced" the piece and the latter as the man "who helped to 'produce'"; five years later appeared a notice of *Arsène Lupin*, "which Mr. Frohman has produced", yet elsewhere the same notice refers to the play as "produced under the direction of Mr. Dion Boucicault"; the following year *The Glad Eye* has the names of E. Dagnall as "The Producer" and of Louis Meyer as "Sole Director", while in 1912 Arnold Bennett's *Milestones*, presented at the Royalty when that playhouse was managed by J. E. Vedrenne and Dennis Eadie, was said to have been "produced under the Direction of Frank Vernon".

Whatever the uncertainties about nomenclature, the fact of the directors' theatre, particularly after the seasons for which Granville-Barker had been responsible, was commonly accepted – so commonly accepted, indeed, that many of the readers of Palmer's book in 1913 probably experienced a sense of surprise and shock on being reminded that the new dispensation was then only about ten or a dozen years old. By that time the "producer" or "director" had established himself as an important theatrical functionary, and his control of the stage was made the firmer both by the operation of outside forces and by the activities of the related scene-designers. The first visions of the Russian ballet made rapt spectators realise immediately that these performances owed their being to strict and precise directorial control. In January 1911 Max Reinhardt, the master-director, presented a condensed version of the wordless musical drama *Sumurun* at the Coliseum, following that with a lengthier performance at the Savoy in October and with the production of *The Miracle* at Olympia in December, while in January 1912 spectators at Covent Garden saw Martin-Harvey in his production of *Oedipus Rex* – and thus the Austro-German theatrical wizard and his designer Ernst Stern were added to topics of excited debate. About the same time Granville-Barker's presentations of *The Winter's Tale, Twelfth Night* and *A Midsummer Night's Dream* not only gave further stress to what a director might achieve but also introduced the names of Norman Wilkinson and Albert Rutherston or Rothenstein. The director thus came on stage arm-in-arm with the new kind of designer. More than one critic observed that "this innovation of scenery" was "a vital feature" of the years 1911–12, and quite appropriately *The Stage Year Book* for 1914 found space for a novelty – a symposium on "Modern Scenic Art", introduced by Arthur Scott Craven, with contributions from several artists such as Rutherston, Wilkinson and Joseph Harker.

Thus was a new world created, and naturally, as the years advanced, other stage innovations were brought before the public and further discussions ensued. In the early twenties men such as Aubrey Hammond, Norman Macdermott, Paul Nash, Herbert Prentice, Charles Ricketts, George Sheringham and Paul Shelving aided in enriching the staging of plays; novel artistic endeavours, such as expressionism, were introduced into the theatres; and a new informed public was seeking for information about all kinds of Continental and American experiments. A. S. Craven's modest symposium of 1914 was followed by dozens of books dealing with what John Mason Brown called *The Modern Theatre in Revolt* and by 1928 the beginnings of this revolt seemed to lie far back in the past when René Fuerst and Samuel J. Hume published their comprehensive survey, *XXth Century Stage Decoration.* Six years earlier than that a clear reflection of the lively interest which was being taken in the work of the scenic artists appeared in the exhibition of theatrical designs arranged at the Victoria and Albert Museum: even at the very close of the old Queen's reign hardly any save one or two professionals could have given the names of those responsible for preparing the sets displayed in the theatres of Paris, Berlin, Munich and Vienna, and no more than a few stragglers would have troubled to visit an exhibition of sketches and drawings on which these sets had been based. Now, all was changed.

And this exhibition reminds us that, in addition to the animated discussions concerning current scenic experiments, there was an accompanying interest in the exploration of all theatrical activities in times past. For many long years, of course, classical scholars had been active in their attempts to reconstruct the ancient playhouses of Greece and Rome, but for the most part these attempts might most fittingly be described as archeological and scholarly: what the early years of the twentieth century witnessed was both an expansion of these studies and an approach which tended to bring the specialised information close to the modern stage: Roy C. Flickinger's *The Greek Theater and its Drama* (1918) and J. T. Allen's *Stage Antiquities of the Greeks and the Romans* (1927) were scholarly in execution but theatrical in interest. And much the same comment may be made concerning studies of play-production in other periods. The six volumes compiled by Sir E. K. Chambers – the *Medieval Stage* (1903) and *The Elizabethan Stage* (1925) – were, from the scholarly point of view, the age's greatest achievements in the analysis of evidence relating to the presentation of dramatic writings from the earliest, primitive liturgical scenes on to Shakespeare's final dramas; yet maybe the spirit animating these first thirty years of the century is even more powerfully reflected in the fact that the indefatigable W. J. Lawrence was able, because of the widely spreading interest in these subjects, to make his living largely through the penning of articles and books on old playhouse days and ways.

It must, of course, be admitted, first, that in Renaissance Italy the Graeco-Roman stage was the model eagerly studied and imitated by theatre architects and, secondly, that from the middle of the sixteenth century, when Sebastiano Serlio published his *Architettura*, scores of volumes were issued dealing with playhouse construction and with scenic design. At the same time it is essential to observe that the early enthusiasm which had led to the building of the Teatro Olimpico at Vicenza soon passed away and that almost all the volumes referred to above were, in their expensive format, not addressed to general readers and often were not easily obtainable even by practising professionals. What distinguishes the first thirty years of the present century is the growing demand for reasonably inexpensive studies aiming at the disinterring of long-vanished stage conventions, at an assessment of what these had meant for spectators in the past, and at suggesting new experiments.

It was against this background that the new productions were examined, and where doubts were expressed these generally were motivated by practical consideration of the relationship between the work of the producers and the plays, original or revived, with which such producers were dealing.[1] While the gradual banishing of the old Charles Kean–Henry Irving–Beerbohm Tree spectacularism was almost universally welcomed, many more critics than sometimes we are inclined to admit discerned disadvantages in the fresh styles of presentation which were being put in their place. Nowadays, we have become accustomed to

[1] The late arrival of the "modern" producer or director in England meant that not until towards the close of the present period were any notable English studies written on the subject of directorial practice. Some such studies were available in other languages, but the majority of these remained known only to a very limited circle of readers. Among the few which succeeded in finding a certain number of readers, perhaps the most important was the *Geschichte der Regie* (1925) in which Adolf Winds sought to trace the practice of play production from the days of ancient Greece on to those of Jessner and Reinhardt.

hearing that Granville-Barker's Shakespearian productions were the finest of their kind during the entire course of the twentieth century, but actually there were numerous thoughtful spectators who were troubled by doubts. They questioned whether, in Palmer's words, "the total aesthetic effect of Mr Barker's *Twelfth Night*" was greater than "the total aesthetic effect of Sir Johnston Forbes-Robertson's *Hamlet*", even although the former had beautiful scenery and costumes, while the latter, visually, was dull and tawdry: they pointed out how Granville-Barker's literalism could injure the quality infused by Shakespeare into the first scene of *Twelfth Night* and into *A Winter's Tale*'s sheep-shearing episode: they noted, too, that the advent of fresh productional methods, although it introduced some things worthy of praise and admiration, might easily ruin the drama. Thoroughly characteristic is James Agate's review of Georg Kaiser's *From Morn to Midnight* at the Regent in 1926. Being a penetrating critic, he immediately recognised the essential merits of the expressionistic scenic approach and adroitly set these merits forth. In older days, he said, when

> you glanced down at your theatre programme and saw the words "Bathroom in the Palace of the Emperor Hadrian", you fell at once to wondering two things – first, what cranes had been used to haul those giant and marble blocks so noiselessly into place, and second, why the programme should fib, since you were obviously enjoying an expensive set in the beautiful London theatre of the Emperor Beerbohm. But when they tell you at the Regent that the scene is the "Interior of a Small Bank" you quite perfectly believe it. The actors, sharply defined against the vague background – in which there are neither walls nor doors – can these be characters in a bank? Yes, because there is a square yard or so of tortured grating to suggest the cramped lives of those who must spend their lives raking in and paying out other people's money. Can cavernous gloom with a few dimly flying flags and four excited gentlemen in evening dress waving top-hats suggest a "Velodrome during Cycle Races"? Again, yes; because the top-hats are semaphores keeping us in touch with the crowd on the stands and signalling messages of cupidity and

greed. All expressionistic scenery has this two-fold appeal; it stimulates the eye by the little which it puts in, and the mind through all that it leaves out.

Yet, despite his enthusiastic praise of "the peculiar virtue of expressionism" whereby it "goes one better in the way of presenting things to the mind than the representational method which presents them to the eye", he finds himself compelled to enter a caveat: "the fact that a dramatist should have found a magnificent way of saying something must not bluff us into the belief that the thing said is magnificent". "I tried with might and main," he informs us, "to see spiritual significance in Mr. Kaiser's turgid bombinations, but all I could see, or rather hear, was a small cashier talking at enormous length through a very large hat...I take off mine to the setting, which whetted the appetite to an extraordinary degree, though, with all respect to everybody concerned, I could not find that there was much of a meal."[1]

Beyond the doubts which derived from attending particular productions, however, there was something more – a doubt philosophical concerning basic issues. In 1912, among the multitudinous theatrical associations, one group was founded with the unqualified and uncompromising title of The Society of the Theatre. Its prospectus listed an impressive "International Committee" which included the names of Augustus John, R. B. Cunninghame-Graham, Albert Rothenstein, Gilbert Cannan, William Poel, J. Martin Harvey, W. B. Yeats, Lord Dunsany, Constantin Stanislavski, Tomasso Salvini and Matsumoto Koshiro, as well as a correspondingly impressive "Executive Committee" which consisted of Gordon Craig and his wife, John Cournos, Elsie Fogerty, Lovat Fraser, Holbrook Jackson, Walter Crane, Yeats, Cecil Sharp and Ezra Pound. The text of this prospectus declares that the Society

aims at creating a dramatic movement which shall appeal to the theatrical rather than to the literary aspects of drama. By "theatrical" is meant that form of stage production which makes an

[1] *The Contemporary Theatre, 1926* (1927), pp. 79–82.

appeal to the senses through the imagination rather than to the intellect.

The Society has adopted the idea of Gordon Craig, and is formed to promote discussion of that idea, and to try to establish a School for the Art of the Theatre, with Gordon Craig as authoritative director.

These two brief paragraphs, which quite possibly may have been penned by Craig himself, contain at least four highly significant words or phrases. First of all, the term "idea" attracts our attention. Paradoxically and yet typically, the man who came to be regarded as the prime symbol of the director's theatre derived his fame, not from practical work in the playhouse, but from the enunciation of a philosophy. In an introduction to the 1967 Craig Memorial exhibition arranged at the Lincoln Center in New York, Donald Oenslager has rightly used the epithet "astonishing" to describe the fact that six London productions between 1900 and 1903, "plus only four which were to follow later in his career, represent the sum total of his experience in the Theatre".[1]

[1] *Edward Gordon Craig, Artist of the Theatre, 1872–1966*, a catalogue prepared by Arnold Rood (1967). With this catalogue should be associated that prepared by George Nash for the 1967 Victoria and Albert Museum's Craig exhibition. Studies of all kinds relating to Craig's career now abound. Enid Rose's *Gordon Craig and the Theatre* (1931), the first attempt at a comprehensive record, has lately been superseded by the more detailed accounts presented by Ferruccio Marotti in his excellent *Gordon Craig* (1961) and by Denis Bablet in his *Edward Gordon Craig* (1962; English translation, by Daphne Woodward, 1966). A comprehensive bibliography of his writings, prepared by I. Kyrle Fletcher and Arnold Rood, was published by the Society for Theatre Research, 1967. Craig's very early productional efforts, chiefly those associated with the Purcell Operatic Society, are excellently documented and discussed by Michael Peter Loeffler in *Gordon Craigs frühe Versuche zur Überwindung des Bühnenrealismus* (*Schweizer Theaterjahrbuch*, 35, issued by the Schweizerischen Gesellschaft für Theaterkultur, 1969). On this subject Arnold Rood, in an article entitled "'After the Practise the Theory': Gordon Craig and Movement" (*Theatre Research*, xi, 1971, 81–101), interestingly adds more information, and still further information is presented in Denis Bablet's "Edward Gordon Craig and Scenography" (*Theatre Research*, xi, 1971, 7–22). The impress which Craig made on European stages can be gauged by the number of references to him in the eighth volume of Heinz Kindermann's extensive *Theatergeschichte Europas* (1968), a detailed account of German, Austrian and Swiss productions during the period of "Naturalismus und Impressionismus".

This sense of astonishment is increased when we recall that three of the 1900–3 productions[1] were performed for only a few days each before tiny subscription audiences supplied by the Purcell Operatic Society, founded by Craig and his friend Martin Fallas Shaw; that a fourth[2] was another semi-private production prepared by the same two collaborators; and that consequently his only two professional productions were those which he undertook for his mother, Ellen Terry, when she assumed her rather disastrous management of the Imperial.[3]

It is true that among the few contemporary comments on these productions there were two which appreciatively called attention to the revolutionary quality of Craig's work.[4] It is also true that his designs early won him the esteem of pictorial artists: in 1903 he was elected a member of the Society of Twelve[5] and showed some of his work at their 1904 exhibition; during the following year several of his designs and etchings were on display at exhibitions in Germany and Austria. To these facts must be added another: through the enthusiasm of Count Kessler, who had been introduced to him by Rothenstein, he was invited in 1904 to assume responsibility for a production of Otway's *Venice Preserved* at the Lessing Theater in Berlin – although perhaps the less said about that the better.[6] Yet even when all these

[1] *Dido and Aeneas* (Hampstead Conservatoire, May 1900), *The Masque of Love* (concocted from Purcell's *Dioclesian*, Coronet, March 1901), and *Acis and Galatea* (Great Queen Street, March 1902).

[2] Laurence Housman's *Bethlehem* (Imperial Institute, December 1902).

[3] Ibsen's *The Vikings of Helgeland* (April 1903, with a three-weeks' run) and *Much Ado about Nothing* (May 1903, not successful but later taken on tour). For Fred Terry's production of *For Song or Sword* (Shaftesbury, January 1903) he provided only some designs.

[4] Haldane Macfall, "Some Thoughts on the Art of Gordon Craig with particular reference to Stagecraft" (*The Studio*, xxiii, Sept. 15, 1901, 255–7) and Dion Clayton Calthrop, "*Acis and Galatea* by Handel, and *The Masque of Love* by Purcell" (*The Artist*, i, May 1902, 57–8).

[5] This important group included, among others, Augustus John, William Strang, Sturge Moore, William Rothenstein, Charles Ricketts, D. Y. Cameron and Muirhead Bone.

[6] The effort ended with recriminations between Craig and Otto Brahm, the theatre's Intendant: Craig abandoned the production. His later practical work on the stage included: the supervision of *Rosmersholm*

facts are freely admitted, it must be obvious that the excitement aroused in certain circles by the appearance of *Die Kunst des Theaters* in Germany and of its English version, *The Art of the Theatre*, in 1905 cannot be explained by assuming that Craig's practical theatre activities were so widely known and so effective as to make readers clamour for an enunciation of his basic concepts.

Fundamentally, the excitement was connected with, and indeed dependent upon, the final term used in the prospectus of the Society of the Theatre, "authoritative director": this was the true foundation of Craig's "idea"; and, although several theatre-men in Europe had been secretly dreaming about the concept, hardly anyone had dared to put the vision into words or to suggest the identity of this "authoritative director" with "the art of the theatre".

The new philosophy enunciated by Craig, in effect, demanded that this director should be regarded as the only artist in the playhouse, and the impact made by his volume derived from the fact that uncompromisingly and forcefully he confronted the implications arising from his basic assumption. Although his words had the more force because they flowed from his pen in an apocalyptic style, a style emotionally appealing even when at times his thoughts were expressed in a form abstruse and necromantic, these thoughts are to be seen as essentially simple. We must, argued Craig, set the theatre, as an art, alongside the other arts. The Painter, for example, is a man whose imagination must be permitted as complete independence as possible and who must have total control of his material. (Here he disregarded the fact that a Raphael or a Michelangelo may find stimulation in accepting a commission to paint a particular subject within a predetermined area, and that, consequently, neither absolute freedom nor permissiveness are necessarily, in themselves, to be looked upon as virtues. But that is by the way.)

for Eleonora Duse, Florence, 1906; *Hamlet*, at the Moscow Art Theatre, 1912; Ibsen's *The Crown Pretenders*, Royal Theatre, Copenhagen, 1926; and an unsatisfactory *Macbeth*, prepared for George C. Tyler, New York, 1928, for which Craig only supplied the designs.

The theatrical director, as an artist, Craig declared, must be similarly granted paramount supremacy, must have corresponding independence and untrammelled authority. Thus, any drama with which he is concerned has to be seen as part of his working material, not something simply to be "interpreted" but an object which he may be permitted to mould in any way he cares in order to render it an harmonious element in his total inspired vision. Ideally, this theatre artist should be not merely the "authoritative director" but also author of the play contributing to the effect which he is intent upon creating: but even Craig was compelled to admit that such conditions could exist only in an impossible dream-world, and as a result he found himself forced, in his own practical stage efforts, to cope with dramas written by others. Astutely, he was very careful to make his own choice of scripts: in Donald Oenslager's words, he completely "put aside the contemporary playwright". This procedure his disciples explained by declaring that "his singular ego made alliance with living playwrights impossible" because his genius was so much mightier than their poor talents: he was unable, they said, to find in the contemporary theatre any dramas sufficiently powerful and imaginative as to make them worthy of his attention, so that his preference for the works of Sophocles, Euripides, Shakespeare, Otway and Ibsen was due entirely to the fact that these authors' writings measured up better to his own vaster conceptions. Nevertheless, we must not delude ourselves. His choice was in strict accord with his own basic philosophy: all the dramatists mentioned above were dead dramatists, and with their works he could do anything he liked: in striving for an "appeal to the theatrical rather than to the literary aspects of drama", he could treat these plays as malleable material for the artist–director, something which he could not do with plays written by living authors. His logic here was impeccable.

The other troublesome element for the supreme artist–director was the company of performers. A painter has his tubes of colour, his brushes and similar professional instruments and materials: these brushes and tubes of colour remain entirely within his command: they are completely inanimate: they can never stand up and answer back or determine to pursue their own courses. But stage performers are men and women: some of them may be prepared to accept commands, but others, endowed with visionary gleams of their own, will refuse to follow the directions given to them: and, apart from this, since they are human, their performances will incline to vary from presentation to presentation: if no philosopher can suffer the toothache patiently, no actor can so rid himself of his own humanity as to give precisely the same performance from one night to another. The artist–director, therefore, is being placed in an impossible position: it is almost as though a painter were to discover that his reds, his yellows and his blues were assuming vitality of their own, were refusing to remain strictly in their appointed places, were subtly changing their shades, were disturbing the creator's over-all design. Many attempts have been made to argue that what Craig wrote in his essay,[1] published in 1907, "The Actor and the Uber-Marionette", must be interpreted as meaning only that he sought for a new histrionic style, or that he was thinking here of the use of masks on the stage: but when we relate this much-discussed essay to his total philosophy one conclusion alone seems possible – that he literally meant what he said. For the artist–director, actors were a troublesome and unstable element in the theatre, and they must either go or be reduced to insignificance.

Such a lively, enthusiastic, outwardly persuasive expression of the principles involved in the concept of the director's theatre could not fail to attract attention; and, rightly, this was associated with, and increased by, the various exhibitions of his designs, by the sale of his etchings and lithographs, and, later, by the publication of such volumes as *Scene* (1923), the Cranach Press *Hamlet* (1928) and *The Pretenders*

[1] It seems possible that in writing this essay Craig may have been inspired by Arthur Symons' "Apology for Puppets" originally written in 1897 and printed in *Plays, Acting and Music* (1903).

(1930).[1] Although he never had had any professional training in art, he was manifestly a master of line, and these designs, with their simple masses of light and shade, their delicate contours and their bold effects, exerted wide influence in advanced theatrical circles throughout the whole of Europe and America.

In this connection, it is important to consider Craig's reputation and influence within his own country, and here once more we must return to the 1912 prospectus issued by the Society of the Theatre. The lists of supporters are, as has been said, impressive, yet an analysis of the names reveals something peculiar: with the exception of Martin-Harvey, the only prominent theatre-men who appear here are a Russian, an Italian and a Japanese: most of the individuals mentioned are pictorial artists, poets and literary men only marginally associated with the stage, and one or two others, such as Cecil Sharp, whose interests were not specifically theatrical. Certainly Elsie Fogerty and William Poel are present, but it may reasonably be wondered whether they and some of their companions really had grasped the implications of Craig's "idea". The restricted range of Craig's disciples thus revealed in the lists may well be accepted as symbolic. They, and a few other enthusiasts, bitterly complained that the English theatre was ignoring its prophet, and from the factual point of view they were correct, since in general Craig had no large following in England. On the other hand, we must be careful not to give the proverb about prophets and countries an automatic value-significance: not all prophets are divinely inspired, not all the countries which have rejected them were crassly stupid and imperceptive.

The plain fact is that, amid all its vicissitudes, the English stage, from the times of Burbage and Shakespeare onwards, has derived its strength from the words created by its dramatists and interpreted by its long line of distinguished

[1] *A Production being thirty-two collotype plates of designs projected or realised for The Pretenders of Henrik Ibsen and produced at the Royal Theatre Copenhagen 1926.*

actors and actresses. The attitude towards Gordon Craig during the early twentieth century springs directly from this tradition. There may have been some who wished to see his logic applied to the London theatre, but against this operated a force which embraced a majority of the playwrights, of the players and of the public. And the power inherent in this force was shown by the fact that, apart from a scattering of newspaper articles and comments in a few books, little was published during those years in an attempt to rebut his own often petulant and provocative articles in *The Mask* or the emotional pleas of his supporters. There was ample credit given to him for what he had done to release the theatre from the trammels of scenic naturalism, while at the same time there was a refusal, more frequently implied than directly expressed, to accept the "idea" cultivated by the members of the Society of the Theatre. Rightly or wrongly, the English stage of this period remained true to its tradition of reliance upon its dramatists and its actors.[1]

[1] If there is any truth in these comments, perhaps it may be profitable to relate them to a conclusion reached on September 28, 1970 during a radio discussion by John Russell Taylor and Martin Esslin concerning the theatre of today. In the course of this discussion it was observed that during recent years England seems to have been the only country to maintain an effective "Writers' Theatre" and to produce a series of plays interesting in themselves: elsewhere the stage more and more has relied not on words but on action. And from the observation of this fact arose a basic question – whether this was not the natural expression of something inherently peculiar and proper to the English playhouse. In considering this question, perhaps we should do well to remember that, while Italy and other continental lands in Renaissance times found glorious expression in pictorial and sculptural art, England had but little in this kind of which it might truly boast, but that, on the other hand the works produced by Italian dramatists, while no doubt interesting, are manifestly creations far inferior to the paintings and sculptures of those times, whereas Shakespeare's plays soar far beyond all other contemporary stage writings. Not surprisingly, the Italian theatres began early to experiment in stage settings and productional effects; in England, such things did not take control until many generations had passed by.

CHAPTER III

THE DRAMA: INFLUENCES, PATTERNS AND FORMS

FOR an understanding and appreciation of the plays which were written during those three decades clearly a consideration of the theatrical conditions amid which the authors worked is obligatory, but of equal, and perhaps even of greater, importance is a survey of what may be called the dramatic conditions prevailing at that time. An understanding of these dramatic conditions involves consideration of a variety of different forces, tangible and intangible, theoretical and practical, among which it would seem proper that the first to be examined should be the connections between the English dramatists and the dramatists of other countries.

1. *Dramatic Internationalism*

Throughout the entire course of its career, from the days of the medieval mysteries onward, foreign influences were never absent from the English stage, and as the decades passed by the impress of these influences increased rather than diminished, so that in the nineteenth century so many playwrights freely borrowed their themes, plots and characters from French and German sources that the relatively few dramatists who took the trouble to invent their own subject-matter were generally forced to draw special attention to the fact that their works were "Original". It can, therefore, hardly be said that such influences from abroad were greater during the first years of the present century than they had been in the past. Nevertheless, it must be emphasised that after about 1900 three changes of such a kind developed in the relationship between the English stage and the stages of other countries as completely to alter the general pattern.

Of these changes two are conveniently and effectively illustrated by a collection of *Modern Plays* issued by the publishing firm of Duckworth at the turn of the century. If we exclude the works of Ibsen, it may be said with assurance that almost all the foreign dramas introduced into England during the latter part of the nineteenth century came from France, Germany and the United States and that almost invariably they were of a popular kind. The significance of this series of *Modern Plays* is immediately underlined by the publisher's advertisement, which stresses the fact that the volume was designed to give English readers an introduction to "the activity of the modern drama" in lands other than their own, which proceeds to assert that "the greater number of the Continental dramatists are at present little known in this country", and which confidently expresses the belief that, for example, "the name of Strindberg will be almost new to the English public".[1]

The list of titles is sufficiently interesting to warrant recording: Ibsen's *Love's Comedy*, Strindberg's *The Father*, Verhaeren's *The Dawn*, Ostrovski's *The Storm*, Maeterlinck's *L'Intérieur*, *La Mort de Tintagiles* and *Alladine et Palomides*, and Hauptmann's *The Coming of Peace*. The first thing we notice is the inclusion of dramatic works emanating from lands – Sweden, Russia, Belgium – which rarely, if ever, before had been deemed worthy of any such attention; and the second is that these plays are described, characteristically, by the term "modern", obviously used in the sense of "up-to-date", "new in style" and "advanced in subject-matter". Generally a publisher who issues an anthology of plays hopes that some of them will be performed, but when this collection was thus advertised in 1900 no one could really

[1] The collection was edited by R. Brimley Johnson and N. Erichsen: the date given on the title-page is 1898, but apparently it was not actually put on sale until the following year: the quotations given here are derived from the publisher's advertisement of 1900.

have expected that its contents were likely to be deemed stageworthy: every one of the dramas was of a "special" kind, not calculated to appeal to contemporary London audiences. Instinctively, as it were, those responsible for the series were dreaming ahead towards an as yet unseen future, towards the time when the scores of play-producing societies and the repertory theatres were to be searching for dramatic texts of a particular, exclusive and even esoteric kind.

To the two changes exemplified by this collection must be added a third. During the latter part of the nineteenth century numerous foreign actors had visited London, bringing with them plays of their own countries, but, numerous though they may have been, they can in no wise be compared with the range of foreign companies which from 1900 onwards presented their repertoires in the West End. Improved methods of travel now meant that New York's latest successes could, if desired, be transferred to London within a matter of weeks, and they made easier and more pleasant the journeys made by the increasing flock of visitors from Paris and (up to 1913) from Berlin. The London public actively responded, so that by 1909, for example, Gaston Mayer could open the Royalty as the "Théâtre Français de Londres", and critics could draw attention to a "new" development which meant that the modern reviewers of performances had almost to become "polyglot archangels". "During the last few years," writes E. F. Spence in 1910,

> we have had plays in Russian, Japanese, Bavarian *patois*, Dutch, German, French and Italian, to say nothing of East End performances in Hebrew and Yiddish....A Greek company came to the Court but did not act. A Chinese has been promised, and a Turkish drama threatened; Danish has been given; there are awful hopes of Gaelic and Erse; and goodness knows why we have escaped Echegaray, Lope de Vega and Calderon in the original.[1]

Clearly, the spirit of theatrical and dramatic internationalism was enveloping the theatres. When *The Stage Year Book*

[1] *Our Stage and Its Critics* (1910), p. 1.

designed to cater largely to professional readers, was established in 1908, it made a feature of informative articles dealing with the latest trends in various national playhouses; very soon the dailies and the monthlies began to show their awareness of an expanding public interest by reporting outstanding theatrical events here, there and everywhere; and at the same time lengthier and more comprehensive studies, such as Ashley Dukes' *Modern Dramatists* (1911), Archibald Henderson's *The Changing Drama* (1914), Storm Jameson's *Modern Drama in Europe* (1920), Graham Sutton's *Some Contemporary Dramatists* (1924), Barrett H. Clark's *A Study of the Modern Drama* (1925) and John Palmer's *Studies in the Contemporary Theatre* (1927), were eagerly welcomed and multiplied apace as the years advanced.

It hardly needs to be said that it would be improper, indeed impossible, to make a particular survey here of all the various influences from abroad which made their impact upon English playwrights; but a few of these are so important that they deserve at least brief individual mention. The discovery of the delicate, sharp, appealing and slightly melancholy tone of the Austrian Schnitzler was one of these; a second was the advent of German expressionism represented in the writings of Toller and Kaiser; a third was the fresh prominence given to another European theatre which in earlier times had exerted a fitful influence on the English stage, a prominence which came when Granville-Barker took Sierra's *Romantic Young Lady* by the hand and induced her to bow to the West End public. There was, too, the attention and even admiration extended at the very beginning of the century to D'Annunzio's violent and rather melodramatically poetic pretentiousness, the excitement when in 1908 the Sicilian players exhibited in London their fierce native naturalism, the puzzled and dazzled reception of Pirandello's theatrical–philosophical probing of reality, and – maybe of greatest significance – the widespread realisation of the power of the *commedia dell'arte*.[1]

[1] This encouraged the writing and performing of dozens of one-act playlets, extending in style from music-hall sketches to poetically-

Russia also provided wide variety – the uncompromising realism of Gorki, the innovating subtlety of Chekhov, the experimental forms of Andreev and Evreinov, and the wonders of the Russian ballet.[1] Not until 1928 did London audiences have an opportunity of attending performances given by the Moscow Art Theatre, but for a long time before this the Stanislavski "system", as explained by émigrés and knowledgeable visitors to Russia, had been a prime topic of discussion in numerous professional circles, and in 1924 a translation of the director's *My Life in Art* set forth its principles in his own words. It was between 1909 and 1911 that the Russian ballet first appeared over London like a blazing meteor which, instead of vanishing or exploding into darkness, continued to throw forth its

conceived scenes such as Drinkwater's *The Only Legend: A Masque of the Scarlet Pierrot* (1913) and to romantic–realistic fantasies such as Barrie's *Pantaloon* (1905). It is worthy of note that during this time, while scholarly-theatrical volumes explored the history and scope of the *commedia*, many new plays sought to give new stage life to Arlecchino, Colombina and Pierrot, either directly or by implication. Among these writings three may be particularly mentioned here. In 1913 Granville-Barker and D. C. Calthrop collaborated in composing *The Harlequinade*, a fanciful dramatic history which started with the Greek gods, showed them transformed into the comedy figures of the Renaissance, then carried them on into the eighteenth century and even into the new, apparently alien, "modern" theatrical realm. Another collaborative venture, *The Tragedy of Mr Punch* (1920) by Russell Thorndike and Reginald Arkell, cleverly proceeded to psychoanalyse the descendant of Pulcinella, finding him a person who desires to be feared by others but who is constantly tormented by the thought that "the more people you kill the more they will laugh". And in 1924 Arnold Bennett, in *The Bright Island*, went still further, presenting an imaginary country in which a British naval officer and his sister become involved in the political life of a community ruled by King Pierrot, wherein the Captain and the Doctor are court officials, Pantaloon a democratic rebel, and Isabella an ardently militant feminist.

[1] The interest in the later revolutionary drama and theatre is reflected in the many critical–historical studies devoted to its development and aims. Among these volumes may be mentioned: Alexander Bakshy's *The Path of the Modern Russian Stage* (1916) and *The Theatre Unbound* (1923); Huntly Carter's *The New Theatre and Cinema of Soviet Russia* (1924) and *The New Spirit in the Russian Theatre, 1917–28* (1929); and the pictorial record gathered by René Fülöp-Miller and Joseph Gregor in *Das russische Theater* (1928: translated into English in 1930 as *The Russian Theatre... With Especial Reference to the Revolutionary Period*).

effulgent radiance for many years.[1] Although the ensuing balletomania might be thought to have been a force inimical to the appreciation of plays, in fact the Russian dancers opened up for the English public a whole new world of aesthetic experience, an experience well reflected in the excited words of Gilbert Cannan:

> The Russian Ballet, passing from capital to capital, has given the workers in the theatre the inspiration and the revelation that they needed to lift them beyond their experiments in realism and analysis, and it has given a new zest to the public by providing them with a pleasure keener than any that has been known in the theatre for generations, a pleasure so keen that critics and public are beginning a little unjustly to ask if there is really any greater merit in the politico-intellectual realism of the modern school than in the clever trickery of Scribe and Sardou.[2]

If we wish for other signs, we need hardly go further than the observation that Geoffrey Whitworth, founder of the British Drama League and active proponent of the idea of a national theatre, was the author of an enthusiastic account of *The Art of Nijinsky* (1913) and that Barrie composed his *Truth about the Russian Dancers* (1920) especially for Tamara Karsavina.

[1] The first harbinger seems to have been Tamara Karsavina, who appeared at the Coliseum in 1909: the following year no fewer than four of London's great music-halls welcomed Lydia Kyasht, Anna Pavlova, Olga Preobrajenska and others. One of the earliest signs of the balletomania to come is to be found in the historically important special issue (xviii, 74) of the *Play Pictorial* issued in 1911: only slightly less important is the illustrated booklet published by Covent Garden during the same year – *Royal Opera and Imperial Russian Ballet* – which describes the dances, reproduces photographs of many performers and provides sketches of their lives. A particularly interesting record of the current excitement is presented in A. L. Haskell's *Balletomania: The Story of an Obsession* (1934). The literature on this subject is extensive: W. A. Propert narrates the history of *The Russian Ballet in Western Europe, 1909–1920* (1921) and extends his account in *The Russian Ballet, 1921–1929* (1931): Cyril Beaumont has a lively "personal record" of *The Diaghilev Ballet in London* (1940; enlarged second edition 1945), and this is supplemented by Prince Peter Lieven's *The Birth of the Ballets Russes* (translated by L. Zarine, 1936) and Alexandre Benois' *Reminiscences of the Russian Ballet* (translated by Mary Britnieva, 1941); Serge Lifar, in *Serge Diaghilev* (1940), deals both with the life and with the professional career of the great director.

[2] *The Joy of the Theatre* (1913), p. 49.

The internationalism which thus brought forward so many fresh things to notice was by no means confined to exploration among the theatres of Europe and America: spreading still further, it aroused a fresh interest in the ancient Sanskrit plays, and, much more importantly, it provided intimate information concerning the Japanese Nō dramas, thus deeply influencing numerous English playwrights, not all of whom belonged to the rather exclusive school of W. B. Yeats. The movement at first was slow. In 1880 B. H. Chamberlain's *The Classical Poetry of the Japanese* had been published in Boston, but it would appear to have remained almost completely unknown in England until a revised edition was issued in 1911; Osman Edwards found a few, but only a few, readers for his *Japanese Plays and Playfellows* (1901); presumably F. V. Dickins' *Primitive and Mediaeval Japanese Texts translated into English* (1906) attracted still fewer readers, and only one or two professional orientalists were aware of a tiny number of other versions printed in learned journals. When Marie Stopes and Joji Sakurai collaborated in producing *Plays of Old Japan: The Nō* (1913) they could correctly claim that out of the total of nearly two hundred and fifty Nō dramas there were available for English readers only half-a-dozen complete texts, together with portions of a few others: thus, they stated, "these treasures are practically unknown to the reading public of the West, notwithstanding the interest that has been taken in 'things Japanese'".[1] "*Noh*", *or Accomplishment* and *Certain Noble Plays of Japan*, by Ezra Pound and E. F. Fenollosa, did not appear until 1916; not until 1921 came A. D. Waley's more widely popular *The Nō Plays of Japan*, and seven more years passed by before the appearance of F. A. Lombard's *Outline History of the Japanese Drama*.[2] Even although the spread of this

[1] Pp. 1 and 26.

[2] On the influence of these plays see Makoto Ueda, *Zeami Busho, Yeats, Pound: A study in Japanese and English Poetics* (1956) and Shotahara Oshima, *W. B. Yeats and Japan* (1965): John Rees Moore has a general, but not complete, account, in *Masks of Love and Death* (1971), of what the poet hoped to achieve within this dramatic form. Hiro

knowledge was slow, it had considerable influence as a force opposed to the current realistic style: its impact, for example, may be seen in the note with which W. J. Turner prefaced the revised text of his *Man Who Ate the Popomack* (1929) in which he informed his readers that his aim had been to devise a new dramatic form based on ancient and oriental models: "the first beginnings of this new art," he wrote, "may be traced back in the past, as far as the fifteenth century in Japan", and he proceeded to express his fervent belief that this "new art" could offer a "freedom of expression beyond what" could be discovered "in the ordinary realistic play of our time".[1]

Turner's emphasis upon the fifteenth century reminds us that the theatrical internationalism of this period – which may be regarded as a kind of horizontal force – was closely associated with a concurrent vertical force, the newly awakened interest in dramatic forms which belonged to the remote past of the English stage. The inauguration of W. Bang's *Materialen zur Kunde des älteren englischen Dramas* in 1902, of J. S. Farmer's *Early English Dramatists* in 1905 and his *Tudor Facsimile Texts* in 1907, and of W. W. Greg's *Malone Society Reprints* in 1907 no doubt

Ishibashi, in *Yeats and the Noh* (1969), interestingly shows how limited and defective were the poet's sources of information on this subject. Interest in the Japanese stage was reflected in, and stimulated by, the growing appreciation of Japanese pictorial art: this is well indicated in the title of Basil Stewart's *Subjects Portrayed in Japanese Colour-Prints: A Collector's Guide to all the subjects illustrated including an exhaustive account of the Chushingura and other famous plays, together with a causerie on the Japanese Theatre* (1922). Knowledge of the intricate conventions of the Nō was, of course, restricted at this time to a small intimate circle of poet–playwrights, but at least some flavour of the modern Japanese stage had been brought before the general public when a Japanese company under the direction of Kawakami Otojiro performed at the Court Theatre in 1900. A few years later a popular musical comedy at the Prince of Wales's incorporated within its structure a short burlesque called *The Darling of the Guards*, described as "a skittle, in one throe and seven Japanese screens".

[1] That Turner was not alone in his search for a fresh dramatic structure and that he was by no means the first to aim at such a discovery is shown by a much earlier effort made by "Dean Ballyn" who, in publishing *The Price of Freedom* in 1910, described that drama as "creating an entirely new literary form".

seems at first to be something which belongs entirely within the academic sphere, yet, when examined more closely, its interest must come to be seen as being of wider application: the selection of the sixteenth-century *Youth* by Birmingham's Pilgrim Players, associated with the way in which the ancient terms "interlude" and "morality" were again being brought into familiar use, compels us to the realisation that academics, actors and dramatists were breathing the same air.

Between 1903 and 1905 summer-time audiences attending the open-air "theatre" in Regent's Park were given the privilege of savouring rarities such as Lyly's *Gallathea*, Jonson's *Hue and Cry after Cupid* and Fletcher's *The Faithful Shepherdess*: from that time on to 1914 various play-producing groups offered to their subscribers a long list of early dramatic works extending from the sixteenth to the eighteenth centuries; the Pilgrim Players were by no means alone in their devotion to early interludes; spectators at the Great Queen Street Theatre in 1907 (although certainly they remained unaware of their peculiar privilege) may quite possibly have been attending the public première of Shakespeare's *Troilus and Cressida*; and there is nothing strange in the fact that when an all-star performance was being arranged at Covent Garden in 1915 the play selected should have been *The School for Scandal* – and if the author could have looked down at this event he would unquestionably have rejoiced in the glittering galaxy of Beerbohm Tree, Louis Calvert, Henry Ainley, Owen Nares, George Alexander, Arthur Bourchier, H. B. Irving, Weedon Grossmith, Irene Vanbrugh, Lady Tree, Constance Collier, Ellaline Terriss and Eva Moore. The Stage Society discovered that there was such demand for revivals from the past that it created the Phoenix Society specifically for the purpose of resuscitating older plays, and, although the success of Gay's *Beggar's Opera* at the Lyric, Hammersmith, in 1923 was rivalled by no other kindred production, the West End stages showed increasing interest in the national dramatic heritage. An energetic London playgoer during those years was, in fact, being offered a much greater opportunity than that enjoyed by any playgoer in the past of seeing a wide diversity of older comedies and tragedies extending from the medieval period to the early nineteenth century.[1] The loss sustained by the vanishing of the stock-company system was now much more than remedied.

Before leaving this question of London's dramatic and theatrical internationalism, one final comment must be made. In 1931 a Danish critic, Martin Ellehauge, publishing a volume entitled *Striking Figures among Modern English Dramatists*, stated uncompromisingly at the beginning of his preface that "the dramatic work of the authors we are going to review shows Continental subjects making their way into the maturing English problem-play, and Continental methods followed in their treatment".[2] And when we look at the general context within which this sentence is placed and particularly when we read the judgment expressed in Ellehauge's following words – "Yet Continental realism is only exceptionally approximated" – we realise that here we are confronted by a bold assertion, not unreflected in the writings of some other contemporary critics, which depends upon a series of unsupported or debatable assumptions. The author takes for granted that English drama of the new age from 1900 to 1930 owed its entire growth to Continental example, that this Continental example belonged to the sphere of the problem play, that the problem play, being modern, represented the highest form of dramatic writing, and that, however "striking" some of the early twentieth-century English authors might be, they had almost completely failed to rise to the heights attained by authors elsewhere.

While it would not be appropriate here to challenge the reliability of these assumptions, something must be said about the resultant conclusion. Certainly the English playwrights received inspiration and encouragement from their

[1] Harold Child has a very useful and informative record of "Revivals of English Dramatic Works 1919–1925" (*Review of English Studies*, ii, 1926), but unfortunately there is no similar list relating to the later years of the period.

[2] P. 7.

knowledge of what was being done abroad, but frequently when they refused to do more than "approximate" foreign examples, it is evident that this refusal was deliberate – a reflection within the dramatic world of the very general repudiation in England of such other artistic movements as the dead-end destructiveness of Dadaism and the frenetic follies of Marinetti's Futurismo. Still further, another thing should be kept firmly in mind. Notwithstanding the devastatingly superior tone of Ellehauge's remarks, there were numerous early twentieth-century English playwrights whose inspiration was native and individual, who were regarded by their fellows in other countries with genuine admiration, and who made definite contributions to the European stage. George Bernard Shaw was at that time a name to conjure with, and, even although he stood high above his companions, he did not remain by any means a solitary figure whether at the start of his career or at the time of his greatest eminence. One of his latest fellows was Noël Coward, and regarding him there is evident truth in a comment recently made by the director Leonard L. Schach: "Bertholt Brecht", says Schach, "Giraudoux, Anouilh, O'Casey, Tennessee Williams and Arthur Miller may have made, each in his own way, a more profound impact on Modern Drama than has Noël Coward, yet none has reigned so long nor proved himself so versatile in his creativity."[1] And between Shaw and Coward there were many English dramatists who made significant contributions to the world's stage. Occasionally, it might be thought that things more exciting were to be found elsewhere, but exciting things do not always have an enduring quality; and in the best English contributions of this time there was a firm sense of assurance.

[1] Programme note for his production of *Hay Fever* at the Cameri Theatre, Tel Aviv, 1967. Opinions, of course, may differ. Thus, for example, Bamber Gascoigne, in his penetrating study of *Twentieth Century Drama* (1962), completely ignores the Edwardian theatre, devotes only two or three pages to the twenties, merely mentions Shaw and Coward in passing, and does not discuss the work of English dramatists before the arrival of Osborne.

2. *Dramatic Architecture and the Vogue for One-Act Plays*

The influence of at least some among the foreign dramatists, the realisation that Elizabethan dramatists planned their stage writings in a characteristically expansive manner (sometimes, indeed, probably ignoring act divisions altogether) and the widespread desire to develop things fresh and novel combined at this time to evoke a new attitude towards dramatic architecture. When in 1922 W. J. Turner sought to plan his *Man Who Ate the Popomack* in a novel manner, he explained that he did so because of his "belief that the dramatic principles inculcated by all writers on the theatre", having "only a narrow, logical foundation", were "aesthetically worthless"; and this opinion excellently indicates the general trend of thought which is to be found among many theatrical circles at the beginning of the twentieth century. Before proceeding to examine individual dramas emanating from those circles, therefore, it is essential to scrutinise the milieu amid which this new dramatic philosophy developed.

Here, it would seem, a start must be made by observing the truly enormous number of one-act plays written during the extent of those thirty years. Even the most cursory glance at the hand-list which forms part of the present survey will indicate how numerous they were.[1] It may be argued with some justification that one-act pieces proliferated during the entire course of the nineteenth century, yet there can be no doubt that during the Victorian age there existed nothing in any respect comparable with the scope, the variety and the import of the corresponding plays produced during the Edwardian–Georgian epoch. This wide range, qualitative as well as quantitative, resulted from the fact that within the later years various forces of diverse kinds combined to encourage their multiplication and their importance. Within the sphere of the commercial stage the first thing to be taken into consideration is the cult of the

[1] In looking at this hand-list, moreover, it must be remembered that it deliberately excludes even more one-act play titles than it includes.

"curtain-raiser". This cult, it is true, was an inheritance from the preceding century, and it is even necessary to admit that it was beginning to lose its force in Edwardian times; but even while it was gradually passing away in the West End theatres, several other new movements contributed towards not merely maintaining its popularity but actually making that popularity stronger. During the very first years of Edward's reign, as has been seen,[1] the hundreds of music-halls began to include short dramatic sketches among their acrobatic, clownish and musical turns: the lovely golden guineas with their comfortingly sterling ring attracted the star actors, and the dramatists, even the most distinguished, found equal profit, as well as occasionally stimulating challenge, in providing them with suitable texts. So popular were these playlets that at least a few theatre managements were actually induced to experiment in the presentation of triple or quadruple bills. And just as the music-halls started to sink and as such experiments were losing the gloss of novelty the popular revues began to make constant demands for more and ever more brief sketches with which to delight their public. Certainly it must be admitted that these revue sketches were very brief indeed and that the majority, constructed so as to make a sharp epigrammatic point rather than to develop characters, hardly assumed the shape of plays at all, yet their often skilful, ingenious dialogue and clever construction still render them quite as important as the multitude of "duologues" which formed a great part of the one-act activity in earlier years.

The commercial theatres and the music-halls thus offered wide encouragement for the penning of these short playlets, but this encouragement must be accounted slight when it is set against the broader and even more urgent demands of the societies and the repertories. Hundreds of amateur and even semi-professional associations found these short pieces easier to handle than full-length dramas, and many of them sought for short pieces with at least some measure of literary

[1] See pp. 43–6.

distinction. Hundreds of amateurs, no doubt, asked for no more than easily-managed pieces in any style and on any theme; but there remained numerous associations whose requests were more exacting and more specific. Some wanted poetic pieces; some of them desired grim realistic scenes; some inclined towards fantasy. The village groups asked for the dramatic treatment of rustic life; those associated with the cult of interludes and moralities made search for original playlets infused with moral and "philosophic" aims; there were those who looked only for plays with a religious content, for plays socialistically inclined or for plays apt to appeal to children. To the range of the demands hardly any frontiers can be found. And, to add to all this, there was the important fact that the writing of successful one-act pieces could be most profitable. In 1924, St John Ervine drew italicised attention to the "financial inducement" offered to authors by the amateur clubs: "people of the theatre," he emphasised,

> hardly realise that many dramatists earn considerable sums of money from the performance of their plays by amateurs. Two well-known dramatists have personally told me that they earn something like a thousand pounds a year from amateur performances of their work. The author of a popular one-act play told me that it brought him a steady income of two hundred pounds a year from amateur performances.[1]

As we move on from the earliest years of the century to the twenties we can easily see how the picture altered without losing its impressive central design. At the start "one-act plays had professional standing" and were frequently to be seen in the theatres of the West End: by the close of the period, they had virtually disappeared in that area, save for the programmes presented by the Grand Guignol company and for the tiny sketches introduced into revues. Thinking of this change, John Pollock was fully justified when in 1926 he declared that "in London one-acters practically do not exist".[2] Nevertheless, it was during this latter period that

[1] *The Organised Theatre* (1924), p. 150.

[2] *Twelve One-Acters* (1926), preface, p. 9.

the short play truly came into its own: it was then that dozens of anthologies of such dramas, both American and English, fed the growing demand: it was then that the short playlet could truly be accepted "as a legitimate form of dramatic art – as legitimate as the short story or the miniature":[1] it was then that there could be developed what may be called an aesthetic of this miniature dramatic form, as exemplified by Percival Wilde's *The Craftsmanship of the One-Act Play* (1923) and other similar studies, both in book and article form: it was then that "the nineteen-twenties jazz" was opposed not only by a *St Joan* and a *Juno and the Paycock* but also by the combined force of almost innumerable more lightly-armed auxiliaries.[2] Narrating the story of the Arts League of Service Travelling Theatre, Eleanor Elder recorded that when this notable venture was first launched in 1919 "the list of available one-act plays was a comparatively small one", whereas just a decade or so later "among the hundreds that" were published annually, "in addition to the thousands" being written, a producer was confronted by an embarrassment of riches. If we wish to have further evidence of what the theatre then meant to hundreds of spectators throughout Great Britain, we need only glance at the programmes of this Travelling Theatre from 1919 to 1930:[3] despite the fact that this organisation worked under severe handicaps, mechanical and meteorological, the number of interesting plays given "for the first time on any stage", or "for the first time in this country", or for the first time in public, is truly astonishing.

The establishment of a critical aesthetic for the "one-acter" is of double significance. Not only does it testify to the fact that the miniature play had attained to a distinctive and honourable position of its own, it also indicates how these short pieces tended to exert a pervasive influence on the structural forms assumed by the full-length drama. This

[1] J. W. M. Marriott (editor), *One-Act Plays of To-Day* (1924), foreword.

[2] Harold Brighouse, *What I Have Had: Chapters in Autobiography* (1953), pp. 38–9 and 99–100.

[3] These are summarised in Eleanor Elder's volume, pp. 252–8.

influence was both indirect and direct, and, whether the one or the other, the results were unfortunate. First of all, it may be observed that, while some of the major authors possessed the power of keeping the requirements of the short play distinct from those of the longer, many lesser writers were apt to confuse the two, and that, in particular, numerous younger apprentice playwrights had their talents sadly injured by starting their careers with the composition of one-act pieces. The planning of a full-length drama clearly calls for a large, sure architectural sense; and experience in the shaping of short playlets may well be thought to be as inappropriate for the gaining of such an architectural sense as application to the art of the miniature would be for a painter whose ultimate aim was to apply himself to large canvases or extensive murals. Again and again in this period we encounter dramas which clearly had been originally conceived in smaller terms and which had been given larger bulk only with an effort – dramas which were no more than good one-act play liquor inordinately diluted with tasteless water. Indeed, we might even be prepared to go further than this and accept John Pollock's judgment that "the more perfect a play in one act, the less likely it is to be good in three".[1]

Far more important than this, however, are other related considerations. During the earlier part of the nineteenth century (to go no further backwards in time) the traditional five-act structure for dramas both tragic and comic was almost obligatory. There were, certainly, numerous lesser pieces penned in three acts, but the more ambitious and "literary" authors always donned the toga cut in quinary form. As the century advanced, however, two changes occurred: gradually the five-act pattern gave way to a pattern in four acts, and even, at times, to a simpler three-act plan; and concurrently, through the practice of Scribe and Sardou, the *pièce-bien-faite*, the well-made play, with plots carefully presented in neat logical manner, came into common use.

By the beginning of the twentieth century, however, a

[1] *Twelve One-Acters* (1926), preface, p. 11.

number of playwrights started to introduce variations of divers kinds, and it is important to note that this disruptive trend developed both among those who liked to consider themselves "advanced" and among those whose eyes were set on the popular commercial stage. In 1903, for example, Henry Arthur Jones, an author who at that time may be considered as belonging to the old guard, designed his *Whitewashing Julia* in three acts and an "epilogue" – the epilogue being, not an address to the audience in the style so popular in the seventeenth and eighteenth centuries, but a concluding dramatic scene; and, when we examine its content and structure, we realise that, while of course its theme is related to the events dealt with in the main part of the comedy, its planning is reminiscent of what can be found in hundreds of independent one-act sketches. These sketches might be described as "episodes", and Jones' epilogue is of an episodic kind. Five years later, J. K. Jerome described his *Passing of the Third Floor Back* as "An Idle Fancy, in a Prologue, a Play and an Epilogue", thus in effect planning his action, with a kind of "framework" effect, as an introductory episode followed by the central part of the plot and concluding with another episode.

The practice exemplified in these two plays became commonly adopted by numerous dramatists, not only during the earlier years of the period but on to its conclusion, with various modifications and novel deviations from the simple norm. In 1908, for instance, Cicely Hamilton's *Diana of Dobson's* opened with what she called a first act, but which was, in fact, a separate short introduction to the play as a whole, an atmospheric picture of resident work-girls in a dressmaking establishment. Shortly afterwards Jeanette Steer, in *The Sphinx* (1914), introduced a new term to the theatre by designing her drama in three acts and what she described as an "apotheosis". In 1924 Temple Thurston seemed to be following older traditions by planning his *Blue Peter* in four acts, but when we examine the plot we realise that the main action, placed in a Liverpool domestic setting, does not begin until the curtain rises on act 2; the first act takes shape as a "prologue", which itself is planned as a short playlet – an episode in a remote mining camp where friendly natives bring a young girl as a present to the hero and where, at the end, there is an exciting attack by a savage tribe. Two years earlier than this, Rudolf Besier and May Edginton in *Secrets* (1922) adapted the device to the requirements of a dream play, first showing an episode in which a wife is seen sitting dozing by the bedside of her husband, who is critically ill and like to die, then carrying the audience back in time to their marriage and to their domestic trials and tribulations, and finally returning to the sick-room.

In most of the earlier plays the pressure of custom and convention caused the playwrights to describe the main sections of their dramas as "acts", but as the years advanced even that time-honoured term was often abandoned. In this connection Arnold Bennett's *Great Adventure*, presented in 1911, is particularly interesting: the title-page calls it a play "in four acts", but immediately below the register of the dramatis personae there are listed four "SCENES", in the sense of settings, and this is followed by a "SPECIAL NOTE – Each act is divided into two scenes, separated by a passage of time more or less short". Acts, scenes, settings are placed here in admirable confusion, and all of them remind us of the episodes presented in one-act playlets. If we want another example, and a further extension, of this device, we need go no further than Shaw's *St Joan* (1923): this is described as "A Chronicle Play in Six Scenes, and an Epilogue", and as we examine it we may well be tempted to see the first scene as a kind of episodic introduction and the epilogue as a separate episodic commentary.

These novel planning designs, so far from having been imitatively based on the invention of a single master-dramatist, must be seen as resulting from the prevailing stage conditions of the age and, particularly, as drawing both their basic strength and their varied forms from many different sources. The first of these is typified by the fact that the author of *The Great Adventure* was a novelist. In looking at the dramatic records of the time we must be struck by two related facts – the increasing number of novelists who also applied themselves to writing for the stage, and the increasing number of such authors whose prose narratives were dramatised, not by theatrical adapters, but by their own, often unaided, efforts. Arnold Bennett, Hall Caine, John Galsworthy were merely a few prominent figures standing at the head of a larger roster. Now, although clearly there are close connections between the novelist and the dramatist, the art of prose fiction and the art of the play had previously tended to be kept distinct: whereas the former had never accepted the application of any formal conventions, the latter had from earliest times shown a willingness, even a desire, to be bound within particular forms. This might be put in another way by saying that, while each great novel had developed its own peculiar shaping laws, each great play had inclined towards the acceptance of laws already established.

Along with the influence of the novel must be taken that of the film. With increasing frequency, especially after the year 1919, plays are to be encountered which deliberately attempted to make theatrical use of structural experiments inspired by what had been viewed on the silver screen. Numerous instances of this trend will have to be mentioned later, but for the present it may be sufficient merely to refer to four or five typical examples: in his *Man Born to Be Hanged* (1924) Richard Hughes combined direct action with narrative in a manner patently imitative of the silent screen's pictures and captions: Monckton Hoffe used flashbacks in *Many Waters* (1928); and cinematic technique is clearly evident in W. Hackett's *77, Park Lane* (1928) and W. Walter's *Happy and Glorious* (1930). Even before any of these pieces had appeared, Somerset Maugham, always an acute observer of the latest modes, had shaped his *East of Suez* (1922) in a novel manner by starting with a scene which consists entirely of a wordless picture of a Peking street, with cooks and coolies, carts and rickshaws, Manchu ladies, musicians and Mongols passing by: this atmospheric picture, innocent of dialogue, was no more than a stage aping of the kind of opening which by the early twenties had become so familiar on the screen. Between the year when this play of Maugham's was presented and the arrival of the thirties the silent films had been succeeded by the talkies, and the effect of the latter on the dramatists is amply made apparent in one of Daphne Du Maurier's passing comments. "In the June of 1930," she records, Gladys Cooper and her father, Gerald,

> remembering the enormous success of their last venture, *Cheyney*, joined forces once more and acted together at the Playhouse. The play was *Cynara*, by H. C. Harwood and Gore Browne, and with the competition of the talkies on every hand the authors had borrowed something of the cinema's technique. The play was chopped up into several scenes for variety, one or two of which, if amusing, were superfluous, and it was obvious that the play had been adapted from a novel.[1]

The influences of novel and film here were combined: and there is still one other earlier and not dissimilar force to be considered. At the beginning of the century the active Louis N. Parker invented a new kind of outdoor entertainment – the civic "pageant";[2] and a few years after the first of these displays had been presented to the public he went further by inventing the "Pageant Play". This term, he remarked,

> which is new, may require a word of explanation. A Pageant Play, as I conceive it, is written on the same principles as my English Pageants. In those the towns in which they took place were the heroes, and I tried to tell their entire histories. In my Pageant Plays ("Drake"; "Joseph and His Brethren") I try to tell the entire history of the man whose name the play bears. The unities of time and locality go by the board, and are replaced by the unities of idea and personality.[3]

And he might have added that, with the dismissal of the "unities", these plays naturally tended to have their themes presented in a series of episodes.

While Parker's example cannot be deemed the only force

[1] *Gerald: A Portrait* (1934), p. 286.
[2] See pp. 92–3.
[3] *Joseph and His Brethren* (1913), introductory note.

which led later to the widespread cultivation of the biographical drama, unquestionably he was largely responsible for the multiplication of such plays – and in most of them the authors inclined towards episodic methods in presenting their subject-matter. Clemence Dane's *Will Shakespeare* (1921) was, it is true, described as "An Invention in Four Acts", but the splitting of the two middle acts into four scenes gives it a form akin to the "Five Episodes" in the *Shakespeare* (1921) written by H. F. Rubinstein and Clifford Bax; *Churchill* (1925), by Rubinstein and A. J. Talbot, is called a "Chronicle-Comedy in Eight Scenes"; Drinkwater uses sets of scenes with intermittent duologues by "Chroniclers" in shaping his *Abraham Lincoln* (1918); and Shane Leslie in his *Mrs Fitzherbert* (1928), even although he returns nominally to the pattern of *The Passing of the Third Floor Back* by describing his drama as written in a prologue, five "acts" and an epilogue, follows the same general style.

Nor should we neglect to notice that the pageant plays and the biographical chronicle dramas expanded beyond the treatment of individual heroes, literary or political. Arnold Bennett's *Milestones* (1912), for example, brought the notion of "generations" to the fore. The title of H. F. Rubinstein's *The House* (1926) indicates that an inanimate object, the dwelling itself, is the focus of interest, and this may be associated with other similar examples, such as F. Tennyson Jesse's *Anyhouse* (1925) and Reginald Berkeley's *The White Chateau* (1925). As early as 1914 E. Knoblauch made his hero (or should it be heroine?) *My Lady's Dress*, binding thus together what are really a series of separate episodes by relating them all to the manufacture of this frilly object. When C. K. Munro later presented his *The Rumour* (1922) and *Progress* (1924) he was, in fact, following the same pattern even although his central binding object was an intangible essence rather than something material. And in *Cavalcade*, which came just outside the limits of this period, Noël Coward adroitly made a combination of many things, both tangible and intangible, when he devised his architectural plan of three "parts", the first consisting of eight scenes, the second of eleven and the third of one, followed by an "epilogue".

It cannot be denied that the impact of these forces – novels, films, pageants – stimulated occasionally by the discovery of foreign experiments and constantly influenced by the masses of one-act playlets, created an atmosphere certainly full of excitement. The well-made drama whose impress had been so potent in the past now was largely despised, and a new-found freedom ruled. Nevertheless, when we look beyond the flag-waving, we become conscious of a vague underlying feeling of disappointment and anxiety. Although many of the enthusiasts for things fresh and untried did not consciously realise what was happening, the truth is that a severe strain was being placed upon young apprentice playwrights: these were now left without guides, and each one of them, as it were, was forced to devise his own dramatic conventions. Sometimes, this or that author was successful in his efforts, although only too often the design contrived satisfactorily by a single dramatist to suit his own needs proved useless and unsatisfactory for others; while furthermore it becomes quite clear that frequently the efforts themselves inclined to use up energy which otherwise might have gone into the deeper development of themes and characters, and into invigorating the dialogue. Nor was this entirely confined to apprentice playwrights engaged in learning the technique of their craft: there would seem to be no doubt but that even such an experienced author as John Galsworthy was led sadly astray when in his later plays, *The Forest* (1924), *Escape* (1926) and *The Roof* (1929), he sought to be "with it" by experimenting in the episodic style.

At least a few perceptive critics saw the dangers clearly. In 1922 James Agate gave a clear warning of what was being lost amid the shapeless welter of freedoms. "It is difficult," he wrote, "to understand the intellectual's stern dislike of the well-made play. All the world's best plays have been well-made, even if *Hamlet* seems to first sight untidy and sprawling like some overgrown cathedral" – and to this he added a further observation, that the growth of the director's power, with its stress upon the "theatrical", had paradoxically resulted in the conclusion that "plays written for the theatre should be badly written and non-theatrical". Similarly, B. W. Findon, the founder and editor of *The Play Pictorial*, after having declared his belief in 1919 that playgoers were becoming bored with shapeless plays and yearning for a return to the well-made drama, uncompromisingly declared three years later that "We have cast aside the old models, our old ideas of what constituted a good play, and appear to have formed a drama more or less based on the lines and conventions of a film production with its inconsequent procedure and incidental trivialities."[1] In this connection is it not significant that almost without exception the dramatists of this time who are still remembered now are those who devoted most time in their youth to the intimate study of dramatic form? Maugham has recorded how seriously he applied himself to the task of learning how to be an effective playwright, and Coward's recent comments on his early training are of the same kind.

3. *The Dramatic Kinds*

In 1925 Bonamy Dobrée, in his *Timotheus*, published an entertaining imaginative account of a journey into the world of 2100. Eagerly, he tells us, he sought for information concerning the kind of drama that existed in this realm of the future and those to whom he was speaking questioned him as eagerly about the stage as it had existed in his time. "I laid myself open to much banter," he remarks, "by asking whether" one of their latest dramas was "a tragedy or a comedy". "Such a crude distinction," these denizens of the future confidently assured him, "was typical of the muddle-headedness of our age, on a level with the antitheses classical–romantic, conservative–liberal, matter–mind, and even intellect–emotion we were so fond of making, and which for absurdity were only equalled by our craze for dressing men and

[1] *The Play Pictorial*, xxxv, no. 213, 93, and xlii, no. 250, 1.

women in different sorts of clothes."[1] While a movement towards the breaking-down of traditional dramatic categories may be traced as far back as the days when Polonius was created and while this movement can be seen gathering expanding force throughout the whole of the nineteenth century, Dobrée's satiric picture of the theatre of tomorrow has particular pertinence when we consider the theatre's development from 1900 to 1930. And, since the categorising labels given to stage-pieces are always of great importance as indicating the aims and attitudes of their authors, a general survey of this theme also becomes almost obligatory before we proceed further.

Such a general survey, in fact, demonstrates at once that the pattern during those years was a peculiarly complex one, with lines criss-crossing each other in what at first appears to be mere confusion. Gradually, however, the eye begins to discern a large central basic design incorporating three or four principal elements.

Of these elements the first is the vanishing or the twisting in meaning of several descriptive technical terms which even in the nineteenth century had still retained much of their original significance. Within the popular sphere, a limited few – such as "farce", "musical comedy", "pantomime", "melodrama" – remained in current use, but others either disappeared or were rarely employed or else had ceased to have an exact significance. The fate of "tragedy" at this time provides us with a prime example of what was happening. It is difficult to find more than about a score or so of plays so designated between 1900 and 1930; most of these were one-act pieces, as though Melpomene's majestic robes had been drastically cut down; and in general it becomes clear that among those who did use the term there was little or no sense of what the word "tragedy" signifies. When an author designated his play in this manner, he was doing no more than informing his readers or audiences that his was a drama with an unhappy ending, death being its conclusion: in no wise was he suggesting that he had taken a particular attitude towards his characters and his theme.

[1] *Timotheus: The Future of the Theatre* (1925), p. 12.

Along with "tragedy" various other descriptive terms fell into disuse, while at the same time the words "play", "drama" and "dramatic" came to dominate over the stage. Fully half of the scripts written during those thirty years are distinguished by no more informative a generic term than "play", usually followed by a phrase such as "in four acts" or "in seven scenes". At first it might be thought that the use of a formula like this was otiose if not absurd, since the public was merely being told what it already knew – that the piece in question was not, let us say, a novel, and that it was framed in a form suitable for stage performance. Closer examination, however, suggests that it did have some interpretative significance, even if rather vague and general. This may be explained by observing that, along with the word "farce", the term "comedy" was among the relatively few standard dramatic terms which remained in frequent use. Obviously "comedy" meant a play the scenes of which were intended to be amusing, while "farce" indicated that the author hoped that his stage action would be regarded as hilariously funny: with these two terms in mind, when we examine the texts to which the word "play" was attached we realise that here the authors were trying to indicate that their writings were so planned as to stand well above "farce", but to bear a definite relationship with "comedy". In the typical "play" the audience might expect a very slight modicum of the laughable, just enough to provide variety and arouse a feeling of enjoyment; they might expect a main theme which was serious, but not too serious; they might expect, too, that such passions as were displayed would not have any very great depth or tension; and, above all, they might confidently assume that none of the characters would end in death. Thus, in effect, the employment of this word indicated that the playwright was intent upon pursuing a middle course, with "comedy" and "farce" on one side, and on the other side with "drama" as a term of almost equally common employment. At first glance, such a frequent description as "dramatic play" seems to be foolishly conceived, meaningless and absurd; yet when it is put alongside a variety of associated descriptions it must be realised that here "dramatic" is being used to suggest gripping situations, startling scenes, tense episodes, even murders – its import deriving consciously or unconsciously from the implications of the term "melodrama".[1]

One of the chief movements during this period, then, was the abandonment of several traditional dramatic terms and the wide employment of the unadorned and frequently indeterminate "play" and "drama" – in fact, a blurring of the traditional categories. Paradoxically, however, numerous authors, even those who most freely used these ill-defined descriptions, started to indulge in a new movement which may be described as the cult of the non-theatrical descriptive term and of the qualifying adjective. Jerome's *The Passing of the Third Floor Back* again provides a convenient and suggestive example. This, as has been seen, was announced as "An Idle Fancy". From one point of view the author's descriptive label might be construed as an attempt to indicate the peculiar quality of his plot, or perhaps even his attitude towards his invented theme – as an effort to inaugurate a new, or nearly new, dramatic category. That there might be some justification for so interpreting it is shown both by the employment of "fancy" by some other authors and by the fairly frequent utilisation of kindred terms by others. "Fantasy", "fantasy drama", "fantastic comedy" and the like appear frequently, and these are associated with related terms such as "dream fantasy", "dream drama", "impressionistic drama", "psychological drama", while at times other seemingly distinct descriptive labels, like "morality" and "drama of the soul", may reasonably be thought to bear allied connotations.

Nevertheless, when we look at this "idle fancy" from

[1] While "drama" was frequently used at this time with at least suggestions of a kinship with "melodrama", it may be noted that occasionally the idea of the latter was expressed by employment of the first element in that word: thus Cecil Raleigh's label of "melo-farce" for his *Flood Tide* (1903) does not mean, as might have been thought, a farce with musical accompaniment: it indicates a farce which includes some theatrically startling incident.

another point of view, we cannot escape noticing that it is connected with a tendency, freely exhibited in the work of many playwrights, to devise self-consciously clever labels for their compositions: one piece is an "uncomfortable play", another is an "unusual comedy", another a "bas-relief", another a "symbolic symphony", another a "quaint adventure", another an "invention", another a "peep-show into Paradise". And still others freely characterised their plays by terms such as "sermon", "discussion", "disquisitory play", "conversation", and "debate"; while the same trend towards the exhibition of cleverness in nomenclature can be seen in the fashion for what can be described only by the use of the phrase "quotation titles" – *Dear Brutus*, *Such Men Are Dangerous*, *Many Waters* and the like. Even although we might well be prepared to say that fundamentally it does not really matter what name or description a dramatist gives to his work, we are compelled to acknowledge that in many instances, if not in all, the impression of self-conscious ingenuity does not derive from these alone – that, in fact, title, label and play reflect the same mood or approach, and that basically none of these is in accord with what the stage seems basically to demand.

Clever descriptive terms abounded, but still more numerous were those which, instead of indicating the attitude of the authors towards their writings, merely drew attention to their subject-matter. Frequently these were of a broad kind: the scores of "costume dramas" and "romantic dramas" advised the public that here they would witness scenes exotic or historically remote. And at the same time a very large number of stage pieces were sign-posted with qualifying adjectives denoting the nationalities or local environments of the characters being dealt with: here we encounter "Russian drama", "Anglo-Russian drama", "Russian-Jewish drama", "American drama", "oriental drama", "modern Chinese drama", "gipsy play", "Irish comedy", "Lancashire comedy" and a host of similar descriptions, all pointing, not to the sources from which the plays were derived, but to the milieux with which they were concerned.

Slightly different, and yet expressive of much the same trend, were also many pieces whose descriptive titles drew attention to their basic subjects or to the nature of their action: here "smuggling drama" may be taken as an illustrative instance. Most of these may be deemed to possess little significance, but one, because of its increasing popularity, deserves a passing comment. During the first years of the century several plays, mostly one-acts, were given the epithets of "crook" and "mystery", and by 1907 the term "detective play", or "detective drama", had stepped on to the stage, albeit with a tread which was appropriately cautious and rubber-soled. Soon, however, writings of this sort came to make wide appeal; eventually they found companions in various forms of "spy play", while at the very close of the period several authors, such as Patrick Hamilton, sought to make the "thriller" into a recognised dramatic category.[1]

The general pattern which takes shape before our eyes as we consider these criss-crossing lines is one which suggests that the dramatic authors of the period were being granted a new sense of liberty, were being encouraged to indulge in experiments, and at the same time were often baffled in their efforts by the vanishing of those supports on which their predecessors had leaned. True, there was a general disappearance of such descriptions as, for example, "a grand comic, romantic, operatic, melodramatic, fairy extravaganza" of the kind so commonly used by the Brothers Brough, H. J. Byron, J. R. Planché and others during the nineteenth century, but it must be remembered that these belonged exclusively to the world of the "minor drama" and the "burlesque" and the "burletta": they did not intrude into the realms of the more serious drama even when, as sometimes occurred, the older standard dramatic categories were becoming frayed and insecure on their frontiers. It must be freely admitted that, in the nineteenth century, young writers were not offered much vital inspiration and that the dramatic supports on which they leaned had become shaky and

[1] See below p. 211.

insecure; yet their position, if by no means happier, was at least completely different from that of their descendants, the worried and troubled apprentice playwrights of the twentieth century who, without firm aid, found themselves forced to design and construct their own individual theatrical foundations.

4. *Copyright, Criticism and Censorship*

If these young dramatists, in the midst of the modern iconoclasm, were often confronted by incertitudes, distracted by conflicting theories, perplexed about the very nature of the theatre and particularly about the relationship between the play and the production, one thing is sure – that the writers were now being given certain opportunities and encouragement such as none of their predecessors in the nineteenth century had enjoyed.

Obviously the prime necessity for an apprentice playwright is that he should have the chance of watching his scenes presented on a stage before an audience. During the latter part of the preceding century, as we have seen, this chance was frequently very slim indeed: the conditions operative within the circle of metropolitan playhouses naturally made managers, whether they were star actors or not, duly cautious when they were asked to consider a drama by an unknown author, and induced them to rely, in the main, upon the works which came from members of the "dramatic ring", men whose writings had already stood the test and whose reputations were firmly established. Now, on the contrary, all this was being steadily and surely changed through the activities of the repertories and the play-producing societies: now young playwrights lived in a happy land where almost everything of any worth was given the prospect of stage production in some form or another.

Nevertheless, this encouragement and these opportunities raised problems of their own: difficulties and distractions remained. Let us suppose, for example, that some youthful provincial writer, observing that his local repertory exhibits a desire to assist local talent, pens a dark, grim dramatic study of life within that district; let us suppose that this has been accepted and that its production has met with a certain measure of success. The young playwright is no doubt overjoyed; he has been granted the privilege of watching his scenes taking three-dimensional shape on the stage: yet he now finds himself confronted by a dilemma. He probably realises that part, at least, of his success depended upon his selection of regional material and that such regional material might have made no appeal to audiences unfamiliar with the real environment whereon the dramatic action had been founded. The dilemma for this hypothetical young author, therefore, is whether he should continue to write other similar plays for the local theatre which had given him his first opportunity or whether he should risk breaking away, dealing with themes and characters less intimately familiar to him, and trying his fortune in a wider sphere.

This dilemma, basically an artistic one, was complicated by economic considerations. In general, dramatists now found themselves in a world much more comfortable than that which existed in Victorian times. Certainly, a great deal had been done to protect authors since the passing of the Dramatic Copyright Act of 1833, but even as late as 1907 it was found necessary to establish a Copyright-Play Protection Society because there was so much piracy in the provinces, while five more years had to pass by before playwrights were relieved of the necessity of actually putting their scripts into production before they could claim what then was generally known as "stage-right':[1] but conditions generally had improved, particularly after the signing of an International Copyright Convention on November 13, 1908 and the passing of the American Copyright Act of March 4, 1909. Despite all of this, however, the young – and sometimes even the not-so-young – dramatists, especially those who were attached through circumstance or inclination to the repertory theatres, found themselves confronted with a serious question. While most attractive sums of money could come from

[1] This was effected by the Copyright Act of 1911, the provisions of which did not become operative until July 1, 1912.

a London success, only trifling remuneration might be expected from local playhouses, themselves struggling to make ends meet, where runs were deliberately rejected. St John Ervine offers a pertinent personal illustration. In 1922, he tells us, he gave a new drama, *The Ship*, to the Liverpool Playhouse: it was acted for a fortnight, and in royalties he received a sum totalling £48. 15*s*. 3*d*. "The play," he continues,

> was not performed again until the beginning of 1924, when it was included in the programme of the Little Theatre at Bristol, which is about half the size of the Playhouse. It was performed there for a week, and the royalties amounted to £14. 12. 8....The managers of both these repertory theatres tell me that "The Ship" was a financial success, in that it more than paid its way, but no one can say that it has been a financial success, so far as its author is concerned, when his total earnings from it in three years, counting from the time it was written, amount to £63. 7. 11, out of which he has to pay an agency commission of ten per cent. I have not, in fact, earned ten shillings per week from "The Ship", although it took longer to write and cost me more trouble than a popular piece out of which I earned several thousand pounds.[1]

It would seem certain that it was the realisation that all was not quite satisfactory in this new theatrical realm which caused several individuals and institutions at this time to offer a new kind of encouragement to young dramatists. This was the age when the concept of dramatic prizes was born, and, although these were not so many or so financially rewarding as those with which we are now familiar, they certainly did give some stimulus and occasionally substantive support to writing for the stage. Stratford-upon-Avon appears, appropriately, to have been first in the field when in 1910 Josephine P. Peabody's *The Piper* won a public award.[2] Two years later the periodical *Tit-Bits* selected William Wade's one-act play *Tracked* as its "Prize Sketch"; and during the same year a Welsh Drama Competition was

[1] *The Organised Theatre* (1924), pp. 153–4.

[2] This prize was offered by the Governors of the Memorial Theatre, and its amount – £300 – was for that time surprisingly generous.

inaugurated by Lord Howard de Walden, the first choice going to J. O. Francis for his *Change.* In 1913 the judges of the Lyceum Club Prize Play Competition selected Winifred M. Ardagh's *As the Law Stands* for a "general award" and gave a special "costume-play prize" to Priscilla Craven and Sybil Ruskin for their collaborative *The Painted Nun.* When the war came to an end, a Charles Gulliver £50 prize was offered for the best variety playlet; the British Drama League established an award associated with guaranteed trial performance and publication; and other similar ventures, such as the Sheffield Playgoers' Play Competition, carried the concept into the provinces.[1]

When an examination is made of contemporary critical writings, from those in the daily and weekly columns of periodicals to those in the many books which sought to explore the latest trends in the new drama, it becomes clear that, in general, there was a corresponding endeavour on the part of dramatic critics to welcome and encourage the creative authors who were seeking to give novel material to the stage. This statement, of course, requires to be qualified by noting the obvious fact that the dramatic critics who were attached to daily newspapers and weekly journals naturally regarded it as their duty frankly to condemn any diversions which seemed to them inimical to the interests of the stage – and it hardly needs to be said that some of the enthusiasts, like the enthusiasts of other times, expressed annoyance and anger when adverse judgments were passed on any of their latest endeavours. On looking back from our own vantage point in time, however, we must freely recognise the excellence displayed by the majority of the reviewers, the seriousness with which collectively they viewed their mission and the generally sympathetic support which the "modern" drama received in their writings. During the earlier part of the nineteenth century there had been brilliant commentators on plays and productions, but for the most part these men had worked alone, giving their solo performances on the

[1] For this see the prefatory note in Alma Brosnan's *At Number Fifteen* (1927).

critical stage. There were some signs of a change towards the close of Victoria's reign when, significantly, "schools" of critical thought began to take shape,[1] yet, even so, whatever was done within those decades must be regarded as merely an anticipation of things to come. In 1923 William Archer, than whom there could be no better witness, had full justification for his assured statement that "the theatrical criticism of to-day is immeasurably more competent and brilliant than that of forty years ago when I was a beginner."[2] Throughout this period penetrating and lively assessments and explorations were being made by a body of reviewers stretching from Max Beerbohm, A. B. Walkley, Harold Child, James Agate and St John Ervine to Ivor Brown, Charles Morgan, Horace Horsnell, W. A. Darlington and M. Willson Disher, and also including several of their fellows in the provinces, such as the brilliant C. E. Montague of *The Manchester Guardian* and Crompton Rhodes of *The Birmingham Post*.[3] The quality of their work is clearly demonstrated by the fact that we can turn back to so many of their reviews, even of plays which have absolutely no meaning for us, and read what they have to say with pleasure (deriving from an appreciation of their style) and profit

[1] See *H. E. D.*, v, 21–7, 776. [2] *The Curtain*, i, no. 3, 1923, 27.

[3] A list of the more important writers and their affiliations may prove useful: Max Beerbohm (*The Saturday Review*), A. B. Walkley (*The Times*), Harold Child (*The Times* and *The Observer*), James Agate (*The Sunday Times* and *The Manchester Guardian*), William Archer (*The Tribune*), St John Ervine (*The Morning Post* and *The Observer*), Horace Horsnell (*The Observer*), W. A. Darlington (*The Daily Telegraph*), E. A. Baughan (*The Daily News*), S. R. Littlewood (*The Daily Chronicle*), H. M. Walbrook (*The Pall Mall Gazette*), Hannen Swaffer (*The Daily Express*), J. T. Grein (*The Illustrated London News*), H. Chance Newton (*The Referee*), M. Willson Disher (*The Sunday Times* and *The Empire News*), A. V. Cookman (*The Times*), Ivor Brown (*The Manchester Guardian*, *The Saturday Review* and *The Observer*), Sydney Carroll (*The Sunday Times*), and Charles Morgan (*The Times*). G. W. Bishop was for many years the dramatic critic of *The Era*, and between 1928 and 1931 its editor. Although the work of J. C. Trewin belongs mainly to the period after 1930, he was dramatic critic of *The Western Independent* from 1928 to 1932 and his reviews of productions at the Plymouth Repertory Theatre are a valuable record of the activities of that playhouse. C. L. S. Earley has a survey of *English Dramatic Criticism, 1920–1930* (1952).

(arising from their keen appreciation of dramatic values). And at the same time, the broadly-spread public interest in things theatrical and dramatic is perhaps nowhere more clearly exemplified than in a second fact – that a surprisingly large number of these men not only had followings of readers for their current criticism but also found a ready market for substantive volumes, some containing anthologies of selected reviews and some of an historical kind. Besides his *Nights at the Play* (1911) and *A Playgoer's Wanderings* (1926), H. M. Walbrook thus published a history of Brighton's Theatre Royal (1919) as well as an account of *J. M. Barrie and the Theatre* (1922) and a "history and comment" devoted to the Gilbert and Sullivan operas (1922); A. B. Walkley issued three collections of dramatic "prejudice";[1] "E. F. S." (who was Edward Fordham Spence, critic of *The Westminster Gazette*) surveyed *Our Stage and Its Critics* (1910); J. T. Grein in several volumes gave particular attention to experimental efforts in the "modern" style;[2] and James Agate was responsible for an entire shelfful of books in which, with theatre and drama as the core, he discussed almost everything.[3]

Diverse in personality and opinion as these men might be, it was typical of the time that collectively they should seek to link themselves together. Among the welter of clubs, societies and professional associations is to be found the

[1] *Pastiche and Prejudice* (1921), *More Prejudice* (1923) and *Still More Prejudice* (1925).

[2] Particularly *The World of the Theatre* (1921), *The New World of the Theatre* (1924) and *Miniatures of Playwrights and Players* (1922).

[3] These are merely a few examples of what was a general trend and they do not include numerous books of a more general and philosophic kind, several of them published after 1930, by critics who were already active during the earlier period. Among others, especially important are C. E. Montague's *Dramatic Values* (1911; revised edition 1925), significant because it goes beyond immediate reviewing into the sphere of "dramatic theory"; Ivor Brown's *Masques and Phases* (1926); Sydney Carroll's *Some Dramatic Opinions* (1923); and St John Ervine's *The Theatre in My Time* (1933). In 1960 W. A. Darlington gave, in his *Six Thousand and One Nights: Forty Years a Critic* a thoughtful and entertaining account of the drama from 1920 onwards. The significance of *The Dramatic Criticism of William Archer* (1964) is discussed by Hans Schmid.

Society of Dramatic Critics, created in 1906 with A. B. Walkley as its president and William Archer as its vice-president, and this was followed in 1923 by the better-known Critics' Circle. Neither of these two societies, of course, ever had in any respect the objective of establishing a common platform of thought – that would have been impossible to achieve, and, even if it had been possible, would have been either absurd or dictatorially dangerous: what they did was to reflect the seriousness with which the critics viewed their position within the theatrical world as a whole, their eager interest in the contemporary drama and, above all, their deep sense of responsibility.

In all their writings we feel their deeply-rooted desire, as critic-spectators, to be able to praise what they went to see and hear; but, like many other non-professional members of the play-going public, this only too often proved impossible: there had to be the admission that, in actual fact, many of the age's experiments were proving unsatisfactory. Thus there arose what might be called the well-wishing alibi: the modern dramatists had to be encouraged, and, although honesty in judgment must prevail, excuses had to be advanced when they failed to come up to their promises. The alibis were, of course, various, rising and falling in accordance with the theatre's development: some writers at the beginning pointed their accusing fingers at the supposedly vicious actor–manager system,[1] some later attacked the commercial managements; some, with duly cautious politeness, girded at the music-hall's competition or, more forcefully, attacked the "movies" and the "wireless"; many deplored London's entertainment-seeking spectators and provincial public apathy.

Amid this rising and falling of alibis, however, one excuse remained as constant as Caesar's northern star: almost all could shake hands in agreeing that, whatever other inimical forces might be to blame, the censorship was largely responsible.[2] Repeated attempts to abolish the control of the Lord

[1] See above pp. 30–2.

[2] A useful early booklet is that by "G. M. G.", *The Stage Censor: An Historical Sketch* (1908). A fuller account appears in John Palmer's

Chamberlain's Office were made all through these thirty years, and at the start it looked as though the efforts might end in success. In 1907 a deputation of prominent authors presented a petition to the Home Secretary, and a bill designed to modify the provisions of the 1737 Act was introduced into Parliament. As a result, a Select Committee was appointed; the hearings began on July 29, 1909, a Report was issued on November 11 of the same year – but no further action was taken. Three years later, in 1912, the banning of Eden Phillpotts' *The Secret Woman* occasioned a flurry of excitement in intellectual quarters; a fresh petition was prepared – addressed this time not to the Home Secretary, but actually to Majesty itself; and the London managers, alarmed as to what might happen and afraid lest the abolition of the Lord Chamberlain's powers might place them in an insecure position, hurriedly put forward a counter-petition. Already, however, the Lord Chamberlain himself had taken protective action: in 1911 he had quietly invited an advisory committee, consisting of Sir Edward Carson, Sir Squire Bancroft, Sir John Hare, Walter Raleigh and S. O. Buckmaster, to make recommendations concerning such particular thorny questions as might arise from the consideration of doubtful plays, and this action, when publicly known, tended to quieten the protests of the abolitionists. Later, after the end of the war, the adoption of a less rigid policy than that which had prevailed in previous years kept the simmering pot from boiling over.

These facts concerning positive action are significant, but

The Censor and the Theatres (1912), and recent surveys of the whole subject appear in R. Findlater's *Banned: A Review of Theatrical Censorship in Britain* (1966) and Donald Thomas' *A Long Time Burning: The History of Literary Censorship in England* (1969). The subject was much discussed in the periodicals of the time: G. S. Street's "The Censorship of Plays" (*Fortnightly Review*, dccv, Sept. 1925) is especially noteworthy if only because the author, a one-time Reader of Plays, was writing from the inside. In 1908 a privately printed booklet entitled *The Censorship of Plays* collected together a number of statements on this subject made by a number of persons associated with the theatre: in *The Censor, the Drama and the Film, 1900–1934* (1934) Dorothy Knowles set the debate within a wider context and included a representative "bibliography".

far more significant is an appreciation of the attitude adopted towards the censorship by many advanced critics at this time. Not all, of course, agreed that the theatre should be made completely free: it is, for example, most interesting to observe that no less ardent an innovator than J. T. Grein declared in 1923 that "if the Lord Chamberlain were to lose his control we should come under the heel of the police, and what that means can only be realised by those familiar with the procedure abroad";[1] and hardly less interesting is the attitude taken with regard to this subject by the very liberal Frank Vernon who, in 1924, after listing the minute number of plays which had been banned, refused to permit himself to get all hot and bothered over a matter which seemed to him of no real importance. On the other side, however, as Grein noted, there were hundreds whose first thought, on considering "the enemy of the theatre", was of the Censor. Thoroughly typical is a slim booklet, *What is Wrong with the Stage*, published by William Poel in 1920. In this he rightly started off by stressing the way in which finance ("Threadneedle Street") was coming to dominate over the playhouses, so that, in his opinion, "the condition of the English Theatre has moved steadily downward" until "to-day it may be said to have reached its lowest level on record". So far, so good: but, after a few pages devoted to an elaboration of this thoroughly pertinent theme, when he turned to enumerate the evils which required to be eradicated if the stage and drama were to flourish again, unexpectedly and illogically he placed at the top of his list "abolition of the Lord Chamberlain's office".

Poel's booklet may give us a clue for an understanding of the particular attitude adopted towards this subject at the beginning of the century. In recent discussions of the censorship problem, particularly those which filled so many columns in the newspapers and weeklies between 1968 and 1969, the main stress was, properly, placed on the basic issue of freedom of expression: even although various

[1] *The New World of the Theatre* (1924), p. 51 (essay dated May 12, 1923).

instances were adduced of annoyances occasioned to individual authors by the demands made by the Reader of Plays, there was hardly any attempt to argue that with the disappearance of that officer a new future for the drama would begin. In contrast with this, the abolitionists of the years 1900 to 1930 tended to make three fundamental suggestions – that such weaknesses as were to be found in the drama of their own times derived largely from operation of the Lord Chamberlain's control,[1] that many masterpieces had been condemned and were thus lost to the stage, and that the banishing and vanishing of the censorship would assuredly release a great flood of dramatic energy. Even while we may agree that the Lord Chamberlain's Reader had, during the early years of the century, been acting foolishly and over-severely and that there is justification for those who logically have argued, on the principle of freedom of speech, for termination of the Lord Chamberlain's control, it is also necessary to admit that the emotional attacks so frequent at the beginning of the century had often, indeed generally, been falsely inspired because they were, often unconsciously, put forward as an alibi and even as a confidently prescribed panacea. Those who argued for the abolition of the censorship in 1968 were quite prepared to believe that this might result in little more than an *Oh! Calcutta!*:[2] their predecessors fifty years earlier promised wonders and would have been bitterly disappointed if the air, freed from all restrictions, had not been filled with greatness. There was, of course, absolutely no justification for their claim that, if this "enemy" were vanquished, great plays by the score would march triumphantly onto and round the stage; there was no justification for the assumption that numerous masterpieces

[1] This argument appeared as late as 1947 in Norman Marshall's survey of *The Other Theatre*, p. 13: the English stage, he declares in that volume, "was saved from stagnation and sterility by the small group of producers, players and playgoers who, supported by many of the dramatic critics, refused to accept the drab monotony imposed upon the theatre by the managers and by the Censor".

[2] At least, so they said at the time; but several recent comments suggest that some of them are suffering from disappointment and even from qualms of conscience.

were being denied to contemporary audiences; there was absolutely no justification for inflating such a dull and mediocre drama as *The Secret Woman* into a supposed masterpiece simply because it had been refused a stage licence; there was no valid reason for suggesting that Edward Garnett's *The Breaking Point* (1907) – which was printed with the advertisement of "*A CENSORED PLAY*" at the top of the title-page – or Hubert Griffith's *Red Sunday* (1929) – with its "*BANNED!*" flaring in large red capital letters across its cover – merited any particular praise simply because they had been denied approval in the Lord Chamberlain's office. Frank Vernon was simply speaking the obvious truth when he remarked that "under Censorship the greatest drama since Elizabeth was written in England in the pre-War years of the twentieth century. It would have been no greater had there been no Censor."[1]

Actually Vernon's declaration is saying two things. First, it asserts that, if any alibi is needed, this particular excuse is just not good enough and, secondly, it insists that, as the prisoner standing in the dock is innocent of the crime imputed to him, no alibi at all is demanded. Here Vernon reminds us that according to English justice no persons are to be deemed guilty unless there is firm evidence against them and that therefore it behoves us now to leave this consideration of theatrical and dramatic conditions for the purpose of examining, in as unprejudiced a manner as possible, the plays produced by the dramatists of this time.

[1] *The Twentieth-Century Theatre* (1924), p. 117.

CHAPTER IV

POPULAR ENTERTAINMENT: MUSICALS, REVUES AND MELODRAMAS

IF we exclude the many hundreds of "sketches" and "scenes" written for presentation in the music-halls, most of the plays composed between 1900 and 1930 may be considered as belonging to one or another of three fairly clearly-marked areas – to have taken shape from one or another of three points of view.

Of these areas, the largest and fundamentally the most important occupies an extensive central position. This area was associated with the activities of the majority of London's West End theatres, whether managed by prominent actors or controlled by impresarios and entrepreneurs, and to it belonged the majority of those playwrights, from Pinero and Barrie to Maugham and Coward, whose reputations, even if all are not so glittering as once they were, still endure. These men almost always aimed at appealing to as large and representative an audience as possible, the educated and uneducated, the intellectually brilliant and the obtuse, the rich and the poor. No doubt there was much within this central area which was trivial, dull and uninspired, yet nevertheless, even before we proceed to examine some of its productions, we must realise that it was not only the widest in extent but, more importantly, the most intrinsically interesting. Should we wish, for convenience, to give it a name, we could not do better than take our cue from Hamlet and call it the "general".

To each side of it stand two flanking areas – one to the

left, usually caviare to the general, which for the moment may be styled the "progressive", and one to the right which may be called the "popular". The theatres associated with the former were various, the repertory playhouses and the stages occupied erratically by the teeming bevy of play-producing societies, but within this area was also the greater part of what may be described as the stageless drama – the scores of plays which, although published, never succeeded in securing a performance or which never were intended for theatrical representation. Easier to list and define are the theatres associated with the "popular" drama. Here stood the most honoured of all England's playhouses, Drury Lane, companioned by the Lyceum and the Prince's as well as by those other houses, such as the Gaiety, which specialised in musical comedy:[1] here also were many of the suburban stages, together with a large number outside the metropolis. Here the managers, the actors and the playwrights set their gaze, not on the broadly representative "general" audience, but on spectators of a more limited range, spectators who were emblematised in the West End by the young men about town who, despite the fact that many had just come down from Oxford, were essentially brainless and whose counterparts in the East End were the uneducated workers and their worthy spouses. It should hurriedly be said that this condensed definition of the term "popular" is by no means intended to be derogatory: these simple-minded playgoers, as will be seen, had much to give to the stage – sometimes far more than what was contributed by spectators more self-assured and intent upon things of an intellectual kind.

While the independent existence of these three areas must be kept prominently in mind, and while therefore it is convenient to examine them separately, it must always be remembered that none of them had inviolable frontiers, and that playwrights who might seem to be firmly attached to one could easily move over into another. These inter-relationships exhibit themselves in divers ways. It is, for instance, obvious that the playwrights who belonged to the central area found

[1] See pp. 24–5, 153–4.

themselves influenced, as season succeeded season, by the writings of those who belonged to the "progressive" territory, while there were at least some occasions when these "progressives" found themselves taking over styles which had belonged to the "popular" authors. Some dramatists – of whom John Drinkwater and St John Ervine may be taken as examples – attached to the "progressive" repertories turned in later years to make their appeal to "general" audiences; and, conversely, other authors, such as Clemence Dane, could address themselves in their earliest dramas to broadly popular audiences and then gradually develop a taste for caviare. Within each of these three areas characteristic types of plays sprang into being, but, as again will be seen, a particular style which at first seemed attached firmly to one might surprisingly find its most effective expression within the range of another. It must, accordingly, be clearly understood that, although the following three chapters are devoted, respectively, to the "popular", the "progressive" and the "general", there must be occasions when in each of them the frontiers have to be deliberately crossed. To give just one example, it would be confusing and absurd to deal in three separate sections with the various attempts made during this time to cultivate a poetic drama: the only proper procedure, here and elsewhere, is to feel free when occasion demands to move from one area to another.

Just at first, it might appear that the central area, since it is the largest and the most important, ought to be dealt with before an examination is made of the smaller areas on its two sides; but unquestionably the more profitable course will be to examine the territories of the "popular" and the "progressive" before turning to consider the larger body of dramatic material incorporated within the first, even although at times anticipatory comments must be made regarding certain developments which, originating within the "popular" or "progressive" areas, spread out to take possession of the West End stages catering to wider audiences. And, in making choice between the two flanking areas, it seems proper to begin with the "popular", partly because its significance has been so often ignored and partly because it is, historically, most firmly attached to the kind of theatre which flourished during the latter years of Victoria's reign.

We start, therefore, with the musicals, the revues and the melodramas.

1. *The Musical Comedy and its Companions*

It may indeed seem most peculiar, in a survey of drama, to make one's first step into the realm which in that period was the least serious, the most intent upon entertainment for its own thoughtless sake. There are, asserted one discerning critic in the year 1924, "two theatres, the theatre of drama and the theatre of musical comedy and revue" – and, he added, these are not only different, they simply "don't mix". In making this declaration he was, of course, by no means alone: thousands there were who thought alike.

Most readers now, recalling the long lists of wretchedly trivial shows which came and went, and went and came, during those years, are likely to accept this view as expressing a basic truth, and they are equally likely to receive with silent approbation the numerous vitriolic attacks which ardent theatrical reformers directed at those spectators who found pleasure in performances which confessedly aimed only at providing light senseless entertainment. Nevertheless, a second thought may possibly come to mind – that this period is known familiarly as "The Singing Years" and that many among its tuneful ditties still continue to make their appeal, have become indeed part of our heritage. "The theatre of drama" may be that which is of particular and serious significance, but at least a brief glance has to be given to the qualities of this other stage which proved so popular; and, as a prelude to a consideration of these qualities, it may be wise to remember that the historian of the Gaiety Theatre, W. Macqueen-Pope, did not hesitate in 1949 to capitalise on his title-page the descriptive words "*THEATRE OF ENCHANTMENT*".[1]

It is important to recognise at the start that the term "musical comedy" had, and still has, both a specific and a widely general application. In so far as the former is concerned, there is comfort in knowing that all contemporaries were agreed about its original conception, everyone giving credit to one man – the great George Edwardes who, after having been business manager at the Savoy for several years, had taken over the management of the Gaiety in 1886. Already by that time this playhouse had achieved considerable distinction under the control of John Hollingshead, and what Edwardes did was, as it were, to fuse together the tradition set by his predecessor and the experience which he had gained in working with Gilbert and Sullivan. The Gaiety thus flourished, and not so long afterwards Edwardes was

[1] Besides his *Gaiety: Theatre of Enchantment* (1949), Macqueen-Pope has an informative volume of wider scope, *Nights of Gladness* (1956). The original Gaiety was opened in 1868 and played a notable part in London's theatrical life until it was torn down in 1903 during the time when the Aldwych–Kingsway area was rebuilt. A second Gaiety, located at the Strand corner of Aldwych, was opened a few months later and enjoyed a prosperous career, hardly less distinguished than that of its predecessor, until it was closed in 1939. A summary historical account of the two houses is to be found in Raymond Mander and Joe Mitchenson, *The Lost Theatres of London* (1968), pp. 80–119: on the activities of the first theatre John Hollingshead's "*Good Old Gaiety*" (1903) is particularly interesting: and S. Naylor examines the second in his *Gaiety and George Grossmith* (1913). D. Forbes Winslow deals with musicals at *Daly's* (1944): the rise and fall of this house is also entertainingly dealt with by H. G. Hibbert in his *Fifty Years of a Londoner's Life* (1916). The general atmosphere amid which these playhouses flourished is discussed in A. E. Wilson's *Edwardian Theatre* (1951), J. C. Trewin's *The Gay Twenties* (1958), P. Noble's *Ivor Novello* (1951) and several similar general and specialised studies. The development of the American musical is traced by J. Walker McSpadden in *Light Opera and Musical Comedy* (1936) and by C. Smith in *Musical Comedy in America* (1950): Abe Laufe's more recent *Broadway's Greatest Musicals* (1969) contains a lively and perceptive record of its best achievements. Obviously, the English musicals of the time made great use of Continental material, and consequently reference should be made here to *Die Wiener Operette* (1947) by F. Hadamowsky and H. Otte, Louis Schneider's *Les maîtres de l'opérette française* (1921–1924), and *Operettenführer von Offenbach bis zum Musical* (1958) by H. Steger and K. Howe.

able to extend his empire by assuming the management of two other houses, the Prince of Wales's in 1892 and Daly's in 1895.[1] Shortly before this expansion of his activities he is known to have been dreaming of a new type of musical entertainment adapted to what he believed were changing tastes among the public, and it was his inspiration that had induced Adrian Ross and James T. Tanner, associated with the composer Osmond Carr, to create a "musical farce" entitled *In Town*: originally presented at the Prince of Wales's in 1892, this proved to be a remarkable success. Although some purists have sought to argue that it was not a musical comedy proper, there can be no real doubt but that this pioneering effort established in all its basic essentials a fresh pattern, the lines of which were soon made firm by the accomplished group of writers and musicians whom Edwardes astutely engaged as his associates. To Adrian Ross, J. T. Tanner and Osmond Carr, all of whom remained active well into the twentieth century, were added others of like calibre and interests. The popular *Shop Girl* (1894) had a libretto written by H. J. W. Dam, lyrics by Ross and Lionel Monckton, music by Ivan Caryll; Tanner wrote the book of *My Girl* (1896), Ross contributed the lyrics, Carr the music; Tanner took W. Paling as a collaborator in preparing the script of *The Circus Girl* (1896), the lyrics were supplied by Ross and Harry Greenbank, the music by Caryll and Monckton. And so we move on to *The Messenger Boy* of 1900, prepared by almost the same team: Alfred Murray joined Tanner in writing the book, the lyrics were penned by Ross and Greenbank, and, once more, music by Caryll and Monckton graced the show.

Edwardes' plan, variously exemplified in these nineteenth-century musicals, was based on some four or five principal demands. He asked that musical comedy should have a plot sufficiently strong to hold the audience's interest, but he

[1] Actually Edwardes was responsible for building this house in 1893, when he leased it to Augustin Daly. The following year he transferred his production of *A Gaiety Girl* to its stage, and, although for some time Daly technically remained the lessee, in effect Edwardes controlled the theatre thereafter.

insisted that this plot should not be a dominant element or make any deep emotional appeal. Every endeavour should be made to keep it attractive, but slight and light. There were to be no villains here to occasion dramatic "scenes". There was to be no satire – or, if occasionally satiric touches were to be introduced, they had to be kept muted, polite and gay. Significant is the fact that it was in these musical comedies that George Grossmith jr, prime exponent of the feckless yet genially good-natured man-about-town, won his greatest successes. "I'm an awf'lly simple fellow," he characteristically sang in *The Toreador* (1901),

I'm an awf'lly simple fellow
As I'm sure you'll all agree,
And I don't know what
My various friends can see in me:
My acquaintances are endless
And their names I quite forget,
For one half I only know by sight
And the rest I've never met.

But everybody's awf'lly good to me,
Don't you know;
I'm just about as spoilt as I can be,
Don't you know;
If I go out, say to Prince's, and alone I chance to dine,
Why, it's ten to one I meet some dear old Oxford friend of mine:
Well, not only does he join me, but he orders all the wine;
Everybody's awf'lly good to me.

Sociologically most reprehensible, no doubt, but merrily charming.

The second demand was that this story should be cast in such a way as to permit the introduction of diverse numbers of an apparently extraneous kind, and that it should allow for the lyric treatment of topicalities. Thus, for example, the romantic adventures in Corsica and Venice which formed the main theme of *A Runaway Girl* (1898) permitted the exotic escapades to be related to the current familiarities of the time: perhaps its most effective song was:

Oh, follow the man from Cook's,
The wonderful man from Cook's,
And whether your stay be short or long
He'll show you the sights, he can't go wrong.
Oh, follow the man from Cook's,
The wonderful man from Cook's,
It's twenty to one
You've plenty of fun,
So follow the man from Cook's.

The Spring Chicken[1] (1905) set its characters in Paris, but, as we have seen, that did not prevent Grossmith from dressing up in doublet and hose in order to sing his own song about Sutro's latest play, *The Walls of Jericho*, about performances of Shakespearian scenes in the music-halls, about plans for a National Theatre, and about Tree's support for the Academy of Dramatic Art:

The drama of Britain is limping
  Outside of the Jericho Walls,
Of all they've bereft us
There's nothing now left us,
  For Shakespeare is going on the halls.
The day of the National Theatre
  Enthusiasts tell us is near,
There's hope for to-morrow
To-day all our sorrow
  We'll drown in a bumper of beer.

Beer, beer, beautiful Beerbohm!
Oh, 'Business is Business', it's true,
If you your way can see
Find me a vacancy
In your Academy, do.
How's your pretty Miss Viola?
Fair and so charming is she,
A very short time
It will take her to climb
To the top of the Beerbohm Tree.

[1] Book by George Grossmith jr, additional lyrics by A. Ross and P. Greenbank, music by I. Caryll and L. Monckton.

"Plenty of fun" was promised by the man from Cook's, and plenty of fun in general was Edwardes' third demand. Whatever the theme of the plot, ample opportunities had to be provided for comedians debonaire and grotesque. And, above all, there was his fourth demand, that free space on the stage should be left both for one single beautiful Girl, centrally placed, and for the surrounding bevy of the famous Gaiety Girls in the plural. How emphatic was this demand, and how acutely Edwardes had gauged what the public wanted, is clearly shown by the number of his plays which stressed the importance of a "Girl" in their titles, and also by the way in which other managers, English and American, followed his lead. Nor was his perspicacity less clearly manifested in the care with which he selected, trained and controlled the chorus. He insisted that his team of maidens should be lovely, graceful, talented and circumspect, and his skill was such that, although other musical comedy producers sought to imitate what he had made so popular, not a single group elsewhere achieved the position enjoyed by the Girls of the Gaiety.

The Edwardes style was carried on into the twentieth century; in 1901 the old Gaiety had a winner in *The Toreador*, which ran on until the theatre closed on July 4, 1903; and within a very few months, on October 26, the new Gaiety opened with the merry wit of *The Orchid*, in which the standard formula was given a new look by the old team; the Tanner–Ross–Greenbank trio provided the words while the other trio of Caryll–Monckton–Rubens prepared tuneful music, and Gertie Millar consolidated her position as darling of the town with her "Little Mary" ditty.

It need hardly be said, however, that no formula of this kind could endure for ever, and there were several forces operative at this time which made change inevitable. Strangely, one of these forces came from Edwardes himself. He was responsible for creating and maintaining the Gaiety pattern, but one of the surest testimonies to his skill was his adroitness in contriving, carefully and cleverly, to keep the qualities of the shows presented on his other stages subtly distinct.

During the early years, for example, it was noted that there was "an atmosphere about Daly's, different from the atmosphere of the Gaiety. It is difficult to describe it. If one gave the best velvet, the other gave the best silk – both magnificent materials but different in texture."[1] Later, when he took over the Adelphi in 1908, contemporaries similarly observed the delicate variations in style which set his *Quaker Girl* (1908) and *The Dancing Mistress* (1912) apart from his Gaiety pieces.[2]

A second force might almost be described as unintentional rebellion on the part of some among Edwardes' own protégés. Not all the members of his company could avoid indulging in deviations from his formula, particularly by allowing elements of contemporary "comic opera", "operetta", "comedy with music" and even "musical extravaganza" to intrude into the pattern. A pertinent example of this process is *Havana*, presented at the Gaiety in 1908:[3] when Adrian Ross, the author of the lyrics, was asked to categorise this piece, all he could do was to call it "a musical comedy overflowing into opéra comique and very nearly into grand opera".[4]

Still more powerful were the influences which came from the west and from the east, the American and the Viennese. Already in 1898 *The Belle of New York*[5] had excited such interest that its run at the Shaftesbury almost reached to the seven hundred mark, and from this time on more and more transatlantic successes were brought from Broadway to the West End: *The Whirl of the Town* – the title of another musical comedy by the same librettist and composer,

[1] W. Macqueen-Pope, in D. Forbes-Winslow's *Daly's: The Biography of a Theatre* (1944), p. 209.

[2] Both these musical comedies were prepared by the same collaborators: Tanner was responsible for the books; Ross and Greenbank wrote the lyrics; the composer was Monckton. Between these two came another production of an individual kind – *Autumn Manoeuvres* (1912) – which was described as "a play with music", adapted from the German by Henry Hamilton, with the original music of Emerich Kalman for which Greenbank penned the lyrics.

[3] The book was written by George Grossmith jr and Graham Hill; Ross contributed the lyrics; the music was by Leslie Stuart.

[4] Letter contributed to *The Play Pictorial*, xii, 1908, 30.

[5] The book was by Hugh Morton and the music by Gustave Kerker.

presented at the New Century in 1901 – might be taken as a motto indicating how the same rhythms proved alluring both to Americans and to Londoners. Within a year or two jazz music was the rage on both sides of the Atlantic, and during the twenties many London stages were triumphantly graced with musicals from overseas: in 1925 spectators crowded in to the Palace in order to applaud *No, No' Nanette*,[1] and still more at Drury Lane gave a triumphant run to *Rose Marie*;[2] in 1926 came the popular *The Student Prince*[3] at His Majesty's; during the following year *The Vagabond King*[4] was much admired at the Winter Garden, and *The Desert Song*[5] at Drury Lane; a few months later, in 1928, the last-mentioned theatre presented *The Show Boat*,[6] when Paul Robeson's magnificent rendering of "Ole Man River" won excited plaudits.

The Viennese influence – which really ought to be styled the "Continental" – proved even more pervasive, and certainly it is far less easy to define because of the manner in which it was introduced to the English stage. For the most part, the American musicals, even when presented by English companies and even when occasionally they suffered modifications designed to fit them for London audiences, retained their original basic features, whereas more frequently than not the stage versions of Continental musicals were so freely altered as to make them virtually new. The English "book" of *The Merry Widow*, which ran for nearly 800 performances

[1] The book and lyrics were by Frank Mandel, Otto Harbach and Irving Caesar, the music was by Vincent Youmans.

[2] The book was by Otto Harbach and Oscar Hammerstein II, while Rudolf Friml and Herbert Stothart were responsible for the music.

[3] Dorothy Donnelly was responsible for the book, the music was by Sigmund Romberg.

[4] The book and lyrics were written by W. H. Post and Brian Hooker: the music was composed by Rudolf Friml.

[5] The book was by Oscar Hammerstein II, Otto Harbach and Frank Mandel: the music was by Sigmund Romberg (a composer born in Hungary, but from 1913 identified with the New York stage). Both *The Vagabond King* and *The Desert Song* reached almost exactly the same number of performances – 480 for the former, 432 for the latter.

[6] Oscar Hammerstein II was responsible for the book, Jerome Kern for the music.

at Daly's in 1907, may have kept reasonably close to its source, *Die lustige Witwe*,[1] but dozens of other pieces taken from abroad veered far away from their originals. Basil Hood, one of the most active among the writers of musical plays, spoke from wide experience when he emphasised the fact that mere translations from German and other sources "would not suit or satisfy the taste of our English audiences", instancing as an example his own *The Count of Luxembourg*: this was billed at Daly's in 1911 as "A New Musical Play in Two Acts by A. M. Willner and Robert Bodansky", but in fact, although the music by Franz Lehár remained with little adaptation, Hood pointed out that fewer than thirty lines of dialogue were actually taken from the German text; he and his associate Adrian Ross had completely reworked the plot, built up some of the characters and reduced others in stature, invented new scenes, and thus were almost wholly responsible for the English libretto.[2]

Other influences making for change came, too, from within the London stage itself: thus, for example, Seymour Hicks and his wife Ellaline Terriss established a new model at the Aldwych in 1906 and 1907 with *The Beauty of Bath*[3] and *The Gay Gordons*[4] and for both of these musicals they were rewarded with outstanding success. Nor was it merely from the ranks of those unassociated with Edwardes that other forms came. Basically, Edwardes' ideals were carried on by Edward Laurillard and Robert Courtneidge, yet the latter was responsible for producing a "fantastic musical play", *The Arcadians*,[5] at the Shaftesbury in 1909, a piece which ran for two years, while shortly afterwards he collaborated with

[1] Written by V. Léon and L. Stein, with music by Franz Lehár. The English version was originally attributed to Edward Morton, but later his name ceded place to that of Basil Hood: the lyrics were by Adrian Ross.

[2] Letter printed in *The Play Pictorial*, xviii, 1911, 50–1.

[3] Written by Hicks himself in collaboration with Cosmo Hamilton; the lyrics were by C. H. Taylor, the music by H. E. Haines.

[4] Hicks was responsible for the book, with lyrics by Arthur Wimperis, C. H. Bovill, P. G. Wodehouse and Henry Hamilton; the music was composed by Guy Jones.

[5] Written by A. M. Thompson and Mark Ambient, with lyrics by Arthur Wimperis, and music by Monckton and Howard Talbot.

A. M. Thompson in preparing the text of the attractively charming *The Mousmé*,[1] another popular triumph. Both of these introduced elements which went beyond the pattern so clearly outlined by Edwardes.

Assuredly, then, some of the best musicals of that period drew at least some of their liveliness and beauty from abroad; assuredly, too, popular designs often tended at times to be unadventuresomely imitated; yet the constant changes within the larger pattern fully testified to the vitality with which the musical comedy was endowed. The Japanese and oriental mode which had been represented in Owen Hall's *The Geisha* (1896) and Edward Morton's *San Toy* (1899), while it still had some slight following during later years, gradually declined; from *The Merry Widow* (1907) to Adrian Ross' *Lilac Time* (1922) the haunting charm of Viennese and other Continental melodies, associated with delicately romantic scenes of love, intrigue and sentiment, made their own strong appeal; Henry Hamilton's early *Duchess of Dantzic* (1903), with music by Caryll, may be taken as representative of those many pieces which exploited the fanciful dreams of Ruritania and the no less fanciful dreams associated with historical characters belonging to lands with firmer frontiers; the Dutch charm of *Miss Hook of Holland* (1907)[2] and the French rusticity of *The Belle of Brittany* (1908)[3] added variety of an engaging kind; more boldly dramatic – indeed almost melodramatic – episodes enriched other kindred pieces. Interesting experiments were numerous. Rightly, the Gaiety's early *Miss Gibbs* (1909)[4] had drawn admiring audiences by its realistic scenes, a style carried further when J. H. Turner, in *Merely Molly* (1926),[5] actually

[1] The lyrics were by Wimperis and Greenbank, the music by Monckton and Talbot.

[2] Written by P. A. Rubens and Austen Hurgon, with music by Rubens.

[3] Written by Leedham Bantock and P. J. Barrow, with lyrics by Greenbank and music by Talbot.

[4] This had appeared originally as by "Cryptos" (a composite pseudonym for Ross, Greenbank, Caryll and Monckton), with the additional statement that it had been "constructed" by Tanner.

[5] The lyrics were by Harry Graham, the music by Herman Finck and Joseph Meyer.

presented a first-act scene set "naturalistically" in the slums. At the same time there came essays in the fantastic which by no means are unworthy of note. Already, mention has been made of *The Arcadians* (1909): in this almost Gilbertian work a prosaic James Smith strays into a pastoral realm, encounters a beautiful Sombra, and is eventually influenced by her to "set up the truth in England for ever more, and banish the lie". Gladys Unger, taking her start from *Die Fledermaus* and adapting her book to the music of Johann Strauss, produced her rather strange *Nightbirds* in 1911: this introduced a model prison so excellently conducted according to the best social reform principles that its inmates are cast into a miserable state of dismayed gloom as their sentences begin to come to their end and the chill world outside threatens them. A few years earlier, in *Butterflies* (1908),[1] the librettist, none other than the novelist–playwright W. J. Locke, created as his central characters three very dull, but at the same time very honest, suburbanites who are induced by Puck to see the beauty of the world and thus to escape from the suffocating atmosphere of their dreary, drab surroundings, while in *My Lady Frayle* (1915)[2] the place of the lovely nymph and of the cheerful Robin Goodfellow is taken by a most fashionable devil, Lucifer D. Nation, who tries to insinuate his temptations into the breast of the heroine and is duly thwarted by her innate honesty.

In considering these musicals as a whole, two questions arise – one concerning their general worth, and another concerning their relationship to the drama of their time.

In general, the more vocal *avant garde* theatrical enthusiasts during this period ruthlessly attacked the musical comedy, but it is necessary to set against their denunciations the vindications put forward by others belonging to

[1] The book was adapted from Locke's own "fantastic comedy", *The Palace of Puck*, which had been presented at the Haymarket during the preceding season: the lyrics were contributed by T. H. Read and the music by J. A. Robertson.

[2] Written by Wimperis and Max Pemberton, with music by Talbot and Herman Finck.

different ideological groups. "We are told by so-called artistic persons," declares Basil Hood, "that musical comedy is an abomination of which the theatre must cleanse itself. These attacks are nearly always arrogant and frequently insolent, while the ignorance of those who make them is amazing."[1] If we listen to the objectors, into our minds comes thought of the uninspired musical trivialities which won esteem during those years, of the sheer "escapism" manifested in spectacular show after spectacular show, of the playgoers magnet-drawn in their hundreds and thousands from more serious dramatic efforts. If we listen to Basil Hood, then we think once more of that phrase, "The Singing Years", and maybe we permit some of their melodic tunes to return nostalgically to our memories. Perhaps, however, before trying to reach a balanced judgment we may decide to listen to still a third voice, none other than that of George Grossmith jr. In 1926, writing an essay entitled "Musical Comedy as – is now – and . . . ",[2] he declared:

> Crowds flock to the Prince's Theatre to see the Gilbert and Sullivan revivals, but I undertake to say that if a company existed able to perform a repertoire consisting of The Shop Girl, The Circus Girl, The Toreador, The Orchid, Our Miss Gibbs, The Gaiety Girl, The Spring Chicken, The Girls of Gottenburg, The Sunshine Girl, Havana and The Arcadians, the crowds would be equally as great.

Undoubtedly, his implied praise of these pieces is fully justified, yet his basic proviso must certainly not be ignored. "If a company existed able to perform" these musicals, he asserts, they would attract many spectators; but immediately afterwards he proceeds to destroy his fundamental condition: "Alas!", he admits, "there is no company capable of adequately performing such a repertoire, as much of the success of these plays depended on the personality of the players." Even a cursory examination of the significance of his words reveals the essential difference between the

[1] D. Forbes-Winslow, *Daly's* (1944), p. 107.
[2] *The Play Pictorial*, l, no. 300, 1926, viii–x.

musical plays presented during these three first decades of the twentieth century and the productions of Gilbert and Sullivan. Of course, the D'Oyly Carte company was a brilliant one; of course, Gilbert's own painstaking devotion to the niceties of stage-management contributed materially to the original success of the Savoy productions: yet the performances merely gave a final theatrical grace to something which had achieved its own measure of perfection in text and score. Gilbert's words on the printed page can be read with pleasure, Sullivan's music by itself, without these words, can be savoured with delight, and playgoers can enjoy performances of *The Mikado* or *The Gondoliers* even when these are interpreted by companies and orchestras less than brilliant.

The distinction between the two kinds of musical plays is epitomised effectively in one of Grossmith's following comments wherein he contrasts the Savoy libretti with those belonging to the later musical comedies: if we turn from the former to the latter, he remarks, "in lieu of the Gilbertian dialogue" we should be apt to "find in the author's MS, 'Enter So-and-So' and 'So-and-So' (indicating the two chief comedians) 'comic scene, business, and exeunt'." The later actors, like their improvising predecessors in Renaissance Italy, no doubt gave an appealing vitality and effectiveness to the productions, yet we are bound to admit that without the George Grossmiths, the Gertie Millars and all their numerous talented associates the musical plays which so attracted London's theatregoers to the Gaiety, the Adelphi and the Lyric can, in general, now be little more than a pleasant dream of the past.

The second question suggested above has, however, still to be answered. The intellectuals not only condemned the musicals: they declared that the two theatres, that of musical comedy and that of drama, could not mix. As a matter of fact, when we look at the stage during those years in its entirety, we find that in many ways they did actually mingle with each other, and that this process of mingling tended to increase as the decades passed by. In the beginning, the majority of musical comedies were the results of team-work involving the efforts of some four to six men: the books were often written by two authors in collaboration, two rhymsters frequently joined in preparing the lyrics, and as frequently a couple of composers prepared the music. Moreover, comparatively few of those who were engaged in these activities moved far beyond the circle of musical comedy theatres: a librettist in general remained a librettist, and, if occasionally one member of the group turned to write a non-musical play, his dramatic efforts were half-hearted.

Gradually, however, this pattern began to be altered, and as an indication of the way in which it was changing we may take the career of Frederick Lonsdale. Nowadays this writer is remembered as the author of comedies which, if not the greatest of masterpieces, are eminently deserving of attention and revival. Only seldom is it recalled that his first stage piece was a musical play called *The King of Cadonia* (1908)[1] and that thereafter he alternated the composition of plays with that of musicals. To him we owe not merely *The Last of Mrs Cheyney* (1925) but also *The Maid of the Mountains*[2] which, when presented at Daly's in 1917, had a lengthy run of nearly 1,400 performances. And throughout these years are to be encountered many other writers with careers not dissimilar – men such as P. G. Wodehouse, J. H. Turner, Dion Titheradge, Ronald Jeans and Reginald Arkell. Thus the stage was set for Sir Alan P. Herbert's amusing *La Vie Parisienne*[3] and, more importantly, for Noël Coward's pathetically touching *Bitter Sweet*, both presented in 1929.

Through the work of such authors the theatre of musical comedy and the theatre of drama came together – and perhaps it may even be suggested that there were other ways in which their styles mingled. George Bernard Shaw,

[1] This had lyrics by Ross and music by Sidney Jones.

[2] The lyrics were by Harry Graham, F. Clifford Harris and "Valentine"; Harold Fraser-Simson was responsible for the music, and some additional numbers were contributed by J. W. Tate.

[3] Although this author added to the theatre's gaiety from 1926 onwards, his major contributions did not come until the thirties. His autobiography, *A. P. H.: His Life and Times*, was published in 1970.

although he was so deeply interested in music, never matched Coward by penning a musical play; but he well might have done. When the structure of his *Arms and the Man* is examined in the light of current playwriting styles, it must be acknowledged that its scenes and characters are strangely similar to those of Ruritanian musicals, so closely akin indeed as to provide Leopold Jacobson and Rudolph Bernauer with material ready-made for *The Chocolate Soldier*, a musical which, after its success at the Lyric in 1910,[1] has become even more widely familiar than the original comedy. Possibly, too, we may be prepared to go further and see a similar spiritual kinship between *Pygmalion* and *My Fair Lady*. Shaw took suggestions from many sources, and among these he did not neglect the popular theatre which so many worthy "artistic persons" so roundly condemned.

2. *The Revue*

"Musical comedy" is clearly an elusive term, and still more elusive is the term "revue". Far back in the nineteenth century the prolific innovator J. R. Planché produced a piece called *Success; or, A Hit If You Like It* (Adelphi, 1825) which he described as "A New Grand Mock-heroical, Allegorical, Operatical, Melodramatical, Magical, anything but Tragical Burletta, in One Act, Founded on Fact." Half a century later he seized two opportunities of referring back to this early dramatic effort: in his *Recollections* (1872) he drew attention to the fact that this was "the first attempt in this country to introduce that class of entertainment so popular in Paris called 'Revue'", and seven years afterwards, in his preface to his collected *Extravaganzas* (1879)[2] he expanded his brief comment by remarking, first, that his "visits to Paris made" him "acquainted with two classes of drama" of which hitherto he had been "totally ignorant – the 'Féerie Folie' and the 'Revue'", and, secondly, that from imitation of these French pieces derived his own long

[1] English version by Stanislaus Stange, music by Oscar Straus.
[2] See *H. E. D.*, iv, 135–6.

series of "extravaganzas". At first glance, it might seem that here is to be discovered the true fount from which flowed those great streams of revues so popular from the beginning of the twentieth century on to 1930. It is, however, necessary to observe that neither were Planché's extravagant burlettas in any true respect akin to those later productions, nor were the early 'fairy' *folies* and the associated French "revues" more than dim ancestors of the widely spawning breed which flourished in Edwardian and Georgian days. *Success* had been concerned solely with satirical comments on certain recent popular theatrical productions; Planché's subsequently penned extravaganzas for the most part exploited purely imaginative, fairy-tale material; although it has been stated several times that a much later production, *Under the Clock* (1893), by Charles Brookfield and Seymour Hicks, was "the first real revue" presented on the London stage,[1] even this "musical extravaganza" hardly went beyond the theatrical burlesque which had been the chief feature of Planché's early experiment; in any event during the whole of the nineteenth century the descriptive term "revue" failed to establish itself in England.

It would appear that the time when this word was introduced to the London stage can be determined with fair precision. During the year 1905 J. B. Fagan's *Shakespeare v. Shaw* was so labelled when it appeared at the Haymarket, and the same term was applied by George Grossmith jr to his show, *Rogues and Vagabonds*, at the Empire music-hall: during the following year Grossmith's second Empire show, *Venus*, was similarly described, J. M. Barrie did not hesitate to apply the term to his *Josephine* at the Comedy, and *The Revue* was employed as the title of an entertainment at the Coliseum. Thereafter its use became more and more frequent, and very soon it had grown as familiar to the general public as the words comedy and farce. With assurance, then, we

[1] Joe Graham, in *An Old Stock-Actor's Memories* (1930), p. 249, calls it "one of the earliest revues"; in *Daly's* (1944) D. Forbes-Winslow categorically states that it was "the first real revue produced in London" (p. 152).

may say that the term "revue" entered our theatrical vocabulary during the years 1905 and 1906.

The term itself, of course, came directly from France, so directly indeed that in its transportation across the Channel not the slightest attempt was made at anglicisation of its spelling. At the very start, as is demonstrated by the examples cited above, there was a certain vagueness and uncertainty concerning its exact significance, but within a very short time everyone came to know what it meant: a "revue" was an evening's entertainment made up of numerous "turns", generally short, some pointedly topical and some spectacular, presented in swift, kaleidoscopic rotation. And this basic interpretation of the word exactly applied to the particular types of revue which had developed in Paris around the turn of the century. Some revues inclined to stress wittily satiric comments on the current social scene; in some the spectacular took chief place; the majority sought to win success through a combination of these two elements.

Considering these facts, it might be thought that the English examples of the form were nothing more than imitations of French originals and that their appeal derived from their novelty. Yet, when they are examined more closely, it seems to become apparent that this appeal would not have been so great had they not been intimately related to what was happening within the English theatre itself and that many influences besides the French played a part in their composition. The word "revue" may have come from Paris, and the concept of the "revue" may have been an importation, but it is significant that the first show of this sort was devised by George Grossmith jr, one of the principal leaders in the musical comedy world, and that it was presented in a music-hall. If we bear these two facts in mind, several reflections follow. In a sense, a revue is akin to a music-hall programme in which the various turns, instead of being separate and distinct, are given a general common sense of direction; this was a time when the music-hall world was nearing a great period of crisis and when it was searching around for novelties wherewith to attract its customers; the welcome given to the revue by the Empire and other prominent metropolitan halls may thus be looked upon as largely motivated by the desire to find something which would be more than the old-established series of unrelated turns. That Grossmith should have been responsible for this inaugural effort is not surprising, since all through his life he displayed an interest in the Parisian stage: he had, in fact, received part of his early education in that city, in 1910 he took part in a revue at the Folies Bergères, and the next year saw him acting at the Théâtre Réjane. What, however, is important to remember is that the Edwardes type of musical comedy in which Grossmith won his fame might almost be thought of as a revue with a dominant central story. Putting this in a different way, we might say that if the story were cut out of one of these musicals and the comic topical part were extended, then a revue could easily result. As a matter of fact, revues actually were fashioned in such a manner during the period when the vogue of this kind of entertainment was at its height; and the intimate connection between the two popular forms of entertainment is further emphasised in the appearance of descriptive terms such as "musical comedy revue" and "revuistical musical comedy".

At the start, then, it can be confidently asserted that the earliest English revues resulted from a combination of three elements – the influence of the contemporary French type, the adaptation of native music-hall practice, and the utilisation of material culled from the musicals, with Grossmith one of the chief encouragers of the new theatrical genre. During the course of the following years these forces remained basic, yet it is easy to see how other elements, both native and taken from abroad, introduced modifications which made the later examples of the form differ markedly from their predecessors. It would, of course, be quite improper here to deal with these various influences as a whole and at length; all that can usefully be done is to refer briefly to a selected few.

The close ties between the American and English stages meant that what was happening on Broadway became rapidly known to the professionals working in Shaftesbury Avenue and that at least some characteristic developments within the world of the transatlantic revues were directly imported for the delight of English audiences. The so-called "American Institution", the lavish Ziegfeld Follies which pursued a popular career from their establishment in 1907 until the close of this period, became familiarly talked about; and similar familiarity was later accorded to the various editions of the *Passing Show* sponsored by the Shubert Brothers and to George White's *Scandals*; necessarily the political hits which appealed to New York's spectators could not satisfactorily be transferred to London, but it was not long before rag-time and jazz, musical forms which were to become identified with many English revues, became as popular here as there.

Ziegfeld had entitled his entertainments "Follies", presumably taking his inspiration from the Parisian Folies Bergères, and in so doing he had been anticipated by the genial Harry Gabriel Pélissier, whose *Follies* first appeared at the Palace in 1904, came to the Royalty in 1907 and later established themselves at the Apollo.[1] During the years when many revues were tending to lose their powers of speech in their frantic endeavour to exploit luxurious spectacle and to provide sexual titillation,[2] the influence of this charming group was by no means negligible: they relied not at all upon visual display, but held their audiences solely by their witty sketches and their accomplished histrionic skill. Nor did they stand entirely alone. *The Co-optimists* carried on much of the same tradition,[3] and, although cabarets did not flourish so freely as they did in France and Germany, at least some of the private shows of this sort made their own interesting contributions.[4]

[1] Gardner Fitzroy, *Pure Folly. The Story of Those Remarkable People, The Follies* (1909).

[2] Frank Vernon has at least some justification for his declaration that many spectators went to the revues "to procure the emotions of mixed bathing in a place where these emotions are not corrected by cold water" (*The Twentieth-Century Theatre* (1924), p. 8).

[3] See Ashley Sterne, *The Comic History of the Co-optimists* (1926).

[4] Information on London's cabarets is not always easy to find. As early as the beginning of the year 1912 a show of this kind was opened at

In England, as in other countries, the revues progressed in a constant struggle between scenic display and the exhibition of wit, and in a ranging variety which embraced everything from the stupidly vulgar to the exquisite. Many shows were hurriedly thrown together without any sense of purpose, with costumes and sets garishly tatty, with dialogue deplorable and lyrics beneath contempt: in others the spectacles offered to the public were magnificent, the dialogue of the short sketches was pointed, and the songs frequently memorable. In *Hullo, Ragtime!*, presented at the Hippodrome in 1912, Albert De Courville showed his skill in devising these entertainments: during the twenties André Charlot sponsored numerous lively and beautiful productions; and, above all, C. B. Cochran brought forward a series of splendid entertainments, from *Odds and Ends* in 1914 to *Wake Up and Dream* in 1929, which could hardly have found their match in any other metropolis. Nor should our attention be directed solely at these more elaborate and costlier productions. The revue had clearly caught the imagination and interest of the time, and there might be justification for regarding it as one of the most characteristic theatrical developments in England between its introduction in 1905 to the close of this period. Although its major manifestations were definitely "popular", although it was closely allied to musical comedy and although some critics dismissed it as belonging to a kind of stage which they regarded as inimical to the "theatre of drama", it extended its appeal far beyond the larger music-halls and playhouses of the West End. The presentation of Ronald Jeans' *Hullo, Repertory!* at Liverpool in 1915 may be taken as symbolic of the way in which its appeal was spreading into the sphere of the new civic theatres; the vogue of the "intimate revue" soon was established; the "highbrow" revue, which perhaps reached its finest expression in

the Boudoir, Pembroke Gardens, and described as "the first artistic cabaret in England". The true vogue, however, would not seem to have come until about 1920, when several large restaurants introduced "supper entertainments" and when night-clubs started to flourish: by 1925 numerous such associations could be listed, and their success was so great that there was even talk of inaugurating a "People's Cabaret".

A. P. Herbert's *Riverside Nights* at the Hammersmith Lyric in 1926, flourished alongside the more elaborate productions; in the suburban and provincial houses, titles such as *Bill out o' Work*, *Capital and Labour*, *The Capital Levy*, *On the Panel*, *Workshy*, *Why D'Ye Work?* and *The Never Works* indicated how a number of now completely forgotten revues reflected the social conditions and troubles of the age; and those enthusiasts who directed their attention at special forms of theatrical performance discovered that this novel form could easily be adapted to their own purposes; as, for example, is demonstrated in the appearance of A. A. Milne's *Make Believe* (1918), described as a "Children's Revue".[1] While, therefore, the revue was very definitely a "popular" form of entertainment, its impact was felt far more widely than in London's larger theatres and music-halls which were its principal home.

The extensive range of these productions would have demanded much more detailed examination if the theme of this survey had concentrated upon the theatre, but since the focus here is on the drama immediate consideration has to be given only to those elements which have a connection with playwriting. In particular, one fundamental question must be asked – a question, however, which requires a preliminary introduction. While everyone would agree that scores of these shows were not only stupidly vulgar but also chiefly made up of spectacular and similar turns, with absolutely no relationship to the drama, both the larger West End revues and those categorised by the term "intimate" did call for the services of men whose talents equipped them to organise the productions as a whole and enabled them to give to these productions a measure of unity by themselves penning the dialogue scenes which were intermingled with the revue's other components. It is, therefore, by no means surprising that within a few years a group of bright young authors – some of them, like Noël Coward, belonging to the

[1] Milne's title was not a complete innovation: already the Hippodrome at Golder's Green had presented a "children's revue", *Twinkle, Twinkle, Little Star* by B. Landeck, in 1915.

London stage, and others, like Ronald Jeans, with strong repertory affiliations – should have been encouraged to apply their efforts to this form of entertainment. This is the fact: the question which follows must inquire whether the experience gained in the preparing and writing for the revue stage was propitious for the drama or not.

To a certain extent it might seem that the answer to such a question must be much the same as that which results from a consideration of the related realm of musical comedy. Yet a further difference in its terms is inevitable. Most of the musicals, no doubt, were flimsy things of a moment, yet some at least were possessed of sufficient substance and vitality as to render them suited for occasional revival: they may not possess the quality inherent in the Savoy operas, but they still exhibit a quality and flavour worthy of remembrance. All the revues, no matter how splendid and enjoyable in their own time, were merely transitory and ephemeral. To this must be added a further reflection. However much the musical comedies introduced extraneous matter, the majority of them – and certainly the entire range of those whose titles remain in our minds – had palpable form and shape: to all the revues, even the very best, might have been applied the title used for Cochran's first production – *Odds and Ends*. Things of shreds and patches, bits and pieces, they were made up generally of unrelated turns, and as a result not a single example can now be completely reconstituted in our imagination. With delight we may recall Coward's clever lyric about mad dogs and Englishmen, but his revues in their entirety have gone for ever: it is significant that even he himself, in the explanatory preface to his *Collected Sketches and Lyrics* (1931), makes a pregnant confession: "Personally, I should imagine that for the layman a large portion of the following pages will be extremely bewildering if not actually unintelligible." In seeking to grasp the nature of any single revue we can do no more than tantalisingly grope our way through contemporary critiques, realising constantly that even the most brilliantly penned critical notices, whether or not assisted by printed texts of selected lyrics and sketches, must inevitably fail to bring any of these pieces to life for us.[1]

Naturally, then, we are forced to say that in their entirety these entertainments could offer little of value to the development of the drama: indeed, we may go further and declare that, while of course it was excellent that the group of bright young authors were offered the theatrical opportunities given to them by Cochran and his fellow managers, the fact that they became thus engaged in spending their time upon basically formless immoment toys ill served them for the writing of plays. A good drama demands integrated architectural form: no corresponding architectural form was demanded by, or in fact possible for, a revue. Perhaps the suggestion may be made that if Noël Coward had not had the experience of preparing the text and music for *This Year of Grace!* in 1928, he might never have produced either *Bitter Sweet* in 1929 or *Cavalcade* in 1931; but, after all, such a suggestion can be only a guess at the very best, and Coward himself was an exceptional figure among his companions, gifted with qualities and powers not shared with the others. Fundamentally, planning of revues cannot be regarded as having provided a fruitful apprenticeship for authors intent upon the composition of full-length dramas.

If we turn from the planning of revues in their entirety to look at the few remnants of their written texts that have come down to us, a second doubt arises. Some half a dozen authors besides Coward succeeded in finding publishers for selected specimens of their work, and the very titles of some among their collections sufficiently indicate their attitude

[1] For such critical notices direct reference to the periodicals in which they appeared is generally necessary: few have been collected, the only notable exception, indeed, being the small group gathered together in James Agate's *Immoment Toys* (1945). Accounts of some individual revues are to be found in biographical and autobiographical volumes, but the records rarely have substance. Perhaps the most vivid impression of these vanished performances is to be gained from the various essays assembled under the editorship of C. B. Cochran in *A Review of Revues and Other Matters* (1930). Cochran's own *A Showman Looks On* (1945) and a recently published picture-book by R. Mander and J. Mitchenson (*Revue*, 1971) also help to evoke their spirit.

towards these compositions. A few such titles, but only a very few, are either vague – such as Douglas Furber's *From London and New York* (1927), Ronald Jeans' *The Stage is Waiting* (1931), Dion Titheradge's *From the Prompt Corner* (1925) and J. H. Turner's *Evenings at Eight* (1925) – or else fall back upon the word "sketches" and its variants – such as Ronald Jeans' *Vignettes from Vaudeville* (1924), *Sundry Sketches* (1924) and *Charlot Revue Sketches* (1925), Austin Melford's *Revue Sketches* (1924) and the similarly-titled collection by Harold Simpson (1924). Others, however, have authorial attitudes suggestively incorporated in their wording: three of Jeans' collections are called *Bright Intervals* (1927), *Odd Numbers* (1927) and *One Dam' Sketch after Another* (1928), Mackenzie Lee has *For Chaps and Chits* (1930), the title *Nonsense* (1930) is used by Austin Melford, Harold Simpson employs *Straws in the Wind* (1925) for one collection and *Oh – By the Way* (1926) for another, while J. H. Turner thinks of pieces *Rescued from Revues* (1923). The general trend here is patently obvious: the authors recognise that these writings are trivialities merely, that the revues encouraged, in fact positively demanded, sketches as brief as possible and conventionally stereotyped in structure.

In so far as their brevity is concerned we may discern here the ultimate development of the short play which was so representative a feature of those years. The repertories had stimulated the modish cultivation of "artistic" one-acts; some of these were on occasion transferred to the music-halls, but for the most part the variety programmes were better suited by somewhat shorter pieces, and hence there was a proliferation of innumerable abbreviated sketches and skits. The revues required things shorter still, and as a result the music-hall skit was abbreviated into a miniskit. And naturally the curtailment in length inevitably imposed upon these miniskits conventionally standard forms: they were not "plays" but rather short, sharp jokes presented in dialogue, and they tended to assume one of two forms. Some were truncated "witty" pieces, abrupt in their openings and with equally sudden endings, epigrammatic, paradoxical or simply unexpected. Others might be described as consisting of a number of vignettes separated from each other by sudden black-outs which kept the electrician as busy as the actors. As an example of this latter form Ronald Jeans' "Incredible Happenings", included in the Vaudeville revue, *Rats!* in 1923, may be cited. This opens with a "Preliminary Speech":

Ladies and gentlemen, the next scene is an attempt on our part to give you something completely different from anything you can see in any other theatre in London. As you know, all the plays you've ever seen have set out to reproduce events which happen, or might conceivably happen, in real life; so we thought it would be rather a change for you to see a few things that never happen in real life. The following episodes we have therefore selected because they have never actually happened, and what is more, we are willing to guarantee that they never will happen.

Ten such "episodes" are then presented, so brief that they occupy only five pages in the printed text, and the quoting of three or four will indicate the style of them all:

(*A man and a girl, in evening dress, seated at a table. Enter to them a* WAITER, *bearing change on plate. The man takes the change, selects some silver, and hands it to the* WAITER.)

WAITER. It's very kind of you, sir, but I really couldn't take it. I have served your dinner both clumsily and slowly, sir, and I am about to report myself to the Head Waiter.

BLACK OUT

(*During which replace table covering with whisky bottle, siphon and glasses.*)

(*A* BARMAID *discovered standing behind table.* MR SMITH *and* MR CAMERON *enter.*)

MR SMITH. Will you have a drink?

MR CAMERON (*in broad Scotch*). Not for me, Mr Smith. But ye'll hae a wee drappie ye'sel'?

MR SMITH. Thanks, I don't mind if I do.

MR CAMERON. A large whisky, please, for my friend here. (*Puts half a crown on counter.*) That's all richt. Ye can keep the change!

BLACK OUT

(HUSBAND *and* WIFE *are discovered seated. A* MAID *enters and hands the* HUSBAND *an envelope.*)

WIFE. What is that, darling?

HUSBAND. It's the bill for that hat you bought last week. I'm so glad you decided to buy it after all.

WIFE. I think it was very extravagant of me, Jack.

HUSBAND. Not at all, darling – I'm only sorry you didn't get the dress as well.

WIFE. I would have – but I thought we ought to spend the money on a new suit for you.

HUSBAND. Absurd! What should I do with a new suit? I have only had this one ten years.

WIFE. But I like you to look smart, Jack. That reminds me, I've asked that pretty Miss Willoughby in to-morrow night.

HUSBAND. To-morrow night? I thought you were going to Aunt Emily's to-morrow night.

WIFE. So I am, darling. That's why I asked Ruby Willoughby in to keep you company. I know you like her; you even noticed the dress she wore at the theatre the other night.

HUSBAND. I couldn't help it – there was so little of it –

WIFE. She promised me she'd wear it to-morrow night just to please you.

HUSBAND. Good Heavens! I shan't know where to look!

WIFE. Oh! yes, you will, darling. And listen, Jack, I shan't be back till midnight – and I'm sending the maids to the pictures!

HUSBAND. Now that's very kind and thoughtful of you, darling!

BLACK OUT

(*A* GENTLEMAN *discovered seated in a* BARBER'S *chair having his hair cut.*)

THE BARBER. Your hair's in splendid condition, sir, and if you take my advice, you'll never put anything on it!

BLACK OUT

(*A* BOOKMAKER *is discovered, with satchel and board.*)

BOOKMAKER. To win or a place! To win or a place. I'll lay 3 to 1 bar one!

(*Enter harassed* RACEGOER)

RACEGOER. I beg your pardon, but can you tell me – did Stoneflint win the last race?

BOOKMAKER. He did, sir. At 33 to 1.

RACEGOER. Now, isn't that annoying? I meant to put £5 on it, and I forgot.

BOOKMAKER. You really did mean to, sir?

RACEGOER. Certainly I did.

BOOKMAKER. All right. I'll take your word for it. (*Pays out.*)

BLACK OUT

(*A* BRICKLAYER *discovered laying bricks.*)

BRICKLAYER (*sings*). Work – boys – work – etc.

(*A whistle blows. Enter his* MATE.)

MATE. Knock off, Bill! Dinner-time!

BRICKLAYER. Dinner be blowed! I'm going to finish this job!

BLACK OUT

Many of the revue sketches were amusing – no worse, and indeed for the most part more neatly adroit, than the similarly-planned sketches and vignettes presented to today's television viewers in so many dull "guest star shows". But our basic concern here is not to institute any comparison between scripts past and present: it is to inquire whether the revues offered to young authors anything of value except financial opportunities – and the answer to that question seems to be clear and unequivocal. Writing for the revues provided the apprentice playwrights with ample opportunities for the display of cleverness and wit, but beyond that little or nothing. In fact, it tended to lead them astray. Noël Coward was able to balance himself with exquisite ease between the worlds of revue and drama; but there are several of his companions who appear to show that promising potential dramatic skill was often injured by indulgence in composing the light trivialities which helped to attract popular audiences to this new form of entertainment.

3. *The Melodrama*

When reference is made to "melodrama" almost certainly there is immediate thought of the nineteenth century, of *Maria Marten* and its multitude of companions both early and late. There is realisation, of course, that during the first decades of the twentieth century Drury Lane attracted audiences by means of elaborately presented, exciting shows to which the same generic term is applied, but generally these tend to be separated off in our minds from the pieces which in previous years had flourished on the Surrey side and elsewhere. Except for revivals (usually executed tongue in cheek) of such selected plays as *Ten Nights in a Bar-room*, we generally assume that the melodrama, as a popular form, disappeared with the passing of the old century, and that the prolific authors of such pieces had vanished for ever.

Playgoers, we believe, were now thinking of playwrights from Barrie to Bridie, from Sutro to Shaw, from Maugham to Milne and Munro. No doubt this supposition is correct if our attention is directed solely to the more important dramatic theatres in London's West End and to the new repertory playhouses; but if we extend our gaze to include theatrical interests beyond these restricted areas, we must recognise, perhaps to our considerable surprise, that hundreds of thousands of regular playgoers thought in terms of other authors and authoresses, and that these authors and authoresses, generally prolific in their output, were responsible for producing a very large proportion of the plays written between the start of the century and 1930.

Mere lists of names must always be dull, and usually are to be avoided; but here perhaps it is desirable to break a customary rule, because only in such a way can the extent of this playwriting activity be demonstrated. We all know the names of the "literary" authors cited above, and to those we can easily add the names of a score of others from Galsworthy to Sherriff – but who has heard of the names in the following list – a list so lengthy that it may best be given in double column?

Stuart Lomath
Myles Wallerton
Fred Jarman
J. A. Campbell
Joseph M. Wharncliffe

Fred Moule
C. Watson-Mill
Max Goldberg
Edward Thane
Harold Whyte

Frank M. Thorne
Matt Wilkinson
Frederick Melville
Rev. A. J. Waldron
Clifford Rean
W. W. Saltoun
F. A. Scudamore
Royce Carleton
W. P. Sheen
Frank Lindon
I. P. Gore
T. G. Bailey
W. A. Brabner
Jack Denton
R. H. Douglass
Herbert Fuller
Horace Stanley
James Willard
Walter Melville
Rev. John Maclaren
C. Vernon Proctor
Frank Price
Lionel Scudamore
Charles Darrell
Owen James
A. Myddleton-Myles
Ronald Grahame
H. F. Housden
Walter Howard
C. A. Clarke
J. Douglas
E. V. Edmonds
W. V. Garrod

Who has heard of their associated lady-companions?

Mrs F. G. Kimberley
Florence Marriott-Watson
May Dana
Sheila Walsh
Aimée Grattan Clyndes
Emma Litchfield
Dorothy Mullord
Eva Elwes
Gladys Hastings-Walton
Nita Rae

Who knows anything about that pair of writers, Henrietta Schreier and Lodge-Percy, whose extensive dramatic output almost vies with that of some early nineteenth-century authors?

All of these, notwithstanding the aristocratic-seeming hyphenated names borne by some of them, devoted their time and energies to the providing of plays for the delectation of "popular" audiences. Among their hundreds of scripts not a single one has come down to us in printed form; not one could now be considered worthy of revival; in their own time only a few penetrated into the West End; if these pieces are taken separately, without doubt they must be regarded as having no value. And yet, collectively, they cannot be ignored.

The lineage of all these plays is to be traced clearly in the melodrama's genealogical tree, and their true theatrical homes are to found in the provincial and suburban playhouses. A certain number appear to have been penned with the latter group of theatres directly in view, but for the most part they started their stage careers well outside of London and gradually travelled down to within sight of the metropolis – *en route* frequently changing their names. Thus, for example, a drama called *Soiled*, presented at the Hippodrome at Maidenhead on January 6, 1919, soon afterwards appeared at Stratford E. as *The Girl Who Took Drugs*, and later still was given under the title of *A Man's Plaything*; what originally bore the title of *What is Home without a Mother?* was re-christened as *The Curse of Marriage* and *A Bad Woman*; one of Edward Thane's plays, *The Slave of Sin*, became, during the course of its peregrinations, *The Worst of All Women*, then *A Daughter of the Devil*, and finally *The Love that Lasts for Ever*.

The examples given above may serve also for another purpose. These plays were certainly melodramas, but in general they were restricted to one particular branch of that dramatic form. It is true that occasionally the authors turned to deal with romantic themes, but the larger proportion of their writings dealt with domestic topics and familiar characters, and among these characters there was as much emphasis on the feminine as there was in the musical comedies. "Girls", as we have seen, preponderated in the titles of the lyrical shows, and girls were almost as common in the melodramas. Plots of a novelette type obviously made great appeal. Very occasionally a success-story might feature a male personage – as in *From Miner to M.P.* – but much more frequent were tales which narrated the adventures of ladies *From Shopgirl to Duchess*, *From Washerwoman to Duchess*, *From Convent to Throne*, or *From Mill Girl to Millionairess*.

Nevertheless, while observing this characteristic trend, it is interesting to note that the authors did try their best to appeal to all their public, the male spectators as well as the female, by preserving a kind of balance; and this is to be seen both in the melodramas as a whole and within the range of writings by individual authors. Stuart Lomath, for instance, pens a *Come Home Daddy*, counterpoises this with *The Wife Who Sinned*, and brings the two together in a play entitled variously as *Whom God Hath Joined* and *Wife or Mistress?*. If Nita Rae writes *For Love of a Woman*, T. G. Bailey presents *How Women Ruin Men* and follows this immediately with an almost apologetic *How Women are Slandered*. Mrs Morton Powell tells *How Girls are brought to Ruin*, C. Watson-Mill inquires *Can a Woman Be Good?*, C. Darrell counters with *What a Man Made Her*, Mrs Kimberley lugubriously traces *Her Path of Sorrow*, W. Melville narrates the sad story of *The Shop-Soiled Girl*, Augusta Tullock deals with *The Woman who Sinned*, and Mrs Kimberley anxiously enquires *Was She to Blame?*.

During the nineteenth century, as is well known, hundreds of melodramas were presented to the public in printed form: no one is likely to ignore the popularity they enjoyed at that time, and anyone who, in an attempt to illustrate their conventions and styles, starts to look round for quotable representative examples is certain to find himself confronted by a tantalising embarrassment of riches. After the year 1900, however, came a marked change. While melodramas certainly remained popular fare in many theatres, hardly any publisher considered their texts worthy of being put into print, and, in general, it may be said that the only writings of this kind which are now readily available are, with one exception, a few odd manuscripts or typewritten copies which have by good fortune escaped a general holocaust.[1] The exception consists of some thirty plays the typescripts of which have recently come to light and which represent

[1] All the plays which had previously been submitted to the Lord Chamberlain for licensing are now, of course, housed in the British Museum. Not infrequently, however, the task of locating particular dramas within this enormous collection proves tiresomely laborious, and, when eventually found, these texts seldom prove so informative as Garrod's typescripts – all presented in forms carefully prepared for stage production.

practically the whole work of a single melodramatic author, W. V. Garrod, extending from a piece written originally in 1909 and characteristically called by several names, *Murder Will Out*, *A Mother's Vengeance* and *Love Levels All Ranks*, on to *The Verdict of the Jury* (1928) and *The Man from the C.I.D.* (probably about 1929).[1]

Although it certainly cannot be asserted that these scripts have any great intrinsic value, the unique nature of this comprehensive collection gives it considerable historical interest and significance. Garrod seems to have been a man intimately and professionally acquainted with stage affairs, and as a writer he was rather a follower of popular fashions than a bold innovator. Thus, taking his plays as a whole, we can reasonably regard them as a kind of microcosm reflecting the larger movements within the area of the popular drama in general. *Murder Will Out* was followed by various other similar plays with characteristically melodramatic titles, such as *A Wife for a Day* (1910), *The Love Marriage* (1915), *The Heart of a Thief* (1917), *One Law for Both* (1919), *The Right to Live* (1919), *A Riddle of the Night* (1920), *Child o' My Heart* (1924), and *A Man without a Past* (1924). About this time, however, the middle twenties, we can see how his earlier melodramatic themes gave way to themes dealing with crimes and detectives – *The Ragged Millionaire* (1924), *The Law Breakers* (1927) and the two dramas referred to above, *The Verdict of the Jury* and *The Man from the C.I.D.* Even more significant is the fact that at the same time he started to experiment with the writing of plays wholly different in kind. In 1921 his *Pretending to Be Cinderella* was a comedy actually selected for performance at Liverpool's Repertory Theatre; another comedy, *Blissful Ignorance*, was presented by the high-minded Altrincham Garrick Society; and apparently soon after 1930 came several other comedies, such as *Happiness*, *Adam and Evil* and *The Years of Indiscretion*, as well as some farces, *Dear Sir, Unless –*, *Too Much Marriage* and *The Prince's Bride*. Hardly anything could more clearly demonstrate how the old

[1] For the titles of these plays see the Hand-list, pp. 662–3.

melodrama continued to flourish during the greater part of the period 1900–30, how it began at the end to fade into the "detective play" and how eventually, during the thirties, it vanished.

By no means, however, is that the only interest inherent in this collection. When we proceed to examine Garrod's melodramatic texts, perhaps the first thing to impress us is what may be called the antiquated nature of their dialogue: we seem, indeed, to have been suddenly whisked back in time to the beginning of Victoria's reign. In some scenes Garrod shows himself capable of listening to ordinary speech and of reproducing its tones, as, for instance, he does in *The Ragged Millionaire* when he brings in the person of Mrs Buck. "Ho!" she ejaculates as she finds her son Sam with a girl in Hyde Park,

Ho! Jest as Hi sexpected! Somefink told me hif Hi strolled frough the Pork during the dinner-hour I should find you two tergether.

"We ain't doing no harm," Sam protests, and she proceeds in her tirade,

P'raps not – *hat* present. But Hi'm goin' ter keep yer hout of 'arm's way. You'll jest get back to your shop along o' me, my lad: an' I shall harsk your boss to maike yer dinner-*h*our a dinner *'arf h*our in fucher. That'll put a stop to hassassinations in the Pork wiv young pussons has ought ter be hold henough ter know better.

This reproduces the terms of Cockney speech with almost as exact precision as does Shaw's opening scene in *Pygmalion*. In Garrod's comedies, too, the words which he puts into the mouths of several of his characters – Janet Bradstone, for example, the alertly wise old grandmother in *Blissful Ignorance* – often prove effective means of revealing the inner natures of the speakers. While there is no brilliance here, there certainly is competence and there is also evidence that the author could effectively use his ears and eyes in his observation of life.

What immediately attracts our attention, however, is that

when he turns to melodrama his method is completely different. His persons in such plays are obviously stereotyped according to the forms which had been established a hundred years earlier. In *One Law for Both*, Jack Kingsley is the typical hero – a youth who can gamble and occasionally drink too much but who is essentially noble; Marjorie Drew is the equally typical heroine – and, according to tradition, an orphan; Mortimer Gloade and his deceitful daughter, Ethel, combine to provide the force of villainy essential in this form of dramatic composition. So, in *The Ragged Millionaire* the almost impeccable hero is a Ronald Kendrick who some years previously had taken the blame (in order to protect his sister) of forging his father's name on a cheque and who had consequently been disowned by the irate parent; Nellie Howard, who is shown in the distressful position of having lost her secretarial job, is the heroine; while once more the rôle of villainy is strengthened by the association between the elder Kendrick's son-in-law, Lawrence Wilde, and the avaricious housekeeper Lola Casson. And, of course, in addition to the inevitable trio of hero–heroine–villain, both these pieces introduce another almost obligatory person, the low-comedy character – Snidd Proll in the former play and Sam Buck in the latter. Still further, it is to be observed that in all these melodramas Garrod carefully underlines the "stock" quality of his cast by defining them in terms which we might well have thought to have then been long defunct: thus, for instance, *One Law for Both* starts with a page in which are listed

THE PERSONS IN THE PLAY:–

1. MRS KINGSLEY	*A wealthy widow. Aristocratic old woman.*
2. JACK KINGSLEY	*Her son. Lead.*
3. MORTIMER GLOADE	*A distant relation. Aristocratic old man.*
4. ETHEL GLOADE	*His daughter. Juvenile heavy.*
5. MARJORIE DREW	*An orphan. Juvenile lead.*
6. JACOB PARRAS	*An inn-keeper. Heavy lead.*
7. COLIMA DURANGO	*His mistress. Heavy lead.*

8. SNIDD PROLL	*A servant at Parras's inn. Low comedy.*
9. MAMIE ATWOOD	*Another servant at Parras's inn. Chambermaid. Character comedy.*
10. SILAS Q. TURNBULL	*A silver miner. Responsible.*

Contemplating this and the accompanying lists we might well be justified in believing that we were back in the days of Moncrieff, Pocock and Dimond instead of considering the stage during the years when Coward and Milne were taking command, when London audiences were welcoming *Heartbreak House* and *Saint Joan.* And it hardly needs to be said that characters so described had to be given language of a correspondingly stereotyped kind: asides are plentiful in the dialogue, and emphatic melodramatic capitals are freely used to give force to the scenes. Speech after speech echoes the tone of Simon's tirade in *Out of Wedlock:*

Leave my house, you nameless cub! Who are YOU to dictate to me? All that you've had of me had been obtained by your mother's false pretences. Go to your FATHER! Get what you can from HIM – he can't give you his NAME! And, by heaven, you shall never use MINE again!

Passage after passage reflects the pattern of the hero's and heroine's confrontation in the same play:

DAVID. Fay, I must ask a big thing of you: I can't tell you the reason; I want you to trust me.

FAY. Yet *you* distrust ME – or you'd confide in me. Have I given you cause? Have I been false to my promise to keep our engagement a secret?

DAVID. No, no – my faith in you is absolute: but to tell you why I go would be to betray another.

FAY. Since you are trusted with this secret, why should not I be? Will you EVER confide in me?

DAVID (*after a pause: regretfully*). No.

FAY. You're spoiling your chance of happiness. What is marriage worth without complete confidence? (*A pause*) Will you tell me WHOSE secret you are keeping?

DAVID (*distracted*). God help me – I can tell you nothing.

FAY. Then I do not come FIRST with you.
DAVID. You do, you do –
FAY. Yet you will not give me proof of it.
DAVID. THAT proof I CANNOT give.

Taking all these facts into consideration, it might seem that this author W. V. Garrod was writing tongue in cheek when he was engaged in the composition of his melodramatic scenes: yet, if his scripts are examined carefully, it must be recognised that these plays were, in fact, concocted with meticulous care. Each text is prefaced with detailed production notes – a dress-plot detailing the various costumes to be worn in the various scenes, a property-plot, a hand-property plot, a scenery-plot and a (very expert) electric-lighting-plot – followed by plans of the settings. And, since most of the melodramas had clearly been designed to be performed both in full and in "twice-nightly" versions, the author had obviously spent a very great deal of time in marking the cuts and changes necessary for the latter. In fact, the impression which we receive is that Garrod regarded these writings very seriously indeed; there is not the slightest sign that he composed his plays hastily, nor is there any sign that he treated them with contempt, however good-natured; it seems obvious that his heart and mind were firmly engaged in accomplishing a task which seemed to him to be worthy and important.

That he was not alone in mingling artificiality of dialogue with obvious sincerity is happily proved by some interesting and revealing comments made by H. F. Maltby in a section of his autobiography wherein he recounts his association, about 1904, with the Melville family, then owner–managers of the Standard Theatre, Shoreditch, as well as of at least two provincial houses.[1] Two brothers, Walter and Fred, he records, "used to write all their own dramas in those days", these being "'scissors and paste' affairs, the situations suggested by pictorial posters they might have in the bill room, or remembered from the old dramas they had seen". Yet, he proceeds,

[1] *Ring up the Curtain* (1950), pp. 104–5.

in spite of all that there was an element of, if not originality, fresh thought about them. And let me mention here to the high-brow who imagines that it is simple to turn out a clap-trap, blood-and-thunder drama, that they are no easier to write than any other forms of dramatic work. One must be sincere and believe in what one is writing; people would sneer at the Melville dramas, but to Walter and Fred they were works of art; they believed every word of them.

And that, of course, is precisely why they made so broad an appeal and so deep an impression upon their popular audiences.

These audiences, as we have seen, were mostly outside of London's centre, yet it is necessary to remember that during the first decade of the century metropolitan spectators were able to welcome – and in fact did warmly welcome – not only melodramas of the domestic kind but also of other kinds as well. In 1910 the two Melville brothers moved westwards from the Standard to assume management of the Lyceum, and, as Maltby remarks, "their magic touch" turned it into "a gold mine"; and two years later they went even further by building the Prince's theatre, where "more money flowed into their pockets". Perhaps, however, even greater significance attaches to a still earlier venture at the Lyceum when, in 1907, H. R. Smith and Ernest Carpenter took over its management and were rewarded for their efforts by what one contemporary critic called "a remarkable popular success". Their first play was Walter Howard's *Her Love against the World*, which Manchester playgoers had seen during the preceding year; this was followed by another Manchester drama written by the same author, *The Midnight Wedding*; and the third was Hall Caine's *The Christian*.

Maybe not very much of good can be said about Hall Caine as a playwright; indeed it is possible to deem his dialogue no less artificial than that written by the Melville brothers; yet he carried their obvious sincerity a stage further, and it cannot be denied that the association of his name with those of the now-long-forgotten names of the provincial dramatists is a matter of some considerable importance. Here the melodrama was being made "literary" and respectable.

Already in the nineteenth century Caine had established himself as one of the most popular novelists in England: *The Deemster* (1887), *The Bondman* (1890), *The Manxman* (1894) and *The Christian* (1897) were titles familiar to all readers, and to those titles were soon added those of *The Eternal City* (1901) and *The Prodigal Son* (1904). When this shelf of narrative fiction is set alongside the productions of the popular stage, there becomes immediately evident an inner affinity between them, and hence we need feel no surprise in finding that at an early date Caine not only planned theatrical versions of *The Deemster* and *The Manxman* but actually wrote their scenes in collaboration with one of the most melodramatic actors of that time, Wilson Barrett. Novelist and player were spiritually well suited to each other: both loved the bold passions, the thrilling episodes and the strong strain of moralism which had been characteristic of the popular playhouse throughout the whole long course of its career.

Wilson Barrett died in 1904, but Caine actively pursued his theatrical efforts unaided, producing both dramatisations of later-published novels and, interestingly, recasting entirely some of his earlier adaptations. In these endeavours he won resounding success. *The Prodigal Son*, with its emotion-laden plot set in Iceland, created a sensation at Drury Lane in 1905, and the following year at the same theatre a similar sensation attended the production of *The Bondman*: its strong story of two half-brothers, Michael and Jason, who were designed deliberately to "illustrate the conflict of the Pagan ideal of vengeance with the Christian ideal of love", so captured the interest of the public and made it so newsworthy that the *Daily Mail* decided to publish the play in a fat, thick-paper, illustrated edition. And the excitement was to endure for some time. A version of *The Christian*, prepared by Caine himself, had been presented on the stage as early as 1898, but its reception then was as nothing compared with the almost frenetic rapture which greeted his new version at the Lyceum in 1907.

This success can, if we wish, be attributed to the fact that during the intervening years the author had profited considerably from his stage experiences, so that, while his dramatic language tended to remain rather stiff and melodramatically artificial, his scenes were now re-channelled in such a way as to make them flow more easily than they had done in the past. Yet such an explanation seems, on closer examination, to be unsatisfactory: we must decide that the praise accorded to the Lyceum production cannot be ascribed solely to an improved theatrical style. Rather must it be considered to result from what may be regarded as a further extension of the melodramatic pattern. Here the sincerity which Maltby discerned in the writings of the Melville brothers has been made more intense; here the general melodramatic trend towards the introduction of crudely but boldly expressed social ideas has become more self-conscious; here the moralism is more pronounced. The second version of *The Christian*, Caine said, was written designedly "in order to introduce without any kind of restraint a new social propaganda on which" he "had long felt deeply".[1] With a precisely similar objective he proceeded, in collaboration with L. N. Parker, to replace the original dramatisation of *The Manxman* by a new rendering under the title of *Pete*. As presented at the Lyceum in 1908, this play also attracted much popular attention, and its appeal may likewise be explained by the broader social overtones which had been added to the sentimentally melodramatic story of a noble hero who, after having spent time abroad making money for his marriage to Kate, weds his bride, after some months discovers that the babe to which she gives birth had been fathered by the hypocritical "Deemster", Philip, and, following a number of stormy passionate scenes, magnanimously forgives those who have wronged him.

In the same manner, too, he virtually transformed the action of *The Deemster* when he turned it into *The Bishop's*

[1] Letter printed in *The Play Pictorial*, xi, 1907, 1.

Son (1910), and here it is particularly interesting to observe that paradoxically, while the action is made to agree more closely with the plot of the original novel, the episodes are dealt with in a manner more boldly melodramatic in style. The story is mainly concerned with the Mylrea family. Gilchrist Mylrea, by nature kindly and understanding, is Bishop of Sodor and Man; his hard, selfish, puritanical brother, Thorkell, is the "Deemster". The former's son, Daniel, is the hero, cast in a mould beloved by popular audiences – careless, good-natured but with a reputation for profligacy: he truly loves the equally typical heroine, Thorkell's daughter Mona, but is forbidden to meet her. The lovers have their secret trysts; Thorkell, in a rage, arouses his son, Ewan, to confront Daniel; there is a struggle; Ewan falls on the ground and is killed. This might easily have been almost, if not quite, the end of the drama, but much more is to come. The dour Deemster brings Daniel before his court of law and is about to pronounce sentence for murder, when the Bishop intervenes; having the right to take a felon out of the hands of the civil judge, he demands that the punishment should be left to him. "It is not," he declares in a "dramatic" speech,

It is not the way of God's worst chastisement to take an eye for an eye, a tooth for a tooth, and to spill blood for blood that has been spilled. When the sword of the Lord goes forth it is sometimes to destroy the guilty man, and sometimes to cut him off from the living, to banish him to the parched places of the universe, to end the days wherein his sleep shall be sweet to him, to blot out his name from the names of men, and to give him no burial at last when the darkness of death shall cover him. Daniel Mylrea, this is to be your punishment!

The scene ends appropriately. The courtroom empties:

(*When everybody has gone, black darkness falls on the scene; there are fierce flashes of lightning and loud claps of thunder. In the midst of the tempest* DAN. *is seen to rise and to stagger out, with the lightning coming and going on his face, and crying* –

Alone! Alone! For evermore alone!

Time passes, and a strange thing happens. A wave of mortal sickness sweeps over the whole community; men and women are dying daily, and in desperation the Bishop suggests that they send out a call to Ireland for a certain "holy man" who seems to "have been blessed, under God, with miraculous powers of curing" just such awful maladies as this. The priest duly crosses the sea, but his boat is wrecked on nearing the shore and he himself is heavily struck by the shattered mast. In pain and travail he struggles ashore, finds Daniel's lonely cabin and tells him about the sickness:

After fruitless efforts to combat the disease, your good Bishop sent for me, hearing that the Almighty had blessed my efforts in a like terrible scourge which broke out over the bogs of Ireland two years ago. But much I fear my coming is useless. As I was thrown ashore a falling spar struck me. My head is injured – my errand will be fruitless.

Passionately he begs Daniel to go to the people in order to tell them how they can escape from the epidemic; and, lest the young man should himself fall sick, he gives him a small quantity of some "powder that is very potent in such maladies". Dressed in the priest's cloak, Daniel accepts the mission, helps to save the people, feels the illness coming upon him, is about to take the last few remaining grains of the powder, and is confronted by the Deemster who, feeling in terror that he is seriously ill, acts as any properly behaved villain should by confessing his sin. Nobly Daniel sacrifices himself, gives the last of the powder to the Deemster and returns to his cabin. As he grows weaker and weaker, there is heard the faint sound of church bells ringing at a distance mingled with voices singing a joyful hymn. Mona and the Bishop come to visit him:

MONA (*In a broken whisper*). Dan!

(*A shaft of brilliant sunlight falls on his upturned face and fills the place with radiance.*)

DAN. (*His face full of rapture, putting one arm round* MONA, *pointing to the sunbeam*). Look! Look upward! What a throng. They are coming. The millions of the angels of heaven! See how graciously they stretch down their arms to us!

MONA (*With awe*). Dan.

(*The same voices seem to be singing very softly the joyful hymn.*)

DAN. (*Drawing closer to* MONA *until their faces touch*). Hark! What a joyful sound! They are singing the songs of my forgiveness! Hush! "Though your sins were as scarlet they are washed whiter than snow!"

MONA (*Barely audibly*). Dan!

(*The sunshine is now upon him, and his face beams with celestial joy. The cabin is full of glory.*)

DAN. Hush! Hush! Hark again! All the bells of heaven are ringing. They are ringing a penitent soul to his salvation. Yes, yes, God has spoken, his wrath is appeased, Daniel Mylrea is pardoned and is going back in peace – (*There is a distant sound like that of a heavenly trumpet.* DAN. *rises suddenly as if to the call.*) Mona!

MONA (*Rising and holding him*). Yes?

DAN. Give me your hand, beloved.

MONA. Here is my hand, Dan.

DAN. Are you ready?

MONA. Yes, I am ready.

DAN. (*With great exaltation*). Then we two will go together. Home! Home at last, by right of God's law and man's.

(*He stands erect for a moment. The bells and the anthem swell up. He sinks back to the bed. With a rapturous smile and exclamation he closes his eyes as if to listen.* MONA *tightens her arms about him.... The* BISHOP *steps forward and raises his hand as if in benediction.*)

BISHOP. For this my son was dead and is alive again – was lost and is found.

DAN. (*Opening his eyes, half rising and holding out one hand towards the* BISHOP *rapturously*). The Vision! The Vision! (*Then reverently, in a soft whisper, with a radiant smile, as if his spirit already reaches heaven.*) Father! (*The anthem and the bell-ringing continue, growing gradually louder and more joyful. The rude old cabin shines with celestial light.*)

And the curtain falls.

This conclusion, eminently in keeping with the entire tone of the play, is hardly surpassed by the final acts of any nineteenth-century popular dramas; a contemptuous smile may form on our lips, but before it is permitted to assume full expression maybe it is well to recall the close of another much earlier popular play –

Now cracks a noble heart. Good night, sweet prince,
And flights of angels sing thee to thy rest.

The one scene may be peerlessly written, the other may be rather crude, but in intended effect do they not come close together?

Sufficient has been quoted here to provide an indication of Hall Caine's style, but one other of his dramas demands brief comment. In 1910 he brought forward *The Eternal Question*, a play which, he claims, owed nothing to his much earlier *Eternal City* "except the material which that play owed to the novel of the same name. It omits some of the scenes of the earlier drama, substitutes other scenes, and does not... contain a single page that is quite the same". His purpose in preparing this second text is made fully clear: he did so, not to improve the dialogue, but in order "to present the general features of two problems of life" which had come into prominence since he wrote his novel – "the problem of socialism" and "the woman question". Religious sentiment had pervaded *The Bishop's Son*: here, instead, he concentrated on secular issues – and the two themes, taken together, demonstrate once more the sources of his inspiration. From the start, despite its theatricality, the melodrama had always been moralistic, had praised goodness and denounced evil, had frequently sought to deal with social issues, had always attempted, in its own manner, to be up-to-date – and here in its latest stages it was remaining true to its ancestral traditions. Quite appropriately, for instance, when the management of Drury Lane in 1912 looked round for a play which might form the basis of its annual spectacle, it seized upon a melodramatic "modern morality play" called *Everywoman*, composed by the American author Walter Browne "in five canticles" and graced with music by George Whitfield Chadwick (produced at the Herald Square Theatre, New York, on February 27, 1911): appropriately, too, this was put into the hands of Stephen Phillips for revision, and when it was presented as *Everywoman: Her Pilgrimage in Quest of Love*, it had a run of nearly a hundred performances.

The bills announcing *Everywoman* had stressed its "modern" quality, and unquestionably the style and tone of Hall Caine's dramas were derived from the genre of domestic melodrama, yet two features in his plays carry them into different, although related, realms. Certainly, their main actions concentrate upon a limited number of individuals, but there is here an impression of largeness, even of grandeur, and it was no doubt partly because they possessed this quality that two of them were selected for production at Drury Lane. Under the régime of Augustus Harris at the close of the nineteenth century and during the first years of management by his successor, Arthur Collins, the great Theatre Royal had specialised in that type of melodrama which has been called variously "realistic" and "spectacular" – the type which found its fullest development in the plays of Cecil Raleigh – *The Great Millionaire* (1901), *The Sins of Society* (1907) and *The Whip* (1909). Just at first it might appear that Caine's dramas were hardly the same as these productions of Raleigh, but Arthur Collins was astute; he knew what he was doing; he realised that *The Bondman* and *The Prodigal* had something still more to offer; and the success of those dramas fully proved that he had assessed aright the tastes of the spectators who in their thousands flocked to Drury Lane.

The something more that Caine had to give was the environment in which he placed his characters. For the contemporary public, Iceland was a grim unknown territory of snow-covered mountains and treacherous ice-floes; at that period even the Isle of Man was almost equally strange, and Caine made it stranger still by setting his action in an indeterminate past; only a limited, favoured few among the spectators had had the chance of visiting Italy, so that this country too had about it an aura of wonder. It would, of course, be going too far to suggest that such settings might properly be termed romantic, yet they were sufficiently far-off to warrant the surmise that in selecting them the play-wright was influenced by the second type of melodrama, the romantically-historical, a type which still remained popular in many of the provincial playhouses and which, from the point of view of Drury Lane's manager, had the added attraction of linking up with a popular trend amply exemplified in numerous West End theatres. During those years the stage was certainly veering more and more towards the realistic, but several distinguished star performers persisted in keeping the romantic style alive on the boards, delighting audiences with colourful scenes, costumes, adventures and acting – developing and exploiting what several contemporaries dubbed "decorative melodrama". John Martin-Harvey's three great stand-bys – Freeman Wills' *The Only Way* (1899), Charles Hannan's *A Cigarette Maker's Romance* (1901) and John Rutherford's *The Breed of the Treshams* (1903) – might politely be classified as romantic plays but in fact they were of melodramatic texture. Fred Terry, debonaire hero of *The Scarlet Pimpernel* (1903), in the version by M. Barstow and Baroness Orczy, delighted in episodes of a similar sort: as the central character in "*Matt*" *of Merrymount* (1908) by B. M. Dix and E. G. Sutherland he is a man who believes he has killed his cousin, takes flight and lives a kind of Robin Hood existence until his name is cleared; he is a gallant Henry de Bourbon during the days of Catherine de Medici in William Devereux' *Henry of Navarre* (1908); and, after many changes of costume and countless hair-breadth escapes, in 1921 he is still the same flamboyant hero (on this occasion called Bothwell), when he shares honours with Julia Neilson as Mary Queen of Scots in the cloak-and-dagger action of *The Borderer* by Madge and Leslie Howard Gordon. And alongside these two excellent romantic players stood another – Lewis Waller, creator of the title-rôle in *Monsieur Beaucaire* (1902) by Booth Tarkington and E. G. Sutherland, of that of Mohun in *His Majesty's Servant* (1904) by S. Elliott and Maud Hosford, and that of Henri de Lagardère in J. H. McCarthy's *The Duke's Motto* (1908).

Audiences loved these plays, numerous authors turned them out apace, and in general it may be said that their influence was even longer-enduring than that of the domestic genre of melodrama. Here, however, care must be taken to interpret their appeal correctly. Although some of these romantic plays had a Ruritanian setting, most were given a flavour of historicity, and at least a few were disfigured by deplorable attempts on the part of their authors to make the dialogue seem "archaic". Yet it is reasonably certain that this historicity deluded nobody – playwrights, actors, audiences all recognised it for what it was, a means of giving colour to the action. The dramas which gave Martin-Harvey, Terry and Waller their greatest triumphs were made up of substance and sheen: the substance was the melodramatically conceived plot, the sheen was simply the atmosphere suggested by different costumes and colourful sets. During the first half of this period the two elements remained closely attached to each other, but during the second half they tended to become disjoined. Erratically romantic historical dramas continued to appear, but almost all of these, such as Mrs Clifford Mills' *In Nelson's Days* (1922) or *The Yellow Poppy* (1922) by D. K. Broster and W. E. Stirling, were poor things, somehow seeming out-of-date and lacking the drive necessary to give them stage appeal. The sheen no longer possessed its earlier attraction – or rather it might be said that it had been taken over by a number of new writers who did not belong to the melodramatic sphere and had, in effect, itself been transformed into substance. During the twenties true historical plays flourished, with particular emphasis on the dramatic presentation of individual characters, but in these care was generally taken to avoid action of the cloak-and-dagger kind: and with the development of these biographical-chronicle plays, seriously based on study of the historical periods selected, the gloss and the gleam of period costumes in the melodramatic theatre rapidly lost its earlier allure.[1]

Such a disjunction between substance and sheen, on the

[1] Robert Fricker has a study of *Das historische Drama in England bis zur Gegenwart* (1940).

other hand, by no means checked the course of the romantically inclined melodrama: all that happened was that, while the substance was preserved more or less in its pristine form, a different sheen was chosen to replace that which had previously been so popular. Still further, it may be observed that the melodramatic force remained so potent that it often penetrated beyond the range of "popular" authors into the ranks of those attached to the *avant garde*. One single example of this may serve as a kind of symbolic illustration. The name of William Archer is well known, and when we think of him we have in our minds a picture of the serious, devoted exponent of the "new theatre", the translator of Ibsen, the enthusiastic advocate of the stage as a platform for the discussion of social and related problems. This picture is not a false one, yet it needs to be qualified by consideration of a second, companion portrait. Towards the close of his career something happened to Archer. In 1921 New York audiences flocked to see his play, *The Green Goddess*, and two years later the London public followed suit when it appeared at the St James's.

The success was, of course, due to the fact that the author had decided to cast his Ibsen completely overboard, to turn for inspiration to the melodramatic form, and, surprisingly, to exploit the theatrical appeal of a sheen distinctly romantic. The setting of *The Green Goddess* is a remote native state in India ruled by a young Rajah who, although educated at Oxford and thoroughly adept in the use of its speech, has developed a bitter hate of England because three of his near relatives have been condemned for the murder of a British officer. Unexpectedly, an aeroplane in distress has to make a forced landing near his palace and its occupants – Lucilla, her husband, and the husband's friend Traherne – find themselves in the Rajah's power.

The melodramatically-conceived company is thus complete, and the action proceeds along well-established lines. The Rajah decides to hold the unexpected visitors to ransom and becomes still more threatening by his open assault on the heroine's virtue. The hero turns out to be Traherne, a man deeply devoted to the heroine, who has hitherto nobly concealed his passion but who is able to confess his love when the husband is killed. For this pair of lovers all hope of escape seems lost when suddenly an unanticipated opportunity comes: they gain their freedom just at the moment when military planes are about to bomb the palace – and the villain is foiled.[1]

If *The Green Goddess* had stood alone, its sole interest would relate to its place in Archer's long and notable career; in fact, however, the success of this drama arose from its author's awareness of what the public wanted and from his ability to deal with its exotic, melodramatic theme in an expert manner. Instead of standing alone, it is representative of a general trend which was of considerable theatrical, if not dramatic, interest. This development within the melodramatically romantic sphere, however, requires to be considered in association with still another kind of melodrama which shaped itself during the first three decades of the century – a variety which sometimes ran parallel with the exotic and sometimes coalesced with it.

In 1901 the American actor William Gillette brought to the Lyceum a play, *Sherlock Holmes*, which he and Conan Doyle had written in collaboration. It proved one of the greatest successes of the season,[2] and there is justification for regarding it as the foundation for the whole of that popular school of drama to which are variously attached the terms "crook", "crime", "detective", "mystery" and "thriller". The

[1] Although *The Green Goddess* seemed in 1921 to be such an extraordinary play for Archer to write, a posthumous volume published in 1927 with a most interesting preface by Bernard Shaw demonstrates that towards the end of his life he was indulging in experiments outside of the Ibsen sphere. *Martha Washington* is an eight-scened biographical chronicle play rather reminiscent of those produced by John Drinkwater, while *Beatriz Juana* and *Lidia* are blank-verse reworkings of Middleton's *The Changeling* and Massinger's *The Great Duke of Florence*. None of these reached the stage, and their exact dates of composition appear to be uncertain, but the probability is that they belong to about the year 1920.

[2] How great a success is clearly reflected in Malcolm Watson's *Sheerluck Jones* (1901), described as "a dramatic criticism in four burlesque paragraphs".

souvenir of *Sherlock Holmes* printed in *The Playgoer* concisely and correctly defines its position:[1] this play, it states, "is a melodrama pure and simple"; it is by no means the first of its kind to deal with criminals, police and detection; it gains its distinction from the fact that here the melodramatic style is so raised in quality as to give it "a position by itself, where it stands unique as a play and as an inciter of intense interest. It may be said to be in a class by itself".[2]

If in 1901 *Sherlock Holmes* was indeed in a class by itself, very soon it found numerous companions. Five years later, Gerald Du Maurier created considerable excitement when he took the chief part in another transatlantic drama, *Raffles* (1906) by W. Hornung and E. W. Presbrey. Although his daughter Daphne was hardly justified in declaring that he was thus responsible for introducing "the first crook play to herald the American invasion",[3] he certainly made popular the rôle of the suave, well-born, amateur cracksman who held everyone enthralled by his unruffled calm and unfailing dexterity: in the English version of *Arsène Lupin* (1909) he repeated his triumph by interpreting the part of the "swell mobsman", the Duc de Charmerace, and the following year appeared as the equally adroit Lee Randall in Paul Armstrong's *Alias Jimmie Valentine*. And it may further be noted here that, as plays dealing with murder took the place of those in which the central character was a light-fingered "mobsman", he continued to stay in the lead. In George Pleydell's *The Ware Case* (1915), almost the first of those numerous dramas which concentrated on the suspense of trial scenes, he was Sir Hubert Ware, cold-blooded slayer of his wife's brother, who succeeds by his aplomb in persuading a jury to acquit him, and then, afterwards, breaks down in violent self-accusation. Seven years later Du

[1] *The Playgoer*, i, no. 2, Nov. 1901, 79–86.

[2] The close connections between melodrama and detective play could be exemplified by reference to many authors, of whom Fred Moule may stand as representative. Almost all his earlier pieces were melodramas; in 1911 he was responsible for a "detective drama", *The Black Hand*, and later concocted several other similar works.

[3] *Gerald: A Portrait* (1934), p. 114.

Maurier transferred his allegiance to the forces of law and order when he appeared, amid plaudits from all parts of the house, as Captain Hugh Drummond in the exciting scenes of *Bull-Dog Drummond* (1922) which he himself wrote in collaboration with "Sapper", while five years after that success his part in *Interference* (1927), by Roland Pertwee and Harold Dearden, placed him, as it were, midway between crime and the law – here he was John Marley, a famous medical specialist, who thinks his wife has committed a murder, deliberately rearranges the scene so as to suggest that the dead man had killed himself, and, when that ruse fails, actually brings suspicion upon himself, prepared to go in silence to his doom – when unexpectedly it is discovered that the murderer was in fact his wife's former husband. Du Maurier's influence in this area was widespread, and numerous other dramas rang the changes on these basic themes.

Interference, however, takes us far ahead, and, before looking at any of the later plays of this kind, it is necessary to observe that if Du Maurier cashed in on this appeal of the crook play, there were others who were equally fortunate in realms far removed from the West End. The example of one single venture may here stand as representative. In January 1908 John M. East and Brian Daly completed a drama called *Sexton Blake, Detective*, were thoroughly pleased with its reception at a "copyright" performance, and, with two or three associates, formed a company called The Melodramatic Productions Syndicate Ltd., with the object of making a kind of "corner" in Sexton Blake themes. No fewer than seven tours were arranged for the original drama, and it itself was followed by others such as *Hush Money, or, The Disappearance of Sexton Blake*, *Convict 99*, *After Midnight*, *Master of the Mill* and *Tracked by Wireless*.[1]

As the crook drama continued on its course, whether in London or in the provinces, it gradually inclined to develop into the thriller. The gentleman-detective mixing with gentlemen-crooks, as in Noel Scott's *The Joker* (1927) or

[1] For this information my thanks are due to Mr John M. East, author of *'Neath the Mask: The Story of the East Family* (1967).

the story of Pierre Boucheron and his faithful Odile in the Paris underworld of David L'Estrange's *The Rat* (1924), provided ample opportunity for the free use of concealments, sudden unexpected discoveries, twists and turns, thrills and excitements; and these stage tricks, like all stage tricks of an exciting nature, had constantly to become more and more exaggerated as play followed play: in the advertisements such terms as "stunts", "shocking", "horror" and "thriller" were ever more and more emphatically stressed. Some of the authors who applied themselves to the writing of dramas in this style did, it is true, seek to make their stunts and shocks outgrowths of the situations which they devised and, at the same time, to keep the "thriller" element within such bounds as to permit the spectators to take at least a little interest in the characters. As examples two playwrights may be treated as representative. In 1925 Arnold Ridley wrote his *Ghost Train*; not only was this "non-stop thriller" an immediate success, but for a considerable time thereafter it almost seemed as though it might be vying with *Charley's Aunt* in longevity. The reasons for its appeal seem obvious: while no great masterpiece, it cleverly accomplishes its basic aim of keeping its audiences in suspense without the employment of extravagant tricks; its little group of characters is held together as one assembled unit; and, despite this, the individuals composing the unit are effectively individualised as independent stage personalities. If we are prepared to accept the possibility that criminals may, for their nefarious purposes, be running trains at night along a deserted line and that a number of passengers may be marooned in the waiting-room of a lonely small station, then all the action follows quite naturally. Similar qualities are to be discerned in those numerous plays by Edgar Wallace which kept the public excited in the late twenties. Most of them freely employ sensational elements – doors ominously creak, windows mysteriously open, there are revolver shots in the dark, yet all these things may, in a sense, be regarded as natural phenomena within the particular crook world of Wallace's imagination, and they do not completely destroy interest in the persons and the plot. *The Ringer* (1926), with its vengeful master-criminal, *The Terror* (1927), exploiting its insane malefactor, *The Flying Squad* (1928), interesting because of the sympathetic pity with which the crooks are presented, *The Squeaker* (1928) and *Persons Unknown* (1929) all, in their own way, deserved their popularity. They are infused with the same kind of spirit which Maltby discerned in the crude melodramas penned by the brothers Melville.

Gradually, however, particularly in the hands of a number of young authors, the seach for clever novelties and the desire to exhibit out-of-the-way stunts swamped the stage with pieces which had nothing save thrills and unexpected tricks to recommend them. Eagerly the playwrights sought for new general devices: Harold Holland, for example, sets his *Big Drum* (1927) within a fictional theatre, has an actress shot on the stage and eventually makes a man in the audience give himself up to the police; in *Murder on the Second Floor* (1929) Frank Vosper shows a youthful intellectual writer persuaded by his landlady's daughter to turn from the poetic play on which he is engaged to contrive a thriller in which his fellow-boarders are surrounded with an atmosphere of mystery, while in *People Like Us* (1929) he seeks to explore a new area by basing his plot on the notorious Bywater case and by styling his rather sentimental drama a "symbolic play".[1] Insane doctors and charlatans made good hunting. In *The Man Responsible* (1927) a physician, believing that a fellow-practitioner has been responsible for the death of his daughter, dopes and hypnotises his victim, causing him in this state to perform a fatal operation on his mother (who, for the sake of placating possible audience reactions, is said to have been suffering from an incurable disease);[2] while in Carl Glick's *The Devil's Host* (1928) a quack psychologist, pretending to be the very devil himself, torments and tortures a group of men and women who fall under his evil

[1] This play was banned, but presented on the stage in a Sunday performance: recognising its news-worthiness, the *Evening Standard* gave it considerable publicity by publishing its scenes in serial form.

[2] This play seems to have been announced as by Julian Frank in one production, and in another as by Brian Marsh.

spell. And there was good hunting, too, among spooks both supernatural and simulated. Vernon Sylvaine and Sydney Lynn thus aim at terrifying their audiences in *The Phantom Fear* (1928); Percy Robinson and T. de Marney empty all their bag of tricks – phosphorescent hands, ghostly susurrations and the like – in *The Whispering Gallery* (1928); in his *Dracula* (1925) Hamilton Deane goes back for inspiration (if inspiration it may be called) to Bram Stoker's sensational nineteenth-century novel; in *A Murder Has Been Arranged* (1930), described as "a ghost story", a young Welsh actor–author, Emlyn Williams, gave an indication of his later dramatic skill by setting his clever plot within the eerie bounds of a spook-ridden playhouse. Not without reason the gay Co-Optimists introduced into their 1926 programme a skit in which a Ghost Union is formed under best trade-union rules to insist that hauntings should last no longer than four hours a time, and that passing through walls and carrying heads under arms should be treated as skilled labour, with appropriate increases in salaries.

Although there were some worthy examples of this genre, most of the ghost thrillers were silly enough; but the absolute nadir seems to be reached in the plays, American and English, which exploited oriental, usually Egyptian, characters, strange cults and sacred scarabs.[1] *The Creaking Chair* (1924) by Allene Tupper Wilkes and revised by Roland Pertwee, manufactures a concoction in which ancient jewels unearthed by an archeologist, murder, ominous Egyptians, an astute detective and a villain in the person of a journalist who is animated by the best of liberal principles are stirred up into a witch's brew: as the handcuffs are slipped on to the journalist's wrists he stands facing the other persons – and of course the spectators as well: "One moment," he declaims,

> I wonder if your Government would grant me a favour in the cause of science. A little thing for a man to ask who has to die.... An hour with a pick and a spade in the Poets' Corner of Westminster Abbey – an hour to prize open the sepulchres of a few

[1] Many of these, it may be noted, were deliberately described as melodramas.

of your English kings – the right to scatter their remains for children to play knucklebones with at street corners, and mumbling old men to label and put into glass cases. A letter to the Home Office would not take very long to write, Mr Latter, or are *your* dead too precious to disturb?

John Willard's *The Green Beetle* (1929) has a Chinese background,[1] but in general beetles were regarded as the peculiar property of the land of the Nile – and as an example one may take a theme selected in 1928 by the collaborative team of J. B. Fagan, C. Freeman and G. S. King for *The Beetle*, in which a young Englishman is shown captured by a mysterious Egyptian religious sect, killing their priestess and being haunted for years by (apparently) the spirit of this defunct lady in the likeness of an active, elusive and tormenting virescent scarab.

This last play was derived from a novel by Richard Marsh, and this reminds us that sensational fiction exerted a most unfortunate influence upon the stage during these years – unfortunate because frequently what might be perfectly acceptable on the printed page proved sadly unsuited to any kind of presentation on the stage, except, perhaps, for the purpose of arousing artificial shrieks from young ladies who sought the manly comforting of their escorts. Still further, the fact that *Dracula* was presented at the Little Theatre brings to our minds something else – the notable "Grand Guignol" seasons sponsored in that playhouse by José G. Levy between 1920 and 1922,[2] seasons which, however brilliant in acting and production, however nobly supported by Sybil Thorndike and her husband, must be seen as having had effects almost equally unfortunate. The programmes, of course, consisted of short plays in varying styles, but those which made most impress on the public mind were clearly those which may be exemplified by Christopher Holland's

[1] This was originally performed in the U.S.A. in 1924.

[2] The vogue created by this theatre is exemplified by the publication of a *Grand Guignol Annual Review*, edited by Mervyn McPherson. The first issue is particularly important because it contains articles by Lewis Casson, Sybil Thorndike and Russell Thorndike, the leaders of the company.

The Old Women (1921). When this is compared with, let us say, *The Ghost Train*, we realise that the best, the most satisfactory and indeed one might almost say the most salutory of the thrillers were those which did not base their theatrically exciting or terrifying scenes on physical torment and torture. The "Grand Guignol" playlets which achieved most notice were composed with a sort of spurious, pretentious seriousness, and freely concentrated upon scenes of realistically horrifying suspense. In themselves, no doubt, many were dramatically effective within their limited scope, and certainly they provided opportunities for the very distinguished players who presented them to the public: but their consequences were by no means happy since they induced a number of talented authors, who might well have applied themselves to more profitable styles, to expand the brief terrors of the "Grand Guignol" one-acts into full-length dramas, and, in doing so, to treat their artificially-concocted subject-matter with a solemnity peculiarly inappropriate.

The combined influences of prose fiction and "Grand Guignolism" were widely spread, but again a few examples may stand for many. A. E. W. Mason was a novelist–playwright who, when he wanted, could compose detective plays as honestly and effectively planned as his detective stories: his *House of the Arrow* (1928), for instance, based on the question "Who murdered Mrs Harlowe?", skilfully keeps attention alert as the action moves from doubt to clarification. By no means, however, can such esteem be expressed for *At the Villa Rose* (1920) or *No Other Tiger* (1928), both rather wasteful exercises in the ostentatiously sinister: the former tediously deals with an old lady's spiritualistic activities and with her maid's designs to steal her jewels in the midst of a séance, while the latter, in a correspondingly tedious manner, plays continuous variations on treachery, greed and murderous passion, with an ominous oriental touch brought in for good measure. With these dramas may be associated *A Man with Red Hair* (1928), written by Benn W. Levy on the basis of a novel by Hugh Walpole. A lonely Cornish house inhabited by the grotesque maniac

Crispin, his equally maniac and grotesque son Herrick and three Japanese servants – a heroine, Hesther Tobin, and her drink-sodden father – a faithful David Dunbar, the lover unloved – the timid American tourist, Charles P. Harkness, who strays into this ménage – these are the characters by means of which an effort is made to secure an impression of suspenseful dread. Appropriately, the drama ends with no fewer than four pages of dialogueless stage-direction: Harkness is shown closely and cruelly bound to a pillar; Crispin enters cracking a whip in the air and

then with all his force, sends the lash with a resounding noise curling round HARKNESS'*s chest and the pillar;*

Dunbar, who has also been tied up, releases himself, grapples with Crispin and both conveniently crash through a window, fatally falling on savage rocks far below: "*one hears a long, wailing treble cry as the two bodies*" descend; Hesther fumbles at Harkness's cords, and

all the time, dry-eyed, she whimpers – whimpers in a strange, hurt, childish fashion. She leads HARKNESS *to a chair, and, still whimpering softly, crushes his tired head to her breast, tight, tight, her fingers jerkily smoothing his hair, her eyes staring out of the window.*

The clock strikes six, and at that moment the first golden rays of the morning sun creep in through the window, blinding the candle-light with their brilliance.

What is wrong here? Even the words of the stage-directions ring false. The answer, it would seem, may be found by comparing this descriptive coming of light with that other description which has already been quoted from Caine's *The Bishop's Son* and by relating both to what Maltby had to say about Melville. Melville honestly accepted his melodramatic actions and scenes as possessing their own worthiness: his attitude might be described as simple-minded, akin to the simple-mindedness with which audiences in the melodrama theatres accepted the plots presented before them. Caine cannot, of course, be said to have been without a measure of intellectual acumen, yet his acceptance of the melodramatic material was as honest and as whole-hearted as Melville's. By contrast, we cannot escape feeling that both Mason and Levy are intellectuals who realise that the thrilling episodes with which they deal are in essence absurd. And why two men of such genuine ability as Walpole and Levy should have expended their labours on such a novel and on such a play seems an insoluble enigma.

Nor does the enigma remain a solitary one. Why, for instance, did Ashley Dukes choose a spurious play, *Der Patriot* (1927), by Alfred Neumann and translate it in an equally spurious manner as *Such Men Are Dangerous* (1928)? With almost incredible stiffnesses this "psychological" story of Paul I of Russia and the plotter Count Pahlen is put before us. Pahlen's eyes, says Anna, "tell me why I came to you tonight. I must have felt a longing, a homesickness for you. Yes, I have such foolish weaknesses at times." "Do you know what you are saying, Baroness?" enquires Pahlen, "Have you forgotten that in this country a thoughtless word may cost a life?" To the conspirator is given a soliloquy or two, like this:

> If my politics are the devil, this woman is the deep sea. She knows me too well, for she sees me with my own eyes. And still I am a match for her, because I spell necessity. And if need be... (*He seems to shiver.*)

This is truly deplorable, coming from the author of *The Man with a Load of Mischief*.

And what about Charles Bennett's *The Last Hour* (1928)? This playwright, in his *Blackmail* (1928), demonstrates that he is able to deal effectively with a relatively straight-forward "detective" plot, even although it ends up with a rather trite twist and solution. Peter Hewitt, meeting Alice Jarvis at a dance, invites her to come to his studio; she accepts; he tries to assault her; she struggles, and he falls dead. Harold Webber, Alice's fiancé, is a young detective who is ordered to deal with the case; he finds Alice's gloves in the studio, and suppresses this piece of evidence; but unfortunately a ne'er-do-well named Tracy knows of her visit to the studio and starts to blackmail the pair. The scenes become tenser and tenser until the announcement is made that a post-mortem has revealed that Hewitt had died of a heart attack. This play does not seem to have very much significance, yet it might be accounted a masterpiece when compared with *The Last Hour*, a stupidly absurd spy drama in which Prince Nicola de Kovatch and the evil Carol Blumfeldt, alias Dr Hoyt Logan, try to steal the plans of a "death ray machine" which would have the power to destroy whole nations. They are, of course, appropriately foiled by two secret service men, Peter Byron and "An Unexpected Visitor", but it is not really the plotting and counterplotting that matters: conflagrations, stranglings and horrors dominate the stage – as indeed is shown by the author's preliminary "Notes" designed to explain how the "stunt" effects can be secured in production. As for the play, perhaps quotation of its final lines will be sufficient to suggest its quality:

PRINCE (*At door, his eyes gleaming*). Is he not? Gentlemen, good night.

(*He turns to go through the door. His body is half-way through. But at the same moment, Tregellis, wild with rage and fear, falls on the ray. He does not know what he is doing. He only knows that before him is the instrument of death. His hand descends on the lever.*)

(*The Ray takes effect.*)

(*There is a blinding flash, the crash of falling masonry and a deafening roar.*)

(*The charred and unrecognisable body of what was once the Prince staggers and falls back into the room, C.*)

(*See Note at beginning of script.*)

(*Mary and Lister are in each other's arms, Mary hiding her eyes from the horror below the door.*) (*General picture, horror and consternation as*

THE CURTAIN FALLS.

There were some writers who saw clearly the uselessness, the wastefulness, of spending time on such devices, yet even they, when trying to do better, failed. A prime example here is Patrick Hamilton, author of *Rope* (1929). For the printed version of this play he wrote a special "Preface on Thrillers", in which he stated boldly that for him,

in the ordinary thriller and Grand Guignolism of this decade, the incessant round of throat-slicings, eye-gougings, thumb-screwings, floggings, burnings, brain-twistings, charred bodies and the like is merely aimless and sickening.

"This sort of thing," he thought, "can only derive either from pure unimaginativeness or real unpleasantness of mind." Yet when he essayed to demonstrate what a thriller might be, all he could do was to invent a contrived macabre situation in which two undergraduates strangle one of their companions for no ostensible reason save to plume up their wills by committing "passionless – motiveless – faultless – and clueless murder", while, not content with this basic situation, the playwright further proceeded in a grisly manner to show how they place the body in a chest and then deliberately invite the dead youth's father and aunt, together with three of their friends, to come round for a party in what might be regarded as the parlour–mortuary.

We have moved far here from the old melodrama, and yet unquestionably these thrillers, even although in style they are often more polished and polite than the earlier popular plays, even although now they were being written by clever young highbrows, belonged to the same tradition. The only trouble was that, while both the melodramas and the thrillers abounded in plots that were absurd and episodes of a ridiculous kind, the emotions introduced into the former were sincere, the emotions introduced into the latter were essentially false.

The date on the tombstone of the true melodrama is the year 1930. Even as late as 1923 the Lyceum could present a piece written by Arthur Shirley and Ben Landeck called *What Money Can Buy*: it was described in fashionable terms as a "drama of modern life", but in fact its plot went far back in time to the days when the nineteenth-century melodramas were based on a scheme wherein a virtuous young heroine suffered hairbreadth escapes from peril-scene to peril-scene; and this play's melodramatic ancestry was further stressed by the fact that it was actually performed against a background of music, specially composed by Guy Jones. From beginning to end the heroine here is pursued by a trio of villains, and constantly, each time they trap her, she is saved by the noble hero, the Rev. Denzil Norton, none other than the handsome Dennis Neilson-Terry. This production, however, was near to the end. A few years later, between 1927 and 1929, an effort was made to revive some of the more lurid examples of the older melodramatic stage – *Sweeny Todd*, *Maria Marten*, *The Dumb Man of Manchester* and *Jack Sheppard* – and audiences were thus attracted to the Elephant and Castle: but they went there, not to be gripped by emotion, but to indulge in superior laughter.

Here, at the Elephant and Castle, the melodrama finally died, but its demise was not unaccompanied by expressions of regret and even by an effective obituary. On both sides of the Atlantic there were many sympathetic mourners who could not easily forget its power of appeal. In his early concerts organised in connection with the Yale University Glee Club, one of Cole Porter's favourite solos was one which he called "Yellow Melodrama":

I'm so bored at going to the theater,
Modern drama isn't worth a penny.
Rostand has no charms for me,
Maeterlinck I cannot see –
Chanticleer and bluebirds are too many.
Oh, I know, it's hardly *comme il faut*
But a melodrama fills my soul with bliss.
My tastes may be plebeian
But efforts herculean
Can never change my taste for plays like this...

Oh, oh, that yellow melodrama
Nowadays considered out of date
I really fear that no more we'll hear
The distant mail train calling to its mate.

No more we'll see the villain cutting capers
With Lady Vere de Vere
Because he knows she has the papers.
They were grand old days.
They were wonderful plays.
Oh, that yellow melodrama for me.[1]

Cole Porter's tone was light, but below the lightness was a serious thought; and this serious thought received serious enunciation from the pen of James Agate. Defining melodrama as "tragedy for a popular audience" and declaring that "its saving grace...is that it reiterates in and out of season that which popular audiences most wish to hear", he ends with a notable pronouncement: "*A Royal Divorce* is not a work of high art, *The Master Builder* is; but I have little doubt which contains the better theme for theatrical exposition, and none at all as to which Shakespeare would have chosen." On true melodrama this may well be taken as the final word.[2]

[1] Robert E. Kimball, "The Cole Porter Years", in the *Yale Alumni Magazine*, March 1969, 52–6.
[2] *Alarms and Excursions* (1922), pp. 211–23.

CHAPTER V

THE MINORITY DRAMA

THE territory of the musicals and the revues, the melodramas and the thrillers, clearly found its antithesis in what has been styled above as the "progressive drama".[1] This descriptive epithet, however, although useful and in many respects appropriate, seems on consideration not to be the term which is most fittingly and comprehensively capable of embracing all the manifold forms of playwriting which belong in this chapter: indeed, some of these forms, as will be seen, may well be regarded as retrogressive rather than as endeavours reaching forward towards the achievement of things novel and inspiringly fresh. It might be thought that "the other drama" would be an apposite designation, on the analogy of "the other theatre" – the general title given by Norman Marshall to those playhouses and producing organisations with which a large number of these plays were associated: yet this term, too, must be deemed equally unsuitable because, paradoxically, its connotations are both too narrow and too wide – too wide, since at least some of the "other theatres", so far from offering encouragement to young authors, tried vigorously and firmly to put the drama in its supposedly proper place as something the sole value of which was to provide raw material for the artist–director's moulding hands; and too narrow, since by no means all the experimental writers lived and worked within its ambience.

The range of diverse and disparate interests is indeed so wide that at first it might appear as though any attempt to reach an effective comprehensive denomination must inevitably be doomed to failure. It is, of course, easy enough to make a broad contrast between those playwrights, such as

[1] See p. 150.

J. M. Barrie and Somerset Maugham, who consistently directed their attention to the West End's commercial playhouses and the other group of dramatists whose activities belonged wholly or largely to the sphere of the repertories and the play-producing societies, but just as soon as we move from generalisations to particulars the picture becomes confused. Here, for example, we encounter not a few authors who may well be represented by Ronald Jeans, R. C. Sherriff and James Bridie – all of whom gained their early training among the societies and the repertories but all of whom had their gaze set, even at the very beginning, upon larger things. Jeans had been largely responsible for the establishment of the Liverpool Playhouse, yet almost from the start of his career he can be seen moving towards cultivation of what was to be his chief contribution to the stage – the light and gay skill which provided at least some vitality and interest to several of the most important revues of the twenties, *London Calling* (1923), *Charlot's Revue* (1924), *Cochran's Revue* (1926), *The Charlot Show of 1926*, and *The House that Jack Built* (1929): even when Sherriff was penning plays for an obscure provincial amateur club he evidently was thinking of performances by more accomplished actors and of an appeal to a broader playgoing public: and so James Bridie, while he was writing his *Sunlight Sonata* (1928) for amateurs further north, indeed while later he continued his active association with the Glasgow Citizens' Theatre, patently was displaying both the outlook and the qualities which enabled him to capture the esteem of metropolitan audiences. Still another group of dramatic writers may find their representatives in St John Ervine and John Drinkwater: these are the men who, as it were, combine two careers within their single beings: the Ervine who wrote *Mixed Marriage* (1911), *Jane Clegg* (1913) and *John Ferguson* (1915) appears to be a person quite distinct from the author of *The First Mrs Fraser* (1929), and similarly there was a John Drinkwater of early poetically-tragic days and another John Drinkwater who wrote *Bird in Hand* (1929). A fourth group, although a much smaller one, finds an example in Harold

Brighouse: even the most rapid and cursory glance at a list of his dramatic writings shows clearly that from the beginning to the end of his career he breathed the air of the provincial repertories, yet with his *Hobson's Choice* (1915) he suddenly and unexpectedly captured general attention and acclaim. Nor are these groups by any means all. There were authors like Gordon Bottomley who not only never came to the knowledge of a larger public but who barely touched even the fringe of repertory playgoers, men whose focus was set entirely upon very small societies whose artistic aims coincided with their own. There were poets as precious as W. B. Yeats who came to despise any audience larger than that consisting of a few appreciative friends gathered in a drawing-room – an audience hopefully fit if assuredly few. And there were numerous others who rejected audiences completely and who elected to prepare their scenes for the delight of readers only, cultivating what W. A. Darlington has called "the theatre of the mind".

When all of these are considered together, there appears to be one way – and only one way – of satisfactorily classifying them, and that is by considering their objectives. The "commercial" playwrights obviously aimed at appealing to general audiences, as widely representative as possible; those who composed the books for musical comedies thought primarily of the fashionable but unintellectual spectators who flocked to the Gaiety Theatre and its companion houses, or of the by-no-means fashionable yet similarly unintellectual suburban and provincial playgoers avidly seeking amusement; the Melville brothers penned their melodramas for audiences of a similarly unintellectual kind, and clearly at that time such audiences were sufficiently large to fill scores of theatres throughout the country. The plays with which we must concern ourselves in this chapter are undoubtedly widely diverse in character, but one thing binds them together – they were all composed with restricted and limited audiences in mind. No matter whether Jeans and Sherriff in their youth were associated with repertories and societies, their fundamental attitude proves that they do not belong within this realm: neither does the Ervine of *The First Mrs Fraser* or the Drinkwater of *Bird in Hand*. But all the others are gathered together in one large assemblage paradoxically because they are concerned not with large auditories, whether "general" or "popular", but with scores, hundreds, of little coteries. "Coterie drama" is, indeed, a term which well might have been applied to the plays within this area were it not for the fact that not always did the authors have a particular coterie or group of spectators (or readers) in mind. Members of a society founded for the purpose of producing early morality dramas or modern works of a similar kind could assume that their fellows were animated by kindred interests, but in many other instances no such assumption could possibly have been made.

The cult of the coterie, in fact, was often negative rather than positive, the result of a distrust of the general public. During this period continual complaints were being made that general and popular audiences wanted nothing save "mere entertainment, usually frivolous, often wanton";[1] and there was pleading for the development of small intelligent audiences distinct from the dull, crass playgoers who filled the auditoriums of the commercial playhouses. This being so, one appropriate descriptive term does come to mind for the plays which these men wished to put on the stage – "the minority drama": all the authors engaged in composing pieces of this kind had their minds fixed on small, selective, élite gatherings of men and women likely to appreciate the flavour of dramatic caviare.[2]

[1] St John Hankin, "Puritanism and the English Stage" (*Fortnightly Review*, Dec. 1906; reprinted in his *Dramatic Works* (1912), iii, p. 132).

[2] In suggesting the use of the term "minority" there should, perhaps, be reference to the way in which the word "little" was being employed during these years. Although in this country the term "repertory" was the familiar designation of the rising non-commercial playhouses, it is well known that in the United States "Little" was the adjective commonly applied to corresponding playhouses, occupied mainly by amateurs: and of course even London had its own Little Theatre, as well as others, such as the Bijou, with titles designed to emphasise their minuteness. And, when we look round further, we cannot escape from noticing how frequently in play-titles and in character-descriptions

Very great care, however, has to be taken in tracing a path among the many varied stages on which were presented the scores of new plays at this time. Of course, when a spectator went to His Majesty's, in general he knew what to expect, unless he were attending one or other of the special "Afternoon Theatre" performances experimentally sponsored by Sir Beerbohm Tree. Similarly if he happened to be one of W. B. Yeats' intimate associates invited to attend a drawing-room performance of the poet's latest composition, he could be equally sure of the kind of fare which would be presented before him. And, as the century brought repertory theatre after repertory theatre into being, almost everyone recognised that, even although these repertories differed widely from each other and even although their stages frequently welcomed comedies and dramas which had won success in London's West End, there was indeed something which, breathing a special air of its own, could appropriately be called "the other theatre".

Nevertheless, it must certainly not be assumed that all the out-of-the-way theatrical ventures of this period are to be regarded as spiritually belonging to the world of the minority drama. A prime example of the dangers involved in any such automatic association of the two is, indeed, put before us at the very start of the modern movement when the Court Theatre made stage history during those five years from 1904 to 1909 by the series of productions offered in a semi-repertory manner under the management of Granville-Barker and Vedrenne.

Already in the brief general discussion of the "minority theatre" movement of the period, this venture has been singled out as the earliest, the principal and the most influential London endeavour of its kind.[1] But, in fact, did it ever deserve to be regarded in this manner? Certainly it brought to the stage a few plays by young dramatists whose early

similar stress was laid on smallness: Galsworthy (when in what might be described as a "minority mood") had his *Little Dream* and *Little Man*, Calderon had his *Little Stone House*, and Housman produced his lengthy series of *Little Plays*.

[1] See above pp. 70–1.

efforts might have been overlooked by the professional managers, but, with the rather strange exception of Granville-Barker himself, of his collaborator Laurence Housman and of that odd man out in this company, the poet–professor Gilbert Murray, it may be said with assurance that all the playwrights included in the Court repertoire had more than "minority" ends in view.

This fact is significant, but of far greater significance is the apparently extraordinary disposition of the repertoire. Already attention has been drawn to the fact that between the opening of the Granville-Barker–Vedrenne management on October 18, 1904, and its conclusion on June 29, 1909, nine hundred and eighty-eight performances were placed before the public[1] – and of these no fewer than seven hundred and one consisted of writings by a single dramatist, George Bernard Shaw. The discrepancy between these two totals is assuredly startling, and at first it might seem as though the only explanation must rest in the presence during those years of just one solitary prolific playwright of an "advanced" kind, the single author capable of providing dramas sufficiently diversified to attract audiences to the Court Theatre. If, however, we are to think of these seasons aright, we must bear two things in mind – one, a possibility, and the other, a certainty. The possibility is that the commonly accepted account of the inauguration and conduct of those seasons may require at least some emendation: no doubt they came into being largely because of Granville-Barker's enthusiasm, but the extraordinary preponderance of Shavian dramatic writings in the "repertory" is not by any means the only hint we have that the *éminence rouge* of G. B. S. stood behind both Granville-Barker and Vedrenne. As yet Shaw's correspondence with Vedrenne has not been published, but, even without this, there is ample evidence to justify C. B. Purdom's categorical statement that "it was, indeed, Shaw's practical theatrical sense as well as his plays, to say nothing (as nothing was ever said) of his money, that provided the

[1] This total includes a number of shorter plays given in double and triple bills.

basis for the undertaking".[1] From all that is known about this venture it would appear that, whatever aspirations stimulated others, the author of *Man and Superman* looked upon the Court experiment as an endeavour likely to benefit himself. Until the totality of his voluminous correspondence has been printed, this must, of course, remain as a possibility only, but an accompanying certainty remains incontrovertible: although Shaw put many new things upon the stage, he belonged in no wise to the "minority" movement. Just at the very start of his career during the last decade of the nineteenth century he certainly wrote a play or two which could not then have been brought on the stage before the public, and even after he had become fully established he could still permit himself, with a kind of careless abandon, to pen such pieces as *Getting Married* (1908) and *Misalliance* (1910), but it is obvious that his chief aim at the beginning of the century was to find an opportunity for the presentation of dramas which might attract the attention of some of the more prominent actor–managers of the time. When we come across such a letter as he wrote to Vedrenne in 1905, angrily scolding both partners for having put Hankin's *The Return of the Prodigal* into the repertory, we must be struck by the way in which he accompanied his scolding with emphasis upon his own contributions to the venture. "I have given you", he wrote, "a series of first-rate music-hall entertainments, thinly disguised as plays, but really offering the public a unique string of turns by comics and serio-comics of every popular type."[2] That he had experienced difficulty in persuading the commercial managers to accept his works in the past may freely be admitted, but the difficulty did not arise from any tendency on Shaw's part to seek for any limited, minority appeal: always he had hoped that popular stars would interpret his major rôles and that the general public would acclaim his eminence as a dramatic author.[3]

[1] C. B. Purdom, *Harley Granville-Barker* (1955), p. 66.

[2] For this statement see also C. B. Purdom's study, p. 62: and for the reference to a "profitable investment" below, see p. 87.

[3] On this see below pp. 352–3.

In effect, then, the famous Court seasons may be considered not as an attempt to create an audience induced to welcome plays of an exclusive kind written for the elect by a number of intellectually-inclined young dramatists, but as an effort on the part of one man, George Bernard Shaw, to win popular support for himself. In this effort he was, as is well known, eminently successful. Before 1905, despite the fact that his name was becoming familiar on the American stage, practically no one of any distinction in the London West End scene paid any attention to his work; after 1910 several of the most distinguished actors were prepared to humble themselves by asking for plays from his pen, and very soon he had established himself as the most prominent of all contemporary English dramatists. Once again, C. P. Purdom is fully justified in declaring that "he had, in fact, made a profitable investment, as he well knew".

This brief examination of the significance of the Court seasons demonstrates how careful we must be in considering the nature of the minority drama, and perhaps it may also serve to remind us again of something else – that the present chapter, even although it is concerned primarily with the contributions made to this "minority" drama, cannot be restricted entirely to discussion of the works of those who deplored what the commercial playhouse had to offer: for several reasons, which will, it is hoped, become amply apparent later, it would be wholly improper to restrict the survey in any such manner. In certain areas the general drama veered far away from the minority, but in others, even although their styles might be different and although each continued to fix its attention upon its own chosen kind of audience, they came together – and in such instances it would clearly have been unreasonable to examine their respective contributions separately. Already it has been pointed out that, for example, it would be both confusing and unjust to separate the poetic drama put before West End audiences from the similar endeavours made by enthusiastic members of the minority movement.[1]

[1] See above, pp. 151–2.

In the present chapter, then, while attention must be devoted principally to dramatic writings of which the general metropolitan public remained entirely unaware, consideration must from time to time be given to related plays which, whether influenced by minority experiments or not, were motivated by similar aims.[1]

1. *Miscellaneous New Forms and Objectives: Propagandist Plays; Religious Dramas; Plays for Children and for Villagers*

In approaching the minority drama as a whole, no doubt our first thoughts are likely to be of the regional plays which were being written on and around local themes in almost every part of the British Isles and of the valiant, extensive but so frequently disappointing attempts to encourage the debilitated and well-nigh moribund poetic theatre. Before turning to consider what was accomplished within these two areas, however, it may be well to examine cursorily a number of movements which, although often passed by unheeded, are

[1] As has been noted above, the development of the "modern" drama was a subject which attracted the attention of numerous critics and scholars during this period, and only a few of the studies published then can be referred to here. Some of the volumes were wide in scope – such as *A Study of the Modern Drama* (1925) by Barrett H. Clark, *The Changing Drama* (1914) by Archibald Henderson, *The Twentieth Century Theatre* (1918) and *Essays on Modern Dramatists* (1921) by W. L. Phelps, *The Drama in Europe* (1924) by Eleanor Jourdain, and *The Modern Drama in Europe* (1920) by Storm Jameson. Mario Borsa's *The English Stage of To-day* (1908) has already been cited: this draws attention to at least a few of the innovating dramatists active at the very beginning of the century. T. H. Dickinson's *The Contemporary Drama of England* (1917) attempts to be more comprehensive, but most of the books dealing with this subject were, like Borsa's, selective – as indeed their titles indicate (A. E. Morgan's *Tendencies of Modern English Drama* (1924), *Some Contemporary Dramatists* (1924) by Graham Sutton, *Dramatic Portraits* (1913) by P. P. Howe, and *Striking Figures among Modern English Dramatists* (1931) by Martin Ellehauge). Among later works attention should be drawn especially to the stimulating wider survey of *Twentieth Century Drama* (1962) by Bamber Gascoigne, the perceptive *Theatre since 1900* (1951) by J. C. Trewin, and the general conspectus (of particular reference to the present chapter), *Modern English Drama: A Survey of the Theatre from 1900* (1949) by Ernest Reynolds.

thoroughly characteristic of the intense and extensive interest in things theatrical which proved so attractive during this period.

An introduction to such trends may be provided by a rapid examination of a development which at the time produced little of any great positive worth and yet which was basically symptomatic of the new spirit operative almost everywhere. For convenience this can be described as the propagandist drama, and it is relatively easy to see how it came into being. From one point of view this was nothing new. If we look back on the history of the stage, it is obvious that from the earliest days of the medieval mysteries the drama had been used not merely to delight but also to instruct, and that at various times (as, for example, in the sixteenth century when moral interludes flourished) many dramatists had applied themselves to the use of the stage as though it were a platform or a pulpit: during the reign of Mary Tudor the moralities had sought to present the theological principles and practices of the Old Faith; during the reign of Elizabeth they preached the philosophy of the New. Thus, from this point of view, the development of a propagandist drama within the early years of the twentieth century may be looked upon simply as a continuation of a long-standing tradition. On the other hand, if, instead of casting our eyes over the entire range of the theatre, we consider merely its career within the preceding century, we realise that, except for a limited number of political plays intended merely for perusal by readers and for an equally limited number of melodramas which in their own crude manner commented on some current social evils such as rack-renting and the insidious temptations of the bar-room, the Victorian age had almost nothing of this kind – and consequently we need not be surprised to find numerous commentators in Edwardian days drawing attention to the growth of propagandist playwriting as something which seemed to them an absolutely novel development.

What was happening is easy to explain. The appeal of the theatre had spread widely, far beyond the limits of the established playhouses. Many of those who were gripped most powerfully by its attractions were young intellectuals whose social, philosophical and religious beliefs were both strongly-held and unconventional, and these beliefs they incorporated into their plays. The way in which beliefs and ideas were thus being exploited in dramatic writings soon attracted the attention of others who originally had not been aware of the possibilities offered by the stage for propaganda, and it was not long before political and other similar organisations began to establish their own dramatic groups, designed specifically to spread knowledge of their aims and principles.

In discussing this development, several of the contemporary commentators expressed the belief that the innovators were for the most part women playwrights. Looking back in 1910, for instance, E. F. Spence thus drew attention to "a curiosity" – "that it is the woman rather than the man dramatist who appreciates the utility of the stage as a means for seeking reform" – and he added the wry reflection that "no doubt, we shall suffer for a while from a lot of bad plays with a good purpose".[1] Some fourteen years later, Frank Vernon remarked that "it is the smaller writers of the period, it is especially the women writers, who took the view that their business was not merely to state cases, but to propose remedies."[2] Unquestionably these two observers of the current scene were correct both in locating the source and in assessing the quality of these plays and playlets. The short pieces sponsored by actresses active in the Votes for Women movement can all be dismissed; other kindred one-acts which came from the devoted pens of social workers are no doubt worthily inspired, but of dramatic value they are innocent; and various patriotic dramas of the kind represented in Winifred Dolan's "*Wake Up, John Bull!*" (1912) clearly are of no theatrical concern. Slightly more significance attaches to the fairly numerous plays inspired by a

[1] "E. F. S." (Edward Fordham Spence), *Our Stage and Its Critics* (1910), pp. 115 and 117.

[2] *The Twentieth-century Theatre* (1924), pp. 39–40.

faith in socialist ideals, sponsored mainly by Labour organisations, but the majority make painful reading precisely because they are so humourlessly intent on their political mission. Ralph Fox's *Captain Youth* (1922), called "a romantic comedy for all socialist children" and published in the series of *Plays for a People's Theatre*,[1] reveals itself as a rather silly story of a boy who dreams of defeating wicked pirates and who, when he comes to adolescence, takes sword in hand to battle for a new and better world, while *Foiling the Reds* (1926) by "Yaffle" takes shape as "a revue in one or more scenes" conceived in a spirit of pitifully inept and clumsy caricature. Almost equally distressing to read is a related group of historical dramas treated with strong political sentiments. Hubert Griffith's *Red Sunday* (1929)[2] thus deals with real or supposed episodes in the careers of Trotsky and Lenin; W. H. Terry goes further back in time in composing his three-part *Interregnum* (1928) as a stiffly written eulogy of Oliver Cromwell, as a general attack on "Politicians, Lawyers and State Officials" and as a piece of propaganda designed to demonstrate how much Britain needed a dictator – socialism shading into National Socialism. While political beliefs, whether belonging to the left or to the right, provided the most fertile soil for the burgeoning of the propagandist drama, there were also many other authors anxious to exhibit their pet philosophical excogitations in dialogue form. Typical are the six one-act pieces offered to the public by someone who called himself "Robot" (*The Secret and Other Plays*, 1926). This collection has a dust-jacket on which is prominently featured a reproduction of Rodin's "The Thinker", and the little dramas are prefaced by a lengthy introduction divided into three parts – the first dealing with "The Standard of Modern Plays", the second, called "Evolution", discussing "The World", "Man", "Thought" and "Sex", and the third reaching what the author believes is an original and profound "Conclusion". Characteristically, the opening section of the introduction (which is described by the writer as "a candid criticism and discriminative

[1] See pp. 72 and 89.

[2] For its publication, see p. 149.

appreciation of the modern drama") begins on a familiar note: "The average dramatist writes plays with only one express object in view – namely, to supply a saleable article to theatrical producers; and producers, in turn, endeavour to present plays which will enhance their bank balance. In both cases money is the root of the evil these two classes of men are perpetrating in our midst." And the "Conclusion", naturally, implies that the plays which follow are representative of the kind of drama which "Robot" would wish to substitute for the theatrical entertainments which he so roundly condemns.

Plays of this kind, of course, remained for the most part either unacted, or, if given stage presentations, performed within the limits of the clubs whose basic objectives were to promote particular social philosophies. Nevertheless, the term "play of ideas" was one which was being continually heard within advanced circles, and there is evidence to show that only too often, in its stress upon the intellectual, part at least of the repertory movement tended to lead some young playwrights from the dramatically emotional into a realm of arid doctrinaire homilies or of cerebral debate. For this, no doubt, there was much justification, since a great deal of writing for the commercial stage had been, and indeed still remained, blissfully mindless; yet we cannot close our eyes to the facts that for those young writers there was thus added a further element of confusion and uncertainty, and that many theatregoers were being alienated through being confronted by such a large number of dramas which, while no doubt worthy in intent, were more of sermons than of scenes. It was not only Bernard Shaw who boldly used that word "sermon" as a descriptive term for one of his plays. Even such an avowed "repertory theatre man" as St John Ervine, looking back in 1924 at the failure of several non-commercial theatres to attract larger audiences, declared that "we cannot exonerate the directors of them from blame when we remember that they were more eager to instruct than to entertain".[1]

[1] St John Ervine, *The Organised Theatre* (1924), p. 173.

Certainly, as the years advanced, many of the dramas presented in West End playhouses tended to introduce reflections on current problems, both domestic and political, so that it cannot be said that the "play of ideas" was wholly confined to the sphere of the minority theatre, but only very rarely did straight propaganda afflict London's playgoing public. The two or three odd exceptions owed their presentations not to any dramatic power exhibited by the authors but to the sensational nature of their themes. The relatively few playgoers, for instance, who in 1923 bought tickets at the Court for Marie Stopes' *Our Ostriches* almost certainly paid out their money, not because they anticipated any theatrical pleasure or because they sought for intellectual enlightenment, or because they thought that they were giving support to a "cause", but simply because they wished to share in the mild shock of listening to the exposition of its then rather daring theme – the need for methods of birth-control and an attack on the dangers of uncontrolled propagation of the poor and unfit.

So far as can be determined, the only propaganda play which created a real stir was the patriotic *An Englishman's Home*, written by Guy du Maurier and produced in 1909 by his actor-brother Gerald: and even this illustrates the fate of the propagandist drama in general. When it first appeared, the story of quiet little middle-class Mr Brown who in shocked disbelief sees his house suddenly occupied by an invading foreign army (apparently intended to be Russian) aroused a "frenzy of enthusiasm", but, once the sensational plot had lost its novelty, "the bubble burst, evaporated, and was lost; the excitement died down; the Press lost interest; the men returned to their football and the women to their fashion articles. *An Englishman's Home* became no more than one other crumpled manuscript in a dusty drawer."[1]

Of considerably greater interest and significance was another movement which, although in general it cannot properly be styled propagandist, was at least largely inspired by extra-dramatic concepts and sense of purpose. The

[1] Daphne Du Maurier, *Gerald: A Portrait* (1934), pp. 123–9.

nineteenth century had carried on the tradition which had been established at least three hundred years previously whereby religious plays were exiled from the confines of the church and rigorously banned from the stage. From time to time, of course, a few individual poets, most of them undistinguished, had followed Milton's example by dealing with biblical themes in closet dramas intended solely for readers,[1] but the closest the theatre approached to this area was when, towards the very end of the century, Wilson Barrett presented his sensationally spectacular *The Sign of the Cross* (1896) and *The Daughters of Babylon* (1897); and these garish exhibitions of often spurious religiosity hardly deserve mention in this connection. Of more humbly sincere performances of genuine religious plays there was absolutely nothing.

The minority quality of the new theatrical movement which arrived at the very beginning of the new century is perhaps nowhere more clearly symbolised than in William Poel's presentation at the Charterhouse in 1901 of the sixteenth-century *Everyman* and the still older Chester *Sacrifice of Isaac*. Needless to say, this performance reminds us of the way in which numbers of eager amateurs – the Pilgrim Players, for example – were at this time instinctively turning to seek inspiration in the early moralities. Poel's production of 1901 was not simply a model which was imitated by others: probably, indeed, only two or three persons outside the range of the little audience at the Charterhouse had heard of his venture; the various efforts of a similar kind, as

[1] This whole subject has been expertly surveyed by Murray Roston in his *Biblical Drama in England* (1968). In that work he expresses surprise that apparently there was one extraordinary exception to the general rule forbidding the theatrical representation of biblical material on the stage when, as he says, formal approval seemed to have been given for the presentation of Elizabeth Polack's *Esther: the Royal Jewess* at the Royal Pavilion in 1835. Of course, it would indeed have been most surprising if the Reader of Plays had deviated from established practice by giving a licence for this lady's work; but it seems almost certain that, like all the "burlettas" presented at the Pavilion, no script was submitted at the Lord Chamberlain's office. What many interested churchmen hoped to achieve through the cultivation of this kind of play is indicated in Gordon Crosse's *The Religious Drama* (1913).

has already not only been tentatively suggested but actually proved, came into being in an entirely independent manner: they were instinctive movements, uninfluenced by any forces from without. The initial compulsion which led to this backward sweep over the centuries no doubt was the realisation that between the modern amateurs, conscious now of a mission wholly lacking among their spouting predecessors, and the small groups of Tudor interluders there was a spiritual kinship, and this sense of kinship was considerably deepened when discovery of the dramatic interest inherent in the moralities carried attention still further back in time to the larger and even more definitely amateur mystery cycles of the medieval town guilds. This, in turn, led, at least in certain circles, to a re-examination of the original significance of the ancient religious plays and stimulated a desire to make the drama once more serve a similar purpose. Thus there came together three groups which at the start had been completely separate and which, even after the passage of several decades, only rarely coalesced – those who sensed the connection between the early amateurs and the new; those who, although not inspired by religious beliefs, discerned the simple and impressive effectiveness of the moralities and mysteries; and those connected with the churches who either were caught up in the current wave of theatrical enchantment or realised how much the stage exposition of their beliefs might aid their cause.[1]

The progress of the movement was extraordinarily rapid. In 1901 Poel was forced to use the Charterhouse for his production of *Everyman* because the ecclesiastical authorities both at Westminster Abbey and at Canterbury Cathedral had curtly refused permission for its presentation within any precincts under their jurisdiction; yet only a year or two had passed by before many members of the clergy were to be found not only enthusiastically supporting, but even themselves composing, Nativity and other kindred dramas; in

[1] In addition to the later chapters of Murray Roston's comprehensive study, reference may here be made to the survey of *Religion in Modern English Drama* (1961) by G. Weales.

1921, by an ironical twist, the Westminster Abbey Restoration Fund was materially aided by a series of performances of *Everyman* given in Church House; and nearly two decades before, in 1904, the truly amazing, although now little-known, success story of Alice Buckton's *Eager Heart* had its beginning.

Eager Heart was a not ineffective pageant-like playlet which adroitly combined mystery and morality patterns by showing a symbolic heroine, Eager Heart, waiting for the arrival of some great king. Her two sisters, Eager Fame and Eager Sense, do their best to ridicule the simple preparations which she has been engaged in making, while, with apparently impeccable logic they seek to persuade her that of course such a great monarch will arrive in rich panoply and gorgeous splendour. "But wherefore linger here?" asks the former,

Think you He deigns
Beneath so small a roof to bend His head?
How should He find this quiet street, where no
Great chariots pass, no victory-pageants roll?
Kings are not wont to come in these *our* days
To poor and beggared doors! This foolish freak
To sit at home, and wait Him in the house
Is bygone fashion! Come with me, away
Up to the terrace of the capitol,
Where famous deeds are done, and tapestries
Blazon the walls with tales of heroes dead!
There, Fame, her golden trumpet at her mouth,
Governs the winds that sweep the echoing world:
And men, amazed, bow lowly, worshipping!

And Eager Sense points her finger mockingly at the meagrely set table –

Behold the childish meal, set bravely here
To tempt the Royal train! Water, and bread!
Ha! Ha! and peasant grapes! that scarce have won
The faintest flush of crimson, trained by herself
Upon the walls, and pressed with her own small hands!...

Come to the palace, in the orange groves!
There the loud viol plays the night away;
And none is sick, or fasting! Come, poor child!
I'll lend thee other garb and jewels! See!
This brow should bear a diadem!

So distracted is Eager Heart by these rather exclamatory arguments that when two ragged, wretched vagrants with a babe come begging for shelter she is at first much too preoccupied to be able to offer them her aid. Yet some inner prompting, a feeling of pity, causes her to reverse her decision; they are brought into the house, and, almost at once, to her wondering amazement, three shepherds and three kings arrive to adore them.

Although it cannot be said that the piece is written in a masterly manner, its scene and characters are put before us with manifest sincerity and even with a simple skill which seems not too far removed from the style of the early mysteries. Not only did it prove to be an immediate success, it was still going strong thirty years later, with hundreds of performances and with the published text exceeding its forty-first thousand copy: an Incorporated Company of Eager Heart was established, complete with its own Vice-Presidents and Council, their mission being to decide which among the numerous acting groups anxious to present the play satisfied the conditions set out in its constitution – that no payments should be made to any performers, the sole salaried participator being "a Professional Adviser or Producer, or Stage Manager".[1]

Mabel Dearmer, wife of the active priest–playwright Percy Dearmer, founded the Morality Play Society in 1911; the following year the Rev. B. P. Boulter seems to have made history in his own modest way when he produced his own *Mystery of the Epiphany* in St Silas Hall, Kentish Town;[2]

[1] Alice Buckton later produced her *Kings in Babylon* (1906) and her "pageant play", *The Coming of Bride* (1914), but these created no such stir as was aroused by her primal effort.

[2] It cannot be asserted with absolute assurance that this clergyman was the first to pen and present a mystery play, but I have been unable to

and his example was followed by authors so numerous that only a few of their names can be even cursorily mentioned. Among them, May Creagh-Henry was particularly industrious: after penning some four non-religious playlets, she turned out many capably-written short dramas dealing with biblical themes – such as *The Star* (1925), *The Crib* (1929) and *The Victory of the Cross* (1929) – as well as a "modern mystery play", *The Gate of Vision*, which was performed at Church House, Westminster, in 1922. F. J. Bowen was responsible for *Emmanuel* (1925), *The Three Kings* (1928) and *The Blessed Thomas More* (1930); Irene Caudwell for "*By Thy Cross and Passion*" (1927) and *The Mystic Tree* (1921); C. Kate Chadwick for a "Christmas mystery", *The Wassail Bough* (1923); Una M. Goodwin for a Nativity play, *I Was a Stranger* (1923), notable for its appealing simplicity.

"Appealing simplicity" may not be considered a very high term of praise: indeed, it might be thought that it is being used in a slightly condescending and even derogatory manner. It must, therefore, be emphasised that it is here being employed approvingly as a phrase designed to make a contrast between these unassuming playlets and the group of longer, more ambitious dramas which, following the tradition established by numerous poets in the past, dealt in a "literary" manner with biblical material. During this period hardly any of these plays could be said to be appealing, and rarely can one be found which exhibits the honest faith which had inspired the others. For the most part, we find here a collection of usually dull, tendentious works in which the various writers were chiefly intent upon using the familiar stories for the purpose of enunciating their own pet philosophic ideas and political beliefs. Of course anyone whose objective is exploration of the work of individual authors has to give such dramas close attention, but hardly a single one of them has any real relevance for an historian of the drama. A critic concerned with an examination of Yeats' poetry

find any earlier record of an event of this kind. It is to be observed that even he refrained from bringing his scenes into his church: that was a development which came later.

must clearly give due attention to his *Calvary* (1920), and in the same way a critic engaged in examining the thought and style of D. H. Lawrence must place his *David* (1926) within the context of all his compositions in prose and verse; but anyone concerned with the progress of the drama may safely, and profitably, and cheerfully, dismiss almost all those prevailingly humourless works written by the companions of Lawrence and Yeats – works in which miracles are treated as adroit politically-motivated legerdemain, heroes are turned into fools or villains or men with a lust for power, murderers are condoned, and heroines either are transformed into nymphomaniacs or endowed with the fervency of a Mrs Pankhurst.[1] Although it must be freely acknowledged that several of these dramas have an ambitious range and a literary style going far beyond the modest scope of *Eager Heart* and its successors, when we bear in mind the way in which the hundreds of enthusiastic amateurs were attaining a rôle much wider than any they had aspired to in the past, we may be willing to believe that even the most humble and unassuming of the Nativity scenes had at least some share, however tiny and apparently insignificant, in the twentieth-century dramatic world, whereas almost all those literary efforts had none.[2]

In considering these movements, one other category of

[1] Aptly, Murray Roston indicates some of the chief general trends by the titles he gives to two of the main sections of his survey – "Biblical Suffragettes" and "The Nietschean Moses".

[2] Note may further be taken of the fact that, within this period, the ban on performances of biblical dramas was slowly being lifted. Gwen Lally's *Jezebel*, which was given a copyright performance in 1912 and which was the first play written on a biblical theme to be licensed by the Lord Chamberlain, obviously had been written with the hope that it might be accepted for public presentation; the following year saw the appearance of L. N. Parker's *Joseph and His Brethren* at His Majesty's; and this was followed in 1914 by T. W. Broadhurst's "scriptural drama", *The Holy City*. The last of these included in its lengthy list of characters most of the disciples as well as Mary Magdalene and Martha: virtually the only fixed ban remaining was that which prohibited the impersonation of Christ on the stage. As usual, the Lord Chamberlain's policy was being adjusted to changing public attitudes, and here it must be thought that the spread of interest in the amateur Nativity playlets had much to do with the gradual relaxation of the rules.

dramatic writing, even although at first it might seem to have even less to do with the development of the religious play than some of the dramas with biblical themes treated in a "modern" manner, deserves brief mention. When Mrs Frances Chesterton devised her *Piers Plowman's Pilgrimage* (1925) we may confidently assume that she never had thought of anything more than a possible local amateur production; but the *Magic* (1913) written by G. K. Chesterton was clearly cast in a different mould and intended for public presentation. Characteristically styled a "fantastic comedy", this piece might appear to have nothing whatsoever to do either with the dramas, whether amateur or "literary", the plots of which were derived from the Bible, or with the related plays which belonged to the morality tradition: yet obviously its central enigmatic figure of the Stranger – an accomplished conjuror? or one gifted with supernatural powers? or perhaps even a spirit in disguise? – has been born of religious questioning. Chesterton's play, in turn, calls to mind an earlier "idle fancy", Jerome K. Jerome's *The Passing of the Third Floor Back* (1908), a work which nowadays may readily be condemned to oblivion as being mawkishly sentimental, yet nevertheless a strange, sincerely-written piece which is of peculiar theatrical interest because its contemporary success shows how the general London public of that time was, on occasion, willing to welcome dramas out of the ordinary. Here the author starts with an introductory scene set in a shabby-genteel Bloomsbury boarding-house peopled by inmates spiteful, vicious, artificially snobbish, depraved, forlorn. A Stranger arrives, looking for a room. At first the landlady hesitates, since his clothes are shabby, but later she agrees that there is one bedroom available, which she offers, first, at two pounds ten and then, without precisely knowing why, reduces to two pounds. She and the Stranger have a brief conversation, within the course of which he causes her to recall her earlier life, when her husband, a solicitor, had been alive and when she had not needed to be a grasping keeper of the lodging-house. Suddenly her mind comes back to the present. "Would you like to go up to your room now?" she asks, "We dine at six-thirty":

STRANGER (*rising*). Thank you. That will just give me time. (*They go up stage.*)

MRS SHARPE. I'll just see first that everything – (*He has taken his hat and stick, and is moving towards the door. She pauses* R. *of table.*) Did I say two pounds a week? (*Something is worrying her; it causes her to speak in an angry, aggressive tone.*)

STRANGER (*up* R.C. *turns to her*). It was to have been two pounds ten. You were kind enough to reduce it.

MRS SHARPE. I must have been thinking of some other room. It should have been one pound ten. (*By chair* R. *of table.*)

STRANGER. Then I decline to take it. The two pounds I can well afford. (*Turns to go out – up a step to door* C.)

MRS SHARPE. One pound ten are my terms. If you are bent on paying more, you can go elsewhere. You'll find plenty to oblige you.

STRANGER (*looks at her*). Women are so wilful. (*Smiling*) And you kind women are the worst of all.

At first, this new arrival is regarded by the boarders with a certain amount of contempt, since obviously he is poor; yet gradually, sometimes by his gentleness, sometimes by his uncanny perception, he begins to evoke all their concealed good qualities, so that soon they are no longer the same persons revealed at the start of the play; and at the conclusion, as he departs, all are left wondering whether this guest was just an ordinary man or a being divine. Sentimental? Assuredly, yes: but there are two kinds of sentimentalism – the intellectually superior, and the humbly, emotionally, honest – and Jerome's play is of the latter sort.

The enigmatic atmosphere which surrounds the actions of *Magic* and *The Passing of the Third Floor Back* is not by any means confined to these two plays: its presence is to be traced in numerous other dramas of the time, and in these dramas it is used to produce many variant effects. In 1921 Laurence Housman wrote his short play *Possession*, where, in what appears at first to be an ordinary "comfortably furnished Victorian drawing-room", we listen to gentle (but very domineering) Julia Robinson chatting with her old maid-servant Hannah, and where only gradually do we come to realise that they are both dead, that this is the after-life. Here, of course, there is no sentimentalism: we are in the presence rather of mildly affectionate cynicism. The first lines are:

> JULIA. How the days are drawing out, Hannah.
> HANNAH. Yes, Ma'am; nicely, aren't they?

and we learn that they are awaiting a visit from Julia's sister, Laura. Laura arrives: there is conversation, combined with some rather puzzling events; and then comes the conclusion:

LAURA. What is this place we've come to?
JULIA (*persuasively*). Our home.
LAURA. I think we are in Hell!
JULIA (*going to the door, which she unlocks with soft triumph*). We are all where we wish to be, Laura. (*A gong sounds*) That's supper. (*The gong continues its metallic bumbling.*)

Possession, although in its own delicate way it effectively shows earth's petty sentiments, desires and envies stretched out to infinity, is not a very important drama, but clearly it is related to, and possibly inspired, Vane Sutton-Vane's *Outward Bound* (1923), a play much better known. Here, too, there is a similar surprise. The curtain rises to show the saloon in a great ocean liner, and the passengers, although they are strangely few and although occasionally they behave in a peculiar manner, seem at first to be ordinary travellers voyaging across the Atlantic: then, slowly but with growing intensity, doubts begin to arise, and they increase until suddenly the audience is made to realise that this ship is the modern equivalent of Charon's boat which ferried the dead across the Styx. The author may not have been able to sustain the technical brilliance displayed in this opening act or to bring his drama to a thoroughly satisfactory conclusion, but *Outward Bound* remains still a play possessed of its own considerable importance. Rightly, a contemporary critic declared it to be "pure Morality: *mutatis mutandis*, it is as mediaeval (and modern) as Everyman or the best of the Nativity plays – of all of which indeed, it is a compendious twentieth-century edition".[1] And, in looking at these works, perhaps it is not wholly fanciful to see the same impress obliquely reflected in other dramas which might almost be described as moralities in reverse. Frank Birch's cynical *Mountebanks* (1925) may serve as an illustration: in this play a pious monk succumbs to the temptations of a dancing-girl and her stroller-companion – whose names, if they had appeared in ancient moralities, might well have been Lechery and Fraud; the pair endeavour to steal some jewels from the chapel, and during the course of this attempt the monk is stabbed; because of a mistaken interpretation of the circumstances connected with his death, however, he ironically becomes enshrined in the monastery's collective memory as a saint.

This saint, even if he be a false one, serves to introduce another genre of related drama. In 1905 William Poel presented a play of his own called *The First Franciscans.* In itself, this piece has but little importance, but quite possibly Poel's innovating effort had some influence on Laurence Housman when, some seventeen years later, that author composed his *Little Plays of St Francis*, once very popular among readers and members of amateur acting groups,[2] and not entirely forgotten even in our own times.

Since Housman is, so to say, the first "major" dramatist whom we have encountered in the minority field, and since he was a most prolific author, his plays may be taken as a picture in little of the many diverse interests displayed by his fellows during this period – and it may be added that it is

[1] Graham Sutton, *Some Contemporary Dramatists* (1924), p. 184. In this way *Outward Bound* links up with the numerous "modern moralities" written during this period (see above pp. 136 and 195) – plays such as Blanche G. Vulliamy's *Give Heed* (1909), or A. J. Waldron's *The Carpenter* (1914), or M. Wadham's *The Hill of Vision* (1923), or G. V. Hobart's *Everywife* (1910).

[2] How popular they were is demonstrated by the fact that Housman found it worth his while to prepare a "*Little Plays' Handbook: Practical Notes for Producers of Little Plays of St Francis*" (1927). On his writings generally see A. Rudolf, *Die Dichtung von Laurence Housman* (1930).

impossible to assess the significance of these *Plays of St Francis* without relating them to the entire range of his other writings. Already, *Possession* has been referred to, but that was a piece published in 1921, and almost two decades before, in 1902, his *Bethlehem* had been given a private performance in the hall of the Imperial Institute.[1] For a few years after this it looked as though he might be thinking of shifting his theatrical allegiance from the amateurs to the professionals: a half-step in that direction was taken when he collaborated with Granville-Barker in writing *Prunella; or Love in a Dutch Garden*, certainly not a "commercial" piece but one which at least could be included in the Court's 1904 season; and a very definite stride followed when he made himself responsible for preparing the text of a "romantic opera", *The Vicar of Wakefield*, which, with music composed by Liza Lehmann, was produced at the Prince of Wales's Theatre in 1906. This toying with the commercial stage, however, did not last for long, and from 1910 onwards almost all his plays were "minority" in theme and structure. A "morality", *The Lord of the Harvest*, came in 1910, and a *Nazareth* in 1916; he penned several "fairy plays", a "political skit" called *Alice in Ganderland* (1911) and a collection of "dialogues", *Cornered Poets* (1929); rather unexpectedly he translated (with polite caution) Aristophanes' *Lysistrata* (1910) and, more predictably, dealt with some "tragic" classic material, *Apollo in Hades, The Death of Alcestis* and *The Doom of Admetus* (published as a "trilogy" in 1919). Although he must have been well aware that one of the Lord Chamberlain's fixed rules forbade the stage presentation of living or recent royalty, he spent time in penning his "defence of Queen Caroline", *Pains and Penalties* (1911), and this led him to his well-known one-acts showing episodes in the life of Queen Victoria. Others of his plays might be listed here, but these few selected titles are sufficient to indicate the diverse nature of his subject-matter and to demon-

[1] This was not entirely forgotten after its original presentation: in 1923, revised as a "music drama" in collaboration with Rutland Boughton, it was revived at the Regent Theatre.

strate that his structural power never went beyond the limits of the one-act "episode". It is true that when *Pains and Penalties* was presented privately in 1911 it was described as a "four-act play", but, when it is compared with the *Victoria Regina* which was constructed from a number of his short sketches in 1935, it is patently clear that the dramatic architecture of both is the same.[1]

Within this variegated pattern come the *Little Plays of St Francis* (1922), a collection which proved so attractive that many other playlets were added later to the original series of sixteen short episodes. Here we are carried back to the spirit of the earlier Nativity playlets. There is no cynicism here, no attempt to preach an author's personal philosophy. Housman's own claim that the *Little Plays* had been sincerely written in an attempt to "present a spiritual interpretation of character" may be taken at its face value,[2] and it was this sincerity which gave them their appeal. As Granville-Barker observed, they were the result of the new conditions operative at that time, when there was an "upspringing all over England of bodies of people so hungry for a little simple, wholesome, unhocussed dramatic art, that, denied it by the professional producers, they are ready to see to the supply themselves".[3]

Granville-Barker is correct in the presentation of his facts, yet two qualifications must be made concerning what he implies. First, while Housman's playlets on Franciscan legend deserve esteem for their simplicity and adroitness, they cannot be raised, as he here suggests, to the level of

[1] *Victoria Regina* was first produced at the Gate Theatre in 1935, where, as Norman Marshall, the director, reports, it "made a profit of exactly £5" (*The Other Theatre* (1947), p. 110). Later it was a great success in a Henry Miller production in New York and ran for more than three hundred performances at London's Lyric in 1937. In spite of this general triumph, however, note should be taken of a comment by Marshall: "I think," he remarked, "the play was seen at its best at the Gate. It is essentially a chamber play, ideally suited to the intimacy of the Gate where Roger Furse succeeded brilliantly in suggesting the palace settings in spite of the smallness of the stage" (p. 110).

[2] Author's preface to the first collection (1922), p. xvii.

[3] Granville-Barker's preface to the first collection (1922), p. xi.

great dramatic achievements: whatever their virtues, they remain very much minority writings. And secondly, both here and in other related comments made by Granville-Barker we cannot accept his suggestion that the "professional producers" of that period had nothing of value to offer. A sense of balance must be maintained. On the one hand, there has to be clear recognition of what actually was accomplished by the minority playwrights, whether the unassuming and unambitious authors of little Nativity playlets or those, such as Laurence Housman, who were more "literary" in their approach, more varied in their themes and more skilful in the presentation of character. Yet, on the other hand, it must be admitted that "hocussing", the expert display of leger-demain, the conjuring skill of the dramatist, has always been an important part of the theatre's power and strength. Much of the professional dramatic fare put before West End audiences was certainly poor and shoddy and contemptible, but at the same time we must be prepared to admit that, even within areas where we might have expected the minority playwrights to have had especial advantages, professional West End authors catering for a general public often far exceeded their efforts. The truth of this becomes patently evident when a scrutiny is made of two other minority movements by no means unallied to that which encouraged the composition and performance of the Nativity and related playlets – and to these two movements Housman also may be taken as a guide. Towards the beginning of his dramatic career he had written two "fairy plays", *The Chinese Lantern* (1908) and *Bird in Hand* (1918), while in 1928 he published *Ways and Means: Five One Act Plays of Village Characters*. Thus does he introduce us to the Village Drama movement and the various attempts to establish a Children's Theatre.

Both of these developments belong essentially to the twentieth century, even although for both it is possible to unearth records of a few earlier experiments which pointed the way towards things to come. Before 1900 there had certainly been numerous playlets devised for performance by children in drawing-room or parlour, and occasionally efforts had been made at giving advice concerning their production; Mrs Hugh Bell's *Fairy Tale Plays, and How to Produce Them*, published in 1899, was by no means the first book of its kind. Nevertheless, the concept of a Children's Theatre, as yet unthought of, remains a characteristic invention of the later period. Similarly, we can find various odd Victorian plays intended for rustic interpretation, yet no one at that time could have dreamed of establishing a Village Drama Society. The scattered early anticipatory experiments in both fields had come from individuals only, whereas now, in the new age, the efforts were being co-ordinated, with numerous authors associating together and gaining strength in purposeful endeavour to reach commonly determined ends.

The term "Children's Theatre", of course, embraces two entirely distinct kinds of play – simple scripts planned for acting by the very young, and more elaborate dramatic works, designed for professional production before audiences consisting largely of children. In the former category hundreds of playlets were hurriedly turned out by dozens of authors, most of them amateur and many of them ladies. As the years advanced, there was a marked tendency towards specialisation in the nature of the scripts: formerly the majority of these pieces had simply been labelled "for children", whereas now some were advertised as suitable for boys, some for girls, some for Brownies and some for Scouts.[1] At the same time it is possible, at least occasionally, to detect an enlargement and extension of the playwrights' aims. Originally designed purely for amusement, the children's drama was now being seized upon by educationalists who saw an opportunity here of sugaring the scholastic pill, as well as by propagandists who thought they saw a chance of furthering their particular objectives.

Fairies abounded here in profusion, amply supplied with

[1] It should be borne in mind that it was not merely the very amateur authors who indulged in penning such pieces. Charles McEvoy, for example, wrote *The Dew Necklace* "for Brownies", while the first dramatic works composed by serious-minded Githa Sowerby were *Little Plays for School and Home* (1910).

toadstool props; Hans Andersen's tales and Andrew Lang's multicoloured collections of folk stories were eagerly scanned for suitable material; most of the authors thought of indoor performances, but certain writers – Grace James and Harold Brighouse, for example – had in their minds visions of the outdoors, of gardens and lawns and meadows. The variety here was legion, obviously the central inspiring aim was admirable, but sadly it must be admitted that hardly any of the individual texts are worthy of even cursory individual attention. It is, no doubt, to be presumed that the authors of these ingenuous, unassuming playlets would have made claim to no other judgment, yet we may feel some surprise on observing that not even one or two purveyors of the pieces suitable for children's interpretation displayed any real originality in theme or in style.

Naturally, the plays written for children to watch in the theatre had to be considerably more ambitious, but here again a peculiarity, of a different sort, has to be noted. One might have expected that in this realm the minority dramatists would have triumphed, yet hardly any of them had much to offer, despite the large number of "fairy" and other pieces which they turned out. The surprising fact is that the only two works of this kind which deserve serious consideration were the creation of authors whose affiliations belonged almost exclusively to the London stage: J. M. Barrie and A. A. Milne both were professional West End dramatists, and where the minority writers failed they succeeded. *Peter Pan* (1904) still remains one of the best-known plays in the English theatre, and *Toad of Toad Hall* (1929) is now fully forty years of age. Seriously-inclined intellectual critics and directors may seek to argue that the former appeals more to parents than to children, or else may try to give it the treatment which has recently been meted out in television to *Alice in Wonderland*; nevertheless, tens of thousands of youthful spectators have been held spell-bound by its scenes and, if J. B. Priestley is right in seeing audiences as childlike in their appreciation of performances, the appeal to parents as well as to their offspring can mean only that

Barrie's adroitness is even greater than we commonly suppose.

A single short passage may be taken to illustrate whence this double quality derives. The pirate ship is the setting for the first scene of the fifth act, and this is how Barrie presents it:

THE PIRATE SHIP

The stage directions for the opening of this scene are as follows: – 1 Circuit Amber checked to 80. Battens, all Amber checked, 3 ship's lanterns alight, Arcs: prompt perch 1. Open dark Amber flooding back, O.P. perch open dark Amber flooding upper deck. Arc on tall steps at back of cabin to flood back cloth. Open dark Amber. Warning for slide. Plank ready. Call HOOK.

In the strange light thus described we see what is happening on the deck of the Jolly Roger, *which is flying the skull and crossbones and lies low in the water. There is no need to call* HOOK, *for he is here already, and indeed there is not a pirate aboard who would dare to call him. Most of them are at present carousing in the bowels of the vessel, but on the poop* MULLINS *is visible, in the only great-coat on the ship, raking with his glass the monstrous rocks within which the lagoon is cooped. Such a look-out is supererogatory, for the pirate craft floats immune in the horror of her name...*

HOOK (*communing with his ego*). How still the night is; nothing sounds alive. Now is the hour when children in their homes are a-bed; their lips bright-browned with the good-night chocolate, and their tongues drowsily searching for belated crumbs housed insecurely on their shining cheeks. Compare with them the children on this boat about to walk the plank. Split my infinitives, but 'tis my hour of triumph!

Compare this with most scenes of a similar kind in the minority dramas. The minority authors write down and, when whimsically fanciful, remain superiorly above their material: Barrie writes up, and his whimsicality, openly displayed, is honest. The former frequently possess no theatrical sense or, if they do, try to conceal it: his theatricality is frank and unashamed; for him the amber lights are an essential part of his vision. He is not a self-conscious airy-fairy writer: he is a practical professional author, and the very fact that he does not conceal this gives to *Peter Pan* its peculiar quality and strength. Barrie knew that the average child's mind is apt to possess a strange duality – on the one hand, an inquiring practicality ("What's that spoon *for*?" or "What's that word *for*?"), and, on the other, a free-ranging power of imaginative acceptance. Successive audiences of children watching *Peter Pan* have shown that they were perfectly well aware that they were seated in a theatre and that they knew what a theatre is *for*, while at the same time they have carried from the stage-experience things about which they could dream. And the adults who accompanied them, even those who might have started by feeling superior, have been caught up by Barrie's skilful sops to their intelligence. Hook's description of the "belated crumbs" of the goodnight chocolate and his "Split my infinitives!" were likely not to be appreciated by the children – whose minds at that moment would be all a-gog in expectation of the imminent walking-the-plank episode; realising that that episode might hardly cause such excitement in the parents, the author thus skilfully exercises his craft, keeping the adult attention alert by Hook's parody of the melodramatic style.

When, some fourteen years later, A. A. Milne wrote his *Make-Believe* (1918) he confessed that "the difficulty in the way of writing a children's play is that Barrie was born too soon –" and his work, charming though it may be, demonstrates the truth of his statement. The idea of introducing some children who decide to "think up" a play which will include a fairy-story, a desert island and Father Christmas grows, as it were, out of Barrie's fancy, and at least one stage-directional comment concerning James the butler (who collaborates in the children's game) shows that Milne had clearly grasped, and delighted in, the basic secret of the success attained by *Peter Pan:*

The truth is that JAMES, *who wasn't really meant to be in it, thinks too. If there is anything in the play which you don't like, it is* JAMES *thinking.*

Make-Believe is delightfully charming and felicitous although without manifesting any clear individuality of its own:

Milne was able to escape from Barrie's fascination only when, years later, he took Kenneth Grahame's *The Wind in the Willows* for his material and wrought it into *Toad of Toad's Hall* (1930), thus in his own right establishing a new type of children's drama.

Not one of the minority playwrights came even within hailing distance of the Pirate Ship, or knocked at a door such as that which led into Toad Hall, or even drew close to Milne's make-believe. Walter de la Mare's *Crossings* (1919), one of the best in this kind, is sensitively written, yet it stands far off from the achievements of Milne and Barrie, even from the lesser achievements of other authors whose eyes were fixed on the West End theatres. In 1901 the Prince of Wales's saw a production of *Katawampus*, the collaborative effort of Louis Calvert and Judge Parry (himself almost a professional dramatist); at the Vaudeville during the same year came the "musical dream play", *Bluebell in Fairyland*, written by Sir Seymour Hicks, with lyrics by Aubrey Hopwood and music by Walter Slaughter; in 1911 the still-remembered *Where the Rainbow Ends*, by Mrs Clifford Mills and John Ramsey, with music by R. Quilter, was presented at the Savoy; the year following, audiences at the Birmingham Repertory saw the "fairy frolic" called *Fifinella*, contrived by Barry Jackson and Basil Dean; and during the twenties Harcourt Williams wrote eight or nine effective pieces for his wife's "Children's Seasons".[1] All of these, even although they do not rise to the level of *Peter Pan*, far surpass anything devised in a kindred strain by authors who did not look beyond restricted audiences.

Housman's *Ways and Means* is thoroughly in keeping with the dramatic activities of numerous other minority authors who carried their interest from children's plays into the sphere of the village drama, and here again all that can be said is that these various individual efforts which eventually were co-ordinated within the work of the Village Drama

[1] Already in December 1913 there had been a "Children's Theatre" at the Court.

Society deserve praise for their meritorious aims, but cannot, with the best will in the world, be deemed of any significant dramatic value. Some of the writers sought to exploit local dialects, legends and historical associations;[1] others invented or adapted situations of a "folk" kind involving rustic characters; still others attempted to combine such material with objectives which almost deserve to be styled educational. Although there were a few male authors active in this area, the majority of these simple one-acts were the work of ladies, many of them titled, whose contributions were intended mainly for the people of the several districts in which they resided.

For the moment the dialect plays must be set aside, since they belong within the larger pattern of the regional drama, but a very brief glance may be cast here at a few other examples illustrative of what was being attempted in this sphere. In looking at these, we must, of course, realise to the full that the past thirty or forty years have wrought a complete change in the countryside, so that a large proportion of the "Plays for Villages" issued by the Village Drama Society or, with the Society's "recommendations", by interested publishers, seem now to be separated from us by centuries. Many, such as Vera Bannisdale's *Moggeridge's Cow* (1922), or *The Old Miser* (1920) by Elfrida and Clarence Derwent, appear not merely time-worn but things of a far-distant and forgotten past. On the other hand, at least a few authors succeeded in reaching somewhat further by turning to historical subject-matter: already in 1903 Marie Boileau had written "*When Anne was Queen*", and this playlet retained sufficient vitality to warrant its reprinting by Samuel French in 1920; Mary Pakington's *The Queen of Hearts* (1926) not ineffectively showed Queen Elizabeth visiting Hartlebury Castle and talking to villagers of the surrounding countryside; and Mrs Clifford Paul's *The Fugitive King* (1926), dealing with the adventures of the future Charles II after the battle of Worcester, has a kindred

[1] For the development of the Village Drama Society and related ventures see pp. 85 and 245–7.

flavour. Moreover, while the majority of the authors took their self-appointed duties with an excess of seriousness, there were some who agreeably smiled at themselves and at their companions, the rustic performers: E. U. Ouless, for instance, in *Our Pageant* (1926) – an amusing picture of the bumbling confusions and mistakes made during the rehearsing of a local show – justifying her "motto" which relates her scenes to those in which Bottom the Weaver played his heroic rôle. Even so, however, there is nothing to be encountered here equivalent to, let us say, Cyril Roberts' *Village Industries* (1928) – a piece to which the Village Drama Society might not have given its recommendation – which introduces us to an out-of-the-way Cotswold inn where the landlord stages a little "old-world" scene for his own benefit and for the wondering admiration of some conveniently-stranded American tourists.

Mary Kelly, in 1939, concluded her general survey of *Village Theatre* with a bold statement of purpose and belief, nothing less than

> putting into the hands of the countryman those tools by which he will be able one day to create for himself a theatre which will give a true expression to all that he has learnt from the great teacher, Nature, to all that he has suffered, to his philosophy, to his humour, and to his abiding faith in the ultimate triumph of life. And when he has built this theatre, he will have made a great contribution to the universal art of the drama, a contribution which none but he can make.

No more can be said in comment save that the confident faith thus expressed was widely reflected in other ways (as, for example, in the fact that one publisher issued a series of playlets under the general title of "Modern Plays & Comedies for Women's Institutes, Girls' Clubs, Village Performance, etc." and then changed the descriptive heading to "Plays for the New Era"); that this faith and this objective still continue to fascinate some theatre-lovers of today; that the objective, in its complete formulation, was a creation of the first three decades of the present century; that despite the enthusiasm with which it was cultivated nothing positively significant and enduring was at that time fashioned in its image; but that possibly a full appreciation of its force can be gained only when it is considered within a still larger concept and framework – that of the regional drama.

2. *The Regional Drama*

Except in one respect the regional drama movement stands absolutely separate in concept and procedure from that which concentrated its efforts on the cultivation of village drama. Mary Kelly's ultimate hope was that some day the means might be given to the countryman for writing and for acting plays of his very own. The first clearly-defined manifestation of the spirit of the regional drama came in May 1899 when the newly-formed Irish Literary Theatre presented *The Countess Cathleen* by W. B. Yeats and *The Heather Field* by Edward Martyn: and the very last thing which the people responsible for this venture would have wished to do would have been to give to countrymen the opportunity and the ability to compose dramatic works and to present them to the public. Countrymen, peasants and small farmers may have been the characters most commonly dealt with by the Irish Literary Theatre, but they were presented, not by and to members of their community, but by professional authors and by eager civic amateur actors, before Dublin spectators.

The only thing, apart from interest in and affection for the bucolic characters, which bound the village theatre movement and the regional theatre movement together was, in fact, the cultivation of dramatic dialogue freely employing dialect speech. It is of such dialect speech that we think first when we call to mind the plays performed under the auspices of the Irish Literary Theatre, whether presented in hired halls or within the Abbey playhouse; and unquestionably the example thus set exerted a powerful and long-continuing influence on the minority drama as it took shape in districts far removed from Ireland.

In approaching this subject, however, we must be very cautious. It is tempting to say that the whole of the minority drama movement took its inspiration from the venture which found a permanent home in the Abbey; but in fact there is nothing else to be found within the entirety of this period which in any real respect may be regarded as akin to what was accomplished by Yeats and his companions. We shall have occasion to see how the drama in England spread far beyond the purlieus of London into the provinces – and presumably from one point of view Dublin was looked upon by members of the theatrical profession as provincial. Nevertheless, from every other point of view it has a distinction all its own. It was the capital of a country separated by a stretch of sea from England; it rejoiced in having its own independent culture; not only could it boast a long and distinguished theatrical history from the beginning of the seventeenth century, it had richly contributed to the London stage both players and playwrights. If Dublin was provincial, it was provincial in a grand manner; and there is no other city with which it can be compared – not Birmingham, Liverpool or Manchester, not even an Edinburgh which, whatever independent culture it had exhibited in the past, could not make many vaunts concerning its achievements in the theatre.

The Abbey Theatre thus stands in a peculiarly anomalous position. When its doors were first opened in 1904, it could be, and indeed was, regarded as the first of the British repertories: twenty years later it had become, in spirit if not in title, virtually a national theatre set in the capital of an independent country; and even although in 1904 the Republic of Ireland was not to be formally established for some time to come, those who were active in the Irish Literary Theatre movement and in this newly-founded playhouse of their own had already dreamed themselves into political independence. No doubt its early plays may, not improperly, be considered as part of English literature; yet it is impossible to set up an arbitrary barrier between this Abbey of 1904 and the Abbey of 1930: the plays presented in both belonged to Irish literature, and however close, both geographically and spritually, these plays might be to the plays being produced in London, it would seem to be no more proper to introduce here any historical account of Irish dramatic activity during those years than it would be to incorporate an historical account of contemporary playwriting in the United States of America.[1]

Perhaps the most immediately characteristic feature of this Irish theatrical movement during its first twenty years was the way in which it built its repertory almost entirely from native plays. From the start, with Yeats, Lady Gregory, Martyn, T. C. Murray, J. M. Synge, William Boyle, George Fitzmaurice, Padraic Colum and the young Lennox Robinson, embracing in its course such Ulster authors as Rutherford Mayne, St John Ervine and George Shiels, onwards until, as these thirty years were drawing to a close, came the meteoric advent of Sean O'Casey, audiences at the Abbey might well have thought that no dramatic literature was being written – or indeed had been written – anywhere save within the frontiers of Ireland. For this, no doubt, there was ample justification, since Ireland was in the midst of an extraordinary literary renaissance; but for our present purposes, from our present point of view, what is of paramount significance is not this development in itself but the influence it exerted upon the development of the English stage. Considered thus, it is obvious that numerous Abbey authors (William Boyle may serve as an example) remained practically unknown across the Irish Sea and that it is only the earliest dramas, especially those which came within the century's first decade, which for our present purposes are of particular significance. And here some four or five of their characteristic aspects, in form and in subject-matter, demand at least brief comment.

In turning to deal with local themes and characters, the

[1] It may be mentioned here that many, if not all, of the plays presented at the Abbey have been recorded in the Handlist of Plays. Although there is an inconsistency here, this procedure seemed to be desirable because of the close connections existing between the London and Dublin theatres during at least a considerable part of this period.

Irish authors were granted a peculiar advantage: they found themselves in an environment rich in various forms of native speech, not dulled and deadened but vital, exuberant and vital, coming easily to the lips of men who, themselves naturally loquacious, were apt easily to be charmed by a wondering faith in the magical power of words. Some of these authors – Fitzmaurice, for example – needed to do little more than listen acutely to the conversation of peasants and reproduce the forms of their conversation in dramatic dialogue; others more highly gifted, such as Synge, were able to build from this peasant foundation a rich and new literary expression of their own.[1] Without any doubt, the development in England of plays in which local dialect forms took possession of the stage largely owed its being to the inspiration which came from Dublin, but for those admirers of Synge who had hoped that a following of his example would lead towards the releasing of a fresh flow of exciting dramatic eloquence in other districts the results were disappointing. We must ever bear in mind what so many of the early enthusiasts ignored, that the peculiar flavour of Irish speech was, in fact, absolutely unique, that its musical and gustful abundance derived, as St John Ervine observed, "not from the ancient Gaels, but from the Elizabethans",[2] and that no attempts made elsewhere to imitate its stage use could hope to prove truly successful.

In addition to this still rich and unimpaired native speech, too, the Irish playwrights discovered folk legends which had not lost their hold on the communal memory, and, even more important, they found themselves in the living presence of a myth-making power such as had created these legends centuries before. Past and present could, therefore, merge

[1] It is true that Irish-speaking characters had been freely introduced into numerous plays from the seventeenth century onwards, but in these dramas there had been little beyond the seizing of a few particularly peculiar and outstanding dialectal features likely to prove interesting on the stage. For the earlier periods J. O. Bartley, in his *Teague, Shenkin and Sawney* (1954), provides a useful and interesting account of the various types of language given to Irish, Scottish and Welsh dramatic characters.

[2] St John Ervine, *The Organised Theatre* (1924), p. 83.

into one within this environment: Yeats' *Cathleen Ni Houlihan* (1902) is supposed to be set in the eighteenth century, but the peasant characters are made to speak in terms to which the poet himself might have listened in the countryside of his own time, while, without any feeling of incongruity, there is brought into their midst a mythical figure – a decrepit old woman who yet could seem to have the walk of a queen. Nothing like this can be found elsewhere.

Next to the influence exerted by the dramatic use of dialect speech may be placed the inspiration which Yeats offered to a limited number of poets who dreamed of supplanting the realistic prose plays of their time with dramas richly and nobly framed in verse dialogue; but perhaps this is something which may most conveniently be considered later in connection with the verse-drama movement as a whole. Of considerably wider significance in the spread of the minority drama was the way in which the Irish dramatists, partly because they found short plays easier to write than long and partly because they realised that such short plays were best suited for interpretation by their amateur actors, gave distinction and richness of quality to the one-act theatre. Some of these one-acts, such as Synge's *Riders to the Sea* (1904), absolutely defied the possibility of even tentative imitation, but many of them, even a surprisingly large number worthy of high praise, were of a kind which allowed other authors to think of emulating what they had accomplished. Here, instead of the poetic Yeats – although it must be remembered that he too had that aberration among his poetic writings, *The Pot of Broth* (1902) – we think of the active Lady Gregory as the chief potent force: it can indeed be argued that, during the earliest days of the minority drama movement in England her playlets were more widely read and followed than those of any other Irish dramatist.[1]

[1] It is of interest to note that within the past few years there has been renewed appreciation of the dramatic accomplishments of Lady Gregory. Although these had never been completely neglected, the title of Ann Saddlemyer's study, *In Defence of Lady Gregory, Playwright* (1966), clearly reflects a feeling that she had not previously received the credit

When an attempt is made to secure an over-all conspectus of the Irish repertoire, we must feel surprised to note how solemn most of the authors were. It is well known that during the Abbey's earliest years the management experienced great difficulties in securing suitable comic scripts, and probably their scarcity derived from the same sense of abashed humility which made Lady Gregory, a much more skilled dramatist than Yeats, look upon his "serious" works with awed admiration.

The general impression we receive is of a series of dark dramas, mostly concerned with clash and conflict within family circles, with the destructive force of age over youth, and sometimes with the evils consequent upon religious bigotry. One special feature in these plays may be noted. In a sense they are akin to those English minority dramas which concentrated upon the struggle between youth and age; but, whereas the playwrights in England tended to concentrate their interest upon the daughter who struggles to gain her freedom, the Irish authors nearly always concerned themselves with a son oppressed by family pressure and, in particular, by the domineering selfishness of a father. The dour, dictatorial, self-opinionated old Morrissey in Murray's *Birthright* (1910) is thus made responsible for a series of disasters culminating in dismal fratricide; in the same author's *Maurice Harte* (1912) family compulsion drives a sensitive youth to near-madness because he is being forced to enter a priesthood for which he is utterly unqualified; Padraic Colum's *Thomas Muskerry* (1910) varies the pattern somewhat by making the title-character an elderly Master of a Workhouse, but otherwise intensifies rather than relieves the drab depression in which the action is immersed; St John Ervine, reflecting conditions in his native Ulster, chooses in *Mixed Marriage* (1911) a city setting for his gloomy study of the young in the grip of the religiously fanatical old, and even when in *John Ferguson*

due to her and this feeling has been further marked by the appearance of Elizabeth Coxhead's biographical–critical *Lady Gregory* (1966) and of Anne Dedio's *Das dramatische Werk von Lady Gregory* (1967).

(1915) he moves his scene to "the kitchen of a farm-house in County Down" in "the late summer of 188–", the same familiar features are reproduced – violent passions, dismal coincidences, melodramatic actions combining to create an atmosphere of dull and universal gloom; and the same admixture of what often seems to be forced theatricality and stark emotion is repeated in the first dramas of Lennox Robinson – *The Clancy Name* (1908), *The Cross Roads* (1909) and *Harvest* (1910).[1]

By far the greatest of all the Irish playwrights was J. M. Synge, and since his influence on the English theatre was particularly strong, it seems proper that some further attention to his work should be given here, the more particularly because among his prevailing themes was one which found varied forms of expression in the writings of his fellow dramatists and which has an interesting connection with a related although differently expressed topic popular among the theatres in London and elsewhere in England.

If we put aside *Riders to the Sea* and the unfinished *Deirdre of the Sorrows* (1910), we are inclined to look upon Synge as a richly comic author: yet when we examine his scenes more carefully we are compelled to recognise that, in fact, we are confronted here by something peculiarly complex and born of several sombre emotions – a sense of disillusionment, a keen awareness of the painful contrast between man's dreams and the reality surrounding him, a wry acceptance of inevitable disappointment and, above all, a desire to escape from dull material values. Comedy undoubtedly; but comedy of a very special kind.

Outwardly, *In the Shadow of the Glen* (1903) appears to be simply an adroit and cleverly devised amusing sketch, but closer examination convinces us that its quality derives from something which rests far below the almost farcical action. The young wife, Nora, is driven out of her cottage, and yet she departs of her own volition; she is fully aware that outside the shelter of those walls the wind is keen and the rain

[1] On this author's career see Michael J. O'Neill, *Lennox Robinson* (1964).

bitter; but the dream, expressed in the Tramp's words, is of greater import to her than any material comfort. There is no wild romantic passion here, but a deliberate and clear-eyed choice made between two values:

TRAMP (*at the door*). Come along with me now, lady of the house, and it's not my blather you'll be hearing only, but you'll be hearing the herons crying out over the black lakes, and you'll be hearing the grouse and the owls with them, and the larks and the big thrushes when the days are warm, and it's not from the like of them you'll be hearing a talk of getting old like Peggy Cavanagh, and losing the hair off you, and the light of your eyes, but it's fine songs you'll be hearing when the sun goes up, and there'll be no old fellow wheezing, the like of a sick sheep, close to your ear.

NORA. I'm thinking it's myself will be wheezing that time with lying down under the Heavens when the night is cold; but you've a fine bit of talk, stranger, and it's with yourself I'll go.

The Tramp here is not just a flattering blatherer: he is kin to the Tramp in Lady Gregory's *The Travelling Man* (1910), a mystical symbol of an emotional force more potent than any material considerations, wandering along a road leading away from the trammels of society. That the mood thus expressed in *The Shadow of the Glen* was not simply born of the theme of that playlet is shown doubly when we turn to *The Well of the Saints* (1905). Martin Doul is a "weather-beaten, blind beggar", his wife, Mary, is a "weather-beaten, ugly woman, blind also": a Saint miraculously grants them the power of sight: they look upon each other, and, instead of the images in their minds – he a fine upstanding lad, and she a young "beautiful dark woman" – they see only the harsh truth of reality: bitter, angry words come to their lips, and they part. Time goes by, their blindness returns, and with the blindness come reconciliation and renewed dreaming:

MARTIN DOUL (*bursting with excitement*). I've this to say, Mary Doul, I'll be letting my beard grow in a short while, a beautiful, long, white, silken, streamy beard, you wouldn't

> see the like of in the eastern world....Ah, a white beard's a grand thing on an old man, a grand thing for making the quality stop and be stretching out their hands with good silver or gold, and a beard's a thing you'll never have, so you may be holding your tongue.

The Saint comes to them again and proposes once more to apply his holy water in order to renew their cure and make it permanent, but Mary begs him to refrain:

> Let us be as we are, holy father, and then we'll be known again in a short while as the people is happy and blind, and be having an easy time, with no trouble to live, and we getting halfpence on the road.

The ordinary hard-working peasants around them try to teach them common sense; the Saint prepares to exercise his authority; but Martin dashes the bowl of water from his hand, crying out

> If it's a right some of you have to be working and sweating the like of Timmy the smith, and a right some of you have to be fasting and praying and talking holy talk the like of yourself, I'm thinking it's a good right ourselves have to be sitting blind, hearing a soft wind turning round the little leaves of the spring and feeling the sun, and we not tormenting our souls with the sight of the gray days, and the holy men, and the dirty feet is trampling the world.

And if one considers the innermost theme of Synge's greatest dramatic achievement, *The Playboy of the Western World* (1907), it must surely be recognised at once as possessing much of the same mood. On the surface all we discern is a story of a wretched youth who, having quarrelled with his father and given him a blow, comes to a village, confesses that he had "let fall the edge" of his spade "on the ridge" of his parent's skull, and finds that his sorry narrative, instead of exciting horror, is regarded with admiring awe and admiration as an heroic tale. This, however, is not the true theme of the play: if we look beyond, we see three dreams or illusions taking shape, interacting one upon another. The villagers, amazed with wonder at his boldness and, more particularly, at his independent breaking away from accepted conventions, look upon this Christy Mahon, not as he is in reality, but as he is fashioned in their imagination; he himself enters a dream world of his own, embellishing his original story in almost epic manner; and the prettiest, liveliest of the village maidens, Pegeen, becomes infatuated with the heroic vision created in her mind. Particularly significant is the close of the play. The irate father comes tramping in, and Christy is reduced to the wretched youth of the first act. For Pegeen there remains, after the glory of the dream, only the old, familiar, depressing reality. She is, in fact, almost a thwarted Nora, and her final words express her sense of loss; she had dreamed of going off with Christy into a rare world, far apart from the commonplace conventional, and now all she can think of is that the "only playboy of the western world" is gone.

If we regard *The Well of the Saints* as simply "an excellent piece of comedy", based on "a delightfully absurd idea", or if we discern no more in *The Playboy of the Western World* than a satire of hero-worship and simple-minded credulity, we shall certainly remain far away both from a true realisation of what Synge had to offer and from an appreciation of the mood which he shared with so many of his companions, even with some whose spirit might seem, at first glance, far removed from his. Rutherford Mayne's *The Turn of the Road* (1910), for example, might appear to be as distant from *The Playboy of the Western World* as we could possibly imagine – just one other gloomy drama of a familiar and conventional kind, showing a lonely farm ruled by a grasping, domineering, hard-working father, William Granahan, and a generation conflict between him and his son. This son, however, may be looked upon as a sort of symbolic figure: he does not want to work; the only thing that gives him pleasure is idle fiddling – not because he is a frustrated musical genius, but solely because he has no interest in his father's material values. Indeed, the very title of the play is in itself symbolic: at the close, the boy breaks entirely with the environment which means less than nothing for him, and off he tramps round the turn of the road to a life of vagrancy. In a short epilogue the moral is stressed in the words of the old Grandfather, speaking in the wisdom of his years:

> Ye thought he was wasting time and money. D'ye think there's nothing in this life beyond making money above the rent? I tell you it's not the money alone that makes life worth living.

Both youth and great age share in these dreams: it is the middle range which is dragged down by reality. So the wrinkled and hoary Conn Hourican in Padraic Colum's *The Fiddler's House* (1907) is as much fascinated by the thought of freedom, the open road and the vagrant life as is Synge's Nora; and at the end of the play we see his daughter Maire handing him his fiddle, prepared to trudge off with him towards the fairs.

Numerous other dramas, both heavy and light, could be cited to stress the prevalence of this mood, as expressed in various ways. Occasionally, for example, we find almost merry attempts to justify the loafing work-shy spirit in the very terms of what it sought to reject. Rutherford Mayne's *The Drone* (1911) thus moves from the passion-fraught atmosphere of *The Turn of the Road* to present an amusing sketch of another toiling farmer, John Murray, diddled by his indolent, blathering brother Daniel who enjoys a life of ease by sporadically toying with an "invention" – but who ultimately (and rather unbelievably) finds the fruits of his idleness bringing in a considerable monetary reward; while Lennox Robinson, a few years later, contrived in *The White-headed Boy* (1916) a joyous comedy about an idle, pampered but charmingly sympathetic youth, Denis, who has been living comfortably in London, ostensibly training to be a doctor, who is called back by the irate industrious family which had been supporting him, who is about to be shipped off to Canada, and who ends up re-instated by his relatives in a life of ease.

These last two plays are jests, but the jest itself stems from something serious – something indeed which was mystically expressed by Yeats at the very beginning of the century in his

Where There is Nothing (1903). In that drama, a young man, weary of conventional, orthodox values, gives up his material possessions, joins a monastic group, has a vision wherein he is told that God may be discovered only "where there is nothing that is anything and nobody that is anybody", and proceeds to preach an anarchist creed of universal destruction. This youth, Synge's Nora and the Tramp, his two blind beggars and Pegeen, Mayne's idle fiddling youth and Colum's Conn Hourican and Robinson's White-headed Boy all are denizens of one and the same spiritual world.

In looking at this trend several things seem particularly noteworthy. It is strange that the direct or implied rejection of established social values, together with the acceptance of discomfort for the sake of a dream, should have come, not from playwrights contemplating an industrialised society, but from those whose lives were usually set in the countryside: it is strange that, despite the widespread influence exerted by the Irish drama upon minority playwrights elsewhere, this was a mood which found but faint reflections outside of Dublin, and then more commonly on the commercial stage:[1] and it is equally strange that what was enunciated philosophically by Yeats and emotionally by Synge did not find any true counterpart until we reach the world of youth in our own times.

This Irish drama, as properly it must be called even during the first two decades of its existence, thus clearly occupies a dualistic position: on the one hand, it was born of national sentiment and shows hardly any interest in theatres outside of Dublin, but, on the other, it assumes form as an

[1] Such reflections usually appear in connection with plays which introduced "passers-by" and "artists": see pp. 332–6. While the "passer-by" is a dramatic character not unknown in Ireland, hardly any of the Abbey dramas dealt with "artists" as such: the fiddling, as has been suggested above, was merely an excuse for idleness. Discussion of Sean O'Casey's plays is omitted here because they came too late to exercise any marked influence within this period. Both *Juno and the Paycock* (1924) and *The Plough and the Stars* (1926) made a deep theatrical impact, but there is little evidence before 1930 of his influence upon English dramatists.

early and prime expression of a movement which affected almost all areas within the British Isles. Because it arrived so early and because of the rich quality of its plays, its influence is widely manifest, yet it must be repeated that we shall go far wrong if we suppose that regional and associated developments elsewhere were all initially inspired by its example. These developments would certainly have come into being even if there had been no Irish Literary Theatre and no Abbey playhouse. The impress of Lady Gregory and Synge may be apparent almost everywhere, yet equally patent is the way in which the various areas cultivated characteristic styles of their own.

The ideals which inspired small groups of enthusiasts in Wales and Scotland may be regarded as coming most close to those which had stirred and animated the Irish dramatists, yet recognition of this closeness has the paradoxical effect of emphasising and underlining the peculiar advantages which the latter enjoyed. Nowhere in Wales, for example, was there any such long-standing theatrical tradition as had given to Yeats and his companions a firm foundation for their efforts. Instead, those Welsh authors who sought to establish a local drama of their own were compelled to fight against two inimical forces.[1] General disapproval of the stage was one of these, largely stimulated by the many puritanical preachers who, following seventeenth-century example, denounced the theatre as the Devil's true home. The second, peculiarly, also derived from the same source, since at least some of these preachers, recognising – however unwillingly – the appeal of the drama, tentatively tried to beat this Devil at his own game by encouraging amateur

[1] Numerous interesting articles have been written both on the earlier theatrical activities in Wales and on the twentieth-century dramatic movement: some of the more important are conveniently listed by Alfred Loewenberg in *The Theatre of the British Isles* (1950), p. 63. Cecil Price's *The English Theatre in Wales in the Eighteenth and Early Nineteenth Centuries* (1948) ably presents a record of stage activities, both amateur (as at Wynnstay) and professional, up to about 1840; the new movement is examined by Olive Ely Hart in *The Drama in Modern Wales* (1928), and an account of the general literary renaissance appears in Gwyn Jones' *The Dragon has Two Tongues* (1968).

performances of short plays informed with highly moral and religious sentiment. Thus those who directly disapproved joined forces with those who sought to convert the stage into a pulpit.

Nevertheless, despite the unpropitious conditions, the relatively small group of theatre-lovers struggled on, and a prime symbol of what was happening may be found in a play called *Change*, by J. O. Francis, which in 1912 had the distinction of winning the prize at a Welsh Drama competition instituted by Lord Howard de Walden, of being the first work by a local author presented by a newly-formed Welsh National Drama Company, and of bringing knowledge of this Welsh movement to London when it was produced under the aegis of the Stage Society in 1913. Another "literary theatre" was thus launched, and soon the Portmadoc Players were actively engaged in an effort to encourage native young dramatists.

During the period with which we are concerned, however, it cannot be claimed that these dramatists achieved anything comparable with what had been created in Ireland. Francis' various plays from 1912 on to 1929 – the one-acts, *The Bakehouse* (1913), *The Poacher* (1914) and *Birds of a Feather* (1927), and the full-length farcical comedy, *Antony Settles Down* (1922) – show him possessed of an engaging comic sense and occasionally a keen power of observation, but not of distinctive originality. Among his companions almost the only one who had something of that quality was Richard Hughes, and even his contributions seem, in retrospect, disappointing. His *The Sisters' Tragedy* (1922), although replete with symbolic overtones and despite the author's declaration that it "is not essentially a Grand Guignol play", may in fact be thought to have found its appropriate place when it was included in the Little Theatre's horrific repertoire: its setting in the gloomy mansion of a degenerated county family, its initial scene showing a girl, Charlotte, killing a rabbit which had been mauled by a cat and its final episode wherein this girl's young sister Lowrie murders her blind-deaf-mute brother were all in harmony with the Guignol style.[1] More ambitious, more interesting, but unfortunately somewhat heavy-handed is his *Comedy of Good and Evil* (1924): there may be appreciation here of the dramatist's endeavour to achieve something significant in his strange story of a Welsh clergyman and a woman possessed of a devil, and yet there must be the impression that he had become lost in a morass of obscure questings.

Numerous other plays – most of them in one-act form – were produced during those years by Welsh authors, and among them may be found not a few endowed with original qualities. There is, for example, an appealing strangeness in A. O. Roberts' *Cloudbreak* (1923), which brings together past and present, the real and the imaginary. We start here in the midst of an ordinary remote village and are introduced to a poverty-stricken woman who does not possess even a small coin for the plate in her chapel; the Devil tempts her, so that she sells her soul for a tiny piece of silver, but she is saved from damnation because, going along the road, she meets a wandering beggar to whom she gives the coin; and at the end of the play we discover that this beggar is, in fact, Judas Iscariot, doomed to walk the earth until he can find the thirty pieces of silver for which Christ had been sold. Obviously, this is a story difficult to make credible in dramatic form, and Roberts' skill is shown by the fact that he has wrought what might seem to be an almost impossible stage plot into an effective pattern. It must, however, be confessed that the Welsh movement as a whole produced comparatively little of intrinsic excellence, largely because so few of the authors were able to give to their dialogue the vigour, variety and ease which enlivened so many of the

[1] Similarly Guignolesque is *The Man Born to be Hanged* (1924), notable for its experimental use of narrative combined with "here-and-now" action. Hughes' interest in this kind of play enabled him in *Danger* (1924) – apparently the first "Listening Play" commissioned by the B.B.C. – to write an effective sensational sketch with a situation eminently proper to the conditions of broadcasting: the scene is in the darkness of a mine into which a group of visitors have descended, and the author displays his skill by the evocation in words of a sudden accident, a scrambling escape in the blackness and the noble self-sacrifice of a member of the group.

Irish dramas – and that failure, in turn, may be seen to be consequent upon a quality less rich in the native speech of the country. Perhaps such a prolific writer as Naunton Davies may be taken as typical. Although some of his dramas deal with trite subject-matter, others display interesting efforts to tackle new themes: among several plays published in 1920, for instance, *The Crash* treats of chicanery and corruption in a largely fraudulent business organisation, "The Universal Commission Company", *The Schemer* is mainly a study of an intriguing engineer who is prepared to let no moral scruples interfere with a determination to reach his own selfish ends, *The Human Factor* has a savage industrial strike as its core, and *The Arrogance of Power* introduces a novelty by setting its action several years in the future when a revolutionary organisation has established a Republic in Britain and is defeated in its aims by its own inner corruption and brutality. Even if we give full credit to Davies' subjects, however, not the best will in the world can regard his dialogue – whether in straight English or in local dialect – as anything but dull, antiquated and artificial. On the other hand, it must be added that he was also the author of several writings in Welsh which cannot be dealt with here. In this he was typical. The English plays written by some of his companions may seem, like his, lacking in liveliness, but we must bear in mind that these authors were frequently as much intent, or even more intent, upon developing drama in the Welsh language. For any true appreciation of what was being accomplished theatrically within Wales as a whole during the early years of the century the two must be taken together, although obviously here only the former can be considered. In truth the dragon had two tongues, and this, dramatically, may have taken away some of its power.[1]

For those intent upon promoting the drama in Wales

[1] The scope of this dramatic writing in the two tongues may be gauged by looking at the long list of plays published from 1910 onwards by the Educational Publishing Company of Cardiff in association with Samuel French.

conditions certainly were not propitious, and it might have been thought that Scotland, where anti-theatrical sentiment, although still present, was largely a thing of the past, and where there had been a fairly lengthy and not undistinguished stage tradition, would have been first in the field. Certainly the Glasgow Repertory came early and was indeed the first playhouse of its kind to be supported, not by an individual sponsor, but by public subscription; yet it must be borne in mind that this theatre was forced to tread a very difficult path which constantly skirted the edge of the abyss of bankruptcy and that a real start was not made towards the development of a Scottish drama until the appearance in 1914 of J. A. Ferguson's *Campbell of Kilmohr*, in which with economic effectiveness the author shows a Highland woman prepared to sacrifice her own son in order to protect the fugitive Bonnie Prince Charlie. The outbreak of war was responsible for preventing further immediate experiments of a similar kind, so that it was not until the twenties, and even then somewhat hesitatingly, that firmer steps were taken in this direction – a progress which was aided by the formation of the Scottish National Theatre Society in 1927[1] and by the establishment in 1924 of *The Scots Magazine*, a journal which enabled many authors to see their plays in print.[2]

Ferguson followed his early piece with a not unamusing comedy, *The Scarecrow* (1921), especially composed for the Arts League of Service Travelling Theatre. Although only a one-act piece, its characters – the crofter's wife who thinks milk is being stolen from her cow by witchcraft, her lively daughter who hides her lover, a sailor trying to escape from bondage, by (as it were) setting him up in the barn in the guise of a derelict scarecrow and a hesitant policeman who is driven almost frantic by the girl's tales of ghosts and goblins –

[1] See pp. 61–3.

[2] In contrast with Wales, Scotland produced very few plays written in Gaelic – although one such, *An Gaod a bheir Buaidh*, by Hector MacDougall, was presented in 1911 at the Scottish Exhibition. Apparently the first drama specifically described as "a play in Scots" was H. S. Roberton's *Christ in the Kirkyard* (1921).

are portrayed with incisiveness, consistency and skill. This laughable playlet was followed by another quasi-historical drama, *The King of Morven* (printed 1922, acted 1926), and it joined his other two stage writings to provide the chief inspiring force which made a Glasgow doctor, John McIntyre, turn into "John Brandane", a dramatist who proved much more prolific and more varied in his choice of themes. *Glenforsa* (written in collaboration with A. W. Yuill, 1921) and *The Lifting* (1925) follow Ferguson's lead, but *The Glen is Mine* (1923), *Full Fathom Five* (1924), *The Treasure Ship* (1924), *The Inn of Adventure* (1925) and *Heather Gentry* (1927) show that, like Lady Gregory, he had, in addition to a skill in devising and handling strong dramatic situations, a lively sense of the comic – and in this connection it is interesting to note that he, again like her, recognised how aptly early French farce could be adapted into modern peasant terms.

Ferguson's influence can readily be traced on several of Brandane's companions, in whose hands themes historical and fictional–historical flourished apace: C. S. Black thus produced a *Châtelard* (1921), a *Knox* (1925) and a *Stewart of Ardbeg* (1927), Donald Carswell has a *Count Albany* (1926), and there were others who cultivated the same area. Comparatively rare were attempts to emulate the "grim" rustic plays of Ireland – indeed, the only notable example appears to be *Soutarness Water* (1926), by G. R. Malloch, wherein discovery of an incestuous marriage leads to suicide of mother, son and wife. Also rare were dramas dealing with city life. Joe Corrie might deal realistically with contemporary urban surroundings, Robins Millar might place *The Shawlie* (1924) in a Glasgow slum, and George Blake might write a *Clyde Built* (1922), but in general a scanning of these Scots plays suggests that the prevailing interests lay in an atmosphere of romance and in the realm of moor and glen.

Just as Ferguson's example caused Brandane to turn to the stage, so the latter in turn was the acknowledged inspirer of another Glasgow doctor, O. H. Mavor, an author who, however, stands in an entirely different position from that of his companions. While it is true that his first efforts belonged to the minority regional drama movement and that he remained one of the chief supporters of the Glasgow Citizens' Theatre, his fundamental outlook was by no means local, as is amply apparent even from a consideration of the first four plays which he brought to the stage. *The Sunlight Sonata* (1928), described as a "farcical morality", and *The Girl who did not want to go to Kuala Lumpur* (1929), both presented as the work of a "Mary Henderson", were clearly written with performance by the Scottish National Players in mind, but when, as "James Bridie", he wrote *What It Is To Be Young* (1929) and the final version of *The Switchback* (1929) he was clearly reaching out to a larger audience: his ultimate goal, in fact, was London's West End. One step towards that goal was taken when the last-mentioned play was performed at the Birmingham Repertory in 1929; a second step was its inclusion in 1931 within the Malvern Festival repertory; the third, and final, step was reached with the success of *The Anatomist*, with which the Westminster Theatre opened two months later. From that time on he ceased to be a minority playwright, becoming instead one of the most popular West End authors, and it is as such he will chiefly be remembered.[1]

Perhaps the only other activities which may even remotely be related to those in Scotland and in Wales were the attempts made by a few ardent souls in Cornwall and in the Isle of Man, but these produced hardly anything of genuine dramatic worth. Elsewhere, it is true, the desire to foster and encourage plays dealing with local subject-matter expressed in dialect speech was widely spread, but the spirit animating these efforts was not nationalistic. A large number of playlets must, of course, be set aside here as belonging to the village drama movement; and when we examine the more ambitious works we realise that, in the main, they came, not from groups of like-minded enthusiasts, but from a few

[1] On his career see Winifred Bannister's *James Bridie and His Theatre* (1955) and Helen Luyben's *James Bridie, Clown and Philosopher* (1965).

individual authors working alone and indeed sometimes not directly in contact with the districts whose language and characters were brought into their scenes.

A few examples will make this clear. For a time the so-called Greenleaf Theatre was active in the Cotswolds, but this was essentially the creation of two writers, Anne C. Smedley and her husband M. Armitage – a worthy endeavour, certainly, although dramatically productive of hardly anything save the *Greenleaf Rhythmic Plays* published between 1922 and 1925. If we seek for distinction in the Gloucestershire–Herefordshire area we must turn to just one solitary play – John Masefield's *The Tragedy of Nan* (1908), a drama not written for local presentation, first produced by the Pioneer Players at London's Royalty.[1] Similarly, the *Six Plays* (1921) by Lady Florence Darwin, despite their description as "country" dramas and despite their attractive handling of local dialect speech, seem not to have been associated with any regional acting group. Donald Colquhoun's effective Lancashire playlet, *Jean* (1910), made its first appearance at the Glasgow Repertory. Just at first it might seem as though a firmer and broader movement was at work in Yorkshire, but closer examination of the evidence hardly bears out this impression. John Metcalfe's little collection of plays in Yorkshire dialect (*Bunderley Boggard, and Other Plays*, 1919) belong rather to the village drama movement than to the regional, and much the same judgment may be expressed concerning the *Dale Dramas* (1923) written by Dorothy Una Ratcliffe, although the very short pieces in her collection have an appealing verve and sincerity. Considerably more ambitious were F. W. Moorman's *Plays of the Ridings* (1919), but it may reasonably be assumed that the author, in composing them, had no particular thought of their performance before an audience. Perhaps the nearest we can come to the theatre is in Gwen John's *Plays of Innocence* (1925), and even when these are taken into consideration we realise that one of her playlets was apparently never acted, two were given per-

[1] See also p. 82.

formances by London societies, and the fourth attained to no more than amateur production in Manchester.

One thing in connection with such scattered efforts, however, deserves attention. Collectively these many plays and playlets, whether acted or not, were stimulating an alteration in attitude towards the dialect drama and were encouraging further developments in areas far removed from the rustic scenes which they exploited. In the past, London audiences had shown but little interest in plays of this kind, and consequently managers had looked upon them askance; but change was in the air when an amusing "Scottish comedy", *Bunty Pulls the Strings*, ran for more than six hundred nights at the Haymarket in 1911 and when, in 1924, the equally amusing Somerset comedy of *The Farmer's Wife* more than doubled that record at the Court. Both these plays were written by authors not connected with any regional theatre groups: Eden Phillpotts was a professional novelist–dramatist; in the records of the movement towards the establishment of a Scottish national theatre the name of Graham Moffatt is never mentioned – he was a successful professional platform entertainer who in his forties suddenly discovered a hitherto latent playwriting talent.[1] The appeal of the dialect play was certainly stimulated by the activities of the regional groups, sometimes amateur or only semi-professional, but in giving due credit here to their inspiration it would seem unwise and improper to disregard the significance of others who did not directly belong to the minority stage.

Nor should interest in the Scottish, the Welsh and the English regional plays cause us to ignore another "regional" development which paradoxically grew independently, without any formal group to guide its course, in the metropolis itself. Cockney characters, of course, had frequently been put upon the stage in the nineteenth century, but it was only after 1900 that attempts were made to go beyond stereotyped

[1] Graham Moffatt has an entertaining record of his career, *Join Me in Remembering: The Life and Reminiscences of the Author of "Bunty Pulls the Strings"* (1955).

patterns and to draw material from real life. No doubt the early Cockney plays, most of them one-acts, may now appear to be somewhat sentimental in tone: as examples may be cited Edward Granville's *'Enery Brown* (1901), of particular interest technically because the title-character never appears on stage but is, as it were, evoked through the conversation of others, the effective little sketch of romance in a London laundry, *'Op-o'-Me-Thumb* (1904), by Frederick Fenn and Richard Pryce, and George Paston's *Tilda's New Hat* (1908). But soon others were applying themselves with more determination and more conscious artistry to these city scenes, besides providing variety by including more than characters who might properly be described as "Cockneys". The kindly and sad atmosphere within which Harold Chapin enveloped *The Dumb and the Blind* (1911) made this short piece a notable miniature: Elizabeth Baker's still-remembered *Chains* (1909) rightly won critical praise for its unrelenting picture of a poverty-stricken young clerk whose dreams are inexorably eroded by the compulsions of domestic life; and Hermon Ould, in *Between Sunset and Dawn* (1913), produced one of the first plays to treat slum life with absolute realism – the scene a filthy dosshouse to which Liz Higgins has come to escape from her vicious husband and where her lover, Jim Harris, almost motivelessly murders her.[1]

Notwithstanding its strong action, Ould's drama might almost be called an atmospheric study, and this style was taken up by various playwrights in the twenties. Gilbert Cannan's *In the Park* (1923) is a sketch of such a kind, introducing two wretched creatures, Misterobbs and Missisobbs, each trying to find solace in illusions and each, in the end,

[1] Unfortunately Ould made no further attempts to exploit such material. His later plays, in their variety and in their failure to match accomplishment with aim, are thoroughly typical of the work of numerous other minority writers – a "folk music play" called *Christmas Eve* (1919); a peculiar and strained drama of dark passions, *The Black Virgin* (1922); a pretentious *Dance of Life* (1924); a rather poor study of an actor who marries a girl of easy virtue, *The Light Comedian* (1928); and an excursion into the world of expressionism, with a translation of Ernst Toller's *Hoppla!*

accepting the depressive reality which surrounds them and from which they cannot escape. About the same time appeared two not dissimilar plays, Alma Brosnan's *The Street* (1926) and Beatrice Mayor's *Thirty Minutes in a Street* (1922), in both of which the location itself becomes, as it were, the chief "character". The attempt to develop something novel in structural form is interesting, but the limitations in this dramatic style are obvious: in a short piece it may prove effective, but manifest dangers and difficulties arise when an attempt is made to apply it to a full-length drama. Two of Beatrice Mayor's works illustrate this clearly. *Thirty Minutes in a Street* is, as its title indicates, a one-act piece, and within its limited scope the authoress has been able to present an effective "atmospheric" scene showing many people passing by, while a Stray Man, blind, vainly tries to get help so that he may deliver an urgent letter at number 185. Two years later she essayed a full-length *The Pleasure Garden* (1924), evidently fashioned with her earlier playlet in mind, and the result can hardly be described as satisfactory. Here, instead of introducing a few disparate and unconnected individuals, she has, of course, to link her characters together – and this she does in a rather uninteresting manner by simply making them all discontented with the two exceptions of an old man about to die and a young wife engaged in sewing baby-things; while, in order to keep the various persons within the group distinct from each other, she boringly presents them as mere types – a "Gentlewoman", an "Actor", a "Poet", an "Intellectual", and so on.

Thus, in various ways, divers playwrights belonging to the minority movement sought to explore – sometimes fruitfully, sometimes without success – aspects of London life which the theatre had largely ignored in the past, and at least some of these dramas were able to move beyond the restricted audiences of the little playhouses and to capture wider public attention. Charles McEvoy's vivid picture of coster life in *The Likes of Her* (1923) made dramatic history when, after having been performed by Lena Ashwell's Once-a-Week Players at Battersea Town Hall in January

1923, it was taken to the St Martin's during the following August, and, to everyone's surprise, ran there into the spring of 1924. This success was fully justified: although slightly sentimental at moments, the simple plot of a crippled soldier returning to his girl, Sally, is handled with dramatic effectiveness and the characters are revealed with sensitive insight. The stages which hitherto had been inclined to restrict themselves to displaying scenes within opulent mansions now were prepared to show pictures of humbler sort. *The Likes of Her* had barely ended its run when the Everyman Theatre presented Ernest George's *Low Tide* (1924), a tense delineation of action on a Thames wharf at midnight. Monica Ewer's *The Best of Both Worlds*, although published in 1925, took longer to reach the stage: not until 1930 did the public have an opportunity of viewing its picture of slum life as seen by a cultured and art-loving woman, Ruth Allison, who, in spite of her cravings for other things, stays by the side of her dedicated socialist husband amid dirt, poverty and crime. During the same year appeared Alma Brosnan's *At Number Fifteen*, a drama which, originally brought forward by the Repertory Players in 1927, interestingly presented a decaying house which seems to be observing compassionately the gradual degradation of a poverty-stricken family. Although this drama deals with a milieu which, however indigent, differs from that of the other plays mentioned above, reference to it here is justified, partly because its author had been responsible for *The Street* in 1926, partly because it was sufficiently interesting to be brought before the public, and partly because it illustrates the wide sweep of lower-class London life which had not previously been included in the theatre's range.

And, strangely, it seems entirely proper to mention these London plays before discussing what many critics then thought, and what some theatrical historians still think, to be the most significant dramatic development during this time – the widespread development of playwriting in the Midlands. Despite the mention here of Elizabeth Baker, Charles McEvoy and Harold Chapin, playwrights commonly associated with this Midlands movement, we may well think that most of the London plays are closer in style and intent to those which came into being from Cardiff, Glasgow and Edinburgh onwards to the Yorkshire dales than they are to the style and intent of the dramas which gave a characteristic tone to the theatre in Manchester and related cities.

3. *Social Drama: The "Manchester School" and Others*

Whenever the phrase "English regional drama" is referred to, immediately we are apt to think of the Manchester School of writers encouraged by Miss Horniman's management of the Gaiety Theatre. In many respects the thought itself is justified by the fact that Miss Horniman was responsible for establishing the first of England's regional repertory playhouses. Standing for a time alone in this unique position, its seasons attracted special attention from critics, playwrights and informed playgoers; its performances brought forward a wide range of new plays; and through its various visits to London it materially assisted in making West End spectators aware of what the provincial minority dramatists were striving to accomplish.[1]

If, however, it is eminently right and proper to give such precedence to this playhouse, it is also necessary to keep in mind several other considerations. In the aid it gave to young authors the Gaiety by no means stood alone: other repertories soon began to make their own contributions in this direction: and, in addition to the way in which these provincial playhouses brought new plays before the public, we must give full praise to the manner in which numerous London societies, such as the Play Actors, devoted themselves to the encouragement of apprentice young authors, many of whom actually came from the provinces. Even a cursory glance at the careers of some among the more

[1] An excellently acute essay on this "Manchester School" appears as a preface to Harold Brighouse's *Three Lancashire Plays* (1920).

prominent minority dramatists is sufficient to demonstrate the desirability, indeed the necessity, of thinking in terms considerably wider than those implied in the use of the phrase "Manchester School". The Gaiety opened in 1908 with McEvoy's *When the Devil was Ill*, but not only was this author a Londoner, his first introduction to the theatre was the production of *David Ballard* by the Stage Society in 1907. Although Elizabeth Baker's *Chains* was given its earliest public performances at Manchester in 1911, originally it was a discovery of the Play Actors; and although she had later affiliations with Miss Horniman's theatre, she also had associations with the Birmingham Repertory. The Play Actors, too, were responsible for bringing Harold Chapin to notice, and it was at the Glasgow Repertory that he was accorded a first public performance of any of his dramatic writings. Even when we look at the careers of authors more local, a similar pattern is apparent. The earliest three plays of Allan Monkhouse were given at the Gaiety, but his interesting *The Education of Mr Surrage* (1912) was introduced by the Liverpool Playhouse. Harold Brighouse's earliest unimportant playlet, *The Doorway*, was given at Manchester in 1909, but it was the Glasgow Repertory which, during the same year, presented the much more impressive *The Price of Coal*, and, two years later, produced the sensitive *Lonesome-like*; true, *Garside's Career* and *The Northerners*, both in 1914, were Manchester productions, yet on the other hand *Hobson's Choice* (1916) made its earliest English appearance in the West End. Even Stanley Houghton, so intimately connected with the Gaiety at the beginning, saw his best play, *Hindle Wakes*, given under the aegis of the Stage Society before its public performance at the Aldwych Theatre.

These facts are not cited here for the purpose of slighting the Gaiety's achievements: indeed, essentially they agree with the judgment expressed by Rex Pogson, an enthusiastic admirer of what this playhouse accomplished, when he points out that "the value of the Gaiety's discoveries cannot legitimately be judged merely by the plays produced there in

Miss Horniman's time".[1] The facts are presented here solely for the purpose of indicating that, while Miss Horniman's Gaiety was unquestionably the start, neither did that start belong exclusively to itself nor was a conclusion reached in its efforts: consideration of the movement as a whole demands that attention be given not simply to Manchester but to a development of much wider scope.

When thought is given to this larger development, and more particularly when there is reference to the "Manchester School", there is generally a mental image of a preponderance of hard, grim, grey, depressing dramas of the kind which Agate so heartily opposed.[2] This mental image is at once right and wrong. That it is patently false, or at any rate misleading, becomes manifest just as soon as our eyes run down the theatre's annual programme lists. Miss Horniman's productions were varied and well-balanced, plays comic and fantastic contrasting with others dark and tense: and the same is true of the seasonal offerings at Glasgow, Liverpool and elsewhere. Nevertheless for this mental image there is some considerable justification. At the Gaiety and elsewhere there is amply apparent a tendency to regard the "serious" drama as in itself more significant and more important than lighter fare, and this inevitably resulted in the selection of a fair number of poor plays solely because of the subjects with which they dealt. Although an excuse may be offered for this trend – that an attempt needed to be made to expand the theatre's scope beyond the limitations of the West End's familiar frontiers – we now, looking back, must see that many of these serious dramas have far less vitality, are peculiarly more imitative and are often more artificially contrived than numerous comedies and other plays less rigidly confined to the exposition of serious thoughts.

Of this, two among Houghton's earliest playlets may be taken as examples. *The Dear Departed* (1908) is set in a parlour where relatives have gathered after hearing that Grandfather is dead upstairs. Angrily and greedily their

[1] *Miss Horniman and the Gaiety Theatre, Manchester* (1952), pp. 183–4. [2] See pp. 132–3.

clutching hands stretch out to grab his possessions – when suddenly Grandfather, risen from his supposed death-bed, tramps downstairs and shocks them all by announcing, that not only is he feeling quite well, thank you, but he has decided to marry the lady who keeps the nearby pub. This is excellently adroit comedy. The companion play, *The Master of the House* (1910), although also, ironically, styled a comedy, is a different matter altogether. Again there is a parlour setting, where two persons are seated in silence – Mr Ovens, supposedly asleep, and his second wife, eagerly awaiting the arrival of a solicitor who is due to bring a new will which should leave her all her husband's goods. Mr Ovens, however, is not sleeping, but dead; his ne'er-do-weel son, his father's heir by an earlier will, arrives, turns his step-mother summarily out of the house and gloats at remaining its master. His good fortune, he thinks, must be celebrated with a drink at the pub; he puts out the light and goes to the door, remembers he is penniless, returns to grope in the dark for money:

He takes a cash-box and turns towards the window with it to examine it carefully. As he turns he comes full on the silent figure of Mr. OVENS, *sitting rigid in his chair, shrouded in white, ghastly in the glare of the moon.* FRED *starts back with an oath and drops the cash-box.*) You can't frighten me. You shan't turn me out, I tell you. I'm master of the house. (*He sits on the edge of the table looking at the figure for a long space. Then he speaks in a low, strained voice.*) Don't look at me like that!...(*Another pause: he shudders and covers his face with his hands.*) God! I can't stand it. (*He steals silently out of the room. Mr.* OVENS *sits in his shroud in the moonlight, master of the house.*)

This is sorry stuff, contrived and forced.

In both these playlets the theme concerns a family, and indeed generally within this dramatic area family circles form the chief focus of attention, sometimes, as here, showing the jealousies and greed of its members, sometimes varying this by presenting it as a group united in hypocritical isolation, sometimes introducing the clash between the iconoclastic ideas of modern youth and the traditionalism of age. On occasion, it is true, we find plays of ideas here, such as Brighouse's *The Polygon* (1911) which deals with the subject of housing, but these are comparatively rare; and equally rare are dramas like the same author's *The Price of Coal* (1909) concerned with conditions of work. It is the Family that is dominant, and, once this is realised, we become conscious of the fact that the master-model of these authors is not, as might have been expected, Bernard Shaw but John Galsworthy, Harley Granville-Barker and, to a certain extent, Arnold Bennett.

Allan Monkhouse's *Mary Broome* (1911) tackled a situation which, in a variety of forms, attracted several other playwrights of the time – a respectable middle-class household confronted by the discovery that the eldest son has had an affair with a girl: here the girl is a housemaid, and the irate father, believing righteously that he must marry her, is shocked when she rejects the forced offer. The same author's *Sons and Fathers* (1925) dealt with a family man desirous of giving up work and possessions in order to gain "a change of heart" who finds he can do so only when he outlives all his family and is thus freed from his "chains";[1] *Chains* (1909) by Elizabeth Baker concentrated, as we have seen,[2] on a poor clerk planning to escape from his boring surroundings by emigrating, but thwarted by domestic commitments; the same author's *Edith* (1912) exposed the rapacity of relatives eager to snatch the wealth of a dead man, contrasting these vultures with the only honest and magnanimous member of the family – a girl who, years before, had rebelliously deserted her home in order to make her own way in the world; in *The Waldies* (1912) G. J. Hamlen made his central character a severe and self-made man who, by constantly forbidding his son Alick this and that, turns the lad into a thief; Githa Sowerby's *Rutherford and Son* (1912) darkly studied family pride and conflict. All of these, within their own limits, were

[1] It should be noted that this comparatively late play is one of the very few English dramas which reflects the attitude so characteristic of numerous Irish dramas: see p. 259.

[2] See p. 269.

well written and, in their own time, of some significance, yet all now are dead. It is interesting to observe that the few serious plays of this kind which still preserve some vitality today are those which may be exemplified by Elizabeth Baker's *The Price of Thomas Scott* (1913), where the playwright was forced, almost against her will, to admire the strength of character which kept an old, prejudiced and bigoted father true to his principles, and J. R. Gregson's *T'Marsdens* (1917), where the divisive trends in a family circle are replaced by an unexpected solidarity when the group is threatened from without.

Fortunately, however, some of these repertory authors were gifted with a pleasant sense of humour and dared at times to let it find expression on the stage. Already in *The Younger Generation* (1910) Stanley Houghton had allowed a few ripples of laughter to appear in what was a stern father–rebellious son drama, and it was the free range given to this thoughtful laughter that gave *Hindle Wakes* (1912) its power to withstand the passage of the years. Here there was no attempt to expose the darkness of curtained parlours or the evils wrought by petty domestic tyrants; quite clearly the play had been designed not to impress small audiences of high intellectual content but to appeal to larger and more balanced groups of playgoers. In it the new woman not only finally asserts her independence: she steps on stage as a likeable and believable human being. This Fanny Hawthorn has just returned from a weekend she had enjoyed with Alan Jeffcote and has discovered that their secret affair has become known to both their families. Everyone agrees that, of course, the lad must marry her, and, although he is already engaged to another girl, eventually he is persuaded – or persuades himself – that this is the correct thing to do. To his rather dismayed astonishment she refuses. "You *do* like me?" he asks:

> You wouldn't have gone to Llandudno with me if you hadn't liked me?

FANNY. Oh yes, I liked you.
ALAN. And don't you like me now?

FANNY. You're a nice, clean, well-made lad. Oh ay! I like you right enough.

For a while they argue further, and at last the truth sinks into Alan's mind:

ALAN. But you didn't ever really love me?

FANNY. Love you? Good heavens, of course not! Why on earth should I love you? You were just some one to have a bit of fun with. You were an amusement – a lark.

ALAN (*shocked*). Fanny! Is that all you cared for me?

FANNY. How much more did you care for me?

ALAN. But it's not the same. I'm a man.

FANNY. You're a man, and I was your little fancy. Well, I'm a woman, and *you* were *my* little fancy. You wouldn't prevent a woman enjoying herself as well as a man, if she takes it into her head?

ALAN. But do you mean to say that you didn't care any more for me than a fellow cares for any girl he happens to pick up?

FANNY. Yes. Are you shocked?

ALAN. It's a bit thick; it is really!

FANNY. You're a beauty to talk!

ALAN. It sounds so jolly immoral. I never thought of a girl looking on a chap just like that! I made sure you wanted to marry me if you got the chance.

FANNY. No fear! You're not good enough for me.... You're not man enough for me. You're a nice lad, and I'm fond of you. But I couldn't ever marry you. We've had a right good time together, I'll never forget that. It *has* been a right good time, and no mistake! We've enjoyed ourselves proper! But all good times have to come to an end, and ours is over now. Come along, now, and bid me farewell.

There is real skill in this dialogue. Other authors dealt with much the same theme, but lacking Houghton's delicacy and theatrical effectiveness. Considered from one point of view Fanny's words here can be taken as a serious declaration of feminine emancipation, uttered in a drama solemnly exhibiting a new world of youth wherein "the right to joy is no longer a burning issue":[1] regarded from another point of

[1] T. H. Dickinson, *The Contemporary Drama of England* (1917), p. 219.

view, they can be taken as a straightforward expression of her attitude to Alan; and, looked at from still a third viewpoint, perhaps they might seem to have just a flavour at least of regret that what might have been is impossible.

There was a special individuality about Houghton which makes his plays worthy of remembrance, and this individuality was shown not least in his short *Fancy Free* (1911), with its lightly-drawn picture of the Hotel Cosmopolitan, Babylon-on-Sea, whither Fancy has run off with Alfred, and Ethelbert with Delia. The couples know each other, and gradually they re-form in a new pattern. When we reach the close and find Delia cosily seated beside Alfred while Fancy and Ethelbert become absorbed in each other, when we hear Delia's words to Alfred as the curtain is falling – "Do you know, you've got the most delightfully wicked eyes", and when we read the author's final instructions –

This play should be acted with the most perfect seriousness and polish. It should not be played in a spirit of burlesque. It should be beautifully acted, beautifully costumed, and beautifully staged –

can we avoid thinking of *Private Lives*? Coward's play did not come until 1932 and we are inclined to think of it as expressing the atmosphere of that later age, yet here, more than twenty years earlier, the atmosphere is nearly the same: those who assert that a complete break with the past came in the twenties have indeed much to explain, or, rather, to explain away.[1]

The talent of Harold Brighouse, too, flourished at its best either in an atmosphere of laughter or in an ambience where laughter is made the more rich by being linked with compassion – the worlds of *Lonesome-like* (1911), where a sense of fun is combined with pity as lonely Sam Horrocks saves crippled old Sarah Ormerod from going to a workhouse by "adopting" her as his mother, and of *The Oak Settle* (1911),

[1] A few years later, Houghton used the plot of *Fancy Free* for a full-length comedy called *Partners* (1914), but, even although he introduced an epigram into every second line, this play completely lacks the flavour of the one-act piece.

which shows an agreeable country couple busily stocking their little farmhouse with fake antiques designed to be sold to innocent tourists at exorbitant prices. It must, of course, be freely admitted that Brighouse's range is surprisingly wide. In *The Game* (1913) he could entertainingly anticipate the world of 1971 by dealing with the mass-hysteria over footballers and with the "transfers" by which they might be "sold" from club to club; in *The Price of Coal* (1909) he could poignantly present a picture in miniature of mining life; in *Plays for the Meadow and Plays for the Lawn* (1921) he could move out of the professional theatre into a realm of audience-participation; in *The Northerners* (1914) he could move back in time by a full hundred years and produce a trenchant panorama of industrial strife which well may be thought to be a better play than Hauptmann's more widely-known *The Weavers.* Nevertheless, it is in quiet comedy that he truly excels. When he tries to be serious and "significant" the result tends to be a falsely melodramatic piece such as *The Odd Man Out* (1912); when he keeps his sense of laughter unimpaired the result is the delightfully pleasant *Hobson's Choice* (1915). The characters in the former of these two plays are stock figures, Barbara the innocent heroine, Dick the bronzed athletic hero, Laurence the luckless lover; the latter owes its deserved reputation to its mellow humour, to its intimately drawn persons and to its light treatment of a "family" theme wherein a young girl not only defies authority by seizing upon her worker-husband but also succeeds adroitly in taming her crotchety old father and in making him toe the line.[1]

Nor is the record of Allan Monkhouse's dramatic career much dissimilar. The short "tragedy", *Reaping the Whirlwind* (1908), which first introduced him to the stage is of no particular value, and his second effort, a "problem-play" called *The Choice* (1910), is mawkishly serious. Greater quality may be found in *Mary Broome* (1911), a domestic study which has already been mentioned in connection with

[1] Brighouse has a lively autobiographical record of his career in *What I Have Had* (1953).

Hindle Wakes, yet its characters can be regarded as little more than stereotypes. Among all his dramatic writings *The Education of Mr Surrage* (1912) appears to have greatest chance of maintaining an enduring appeal because it treats the familiar theme of youth and age in a fresh and even gay spirit. Here is the shocked father opposed to "modern" youth, but, instead of being a dummy figure of old-fashioned repression, this Mr Surrage anxiously seeks to understand his children. In an effort to educate him they decide to invite some of their "artist" companions to visit the house – a playwright, an "advanced" woman and a painter – but the first of the trio reveals himself as a "puppy", the advanced woman is seen to be a crashing bore, and the painter turns out to be a thief. This play does not possess the quality of *Hindle Wakes* or *Hobson's Choice*, largely because Monkhouse, even here, cannot quite escape from his tendency to indulge in argumentative dialogue, but it has more of a living essence than any of his serious dramas.[1]

Among this group of authors Harold Chapin occupies a somewhat peculiar position of his own, his originality and deft technical skill introducing a welcome variety both to the repertory stages and to those of the West End. His lower-class, tenement-set playlet, *The Dumb and the Blind* (1911),[2] and *It's the Poor that 'Elps the Poor* (1913) might seem to suggest that his talent lay in the sphere of serious drama, yet it was in comedy that he wrote most easily and felicitously – the signpost pointing toward his highly individual style and vision being clearly set up both in *The Marriage of Columbine* (1910), with its cleverly-handled *commedia dell'arte* material contrasting with commonplace reality, and with its balanced conflict between joyful innocence and bourgeois puritanism, and in his *The Philosopher of Butterbiggins* (1915) which shows an elderly Scottish sea-captain retiring from his posi-

[1] His later plays, *The Conquering Hero* (1923) and *First Blood* (1924) may be regarded as worthy efforts, yet here, as in his earliest stage pieces, his seriousness drove him to make his characters mere abstractions: in the former, an "artist", a "pacifist clergyman" and a "soldier" and, in the latter an "industrialist", a "rebel" and a "shop steward".

[2] See p. 269.

tion of command and entering the home of his married daughter – where, by exercising his adroit philosophy of life, he still remains commanding master on the bridge. Neither of these, perhaps, can be considered a great play, yet they help us towards an appreciation of the still more characteristic comedies in which he gave prominence to a heroine, "baffling", "charming" and clever. In *Art and Opportunity* (1912) this lady is a widow, Mrs Cheverelle, who, spritely and truth-loving, slips from the outstretched arms of a duke and an earl and accepts the hand of the former's secretary; truth-loving and unconventional, too, is the heroine who gives her name to *Elaine* (1912); and in a final appearance she becomes the Betty of *The New Morality* (1920), unquestionably Chapin's most interesting play. A cerebral idea – that morality is something spiritual and not legalistic – underlies this comedy, but, when Betty is shown flying into a tempestuous rage on seeing her stupid husband dancing attendance on another lady, the idea as such is subsumed into the dramatic: the intellectual purpose is transformed into emotional and theatrically effective terms as we watch her, "a jealous materialist and an exacting idealist", lashing out in her idiosyncratic yet logical wrath – she would not have minded so much if her husband had been passionately unfaithful, her rage arising from seeing the silly fool transforming himself into an idiotic lapdog.

In considering all these plays as a whole it becomes evident that long before 1913 the stage was reflecting a revolution in society which commonly is thought not to have arrived before the twenties. Play-titles such as *Change* and *The Younger Generation* tell their own story, providing labels for a general movement embracing the rebellion of youth against traditional restrictions, the breaking-up of the class barriers and, perhaps most significant of all, the advent of this New Morality.

4. *The Poetic and Literary Drama*

Among the many varieties of dramatic writing cultivated within the range of the minority style by no means the least interesting were the plays which strove to bring poetic colour and fervour into the theatre. This, however, is a subject of peculiar complexity and requires very circumspect examination.

First of all, of course, it is necessary to give full consideration to the fact that the new century inherited from its predecessor a realistic tradition within which men such as Pinero and Jones had established a capable, sometimes not ineffective but generally rather commonplace style – a style which, no matter whether the characters were selected from London's aristocracy or from the provincial bourgeoisie, might reasonably be described as middle-class. This style, because it had got rid of the patent artificialities which had abounded in earlier attempts at realism and because it was effectively theatrical (in the sense of providing good material for actors) had proved very exciting in the days when *The Second Mrs Tanqueray* and *Michael and His Lost Angel* had first been brought before the public, but even within the short period of time between the production of those dramas and the opening of the new century the style itself was beginning to lose its first appealing force, and, although it remained dominant on the stage during the Edwardian period, the last years of Victoria's reign exhibited ample signs that there was now a craving among authors and audiences for something different and more exciting. Even if we look merely at a selected number of West End productions we cannot fail to see in the success of many romantic costume plays a desire on the part of playgoers to escape from this dully middle-class medium into a different, more richly-coloured environment.

It is certainly true that, save for one notable instance, no professional author engaged in contributing plays for the West End theatres essayed the poetic style. That must fully be acknowledged, but at the same time sufficient experiments in the production of verse dramas were made by prominent managements to indicate that there existed a readiness within the confines of the commercial playhouses to encourage efforts of such a kind, and the applause which greeted at least a few of these experiments openly manifested the need for a stage removed from the drabness and ordinariness of the "true-to-life" – one is almost tempted to say – "theatre of fact".

Interestingly, the very first years of the new century provide a prime example of this in what must be one of the most extraordinary events in the history of the English theatre – the almost frenetic chorus of adulation which hailed the appearance of Stephen Phillips. Towards the close of the year 1900 Beerbohm Tree presented *Herod* at Her Majesty's, and promptly numerous playgoers and critics ran as mad as did the hero of the play after the slaying of his beloved Mariamne. When Max Beerbohm declared that this play was "so fiery coloured, so intense, the character so largely projected, the action so relentlessly progresses till the final drops of awe are wrung from us, that only the greatest of dramatic poets could accompany with verse quite worthy of it", it might be thought that he was influenced by affection for his brother in thus confusedly pulling out all the stops in his critical vocabulary, but Max was only one among many. Another reviewer claimed it to be "a noble work of dramatic imagination dealing greatly with great passions"; a second associated the author with Marlowe; a third thought of Webster and Chapman; dour William Archer compared Phillips with Milton. The excitement became even greater when, two years later, George Alexander produced *Paolo and Francesca* at the St James's. This drama, according to Churton Collins, made its poet-author worthy of claiming "kinship with the aristocrats of his art – with Sophocles and with Dante" – a statement which may be taken as summing-up the general praise accorded to it by the intoxicated reviewers.

What must have been a cruelly devastating experience for poor Phillips was that within a few years after his triumphant success those who had been offering him these wreaths of laurel suddenly fell into an embarrassed silence.[1] His days of glory were pitifully brief, and despite a series of rather poor later efforts he soon sank into almost complete oblivion. Nowadays, of course, it is easy to see how utterly mistaken the critics had been in their initial paeans of praise. Apart from the fact that Phillips belonged to a decaying and indeed decayed tradition in poetic drama, he himself was decidedly not gifted with any great power: even his highest reaches may be described only by the damning epithet "competent" and frequently he descended to the abyss of dull artificiality. "Remember," advises the Physician at a moment of tension towards the conclusion of *Herod*,

> Remember, if we can but bring him safe
> Through the sharp crisis of his malady;
> If for the first few hours of his return
> We can with music and with gems divert him
> From realising Mariamne's death,
> Then is there hope that he, with stealing time
> And reconciling lapse of quiet hours,
> May come to acquiesce and to submit
> To the dread fact of Mariamne's death.

The pages are spattered with speeches of this kind and with passages of dialogue such as that of the three Messengers towards the start of the drama:

FIRST MESSENGER. Is the king risen? From Samaria we,
Breathless, and with a burning tale to tell.
SOHEMUS. My place is here: to sentinel this door.
SECOND MESSENGER. But these are tidings –
SOHEMUS. Here I stand and stir not.
THIRD MESSENGER. Believe it, sir – look on this dust and haste.
SOHEMUS. I am a soldier, and obey.

[1] Strangely, one of the few later favourable comments on Phillips came from Arthur Waugh in 1919. "But," he wrote, "when criticism has said all it can, it remains indisputable that 'Paolo and Francesca' is simply alive with beauty and with beautiful lines" (*Tradition and Change*, 1919). It would indeed be difficult to find any other author at that time prepared to endorse these sentiments.

FIRST MESSENGER. But, sir –
'Tis Herod's throne – his life perhaps – this news –
SOHEMUS. Must wait.

It may appear almost incredible that plays so turgidly written could have been acclaimed as masterpieces, but the fact remains that they were; and this fact is of not inconsiderable significance. Some slight excuse for the extraordinary over-valuation may certainly be adduced: whereas the majority of nineteenth-century poetic dramas had been composed by authors, both major and minor, who knew little or nothing about the theatre, Phillips had spent several years as an actor in F. R. Benson's company; approaching the drama from within rather than without, he was thus enabled to invest his scenes with a theatrical spirit often sadly lacking in the works of his predecessors, and the presence of that spirit undoubtedly distracted attention from his other deficiencies. This excuse, however, by no means offers a full explanation for the excitement occasioned by his early plays: that is to be found not so much in the dramas themselves as in the attitude of those who listened to them. The ears of the critics and the playgoers, as it were, brought to the productions what they wanted to hear. Unconsciously yearning for something beyond the old grey solitary nothingness of the current dramatic prose dialogue, they stretched forwards avidly towards *Herod* and *Paolo and Francesca*, believing that here was what they sought.

The belief, of course, was a mistaken one, and when they came to realise their error, their disappointment on realising the truth had the immediate effect of making many of them question the validity of their dream. Nevertheless, there are still signs to be found indicating that the dream continued to persist both among those practically concerned with the stage and among playgoers. When J. E. Flecker's *Hassan* was sumptuously panoplied at His Majesty's in 1923,[1] its run of nearly three hundred performances was consequent

[1] For biographical records of this poet's career and critical assessments of his writings see the studies by Douglas Goldring (1922), Geraldine E. Hodgson (1925) and Thomas S. Mercer (1952).

not only upon the appeal of its romantically exotic theme but also upon appreciation of the quality of its poetic-prose dialogue. For the praise given to this play there was much greater justification. Even if now we can look somewhat coolly upon much of the contemporary praise which prophesied that "critics of a future age" would assuredly point "to *Hassan* as the greatest achievement in imaginative drama since the days of the Elizabethans",[1] we are bound to recognise that its author possessed a dramatic power which Phillips, in spite of his theatrical training, sadly lacked. It is indeed most unlikely that anyone would dream today of reviving *Herod and Mariamne*, but *Hassan* still offers challenges to the greatest among our actors, and still it holds the attention of audiences. Wisely, Flecker avoided the use of blank verse. The greater part of his dialogue is in prose, enriched and enlivened by phrases which appropriately can be put in the mouths of his eastern characters. Selim quite properly may say,

Plunge not the finger of enquiry into the pie of impertinence, O my uncle.

"When did you learn poetry, Hassan of my heart?" demands the Caliph, and Hassan replies,

In that great school, the Market of Bagdad. For thee, Master of the World, poetry is a princely diversion: but for us it was a deliverance from Hell. Allah made poetry a cheap thing to buy and a simple thing to understand. He gave men dreams by night that they might learn to dream by day. Men who work hard must have special need of those dreams.

Within this verbal setting Flecker could, with entire consonance, introduce lines of a purely lyrical kind – such as Hassan's plea to Yasmin when he stands below her window, beginning with its

How splendid in the morning glows the lily; with what grace he throws
His supplication to the rose: do roses nod the head, Yasmin?

[1] *The Curtain*, ii, no. 23, 1923, 109.

and ending

Shower down thy love, O burning bright! for one night or the other night
Will come the Gardener in white, and gathered flowers are dead, Yasmin! –

and he could effectively and harmoniously close his action with the departure of the caravan to Samarkand:

ISHAK

We are the Pilgrims, master; we shall go
Always a little further: it may be
Beyond that last blue mountain barred with snow
Across that angry or that glimmering sea.

White on a throne or guarded in a cave
There lives a prophet who can understand
Why men were born: but surely we are brave,
Who take the Golden Road to Samarkand.

THE CHIEF MERCHANT

We gnaw the nail of hurry. Master, away!

ONE OF THE WOMEN

O turn your eyes to where your children stand.
Is not Bagdad the beautiful? O, stay!

MERCHANTS

(*In chorus*)

We take the Golden Road to Samarkand.

AN OLD MAN

Have you not girls and garlands in your homes,
Eunuchs and Syrian boys at your command?
Seek not excess: God hateth him who roams!

MERCHANTS

(*In chorus*)

We take the Golden Road to Samarkand.

HASSAN

Sweet to ride forth at evening from the wells,
When shadows pass gigantic on the sand,
And softly through the silence beat the bells
Along the Golden Road to Samarkand.

ISHAK

We travel not for trafficking alone;
By hotter winds our fiery hearts are fanned:
For lust of knowing what should not be known,
We take the Golden Road to Samarkand.

Not only does Flecker display ingenuity and power in his dialogue, at times he exhibits a keen theatrical sense. Impressive, for example, is his constant emphasis upon the image of a fountain, real and metaphorical. The second scene is set in "The Street of Felicity by the Fountain of the Two Pigeons": there Selim, above at a window, is seen embracing Yasmin, as he plagues the wretched Hassan below,

Could'st thou but see, O my uncle, the silver hills with their pomegranate groves; or the deep fountain in the swelling plain –

and Hassan sinks down in despair, putting his hands to his head,

The fountain, the fountain! O my head, my head!

In itself, this may appear to have only passing significance, yet Flecker binds it up with what perhaps is the most effective scene in the drama, that in which the Caliph leads Hassan through the wonders of his palace garden. As they are talking, the former notices that his guest has become distracted: "At what are you gazing as if enchanted?" he asks:

HASSAN

What a beautiful fountain, with the silver dolphin and the naked boy.

CALIPH

A Greek of Constantinople made it, who came travelling hither in the days of my father, the Caliph El Mahdi (may earth be gentle to his body and Paradise refreshing to his soul!) He showed this fountain to my father, who was exceptionally pleased, and asked the Greek if he could make more as fine. 'A hundred,' replied the delighted infidel. Whereupon my father cried, 'Impale this pig.' Which having been done, this fountain remains the loveliest in the world.

HASSAN

(*With anguish*) O Fountain, dost thou never run with blood?

CALIPH

Why, what is the matter, Hassan?

HASSAN

You have told a tale of death and tyranny, O Master of the World.

And later, in the terrible scene of "Protracted Death", almost the only sound is the splashing of the fountain's water, which runs forth crimson-red.

This is the kind of device which Phillips could never have imagined. In *Hassan*, we are bound to recognise the presence of an author of true talent, one whose poetically dramatic style and vision were far more intimately adjusted to the contemporary dream than any of his predecessor's biblical, classical and renaissance wanderings.

Less easy is it, however, to guess what he might have accomplished had he not died miserably of tuberculosis at an early age, in 1915. His only other play was *Don Juan* (1925), but this he had completed, in 1911, before applying himself to the composition of *Hassan*. Were that all, we could, of course, treat it as an apprentice effort and thus disregard it: the trouble is that, after *Hassan* had been completed, he not only devoted himself to a revision of the earlier script but expressed his own admiring surprise at the "excellency" of much in the original text. It must be assumed, therefore, that if he had lived his writings for the stage would have resembled *Don Juan* rather than *Hassan*, and should we decide that such an assumption is justified we may well wonder whether he was likely to build any sure foundation for a modern poetic drama. To a friend he wrote:

I shall portray Don Juan utterly disappointed in his grande passion seeking refuge from sickly and decadent despair first in the world and in the passion for humanity and justice, then questioning religion, then ordinary morality until finally he becomes an utter sadist. Then comes the statue which is the miracle, to make him doubt reason itself.

This suggests a disappointingly intellectualist approach (Flecker himself declared that his "conception will be modern"), but, even so, it hardly agrees with or explains the strange farrago of diverse elements which are jumbled into his text – Don Juan wrecked on a Welsh coast, swimming to safety in the company of Owen Jones, being rescued by a fisher-girl named Tisbea, tramping the roads until he arrives, *mirabile dictu*, at Gloucester where he protects a wretched blackleg from an irate mob of trade-unionists, debating in the street with a socialist labour leader, becoming engaged to the daughter of a conservative prime minister, finally shooting both that gentleman and his fiancée's sister. It is hardly probable that such a confused and confusing work could ever have come on any stage, large or small.

The welcome given to *Hassan* does not stand alone. These were the years, for example, when Gilbert Murray enjoyed his greatest popularity, not only among countless readers but among playgoers as well. His *Andromache*, a not very successful attempt to deal with a Greek theme in modern style, did not attract much praise when it was presented at the Garrick in 1901, but his translations from Euripides were still to come. In 1904 *Hippolytus* was given at the Lyric, and several other Euripidean dramas were included in the Granville-Barker–Vedrenne seasons at the Court; it was his version of Sophocles' *Oedipus Rex*, directed by Max Reinhardt, which Martin-Harvey impressively presented at Covent Garden in 1912.

Twelve years later, in 1924, Covent Garden saw a production of still another of Gilbert Murray's translations, that of Euripides' *Alcestis*, with music composed by Rutland Boughton. *Alcestis* had had its first performance at Glastonbury in 1922, and this was the year when the words of Fiona Macleod and Boughton's music in Barry Jackson's production of *The Immortal Hour* not only attracted thousands of spectators to the Regent Theatre but even magnetised many of them into making a habit of attendance at numerous successive performances. Here audiences gladly submitted themselves to the magical fascination of Celtic myth – but discussion of this realm of Celtic myth must be left aside for the moment since it requires to be placed within a larger framework which carries us away from the London theatres into the furthest reaches of the minority drama. We may, however, place alongside the dramas of Phillips, Flecker and Fiona Macleod a limited number of others which came and went on the stage. There was, for example, J. B. Fagan's rather bombastic blank-verse religious play, *The Prayer of the Sword*, which appeared at the Adelphi in 1904, followed a couple of years later by Rudolf Besier's reasonably effective *The Virgin Goddess* and J. Comyns Carr's *Tristram and Iseult*, a piece not un-stageworthy, but with verse dialogue which, in its excitement, frequently loses its breath:[1] in 1910 Josephine Peabody's *The Piper* was presented both at Stratford-upon-Avon and at the St James's: a decade later Clemence Dane cast part of her *Will Shakespeare* in verse form: and in 1927 the posthumous printing of *Three Plays* by William Archer surprised most readers because it demonstrated how even the most confirmed Ibsenite of the age – and the author of the uncompromisingly "modern" *Old Drama and the New* (1923) – had been sufficiently influenced by the spirit of the age to toy with blank-verse scenes.[2]

Such a background of endeavour and interest must be fully appreciated even although nearly all the scores of poetic dramas are of small value, although most of their authors clearly had no expectancy of seeing their dramas put upon the stage, and although many of them unadventuresomely pursued the paths taken by the nineteenth-century closet playwrights, dealing with hackneyed themes secular and religious, medieval, renaissance, exotic and occasionally classical. Numbers of these writings were the only plays attempted by their authors, such as Sir Oliver Lodge's *The Labyrinth* (1911), Gertrude Leigh's *Tasso and Eleonora* (1912), Frederic Harrison's *Nicephorus* (1906), C. W. Hay-

[1] Alice Comyns Carr has an interesting biographical account of her husband's literary career (1920).

[2] See p. 200.

ward's *Anthony* (*The Philosopher*) (1910), and James Barton's *Denys of Auxerre* (1912): the majority were composed in uninspired verbose blank-verse – of which a few lines from Hayward's drama may be taken as a fair specimen –

> Oh, brave, true heart! methinks that these assaults
> Which they do futile make, do but recoil
> On their own heads, and sap their boasted strength,
> That freedom sooner come than we did hope.

Some other writers were more persistent in their dramatic efforts, composing numerous long and short poetic pieces and occasionally having these published in collections – for example, Arthur Symons' *Tragedies* (1916), Adolphus Jack's *Four Plays* (written from 1908 onwards, printed separately and collected in 1935), W. L. Courtney's *Dramas and Diversions* (1908) and Mabel Dearmer's *Three Plays* (1916). In dozens of these dramas the influence of Stephen Phillips is manifest. Adolphus Jack's *The Prince* and *Mathilde*, for example, take renaissance Italy as their setting, while *The Angry Heart* deals with a tale from the Icelandic sagas transferred to Scotland; and, although the author suggests in his preface how he had sought to develop and improve his dramatic style, they all follow the same old pattern. We know immediately in what milieu we are set when we read (in *The Prince*)

> ACT I
>
> SCENE I
>
> CORRIDOR IN THE PALACE OF SALUZZO
>
> *Enter two doctors, one from a room within, closing the door behind him, the other approaching to meet him.*
>
> 1ST DOCTOR. The Prince sleeps sound?
> 2ND DOCTOR. This moment fallen asleep,
> And in the embraces of the drowsy night
> Lies like a play-tired child, which good sleep past,
> We sage physicians are dismissed with thanks
> And courtly tributes to our saving art
> Where art was none but Nature's –

or (in *The Angry Heart*)

ACT I

SCENE I

THE NORTH-WEST COAST OF SCOTLAND

Gertrude and Kenneth sitting on the hillside by the sea.

GERTRUDE. The waves, how wearisome a lutany
To ears not glad, or jaundiced with some sorrow,
In their dead repetition would they now
Be ever sighing!

This Phillipsian influence was frequently associated, too, with the patent impress of the widespread "morality" style. Thus Antonia R. Williams' "New Telling" of *Isolt* (1915) identifies the characters with rather complex personified qualities such as "Human Fear and Sorrow" or "Fear of True Values, embodied in Cheap Success". More common was the simpler style adopted by Lady Alix Egerton, a style obviously inspired by the old moralities, in a series of plays extending from *The Masque of the Two Strangers* (1907) to *The Were-Wolf* (1926).[1]

The seriousness of purpose inherent in the writings of Lady Alix Egerton well reflects the spirit manifested in the majority of these attempts at the poetic drama. Nearly all the authors, even the least ambitious, were animated by the hope that they might, in however humble a manner, aid the cause of the verse play – although, in making such a general assertion, it is necessary to add that on occasion we are confronted by curious puzzles. What strange motive, we well may ask, induced a distinguished writer such as John Middleton Murry to spend effort and time in composing his feebly absurd blank-verse satire of contemporary life and

[1] One of the most extraordinary performances within this period must have been the presentation of *The Masque of the Two Strangers* at Stafford House, with the characters interpreted by a roster of the theatrically great and distinguished, including Italia Conti, Lily Brayton, Harcourt Williams, Matheson Lang and Henry Ainley. No doubt this must be regarded as a very special occasion; but it seems likely that a fair number of these poetic plays had at least dramatic readings in the drawing-rooms of friendly mansions. We know, for instance, that B. L. Bowhay's *As Hand with Hand* was so presented under the auspices of the Poetry Society at Mitford House on November 27, 1928.

politics called *Cinnamon and Angelica*? What peculiar and eccentric force exerted its power on the mind of the obscure Walter Broadsworde, urging him to compose his five-act drama, *Junius Brutus*, the text of which clearly indicates that he had hardly any dramatic sense, that he was insensitive to verse rhythms and that even his knowledge of grammar was deficient? This play starts thus:

KING: Nay, tell me Brutus is not this the day
That keeps the service of Lemuria?
BRUTUS: Aye. Let he that hath a conscience answer it,
Before hobgoblins of the netherworld
Make answer for him –

and jerkily the characters lead us on through speeches such as Valerius' soliloquy:

This disaffected document is mine;
It is most damning. The captain I despatched,
To seize the palace round, I hope has won,
I told him to bring, drive or carry them
(*Noise outside.*)
To the forum. There he goes along!
And judging by the great dishevellment
He is the victor; Mars be praised.
I will along a nearer way than he
To reach the forum. On the way
I will despatch a feathered messenger
To both the praetors. O, Brutus,
That I of all the Romans should do this
That brings the most discredit to your gens.
The gods deal gently with his progeny
So lately fleshed in manhood, now a villain!
O Jupiter! It is not! Yet look here!
The superscription of that noble gens;
Cozened by a promise made by Tarquin's self
To give his daughter's hand in marriage vow.
O heinous and most prostitute of words,
To lead such green and suple youth to death
That held the earth a pupil to his virtue;
Set honour her instruction; shew the gods
Their duty; and be tutor of the world,

That would breed yellow jealousy among them.
O Brutus! what shall Rome require of thee
That hast already had thy soul before?

Efforts such as these may, of course, be completely ignored, but it is necessary to observe that, even when pieces of this calibre are set aside, much still remains; and we must endeavour to get at least a general picture of what so many zealous writers were anxiously, although rarely successfully, seeking to achieve.

Sometimes novel experiments in style are to be encountered in this realm, such as Elizabeth Hall's utilisation of rimed couplets for her *Revolt of Siena* (1927) or Robert Vansittart's attractive although untheatrical design for his verse comedy, *Foolery* (1912), but in general a stroll through these poetic bowers is apt to bring disappointment only. We can say that W. L. Courtney's *Bridals of Blood* (1908), set in the time of Catherine de' Medici, has some vitality in its characters and occasional felicities in its dialogue – without, however, being able to go further and claim it as a truly effective drama. Mabel Dearmer displays some originality in her treatment of *Don Quixote* (1916) as both completely mad and yet, in this evil world, as eminently sane: nevertheless, her play has but slight value. In *Eugene* (1928) Campbell Fletcher takes us to Palermo about the year 1500, introduces us to his hero, a "Vagrant Poet", iconoclastic and revolutionary, shows him stimulating an insurrection and finally ending in destruction when his love for the daughter of a rich merchant conflicts with his political ideals – a plot by no means uninteresting, told in a blank-verse dialogue which at times has real vigour, but somehow leaving us in the end unimpressed. What seems most peculiar is that even authors possessed of liveliness and skill often became men completely changed when they turned to the dramatic form. There are, for instance, numerous readers who have gained pleasure from perusals of Maurice Baring's untheatrical *Diminutive Dramas* (1911)[1] and these readers might well have expected

[1] These brief skits were originally contributed to *The Morning Post*. Dame Ethel Smyth has a biographical–critical study of this author (1938).

to discover kindred qualities in his fairly extensive dramatic writings. "Might well have expected" is the operative phrase, since any such expectations must certainly vanish in the midst of puzzled disappointment. *Mahasena* (1905), set in an imaginary "Island of Lanke", dully puts before us a hero who, in an entirely unoriginal manner, boringly preaches peace and mercy; equally boring is the tale of *Desiderio* (1906), a tramp whom an ambitious Cardinal and Count, after they have assassinated their king, put upon the throne for their own political purposes. Nor is there any greater virtue in Baring's prose, or poetic-prose, plays which he wrote after these sad and sorrowful early pieces: when an author can pen speeches such as

> I once asked her to do something for me. When I was young and struggling to find an opening, I asked her to get her husband to send an article of mine to the editor of *The Coming Age*, who was a great friend of his. She said her husband would certainly have done so if he had considered the article good enough to recommend, but that he was too busy during the next three months to read it. She was sure I would understand –

it seems clear that he has no right to be toying with drama. And when we glance at the unplanned mixture of prose and verse in *Manfroy Duke of Athens* (1923) we realise, with bitter regret, that this was what the poetic play had come to – a sorry thing of shreds and patches exhibiting neither dramatic interest nor effective dialogue.[1]

Here there is only dulness, but sometimes the dulness, in its parrotry of old-fashioned absurdities, can prove unconsciously amusing. W. G. Hole's *Queen Elizabeth* (revised in 1928 from a play published in 1904) thus begins:

> See, here we stand, six proper men and bold,
> A-tremble lest her Grace's farthingale
> Should rustle in the passage ere arrives
> Our spokesman, Burleigh.

[1] "Pleasant to Know Mr Baring" is the heading given by Frank Swinnerton to his review of Paul Horgon's anthology, *Maurice Baring Restored* (1970) (*The Sunday Times*, September 20, 1970) – but this heading could hardly have been made to apply to these "poetic" dramas.

Harrison's *Nicephorus* descends to even further depth.[1] This Byzantine "tragedy" starts with the entry of Lord Sisinnios and Lord Theophylact, and it would be a pity if we were to refrain from eavesdropping on their conversation:

SISINNIOS. Hail, Lord Theophylact! How fares his Grace?
THEOPHYLACT. Illustrious Senator! Our gracious Sovereign,
Born-i'-the-Purple, draws to his end, we fear,
In the Porphyry Chamber – where his life began!
SISINNIOS. And his gay and gallant heir, the Prince Romanus?
(THEOPHYLACT *draws the Senator aside.*)
THEOPHYLACT. Gallant and gay! – still cares for naught on earth
Save sport and revels –
SISINNIOS (*aside to* THEOPHYLACT). Ah! all this bodes ill!
THEOPHYLACT. Hush! hush! my Lord – the days seem darkening round us,
Big with the fate of this Imperial House!

Thus could a not undistinguished author plunge downward into dramatic bathos – and in his crashing descent thus he could be accompanied by a fairly well-known poet, John Davidson.[2] In the preceding century Davidson had made a certain name for himself partly because of the quality of his verse style and partly because of his attacks on Christian virtues, chastity in particular; and now in this later period he launched forth with his long, confused, bombastic "tragic play of Church and State", *The Theatrocrat* (1905). The introduction to this drama, evidently penned by an admiring friend, declares that it and Davidson's other dramas are "the likeliest poetical plays written for the English stage in these times" – a judgment which must be deemed truly extraordinary, indeed almost incredible, when

[1] See above p. 292.

[2] The esteem with which this writer is regarded in some quarters is indicated by the various critical studies devoted to his work – particularly H. Fineman's *John Davidson: A Study of the Relations of his Ideas to his Poetry* (1916); Gertrud von Petzold, *John Davidson und sein geistiges Werden unter den Einfluss Nietzsches* (1928); Robert D. Macleod, *John Davidson: A Study in Personality* (1957); and James B. Townsend, *John Davidson, Poet of Armageddon* (1961).

we turn to almost any page of his dialogue. What characters are speaking hardly matters at all, and blank dashes may stand for the immaterial names:

—: This makes my whole life horrible.
—: Most lives
Confronting this, will shrivel into dust.
—: I've never lived.
—: That is, you've never thought,
Never imagined.
—: Never! A phantom life,
The actor's; a spell-bound drudgery chained
And eyeless. What a ruthless tyrant public
Opinion is – an armed automaton
That fells its victims blindly! Entertain
A motley audience for a livelihood
You never make; be this, be that – a fop,
A fool, a hero, or a villain; lose
Conceit of everything except applause;
Be certain of success when self-contempt
Assures you that you play a popular part;
Be courteous to the bully, bland with fools –
The dreadful folk that haunt celebrities,
That haunt theatrical celebrities –

but nothing can be gained by proceeding further with such minority drama balderdash.

As has been suggested above, most of these verse plays were the work of individual poets (if poets they may be called) working alone, and most of them in style followed the impoverished rhythms of nineteenth-century blank verse. Occasionally, however, we catch glimpses of small "schools" of like-minded authors with kindred aims. One such carries us back to the world of Celtic myth to which passing reference has already been made.[1] In 1905 the small Coronet Theatre saw the presentation of a "Celtic music drama", *Gwenevere*, written by Ernest Rhys, with music by Vincent Thomas; three years later came the publication of the poetic drama *Lanval*, composed by "T. E. Ellis" (Baron Howard de Walden); and these two works may be taken as introduc-

[1] See pp. 291–2.

ing a movement which sought to exploit Arthurian themes and to popularise verse plays by associating the "poetry" with music. Not always were the two endeavours interconnected: as in *Lanval*, the Arthurian characters sometimes appeared within a framework wholly innocent of musical accompaniment; sometimes, as in R. C. Trevelyan's *The Bride of Dionysus* (1912) a "music-drama" might deal with themes other than Arthurian – yet even so there is a strong bond between these two endeavours, a bond which Rutland Boughton strove to forge into more powerful links at his Glastonbury Festival.[1] There, appeared Reginald Buckley's *The Round Table* (1916) and *The Birth of Arthur* (1925): neither of these, however, would seem to have aroused more than a faint ripple of interest: the only considerable success inspired by Boughton's experiments came when Fiona MacLeod's Celtically-mystical *Immortal Hour* won its brief hour of fame.[2] Divers other composers and poets attached themselves in various ways to this movement. Already in 1906 Dame Ethel Smyth had taken H. B. Brewster's "Cornish drama", *The Wreckers*, as a subject for music,[3] and during the twenties there was a very definite flutter of interest in works of a similar kind: W. H. Davies' "tramp's opera", *True Travellers*, was printed in 1923; the following year came a production of *Hugh the Drover*, by H. H. Child, with music by R. Vaughan Williams; in 1928 the Old Vic performed Clemence Dane's "music play", *Adam's Opera* – the music composed by R. Addinsell. The forces combining at this time to promote works of such a kind are clearly exemplified in the association between Sir John Martin-Harvey, Laurence Binyon and Sir Edward Elgar, which

[1] On the Glastonbury activities see Rutland Boughton's own contribution to *Somerset and the Drama* (1922), edited by S. R. Littlewood.

[2] This play was originally published in 1900, and fourteen years later the musical version was performed at Glastonbury. The strange double career of its author, under his own name and under his feminine pseudonym, is well-known. *The Immortal Hour* and *The House of Usna* (also published in 1900) had been planned as part of a series to be called "The Theatre of the Soul" or "The Psychic Drama".

[3] Originally this was presented at Leipzig in 1906; its English première was at His Majesty's three years later.

resulted in the production of a "tragedy", *Arthur*, at the Royal Victoria Hall in 1923.

At Glastonbury Rutland Boughton had sought, perhaps not with very great success, to establish what might almost be called a poetic community. This attempt was the solitary effort of its kind during the first three decades of the century, but naturally there are several examples of loose associations of minority dramatists drawn together by personal friendships and kindred interests. One such stemmed from the influence of W. B. Yeats – but this unfortunately proved itself to become negatively anti-theatrical. Of course, Yeats was absolutely correct in his realisation that the old blank-verse tradition had lost its validity and that there was little or no hope of its possible resuscitation: he was absolutely correct, too, in searching round for some fresh source of inspiration. Unfortunately, however, his cultivation of the Japanese Nō drama must be thought to have been misconceived and inexpedient. The Nō drama in itself is certainly one of the most interesting developments in the entire history of the theatre, but it was always an "aristocratic" form, enshrined within the limitations of its own period and milieu. Even in Japan today, although rightly it is preserved as a precious record of the past, it lacks direct inspiring power, and, even if it were to have had any inspiring power, that would have had to depend upon what might well be styled theatrical antiquarianism – a working within its own peculiar stage structure and its highly conventional histrionic traditions. For the individual poet who, like Yeats, felt a revulsion towards the ordinary audience it may possess some attraction and value: for the creative theatre it has neither.

The effect of Yeats' influence is well illustrated in the career of Gordon Bottomley. This romantic poet, gifted with vivid imagination and delight in evocative words, had always been interested in the drama, and at the start it seems evident that he had hopes that at least some of his writings might appear on repertory stages. Even then, however, he failed to take sufficiently into account the sensibilities and interests of possible spectators no matter how few in number and how élite. *King Lear's Wife* (1915), for example, may properly be deemed one of the most inventive plays written at this time, yet it is obvious that, in penning its final episode – the laying-out of the queen's body for burial – Bottomley either banished from his mind the very thought of a theatrical public, or else sought to give such a public a most disagreeable (and dramatically self-defeating) experience.[1] And very similar comments may be made concerning lines and episodes in all these dramatic writings – the primitively Icelandic *Riding to Lithend* (1909), the esoteric *Midsummer Eve* (1905), even the later, and interestingly novel, *Gruach* and *Britain's Daughter* (both 1921). All these works must be regarded as too grim, too lacking in variety, often too allusive, to make a strongly favourable appeal even to dedicated repertory playgoers. Yet, in so far as they were considering at least some kind of a theatrical audience, dreaming of actors enunciating their lines, they were clearly moving in the right direction. During the twenties, however, Bottomley permitted himself to come ever more and more under the influence of Yeats, and by 1929 he was deliberately writing his *Scenes and Plays* as "chamber drama", completely abandoning thought of the playhouse, substituting for it a vague concept of any "room large enough for a gathering place", and, in so far as possible performers were concerned, thinking of no more than obscure amateur groups who found choric speaking, because of its comparative novelty, an attractive exercise. Unquestionably the individual playlets in this collection, such as *Towie Castle*, *Ardvorlich's Wife* and (particularly) *The Singing Sands*, are interesting experiments; they show unquestionably a maturing and deepening poetic power: but they have abandoned the theatre.[2]

[1] On this see above p. 12.

[2] In various comments on the contemporary drama, Bottomley argued that, since the theatre had become wholly "realistic", the only hope for a revival of poetic quality on the stage rested in, so to say, "training" an audience to welcome verse dialogue: and this, he averred, was precisely what he aimed to do in writing these choric plays for amateur performance. In considering these remarks, however, it is essential to observe how eagerly the general public welcomed the several attempts, from those of Stephen Phillips onwards, which were made by West End

Much of the same trend towards increasing exclusiveness can be traced in the work of Bottomley's friend, Lascelles Abercrombie, a writer who stylistically made very considerable contributions towards the establishment of a new theatrically viable verse form.[1] Although it cannot be said that his particular kind of exclusiveness derived from the influence of Yeats, or that he moved from the repertory stage to the drawing-room, or that he cast aside thoughts of scenery in favour of Japanese screens and the ritualistic unfolding of curtains, spiritually at least he gained support for his uncompromising stand from the example of the Irish poet. He did hope for repertory, or at least for society, production of his writings, and this indeed he secured for the four short plays which he published in 1922 and for his longer *Phoenix* (1923), yet he was not prepared to make any concessions: an audience, no matter how hand-picked, does not consist of a lecture-hall assemblage prepared to listen to a logically-conceived argument, and only too often Abercrombie was inclined to preach a peculiar kind of sermon and to express that sermon in a form unlikely to appeal in a theatre. This trend in his writing has been well examined by Martin Ellehauge,[2] who rightly observes that the poet is constantly concerned with the question of "what distinguishes man from the animal" and that this questioning leads him to conclude "that it is chiefly sin which is the mark of humanity". *The Adder* thus becomes a "hymn to the glory of sin", and *The End of the World* presents its potent "metaphor" illustrating the warped and stunted nature of the sinless life:

> My good life!...
> A caterpillar munching a cabbage-heart,
> Always drudging further and further from

managements to present poetic plays. The fact that most of these were soon forgotten is to be explained not by indifference on the part of the audience, but by the dramatic weakness of the authors.

[1] See Oliver Elton, *Lascelles Abercrombie, 1881–1938* (1939) for intimate comments on the quality of this poetic style. J. Cooper has a *Bibliography and Notes on the Works of Lascelles Abercrombie* (1968).

[2] *Striking Figures among Modern English Dramatists* (1931), pp. 89–99.

The sounds and lights of the world, never abroad
Nor flying free in warmth and air sweet-smelling:
A crawling caterpillar, eating his life
In a deaf dark – that's my gain of goodness!

The combination of "abstract thought and imaginative poetry", Ellehauge further observes, is associated with a combination of "beautiful and ugly elements" in the imagery. Thus, "the beautiful and the ugly amalgamate in a fisherwoman's imagination when she describes the plague which is raging in *Deborah*":

But I within me
Can see the thing, a ghost as grey as rain,
Fleeces of shadowy air wrapping his shape,
Tall as the winds, standing up over us,
Smiling and idly bandying with his feet
This way and that the writhing bodies like
A man turns rats that have taken the bane he laid.

All of this is difficult for an audience to accept, and, even although there is more of a directly-appreciable dramatic quality in *Phoenix*, the theme of that play too is somewhat difficult to follow as the lines come flowing from actors' mouths. No doubt there is significance in the fact that Abercrombie's last play was designated a "dramatic poem", intended only for readers.

In his notes to *Scenes and Plays* Bottomley makes reference to two other poets, T. Sturge Moore and John Masefield; and the close association between these three authors and W. B. Yeats is underlined in a comment made by Moore – a formal note in his *Tragic Mothers* (1920) acknowledges that his dramatic efforts were inspired and encouraged by what had been accomplished by the Irish poet – and by the fact that the first among the three short dramas printed in that volume, *Medea*, was performed at Masefield's Oxford home, with Bottomley seated in the select group of spectators. "My friend Mr. W. B. Yeats", wrote Moore, "asked me to try my hand, having himself achieved brilliant success, in this new form of drama, independent of stage and scenery and suitable for chamber presentation. The idea had come to him while reading about the Japanese Noh plays." When we encounter the first words in *Medea*:

Enter one bearing a folded curtain. He bows to the assembly and then addresses them:

> You doubt of ghost and angel god and jinn,
> You think those bodied like you, the sole speakers
> Who put a show of wisdom into words
> Here on this planet piebald with pale seas.
> But those less hood-winked with to-day, still hear
> Voices in chancelled wood and panelled room;
> Since thought can run too long on such smooth rails,
> I ask your minds to shake off their stale faith
> That things are always merely what they seem –

we know precisely where we are: we are in the company of a few choice souls invited to listen for an hour or so to the precious words of a poet intoxicated with Japan and we are almost certain that at no moment in the course of this recitation will there be any genuinely dramatic experience. And if this is true of *Medea*, *Niobe* goes even further in anti-theatricalism by being composed as "*a drama for three voices overheard behind screen or curtain*". An undated manuscript note by Rutland Boughton on the flyleaf of his own copy of *Tragic Mothers* stresses his belief that "the later works of Yeats and Sturge Moore" are "another sign of the growth of a real music-drama", but a bracketed addition to this note, reading "(also Binns)", suggests how potentially destructive of the stage this whole movement was. "Binns" presumably was H. B. Binns, and Boughton was thinking of that author's insignificant *The Adventure* (1911), described as "a romantic variation on a Homeric theme": only a minority enthusiast could so have lost his critical sense as to permit him to see in such a piece anything of slightest theatrical worth.

During these years another poet was active, and without doubt this author's contribution to the stage was of considerably greater significance: yet when John Masefield's numerous writings are examined against the background of the minority drama as a whole three qualifications become evident: first, the truly extraordinary diversity to be found here in theme, character and style seems to show that he himself did not have any clear inner sense of what course he ought to take; secondly, although in several of his plays he displayed some innate originality, only too often he followed the lead of this author or of that, so that his stage writings as a whole might be regarded as an epitome of almost all the current contemporary trends; and, thirdly, even when the quality of *The Tragedy of Nan* (1908) is freely acknowledged, it must be admitted that its author had but little of true worth to offer to the drama as a whole.[1]

At the very start of his dramatic career he obviously was deeply influenced by the Irish plays – although fortunately not the exclusive style of Yeats, but rather that cultivated by Lady Gregory. The playlet called *The Sweeps of '98* (not acted or published until 1916, but written in 1906) openly displays its indebtedness to the work of that authoress and to her it owes its unquestioned effectiveness. During the same year, too, Masefield composed the play by which he is best known, *The Tragedy of Nan*, and it can hardly be doubted that he was inspired in this drama to do for his native Gloucestershire–Herefordshire speech what had been achieved for the speech of the Irish peasantry by the early members of the Irish Literary Society. In comparing these dramas, however, we cannot escape realisation of the advantages possessed by Lady Gregory, Synge and their companions but denied to him: in the rustic dialects which they utilised for their dialogue there was a combination of vigour, effective strength and beauty, whereas quite clearly Masefield was often working against rather than with the utterance of the countryside which he had selected as the scene of the plot: while the characteristic Irish inflections and turns of phrase (even when, as in the plays of some

[1] W. H. Hamilton (1922) and C. Biggane (1924) have serviceable surveys of Masefield's career and poetic style: a bibliography of his writings has been compiled by I. A. Williams (1921).

authors, they appear to suffer from inordinate repetition) generally give an impression of reality, by no means the same comment may be made concerning the words which Masefield puts into the mouth of his old Gaffer. *The Tragedy of Nan* was a notable early twentieth-century play, yet it has about it an atmosphere of artificiality.

Even at the time when the poet was thus under the spell of the early Irish dramas the dark world of the northern sagas began to influence him as they had influenced Bottomley, but neither *The Locked Chest* (written in 1906, published ten years later) nor *The Witch*, a version of a Norwegian drama by Hans Wiers-Jenssen, can be accorded any great praise; nor can two other plays dealing with peasant passions in the Gloucestershire countryside – *The Campden Wonder* (1907) and *Mrs Harrison* (printed in 1909 but written some time earlier) – be thought to possess the quality exhibited in *The Tragedy of Nan*.

What may be described as Masefield's artistic restiveness was to be exemplified a few years later by his turning, in *Pompey the Great* (1910), to classical subject-matter and, in *Philip the King* (1914), to early Spanish – both plays memorable for a few impressive passages but neither consistently effective. The current interest in the Japanese stage then captured him, as it had captured so many others, and *The Faithful* (1915) was the result. Next came the biblical phase, expressed in *Good Friday* (1916) and, much later, in *A King's Daughter* (1923), *The Trial of Jesus* (1925) and *The Coming of Christ* (1928) – a phase oddly intermingled with a sudden interest in Racine, which inspired him to prepare his own versions of *Esther* and *Berenice* (1921). In the midst of these plays *Melloney Holtspur, or The Pangs of Love* (1922) may appear to be a strange aberration, but when the structure of the play and its theme are carefully considered in association with a number of not dissimilar fantastic contemporary dramas we again get the impression that Masefield was still groping vainly for a style which might suit his purposes. The technical device of overlapping scenes set in present and in past, the "philosophic" treatment of sin and redemption, the analysis of an artist's soul, and the pervading atmosphere of the supernatural – all of these can be found elsewhere in the writings of other contemporary playwrights, and it cannot honestly be averred that Masefield's handling of such matters is superior to that of his companions.

For some extraordinary and inexplicable reason this *Melloney Holtspur* was dedicated to Gordon Craig, although no apparent spiritual or artistic kinship exists between the play and its recipient – but Masefield's movement from influence to influence was by no means done: *Tristan and Isolt* (1927) showed him captured by Celtic magic, while *Easter* (1929), described as a "play for singers", carried him to its centre in Glastonbury.

In viewing his work as a whole, we may perhaps discern the chief obstacle to his success as a dramatist arising from the peculiar uncertainty he displayed concerning the form or forms which might best be suited to his talents, an uncertainty which kept him constantly drifting from one object of admiration to another and which no doubt was also responsible for his puzzling experiments with varying styles which offered little or nothing either to him as an individual poetic dramatist or to the English stage in general. Apart from this incertitude and from a resultant vacillation, however, there was something else which prevented him from contributing more to the stage: whenever he took pen in hand to compose a theatrical scene, we get the impression that no hint of a smile softened his face; always his thoughts were rather monotonously grim, and in our imagination we see him with eyes staring darkly at the paper on his desk.

Much the same sort of undeviating grimness enveloped nearly all the work of another aspiring poet, Wilfred Gibson, who, although never attaining anything that approached the reputation of Masefield, was esteemed in certain "literary" circles. In the series of short plays which he called *Stonefolds* (1907), he dealt mainly with the stark bitter life of men who spent most of their time braving the elements as they tended their flocks – shepherds old and young who are made to speak in a peculiarly jerky, unflowing blank-verse measure –

> I did not wake till you had gone this morn.
> I must have slumbered soundly, though I slept
> But little in the night. I could not sleep.
> I lay awake, and watched the dark hours pass.

Gradually, however, he moved away from such themes into the still darker world of industrialism. The collection called *Daily Bread* (1910) contained plays, such as *The Furnace* and *The Night Shift*, in which workers of a different kind appeared, and these were made to express themselves in irregular, but generally short, lines which obviously brought the tone of their dialogue closer to that of prose. Gibson's importance, rightly declares Ernest Reynolds, "lies in the fact that he attempted to do for poetic drama what Stanley Houghton and the Manchester School were doing in prose – that is, to bring the life of the English workers into the theatre".[1] Interesting although this attempt may have been, however, the fact remains that neither in these two collections nor in the contents of his *Kestrel Edge and Other Plays* (1924) did his writings have any real connection with or influence upon the stage.

Verse in the theatre was something dreamed of and desired by so many: yet at the same time this verse dialogue had lost its pristine spirit and power. These two facts – and they are incontrovertible – explain why there were so many authors of the time who, as it were, divided their lives into two – spending their earlier years as ardent devotees of the poetic drama and later abandoning it almost completely. Of this group John Drinkwater may be taken as a typical representative. From 1911 to 1917 he remained consistently within a spiritual atmosphere which was youthfully romantic, yet fatalistically ironical, expressed in a verse form which, it must be admitted, in its simple unelaborated directness was much more apt for stage utterance than, let us say, the more distinguished but often "difficult" poetic form employed

[1] *Modern English Drama* (1949), p. 83.

by Lascelles Abercrombie. There was, too, in his writings a corresponding simplicity. In reading the latter's *Phoenix*, for example, we find ourselves in a milieu puzzling and at times even incredible; if we turn from this to Drinkwater's *Cophetua* (1911) we have the feeling that we have moved from a poet–professor's desk to a table and chair conveniently set close to or even on the stage: Abercrombie's theme is intricate and somewhat perplexing, Drinkwater's is simple – that of a king who, refusing to prostitute himself to a royally-arranged marriage, gives his love to the traditional beggar-maid, realising that, although she is "not dowered as a queen might be", she brings him

> a soul
> Not alien before the Lord,
> A will unbent, a purpose whole,
> A passion shining as a sword.

Rebellion (1914) may be slightly more complex, but even it, with its Blakean motto concerning the tigers of wrath, has a plot easy to interpret – a passionate queen and a revolutionary poet–insurgent as hero and heroine, both ultimately defeated yet glorified in their fervent testimony to love as life's only true value. Interestingly, the atmosphere of this play is strangely anticipatory of those youthful despairs and ecstasies with which, more than half a century later, we are so familiar. Ironically bitter anger at Man's thraldom to fate and at some men's insensitivity provides the basic theme of *The Storm* (1915), while in *The God of Quiet* (1916) and $x=0$ (1917) the ironic finger is pointed towards the uselessness and yet the apparent inevitability of war.

Taken together, these may be accepted as among the most stageworthy verse plays of the period, and it is interesting to speculate whether Drinkwater might have been able to create something still more effective in the same style after the war if $x=0$ had not been the mathematical conclusion of this section of his work as a playwright. Chance, or fate, however, led him in a different direction, and if indeed a Greek moira was responsible for urging him to take a different path, he made rich use of its bidding. Although *Abraham Lincoln* (1918) may not appear to us to be the great masterpiece which many thought it in its own time, it still remains one of the most important plays of the period – and obviously it carried its author from a relatively obscure repertory career into the world of the West End.

The dramatist who approached nearest to Drinkwater was Clifford Bax, even although there were numerous differences between them. During his earlier days the former was manager of the Birmingham Repertory Theatre: Bax had no stage affiliations, and we think of him in his youth, not as a playhouse manager, but as editor of and contributor to *Orpheus*, a privately-printed quarterly magazine described as being devoted to "mystical art". This association with *Orpheus*, however, is deceptive. *Antique Pageantry* and *Polite Satires* (1921 and 1922), the titles given to his first collections of one-act plays, effectively suggest the prevailing tone of his earliest writings for the stage – deft, light and sparkling – extending from *The Poetasters of Ispahan* and *Aucassin and Nicolette* to *The Volcanic Island* and *Square Pegs*. There is no grimness here, there are no serious reflections on life, morality and politics: throughout we are in a world of laughing pleasure, delighting gaily in verbal dexterities and not unduly disturbed by the pricks of a few satirical, but not too painful, barbs. The verbal dexterities are excellently illustrated by a magnificent compound literary pun in *The Unknown Hand* – "Squire Turner pounds on Shanks's de la Mare"; the Freudian skit in *The Volcanic Island*, with its conversation between the contrasting identities of Dorothea Wylde and Dorothy Wild, exemplifies the peculiar quality of Bax's good-humoured satire; and in *Square Pegs* the laughing delight is amply revealed when a modern girl is made to converse with a sixteenth-century Gioconda. These are, no doubt, merely poetic trifles, but not only is their light tone most welcome after the all-too-pervading gloom of the minority poetic drama as a whole, they also serve to explain Bax's later success as a dramatist possessed of reasonably wide appeal. At times he permitted the minority idea to take possession of his mind – as, for instance, in the dull *Up Stream* (1922) and the undramatic (although interesting) *Socrates* (1930); but his reputation as an author with power to attract a general audience was demonstrated in his versions of four of Goldoni's Venetian comedies, in his *Midsummer Madness* (1923) – the most delightful of all the many *commedia dell'arte* plays of the time – and in the amusing ballad opera of *Mr Pepys* (1926). Although his greatest success did not come until 1932 with his *Rose without a Thorn*, in these earlier plays he had already conjured up a welcome oasis of lyric laughter and had demonstrated in his own distinctive manner that he was an iconoclast in the realm of the seriously-minded little men.

The revolt clearly evident in Bax's writings against the prevailing "literary" style of the contemporary poetic drama was accompanied in the twenties by what might be defined as a transference of the "poetic" spirit from the verbal to the practical – a transference which at that time received philosophical explication in Halcott Glover's *Drama and Mankind* (1923). In this study the author's thesis is simple. First of all, he expresses his conviction that the realistic play no longer has any power to inspire or to excite theatrical audiences. In effect he expounds at some length what was, by a coincidence, expressed more succinctly during the same year by the editor of *The Curtain*: "Realism in the theatre has reached such a pitch that it has almost killed the art of the Drama.... Unless the present method is changed, the art of the Drama will be lost and the reason for the theatre will cease to exist."[1] Glover then proceeds to consider what might be put in the place of this outworn realistic play, and he shows himself sufficiently perceptive to acknowledge that "the blank verse drama has had its day", supporting his argument not merely by pointing out that the blank-verse measure had become old-fashioned, but also by declaring that in the past this poetic measure had belonged to a type of play written by authors who "made humanity their theme", whereas in these his own days "the theme of

[1] *The Curtain*, ii, no. 18, 1923, 62.

the modern poet is himself". Thus he is confronted by a dilemma: on the one hand, there is the conclusion that the present age "being an age of prose, prose is the proper medium for the theatre"; on the other hand, he insists that truly effective drama must itself be "poetic". And thus he reaches his final solution: prose, he agrees, must be the proper medium, but "if the prevailing prose drama is to have any value, this value must somehow derive from its share in the poetic". That, in essence, means that the "poetic" quality should, indeed must, derive not from the style of dialogue but from the choice of enriching subject-matter.

In thus arguing, Glover did not stand alone, nor was he even an innovator; yet his *Drama and Mankind* has a definite importance because it sums up what many were thinking at that time and also because he himself was intimately associated with several other minority authors. His own early plays, *Wat Tyler* and *The King's Jewry* (both published in 1921), despite the fervent expression of his high hopes for the theatre, unfortunately cannot be deemed to have much to contribute to the stage, but it is of interest to observe that he collaborated with H. F. Rubinstein in the writing of *Exodus* (1923) and that Rubinstein, responsible later for a "chronicle comedy" on the life of *Churchill* (1925), collaborated with Clifford Bax in the composition of *Shakespeare* (1921). There was much like thinking at this period, and not merely within the limits of small groups of writers. As an example of this, mention may here be made of Reginald Berkeley, an author who started by attaching himself firmly to the minority style, but who later won wide acclaim for his biographical *The Lady with a Lamp* (1929). Both he and Rubinstein, without any influence exerted by one upon the other, mingled their biographical–historical dramas with plays which concentrated, not on themes, but on buildings. Berkeley's *The White Chateau*, one of the most effective dramatic compositions of the period, was written for broadcasting in 1925, but did not appear on the stage until two years later: in 1926 Rubinstein's *The House* attempted, independently, to achieve something correspondingly novel. Berkeley's chateau was a French mansion whose fortunes he traced through successive turbulent events; Rubinstein's house was an ordinary city dwelling whose chequered career he depicted from "the present" backwards to "fifty years before".

Other dramas of kindred sorts will be cited later, but here these few examples will sufficiently indicate how much the playwrights were attracted by people of the past – Shakespeare, Churchill, Florence Nightingale – and by the buildings in which they lived and worked. Such interests were pervasive in both the minority and the general theatre, so that if we think of the play which won more applause than any other in this kind – *The Barretts of Wimpole Street* (1930) – we may not be mistaken in believing that Besier gained his wide public esteem not merely by his adroitness in choice of plot but also by his skill in selecting that most felicitous title which bound together the people and the place.

Dramatists a-plenty followed similar paths, eagerly seeking topics and characters which, in Glover's terms, might be regarded as having something of the "poetic" about them. Oliphant Down starts in the *commedia dell'arte* style with *The Maker of Dreams* (1910) and pursues it further in *Bal Masqué* (1923), pens a short, rather pretentious "'psychological' piece about a peasant couple longing for the birth of a son – *The Dream Child* (1913), and in *The Quod Wrangle* (1914) treats himself to a little mild satire when he shows a work-shy Bill Jenks listening with avidity to his friend Snippy, who, having just returned to his tenement home after a month in jail, dilates on the advantages it offers – warmth, food, and a new set of clothes: Bill, dazed and inspired by this account, is just about to go forth in an attempt to steal something, anything, when a bossy suffragette social worker greets him, compels him to have a bath and drags him off to do a spot of work. Rather more serious in her satire is Gwen John, with her cynically-titled *Plays of Innocence* (1925) and with her strange "mystery", *Mr Jardyne* (1925), equally cynical, apparently written as a personally-felt attack upon commercial theatre management (its central character is a poor playwright who dies of starvation after his scripts are returned to him and who makes a re-entry as a ghost – and the moral seems to be that no producer should turn down any drama unless he wants his stage to be spectrally haunted). Gwen John's interests are shared by a companion woman playwright, Kate O'Brien, who dedicates her *Distinguished Villa* (1926) – still another piece in which the central "character" is a house – to the "Repertory Players" who first presented this dark domestic documentary upon the stage. Chiefly at the Liverpool Playhouse Philip Johnson offered to the public a series of short plays varying in style from the preciously sentimental (*The Lovely Miracle*, 1929) to the somewhat morose (*Afternoon*, 1928). A journey throughout these 'repertory' areas is by no means unpleasant, and at times it can even prove stimulating; but it must be confessed that only rarely do we feel tempted to remain for long in the company of the playwrights who were directly or indirectly inspired by objectives akin to those set forth by Halcott Glover and that among their numerous writings it is difficult to think of any which are worthy of unqualified praise.

One might have thought that Gilbert Cannan, who had so warmly expressed his philosophic beliefs and his ardent hopes in *The Joy of the Theatre* (1913), might have been able to achieve things somewhat better, but any such anticipations must be dashed to the ground by perusal of his rather stiff dramatic writings. Among his earliest plays *Miles Dixon* (1910) shows a tramp who loves a free, untrammelled life being crushed by social circumstance, *James and John* (1911) offers a picture of a father who had been guilty of fraud being driven out of his house by his sons when, after having made expiation for his crime, he returns home, and *Mary's Wedding* (1912) deals with a "cured" alcoholic who arrives drunk at his marriage ceremony. And even when in his later efforts he turned from this gloomy picture-gallery of failures, he could find no substitute for the dismal atmosphere save sad, disillusioned and sardonically-expressed sentiment. Dark reality takes the place of broken dreams; laughter is almost completely absent; Columbine is here presented as a worn-out, toiling, despondent married woman, and Pierrot dies in the knowledge that his days of frolicking are irretrievably vanished (*Pierrot in Hospital*, 1923); another play presents two characters – a young husband, after finding out that his wife has been having an affair, comes seeking sympathy from his father, but the sole comfort that the latter can offer is that his mother had behaved in the same way, so that indeed all is *The Same Story* (1923); even the most effective of these playlets, *Everybody's Husband* (1917) shows a girl on the night before her wedding, afraid of losing her dreams, almost eloping with a Domino who enters her room by the window, and being checked in her romantic desire only when the spirit of her great-grandmother appears to snatch off his mask, revealing thus "*a perfect type of Victorian husband standing with his legs straddled and his arms under his coat-tails*"; in *The Fat Kine and the Lean* (1923) a Fat Man and a Fat Woman are denied entry at Heaven's gate because they had committed no sins – a kind of echo of Abercrombie's philosophy.

This last play has as its setting the threshold of the other world, and it calls to mind that fourteen years earlier Lord Dunsany's *The Glittering Gate* (1909) had shown two deceased burglars confronted by a great, massive portal, forcing its lock, gleefully and expectantly pushing it open, and in dazed dismay staring out at complete emptiness. Long before Cannan's work the sardonic mood was thus being exploited, although for the most part Dunsany, consciously avoiding the realistic, preferred to associate it with themes mysterious and often strangely cruel.[1] Sometimes he succeeded in making these themes appear to be sincerely felt, but often they give an impression of false, because forced, theatricality – which may perhaps be considered somewhat peculiar in view of his frequently-quoted statement, "I know nothing about the theatre: I never see my own plays."

[1] E. H. Bierstadt has a study of *Dunsany the Dramatist* (1917; new edition, 1920).

The title of his "tragedy", *The Laughter of the Gods* (1917), expresses succinctly his favourite attitude: just as his first playlet closed amid the sound of ironic celestial merriment, so this tale of a city which endeavours to cheat the divine power ends as we hear peals of "demoniac", sarcastic laughter. *The Golden Doom* (1912), set in Babylon, shows Man's pitiable folly in trying to penetrate the secrets of space and the stars. In the tense *A Night at an Inn* (1916) "a hideous Idol" from the East gropes its way blindly, but inexorably, until it wreaks its terrible vengeance on the men who had stolen its ruby eye. "I did not forsee it", are the last words spoken by The Toff, chief of the depredators, as he, the last of his gang, is forced to go out to meet his doom. In an ancient Egyptian setting, *The Queen's Enemies* (1916) grimly tells the story of a predecessor of Cleopatra who destroys her opponents even although they were confidently certain that they had taken all precautions for their own safety and for her discomfiture. In *The Tents of the Arabs* (1914), at some "uncertain time" a King goes in disguise to the desert, falls in love with a girl he meets there, and allows a humble camel-driver who is almost his double to assume his place on the throne. Even Dunsany's *Seven Modern Comedies* (1929) are invested with the same atmosphere: in *The Raffle* held in aid of church funds it is a vicar's soul which unexpectedly becomes the prize for which tickets are being sold and bought; a father puts his daughter in the bedroom of *His Sainted Grandmother*, hoping that the girl, rather "modern" in some of her attitudes and concepts, will be influenced by the spirit of that devout lady's pious morality, but when her ghost materialises the grandmother turns out to be a gay old thing, most unbecomingly advanced in her views; in *The Jest of Hahalaba* Sir Arthur Strangways engages an Alchemist to call up "the Spirit of Laughter", is offered a boon, asks to see next year's *Times*, hoping, of course, thereby to make a fortune from the knowledge he will thus acquire – and instead reads his own obituary. This last theme, in an altered form, gave Dunsany the plot for the only play, *If* (1921), which brought him a measure of general public success, and, since it did attract public audiences it is perhaps worthy of notice that in its scenes the ironic tone is muted and subdued. Here too, a man, John Beal, is offered a boon – the only essential difference being that, whereas Strangways had asked to penetrate into the future, Beal more modestly asks to be permitted to go backwards in time for ten years so that he might catch a train which once he had missed. The boon is granted. In the carriage which he enters he meets a girl who, asking for his help, leads him onwards from the even tenor of his humdrum suburban life into a world of oriental adventure. At the end he suddenly wakes up to find it had all been but a dream – or was it? The ironic laughter is gentle here – at the close of the final scene the magician Ali "throws his head up and laughs", but laughs "quite silently".

Dunsany's numerous writings have been described as "decorative drama", and this term may be given wider application by attaching it also to the works of those numerous authors who sought to deal with patterned themes which might either compensate "poetically" for their prose dialogue or else provide an excuse for its stylisation. Dunsany himself, as has been seen, tended to remain within the sphere of the mysterious, and especially within that of the mysterious orient, generally seen in the light of ancient days or of uncertain time: others travelled back into divers historical periods, explored the biblical narratives, dealt with the lives of poets English and foreign, allowed themselves to dream further of Pierrot and Columbine, made strange journeys into worlds of fantasy. Already, of course, within the range of Laurence Housman's dramatic compositions almost all these various trends have been seen exploited, and all through this period numerous quite distinct contributions to the general trend were made by other minority authors belonging both to greater and to lesser literary circles. George Moore applied his polished style, although not with any marked success, to plays as different as *The Apostle* (1911), an essay in literary dialogue which shows Christ killed by a blow delivered by Paul, and *The*

Coming of Gabrielle (1920), a rather garrulous comedy concerning a famous dramatist, his secretary and the complications of their life in Vienna. India entered this sphere with Rabindranath Tagore's short pieces penned in his special brand of poetic prose, and, in a different way, with Edward Thompson's *Krishna Kumari* (1924), set in the early nineteenth century, and *Atonement* (1924), "a play of modern India". One of Arthur Symons' plays was a version of the Sanskrit *Toy Cart* (1916); among his other works, quite characteristically, were a "morality", *The Fool of the World* (1906), a playlet dealing with *Cleopatra in Judea* (1907) and an individualistic treatment of the old Celtic story of *Tristan and Iseult* (1917).

Few of these dramatic essays are invested with any intrinsic value; most of them were written by authors unconnected with the stage; and, even when we come across some who had a little theatrical experience, as often as not we see them reverting to closet worlds of their own. Of the last-mentioned group, W. B. Nichols may be taken as an example. In 1916 was published a drama, *Coloman*, which he had composed in collaboration with Edward Percy. From the dedication it seems to have been originally inspired by Laurence Irving, and, somewhat surprisingly, it was actually chosen for production by the Repertory Players in 1923. Surprisingly, because its prose dialogue reads as falsely as the false verse cultivated by others. "I have spun a plan", declares Simon Szvela, and Coloman interrupts him:

COLOMAN (*stopping him with a gesture*). Master Szvela, I had a horse caught in a quicksand. I watched him struggling – as you are watching me. But he freed himself. Get you gone.

SIMON SZVELA (*Abruptly, with a fantastic bow*). I am snuffed out. (*He makes as if to withdraw, then stops with a sidelong glance at the* BISHOP). What of your mistress?

COLOMAN (*Slowly*). You omnipotent devil... (*A pause, then eagerly*) What of her?

SIMON SZVELA. She would have her love set high. Love is always for the height...

COLOMAN. How much do you know of – us?

SIMON SZVELA. Enough to be your pander.
COLOMAN. How came you by your knowledge?
SIMON SZVELA. I threw a casual javelin into the dark...

and so on, and so on. This drama set in eleventh-century Hungary may have some of the "poetic" material demanded by Glover, but it is chilly dull; and it is without any wonder that we find the author, in 1922, producing a "trilogy" on *Earl Simon*, with no thought other than that of publication.

Amid this company such a minority dramatist as Ashley Dukes, actively interested in the practical stage and endowed with the power to produce at least one successful, widely applauded play, stands almost alone. Yet, even so, that one play remains solitary among his dramatic writings, an oddity, an anomaly. Almost all the others, whether original or translated, were of a "special" kind, unapt to make an appeal beyond the limited range of a circle of like-minded litterateurs – pieces such as *The Song of Drums* (1926), based on the Ulenspiegel story, and *The Fountain Head* (1928), with its somewhat hackneyed theme of a magic well from which men and women might learn the truth about themselves. In the midst of these plays *The Man with a Load of Mischief* (1924) stands unique, a polished costume comedy, delightful and sparkling, telling the story of a minor Regency actress fleeing from her royal lover and escaping from his clutches as she makes her exit in the company of a romantically devoted, but practically minded, servant: not only was it a great success in its own time, not only was it recently turned into a musical, its several revivals since 1933 onwards amply testify to its appeal. That appeal derives, no doubt, from the fact that here Ashley Dukes was able successfully to accomplish the aims which he explained in the preface to his *Five Plays of Other Times* (published 1931). "These pieces", he explains, "have arisen from an interest in the theatre stronger than any interest in literature or thought or the action of the world at large": in them he sought to deal with modern characters concealed under the costumes of past periods, "in order to remove the *dramatis personae* from the ordinary plane of realist expression", and to provide himself with an environment which might harmonise with a prose dialogue richer and more delicately adorned than the dull conversational tones of contemporary life. In four of his *Five Plays* he failed to give satisfactory expression to his imaginative dream, but momentarily at least that dream became reality in *The Man with a Load of Mischief*.

There were at this time several other authors inspired by a kindred desire to release the stage from the grip of current realistic models who elected to proceed towards their objective by different paths. A present-day enthusiastic explorer of the origins of the theatre of the absurd, for instance, may well pause to consider W. J. Turner's "tragi-comedy of love", *The Man Who Ate the Popomack* (1923). Here there is no attempt at stylisation, nor is there any effort to move away from the present into ages past – although it must be admitted that the introduction of an oriental flavour suggests that the author may not have remained uninfluenced by Dunsany. If, however, something of Dunsany's spirit is to be traced in the play, the tone of dialogue and the development of action are both entirely different: instead of grimness and cruelty there are fanciful extravagances and impossibilities. The "popomack" of the title is a strange, rare fruit, a single specimen of which is exhibited at a party in the house of Sir Solomon Raub. On encountering it, Sir Philo Phaoron, a "famous Egyptologist", jumps up excitedly, "*holding his handkerchief to his nose*":

> That's it! That's it! I remember now! It smells! *Une odeur épouvantable*, Lefebure translates it. It's quite correct. It's the real thing! Wonderful! A divine colour, lapis-lazuli blue, and a smell like the plague!

Although all the others in the room back away from this object, Sir Philo and Lord Belvoir devour it greedily, with the result that they develop atrocious odours to which they themselves remain impervious. The former decides to don a diving suit, and discovers that this metallic means of separating himself from the rest of humanity has its decided advantages. At the close of the play, the author, rather feebly, introduces a brief scene for the purpose of stating that everything has been just a dream; but up to this rather lame conclusion he does unquestionably hover at least at the threshold of the drama of absurdity.

Nor was Turner a wholly solitary figure standing before that doorway. Something of the same mood as that which pervades *The Man Who Ate the Popomack* may be sensed in the work of G. D. Gribble, although it must be confessed that the fantastic elements introduced into his *The Masque of Venice* (1924) appear rather dull and that his "tragi-comedy in one act", *The Scene that was to Write Itself* (1924), is decidedly ineffective. And much the same may be said of Ewan Agnew's *The Shingling of Jupiter* (1924), described as "a fantastic play for serious people", which loses much of its effect because of too determined a straining after ingenuity – although here it may be added that the episode in which the idealistic Patricia, dreaming romantically of an enchanted existence among the planets, is whisked up to Jupiter, only to find it as dully unexciting as earth, has its own contemporary relevance for ourselves.

There is a certain measure of interest in these and in a number of related plays, yet in all of them this painful quest for the clever situation takes away from such genuine values as they possess. Perhaps the best way of stressing this, and also the best way of concluding the brief survey of the poetic and "literary" drama of the age is to end with a contrast. In 1922 George Calderon joined the company of minority dramatists by writing an "historical play", *Cromwell: Mall o' Monks*.[1] If this had been his sole dramatic essay even his name would hardly warrant citation here. In fact, however, this piece was a kind of oddity, perhaps merely occasioned by an attempt to follow the current literary–poetic trend. Certainly Calderon remained throughout his all-too-short career associated with the repertories; certainly, too, he was, during this brief period, unable thoroughly to master the dramatic form; yet he showed a remarkably fruitful independence. His very first play, *The*

[1] See Percy Lubbock's study (1921) devoted to this author.

Fountain (1909), revealed an interest and a depth of thought richer in quality than the majority of the historical–fantastic–eccentric writings of so many of his companions – and clearly this drama was a determined effort to achieve an effect, not by means of smart tricks and out-of-the-way settings, but by an enrichment of the realistic style. Even more was this endeavour displayed in *Revolt* (1912), from the technical point of view by no means a successfully-wrought drama, and yet one of the more remarkable anticipatory dramatic experiments made during this period. From the very first lines of apparently inconsequential dialogue, its originality is made obvious and the second act, with its picture of a mathematical genius, Vernon Hodder, dying wretchedly in a Glasgow slum, immediately points forward to Bridie's *The Sleeping Clergyman*. After his demise, it is discovered that this man had discovered the formula for producing atomic power. Says one technological industrialist:

It's time we began looking about for some new source of energy for succeeding generations. Coal's running short; petroleum may give out; and where shall we be then?...Think what it means! An inexhaustible supply of motive power for our engines, cheap electric light, cheap heating for the poor in winter –

and to this his companion replies as enthusiastically:

It may supply us with an explosive of a more destructive kind than anything hitherto discovered.

At the end, during the course of a strike, the laboratory is blown up. We may agree that *Revolt* is structurally weak and that much of its dialogue seems monotonously unimaginative and trite – clearly not a great play, yet somehow possessing a substance which so many of the minority dramas lack. This substance does not depend merely upon the talk about atomic power, interesting although that may be in a play of such an early date: rather it derives from Calderon's fundamental attitude, his rising above pettiness, whether the pettiness of the grim Manchester interiors or of the artificially conceived and crepuscular "poetic" fancies – and in this it reveals by contrast wherein the other plays ultimately failed.

CHAPTER VI

THE "GENERAL" DRAMA

In moving onwards from the dramatic realms which have been discussed above, it is essential, even if this involves a slight amount of repetition, to present at least a broad definition of the way in which the term "general" is here being used. The musicals and the melodramas have been described as "popular", in the sense that, although the audiences at the Gaiety's tuneful spectacles differed almost completely from those which flocked to Melville's melodrama houses, these two completely diverse forms of theatrical production were alike in attracting spectators who sought primarily for entertainment. The entertainment provided by the melodramas derived from thrilling incident, boldly presented characters, essentially simple plots which nevertheless were replete with scenes of an exciting sort; the entertainment served up by the musicals offered pleasant melodies, plenty of laughable episodes, rich scenery and, above all, their skilful, lovely, singing and dancing choruses. By contrast, the "minority" drama as a whole tended to be rather serious, to invest even laughter with significance, to dwell upon problems social and personal, and generally to appeal to the intellect of more select "thoughtful" audiences: this was the form cultivated by those many young modern enthusiasts who despised alike what they regarded as the crass interests of the "popular" and the compromises necessarily adopted by the playwrights who endeavoured to attract "general" audiences.

Instead of the term "general," the descriptive adjective "West End" might have been employed since this directs attention to the familiar habitat of dramas of such a kind. If this descriptive epithet were to be employed, however, its usual scope would necessarily demand both narrowing and expansion. It would, in so far as this chapter is concerned, have to be applied in a very special way, since already a fair amount of theatrical entertainment in the metropolis – the musicals, the melodramas, the revues and the thrillers – has been separately discussed elsewhere: it would also have to be extended so as to include not merely the productions presented in the larger commercial playhouses situated between the Haymarket and Drury Lane, but also performances at the Court in Chelsea, at the Lyric in Hammersmith (when that playhouse came under the aegis of Sir Nigel Playfair), at the Hampstead Everyman and at the far-off Q. Nor do even these playhouses mark the outermost limits: despite the fact that the new theatrical conditions had largely destroyed the old professional provincial stages, at least a few plays of the "general" sort started their careers in theatres far removed from London's glittering centre of entertainment. No doubt the managements responsible for the conduct of the Everyman and the Q were prepared to be more daringly experimental than the ordinary commercial managers; no doubt numbers of spectators who belonged to the "minority" were to be found voyaging northwards to Hampstead and westwards to Kew when they would have thought it far beneath their dignity to attend performances in at least some of the West End houses; yet essentially all the theatres above-mentioned belonged to the same circle. Some were more venturesome than others; some had a more "intellectual" tone than their companions; but all stood apart both from the "popular" and from the "minority". Despite the fact that Norman Marshall has classified a few of them under his heading of "the other theatre", all of them were, in their own ways, commercial.

A second preliminary comment, even although it also repeats what has been said before, must here be made. While "West End" or "general", "popular" and "minority" may on the whole be kept more or less distinct, it is obviously impossible to set up absolutely clear and precise lines of demarcation between them. Already, in scanning the range of the minority drama we have encountered more than a few playwrights moving from the narrower sphere to the larger: indeed, we have on occasion found plays which proved capable of making an appeal both to members of minority groups and to a wider and more variegated public. And, at the opposite extreme, among the "West End" authors there are to be discovered several who deliberately introduced among their "popular" or "general" writings at least a few pieces so special and even precious in style as to guarantee that they would have no chance of finding any London producers willing to put them on the stage.

Finally, a third general introductory remark must be made here. During the thirty years from 1900 to 1930 there were marked developments in the social content of the dramas presented before the public; and of course it is well known that, in the "general" as well as in the "minority" sphere, this was the period when the "play of ideas" gradually assumed a prominent position on the stage. Because of that, it might have been thought that in seeking to survey the growth of the "general" drama as a whole the most effective procedure – perhaps we might almost believe, the only proper procedure – would have been to lay stress upon the content, and especially the sociological content, of the plays which stretched forwards from those produced at the beginning of the period by Pinero and Jones to those written during later years by Maugham, Coward and their companions. Nevertheless, what may be called the "ideological" approach does not, on closer consideration, appear to be the one best fitted to create an effective general picture of the developments in the Edwardian and Georgian drama. After all, the present study is not designed to be a sociological one; after all, too, theatrical works are, or should be, composed by playwrights, not by philosophers; and it has seemed more appropriate to plan this chapter by placing major emphasis upon the styles of the various dramatists – normally dealing with these writers individually, but at times introducing digressions designed to draw attention to especially interesting forms, conventions and themes of a broader kind.

I. *The "Established" Dramatists: H. A. Jones and A. W. Pinero*

As everyone is aware, the last decade of the nineteenth century had witnessed a vigorous revitalisation of the stage, and with this revitalisation was associated the formation of a kind of dramatic aristocracy, consisting of a limited group of authors, sometimes designated as "established" or "representative" and sometimes, less politely, categorised collectively as the "dramatic ring", men of varied talents whose previous theatrical successes had induced the managers to regard their scripts with special favour. There was, of course, nothing strange or peculiar about this: in all ages in the theatre's history there have been playwrights who, after having presented one or two particularly successful plays, came to be treated with deference and respect when they brought new scripts to the managers. During the early years of the century, however, the presence of such playwrights attracted many complaints from disgruntled young stage aspirants, and it is not difficult to determine why this should have been so. We may lay aside the stock complaint that, because of the existence of the "Ring", the managers would not trouble themselves even to glance at any manuscripts submitted by unknown writers: so far as can be determined this accusation was simply not true. The explanation lies elsewhere, partly in the theatrical conditions prevailing at the time, partly in the relationship between the playhouse managements and their public, partly in the intents of the young stage aspirants themselves. Until the establishment of the play-producing societies and of the repertories, it was certainly true that these young authors could find only a very restricted number of theatres to which their works might be submitted.[1] True also was the fact that, despite the reinvigoration of the stage, the general public was, on the whole, conservative and that the actor-managements naturally sought to give this public what it wanted. And there is also the third truth that many, indeed

[1] On this see p. 50.

most, of the plays being penned by the ambitious young dramatists tended to be of the minority kind and were therefore unsuited for West End presentation.

Thus, when we approach the theatre during the first seasons of the present century, it is the work of the established authors, of the dramatic ring, which primarily, and indeed almost exclusively, demands consideration here.

Of the more prominent playwrights who had given distinction to the late Victorian theatre, three effectively closed their careers with the century's end. Wilde's brilliantly eccentric sparkle was suddenly extinguished in 1895. During the very first few years of the new century, Sydney Grundy continued active, but his heavily sentimental style had already lost its appeal, and out he spluttered like a damp squib, discontentedly prophesying a gloomy future for the English stage.[1] The long and glorious career of the Savoy operas had ended, and W. S. Gilbert had, after 1900, only a few oddments to present to the public. None of these oddments is of particular significance, but the "domestic pantomime" called *The Fairy's Dilemma* (1904) perhaps deserves to be recorded here since it now remains unknown even to the majority of Gilbertian enthusiasts. In this eccentric Christmas show the Demon King, Alcohol, has a running fight with the Fairy Queen, Rosebud. After the conventional pantomimic opening, the scene turns to the vicarage of St Parabola, where the incumbent, the Rev. Aloysius Parfitt, M.A., is about to wed Lady Angela Wealdstone, daughter of the Earl of Harrow, while his friend, Col. Sir Trevor Mauleverer, is similarly planning his union to Clarissa, daughter of Mr Justice Whortle. The Fairy Queen endeavours to do her best for the lovers, but, being unfortunately (and unexpectedly) inept at her job, she succeeds in landing everyone in a muddle, and, in order to rectify her mistakes, she is forced to transport the whole company to "The Revolving Realms of Radiant Rehabilitation" – where the Colonel becomes the Clown, the Justice is transformed into Pantaloon, Aloysius becomes Harlequin, and Angela is

[1] *The Play of the Future. By a Playwright of the Past* (1914).

Columbine. Thus, with characteristic humour and a return to his early fairy world, Gilbert took what was almost, if not quite, his final bow before the public.

Naturally, the remaining members of the establishment varied in quality and dramatic interests. Some were serious, almost solemn in purpose; some were intent merely on the securing of temporary success; some were little more than skilful imitators of other authors gifted with an originality beyond their range; some possessed distinctive styles of their own; some made only a brief, quickly passing, impress on the stage; some, to a greater or a less degree, left their memories in the playhouse world. Various though they may be, however, even the least of them can hardly be completely neglected. As an illustration, let us consider H. V. Esmond. This actor–author might readily be dismissed as no more than a concoctor of shallow, sentimental comedies lacking any real significance. Yet even he could create the quiet, charming atmosphere of *The Dangerous Age* (1913), with its sensitive study of a middle-aged woman who falls deeply in love with a youth hardly more than half her years. When, in *Billy's Little Love Affair* (1903), we hear an aspirer to holy orders saying,

I remember writing a sermon once, and when I read it aloud to myself I was quite sorry I was present –

or when we hear another character declaring,

I don't think a man who is a baronet and has £10,000 a year has any right to have any principles at all. Principles belong to the poor. Why should the rich man have everything? It seems selfish –

or when we listen, in his *Eliza Comes to Stay* (1913) to a young playwright's description of the concluding scene in what is obviously a minority drama,

The man says: 'Misery, misery – that's all our lives have led to!' and then his wife says: 'My God, and we've tried so hard!' And he says: 'We *have* tried, Mary', and she says 'Is this the end?' and he says: 'I wonder' – and the curtain comes down very slowly –

can we refrain from according to Esmond credit for a very pretty gentle wit? And, still further, when we consider the theme of this last comedy, noting how a very dowdy Eliza enters unexpectedly into the household of the Hon. Sandy Verrall, how by his orders she is more appropriately dressed up, how she is tutored to act as a lady, how she falls in love with her guardian, how his aunt, Lady Pennybroke, sympathises with her in her difficult situation, and how, in speaking excitedly to this lady, she ejaculates, in carefully enunciated syllables, "There's a hell of a lot going on inside me" – can we possibly escape from associating this Eliza with that other more famous Eliza who captivated audiences at His Majesty's Theatre just fourteen months later and who stayed on the stage as My Fair Lady even until our own times?

The example of H. V. Esmond may stand as fairly representative of the interest to be found in the writings of the company of dramatists who were already established at the close of the nineteenth century. Some, like Harriet Jay ("Charles Marlowe"), had almost reached the close of their careers and had not much to offer to the new century, yet even such a minor dramatist as this deserves to be remembered: her popular, merry farce, *When Knights Were Bold* (1906), may not be a masterpiece, but because of its clever linking-together of the colourful scenes of the costume drama and of farcically laughable situations it definitely created its own niche in theatrical history. How can we dismiss the light airy figure of Sir Seymour Hicks, already an active author of dramas and musical comedies during Victoria's latest years and proving even more active during the first years of the new century, passing on something of his own characteristic style to Ian Hay? Or R. C. Carton, who had started his career in 1885 and who similarly carried on vigorously until 1922, producing comedies and farces which, although no doubt possessing little true originality, abound in humour and easy dalliance? His fast-moving *Public Opinion* (1905) is gaily amusing with its merrily-told story of a young music-hall starlet who, being in possession of a number of indiscreet letters, sends their respectably prominent writers into a dither when she proposes to use these epistles for the purpose of furthering her marriage to a viscount; his amusingly appealing main character in *Mr Hopkinson* (1905) is a stage persona out of the ordinary; the mock-serious satire directed at contemporary novelettes is skilfully handled in *The Eccentric Lord Camberdene* (1910); his *The Bear Leaders* (1912) is called a farce, but its presentation of the household run by Mr and Mrs Molyneux for the training of socially awkward young aristocratic cubs is dealt with so adroitly as to make it a farce with a decided difference. Jerome K. Jerome, who first made a stage appearance within a year of R. C. Carton and whose latest play, the strange piece called *The Soul of Nicholas Snyders*, did not come until 1927, no doubt enjoyed only one very great success – *The Passing of the Third Floor Back* (1908)[1] – and even this work is now generally sneered at; yet in his dramatic writings, taken as a whole, he may be thought to have had something worthy to give to the theatre. *The Master of Mrs Chilvers* (1911) can justly be styled sentimental, yet this "improbable comedy" skilfully reflects in many of its scenes the frenetic atmosphere enveloping the Votes for Women movement of its time; and *The Celebrity* (1917, as *Cook*; revised 1926) by no means ineffectively presents its main character, John Parable, the illustrious spokesman of the liberal left. Perhaps Robert Marshall among his numerous dramatic writings after 1900 had nothing so lively to offer as his wittily fantastic *His Excellency the Governor* of 1898, yet the "farcical romance" of *The Duke of Killiecrankie* (1904) has a fascinating sparkle in several of its scenes, while *The Alabaster Staircase* (1906) exhibits genuine novelty in its sardonic plot wherein a severely rigid Tory Prime Minister, after an accident in which he receives a severe blow on the head, becomes a man completely changed in character, one indeed who mightily dismays his colleagues by becoming sympathetically, indeed almost socialistically, advanced in his views and actions.[2] Even although Cosmo

[1] See above pp. 234–5.

[2] In its own time this play proved a complete failure: the first performance, according to Herbert Swears (*When All's Said and Done*, 1937, p. 199), ended with the actors delivering their lines to a stonily unreceptive

Hamilton, despite his occasional excursions into reasonably amusing farce, tends on the whole to be rather sentimentally serious, there is sufficient in the total range of his varied writings to make him at least historically interesting. Equally sentimental, and inclined to rely on those strained coincidences which currently beset the realistic style inherited from the last years of the nineteenth century, C. Haddon Chambers nevertheless shows his individuality in his sometimes truly excellent handling of pregnantly laconic dialogue, as exemplified in *The Awakening* (1901).

With Haddon Chambers it may be profitable to pause for a moment since, besides his stylistic skill, he has a particular interest for us as illustrating something else.[1] His *Passers-By* (1911) no doubt cannot be honestly praised as a great play, or even as one which in general rises above a rather mediocre level, but it may be taken as another instance of a prime element of importance in the work of these lesser dramatists – and this is of sufficient significance to justify, even to demand, the introduction of a general digressional comment.

In Haddon Chambers's play the scene is a room in the house of a rich Peter Waverton into which his servant, Pine, on a bitterly cold night, brings a half-frozen cabby, nicknamed Nighty, and Burns, a simpleton tramp – and it is difficult not to see here a direct anticipation of Galsworthy's *The Pigeon*, presented on the stage just one year later, where a well-to-do artist brings into his studio a homeless vagabond, a pitifully bedraggled flower-seller, and a drunken cab-driver. But the interest of the play does not rest merely upon any connection it may have with Galsworthy's better-known work: it depends upon the fact that here, in title, in plot and in treatment, Haddon Chambers presents, as it were, a symbol of what is to be traced as a constantly recurring element in the drama of this period.

house and finally bowing to such a silence as "chilled the blood". Maybe *The Alabaster Staircase* was a little before its proper time.

[1] In connection with the dramatic devices briefly discussed in the following pages, reference may be made to an article, "Somewhat in a New Dimension", contributed to *Contemporary Theatre* (*Stratford-upon-Avon Studies*, no. 4, edited by John Russell Brown and Bernard Harris, 1962).

The introduction of a catalytic stranger or strangers into a comfortably ordered household is, of course, a dramatic device which can be traced back in its origins to antiquity, and particularly during the latter part of the nineteenth century it can be found familiarly employed in plays as various and diverse as François Coppée's *Le Passant* (1869)[1] and several among Ibsen's writings: indeed, of Ibsen Somerset Maugham observed in his *Summing Up* – "It is not a gross exaggeration to say that his only gambit is the sudden arrival of a stranger who comes into a stuffy room and opens the windows."

In the English theatre, however, it was not until after 1900 that this device became common, and its frequent utilisation from that time on to 1930 makes it peculiarly characteristic of the period. It cannot, of course, be said that Haddon Chambers was personally responsible for its introduction, but the title which he gave to his play makes him, if not the sole innovator, at least the man who drew general attention to the dramatic interest inherent in these persons who are brought in, as it were, from outside; and, when his scenes are compared with those of other authors it becomes evident that his treatment of the passers-by proved a direct inspiration to his successors.

The theatrical strangers assumed all sorts of guises. Chambers's, as has been seen, were poverty-stricken individuals picked up from the street; so were Galsworthy's; and so, too, was the girl waif whom H. H. Davies brought into his *Outcast* (1914). During the first years of the century plays and playlets featuring burglars were particularly numerous, and, although naturally most of these are to be associated with the growing cult of the "detective" and "crime" drama, there still remain many, such as St John Hankin's *The Burglar Who Failed* (1908), in which the nefarious stranger acts as a catalytic agent. In the same author's *The Return of the Prodigal* (1905) the unexpected intruder, even although he is a ne'er-do-well son who, after

[1] It may be noted here that this piece was translated by Rathmell Wilson in 1913 as *The Passer-By*.

his banishment, forces his way back into the family circle, is a figure not far removed. At the opposite extreme, in J. K. Jerome's *The Passing of the Third Floor Back* (1908), the stranger becomes potent and divine. In 1909 Maugham's *Smith* introduces the type as a visiting "Colonial", and shortly before this Keble Howard brings a down-and-out vagrant into *The Cheerful Knave* (1908) in order to unravel the sentimental complexities of his plot, while R. Warren Bell, in his *Company for George* (1910), invents an interesting variant – a penniless Cambridge student who, after he has been kindly received by a sympathetic household, clings like a limpet to the position from which the good-natured husband and wife now seek to detach him. If we want a corresponding play of later date we have only to turn to a comedy by Vernon Woodhouse and Victor MacClure, actually entitled *The Limpet* (1922), which shows an unpleasant, fat, lazy Percy Sheepwell firmly determined not to abandon his comfortable room and good food in the country house where he has installed himself. *The Man Who Came to Dinner*, the American comedy by George S. Kaufman and Moss Hart, was thus well and truly anticipated some twenty years before its appearance. A. A. Milne's *Mr Pim Passes By* (1919), echoing the title which had been employed by Haddon Chambers so many years before, extended the stranger's rôle; the extension was carried even further by F. T. Jesse in *Anyhouse* (1925); while Benn W. Levy gave the device a further twist in *Mrs Moonlight* (1928) by making his "down-and-out" Visitor at the close of his play none other than the gentle heroine of the first act.

This exploitation of the passers-by can be explained in various ways. Their catalytic function is obvious, but, in addition to this, these intruders have two other main parts to play: the destitute waifs serve to focus at least some attention upon social problems, while the characters of the "Colonial" type suggest the existence of values different from, and possibly better than, those operative in conventional English society circles. And precisely here this brief digression must be extended in order to include another and related theme which played a truly extraordinarily potent rôle in all kinds of drama during those thirty years.

Naturally, in the drama's picture-gallery from Elizabethan days onwards the diversity of characters put upon the stage is legion, but, peculiarly, if we exclude a few satirical plays such as *The Rehearsal* and *The Critic*, we must be struck by the fact that amid this teeming multitude which embraces almost all kinds and conditions of men, the "artist" is almost if not entirely non-existent on the stage: apart from a very few odd plays such as Frederick Reynolds' *The Dramatist* in 1789 and H. J. Byron's *Cyril's Success* in 1868 it is difficult to call to mind any dramas in which the central characters are writers, painters or musicians, and it is almost equally hard even to find plays in which such persons take minor parts. What must immediately call for attention is that suddenly, during those early years of the present century when the "passer-by" theme was being so freely exploited, stage poets, musicians and painters came into their own and that not infrequently the two new patterns were combined. Haddon Chambers, who brought his waifs and strays into *Passers-By*, makes the heroine of his *The Awakening* (1901) an unconventional artist's daughter, Olive Lawrence, whose attitude to life, influenced by her father's views, is contrasted with that of the ordinary well-brought-up society girl. Lechmere Worrall's *Ann* (1912) is an authoress and the man she loves is a novelist; a painter, Christopher Wellwyn, is the hero of John Galsworthy's *The Pigeon* (1912), and a novelist is the central character in *Windows* (1922).

So luxuriantly do these artists proliferate during the first three decades of the century that no attempt can be made to list all their appearances, but if it would be improper to encumber the main text with a catalogue of all (or even of many) plays in which they have important rôles, at least a few characteristic examples may be recorded in a note.[1]

[1] In 1903 Herbert Swears deals with a woman painter in *Pansy*, and during the same year H. H. Davies in his *Cousin Kate* places a painter and a woman novelist, with their free ideas, in opposition to a rigidly conventional clergyman. Alfred Sutro concentrates upon a novelist in *The Cave of Illusion* (1900), sets a dramatic critic centre-stage in *The*

What is of especial importance to remember is that their introduction and development belonged mainly, if not entirely, to the often-despised members of the dramatic ring.

From this digression occasioned by Haddon Chambers' *Passers-By* we must return to a further consideration of numerous other contributions made to the theatre by several of his companion "representative" authors. It must be

Man in the Stalls (1911), and in *John Glayde's Honour* (1907) gives prominence both to a painter and a columnist. In 1909 R. C. Carton actually calls a play *Lorrimer Sabiston, Dramatist.* A composer is dealt with by Israel Zangwill in *Merely Mary Ann* (1903), and a travelling showman is the dominant figure in H. A. Jones' *The Chevaleer* (1904). Harold Chapin has a poet in *Elaine* (1912); another appears in B. Macdonald Hastings' *The New Sin* (1912); a painter is elevated to a high position by Arnold Bennett in *The Great Adventure* (1911) and the same author concentrates upon pianists in *Sacred and Profane Love* (1919). H. H. Davies has a painter in *Doormats* (1912) and an author in *A Single Man* (1910); both a dramatist and a painter have prominent rôles in Allan Monkhouse's *The Education of Mr Surrage* (1912). In the last-mentioned play the artist types are not drawn very flatteringly, but during the early period most commonly they are used for the purpose of stressing ideas different from those prevalent in conventional society circles: a sharp contrast between the "artist" and the "Philistine" (or simply the "bourgeois") provides the central theme of H. A. Jones' *The Hypocrites* (1906); Harold Chapin's *The Marriage of Columbine* (1910) introduces a similar contrast between an artist and a provincial puritan; H. M. Paull calls his *The Painter and the Millionaire* (1912) a "modern morality play"; and the conflicting attitudes to life form the core of J. R. Gregson's *T'Marsdens* (1917). During the twenties, these stage artists increased in number, and in general their function remained the same, as, for example, in Frederick Lonsdale's *Spring Cleaning* (1923) and Noël Coward's *Home Chat* (1927). On the other hand, it is noticeable that in the twenties the setting-up of "artistic" values against "ordinary social" values was at times made more complex. The spirit of *The Education of Mr Surrage* was almost unique when that play appeared in 1912; but now there were many authors who were prepared to acknowledge that not all the good was to be found among the Bohemians. It is this awareness, for instance, which gives rich quality to *Hay Fever* (1925) and in some other plays, such as A. A. Milne's *Mr Pim Passes By* (1919) and Zangwill's *We Moderns* (1922), art's follies could be made the target for arrows, both soft-tipped and dangerously barbed. In *The Truth about Blayds* (1921) Milne could actually dare to present a poet of highest esteem as a complete fraud. A fair proportion of the dramas listed above will, of course, receive further notice in association with their authors' dramatic careers, and in the following pages many other examples of this theme will be cited.

obvious to everyone, indeed, that so far the greatest and most influential members of this group have been no more than cursorily mentioned, and it is to these in particular that attention must now be given.

When thought is given to the theatrical revival which characterised the final years of Queen Victoria's reign, two names immediately and inevitably come to mind – Henry Arthur Jones and Arthur (later Sir Arthur) Wing Pinero. As the old age ceded place to the new Edwardian era both continued actively to supply the West End theatres with plays both serious and comic: they remained notable and esteemed dramatists, even if their fates were by no means similar.

The position occupied by Jones proved to be peculiarly anomalous.[1] In 1900 his *Mrs Dane's Defence* proved that his constructive power remained unimpaired, fully as expert as it had been in the past, and that his skill in the penning of tense, terse dialogue was even more adept than it had been before; and from the date when this play was presented to the public on until 1923 he continued to write prolifically for the stage, producing nearly thirty works of diverse kinds, some deeply serious, some entertainingly light. In themselves these facts might suggest that within this period his popularity and fame must have been second to none; yet the truth is that, however active and adroit he remained, whatever occasional successes he enjoyed, his previous firm grip on the public had been lost. Gradually – and increasingly as year succeeded year – this man who before the advent of the present century had been so largely responsible for arousing audiences to appreciation of new dramatic themes came to appear old-fashioned, and towards the close of his career he stood neglected, almost completely forgotten. In *Whitewashing Julia* (1903), despite its occasionally amusing situations, his familiar satire of moral hypocrisy seemed just a

[1] Jenny Doris Jones' *Life and Letters of Henry Arthur Jones* (1930) well outlines the chief facts relating to his career and contains much material bearing upon his dramatic aims. An excellent survey of his achievements is provided by Richard A. Cordell in his *Henry Arthur Jones and the Modern Drama* (1932).

little stupid; the artificialities of *Joseph Entangled* (1904) were more evident than its virtues; in *The Chevaleer* (1904) the presentation of the passing-by travelling showman gave to Arthur Bourchier one of his most effective parts, yet the general theme of the play was thought by many to be merely silly; we today may find a slight interest in *The Hypocrites* (1906), the more particularly since its plot anticipates those of two significant plays of 1912 – Galsworthy's *The Eldest Son* and Houghton's *Hindle Wakes* – yet for us and for Jones's contemporaries alike the narrowness of his vision leaves his own scenes dull and ineffective. It is true that when *Dolly Reforming Herself* appeared in 1908 one still-esteemed critic (whom charity may here leave anonymous) referred to its "lifelike" characters, while one of his companions, equally distinguished, actually compared the author with Sheridan; it is also true that even now we can admit it as belonging to Jones's more successful efforts – yet at the same time there must be a more serious admission, that its planning is mechanical and its persons rather caricatures than characters. Nor can we accept the rather poor drama of provincial politics and rivalries, *Mary Goes First* (1913), as being, in the words of still another well-known critic, a "notable achievement" in the style of "high comedy".

Jones, in fact, suffered the fate of not a few playwrights in the history of the theatre – men whose abilities by no means can be questioned, men whose purposes were sincere and serious, but at the same time men whose own intelligences were not deep and who, as a result, after making considerable impact in the theatre during their earlier days, soon found that the relatively simple things which they had preached were later become old-fashioned, obsolete and even at times not a little ridiculous. Fundamentally, the dominant "idea" which Jones constantly incorporated in his plays may be described simply as a hatred of hypocrisy; beyond this it proved difficult for him to go, while the hatred itself tended, as the years advanced, to become blindingly rigid. One really anonymous reviewer summed this up when, in 1907, he declared that Jones exhibited "a narrowness of mind exceeding...the narrowness of mind" which he set out to castigate. Certainly it must be admitted that among his later writings he composed some comedies in which he introduced divers versions of charming ladies who by the exercise of sheer audacity managed to get their own way in everything, or who were delightfully irresponsible over money matters, or who complicated the lives of all around them by their feminine whims and fancies and follies; also to be admitted is the fact that in these comedies appear several skilfully written scenes – yet, even so, there is comparatively little here that can be compared with what he had to offer earlier audiences in *The Masqueraders*, *The Triumph of the Philistines*, *Michael and His Lost Angel* and *The Liars*.

In several respects A. W. Pinero's historical position in the twentieth-century playhouse, although considerably happier, parallels that of Jones. The success of *The Second Mrs Tanqueray* in 1893 – a success for which the epithet "tremendous" seems to be appropriate – almost exactly coincided with the impact made by the latter's serious dramas: at the beginning of the new century *Iris* (1901) corresponded with *Mrs Dane's Defence*; in spite of the excellence of some among their later writings, both authors found their original appeal beginning to fade towards the end of the century's first decade, and both were forced at times to seek American instead of English production for several among their later works.[1] However, although these facts may suggest that the lines of their dramatic careers ran along the same tracks, they diverged in several marked respects. Jones's plays declined in their appeal largely because they owed their main being to what must be styled their propagandist quality: they were, in fact, dramas in which an idea or at least an attitude was more important for him than either characters or plots – and the word "idea", or "attitude",

[1] Wilbur D. Dunkel has a "critical biography" of this author (1941). Interesting contemporary assessments of his work appear in P. P. Howe's *Dramatic Portraits* (1913), pp. 11–52 and in Ashley Dukes' *Modern Dramatists* (1911). A more detailed examination of Pinero's style appears in Wilibald Stocker's *Pinero's Dramen: Studien über Motive, Charakteren und Technik* (1911).

must remain in the singular, for he had virtually only the one thought to expound. Pinero, on the other hand, generally avoided ideas, concentrating instead upon expert planning of his scenes and elaboration of his characters; and for that reason his plays, their restricted scope notwithstanding, continued to have an appeal which extended further than that of Jones's – an appeal, indeed, which makes them retain an interest for us now, even after the passage of so many years. While both these authors often stood condemned together in the *avant-garde* critical court-rooms of 1910, Jones never succeeded in rehabilitating himself after his sentence, whereas in more recent years, within some quarters at least, there has frequently been evident an uneasy feeling that perhaps the condemnation of Pinero had been over-severe. During the forties some of his works were actually brought forward on the stage, and, watching them, J. C. Trewin found himself forced to declare his opinion that "play after play from the shelf, instead of emerging as a prehistoric peep, has had qualities that any modern dramatist might envy". In its 1945 production, he wrote, *The Thunderbolt* "fell indeed like a thunderbolt into the company of our go-as-you-please dramatists, all local colour and very little play", while in 1947 *Mid-Channel* "also showed itself to be work to shame our tinkerers in flimsy plywood",[1] and some ten years later Cecil W. Davies could firmly express his belief that Pinero, despite his limitations, "remains one of the most neglected of the major English dramatists".[2]

We are, of course, bound to agree that a few of his later works deplorably display several of his basic weaknesses. *Preserving Mr Panmure* (1911), instead of arousing any genuine interest and laughter, strikes us as merely absurd. *The "Mind the Paint" Girl* (1912) can be viewed as nothing save a sentimentally-ridiculous reflection of Tom Robertson's *Caste* (with a few suggestions taken from *Trelawny of the "Wells"*) – a play so dully written that its rather forced curtain-line might almost be deemed to be a sparkling jewel

[1] *The Theatre since 1900* (1951), p. 35.
[2] "Pinero: The Drama of Reputation", *English*, xiv (1962), 13–17.

of wit: there the Pantheon Theatre girls whom lords and other aristocrats are anxious to marry are advised by the star's mother to

Think – think wot a lot o' good you're all doin' to the aristocracy!

The Big Drum (1915) ineffectively contrasts a number of rich social climbers with Mackworth, "a novelist, a poet, and would-be playwright", who, in outlining the theme of his latest book, is made to speak in such artificial terms as may fairly be exemplified thus:

It's an attempt to portray the struggle for notoriety – for self-advertisement – we see going on around us to-day.... It shows a vast crowd of men and women, sir, forcing themselves upon public attention without a shred of modesty, fighting to obtain it as if they are fighting for bread and meat. It shows how dignity and reserve have been cast aside as virtues that are antiquated and outworn, until half the world – the world that should be orderly, harmonious, beautiful – has become an arena for the exhibition of vulgar ostentation or almost superhuman egoism – a cockpit resounding with raucous voices bellowing one against the other!

And, if Pinero loses himself in this way when he is dealing with serious matters, almost abandoning dramatic dialogue completely and substituting for it passages which might be considered more proper for public speeches at Blackpool conferences, his corresponding failure in many comic scenes is made painfully evident when he follows feeble witticisms with a "Ha, ha, ha!", or a "Ho, ho, ho!", or, for variety's sake, with a "He, he, he!" Still further, we recognise that among these later plays are some, such as *The Enchanted Cottage* of 1922, which demonstrate the restricted boundaries of his dramatic vision: his handling in this drama of a dream world peopled by witches and goblins and replete with miraculous incident can be described only as fumbling and awkward.

Yet all these failures taken together cannot submerge his genuinely imaginative qualities and his dramatic expertise. Although perhaps *Iris* may not have so much interest today in our world of feminine emancipation, the study it presents of a weak woman caught in a legal trap and besotted by love of a saturnine author, Malaise, possesses in its own way an enduring value: the sad tale is fashioned with skill, the author has refused to indulge in any sentimental conclusion, and, despite the fact that we see quite clearly that the fate of his heroine could not be exactly reproduced in our own times, we must acknowledge that the pattern, if not the precise circumstances, might well find parallels within the freer range of present-day social life. So, too, although maybe we are prepared to see *A Wife without a Smile* (1904) as a somewhat unfortunate "biter-bit" comedy-farce, Pinero's resolute refusal to take the easy sentimental path is once more displayed: at the close of the play, the hero's wife, who had been preparing to go off with an artist, Vivian Trood, suddenly and realistically decides that she cannot give up her husband's wealth and inveigles him, even forces him, to take her into his arms again.

Clearly, however, it is not even these plays which come to our minds when we think of Pinero's true achievements after the start of the century: the dramas which we recall are *His House in Order* (1906), *The Thunderbolt* (1908) and *Mid-Channel* (1909). The first of these introduces to the stage a household made dismal through its domination by the self-interestedly sanctimonious relatives-in-law of a husband mesmerised by memory of the supposedly saintly reputation of his first wife: with excellent dramatic effectiveness Pinero shows this picture being torn down by the husband's worldly-wise brother so that eventually it is completely destroyed. Sometimes the dialogue is not of the best, but life has been given here to what might well have been a dull domestic drama. In *The Thunderbolt*, described as "An Episode in the History of a Provincial Family", he focussed attention upon the familiar figure of an "artist" who at the same time has some of the qualities of an intruder, and once more life is infused into material which could easily have been nothing save tediously conventional and hackneyed. A rich man dies, surrounded at his bedside by a number of relatives from whom he had long been estranged.

No will can be found, and this puzzles everyone, for apparently he had been devoted to his illegitimate daughter, Helen Thornhill, at that time resident in Paris studying art. Reluctantly, the members of the family, who assume that in the absence of a will, all his money will come to them, are cajoled into agreeing to offer her at least a small amount from the estate: but, when this offer is actually conveyed to her, she bluntly refuses. The group then start to make plans in expectation of the wealth coming to them, when suddenly a discovery is made. The only relatives with whom Helen had felt sympathy were Thaddeus Mortimore, a poverty-stricken music-teacher, Phyllis, his hard-working wife, and their two children. Phyllis obviously is in an exceedingly nervous state, and eventually she breaks down, confessing that indeed there had been a will, a will which left everything to Helen, and that this she had destroyed. The true nature of the "artist" quality now takes centre stage. Largely in order to save Phyllis from arrest for having burned the document, Helen agrees to a share-out: Thaddeus (who as a music-teacher presumably participates in the "artist" nature) refuses, but the girl decrees that his portion will go to the two children. This plot is handled with dramatic deftness and skill; the characters are all invested with substance and individuality; the group-picture is dealt with firmly and effectively; and here Pinero, perhaps realising how prone he was to indulge in "literary" speeches of the kind illustrated above, interestingly keeps his dialogue simple, concise and eminently natural. Darker in tone is the theme of *Mid-Channel*, but it is no less impressive. This is a drama dealing mainly with two characters – a businessman and his wife whose marriage is doomed. The husband has always been occupied with his stockbroking affairs, spends but little time at home, and, even when he is at home, clearly has his thoughts elsewhere. She is still pretty and lively; young admirers cluster round her; and her attention is directed constantly towards these, her "tame robins". The husband objects; she is led more and more to realise that she cannot continue in her essentially false position. Since, basically, deep down, the pair retain affection for each other, for a moment it seems that reconciliation is a possibility; but once again the author remains resolute – this heroine ends as Iris had done.

Pinero's strength thus depended upon his intimate knowledge of, and lively interest in, characters set within their social environment. "Ideas", as such, either attracted him not at all, or else, if he did admit them into any of his plays (*The Big Drum*, for example), he found these plays collapsing in ruins about him. Maybe the true quality and strength of his best work is negatively reflected in his little "domestic episode" called *Playgoers* (1913), in which a Mistress, having engaged a new set of servants, decides to win their favour by offering them all, as a treat, a visit to the theatre:

THE MISTRESS. What you will see is a play of ideas, something to stimulate your imaginations and make you think.
THE COOK. Ideers!
THE PARLOURMAID (*with a sickly expression*). Make us think!
THE ODD MAN (*gloomily*). Crickey!
THE MISTRESS. A slice cut clean out of life, in fact....
THE HOUSEMAID. Souns 'orribly crool....
THE COOK. Well, any 'ow, gals, it strikes me we're in for a preshus dull evenin'.

In fact, however, they are not: all save the Odd Man prefer to hand in their notices rather than suffer such a dismal fate.

2. *J. M. Barrie and G. B. Shaw*

There still remain from this group of dramatists two men either of whom would by himself have given true distinction to the theatre of any period.[1] Both of these, strangely, pursued careers closely parallel in time if not in substance. Barrie's first twentieth-century play appeared at the Criterion in April 1901, Shaw's first was presented at the Royalty two years later: within the next quarter-century all

[1] It is, of course, true that before 1900 Shaw could hardly be described as a member of the dramatic ring. Nevertheless he had already made a name for himself by his published plays and had even then started to move onto the stage: see pp. 351–3.

their greatest dramas were written. The parallel movements in time, however, merely serve to stress their basic differences – differences already shadowed forth in 1891 when Shaw published his enthusiastic *Quintessence of Ibsenism* and when Barrie produced his gay irreverent skit of *Ibsen's Ghost*. Both men had a sense of fun: but whereas Shaw united an effervescent Irish wit with a serious sense of purpose, Barrie was completely possessed by the spirit of Scottish humour, and of a serious sense of purpose he owned little or none. Both men, of course, were essentially sentimental, but their sentimentalisms derived from disparate sources: Shaw's was the sentimentality of the mind, Barrie's of the heart. Shaw's intellect had a flashing brilliance, a brilliance hardly to be matched in his age – and certainly not anywhere else in the contemporary theatre – but intellectual brilliance does not always imply wisdom, and of wisdom, save in one or two of his plays, there are only occasional glimmerings: Barrie had wisdom, but not the mental force by which wisdom attains power. Barrie had no new ideas to express: Shaw so habitually dwelt in a world of ideas and concepts that often human beings became lost amid the notions. In life, as on the stage, Shaw was ever attracted by extravagant oddities of all kinds, whereas Barrie quietly delighted in the fascinating complexities of the ordinary and the seemingly commonplace.

The principal works of these two authors, of course, are familiar to all who are in the least interested in the drama, and thus, paradoxically, in a survey of the present kind they may be examined more briefly than many lesser plays by dramatists now forgotten or but barely remembered. Before 1900 Barrie had won success both as a novelist and as a popular playwright, but his true and characteristic impact upon the stage did not come until, between 1902 and 1904, his *Quality Street*, *The Admirable Crichton* and *Peter Pan* brought audiences flocking to the Vaudeville and the Duke of York's.[1] If *The Admirable Crichton* had been written by

[1] This statement must, of course, be qualified by observing that *Walker, London* and *The Little Minister* both had had fairly lengthy runs

Shaw, or indeed by any one among a dozen of contemporary authors, it would have taken shape as a social document, with some more or less severe comments upon prevailing social errors and injustices and with stock-figures clothed in ideological garments. What Barrie is interested in is the half-real, half-impossible situation, in the imaginative flight from the ordinary world into a realm of the might-have-been, and, above all, in the characters conjured up by his imagination – characters created out of what might be called ordinary interests. "The success of J. M. Barrie in the theatre", said P. P. Howe perceptively, "is the success of simplification...our pleasure is the pleasure of recognition."[1] Because of this ordinariness and simplication, it was, of course, easy for some of the minority playwrights and their attendant critical followers to dismiss him merely as an unthinking sentimentalist and to ignore the peculiar and subtle qualities he possessed – and here perhaps it may be wise to refer to an equally perceptive comment made by James Agate:[2] "Once there was a mother star gathered little baby stars round her knee to tell them a fairy-story, and during the telling the genius of Barrie was born. For genius it is, despite a passion for literary baby-ribbons only too easily parodied."

at the close of the nineteenth century: but, although both are coloured by the tones in the use of which Barrie excelled, neither exhibits to the full the elements so clearly expressed in the three dramas presented immediately after 1900. The Barrie literature is extensive, including numerous volumes devoted to appreciation of his writings and scores of articles. The earlier biographies, notably that by D. G. Mackail (*The Story of J. M. Barrie*, 1941), have recently been completely superseded by Janet Dunbar's *J. M. Barrie: The Man Behind the Image* (1970), which makes use of much hitherto unpublished material. The complicated record of the printings of his works is examined both by B. D. Cutler (1931) and Herbert Garland (1928). W. Eschenhauer has a technical study on the theme of *Sir James Barrie als Dramatiker* (1929), and significant appreciations of his contributions to the stage have been published by H. M. Walbrook (*J. M. Barrie and the Theatre*, 1922), Thomas Moult (1928), F. J. H. Darton (1929), J. A. Hammerton (*Barrie: The Story of a Genius*, 1929), J. A. Roy (1937) and W. A. C. Darlington (1938). Among the almost innumerable articles concerned with criticism of his work attention may be drawn to H. Granville-Barker's "J. M. Barrie as Dramatist" (*The Bookman*, xxxix, 1910, 13–21).

[1] *Dramatic Portraits* (1913), pp. 115–32.

[2] *At Half-Past Eight* (1923), p. 69.

The literary baby-ribbons are plainly to be discerned in *The Admirable Crichton*; even more clearly are they exhibited in the now-vanished interiors of *Quality Street*; and colourfully they wrap up the joyous adventures presented in *Peter Pan*. But, in taking note of them we must always bear in mind what Agate so patently observed – that these baby-ribbons are introduced as part of what Barrie's genius had to offer: they are brought in consciously and deliberately, with full realisation of what they are. Your commonplace sentimentalist generally remains blissfully unaware of his sentimentalism and, in pursuing his own path, is often as grimly serious as any rabid puritan; and most dramatists, sentimental or not, somehow seem to stand over and apart from the scenes they create and fashion for the stage. Barrie's genius gains its distinctive quality from his utter simplicity, from a frank acceptance of, and indeed emphasis upon, the fact that a play is no more than a figment, and on his ability to mingle with his characters on the boards, unseen yet omnipresent. When we consider the matter carefully, perhaps we find ourselves forced to agree that from Shaw downwards there lived at that period no playwright save Barrie who honestly could share with Shakespeare the truth which the Elizabethan dramatist puts into the mouth of his wise Theseus:

> The best in this kind are but shadows: and the worst are no worse, if imagination amend them.

Characteristically, the opening lines of *Peter Pan* start with a matter-of-fact stage-direction and then proceed paradoxically both to underline the unreal, imaginary nature of the setting and to make it assume the quality of reality:

> The night nursery of the Darling family, which is the scene of our opening Act, is at the top of a rather depressed street in Bloomsbury. We have a right to place it where we will, and the reason Bloomsbury is chosen is that Mr Roget once lived there. So did we in days when his *Thesaurus* was our only companion in London; and we whom he has helped to wend our way through life have always wanted to pay him a little compliment. The Darlings therefore lived in Bloomsbury.

It cannot, of course, be denied that quite frequently Barrie's genius led him astray, so that many of his plays, especially the one-act pieces, deserve scant attention as a whole – although there is hardly one of them which does not reflect his fundamental concept of the theatre and exhibit instances of his quiet wisdom. While others around him were solemnly preaching the perfectability of man and expressing confidence in the supposedly magical properties of social science, he proceeded quietly on his own path, observing men and women from the inside, marvelling at their often unexpected good qualities yet always aware of their unpredictable weaknesses and vices – aware that the imagined happiness of which men dream is an illusion even while the possibility of grasping real happiness so often lies neglected within their reach: continually he kept himself within the company of his characters, romance and reality fading so imperceptibly into each other that the substance might hardly be distinguished from the shadow: and always, too, he looked upon himself, and upon the theatre for which he wrote, with a mild and often self-derogatory humorous smile. In *Alice Sit-by-the-Fire* we are introduced at the very beginning to two young girls, innocent of the world (who have been making up "for lost time", as they themselves say, by a secret bout of theatre-going) and who now are discussing their impressions. "Every night since Monday," declares Amy, "including the matinée, has been a revelation":

(*She closes her eyes so that she may see the revelations more clearly. So does* GINEVRA.)

GINEVRA. Amy, that heart-gripping scene when the love-maddened woman visited the *man* in his *chambers*.

AMY. She wasn't absolutely love-maddened, Ginevra; she really loved her husband best all the time.

GINEVRA. Not till the last act, darling.

AMY. Please don't say it, Ginevra. She was most foolish, especially in the crêpe de chine, but *we* know that she only went to the man's chambers to get back her letters. How I trembled for her then.

GINEVRA. I was strangely calm.

AMY. Oh, Ginevra, I had such a presentiment that the husband would call at those chambers while she was there. And he did. Ginevra, you remember his knock upon the door. Surely you trembled then?

(GINEVRA *knits her lips triumphantly.*)

GINEVRA. Not even then, Amy. Somehow I felt sure that in the nick of time her lady friend would step out from somewhere and say that the letters were *hers.*

AMY. Nobly compromising herself, Ginevra.

GINEVRA. Amy, how I love that bit where she says so unexpectedly, with noble self-renunciation, 'He is my affianced husband.'

AMY. Isn't it glorious! Strange, Ginevra, that it happened in each play.

GINEVRA. That was because we always went to the thinking theatres. Real plays are always about a lady and two men; and, alas, only one of them is her husband. That is Life, you know. It is called the odd, odd triangle.

This is not satire: it has about it the flavour of delighted impish acceptance. Even when, in *What Every Woman Knows* (1908) the plot proceeds to deal with politics, high life and troublesome domestic wrangles, Barrie clearly could not have been happy had he not started his play with its scene of fantasy and had he not conceived his situations and his persons in such a manner, uniquely his own, as permitted them to be at once more and less "theatrical" than those which his companion-authors introduced in their current society and problem dramas. Bodie, the novelist, in *A Kiss for Cinderella* (1916), described in the stage-directions as "the least distinguished person in *Who's Who*", is almost an image of Barrie himself, one who has "a weakness for persons who don't get on". He "has escaped, as it were, from" the "fashionable crush, and is spending a quiet evening at home". But home becomes romance and the playhouse and the fairy-tale – and in its own way a more genuine reality than the fashionable world of social functions. And so we proceed to the greatest of all the might-have-been dramas,

Dear Brutus (1917), wherein men and women who seem to be as substantial as ourselves pass through a palpable stage-door, are offered realisation of their inner dreams and longings, and end up as they had begun.

Perhaps the true key to an understanding of Barrie the man and the dramatist is to be found in eight lines which Thomas Hardy scribbled down at a rehearsal of *Mary Rose* (1920) and which appropriately are printed as a caption beneath the portrait-frontispiece of the *Collected Plays* (1928):

> If any day a promised play
> Should be in preparation,
> You never see friend J. M. B.
> Depressed or in elation,
>
> But with a stick, rough, crooked and thick,
> You may sometimes discern him,
> Standing as though a mummery show
> Did not at all concern him.

The photograph shows Barrie steadily staring out as if in quiet resignation at something which lies beyond our view, but which from his plays we realise was the entire mummery show of life.

Whatever the correspondence in time between this calmly placid Barrie and the energetic Shaw, with his restless fiery exuberance, the contrasts, both inner and outer, between the two men might well seem to be so great as to make ridiculous any attempt at a conjunctive consideration of their writings. The former was, in 1900, indeed one of the chief among the established or representative playwrights and within the following two or three years he had made his already firm position in the theatre even firmer. By comparison the latter seemed to belong in a different world, to belong – not to any established group of popular authors, but to the number of those playwrights who were bent on setting up what Norman Marshall was to style the "other theatre".[1]

[1] The literature on Shaw is so vast that only a very few titles can be cited here. Biographical studies abound. Among the earlier works of this kind that by Archibald Henderson (1912) deserves notice since it

During the latter years of the nineteenth century and the early years of our own, ardent members of the intelligentsia, of course, were eagerly perusing *Plays Pleasant and Unpleasant* (published 1898) and *Three Plays for Puritans* (1901): tiny audiences had seen *Widowers' Houses* at an Independent Theatre Society performance in 1892: later, Stage Society affiliates witnessed performances of *You Never Can Tell* in 1899 and of *Captain Brassbound's Conversion* in 1900: through the sponsorship of that heroine of the repertory movement, Miss Horniman, *Arms and the Man* had a short run and a mixed reception at the Avenue Theatre in 1894, while in 1897 certain provincial audiences had the privilege of seeing *Candida* as acted by Janet Achurch's Independent Theatre Company; in 1897 the one-act *The Man of Destiny* was, strangely, performed at the

includes material contributed by the author himself, and some further information of a similar kind appears in Henderson's later *Bernard Shaw: Playboy and Prophet* (1932). Especially important is the *Bernard Shaw: His Life, Work and Friends* (1956) written by one of the closest among these friends, St John Ervine. There is, too, much of real value in the interesting compilation made by Stanley Weinraub in his *Shaw, an Autobiography 1856–1898* (1970) wherein the dramatist's own comments on his earlier years are adroitly brought together. The critical literature dealing with the plays is so diverse that only a very few comments of a personal kind can be introduced here. For the present writer the volumes written by Kenneth Pearson (*Bernard Shaw*, 1942, and *G. B. S.: A Postscript*, 1951) contain some of the most balanced and carefully considered assessments of his work. During recent years there has been a tendency for academic writers to concentrate rather upon his "philosophy" than upon his attainments as a playwright: but perhaps the most serviceable contributions to a full appreciation of his achievements are the several volumes (among which Dan H. Laurence's *Collected Letters* is most significant) which aim at providing us with full background material. Special attention may be directed to *The Shaw Review*, a periodical which not only presents interesting assessments of critical studies on G. B. S. and his works but also prints a considerable number of original essays on diverse aspects of his writings. An active member of the editorial board of this journal, Sidney P. Albert, has lately been making valuable contributions to our knowledge of Shaw as a "producer" of his own works, contributions which support and extend the statements made on this subject by William Armstrong, "George Bernard Shaw: the Playwright as Producer", *Modern Drama*, viii, 1966): of particular interest are "Shaw's Advice to the Players of *Major Barbara*" (*Theatre Survey*, x, 1969) and "'In More Ways than One': *Major Barbara's* Debt to Gilbert Murray" (*Educational Theatre Journal*, xx, May 1968).

Grand Theatre in Croydon. And that was all. To the public at large Shaw remained virtually unknown until between 1904 and 1907 the Granville-Barker–Vedrenne seasons at the Court directed the spot-light on his fiery Irish beard.

In one sense, then, it might well be said that in 1900 no author could be found less "established" in the theatre than G. B. S. and that his activities to date suggested that he definitely belonged in spirit to the early school of the minority drama. The only people who were intimately acquainted with his writings were the young intellectuals. Yet even at that time he cannot appropriately be considered as belonging in spirit to the company of those who despised the West End actors and who looked with disdain at the popular audiences which flocked to give them applause. He must, of course, have been well aware that *Widowers' Houses* dealt with a theme which could have appealed to only a limited few, but there is plentiful evidence to show that, apart from this drama, he was thinking in terms of sponsorship, not by enthusiasts such as Annie Horniman or Janet Achurch, but by actors beloved of the general public. St John Ervine shows that in penning *The Man of Destiny* he "had one eye on Richard Mansfield, and the other eye on Ellen Terry",[1] and that, when the former declined the play he was deeply distressed: "I was much hurt by your contemptuous refusal," he wrote, "not because I think it is one of my masterpieces, but because Napoleon is nobody else but Richard Mansfield himself." "I studied the character from you," he assured the actor, "and then read up Napoleon and found I had got him exactly right." Already, even during the early days of his neglect, he was doing what most popular authors do – he was creating his stage characters with the personalities of living performers in mind. The Court seasons, during which he worked so hard at perfecting the staging of his plays, were a deliberate attempt to capture the attention of the general public and, through these spectators, of the more prominent players of the age: and the attempt was successful. In 1906 Cyril Maude was among

[1] *Bernard Shaw* (1956), p. 283.

others who condescended to ask him for a script, and the letter of November that year which Shaw wrote in reply tells its own story. No doubt we must, in reading its lines, remember that three years previously Maude had refused *You Never Can Tell*, and we must believe that this thought gave edge to Shaw's words, but there is obvious truth expressed in his statement: "Nothing would please me better than to do a comedy for you, a fantastic masterpiece for Tree, a problem play for Alexander, and another *You Never Can Tell* for Harrison, not to mention a romantic melodrama for Waller and a musical comedy for Edwardes."[1] Equally significant is an article which he contributed the following year to *The Play Pictorial*.[2] *Caesar and Cleopatra*, he declared, was his attempt "to pay an instalment of the debt that all dramatists owe to the art of heroic acting". Forbes-Robertson he lauds as "the classic actor of our day"–

> He stands completely aloof in simplicity, dignity, grace, and musical speech from the world of the motor car and the Carlton Hotel, which so many of the others, clever and interesting as they are, very evidently prefer to the Olympian region where the classic actor is at home....Without him Caesar and Cleopatra would not have been written; for no man writes a play without any reference to the possibility of a performance.

Quite clearly Shaw's outlook and aims were entirely different from those of the minority authors, and odd performances on special occasions or, later, at the repertories were not for him.

It may seem absurd to suggest that, in trying to place Shaw's works within their contemporary setting, his own philosophical, sociological and economic pronouncements ought to be banished from our minds. The suggestion appears particularly absurd both because in his earlier years he stood at the head of that band of innovators who aimed at establishing the play of ideas upon the English stage and because throughout his whole career he continually sought in his lengthy prefaces to propound his theories concerning

[1] Cyril Maude, *Behind the Scenes with Cyril Maude* (1927), p. 153.

[2] *Play Pictorial*, x, 1907, 110–11.

the universe in general and political life in particular. Yet this suggestion must be made if the true dramatic quality of his idiosyncratic contributions to the stage are to be appreciated. Without the slightest doubt he possessed a brain peculiarly brilliant, alert and scintillating; without doubt, too, ideas of all kinds fascinated him; on the other hand, it is essential to recognise that in his own individual thinking he was strangely simple-minded, apt to seize upon conclusions without considering their implications, inclined to lose sight of humanity in the process of ratiocination.[1] Rightly he deplored the evils of poverty, but only in the abstract, and never for a moment did he proceed to ask himself whether there might not be evils in more widely spread affluence. His belief that the unfit should be disposed of is well-known: he was even prepared to argue that all individuals should be made to appear periodically before tribunals in order to apply, as it were, for certificates of life-worthiness; and St John Ervine is fully justified in his caustic comments on that particular idea. Pointing out that a vast number of men and women would fail to pass the test and that no conceivable tribunal could be fit to take responsibility for judging "who should be slaughtered and who should be permitted to survive", he proceeds to ask a series of basic questions:

What is the survival value of Beethoven, Shelley, Lord George Gordon, Napoleon Bonaparte, Peter the Great, Nelson, Voltaire, Robespierre, Frederick the Great, Goethe, George IV, Mrs Siddons, Balzac, Torquemada, any Pope or Archbishop of Canterbury, and a butler, a footman, a carpenter, a tramp, and a shiftless fellow who drifts from job to job?

Perhaps we may think that a project so patently absurd does not need to be lengthily argued, yet there is still the fact that Shaw made the proposal seriously: as Ervine points out, he never for a moment considered that "a man may be a highly skilled carpenter and a bad husband and worse father".[2]

[1] There is very much more than a single grain of truth in the preface which George Calderon attached to *The Fountain* (1911), in which he stressed the fact that Shaw's ideas in *Widowers' Houses* were "naif and old-fashioned".

[2] *Bernard Shaw* (1956), pp. 533–4.

In his weightiest statement of belief, the diffuse *Back to Methuselah* (1922), the flimsiness, the inconsistencies and the ill-considered conclusions of his thought must be glaringly apparent to even the least philosophical of readers. When we reflect upon these inadequacies, we become less surprised on realising that the admiration he expressed for dictators from Stalin to Mussolini and Hitler was not simply an exhibition of paradoxically Shavian perversity, but that it was a genuine expression of esteem: despite the kindliness and generosity which Shaw so often displayed in his private life, he was always a pathetically perpetual dupe of ruthlessly brutal dictators: if in 1940 he had been a German instead of an Anglo-Irishman he would almost certainly have been a fervent propagandist for the National Socialists, and had he been living in England in 1970 he would have been eagerly looking round for some logically-illogical demagogue, no matter whether left or right, whom he might applaud. Actually, during his last years he came to despair of man, not because of the terrible atrocities inflicted by fascists and communists upon those of whom they did not approve, but because the mass of humanity stubbornly refused to be inhuman enough to fit into his mechanical concepts.

There is, assuredly, every reason for rejecting outright his individual thought on almost all subjects as being both wayward and capricious.

Fortunately, however, Shaw's rather jejune but dangerous personal philosophisings were accompanied by other qualities, and especially by his effervescent sense of fun, by his magnificent stylistic virtuosity, by his innate theatrical skill and, perhaps most important of all, by his idiosyncratic treatment of his stage figures. The sense of fun was sufficiently powerful to break in upon his own more solemn reflections, not only sending flashes of mirth across scenes which otherwise might have appeared to be either dully propagandist or essentially stupid, but also at times happily shattering the course of his own arguments. The style which he evolved for himself, although fundamentally based upon a close adaptation of eighteenth-century prose measures, especially those of Dean Swift, was instinct with rich variety, so that he was able to use it for giving effective expression to persons of all kinds and conditions as well as to episodes of the most diverse tones: no dramatist of his time ranged so widely, at one moment keeping attention riveted upon the cut and thrust of intellectual debate and at another enthralling listeners with such almost operatic arias as that which closes *Back to Methuselah* or with such diapasons as roll richly through *Don Juan in Hell.* Concerning his innate theatrical skill there would seem to be no doubt. Certainly it has been said of him that he had very little interest in the stage itself, the theatre being "always a means to an end with him",[1] and the end itself being "not artistic but sociological"; certainly, too, it has been implied that his plays read better than they act;[2] but, even although it is hazardous to challenge the opinions of such experts in dramatic affairs as Darlington and Trewin, it may be suggested that in these categorical statements what undoubtedly applies to some of Shaw's writings has been unjustifiably extended into a universal generalisation. To a few of his dramas such a judgment applies, but when we examine these we realise that they are his least effective productions: although he deluded himself into believing, and declaring, that *Back to Methuselah* was his best play, clearly we must decide that, despite its tremendous range and despite the quality inherent in some of its individual scenes, it is a mighty failure precisely because the author had allowed himself for the time being to veer away from the theatre which was his true inspirational home. And if we wish to have evidence of a different kind concerning his stage sense we need only turn to the records of his painstaking directional methods and to the crisp, emphatic, penetrating little letters which he was in the habit of addressing to his actors during the course of their rehearsals.

A peculiar problem, and difficulty, arises when considera-

[1] W. A. Darlington, *Six Thousand and One Nights* (1960), p. 39.
[2] J. C. Trewin, *The Theatre since 1900* (1951), p. 60.

tion is directed towards his stage figures. The drama, of course, is a house of many mansions, and among these mansions are some wherein the inhabitants through whom the purport of the scenes is conveyed to the audience have not the semblance of human beings. The strange and individual nature of the particular dramatic mansion created by Shaw is that it comes, as it were, between the "real" and the "ideological". If we consider his plays as a whole from one point of view they may seem to be peopled by a vast array of diverse characters each possessed with an individuality of his own: Jack Tanner, Eliza Dolittle, Major Barbara...we can easily reel off their names and in our mind's eye see them passing in procession before us. Yet, if we go on a little further, we are bound to realise that the "reality" which these characters seem to possess is specious. They have been conceived in a manner decidedly Shaw's own, and in the terms of this manner they require to be construed: diverse as they are, these dramatic persons are put before us in such a way as to make us realise that of "character" Shaw has virtually nothing to offer us. Barrie's Maggie Shand may not be a profound and penetrating study of a particular woman, but she is presented as a living personality, without any ideological or symbolic overtones, made palpable and unique by subtle observation and delicately emotional sympathy: Shaw's Major Barbara lives in an entirely different world – no less effective a stage figure, but one conceived in intellectual rather than in emotional terms. The truth is that, while Shaw, in penning his plays, was of course intent upon his own personal ideas, at the same time his continually active brain was also fascinated by the ideas of others; as a dramatist it was upon these ideas that he concentrated, and sometimes at least the result was a confusion between his own interests and the dramatic milieu which his imagination had created. Maybe this clash can best be exemplified by a particular instance. In 1970 *Arms and the Man* was revived at Chichester, and, in reviewing the production, Harold Hobson drew attention to the fact that "not a single speech in the brief entertainment" rang true. The reason, he says, is obvious. Theoretically Shaw attacks military glory in the person of the flamboyant Saranoff and extols the prosaic Bluntschli. But the simple fact is that, Shaw being what he splendidly was, the attack should have been the other way round. Bluntschli was an ordinary man: that is, someone Shaw never understood. The man he was fitted to admire was the show-off, the braggart, the swaggerer Saranoff, since it was Shaw's brilliant literary uniqueness to be all these things himself....Conversely his complete want of temperamental sympathy with the common-sense Bluntschli was the sort of thing that made him one of the few men in history incapable of writing a viable will.[1]

In this connection a glance at a few passages in some of his private letters is instructive: there, being as it were off his public guard, he sometimes unconsciously let the truth about himself become apparent. Thus, writing to Frank Harris in 1930 he declared – "I am of the true Shakespearean type. I understand everything and everyone, and am nobody and nothing." These words may seem not only a mere extravagance but also an essential contradiction of what Harold Hobson divined in *Arms and the Man*: but they present at least part of the truth. When Shaw temporarily forgot his own ideas he could understand the ideas of others. The allusion to "the true Shakespearean type" receives further elaboration in a second chance statement in which he declared that his "practice" had always aimed at

making my characters say, not what in real life they could ever bring themselves to say, even if they understood themselves clearly enough, but the naked soul truth, quite objectively and scientifically presented, thus combining the extreme of unnaturalness with the deepest attainable naturalness.[2]

As an example he here alludes to the British sergeant introduced into *Too True to Be Good* (1932), explaining that, as an author, his

aim is to reach the real sergeant in the audience and make him say "That's me all right enough; but I never could have put it as straight to myself." The Shakespearean soliloquy, in so far as it

[1] *The Sunday Times*, July 12, 1970.
[2] In a private letter of September 17, 1932.

was not merely an "aside" for the information of the audience, was an attempt at this. The highest drama is nothing but a striving towards this feat of interpretation.

A third instance is not a direct statement such as in the above epistles, but is something which emerges from the general content of several letters written to Gilbert Murray in 1905[1] – and here we are carried beyond the Shakespearian comparison to a consideration of Shaw's specific procedure. In the process of rewriting *Major Barbara* he had told Murray that he proposed to use him as a model for the character of Cusins. This in itself seems to be no more than common and almost inevitable dramatic practice: the number of living men and women whom authors have introduced into plays and novels must be legion. What matters, however, is the light which the correspondence throws upon Shaw's particular method. This demonstrates that he was not really interested in Murray as a man, as an individual, as a unique personality: instead, his interest concentrated on Murray's thought, on what might be called his intellectual attitude as a Professor of Greek at Oxford.

Such is his procedure throughout the greater part of his writing, and if we seek for some term to express his peculiarly individualistic and eccentric kind of drama we might well describe it, on the analogy of the comedy of manners, as the comedy of mental attitudes. Of emotions Shaw's plays are almost completely denuded. Certainly an actress playing the part of St Joan may infuse into the character a warmth and passion of her own, but for the author Joan is conceived in terms of her political position and of her beliefs: only for a short moment do her individual emotions find expression. So it is with all. The most memorable scenes in the plays are those in which the flash and gleam of conflicting mental postures flicker in duels of the mind. These Shaw directs with consummate skill and artistry, deliberately ignoring any of the intimate emotional glimpses and suggestions

[1] These have been printed in an article, "'In More Ways than One': *Major Barbara*'s Debt to Gilbert Murray", contributed by Sidney P. Albert to the *Educational Theatre Journal*, xx, May 1968, 123–40.

which would have been proper to the creation of a dramatic character as commonly interpreted, but which would have destroyed what, consciously or unconsciously, he set out to achieve.

Elsewhere in the course of the theatre's history, of course, there are to be found persons and scenes which remind us of the Shavian practice, but it is almost impossible to think of any series of plays which so rigorously hold to this special form. His method may be accepted as particular and peculiar to his own individual genius, and this fact is reflected in the position he occupied in the playhouse of his time. Naturally no dramatist of such eminence could remain without strongly influencing his contemporaries, yet when he is compared with others – with, for example, J. M. Barrie – that influence is seen to be rather peripheral than central.[1] Again and again in the plays penned during those years are to be found scenes and characters dealt with in a manner which can be described only as "Barriesque", but of plays and characters which might be styled "Shavian" there are remarkably few. His comedy of mental attitudes demands for its creation and successful exploitation a stern and stringent rejection of everything which might disturb its essential being, and there is hardly any other author of that age who could pursue a course so inflexible.

Before leaving this dramatic colossus a brief glance at the course of his career is necessary. What the public was offered during those seasons at the Court between 1904 and 1907

[1] This statement, it must be admitted, clashes with contrary assertions made by several others: Gerald Weales, for example, in "The Edwardian Theatre and the Shadow of Shaw" (*English Institute Essays, 1959* (1960) pp. 160ff.) argues that "1914 puts the most emphatic full stop to an era", that then the authors marched forward under the influence of Shaw, that he gave them a new faith in the power of the stage, that he taught them what a mighty instrument the theatre might be for the purpose of spreading ideas sociological and political. Perhaps sufficient evidence has been given in the preceding chapters of the present volume to suggest that these arguments take their form from wishful thinking: the process which Weales describes is, as it were, what ought to have been – the greatest dramatist of the age directing the whole course of playwriting during his lifetime: but careful examination of the available facts fails to substantiate such an historical account.

was a number of plays which had been written within the last years of the nineteenth century, together with a few later works, notably *Man and Superman*, *John Bull's Other Island*, *Major Barbara* and *The Doctor's Dilemma*. These, as has been suggested, made him a master of the theatre, and thereafter, presented at various theatres and by divers star performers, came a series of about thirty comedies and dramas, including among their number most of Shaw's greatest achievements. Some of them, certainly, may be dismissed as of no account – pieces such as *The Inca of Perusalem* (1916), and *Annajanska, the Wild Grand Duchess* (1918), for instance – although even in these lighter realms he could at times brilliantly demonstrate, as in *The Dark Lady of the Sonnets* (1910), the qualities which gave distinction to his more ambitious works. In 1911 came *Fanny's First Play*, originally said to have been penned by "Fanny O'Dowda" or else by "Xxxxxxx Xxxx"; *Androcles and the Lion* was presented in 1913, and *Pygmalion* in the year following; in 1921 *Heartbreak House* had its London première and *Back to Methuselah* was published; three seasons later, in 1924, came the triumph of *Saint Joan*, and in 1929 *The Apple Cart* was presented at the Malvern Festival. To discuss any one of these plays separately here would be inappropriate, but one general comment may be made on a feature of his writing which has direct pertinence to a panoramic view of the theatre during these years. In considering Shaw, we are often inclined to think of him as a playwright who, following in his own eccentric manner the path pursued by the later Ibsen, found his true power when he stood with his lengthy legs firmly planted in the world of the present. We remember *Saint Joan*, of course, but frequently we are apt to forget just how much of his writing is set either in the historical past or in a no-man's land of fantasy. Among the plays which he had composed in the nineties, *Arms and the Man* has its action placed in a Ruritanian Bulgaria, *The Man of Destiny* deals with a fictional Italian episode in Napoleon's early life, *The Devil's Disciple* presents a comic–melodramatic action supposed to have taken place during the American

War of Independence, *Caesar and Cleopatra* goes back to classical times, *Captain Brassbound's Conversion* travels across to Morocco – no less than five plays out of ten. Among those composed during the first thirty years of the present century *The Shewing-up of Blanco Posnet* (1909) melodramatically associates itself with *The Devil's Disciple*, *The Dark Lady of the Sonnets* (1914) deals with Queen Elizabeth and Shakespeare, *Androcles and the Lion* (1913) is a classical fantasy, the atmosphere of *Heartbreak House* is visionary even if its furnishings are realistic, *Back to Methuselah* starts at the very beginning of things in the Garden of Eden and proceeds into the future as far as thought can reach, *Saint Joan* has its action set in late medieval times, and *The Apple Cart* exists in a world of pure extravaganza with its King Magnus, its Boanerges, its Pamphilius and its Sempronius. Inhabiting such worlds of the imagination, it may be suggested, Shaw was happiest. These worlds permitted him, as the realistic environments did not, to give full range to his verbal virtuosity, while essentially their atmosphere was more harmoniously in keeping with the particular and peculiar comic spirit which was distinctively his own. Something like *Man and Superman* (although decidedly not the scene of *Don Juan in Hell*) might have been created by another playwright: *Androcles and the Lion* is uniquely Shaw. In these realms his genius flourished, and the things he wrought in them are those which retain their worth. Reviewing a number of plays presented in March 1970 J. W. Lambert succinctly began his article with a "Tiresome to have to report that the week's most amusing, stimulating and – to drop into current cant – relevant offering is *The Apple Cart* (Mermaid), over forty years old, and one of Shaw's lesser works at that."[1] In these words, we may think, there is enshrined a symbolic quality.

[1] *The Sunday Times*, March 8, 1970.

3. *New Members of the Establishment: Davies, Sutro and Maugham*

At the turn of the century the dramatic theatre thus found itself moving forward on certain clearly marked lines. Farce and light comedy, frequently dealing with characters at least titularly belonging to the aristocracy or with others belonging to the upper middle class, flourished; the public also thoroughly enjoyed romantic dramas with strong situations and melodramatic in action; and apart from these they revelled in the newer forms of the so-called "realistic" society play, sometimes tensely serious, sometimes unashamedly sentimental, sometimes concentrating upon heroines whose lives occasionally ended in utter disaster but who more often were rescued from the scrapes into which their charming follies had plunged them, or who succeeded, against odds, in seizing upon the men upon whom their hearts had been set, sometimes placing chief stress upon heroes, masculinely obtuse, who only with difficulty were brought to a realisation of where true love resided and where genuine happiness could be found. Love, in fact, formed the staple element in the majority of these offerings, the audiences taking almost equal delight in being able to weep at distressful situations and in having the vicarious thrill of watching hero or heroine eventually finding bliss in the arms of heroine or hero. The more prominent, and the more skilled, among these authors were able to give to their "realistic" society plays individual qualities of their own, but it must be acknowledged that many of the stage writers popularly established during the latter years of the nineteenth century owed their position to the fact that they were able with unadventuresome ease to repeat familiar patterns.

In thus examining the development of the stage in the twentieth century, it is of course absolutely essential to bear in mind two things–that the representative authors did not suddenly abandon the theatre in the year 1900 and that the best of them did not merely repeat what they had been writing in late Victorian times but materially aided in shaping the drama presented to Edwardian and Georgian audiences.

Nevertheless, it is equally important to observe how many younger authors began to knock at the establishment's door within the first half-dozen years of the new century. Of these, numbers were simply sedulous and often not very accomplished apes, copying with minor variations the designs already made familiar or else searching for material abroad (and "abroad" for them generally meant Paris) which, suitably toned down, might prove acceptable on the London stage: there were dozens of writers such as Cosmo Gordon-Lennox who kept the theatres supplied with pieces of this kind filched from the French. Yet even among these lesser authors there are to be found things of interest. The work of H. F. Maltby may serve as an example.[1] First appearing as a dramatist in 1905 and carrying on to the close of the present period, he never attained real eminence and, as a result, he might readily be dismissed. Looking at his *The Right Age to Marry*, for instance, it may seem extraordinary that as late as 1925 he could repeat such an old-fashioned comedy-drama formula as that which here shows a middle-aged Lomas Ramsden almost trapped into a loveless marriage by an intriguing Mrs Carlisle, and then, just before the final curtain, suddenly realising that his warm-hearted and virtuous housekeeper, Ellen Marbury, is devotedly in love with him. Others of his plays are of a similar kind, but, if we examine his work as a whole, rather unexpectedly we come upon his *The Laughter of Fools* (1909) which not only has its delightfully attractive portrait of the half-dithering, half-perspicacious Colonel Grieg, but also presents, in a quietly unassuming manner, a skilfully-drawn family picture of pretentiousness, incorporating a critical view of society's artificial values. Proceeding further, we also find his "tale of a respectable family", *The Rotters* (1916), which, if it cannot quite be accorded the current cant label of "black comedy",

[1] Maltby's own record, *Ring Up the Curtain* (1950), is of particular value not only as a picture of his own career but as an impressionistic sketch of the theatre during his lifetime.

must be regarded as decidedly and innovatingly brown – a comedy designed to expose all the vices and deceptions festering beneath the foundations of a family seemingly virtuous. This, as the author himself has stated, was the first play in English dealing with "nasty" people – and in this respect may we not even say that it is the first of all plays constructed on the principle of "alienation"? Can it be that Maltby, and not Brecht, was the true innovator?

In his own way, Maltby, although confessedly not one of the outstanding authors of this period, was thus playing his part in the development of the twentieth-century theatre, and he was accompanied by others, such as "George Paston" (Emily M. Symonds) and Frederick Fenn, endowed with similarly original inventive skill. Collectively these dramatists provide an effective illustration of the way in which diverse forces were at work on the popular stage – forces old and forces new: and it is important to observe how many of the young writers appeared before the public in or about the year 1900 and bowed their way out either just before or just after 1930. J. B. Fagan thus began his career in 1899 (with a "romantic drama") and ended it in 1931 (with a comedy, *The Improper Duchess*). In 1904 he presented, ambitiously but not very successfully, a rather old-fashioned blank-verse *Prayer of the Sword*, romantically religious in tone. Fortunately, however, he soon abandoned plays of such a nature, and five years later, in *The Earth*, he (quite appropriately) broke fresh ground by electing to take as his main character a press tycoon, Sir Felix Janion, passionate for power and prepared to employ any device, even the blackmailing of a government minister, to gain his own ends. Two years after that, Fagan gave strong parts to George Alexander and Mrs Pat Campbell in his sultry *Bella Donna* (1911) while a long time afterwards he provided Yvonne Arnaud with a rôle equally popular but delightfully comic in *And So to Bed* (1926). None of these, perhaps, can be deemed great plays, yet they have value and interest both individually and in combination. Not dissimilar, although outwardly far different, was the career of Cicely Hamilton, an authoress who in her own way might be taken as a prime instance of the dramatist who stood hesitant between the minority drama and that of the West End – or maybe even as an instance of the playwright who, with the desire to appeal to the general public, enriched her works with scenes and concepts which had about them a minority flavour. Success came to her early in life with the production of *Diana of Dobson's* (1908), described as a "romantic comedy", but one invested with decidedly original features. Starting with a kind of first act prologue realistically depicting the dormitory of a large drapery store, she succeeded in establishing its boringly depressive atmosphere – an atmosphere which provided a background for, and which explained, the girls' excitement when the popular Diana, hearing that unexpectedly she has been left a legacy of £300, boldly and daringly announces that she is prepared to spend it all in one wild fling. Off she goes to an hotel, where a Mrs Cantelupe, believing that she is a rich widow, is delighted when her impecunious playboy nephew, Captain Bretherton, falls in love with her. Eventually Diana tells him the truth and berates him for being a mere sluggard and adventurer, so that, stung by her taunts, he determines to try to earn his own living. Save for the opening prologue, all of this may appear to be sentimentally novelette material, but the end of the play carries us back to the beginning: on an Embankment bench the pair meet again, and reality takes the place of artificial dreaming. After a number of less penetrating and less effectively penned long and short plays – some designed for the London stage, some for repertories – and at least one Nativity drama, Cicely Hamilton once more captured the lively spirit which had animated her earliest work: her imaginative drama of *The Old Adam* (1914) displays originality in concept and execution.[1] This concerns a state of cold war which has been a dominant element in the foreign policy of two countries – England and a judiciously named Paphlagonia – and of late there have been speeches wherein the coolness has assumed more than

[1] This, as is recorded in the hand-list, was first called *The Human Factor*.

a little warmth. An English inventor, Athelstane Lilley, makes an unexpected discovery – an instrument by the operation of which all machinery within a selected area can be put out of action – and the secret of this instrument he hands over to his government. Immediately the Prime Minister declares war. To everyone's dismay, however, it is found that precisely the same discovery has been made in Paphlagonia: all machines in both countries are effectively immobilised. Instead of the conflict being brought to a halt, however, the war proceeds with recourse to mankind's most primitive weapons – staves, and stones, and scythes. The Navy, of course, has been rendered useless, but the fishermen bitterly carry on in bloody battle. By no means has the Old Adam been exorcised. While Cicely Hamilton's dramatic talent may not be deemed to have been very great, her inventiveness and originality, together with the skill shown in the writing of individual scenes, as exemplified in these two plays, the one early and the other late in her career, certainly are not undeserving of notice.

Much more firmly set within the sphere of the ordinary realistic tradition stand two other contemporary playwrights the value of whose work, for diverse reasons, is somewhat difficult to assess. Writing in 1921, Hugh Walpole expressed his firm belief that the serious comedies composed by H. H. Davies would "be delighting theatre-goers of a hundred years from now".[1] Although the time limit of a century has not yet been completed, it may well be thought that here is one of those shattered prophecies with which the stage's story has been littered, and there may be a resultant tendency to thrust Davies aside. Yet that would be a mistake. After one or two early and obscure efforts, this playwright suddenly soared to fame in 1903 when no fewer than three of his full-length comedies – *Mrs Gorringe's Necklace*, *Cousin Kate* and *Cynthia* – caught the attention of the public; and during ensuing seasons these were supplemented by a number of other works which proved no less appealing and among which one, *The Mollusc* (1907), attained to the long-run list. With-

[1] Introduction to Davies' *Plays* (1921), pp. xix–xx.

out any doubt whatsoever their author possessed a lively and inventive mind and a pleasantly effective style; equally without any doubt he displayed an uncertainty in the handling of dramatic situations, his general following of contemporary patterns in the sphere of the social drama conflicting with his own original insights into human nature. His plays thus exhibit a pecular mixture of evasions and confusions, liveliness and warmth. This mixture is, for example, clearly exemplified in the structure of his first important play, *Mrs Gorringe's Necklace.* The main theme here is the story of a weak youth, Lieutenant David Cairn, who steals the jewels which give the title to the drama, who is protected by an older friend Captain Mowbray, a man nobly (but perhaps not very convincingly) willing to assume the blame, and who ultimately shoots himself. Even although Mowbray provided a nice sympathetic part for Charles Wyndham, the theme itself must be regarded as trite, its elaboration as forced, and the dialogue with which it is put before the audience as no better than what commonly accompanied this particular kind of drawing-room drama. Running parallel with its rather artificially conceived plot, however, goes the wholly delightful comedy which envelops Mrs Gorringe herself, a woman whose mind is a "morass", one who fecklessly bumbles on although there is no one to listen to her. Just as the final curtain is nearing its fall we see her standing there, happily oblivious of the fact that the backs of all her stage companions are turned towards her, as she rambles on blissfully:

That shows you the kind of man he is – He's the sort of man to lead a woman on and make her say things that – well, I don't think I know you well enough to explain – (*She looks at the others and sees that no one is paying any attention to her*) If you've all done with me I'll go.... Did I ever tell you how I came in and closed the door? It's as if the dressing-table were there – (*Points to the window*) No, there. (*Points somewhere else*) And the door – (*Coming toward the door*)....

And so on. In its own setting all of this is excellent fun.

Cousin Kate, which had a central male lead admirably suited for Cyril Maude, likewise falls into two parts, but here these parts are better adjusted to each other than in the earlier play. What should attract particular attention is the way in which Davies has taken a topic popular among minority playwrights – the narrow, sanctimonious atmosphere of a rural community – and has rendered it dramatically appealing for a general audience. The action starts with trouble at the home of Amy Spencer, a girl whose fiancé, Heath Desmond, a painter, had suddenly taken fright and decamped just before the intended wedding: in their distress the family decide to call in Cousin Kate, a young novelist, who has always shown herself ready to lend a helping hand in times of distress. During her train journey from Town, Kate (who, of course, knows only the family's side of the story and who is picturing Heath as a selfish monster) finds herself talking to and being much attracted by a man with whom she shares her carriage. After her arrival, she discovers, to her dismay, that this stranger is Heath himself: a further meeting with him makes her realise that indeed she has fallen in love with him – and a heart is preserved from breaking only when the brainless and fickle Amy unexpectedly announces that, after all and taking everything into consideration, she finds she would prefer to marry the prim young local clergyman. Once more, we must stand hesitatingly uncertain regarding our judgment on this play. The plot steps dangerously close to the crumbling edge of slushy sentimentality, yet Davies does not quite lose his balance. He displays real ability in giving his characters living qualities, and beneath the course of the action we must be aware of a central informing force. There is no intellectually conceived sense of purpose, no idea, here, nor is there any satire – not even in the presentation of the dim-witted and hide-bound clergyman: and the association of the two "artists" is treated adroitly and with true sensitivity. *Captain Drew on Leave* (1905) hardly merits so much attention, but *The Mollusc*, Davies' best play, was still to come. This, an excellent comedy of four characters, concentrates mainly upon one central figure representative of the genus molluscry – that particular class of humanity which is to be distinguished from the merely lazy – those who are purely passive – by the active exercise of force to resist pressure. "It's amazing," remarks one of the characters, "the amount of force a mollusc will use, to do nothing, when it would be so much easier to do something." No doubt for many of the *avant garde* this comedy must have seemed sadly lacking in theoretical social comment, but it is penetrating in its observation of life, and it is entertaining. The kind of drama which Davies himself decidedly did not care for is suggested in his portrait of a young, suddenly successful author, Paul Hughes, who at the start of *Lady Epping's Lawsuit* (1908) is shown talking to an interviewer. The success which has come to this gentleman is a comedy, but he explains that he wants to write a "serious play": no one, he avers, believes that a play can be serious

> unless it's about unpleasant people. However, if you'll give me time I'll show you some most objectionable specimens of both sexes, and prove that all our English principles are wrong. I don't want people to think I have no ideas.

In a period when the drama of ideas was the fashionable craze in several of the more prominent circles this must have seemed a deplorable sentiment, yet when we read Davies' plays we realise that he did have things of significance to say about human nature perhaps of greater value than many of the solemn and sometimes angry theorisings of others, and that his humanism, which led him so often to make an "artist" his hero (Heath in *Cousin Kate*, Noel Gale in *Doormats*, 1912, Robin Worthington in *A Single Man*, 1910) has genuine and enduring worth. Even although hardly anyone now could be found willing to endorse Walpole's judgment – a judgment which that author rendered even stronger in his declaration that these plays by Davies "must surely endure in the line of great English comedy so long as the English stage endures at all" – there may at least be some critics prepared to acknowledge his virtues within his own period and even to admit that some of his scenes and characters have a quality which goes beyond what may be found in not a few later dramas better known.

An entirely different problem presents itself when we turn to the voluminous writings of Alfred Sutro. Strangely this widely popular author started with a lengthily verbose "psychological" and prevailingly dull drama, *The Cave of Illusion* (1900) – a work which, no doubt fortunately, never reached the stage. Thoroughly in the style of the minority drama, it presents as its hero a novelist, David Hollesdaile, who, when he finds that his publisher, liking the script of his latest book, expresses the belief that it will prove a great popular success, is cast into a dismayed and agonised torment of despair: if any book is popular, it must be bad. The general theme of the play's plot – that of the married artist who finds inspiration in another woman, tires of her and then finds she is to have a child – is a commonplace one told in language artificially frenzied: the woman's cry, "O God, O God, have mercy on us both!", brings it to an appropriate end. The whole thing is, in fact, rather absurd, and its "minority" inspiration is clearly revealed in the terms of the lengthy and praiseful introduction by Maurice Maeterlinck which starts with the striking of a familiar note:

La pièce qu'on va lire appartient à un genre ingrat et difficile, mais il semble bien que ce genre soit aujourd'hui le moins artificiel, le plus vivant, le plus sincère, et qui sait? le seul qui réponde à toutes les réalités, et surtout aux plus hautes, de notre vie.

Fortunately for himself, Sutro, even although his passion for the creative work of Maeterlinck led him to prepare translations of many of the Belgian's plays, had other less delicate and fragile strings to his bow. A fairly skilful one-act piece, *A Marriage Has Been Arranged* (1902), served as a signpost pointing directly towards the enormously successful *The Walls of Jericho* in 1904. The one-act is a simple duologue between a self-made millionaire Harrison Crockstead and a Lady Aline de Vaux: the latter's aunt (a Duchess) and her mother (a Marchioness) have arranged their engagement, but when he proposes to her she refuses him; he speaks out bluntly, in phrases not usually heard in the polite society language of the time, and she is shocked – but shocked, as it were, into a sense of reality. What had been begun as an artificially contrived, loveless union suddenly is warmed by her appreciation of his honesty, so that, when he abandons his suit but asks her to choose him a wife, she tells him she wishes him for herself. This simple story, cleverly told within the brief scope of a one-act play, becomes, in the full-length drama, an exposure of the follies and vices of the smart set revealed in the contrast between a rich Queensland sheep-farmer, Jack Frobisher, and his wife, Lady Alethea. She spends most of her time with an idle circle of society friends, and, after suffering her follies for a time, he eventually explodes in an outburst of rage:

> I've had enough of these companions of yours, these wretched sexless women who do nothing but flirt and gamble, those childless wives, who grudge the time that it costs them to bring a baby into the world.

In his anger he tells her that he has decided to return to Australia, and eventually she finds herself compelled, partly through thought of her child and partly through a new-found appreciation of his virtues and standards, to accompany him.

From this time on to 1929 Sutro turned out nearly forty plays long and short, of varying kinds and of varying values. That he had an adroit constructive ability is certain, and this we can esteem even while we recognise that his ability was somewhat restricted in scope. Several of his one-acts are thoroughly masterly. If, for instance, one looks at his *The Man in the Stalls* (1911) and analyses its action impartially, one is bound to agree that in artful accomplishment it can hardly be matched by any other play of its time. From its opening lines (ultimately laying the ironic basis for the entire action), through its cleverly managed transformations, on to its cynical conclusion it is indeed a gem of its kind, anticipating all the basic features of Somerset Maugham's short-story technique. We cannot fail here to applaud Sutro's skilful and astringent treatment of his plot, nor can we fail to admire the way in which he has brought a fundamentally complex story within the simple limits of a one-act piece. At the same time we are no doubt forced to agree that he did not have the power to create lifesize portraits in his longer plays or to handle their movement with equivalent skill. They, indeed, contain interesting and appealing scenes and acts, but rarely do we feel satisfied throughout the entire course of his actions: within the epigrammatic limits of a playlet Sutro can be admirable, but in the length of a three-act or four-act drama there are always stretches of boredom: he can tell a short story, tense or amusing, in a lively, entertaining and gripping manner, but in more extended narratives his style falters and palls.

Thus, for example, the "artificial comedy" of *Mollentrave on Women* (1905) is affectedly and rather tediously contrived; thus, in spite of its directness and dramatically tense situations, *John Glayde's Honour* (1907) must be considered largely a replica of *The Walls of Jericho*, with its magnanimous strong-man hero and its erring wife; thus the passions depicted in *The Barrier* (1907) seem artificially false. The same strong-man, who angrily spurns the heroine and then sentimentally takes her into his arms, reappears in *The Builder of Bridges* (1908) and, in a form still more extreme, in *The Choice* (1919) – in this last-mentioned drama audiences were startled on seeing powerful, masterful John Cordways (Gerald Du Maurier) displaying his affection for the woman he loved by giving her a hearty smack on the face. Certainly Sutro provided his heroes with considerable excuse for their outbursts by showing his ladies stupid, if charming; Dulcie Elsted in *The Perplexed Husband* (1911), infected by "Ibsenism", Isabel Jervoise in *The Two Virtues* (1914), Margaret Verrall in *The Barrier* and Mrs Ruth Tedcastle in *Far Above Rubies* (1924) are all diverse mirror-images of the same person as she turns her face this way and that. Occasionally, it is true, Sutro tries to break new ground – as, for example, in *The Firescreen* (1912), where the hero is a dedicated medical researcher, or in the somewhat silly *Freedom* (1916) with its uncompromising presentation of a devoted wife and mother who, being an "intellectual", believes in woman's rights, and in a manner coldly deliberate enters into a loveless affair – but his questings after novelties rarely appear satisfactory.

In these plays the dialogue usually moves forward with a steady and rather monotonous pace. In some scenes, particularly when two women are politely and cattily talking to each other, there are moments of lightness –

LEONORA. Mrs Jervoise, it was under a – misapprehension – that I mentioned my Tuesdays to you.

ISABEL (*Loftily*). Please don't let that disturb you. I shouldn't have dreamed of going. We prefer brains to money.

LEONORA (*Placidly*). I wish, with all my heart, that you may one day possess both –[1]

but commonly his attempts at wit are almost painfully laborious –

It's a terrible thing to say about any man – and I beg that you won't repeat it – but I've the profound conviction that Daniel – in the twenty odd years that he has been married – has never once been unfaithful to his wife! –[2]

or, in would-be satiric vein –

SIR ALGERNON (*With a great sigh of relief*). Thank Heaven for that! Then the blunder is not so serious (*He turns to* CON) in it's effects, sir – merely in its effects! And fortunately Tamhouse will be returning soon – eh, Martindale?

MARTINDALE. In a fortnight, Sir Algernon. And we shall all be very glad. However much we may like Tedcastle personally – his mania for insisting that letters shall be answered the day they're received –

SIR ALGERNON (*In blank amazement, as he turns to* CON). What, sir, what? Can this be true?

CON. Certainly, Sir Algernon.

SIR ALGERNON (*Bending forward impressively*). Are you aware, sir, that this is a Government Department – and that it is the ritual, handed down to us through the centuries, that at

[1] *The Two Virtues* (1914).

[2] *The Laughing Lady* (1922).

least a week shall pass before a communication is acknowledged – and a month before the matter is dealt with?

CON (*Pleasantly*). I am aware, Sir Algernon, that this is the usual practice. But it seemed to me that, in the interest of the public –

SIR ALGERNON (*Completely overwhelmed, rising solemnly*). The interest of the public! Sir, has it occurred to you that if your impetuous and indecent – yes, sir, indecent – haste became general, Government Departments could be run on HALF THEIR ACTUAL STAFF? You have no answer: for once you have no answer. Ponder it, sir: ponder it: and mend your ways.[1]

Possibly Sutro's work might have been more kindly treated by the critics had it not been for the fact that his career – in time sequence, in choice of themes, in style and to a large degree in technique – coincided with that of a much more accomplished dramatist, Somerset Maugham. The connections between them may be illustrated by two examples. Sutro's first significant play was *The Walls of Jericho* in 1904. Five years later Maugham presented his *Smith* in which the same basic situation is dealt with. Living in an artificially smart Kensington circle, Herbert Dallas-Baker, K.C. and his wife Rose will not have any children because they are not prepared to undertake the expense and bother of bringing them up; Algy Peppercorn is a parasite who dances attendance on Rose, and Emily Chapman is a family friend who gains her livelihood by playing bridge. Into this ménage arrives Rose's brother, Thomas Freeman, who has been nine years abroad in Rhodesia and who is shocked by all their flippancy. Wishing to marry, and seeking for a "natural woman", he, in turn, shocks the whole group by proposing to Smith, the parlourmaid – yet the shock is sufficiently salutory to induce Emily to set off working her way to Australia, to make Algy offer his parasitical hand to an American girl, and to leave Rose in lonely despair. Actually, inverted sentimentalism runs riot here, and Sutro's might well be esteemed the better play; yet the facts that Maugham

[1] *Far Above Rubies* (1924).

was thus moving in the same environment and that, notwithstanding the deplorable qualities exhibited in *Smith*, he was as a writer the more richly talented of the two, may have disturbed the course of what Sutro was bringing to the theatre and certainly influenced those many critics who came to compare him unfavourably with his rival.

The title of Maugham's first "modern play", *A Man of Honour* (1903)[1] reminds us already of Sutro's style in certain of his dramas. It is a rather unexpectedly grim, supposedly realistic, play, pessimistic in tone, dealing with the marriage of a barrister to a barmaid and ending with her final suicide. Such a style, however, was not that destined to make him so widely popular a playwright: perhaps we may think of it as bearing much the same relationship to his later works as *The Cave of Illusion* does to those by his rival. Success came to Maugham with *Lady Frederick* (1907) and *Mrs Dot* (1908), both concentrating, like Sutro's, on the exposure of society's foibles, but displaying much greater sensitivity and, at times, much more penetrating sympathy, besides sparkling occasionally with true wit. Lady Frederick is outwardly a frivolous flirt, aged about thirty-five, and thus not markedly different from, say, Sutro's Rose: where Maugham scores is in the enrichment of this lady's character; beneath her modish veneer she is shown to be good-natured and sensible – qualities which become clearly evident when she decides to reject the callow devotion of a youthful Marquess in favour of the love brought to her by an older man of the world: in doing so, she is motivated, not by practical considerations but by the dictates of her own heart and nature.[2] And, in place of the laborious wit, the scenes are diversified by lines such as the comment on a Marchioness' title –

[1] Written in 1898. Maugham himself has indicated, in *The Summing Up* (1938), the order in which his earliest works were composed.

[2] A recent (1970) revival of this play was not greeted by the critics with overgreat enthusiasm; but perhaps this was due to the fact that they were adversely swayed by the general picture of upper-class insolence and by the toadyism displayed by those less happily born. Notwithstanding the general critical condemnation of the drama, Maugham's skill in drawing his portrait of Lady Frederick is still worthy of esteem.

Unlike a duchess, it's cheap without being gaudy –

or the rueful remark –

It's one of the injustices of fate that clothes only hang on a woman really well when she's lost every shred of reputation.

Mrs Dot, with its small, gay, rich Mrs Worthley who gains her man by a trick, is confessedly more farcical, but equally sprightly in its dialogue, the goodhumoured tones of which may be summarised in a single comment:

No man is quite safe from the toils of woman till he's safely in his grave. And even then a feminine worm probably makes a dead set at him.

Here certainly Maugham was going far towards establishing the basis for a modern comedy of manners out of the society drama of his time: the attitude of a Dorimant and a Mirabel, intellectually perceptive moths who are perfectly well aware of the candle's danger and yet are drawn towards its perils by a force beyond their comprehension, might well have given the cue for these words.

This style Maugham pursued in several later plays. *Penelope* (1909) varies the pattern by making its heroine a loving wife who succeeds in disentangling her husband from the web-like mesh of another woman and by introducing the excellently-drawn character of the wise and wily old professor of mathematics, Golightly. *Caroline* (1916), designated as a farce, deals with the "frilly adorable" Caroline Ashley (married, but with a husband who has been rather mysteriously absent for some ten years) and her devoted lover, Rex Cunningham: when news comes of the husband's death, the pair suddenly begin to have doubts about their possible marriage – and Caroline realises that only in the unattainable is there a real attraction. A second farce, *Home and Beauty* (1919), has in its Victoria another "dear little thing" as heroine. Dear little thing she may be, but she is hell to live with: her present husband is Fred, but unexpectedly her former spouse, Bill, turns up alive and well after having been reported dead: the two husbands have a fine old quarrel as to which of them will escape her clutches, and then, joining forces, succeed in foisting her off on an unsuspecting, susceptible business-man. The final curtain falls on the pair of them toasting their good fortune in champagne.

Gradually, however, the current of Maugham's underlying cynicism surged to the surface: it is as if we were seeing a recrudescence of Wycherley's movement from laughing comedy to the bitterness of *The Plain Dealer*. In *Our Betters* (1917) this cynicism almost completely submerged the spirit of laughter, a sardonic anger taking the place of the earlier largely resigned comic irony. It is true, however, that out of this new mood Maugham was able to create his best "modern comedy", *The Circle* (1921) as well as *The Constant Wife* (1926) and *The Bread-Winner* (1930). The first of these shows an elderly couple, Lord Porteous and Lady Kitty Champion-Cheney, once romantic lovers who had deserted their married partners in a joyous ecstasy, but now an ugly, bickering pair, he flabby and she bepainted, and as a later parallel to them, the younger Champion-Cheney's wife, Elizabeth, who has fallen passionately in love with an Edward Luton. The father, Champion-Cheney himself, thinking himself very wise, counsels his son to make a show of generosity towards his Elizabeth, to propose that he should open all bars in the matrimonial cage: but his wisdom comes to naught: the generosity of the husband, even while it touches the heart of the wife, cannot compete with romantic passion, and as Elizabeth looks on the decrepit Lord Porteous and his mistress, she cannot see them as they are, her thoughts going back to the time when they too were passionately devoted to each other and were prepared to dare the whole world for the sake of their love. *The Circle* thus ends where it had begun: the young lovers decamp. And the same mood prevails in *The Constant Wife*. Constance Middleton, knowing that her husband has been unfaithful to her, decides to make herself independent and go off with a lover of her own – not because she wishes to have her marriage dissolved but because she wants to preserve it, if not intact, at least not permanently shattered. The dialogue, with its angry laughter, is thoroughly in accord with the theme: Mrs Culver is speaking to her daughter –

MRS CULVER. After all, what is fidelity?
CONSTANCE. Mother, do you mind if I open the window?
MRS CULVER. It is open.
CONSTANCE. In that case do you mind if I shut it? I feel that when a woman of your age asks such a question I should make some kind of symbolic gesture –

or,

MRS CULVER. Are you in love with Bernard?
CONSTANCE. To tell you the truth I haven't quite made up my mind. How does one know if one's in love?
MRS CULVER. My dear, I only know one test. Could you use his tooth-brush?
CONSTANCE. No.
MRS CULVER. Then you're not in love with him.

An almost Thurber-like atmosphere envelops *The Bread-Winner*, which concentrates on a father who, tired of laboriously earning money for his thoughtless and irksome children, determines to make a complete break with his family – and in harmony with this domestic picture, the dialogue becomes still more strongly impregnated with ironically savage bitterness. From this play comes the often-quoted lines:

Don't you know that since the war the amateurs have entirely driven the professionals out of business? No girl can make a decent living now by prostitution.

This realm of comedy, whether good-natured or sardonic, glittering or dark, was that in which Maugham's genius most happily flourished, but unfortunately he had in him the comedian's desire to triumph in tragedy. *The Tenth Man* (1910), with its central character of a financial magnate who eventually commits suicide, is almost absurdly melodramatic; *Grace* (1910), with its "big" scenes, inflated like the frog in the fable, could have been written by any one of half-a-dozen contemporary minor playwrights; the study in *The Land of Promise* (1913) of Norah Marsh, who, going to Canada, asks a hired hand to marry her and is brutally tamed by him, is equally disappointing; *Caesar's Wife* (1919) has as its main figure a magnanimous husband who might have been the brother of a Sutro strong-man hero. The strange aberration called *The Unknown* (1920) is nothing but a dull and rather stupid drama of religious attitudes – professional conventional Christianity, true simple devotion, passionate intensity, half-belief and lost faith: Shaw could have made these walking ideas interesting – Maugham's treatment of them is utterly boring. *East of Suez* (1922), once a popular success, can nowadays be regarded as no more than a fairly skilfully devised but essentially contrived grim drama of love in the Orient, and one wonders whether originally it may not have been inspired (if that is the proper word to employ in this connection) by a wish to emulate Robert Hichens' Drury Lane spectacle of 1920, *The Garden of Allah*, replete with all the eastern stage props – desert sand, prayer carpets, donkeys, horses, and of course the inevitable camels. Almost the sole interest in Maugham's play is purely historical – the introduction on the stage of the opening wordless pantomimic street scene in Peking, a patent aping of cinematic style.[1] So, too, the filmic flash-back at the close of *The Letter* (1927) might be regarded as the solitary noteworthy element in that sensational Malaysian farrago of murder, deceit, adultery and blackmail. Even in the drama which gives the impression of having been the most sincerely felt among these later plays, *The Sacred Flame* (1928), this melodramatic quality remains a central element, and Maugham's deliberate attempt to deal with his subject-matter in a "literary" manner is a hopelessly dismal failure. It was not successful in its own time, and Irving Wardle's review of its revival in 1967 may be taken as reflecting in general its impact on those who attended its later performances:

[1] See pp. 129–30.

> The play is part thriller and part moral drama. An incurably crippled test pilot, chairbound in the midst of his adoring family, is found dead in bed: his nurse demands a post-mortem examination for poisoning, and the whole family are enmeshed in a web of guilty responsibility before the accuser finally drops the charge.

Maugham, he says, made an eloquent defence of the play in *The Summing Up*,

> but after five minutes of the thing itself it seems that little has changed. The same collection of stuffed shirts assemble in a middle-class living room and hardly a line clatters by without its supporting cliché; blushes rise to maiden cheeks, situations are fraught with danger, passions are hopelessly cherished. We are still in the company of Maugham the narrative craftsman and dialogue hack.[1]

Perhaps the essential point to observe here is that in the plays which were best suited to Maugham's genius he was precisely *not* a dialogue hack: only when he selected a theme of such a solemn nature did he fail: he might have made of this situation an effective short story; as the theme of a full-length play it was, at least for him, hopeless.

The fact that Maugham combined writing for the stage with the writing of novels and short stories is perhaps to be considered the fundamental explanation for the artistic weaknesses discernible in some of these later plays – and the thought reminds us that he belonged to a company of novelist–dramatists who formed a characteristic group from the beginning to the close of this period. There was, admittedly, nothing particularly new in the presence of authors who thus divided their literary activities between narrative fiction and dramatic dialogue: from Fielding onwards to Lytton and Reade dozens of such writers readily come to mind: but even so their increasing numbers were sufficient to make many contemporary critics call attention to their presence, while at least a few of them, not content merely with preparing dramatic versions of their own fictional works or with composing plays in already well-established styles,

[1] *The Times*, February 4, 1967.

consciously set about the task of introducing structural innovations within the theatrical form.

The select company of "representative dramatists" who stepped from the last years of the nineteenth century into the twentieth included several authors of this sort. Already, the work of Hall Caine has called for attention, and with him may be associated Arthur Conan Doyle, even although the latter's boxing melodrama set in the reign of George III, *The House of Temperley* (1909), is less original than the Manx plays of his companion, and although his *Fires of Fate* (1909), despite its interesting description as a "modern morality", has no intrinsic value. From time to time enthusiastic admirers of Henry James have sought to suggest that this novelist's dramatic efforts had been unjustly and over-harshly treated by the theatre, but recent presentations on stage and on the television screen have tended to emphasise the peculiar fact that while a few of his novels and stories have offered excellent material for dramatisation, his own theatrical attempts are utter failures: *The Outcry*, for example, which apparently never got beyond a Stage Society performance in 1917 until its revival in 1968, reveals itself as a laboriously-penned ironic drama which might easily have come from one of the lesser playwrights of the age,[1] while at the same time television serials constructed from *The Spoils of Poynton* and *The Portrait of a Lady* have had unquestioned appeal.

Various other dramatic efforts made by later novelists may be cursorily dismissed. From the pen of W. W. Jacobs came nothing save a collection of one-acts. Among the numerous writings of Horace Vachell are various trivial farces, such as *Plus Fours* (1923), and artificially conceived dramas, such as *The Case of Lady Camber* (1915): only in *Quinney's* (1915), his attractive story of an antique dealer, does he rise above mediocrity. The sole full-length play by Joseph Conrad which reached the stage, *The Secret Agent* (1922), was an

[1] On this play see L. Edel, *Henry James and "The Outcry"* (1949): the same critic has a general commentary on James as a dramatist in the introduction to his edition of *Guy Domville* (1961).

almost complete failure. Divers polite critical remarks have been accorded to recent performances of D. H. Lawrence's essays in dramatic form, yet, except perhaps for *A Collier's Friday Night* (printed in 1934), it seems most probable that, if they had not borne his name, they would never have been dug out of their dusty obscurity. Although some strength may be found in his scenes, no author could be considered well fitted for the playhouse who wrote speeches such as:

> No, Oliver – I was *awfully* fond of you. I trusted you – and I trust you still. You see I knew how fond Gerald was of you. And I had to respect this feeling. So I *had* to be aware of you: I had to be conscious of you: in a way I had to love you. You understand how I mean? Not with the same fearful love with which I loved Gerald.[1]

Neither *The New Sin* (1912) nor *Advertisement* (1915) by another, but less well-known, novelist, Basil Macdonald Hastings, has a clear focus: the best we can say of him as a playwright is that he was responsible for the highly successful adaptation of A. S. M. Hutchinson's once-popular *If Winter Comes* (1922).

Certain original and appealing features in the writings of some five other members of this group do, however, call for attention. The first, and no doubt the least important of these, is Monckton Hoffe. The structure of *The Little Damozel* (1909) may seem more than a trifle amateurish, but, when it is considered in relation to the general dramatic work of its time, interest attaches to the crisp, neatly compact, quality of its dialogue; a polite anticipation of a recent play may be found in *Pomp and Circumstance* (1922), which shows a married pair, bored with each other and yet with some mutual affection still latent in their hearts, agreeing to effect a divorce, with the wife disguising herself in order to act as co-respondent – but when she arrives at her assignation she finds him clad in eighteenth-century clothes, and this so titillates her that, falling into his arms, she protests she will love him for evermore; and in *Many Waters* (1928) Hoffe succeeded in writing a drama which, although it

[1] *Touch and Go* (in *The Plays of D. H. Lawrence*, 1933, p. 109).

cannot be styled a truly great work of art, is quietly delightful in its atmosphere and exhibits a number of novel features. It starts with a conversation between a producer Delauney and a playwright Schloss concerning what the public wants. As a test they take an ordinary humdrum couple, James and Mary Barcaldine, offering them free tickets to go to any one of three shows – *Putrefaction*, which provides the attractive promise of a prominent star actress in the chief rôle, *Soda and Water*, which the critics have excitedly acclaimed as a most clever comedy, and *The Cinderella Princess*, the title of which amply testifies to its style. Because the couple protest that they have had no romance and excitement in their own lives, they agree to choose the last. This opening episode, however, is merely an introductory prologue. The play proper takes shape as a dramatic presentation, in many short scenes, of Barcaldine's account of what has happened to his wife and himself, from their courtship to their marriage, through the times when they came near to bankruptcy and when in misery they watched over their beloved daughter as she lay on her sick-bed, and so on through domestic episode after domestic episode up to the present. After all this narrative of joy and sorrow, of emotions dark and emotions light, comes the epilogue:

DELAUNEY. Now that's what you're up against.
SCHLOSS. What?
DELAUNEY. That's your bloody British public! Can you beat it?
SCHLOSS. Perfectly appalling! They're nice people, too!
DELAUNEY. Of course they are. They simply *don't know*. These sort of people don't live, my dear chap, they just exist.

The characters here may not be developed intimately, but the combination of play-within-play, flashbacks and short, almost cinematic, scenes does succeed in making *Many Waters* what the author called it, "a new play".[1]

[1] For the influence of cinematic technique on dramatic structure see pp. 129–32. Among the various authors who were particularly influenced by this was E. Temple Thurston, although neither in plays of contemporary themes, such as *The Blue Peter* (1924) nor in such a "dramatic chronicle" as *Emma Hamilton* (1929), did he display any noteworthy expertise in the handling of these devices.

Among these novelist–dramatists Eden Phillpotts occupies a different, and very peculiar, position. In the theatre his name is, of course, remembered as that of the creator of the long-run *Farmer's Wife* in 1924[1] and of *Yellow Sands* in 1926 – but for hardly anything else is he worthy of mention: certainly not for the disastrously pretentious *The Blue Comet* (1926), or for the symbolic *My Lady's Mill* (1928), or for the absurd gipsy drama *Buy a Broom* (1929). Probably there are few persons, even among those particularly interested in the drama of the present century, who are aware that in distant days he was responsible for *The Secret Woman*, a play the banning of which inexplicably aroused fierce anger among intellectuals in 1912: simply because it had been censored this stupid piece was treated by those who belonged to the minority as a persecuted dramatic masterpiece: sufficient to indicate its quality is a random quotation from one of its stage directions:

Her face indicates that she is thinking of old times. Emotions cross it. Grief fades to indifference, which anger banishes. Her expression grows inert, and then quickens into a momentary happiness. Looking into the bygone years, she smiles. For a moment she forgets. Then her face grows tender and yearning.

It seems incredible that this dull drama, conceived in completely untheatrical terms, together with its companion piece *The Mother* (1913), and *The Farmer's Wife* could have come from the same man.

A peculiar position, too, but one of an entirely different kind, is occupied by Israel Zangwill. Starting with comedy, he won attention in 1904 with his *Merely Mary Ann*, in which a poor little slavey finds herself in a boarding-house

[1] This had originally appeared at Birmingham in 1916. It is especially notable because of the fact that when it was first presented in London its reception was decidedly lukewarm. For nearly six months business at the box-office was so bad that it was kept on the stage only because of the pertinacity (and financial means) of its producer, Sir Barry Jackson: then suddenly and inexplicably it became all the rage, and finished up with a run of 1,324 performances. C. W. Meadowcroft discusses *The Place of Eden Philpotts in English Peasant Drama* (1924).

for "Bohemians": there she is treated kindly by Lancelot, an impoverished composer ignored by public and critics because he is ahead of his time. Unexpectedly she becomes an heiress: six years pass by: she is now Marian, mistress of a large estate: and of course she meets her Lancelot again, an artist whose contributions to music are widely recognised and on whom the sun shines brightly. Such simple fairy tales, however, were hardly for Zangwill: more closely in harmony with his nature was the "high comedy in three movements", *Plaster Saints* (1914), and *We Moderns* (1922), a bitter denunciation of "our turbulent and jazz-ridden age" in which "modern" painters and "modern" ideas are pilloried in a style sometimes heavy-handed, sometimes illumined by satiric wit.

Although these two comedies came nearer to his inner spirit, Zangwill's mind was almost always seriously occupied with thoughts of deeper problems than comedy, no matter how satirically bitter, could express: indeed, he was consumed by passions which, while rarely profound, were at least intense, and with dramatic ambitions so grandiose as to carry him beyond the theatre's range. The well-known and, for its time, effective *The Melting Pot* (1908) certainly was written in a style which won it considerable success, but the attempt to extend this into a trilogy by adding *The Cockpit* (1921), a sincerely felt but rather wordy drama dedicated "with the author's compliments to the Washington Conference", and *The Forcing House* (1922), a vigorous denunciation of the results of the Russian revolution, failed to make any theatrical impact: the same fate attended *The War God* (1911), even although several advanced writers greeted it as, in the terms attributed to Alice Meynell, "a very great tragedy, full of genius", while *The Next Religion* (1912), a work which joined the exclusive club of banned plays of this period, has little to recommend it save sincerity of purpose.

Two dramas worthy of note and praise both for their themes and structures give to Arnold Bennett a considerably greater theatrical significance. This novelist's first approach to the writing of plays, three now long-forgotten pieces published in 1900 as *Polite Farces for the Drawing-room*, might have suggested that in his later years he would have attached himself to the lesser branch of the minority company: these sketches may be penned in a sprightly manner, but confessedly they are intended for interpretation only by amateurs. In contrast, his first full-length drama, *Cupid and Commonsense* (1908), might have suggested that, if he were to proceed further with playwriting, he would attach himself to the "Manchester school". And if we knew only some of his later works – *The Title* (1918), for example, or *Sacred and Profane Love* (1919), or *The Love Match* (1922), or *Body and Soul* (1922), or *London Life* (1924), or *The Return Journey* (1928) – we might readily tend to dismiss him as a rather inflated, verbose and pretentious author with a style akin to that exemplified in some of Sutro's less successful efforts. True, on reaching *The Bright Island* (1925) we might pause for more than a moment on encountering there the inventive mingling of *commedia dell'arte* and real-life characters;[1] and possibly we might be attracted by the enjoyable good humour of *Mr Prohack* (1927). And this would probably be all. From a scrutiny of these plays we could hardly have imagined that between the earlier pieces and the later came the widely popular and influential *The Great Adventure* (1911) and *Milestones* (1912).

The Great Adventure concentrates upon a prominent artist, shy and retiring, who hates public adulation, who detests parties and dinners arranged by lion-hunters, and who, as a result, prefers to spend most of his time abroad in obscurity. Making one of his rare visits to his London house, his valet suddenly dies, and the doctor who is called in makes the mistake of assuming that the defunct servant is in fact the master. The press is alerted, and after some moments of doubt and feebly diffident attempts at an explanation of the truth, the artist begins to take a whimsical delight in allowing himself not only to be considered dead but actually to be vicariously entombed in Westminster Abbey, while he

[1] See above p. 115.

settles down in a suburb as the husband of a Janet Cannot.[1] Not only is the tale given sharp dramatic focus, with dialogue alert and humorous, but the central characters of Ilam Carve, the painter, and of simple, sensible, affectionate Janet Cannot are depicted with warmth, sensitivity and precision. No doubt the play in a present-day revival might appear somewhat dated, yet in all probability at least some of the quality which brought it its original success would still remain. Almost equally popular,[2] and of considerably greater influence, was *Milestones*, written in collaboration with Edward Knoblock,[3] in which the clash of youth and age, of old-fashioned conservatism and the spirit of invention, of the force of love and the pressure of expediency, are dealt with in three stages during the course of a family's progress: the first part is set in the year 1860, the next in 1885 and the third in 1912, with two individuals, John and Rose Rhead, serving as links between them. Somewhat strangely, this sweeping chronicle style was offered to the public at the very time when L. N. Parker was developing his related "pageant-drama" in *Disraeli* (1911), *Drake* (1912) and *Joseph and His Brethren* (1913). There was thus a strong double force operating upon the playwrights of the period and drawing them away from the older dramatic forms, and, in particular, from the restricted patterns of the realistic three-act play. Parker's dramas may not be thought to possess very great merit, but *Milestones* was boldly planned and expertly written; and it may well be thought that here was the prime, if not the sole, source of that movement which, modified by devices borrowed from the contemporary cinema, led directly towards *Cavalcade* and beyond.[4]

[1] The story was first told by Bennett in his novel, *Buried Alive* (1908), but there are few who would disagree with the assertion that his dramatic version is considerably superior to his prose narrative.

[2] By a peculiar coincidence, *The Great Adventure* had a run of 673 performances at the Kingsway while *Milestones* ran for 607 performances at the Royalty.

[3] This author has an autobiographical account of his career in *Round the Room* (1939).

[4] See above pp. 129–32. There is interest in noting how, at a much later date, Parker's *Angelo* (1922) clearly displayed the influence of

This "Milestones" pattern, with many individual variations, spread widely. Already reference has been made to some examples such as Hoffe's *Many Waters*; Barrie's *Mary Rose* was clearly influenced by the form; and numerous other similar instances abound, instances which may find typical illustration in the work of the last of the novelist–dramatists here to be considered. Rudolf Besier is still remembered for his *Barretts of Wimpole Street*, with its lengthy run in 1930, its success in the United States, its subsequent revivals and its transformation into a musical; but perhaps only a few are aware (or, if once they were aware, still remember) that this author first came to the stage nearly a quarter of a century earlier, in 1907, with an ambitious, and not wholly to be despised, *Virgin Goddess*. Three years later he won some considerable praise for his comedy *Don*, which, although now appearing rather stilted in its dialogue and certainly more than a little sentimental, draws an attractive and bold portrait of its eccentric and kind-hearted protagonist (inevitably, an "artist", a poet). True success, however, did not come Besier's way until the appearance of his attractively-written *Secrets* in 1922. In that play, a prologue showed old Lady Carlton, worn out tending her sick husband, falling asleep in an arm-chair by his bedside; and the drama itself took shape in the form of a "dream" presented in an extended series of flashbacks in which the lives of the couple are presented from the start of their marriage in poverty onwards to a period of affluence, including the time when he took up with another woman and when she, although bitterly jealous and deeply wounded, forgave him because of her realisation that he needed her.[1] Sentimental this play also may be called, yet sentimentalism, if sincere, is not without virtue; and the original success of *Secrets* and its revival several years later were fully justified by its quietly keen insight into the inner beings of its two main characters. Although many playgoers expressed surprise when *The*

narrative film technique. His autobiography, *Several of My Lives* (1928), gives a vivid picture of his enthusiastically experimental career.

[1] See p. 128.

Barretts of Wimpole Street achieved its wide popularity, the facts that Besier at the very start of his career had successfully drawn his portrait of an eccentric poet, that in *Secrets* he had displayed an acute and sympathetic awareness of human sentiment and that in several of his stage writings he had demonstrated an ability to seize upon the basically essential virtues of the melodrama clearly indicated that this play of Robert Browning and Elizabeth Barrett was not something unexpected and extraordinary. In essence, *The Barretts* is indeed a melodrama, with the stock characters attractively disguised – the villain is a Victorian father, the heroine is a frail poetess and the hero is a poet of outstanding fame; Besier had already indicated that he was gifted with sufficient fineness of temper to deal satisfactorily with his hero and heroine: and his very first play, *The Virgin Goddess*, suggested that he was eager to bring colour back into a stage dialogue which had tended, ever more and more, to become drably dull.

4. *The Play of Ideas: Harley Granville-Barker, St John Hankin and John Galsworthy*

Concerning the basic attitudes and aims of the dramatists so far considered there can be little or no doubt. They all looked towards the West End theatres and sought to compose plays likely to appeal to their managers. We may encounter here a number of oddities – the later dramas written by Israel Zangwill, for example, or the more eccentric pieces on which Bernard Shaw was self-induced to spend his time – but rarely, if ever, did any of these men think of making a special appeal to coterie audiences. Whether they penned farces or serious plays, they were concerned with producing theatrical works designed to offer general entertainment: occasionally, they found themselves captured by some thought or philosophical concept of a serious kind, but when this occurred they were inclined to address their words towards readers rather than towards a public assembled in a playhouse; not for a moment did Shaw believe that *Back to*

Methuselah could be presented on the stage, but, in making this observation, we must add another – that never did he think of addressing his metabiological pentateuch to any small, restricted circle of the intellectual élite.[1]

The farces, of course, required nothing save cleverly contrived plots, boldly presented type characters and dialogue as amusing as possible. The serious plays, however, were another matter. Already in the nineties of the preceding century, Pinero, Jones and their companions had accustomed spectators when they attended such serious plays to look for more than plots and characters, and the "drama of ideas" thus adumbrated in their writings was still further cultivated and developed during the first years of the Edwardian period. Pinero's little skit called *Playgoers* may have been planned to show how horrified the servants were at the thought of listening to the dialogue of a play designed to offer them any "ideers", but incidentally the skit is also of interest because it shows an ordinary upper-middle-class housewife assuming that these ideas ought to be expected and encouraged on the stage. If, however, this lady (and no doubt her husband) welcomed a certain amount of social and philosophical comment in the dramas which they elected to patronise they positively did not want too much of it: they expected the comment to be the salt or spice added to the dish, not the dish itself: and, furthermore, they did not wish to have so much of this spice as might destroy the emotional flavour of the plays to which they listened. A little exercising of the mind was, for them, an excellent thing, but basically they knew that the experiencing of a theatrical production ought to come from heart and not from head. And in this they differed markedly from numbers of minority authors who, believing that they had something important to say, made their dramas intellectual exercises merely.

On the whole, then, we can distinguish at this time two kinds of "play of ideas" – the kind to which the general public had been made accustomed, and the other kind which made many critics think of sermons or lectures. "On the

[1] His surprise when it was produced is both well-attested and genuine.

whole", yes; but not completely, since during this period there were at least a few dramatic authors who stood, as it were, ambiguously in the middle, half-general and half-minority: and in this company no man was more ambiguous than the actor–author who had been so largely responsible for the Court seasons of 1904–7 – Harley Granville-Barker himself.[1] If Shaw frequently seems to be an enigma, his nature and literary compositions might almost be thought to be patently clear and simple when they are contrasted with those of his early associate and friend. There is the puzzle presented by Granville-Barker's abandonment of the theatre to which he had seemed so surely and intricately bound: there is the puzzle arising from consideration of his three or four separate lives as actor–producer, dramatist, scholar, critic and translator – a puzzle which certainly cannot be resolved in a facile manner by reference to his second marriage: and there is the still more perplexing puzzle concerning the essential quality and worth of his own original plays, particularly when these are taken in conjunction with the Spanish comedies which he selected for translation into English.

From what we know about his early life and interests we should undoubtedly have expected him to have been a prolific playwright, yet, if we leave out of account his few odd collaborative efforts composed in conjunction with Berte Thomas before 1900, together with his translations and his two unimportant "experiments" written in 1901 and 1902, his total body of dramatic work consists of no more than four full-length plays and a couple of one-acts before be published his *Farewell to the Theatre* in 1917. It would, of course, be wholly absurd to judge an author's value by the quantity of his writings, but at least we should have assumed that all Granville-Barker's plays, no matter

[1] C. B. Purdom's *Harley Granville Barker: Man of the Theatre, Dramatist and Scholar* (1955), although presenting many interesting critical comments on the plays, devotes most of its space to his stage activities. Margery M. Morgan's *A Drama of Political Man* (1961) is entirely concerned, as its sub-title indicates, with "A Study in the Plays of Harley Granville-Barker".

how few in number, would have been eminently stageworthy. Our expectation, however, remains almost wholly unrealised. To his meagre pre-1917 list he later added only two original dramas – *The Secret Life* (1923) and *His Majesty* (1928) – but these can be dismissed from consideration here since, surprisingly, they appear to have been composed with little or no thought of possible theatrical presentation. Among the earlier works, *Waste* (1907) was prevented by the censor from being performed, so that it was at that time seen only by the members of the Stage Society at a "private" production. Clearly Granville-Barker was not to be blamed for its failure to reach the stage, but it does seem strange that a man so intimately acquainted with theatrical conditions in 1907 should have been mightily surprised and upset when this gloomy tale of illicit love, unwanted child, abortion and suicide was looked upon askance at the Lord Chamberlain's Office. It is we who should feel surprised that the theatrically expert author could ever have imagined that such a drama could make any strong impact upon an audience: in so far as the plot is concerned, it is one of the simplest of Granville-Barker's plays, and its dialogue is clearer and more comprehensible than that in most of his other stage writings, but unfortunately, as a whole, it lacks interest and variety. Even the revised version which was staged in 1936, many years after the censor's ban had been removed, failed to appeal.

As a dramatist, then, his reputation must depend on just three plays. The first of these, *The Marrying of Ann Leete* (1902), with its complex story which ends with the heroine, a well-brought-up, relatively rich girl, suddenly calling out to the family's gardener with an inquiry as to whether he will marry her, completely baffled those who saw it at the Royalty in 1902, and it must prove as baffling to readers today. In a vague kind of way we can see what the author was aiming at but it is impossible to think that this is an important drama. Thus, in the end, we come down to two works, *The Voysey Inheritance*, presenting its pathetic picture of an honest Edward Voysey who, inheriting his father's business, finds that it has been built up on trickery and deceit, and *The Madras House*, with its kindred picture of an idealistic young man thwarted by the force of society. These unquestionably are both works which we cannot ignore, yet even here we find ourselves confronted by doubts, since neither has had a distinguished playhouse career: *The Madras House*, after its original meagre ten performances at the Duke of York's Theatre in 1910, has apparently had only one, surprisingly disappointing, London revival, directed by the author himself, in 1925; nor has the fate of *The Voysey Inheritance* been more than slightly happier, its original production at the Court in 1905 having been followed by just two London revivals, in 1944 and 1953.

Obviously there is something wrong here. C. B. Purdom in 1955 suggested that "when we have a National Theatre" Granville-Barker's dramatic works "should be played regularly for their particular values", firmly asserting that in his judgment "they will remain in the repertory of English plays";[1] but so far no move has been made by our National Theatre's management to act on this suggestion, and it is hard to believe that, even if one of them is put into production, its appeal would be so wide as to warrant "regular" performances. There is, then, the paradox that the man who devoted so much time and effort to propaganda for the establishment of a National Theatre has, in his own writings, completely failed to leave us any dramas which might grace such a stage. And the causes of this failure are to be found in the very words used about them by the most enthusiastic among Granville-Barker's admirers. When we are informed, rightly, that his virtues are to be discovered in "his subtlety, his intellectuality, his many-sided characterisations, the strange mixture of irony and sympathy with which he approaches men,"[2] we realise two things – first, that these qualities are precisely those which may impress readers, particularly readers who are critics, but are almost certain

[1] C. B. Purdom, *Harley Granville Barker* (1955), p. 214.

[2] This comment is made by Gerald Weales – "The Edwardian Theatre and the Shadow of Shaw" (*English Institute Essays, 1959* (1960), p. 186).

to leave ordinary spectators either cold or at a loss, and, secondly, that the qualities themselves are often, surprisingly, handled in a manner untheatrical. Subtlety, certainly; but Granville-Barker's subtlety is only too frequently over-fine and over-delicate for this workaday world: many-sided characterisation, also certainly; but so many-sided that, within the limited range of the dramatic form, it becomes confused and confusing: intellectuality, again certainly; yet an intellectuality which somehow remains alien to the stage, giving the double impression that the author is too inward-looking and that he stands aloof from us. So, too, when we are told, and correctly told, that in his group scenes he invites his audiences to enter "like a guest at a party, where everyone, including the host, is a stranger to him, and it takes most of the act to find one's ways through what is being said", we must decide that here we are far from the playhouse. Perhaps Alec Clunes, with the penetration of an actor, has expressed this with greatest precision: "at their best," he has said, "there is in the plays something akin to the joy of a Torquemada cross-word, at their worst something akin to sewing little beads meticulously on to embroidery".[1]

It is tempting to think that Granville-Barker's apparent weaknesses were due to the fact that deliberately he addressed himself to a minority and that we do him wrong in putting stress upon his failure to capture the attention of any large general public. In support of this thought may be cited several of his scathing remarks concerning commercial managers, his constant belief in the prime importance of the "repertory" theatre, his friendship and, indeed, collaboration with such minority authors as Laurence Housman. Nevertheless, even after taking all such things into consideration, we must in the end be forced to believe that he did not belong to the dim galaxy of those true minority playwrights whose aims and achievements have been examined in the

[1] This remark was made by Clunes in a letter addressed to Margery M. Morgan, who quotes it in her commentary on Granville-Barker's dramatic work, pp. 303 and 323.

preceding chapter. Certainly we must pause for a moment on reading the extraordinary cast-list for the copyright performance of *Waste* at the Savoy in 1908:

Walter Kent...	Mr Gilbert Cannan
Mrs O'Connell...	Mrs Bernard Shaw
Lucy Davenport...	Mrs H. G. Wells
George Farrant...	Mr St John Hankin
Russell Blackborough...	Mr J. Galsworthy
Henry Trebell...	Mr Laurence Housman
Gilbert Wedgecroft...	Mr H. G. Wells
Lord Charles Cantelupe...	Prof. Gilbert Murray, LL.D.
The Earl of Horsham...	Mr Bernard Shaw
Justin O'Connell...	Mr William Archer –

and, in thus pausing, we must ask ourselves whether the list in itself is not symbolic. The question, however, may readily be settled: this does not indicate that Granville-Barker belonged to a minority public; it simply testifies to the fact that, perhaps not entirely for his own good, he was, as an individual, the pet of a creative literary coterie.

Among the authors who took part in the reading-performance of *Waste*, the stage activities of some have already been glanced at, but so far only indirect references have been made to St John Hankin, the writer who may be thought closest to Granville-Barker himself, even although in spirit and technique a great gulf lies between the two. Perhaps the best way of appreciating Hankin's characteristic quality is to start by considering his delightful *Dramatic Sequels* (published in 1901) in conjunction with one of his later one-acts, *The Constant Lover* (1912). The *Sequels*, originally printed in *Punch*, indulge in speculations concerning what happened to the characters in various well-known plays after the final curtain had descended upon them. Thus in "The New Wing at Elsinore" poor Horatio and Fortinbras are plagued by Shakespeare's ghost; in "Still Stooping" the unfortunate heroine of *She Stoops to Conquer* discovers that, if she hopes to retain her husband's affection, she must go about constantly in the clothes of a domestic servant, broom in hand; and in "The Third Mrs Tanqueray" Pinero's husband–hero lands himself in trouble once again. These brief sketches amply demonstrate the author's wit – a wit which sometimes is merely epigrammatically amusing, sometimes decidedly caustic, and which always displays him as intellectual – not coldly aloof in the Granville-Barker manner but equally lacking in the emotional warmth attractive to public audiences. After having read these short sketches, we have no difficulty in understanding the mind and qualities of the man who, twelve years later, wrote the one-act *The Constant Lover*. This simple "comedy of youth" is wholly concerned with a meeting between an Evelyn Rivers and a young man, Cecil Harburton, in whom she is interested – the latter being presented as the truly constant lover because he is always in love, although hardly ever with the same lady from one week to another. No doubt this piece aspired, in its own time, to nothing higher than the majority of the sketches written for today's television screens, yet in its very simplicity it amply reveals the main features of Hankin's dramatic style. Here there is nothing of Granville-Barker's elusive subtlety; his dialogue confronts the audience with no difficulties; all the lines are effectively pointed. On the other hand, it is obvious that this very clarity owes its being to a rather chilly intellectual approach, so that neither spectators nor readers can escape an impression of planned contrivance; and this impression becomes the more powerful as we make ourselves aware of the author's general attitude to life. All his dramas have the same quality – the neatly planned action with its contrasted characters, the prevailing cynicism and the intellectually clever twisting of familiar situations. In *The Two Mr Wetherbys* (1903) these features are to be seen in their most mechanical forms: a "good" James Wetherby is married to a rigidly sanctimonious Margaret, and a "bad" Richard Wetherby is thoroughly enjoying life in separation from his wife, Margaret's sister Constantia. As we proceed through the scenes, the mechanical patterning and the exaggerated sardonic satire become positively oppressive.

Like *The Constant Lover*, the title of *The Return of the Prodigal* (1905) is sarcastic: no fatted calf is sacrificed here, no poor wanderer, weary and contrite, is welcomed back into the fold: the story is simply that of a wastrel who, after having been shipped off to Australia, comes back home to blackmail his father and makes himself such a nuisance that he is given an allowance on condition that he should pack off again. *The Charity that Began at Home* (1906) in much the same cynical manner introduces another vagabond type, while *The Cassilis Engagement* (1907), unquestionably Hankin's best play, makes an almost geometrical design of a difficult and complex domestic situation: excitement and dismay rule at Deynham Abbey when news arrives that young Geoffrey Cassilis has become engaged to a girl with the dreadfully plebeian name of Ethel Borridge. Mrs Cassilis, surrounded by distressed and sympathetic society friends, not only invites the girl and her mother for an extended visit at the Abbey but is saccharinely sweet to them both; the result is that Ethel finds herself unutterably bored, breaks off the engagement and, with a sigh of relief, departs for the joys of suburban London. All these plays are clever; all are clearly and expertly written; yet all are dependent upon artifice and lack true warmth. When Hankin published three of them (*The Return of the Prodigal, The Charity that Began at Home* and *The Cassilis Engagement*) in a single volume under the title of *Three Plays with Happy Endings* he provided them with a general preface in which he sought to explain his dramatic method. "I select an episode in the life of one of my characters or of a group of characters," he wrote,

> when something of importance to their future has to be decided, and I ring up my curtain. Having shown how it was decided and why it was so decided, I ring it down again. The episode is over, and with it the play. The end is "inconclusive" in the sense that it proves nothing. Why should it? It is the dramatist's business to represent life, not to argue about it. It is however the "ending" of that particular episode, and, as such, forms a fitting termination for a play.

This explanation seems eminently reasonable, and, of course, it correctly replies to the arguments of those who had wanted him to provide "happy endings" for his comedies: yet there still remains a doubt. Even while he seeks to suggest that he simply reflects actual life, we are uncomfortably aware of the fact that he has contrived his selected "episodes" and that he has determined the "ending" in a deliberately rational manner. These are plays of ideas, not in the sense that Hankin has any pet sociological concepts to place before his spectators, but in the sense that from start to finish his comedies are cerebrally inspired.

A third dramatist who was first introduced to the London public at the Court was John Galsworthy.[1] That he was a true playwright of ideas in a style distinct from that of Hankin is immediately evident from the characteristic titles he gave to so many of his dramas from *Strife* and *Justice* on to *Loyalties*, yet peculiarly these plays reveal what was lacking in so many examples of this dramatic genre. Granville-Barker gives us either a feeling of cold exclusiveness and superiority, a clinical assessment of life – almost as though he were an Olympian super-consultant, stethoscope in hand, diagnosing social ills – or else, paradoxically, an exploration of human thoughts and feelings which becomes so intricate and involved as to be dramatically meaningless. What impresses us in Galsworthy's dramas, apart from their "ideas", is their warm humility and compassion. Granville-Barker tended to look at the characters in *Madras House* not merely from the outside but from a perch up in the flies; Hankin's contemplation of life's vagaries is deliberately frigid, as though he were seated alone in a box; in Galsworthy's plays, as in Barrie's, the author seems to be placing himself alongside his persons on stage.

[1] Studies of his structural style and dialogue methods appear in A. C. Choudhuri's *Galsworthy's Plays* (1961) and Johanna Kroener's *Die Technik des realistischen Dramas bei Ibsen und Galsworthy* (1935). H. V. Marrott has *A Bibliography of the Works of John Galsworthy* (1928). Victor Dupont's *John Galsworthy: The Dramatic Artist* (1942) presents a careful record of his career and includes a keen, balanced assessment of his worth. Dudley Barker's life of the author – *The Man of Principle* (1963) – is an excellent biographical study.

This quality gave to his theatrical writings a peculiar appeal. The works of some among his tendentious companions may have had longer runs than his did, but it may well be thought that they induced their audiences to "think" less than his. Shaw's wit aroused delight and laughter, but we are probably justified in believing that none save intellectuals were really swayed by his philosophical and sociological notions – whereas Galsworthy's sympathy could stimulate others, often against their will, to reconsider their views of the life around them. It is not without significance that the solitary drama produced during this period which truly effected a direct and significant social reformation was *Justice* (1910), when a Home Secretary, who was later to become England's most famous personality, was so moved as he sat watching the drama, and was so conscious of the fact that all around him were similarly moved, that within a short time he had abolished the indiscriminate practice of penal solitary confinement.

Nevertheless, after all this has been said, Galsworthy's dramatic writings, interesting as they are, just failed to achieve complete success; and, when his work is considered in its totality, it would seem as if this failure was resultant upon a triple bafflement which continually perplexed his mind – bafflement with himself, bafflement with humanity, and bafflement with the limitations of the dramatic form itself. In his own attitude to the human world around him is evident a marked dichotomy – and there are ample signs to indicate that he himself was aware of this, and deeply troubled by it. On the one hand, he had a strong personality, and quite clearly strength of character as exhibited in others greatly appealed to him: *Old English* (1924) might have been thought to be a strange piece to have come from his pen if we were to fail to appreciate the vigorous and delighted fascination manifest in his treatment of the grand, individualistic old rogue whose nickname gave its title to the play. Nor was this work an exception: part of the basic quality of his early *Strife* (1909) derives from the evident admiration with which his two main characters, John Anthony and David

Roberts, despite their obvious wrong-headedness, are contemplated. On the other hand, there were two other kinds of human beings for the one of which he had deep and sincere compassion and for the other a special sort of esteem. The little man, the weak man, the down-and-out man who is caught inexorably in the satanic mills aroused both his pity and his understanding: it was as if he continually looked upon such persons with one dominant thought in his mind – "There but for the grace of God go I." The unfortunate wives in *Strife*, the miserable Falder in *Justice* (1910), the waifs and strays befriended by the artist Christopher Wellwyn in *The Pigeon* (1912), the unfortunate Clare Dedmond in *The Fugitive* (1913) and many other kindred figures are recurrent persons in his works. Here, however, he encountered several difficulties. He sternly refused to sentimentalise these characters, so that, for example, Falder is made at least partly responsible for his own miseries, and Clare herself takes the step which eventually leads to her suicide. In addition to this, all these little men and women belonged to the anonymous mass of humanity, and above all other things Galsworthy hated and despised those who, losing their personalities in the crowd, allowed themselves to be transformed into an insensate mob. Such a hatred of the crowd was, in turn, associated with a third group of men and women for whom he had esteem, compassion and admiration – those whose whole beings were ruled, not by principle, but by native and often unconscious humanitarian feelings – Edgar Anthony in *Strife*, Wellwyn in *The Pigeon*, Geoffrey March in *Windows* (1922), above all Stephen More in *The Mob* (1914). In general Galsworthy sought to be impartial, or at least to avoid sentimentalist excesses, yet there were times when he could not conceal the strength of his own emotions. Stephen More is made to sacrifice his career and completely to ostracise himself from his community not because of a concept, an idea, a political belief, but because of an inner force which is at the most only half-conscious – and against him the insensate mob howls in its thoughtless rage: and we may think that into More Galsworthy has put much of himself. The latest and most detailed biography of Galsworthy is entitled *The Man of Principle*, but in reality it was not principle which ruled his life: he might have been more appropriately described as the man of sympathetic conviction.

The result of all this was one kind of confusion in his mind, and the bafflement was increased by his despondent contemplation, not of individual men but of humanity as a whole. The world should, he feels, be ruled by justice and sympathy, and the fact that it is not so ruled leads to the sense of puzzlement which appears so often in his dramas, sometimes merely implicit, sometimes expressed overtly and emphatically, as in *Windows*. Thus his plays are invested with a rare distinctive quality. A satirist would have lashed out in bitter anger, but neither did Galsworthy have the contemptuous and often arrogant mind of the satirist, nor had he the stylistic precision which alone can make satire effective. He was far too keenly aware of his own failings and inadequacies, real or imagined, to stand apart, sneering and lashing at humanity – yet this virtue paradoxically meant that often in his plays he was unable to present such a clear vision as might grip and appeal to his audiences, or, indeed, such as might have been secured by a far lesser man untroubled by inner doubts.

These two qualities were singular to himself, but there was another double problem confronting him which derived from the kind of drama he elected to adopt. Galsworthy was fundamentally a realist; perhaps more potently than any other playwright of his age he revealed the curbs, restrictions and dangers inherent in that currently dominant style; and his own awareness of the difficulties involved in the exploitation of this style is made manifest in various ways, both positive and negative. The first of two chief obstacles which have to be overcome by the author who decides to write serious realistic plays is that the presentation of ordinary commonplace scenes may so easily become theatrically dull and even boring. Several of Galsworthy's contemporaries sought to surmount this obstacle by intermingling their serious plots with episodes of a humorous kind, but he himself was a writer possessed of but little aptitude for comedy, whether expressed in laughable actions or in pert epigrams. Instead, he frequently permitted himself to seek an escape from possible drabness and dulness by indulging in several varieties of what can only be called melodramatic themes. This melodramatic trend has been noted by several critics, and generally it is asserted that it derives from his practice as a novelist; but it appears much more likely that the true explanation depends upon his recognition of the needs of the stage. Some of his dramas are thus directly or indirectly concerned with a "crime" – a theft provides the title for his first theatrical work, *The Silver Box* (1906); *Strife* may introduce no action which goes against the law, but sensational elements are an essential part of its plot; forgery and suicide are brought into *Justice*; self-poisoning ends the story of *The Fugitive*; there is an attempted suicide in *The Pigeon* and homicide at the close of *The Mob*; unexpected revelations consequent on the suicide of a famous aviator provide plenty of melodramatic material in *The Show* (1925); and there is another attempted suicide in *The Skin Game* (1920). Somehow, however, the amount of such material introduced into his dramatic writings does not seem to be natively proper to Galsworthy, to arise from an inner compulsion, in the same way as the sensational episodes of, say, *The Bondman* appeared entirely in harmony with Hall Caine's objectives: there is a decided artificiality, and consequently falseness, in their use.

Associated with the obstacle which he thus sought, sometimes not very effectively, to surmount, was another – the problem of finding means for the expression of emotions too deep for utterance in the ordinary commonplace language of real life. Here, too, his solution cannot be deemed truly satisfactory. This solution, expressed in numerous scenes, is the replacing of dialogue by wordless, or almost wordless, episodes which clearly he hoped might imaginatively evoke the desired emotions, but which unfortunately only too often savour of sentimentality. In *The Silver Box*, for example, when he can find no fitting words for the conclusion of an act, stage-direction takes the place of dialogue:

MRS BARTHWICK *turns her back to the window. There is an expression of distress on her face. She stands motionless, compressing her lips. The crying begins again.* BARTHWICK *covers his ears with his hands, and* MARLOW *shuts the window. The crying ceases.*

The Fugitive, too, ends with a lengthy pantomimic scene of this sort, and the device is even more fully developed at the close of *The Mob*. Here the independently-minded Stephen More faces the brainless crowd which has gathered in anger outside his house:

CHIEF STUDENT (*Checking a dangerous rush*). Hold on! Hold on! (*To* MORE) Swear to utter no more blasphemy against your country! Swear it!

CROWD. Ah! Ay! Ah!

MORE. My country is not yours. Mine is that great country which shall never take toll from the weakness of others. (*Above the groaning*) Ah! you can break my head and my windows; but don't think that you can break my faith. You can never break or shake it, if you were a million to one.

(*A girl with dark eyes and hair all wild, leaps out from the crowd and shakes her fist at him.*)

GIRL. You're friends with them that killed my lad! (MORE *smiles down at her, and she swiftly plucks the knife from the belt of a Boy Scout beside her*) Smile, you – cur! (*A violent rush and heave from behind flings* MORE *forward on to the steel. He reels, staggers back, and falls down amongst the crowd. A scream, a sway, a rush, a hubbub of cries. The* CHIEF STUDENT *shouts above the riot:* "Steady!" *Another:* "My God! He's got it!")

CHIEF STUDENT. Give him air!

(*The crowd falls back, and two* STUDENTS, *bending over* MORE, *lift his arms and head, but they fall like lead. Desperately they test him for life.*)

CHIEF STUDENT. By the lord, it's over!

(*Then begins a scared swaying out towards the window. Someone turns out the lights, and in the darkness the crowd fast melts away. The body of* MORE *lies in the gleam from a single Chinese lantern. Muttering the words:* "Poor devil! He kept his end up anyway!" *the* CHIEF STUDENT *picks from the floor a little abandoned Union Jack and lays it on* MORE'*s breast. Then he, too, turns, and rushes out.*

(*And the body of* MORE *lies in the streak of light; and the noises in the street continue to rise.*)

The effect aimed at in this scene is, when we consider it carefully, almost the same as that which was to be found in many of the old silent films, when pantomimic action was interspersed with a few brief captions, many of them putting quotation marks round phrases supposed to be spoken by the characters: and somehow the pattern in both tended towards the sentimental. The laying of the small Union Jack on More's breast, "Smile, you – cur!" and "He kept his end up anyway!" are precisely what we might have expected to see on the silent screen. And to add to this cinematographic effect, Galsworthy brings in something more. Of course, "*the curtain falls*" on the stage picture as "*the noises in the street continue to rise*", but almost at once up it goes again to reveal an

AFTERMATH

A late Spring dawn is just breaking. Against trees in leaf and blossom, with the houses of a London Square beyond, suffused by the spreading glow, is seen a dark life-sized statue on a granite pedestal. In front is the broad, dust-dim pavement. The light grows till the central words around the pedestal can be clearly read:

ERECTED
To the Memory
of
STEPHEN MORE
'Faithful to his ideal'

High above, the face of MORE *looks straight before him with a faint smile. On one shoulder, and on his bare head, two sparrows have perched, and from the gardens behind, come the twittering and singing of birds.*

Reading this, we may well be reminded, too, of something other than the silent film. The statue of More, with the sparrows patiently trained to perch on its head and shoulder, finds an apt counterpart in those figures of Lenin, in three-dimensional bronze and two-dimensional paint, which are so beloved in Moscow and Leningrad. Galsworthian realism and Socialist Realism tend to suffer from the same pathetic complaint – deplorable and even tawdry sentimentalism. The body of More is described as being dimly seen in "*the gleam from a single Chinese lantern*": at the close of *Joy* (1907) Mrs Gwyn and Colonel Hope stand on a stage fitfully illuminated by some other paper lanterns, and in the distance the moon can be seen rising in the sky. The Colonel speaks:

Don't like these Chinese lanterns with that moon – tawdry! eh! By Jove, Molly, I sometimes think that we humans are a rubbishy lot – each of us talking and thinking of nothing but our own petty little affairs, and when you see a great thing like that up there – (*Sighs*)

Realistic, no doubt, but not really good enough when a sigh has to take the place of the words for which the scene is desperately crying. If the statue of More reminds us of the statues innumerable of Lenin, the Colonel's speech inevitably reminds us of the pitiful dialogue with which so many post-Revolution Russian plays are so freely bespattered.

It is, of course, important – indeed, it is essential – to recognise here that Galsworthy by no means stood alone:[1] his difficulties were, indeed, those confronting most of the serious dramatists of the time, and like many of them he occasionally sought in a rather ineffective manner to escape from the trammels in which he was imprisoned. Early in his life he experimented, rather unhappily, with the fantastic in his short *Little Dream* (1911); in *Windows* it would seem that he tried to imitate the inimitable Chekhov; *The Forest* (1924) perhaps owed something to the experimental forms introduced by C. K. Munro;[2] *Escape* was an episodic play, and *The Roof* (1929) showed in its seven scenes several different situations supposedly coincident in time. None of these variations from the realistic norm, however, gave him

[1] On this, see also pp. 312–13.
[2] For these see p. 436.

real assistance. To the end he stood forward as an author of strength and sensitivity, striving to make his audiences interested at once in social problems and in the personalities of his imagined characters, yet generally failing to reach completely satisfying results because he was defeated by the very form in which he had chosen to work.

In considering his writings we tend to think of two opposed contemporary attitudes towards the drama of the age. Writing in 1924 Frank Vernon made a bold pronouncement:[1]

> Some things are beyond argument, and it is not to be questioned that since the Elizabethan outburst no such number of the right play-words has ever been written and spoken in England as during the pre-War years of the twentieth century. Decidedly we may differ about the individual merit of this play and of that, but as to the collective merit of the drama of this our great post-Elizabethan period there is no disputing.

In its broader terms this statement may be accepted without much quarrelling, but Vernon's emphasis is placed upon the "right play-words", and here we cannot avoid thinking back to statements which already have been quoted from the pen of Ashley Dukes – of thinking back, too, to the various efforts made by minority authors to enrich the verbal qualities of the stage – and, particularly, of considering the way in which a writer such as Galsworthy found himself thwarted in his efforts by the style which, in his choice of "realism", was imposed upon him.

5. *The End and the Beginning: Ervine, Drinkwater, Lonsdale, Coward, Milne*

All these authors, whether they were intent upon ideas or not, had started their careers during the first years of the century, and the majority of them continued active after the end of the war. Inevitably, therefore, the references to their later writings have led us from the first decade of this period onwards into the decade which was its third and last. These

[1] *The Twentieth-Century Theatre* (1924), pp. 18–19.

men, therefore, together with at least a few who had become established even before their time, were thus engaged in helping to shape the drama of the twenties.

It is, however, important to repeat what has already been observed – that, in general, their productive contributions terminated round about the year 1930. The dedication to Shaw of the Malvern Festival in that year was in more than one sense symbolic: it testified to the dominating eminence attained by the author of *Heartbreak House* (1920) and *Saint Joan* (1924), while at the same time in *Too True to Be Good* it decidedly hinted at the declining of his creative power. The general strength and particularly the architectural vision which had so distinguished his earlier writings and through which he had won both popular esteem and critical approbation were now losing their vigour. J. M. Barrie's last play, *The Boy David*, did not come until 1936, but it is abundantly clear that this piece was a belated unsuccessful aberration: with *Mary Rose* (1920) and the puzzlingly adroit *Shall We Join the Ladies?* (1921) his work was finished. Somerset Maugham's activity as a stage-writer, beginning with his first great triumph in 1908, continuing on to *The Constant Wife* (1926) and even *The Sacred Flame* (1929), had made him one of the most popular and skilful among the playwrights of his age, but this was the end: although he carried on his theatrical activities briefly into the century's fourth decade with *For Services Rendered* in 1932 and *Sheppey* in 1933, his characteristic contributions to the drama had already been completed. And the year 1929 saw the last of Galsworthy's significant dramas, *Exiled*.

If these facts had stood alone, it might have been thought that they were due merely to coincidence; but similar features become evident when consideration is given not only to the careers of two other authors, John Drinkwater and St John Ervine, who, after having started in the field of the minority drama, had moved over to the West End, but also to the careers of several other playwrights who came to the stage during the years immediately preceding the outbreak of war. There are two or three exceptions, certainly, but they are exceptions which count for comparatively little when set against the general trend.

St John Ervine, who had at first been mainly devoted to grim studies of Irish life,[1] and who had carried this preoccupation with grimness to the English scene in *Jane Clegg* (1913), developed a fresh serious inspiration when he wrote *The Ship* (1922) and then suddenly flourished forth in *Mary, Mary, Quite Contrary* (1923) and in the delightful *The First Mrs Fraser* (1929) with unexpected laughter. The former comedy, making its chief character an actress for whom stage artificiality has become the natural, deals largely with the now common admixture of "love" and "matter-of-factness": "we modern girls," remarks a vicar's daughter, "know perfectly well that men don't really love us, and the best we hope for is that they'll get accustomed to us and won't mind our being married to them". The latter play, one of the numerous comedies written for Marie Tempest, has a peculiar Barriesque flavour – almost as though it might have been a sequel to *What Every Woman Knows* if John Shand had indeed been divorced from his Maggie and married to Lady Sybil. And to these plays may be added what was in fact a deliberate sequel planned by the author, *The Lady of Belmont* (1923), which, although now but seldom remembered, is one of Ervine's most penetrating dramas, showing what might have happened to Shylock and Portia, Lorenzo and Jessica, some years after the clashing words at the court scene and the lyrical strains heard in the midst of moonlight at Portia's mansion. It is true that other plays, including *Robert's Wife* (1937), continued to come from Ervine's pen even as late as 1957, so that the pattern here is, on the surface, considerably different from that which emerged from consideration of his companions: yet it may be thought that his truly creative period ended about the same time as theirs.

With Ervine's movement from the minority regional to London's general is to be associated the similar movement of John Drinkwater, whose *Abraham Lincoln* drew spectators to nearly five hundred performances at the Lyric Hammersmith

[1] See pp. 250–1.

in 1919. The success of this piece was, of course, partly due to the circumstances of the time: it capitalised on the interest in America and on the thoughts concerning war; but basically it made its impact by its structure and its style, both breaking away from the now dull realistic pattern set by the "Ibsenite" drama. Its presentation of a mighty and terrible problem confronting a great man, so far removed from the small domestic dilemmas faced by the lesser characters in the society plays, its series of short episodic scenes instead of formal acts, and the poetic flavour provided explicitly by its chorus of chroniclers and implicitly by its setting in the past – all these gave the public a spectacle for which it had been craving. These things, certainly, were not new; already, as we have seen, Parker's pageant-plays[1] had been looking forward to something of this kind, and the various dramas devoted to the lives of Shakespeare, Marlowe, Thomas Cromwell and other kindred historical figures were indicative of a largely unconscious desire to escape from the restrictions of the immediately contemporary scene and all its accompanying dreariness. Thus, in a sense, *Abraham Lincoln* may be looked upon as the practical realisation of something about which many other writers before its time, particularly during the years from 1910 to 1913, had been dreaming. Nevertheless, if Drinkwater is to be regarded in one way as a culminator he must also be looked upon as a leader in a new style. True, this drama of his now seems much less impressive than it appeared half a century ago; and it is also true that his later *Mary Stuart* (1921), *Oliver Cromwell* (1923) and *Robert E. Lee* (1923) disturbingly showed up his limitations both in vision and in style. Even in 1921 Agate indicated his clear awareness of such deficiencies: after giving him full credit for his seriousness of purpose, he drew attention to the fact that the dramatist's outlook was, in fact, narrowly circumscribed – "It is unfortunate...that he cannot resist whitewash. As soon as his eye lights upon an historical figure it is filled with the gleam proper to the blanching of sepulchres –" and, as for language, he decided that such a

[1] See pp. 130–1 and 338.

person as Drinkwater's Mary Queen of Scots "turned out to be a woman magical with platitudes and copy-book maxims". In noting these things Agate was ahead of most of his companion critics, but within a few years many others were observing similar weaknesses, pointing out, for example, that of the eight scenes in *Oliver Cromwell* seven were simply narrative, only one dramatic, and remarking on the sentimentally doctrinaire treatment of the central character. When all has been said, however, *Abraham Lincoln* stands at the head of a lengthy line of historical–biographical plays, the number and success of which were so characteristic a feature of the theatre in the twenties. Authors already well established and authors who made their first bows to the public at this time turned to experiment in plays of this kind, and with the kind itself should be associated other dramas of inspiration not far different. St John Ervine's Portia, for instance, was originally a figment of Shakespeare's imagination, not a living person, but in effect *The Lady of Belmont* offered him the same opportunities as were being offered to those who set real historical persons on the stage.

Like the careers of so many of his contemporaries, Drinkwater's active contributions to the theatre virtually ended in the twenties. In 1927 he won fair success with his comedy *Bird in Hand*, but after that came nothing save the somewhat shaky and wholly unimportant *A Man's House* in 1934.

Ervine's first play had appeared in 1911, Drinkwater's first in 1905, but in considering their work from those earlier years to 1930, it is important not to forget that during the years between 1912 and 1914 a fresh company of young authors was making its appearance and that during this time numbers of noteworthy plays, presented both on minority stages and in the West End theatres, indicated the presence of an expanding, if not of an entirely new, dramatic spirit – a spirit which is often thought to belong specifically to the post-war years.

Two or three selected authors may serve to illustrate this

development. H. M. Harwood's first play, the one-act *Honour Thy Father*, was presented in 1912; although of no very great intrinsic importance, its setting – poor furnished rooms in Bruges – is interesting, as are its characters – a poverty-stricken father, a mother and a younger daughter receiving a visit from an older daughter, whose loose life has well supplied her with money; the father, shocked by her ways, first abuses her and then accepts the assistance she offers. The tone of this piece introduces something new: so does the same author's study, in *Interlopers* (1918), of a wife's neglect of her husband because of her excessive devotion to their children. Even in the lighter *Please Help Emily* (1916) the portrait of the emancipated young minx who takes centre-stage has elements of novelty. In spite of the fact that there are few particularly memorable qualities apparent in these or in Harwood's later plays, interest attaches to the way in which the cynical aspects of the earlier works lead on to those of *The Grain of Mustard Seed* (1920), a study of a conservative political family, and of *The Transit of Venus* (1927), in which there seems to be enshrined a general critical assessment of Western civilisation.

In time, Norman Macowan's career ran almost exactly parallel, starting in 1912 with a Stage Society production of *The Travellers* and a presentation by the Play Actors of *The Demagogue*, proceeding through the cinematically-inspired adaptation of *The Blue Lagoon* (1920) on to the once much-praised but now neglected *The Infinite Shoeblack* (1929). Since there were other young authors, such as Harold Chapin and B. Macdonald Hastings, who also made their first appearances on the London stage in 1912, there was justification for the employment by at least two critics during that year of the phrase "renascence of the English drama". During the following season came Miles Malleson's *A Man of Ideas*, the wry tale of a materially unsuccessful intellectual, and later he too was to compose many diverse plays from the "fantastic scrap", *The Little White Thought* (1915), the "little fairy play", *Paddly Pools* (1916), the bitter war pieces, '*D*' *Company* (written 1914) and *Black 'Ell* (1916), and the no doubt introspective *Youth* (1916)[1] on to the mordant *Conflict* (1925), which shows a down-and-out socialist Cambridge graduate who wins a parliamentary seat from a hitherto entrenched conservative party and gains the devotion of the heroine (who had for years been an aristocrat's mistress), and the thoughtful *Merrileon Wise* (1926). In this last play the central figure is another rebellious girl, and fundamentally the theme of the drama is anger at society's structure: one speech may serve as its motto –

> Somebody's got to break through that sometime. This generation has got to. I tell you this generation owes more to the future than to the past.

This same uncompromising attitude becomes symbolised in the titles given to the acts of *The Fanatics* (1924) – "Downstairs", "Upstairs", "Downstairs Again" – downstairs living an affluent businessman, upstairs in an attic residing his son John, an idealist who wants to be an author, and who influences his sister Gwen, so that she refuses to wed the man she loves (a popular playwright named Colin Mackenzie) unless he agrees to his going off with her first on a kind of trial marriage. All of this certainly expresses the spirit of the age, yet we must not make the mistake of believing that this spirit belonged exclusively to the twenties or came into being only at that period. The mood was already presented clearly in Malleson's first play, *The Man of Ideas*, and numerous examples have been cited above to prove that the battle between a new generation and an old and the appearance of a youthful demand for freedom date back to the very beginning of the century.

F. Tennyson Jesse's first playlet, *The Mask* (1915) had been written in collaboration with Harwood. Once again marriage questions form the theme, with rebellious actions taken against conventionally accepted values. Expressed ironically, the same topics are treated more seriously in *Quarantine* (1922), in *The Pelican* (1924, another play penned

[1] Historically this has interest as a life-like picture of a small contemporary repertory company at work.

in collaboration with Harwood), and in *Anyhouse* (1925). The title of this last-mentioned play bears almost the same application to what is the author's mental picture of the universal domestic interior as the late medieval *Everyman*'s does to its writer's image of universal man, and in so far it shows itself as a later development of that interest in the "morality" which played such a potent part in the advanced theatre of the century's first decade. "We all pretend in this house", says the girl who stands centrally in the course of the action,

> we pretend to be happy and prosperous and to love each other and be a united family – but we are nothing of the sort. We always sacrifice everything to keeping up appearances – that's what's the matter with us.

As Agate remarked in his review of this work – "It is extraordinary how popular Ibsen is whenever he is played under another name." Obviously the sentiments expressed in *Anyhouse* might seem to be the result of war's impact upon society's foundations, but another remark in *The Pelican* deserves to be noted and remembered:

> Morality depends on mechanics. It always has, especially when it is artificial, as in the case of women. Victorian morality began to wilt with the introduction of the safety bicycle, the motor-car was its death-blow, and there is still the aeroplane. St Paul and John Knox have proved no match for Dunlop and Daimler.

This statement may well be looked upon as being one of the most socially percipient to be discovered in the entire range of early twentieth-century dramatic dialogue, not excluding that of Shaw's; and it might almost be applied as a kind of emblematic summation, not merely of attitudes to morality, but of the general trend in dramatic atmosphere during this period. In 1900 the safety bicycle was indeed becoming widely popular; in 1912 the motor-car was in the process of extending its range from the domains of the very wealthy to those of at least the upper middle-class, and during the same year dare-devil aviators were giving displays of their skill to gaping crowds whose eyes – even although their heads were turned up towards the heavens – were set not upon the ineffable wonders of the empyrean but upon the whirring wonders of technology: during the twenties the automobile had been made popular, and the hitherto peaceful skies were being shattered by the roar of planes.

Harwood, Jesse and Malleson, notwithstanding their various comedies, all tended to be not only rather serious in their efforts but also on occasion to direct their attention towards limited audiences when they felt they had things to say which might not appeal to a general public. It is, therefore, of very considerable interest to observe how a fourth dramatist of this time, concentrating entirely upon the ordinary general public and usually writing in lighter vein, reflected sentiments akin to those of this companions. During his earlier years he had won success chiefly from the libretti he wrote for musical plays, although it is not to be forgotten that one of his very first contributions to the theatre was a comedy which, dealing with the vagaries of the smart set, bore a title, *The Best People* (1909), anticipating that of Maugham's *Our Betters* by fully ten years and which was penned in such a style as to enable it, with only slight revision, to win success as *Aren't We All?* in 1923.[1] The theme and dialogue of this comedy are thoroughly typical of Lonsdale's work as a whole: its first act shows a wife, Margot, on her return from a holiday abroad, finding her husband toying with another woman; in the second act, her father-in-law, the good-natured and wordly-wise Lord Grenham, on discovering that she herself had nearly had an affair during her vacation, politely blackmails her into expressing her forgiveness; and at the end comes a surprise, when Margot gives Grenham tit-for-tat by placing in *The Times* an announcement of a forthcoming marriage between him (a somewhat unwilling victim) and a Lady Frinton (who for some time had been trying to catch him). The plot is clever; the play's structure is excellently

[1] For his career see Frances Donaldson, *Freddie Lonsdale* (1957). Incidentally it may be observed here that in his "books" for musical plays Lonsdale introduced an innovation by placing considerable emphasis on the plots.

contrived; a cynical attitude towards life is nicely blended with a humorous kindliness; and the lines flow easily with constant flashings of gentle wit. Later the same year *Spring Cleaning* employed the same methods to deal with a situation rather more serious. Here a husband, disturbed by finding that his wife is spending too much time with dissipated fashionable companions and is being courted by a notorious roué, suddenly decides on a drastic course of action: he instals a prostitute in his household, and thus achieves happiness by means of shock treatment.

These plays well illustrate both Lonsdale's strength and his weaknesses. Concerning his theatrical skill there can be no doubt; his individual scenes are usually attractively presented, and, if at times his epigrams seem to derive rather from the exercise of conscious art than from spontaneous wit, he definitely has the gift of writing easy dialogue. Had he stood alone in his own particular style, his qualities might perhaps today be more amply, and more justifiably, admired; but, unfortunately for him, he has had to suffer comparison, on the one hand, with Maugham, whose view of the human comedy was deeper, and, on the other, with Coward, whose wit was more scintillating and spontaneous. Nevertheless, his contributions to the stage of this time ought not to be ignored, nor should we neglect to take note of his originality in attitude. In *On Approval* (1926) for instance, he created a comedy which has had sufficient strength to warrant several revivals. For Malleson and others the idea of a "trial marriage" had been a serious (for some even a solemn) affair, a fervent expression of women's rights, and, implicitly if not explicitly, treated as a necessary prelude to future marital happiness. Lonsdale here turns the situation around by taking two couples, an unselfish Richard in love with an egotistical Maria and an equally unselfish Helen in love with an egotistical George, Duke of Bristol; marooned for a month in a snow-bound Scottish house, the incompatability of the pairs is made evident, and with manifest agility the author has kept interest awake in the adroitly conceived permutations among his four characters. The process of inversion exhibited in this comedy, combined with the theme of polite blackmail shown in *Aren't We All?* and *Spring Cleaning*, appears, differently handled, in his most characteristic play, *The Last of Mrs Cheyney* (1925), where at the start we seem once again to be in the midst of the usual aristocratic circle, and where, to our surprised delight, we discover that the charming Mrs Cheyney is in reality a crook among crooks – although one gifted with the grace of repentance – ultimately the fit companion of the equally charming roué – also willing to turn over a new leaf – Lord Arthur Dilling. Inversion, too, and comic irony rule in *The High Road* (1927). A common theme in earlier plays had been the passion of a rich peer for a poor chorus-girl: here the impecunious son of a not-too-wealthy lord aspires to the hand of a highly respectable actress; the family, worried by thought of the girl's low-born origins, send for her father with the object of finding out what he will accept to have the intended marriage broken off, but to their surprise and discomfiture they discover that he is anxious to have them exert pressure on the young man with the same objective; all he is concerned about is that his daughter's promisingly brilliant stage future should not be destroyed. And another variant appears in *Canaries Sometimes Sing* (1929) where, as in *On Approval*, Lonsdale skilfully juggles with four partners – Ernest Melton, a peer's son, irritated with his unconventional ex-chorus-girl wife, Elma, and Geoffrey Lymes, a popular dramatist inclined to think himself unconventional, bored with his socially-pretentious wife, Anne. The two men are friends, and as the play develops Lonsdale cleverly allows us to think that this will be simply another comedy of swapped partners – but at the close we discover that Lymes, inwardly conventional, is landed with his detested Anne again, while Ernest remains alone – Elma having decided to get herself divorced from him. The comic point of the play rests in the fact that, although this Elma behaves in a thoroughly "immoral" manner, she impresses us as being the only one of the quartet gifted with magnanimity and warm human emotions.

Lonsdale the dramatist, then, inevitably stands associated with two writers who, each in his own particular manner, have styles akin to his own: on the one hand, he had to vie with his elder contemporary, Somerset Maugham, and, on the other, he was forced into rivalry with the young Noël Coward,[1] who in 1923 made an extraordinarily sudden advent, winning both notoriety and esteem for his *The Young Idea* – and this, as is universally known, was followed by a long series of plays bewildering in their variety, and, it may be added, rather perplexing in their erratic qualities. The joyous *Hay Fever* (1925) has thus to be set against the dull and artificially contrived *Home Chat* (1927); already in the year when *The Young Idea* brought him to public notice his collaboration with Ronald Jeans carried him into the world of revue, a world in which he proved a master and one to which during this period he made distinctive contributions terminating in the triumphant *This Year of Grace!*; in 1924 an utterly different world, a world dark and painful, attracted him to produce *The Vortex* and *The Rat Trap*; in 1926 with *The Queen was in the Parlour* he induced himself to purchase a ticket to Ruritania, a voyage during which he exploited romance with more than a tang of bitterness and also one which led him to extend his travels by making a trip to eighteenth-century France in *The Marquise* (1927) and to melodious Vienna in *Bitter-Sweet* (1929). His own fortunes were as diverse as the nature of these plays: the frenzied, shrieking, hysterically ecstatic reception at the first night of *The Young Idea* finds its complete contrast in the boos and hisses which greeted his peculiarly inept *Sirocco* just five

[1] R. Mander and J. Mitchenson, in their *Theatrical Companion to Coward* (1957), present a most useful record of his plays and their productions. The author's own *Present Indicative* (1937) is a pleasant autobiographical account of his earlier years. In 1933 Patrick Braybrooke published *The Amazing Mr Noel Coward* – its title well reflecting the public wonder at his extraordinary variety; Rose Snider's *Satire in the Comedies of Congreve, Sheridan, Wilde and Coward* (1937) and Robert Greacen's *The Art of Noel Coward* (1953) demonstrate how he became accepted, not simply as a flashing comet, but as a permanently-shining theatrical luminary; in 1969 Sheridan Morley's *A Talent to Amuse* suggests an appropriate fusion of delight and serious contemplation.

years later. The contemporary critics engaged in reviewing his contributions to the stage were repeatedly forced to alter their organ-stops from a high "Masterpiece" to a denunciatory bass "Utter Failure".

The strange lapses from brilliant concept and sparkling dialogue to boring dulness of theme and language need not concern us here. Unquestionably during those years Coward was in a frantic, desperate haste as though some yapping hound of heaven were at his heels, and at least half of his total early dramatic efforts can be dismissed as insignificant. Still further, to his haste must be added his uncertainty concerning the style which would best be suited for the exploitation of his genius – an uncertainty which was shared by several of his fellow-dramatists and one which was not finally put to rest until he presented *This Year of Grace!* and *Bitter-Sweet*: in these he truly found himself, and his *Private Lives* (1930), *Cavalcade* (1931) and *Design for Living* (1932) were their triumphant successors.

While any attempt to consider merely a small section of any writer's work must inevitably be unsatisfactory, Coward's position in the theatre of the twenties is such that these earliest plays, however hurriedly they were written and much as he remained unsure as to how his talents might most effectively find expression, demand careful assessment. As with Shaw's works, the obvious approach to them might at first seem to be the sociological – particularly today when the fashionable style of dramatic criticism generally tends in this direction. *Hay Fever*, for example, has lately been analysed as a picture, almost symbolic, of a country house which, following the destruction of the older society, is now occupied by a new kind of family, the Blisses, whose artificiality is so dangerously threatened by commonplace visitors from without that they are compelled to hound them out of their little circle. This interpretation, entirely in keeping with current analyses of Shakespeare's plays and of Congreve's, hardly agrees with the content of a delightful comedy whose author almost certainly had no such serious thoughts in his mind when he was composing it. Coward was a keenly acute observer of the human scene, but assuredly his attitude never approached that which prompted Galsworthy to write *The Foundations* – or, for that matter, which prompted Shaw to write *Heartbreak House*.

In the young Coward three basic qualities can be discerned. First, and paramount, is the fact that he was, in a double sense, a one-man total theatre. It is almost impossible to think of anyone before his time who so actively and expertly combined in himself almost everything appertaining to the stage – he was actor, singer, dancer, director, producer, composer, playwright – or who applied himself at the same time to so many different forms of theatrical entertainment, comedy light and comedy satirical, grim drama, glittering revue and pathetically-charming operetta. And besides this diversity there was something else – his absolute and complete devotion to the playhouse. Whereas so many other dramatists in choosing their themes were at least partly intent upon what they, as individuals, had to say on social life, on politics and on related subjects, his gaze was continually set on theatrical appeal. *The Mob* was a failure because Galsworthy was so deeply concerned with its subject-matter that he almost lost sight of his audience: Coward's *Sirocco* was an even greater failure – but not because the author was over-concerned with any "idea"; the failure simply and plainly was the result of miscalculation. Coward had been acclaimed for *The Vortex* in 1924; the following year the London public was animatedly talking about *Fallen Angels*, a play possibly influenced by the desire to rival another new author, Michael Arlen, who was also becoming the talk of the Town because of *The Green Hat* (1925); and in *Sirocco*, with its story of a young English businessman's wife who absconds with an Anglo-Italian artist and miserably regrets her action, he no doubt hoped that he would repeat or recapture his success by riding on the crest of a new wave. Unfortunately, however, six years separated its original composition from its performance in 1927. Although revised, the text showed that the author was only a dramatic apprentice and that the entire planning of the piece belonged to a mode which had been novel in 1921 but which, possessing no enduring power, soon seemed irritatingly absurd. Thus "catcalls and various other animal noises" punctuated nearly all the actors' lines.

No doubt Galsworthy was most distressed because the public would not fully sympathise with the humanitarian thesis of *The Mob*; Coward, not having any philosophical or social concept in his mind, could have felt distress only because he had made a theatrical blunder: and *This Year of Grace!* and *Bitter-Sweet* might well be regarded as the result of the playhouse lesson he had learned.

We must, of course, be circumspect. The absence of social criticism in Coward's writings by no means implies that his best plays existed solely in a realm of popular amusement or entertainment. While it is certainly inadvisable to read into *Hay Fever* any deep commentary upon what was happening to English society, there can be no doubt but that in his finest plays Coward exhibited the true dramatist's eager and penetrating insight into human idiosyncrasies and into social behaviour – and the titles he gave to his writings indicate clearly that at which he aimed: Galsworthy found *Justice* and *Loyalties* indicative headings for his scenes, whereas for Coward *Private Lives* and *Design for Living* were titles thoroughly appropriate as an expression of his purposes. And as a third quality, although not one which requires any lengthy and elaborate discussion, we must bear in mind that the special kind of insight which he possessed was all-embracing and objective.

His first two successes in themselves fully illustrate what he had to offer to the stage. *The Young Idea* came into being not as something new but as an exceedingly clever adaptation and extension of several themes which, as has been seen, were freely exploited in the theatre between 1900 and 1913 – first, the contrast between "aristocratic" or "upper-middle-class" society and the world of the "artist"; second, the ever-increasing rebelliousness of youth; and, third, the contrast between society's values and those which were to be found, for example, in "Colonials". Many of the dramas which had exploited these elements had inclined towards the serious (and, worse, towards the solemn), and the majority had presented their main characters in a narrow and ultimately uninteresting manner: the "Colonials", for example, introduced to show up society's follies and vices were uncut diamonds and, like diamonds uncut, they were often almost incredibly dull. What Coward did in *The Young Idea* was to take the three staple elements, arrange them in a different and attractively novel way, and deal with them joyously. His scene he sets in the midst of a county hunting social environment, with the central figure a middle-aged George Brent who, years previously, had separated from his first wife, an artistically-inclined Jennifer; now he finds that his second wife, Cicely, is a stupid, deceitful, disagreeable, socially smart and thoroughly disappointing encumbrance. His children by his first wife, the irrepressible Gerda and Sholto, after having spent almost all their years abroad, arrive to pay him a visit – thus introducing a combination of "youth", the "artist" and the "colonial" to show up the pretensions, the absurdities and meannesses of the hunting set, to disentangle their father from his unwanted Cicely and to bring him back to his old love, Jennifer. Quite clearly for Coward this plot has an interest almost exclusively theatrical: no doubt it does permit him to make fun of the conventional, useless, hypocritical, contemptuous and contemptible English society which is smothering George Brent, but this fun, even although it is invested with a certain satirical force, has a purpose rather entertaining than sociological – and, in order to preserve his balance, the author allows some of his laughing barbs to be directed against the youthful iconoclasts. *The Young Idea*, as a title to the comedy, refers to the tricks by means of which the father is rescued, not to any dramatic presentation of a new social concept.

The same approach gave to *Hay Fever* its enduring quality. It is said that the play was written, within the course of but a few days, after Coward himself had spent a bewildering week-end in the midst of a household very closely akin to that of the Blisses – and there is no reason for disbelieving that thus indeed it came into being. The twin sprites of amusement and joy were its creators. No social comment is present here, simply the gleeful contrasting of a self-centred artistic (and, in particular, a theatrical) family and of other individuals – Richard Greatham, a Foreign Office man, Sandy Tyrell, a boxer, and Jackie Coryton, described by the novelist David Bliss as "an abject fool, but a useful type" whom he wants to study "in domestic surroundings" – all of whom are utterly lost in a world bafflingly alien to them. Coward's success here depends upon two things. The first of these is his complete objectivity: the Blisses are charmingly delightful in their make-believe existence, yet they are absurd; their guests – who at the end dazedly steal away, hardly noticed, at breakfast-time – are ordinary persons, pleasant enough no doubt, yet of delightful charm possessing nothing. Secondly, there is his style. Since the time of Oscar Wilde, comedies had tended to be full of fire-crackers, of epigrams which usually could be seen for what they were – deliberately concocted witticisms, lines belonging to the authors rather than to the characters: even Somerset Maugham, who sought in general to make his dramatic persons express themselves in their own ways, has numerous smart sayings which give us the impression of having been contrived with pain and effort, while dozens of apprentice playwrights deemed it essential to pile joke upon joke. Coward, of course, has a fine wit, but generally he uses it with effective restraint and makes the jest fit the speaker; and, more significantly, he introduces something novel – amusing lines in which not a single epigram is present but which achieve their comic effect from a condensation of ordinary talk and from exquisite pointing. Among scores of examples a short conversation between Richard and Jackie may be taken here as an illustration. Jackie is nervous, timid, ill at ease, and Richard, diplomatically and good-naturedly, seeks to calm her sense of awkwardness:

RICHARD. I do hope the weather will keep good over Sunday – the country round here is delightful.

JACKIE. Yes.

RICHARD. There's nowhere like England in the spring and summer.

JACKIE. No, there isn't, is there?

RICHARD. There's a sort of *quality* you find in no other countries.

JACKIE. Have you travelled a lot?

RICHARD (*modestly*). A good deal.

JACKIE. How lovely.

(*There is a pause.*)

RICHARD. Spain is very beautiful.

JACKIE. Yes, I've always heard Spain was awfully nice.

RICHARD. Except for the bull-fights. No one who ever really loved horses could enjoy a bull-fight.

JACKIE. Nor anyone who loved bulls either.

RICHARD. Exactly.

JACKIE. Italy's awfully nice, isn't it?

RICHARD. Oh, yes, charming.

JACKIE. I've always wanted to go to Italy.

RICHARD. Rome is a beautiful city.

JACKIE. Yes, I've always heard Rome was lovely.

RICHARD. And Naples and Capri – Capri's enchanting.

JACKIE. It must be.

RICHARD. Have you ever been abroad at all?

JACKIE. Oh, yes; I went to Dieppe once – we had a house there for the summer.

RICHARD (*kindly*). Dear little place – Dieppe.

JACKIE. Yes, it was lovely.

This is impeccable, revealing the characters who are speaking, exuding a warm sympathy with both, and at the same time offering to two skilled performers material apt to keep an audience in a mood of amused delight.

In subject-matter as in dialogue, the balance kept by Coward is constant. The ageing actress in *Hay Fever* is eccentrically alluring; the ageing mother in *The Vortex* lives a selfish, messy and even slovenly existence, and thus virtually destroys her son. On the first night of *The Young Idea* the teen-age spectators shrieked themselves hoarse in their approbation of Gerda and Sholto, yet very soon they came to be dismayed on finding their pop-idol criticising youth for its brainless self-centredness. In *Hay Fever* Judith Bliss and her novelist-husband dwell reasonably happily and contentedly in their artificial ambience; in *The Rat Trap* a playwright and his novelist-wife are at odds with each other and their shattered marriage is mere misery. In general, his "artists" are individualistic oddities whose way of existence is contrasted with respectable commonplace standards, but this does not mean that Coward is completely content in the company of these oddities: at times they may bring disaster upon themselves and others, and occasionally, as with the novelist in *Home Chat*, they may become almost unbelievably dreary and conventional.

These comments on the work of the young Coward are necessary if only because he, more than any other playwright, stands as the symbol of the theatre during this decade. At first glance he seems to be expressing something essentially new, something different from what had come upon the stage before 1913, and yet closer examination makes us realise that almost all his plays, whether comic or serious, are planted on ground which had been similarly cultivated for fully twenty years before he applied himself to its tilling: his two excursions into period and Ruritanian drama, *The Queen was in the Parlour* and *The Marquise*, might perhaps be called old-fashioned in atmosphere and even in execution; indeed, it is possible to go still further and find at least partial justification for a contemporary critique of *Bitter-Sweet*: "To the most daring it is given to be the most retrogressive. 'Bitter Sweet' might have been written by A. W. Pinero, composed by Paul Rubens, and produced by George Edwardes in the glorious nineties."[1] Only partial justification, of course, and uttered tongue in cheek, because it obscures the new note of a Coward who, building his plays on the models of the past, was at the same time preparing to lead the drama into something fresh: the double process of culmination and revolution is clear even in these his earliest plays.

Among the other new playwrights who made their appearances at this time the one who most deserves to be placed

[1] *The Play Pictorial*, lv, no. 330, 1930, 38.

alongside Coward is A. A. Milne, and here once more we find an author whose inspiration clearly derived from the past and yet who stands not only as thoroughly representative of the theatre between 1920 and 1930 but, also, as one who gave not a few suggestions to the playwrights following him.

If Somerset Maugham (among others) was Coward's acknowledged master, there can be not the slightest doubt that Milne was the spiritual heir of J. M. Barrie. Although later in his career he expressed regret at being labelled a "whimsical" dramatist,[1] from the very start of his career his plays were patently inspired by the style which had been so fully exploited by the author of *Peter Pan* and *A Kiss for Cinderella.* Even in his earliest comedy, *Wurzel Flummery* (1917), the character of Clifton, the young solicitor anxious to write for the stage, may be regarded as at least a partial self-portrait: when one of this Clifton's companions pompously refers to his scripts as farces, he immediately interjects –

> Pardon the interruption. But you said farces. Not farces, comedies – of a whimsical nature.

This unconcealed indebtedness raises a serious obstacle to our obtaining a true appreciation of Milne's independent contributions to the theatre. That his attunement to Barrie's personality and style materially aided him is certain: from this source he gained much in the subtle handling of his plots and scenes, in delicate methods of characterisation, in finely textured dialogue. But, however beneficial this may have been, the result has been unfortunate for his reputation – and that for two reasons. The first is immediately obvious: even if we are not familiar with his writings, we are apt (having listened to the words of unsympathetic critics) to dismiss him simply as a mere imitator; we do not bother to inquire into the possible ways in which he modified and elaborated the earlier patterns which he had taken as his models, producing plays which were at once like and unlike

[1] Preface to *The Ivory Door* (1930).

those of his masters. The second obstacle, while not so obvious, is still more serious. Regrettably, Milne swallowed Barrie whole, including those well-known characteristic stage-directions which, as it were, took the reader into the author's confidence and "whimsically" made comments on the play's actions and persons: and with even greater regret we are forced to realise that Milne has not been content merely to follow this style but has deplorably exaggerated it – with the result that his own stage-directions must frequently seem absurdly sentimental and conceited. Now, lengthy stage-directions, printed in arresting italics, are apt to catch the eye of a reader, and anyone unfamiliar with Milne's work is in danger of throwing his comedies aside simply because what first catches the attention is admittedly ridiculous. Since there are now few if any opportunities of seeing these comedies presented on the stage, it may be suggested that our only possible way of appreciating their quality is to ignore, rigorously and completely, all the author's comments and concentrate exclusively upon the dialogue.

If we do so, perhaps we shall find ourselves induced to acknowledge that Milne has a subtle ingenuity, a quiet humour, a gentle sympathy all distinctively his own: and distinctive, too, is his central vision, a sad and resigned acceptance, tempered by humour and deep benevolence, of life's crushing littleness: shadow and substance, appearance and reality, truth and illusion, are the contrasting opposites of this world. These qualities are amply evident in his first successful play, *Mr Pim Passes By* (1919). Its title unashamedly testifies to its dramatic ancestry: the very name of Mr Pim is Barriesque, and the fact that this character's main dramatic mission is, indeed, simply to pass by carries us back to those intruders who so fascinated earlier playwrights. The emphasis upon the ancestry, however, should not be allowed to conceal from us Milne's independent dramatic skill and originality. The household to which we are introduced is that of a very respectable George Marden J.P., a man perhaps somewhat heavy, if kindly, whose delightful wife, Olivia, had previously been married to a disagreeable rotter named Jacob Telworthy, confidently assumed by all to have died in Australia many years previously. Inconsequent Mr Pim happens to visit the house, hears the name Telworthy mentioned, and, completely without malice, shocks everyone by saying that on the ship which had just brought him to England he had encountered one of his former employees, a drunken cheat, whose name he *thinks* was Telworthy. In distress George and Olivia try to get further information from Mr Pim – "But – didn't I tell you", says the passer-by, "of the curious fatality at Marseilles – poor fellow – the fishbone?...Yes, yes, a herring, I understand...Oh, undoubtedly, undoubtedly. A fishbone lodged in his throat." George, the conventional man, decides that he and Olivia must secretly wed again, and this gives the merry Olivia her chance for a bit of play-acting. She demands from him a fresh proposal of marriage, and there is considerable debate – when Mr Pim, about to pass still further on, calls in to correct a slight error: after having thought things over, he has recalled that the man's name was Henry Polwittle, not Jacob Telworthy. Even so, however, we are not finished with Mr Pim: at the very close of the comedy he makes a final appearance in order to acknowledge a mistake: "Mrs Marden!" he declares beamingly, "I've just remembered. His name was *Ernest* Polwittle – *not* Henry." And happily off he goes. When we realise that this adroit and original adaptation of the passer-by motif is in itself chiefly a means for introducing an intimate character portrait of husband and wife, that the picture is enlarged and diversified by equally intimate portraits of the niece Dinah and her boy-friend Brian, and that almost every section of the dialogue is intricately varied and humorously pointed, we must concur in recognising *Mr Pim Passes By* as a minor comic masterpiece. It has positively nothing to say about social or political questions, but it has much to say about human nature.

The complications introduced here into what might have been just a simple slightly farcical action point to an idiosyncratic feature of Milne's plays: in general, he loved to confront himself with dramatic problems. Even in electing to write a detective play, *The Fourth Wall* (1928), it gives him pleasure to make his task peculiarly difficult by introducing a daringly novel device. The first act shows the audience not merely a murder but also who commits that murder and why; and thus the last two acts are left with the problem of holding interested attention without reliance upon the usual puzzled suspense peculiar to this theatrical genre. His originality, in structure, style and character delineation, is nowhere more apparent than in *The Truth about Blayds* (1921), a drama which is again both an imaginative transformation of what Milne found in the theatre of previous years and something markedly novel. Here the theme of the "artist" is expanded into what seems to be the first important theatrical presentation of the "grand old man" – a poet named Oliver Blayds, now aged ninety and universally acknowledged by critics and by public as the "Supreme Songster of an Earlier Epoch", a master whose peers could be found only among the Tennysons, the Brownings and the Swinburnes. During some three-quarters of the play the audience is led to believe that Milne's only object is to make a study of this man's relationship with the members of his family – his younger daughter Isobel – a woman who eighteen years before had refused marriage because she believed it was her duty to care for her father – her sentimentally stupid married sister whose husband, William Blayds-Conway, dreaming always of eventually winning fame as the great poet's biographer, acts as his secretary-amanuensis – and the two grandchildren, Oliver and Septima, who feel that their lives are being ruined in this temple of awed veneration. Then, suddenly, the picture changes. The old poet dies, and Isobel gives a chilling shock to everyone by revealing that the supposedly mighty poet had, in fact, been a thieving fake: the poems which had made him famous had all been written in the far-off past by his then closest friend, a shining genius who after a few years of frenzied unpublished lyrical writing had died young. And here becomes apparent Milne's basic purpose – the effect, not of the illusion, but of the truth. Even although we may feel that at moments the play veers towards the sentimental, when taken all in all it must be accepted as one of the most interesting works of its time.

Throughout all his dramatic writings Milne's dominant vision prevails – now boisterously farcical and exuberant, as in *The Great Broxopp* (1921), now reflectively sad, as in *Success* (1923), and now humorously fanciful, as in *Ariadne* (1925). Among all these plays three deserve particular mention, but for vastly different reasons – *The Dover Road* (1921), *Success* and *The Ivory Door* (1929). All show how deeply impressed was this author's imagination by the combined contrast and inter-relations between the dream and the reality. In looking at the first of these three works, however, one becomes aware of something unexpected – that Milne is not, after all, so far removed from Coward, nor is Coward so far off from Barrie. Mr Latimer's house, "a little way off the Dover road", has in it something of a whiff of "an Arabian-night-adventure air", and when we find that its owner delights in intercepting run-away couples on their surreptitious flights to Paris, we are perhaps inclined at first to dismiss the whole fantastic story as little more than Barrie and water. Yet maybe will come a second thought, that the house off the Dover road is not so unlike the French hotel to which Chance, following the lead of Mr Latimer (just as he had followed the lead of Mr Lob) brings his two cross-related couples of runaways in *Private Lives* (1930): and, if that thought does arise, then possibly there may be found at least some passages of Milne's dialogue which have a flavour of Coward's wit in the midst of their fantastic humour.

Unfortunately, however, Milne did not realise wherein lay his true strength. His characteristic and original contribution to the theatre rested in his special kind of humour, but regrettably he could not prevent himself from making many of his plays over-serious. When in 1939 he was asked by Faber and Faber to choose his "best play" he selected

Success, and it is known that, despite its failure on the stage, he highly esteemed *The Ivory Door* – and both of these, although they interestingly carry us deep into the author's mind, lack entirely any lighter touch in their scenes. In the "legend" which forms the plot of the latter drama a young prince ("once upon a time") on the day before his intended marriage, sits wondering – as he had wondered from his earliest boyhood – about a mysterious door in the castle through which, says legendary myth, his grandfather Stephen and others had passed and disappeared. Boldly he decides to open it, and, after groping his way along a dark passage, he emerges, all dusty, dirty and dishevelled, outside the castle's walls. So changed in appearance is he that the people whom he meets refuse to recognise him as their prince: he encounters a Mummer, and this man, who as an accomplished actor is certain he knows how a king ought to behave, dismisses him contemptuously as a mere amateur counterfeiter. Back he returns the way he had come and, entering the castle again, meets his bride-to-be: after some talk the pair, hand-in-hand, go through the portal, and this time utterly vanish. Illusion and reality, legend and truth, sincerity and make-believe all are here intermingled to make up the content of the drama, and, although we recognise Milne's seriousness of purpose, we cannot deem the result truly stageworthy.

Not far different is *Success*, which may be regarded as a kind of antidote to Granville-Barker's *Waste*, since the "waste" presented here is precisely "success" itself. The Rt Hon. R. Selby Mannock, M.P., is a prominent politician, but one day he meets his old school-chum Eversley and this recalls to his mind thought of the girl, Sally, who had been their companion in holiday games and whom as a boy he had loved. Chance causes Mannock and his Sally to meet again; the old love grips him once more, and his "success" suddenly appears empty and vain; he determines to give up everything and go off with her, and his letter of resignation is sent to the Prime Minister. A reply arrives delivered by hand, and to his amazement it contains, not a message of acceptance, but an appointment as Chancellor of the Exchequer. "Success" grips him once more – and characteristically the play ends with a stage-direction:

MANNOCK *walks slowly to his desk. For a little while he sits there, holding the letter in his hand....* SALLY *is dead. He has killed her. No good explaining, apologizing, whining, to a person whom you have killed. Let him be man enough to spare her that last insult. No, there's nothing to say. It was* EVERSLEY *and that damned tune that got into a man's head, and made him dream....The sweetness of her in his dream! But that was twenty-five years ago. They're dead now; both dead....But – Chancellor of the Exchequer! It will be in all the papers to-morrow. Chancellor of the Exchequer! What will the papers say? What will people say? Everybody will see it....* SALLY *will see it. Will know, will understand. No, there's nothing to be said. That damned tune, that damned dream. O Sally, Sally, Sally! Don't! Don't come into my dreams again....So for a little he sits, thinking. Then, with a bitter, contemptuous laugh, he tosses away his thoughts and comes back to the letter. Chancellor of the Exchequer! Briskly he dips his pen into the ink, and writes to the Prime Minister.*

The Ivory Door is not a good play, nor is *Success*, whatever high opinion Milne himself may have had of it; and this author has many other dramas which must be regarded as failures. Yet his better works claim the right to remembrance. Social problems find no mention in these: there is nothing of cynicism in his scenes: and the absence of "problems" and satire may make him antipathetic to our age – but in humility we must bear in mind that this our age is not necessarily the be-all and the end-all of everything. Milne is as much a votary of youth's dreams as is Coward, but whereas the latter deals with the modishly fashionable, idly rebellious or intellectually eccentric young men and women of the period, Milne is interested in those whom the others might have dismissed as "ordinary" – the down-to-earth Dinah in *Mr Pim Passes By*, or the dreaming Melisande Knowle of *The Romantic Age* (1920). In effect, the two authors were as complementary to each other as were Shaw and Barrie twenty years before; and, still further, a survey of what was produced in the theatres during the twenties suggests that between them they represented in their combined work most of the outstanding dramatic trends which characterised that decade.

There were, of course, some categories of play, mostly reflections in style of what had already been fully exploited in the past, which neither of them touched. Thus, to select just one dramatist from among many, Edward Percy has but little contact with either. His *If Four Walls Told* (1920) is effectively written, but it belongs to that area of regional theatre which had, as it were, completed its activities several years before. This story of Liz Rysing who has lost her only child, who comes to suspect her husband Jan when he proposes that she should adopt a seventeen-year-old love-child whom a village woman does not want, who almost breaks with him and then is plunged into despair when she believes he has been accidentally drowned is in spirit close to *Nan*, but far away both from *Hay Fever* and from *Mr Pim Passes By*. Reminiscent of the theatre of the past, too, is Percy's *Trespasses* (1923), a "business" study framed according to earlier patterns. Andrew Grayling, owner of a fairly successful firm, marries a girl, Dora, considerably younger than himself; and about the same time his assistant, Quintin Coomber, after having put his savings in the company, is made his partner. Pushed for money, Grayling begins to gamble in goods, losing heavily; financially, Coomber acts generously, but falls in love with Dora. The battle of conflicting interests comes to an end as Grayling, consumed by jealousy, detects a mistake made by Coomber and threatens to ruin him. Although competently written, this is all decidedly old-fashioned. The number of stage authors who thus looked back to the past is large, and often we are surprised on encountering some of those who make up their company. Clemence Dane, for instance, is a writer whose name still remains well-known because of what we consider a very "modern" play, *A Bill of Divorcement*, presented in 1921: yet in fact we are compelled to agree that only the theme of this drama belongs to the twenties; it is "strong" and on the whole well-constructed, yet in essence its spirit is that of the old traditional "play of ideas"; save for the topic with which it is concerned, it might have been written ten years earlier. Nor is this an exception among her writings. The theatre of 1910, too, might well have given birth to her *Will Shakespeare* (1921), a biographical study which, despite some effective scenes, harks back to the antiquated school of the poetic drama. Even more indicative of the world in which she spiritually dwelt is the fact that in her own opinion *Granite* (1926) was her finest work,[1] but how utterly mistaken she was becomes apparent when we realise that its subject, its structure, its characterisation and its language are all poor imitations of the products of the regional theatre which had been an active force many years before and which now had completely lost their strength. The action of this stupidly grim drama is set on the rocky, storm-swept coast of Lundy during the earliest part of the nineteenth century: in a lonely cottage live sensuous Judith and her hard husband Jordan Morris: enters Jordan's handsome half-brother Prosper and she falls in love with him: he is about to leave and she prays to the Devil to make him stay; a water-sodden, half-drowned Man staggers into the cottage seeking succour: there is a fight and Jordan is slain, she marries her Prosper, but he too is killed, and at the close the unnamed Man takes possession of her. Of pieces like this we seek no more.

If, however, the plays produced by such authors as Edward Percy and Clemence Dane exhibit little or no association with the qualities inherent in the writings of Coward and Milne, the characteristic styles of the last-mentioned dramatists are reflected in dozens of those realistic works which dealt with current social life in two contrasting ways, the merrily amusing and the cynically bitter. In so far as the former are concerned we must take note of the increasing popularity of farce during the twenties. Farcical plays, of course, had never been absent from the stage since the beginning of the century, yet perhaps no earlier seasons can

[1] In 1934 she selected it for the anthology of recent dramatic writings published by Faber and Faber under the title of *My Best Play*.

be found in which there were so many performances of this kind offered to the public in the West End, with the Aldwych Theatre established as the temple of the unnamed muse who rules over this form of entertainment. In 1922 Tom Walls and Leslie Henson became that theatre's managers, and from 1927 until 1933 the former carried it on with a stable policy which made it, in a sense, the last relic of the century's earlier actor–manager playhouses. In 1925 he had found in Ben Travers the author who could give him what he wanted, and thus was launched the famous and delightful series of Aldwych farces which kept teeming audiences in a delighted roar of laughter and which even now, almost half a century later, repeat their first successes in television form. *A Cuckoo in the Nest* came in 1925; and this was followed by *Rookery Nook* (1926), *Thark* (1927), *Plunder* (1928), *A Cup of Kindness* (1929) and *A Night like This* (1930). Although the series continued for a short time, we need feel no surprise at finding that it came to its end in 1933: these "Aldwych Farces" properly belong to the late twenties. Nor did they stand alone. Ben Travers may be the most celebrated among the farcical authors, but there were several others who vied with him in popularity – notably Ian Hay, P. G. Wodehouse and Stephen Hall.[1]

With these farces have to be associated the large numbers of "light comedies" which joined with them in attracting large audiences. Some, like W. A. Darlington's clever *Alf's Button* (1924), dealt with themes extravagantly fantastic, but the majority kept within the bounds of common experience. In 1922 Herbert Farjeon and Horace Horsnell won success for their amusing skit, *Advertising April*, concerned with the then new realm of the movie makers. A few years later came Joan Temple's *The Widow's Cruise* (1926), and during the same season Aimée and Philip Stuart began their lengthy dramatic partnership with *The Cat's Cradle*. Nor was it long before Ivor Novello joined them with *The Truth Game* (1928) – a kind of happy *Iris*, in which a young widow, incon-

[1] Hay and Wodehouse collaborated in *A Damsel in Distress* (1928), and the former partnered Hall in *The Middle Watch* (1929).

veniently left a fortune which she will lose if she marries again, fortunately falls in love with the distant cousin, hitherto unknown to her, who inherits her wealth. Among these plays may be noted that strange oddity, *At Mrs Beam's* (1921), a light comedy so original in conception and so skilfully written as to suggest that its author, C. K. Munro, was destined to become a dramatic master; audiences delightedly listened to the boarding-house chatter which he was able to invest with such unexpected charm, and critics excitedly hailed his talent; but unfortunately he could not stay the pace and sank into obscurity.[1]

Both in Coward's and in Milne's dramatic writings laughter abounded, but clearly these two playwrights were interested in the serious as well – and equally clearly they showed their awareness of the fact that it was not only merriment which contemporary audiences desired. In this they reflected a trend readily to be traced in the work of many of their companions. In his *Symphony in Two Flats* (1929) Ivor Novello turned from comic scenes to present a humane and affecting study of two young composers – one who, trying desperately to complete a great musical composition before losing his sight, is deserted by his wife, and another who, after neglecting his wife, suffers from repentant thoughts. From the jesting of *The Widow's Cruise* Joan Temple moved to the dismal atmosphere of *The Cage* (1927) – the cage in question being a household in which restive daughters miserably languish: perhaps it was her fascinated contemplation of such a situation which led her to follow this drama with *Charles and Mary* (1930) wherein is shown a prison of a different kind in which gentle Elia is kept hopelessly confined. In a not dissimilar way the Stuarts also moved from the joyous to the solemn, introducing into their

[1] In all probability his failure was due to a mistaken desire to write "political" plays structured in a novel manner. Some *avant garde* circles praised *The Rumour* when that play was given a Stage Society production in 1922, but interest in Munro rapidly declined when he repeated the same technical device in *Progress* (1924), and it vanished completely after the collapse of his ambitious objective in the "symbolic drama" called *The Mountain* (1926).

Clara Gibbings (1928) a sharply-etched contrast between aristocratic indolence and vice and working-class honesty, and later dragging the capital-and-labour theme into their *Nine Till Six* (1930). A further exemplification of the same movement presents itself in the early work of J. H. Turner: his *Lilies of the Field* (1923) offered to the public a humorous picture of delightfully terrible twins, almost Barriesque in tone, while four years later his *The Spot on the Sun* (1927) was a bitterly cynical exposure of Monte Carlo life, introducing an elderly baroness with a "boy" in tow, a gambler-mother hopelessly in debt and subjected to blackmail, and the latter's daughter who is sufficiently infected by the prevailing atmosphere to be willing to condone these vices.

Play after play thus sardonically or savagely dealt with the darker sides of contemporary social life. Dennis Bradley's *The Sybarites* (1929), otherwise known as *The Amorists*, used its glittering dialogue rather to emphasise than to conceal the ugliness of its theme. Rodney Ackland's *Improper People* (1929) concentrated upon the household of a businessman who had lost all his money, living in such poverty that his wife is forced to go out to work: callously his daughters do nothing to assist, one of them spending all her time imagining (or pretending to imagine) that she is a genius, and the other continually engaged in "dramatising" herself. The presentation of these two girls is interesting because it illustrates the way in which various dramatists were beginning to move from one social attitude to another. Up to this time, as has been seen, the general trend was to laud the revolutionary spirit of youth battling against outworn concepts and, in particular, against the rigid precepts of the middle age and the middle class. Plays of such a kind, certainly, still continued to be written and performed. Thus, for example, *The Best People*, by the American authors David Grey and Avery Hopwood, had a long run at the Lyric in 1926, even although its theme might have been concocted two decades earlier. Here Mr and Mrs Lennox are shown thoroughly satisfied because they think they have arranged a marriage between their daughter Marion and a peer. The girl, however, is determined to wed the family's chauffeur, while her brother creates further consternation by announcing that he proposes to marry Alice O'Neil, a chorus-girl whom the authors are careful to depict as thoroughly respectable. In good old-fashioned manner, the play ends with a sentiment which might have been uttered on the stage in 1910:

> This is the adventure of youth and democracy, and perhaps what this family needs is some new blood.

It is peculiar – in view of the fact that several of his writings somewhat inexplicably fell foul of the censor – that the plays of the very English Earl of Lathom also reflect a style rapidly becoming outworn. At times this peculiarly erratic author could construct effective scenes, as, for example, he does in *Fear* (1927), a tense thriller, and in *Twenty Houses in a Row* (1928), the story of an ageing bank clerk who, dreaming of what he had missed in life, becomes involved in a situation where murder seems to be the only way out. Usually, however, Lathom writes about characters and situations similar to those which had attracted his immediate predecessors. *Ostriches* (1925), which shows a woman's lover transferring his affections to her daughter, may on the surface seem somewhat daring for its time, but if we examine it more carefully it cannot be thought to strike any truly fresh note; even *Wet Paint* (1926), described as a play "about a woman who was unmoral", and *Tuppence Coloured* (1926), "about a man who had no morals at all", are basically reminiscent of the stage in years gone by.

Despite the appearance of numerous writings similar in tone and quality, there can be no doubt but that change was in the air, and perhaps this change is nowhere more clearly expressed than in a sentence which John Van Druten introduced into *After All* (1929). Already, this author had made himself one of the most talked-about dramatists in town because of the then daring theme introduced into his *Young Woodley* (1928), the love affair between a schoolmaster's young wife and an adolescent pupil, but probably he judged correctly when in 1934 he selected this *After All* as his "best play" – a play which shows Ralph and Phyl, a brother and sister, rebelling against their conventional middle-class world. This certainly may seem a very familiar situation, and it is made even more familiar when we learn that Ralph, rejecting the thought of a business life, dreams of becoming an artist and that Phyl is having a secret affair with a married man. All of this would have been admirably "modern" at the beginning of the century; but here, when Phyl first tells her brother, she is not made into an exemplar of the new woman, daringly independent. "Are you shocked?" she asks; and, when he hesitates, she adds quickly, "Ralph, it's not like that. I've not gone all modern. It's serious." Obviously the term "modern", which had been the battle-cry of the young during earlier years, has by 1929 taken on a different connotation, and, in keeping with this, Van Druten's drama ends in a manner quite unexpected: Phyl, wedded to her lover now that he has become a widower, is intent only on conducting her household in most approved conventional order, while Ralph, after having divorced his rakish, restless wife Greta, sits dreaming of a life of quiet bachelor domesticity.

Thus, it might be said, were the late twenties carrying their image of social life into the thirties.

Plays devoted to the presentation of social life, however, formed but a small part of the theatrical picture at this time. What, indeed, must particularly attract our notice is the surprising number of dramas concerned with themes other than those arising from observation of life within town mansions, suburban villas and country houses. In particular, it is important to take note of the way in which the subject of war gradually developed until it became subsumed within something much vaster than itself. As early as 1914 J. E. Harold Terry, in his *General Post*, had anticipated Galsworthy's study in *The Foundations* (1917) of the breaking down of social barriers, and during the years immediately following the Armistice appeared a fairly large number of dramas which sought to depict the effects of war upon selected individuals: these extended from Harry Wall's dramatically impressive *Havoc* (1923) and Monckton Hoffe's *The Faithful Heart* (1921), through J. R. Ackerley's intimate picture of *Prisoners of War* (1925), to H. B. Trevelyan's *The Dark Angel* (1928). One particular aspect of these dramas assumes special significance when they are considered as a group. As the years advanced, the authors began to think of the war itself in a way different from that which at first had been universal: this new way meant that the playwrights were looking upon their themes less in specific terms, that they were frequently turning their gaze from the past to the future, and that, sometimes at least, they were tending to conceive their subject-matter imaginatively rather than realistically. Hubert Griffith's *Tunnel Trench*, published in 1924 although not publicly acted until four years later, with its mingling of the actual and the symbolic may be taken as indicating the start of this new trend; and the larger vision became clearly manifest when Reginald Berkeley's *The White Chateau* was broadcast in 1925 and acted in 1927; although not so powerfully effective, Robins Millar's *Thunder in the Air* (1928) may also be cited as expressive of something similar, showing how thought of the war which had recently ended began to give place to thought of the devastation which still might come in the future.

This new mood, however, could not find free scope until the older style had received its complete fulfilment – and that fulfilment came unexpectedly in 1928 with R. C. Sherriff's powerful *Journey's End.* After the success of that drama no other playwright could hope to find a theme and characters and language able to vie with its scenes. Even although Sean O'Casey introduced his imposing expressionistic scene of the gun into *The Silver Tassie* (1929) the fact that he was dealing with the past which had so impressively been put upon the stage by Sherriff meant that it failed to grip its audiences. The tantalising thought of the future was now dominant – and it is by no means without significance that the year 1928 which had seen the appearance of *Journey's End* also saw the publication of C. B. Fernald's *To-Morrow*, with its prophetic plot showing a man building a private air-raid shelter for himself, the coming of a new war and a glimpse of an afterworld. No doubt Fernald's play is confused; no doubt its failure to reach the stage very materially reduces its significance; yet its groping search for an answer to the "Riddle of Existence" makes it anticipatory of the thirties.

Such a groping search, of course, easily led – perhaps one should say, inevitably led – to the exploitation of the dream world, to the substitution of the imaginative for the realistic and, frequently, to the consideration of social problems far different from those which had attracted attention in the past, problems not concerned with strife between the generations or between middle-class "business" values and the values of the "artist" but those affecting mankind as a whole.

In this connection the career of the author of *The White Chateau* is of special interest. Before writing that drama he had presented, in *The Quest of Elizabeth* (1926), the hallucinatory experience of a patient under the influence of chloroform; in his *The World's End* (1926) he had concocted a fantastic tale of a company of travellers who come to a mysterious inn where a Tibetan magician so works upon them that they are granted all their desires; and his one-act *The Dweller in the Darkness* (1925) was specifically described by him as "a play of the unknown". All of these, like Fernald's *To-Morrow*, were concerned with spiritual questings, but it is important to observe that for such searches Berkeley did not always need to employ "mystical" or "fantastic" devices: his use of the mystical–fantastical was, in fact, a means towards an end rather than an end in itself. Thus, immediately after *The White Chateau* came his *Machines* (1927), described as a "symphony of modern life", in which, dispensing with dreams and symbols, he employs a modified kind of realism for the purpose of posing a question even more serious, more perplexing, more enigmatical than any put forward in his other plays. "Man", he says,

> has succeeded in shackling and subduing Nature by the help of his Machines. He has even put fetters on himself the better to contrive them. Can he succeed in retaining control – or will they ultimately come to rule over and govern him?

In examining these developments comprehensively we realise that several diverse elements are here intermingled, that these elements extend all the way from exploration of the inner self to questionings about the essential nature of being, that theatrical devices which had been established at the beginning of the century – such as, for example, the cultivation of passers-by, the interest in "artists" and the planning of plots spread over many years – are now being employed in different ways, and that the careers of not a few playwrights who first came to the stage in the middle twenties exhibit an uncertainty concerning which dramatic path they should choose for themselves. From this point of view the plays written before 1930 by Benn W. Levy are of considerable thematic interest: in their variety, indeed, they might almost be taken as a symbol of what was happening widely during those years. In 1925 he started with a comedy, *This Women Business*, vaguely reminiscent of *Love's Labours Lost*: a rigid misogynist invites four like-minded friends to enjoy an extended holiday with him in Cornwall; into their select and secluded paradise, however, intrudes a girl who is the embodiment of every feminine virtue – and all come under her spell. This rather thin piece might well have suggested that Levy would join the group of authors who were currently keeping the theatres well supplied with "light comedies", just as his next play, *A Man with Red Hair* (1928), might have caused us to believe that he was preparing to cash in on the vogue for thrillers.[1] Within two or three months, however, this was followed by a drama vastly different, a "shameless tract" called *Mud and Treacle*, and filled not very effectively with much talk about Love and Passion (both clearly demanding initial capitals), in which the central characters are Soloman Jack, a former clergyman turned into a Labour politician, who regards love as a slimy, slithery mixture of mud and treacle, and a vampish Daisy Andrews, who comes into his room clad only in pyjamas, and gets strangled for her pains. Then, towards the end of the same year, 1928, arrived *Mrs Moonlight*, a "piece

[1] For this piece see above pp. 207–8.

of pastiche" which, like Bennett's *Milestones*, carries the action over a great span of years (from 1881 to 1928), presenting as its central figure poor pathetic Sarah Moonlight who, having been given a magic necklace by her Highland maid, retains her youthful appearance, her clear girlish skin and her bright eyes, even as she grows older and older: so impossible does her situation become that at last she forces herself to leave the husband whom she adores, and her final appearance shows her as a down-and-out, very tired old lady of seventy-five, brought into what had been her own house by a boy, Peter, who is all unknowingly her grandson. More than one critic discerned here "the Barrie touch" – and no doubt both this comment and the author's use of the term "pastiche" were fully justified: nevertheless, it is necessary to observe that the Barrie touch is employed in an original manner, that similar originality is displayed in the adaptation of the "*Milestones*" device, that the pastiche includes within itself not a little of the mystical–mysterious–fantastic, and that, as has been suggested above,[1] the passer-by attains here to an apotheosis. The following year, *Art and Mrs Bottle; or, The Return of the Puritan* was produced, and in it the popular "artist" type was given a somewhat similar transformation. The scene is set in the household of George Bottle, a lavatory engineer, from whose uninspiring surroundings his wife, Celia, twenty years previously had eloped with an artist, Max Lightly; Bottle, resigning himself to his position, has allowed himself to be thought a widower, while she, after being callously deserted in Paris by her Max, had become the mistress of a Russian prince. Now, on the death of her lover, she unexpectedly returns "home" where she finds that her children, Michael and Judy, are both rebelliously living in an atmosphere of art – Michael in love with a model, Sonia Tippet, and Judy just on the point of deciding to go off with none other than Max. Paradoxically, she takes command of the situation, and, when Judy refuses to give up Max even when told that this man had been her mother's lover, she is given her big scene. "He is not like

[1] See above p. 334.

other men", declares Judy stubbornly, "He's – an artist", whereupon Celia explodes into a speech delivered, as the author instructs, "*with enormous heat and sincerity*":

> Art and Love! Love and Art! God, when shall we have swept away those twin delusions? The two impregnable excuses of every malingerer that chooses to clog the wheels of Life. I tell you, my child, that one of George's drains is worth more than all the Rembrandts in the world, that one of Charlie Dawes' farm labourers is worth more than the whole of Montparnasse with the Slade thrown in. And it's taken me half my life to find that out.

JUDY. You're judging art and artists by moral standards. You can't.
MAX (*mischievously*). Art for Art's sake, you know.
CELIA. But drains for God's sake. The glory of America is that she has no artists but the finest plumbers. She thinks it is her shame but, I tell you, it is her glory.

In this play the entire plot concerns the theme so popular during the earlier years of the century – the contrast between the restrictive "bourgeois" and the revolutionary, permissive "bohemian" – but the tables have been completely turned: nowhere more clearly than in the young Benn Levy's *Art and Mrs Bottle* can we find emphatic expression of what nowadays is currently labelled with the cant term "backlash". The play points inflexibly towards the thirties, and it is worthy of notice that precisely at the start of this decade, on January 12, 1930, came Levy's next and best play, *The Devil*, described as a "religious comedy" and even more positively pointing towards what was to come. Here the author turns from art and love, middle-class parlour and attic studio, to concern himself with what might be described as the eternal verities, with, as the central figure, the enigmatic Rev. Nicholas Lucy, curate to the Rev. Herbert Messiter. One after another, the various characters in the play come under his influence; apparently he is so devout that the others see him almost as the living semblance of God himself, yet vaguely they are disturbed, until at the end Paul (who, despite her masculine name, is the heroine) bursts out in alarmed fury:

You must be the Devil himself, do you hear! The Devil himself! You look like him! You wanted Dorothy to ruin that poor young author, you wanted Cosmo to steal a dead man's work, and me to betray D.C. and D.C. to imprison me, and Messiter to profit by a blasphemous hypocrisy.

NICHOLAS (*quite unemotionally, almost inhumanly*). Yes; and you all thought you could do it. I offered you all what you thought you wanted most in the world. But you found you had made a mistake. You found to your surprise and humiliation that you all wanted to serve God more. You set your poor, little silly-clever selves up against God and thought you could get away with it. I merely shewed you that you couldn't. That is my work.

His paradoxical and mysterious explanation seems to make him almost into an angel, yet the final words of the play leave us wondering. Towards the close of the drama the spectators for the first time see Nicholas alone on the stage, and they observe that "*his face is utterly without expression*": then Louis Kisch enters, and immediately the "devil" gets to work. "Do you remember," he asks his companion,

also declaring yourself that your one desire in life was to create beauty?

LOUIS. I do.

NICHOLAS. I have been thinking about that; and frankly the idea *has* just flitted across the back of my mind that.... Now how exactly shall I put it?

But before he can put it any way the Curtain has hidden them both from sight.

These quotations from *The Devil* might perhaps be taken to suggest that this play is dully concerned with metaphysical considerations which lie far beyond the reach of effective theatrical expression: but any such thought would be completely wrong. This is indeed a play which stands prominent among the dramatic writings of its time, and it is one which eminently deserves to be revived with a cast worthy to stand beside its original performers.[1]

[1] In the Arts Theatre production of 1930 Norman McKinnel took the part of D. C. Magnus; Diana Wynyard was Paul, Sybil Thorndike was

Apart from its own inherent interest, Levy's "religious comedy" is a prime symbol of what was happening in the theatre towards the close of the twenties. It is allied, for example, with such a dream fantasy as Richard Pryce's *Thunder on the Left* (1928) which shows a boy swept suddenly onwards in time by twenty years so that, while physically he becomes a man, he retains his youthful vision of the world: looking around him, he does not like what he sees there and returns whence he has come. Almost at the same time, the Arts Theatre presented a play by Miles Mander with the revealing title of *It's a Pity about Humanity*. Already note has been taken of the way in which the various efforts made from 1920 onwards to give expression to the emotions aroused by the war reached their culmination in *Journey's End*. That drama was presented by London's Stage Society on December 9, 1928: the following evening, American playgoers attending the latest offering of the Theatre Guild saw a work, written by two English authors, Robert Nichols and Maurice Browne, described as a study of "the discovery of atomic control".[1] The opening act shows a brilliant, Shelley-like young scientist informing a Cabinet meeting that he has stumbled upon the secret of how to split and control the atom. Some of its members are prepared to scoff at the claims of a man whom they call an "infant gasbag", but the act closes with the solemn words of the almost equally brilliant Secretary of State for Foreign Affairs:

Kindly realize that every word that young man said is – I am convinced – literally true....Every word!...And I solemnly say

Dorothy Lister, Ernest Thesiger was Cosmo Penny, Melville Cooper was Kisch, Jean Cadell was Mrs Messiter, Lewis Casson was Messiter, and Dennis Neilson-Terry took the name-part of the Rev. Nicholas Lucy.

[1] Although it had been submitted to the Lord Chamberlain for licensing about the time of its American performance, London audiences did not have the chance of seeing it until it appeared at the Globe Theatre on April 27, 1932. In so far as its theme is concerned, George Calderon had anticipated its two authors by nearly two decades in his extraordinary *Revolt* (1912): see above p. 323. Observation of this fact, however, should not conceal from us a realisation that the whole tone of Calderon's play belongs to the century's earliest years, whereas the tone of *Wings over Europe* belongs definitely to the thirties.

to you all, it would be better for that poor young man and for the world had he never been born.

And the final curtain falls as "*The roar of aeroplanes fills all Europe*". Since it is always difficult, indeed almost impossible, for a playwright satisfactorily to deal with future events and characters, a reader of today, knowing what has actually happened since 1939, may find the scenes of *Wings over Europe* somewhat unconvincing, yet even so there must be full recognition of its significance. And there must also be full recognition of the corresponding significance of another drama written and produced almost at the same time. In October 1931 audiences at Drury Lane witnessed in Noël Coward's *Cavalcade*, not any imaginative flight into the future, but, instead, a broad conspectus of English life from the very start of the century onwards for thirty years – a kind of emblematic summation of an entire age which had now reached its conclusion. These plays, in substance and even more emphatically in their titles, speak of the likelihood of another world war and of technological discoveries likely to alter the entire pattern of human life: thus the years 1928–31 were not only saying the last words about 1914, they were also uttering the first premonitory words about 1939 – and after.

In this manner divers young authors, Noël Coward, Benn Levy and their companions, assumed a position during the late twenties which closely matched that attained by Jones, Pinero and those other dramatists who, during the final years of Victoria's reign, brought a new spirit into the theatre and who carried this new spirit into the Edwardian era. And, just as Pinero and Jones were soon joined by numerous as-yet-untried young playwrights immediately after 1900, many other dramatists were getting ready, after 1930, to join the authors of *The Devil*, *Wings over Europe* and *Cavalcade*. Of these new dramatists, two were of particular importance – one who just before the year 1930 was already tentatively preparing himself for his later theatrical career, and the other who, at precisely the same time, was establishing his popularity as a novelist before turning, a couple of years later, to win a popularity no less great as a dramatist. With the advent of James Bridie and J. B. Priestley in London's West End playhouses the twenties moved quite definitely into the thirties. Without doubt *Jonah and the Whale* (1932), *A Sleeping Clergyman* (1933), *Dangerous Corner* (1932), *Laburnum Grove* (1933), *Time and the Conways*, *I Have Been Here Before* and *I'm a Stranger Here* (all 1937), *Music at Night* (1938) and *Johnson over Jordan* (1939) were the fulfilment of what was being searched for and partly shaped by a few prescient playwrights at the close of the earlier period. It was at this time that a new impulse started in the English playhouses, even while the movement which had taken form at the very beginning of the century was drawing to its end.

Much had happened during those thirty years. Within the theatre, the director or producer had, with startling suddenness, established his authority; the actor–manager system had almost completely disappeared; repertory playhouses came into being for the first time, and there were at least a few men who dared to suggest that society ought to look upon the stage as it looked upon the public library and the civic museum; in the establishment of the Old Vic as Shakespeare's London home the concept of a National Theatre was prefigured, and from the Old Vic, too, came the inspiration which brought a new Sadler's Wells into existence in 1931; what this meant for the development of ballet and opera is known to everyone. In almost all respects the theatre world of our own time was being moulded during those first three decades of the present century.

If this is true of the theatre, what should be our final words concerning the drama? With the development of new styles after 1930 and particularly with the development of still newer styles after 1956, there came a rather general, and perfectly understandable, tendency to depreciate the plays which had attracted audiences during Edwardian and Georgian days, and not a few critical writers felt constrained to refer to these plays in an embarrassed and apologetic manner when they compared them with what had been achieved in other lands during the same course of years.

Latterly, however, there have been some signs of a change in attitude, and justification for such a change is increased rather than diminished the more intimately we examine the achievements of the English drama from 1900 to 1930. That there was a fresh spirit which, becoming evident just before the year 1930, eventually forced the older spirit to give way is certain. This ceding of place, however, came only when the purposes which had given strength to the earlier years had been fulfilled: there was nothing to suggest that a period of weakness and decline was having its inadequacies rectified by a period of advancing strength. No dramatic age which within its course saw the presentation of Shaw's greatest plays and which witnessed the early development of Coward's genius can be lightly dismissed: an amply sufficient number of English dramas written during those thirty years were being exported to the Continent and the United States to convince us that the balance of our theatrical trade figures certainly need not be contemplated with any apologetic gloom: and as we observe how often reflections from the writings of the first "modern" playwrights are to be discerned in our own "modern" drama, we need feel no hesitation in agreeing that hardly any corresponding period in theatrical history has more of interest to offer us than this one has.

HAND-LIST OF PLAYS

1900–1930

Introduction

A great deal of work – perhaps it might be more proper to say, hard labour – has been devoted to the preparation of the following hand-list of plays: yet at the very start it must be emphasised that it neither records, nor aims to record, the titles of all dramatic writings performed and published during its scope of thirty years. Although at first it was indeed intended that the catalogue should be made as comprehensive as possible, such an all-embracing aim had, with regret, to be abandoned, and this for two entirely different reasons – the peculiar nature of the material itself and the enforced necessity of deliberately rejecting large sections of the available evidence. Perhaps this can best be explained, and the frontiers of the hand-list can best be indicated, by describing the procedure which was adopted in gathering the relevant information.

1. To begin with, a complete card-index was prepared of all the titles recorded in the Day-Books of the Lord Chamberlain's Office. This task in itself would have proved impossible (or at least exceedingly difficult) to complete had it not been for the courtesy of the Comptroller at St James's Palace who allowed these Day-Books to be sent to me, volume by volume, so that I might, at my leisure, transcribe the entries. When the card-index was finally completed, the collection of play-titles proved to be alarmingly extensive, very much greater than what might reasonably have been expected, and considerably in excess of the corresponding entries which previously had been gathered for the dramas written within the half-century from 1850 to 1900.

2. Even at this stage, it began to appear likely that some attempt would have to be made to reduce this mass of material,

and likelihood gradually turned into certainty as further work was devoted to the cards already gathered. Obviously, the first task was to search for dates of production. The entries (on the whole, surprisingly accurate) in *The Era Almanack* (or, as it came to be entitled, *The Era Annual*) from 1900 to 1919 and those in *The Stage Year Book* from 1908 to 1928 were all recorded and checked; so, too, were the titles and dates included in *Who's Who in the Theatre* (1912 onwards), both those in the biographical accounts of the various playwrights and those in what came to be known as the "London Playbills" sections.[1] Where any discrepancies were observed, an effort was made to check the entries by reference to *The Era*, or to *The Stage*, or to both; and of course these periodicals had to be employed in the search for information concerning productions after *The Stage Year Book* temporarily ended its run with the volume issued in 1928 (and therefore chronicling no performances after December 1927). In addition to these basic sources of information, reference also was made to dozens of other specialised volumes – biographies and autobiographies of playwrights and actors, histories of individual theatres, and the like – from which occasionally additional information was obtained. When this date-checking process started, it had been confidently assumed that the titles of nearly all the plays would already have been entered on the cards which, in a sense, were an index to the Lord Chamberlain's records, but the completion of the search for production dates left the total mass of cards very materially increased – and it was by no means difficult to realise why that should have been so. This was the age of theatrical clubs and societies,

[1] In the first volume an alphabetical, and very brief, list of "New Plays and Principal Revivals at London Theatres", followed by a correspondingly brief list of "New Plays Produced at Provincial Theatres", was prepared by the active editor, John Parker, but later the information provided was both narrowed and expanded – narrowed by being restricted to London productions, expanded by the inclusion of cast-lists. Attention may be called to the fact that the dates presented in these volumes are, in general, accurately recorded, but that occasionally there are discrepancies between those cited in the biographical entries and those in the lists of performances.

and none of these, because their performances were "private", were required to submit their plays for licensing.[1] The consequence of this increase was that the possible desirability of reducing the number of entries in the hand-list had now been converted into an imperative necessity.

3. And, still further, it was soon found that the accumulation of play-titles was by no means brought to an end when the first two basic tasks had been fully carried out. There still remained the question of printed plays. We are apt to think of the period 1900–30 as one in which the publication of dramatic writings was considerably reduced from what it had been, let us say, during the latter half of the nineteenth century. Perhaps, numerically, it was: but there was a marked difference between the kinds of plays presented to the readers of these two periods. While it is true that divers nineteenth-century publishers brought out a fair number of poetic dramas not intended for performance, the great mass of play-texts put into print during those years came from a few "theatrical" firms, Dicks, Lacy and French, the bulk of whose publications were not unacted or unactable plays, but plays which had already appeared on the stage. In effect, therefore, their titles did not materially add to the titles which had been collected from a scrutiny of the scripts submitted for licensing between 1850 and 1900. On passing from the Victorian into the Edwardian and Georgian era, however, an entirely different picture presents itself. Samuel French still continued to issue acting texts of pieces which had been successful in the theatres; but scores of other publishers, often influenced by the force of the "minority" movement, accepted unacted plays for printing; this was the period when private presses multiplied profitably, many of them electing to issue limited editions of dramatic writings; and there was even the development of what previously had been an oddity – plays set up by local printers either as ventures of their own or else at the cost of

[1] So numerous were these performances that in November 1927 a question was asked about them in the House of Commons: the governmental reply was that no legal action would be taken against them.

their authors. The tracking-down of these out-of-the-way texts presented a peculiarly difficult problem. Commercial publishers, of course, are compelled by law to deposit exemplars of all their productions at six copyright libraries; but just as the play-performing clubs did not require to have the Lord Chamberlain's approval of the pieces put before their members, so the private presses and their authors could frequently dispense with the necessity of following the provisions of the copyright act. While, therefore, a great deal of time has been spent on the endeavour to list as many as possible of the dramas which, whether in commercially-published versions or in private, were made available for readers, there can be no certainty that all such publications have been included: indeed, it would be more proper to express this positively by stating that numbers of them must have eluded capture. Guides are few and limited in content. A few of the more "literary" authors have their own special bibliographies, and the more important private presses issued their own catalogues: but neither of these carry us far. The sole general list seems to be *The Player's Library* (1950, with a supplement issued in 1951) prepared by the British Drama League, but, apart from the fact that this is no more than a catalogue of the League's library holdings, its serviceability is very considerably restricted by the compiler's somewhat surprising decision to omit all dates. For this volume we must certainly be most grateful; yet we are compelled to admit that by no means does it provide an effective chart to what at times seems a labyrinthine and trackless territory. To illustrate the difficulties involved, it may here be noted that, even after the hand-list was nearing completion, examination of four not-too-large collections of early-twentieth-century plays resulted in an unexpected discovery – that each of them contained from half-a-dozen to a score of texts not hitherto recorded – and copies of some of these could not be traced in the British Museum. These searches appeared to indicate that, although of course many plays published between 1900 and 1930 are common enough, at least some are surprisingly scarce and difficult to locate.

Despite all of these problems, however, the search for published texts, even although the list had to be regarded as certainly incomplete, resulted in the accumulation of a further store of titles not included either in the Day-Books of the Lord Chamberlain's Office or in the records of play-performances. And thus further strong support was added to the conviction that the contents of the hand-list must be restricted.

4. With much regret, and after considerable hesitation, it was decided that this restriction could be effected only by regarding various categories of dramatic texts as expendable. First among such categories were the operas, but omission of these offered no really serious doubts since the words sung were mostly in languages other than English, and since it was easy to allow for exceptions to the general rule whereby the list could be permitted to include the very limited number of "English operas" and even a certain number of translations from foreign texts. More difficult was the decision that virtually all pantomimes must be left out, yet further thought strengthened the conviction that such procedure was entirely permissible. The history of the English pantomime has, of course, a value and an interest all its own, but hardly anyone can deny that during the twentieth century this form of entertainment sadly declined, and it seemed that nothing would be lost by omitting lengthy lists of *Cinderellas* and the like, varied only by references to different playhouses and dates. All of them, accordingly, are here excluded with the exception of one or two special items (such as W. S. Gilbert's *The Fairy's Dilemma*) significant because of their authors, or of their styles, or (as in this particular example) of both.

5. A third extensive omission is of a not dissimilar kind. One of the most characteristic developments in the theatre during this period was the growth and expansion of the revue. So dominant, indeed, did this revue become that at first it appeared unthinkable that almost all its teeming activities could be dismissed from the present hand-list. However, anyone who examines in detail the spreading popularity of this type of entertainment is very soon forced to admit that, save for a strictly limited number of exceptions, the mass of

pieces produced under the general descriptive title of "revue" were wholly unworthy of separate citation. Most of these so-called revues were, in fact, little more than "girl-shows" occasionally enlivened with a few jokes and the patter of one or two comedians: still further, scores of these performances, particularly those presented in the provinces, prove on examination to have been nothing more than already-existing musical comedies of the cheaper sort which had been hurriedly, and in general incompetently, broken up into the "revue" form and presented to the public as original works. Beyond even this must we go. Scores of these shows were performed with such kaleidoscopic changes in their titles as to render their cataloguing almost impossible. A single example will serve to illustrate this. A revue entitled *Frills and Flashes* was concocted out of an unidentifiable minor musical comedy; within a month or two, its name was changed to *Bubbly Boy*; then came a transformation into *Here Comes the Girl*; and finally, after another brief period, it turned into *Fizz and Frenzy* – and as such, appropriately and no doubt fortunately, it fell flat and vanished. Since pieces similarly manufactured and entitled were so numerous, no one, it would seem, could object to the decision which has here been made to abandon any general attempt to list their titles and performances. The only exceptions permitted to break the general rule are some of the major London revues for which single authors, such as Noël Coward and Ronald Jeans, were wholly responsible. The decision to disregard most of this material, however, did not, unhappily, provide a complete solution for what may be called the revue problem. If many of the lesser provincial and touring revues were largely "girl-shows", the more important and elaborate productions in the metropolis included many dramatic sketches each of which, although hardly worthy of being classed as a "one-act play", still presented some kind of embryonic plot, characters (even if only of the "He" and "She" variety), and dialogue. When a new revue was about to be presented in a West End theatre or major music-hall, the entire script was, naturally, submitted as a single entity to the Lord Chamberlain's Office, and the official licence, when granted, covered the whole production without any separate listing of the component sketches and skits. Not infrequently, however, as some of these revues ran their courses, alterations were made in at least a few of the items; the scripts of the inserted sketches had then to be submitted for licensing, and consequently their titles were separately recorded in the Day-Books. Careful scrutiny of the cards which had been compiled from this source showed that certainly hundreds of entries were of this sort, and it seemed most probable that, if the almost impossible task of checking all the scripts individually were to be essayed, the hundreds would be found converted into thousands. Quite clearly, any thought of including them in the hand-list had to be dismissed as foolish, useless and inconsistent. Nevertheless, even here provision had to be made for occasional exceptions – fortunately involving no more than about a dozen or a score in all, consisting of those rare contributions to the world of revue by a few prominent authors, such as J. M. Barrie. In thus recording what has been summarily omitted, however, one positive statement may be made – that an effort has been made to provide references to all the known printed collections of revue material.

6. The problem of the revue led to consideration of another problem, not wholly unrelated, which proved even more difficult of solution – that of the one-acts. From the beginning of the century more and more sketches of at least a semi-dramatic sort had tended to intrude into variety programmes, and when H. A. Jones deliberately composed his playlet *The Knife* for music-hall performance, he opened the eyes of his fellow-dramatists to the handsome profits offered to them within this sphere. Previously, the one-acts had freely flourished in the theatres, particularly in the form of curtain-raisers, but now, with their entry into the music-halls, their numbers multiplied almost beyond all belief. It hardly needs to be said that in any hand-list of plays written during those thirty years, *The Knife* could not properly have been omitted from a register of Jones' writings, nor could the

record of Barrie's plays have been considered complete if it left out *The Truth about the Russian Dancers*, planned for performance at the Coliseum in 1920. Concerning hundreds of such pieces there can be no doubts whatsoever: some of them might have been written for minority performance, some might have been intended to serve as curtain-raisers, some might have been composed with variety performance in mind – but they all had to be included. On the other hand, when we proceed to cast our gaze over the entire field, we must decide that the vast majority of the music-hall's sketches merit no individual attention. The nature of many is sufficiently indicated by their titles – *Papering the Parlour*, *Mending a Puncture*, *Repairing the Leak*, *Buying a Bulldog*, and so on – clearly nothing more than vehicles for popular comedians, with a minimum of dialogue so designed as to allow the free introduction of impromptu gags; others were of the "scena" type, depending chiefly upon dancing or acrobatics, even if they did bring in a few lines of dialogue; still others were merely crude musical episodes. It is obvious that, if all their titles and dates were to have been recorded, page after page would have had to be given over to authors now completely forgotten and even in their own days quite insignificant, each of whom was responsible for concocting dozens, sometimes scores, of these wholly trivial and unimportant scripts. Surely everyone must agree that the listing of all such pieces would render any hand-list unduly cumbersome, and – of still greater significance – the accumulated material would have proved of absolutely no use to anyone. Yet a difficult question remains. It is easy enough to decide that all pantomimes should be omitted, but it is not possible to make any such sweeping declaration here. Choice is essential: and the question, naturally, is to determine the principle which should determine which sketches were sheep and which were goats. After much thought had been given to this problem, the only valid solution appeared to be the adoption of a purely empirical procedure. In other words, this means that the compiler, when working within this area, has claimed permission to exercise his own judgment in so far as inclusion or exclusion is concerned. It is impossible to describe or outline the principles governing this procedure, but at least it may be said that, in general, the writings of authors who confined their activities exclusively to the preparation of music-hall sketches have been ignored, that sketches of this kind composed by dramatists whose activities were mainly associated with the theatres have been duly listed, and that particular care has been taken to list odd play-lets (Jones' *The Knife*, for example) which made sporadic appearances among the longer plays of various authors.

7. Even after it was decided to set aside so many categories of dramatic writings, however, one exceedingly difficult decision, perhaps the most serious of all, had to be made. The plays so far selected for inclusion were arranged under the names of their authors, but after this collection of titles had been completed and checked it was found that there still remained some five or six thousand cards recording titles of pieces the authorship of which was unknown. Once more it seemed at first that unquestionably these should be added to the list, but, once more again, further consideration suggested that there could hardly be any profit in burdening the hand-list with such material. If the present work had been specific-ally and exclusively a "bibliography" of English drama from 1900 to 1930, the final decision would, no doubt, have had to be completely different; but in fact this hand-list is, in effect, a statistical supplement to an historical–critical survey, and in the main text there has been no occasion to refer, even in passing, to a single one of these plays of unidentified author-ship, while most of their titles suggested that they were all, or nearly all, of no significance.

8. Naturally, in addition to the leaving-out of these larger groups of dramatic writings, every attempt has been made to present the strictly relevant information in as compact and condensed a form as possible. It should be noted that this has involved the omission of much informa-tion concerning the ultimate source-material upon which various plays and musical comedies were based. This requires some explanation. When there is the entry of a play known to

have been either a direct translation or a fairly close adaptation of a foreign original, reference is, of course, made to its source. On the other hand, such references have been left out for the scores of dramas which, particularly during the first decade of the century, were vaguely described as "based on" or "suggested by" popular pieces presented in Paris or Berlin – such procedure being adopted because the English plays generally deviated considerably from their sources and also because, while many playwrights did not hesitate to acknowledge the suggestions which had come to them from abroad, many of their fellows remained either coyly evasive or else firmly tight-lipped on the subject. In so far as musical comedies are concerned, two observations must be made. Such musicals obviously fall into two groups – those created by English writers and composers, and those which were adaptations of Viennese and other foreign originals. The latter group would seem imperatively to demand the presentation of information concerning their sources,[1] but already it has been noted in the main text that rarely, if ever, were these foreign originals presented on the English stage in faithful adaptations. This being so, it appeared to be entirely proper to save space here by leaving out all references to the titles and authors of the foreign libretti and by referring only to the composers. The bills and programmes relating to the purely English musicals frequently put before the public a lengthy list of credits: as often as not, the "book" was credited to a pair of writers working in collaboration, one or two men might be named as responsible for the lyrics, one or two as composers of the music – and not infrequently there might even be a supplementary note indicating that "additional lyrics" and "additional music" had been contributed by others. In the entries here, all such diverse information has been reduced so as to concentrate entirely upon the names of those basically responsible for the "books" and the music.

9. In the attempt to restrict the length of the hand-list as much as possible, contractions have been freely employed,

[1] See above pp. 160–1.

and these require detailed explanation, the more particularly since the nature of the present subject-matter has demanded the employment of many abbreviations not used in the corresponding catalogues included in *A History of English Drama, 1660–1900*. The plays, as has been indicated above, are in general grouped chronologically under the names of their authors. A preliminary square bracket before an author entry, as in

[*AMES, GEORGE*

indicates that the playwright is American, and it hardly needs to be added that for such American writers record is made only of those dramas which received production in Britain. If an author's name is enclosed in single quotation marks, as in

'*SMITH, THOMAS*'

this indicates that the name in question is a pseudonym, and usually such entries include the proper name of the writer, in square brackets and with a preceding = sign, as in

'*SMITH, THOMAS*' [=*F. L. MANN*]

Normally, the plays are listed under whichever name was used most commonly by the author concerned (with, of course, such cross-references as prove necessary). For dramatists who had started their careers before the year 1900, indication is given of their earlier works as listed in *A History of English Drama, 1660–1900* by the placing of notes immediately under their names in the form of

[For earlier plays see *H. E. D.* v, 243]

10. While in general the writings of the individual authors are arranged chronologically, a single deviation from this practice must be mentioned. One of the peculiarities of play-publishing during this period is the issuing of plays in small collections: usually the contents of these volumes consist of one-act pieces, but sometimes three or four full-length dramas were put before the public in this way. In the preparation of the hand-list, it has been found that,

instead of listing the individual items separately, with necessarily repetitive citations of the titles given to the collections in which they had been printed, it was often more convenient to enter the title of the collection and then to enumerate its contents in a following note, even although, in so doing, the strict chronological order might be disturbed. No excuse is offered here for what may seem to be discrepancies in procedure: whichever practice appeared the more appropriate for any particular entry has been adopted.

11. In order to save space, as much information as possible concerning the nature of each piece, its production, etc. follows the title, all this information being placed within round brackets. Since the contractions employed here are numerous, explanations concerning their significance and objectives must be presented in separate sections. First comes an indication, where this is deemed desirable, of the nature of the piece. The majority of dramatic writings during the period are designated simply as "plays" and "dramas", and in such instances there is no entry in this section: but, if an author has been more specific, then the appropriate information is briefly given, the descriptions appearing in italics within single quotation marks. Quite frequently, the authors delighted in the use of what may be called "clever" descriptions, and these necessarily have to be quoted in fairly full form, as in

'*c. about nothing*'

or

'*mystery pl. of today*'.

Usually, however, it has been found possible to indicate most of these authorial indications by the use of simple contractions, a list of which follows:

'*bsq.*'	(burlesque)
'*c.*'	(comedy, or, in combinations, comic)
'*ca.*'	(comedietta)
'*c.o.*'	(comic opera)
'*d.*'	(drama, or, in combinations, dramatic, as in '*d. poem*')

'*d.d.*'	(domestic drama)
'*ext.*'	(extravaganza)
'*f.*'	(farce, or, in combinations, farcical, as in '*f.c.*' (farcical comedy) or '*f.pl.*' (farcical play)
'*fant.*'	(fantasy, or, in combinations, fantastic)
'*f.m.d.*'	(farcical musical drama)
'*m.c.*'	(musical comedy)
'*m.d.*'	(musical drama)
'*md.*'	(melodrama, or, in combinations, melodramatic)
'*m.pl.*'	(musical play)
'*o.*'	(opera)
'*oa.*'	(operetta)
'*past.*'	(pastoral)
'*pl.*'	(play)
'*r.*'	(romance, or, in combinations, romantic)
'*sk.*'	(sketch)
'*spect.*'	(spectacle, or, in combinations, spectacular)
'*t.*'	(tragedy, or, in combinations, tragical)
'*t.c.*'	(tragicomedy)

Particular note should be taken of the fact that, in the entries of musical plays, citation of the composer's name follows the abbreviations '*m.c.*' or '*m.pl.*', with an 'm.' (not in italics) standing for 'music by', as in

'*m.c.*', m. F. Smith.

A cross – × – preceding the title of a play indicates that this is a one-act piece.

12. Following the indications concerning the type of play comes condensed information relating to performances, and here again various explanations are obligatory. In preparing the entries, it was decided that in general no references would be made to the manuscript or typewritten texts originally in the custody of the Lord Chamberlain and now deposited in the British Museum, since usually the dates of licensing and the production dates more or less were in agreement. For a certain number of scripts, however, the only available indications of possible or at least of intended performance derive from the fact that the plays had been submitted for official approval: in the entries of these dramas the

symbol "LC", followed by the appropriate dates, indicates that licences had been granted, although of course it must be realised that there is no authority for assuming that actual productions followed. Sometimes, too, but far less frequently, an "LC" reference, with citation of theatre and date, is placed before a known date of performance when there is a marked discrepancy between the two.[1] Normally, therefore, only the actual performance date or dates are indicated in the hand-list. A typical entry takes the form of

Scala, 30/11/24,

obviously designating the theatre (the Scala) at which the play was produced, together with the date (November 30, 1924). If a production took place, not in an evening performance, but during a forenoon or afternoon, a following *m.* (as in 30/11/24, *m.*) signifies that the piece appeared at a matinée. Usually, only one performance date is cited, but when a play (as was not uncommon) was given first in a provincial playhouse, then was brought to a suburban theatre and finally was transferred to the West End, information is provided concerning all three productions. When no city is mentioned, it is to be assumed that the theatre referred to was in London; and when the name of a city appears without reference to a particular playhouse, it is to be understood that the performance was at the local Theatre Royal. The names of most cities and localities are given in full, with five exceptions:

B'ham	Birmingham
Edin.	Edinburgh
L'pool	Liverpool
N.Y.	New York
Rich.	Richmond

Among districts in London, Holborn is abbreviated to Holb., and Hammersmith to Hamm. Since there are so many

[1] This means, of course, that in such instances a particular theatre, contemplating the production of a play, had submitted the text for licensing but, for one reason or another, abandoned its original intention, while at a later date the piece was performed at another playhouse.

references to theatres (and other places of performance), however, abbreviations have here been utilised as much as possible, as in the following list:

Adel.	Adelphi Theatre
Alb.	Albert Saloon, Hoxton
Alb. H.	Albert Hall
Aldw.	Aldwych Theatre
Alex.	Alexandra Theatre, Stoke Newington
Alh.	Alhambra (music hall)
A.L.S. Trav. Th.	Arts League of Service Travelling Theatre
Ambass.	Ambassadors' Theatre
Amphi.	Amphitheatre
Apo.	Apollo Theatre
Aquar.	Aquarium
Ass. R.	Assembly Rooms
Ath.	Athenaeum
Aven.	Avenue Theatre
Bed.	Bedford Theatre (or music-hall)
Bij.	Bijou Theatre, Bayswater (*note:* the name Bijou was used also for other places of performance: in such instances the locality is indicated)
Blfrs	Blackfriars
Bor.	Borough (music-hall)
Brit.	Britannia (music-hall)
Broad.	Broadway Theatre, New Cross
Cant.	Canterbury (music-hall: Westminster Bridge Road, Lambeth)
Camb.	Royal Cambridge (music-hall, Shoreditch)
Cent.	Century Theatre
C.G.	Royal Opera House, Covent Garden
Col.	London Coliseum (music-hall)
Coll.	Collins' Music-hall
Coloss.	Colosseum (music-hall)
Com.	Comedy Theatre
Con.	Connaught Theatre
Cor.	Coronet Theatre

C.P.	Crystal Palace
Crippl. Inst.	Cripplegate Institute
Crit.	Criterion Theatre
D.L.	Theatre Royal, Drury Lane
D.P.	Devonshire Park Theatre
D.Y.	Duke of York's Theatre
E.C.	Elephant and Castle Theatre
Emb.	Embassy Theatre
Emp.	Empire Theatre (and music-hall, Leicester Square)
Empress	Empress Theatre of Varieties (Brixton)
Exch.	(in combinations indicates Exchange, as in Corn Exchange)
Fest.	Festival
Gai.	Gaiety Theatre
Gar.	Garrick Theatre
Glo.	Globe Theatre
Gr.	Grand Theatre
Gt. Qn. St.	Great Queen Street Theatre
H.	(in combinations signifies Hall)
H.	Haymarket Theatre
Hippo.	Hippodrome Theatre
H.M.	Her, or His, Majesty's Theatre
Hydro.	Hydropathic
Imp.	Imperial Theatre
Inst.	(in combinations signifies Institute)
K. G's H.	King George's Hall
Kings.	Kingsway Theatre
K's	King's Theatre
K's H.	King's Hall
Ladbr. H.	Ladbroke Hall
Ldn O.H.	London Opera House
Ldn Pav.	London Pavilion
Londesb.	Londesborough Theatre
Lyc.	Lyceum Theatre
Lyc. Club	Lyceum Club
Lyr.	Lyric Theatre
Marl.	Marlborough Theatre
Mem.	Memorial Theatre (Stratford-upon-Avon)

Mem. H.	Memorial Hall
Metro.	Metropole (music-hall)
M.h.	music-hall
M'sex	Middlesex (music-hall)
New X	New Cross
O.H.	Opera House
Oxf.	Oxford (theatre and music-hall, Marylebone)
Pal.	Palace Theatre
Pallad.	Palladium
Par.	Paragon (music-hall)
Pav.	Pavilion
P'cess	Princess's Theatre
P'cess of W.	Princess of Wales's Theatre
P.H.	Public Hall
Playh.	Playhouse
Pleasure Gdns	Pleasure Gardens
P's	Prince's Theatre
P.W.	Prince of Wales's Theatre
Q	Q Theatre
Qns	Queen's Theatre
Qns Gate H.	Queen's Gate Hall
R.	(in combinations) Room, or Rooms
R.A.	Royal Artillery Theatre
R.A.D.A.	Royal Academy of Dramatic Art
R.A.M.	Royal Academy of Music
Reg.	Regent Theatre
Rehearsal	Rehearsal Theatre
Rep.	Repertory
Rot.	Rotunda
Roy.	Royalty Theatre
St G's H.	St George's Hall
St J.	St James's Theatre
St M.	St Martin's Theatre
Sav.	Savoy Theatre
Shaft.	Shaftesbury Theatre
Shak.	Shakespeare Theatre
S. Ldn Pal.	South London Palace of Varieties
Stand.	Standard Theatre
Steiner H.	Rudolph Steiner Hall
Str.	Strand Theatre

Sur.	Surrey (theatre and music-hall)
S.W.	Sadler's Wells Theatre
T.H.	Town Hall
Tiv.	Tivoli (music-hall)
Theatrical Gdn Party	Theatrical Garden Party
Var.	Varieties, or Theatre of Varieties
Vaud.	Vaudeville Theatre
Vic. H.	Victoria Hall
Vic. Pal.	Victoria Palace (music-hall)
W.G.	Winter Garden Theatre
W.L.	West London Theatre
W. Pier	West Pier
Wynd.	Wyndham's Theatre

Reference has already been made to the use of an italicised *m.* as indicating a matinée performance. The majority of these matinée shows were sponsored by one or another of the numerous play-producing societies, and, when these are known, their names appear immediately after the production dates: many of the names are given in full, but a few abbreviations are employed, as follows:

Adel. Pl. Soc.	Adelphi Play Society
Century Pl. Soc.	Century Play Society
English Pl. Soc.	English Play Society
Internat. Th.	International Theatre (Society)
Ldn Welsh St. Soc.	London Welsh Stage Society
Morality Pl. Soc.	Morality Play Society
New Pl. Club	New Play Club
Pl. Actors	Play Actors
Rep. Players	Repertory Players
Scott. Nat. Players	Scottish National Players
Scott. Nat. Th. Soc.	Scottish National Theatre Society
St. Soc.	Stage Society
Sunday Pl. Soc.	Sunday Play Society

The employment of the contraction *amat.* (standing for "amateur performance") means that, although it is known that a particular performance was not professional, information is lacking concerning the name of the association concerned. One other abbreviation which sometimes follows the date is *cpy.* (standing for "copyright performance").

During the early years of the century the copyright law then operative provided protection to a dramatic author only if his play had been presented publicly on the stage. On many occasions dramatists who had not made arrangements for the production of their works by one or another of the theatrical managements made plans for what were called "copyright" or "stage right" performances with the aid of their friends, professional or amateur: frequently, of course, these were little more than readings.

For various dramas included in the hand-list some further information is included within the round brackets. When a play was a collaborative effort, it has been listed under the name of the author placed first in the playbills, the name of his associate being put after the date with a preceding + sign. Thus, if a piece called, let us say, *The Lady's Adventure*, was the joint effort of a T. Smith and a W. Jones, it appears in the hand-list under the name of the former as

The Lady's Adventure (Sav., 22/3/11: + *W. JONES*).

In the entry relating to the collaborator, W. Jones, a cross-reference is given to T. Smith.

13. After the facts thus presented in attenuated form within round brackets, information is provided concerning the printing of such plays as were happy enough to attract the attention of publishers. In order to make a clear distinction between dates of production and dates of printing, the latter are here given in italic type. The contraction (*priv.*) after a publication indicates either that the printing was a "private" one, paid for by the author, or that the issue was strictly limited. In general, these dates of printing stand alone, without any citation of publishers' names: but to this general rule there are two exceptions. First, since the chief theatrical publisher of the period was Samuel French, references to plays printed by this firm take the form of *Fr. 1922*. Secondly, it is worthy of notice that during the early years of the twentieth century a fair number of what may be styled "special" plays were presented to the public in printed form not under the auspices of publishers but under those of

societies founded for the propagation of particular aims: prominent examples of these are the Village Drama Society, the Labour Publishing Co., and SPCK (the Society for the Propagation of Christian Knowledge). Since the play texts thus issued belong to special groups, in these instances the relevant information is added after the publication date.

14. The chronological range of the hand-list (strictly considered) begins with January 1900 and ends with December 1929: allowing for the limitations in subject-matter which have been described above, an attempt has been made to render the catalogue as comprehensive as possible. Both at the beginning and the end of this chronological range, however, there are some special extensions – first, for plays which began their careers before 1900 either in printed form or in out-of-the-way performances but which were not formally presented on the stage until after the start of the new century, and, secondly, for other plays which, although not publicly produced until 1930 or later, had certainly been written before the close of the twenties.

One important final observation must be made. The compiler of a hand-list akin to that which follows cannot but look back upon his work with a wry smile, realising that, even although he has made every endeavour to present the information as accurately as possible, the recording of so many titles and dates cannot be accomplished without at least some errors. In so far as the present list is concerned, the only measure of comfort which may temper such a reflection is that examination of several volumes devoted exclusively to the performances at single theatres (Dublin's Abbey, for example) and even to the writings of individual authors has revealed inconsistencies which, on closer scrutiny, have sometimes proved to be errors.

A., C. S.
The Black Christ. *1901* (Oxford)

A., D. F
Four Fragments. *1924* (Cambridge)
[This includes four short pieces: 1. *Rule Britannia*; 2. *King John Completed*; 3. *Boar at Bay*; and 4. *Snake in the Grass*]

'*A & O*' [or '*ALPHA & OMEGA*' = *OLIVER ST JOHN GOGARTY*]
Blight (Abbey, Dublin, 11/12/17) *1917*

ABBAS, HARRY [see *C. B. WINSTEY*]

ABBOTT, ADA GRACE [*Mrs ERNEST P. ABBOTT*]
The House of Shame (Cardiff, 24/6/07; W.L., 1/11/07, as *The End of the Story*; Broadway, New X, 27/7/08, as *The Man of Her Choice*)
The Sins of the Rich (Darwen, 13/3/11; Stratford, 23/10/11)
The Love Child (Leicester, 31/5/15; Brixton, 19/6/15; title changed later to *Neither Wife nor Maid*)
The Passions (Hippo., Cannock, 21/3/19)
The Wonderful Year ('*m.c.*', m. J. Johnstone: Metro., Glasgow, 7/5/20)
Hearts and Homes (Leicester, 18/8/21; Stratford, 3/3/22, as *Woman and Her Master*)
A Wife in Name Only (LC, Metro., Glasgow, 13/12/21; Stratford, 13/3/22)
The Child Thou Gavest Me (LC, Sunderland, 19/5/23: Stratford, 22/10/23)

ABBOTT, GEORGE [see *P. DUNNING*]

ABBOTT, ALLAN F. [see *CHARLES GARVICE*]

ABBOTT, CHARLES HARRIE
[For earlier plays see *H. E. D.* v, 233]
Where's Bertram? (County, Kingston, 1/12/02) *1902* (*priv.*)
The Just Impediment (Kennington, 27/5/18)

[*ABBOTT, GEORGE* [see also *J. GLEASON* and *P. DUNNING*]
The Coquette ('*t.*': Brighton, 27/5/29; Apo., 3/6/29: + *ANN PRESTON BRIDGERS*) *1928; Fr. 1929*

ABBOTT, H. R.
× The Fortune-Tellers (Cheltenham, 12/9/12; Crit., 17/9/12) *1912*

ABBOTT, W. H.
× Clarissima's Lovers (Goldsmiths' Inst., New X, 1/2/02)
× Whispering Tongues (Pav., 22/4/14)
Felicia (Court, 24/9/14)

ABDULLAH, ACHMED
The Prince's Harem ('*c.*': Q, 17/5/26: called originally *There is No Hurry*: + *R. DAVIS*)

ABELL, FRANCIS M. G.

×Jones in Earnest (Court, 24/10/13)

ABERCROMBIE, LASCELLES

Interludes and Poems. *1908*

[This includes four short pieces: 1. *The New God*; 2. *Blind*; 3. *The Fool's Adventure*; and 4. *An Escape*]

Emblems of Love ('*poetical dialogues*') *1912*

Deborah. *1913*

Four Short Plays. *1922*

[This contains: 1. *The Adder* (Playh., L'pool, 3/3/13); 2. *The Staircase* (Playh., L'pool, 4/3/20); 3. *The Deserter*; and 4. *The End of the World* (Rep., B'ham, 12/9/14). The last of these had earlier appeared in *New Numbers*, vol. ii]

Phoenix ('*t.c.*': St M., 20/1/24) *1923*

The Sale of St Thomas ('*dramatic poem*') *1930*

ACHARYA, SRI ANANDA

Vikramorvasi (adapted from the play by Kalidasa) *1914*

ACHURCH, JANET

[For an earlier play see *H. E. D.* v, 235, 777]

The Coming of Peace (translated from *Das Friedensfest* (1890) by G. Hauptmann: +*C. E. WHEELER*) *1900*

The Lost Paradise (Alex., 1/5/02, *cpy.*; Qns., Manchester, 26/5/02: translated from *Das verlorene Paradies* (1898) by Ludwig Fulda)

Mrs Daintree's Daughter (Manchester, 15/5/03)

ACKERLEY, JOE RANDOLPH

The Prisoners of War (Court, 5/7/25, 300 Club; Playh., 31/8/25) *1925*

ACKERMAN, WILLIAM

×The Outpost (Lyr., 19/1/04)

ACKLAND, RODNEY

Improper People (Arts, 9/10/29) *1930*

Marion-Ella (Players, 30/6/30)

Dance with No Music (Arts, 23/7/30)

ADAIR, FRANK [='*RIADA*']

ADAIR-FITZGERALD, SHAFTO JUSTIN

[For earlier plays see *H. E. D.* v, 369]

Cinq Mars; or, The Conspiracy ('*o.*', m. C. F. Gounod: Gr., Leeds, 27/10/00; Cor., 17/11/01: +*W. VAN NOORDEN*)

×That Sister of Mine (St G's H., 10/12/00: +*W. VAN NOORDEN*)

×Her Answer (Cor., 22/7/07)

One-Act Plays. *1914* (three volumes)

[Each volume contains three plays: 1. *A Jealous Mistake*; 2. *The Forgotten Favourite*; 3. *The Last Wish*; 4. *The Time of Roses*; 5. *Dick and the Marchioness*; 6. *One Goes Out*; 7. *A Friend of the Family*; 8. *The Miser's Revenge*; and 9. *Two Hearts*]

ADAM, AGNES [=*A. WORKMAN*]

ADAM, ANGUS
×The Man fra' Aberdeen ('*c.*': T.H., Sheringham, 4/2/24)

ADAMS, ALFRED DAVIES [see *A. DAVIES-ADAMS*]

ADAMS, ARTHUR HENRY [='*JAMES JAMES*']
×Pierrot in Australia ('*fant.*': Little, 26/1/12)
The Division Bell (P.W., B'ham, 4/12/15: title altered later to *Miss Pretty and the Premier*)

ADAMS, CATHERINE
[For an earlier play see *H. E. D.* v, 235]
Piccallilli ('*Anglo-Japanese m. pl.*'; Drill H., Basingstoke, 10/5/06, *amat.*)

ADAMS, EVE
×A Daughter of Italy (Little, 10/7/13, Stage Players)

ADAMS, HARVEY
Don't Talk in Your Sleep (K's H., 6/2/21, Revival Players)

ADAMSON, MARGUERITE
An April Fool (Rehearsal, 26/6/08, *amat.*)

ADDERLEY, Hon. & Rev. JAMES GRANVILLE
[For an earlier play see *H. E. D.* v, 235]
×Struck (Norton H., Saltley Carlton, 16/11/07)
×Epiphany (Court, 9/2/12, Morality Pl. Soc.)

ADDISON, JOHN
Justice at Last (R.A., Woolwich, 11/4/03)

ADDISON, Miss L. [see *Mrs F. G. KIMBERLEY*]

[*ADE, GEORGE*
The Sho Gun ('*c.o.*': Bij., 24/3/04)
The College Widow ('*c.*': Adel., 20/4/08) *Fr. 1924*
×Mrs Peckham's Carouse (Pav., 17/3/13)

ADELER, EDWIN [see *KENNEDY ALLEN*]

ADKINS, FRANCIS J.
×The Heritage (Temperance H., Sheffield, 7/10/12)
×Education ('*medley*') *1924*

ADRIPOLE, WALTER
Multonomah; or, The White Spirit (Qns., Netherfield, Nottingham, 10/10/12, '*preliminary pfce*': +*J. H. BELL, Jr*)

ADSHEAD, HILDA C.
Ten Shillings (Arts Centre, 8/7/13, Actresses Franchise League)

AGAR, HERBERT [see *ELEANOR CHILTON*]

AGATE, EDWARD
Tales of Hoffman. *1910*
[This English version of *Les Contes d'Hoffman* (1851) by P. J. Barbier and M. Carré, revised in collaboration with Olive Moore and with Offenbach's music, was presented as 'a fantastic opera-ballet' at the Strand on March 2, 1942]
Le Coq d'or. *1911*

[An English version of the opera presented in Russian at D.L. on June 15, 1914 and at the same theatre, in English, on July 19, 1918]

AGATE, JAMES EVERSHED
Blessed Are the Rich ('*c.*': Vaud., 27/8/25: dramatised from his own novel (1914): +*C. E. OPENSHAW*) *1924*

AGNEW, EWAN
The Shingling of Jupiter ('*fant. pl. for serious people*': Q, 2/11/25) *1924*

AGNEW, GEORGETTE
One Day a Gipsy; or The Little Girl who Wanted to See Peter Pan ('*children's pl.*') *1907*
× Two Shadows ('*seventeenth-century idyll*': R.A.M., 2/12/10, *amat.*)

AÏDÉ, HAMILTON
[For earlier plays see *H. E. D.* v, 236, 777]
The Assignation ('*satire*': New, 7/12/05)

AIKINS, CHARLES CARROLL COLBY
The God of Gods (Rep., B'ham 8/11/19) *1919* (British Columbia)

AINES, HUGO
× Blind (Arts Centre, 5/6/14)

AINLEY, ELAINE [see *A. BLACKWOOD*]

AINSLEY, D. [see *A. M. SPENCER*]

AINSWORTH, H. K.
× Dawn. LC, K.G's H., 15/4/18

AITKEN, I.
× Red Carnations (Bij., 21/3/01)

ALAN, LESLIE
× The Sacrifice (Ass. R., Balham, 2/12/01: +*G. STANLEY*)

ALAN-HINESON, C.
Two Men and a Woman (P.W., Mexborough, 4/9/01, *cpy.*; Garston, 16/12/01)

ALBANESI, Mme EFFIE MARIA
Sister Anne (Cor., 5/9/10: dramatised from her own novel, 1908)
Susannah – And Some Others ('*c. of sentiment*': Roy., 22/1/08: dramatised from her own novel, *Susannah and One Elder*, 1903)

ALDEN, MARY E.
× Quits (Emp., Croydon, 19/10/11)
× Ten Days in Blighty (Gr., Brighton, 18/2/20)
× The Scarlet Hour (Gr., Brighton, 18/2/20)

ALDIN, CECIL
The Happy Family ('*children's pl.*': P.W., 18/12/16: +*ADRIAN ROSS*)

ALDIN, CHARLES A.
[For earlier plays see *H. E. D.* v, 238]
A King among Men (P.W., Salford, 11/1/04)

ALDINGTON, MAY
×Love Tokens (Qns, 29/10/20)

ALDINGTON, RICHARD
The Good-humoured Ladies (translated from *Le Donne di buon umore*, 1758, by C. Goldoni) *1922*
French Comedies of the Eighteenth Century. *1923*
[This contains translations of four plays: 1. *The Residuary Legatee* (from Regnard); 2. *Turcaret* (from Lesage); 3. *The Game of Love and Chance* (from Marivaux); and 4. *The Conceited Count* (from Destouches)]
Alcestis (translated from the play by Euripides) *1930*

ALDRICH, T. B.
×Mercedes (Roy., 17/4/02)

ALDWORTH, F.
×Jane in Search of a Husband. LC, Peterhouse Gardens, Cambridge, 7/6/22: +*H. JENNINGS* and *S. TURNER*

ALEXANDER, F. MATTHIAS
×A Question of Time (Cor., 26/10/08: +*E. GLOVER*)

ALEXANDER, HENRY
×The Desperate Lover ('*c.*': Gai., Dublin, 12/5/05)

ALEXANDER, ISABEL
×The White Lady (Scala, 10/7/08)

ALEXANDER, W. M.
Love's Stratagem (Ass. R., Eccles, 12/2/04)

ALFORD, FALLS
Virata ('*m.pl.*': Castle, Richmond, 26/11/07, *amat.*: +*E. HARDY*)

ALFORD, JOHN
Paul I (Court, 4/10/27: +*J. C. DALE*)

ALINGTON, ADRIAN [see also *L. WILSON*]
×No. 13 Paradise Row. LC, Ambass., 4/4/21.
×Two Women. LC, K. G's H., 26/3/24

ALINGTON, CYRIL ARGENTINE, Dean of Durham
King Harrison and Others. *1923*
[Besides the title play, this includes *The Royal Arms*]

ALLAN, HELEN BEATRICE
×The Quest ('*mystery*') *1914* (SPCK)
The Place of Meeting ('*mystery pl. of today*') *1920* (SPCK)

ALLEN, A. WHATOFF
One Little Kiss ('*f.*': Leeds, 8/7/29; Adel., 15/7/29: +*E. DYER*)

ALLEN, ALICE MAUDE
Catherine of Siena. *1921* (Cambridge)

ALLEN, Sir CAERLETON KEMP
×The Woman in Red (Gai., Manchester, 10/8/14)
Brenda (Gai., Manchester, 17/8/14)

ALLEN, CHARLES R.
×The Four Foundlings ('*fant.*': Cent., 18/3/25, Foundlings) *1929* (Oxford)
×Lunch with a Lunatic (Cent., 18/3/25, Foundlings)
×Will and the Witch ('*fant.*': Etlinger School, 20/7/26, Panton Players)
×When Mr Punch was Young ('*fant.*': Etlinger School, 20/7/26, Panton Players) *1929* (Oxford)
[Printed with three other one-act plays: 1. *The Four Foundlings*; 2. *Pierette Cheats the Publisher*; and 3. *The Singing Heart*]

ALLEN, Miss DOT [='*CONSTANCE RAY*']

ALLEN, INGLIS [see also *E. BLORE*]
If We Had Only Known (Little, 13/12/12)
×The Suffragette's Redemption. *Fr. 1913*
×Early Hours (Paisley, 11/10/15)
×The Furry 'Uns. LC, Vaud., 11/3/21
×The Colonel's Manoeuvre (Vic. Pal., 5/12/27: also called *The Colonel Engages His Daughter*) *1935* (in F. S. Box, *Monologues and Duologues of Today*)

ALLEN, KENNEDY
×The Garden of Glitter ('*ext.*': Qns, Poplar, 6/5/07)
×Old Virginia ('*m.ca.*': Olympian Gardens, Rockferry, 8/6/08: +*EDWIN ADELER*)
Anybody's Wife (Hippo., Bolton, 22/11/12, '*preliminary pfce*'; Camb., Spennymoor, 10/11/13; E.C., 6/7/14; Gr., Croydon, 27/5/18, as *Jack on Leave*: +*E. ELWES*)

'*ALLEN, MAX*' [=*H. C. LOMAX*]

ALLEN, OLIVE
[Three short pieces are included in *Home Plays*, edited by C. Bullivant, 1911 – 1. *Aunt Grundy*; 2. *The Little Female Academy*; and 3. *Peter Grief*]

ALLEN, PERCY
The Seekers ('*c.*') *1925*
Tradition and the Torch ('*c.*') *1925*
×Comers Down the Wind. *1925*
×The Life that's Free. *1925*

ALLEN, ROBERT AUSTEN
The Tenth Point ('*c.*': RADA, 11/6/22)

ALLERTON, MARK
[For an earlier play see *H. E. D.* v, 239]
The Girl from Corsica ('*m.pl.*'; m. T. Dickenson: Ath., Glasgow, 25/2/03, *amat.*; O.H., Norwich, 16/5/04)

ALLINGHAM, MARGERY LOUISE
Dido and Æneas LC, K. G's H., 24/4/22
×Water in a Sieve ('*fant.*') *Fr. 1925*

ALLISTER, CLAUD
The Brothers (Str., 28/10/28, Rep. Players)

ALLPORT, N.
×The Lie ('*f.*': Pav., 6/11/13)
The Robber. *Fr. 1930*

ALLWOOD, F. W.
×The Laundrymaids ('*c.o.*': Stand., 1/3/09: +*G. W. FOSTER*)

ALMA-TADEMA, Sir LAWRENCE
Four Plays. *1905* (*priv.*)
[This contains four one-act plays: 1. *The Unseen Helmsman* (Com., 17/6/01); 2. *Childe Vyet, or, The Brothers*; 3. *The Merciful Soul* ('*tragedietta*': Little, 8/11/10); and 4. *New Wrecks upon Old Shoals*]
The New Felicity ('*c.*': Roy., 25/6/05, St. Soc.)

'*ALPHA & OMEGA*' [see '*A & O*']

ALRICOTT, E. J.
Go Chase Me (Hippo., Peterborough, 15/6/16)

[*ALSBERG, HENRY GARFIELD*
The Dybbuk (Neighborhood, N.Y., 15/12/25; Civic, Leeds, 7/3/27; Roy., 4/4/27: from the play by 'S. Ansky' (=Solomon Rappaport): +*W. KATZKIN*) *1926* (New York); *1927*

AMARD, A.
The Triumph of Truth (LC, Vic. H., W. Stanley, 30/11/03; Gr., Walsall, 11/1/04; Dalston, 16/5/04)

AMBIENT, MARK [see also *Lady VIOLET GREVILLE*]
[For earlier plays see *H. E. D.* v, 240]
A Snug Little Kingdom ('*c.*': Roy., 31/1/03) *Fr. 1903*
The Arcadians ('*m. pl.*', m. Lionel Monckton and Howard Talbot: Shaft., 28/4/09: +*A. M. THOMPSON*) *1910*
The Light Blues ('*m.c.*', m. Howard Talbot and H. Finck: P.W., B'ham, 13/9/15; Shaft., 14/9/16: +*J. HULBERT*]
The Net (Scala, 17/10/19)
Oh! Susannah! ('*f.c.*': +*A. ATWOOD* and *R. VAUN*) *Fr. 1920*

AMBLER, BENJAMIN GEORGE
St. Dunstan. *1921*

AMBLER, LEONARD
Saxorra and the Prince (Alb., Brighouse, 14/9/12, '*preliminary pfce*': +*T. STAKE*)
×Vice and Virtue. LC, Alb., Brighouse, 1/10/13

AMES, GERALD [see *F. ROS*]

AMES, HUGO
×The Radical Candidate ('*ca.*': Margate, 18/2/07)
×The Girl in Grey (Metropolitan, 16/9/07)

AMHERST, Hon. SYBIL
×Job (K's H., 28/11/12, Norwich Players)
×Love is Enough (Ethical Church, Bayswater, 8/7/20)
Via Crucis (Mem., Stratford-upon-Avon, 15/12/22; Gar. 5/2/23: +*C. E. WHEELER*: adapted from H. von Hofmannsthal, *Jedermann*)

ANDERSON, ARTHUR [see also *LEEDHAM BANTOCK*]
Two Merry Monarchs ('*c.o.*', m. O. Morgan: Sav., 10/3/10: +*G. LEVY*)
×The Billposter (Emp., Kilburn, 7/10/10; Pal., 31/10/10)
John Berkeley's Ghost ('*c.*': County, Bedford, 27/10/10: +*H. CARRICK*)
×The Daring of Irene ('*m.pl.*', m. M. Reinhart: Tiv., 22/1/12)
The Grass Widows ('*m.c.*', m. G. Kerker: Apo., 7/9/12: +*H. CARRICK*)
×The H'arum Lily ('*m.sk.*': Pav., 9/12/12: +*H. CARRICK*)
The Joy Ride Lady ('*m.pl.*', m. J. Gilbert: New, 21/2/14: +*H. CARRICK*
×Good Company. LC, Pallad., 10/3/14
The Beauty Spot ('*m.pl.*', m. J. W. Tate: Manchester, 26/11/17; Gai., 22/12/17)
×Mr and Mrs? (Emp., Islington, 24/2/19: +*R. COURTNEIDGE*)
Spring Time ('*oa.*', m. F. Lehar: Emp., 8/9/24)

ANDERSON, AUDREY
×A Spring Clean (Aquar., Brighton, 2/3/03)
×Tit for Tat ('*c.*': Aquar., Brighton, 2/3/03)
×Drunk and Disorderly ('*f.*': Pier, Brighton, 20/11/03)

ANDERSON, CONSTANCE POWELL
×The Heart of a Clown ('*autumn fantasy*') *1920*
The Curate of St Chad's (Abbey, Dublin, 20/5/19; Q, 30/7/26)
×The Courting of the Widow Malone ('*c.*') *1922*
The Passing of Peter (Gai., Dublin, 22/2/23, *m.*)
×The Greatest Gift ('*vision*') *1926*
×When Love Grows Up ('*allegory*') *1926*
Barren ('*modern everyday t.*') *Fr. 1926*

ANDERSON, GARLAND
Appearances (Roy., 10/3/30)

ANDERSON, GEORGE F. R.
×Washington (New, Manchester, 19/5/13)

ANDERSON, GRAHAM
The Maiden in Mars ('*m.pl.*': T. H., Aylsham, 27/11/12, *amat.*)

ANDERSON, J.
Regarding a Flight. LC, Glo., Walmer, Deal, 29/8/18: title changed later to *As Ye Sow* –

ANDERSON, J. GRANT
The Ten Commandments (Alex., S. Shields, 17/7/26)

ANDERSON, JOHN REDWOOD
Babel ('*d. poem*') *1927*

ANDERSON, L.
×The Difference. LC, County, St Albans, 31/8/16

ANDERSON, MARY [see *R. S. HICHENS*]

[*ANDERSON, MAXWELL*
Forfeits ('*light c.*': Aldw. 2/12/26, *m.*)

ANDERSON, MILLAR
For Her Husband's Sake (Manchester, 20/5/07; Edmonton, 12/10/08)
Nameless (Metro., Abertillery, 11/09; Stratford 5/2/12)
×The Cottage on the Moor (Pal., Chelsea, 14/11/10; Clavier H., 28/1/12)
The Writing on the Wall ('*r.d.*': Lincoln, 7/11/12)

ANDRÉ, RICHARD
[For earlier plays see *H. E. D.* v, 241]
×Nan ('*oa.*', m. Isidore de Solla: Cor., 12/9/05)
×Red or Blue ('*oa.*', m. Isidore de Solla: Guildhall School of Music, 5/3/12) *1891*

ANDREW, Rev. Father [= *HENRY ERNEST HARDY*]
The Hope of the World ('*Nativity pl.*': Vic. H., 20/12/19) *1920*

ANDREWS, J. B.
×A Clever Deception (Shrewsbury, 15/12/03)

ANDREWS, KENNETH
Bosun 'Enry ('*r.c.*': Huddersfield, 3/9/19: LC, Gai., Manchester, as *Bos'n 'Enry's Luck*: +*L. CALVERT*)

ANGLIN, NORMAN
The Cinder Age (Little, Manchester, 2/11/25, Unnamed Soc.)
Poison Gas. *1928*

ANNESLEY, FRANCIS
[Several sketches and playlets produced at music-halls]

ANNINGSON, G. R. KING
The End of the House of Alard (Rep., Plymouth, 13/6/27: dramatised from the novel (1923) by Sheila Kaye Smith)

ANSLE, PHOEBE
The Motive (Rehearsal, 6/6/12)

ANSON, H. E. [see *M. LANG*]

ANSPACHER, LOUIS KAUFMAN
Daddalums ('*c.*': New Haven, Conn., 6/9/15, as *Our Children*; Maxine Elliott, N.Y., 10/8/15; P'cess, Crayford, 28/7/19; Wimbledon, 13/10/19; Wynd., 15/6/20) *Fr. 1930*

'*ANSTEY, F.*' [=*THOMAS ANSTEY GUTHRIE*]
The Man from Blankley's ('*c.*': P.W., 25/4/01) *1893*; *1901*; *1927*
[This piece was published with twenty other short sketches, mainly reprinted from *Punch*: 1. *One Side of the Canvass*; 2.

The Other Side of the Canvass; 3. *On the Threshold of Themis*; 4. *Boat-Race Day*; 5. *Preserved Venice*; 6. *At a Vegetarian Restaurant*; 7. *At a Hypnotic Seance;* 8. *Wrestling with Whistlers*; 9. *Dilatory Dinners*; 10. *Matinée Mania*; 11. *More 'Pot-Pourri' from the Park*; 12. *The Automatic Physiognomist*; 13. *'Hair-cutting, Singeing and Shampooing'*; 14. *The Menagerie Race*; 15. *Before the Mechanical Models*; 16. *At the Wild West*; 17. *Telephonic Theatre-goers*; 18. *Art in the City*; 19. *At the Confectioner's*; and 20. *Choosing Christmas Toys*]
A Short Exposure ('*f.*': Crit., 3/6/01)
Lyre and Lancet ('*c.*': Roy., 8/11/02: +*F. K. PEILE*)
The Brass Bottle ('*f.pl.*': H., 13/3/07, *cpy.*; Vaud., 16/9/09) *1911*
×A Game of Adverbs (Newcastle, 2/3/08, *cpy.*; Court, L'pool, 9/3/08; Gr., Fulham, 30/3/08)
×Vice-Versa (D.P., Eastbourne, 7/11/10; Com., 10/11/10) *1910*
×A Fallen Idol (St G's H., 25/1/13)
The Would-be Gentleman ('*f.c.*': Lyr., Hamm., 15/11/26: adapted from Molière, *Le bourgeois gentilhomme*) *1926*
The Imaginary Invalid ('*c.*': Old Vic., 28/10/29: adapted from Molière, *Le malade imaginaire*) *1929*

ANSTRUTHER, D. [see *T. FITZROY*]

ANSTRUTHER, Hon. EVA ISABELLA HENRIETTA
[For an earlier play see *H. E. D.* v, 241]
×Old Clothes (Gar., 16/2/04)
Fido (Playh., 26/11/07, *m.*; Playh., 22/2/08)
×The Whirligig (Kings., 19/5/08)
×My Lonely Soldier (Col., 8/5/16)

ANTHONY, FRANK
The Bidden Guest ('*allegory*': W.G., Margate, 10/12/28) *1931* (Margate)

ANTLEY, GEORGE [see *R. H. CURTIS*]

APPLETON, G. W.
[For earlier plays see *H. E. D.* v, 241]
×The Unbidden Guest (Dublin, 13/7/00)

APPLIN, ARTHUR [see also *H. BATH* and *C. THURSBY*]
The Masked Girl ('*t.*': K's H., 22/3/08, Pl. Actors)
×Getting Out of It (Pallad., 24/6/12)
Rags ('*c.*': Court, 2/3/14)
×Le rêve ('*dream pl.*': Court, 2/3/14)

ARABIAN, MICHAEL A.
Trespassers will be prosecuted (Gai., Manchester, 26/4/09)
Love?! (Playh., 4/3/21)
Yeraz ('*a tale within a tale*') *1921*

ARCHER, CHARLES [see also *W. ARCHER*: for other translations see *H. E. D.* v, 242]
Lady Inger of Ostråt (Scala, 29/1/06: translated from H. Ibsen, *Fru Inger til Östråt*)

ARCHER, Mrs F. E.

The Lady from the Sea (Roy., 5/3/02: translated from H. Ibsen, *Fruen fra havet*, 1899)

ARCHER, J.

Judas Maccabeus (Bow Baths H., 5/12/12)

ARCHER, R. L.

×The Model Wife. LC, Little, 3/4/14

ARCHER, WILLIAM

[See also *H. E. D.* v, 242]

When We Dead Awaken (Imp., 26/1/03: translated from H. Ibsen, *Naar vi doede vaagner*, 1899) *1900*

Hannele (Scala, 12/4/08, Pl. Actors: H.M., 8/12/08, *m.*: translated from the play (1893) by G. Hauptmann) *1907*

John Gabriel Borkman (Court, 26/1/11: translated from the play (1896) by H. Ibsen) *1897*

Peer Gynt (Rehearsal, 26/2/11, Ibsen Club: +*C. ARCHER*: translated from the play (1867) by H. Ibsen) *1892*

The Pretenders (H., 13/2/13: translated from H. Ibsen, *Kongsemnerne*, 1863) *1913*

Interior (translated from M. Maeterlinck, *L'interieur*, 1895) *1908*

War is War; or, The Germans in Belgium. *1919*

The Green Goddess (Walnut Street, Philadelphia, 27/12/20; Booth, N.Y., 18/1/21; St J., 6/9/23) [*1921*]

×The Samurai. LC, Hippo., Bristol, 4/12/23

The Joy Ride ('*f.md.*': P's, Manchester, 18/5/25; Q, 8/2/26)

Three Plays. *1927*

[This contains: 1. *Martha Washington*; 2. *Beatriz Juana*; and 3. *Lidia*)

ARCHER-SMITH, F. E.

The Eternal Purpose (Oddfellows' H., Winslow, 26/11/07)

Life's Stepping Stones (Church Inst., Wolverton, 19/4/09)

ARCHIBALD, E. M. R.

Kalliste; or, The Helm of Bronze. *1924*

ARDAGH, WINIFRED MARY

×As the Law Stands ('*modern pl.*': K's H., 12/3/13)

ARDASCHIR, KAI KUSHRON [see also *G. UNGER*]

The Pilgrim of Eternity (D.Y., 12/11/21)

The Magician (Lyc., Newport, 25/2/24: +*W. DICKSON-KENWIN*)

ARDEN, EDWARD C.

The Cornish Girl ('*r.o.*', m. J. H. Wilson and C. Locknane: Pleasure Gdns, Folksetone, 12/11/06)

ARFWEDSON, CONSTANCE A.

Olaf Liljekrans (Rehearsal, 18/6/11, Ibsen Club: translated from the play (1856) by H. Ibsen)

×The Hero's Mound (Clavier H., 30/5/12: translated from H. Ibsen, *Kjaempehöjen*, 1854)

×What's Fair in Love (Rehearsal, 21/7/12)
St John's Night (Margaret Morris, 1/5/21, Pax Robertson Salon: translated from H. Ibsen, *Sancthansnatten*, 1835)
Jack (Bedford H., Chelsea, 19/11/21, Shakespeare Students Soc.)
Judith Renaudin (Bedford H., Chelsea, 26/2/22, Pax Robertson Salon: translated from the play (1898) by P. Loti)
Cousins (Bedford H., Chelsea, 1/4/22, Shakespeare Students Soc.)
Springtime (Bedford H., Chelsea, 29/4/23, Pax Robertson Salon: translated from a play by P. Verlaine)
Isle o' Dreams ('*fant.*': Bedford H., Chelsea, 7/7/23, Pax Robertson Salon: translated from P. Loti, *Pêcheurs d'islande*, 1893)

ARGYLL, ASTRID
×The Infanta (Etlinger, 2/12/26: +*R. M. MORLEY*)

ARKELL, T. REGINALD [see also *R. EVETT* and *L. N. PARKER*]
×Don't (Aldrington T.H., Hove, 23/10/05)
Colombine ('*fant.*': Clavier H., 7/12/11, *m.*; Clavier H., 1/4/12; Str., 27/11/13) *1911*
Oh, Hell!!! ('*revuette*': Little, 1/9/20: +*A. R. THORNDIKE*)
The Tragedy of Mr Punch (Little, 15/12/20: +*A. R. THORNDIKE*) *1922*
Catherine ('*m.pl.*': P.W., B'ham, 30/7/23; Gai., 22/9/23: +*F. DE GRÉSAC*)
Frasquita ('*m.c.*', m. F. Lehar: Lyc., Edin., 22/12/24; P's, 23/4/25: +*F. DE GRÉSAC*)
Reginald Arkell's Latest. *Fr. 1926*
[This contains four revue sketches]
Mademoiselle ('*m.pl.*', m. R. Cox: Epsom, 12/1/26)
The Blue Train ('*m.c.*', m. R. Stolz: K's., Southsea, 14/3/27; P.W., 10/5/27: +*D. TITHERADGE*)
×A Romany Gentleman (Pallad., 14/10/29)
Sending Grandpa to Heaven. *Fr. 1929*

ARKWRIGHT, RUTH
Brownikins and Other Fancies. *1911*
[This includes, besides the title-piece, four short children's plays: 1. *Bibi, or, The Japanese Foundling*; 2. *St Nicholas*; 3. *Fairy Bells*; and 4. *Baby New Year*]

'*ARLEN, MICHAEL*' [=*M. KUYUMJIAN*]
Dear Father ('*c. about nothing*': Scala, 30/11/24, Pl. Actors)
×Why Shelmerdene was Late for Dinner. LC, W.G., 12/12/24
The Green Hat (Gar., Detroit, 29/3/25; Broadhurst, N.Y., 15/9/25; Adel., 2/9/25) *1925*
The Zoo ('*c.*': K's, Southsea, 23/5/27: +*W. SMITH*)

ARLETT, VERA ISABEL
×A Corner in Dreams. *1927*
×The Visitor. *1929*

ARLISS, GEORGE [see also *G. DANCE*]
[For earlier plays see *H. E. D.* v, 243]

There and Back ('*f.c.*': Bath, 7/12/1895, *cpy.*; Bolton, 19/10/00; P.W., 22/5/02)
×Widow's Weeds (Emp., 5/12/10)

ARMFIELD, MAXWELL [see *A. C. SMEDLEY*]

ARMITAGE, HARRY
With Edged Tools (Gai., Ayr, 20/2/07, *cpy.*; Hull, 3/2/08; K's, Hamm., 6/4/08)

ARMOUR, WILLIAM A.
The Best of Her Sex (County, Bedford, 14/9/05, *cpy.*; Coloss., Oldham, 13/5/07; Stratford, 31/8/08: originally called *A Good Woman*: +*R. CHEVAL*)

'ARMSTRONG, ANTHONY' [*GEORGE ANTHONY ARMSTRONG WILLIS*]
Caught ('*f.c.*': Str., 8/12/29, Rep. Players)

ARMSTRONG, CECIL FERARD
The Chair of Love ('*c.*': Court, 13/6/11, *m.*)
×Gentlemen (Pier, Eastbourne, 26/10/16)
×Safe Conduct (Pier, Eastbourne, 13/9/17)
Home Service (D.P., Eastbourne, 22/4/18, *amat.*)
The Understudy ('*c.*': RADA, 18/12/21)

ARMSTRONG, JOAN [see *J. NELSON*]

[*ARMSTRONG, PAUL*
Salomy Jane (Adel., 18/1/07, *cpy.*; Qns, 24/6/25)
Wireless (York, 19/10/08, *cpy.*: +*W. SMITH*)
Alias Jimmy Valentine (Wallack's, N.Y., 21/1/10; Playh., 1/1/10 *cpy.*; Com., 29/3/10)
×Woman Proposes (Adel., 8/3/16)

ARMSTRONG, WILLIAM [see also *A. P. HERBERT* and *F. B. YOUNG*]
A Daughter's Love (Alh., Stourbridge, 17/12/02, *cpy.*: title altered later to *Fetters of Justice*: +*R. LORD*)
The Mad Author (Colne, 18/3/09, *cpy.*)

ARNIM, ELIZABETH
Priscilla Runs Away ('*c.*': H., 28/6/10)

ARNOLD, VICTOR
×Pierrot's Last Adventure ('*wordless pl.*', m. F. Barmann: Col., 11/3/12)

ARTHUR, FREDERIC [see *J. BRANDON*]

ARTHUR, LEE
Eunice (Hicks', 1/6/09: originally called *The Higher Law*: +*F. HALSEY*)

ARTHUR, LILFORD [see *C. WINDERMERE*]

ARTHURS, GEORGE [see also *B. DANSON*, *W. DAVID*, *A. W. FIELD* and *A. A. HURGON*]
The Gay Financier ('*m.c.*', m. B. Scott: Adel., 16/7/04, *cpy.*)
×Maison Decollette ('*oa.*', m. M. Knopf: Pav., 13/1/13)
The Girl who Wronged Her Husband (Bordon, 15/1/14)

×Office Hours. LC, Qns, S. Shields, 5/3/14
×Called for the Rent. LC, K's, Southsea, 28/8/14
×The Village Ne'er-do-weel. LC, K's, Southsea, 21/9/14
×The Magic Touch ('*m.c.*', m. L. Bassett: Pal., Walthamstow, 18/1/15; Oxf., 22/2/15: title altered later to *Go To Jericho*: +*C. DANVERS*)
×Don't Tempt Me ('*m.c.*', m. L. Jerome: Emp., Shepherd's Bush, 19/7/15)
She's a Daisy ('*m.c.*': LC, Pallad., Southport, 14/9/15)
Zuzu. LC, Pal., Manchester, 23/8/16
Peri, the Slave of Love ('*c.o.*', m. W. Neale: Gr., Wolverhampton, 21/2/21; Bor., Stratford, 1/8/21)
The Daughter of the Sheik ('*m.pl.*': LC, Hippo., Balham, 21/4/23)
Archie ('*m.c.*', m. H. Wood and J. Waller: Gr., Hull, 28/7/24; K's, Hamm., 1/12/24: +*W. DAVID*)
A Girl for Sale (Huddersfield, 16/11/25; K's, Southsea, 25/6/28, as *The Revolt of Christopher*: dramatised from the novel (1920) by Mabel Barnes Grundy: +*A. MILLER*)
[Numerous sketches and playlets produced at music-halls]

ARUNDALE, CLAUDE
The Gipsy Girl ('*c.o.*', m. by author: Shak., L'pool, 15/5/05; Waldorf, 28/1/07, '*trial pfce*'; Waldorf, 22/3/07)
×A Ward in Chancery (Emp., Holb., 30/5/10)

ARUNDEL, MARK
Don't Tell Timothy ('*frivolous c.*': Scala, 15/12/25) *1925*

ASCHE, OSCAR [*JOHN STRANGER HEISS OSCAR ASCHE*= '*VASCO MARENAS*': see also *C. O'RIORDAN*]
Mameena (Glo., 30/9/14)
The Spanish Main ('*rd.*': Wimbledon, 6/9/15; Apo., 21/12/15: as by '*VASCO MARENAS*')
Chu Chin Chow ('*m.pl.*', m. F. Norton: H.M., 31/8/16) *Fr. 1931*
Cairo ('*mosaic in music and mime*': H.M., 15/10/21: originally called *Ali Shar*)
The Good Old Days ('*m.pl.*', m. P. Fletcher: Gai., 27/10/25)

ASGOLD, S.
×At the Brig End ('*r.pl.*') *1928* (Village D. Soc.)

ASHBY, EDITH
Miles Standish...dramatised for performance. *1911*

ASHDOWN, F.
×Salt. LC, Watts H., Southampton, 31/10/22

ASHFORD, BERTRAM B.
The Question (Court, 9/1/04: +*J. S. WINTER*)

ASHFORD, CYRIL
×A Question of Duty (Little, 10/7/13, Stage Players)

ASHLEY, OWEN
×The Wrong Room (Ladbr. H., 18/7/07)

ASHTON, HENRY ALLEN

×The King of Borneo ('*f.*': Rehearsal, 23/5/08, *amat.*)
×The Secretary's Wedding Present (Rehearsal, 23/5/08, *amat.*)
×Eileen's Santa Claus (Court, 18/12/13)

[*ASHTON, HERBERT, Jr*

Brothers (K's, Southsea, 26/8/29; Adel., 3/9/29) *Fr. 1934*

ASHTON, KITTY

×The Way Out (Court, 4/12/13; Cosmopolis, 20/3/14, revised as *The Choice*)

ASHTON, TEDDY

[Several sketches produced at music-halls]

ASHTON, WINIFRED [='*CLEMENCE DANE*']

ASHWELL, LENA

The Celluloid Cat. LC, Longfield H., Ealing, 19/2/24: +*R. POCOCK*
Crime and Punishment (Cent.; 7/2/27: dramatised from the novel by F. Dostoievski: +*R. POCOCK*)
Dr Jekyll and Mr Hyde (Bath, 14/3/27; Cent., 28/3/27: dramatised from the novel by R. L. Stevenson: +*R. POCOCK*)

ASKEW, CLAUDE

×A Hair-breadth Escape (Bij., 21/3/01)
×A Little Hobby (E.C., 2/11/03: also called *His Little Hobby*)
×The Shulamite (Sav., 12/5/06: from the novel (1904) by Alice and Claude Askew: +*E. KNOBLOCK*)

ASKEW, MARY

The Kingdom of Dreams (Gr., Brighton, 15/11/24, *m.*)

ASPDEN, H.

The Eve of the Trial. LC, Darwen, 7/10/15

ASQUITH, ELIZABETH

×Off and On ('*c.*': D.L., 9/5/16, *m.*)

ASTON, K. GORDON

×Oh! You Beggar! (Cosmopolis, 17/2/14)
×A Simple Gentleman (Ambass., 26/2/20, *m.*)
×The Stronger Pull (Ambass., 22/4/20, *m.*)
Smoke Persian ('*fant. absurdity*': Little, Kensington, 24/4/22; Everyman, 28/5/29)

ASTOR, A. C.

×Sandy's Return. LC, Connaught H., Worthing, 27/6/19: +*A. LAUDER*

ATACK, FLORENCE N. H.

The Stop-Gap ('*f.*': Aldw., 7/6/22, Playwrights' Theatre)

ATHERSTONE, T. W.

×An Adventure (Str., 25/6/01)

ATHOLL, PEG

×Up the Chimney. LC, Gai. Picture Pal., Tooting, 26/1/25

ATKINSON, F. M.
The Cloud that Lifted, and The Power of the Dead (translation from Maurice Maeterlinck) *1923*

ATTENBURY, C. B.
Enoch Atkins. LC, Emp., Tonypandy, 22/1/19: +*J. A. S. THOMSON*

ATTWATER, HENLEY
Who's Afraid? ('*c.*': Bloomsbury H., 18/10/06)

ATWILL, LIONEL
City of Mystery ('*costume pl.*': Gr., Luton, 9/1/08, *cpy.*: dramatised from the novel (1902) by A. C. Gunter)

ATWOOD, ALBAN [see *M. AMBIENT, L. MONTAGUE* and *R. VAUN*]

ATWOOD, DOROTHY
Kan. LC, Ass. R., Malvern, 3/2/25

AUBREY, A. J. [see *I. L. OSBORN*]

AUBRY, MARC
Jealousy ('*wordless pl.*': Rehearsal, 13/11/08, *m.*, Argonauts)

AUMONIER, STACY
×A Nice Thing (Com., 12/8/20)

AUSTEN-LEE, CYRIL
[For earlier plays see *H. E. D.* v, 245]
×A Man's Idol (Belfast, 25/4/02)

AUSTIN, ALFRED
[For earlier plays see *H. E. D.* v, 245]
Flodden Field ('*t.*': H.M., 8/6/03, Guy's Hospital Entertainment) *1903*
×A Lesson in Harmony ('*c.*': Gar., 16/6/04)
×Achilles in Scyros ('*masque*': Leighton House, 19/7/09)

AUSTIN, AUSTIN B.
The House Next Door ('*f.*': Tolmer's Inst., Hampstead-road, 16/3/05)

AUSTIN, CHARLES [see also *A. ROSE*]
Parker P.C. (Hippo., Islington, 18/5/08, in one act: +*C. RIDGWELL*: expanded to three acts as *Discharged from the Force; or, Parker P.C.*: LC, Dalston, 4/1/09)
[This was followed by a lengthy series of sketches, almost all featuring 'Parker, P.C.' – a kind of comic anticipation of 'Dixon of Dock Green']

AUSTIN, CYRIL [see *T. CRUTCHLEY*]

AUSTIN, FREDERICK BRITTEN
×The Wrong Dressing Room. LC, Lyc., Govan, 5/8/19
The Thing That Matters (Str., 22/12/21)
×Boat Villa. LC, Elite, Bordersley Green, 16/3/23

AUSTIN, GUY K.
The Island Princess ('*m.c.*', m. H. W. David: Lyc., Sheffield, 30/7/28)

AUSTIN, HENRY
× Cry Quits (Brixton H., 16/6/03)
× The Artist's Revenge (Brixton H., 16/6/03)
× Cupid's Dream (Pal., Brighton, 28/5/06)

AUSTIN, JOHN
× How One Woman Did It (Court, 11/3/12)

AUSTIN, MARY [see also *JOHN MACLAREN*]
Margaret Catchpole. LC, Lyc. H., Ipswich, 21/1/21: +*JOHN MACLAREN*

AUSTIN, PHYLLIS [see *E. RIGBY*]

AVELING, CLAUDE [see also *L. C. JAMES* and *W. W. PETRIE*]
× A Very Modern Othello (Emp., B'ham, 19/12/10; Tiv., 26/12/10)

AVERN, ERNEST
The Witch o' Worlebury (Knightstone Pav., Weston, 12/2/14, *amat.*)

AVERY, E. W. [see *F. MOULE*]

AVERY, W. T.
Dolly Dye ('*m. absurdity*', m. K. Morrison: Alex., Pontefract, 20/5/12)

AXTENS, JOYCE
× Impromptu (Crippl. Inst., 23/4/27, Quill Club Players)

AYLMER, HAROLD O.
× A Woman's Deceit; or, The Shadow of a Life (Roy., Glasgow, 26/2/03, *cpy.*)

AYMET, MARAH
× In the Name of the Czar (Kings., 19/3/09, *m.*, *amat.*: originally called *In the Czar's Name*)

AYRE, CHARLES K.
The Skipper's Submarine ('*c.*': O.H., Belfast, 6/12/17)
The Lone Man ('*c.*': O.H., Belfast, 14/11/19)
Loaves and Fishes ('*c.*': O.H., Belfast, 2/11/21; Scala, 4/7/23, Ulster Players)
Missing Links ('*c.*': Gai., Dublin, 15/12/25)

AYRES, HARRY MORGAN
An Ingenious Play of Esmoreit. *1924* (*priv.*)
Mary of Nimmegen (St G's H., 22/2/25, Internat. Theatre Soc.) *1924* (*priv.*)

AYRTON, F. RANDLE
× The King's Minstrel (Cor., 17/2/13)
× A Russian Episode. LC, Rep., Plymouth 28/9/21

'*B. A. B.*'
Those Terrible Twins ('*f.c.*': Cardiff, 25/6/00; Alex., 22/7/00: title altered later to *Mabel's Twins*)

B., W. A. [=*W. A. BRISCOE*]

BACCHUS, REGINALD [see also *H. SHELLEY*]
The Rose of the Riviera ('*m.ext.*', m. F. O. Carr: Eden, Brighton, 25/5/03)
Miss Mischief ('*m.c.*', m. F. O. Carr: W.L., 31/10/04)

BACKHOUSE, JOSEPH
The Lady Companion ('*c.*': Crook, 27/6/11, *amat.*)

BACKUS, Mrs HENRY [*EMMA H.*]
×The Singing Soul. LC, Crippl. Inst., '*Chinese pl.*': 1/11/22. *Fr. 1921*

BACON, F. [see *W. SMITH*]

BACON, ROGER
All the Men and Women (Gar., 20/3/27, *m.*: +*R. R. PRESNALL*)
Barren Gain (Q, 9/12/29: +*J. WOOD*)

BADCOCK, NELLIE B.
Yasodhara; or, The Greater Renunciation. *1923* (*priv.*)

BADDELEY, V. C. CLINTON [=*V. C. CLINTON-BADDELEY*]

BADDELEY, W. H. CLINTON
The Prince of Knaves ('*c.o.*', m. C. Fenn-Leyland: E.C., 10/6/10, *cpy.*)

BADHAM, ALEC
×Odd Numbers ('*f.*': Watson Memorial H., Tewkesbury, 6/11/13)

BAGGE, HENRY
×The Last Rally (Rehearsal, 3/11/09, *m.*: +*F. D. BONE*
×The Truth for an Hour ('*c.*': +*HARTLEY MILBURN*) *1914*

BAGNALL, BERNARD
×Faces in the Fire (Plymouth, 27/5/12)

BAGOT, Mrs CHARLES [*SOPHIA L.*]
×Planchette (Lyc. Club, 12/3/22)

BAGOT, L. [see also *V. H. HILL*]
×Unconditional Surrender. LC, Chelsea Hospital Grounds, 16/7/21: +*V. H. HILL*)

BAILEY, HENRY CHRISTOPHER
The White Hawk (Aldw., 30/5/09, English Pl. Soc.: dramatised from his own novel, *Beaujeu* (1905): +*D. KIMBALL*)

BAILEY, SYDNEY F.
[For an earlier play see *H. E. D.* v, 247]
×A Matrimonial Agency (T.H., Bootle, 21/3/01, *amat.*)
Down by the Sea ('*m.c.*': T.H., Bootle, 5/2/02)
My Lord of Purslow ('*m.pl.*': T.H., Bootle, 14/1/03, *cpy.*)
The Pet of the Embassy ('*c.o.*': Muncaster, Bootle, 3/12/06, *amat.*: Gr., Eccles, 30/3/07)

BAILEY, T. G. [see also *H. CASSELL*]

Love Rules the World (Star, L'pool, 1/7/07; E.C., 14/12/08)
How Women Ruin Men (Vic., Broughton, 9/11/08: Stratford, 28/12/08: title altered later to *Her German Husband*)
How Women are Slandered (Vic., Broughton, 14/1/09)
The Grecian Princess ('*c.o.*', m. Y. Sheffield: Gr., Oldham, 27/11/11)
Anno Domini ('*stage sermon*': Crane H., L'pool, 16/8/16)
× The Ruby Ring. LC, O.H., Barrow-in-Furness, 20/10/16
Romantic Mrs Matchem. LC, Hippo., Maidenhead, 12/5/19

BAILEY, WARD [see also *S. LEE*]

For Wife and Kingdom (Gr., Brighton, 19/11/08, *cpy.*; Smethwick, 8/3/09; Lyr., Hamm., 29/3/09)
× The Bandit's Blunder (W.L., 8/3/09)
× The Mask Torn Off (Empress, 14/3/10: +*E. THANE*)
An Arabian Vengeance (Emp., Southend, 24/6/12; Stratford, 1/7/12)
An Oath of Vengeance. LC, Bristol, 5/7/13
At a Stepmother's Mercy (Metro., Manchester, 6/3/16; E.C., 1/5/16)
The Talisman ('*c.o.*', m. W. Johnson: Emp., Southend, 16/6/19)

BAILEY, WILLIAM, Jr [see also *C. BERTE*]

At Break of Day (W.L., 24/8/03: +*C. BERTE*)
What Women Worship (W.L., 8/5/05: +*C. BERTE*)

BAIN, DOUGLAS

× The Call of May. *1909*
× The Angel of the White Feet (County, Kingston, 22/5/11) *1911*
× Violets (County, Kingston, 31/10/11) *1911*

BAIN, K. MARJORIE

× The Storehouse (Leeds, 24/4/29)

BAIN, ROBERT

The Magic Powder. LC, Porteous H., Crieff, 5/3/13
The Island of Sancho Panza ('*m.c.*', m. J. D. Turner: Porteous H., Crieff, 11/5/20, *amat.*)
The Island of Millionaires. LC, '*m.pl.*': Porteous H., Crieff, 12/3/24
James the First of Scotland (Glasgow, 11/5/25) *1921*
Punch Counts Ten ('*play for children from 9 to 90*': Lyr., Glasgow, 22/12/25)

BAINBRIDGE, JULIAN

The Little Witness (Tonypandy, 2/10/02, *cpy.*; Foresters, 19/6/11, as *The Man from –*; *or, The Little Witness*; sub-title also *or, The Devil's Own Son*)

BAINES, E.

× Be a Sport. LC, Court, 1/5/14

BAINES, FLORENCE

Sally in Society ('*m.f.*': Stratford, 8/1/23)

BAINES, R. T.
A Midwinter's Night's Dream (N. Polytechnic Inst., 2/11/22, *amat.*)

BAINES-AUSTIN, EDGAR H. S.
×Caught Out (Gr., Margate, 14/2/03, *cpy.*)

BAINTON, EDGAR L.
Oithona ('*o.*': Glastonbury, 11/8/15)

BAIRD, H. MORTON
Sin and the Sinner ('*society d.*': Castle, Richmond, 22/4/09)

BAIRNSFATHER, BRUCE
×The Johnson 'Ole. LC, Hippo., Eastbourne, 23/2/17: +*B. M. HASTINGS*
The Better 'Ole ('*m.pl.*', m. H. Darewski: Oxf., 4/8/17: +*A. ELIOT*)
×Lucky Old Bill. LC, Vint's, Llanelly, 19/5/19
Old Bill, M.P. (Hippo., Golder's Green, 17/4/22; Lyc., 12/7/22: +*S. HICKS*)

BAKER, E. C.
×A Cushy Job (Hippo., Sheffield, 7/1/18; Sur., 4/2/18)

BAKER, ELIZABETH
Chains (Court, 18/4/09, Pl. Actors; Gai., Manchester, 1/5/11; Rep., B'ham, 31/10/14) *1911*
×Cupid in Clapham (Court, 20/3/10, Pl. Actors)
×Miss Tassey (Court, 20/3/10, Pl. Actors; Gai., Manchester, 24/2/13) *1913*
Edith ('*c.*': P's, 9/2/12, *m.*) *1927*
The Price of Thomas Scott (Gai., Manchester, 22/9/13) *1913*
×Beastly Pride. LC, Gr., Croydon, 19/3/14
Over a Garden Wall ('*c.*': Rep., B'ham, 20/11/15)
Partnership ('*c.*': Court, 5/3/17) *Fr. 1921*
Miss Robinson ('*c.*': Rep., B'ham, 9/11/18) *1920*
Bert's Girl ('*c.*': Rep., B'ham, 12/9/25; Court, 30/3/27) *1927*
×Umbrellas. LC, Arcadia, Scarborough, 13/3/28. *1927*
Penelope Forgives (Cent., 21/2/30)

BAKER, H. COLE
×A Visit of Inspection. LC, P.W., Grimsby, 23/10/15

BAKER, L. M.
Beryl (Lincoln, 31/10/06, *cpy.*)

BAKER, R. [see *J. EMERSON*]

BALBI, J. L.
Ulysses Brown, or, The Infidelities of a Married Man ('*f.*') *1902* (*priv.*)
Machine Made ('*farcical impossibility*': Bij., 10/10/03, *cpy.*)

[*BALDERSTON, JOHN LLOYD* [see also *H. DEANE*]
Berkeley Square (St M., 6/10/26; Lyr., 6/3/29, *revised*: +*J. C. SQUIRE*) *Fr. 1928*

BALDWIN, CHARLES [see also *F. KARNO* and *H. S. STEPHENS*]
The Withered Hand (E.C., 23/6/04, *cpy.*: +*F. KITCHEN*)
× The Year Dot ('*prehistoric pantomime sk.*': Wallsend, 31/8/05, *cpy.*)
× The First Night ('*f.*': Richmond, 2/9/07)
× Clicked Again. LC, Qns, Castleford, 2/9/19: +*G. PAYNE*
Film Stars (Hippo., Putney, 29/12/19)
[Numerous sketches and playlets produced at music-halls]

BALFOUR, EDITH
× The Faddists ('*f.*': St J., 27/6/05: +*E. STRODE* and *J. CONDURIER*)

BALFOUR, MARIE CLOTHILDE
× Herb o' Joy ('*ca.*': Court, 30/4/12, *m.*; Arts Centre, 10/2/14)
× Mere China (Court, 30/4/12)
× The Pursuer (Arts Centre, 10/2/14)
× Roses of Montignac (Arts Centre, 10/2/14)

BALL, GERALDINE
× A Change for the Better. *1929* (Health and Cleanliness Council)

[*BALLARD, FRED*
Willie Goes West ('*f.*': Castle Square, Boston, 20/11/13, as *Believe Me, Xantippe*; 39th Street, N.Y., 19/8/13; D.P., Eastbourne, 4/10/15) *1918* (New York)

BALLARD, PERCY
Only a Woman (Central, Altrincham, 20/1/08; Qns, Fleetwood, 27/1/08; W.L., 13/4/08)

'*BALLYN, DEAN*' [=*W. R. TROTTER STEAD*]
× The Cash Box (H.M., Dundee, 3/7/05)
The Price of Freedom ('*a tale of today, creating an entirely new literary form*': H.M., Dundee, 27/8/10, *cpy.*) *1910*

BALMAIN, ROLLO [see also *H. WHYTE*]
Monte Cristo (Woolwich, 9/12/12)
× A British Soldier (H.M., Walsall, 28/9/14)
Are We Downhearted? (Junction, Manchester, 1/2/15; E.C., 21/6/15)
A Sailor's Love (Gr., Plymouth, 13/9/15: +*S. MIGNON*)

BALSILLIE, DAVID
[An earlier play is given, erroneously, under 'Balsilio' in *H. E. D.* v, 247]
Becky Sharp (Gr., Croydon, 24/6/01)

BAMBERG, LILIAN
× The Swing of the Pendulum (Crippl. Inst., 9/1/13, *amat.*)
× The Onlooker (Arts Centre, 12/10/13)

BANCROFT, GEORGE PLEYDELL [='*GEORGE PLEYDELL*': see also *A. E. W. MASON*]
[For earlier plays see *H. E. D.* v, 248]
The Little Countess ('*c.*': Aven., 2/5/03)
Lady Ben ('*c.*': Com., 28/3/05)

×Penelope's Lovers (Rehearsal, 17/7/08)
The Princess Clementina (New, Cardiff, 1/12/10; Qns, 14/12/10; as by '*GEORGE PLEYDELL*': +*A. E. W. MASON*: from the latter's novel, *Clementina*, 1901)
One of the Duke's ('*c.*': Playh., 18/3/11: as by '*GEORGE PLEYDELL*')
The Ware Case (Wynd., 4/9/15: as by '*GEORGE PLEYDELL*': from his own novel, 1913) *1915*

BANCROFT, *Lady* [*MARIE EFFIE WILTON*]
[For earlier plays see *H. E. D.* v, 248]
×The Tables (Crit., 3/6/01)
×A Dream (Shak., L'pool, 23/9/03)
×Weather Bound (Pleasure Gdns, Folkestone, 19/11/13)

BAND, GEORGE
×The Visitor. LC, Kennington, 1/5/12

BANKIER, ROBERT
×Whose Zoo? ('*fant.*': Pav., Glasgow, 30/9/07; Roy., Glasgow, 19/5/09, *revised*)

BANKS, CHARLOTTE
Hiawatha (Ath., Glasgow, 10/4/19)

BANNING, H. D.
The Superior Sex ('*c.o.*', m. J. H. Maunder: Emp., Southend, 30/3/09, *amat.*; Crippl. Inst., 9/2/10, *amat.*) *1910*

BANNISDALE, VERA ERSKINE
×Moggeridge's Cow. *1922* (Village D. Soc.)
×A Country Cottage. *1923* (Village D. Soc.)
×Faces and Fortunes. *1923* (Village D. Soc.)

BANNISTER, BERT
The Soul of a Sinner (Oldham, 27/6/21)

BANTOCK, LEEDHAM [see *P. GREENBANK*]
The White Chrysanthemum ('*m.pl.*', m. H. Talbot: LC, Tyne, Newcastle, 23/4/04: Crit., 31/8/05: +*A. ANDERSON*) *1905*
The Girl behind the Counter ('*m.c.*', m. H. Talbot: Wynd., 21/4/06: +*A. ANDERSON*) *1906*
The Belle of Brittany ('*c.o.*', m. H. Talbot and M. Horne: Qns, 24/10/08: +*P. J. BARROW*)
×Man the Lifeboat (Metropolitan, 19/4/09: +*P. GREENBANK*)
A Persian Princess ('*m.c.*', m. S. Jones: Qns, 27/4/09: +*P. J. BARROW*)
Physical Culture ('*m.c.*', m. P. Thayer: Metro., 30/4/17: title changed later to *Frills and Drills*: +*H. SIMPSON*)

BANTOCK, RAYMOND ROBERT MARCUS
Poems in Prose and Verse; and a Play. *1925* (Tokyo)
Children of the Stage. *1927* (Waseda); *1929*
×The Slumberer. *1929*

BANWELL, LOUIE NEVILLE

Alice, Where Art Thou? ('*r.d.*': Jubilee H., Weymouth, 2/3/05, *cpy.*; Emp., Oxford, 18/6/06)

BARBER, ERIC [see also *ARTHUR ROSE*]

×The Village Dramatic Society (LC, Kennington, 21/11/21; Emp., Hackney, 20/7/22, revised with *F. DIX*)

Jill the Giant Killer ('*c.*': Lyc., Newport, 28/5/23)

The Soul of John Sylvester. LC, South Street H., Sheffield, 26/3/25

English Bess ('*r.pl.*': Playh., Newcastle, 4/10/26)

BARBER, HAROLD WORDSWORTH

Mactreth (Guy's Hospital, 12/11: +*A. N. COX* and *E. G. SCHLESINGER*) *1912* (*priv.*)

BARBOR, H. R.

×What Women Want. LC, Midland Inst., B'ham, 11/3/15. *1915* (Birmingham)

×Cortège ('*modern harlequinade*', m. G. Bantock: Court, 11/3/18)

Jezebel ('*t.*') *1924* (*priv.*)

BARCLAY, Lady

×La Révolte (Bij., 7/4/06, New Stage Club: from the play (1870) by Villiers de l'Isle Adam) *1901* (as *The Revolt*)

BARCLAY, Sir THOMAS

The Sands of Fate ('*phantasy*') *1917* (New York)

BARDEN, HUGH

×The Storm (Abbey, Dublin, 22/4/09)

BARDWELL-CHALLIER, A.

My Californian Sweetheart ('*m.c.*': T. H., Burnham, 25/8/08, *cpy.*)

BARIATINSKY, Prince VLADIMIR VLADIMIROVICH

The Career of Nablotsky (Little, 8/12/10, *m.*, in one act; Roy., 28/2/11; Kings., 31/10/11, revised and expanded by *JOHN POLLOCK* to 3 acts, as *The Great Young Man*)

BARING, Hon. MAURICE

The Black Prince. *1902*

Gaston de Foix. *1903*; *1913* (revised)

Mahasena. *1905*

Desiderio. *1906*

Proserpine ('*masque*') *1908*

The Grey Stocking and Other Plays. *1912*

[This contains: 1. *The Grey Stocking* (Roy., 28/5/08, *m.*); 2. *The Double Game* (Kings., 7/5/12); and 3. *The Green Elephant* (Com., 3/7/11)]

Diminutive Dramas. *1911*

[This contains twenty-two short plays: 1. *Catherine Parr* (Hippo., 30/4/12, *m.*; Arts, 27/10/27); 2. *The Drawback*; 3. *Pious Æneas*; 4. *The Death of Alexander*; 5. *The Greek Vase*; 6. *The Fatal Rubber*; 7. *The Rehearsal*; 8. *The Blue Harlequin* (Seaford House, 6/10/24, First Studio Theatre); 9. *The Member for Literature*; 10. *Caligula's Picnic*; 11. *The Aulis Difficulty* (Adel., 6/5/28,

Sunday Pl. Soc.); 12. *Don Juan's Failure*; 13. *Calpurnia's Dinner Party* (Kent House, Knightsbridge, 18/3/10, as *A Tea Party at the House of Calpurnia*; Seaford House, 6/10/24, First Studio Theatre); 14. *Lucullus's Dinner Party* (Seaford House, 6/10/24, First Studio Theatre); 15. *The Stoic's Daughter*; 16. *After Euripides' 'Electra'*; 17. *Jason and Medea*; 18. *King Alfred and the Neat-herd*; 19. *Rosamund and Eleanor*; 20. *Ariadne in Naxos*; 21. *Velasquez and the 'Venus'*; and 22. *Xantippe and Socrates*]

His Majesty's Embassy and Other Plays. *1923*

[This contains: 1. *His Majesty's Embassy*; 2. *Manfroy, Duke of Athens*; and 3. *June and After* (originally called *The Prodigal Daughter*)]

Fantasio (translated from the play (1866) by Alfred de Musset) *1927*

BARING, STEPHANIE

×He Proposed ('c.': Ladbr. H., 31/1/00: +*E. M. LEIGH*)

Kuomi, the Jester (Gr., Luton 12/6/03: +*R. SABATINI*)

×Rose o' Love (Pier Pav., St Leonard's, 20/9/12)

×The Letters of Lady Clare. LC, Emp Middleton, 20/12/13.

BARING, STEPHEN [see *W. BEAUMONT*]

[For earlier plays see *H. E. D.* v, 249]

BARK, C. H. VOSS [see *C. H. VOSS-BARK*]

BARKE, JAMES W.

×Gregarach (Ath., Glasgow, 22/3/26, Scott. Nat. Players)

BARKER, AMELIA M.

×Made Absolute (Arts and Dram. Club., 10/9/13)

BARKER, D. A.

Raleigh (Wynd., 7/6/25, St. Soc.)

BARKER, FRED D.

×A Lioness and Her Whelp (Shaft., 13/2/10, *m.*, St. Soc.)

BARKER, HARLEY GRANVILLE [=*HARLEY GRANVILLE-BARKER*]

BARKER, HENRY W.

×The Man from Paris (Muncaster, Bootle, 22/2/09)

×The Fugitive (Gr., Mansfield, 27/6/12)

BARKLEY, S. REID

×Going West (O.H., Belfast, 28/4/19)

BARLOW, A. I.

×Mr White the Explorer. LC, Central H., Cranleigh, 27/10/25

BARLOW, JANE

A Bunch of Lavender (Hardwicke Street H., Dublin, 18/12/11, Theatre of Ireland)

BARLOW, T.

×Storm Wrack ('*m.pl.*', m. J. Lyon: Shak., L'pool, 15/2/18)

BARLOW-MASSICKS, L.

×The Bachelors' Defence League. LC, Lyc., Sheffield, 7/12/14

BARMBY, BEATRICE HELEN

Gísli Súrsson. *1900*

BARNARD, ALFRED

×Darling Jack (Hippo., Balham, 4/8/13)

BERNARD, PATRICK

A Woman and Two Men (Woolwich, 29/8/10: +*J. BUCKLEY*)

BARNE, MARION CATHERINE (*'KITTY', Mrs ERIC STREATFIELD*)

Tomorrow (*'children's pl.'*: Court, 3/11/10, *amat.*: LC, Crippl. Inst., 18/10/22, *revised*: +*D. W. WHEELER*) *1912*

×Timothy's Garden (*'children's pl.'*: +*D. W. WHEELER*) *1912*

Winds (*'pl. for children'*: D.P., Eastbourne, 18/1/12, *amat.*; Court, 29/11/12, *amat.*: +*D. W. WHEELER*)

Celandine's Secret (*'children's pl.'*: Fairfield Court, Eastbourne, 18/7/14, *amat.*) *1914*

×Peter and the Clock (*'children's pl.'*) *1919*

×Susie Pays a Visit (*'children's pl.'*) *1921*

The Amber Gate (*'pageant pl.'*: D.P., Eastbourne, 27/6/23; Pal., Chelsea, 14/5/27, *m.*) *1925*

×Philemon and Baucis (*'children's pl.'*) *1926*

The Ladder (*'m.fant.'*: Daly's, 20/6/27, *m.*)

×Madge (*'camp-fire pl.'*) *1928*

BARNES, EVA

×Harvest Time. LC, Park, Hanwell, 2/8/17

BARNES, KENNETH

Glass Houses (Glo., 6/6/10: adapted from P. Hervieu, *Connais-toi* (1909))

×War Pageant (Simla, 1918)

×The Sisters (Simla, 1918)

×Undercurrents (RADA, 17/7/21)

The Letter of the Law (Gr., Putney, 22/9/24)

BARNES, LAURA CLIFFORD

God's Heroes. *1910*

BARNES, MARGARET AYER

Dishonoured Lady (Playh., 8/5/30: +*EDWARD SHELDON*)

BARNETT, Mrs [=*MARGUERITE BARRELLIER*]

BARNETT, BEN

×Serving Two Masters (Kennington, 18/7/21)

BARNETT, FRANCIS R.

The Judgment of Pilate (Portsmouth, 9/4/23: originally called *Pontius Pilate*)

BARNETT, H. O.

×The Shadow. LC, Pal., Gloucester, 15/3/13

×No Class. LC, K's H., Cheltenham, 23/10/13

×The Promise. LC, Pal., Gloucester, 8/12/13

×The Protector. LC, Watson Memorial H., Tewkesbury, 10/10/16

×The Ring (K's, Glasgow, 30/3/17)

×The Mind's Eye (O.H., Cheltenham, 25/11/24, *amat.*)

BARNETT, STEPHEN
×When the Mist Comes Down (All Saint's H., Clifton, 8/1/30)

BARNETT, W. GRAHAM
×Kultur (Soldiers' Home, Barry, Carnoustie, 14/7/16, *amat.*)

BARNETT-GARRETT, W. G.
×Poor Punchinello (P.H., Hastings, 24/4/07, *amat.*)

BARNEWALL, JOHN
The Bacach ('*t.*': Abbey, Dublin, 30/10/17)

BARNSLEY, GEORGE D. [see *KATHERINE BARNSLEY*]

BARNSLEY, KATHERINE
The Great Big World ('*fant.*': Court, 26/12/21: +*G. D. BARNSLEY*)

BARR, ROBERT [see also *J. S. JUDD*]
An Emperor's Romance (Gr., W. Hartlepool, 1/1/01: +*C. HAMILTON*: from R. Barr's novel, *The Countess Thekla* (1899))
×The Conspiracy (Dublin, 8/11/07; Adel., 9/9/08) *1939* (in *Short Modern Plays*, ed. S. R. Littlewood, vol. ii)
Lady Eleanor – Lawbreaker (Rep., L'pool, 14/12/12)

BARRELLIER, MARGUERITE (*Mrs BARNETT*)
Estrella ('*wordless pl.*': Guildhall School of Music, 18/12/08)

BARRETT, ALFRED WILSON
[For earlier plays see *H. E. D.* v, 250–1]
Quo Vadis? (Lyc., Edin., 29/5/00; P'cess of W., Kennington, 18/6/00: dramatised from the novel by H. Sienkiewicz)
The Never-Never Land (Vic., Broughton, 9/4/02, *cpy.*; Gr., Hull, 1/2/04; K's, Hamm., 21/3/04)
The Christian King; or, Alfred of Engleland (P's, Bristol, 6/11/02; Adel., 18/12/02; originally called *The King*)
In the Middle of June (Middlesbrough, 11/6/03)
Lucky Durham (Shak., L'pool, 9/6/04; K's, Hamm., 28/8/05)
×The Last Moment (Hippo., Crouch End, 18/4/10)
The Jew of Prague (Colchester, 29/4/12; Whitney, 8/5/12)

BARRETT, DOROTHEA WILSON
×Heber Sayell (P's, Bristol, 24/5/07)

BARRETT, EDWARD F.
The Grabber (Abbey, Dublin, 12/11/18)

BARRETT, JOHN
Why Women Weep (P.H., Haslingden, 30/7/10; Leigh, 1/8/10, as *Brothers*)

BARRETTI, JOSEPHINE
×All Fools' Day (m. C. Carey: Glastonbury, 25/8/21)

BARRIE, Sir JAMES MATTHEW
[For earlier plays see *H. E. D.* v, 251]
The Wedding Guest ('*c.*': Gar., 27/9/00) *1900* (*priv.*); *1900* (in literary supplement of *Fortnightly Review*, Dec. 1900)
Quality Street ('*c.*': Vaud., 17/9/02) *1913*

The Admirable Crichton (D.Y., 4/11/02) *1914* (*priv.*); *1918*
Little Mary ('*uncomfortable pl.*': Wynd., 24/9/03) *1942*
Peter Pan; or, The Boy who wouldn't grow up (D.Y., 27/12/04; D.Y., 26/12/10, *revised*) *1928*
×Pantaloon (D.Y., 5/4/05) *1914* (in *Half Hours*)
Alice Sit-by-the-Fire: A Page from a Daughter's Diary (D.Y., 5/4/05: originally called *The Chaperones*) *1928*
Josephine ('*revue*': Com., 6/4/06)
×Punch ('*toy tragedy*': Com., 6/4/06)
What Every Woman Knows ('*c.*': D.Y., 3/9/08) *1918*
×The Twelve-Pound Look (D.Y., 1/3/10: originally called *Success*) *1914* (in *Half Hours*); *1928*
×Old Friends (D.Y., 1/3/10: originally called *Voices*) *1928*
×A Slice of Life (D.Y., 7/6/10, *m.*)
×Rosalind ('*c.*': D.Y., 14/10/12) *1914* (in *Half Hours*)
×The Dramatists Get What They Want (Hippo., 23/12/12)
The Adored One (D.Y., 4/9/13; D.Y., 28/9/13, *revised*: in the U.S.A. called *The Legend of Leonora*) *1913*
×The Will (D.Y., 4/9/13) *1914* (in *Half Hours*)
×Half an Hour (Hippo., 29/9/13) *1942*
×Der Tag (Col., 21/12/14) *1914*
×The New Word (D.Y., 22/3/15) *1918* (in *Echoes of the War*)
Rosy Rapture, the Pride of the Beauty Chorus (*bsq.*', m. H. Darewski and J. D. Kern: D.Y., 22/3/15)
×The Fatal Typist (H.M., 19/11/15, *m.*)
×The Real Thing at Last ('*surprise*': Col., 7/3/16, *m.*)
A Kiss for Cinderella (Wynd., 16/3/16) *1920*
×Shakespeare's Legacy (D.L., 14/4/16, *m.*) *1916* (*priv.*)
Irene Vanbrugh's Pantomime (Col., 9/6/16, *m.*)
×Reconstructing the Crime (Pal., 16/2/17, *m.*: originally called *A Strange Play*)
×Seven Women ('*c.*': New, 7/4/17: revised first act of *The Adored One*)
×The Old Lady Shows Her Medals (New, 7/4/17) *1918* (in *Echoes of the War*)
Dear Brutus (Wynd., 17/10/17) [*1923*]
×La Politesse ('*international affair*': Wynd., 28/6/18, *m.*)
×A Well-Remembered Voice (Wynd., 28/6/18, *m.*) *1918* (in *Echoes of the War*)
Barbara's Wedding (Sav., 23/8/27) *1918* (in *Echoes of the War*)
×The Truth about the Russian Dancers (Col., 15/3/20)
Mary Rose (H., 22/4/20) *1924*
×Shall We Join the Ladies? (RADA, 27/5/21; Pal., 19/12/21, *m.*; St M., 8/3/22) *1927*
Neil and Tinntinabulum ('*interlude for parents*') *1925* (*priv.*)

BARRIE, RIDGEWOOD [see also *M. DUCKWORTH*]
A She-Devil (Ath., Lancaster, 25/11/02; Carlton, Greenwich, 19/3/06; as *The Queen of Villainy*)
[A few playlets produced at music-halls]

BARRINGTON, E. F.

×Larkin v. Fitzhugh. *Fr. 1920*

The Dæmon in the House (Abbey, Dublin, 19/2/20)

BARRINGTON, RUTLAND

[For earlier plays see *H. E. D.* v, 251]

Water Babies ('*m. fairy pl.*', m. F. Rosse: Gar., 18/12/02)

×Mummydom ('*fancy*': Gt. Qn. St., 25/9/03: +*W. BENDALL*)

Little Black Sambo and Little White Barbara ('*m.pl.*', m. W. Bendall and F. Rosse: Gar., 21/12/04)

×No. 442: His Escape ('*o.*', m. H. M. Higgs: Cor., 15/7/07)

×The Vixen. LC, W.G., New Brighton, 23/1/14

×An Old Actor, LC, Sav., 21/1/21

BARRINGTON, SIDNEY

×Dinna Forget (Burslem, 19/2/01)

[*BARRON, ELWYN A.*

A Prince of the People (Emp., Oldham, 4/6/06)

BARRON, NETTERVILLE

The Three Brothers ('*mystery pl. of the medieval age*': O.H., Blackpool, 22/4/18, *amat.*)

BARROW, SIR FRANCIS

The Island of Tobe-Hang ('*m.ext.*', m. C. Hawley: Gr., Boscombe, 20/10/02)

BARROW, PERCY J. [see also *L. BANTOCK*]

Sadie of Brantome ('*c.o.*', m. P. de Loetz: Pal., Porth, 19/3/07, *cpy.*)

A Daughter of England (Gar., 8/1/15: +*J. G. LEVY*)

×The Grip (Gar., 2/8/15: adapted from *La griffe* (1903) by J. Sartène)

×The Battle of Cressy. *Fr. 1927*

[Several sketches and playlets produced at music-halls]

BARRS, HERBERT

[For earlier plays see *H. E. D.* v, 252]

Life (Swansea, 1894; Stratford, 22/7/01, *revised*)

Repentance (Gr., Leek, 27/10/11; Woolwich, 3/6/12)

BARRY, JOSEPH L.

[For earlier plays see *H. E. D.* v, 252]

×Heads and Tails ('*c.*': St Andrew's Hospital, Northampton, 20/4/00)

Sparkling Eyes. LC, '*m.pl.*': Alex., B'ham, 28/7/20: +*G. PEMBURY*

BARRY, PAUL [see *L. SCUDAMORE*]

[*BARRY, PHILIP*

You and I ('*c.*': Little, 30/12/24) *1925*

Paris Bound ('*c.*': Lyr., 30/4/29) *1929*

BARRY, W.

×The Crooked Way. LC, Woolwich, 12/5/19: title changed later to *The Man From Nowhere*

BARRY-LEWERS, PAUL

[A few playlets produced at music-halls]

BARSTOW, MONTAGU [see *Baroness ORCZY*]

[*BART, JEAN*

The Squall (48th Street, N.Y., 11/11/26; Glo., 15/11/27) *Fr. 1928*

BARTHOLEYNS, A. O'D.

[For earlier plays see *H. E. D.* v, 252, 778]

Swift and Vanessa (Roy., 11/1/04)

Francesca da Rimini ('*t.*': translated from Silvio Pellico's play, 1815) *1915*

[*BARTHOLOMÆ, PHILLIP H.*

Very Good Eddie ('*m.c.*', m. J. D. Kern: Van Curler, Schenectady, 9/11/15; P'cess, N.Y., 23/12/15; Pal., 18/5/18: +*G. BOLTON*)

BARTLE, ARTHUR

× Grandfather ('*c.*': Gai., Manchester, 28/8/16; Court, 23/12/16, *m.*)

BARTLETT, HULBERT

× 'Awkins's Ordeal (Cor., 23/10/11)

All Nonsense ('*m.c.bsq.*': Sur., 13/12/15)

'*BARTON, JAMES*' [=*G. M. COOKSON*]

Denys of Auxerre. *1912*

BARTSCH, HANS [see *G. I. COLBRON*]

BARUCH, E. DE MARNAY

Judith of Israel (Str., 15/2/28)

BARWELL, H. A. [see *C. W. DOCKWRAY*]

BASEL, –

× My Little Maid, since Grown Tall (Tolmer's Inst., Hampstead Road, 16/3/05)

BASEY, GRACE

The Unnamed Play (Lyr., Hamm., 27/4/13: also called *The Play without a Title*)

BASKCOMB, A. W.

× A Cup of Tea (Theatrical Gdn Party, Chelsea, 26/6/23)

BASS, BRODIE

× A Pantomime Dame (W.G., New Brighton, 10/4/11)

× Youth and a Theory (Clavier H., 10/3/12, Arts and Dram. Club)

BATEMAN, Miss [*Mrs CROWE*]

× Sister Helen (Cosmopolis, 27/1/13)

BATEMAN, FRANK

[For earlier plays see *H. E. D.* v, 253]

Sentenced for Life (Qns, B'ham, 17/12/00, *cpy.*; Carlton, Greenwich, 11/2/01; Stand., 24/8/03: +*C. WATSON-MILL*)

At War with Women (Metro., Manchester, 28/7/02; Stratford, 1/6/03)

Sailors of the King (K's, Cardiff, 7/8/05; Terriss, 21/8/05)

No Wedding Bells for Her (K's, Cardiff, 26/12/05: +*J. T. DOUGLASS*)

BATEMAN, JAMES

The Welsh Maid ('*m.pl.*', m. H. Richardson: LC, Ass. R., Balham, 5/7/09: P's, Horwich, 28/3/10)

BATER, Mrs CATHERINE

The Mystery of Desborough (Muncaster, Bootle, 22/1/00)

BATES, FLORENCE

× Her Wedding Night ('*c.*': Col., 9/7/17)
× Retrospective (Lyc. Club, 12/10/24)
Uncle Hiram's Here ('*f.c.*': Q, 12/10/25: +*E. CARTER*)

BATES, HERBERT ERNEST

× The Last Bread. *1926* (Labour Publishing Co.)

BATES, JOSHUA [see also *Mrs HAVELOCK ELLIS*]

× The Decree Nisi (St J., 18/10/04)

BATH, HUBERT

× L'amour et la mort. LC, W.G., 12/5/21: +*A. APPLIN*
× Bubbles ('*r.o.*', musical version of Lady Gregory's *Spreading the News*: O.H., Belfast, 26/11/23; Scala, 11/6/24)

BATH, OLIVER

Naughty Nancy ('*m.c.*', m. R. E. Lyon and W. Davidson: Emp., Southend, 31/3/02; Sav., 8/9/02)

BATHURST, EDITH M. [see *A. H. LINFORD*]

BATLEY, J. ARTHUR

The Gods and Delia. LC, O.H., Harrogate, 24/10/21: +*F. C. BRUNTON*

BATT, HAROLD

× Rights and Wrongs (R.A., Woolwich, 22/3/15)
× A Helping Hand. LC, Pav., Llandrindod Wells, 20/6/16
× The Wrong Man. LC, Pav., Llandrindod Wells, 20/6/16
Orange Blossoms. LC, Pal., Sevenoaks, 23/4/17; title later changed to *Squeaks* and *Keeping Him Busy*

BATTEN, W. S.

Hoppit. LC, '*m.pl.*', Emp., Middlesbrough, 15/1/23

BATTERSBY, HENRY FRANCIS [='*F. PREVOST*']

× The Way of War (Wynd., 8/12/02)
× The Voice of Duty (Com., 23/6/08, *m.*; Col., 24/6/18)

BAUGH, FREDERIC [see *F. MOULE*]

BAUM, LOUISE

× Our Lady's Juggler (translated from *Le Jongleur de Nôtre Dame* (1904) by Maurice Léna) *1911*

BAUM, LYAM FRANK

The Tik Tok Man of Oz. LC, '*m.c.*': Lyr., 30/4/13

BAWTREE, ARTHUR [see *F. LLEWELLYN*]

BAX, CLIFFORD [see also *NIGEL PLAYFAIR* and *H. F. RUBINSTEIN*]

× The Poetasters of Ispahan ('*c.*': Little, 28/4/12, Adel. Pl. Soc.) *1921* (see *Antique Pageantry*, below)
× The Marriage of the Soul (Little, 3/7/13)

×The Sneezing Charm ('*fant.*': Court, 9/6/18, Plough Soc.)
×Square Pegs (Farthingstone, 19/6/19; Edwardes Square, Kensington, 9/1/20, *amat.*; A.L.S. Trav. Th., 1921) *1920*
Antique Pageantry. *1921*
[This includes four short plays: 1. *The Poetasters of Ispahan* (see above); 2. *The Apricot Tree* (Deansgate, Manchester, 23/10/22, Unnamed Society); 3. *The Summit*; and 4. *Aucassin and Nicolette*]
Old King Cole ('*pl. for children*') *1921*
Polite Satires. *1922*
[This includes three short plays: 1. *The Unknown Hand* (A.L.S. Trav. Th., 1926); 2. *The Volcanic Island*; and 3. *Square Pegs* (see above)]
Four Comedies by Goldoni. *1922*
[This collection, edited by Bax, includes two plays translated by him: 1. *Mine Hostess* (Rep., B'ham, 25/10/24, from *La Locandiera*, 1753) and 2. *The Impresario from Smyrna* (from *L'Impresario delle Smirne*, 1759; as well as 3. *The Good Girl* (translated by Marguerite Tracy from *La Figlia obbediente*, 1752) and 4. *The Fan* translated by Eleanor and Herbert Farjeon from *Il Ventaglio*, 1765)]
Up-stream (D.Y., 20/12/25, Rep. Players) *1922*
Polly ('*ballad o.*', adapted from J. Gay's opera, m. F. Austin: Kings., 30/12/22) *1923*
Midsummer Madness ('*m.c.*', m. Armstrong Gibbs: Lyr., Hamm., 3/7/24) *1923*
×Nocturne in Palermo. *1924*
Studio Plays. *1924*
[This includes three short plays: 1. *Prelude and Fugue* (Etlinger School, 7/12/27); *The Rose and the Cross*; and 3. *The Cloak* (A.L.S. Trav. Th., 1923)]
Mr Pepys ('*ballad o.*', m. M. Shaw: Everyman, 11/2/26; Roy., 9/3/26) *1926*
Rasputin (Str., 21/4/29, St. Soc.: adapted from the Russian of A. N. Tolstoi and P. E. Shchegolev)
Socrates (P.W., 23/3/30, St. Soc. and 300 Club) *1930*
Twelve Short Plays. *1932*
[This includes twelve pieces, dated as indicated: 1. *Prelude and Fugue* (1923); 2. *The Summit* (1912, revised 1920); 3. *The Cloak* (1921); 4. *The Rose and the Cross* (1918); 5. *Aucassin and Nicolette* (1914); 6. *The Tale of the Wandering Scholar* (1928); 7. *The Unknown Hand* (1922); 8. *The Volcanic Island* (1921); 9. *Square Pegs* (1920); 10. *The Apricot Tree* (1913); 11. *Silly Willy* (1917); and 12. *The Poetasters of Ispahan* (1912)]

BAXTER, CATLYN
Out of the Darkness ('*r.d.*': Lyc., Stafford, 3/6/05)

BAXTER, JOHN DOWLING
The Witch of Pendle ('*Tudor pl.*': P's, Blackburn, 21/5/09, *cpy.*) *1909*

BAY, WATSON K.
The King's Signet ('*r.pl.*': Gr., Fulham, 17/9/06)

Naughty Nights ('*f.*': Pal., Bradford, 6/12/26)
Husbands Don't Care ('*f.*': O.H., Cheltenham, 13/5/29)

BAYLY, ADA ELLEN [='*EDNA LYALL*']

BAYNES, EUSTACE [see *T. E. MURRAY* and *A. MILLER*]

BAYNES, SIDNEY
× Snatches. LC, Court, 1/5/14

BEAHM, JAY
× Crusoe. LC, Wimbledon, 12/12/13

BEAL, STEUART
× The Dance of Love (Canterbury, 23/6/09)

BEALE, ERICA KATHLEEN
× Princess Suri-Sama ('*fantasia*': Shaft., 19/4/18, *m.*)
[A few sketches produced at music-halls]

BEAMISH, N. DE VIC [see *NORMAN MACDERMOTT*]

BEAN, C.
Blackmail (E.C., 11/2/18: title changed later to *The Voice on the 'Phone*)

BEATTY, CHARLES
× Our Fortune (County, Kingston, 5/6/11)
× The Call of Duty (Pier, Portsmouth, 2/10/11)
× The Question Is? (Pav., 21/1/10)

BEATTY, H. M.
Master Flachsmann (translated from *Flachsmann als Erzieher* (1900) by Otto Ernst) *1909*

BEAUCHAMP, EMILY
[For earlier plays see *H. E. D.* v, 254]
Whips that Scourge (Duchess, Balham, 9/10/00, *cpy.*)

BEAULIEU, C. S. [see *C. S. WATSON*]

BEAUMONT, A. [see *A. LE WARNE*]

BEAUMONT, ALEXANDER S. [see *St J. HAMUND*]

BEAUMONT, MADGE
Sunset Land. LC, Midland Inst., B'ham, 19/4/16

BEAUMONT, WALTER
[For earlier plays see *H. E. D.* v, 254]
A Life for a Life (Gr., Islington, 8/6/03; revised version of his earlier play, 1899): +*S. BARING*)

BEAUMONT, WILLIAM
This Woman (Q, 21/3/27)

BECKDORF, Baroness
× Tomorrow's Dawn (H., 14/11/11, *m.*)

BECKETT, ALFRED
A Face from the Past ('*m.d.*': Emp., Oswestry, 20/5/18: title changed later to *The Girl who Married a German*: +*K. MAYNE*)

BECKETT, ARTHUR

Dacre of the South ('*light o.*', m. J. R. Dear: D.P., Eastbourne, 19/5/26, *amat.*) *1928* (Eastbourne)

BECKETT, DAN

×A Debt Repaid (Rehearsal, 27/11/10)
×The Thief Maker (Rehearsal, 27/11/10)
×Scrooge's Dream (Inns of Court Inst., 1/4/14)

BECKETT, DIANA

The People of Pillarney (St Mary's Schools, Alsager, 8/1/25, *amat.*)

BEDDOW, Rev. SEAWARD

The Challenge. LC, Wycliffe Church, Leicester, 10/11/20. *1920* (*priv.*)
×The Proconsul. *1921* (*priv.*)

BEDFORD, EDWARD H.

×Life for Life (Old Music-hall, Sheffield, 17/5/09)
×How He Did It (Ass. R., Sheffield, 6/7/12)
×My Little Girl (Sheffield Garrick Dr. Club, 12/10/12)

BEDFORD, HENRY LEWIS [see also *A. SHIRLEY*]

[For an earlier play see *H. E. D.* v, 255]
Mafeking: A Romance of the Siege (Carlton, Greenwich, 9/6/02)
[Several sketches and playlets produced at music-halls]

BEEBY, ROBERT

×A Modern Judas (Tiv., Manchester, 15/3/12)

BEECH, EWART

×Fizzical Culture (Surrey Masonic H., 3/1/08, *amat.*)

BEEK, PERCY [see also *N. VEITCH*]

Stalls for Two (People's, Newcastle, 1914: +*N. VEITCH*)
Eunice ('*o.*': People's, Newcastle, 4/28: +*N. VEITCH*)

BEERBOHM, MAX

×The Happy Hypocrite (Roy., 11/12/00)
[A dramatisation of his 'fairy tale for tired men', published in 1897]
The Fly on the Wheel ('*c.*': Cor., 4/12/02: +*S. M. CARSON*)
×A Social Success (Pal., 27/1/13)

BEGBIE, NORAH

Dainty Dresden ('*c.o.*': Vic. H., 20/12/06, *cpy.*: +*P. KNIGHT*)

BEHN, SUSAN

Rampa (Gate, 31/10/28: from a play by Max Mohr: +*C. A. LEWIS*)
Caravan ('*fant.*': Arts, 21/11/28: from a play by Max Mohr: +*C. A. LEWIS*)

BEHR, Rev. G. M.

×Giant Fear. LC, Co-operative H., Colchester, 24/2/14

[*BEHRMAN, SAMUEL NATHANIEL*

The Second Man ('*c.*': Theatre Guild, N.Y., 11/4/27; Playh., 24/1/28) *1927*

BEITH, JOHN HAY [=*'IAN HAY'*]

[*BELASCO, DAVID*

[For earlier plays see *H. E. D.* v, 255]

Zaza (*'m.pl.'*, m. R. Leoncavallo: Lafayette O.H., Washington, 25/12/1898; Gar., 16/4/00)

Madame Butterfly (Herald Square, N.Y., 1900; D.Y., 28/4/00)

Du Barry (Republic, N.Y., 1901; E.C., 4/12/01, *cpy.*) *1928* (Boston)

The Darling of the Gods (N.Y., 1902; E.C., 7/11/02, *cpy.*; H.M., 28/12/03: +*J. L. LONG*) *1928* (Boston)

Adrea (N.Y., 1904: LC, E.C., 14/2/05: +*J. L. LONG*) *1928* (Boston)

The Girl of the Golden West (Pittsburgh, 1905; E.C., 29/9/05, *cpy.*) *1928* (Boston)

A Grand Army Man (Stuyvesant, N.Y., 1906; E.C., 18/9/07, *cpy.*)

Sweet Kitty Bellairs (*'c.'*: H., 5/10/07: dramatised from the novel, *The Bath Comedy* (1900), by Agnes and Egerton Castle)

The Lily (*'modern pl.'*: Stuyvesant, N.Y., 23/12/09; Dalston, 3/12/09, *cpy.*; Kings., 23/2/11: adapted from P. Wolff and G. Leroux, *Le Lys*, 1908)

The Return of Peter Grimm (Holles, Boston, 2/1/11; Belasco, N.Y., 18/10/11: LC, Dalston, 30/12/10)

Timothy (Shaft., 1/10/21: +*W. J. HURLBUT*)

BELL, ARNOLD [see *I. P. GORE* and *R. REDGRAVE*]

BELL, ARTHUR B.

[A few sketches produced at music-halls]

BELL, F. R.

1588. LC, *'c.o.'*: Lecture H., Hull, 25/3/13

Highwayman Love. LC, *'m.pl.'*: Royal Institution, Hull, 4/1/21

Dogs of Devon (*'c.o.'*: Surrey Masonic H., 17/1/28, *amat.*: +*H. ELLIS*)

BELL, Lady, FLORENCE EVELEEN ELEANORE [=*Mrs HUGH BELL*; see also *HARRIE BELL*]

The Dean of St Patrick's. *1903*

×Rumpelstiltzkin (*'fairy pl.'*: Adel., 18/5/03: +*A. CECIL*) *1893* (in *Fairy Tale Plays*)

The Way the Money Goes (Shaft., 13/2/10, *m.*, St. Soc.; Roy., 7/3/10: +*A. CECIL*) *1910*

×Farmer Bates and His Wife. *1917*

The Mother Hubbard Book of Playlets. *1920*

[This contains twelve short pieces for young children]

The Show Room (*'c.'*: Emp., Holb., 19/4/20: called originally *Thornaby's*)

Four Short Plays. *1922*

[This contains: 1. *The Story of Rachel*; 2. *Kirstin*; 3. *The Parachute*; and 4. *A Second-class Duke*]

The Scandal (New, 19/9/22: adapted from *Le Scandale* (1909) by H. Bataille)

The Cat and the Fiddle Book. *1922*
[This contains eight nursery plays]
The Heart of Yorkshire. *1923*
×Fog on the Moor (Art, Leeds, 9/2/25)
Angela (P's, 14/3/27, *m.*) *1926*

BELL, G. S.
×A Flash in the Pan. LC, Church Inst., Lincoln, 10/11/25

BELL, H. R. [see *J. J. BELL*]

BELL, HARRIE
×Miss Flipper's Holiday. *Fr. 1918* (+*F. BELL*)

BELL, Mrs HUGH [see *Lady FLORENCE BELL*]

BELL, J. H., Jr [see *W. ADRIPOLE*]

BELL, JAMES [see also *B. ELLIS*]
A Silent Accuser (Crown, Peckham, 24/7/05)

BELL, JOHN KEBLE [='*KEBLE HOWARD*']

BELL, JOHN JOY
Oh! Christina! ('*c.*': Roy., Glasgow, 6/6/10; Playh., 28/11/11, *m.*, as *Christina*: +*L. THERVAL*) *1909*
×The Best Man (Roy., Glasgow, 18/4/11)
Providing for Marjorie ('*c.*': Roy., Glasgow, 9/10/11)
Wee Macgreegor ('*c.*': Roy., Glasgow, 19/12/11: +*H. R. BELL*)
×The Pie in the Oven (Bury, 10/11/13; Vic. Pal., 25/10/15) *1922*
×Christina's Recruits (Alh., Glasgow, 6/1/15) *1915* (as *Wee Macgreegor Enlists*)
×Wee Macgreegor's Party. *1922*
×Thread o' Scarlet. LC, Pembury, 26/5/25. *1923*
×Courtin' Christina. *1924*
×Wolves (Guildhall School of Music, 19/5/25, Pivot Club) *1925*
×Exit Mrs McLeerie ('*f.c.*') *1926*
×Those Class Distinctions. *1926*
×The Laird's Lucky Number ('*f.*') *1926*
×The Breaking Point. *1930* (in *The Scots Magazine*, xii, 257–64)
×Good Morning, Sir John! *1930*
×A Relapse in 'Consols' ('*f.c.*') *1930*

BELL, MAURICE FREDERICK
Goblin Market. *1923* (Village D. Soc.)

BELL, MAY
What of the Night? and other sketches. *1919*
[This contains, besides the title-piece, five one-act plays: 1. *Britannia Goes to War*; 2. *The Culprit*; 3. *Bluebeard*; 4. *The Strange Physician*; and 5. *Marah*]

BELL, ROBERT STANLY WARREN
[For an earlier play see *H. E. D.* v, 256]
Company for George ('*f.c.*': Kings., 15/10/10) *Fr. 1911*

BELL, STANLEY
There's No Fool (P's, Bristol, 26/4/26; Glo., 29/6/26: adapted from *Les ailes brisées* (1920) by L. Marchand and P. Wolff)
×Our Dogs (Glo., 1/6/26: adapted from a play by A. Savoir) *Fr. 1927*

BELL, VERNON
×Accidents Will 'Appen (Sav., 16/5/14)

BELLAMY, ERNEST
×Wooing by Wire (Brixton, 24/10/04)

BELLAMY, GEORGE E. [see also *B. LANDECK*]
[Several sketches and playlets, mostly written in collaboration, produced at music-halls]

BELLAMY, R. L.
×The Rival Detectives. LC, K. G's H., 12/1/24

BELLINGER, LANCELOT
×The Last Drop. LC, Crippl. Inst., 1/11/22: +*G. MOYSTON*. *Fr. 1921*

BELLINGHAM, G. E. H.
×The Choice (O.H., Dudley, 29/4/01)

BELLINI, GABRIEL
×The Triumph of Remorse. *1916* (*priv.*)

BELLOC, HILAIRE
×The Candour of Maturity (Steinway H., 18/3/12, Molière Soc.)

BELLOC-LOWNDES, Mrs MARIE
The Lonely House (Pir, Eastbourne, 8/9/24: dramatised from her novel (1920): +*C. RANDOLPH*)

BELLOWS, WALTER CHARLES
The Little Christians (E.C., 11/3/03, *cpy.*)

BELTON, A.
[A few sketches produced at music-halls]

BENDALL, W. [see *R. BARRINGTON*]

BENEDICT, SARAH [see also *J. L. SPARKES*]
The Fourth Knave (Bristol, 1/5/22: +*J. L. SPARKES*)

BENGE, WILSON [see also *F. BULMER*]
The Cowboy's Revenge ('*Wild West pl.*': Swansea, 10/3/13; Woolwich, 28/4/13: +*A. RITA*)

BENNETT, (ENOCH) ARNOLD
Polite Farces for the Drawing Room. *1900*
[This contains: 1. *The Stepmother;* 2. *A Good Woman*; and 3. *A Question of Sex*)
Cupid and Commonsense (Shaft., 24/1/08, St. Soc.; Shaft., 26/1/08) *1909*
What the Public Wants ('*c.*': Aldw., 2/5/09, St. Soc.; Roy., 27/5/09) *1909* (*English Review Special Supplement*, July 1909); *1910*

The Great Adventure ('*c.*': Roy., Glasgow, 18/9/11; Portsmouth, 15/7/12; Kings., 25/3/13: from his novel, *Buried Alive*, 1908) *1913*
The Honeymoon ('*c.*': Roy., 6/10/11) *1911*
Milestones (Roy., 5/3/12: +*E. KNOBLOCK*) *1912*
× Rivals for Rosamund (Pal., 16/2/14)
The Title ('*c.*': Roy., 20/7/18) *1918*
Judith (D.P., Eastbourne, 7/4/19; Kings., 30/4/19) *1919*
Sacred and Profane Love (Playh., L'pool, 15/9/19; Aldw., 10/11/19: from his own novel, 1905) *1919*
The Love Match (Pleasure Gdns, Folkestone, 30/1/22; Str., 21/3/22) *1922*
Body and Soul (Playh., L'pool, 15/2/22; Reg., 11/9/22) *1922*
Don Juan de Marana. *1923* (*priv.*)
London Life (D.L., 3/6/24: +*E. KNOBLOCK*) *1924*
The Bright Island (Aldw., 15/2/25, St. Soc.) *1924* (*priv.*); *1926*
× Flora (Rusholme Rep., Manchester, 17/10/27) *1933* (in *Five One-Act Plays*)
Mr. Prohack ('*c.*': Court, 16/11/27: +*E. KNOBLOCK*) *1927*
The Return Journey (St J., 1/9/28) *1928*
× Judith ('*o.*') *1929*

BENNETT, CHARLES
The Return (Everyman, 30/5/27) *1928*
Blackmail (Glo., 28/2/28) *1928*
× After Midnight (Steiner H., 23/6/28)
Midnight (Nottingham, 10/12/28; Com., 20/12/28, as *The Last Hour*) *1928*

BENNETT, F. WILSON [see *J. BRANDON-THOMAS*]

BENNETT, GRAHAM
The Heir of Wenley ('*c.o.*', m. A. Heath: King's Lynn, 1/11/26, *amat.*)

BENNETT, HANNAFORD [see also *M. HENRY*]
The Mystery of the Yellow Room (D.P., Eastbourne, 26/1/20; St J., 26/5/20: adapted from G. Leroux, *Le Mystère de la chambre jaune*)

BENNETT, HARRY DARE
× The Bogey Man. LC, P.H., Streatham, 18/11/13
Beauty and the Beast (Gai., Douglas, 27/9/20)

BENNETT, H. LEIGH
× A Twin Episode. LC, Stanley H., Norwood, 7/10/14

BENNETT, Mrs HERBERT [see *Mrs W. LATHROP*]

BENNETT, J. B. STERNDALE
Minerva's Husband ('*c.*': Rehearsal, 18/2/12, Playfellows)
The Gift Horse (Everyman, 6/11/26)

BENNETT, P. R.
× Mary Edwards ('*anachronism*': Gai., Manchester, 8/5/11, Actresses Franchise League; Aldw., 17/6/12) *1913*

BENNETT, R. D.

×The Scarlet Woman. LC, Temperance H., Sheffield, 25/1/15

A Night in Nursery Land. *1929*

BENNETT, WILSON

×Fragments from France (Pier, Herne Bay, 4/11/18; Dalston, 9/12/18)

[*BENRIMO, J. H.* [see *G. HAZELTON*]

BENSELL, ALARD

The Lady of Haigh; or, A Wife's Penance (Court, Wigan, 1/5/07, *cpy.*; Court, Wigan, 22/7/07)

BENSON, EDWARD FREDERIC

Dodo: A Detail of Yesterday ('*c.*': Scala, 26/11/05, St. Soc.)

×The Friend in the Garden (Sav., 7/3/06)

×Dinner for Eight (Ambass., 23/3/15)

The Luck of the Vails (D.P., Eastbourne, 13/2/28; Hippo., Lewisham, 12/3/28: dramatised from his own novel, 1901)

BENSON, Mrs F. R.

×A Midnight Bridal (LC, Mem., Stratford-upon-Avon, 25/4/05; Cor., 19/2/09: +*Mrs H. NICHOLSON*)

BENSON, HARRY

The Light (Crown, Eccles, 7/6/26)

BENSON, Rev. ROBERT HUGH

The Cost of a Crown ('*A Story of Douai and Durham: A Sacred Drama*') *1910*

The Maid of Orleans (Westminster Cathedral H., 2/1/11, *amat.*) *1910*

The Upper Room. LC, '*d. of Christ's Passion*': Philbeach H., Earls Court, 8/3/21. *1914*

A Mystery Play in Honour of the Nativity of our Lord. LC, Westminster Cathedral H., 9/1/22. *1908*

BENSON, WILFRED H. [see also *J. T. DOUGLASS*]

The Power of Woman (Macclesfield, 7/10/01: +*L. FOSTER*)

The Devil's Own Luck; or The Prince of Rogues (Edmonton, 11/11/01: +*J. T. DOUGLASS*)

Good Women and Bad ('*md.*': Dover, 6/6/04)

×The Halt (Qns, Poplar, 16/11/08)

×The Steam Hammer (S.W., 15/3/09)

The Man who Kept Silent ('*mystery pl.*': Spa, Bridlington, 8/7/29)

[Several sketches and plays produced at music-halls]

BENSUSAN, INEZ

×The Apple ('*episode of today*': Court, 14/3/09, Pl. Actors; The Laurels, Putney, 14/7/11) *1911*

×Nobody's Sweetheart (Little, 29/5/11, Oncomers)

×The Prodigal Passes (Cosmopolis, 20/3/14)

BENTHAM, J. A.

[A few playlets produced at music-halls]

BENTLEY, FREDERICK

My Hat! ('*f.c.*': Canterbury, 16/7/17)

[Several sketches and playlets produced at music-halls]

BENTLEY, H. HODGSON [=*H. HODGSON-BENTLEY*]

BENTON, FRED [see also *G. COMER*]

[For earlier plays see *H. E. D.* v, 258]

A Life's Story (Gr., Nottingham, 12/6/02; Stratford, 9/2/03)

BENTZ, FRANK [see *J. M. LEWIS* and *A. C. TRAVIS*]

BENWELL, ARCHIBALD H.

The Magic Bell ('*fairy fant.*': Ldn O.H., 26/12/12)

BERESFORD, J. DUDLEY [see also *A. S. CRAVEN*]

The Love that Conquers (Bij., 23/11/08, *cpy.*)

The Veiled Woman. LC, Court, 24/10/13

[A few sketches produced at music-halls]

[*BERESFORD, R. S.*

[Several playlets produced at music-halls]

BERESFORD-INGLIS, W.

The Hawaiian Maid ('*c.o.*', m. P. J. Mansfield: Glasgow, 11/10/20)

[*BERGERE, OUIDA*

Suburbia Comes to Paradise (Everyman, 11/6/29: +*G. FERGUSSON*)

BERINGER, Mrs OSCAR (AIMÉE)

[For earlier plays see *H. E. D.* v, 259]

Jim Belmont (Metro., Camberwell, 1/10/00)

×Holly Tree Inn. *Fr. 1905*

×A Bit of Old Chelsea. *Fr. 1905*

×The Agitator (Hicks', 9/12/07)

BERINGER, VERA [see also '*HENRY SETON*']

×Noblesse Oblige. *Fr. 1921*

×The Perfect Pair. *Fr. 1924*

×South-East and South-West. *Fr. 1925*

The Blue Stockings (+*MESLEY DOWN*) *Fr. 1927*

BERKELEY, REGINALD CHEYNE

French Leave ('*light c.*': D.P., Eastbourne, 7/6/20; Glo., 15/7/20) *Fr. 1921*

The World's End and Other Plays. *1926*

[This contains: 1. *The World's End* (Aldw., 8/11/25, Rep. Players; Everyman, 9/5/28); 2. *Eight O'Clock* (Little, 15/12/20); 3. *Mango Island* (P's, 14/6/25, Rep. Players); and 4. *The Quest of Elizabeth* (Playh., 1/3/26)]

Mr Abdullah (Gai., Hastings, 25/1/26; Playh., 10/2/26)

×The Dweller in the Darkness ('*pl. of the unknown*': Blfrs, 25/2/26, Fleetway Players) *1931*

The White Chateau (B.B.C. broadcast, Armistice night 1925; Everyman, 29/3/27; St M., 28/4/27) *1925*

Machines ('*symphony of modern life*') *1927*

×Listeners (Wynd., 9/2/28)
×The Passionate Prince ('*r.m.d.*': Playh., Broadstairs, 13/8/28)
The Lady with a Lamp (Arts, 5/1/29; Gar., 24/1/29: originally called *Florence Nightingale*) *1929*
×The Prince Consort ('*study for a larger frame*': Arts, 24/2/29)
Miss Adventure ('*c.*': D.P., Eastbourne, 2/9/29; Golder's Green, 30/9/29; W.G., 12/10/29: adapted from F. Ganders, *Il manquait un homme*)

BERMAN, L. E. [see *G. GROSSMITH, Jr*]

BERMAN, L. F. [see *F. D. GRIERSON*]

BERNARD, CLARA
×A Dear Old Soul (Granville, 9/8/15)
×Bill's Luck. LC, O.H., Tunbridge Wells, 21/11/16

BERNARD, GEORGE
The Idol of the Studios (Darlington, 10/1/16; Brixton, 21/2/16)

BERNARD, HUGH
The Dawn of Happiness (Dalston, 26/6/16; Alex., Wisbech, 20/1/21, *revised*; Stratford, 23/5/21: dramatised from Ralph Rodd's novel, *Peril*)

BERNARD, JACK [see *TOM GRAY*]

[*BERNSTEIN, HERMAN* [see also *B. MERIVALE*]
Katerina (Barnes, 30/3/26: translated from *Ekaterina Ivanovna* (1912) by L. N. Andreev)
The Chief Thing. LC, ADC, Cambridge, 19/11/27: translated from *Samoe glavnoe* (1919) by N. Evreinov)

BERRELL, BERNARD
[A few playlets produced at music-halls]

BERRISFORD, ALBERT GEORGE
The One Eternal Thing (E. Ldn College. 3/26, *amat.*) *1927* (Oxford)

BERRY, Rev. ROBERT GRIFFITH
×A Frosty Night. LC, H., 8/2/16
×Noson o Farrug (H., 29/2/16, *m.*, Ldn Welsh St. Soc.) *1916* (Cardiff)
×Asgre Lân. *1916* (Cardiff)
×Y Ddraenan Wen. *1922* (Cardiff)
×Dwywaith yn Blentyn. *1923* (Cardiff)
×Yr Hen Anian. *1929* (Cardiff)

BERRYMAN, Miss C. R.
The Fortune of Christina McNab (Crippl. Inst., 21/10/09, *amat.*)

BERTE, CHARLES [see also *W. BAILEY, Jr*]
The City of Millions (W.L., 1/6/03: +*W. BAILEY, Jr*)

BERTON, P. [see *C. E. MAUD*]

BERTRAM, ANTHONY
The Pool (Everyman, 7/2/27)

BERTRAM, ARTHUR

When Woman Strays (P. W., L'pool, 13/12/02; K's, Hamm., 16/30/3, as *The Story of Winifred*: + *P. G. HOLMES*)

[*BERTRAM, FRANK*

The Little Prospector (Gr., Swansea, 24/7/11)
× The Toast. LC, Sav., 28/10/14

BESIER, RUDOLF [see also *H. G. WELLS*]

The Virgin Goddess (Adel., 23/10/06) *1907*
× Olive Latimer's Husband (Vaud., 19/1/09)
Don ('*c.*': H., 12/10/09) *1909*
× Apropos (Alh., 22/2/10, *m.*)
The Crisis (Pav., Hastings, 22/8/10; New, 31/8/10: adapted from *Le rencontre* (1909) by P. F. Berton)
Lady Patricia ('*c.*': H., 22/3/11: originally called *Baldwin*) *1911*
Kings and Queens (St J., 16/1/15: originally called *Regina*)
Kultur at Home (Court, 11/3/16: +*S. SPOTISWOODE*)
A Run for His Money ('*f.c.*': Nottingham, 2/10/16; Str., 7/11/16, as *Buxell*)
Robin's Father (Playh., L'pool, 1/11/18: +*H. WALPOLE*)
The Prude's Fall (Wynd., 1/9/20: +*M. EDGINTON*: originally called *The Awakening of Beatrice*)
The Ninth Earl (Com., 9/3/21: +*M. EDGINTON*)
Secrets (Com., 7/9/22: +*M. EDGINTON*) *Fr. 1929*
The Barretts of Wimpole Street (Malvern Festival, 20/8/30; Qns, 23/9/30) *1930*

BEVAN, WALTER

× Another Dog Story (Lyr., Hamm., 27/7/12, '*preliminary pfce*': +*P. JORDAN*)

BIARDETT, J.

× A Long Journey. LC, P.W., Grimsby, 26/11/17

BIBESCO, Princess ELIZABETH

The Painted Swan. LC, Everyman, 13/3/25. *1926*
Points of View. *1926*

'*BICKERDYKE, JOHN*' [=*CHARLES HENRY COOK*]

Her Wild Oats ('*Thames-side c.*': Corn Exchange, Wallingford, 21/2/06: +*W. G. KING*)

BICKLEY, FRANCIS

× A Moment's Giddiness (Rep., B'ham, 30/11/18)

BIDWELL, PATRICK

Peggy Machree ('*r.c.*': P.W., Grimsby, 7/11/04; Wynd., 28/12/04)
Prince, Pretender or Borrowdene ('*c.o.*', m. E. Barker: Lyc., Sheffield, 7/9/06 *cpy.*)

BIENE, AUGUSTE VAN [see *I. L. CASSILIS*]

BIENE, EDWARD VAN

[Several sketches produced at music-halls]

[*BIGGERS, EARL DEER*
Inside the Lines (Ford's, Baltimore, 1/1/15; Longacre, N.Y., 12/2/15; Apo., 23/5/17) *Fr. 1924*
Three's a Crowd ('*f.c.*': Cort, N.Y., 4/12/19; O.H., Leicester, 6/12/10; Court, 30/1/23)

BINGHAM, FREDERICK
[For earlier plays see *H. E. D.* v, 261]
× Ancient Lights (P.W., Richmond, 19/12/03)

BINGHAM, G. W. RAPER [see *H. A. MARRIOTT-WATSON*]

BINNS, HENRY BRYAN
The Adventure ('*romantic variation on a Homeric theme*') *1911*

BINYON, LAURENCE [*ROBERT LAURENCE BINYON*]
× Paris and Œnone ('*t.*': Sav., 7/3/06) *1906*
Attila ('*t.*': H.M., 15/8/07, *cpy.*; H.M., 4/9/07) *1907*
× Bombastes in the Shades. *1915* (Oxford)
Sakuntala (W.G., 14/11/19, Indian Art and Dramatic Soc.: adapted from Kalidasa's play) *1920*
Arthur ('*t.*', m. Sir Edward Elgar: Vic. H., 12/3/23) *1923*
Ayuli. *1923*
Sophro the Wise ('*pl. for children*') *1923*
The Young King (Hill Crest, Boar's Hill, Oxford, 13/11/24) *1934*
Boadicea. *1927*
Three Short Plays. *1930*
[This contains: 1. *Godstow Nunnery*; 2. *Love in the Desert*; and 3. *Memnon*]

BIRCH, FRANK [*FRANCIS LYALL BIRCH*]
Mountebanks (New, Cambridge, 22/2/26) *1925*

BIRD, RICHARD [see *B. MERIVALE*]

BIRKETT, JOHN, Jr
The Rockylot ('*m.c.*': Roy., Morecambe, 5/2/00)
Nebulista ('*o.*': Roy., Morecambe, 11/4/10)
Myosota ('*c.o.*': Roy., Morecambe, 20/2/11)
The Pick of the Bunch ('*m.f.*': Roy., Morecambe, 12/2/12)

BIRKETT, PHYLLIS
× The Proof (Vaud., 21/6/23, *m.*)
Jane Eyre (Huddersfield, 9/12/29)

'*BIRMINGHAM, GEORGE A.*' [=*Rev. JAMES OWEN HANNAY*]
Eleanor's Enterprise ('*c.*': Gai., Dublin, 11/12/11; Kelly's, L'pool, 7/10/12; Crit., 4/7/23, revised as *Send for Dr O'Grady*)
General John Regan (Apo., 9/1/13) *1933*
× My America (Col., 8/10/17)
The Mermaid ('*light o.*', m. S. H. Nicholson: Guildhall School of Music, 19/5/27, *amat.*)

BISTOLPHI, GIAN
The Sleeping Beauty. LC, '*m.pl.*': Scala, 9/4/23

BITHELL, JETHRO

Turandot, Princess of China ('*Chinoiserie*', m. F. Busoni: St J., 18/1/13: adapted from the play (1911) by Karl Vollmoeller) *1913*
Helen of Sparta (translated from *Hélène de Sparte* (1912) by Émile Verhaeren) *1916*

[*BJÖRKMAN, EDWIN*

[Between 1912 and 1914 Björkman published translations of all Strindberg's plays. Of these the following were performed in England –]
× The Link (Clavier H., 26/1/13, Century Pl. Soc.)
× Simoom. LC, Gai., Manchester, 18/8/13
Swan-White (Bedford H., Chelsea, 2/7/22, Pax Robertson Salon)
× The Stronger (Fest., Cambridge, 31/1/27)
The Spook Sonata (Glo., 14/6/27, *m.*; Str., 27/6/27)
× Creditors (Arts, 20/11/27)

BLACK, CHARLES STEWART

× Châtelard (R. Inst. H., Glasgow, 13/1/21, Scott. Nat. Players) *1925* (in *The Scots Magazine*, ii, 409–16)
× The Guinea's Stamp ('*gentle satire on Glasgow society*': R. Inst. H., Glasgow, 19/1/23, Scott. Nat. Theatre Soc.) *1927*
× Knox. *1925* (in *The Scots Magazine*, iii, 335–46)
× The Treasure Hunt ('*f.c.*') *1926* (in *The Scots Magazine*, vi, 13–33)
× Stewart of Ardberg. LC, YMCA, Paisley, 7/2/29. *1927* (in *The Scots Magazine*, vi, 342–52)
× His Own Country. *1929* (in *The Scots Magazine*, xii, 132–42)
× The Auction Mart. *1929* (Glasgow)

BLACK, STEPHEN

The Brute. LC, Lyr., 16/1/11

BLACKMAN, A. [see *B. WILLIAMS*]

BLACKMORE, GEOFFREY [see also *W. KING*]

Harebell; or, The Wand of White Lilies ('*m.pl.*': St Michael's Parish H., W. Croydon, 7/4/04)
A Fisher Maiden ('*o.*': P.H., Croydon, 14/11/04)

BLACKWOOD, ALGERNON [see also *B. FORSYTH* and *F. K PEILE*]

The Starlight Express ('*m.pl.*', m. Sir Edward Elgar: Kings., 29/12/15: + *V. A. PEARN*) *1914*
Karma ('*reincarnation pl.*': *V. A. PEARN*) *1918*
Through the Crack ('*children's pl.*': Everyman, 27/12/20: + *V. A. PEARN*) *1925*
× The Halfway House (Vic. Pal., 5/12/21: + *E. AINLEY*)

BLAGROVE, CHARLES

× A Double-barrelled Courtship (Bij., 17/5/02)

BLAGROVE, GEORGE HENRY

Love's Magic Power ('*r.d.*') *1901* (*priv.*)

Daniel Dibsay ('*f.c.*': Alb. H., 1/5/05, *amat.*)
×Mumby (Kings., 20/12/08, English Pl. Soc.)

'*BLAIR*' [=*WALLACE WILFRID BLAIR FISLI*]
×Gather Ye Rosebuds. *1928* (Oxford)

BLAIR, TORIN
Officers' Call ('*military c.*': Richmond, 16/9/01)

BLAIR, WILFRED
×Consarnin' Sairey 'Uggins (Gai., Manchester, 16/2/14; Cor., 1/6/14) *1914*
Whimsies (Gai., Manchester, 8/3/15)
×The Private Life of P. C. Pettifer ('*c.*': Gai., Manchester, 16/8/15)
×The Death of Shakespeare. *1916* (Oxford)

BLAKE, GEORGE
×The Mother (R. Inst. H., Glasgow, 13/4/21, Scott. Nat. Players) *1921* (Glasgow)
Fledglings (Ath., Glasgow, 24/1/22, Scott. Nat. Theatre Soc.)
Clyde Built (Ath., Glasgow, 23/11/22, Scott. Nat. Theatre Soc.) *1922* (Glasgow)
×The Weaker Vessel. *1923* (Edinburgh)

BLAKE, GERALD
×His Last Jest (Stand., 19/7/09)

BLAKEMORE, TREVOR
Playing with Love (translated from *Liebelei* (1896) by Arthur Schnitzler) *1914*

BLAND, ALAN
The Comedian (Rep., B'ham, 19/3/27: adapted from *Le Comédien et la grace* by H. Ghéon) *1927*

BLAND, ROBERT HENDERSON [see also *Mrs T. P. O'CONNOR* and *B. TUCKER*]
×The Survivor (Emp., Kilburn, 1911)
×The March Triumphant (Emp., New X, 5/12/11; Qns, 12/12/11: +*A. S. CRAVEN*)
Catherine the Great (Cosmopolis, 11/2/13: +*A. E. M. FOSTER*)
When Friends Fall Out (Brighton, 13/6/21; Kings., 26/3/22, as *The Africander*, Pl. Actors)

BLAND, SYDNEY
The Gamester ('*r. costume pl.*': Emp., Wakefield, 14/7/13)

BLANE, AGNES
A Family Affair ('*c.*': H.M., Blackpool, 28/2/21; Brixton, 5/3/23)

[*BLANEY, CHARLES E.*
Not Tonight, Dearie ('*f.*': Pal., Brighton, 22/3/26: +*N. HOUSTON*)

BLATCHFORD, M. J.
The Highwayman ('*c.o.*': Halifax, 14/4/13)

BLATCHFORD, ROBERT

A Comedy of Bohemia (Socialist Clubhouse, Handforth, 21/5/11, *amat.*)

BLATTNER, L.

×Love and Justice. LC, Scala, 23/11/22

BLEACKLEY, HORACE WILLIAM

The Silver Link ('*c.*': Com., 13/5/02: +*J. A. BLEACKLEY*)

BLEACKLEY, JOHN ARTHUR [see also *H. W. BLEACKLEY*]

BLEICHMANN, RUDOLF

Old Heidelberg ('*c.*': St J., 19/3/03: adapted from W. M. Forster, *Alt Heidelberg*, 1898)

Love's Carnival (Lyc., Edin., 12/11/03; St J., 17/3/04: adapted from O. E. Hartleben, *Rosenmontag*, 1900) *1904*

BLENNERHASSETT, SYLVIA

Nevertheless (Arts, 5/7/27)

BLIGH, H. W.

Pennsylvania ('*hist. d.*') *1924*

BLIN, ERNEST

×Purely Platonic (P.H., Enniskillen, 6/5/05)

BLISS, ERNEST

×Violets (Memorial H., Chesterfield, 8/4/01)

×The Isle of Tears (Terminus H., Littlehampton, 8/5/02)

BLOFIELD, GEOFFREY

Khuzaymah. LC, Actors' Orphanage, Langley, 9/4/21

BLOM, ERIC WALTER

The Trouble Factory ('*t.c.*') *1928*

BLOOD, JAMES J. [see also *G. D. ROSENTHAL*]

[For earlier plays see *H. E. D.* v, 265–6, 779)

Aidan; or, The Warfare of Love ('*historical d.*': Small Heath, B'ham, 20/11/05, *amat.*) *1906* (Birmingham)

BLOOR, JOSEPH

The Sin of Judas. LC, Bij., Rye, 31/7/19: title altered later to *By the Camp Fire*

BLOOR, ROBERT HENRY UNDERWOOD

×The Enchanted Island ('*oa.*', m. R. H. Walthew: St G's H., 8/5/00) *1900*

BLORE, ERIC [see also *A. MELFORD*]

Ring Up ('*intimate rev.*': Roy., 3/9/21: +*A. MELFORD* and *I. ALLEN*)

[Several sketches and playlets produced at music-halls]

[*BLOSSOM, HENRY*

×Once a Thief (Empress, Brixton, 21/4/13)

The Only Girl ('*m.pl.*', m. V. Herbert: Nixon, Atlantic City, 1/10/14; 39th Street, N.Y., 2/11/14; Apo., 25/9/15, revised by *F. THOMPSON*)

The Red Mill ('*m.pl.*', m. V. Herbert: Emp., 26/12/19)

BLOW, MARK

Gay Trouville ('*m.c.*', m. R. Cleveland: O.H., Cheltenham, 24/4/19: +*B. LANDECK*)

BLOW, SYDNEY [see also *W. T. COLEBY*]

Where Children Rule ('*m.pl.*', m. E. Jones: Gar., 11/12/10: +*D. HOARE*) *1909*
×The Little Lieutenant ('*m.c.*': Pav., Glasgow, 23/1/11; Emp., Hackney, 13/3/11: +*D. HOARE*)
Little Miss Llewellyn ('*c.*': Vaud., 31/8/12: +*D. HOARE*)
Oh, I Say! ('*c.*': Bournemouth, 28/4/13; Crit., 28/5/13: +*D. HOARE*) *Fr. 1924*
This Way, Madame! ('*f.*': Plymouth, 15/9/13; Qns, 27/9/13: +*D. HOARE*)
My Aunt ('*f.*': Vaud., 26/8/14: +*D. HOARE*)
×Brides ('*m.bsq.*', m. P. Braham: Hippo., Southampton, 11/10/15; Golder's Green, 20/12/15: +*D. HOARE*)
×Back to Blighty ('*m.bsq.*': Oxford., 7/9/16: +*D. HOARE*)
The Spring Song (Brighton, 30/10/16; Aldw., 22/2/17: +*D. HOARE*)
The Double Event (Qns, 20/2/17: +*D. HOARE*)
The Live Wire (St M., 30/8/18: +*D. HOARE*)
Telling the Tale ('*m.f.*', revised version of *Oh, I Say!*, m. P. Braham: Ambass., 31/8/18: +*D. HOARE*)
The Officers' Mess ('*m.f.*', m. P. Braham: Plymouth, 16/9/18; St M., 7/11/18: +*D. HOARE*)
Lord Richard in the Pantry ('*c.*': Shak., L'pool, 15/9/19; Crit., 11/11/19: +*D. HOARE*: dramatised from the novel (1912) by Martin Swayne) *Fr. 1924*
×Oh, Mr. Dooley! ('*f.*': Metropolitan, 13/6/21: +*D. HOARE*)
Old Jig (Pleasure Gdns, Folkestone, 14/11/21; Str., 19/1/22: +*D. HOARE*)
Enter Kiki ('*c.*': Belasco, N.Y., 29/11/21; Playh., 2/8/23: +*D. HOARE*: originally called *Kiki* and title altered later to *Mam'selle Kiki*: musical version by M. Darewski, Hippo., Portsmouth, 25/8/24; Emp., Stratford, 1/9/24)
Boodle ('*m.pl.*', m. P. Braham and M. Darewski: P.W., B'ham, 26/12/24; Emp., 10/3/25: +*D. HOARE*)
Lady Letty ('*m.pl.*', based on *Lord Richard in the Pantry*: Emp., Glasgow, 18/1/26; Emp., Finsbury Park, 10/5/26: +*D. HOARE*)
The Unseemly Adventure (Chester, 22/2/26; Gar., 26/4/26: from the novel (1924) by Ralph Straus: +*G. WHITEHEAD*)
His Wild Oat (Portsmouth, 29/11/26: +*D. HOARE*)

[Numerous sketches and playlets, many written in collaboration, produced at music-halls]

BLOXAM, E. E.

Little Pageant Plays for Children. *1912*

[This contains twelve short playlets]

BLUMBERG, GUSTAVE

A Code of Honour ('*c.d.*': Com., 9/2/03: +*C. STEPHENSON*)

BLUNDELL, Mrs FRANCIS [=‘*M. E. FRANCIS*’]

BLUNDELLS, Miss A.

The Forged Tombstone. LC, Alex. H., Gt Crosley, 24/3/14

BLUNT, WILFRED SCAWEN

Fand (‘*t.*’: Abbey, Dublin, 20/4/07) *1904* (as *Fand of the Fair Cheek*)

BLYTHE, EDWARD

On the Night of the 22nd (Crippl. Inst., 31/10/24, *amat.*: +*N. MORRIS*, under pseudonym ‘*SANSOVINO*’)

The Nerve Test (Crippl. Inst., 5/3/26, *amat.*: +*T. S. FIELD*)

BLYTHE, J. S.

[For earlier plays see *H. E. D.* v, 266]

A Lost Memory (P’s, Manchester, 4/8/02)

BLYTHE, STEPHEN E. [see *R. L. CAVENDISH*]

BODE, MILTON [see *G. ENGLAND*]

BODEN, HARRY J. [see *E. W. PRITCHARD*]

BODINGTON, P. E.

His Bounden Duty (Court, 30/5/09, Pl. Actors)

BOGUE, J. RUSSELL

[For earlier plays see *H. E. D.* v, 266]

A Trip to Blackpool (‘*f. frenzy*’: Hereford, 9/4/00: title later changed to *A Naughty Husband*)

Ballyhooley; or, A Night on the Big Wheel (‘*f.c.*’: O.H., Doncaster, 5/5/1898, *cpy.*: Workington, 14/10/01: title later changed to *A Warm Member*)

A Fisherman’s Daughter (‘*c.d.*’: Goole, 21/8/02: title later changed to *Molly Machree*)

×Lady Lanigan, Laundress (‘*f.c.*’: L’pool, 9/4/08)

[A few sketches and playlets produced at music-halls]

BOHUN, JOHN

The Hearts (‘*c.*’: Manchester, 29/4/04)

BOÏELLE, E. CLARENCE

The Haunted Man (Oddfellows’ H., St Helier, Jersey, 14/12/08, *amat.*)

The Chimes (Oddfellows’ H., St Helier, Jersey, 4/1/10, *amat.*)

The Battle of Life (Oddfellows’ H., St Helier, Jersey, 3/1/11, *amat.*)

The Cricket on the Hearth (Oddfellows’ H., St Helier, Jersey, 3/1/12, *amat.*)

BOILEAU, MARIE

×‘When Anne was Queen’. LC, Village H., Twyford, 4/2/24: +*J. ERLE*. *1903* (Oswestry); *Fr. 1920*

Deceivers Ever; or, Love-in-a-Mist (‘*rustic c.*’: +*J. ERLE*) *1907* (Oswestry)

×At ye Sign of ye Sugar Heart (‘*past. c.*’: +*J. ERLE*) *1907* (Oswestry)

×Mr Dan Cupid; or, There’s Nowt So Queer as Folks. *1907* (Oswestry)

BOISSIER, FERDINAND
Pierrot's Christmas ('*wordless pl.*': Apo., 21/11/16)

BOLT, T.
A Lovely Lot (Guildhall School of Music, 6/1/26, New Pl. Club)

BOLTON, GUY REGINALD [see also *P. H. BARTHOLOMÆ, G. GROSSMITH, 'IAN HAY', M. MARCIN, G. MIDDLETON, H. M. VERNON* and *P. G. WODEHOUSE*]
Oh, Joy! ('*m.c.*', m. J. Kern: Schenectady, 20/1/17, as *Oh, Boy!*; P'cess, N.Y., 20/2/17; P's, Manchester, 16/12/18; Kings., 27/1/19: +*P. G. WODEHOUSE*)
Kissing Time ('*m.c.*', m. I. Caryll: Apo., Atlantic City, 26/8/19; New Amsterdam, N.Y., 16/9/18; W.G., 20/5/19: +*P. G. WODEHOUSE*)
Sally ('*m.c.*', m. J. Kern (Acad., Baltimore, 29/11/20, as *Sally of Our Alley*; New Amsterdam, N.Y., 22/12/20, as *Sally*; W.G., 10/9/21)
Polly Preferred ('*c.*': Little, N.Y., 11/1/23; Roy., 5/4/24) *Fr. 1923*
Grounds for Divorce (Apo., Atlantic City, 25/2/24; Emp., N.Y., 23/9/24; St J., 21/1/25: adapted from the Hungarian of E. Vajda)
Lady, Be Good ('*m.c.*', m. G. Gershwin: Forrest, Philadelphia, 17/11/24; Liberty, N.Y., 1/12/24; Emp., L'pool, 29/3/26; Emp., 14/4/26: +*F. THOMPSON*)
The Dark Angel (Everyman, 3/11/25)
Tip-Toes ('*m.c.*', m. G. Gershwin: National, Washington, 24/11/25; Liberty, N.Y., 28/12/25; Alh., Glasgow, 16/8/26; W.G., 31/8/26: +*F. THOMPSON*)
Oh! Kay! ('*m.c.*', m. G. Gershwin: Philadelphia, 25/10/26; Imp., N.Y., 8/11/26; Emp., L'pool, 12/9/27; H.M., 21/9/27: +*P. G. WODEHOUSE*)
Blue Eyes ('*r.m.pl.*', m. J. Kern: K's, Southsea, 9/4/28; Piccadilly, 27/4/28: +*GRAHAM JOHN*)
The Five-O'Clock Girl ('*m.c.*', m. B. Kalmar and H. Ruby: Nottingham, 11/3/29; Hippo., 21/3/29: +*F. THOMPSON*)
Rio Rita ('*r.m.c.*', m. Harry Tierney: Colonial, Boston, 29/12/26; Ziegfeld, N.Y., 2/2/27; Prince Edward, 3/4/30: +*F. THOMPSON*)

BOLTON, S. R.
×A Witness to the Will. LC, W.G., 17/2/22

BOND, ACTON [see *Mrs M. F. SHELDON*]

BOND, Mrs ACTON
The Great Galeoto (Steiner H., 1/2/27, International Theatre: adapted from J. Echegaray, *El gran Galeoto*, 1881)

BOND, CHARLES
The Day of St Anthony (Ass. R., Wood Green, 10/11/10, *amat.*)

BOND, JOHN
×Na Poo ('*m. piece*': Worthing, 10/3/19; Bed., 7/4/19: +*F. RAMSDALE*)

×Topping the Bill (Aldw., 7/5/19)
Carmello ('*m.c.*', m. H. L. Norman: Pal., Tynemouth, 24/1/21; Stratford, 31/12/23, as *Gogo*: +*F. RAMSDALE*)

BOND, MERVYN
×The Departure ('*oa.*', m. E. d'Albert: K's, Hamm., 3/9/25: +*A. SKALSKI*)

BOND, STEPHEN
[For an earlier play see *H. E. D.* v, 267]
Yiv and the Blue Wolf ('*r.pl.*', m. A. Collard: Cor., 9/3/03)
×Where the Crows Gathered (Crit., 5/7/05)
×Saved by Little Albert. LC, Pier, Southsea, 24/1/17
[Several playlets produced at music-halls]

BONE, F. D. [see also *H. BAGGE*]
×Pride of Regiment (H., 28/2/08) *Fr. 1908*
×The Sergeant-Major (M'sex, 20/5/08)
×Private Nobody (Court, 2/11/08, *m.*)
×The Topside Dog (Court, 3/11/08, *m.*)
×The Sentimental Bray (Court, 8/11/08, Pl. Actors)
Isaac's Wife (Court, 6/12/08, Drama Productions Club: +*T. SHORE*)
×The New Landlord (Hippo., Margate, 4/9/09; Rehearsal, 3/11/09, *m.*)
×A Daughter of Japan. *Fr. 1914*
[A few playlets produced at music-halls]

BONE, JOHN H.
×The Crystal Set ('*c.*': Pav., Glasgow, 7/7/24, Scott. Nat. Players) *1924* (Glasgow)
×The Loud Speaker. *1927* (Glasgow)

BONETT, NANCY
×Midsummer Madness. LC, Crippl. Inst., 15/10/13

BONNIN, ALFRED
×Palmistry ('*ca.*': Middlesbrough, 19/8/01)

BONUS, AUDREY
×The House that wasn't there. LC, Ass. R., Yeovil, 13/7/20

BOOSEY, WILLIAM
His Highness My Husband ('*fant.c.*': Com., 1/10/04)

BOOTH, A. [see *M. BOOTH*]

BOOTH, JUNIUS
Way Out West ('*c.d.*': Lincoln, 2/9/09; Gr., Fulham, 7/2/10)
The Tavern Knight ('*r.pl.*': P.W., Salford, 29/5/11; Stratford, 31/7/11: dramatised from the novel (1904) by Rafael Sabatini)
×The Wolf (R.A., Woolwich, 11/5/14)

BOOTH, M.
×The Magic Wood ('*fairy pl.*': D.P., Eastbourne, 16/7/25, *m.*, *amat.*: +*A. BOOTH*)

BOOTHBY, GUY

In Sunny Celon ('*f.*': Gai., Manchester, 25/4/04: originally called *The Rickshaw*)

BORGSTROEM, ARTHUR TRAVERS [see *ARTHUR TRAVERS-BORGSTROEM*]

BORLEY, G.

×The Stillest Hour. LC, Gai., Manchester, 6/5/14

BOROS, FERIKE

The Seven Sisters ('*f.*': Sav., 14/5/13: adapted from the Hungarian of F. Herczeg)

BOSE, S. C.

Buddha (Court, 22/2/12) *1912*

BOSWELL, E. S.

×The Empty Chair. LC, Vic. H., Sunderland, 15/4/25

BOTELL, GEORGE W.

×Quits (Newcastle, 19/8/18)

BOTTOMLEY, GORDON

×The Crier by Night (University, L'pool, 21/11/24, *amat.*) *1902* (*priv.*)

×Midsummer Eve (LC, K. G's H., 25/11/24; A.L.S. Trav. Th., 1924) *1905* (*priv.*)

×Laodicë and Danaë. *1909* (*priv.*)

×The Riding to Lithend (Fest., Cambridge, 7/5/28) *1909* (*priv.*)

×King Lear's Wife ('*t.*': Rep., B'ham, 25/9/15; H.M., 19/5/16, *m.*) *1915* (in *Georgian Poetry*, vol. ii); *1920* (printed with *The Crier by Night, The Riding to Lithend, Midsummer Eve* and *Laodicë and Danaë*)

Britain's Daughter (Vic. H., 20/11/22) *1921*

Gruach (Ath., Glasgow, 20/3/23, Scott. Nat. Players; St M., 20/1/24) *1921* (printed with *Britain's Daughter*)

×The Singing Sands. LC, St Luke's H., Reform Club, Clapham, 30/3/27. *1929* (in *Scenes and Plays*)

Scenes and Plays. *1929*

[This contains: 1. *A Parting* (Oxford Recitations, 1928); 2. *The Return* (Oxford Recitations, 1928); 3. *The Sisters*; 4. *The Widow*; 5. *Towie Castle*; 6. *Merlin's Grave*; 7. *Ardvorlich's Wife*; and 8. *The Singing Sands*]

BOTTOMLEY, ROLAND

×Honi soit qui mal y pense (T. H., Chiswick, 9/5/01, *amat.*)

×A Quiet Evening (Brixton, 12/5/02)

The Impertinence of Nancy ('*c.*': Qns Gate H., 26/1/05)

Tompkins's Venus (Pav., St Leonard's, 27/7/06)

Helen's Little Subterfuge (Qns Gate H., 12/6/07)

×The Snake's Kiss (Hippo., Peckham, 25/4/10)

×Present-Day Courtship ('*wordy duologue*') Fr. *1925*

BOULTER, Rev. BENJAMIN CONSITT
The Mystery of Epiphany (St Silas H., Kentish Town, 9/2/12) *1920* (SPCK)
The Mystery of the Passion. *1923* (SPCK)
Paul and Silas. *1923* (SPCK)

BOULTON, CHARLES [see also *G. E. JENNINGS*]
× The Gipsy Girl ('*oa.*': Col., Goole, 7/6/15)

BOULTON, GUY PELHAM
The Joyful Path ('*c.*': Barnes, 30/8/26)

BOULTON, MATTHEW
× The Triumph of Conscience (Ath., Lancaster, 10/5/05, *cpy.*)
× The Burglar and the Girl (Pav., Weymouth, 24/2/13; Bed., 3/3/13) *Fr. 1913*
× His Rest Day (Emp., Shepherd's Bush, 14/12/14) *Fr. 1919*
× The Quest (Altrincham Garrick Soc., 17/11/15)
× Sword or Surplice? (Alex., 24/1/16) *1916*
× The Brass Door-Knob (Alex., 9/10/16) *Fr. 1919*
× The Yorkshire Way. LC, O.H., Manchester, 27/7/22
× The Difference (Col., 28/8/22: originally called *The Obstacle*) *Fr. 1923*
Carpet Slippers (Little Vic., Brighton, 13/4/25)
Silver Threads (Q, 21/10/29)
[Several other playlets produced at music-halls]

BOURCHIER, ARTHUR
[For earlier plays see *H. E. D.* v, 270]
× The Soothing System (Gar., 30/7/03)
× Down Our Alley ('*coster story*': Gar., 25/7/06: adapted from Anatole France, *Crainquebille*, 1903)
The Duel (Gar., 23/4/07: adapted from H. Lavedan, *Le duel*, 1905)

BOURKE, P. J.
For the Land She Loved (Abbey, Dublin, 15/11/15)

BOURNE, C. HAROLD
× Kismas (date uncertain)
× At the Mercy of the Waves (Emp., Camberwell, 25/7/10: + *M. CLEMENT SCOTT*)
The Other Side of Life (B'ham, 5/9/14: + *D. C. CALTHROP*)
× Thais and Talmaæ ('*o.*', m. C. M. Campbell: O.H., Manchester, 13/9/21; C.G., 8/11/21)
What Shall It Profit? (Brighton, 20/12/26; Hippo., Golder's Green, 14/3/27, as *What Shall It Profit a Man?*: + *V. LANGBRIDGE*)

BOURNE, WILLIAM
[For earlier plays see *H. E. D.* v, 270]
Days of Danger ('*spectacular d.*': Gr., Glasgow, 16/4/00; Gr., Glasgow, 15/5/00, as *The Invasion of Britain; or, The Siege of Glasgow*; Broadway, New X, 9/7/00, as *The I. of B., or, The Siege of London*; Dalston, 24/9/00)
The Cry of the Children (Stratford, 9/3/03)
× Ordered to the Front (Emp., Stratford, 6/5/07)

BOVILL, C. H. [see also *F. THOMPSON*]
The Dancing Viennese ('*m.pl.*', m. O. Straus: Col., 1/7/12)
[Numerous sketches and playlets produced at music-halls]

BOWEN, FRANCIS JOSEPH
Emmanuel ('*m.pl.*': St Malachy's H., L'pool, 9/12/25)
The Three Kings ('*mystery pl.*') *1928* (Edinburgh)
The Blessed Thomas More. *1930* (Edinburgh)

BOWEN, HAROLD
The Three Sisters (Court, 8/3/20, *m.*, Art Theatre: adapted from A. Chekhov, *Tri sestri*, 1901)
S.S. Tenacity ('*c.*': Lyr., Hamm., 13/6/20, St. Soc.: adapted from C. Vildrac, *Le paquebot Tenacity*, 1920)

'*BOWEN, MARJORIE*' [=*MARGARET VERA CAMPBELL GABRIELLE LONG*]
Interruptions ('*light c.*': Blfrs., 7/5/27, Interlude Theatre Guild)
×A Family Comedy, 1840. *Fr. 1930*

BOWER, BETTY WYNNE [see *BETTY WYNNE-BOWER*]

BOWER, MARIAN [see also *L. M. LION*]
The Chinese Puzzle (Poli's, Washington, 24/6/18; Shak., L'pool, 1/7/18; New, 11/7/18: +*L. M. LION*) *Fr. 1919*
Homespun ('*c.*': Gai., Manchester, 8/12/19)
The Green Cord (Roy., 2/6/22: +*A. L. ELLIS*)
Comfort (Q, 6/7/25)
×The Solomon Chest (Playroom 6, 15/2/27)

BOWHAY, BERTHA LOUISA
Flower of Grass [and] As Hand with Hand. *1910*
[The second of these two plays had a 'dramatic reading' under the auspices of the Poetry Society at Mitford House, S.W., 27/11/28]
A Happy Christmas (Steiner H., 27/12/26)
Hector of Welcome's ('*c.*') *1927*
I. E. Robinson ('*c.*') *1928*

BOWKETT, SIDNEY
[For earlier plays see *H. E. D.* v, 271]
A Tight Corner ('*f.*': Terry's, 12/10/01) *Fr. 1913* (as *A Squire of the Night*)
Lucky Miss Dean ('*little c.*': Crit., 3/8/05) *Fr. 1906*
The Superior Miss Pellender ('*c.*': Waldorf, 17/1/06) *Fr. 1921*
Audacious Mr Squire (Crit., 19/2/24: +*E. STANNARD*)

BOWMAN, FANNY
×The Ways of a Flirt (D.P., Eastbourne, 21/9/11)
Priscilla – the Rake ('*c.*': Q, 7/2/28)

BOWMAN, FREDERICK H.-U.
Enslaved by a Mormon (LC, Kelly's, L'pool, 14/5/13: Pal., Prescot, 26/6/16)
The Confession (LC, Emp., Southend, 19/1/14: E.C., 23/10/16)
The Woman Who Dared (LC, Kelly's, L'pool, 9/1/15, as *Her Soldier Boy*: Bury, 20/7/17)

×A Cuddlesome Ghost (Park, L'pool, 24/6/18)
Divorce or Dishonour (Gr., Plymouth, 19/8/18)
×Private Pinker on Leave (Westminster, L'pool, 12/12/18)
×Unfit to Marry (P's, Bootle, 16/1/19: originally called *Condemned to Be Childless* and *Her Bitter Pill*)

BOWMAN, ISA
The Girl in the Picture ('*m.pl.*', m. H. Richardson: Deal, 2/9/12; Gr., Clapham, 17/11/13, revised as a 'revue', with *F. FLEXMORE*, called *Who's Got It?*)
Little Miss Ragtime ('*m.c.*', m. W. Neale: Margate, 24/7/13)

BOWMAN, MARK
×A Matter o' Money (Emp., Holb., 17/10/21)

'*BOWSKILL, HENRY*' [=*MARTHA GRAHAM*]
Which? *1924*

BOWYER, FREDERICK
[For earlier plays see *H. E. D.* v, 271–2]
The Drum Major ('*c.o.*': Cor., 1/10/00: +*W. E. SPRANGE*: adapted from Offenbach's *La fille du tambour-majeur*)
×Tricky Trouville ('*m.pl.*', m. E. Woodville: Borough, Stratford, 1/6/05)
The Windmill Man ('*m.pl.*', m. A. H. Behrend and A. Fox: Vic. Pal., 26/12/21, *m.*) *1921*
[Several sketches and playlets produced at music-halls]

BOXER, CECILE F.
×The Call. *Fr. 1929*

BOXES, GEORGE RAPHAEL
It's a Family Affair ('*c.*': Bedford H. Chelsea, 30/4/22, Pax Robertson Salon: adapted from A. N. Ostrovski, *Svoi liudisochtemsia*, 1850)

BOYD, DREDA
×John Feeney, Socialist. LC, Pav., Glasgow, 2/6/15

BOYD, ERIC FORBES
Knight Errant ('*absurdity*': St M., 15/8/28)
Maripesa Bung; or, The Pirate's Daughter ('*pl. for boys*') *Fr. 1929*

BOYD, FOSTER
X.O.3. LC, Playh., Cardiff, 23/1/25

BOYD, Rev. H. J.
The Phantom (Gai., Hastings, 11/2/24)

BOYD, THOMAS JAMIESON LAYCOCK STIRLING
The Case for the Prosecution (Shaft., 18/2/23, Pl. Actors) *1925* (Oxford, as *The Web*)

BOYESEN, ALGERNON
Napoleon ('*historical t.*') *1909*

BOYLAN, GRACE DUFFIE
Yama Yama Land (Ladbr. H., 15/9/09, *cpy.*)

BOYLAN, R. DILLON
Nathan the Wise (Str., 3/5/25, Jewish Dram. League: adapted by *M. J. LANDA*: based on Lessing's play as translated by R. E. Raspe)

BOYLE, DOUGLAS JACKSON
Paul of Tarsus ('*t.*') *1923* (Scarborough, *priv.*)
Marcus Aurelius ('*t.*') *1923* (Scarborough, *priv.*)
Galswintha ('*t.*') *1924* (Scarborough, *priv.*)

BOYLE, GEORGE
× Behind the Curtain. LC, Crippl. Inst., 2/12/19
× The Last Tumbril. LC, Crippl. Inst., 24/2/21

BOYLE, G. W.
The Boomerang ('*c.*': Streatham H., Streatham, 12/12/06, *amat.*: +*F. ROBERTSON*)

BOYLE, LAWRENCE
The First Kiss ('*m.pl.*', m. Pablo Luna: Oxf., 10/11/24: called later *The Butterfly*)

BOYLE, WILLIAM
Never Give In. LC, Glasgow, 31/5/17: called originally *Arms and the Woman*, title later changed to *Arms and the Lady*: +*G. BYAM*)

BOYLE, WILLIAM
The Building Fund ('*c.*': Abbey, Dublin, 25/4/05; St G's H., 28/11/05; Court, 18/6/10) *1905* (Dublin)
The Eloquent Dempsey ('*c.*': Abbey, Dublin, 20/1/06; Court, 6/6/10) *1911* (Dublin)
The Mineral Workers (Abbey, Dublin, 20/10/06; Court, 19/6/11) *1910* (Dublin)
The Love Charm ('*f.*': Abbey, Dublin, 4/9/11)
A Family Failing (Abbey, Dublin, 28/3/12; Court, 27/6/12) *1912* (Dublin)
Nic ('*c.*': Abbey, Dublin, 25/10/16)
The O'Dempsey ('*c.*': O.H., Cork, 4/6/18)

BOYLING, JOSEPH W. [see *F. DAVENPORTE*]

BOYNE, MADELEINE
The Simoun (Q, 18/12/27, Q Sunday Players: +*J. D. O'NEAL*: adapted from the play (1920) by H. R. Lenormand)

BRABAZON, T. B.
London Night Hawks (P.H., Arbroath, 27/9/09, *cpy.*)

BRABNER, W. A.
[For earlier plays see *H. E. D.* v, 272]
For the Colours (Metro., Manchester, 14/8/1899; Carlton, Greenwich, 14/4/02)
The Two Mothers (Metro., Glasgow, 28/6/1899, *cpy.*, as *The Heiress of Daventry*; Metro., Glasgow, 5/3/00; Morton's, Greenwich, 18/6/00; Stratford, 22/12/02, as *The Heart of a Woman*: +*J. M. HARDIE*)

A Busy Day ('*m.c.*', m. H. E. Baker: Blackburn, 22/4/01: title later altered to *Celestine*: +*C. H. TAYLOR*)
By the Hand of a Woman (Carlton, Greenwich, 28/4/02)
Life's Sweetest Sins (Lyc., Eccles, 25/1/04; Stratford, 3/4/05)
The Honour of the House (P.H., W. Didsbury, 28/10/05, *cpy.*)

BRACEY, HENRY GORDON
William the Conqueror and his Fool Berdic. *1925*

BRADFORD, MANSFIELD [see also *HERBERT GORDON*]
×The Stevedore (Gr., Gravesend, 2/6/13)

BRADHURST, CHRISTINE
×Milady's Jest. LC, Colne Priory, Earl's Colne, 11/6/20

BRADLEY, ALICE
The Governor's Lady (Dalston, 24/4/12; Bournemouth, 17/2/19; Kennington, 17/3/19)

BRADLEY, KATHERINE HARRIS [see '*MICHAEL FIELD*']

BRADLEY, CHARLES [see *E. A. PAULTON*]

BRADLEY, F. W.
×The Executioner. LC, K. G's H., 10/4/24

BRADLEY, HERBERT DENNIS
One Sweet September Day ('*f.c.*': St G's H., 1/5/02, *cpy.*)
The King's Cup (Adel., 13/12/09, *m.*: +*E. P. OPPENHEIM*) *Fr. 1913*
Sybarites ('*modern c.*': Arts, 1/6/29; Roy., 3/12/29, as *The Amorists*) *1930*

[*BRADLEY, LILLIAN TRIMBLE*
Out Goes She ('*c.*': Crit., 11/12/28)

BRADSHAW, Mrs ALBERT S. [*ANNIE*]
[For an earlier play see *H. E. D.* v, 273]
×Dearest Friends (Steinway H., 20/6/02)
×Behind a Mask (Steinway H., 20/6/02)
×A Philanthropic Experiment (Exchange H., Nottingham, 23/4/03)
×The Idol and the Husband (Adel., 25/6/07, *m.*)
×The Experiment (Pal., Battersea, 30/11/08; Bed., 28/6/09; K's H., 15/2/13)
×Pattie the Parlourmaid. LC, Bed., 24/10/13

BRADSHAW, A. W.
The Silver Butterfly ('*o.*', m. B. Page: Mechanics' H., Nottingham, 26/4/10, *amat.*)

BRADSHAW, PERCY V.
×H.M.S. Robertus ('*oa.*', m. S. R. Philpot: Emp., Edmonton, 18/7/12: +*D. WALSH*)
Flash Fred (New X, 1/4/18: based on a one-act sketch, LC, Coll., 3/2/13)

BRAHM, MICHAEL [see *A. LLOYD*]

BRAILSFORD, HENRY NOEL [see also *J. E. MALLOCK*]
×A Priest's Honour (Bij., 2/10/01)

BRAND, CHARLES NEVILLE
The Prisoners (St Stephen's H., Hampstead, 23/11/26, *amat.*)

BRAND, OSWALD [see also *B. LANDECK*]
[For earlier plays see *H. E. D.* v, 273–4]
The Fisher Girl ('*m.pl.*', m. W. T. Gliddon: Hanley, 27/5/01; Crown, Peckham, 8/7/01)
Little Nell (Gr., Islington, 23/2/03)
Oliver Twist (Gr., Islington, 30/3/03)
No Thoroughfare; or, The Story of a Foundling (Gr., Islington, 11/5/03)
Bleak House; or, Events in the Life of Jo (Gr., Islington, 1/6/03)
Monte Cristo; or, The Prisoners of the Château d'If (Gr., Islington, 2/11/03)
The Bridge of Sighs; or, A Poor Girl's Love Story (Gr., Islington, 4/4/04)
Black-Eyed Susan (Gr., Islington, 19/9/04)

BRAND, TITA
The Two Hunchbacks (Sav., 14/11/10)

'*BRANDANE, JOHN*' (=*JOHN McINTYRE*)
×Glenforsa (R. Inst. H., Glasgow, 13/1/21, Scott. Nat. Players: +*A. W. YUILL*) *1921*
×The Change House (Ath., Glasgow, 1/11/21, Scott. Nat. Players) *1921*
×The Spanish Galleon (Argyllshire H., Oban, 25/9/22, Scott. Nat. Theatre Soc.: +*A. W. YUILL*) *1924* (in *The Scots Magazine*, i, 117–30)
The Glen is Mine (Ath., Glasgow, 25/1/23, Scott. Nat. Theatre Soc.; Everyman, 5/5/30) *1925* (printed with *The Lifting*)
Full Fathom Five ('*ca.*': Ath., Glasgow, 11/3/24, Scott. Nat. Theatre Soc.)
The Treasure Ship ('*f.c.*': Ath., Glasgow, 11/3/24, Scott. Nat. Theatre Soc.; P's, Manchester, 25/5/25) *1928* (printed with *Rory Aforesaid* and *The Happy War*)
The Lifting (Ath., Glasgow, 3/2/25, Scott. Nat. Theatre Soc.; Q, 14/12/25) *1925* (printed with *The Glen is Mine*)
The Inn of Adventure ('*c.*': Ath., Glasgow, 13/10/25, Scott. Nat. Theatre Soc.) *1933* (printed with *Heather Gentry*)
×Rory Aforesaid. LC, Charing X H., Glasgow, 3/11/25. *1924* (in *The Scots Magazine*, iv, 183–95); *1928* (see above)
Koechlin. 1926 (Edinburgh)
Heather Gentry (Lyr., Glasgow, 24/12/27, Scott. Nat. Theatre Soc.) *1933* (see above)
The Happy War. *1928* (see above)

BRANDON, ALFRED
×The Skeleton in the Cupboard. LC, Rep., Plymouth, 18/4/25
×Miss Emily Makes the Tart (Rep., Plymouth, 23/8/26)

BRANDON, BETTY

×An Old Master ('*f.*': New, Cambridge, 10/5/07, *cpy.*)
×Sister Monica (New, Cambridge, 10/5/07, *cpy.*)

BRANDON, DOROTHY [see also *J. C. SNAITH*]

×Winter Sport (Court, 18/11/08, *m.*)
The Man with his Back to the East (Court, 8/12/12, Pl. Actors: as by '*W. BRANDON*')
×Venus on Earth ('*modern fant.*': Court, 16/11/13, Pl. Actors)
Wild Heather (Gai., Manchester, 27/8/17; Str., 25/10/17, *m.*)
Beau Regard ('*dream of the Dark Ages*') *1920*
The Outsider (Pleasure Gdns, Folkestone, 30/4/23; St J., 31/5/23) *Fr. 1926*
Blind Alley (Pleasure Gdns, Folkestone, 4/1/26; Playh., 27/1/26)
The Black Ace (Glo., 9/5/29: +*N. FARSON*)

BRANDON, H. G.

What Women Suffer (Carlton, Greenwich, 17/7/05: title later changed to *Woman Pays for All*)
×Only an Israelite (Stand., 15/11/09)
×Queen of My Heart. LC, Stratford, 3/12/14

BRANDON, JOCELYN

The Chaperon ('*ca.*': D.P., Eastbourne, 21/4/13; Str., 26/4/13: +*F. ARTHUR*)

BRANDON, JOHN GORDON

A Midnight Mystery (Emp., Camberwell, 22/3/09)
×A Gentleman of Leisure (Shaft., 13/7/20: originally called *The Night before the Derby*)
The Silent House (Emp., Croydon, 27/8/23; Com., 8/6/27, revised with *G. PICKETT*)
[Numerous sketches and playlets produced at music-halls]

BRANDON, PHILIP

×Ships in Sargasso (RADA, 13/1/24)

BRANDON, R. A.

×By Mutual Agreement (P's, Manchester, 11/4/10: +*G. BULL*) *1911*
×The New Life (Aldershot, 15/4/10, *cpy.*; Lyc., 4/10/10, *m.*: +*G. BULL*)

BRANDON, WILFRED E.

Naughty Ninetta ('*m.c.*', m. G. W. Schofield: Star, Swansea, 24/9/10, *cpy.*: +*L. NAPIER*)

BRANDON-THOMAS, JEVAN

×Patchwork. LC, Gr., Oldham, 17/9/25: +*F. WILSON BENNETT*. *Fr. 1927*
The Glory of the Sun (Q, 19/10/25)
Passing Brompton Road ('*f.c.*': Brighton, 11/6/28; Crit., 10/7/28) *Fr. 1929*
'Big Fleas –' ('*f.c.*': K's, Southsea, 18/3/29; Com., 30/3/29)

BRANDT, W. R. [see *H. PEACEY*]

BRANSCOMBE, ARTHUR
The Boy Scout ('*c.*': B'ham, 20/5/12: +*G. FEARNLY:* title later to *Merry Miss Mischief*)
I've Seen the 'Arem ('*m.f.c.*': Empress, 3/8/14: originally called *Morocco Bound*)
Society Ltd. ('*m.pl.*', m. A. Carrington: Scala, 24/3/20)

BRANSON, LEE H. [see also *F. F. SHEPHERD*]
×Phoning for Help. LC, Portsmouth, 14/5/23

BRANT-SERO, JOHN OJIJATEKHA
×Genuine Fellow Savages (Spa, Bridlington, 7/3/05)

BRAUN, Mrs CHARLES
×The Blue Penguin (O.H., Harrogate, 19/1/14: +*H. SIMPSON*)

BRAY, RUTH
Sir Thomas More's House at Chelsea. *1926*

BRENCHLEY, GEORGE [see *V. SULLIVAN*]

BRENNAN, M. M.
×The Young Man from Rathmines ('*c.*': Abbey, Dublin, 6/4/22) *1923* (Dublin)
×A Leprechaun in the Tenement ('*fairy f.*': Abbey, Dublin, 5/9/22)

BRENNER, S. M.
The Girl and the Governor ('*c.o.*', m. J. Edwards: Bij., 2/10/06)

BRENTANO, LOWELL [see *C. F. OURSLER*]

BRERETON, ETHEL C.
×Heartsease ('*m. pl. for children*') *1930*

BRERETON, J. E.
×The Reckoning. LC, K. G's H., 16/6/22. *1924*

BRETT, E. H.
Beauty–A Beast. LC, Alex. Park Pastoral Stage, Hastings, 28/7/21

BRETT, Hon. SYLVIA LEONORA [see *Lady BROOKE*]

'BREVE'
×The Snow Queen ('*children's pl.*') *1925* (Ousley)
×The Fairy Reward ('*children's pl.*') *1925* (Ousley)
×The Pied Piper ('*children's pl.*) *1925* (Ousley)

BREWSTER, H. B.
The Wreckers ('*o.*', m. Ethel Smyth: Leipzig, 1906; H.M., 22/6/09, *m.*, Afternoon Theatre) *1909*

BRICE-WHITE, GORDON W.
The Emergency Exit ('*f.c.*': Little, Brighton, 3/2/27)

BRIDGEMAN [or *BRIDGMAN*], *CUNNINGHAM*
[For earlier plays see *H. E. D.* v, 275]
×Bob ('*oa.*', m. F. Cellier: H.M., Walsall, 8/4/03; Adel., 18/6/03)
×Memories (O.H., Middlesbrough, 12/2/15: title later changed to *Old Memories*)

BRIDGEMAN, SIDNEY
The Stable Door ('*mystery pl.*) *1919* (SPCK)

[*BRIDGERS, ANN PRESTON* [see *G. ABBOTT*]

BRIDGES, ROBERT SEYMOUR
Demeter ('*mask*') *1905* (Oxford)

BRIDGES, T. C. [see *V. BRIDGES*]

BRIDGES, VICTOR [*VICTOR GEORGE DE FREYNE BRIDGES*]
×Cleopatra (Bij., Bedford St., 15/12/07, Pl. Actors)
×Dead Man's Pool (Little, 28/3/21: +*T. C. BRIDGES*) *1929*
×Another Pair of Spectacles. *Fr. 1923*
×The Green Monkey ('*fantastic c.*') LC, St Giles H., Northampton, 17/10/1929. *1929* (Village D. Soc.)

BRIDGMAN, CUNNINGHAM [see *C. BRIDGEMAN*]

'*BRIDIE, JAMES*' [='*MARY HENDERSON*'=*OSBORNE HENRY MAVOR*]
×The Sunlight Sonata ('*f. morality*': Lyr., Glasgow, 20/3/28, Scott. Nat. Players: as by '*MARY HENDERSON*') *1930* (printed with *The Switchback* and *The Pardoner's Tale*)
The Switchback ('*c.*': Rep., B'ham, 9/3/29) *1930* (see above)
×The Pardoner's Tale. *1930* (see above)
What It Is to Be Young ('*c.*': Rep., B'ham, 2/11/29) *1934* (in *Colonel Wotherspoon and Other Plays*)
The Anatomist (Lyc., Edin., 6/7/30; Westminster, 7/10/31) *1931*
The Girl who did not want to go to Kuala Lumpur (Lyr., Glasgow, Scott. Nat. Players, 12/11/30: as by '*MARY HENDERSON*') *1934* (in *Colonel Wotherspoon and Other Plays*)
Tobias and the Angel (Festival, Cambridge, 20/11/30) *1931* (in *The Anatomist and Other Plays*)
[In a private letter, dated July 3, 1933, Bridie states that about 1913 he wrote two plays, *The Duke Who Seldom Smiled* and *Ethics Among Thieves;* some time later came *No Wedding Cake for Her* and *The Baron who Would Not Be Convinced.* Of these, the first was accepted by the Glasgow Repertory, but not produced: the texts of all have been lost. Apart from a burlesque, *The Jackals of Lone Pine Gulch*, performed by a concert party in Mesopotamia in 1918, his next play was *The Switchback*, originally composed about 1924 and 'doctored' three years later by John Brandane]

BRIGGS, HELEN M.
Julius Caesar (translated from *Giulio Cesare*, 1902, by Ennio Corradini) *1929*

BRIGGS, W. H. [see also *F. KARNO*]
Scarlet Runners. LC, '*m.pl.*': Hippo., Gloucester, 8/10/21

BRIGHOUSE, HAROLD [see also '*OLIVE CONWAY*' and *S. HOUGHTON*]
×The Doorway (Gai., Manchester, 10/4/09; Cor., 11/6/09) *Fr. 1913*
Dealing in Futures (Roy., Glasgow, 7/10/09) *Fr. 1913*
×The Price of Coal (Roy., Glasgow, 15/11/09; Playh., 28/11/11, *m.*) *1911*
The Polygon ('*c.*': Court, 5/2/11, Pl. Actors; LC, Lyr., 30/10/11, as *Graft*) *Fr. 1913* (as *Graft*)

×Lonesome-like (Roy., Glasgow, 6/2/11) *1911*
×Spring in Bloomsbury (Gai., Manchester, 3/4/11) *1913* (in *The Manchester Playgoer*); *Fr. 1913*
×The Oak Settle ('*c.*': Dalston, 7/4/11; Rep., L'pool, 16/1/12) *Fr. 1911*
×The Scaring Off of Teddy Dawson. LC, '*c.*', Dalston, 10/4/11. *Fr. 1911*
The Odd Man Out ('*c.*': Roy., 16/4/12) *Fr. 1912*
×Little Red Shoes (P.W., 20/5/12)
The Game ('*c.*': Rep., L'pool, 19/11/13; K's, Hamm., 29/8/21) *Fr. 1920*
Garside's Career ('*c.*': Gai., Manchester, 2/2/14; Cor., 11/5/14) *1914*; *Fr. 1914*
The Northerners ('*c.*': Gai., Manchester, 27/8/14) *Fr. 1920*
The Road to Raebury ('*c.*': P's, Manchester, 12/4/15; Crit., 18/6/15) *Fr. 1921*
×Followers (P's, Manchester, 19/4/15; Crit., 2/6/15) *1922*
×Converts ('*c.*': Gai., Manchester, 23/8/15; D.Y., 6/9/15) *1920*
Hobson's Choice ('*c.*': Poughkeepsie, 16/10/15; P'cess, N.Y., 2/11/15; Apo., 22/6/16) *1916*; *Fr. 1924*
The Clock Goes Round (D.P., Eastbourne, 25/9/16; Glo., 4/10/16)
Zack ('*character c.*': Syracuse, N.Y., 30/10/16; Com., 23/4/22, Rep. Players) *Fr. 1920*
×The Maid of France ('*fant.*': Metropolitan, 16/7/17) *1917*
The Bantam V.C. ('*f.*': St M., 24/7/19) *1925* (Boston)
Other Times ('*c.*': Little, 6/4/20)
Plays for the Meadow and Plays for the Lawn. *Fr. 1921*
[This contains four short plays: 1. *Maypole Morning*: LC, Crippl. Inst., 1/11/22; 2. *The Paris Doctor*: LC, Crippl. Inst., 1/11/22; 3. *The Prince who was a Piper*: LC, Crippl. Inst., 1/11/22; and 4. *The Man about the Place*: LC, Crippl. Inst., 1/11/22]
×Once a Hero ('*c.*': Ambass., Southend, 26/6/22) *1922*
×The Happy Hangman. LC, Crippl. Inst., 1/11/22 ('*grotesque*': Court, 15/6/25, *m.*) *1922*
×A Marrying Man (Playh., L'pool, 28/1/24) *Fr. 1924*
Mary's John ('*c.*': Playh., L'pool, 30/9/24; RADA, 2/10/27) *Fr. 1925*
×The Apple Tree; or, Why Misery Never Dies. *1923*
Open Air Plays. *Fr. 1926*
[This contains five short plays: 1. *The Laughing Mind*; 2. *The Oracles of Apollo*; 3. *The Rational Princess;* 4. *The Ghosts of Windsor Park*; and 5. *How the Weather is Made*]
When Did They Meet Again? LC, Gr., Lancaster, 7/10/26. *Fr. 1927*
×Fossie for Short. *Fr. 1927*
×The Little Liberty. *Fr. 1927*
×The Night of 'Mr H.' *Fr. 1927*
What's Bred in the Bone ('*c.*': Playh., L'pool, 4/4/27) *Fr. 1927*
It's a Gamble ('*Lancashire c.*': Playh., L'pool, 27/11/28)
Safe amongst the Pigs ('*c.*': Rep., B'ham, 27/4/29) *Fr. 1930*

Coincidence. *Fr. 1929*
The Sort-of-a-Prince. *Fr. 1929*
× The Stoker. *Fr. 1930*

BRIGHT, DORA [*Mrs KNATCHBULL*]
× The Dryad (‘*dance pl.*’: Playh., 26/3/07, *cpy.*; H.M., 4/6/09)
× The Portrait (‘*dance pl.*’: P.W., 24/11/10, *m.*)
× The Abbé’s Garden (‘*mimo-drama*’: Glo., 31/3/11, *m.*)
× In Haarlem There Dwelt – (‘*m.pl.*’: H.M., 21/5/12, *m.*; Playh., 22/1/13)
× Poor Pretty Colombine (‘*wordless dance pl.*’: Emp., Kilburn, 3/6/12)

BRIGHT, Mrs R. GOLDING [=‘*GEORGE EGERTON*’]

BRIGHTMAN, STANLEY
Battling Butler (‘*m.f.*’, m. P. Braham: Oxf., 8/12/22: +*A. MELFORD*)
The Haunted House (‘*md.*’: O.H., Manchester, 20/5/27)

BRINTON, J. C.
× Fully Insured (‘*ca.*’: Tetbury Inst. H., Gloucester, 27/4/12, *amat.*)

BRINTON, SELWYN [see *L. N. PARKER*]

BRISCOE, WALTER ALWYN
Three Allegorical Plays. *1912* (Cambridge and London: *priv.*)
[This contains three short verse plays: 1. *Beauty and the Beast*; 2. *The Wild Swans*; and 3. *The Sea Maiden*]

BRISTOWE, SYBIL
A School for Life (Court, 25/3/12)
× On the High Veldt (Lyc. Club, 4/11/13)

BRITTAIN, J.
× Getting the Dinner In. LC, Roy., Chester, 21/4/14

BRITTER, AMYAS
× A Question of Identity (‘*f.*’: Club H., Old Charlton, 11/1/19, *amat.*)
× Sunshine House (‘*health pl.*’) *1925*
The Sins of the Mother (T.H., Woolwich, 23/9/27, *amat.*)
× The Terrible Twins (‘*pl. for children*’) *1929* (Health and Cleanliness Council)

BRITTON, CONSTANCE E.
× Seeing and Believing (‘*Christmas fantasy*’) *1923* (printed in *Two Christmas Plays*)

BRITTON, EDWARD
× In Self Defence. LC, Gr., Southampton, 15/4/14

BRITTON, LIONEL ERSKINE
Brain (‘*pl. of the whole earth*’: Sav., 27/4/30) *1930*

BROADBENT, THOMAS W.
Medea (‘*t.*’: New, Ealing, 2/6/05, *cpy.*)

BROADBENT, UNA FRANCES DELMA RUSSELL
Agis, King of Sparta. *1930*

BROADBRIDGE, FREDERICK C.
× The Doctor (Rehearsal, 4/4/13)

BROADHEAD, WILLIAM B.
Manchester by Day and Night (Metro., Manchester, 17/9/00: called originally *The Black Sheep of Manchester*)
Struck Off the Rolls (Osborne, Manchester, 7/1/01)

BROADHURST, GEORGE H.
× Self-Defence (Hippo., 13/12/10)
Just Like John ('*f.*': York, 23/4/12, *cpy.*)
The Price (Aldw., 21/11/12)
Bought and Paid For (Lyr., 12/3/13) *Fr. 1914*
'The Law of the Land'. *Fr. 1914*
'Innocent'. *Fr. 1914*
He Didn't Want to Do It (P.W., 6/3/15: + *W. HACKETT*)
The Crimson Alibi ('*md.*': Auditorium, Baltimore, 12/5/19; Broadhurst, N.Y., 7/7/19; Str., 29/11/19)
What Happened to Jones ('*f.*') *Fr. 1919*
Why Smith Left Home ('*f.*') *Fr. 1924*

BROADHURST, THOMAS WILLIAM
The Holy City ('*scriptural d.*': Com., 5/5/14) *1904* (Philadelphia)

BROADSWORDE, WALTER
Junius Brutus [*1925*]

BROCK, FREDERICK
[For an earlier play see *H. E. D.* v, 276]
Because She Loved Him (St G's H., 11/2/01, *cpy.*)
Hernani ('*t.*') *1912*

BROCK, LYNN [='*ANTHONY P. WHARTON*']

BROCKWAY, ARCHIBALD FENNER
The Devil's Business ('*c.*') *1926* (I.L.P. Publishing Co.)

BRODIE, WALTER
A Mixed Foursome ('*f.c.*': Bristol, 17/5/26: + *T. JAY*)
A Perpetual Honeymoon (*f.c.*': Pal., Brighton, 18/4/29: + *T. JAY*)

BRODSKY, LEON
The Humour of It ('*c.*': Court, 11/3/12)

BROMFIELD, LOUIS
The House of Women (Q, 3/9/28)

BROMLEY, CONSTANCE
The Ranchman's Romance ('*r.pl.*': Qns, Leeds, 20/6/06)

BROMLEY-TAYLOR, Mrs RICA
× Stolen (St J., 5/7/17, *m.*: called originally *Stop Thief!*)
Aunt Maria ('*f.*': Leamington, 23/5/21)
× Pigeon's Blood. LC, '*f.*': Norwich, 6/12/21
× Two Women and a Telephone (Aldw., 25/5/24, Pl. Actors) *1924*
× The Bitter End. LC, K. G's H., 25/11/24

Five to One, and Other Sketches. *Fr. 1926*

[This contains six short playlets: 1. *Five to One!*; 2. *Poor Old Dad*; 3. *The Bitter End* (A.L.S. Trav. Th., 1924); 4. *Wanted, a Cook*; 5. *Mangold-Wurzel*; and 6. *What Happened to Edward*]

Four Jewish Sketches. *Fr. 1927*

[Numerous sketches and playlets produced at music-halls]

BRONCH, JAMES H.

×A Waefu' Bridal [and] The Reekin' Lum. *1927* (Paisley)

BROOKE, A. EDWARD

The Bolshevik (St Mary's H., Putney, 22/11/19)

The Sin of Ann Stanhope (Roy., Barrow-in-Furness, 17/9/17; Stratford, 26/3/20)

Playing with Fire (S. Shields, 14/7/20)

BROOKE, CHARLOTTE

×Greta (O.H., Harrogate, 22/7/10)

BROOKE, Lady, RANEE OF SARAWAK [*Hon. SYLVIA LEONORA BRETT*]

The Heels of Pleasure (Arts, 22/6/29) *1930* (Allahabad)

BROOKE, E. H.

×The Lottery (Brighton, 12/6/03)

BROOKE, EMMA

The Twins of Skirlaugh Hall (Margate, 17/6/07)

BROOKE, FRED G.

×The World's Opinion (Qns Pal., Poplar, 9/12/07; S.W., 23/8/09: +*D. DEANE*)

BROOKE, RUPERT CRAWNER

×Lithuania (Little, Chicago, 12/10/15; H.M., 19/5/16, *m.*) *1915* (Chicago); *1935*

BROOKE, VIOLET

×Loneliness (Pembroke H., Earls Court, 20/1/24, Sunday Players)

BROOKES, CECILIA F. [see also *N. OLIVER*]

×Unanswered (Terry's, 4/7/09, English Pl. Soc.)

×Pechorin (Bed. H., Chelsea, 5/2/22, Pax Robertson Salon)

BROOKES, HARRY [see *G. A. RILEY*]

BROOKFIELD, CHARLES HALLAM ELTON [see also *B. HOOD*]

[For earlier plays see *H. E. D.* v, 276–7]

Kenyon's Widow ('*c.*': Com., 10/5/00)

×Mafeking Night (Duchess, Balham, 15/10/00: called originally *Mafeking in London*: +*H. FERRAR*)

×The Man with a Past (Gar., 11/12/00)

×The New Regime (P.W., 25/6/03)

×A Lady Burglar (Court, L'pool, 3/11/04; Terry's, 31/3/06)

×Pagliacci (Sav., 6/12/04)

What Pamela Wanted ('*c.*': Crit., 22/4/05)

Dear Old Charlie ('*f.*': Newcastle, 17/5/06; Vaud., 2/1/08:

adapted from *Célimare le bien-aimé* (1863) by E. Labiche and A. Delacourt)
See See ('*Chinese m.c.*', m. S. Jones: P.W., 20/6/06)
×The Young Lady of Seventeen (Crit., 22/2/11)
The Spring Maid ('*m.pl.*', m. H. Reinhart: Whitney, 30/9/11)

BROOKING, CECIL
×Ring Off ('*c.a.*': P.W., Grimsby, 6/2/12, *amat.*: +*A. N. TAYLER*)
×Dressed for Action ('*c.*': Crippl. Inst., 7/4/26, Ingoldsby Club: +*A. N. TAYLER*)

BROOKLYN, THOMAS
×Algy's Advertisement (Hippo., Rotherhithe, 21/2/10)

BROOKS, ALAN
Dollars and Sense ('*humorous t.*': Alh., 8/5/22)

BROOKS, E. OSWALD
×The Simple (?) Life (Gr., Swansea, 29/4/07: +*R. C. JENKINS*)

[*BROOKS, GEORGE SPRAGUE*
Spread Eagle (New, 27/6/28: +*W. B. LISTER*) *1927* (New York)

BROSNAN, ALMA
×The Street. *1926* (Labour Publishing Co.)
Scrapped (Arts, 23/9/27: revised by M. MALLESON) *1928*
At Number Fifteen (Gar., 16/10/27, Rep. Players) *1927*
Billington-Harvey. *1928*

BROSNAN, GERALD
×Before Midnight (Abbey, Dublin, 16/7/28)
×Dark Isle (Abbey, Dublin, 31/12/29)

BROSTER, DOROTHY KATHLEEN
The Yellow Poppy ('*r.pl.*': Rep., Plymouth, 23/1/22; Com., 12/2/22, Rep. Players: +*W. E. STIRLING*)

BROUETT, ALBERT
Around the World in Eighty Days. LC, Guignol, Brixton, 6/5/21

BROUGH, CECIL
×Madame's Holiday (Rehearsal, 4/2/11, English Pl. Soc.)

BROUGH, F. [see *F. MOULE*]

BROUGHTON, MARY
The Moonrakers. LC, Barnes, 6/6/25

BROWMANN, F. M.
An Indian Girl's Devotion (Junction, Manchester, 10/3/13; Emp., Holloway, 26/1/14)

BROWN, ALICE [see *SIBYL CALDWELL*]

BROWN, C. C.
×The Black Knight. LC, '*oa.*': Pal., Battersea, 7/5/19

BROWN, CAMPBELL RAE [see *CAMPBELL RAE-BROWN*]

BROWN, CHARLES
×The Finger of Fate ('*bsq.*': Walsingham Club, 15/1/05: +*A. HILL*)

BROWN, ALBERT CURTIS
Management ('*c.*': Kings., 20/12/08, English Pl. Soc.)
×Mrs Hazenby's Health. *1912*

BROWN, E. B.
The Night-Jaw. *1929* (*priv.*)

BROWN, G. GILBERT [see also *E. GOULDING*]
×Two Ways of Love. LC, Court, 7/11/13

BROWN, IVOR [*IVOR JOHN CARNEGIE BROWN*]
×Smithfield Preserv'd; or, The Divill a Vegetarian. LC, '*interlude*': Holborn Restaurant, 20/6/22. *Fr. 1925*
×Down on the Farm ('*satirical bsq.*': Everyman, 14/6/26) *Fr. 1939*

BROWN, J. R.
×Cat and Dog. LC, Brighton, 29/10/13: +*A. MALLAHEN*

BROWN, JOHN
The Ford of Thorn. LC, Peterhouse Gdns., Cambridge, 7/6/22

BROWN, L. P.
The Potter's Shop ('*c. of mediaeval Persia*': Rep. B'ham, 4/9/20)

BROWN, MARGARET
×The King of Cosmopoland ('*f.*') *1929*

BROWN, MARTIN
Cobra (Hudson, N.Y., 22/4/24; Nottingham, 3/8/25; Gar., 18/8/25)

BROWN, PERCY
Remember Belgium (Woolwich, 10/5/15: called originally *George Grant*)

BROWN, VINCENT
The Greater Love ('*moral pl.*': Brighton, 10/6/01; P's, Accrington, 21/6/09; Edin., 11/4/10)
The Golden Age (Worthing, 7/7/02)

BROWNE, EDITH A. [see also *F. CASTLES*]
×A Farewell Supper (Bij., 11/3/08, New Stage Club; Pal., 13/2/11; Little, 11/3/11: adapted from A. Schnitzler's *Anatol*, 1893: +*A. GREIN*)
[See also under *HARLEY GRANVILLE-BARKER*]
×Literature (Vic. H., 11/3/08, New Stage Club: adapted from A. Schnitzler: +*A. GREIN*)
×The Other Tenth of the Law (Court, 21/3/09, Dramatic Debaters)

BROWNE, ERNEST
×The Recreant Monk. LC, County, Reading, 31/3/13

BROWNE, Miss FRANKIE (*FRANCES*)
Ilsa ('*oa.*': D.P., Eastbourne, 12/5/11, *amat.*)

×Rainbow Ltd. ('*children's fant.*': D.P., Eastbourne, 21/11/11, *m.*)
To Oblige Gertrude ('*c.*': D.P., Eastbourne, 16/12/24, *amat.*)

BROWNE, K. R. G. [see *V. WOODHOUSE*]

BROWNE, MAURICE [see *R. M. B. NICHOLS*]

[*BROWNE, PORTER EMERSON*
A Fool There Was (Qns, 21/3/11)
×In and Out. LC, Oxf., 15/5/14
The Bad Man (Com., N.Y., 30/8/20; Gr., Leeds, 19/2/23; New, 3/3/23) *Fr. 1926*

[*BROWNE, WALTER* [see *S. PHILLIPS*]

BROWNING, HANWORTH STEPHEN [see also *E. BURNABY*]
A Member of Tattersall's (Brighton, 8/10/09; Whitney, 28/2/12)
×Father (Pal., Tynemouth, 17/7/11)
Julian Gets Respectable ('*c.*': W.G., New Brighton, 9/6/13)
The Tame Cat ('*f.*': Q, 4/1/26)
Call Me Georges ('*c.*': Gar., 17/5/28: called originally *The Decline and Fall of the Water-Hens*)
Young Ideas ('*f.c.*': O.H., Blackpool, 7/5/28)

BROWNSON, JACK (JOHN) E.
P.C. Hobbs. LC, '*m.pl.*': Bolton, 11/6/19
[Several sketches produced at music-halls]

BRUCE, GEORGE
×The Blacksmith (Foresters', 10/10/10)

BRUCE, HARRY (HENRY) P. [see *W. BURNOT* and *J. H. DARNLEY*]

BRUMELL, G. HENRY
×Storm Clouds (Bury, 19/6/00)

BRUMFIT, ETHEL
Hinemoa ('*Maori m.pl.*': Ass. R., Surbiton, 25/11/25)

BRUNE, C. M. [see *E. J. LOCKE*]

BRUNNER, ETHEL
The Elopement, or, Celia Intervenes. *1917*

BRUNTON, F. CARMICHAEL [see also *J. A. BATLEY*]
×The Door on t'Chain (Ldn School of Economics, 25/1/24, Half Circle Club) *1928* (Village Dr. Soc.)
×Blind Man's Buff (Arts, 10/11/27) *1933* (in *Eight One-Act Plays*)
×Bet; Better; Best! *Fr. 1930*
×The Door. *Fr. 1930*

BRYANT, E. CRAPTON
An English Girl; or, A Tale of India ('*m.pl.*', m. M. Goyder: K's, Sutton-in-Ashfield, 8/5/07, *amat.*)

BRYANT, EMILY M.
×The Peacemaker ('*c.*': Apo., 22/1/07) *Fr. 1908*
×The Spare Room (Crit., 27/2/09)

BRYANT, KENNETH M.
Herne the Hunter (Vic., Burnley, 26/8/00, *cpy.*)

BUBNA, IRENE, Countess
×The Toast (Everyman, 2/5/21)
Reggie Reforms ('*f.c.*': Everyman, 2/5/21: +*E. CAMILLER*)

BUCALOSSI, BRIGATA
×Moonshine (Hippo., Manchester, 29/5/11; Court, 16/9/11)

BUCALOSSI, ERNEST
×The Head of the House ('*m.pl.*': Scala, 16/10/10)
×A Haunted Honeymoon. LC, Granville, Walham Green, 8/10/20

BUCHANAN, ANDREW
When the Light Came (Little Vic., Brighton, 27/4/25: +*R. WHITEHOUSE*)

BUCHANAN, DOUGLAS
×Robespierre (Vic. H., Weston, 24/4/05)

BUCHANAN, MABEL [see *H. D. G. FOORD*]

BUCHANAN, R. C.
[For an earlier play see *H. E. D.* v, 284]
×Very Very Much Engaged ('*ca.*': T.H., Coatbridge, 13/10/00, *cpy.*: a revised version of his play of 1895)

BUCHANAN, ROBERT
[For earlier plays see *H. E. D.* v, 284–5]
×The Night Watch ('*poetic d.*': Emp., Southend, 8/4/02, *amat.*)
The Maiden Queen ('*c.o.*', m. F. Pascal: Ladbr. H., 6/4/05: +'*CHARLES MARLOWE*')

[*BUCHANAN, THOMPSON*
A Woman's Way ('*c.*': H., 16/4/09, *cpy.*; Com., 14/9/10)
Civilian Clothes ('*c.*': Los Angeles, 29/6/19; Morosco, N.Y., 12/9/19; D.Y., 25/7/22) *1920* (Ottawa)

BUCKHAM, B.
×From Nine till Ten. LC, Glo., 7/5/18

BUCKINGHAM, D. VINCENT
The Hand of Destiny (St Julian's H., Guernsey, 23/8/05)

BUCKLAW, ALFRED
[For earlier plays see *H. E. D.* v, 286]
×Nancy (Str., 11/7/01)
×The Suffragette (Arts Centre, 24/3/14)

BUCKLE, GERARD FORT
×The Contract (All Saints Parish H., Battersea Park, 22/10/12, *amat.*)
×Why Man is Bad (Pier, St Leonards, 17/3/13)
×You—? (Pav., 18/2/14)

BUCKLEY, DONALD
His Sacrifice (Ladbr. H., 26/6/08, *cpy.*)
A Night in June (Everyman, 10/1/28) *1929*

BUCKLEY, JOHN [see *P. BERNARD*]

BUCKLEY, REGINALD R.
Arthur of Britain ('*chronicle d.*') *1914*
The Round Table ('*music d.*', m. Rutland Boughton: Ass. R., Glastonbury, 14/8/16)
The Birth of Arthur ('*music d.*', m. Rutland Boughton: Ass. R., Glastonbury, 27/8/25) *1926*

BUCKSTONE, J. C.
×Scrooge (Vaud., 3/10/01)
×The Postman's Knock (Hippo., Willesden, 22/5/11)

BUCKTON, ALICE MARY
×Eager Heart ('*Christmas mystery pl.*') *1904*
×A Masque of Beauty and the Beast. *1904*
×Kings in Babylon. *1906*
×The Garden of Many Waters. *1907*
The Coming of Bride ('*pageant pl.*') *1914*
×The Meeting in the Gate ('*Christmas interlude*') *1916*
×Dawn of Day. LC, St J., 28/2/1919. *1919*

BUDD, SIDNEY W.
×Stainless Steel (Greyhound, Croydon, 29/7/29)

BUDDEN, PEARCE [see *M. FREY*]

BULGER, GODWIN
×A Shaped End (Balfour Inst., L'pool, 8/1/10, *amat.*)
The Message (David Lewis Club, L'pool, 22/2/12)
×Basil Dunthwaite Comes Home (W.G., New Brighton, 8/7/12)
A Second Spring (Playh., L'pool, 15/7/18)
Millicent and Mr Smith ('*c.*': Playh., L'pool, 13/10/20)

BULL, GEORGE [see *R. A. BRANDON*]

BULLETT, GERALD
Mr Godley Beside Himself ('*c.*': Lyr., Hamm., 28/2/26, 300 Club) *1926*

BULLOCK, SHAN
Snowdrop Jane ('*c.*': O.H., Belfast, 2/2/15)

BULMER, FRED [see also *W. HIBBERT*]
Deadwood Dick (Lincoln, 2/8/13)
For Auld Lang Syne (Junction, Manchester, 29/12/13)
A Gentleman in Khaki (Junction, Manchester, 23/11/14: called originally *A Soldier of the Czar*: +*W. BENGE*)

BUNTIN, Mrs A. C.
×The Japanese Curio (Lyc. Club, 28/1/13)
×With the Publisher's Compliments (Lauriston H., Edin., 6/3/12, *amat.*)

BUONAPARTE, JUAN
The Real Napoleon (Gai., Manchester, 9/3/11: +*A. SHIRLEY*)

BURDEKIN, KATHARINE
Morgan le Fay ('*Arthurian d.*': RADA, 28/10/23)

BURFOOT, J. E

× Drifting Down (Conservative Club, Windsor, 19/4/00, *amat.*)

BURGOYNE, Sir ALAN HUGHES

That Foreigner ('*Tariff Reform pl.*': Vic. H., 27/2/08, *amat.*)

BURKHARDT, ADDISON

[A few sketches produced in music-halls]

BURKE, A. L.

Thank You, Phillips ('*c.*': Apo., 10/11/21)
A Disturbed Night ('*c.*': Q, 16/5/27)
Corporal Cupid ('*c.*': Playh., Walton, 17/10/27)

BURKE, EDWIN

This Thing Called Love ('*c.*': Alh., Glasgow, 17/6/29; Apo., 24/6/29) *Fr. 1929*
[Several sketches produced at music-halls]

BURLES, FRANK

Over the Wall ('*f.*': Margate, 8/5/11)

BURLEY, JOHN

Tom Trouble ('*North-country c.*': Emp., Holborn, 15/3/20) *1920*

BURNABY, EUSTACE

× That Did It! ('*m.c.*': Hippo., Crouch End, 11/5/08: + *H. S. BROWNING*)
× Oh, My Aunt! LC, '*f.*': K's H., Ilkley, 12/8/13

BURNETT, Mrs FRANCES ELIZA HODGSON

[For earlier plays see *H. E. D.* v, 292, 782]
A Little Un-fairy Princess (Shaft., 20/12/02; Terry's, 19/1/03, as *A Little Princess*)
The Pretty Sister of José ('*c.*': D.Y., 16/10/03, *cpy.*)
That Man and I (New, 24/10/03, *cpy.*)
The Dawn of a Tomorrow (Shak., L'pool, 2/5/10; Gar., 13/5/10)

BURNETT, Rev. FRANCIS R.

Divorce (K's, Southsea, 16/12/20)

BURNETTE, CLARENCE [see *S. SPENCER*]

[For earlier plays see *H. E. D.* v, 293]
A Queen of Hearts ('*m.c.*', m. R. E. Irving: Emp., Huddersfield, 2/7/00; rewritten with *H. W. C. NEWTE* and new music by P. Henry, Grand, Rawtenstall, 6/1/02)
When a Man Hates (Ilkeston, 29/8/04; Stratford, 26/6/05)
A Drunkard's Daughter (Blyth, 26/7/05; W.L., 25/6/06, as *A Gambler's Daughter*)
A Soldier of France ('*r.d.*': Woolwich, 13/4/08: + *C. A. CLARKE*)
Her Fatal Marriage (Aston, 28/12/08; Woolwich, 25/1/09: + *A. HINTON*)

BURNEY, ESTELLE

[For earlier plays see *H. E. D.* v, 293]
× The Wisdom of Lord Glynde ('*c.*': D.Y., 28/6/04)
The Greater Glory (Shaft., 19/1/08, Pioneers)

×Off the Cornish Coast (Kings., 2/3/08, *m.*)
×Flo Rigg (Alb. H., 2/6/08)
×The Odd Number (Emp., Kilburn, 17/10/10: +*H. SWEARS*)
The One Thing Needful ('*c.*': Court, 30/3/14, Pl. Actors: +*H. SWEARS*)
The Prodigy ('*f.c.*': Court, 22/12/17, *m.*)

BURNHAM, MARY
×Mother's Bill (Manchester, 10/3/13)

BURNLEIGH, LENA [see *I. L. CASSILIS*]

BURNOT, WALTER
[For earlier plays see *H. E. D.* v, 293]
On Distant Shores (R.A., Woolwich, 18/4/1897; Stratford, 29/4/01: +*H. P. BRUCE*)
Snares of London (Stratford, 16/4/00: +*M. TREVOSPER* and *H. P. BRUCE*)

[*BURNSIDE, R. H.*
The Girl from Cook's ('*m.c.*', m. R. Hubbell and J. Gilbert: Pal., Manchester, 24/10/27; Gai., 1/11/27: +*G. NEWMAN*)

BURRELL, JAMES L. A.
Fata Morgana (Gar., N.Y., 3/3/24; Ambass., 15/9/24: +*P. MOELLER*: adapted from the Hungarian of E. Vajda) *1924*

BURTON, ALARIC
Francesca (Ath., Glasgow, 16/2/03)
Nell Gwyn ('*r.c.*': Ath., Glasgow, 2/11/06)
Queen of Scots (Berkeley H., Glasgow, 1/4/14)

BURTON, B. P.
Prince Fazil (New, 25/3/26: adapted from P. Frondaie, *L'Insoumise* (1922); called originally *Lord and Master*: +*B. LAWRENCE*)

BURTON, G. M. [see *G. M. CARLYON*]

BURTON, GEORGE
×Merry Maid, Marian (Cosy Corner, S. Shields, 29/6/08)

BURTON, H. V. T.
×The Black Crinoline ('*fant.*') *1923*
×Princess Pavona ('*pastoral*') *1923*
×The Bias ('*pastoral*': Scala, 11/6/25, *m.*) *1925* (Leominster)
×Betula ('*fairy pl. for children*') *1925*

BURY, H. G.
Bright and Breezy ('*m.f.*': Emp., Wolverhampton, 27/8/17: called originally *Fitz and Startz*, title changed later to *Some Cocktail*)

BUSH, W. COATS
×Man (Rehearsal, 14/11/11)
×The Weakest Link (Rehearsal, 14/11/11)

BUSHELL, CHARLES
×Smith of the Loamshires (Kilworth, 1/5/18, *amat.*)

BUTLER, RALPH T.
The Maid in the Moon ('*dream fant.*', m. P. H. Hart: Vic. H., 1/2/08)

BUTTS, MARY
×A Mother by Proxy (Edwardes Square, Kensington, 9/1/20)

BYAM, G. [see *W. BOYLE*]

BYATT, HENRY
[For earlier plays see *H. E. D.* v, 295]
King Alfred the Great; or, The First Man (County, Bedford, 10/7/01, *cpy.*)

BYFORD, JOAN
The Rest Home (Pal., Brighton, 13/5/29)

BYFORD, T.
Treasure Trove. LC, Corn Exchange, Hertford, 21/4/22

BYNG, HUGH EDWARD CRANMER
The Success of Sentiment (Court, 27/9/08, Pl. Actors)

BYRNE, A. [see *M. A. COWAN*]

BYRNE, DOLLY [see also *G. VARESI*]
The Land of the Stranger ('*c. of disillusionment*': Gai., Dublin, 8/12/24, Ulster Players)

BYRNE, JAMES
Lords and Masters (Gai., Manchester, 22/5/11: called originally *Your Wife*) *1911*

BYRNE, MURIEL ST CLARE
England's Elizabeth (RADA, 30/9/28)

BYRON, TERENCE
[A few sketches produced at music-halls]

C., E. V.
×The Committee Meeting. LC, Ath., Glasgow, 2/9/19
×The Diamond Ring. LC, Ath., Glasgow, 2/9/19
×A Near Thing. LC, Ath., Glasgow, 2/9/19

CABLE, JAMES
The New Boatswain ('*m.c.*': Hippo., Portsmouth, 2/4/10, *cpy.*)

CADMAN, ANGELA
×We Dine at Seven. *Fr. 1916* (+*P. DAVEY*)

CADMAN, EDWARD
The Wonder-Worker ('*c.o.*', m. A. W. Ketelby: Gr., Fulham, 8/10/00)
The Gollywog ('*m.pl.*', m. J. Greebe: Ladbr. H., 2/11/10, *cpy.*)
×The Royalist (Margate, 8/5/11)

CADWELL, FLORALYN
The Wicked Wang-Pah Meets a Dragon ('*Chinese fant.*') *Fr. 1926*

CAESAR, IRVING [see *F. MANDEL*]

CAINE, Sir HALL [*THOMAS HENRY HALL CAINE*]
[For earlier plays see *H. E. D.* v, 299–300]
Jan, the Icelander; or, Home, Sweet Home (Gr., W. Hartlepool, 24/11/00, *cpy.*; Manchester, 4/9/11, as *The Quality of Mercy*)

The Eternal City (Gai., Douglas, 17/8/01, *cpy.*; H.M., 2/10/02: adapted from his own novel, 1901) *1902*

The Prodigal Son (Gr., Douglas, 2/11/04; D.L., 7/9/05: dramatised from his own novel, 1904) *1905* (*priv.*)

The Bondman (D.L., 20/9/06: dramatised from his own novel, 1890) *1906*

The Christian (Lyc., 31/8/07: new version from his own novel, 1897)

Pete (Lyc., 29/8/08: dramatised from his novel, *The Manxman*, 1894: +*L. N. PARKER*)

×The Fatal Error (Qns, Poplar, 21/9/08)

The White Prophet (Gar., 27/11/08, *cpy.*)

×The Red Shirt (Qns, 29/3/10, *cpy.*)

The Bishop's Son (Gr., Douglas, 15/8/10; Gar., 28/9/10) *1910* (*priv.*)

The Eternal Question (Gar., 27/8/10) *1910* (*priv.*)

The Prime Minister (Atlantic City, 14/1/16, as *Margaret Schiller*; New Amsterdam, N.Y., 31/1/16; Roy., 30/3/18) *1919*

×The Iron Hand (Col., 21/2/16)

The Woman Thou Gavest Me (Shubert, Boston, 9/4/17)

CAINE, WILLIAM [see also *A. D. GRANGE*]

The Island of Pharos ('*c.o.*', m. O. Roberts: T.H., Chelsea, 18/5/04)

×Drinks All Round (Qns, 29/10/20: +*J. A. B. HAMMOND* and *J. P. TURNBULL*)

CAIRNS, J. E.

×The Three Strangers (Little, L'pool, 20/10/27, *amat.*)

CALDCLEUGH, CARTHAGE [see also *A. CLARKE*]

×Man Proposes, God Disposes. LC, Inverness, 20/2/20

The Marble Heart (Sacriston, 3/3/21)

CALDEN, HARRY [see *H. RAY*]

CALDERON, GEORGE [see also *St J. HANKIN*]

The Fountain ('*c.*': Aldw., 28/3/09, St. Soc.) *1911*

The Seagull (Roy., Glasgow, 2/11/09; Little, 31/3/12, Adelphi Pl. Soc.: translated from A. Chekhov, *Chaika*, 1896) *1912* (printed with *The Cherry Orchard*)

×The Little Stone House (Aldw., 29/1/11, St. Soc.; Gai., Manchester, 9/10/11; Court, 19/5/13) *1913*

Two Plays by Anton Tchekov and One by Alfred de Musset. *1912*
[This includes *The Seagull* (see above), *The Cherry Orchard* and *Perdican and Camilla*]

×The Maharani of Arakân (Alb. H., 30/7/12, Indian Dr. Soc.; Rep., Bushey, 29/11/13; Col., 19/6/16)
[In 1914 this play, described as 'adapted from a story by Rabindra Nath Tagore', with 'songs by Rabindra Nath Tagore', was advertised as published, but I have failed to locate a copy]

Revolt (Gai., Manchester, 11/11/12) *1922* (in *Three Plays and a Pantomime*)

Eight One-act Plays. *1922*
[This contains: 1. *Peace*; 2. *The Little Stone House* (see above); 3. *Derelicts*; 4. *Geminae* (D.P., Eastbourne, 3/11/13; Little, 7/11/13); 5. *Parkin Bros.*; 6. *The Two Talismans*; 7. *The Lamp*; and 8. *Longing*]
Cromwell, Mall o' Monks ('*historical pl.*') *1922* (in *Three Plays and a Pantomime*)
Cinderella ('*an Ibsen pantomime*') *1922* (in *Three Plays and a Pantomime*)

CALDWELL, SIBYL
×Their New Paying Guest. *Fr. 1905*
×A Domestic Entanglement. *Fr. 1905*
×Up to Date. *Fr. 1905*
×The Deceitful Miss Smiths'. *Fr. 1906*
×The Ejection of Aunt Lucinda. *Fr. 1907*
×The Misses' Primroses' Deception. *Fr. 1907*
×That Horrid Major. *Fr. 1907*
×The Final Rehearsal. *Fr. 1908*
×Two Aunts at a Time. *Fr. 1908*
Five Sketches for Women's Institutes. *Fr. 1924*
[This contains: 1. *Mary's Dismissal*; 2. *Cousin Lucy*; 3. *Mmes. Fanshaws Ltd.*; 4. *The Diamond Brooch*; and 5. *Lucky Cinderella*]
Quite a Nice Cat: and Other Sketches for Women's Institutes. *Fr. 1927*
[This collection of four playlets, edited by Sibyl Caldwell, contains two pieces by her – *Quite a Nice Cat* and *Sinking*, together with *Joint Owners in Spain* by *A. BROWN* and *Blood Will Tell* by *S. KEMPER*]

CALEY, C. H.
×The Ninth Hour. LC, Little, Bristol, 16/4/24

CALLAHAN, D. T.
Guilty Gold ('*o.*': Dalston, 26/11/06; called originally *Andree*)

CALLENDER, A. ROMAINE
×Over the Hills to the Poorhouse (Gai., Hastings, 24/2/05)

CALLISTER, CHRISTIAN
×A Little Bit of Youth ('*c.*': Abbey, Dublin, 28/5/18)

CALMOUR, ALFRED C.
[For earlier plays see *H. E. D.* v, 300]
The Queen of the Roses ('*c.*': Court, 31/1/00, *cpy.*; Wynd., 13/6/02)
The Mistress of Craignairn ('*r.pl.*': Court, L'pool, 26/2/00)
Dante ('*r.pl.*': Qns, Manchester, 15/6/03; Cor., 28/9/03)
Jevan, the Prodigal Son ('*r.d.*': Qns, Manchester, 30/10/05; Scala, 20/4/07, as *The Judgment of Pharaoh*)
Essex ('*r.pl.*': Qns, Manchester, 7/10/07)

CALTHROP, DION CLAYTON [see also *G. E. JENNINGS*, *A. STRONG* and *C. H. BOURNE*]
×Scaramouch (St J., 1/7/10, *m.*)

×The Great Man (H.M., 28/2/11, *m.*)
×The Gate of Dreams (Col., 31/7/11) *Fr. 1914*
×The Mask (Pav., 22/1/12)
×Trapped (Com., 3/5/13)
The Harlequinade ('*an excursion*': St J., 1/9/13: +*H. GRANVILLE-BARKER*) *1918*
A la carte (Pal., 1/9/13)
×A Private Room (Crit., 16/2/15, *m.*: called originally *Are You There?*)
×The Popular Novelist (Pav., 16/5/16, *m.*)
×A Dramatic Situation (Theatrical Gdn Party, Regent's Park, 11/7/16)
The Old Country (Wynd., 2/9/16)
×The Chance of a Lifetime (Theatrical Gdn Party, Chelsea, 10/7/17)
×Unfurnished (Theatrical Gdn Party, Chelsea, 10/7/17)
A Southern Maid ('*m.pl.*', m. H. Fraser-Simson: P's, Manchester, 24/12/17; Daly's, 15/5/20: +*H. GRAHAM*)
Domes of Silence (Theatrical Gdn Party, R. Botanic Gdns, 25/6/18)
×The King's Majesty (Theatrical Gdn Party, R. Botanic Gdns, 30/5/19)
×Art and Society (Theatrical Gdn Party, R. Botanic Gdns, 30/5/19)
The Daughter of Madame Angot ('*o.*', m. C. Lecocq: D.L., 2/7/19)
×Sweetness and Innocence; or, The Little Liar (Theatrical Gdn Party, Chelsea, 22/6/20)
Out to Win (Shaft., 11/6/21: +*R. PERTWEE*)
×And Did He? (Theatrical Gdn Party, Chelsea, 26/6/21)
Two's Company (Theatrical Gdn Party, Chelsea, 23/6/22)
×Every Tomorrow (Theatrical Gdn Party, Chelsea, 24/6/24)
×The Man with the Whip. LC, Hippo., 22/8/25
×Odfaa; or, Blondes Prefer Gentlemen (Theatrical Gdn Party, Chelsea, 22/6/26)

CALTON, —
The Egyptologist's Daughter (Gloucester, 7/12/00)

CALVADORE, LOUIS
The Way of the Cross (Q, 24/1/27)

CALVERT, CAYLEY [see also *J. M. EAST*]
Saint Augustine. LC, Sandham H., Coldwaltham, 29/12/21
[Several sketches and playlets produced at music-halls]

CALVERT, FRANK
[Several sketches and playlets produced in music-halls]

CALVERT, LOUIS [see *K. ANDREWS* and *E. A. PARRY*]

CALVERT, WILLIAM E.
The Last Word ('*c.*': Steiner H., 4/3/27, Internat. Theatre Soc.: translated from the Danish of Olaf Bang)

CALVOCORESSI, MICHAEL DIMITRI
Love Adrift ('*c.o.*', m. Poldini: Gai., 6/10/26: adapted from E. Vajda, *Szerelem vaśará*, 1920)

CAMARSON, INE [see *C. STORM*]

CAMBRIDGE, J. G.
The Love Thief ('*Canadian pl.*': Qns, 1/3/16: called originally *The Frame Up*)

'*CAMERON, GEORGE*'
Billy ('*f.*': Playh., 6/4/12: called originally *Billy's Tombstones*) *Fr. 1914*

CAMERON, IAIN
× Pot Hooks ('*Highland Harlequinade*': Lyr., Glasgow, 12/11/29, Scott. Nat. Players)

CAMERON, J.
× Certainly Not. LC, Gr., Nelson, 12/3/18

CAMERON, MARGARET
× The Teeth of the Gift Horse. *Fr. 1909*
× The Piper's Pay. *Fr. 1910*
× The Kleptomaniac. *Fr. 1910*
× The Burglar. *Fr. 1917*

CAMERON, RHODA
Great Jupiter ('*c.o.*', m. H. Whermann: Gr., Radcliffe, 20/9/01)

CAMILLE, LUCILLE [see *G. LERONA*]

CAMILLER, EDGAR [see *IRENE, Countess BUBNA*]

CAMP, J.
[A few sketches produced at music-halls]

CAMPBELL, ALAN
Dust of Egypt ('*fant. f.*': Wynd., 6/2/12)

CAMPBELL, ARTHUR
× An Author's Production (Rehearsal, 18/3/13)

CAMPBELL, Mrs CECIL [='*LAURENCE PRITCHARD*']

CAMPBELL, Lady COLIN [see *C. GRAVES*]

CAMPBELL, CONSTANCE
× One of the Old Guard. LC, 13/6/14. *Fr. 1914*
× My Friend Thomas Atkins (Hippo., Manchester, 26/11/14; Col., 14/12/14)
× A Dilemma (Little, 7/3/15, Pioneer Players)
× The Rub (Pav., 25/6/15, *m.*, Woman's Theatre)
× When Woman Wills. LC, Coll., 19/8/15

CAMPBELL, GABRIELLE M. V. [='*GEORGE R. PREEDY*']

CAMPBELL, GERALDINE
× The Wreckers (Richmond, 27/1/08)
× Broken Fetters (Hippo., Woolwich, 14/2/10)

CAMPBELL, H. K.

×The Foreign Butler (H.M., Carlisle, 17/2/06, *cpy.*: +*G. C. SURFIELD*)

CAMPBELL, J. A.

The Sin of Her Childhood (Roy., Barrow-in-Furness, 24/4/03, *cpy.*: P's, Accrington, 14/12/03; Lyr., Hamm., 31/10/04)
The Little Breadwinner (Alex., B'ham, 11/12/05; Stand., 19/3/06)
The Old Folks at Home (Junction, Manchester, 30/9/07; Lyr., Hamm., 5/10/08)
From Convent to Throne (Osborne, Manchester, 31/3/09, *cpy.*; Rotunda, L'pool, 26/7/09; Lyr., Hamm., 6/9/09; P's, 1/8/14, as *A Queen at Seventeen*)
The Hand that Rocks the Cradle (Junction, Manchester, 10/3/10, *cpy.*; Junction, Manchester, 25/7/10; E.C., 14/11/10, as *The Coastguard's Daughter*)
The Queen Mother (Junction, Manchester, 30/10/12; E.C., 1/9/13)
×The Right Thing. LC, Grantham, 23/10/13
Devil-May-Care (Junction, Manchester, 13/4/14)
×The Future Generation. LC, Grantham, 6/12/17
×Robespierre. LC, Grantham, 15/5/18
Ever since Eve (Peterborough, 27/2/22; called originally *The House of Cards*)
×Derek's Wife. LC, Norwich, 28/9/22
[Several short plays produced in music-halls]

CAMPBELL, JOSEPH [=*SEOSAMB MacCATHMHAOIL*]

×Judgement (Abbey, Dublin, 15/4/12) *1912* (Dublin)

CAMPBELL, KANE

The Enchanted April ('*c.*') *Fr. 1927*

CAMPBELL, P. STURROCK

×Trapped; or, One Good Turn (K's, Edin., 14/4/16)
×The Crock of Gold (K's, Edin., 12/11/19)
×The Camerons (K's, Edin., 12/11/19)

CAMPBELL, Mrs VERE (*JOSEPHINE ELIZABETH*]

[For earlier plays see *H. E. D.* v, 301]
×The Gate of Eden ('*r.pl.*': Pav., Eastbourne, 6/11/01)

CAMPBELL-PERUGINI, FLORENCE

Pipeo and the Dryad ('*o.*', m. H. A. J. Campbell: St Alban's Parish R., Acton Green, 27/2/05)

CAMPION, CYRIL [see also *E. DIGNON*]

×Disgrace (P.W., 15/2/25, Green Room Rag)
Ask Beccles (Q, 12/7/26; Glo., 20/7/26: +*E. DIGNON*) *Fr. 1927*
The Lash (Q, 18/10/26; Roy., 26/10/27)
Asleep (Q, 25/4/27; D.Y., 17/5/27: title later changed to *Dope*)
The Admiral's Secret ('*f.m.d.*': Q, 20/8/28; Str., 10/9/28: +*E. DIGNON*)
Watch Beverley (Q, 17/2/30)
The Silent Flyer (Brixton, 19/5/30)

CANNAN, GILBERT [see also *F. KEYSER*]

Four Plays. *1913*

[This contains: 1. *Miles Dixon* (a piece which may be regarded either as two one-acts combined into one medium-length play or as two separate one-acts: Gai., Manchester, 21/11/10; Cor., 8/5/12); together with three one-act playlets – 2. *James and John* ('*t.*': H., 27/3/11); 3. *Mary's Wedding* (which seems to be *Wedding Presents*, LC, Vaud., 27/12/11; Cor., 6/5/12); and 4. *A Short Way with Authors* ('*bsq.*': Cosmopolis, 26/5/13, Drama Soc.)

The Perfect Widow ('*c.*': Gai., Manchester, 18/3/12)

× Three (Little, 4/2/13; Hippo., Croydon, 16/8/15, as *Countess Coquette*, and described as a '*modern c.*': originally called *The Woman*: adapted from a version, by *D. ST CYR*, of *Lui, Lei, Lui* (1887) by Roberto Bracco)

× The Arbour of Refuge ('*c.*': Little, 4/2/13)

Seven Plays. [*1923*]

[This contains the following one-act pieces: 1. *Everybody's Husband* (Rep., B'ham, 14/4/17; Court, 29/6/18, *m.*); 2. *The Fat Kine and the Lean*; 3. *In the Park* (Mary Ward Settlement, 15/10/24, Dr. Art Centre); 4. *Someone to Whisper To*; 5. *The Same Story*; 6. *Pierrot in Hospital*; and 7. *The Polite Art of Conversation*]

CANNON, NORMAN

He Walked in Her Sleep ('*f.c.*': Q, 24/9/28; Vaud., 14/1/29)

CANTAM, ANDREW [see *L. P. NELSON*]

CANTRILL, HAROLD

The Devil and the Hindmost ('*c.*': K's Heath Inst., B'ham, 11/12/12, *amat.*)

× Mesrour (Woolwich, 12/5/19)

CAPEL, GEORGE

[For earlier plays see *H. E. D.* v, 302]

× Little Fay ('*fairy pl.*': Court, 6/4/12, *cpy.*)

× The Sleeping Beauty. LC, Kings., 20/6/17

× Uncle Joe's Will (Kings., 26/6/17, *amat.*)

CAPPER, MABEL

× The Betrothal of No. 13 (Court, 8/10/12)

CARDIFF, MAX

[Several sketches produced at the Alex. music-hall, Stoke Newington, mostly of the revue type or 'Pierrotic' in style]

CARDOW, CHARLES

You Never Know ('*m.c.*': Qns, Leeds, 5/11/17)

CAREY, CHARLES

The Pick of the Bunch ('*m.c.*': County, Kingston, 8/4/07: musical version of *After the Ball* by *E. FERRIS*, *B. P. MATTHEWS* and *N. DOONE*)

CAREY, FALKLAND L.

× The Woman with—. LC, Hydro., Harrogate, 6/10/25

CAREY, H. VERNON

× Kindly Flames (Arts Centre, 24/3/14)

CARLETON, HENRY GUY

A Gilded Fool ('*c.*': Shaft., 10/2/06)

CARLETON, ROYCE [see also *J. MILLANE*]

Her Mother's Crucifix (Emp., Middleton, 24/1/16; Emp., Edmonton, 2/10/16)
His Second Wife (Gr., Stonehouse, Plymouth, 8/5/16)
The House of Fear (Vic., Walthamstow, 29/5/16)
Because Love Made You Mine (Gr., Plymouth, 11/9/16; E.C., 21/1/18)
The Girl and the Blackguard (Pal., Battersea, 26/3/17)
Woman's Calvary (Pal., Battersea, 2/4/17; title changed later to *For Her Boy's Sake* and *A Work Girl's Divorce*)
Queen of My Heart. LC, Pal., Battersea, 5/5/17
×Home Comforts (S. Ldn, 14/5/17)
The Girl who didn't care (E.C., 25/6/17)
The Secret Service Girl (Imp., Canning Town, 16/12/18)
No Place like Home (Gr., Doncaster, 20/10/19; E.C., 27/10/19)
A Flapper's Married Life (Metro., Glasgow, 29/12/19; E.C., 9/2/20: +*O. CRAY*: also called *A War Flapper's Married Life*)
While Love is Sleeping (Hyde, 13/8/23)
Under One Roof. LC, Gai., Methil, 1/2/24
Love and the Sheik. LC, Alex., Hull, 19/3/24
Rose of the Crazy Star. LC, Hippo., Altrincham, 23/9/24
Lucky O'Donovan. LC, Col., Radcliffe, 21/1/25
Nalia of the Coral Seas (Col., Radcliffe, 30/3/25)
Married to Please Mother. LC, Pav., Chorley, 3/7/25

CARLILE, C. DOUGLAS

The King o' the Road ('*r.d.*': Bed., 25/7/10: title changed later to *Romany Love*)
The Sands of the Desert (Aldershot, 31/1/24)
[Numerous sketches and playlets produced at music-halls]

CARLILE, GEOFFREY L. [see also *T. SLAUGHTER*]

The Yellow Streak (Yarmouth, 8/11/18; Stratford, 18/7/19)

CARLTON, A.

The Lost Chord ('*m.pl.*: Worcester, 31/7/22: +*C. WATSON MILL*)

CARLTON, A. P. K. SIDNEY

Dumbell Daisy ('*f.c.*': Gt. Qn. St., 25/9/03)

CARLTON, ARTHUR R. [see also *V. SUTTON-VANE*]

×The Cure (Castle Pav., Aberystwyth, 5/7/16)

CARLTON, ELSIE [see *J. B. STEWART*]

CARLTON, LOUIS H.

The Mysterious Musicians (O.H., Northampton, 2/12/04, *cpy.*)
The Victims of Circumstances ('*sensational c.d.*': O.H., Northampton, 2/12/04, *cpy.*)
×The Wrong Bottle; or, A Jealous Wife's Revenge and its Sequel (O.H., Northampton, 2/12/04, *cpy.*)

CARLYLE, VINCENT W.

The Coward ('*md.*': Gr., Halifax, 13/9/18; E.C., 14/4/19, as *Love, Honour and the Woman*; Pal., Newcastle, 10/5/20, as *The Betrayal*; Stratford, 15/11/20, as *The Betrayal*)
The Man, the Woman, and—? (Emp., Mountain Ash, 13/2/19: title changed later to *The Atonement*)
The Call of the Child (P's, Portsmouth, 22/11/20; Stratford, 28/2/21)
The Man Forgets (Sheffield, 17/6/21)

CARLYON, GLADYS M.

×Salvage (Forum Club, 18/10/25)
Benediction (Everyman, 30/4/26: +*G. M. BURTON*)

CARMICHAEL, ALAN [see *A. SCOTT*]

CARNEY, GEORGE [see also *B. WILLIAMS*]

×The First-Aid Man. LC, P.W., 10/12/21

CAROL, RICHARD

×A Deal o' Thinkin'. *Fr. 1928*

[*CARPENTER, EDWARD CHILDS* [see also *J. L. LONG*]

The Cinderella Man ('*c.*': Belasco, Washington, 23/12/15; Hudson, N.Y., 17/1/16; Qns, 12/6/19) *1915* (New York); *Fr. 1929*
The Three Bears ('*c.*': Detroit, 29/10/17; Emp., N.Y., 13/11/17; Court, L'pool, 4/9/22; Gr., Croydon, 18/9/22) *Fr. 1926*
The Bachelor Father ('*c.*': Golder's Green, 23/9/29; Glo., 30/9/29) *Fr. 1932*

CARPENTER, S. G.

The Christmas Mystery ('*Bethlehem tableaux*': +*E. H. WELSFORD*) *1921* (Cambridge)

CARR, E.

[A few sketches produced at music-halls]

CARR, JOSEPH WILLIAM COMYNS [see also *R. MARSHALL* and *S. PHILLIPS*]

[For earlier plays see *H. E. D.* v, 304]
My Lady of Rosedale (New, 13/2/04: adapted from A. Capus, *La châteleine*, 1902)
Oliver Twist (H.M., 10/7/05)
Tristram and Iseult (Adel., 4/9/06) *1906*
×A United Pair. *1906* (U.S.A.)
The Mystery of Edwin Drood (New, Cardiff, 21/11/07; H.M., 4/1/08)
Dr Jekyll and Mr Hyde (Qns, 29/1/10)
×Sairey Gamp (Pal., 25/3/12)

'*CARR, LYON*'

The Stalking-Horse (Shanklin Inst., Isle of Wight, 20/4/09, *amat.*)

[*CARR, OSMOND*

The Southern Belle ('*m.c.*': Emp., Southend, 7/3/01; Brixton, 20/5/01)

CARR, PHILIP [see also *M. McNALLY*]
Shock-headed Peter ('*children's pl.*': Gar., 26/12/00: +*N. PLAYFAIR*)
×Brer Rabbit and Brer Fox (Court, 26/12/03)
Snowdrop and the Seven Little Men (Court, 26/12/03)

CARR, WILFRED
[For an earlier play see *H. E. D.* v, 304]
The Squatter's Daughter ('*m.c.d.*', m. S. Harris: O.H., Coventry, 5/3/00; Stratford, 1/7/01, as *Dare-Devil Dorothy*; as a 'revusical revue', Granville, Walham Green, 8/11/15)
The Girl from Japan ('*m.c.*', m. C. Dare: Dover, 29/4/03, *cpy.*; Dover, 29/2/04; O.H., Crouch End, 24/10/04)

CARRAGHER, P. CHARLES
The Crock of Gold (Arbroath, 2/1/11)
The Spaewife (Montrose, 18/12/12)

CARRÉ, FELICIEN
La Toledad ('*c.o.*', m. E. Audran: Windsor, 11/4/03; Kennington, 20/4/03: +*A. MOORE* and *J. H. WOOD*)

CARRICK, HARTLEY [see also *A. ANDERSON*, *D. FURBER*, *J. H. TURNER* and *A. WIMPERIS*]
×The Yellow Divil. LC, Little, 13/10/14
×Nellie (P.W., 15/2/25, Green Room Rag: +*E. MAURICE*)
[A few sketches and playlets produced at music-halls]

CARRICKFORD, LILIAN ARDING
The Sow's Ear (Leinster H., Maynooth, 4/9/27)

[*CARROLL, EARL*
The Blue Flame ('*md.*': Stamford, 13/2/20; Shubert, N.Y., 15/3/20; Hippo., Willesden, 19/11/23: also called *The Blue Flare*)

CARROLL, GEORGE
Motives (Q, 30/6/30)

CARROLL, HARRY C. [=*H. C. COHEN*]

CARROLL, SYDNEY WENTWORTH [see also *B. FLEMING*]
Big Game (D.P., Eastbourne, 8/7/12; New, 19/8/13: called originally *Rita*)

CARSE, ROLAND
The Regimental Impresario (Tyne, Newcastle, 5/2/12)
×Only a Dream (Emp., Islington, 23/6/13: called originally *A Dream of the Past* and, later, *Just a Dream*)

CARSON, FRANCES [see *G. EDWIN*]

CARSON, HARRY [see *L. G. R. HOWARD*]

CARSON, J. W. [see *J. SARGENT*]

CARSON, LINGFORD
The Heart of a Hero ('*md.*': Peterhead M.H., 20/10/1897, as *Saved from the Scaffold*; Darwen, 5/8/1899; Pav., 2/7/00)
The Drama of Life (Coloss., Oldham, 21/3/01, *cpy.*; P.W., Mexborough, 27/7/01; Pav., 4/8/02: later called *Undamaged Goods*)

Defending His Honour (Qns, Keighley, 10/11/02; Metro., Camberwell, 17/8/03)
A Modern Adventuress (Qns, Keighley, 26/12/03; Stratford, 21/8/05)
The Great White Chief ('*md.*': Junction, Manchester, 29/1/12)

CARSON, S. MURRAY [see also *M. BEERBOHM*, '*JOHN OLIVER HOBBES*', *L. N. PARKER* and *T. M. WATSON*]
[For earlier plays see *H. E. D.* v, 304]
A Man by Himself (Kennington, 16/11/03: +*N. KEITH*)
When a Man Marries (Wynd., 3/3/04: +*N. KEITH*)
Simple Simon (P's, Manchester, 7/10/07; Gar., 13/11/07: +*N.* KEITH)

CARSWELL, DONALD
×Count Albany ('*historical fant.*': Lyr., Glasgow, 27/12/26, Scott. Nat. Players) *1928* (in *The Scots Magazine*, x, 186–201); *1933*

CARTEN, AUDRY [see also *WALTON TREVOR*]
Fame (St J., 20/2/29: +*W. CARTEN*)

CARTEN, WAVENEY [see *A. CARTEN* and *WALTON TREVOR*]

CARTER, CONRAY
A Bad Name (Q, 11/7/27)

CARTER, R. C. [see *F. KINGSLEY*]

CARTER, EDITH [see also *F. BATES*]
×L'amour de Pierrot ('*oa.*': Clavier H., 17/10/12)
×Treasures in Heaven (Passmore Edwards Settlement, 26/3/15, Kemble Soc.)
×Love and a Thief (Passmore Edwards Settlement, 8/4/16, Kemble Soc.)
×The Wily Widow (Passmore Edwards Settlement, 8/4/16, Kemble Soc.; Emp., Camberwell, 12/6/16)
A Lass o' Laughter ('*c.*': Leamington, 13/3/22; Qns, 29/4/22: +*N. MARRIOT-WATSON*) *1938* (Kingston-on-Thames: *priv.*)
Educating a Husband ('*c.*': Ambass., Southend, 10/12/23; Cent., 8/2/25, Lyc. Club) *1936* (Kingston-on-Thames: *priv.*)
Certified Insane (Castleford, 18/8/24)
Wanted, a Wife ('*c.*': Q, 13/9/26: +*W. CARTER*)
The Lovely Liar (Q, 7/11/27)

CARTER, E. WILLIS
Breach o' Promise ('*f.c.*': Playgoers, Kensington, 2/5/27)

CARTER, J. L. J.
×Darby and Joan (Passmore Edwards Settlement, 8/4/16, Kemble Soc.)
×Sweet Seventeen ('*c.*': Passmore Edwards Settlement, 8/4/16, Kemble Soc.)

CARTER, NOEL
×Hilarion ('*fant.*': Court, 14/6/14, Pl. Actors)

CARTER, WINIFRED [see *E. CARTER*]

CARTLAND, BARBARA
Blood Money (Q, 26/10/25)

'*CARTON, R. C.*' [=*RICHARD CLAUDE CRITCHETT*]
[For earlier plays see *H. E. D.* v, 305]
Lady Huntworth's Experiment ('*c.*': Crit., 26/4/00) *Fr. 1901*
×The Ninth Waltz (Gar., 11/12/00) *Fr. 1904*
The Undercurrent ('*c.*': Crit., 14/9/01) *Fr. 1904*
A Clean Slate ('*c.*': Crit., 10/2/03)
The Rich Mrs Repton ('*c.*': D.Y., 20/4/04)
Mr Hopkinson ('*f.*': Aven., 21/2/05) *Fr. 1905*
Public Opinion ('*f.*': Wynd., 10/10/05) *Fr. 1913*
Lady Barbarity (Com., 27/2/08: dramatised from the novel (1899) by J. C. Snaith)
Mr Preedy and the Countess ('*f.*': Crit., 13/4/09) *Fr. 1911*
×Dinner for Two (Tiv., 12/7/09) *Fr. 1911*
Lorrimer Sabiston, Dramatist (St J., 9/11/09)
The Eccentric Lord Comberdene ('*novelette in 3 chapters*': St J., 19/11/10) *Fr. 1912*
×An Eye Opener (Hippo., Brighton, 1/5/11; Col., 26/6/11)
The Bear Leaders ('*f.*': Com., 1/2/12) *Fr. 1913*
A Busy Day ('*f.*': Apo., 30/1/15)
The Off-Chance (Qns, 19/9/17)
Nurse Benson ('*c.*': Glo., 21/6/18: +*J. H. McCARTHY*)
Other People's Worries ('*light c.*': Com., 29/3/22) *Fr. 1925*
The Incorrigible ('*f.*': Brighton, 30/10/22; Hippo., Golder's Green, 12/2/23, as *One Too Many*)

CARTWRIGHT, CAROL
×Appropriating Anthony ('*f.*': Rehearsal, 11/5/12)

CARTWRIGHT, CHARLES [see *COSMO HAMILTON* and *A. PATTERSON*]

CARTWRIGHT, T. M.
×Robbery under Arms (Shaft., 13/7/20, *m.*: +*T. SHERRATT*)

CARVALHO, A. F. D'ALMEIDA [see *V. LEWIS*]

CARY, FALKLAND LITTON
×Towards Liberty. LC, Hydro., Harrogate, 14/10/24

CARYLL, HOPE
Red Riding Hood. LC, '*m.pl.*': Pal., Chelsea, 15/7/20

CASEY, SADIE
Brady (Abbey, Dublin, 4/8/19)

CASEY, WILLIAM FRANCIS
The Man who Missed the Tide (Abbey, Dublin, 13/2/08)
The Suburban Groove ('*c.*': Abbey, Dublin, 1/10/08; Shak., L'pool, 13/7/16)
×More Respectable (Court, 12/5/13)
Her Sailor Lover (Castleford, 16/8/15; E.C., 24/4/16)

Insurrection (Crit., 16/12/17, Pioneer Players)
Confession (Court, 18/7/26, 300 Club)
As Old as the Hills (Steiner H., 30/1/27; Q, 23/12/27)

CASI, MAURICE
×Domestic Strategy (Ladbr. H., 7/1/03)

CASSARD, VERNON
Ladies Day ('*m.f.*', m. G. Luders: Ladbr. H., 4/10/11, *cpy.*)

CASSELL, H.
[For earlier plays see *H. E. D.* v, 305]
×The Eve of Waterloo (K's, Kilmarnock, 30/10/09, *cpy.*; Hippo., Camden, 4/4/10: +*T. G. BAILEY*)

CASSERLEY, ARTHUR LANGMEAD
The Knocking at the Gate (Crippl. Inst., 28/1/04)

CASSIDY, LILIAN CLARE [*Mrs J. RICE CASSIDY*]
In Holy (?) Russia (P's, Preston, 29/5/05: title changed later to *The Sins of the Mighty*)
The World and the Woman (Pal., Newcastle, 11/5/08; Lyr., Hamm., 10/3/09)
A Rogue at Large (Lyr., Hamm., 19/4/09)
Seaweed (Scarborough, 7/2/10)
The Beggar Princess (Rot., L'pool, 28/3/10)
The Pinch of Another Man's Shoes (Gr., Hull, 17/4/11)
The Home Rulers (Metro., Bootle, 8/1/15)
The Crater (Pal., Redditch, 17/6/15)
His Mother's Son, V.C. (Metro., Bootle, 3/3/16)

CASSIDY, MAUD
×A Family Matter. *1929* (*priv.*)

[*CASSIDY, OWEN*
The Harem ('*f.c.*': Apo., Atlantic City, 10/11/24; Belasco, N.Y., 2/12/24; Gar., 13/9/25, Rep. Players: adapted from the Hungarian of E. Vajda)

CASSILIS, INA LEON
[For earlier plays see *H. E. D.* v, 306]
The Two Misses Ibbetson. *Fr. 1900*
×O.K. (Excelsior H., Bethnal Green, 23/2/01)
The Real East Lynne (R.A., Woolwich, 26/5/02)
A Knight of the Road (Bij., 2/5/04; County, Kingston, 3/6/07)
×A Modern Othello (Tiv., 28/12/08: +*A. VAN BIENE*)
×Karl's Luck (Kelly's, L'pool, 1/7/10: +*L. BURNLEIGH*)
×The Feast of the Wolves (Hippo., Putney, 12/6/11)
×Man and Woman (Sur., 11/8/11)
Is She His Wife? LC, Olympia, Tredegar, 4/10/16

CASSON, ANN
×The Camwells Are Coming (Children's, 31/8/29)

CASSON, Sir LEWIS
×The Unseen (Little, 12/10/21: called originally *The Terror*)
Crime (Little, 28/11/21: adapted from a play by M. Level)
×The Regiment (Little, 25/1/22)

CASSON, R. LOUIS

Lord Jack Intervenes ('*c.*': Court, 27/11/11, *amat.*)
×Double Blank (Emp., Sheffield, 23/6/13)
A Maid of the Midnight Sun ('*m.c.*', m. G. Blackmore: H.M., Carlisle, 24/12/17; Pal., Ramsgate, 1/3/20, as *Maid of Norway*: +*H. C. SARGENT*)
The Girl of the Golden Gate ('*m.c.*', m. G. Blackmore: Hippo., Stockton, 5/5/19: +*H. C. SARGENT*)

CASSON, T. E.

The Wise Kings of Borrowdale. *1914* (Keswick); *1927*

CASTELL, C. A.

×The Battle of the Pump (Rep., B'ham, 25/9/15)
The Best Policy ('*c.*': Gai., Manchester, 6/11/16)
×Snowed Up with a Duchess. LC, K. G's H., 3/3/17. *Fr. 1906*
The Farringdon Case (Gai., Manchester, 18/11/18; Aldw., 4/7/21, as *James the Less*)

CASTLE, AGNES

×Grey Domino (Playh., 30/4/07, *m.*: +*EGERTON CASTLE*)

CASTLE, EGERTON [see also *A. CASTLE*]

The Secret Orchard (Tyne, Newcastle, 14/3/01; Gr., Fulham, 13/5/01)
×At the Point of the Sword ('*fencing sk.*': D.L., 21/11/01)
×Saviolo (Lyc., 14/3/02, *cpy.*: +*W. H. POLLOCK*)

'*CASTLES, FRANK*' [=*F. SCHLOESSER*]

Simoon (Bloomsbury H., 1/12/06, New Stage Club: +*E. A. BROWNE*: translated from *Simoom* (1890) by A. Strindberg)
×The Stronger Woman (Bloomsbury H., 1/12/06, New Stage Club; H.M., 9/12/09 (where author's name given as *F. SCHLOESSER*): +*E. A. BROWNE*: translated from *Den Starkare* (1890) by A. Strindberg)

CASTLETON, ISABEL (*Mrs ROBERT CASTLETON*)

The Tiger Lily (Lyr., Hamm., 31/7/05: +*R. CASTLETON*)
×Vivisection (Emp., Camberwell, 1/6/14)
×The Sin of Murry Lorrimer, M.D. (Ass. R., Balham, 17/10/16)

CASTLETON, ROBERT [see also *I. CASTLETON*]

[For earlier plays see *H. E. D.* v, 306]
The Eleventh Commandment: An Unwritten Law (Margate, 4/12/1899; County, Kingston, 28/3/04)
Slaves of Passion ('*Anglo-Russian d.*': E.C., 25/7/04: originally produced as *The Cross of Olga*, 1896)

CASTON, CHARLES

Are You Married? ('*f.c.*': Pal., Brighton, 4/5/25; Q, 31/10/27)

CATLING, MAUD [see also *C. H. LESTER*]

The Sorrows of Satan. LC, 15/9/15
A Mother but not a Wife ('*md.*': Hippo., Stoke-on-Trent, 18/6/17)
The Splendid Lovers ('*Chinese pl.*': P's, Bradford, 5/8/20)

CAUDWELL, IRENE
The Mystic Tree ('*mystery pl.*') *1921*
'By Thy Cross and Passion' ('*sacred d.*') *1927*

CAVENDISH, JEAN [see *MILES MALLESON*]

CAVENDISH, R. L.
Three Little Hearts of Gold ('*m.pl.*': Metro., Plymouth, 18/7/04: +*S. E. BLYTHE*)

CAVILL, P.
The Test. LC, Newcastle, 12/3/18

CAYSER, CHARLES WILLIAM [='*CHARLES WHITWORTH WYNNE*']

CECIL, A. [see *Lady F. BELL*]

CECIL, EDWARD [see *AUSTIN PHILLIPS*]

CECIL, ERNEST
A Matter of Fact ('*c.*': Com., 27/4/21)
Monica ('*c.*': Everyman, 4/4/24)

CECIL, JOHN
×Good for Evil. LC, Alb., Brighouse, 13/6/13

CELESTIN, JACK
The Man at Six ('*detective pl.*': Q, 16/1/28; Qns, 30/3/29): +*N. DOON*) *Fr. 1929*
The Man in the Dock (Q, 26/11/28: +*N. DOON*: revised with *J. DE LEON*, Hippo., Lewisham, 23/9/29)
The House of Danger (Lyc., 8/11/30: +*J. DE LEON*)
Gamble (Q, 26/12/30: +*J. DE LEON*)

CHADWICK, C. KATE
×The Wassail Bough ('*Christmas mystery*') *1923* (SPCK)

CHALLIS, RASS
The Bells of Old York (Glo., Deal, 17/9/08)

CHALLONER, BROMLEY
The Yellow Cockade ('*r.c.*': Gai., Hastings, 11/11/18; Scala, 27/5/20: +*W. STEPHENS*)
The Garden Folk. LC, Conservatoire, Hampstead, 20/10/22

CHALMERS, BRYN
×Aunt (A.L.S. Trav. Th., 1927)

CHAMBERS, CHARLES HADDON
[For earlier plays see *H. E. D.* v, 307]
The Awakening (St J., 6/2/01) *1902*
The Golden Silence (Gar., 22/9/03)
Sir Anthony ('*c.*': Wynd., 28/11/08) *Fr. 1909*
Passers-By (Wynd., 29/3/11) *1913*
The Impossible Woman ('*c.*': H., 8/9/14: called originally *Tante*)
The Saving Grace ('*c.*': Gai., Manchester, 1/10/17; Gar., 10/10/17) *Fr. 1918*
The Card Players (Sav., 26/4/22)

CHAMBERS, F. OWEN
[For an earlier play see *H. E. D.* v, 307]
The Yellow Peril (Gr., Plymouth, 18/6/20)

CHAMBERS, H. KELLETT
Dan'l Peggotty (K's, Hamm., 11/3/07)
Betsy ('*oa.*', m. A. Johnstone: Ladbr. H., 20/10/11, *cpy.*)

CHAMIER, FRANCIS [see *G. R. NORTON*]

CHAMPION, LEWIS
The Sakeps ('*c.o.*', m. P. Bowie: Ass. R., Balham, 1/5/08, *amat.*)

CHANCE, MALISE
The Lion Tamer (Arts, 9/2/28: adapted from A. Savoir, *le Dompteur*, 1925)

CHANCE, WILLIAM ARTHUR
×Winkle versus Fitz-Allwyn ('*mock trial*') *Fr. 1927*

CHANDLER, BLANCHE WILLS
×A Previous Engagement (Aven., 22/11/00)
×A Born Nurse. *1908*

CHANDLER, JOHN
×An Old Man's Darling (M'sex, 9/12/08)
×Exchange No Robbery (People's, St Pancras, 12/5/27)

CHANDLER, WILLIAM
×Thirteen Eighty One ('*t.*') *1927* (*priv.*)

CHANDOS, G.
A Girl with a Bad Name. LC, Stratford, 9/7/19: +*S. WILLCOCK*

CHAPIN, ALICE [see also *L. WILLOUGHBY*]
[For earlier plays see *H. E. D.* v, 308]
A Knight Errant ('*c.o.*', m. F. Corrie: Gr., Falkirk, 6/8/06: +*H. CHAPIN*)
The Happy Medium ('*c.*': Ladbr. H., 29/7/09, *cpy.*: +*P. GAYE*)
×At the Gates. LC, Alb. H., 13/12/09. *1909*
×A Modern Medea ('*t.*': Rehearsal, 8/7/10, *m.*)
Outlawed (Court, 23/11/11, *m.*: +*M. COLLINS*)

CHAPIN, HAROLD [see also *ALICE CHAPIN*]
Augustus in Search of a Father (Court, 30/1/10, Pl. Actors) *1911*
The Marriage of Columbine (Court, 20/2/10, Pl. Actors) *1911*
×Muddle Annie ('*c.*': Roy., Glasgow, 13/3/11; Court, 19/5/12, Pl. Actors) *1913*
×The Autocrat of the Coffee Stall (Roy., Glasgow, 27/4/11; Court, 19/5/12, Pl. Actors) *1913*
×The Dumb and the Blind (Roy., Glasgow, 20/11/11; Court, 19/5/12, Pl. Actors; P.W., 19/11/12: called originally *Deaf and Blind*) *1914*
×Innocent and Annabel (Court, 19/5/12, Pl. Actors) *Fr. 1921* (in *Three One-Act Plays*)
Art and Opportunity ('*c.*': P.W., 5/9/12) *1921* (in *Comedies*)

Elaine ('*c.*': Gai., Manchester, 23/9/12; Court, 26/5/13) *1921* (in *Comedies*)
Wonderful Grandmamma and the Wand of Youth ('*children's pl.*': Gai., Manchester, 26/12/12)
× It's the Poor that 'Elps the Poor (Court, 19/5/13, Pl. Actors) *1921* (in *Three One-Act Plays*)
× Dropping the Baby ('*fable*': Playh., 12/2/14) *1927*
× Every Man for His Own (Court, 12/6/14, Pl. Actors)
× The Philosopher of Butterbiggins (Qns, 14/12/15) *1921*
The New Morality ('*light c.*': Com., 28/11/20, Pl. Actors; Playh., N.Y., 30/1/21; Aldw., 30/5/21, *m.*; Kings., 29/6/25) *1921* (in *Comedies*)
× The Threshold ('*t.*') *Fr. 1921*

CHAPMAN, ARTHUR
[For earlier plays see *H. E. D.* v, 308]
× A Turkish Bath (Bij., 21/4/03: +*E. L. FURST*)

CHAPMAN, HARRY J.
× The Elocutionist (Redford R., Carmyllie, 2/2/17)

CHAPMAN, WILLIAM
× The Packman (R. Inst., Glasgow, 26/4/23, Scott. Nat. Players)
The Sergeant-Major ('*Lowland c.*': Lyr., Glasgow, 27/12/26, Scott. Nat. Players)

CHARLESON, ARTHUR J.
[For earlier plays see *H. E. D.* v, 308]
The Law and the Man (R.A., Woolwich, 30/7/00)
A Marriage of Vengeance (Clarence, Pontypridd, 21/12/03; Stratford, 8/2/04)

CHARLTON, JOHN
The (K)night of the Garter ('*c.*': Q, 13/5/29)

CHARLTON, THEOPHILUS
Dora Stays the Night (Edin., 21/7/19)
Deceived. LC, Gr., Stockton, 7/2/20
Under Promise of Marriage (Chatham, 9/2/20; E.C., 1/3/20; Stratford, 11/4/21, as *A Hindu's Oath*)
Teddy Wants a Wife ('*f.c.*': Garrison, Bulford, 22/4/20; Borough, Stratford, 22/11/20; Hippo., Golder's Green, 28/8/22, as *Double or Quit*)
The Catspaw (Pal., Brighton, 16/4/23; Stratford, 3/9/23)
× Speaking the Truth. LC, Hippo., Putney, 31/8/23
The Cloven Hoof (Playh., Cardiff, 19/1/25: called originally *A Jest of the Gods* and *Spiritualism*)

CHART, H. J.
× The Discovery of Chelston. LC, Torquay, 17/3/25
× The Thief of Dad's Bags. LC, Torquay, 17/3/25

CHARTER, A. D.
The Camp Cure. LC, Lopping H., Loughton, 21/2/22

CHARTERS, ALAN YORK
× In the Grip of Fate (Cosmopolis, 6/11/13)

CHATAWAY, DENYS

×The Needle's Eye (Pier, Brighton, 19/4/26)

CHATWIN, LESLIE BOUGHTON

×Re Pilgridge (Rep., B'ham, 14/6/13)
×Paying the Price (Rep., B'ham, 13/10/14)

CHAULK, P. J. A.

Sejanus ('*t.*') *1923* (*priv.*)

CHAVANNES, PIERRE

The Hostage (Scala, 23/3/19, Pioneer Players: translated from P. Claudel, *L'Ôtage*, 1911) *1917* (Oxford)

'CHEB'

My Pretty Maid. LC, Gr., Luton, 14/11/22: called originally *An Irish Maid*

CHEEK, T.

×The New Companion (P.H., Gravesend, 10/10/06, *cpy.*)

CHERRY, MALCOLM [see *L. M. LION*]

CHESSON, NORA

Muirgheis ('*Irish grand o.*', m. O. Butler: Dublin, 7/12/03)

CHESTER, GEORGE H.

Jan the Jester ('*m.r.*': T.H., W. Hampstead, 25/10/02, in one act; K's H., 19/5/05, in 2 acts)
×Puncinella; or, The Masked Marriage (Wellington H., St John's Wood, 10/6/03, Apollo Operatic Soc.: +*F. HODSON*)

CHESTERTON, ADA ELIZABETH (*Mrs CECIL CHESTERTON*)

The Man who was Thursday (Everyman, 20/1/26: +*R. NEALE*: dramatised from the novel (1908) by G. K. Chesterton) *1926*
The Love Game ('*c.*': O.H., Southport, 23/8/26; Gr., Croydon, 30/8/26: +*R. NEALE*) *1929*

CHESTERTON, FRANCES (*Mrs G. K. CHESTERTON*)

The Children's Crusade. *Fr. 1924*
[This includes, besides the title-play, two one-acts: 1. *Sir Cleges* and 2. *The Christmas Gift*]
Piers Plowman's Pilgrimage ('*morality pl.*': Pump R., Bath, 8/5/25) *Fr. 1925*

CHESTERTON, GILBERT KEITH

Magic ('*fant.c.*': D.P., Eastbourne, 3/11/13; Little, 7/11/13) *1913* (*priv.*); *1913*
The Judgement of Dr Johnson ('*c.*') *1927*

CHEVAL, ROBERT [see *W. A. ARMOUR*]

CHEVALIER, ALBERT [see also *A. SHIRLEY* and *L. WORRALL*]

[For earlier plays see *H. E. D.* v, 309]
×The Wings of Memory (Small Qns H., Langham Place, 8/4/01)
Memory's Garden (Com., 18/2/02: +*T. GALLON*)
The Scapegrace ('*wordless f.*': D.Y., 3/9/06)
×The Dream of His Life ('*m.pl.*': D.P., Eastbourne, 8/4/07)
×Atonement (D.P., Eastbourne, 8/4/07)

CHILD, HAROLD HANNINGTON

Hugh the Drover ('*r. ballad o.*', m. R. Vaughan Williams: H.M., 14/7/24) *1924*

CHILDE-PEMBERTON, HARRIET LOUISA

'Twenty Minutes': Drawing Room Duologues and Monologues. *1891*; *Fr. 1913*

[This contains: 1. *A Backward Child* (LC, D.P., Eastbourne, 9/1/01); 2. *Chatterboxes*; 3. *Shattered Nerves* (LC, D.P., Eastbourne, 9/1/01); 4. *The Train de luxe from Cannes*; 5. *I and My Father-in-Law*; 6. *A Figure of Speech*; 7. *My Missing Spectacles*; 7. *Nicknames*; and 8. *The Science of Advertisement*]

He, She and the Poker, and Other Dramatic Pieces. *1900*; *Fr. 1913*

[This contains four short plays: 1. *He, She and the Poker*; 2. *Don't Let the Lady Go*; 3. *The Mouse and the Man*; and 4. *Ever Your Friend*]

Carmela ('*poetic d.*') *1903*

Her Own Enemy. *1904*

CHILDERSTONE, CHARLES

× The Sailor and the Nursemaid (Aldw., 27/6/12)

× The Four Jolly Sailormen. LC, Hippo., Exeter, 15/12/19

CHILLINGWORTH, A. ETHEL

× An Academy Picture (Rehearsal, 8/11/09, *m.*) *1911*

CHILTON, ELEANOR

Healthy, Wealthy and Wise ('*c.*': New, 1/3/30: +*HERBERT AGAR*)

CHILTON, HEMAY HERMAN

Grit (Kings., 24/11/08: called originally *The Sparrow and the Lark*)

The Ant (Gai., Manchester, 21/2/16)

CHOLMONDELEY, DIANA

× A Man's Foes (Imp., 26/5/07, Pioneers)

CHOLMONDELEY, MARY

× The Hand and the Latch (Playh., 18/3/11: +*C. MAUDE*)

CHORLEY, HERBERT

The Undercurrent (Grammar School H., Dedham, 8/7/08, *cpy.*)

CHRISTIE, R. A.

× The Dark Hour ('*c.*': Abbey, Dublin, 9/9/14) *1950* (Belfast)

CHRISTMAS, WALTER

Naughty Cupid! ('*c.*': Gai., Manchester, 19/4/20)

CHUMLEY, ALICK

× Little Willie (R.A., Woolwich, 8/3/15)

× The Specialist. LC, Pal., Westcliff, 20/3/15

CHUNDER, K. C. [see *K. N. DAS GUPTA*]

CHURCH, CYRIL M.

The Bones of Men ('*md.*': Sur., 6/4/03)

CHURCHILL, Lady RANDOLPH [see *Mrs GEORGE CORNWALLIS-WEST*]

[*CHURCHILL, WINSTON*
The Title Mart ('*c.*': Shaft., 17/11/05, *cpy.*) *1905* (New York)

'*CIEL, F.*'
Capt'n Jack (Star, Swansea, 26/10/09, *cpy.*; Ilkeston, 15/11/09; R.A., Woolwich, 5/9/10)

CLAIR, H. BUCKSTONE
[For earlier plays see *H. E. D.* v, 310]
Admiral Jack; or, H.M.S. Skylark ('*nautical m. extravaganza*': K's, Walthamstow, 21/7/02: +*W. S. ROBINSON*)

CLAIRE, CYRIL [see *G. ROBINSON*]

CLAPHAM, F. DARE
The Mayor of Montillado ('*m.pl.*', m. L. Butler: St G's H., 9/5/00)

CLARANCE, LLOYD
[For earlier plays see *H. E. D.* v, 310–11]
Jacob Gunston, Agitator (New, Consett, 1/5/02, *cpy.*: +*V. WRAY*)
From the Land of Silence ('*spiritualist pl.*': New, Consett, 19/12/04: +*D. MOORE*)
×What a Life! LC, Glo., Consett, 20/9/17

CLARE, J. W. SABBEN
The Woman who was Dead (Gai., Dundee, 16/3/08; Stratford, 29/5/08: title changed later to *The Power of a Wicked Woman*)
×A Blind Woman (Court, 13/6/11, *m.*)

CLARE, WATSON
True to the Core ('*d.d.*': Qns, Longton, 30/5/02; Croydon, 29/6/03)

CLARENCE, LAURENCE J.
×The Agency (Clavier H., 10/7/12; Rehearsal, 4/7/13)

CLARK, ANDREW
God's Children. *1926*

[*CLARK, BARRETT HARPER*
Danton (Alb. H., Leeds, 14/11/27: adapted from the play by R. Rolland, 1901) *1919* (New York)

CLARK, C.
×A Sporting Knight-Mayor (Bournemouth, 13/4/00: +*M. KING*)

CLARK, DUDLEY
The Gladsome Mind (Little, Bristol, 14/2/29)

CLARK, E. HOLMAN
×The Colonel and the Lady ('*f.*': Playh., 4/11/11: +*D. MILWARD*) *Fr. 1915*

CLARK, G. N.
×Broken Down (Kings., 27/5/21, *m.*, Playwrights' Theatre)

'*CLARK, H. M.*' [=*LAURENCE B. IRVING*]

CLARK, INA KITSON

The Masque of Patience and Hope (+*MARY PORTER*) *1916*
The Children's Christ. *1922* (Leeds: SPCK)

CLARK, MARGERY STANLEY

×An Essay in Matrimony. *1902*
×A Hundred Years Hence (Roy., Glasgow, 18/2/07; Lyr. Club, 27/4/10, *m.*)
The Giftie ('*c.*': Ladbr. H., 18/4/07, *amat.*)
×A Leaf from Life (Lyc. Club, 14/12/09, *m.*)
×Ideals. *1903* (Oswestry); *Fr. 1909*
×The Anniversary (Lyc. Club, 5/12/11, *m.*)
The Fundamental Principle ('*c.*': Crit., 16/2/11, *m.*)

CLARK, THEODORA E.

×Some Dreams Come True. *1910*
×The Wild Bird. *1920*
×The Treasure of Ruydonár. *1927*

CLARKE, A.

×An Eastern Maid. LC, K's, Alnwick, 17/11/19

CLARKE, ALFRED H.

From Prison to Palace (L'pool, 8/5/11)

CLARKE, ALLEN

The People's Rose (K's, Sutton-in-Ashfield, 1/7/05, *cpy.*: +*C. CALDCLEUGH*)

CLARKE, AMY KEY

×Persephone ('*masque*') *1925* (Oxford: in *Three One-Act Plays*)

CLARKE, AUSTIN

The Son of Learning ('*poetic c.*': Fest., Cambridge, 31/10/27) *1927*
×The Flame. *1930*

CLARKE, CHARLES A. [see also *C. BURNETTE*, *W. MILLER* and '*RIADA*']

[For earlier plays see *H. E. D.* v, 311–12]
The Black Vampire ('*md.*': St J., Manchester, 9/4/00; Brit., 10/9/00: +*H. F. SPIERS*)
The Yellow Terror ('*military d.*': St J., Manchester, 1/10/00: +*H. F. SPIERS*)
'Twixt Good and Evil' (Qns, Farnworth, 17/12/00: +*T. M. POWELL*)
A Little Outcast: A Child's Story (Gr., Islington, 15/7/01: +*H. R. SILVA*)
The Mystery of Edwin Drood (Osborne, Manchester, 2/3/08: +*S. B. ROGERSON*)
×Trafalgar Day (Paragon, 10/5/09: +*W. S. HARTFORD*)
His Real Wife (Lyr., Hamm., 16/9/09, *cpy.*; Court, Warrington, 27/12/09; Lyr., Hamm., 15/8/10)
Little Phil's Mother (O.H., Wakefield, 4/10/09; Woolwich, 20/2/11)
Love and a Throne (E.C., 24/3/13)
[Several sketches and playlets produced at music-halls]

CLARKE, CYRIL

×Miss Clementie's Engagement (Rehearsal, 7/5/14)

CLARKE, DELIA

In the Nick of Time (H., 26/8/08, *cpy.*)

CLARKE, DUDLEY

The Portrait ('*r.pl.*': Rep., Nottingham, 30/10/22)
Bluff ('*c.*': Q, 10/10/27)

CLARKE, EDGAR

×The Waking of O'Rourke ('*c.*': David Lewis, L'pool, 16/12/24, *amat.*)
×Robespierre (David Lewis, L'pool, 16/12/24, *amat.*)

[*CLARKE, EDWARD*

De Luxe Annie (Apo., Atlantic City, 30/4/17; Booth, N.Y., 4/9/17; P.W., B'ham, 24/8/25; D.Y., 3/9/25: +*S. LOCKWOOD*)

CLARKE, JOSEPH IGNATIUS CONSTANTINE

Lady Godiva (Imp., 23/4/02, *cpy.*)

CLARKE, JOSEPHINE

×The Spur of Impulse (Lyc. Club, 14/1/24)

CLAUGHTON, H.

×A Woman's Reason. LC, St J., 24/4/15

CLAUSS, PAUL P.

×Matrimonial Misunderstandings (O.H., Cheltenham, 22/12/15, *amat.*)
×Mermaid Land. LC, P'cess H., Cheltenham, 10/12/18

CLAY, BEATRICE ELIZABETH [see also *J. S. MacROBERT*]

Plays from the Arabian Nights. *1913*
[+*C. SPURLING*: this contains two short plays for children: 1. *The Dream Caliph* and 2. *The Jar of Olives*]
×The Magic Mirror (+*C. SPURLING*) *1921* (included in J. S. MacRobert, *The Children of the Year, and Other Plays*)

CLAYE, CHARLES A.

A Joyous Pageant of the Holy Nativity. *1925* (Chelsea)
The Merry Masque of Our Lady in London Town. *1925* (SSPP)

CLAYPOLE, CLARKE

[For an earlier play see *H. E. D.* v, 313]
A Reign of Terror (Qns, Longton, 22/1/03)

CLAYTON, CHARLES

×Lights Out (Oddfellows' H., Crowborough, 26/7/05, *cpy.*)

CLAYTON, CYRIL

×A Fairy Prince ('*ca.*': Cor., 24/4/02)

CLAYTON, HERBERT [see also *H. GRATTAN*, *G. P. HUNTLEY*, '*IAN HAY*' and *D. TITHERADGE*]

Our Liz ('*m.f.c.*': Hippo., Southampton, 13/8/23; Emp., Chiswick, 1/10/23: +*C. WEST*)
Suzanne ('*m.f.*': Pal., Plymouth, 31/12/23; Emp., Chiswick, 11/2/24: +*C. WEST*)

Virginia ('*m.c.*', m. J. Waller and J. A. Tunbridge: Emp., Cardiff, 24/9/28; Pal., 24/10/28: +*J. WALLER*)
[Several sketches and playlets produced at music-halls]

CLAYTON-GREENE, ALICE
The Last Guest (Q, 20/2/28)

CLEAVER, HOWARD C.
Geneviève ('*r.o.*', m. E. S. de Rovigo: Gr., Fulham, 3/8/03) *1903*

[*CLEMENS, LE ROY* [see also *J. B. HAYMER*]
[A few sketches and playlets produced at music-halls]

CLERY, WILLIAM EDWARD [='*AUSTIN FRYERS*']

CLEUGH, DENNIS [see also *C. D. JONES* and *U. KEENE*]
Robin Hood (C.P., 10/12/06: +*C. D. JONES*)
× The Violet under the Snow. *1915*
× Pink Thrift. *1918*

CLEVELAND, ARTHUR RACKHAM
Fenella ('*r.o.*', m. N. Lambelet: Col., 18/12/05)

CLEVELAND, CHARLES
× Charlie's Wedding Day (Sur., 24/1/10)

CLEVELAND, JOHN
His Twin Matilda ('*f.*': Pav., Southend, 25/1/04)

CLIBBORN, Mrs G. M.
The Two Courts (St Gabriel's H., Willesden Green, 7/1/10, *amat.*)

'*CLIFF, LADDIE*' [=*L. PERRY*]
Fantasy. LC, '*m.c.*': Qns, 8/11/21: +*A. E. ILLINGWORTH*

CLIFFORD, BERT
Encore. LC, Gai., Houghton-le-Spring, 5/10/21: title later changed to *The Two Heads*: +*G. B. SILBURN*

CLIFFORD, CHARLES
On Circumstantial Evidence ('*military pl.*': O.H., Perth, 3/4/02, *cpy.*)
The Deserter (Pal., Ramsgate, 24/4/11; Woolwich, 12/6/11)
Sinless ('*c.*': K's, Walton-on-Naze, 29/12/19: from the novel *Ernest Maltravers* by Lord Lytton)
The Eternal Triangle. LC, Stanley H., S. Norwood, 30/1/23

CLIFFORD, E.
× Tantalising Terpsichore (Court, Brighton, 27/1/13; Empress, 24/2/13: +*H. GORDON CLIFFORD*)

CLIFFORD, H. GORDON [see *E. CLIFFORD*]

CLIFFORD, HARRY J.
The Leopard Men (Crown, Eccles, 3/11/24; Pal., Fleetwood, 30/1/28: title later changed to *African Love*)

CLIFFORD, JACK
[Several sketches and playlets produced at Scots music-halls]

CLIFFORD, PHILLIP
Why William Lied ('*f.c.*': Marina, Lowestoft, 11/7/04)

CLIFFORD, Mrs W. K. (LUCY LANE)
[For earlier plays see *H. E. D.* v, 314, 784]
The Likeness of the Night ('*modern pl.*': Court, L'pool, 18/10/00; Gr., Fulham, 12/11/00; St J., 28/10/01) *1900*
A Long Duel ('*serious c.*': Gar., 16/8/01) *1901*
× The Shepherd's Purse. *1906* (Cambridge)
Hamilton's Second Marriage (Court, 29/10/07, *m.*) *1909* (in *Plays*)
[This volume also contains *The Modern Way* and *Thomas and the Princess*, see below]
× The Latch (Kings., 19/5/08)
The Modern Way ('*c.*': Ladbr. H., 11/10/09, *cpy.*) *1909* (in *Plays*, see above)
Thomas and the Princess (Ladbr. H., 11/10/09, *cpy.*) *1909* (in *Plays*, see above)
× A Supreme Moment (Col., 8/8/10)
A Woman Alone (Little, 17/7/14) *1915*
Two's Company ('*c.*': P's, Manchester, 3/5/15)
× The Searchlight ('*t.*') *1925* (in *The Nineteenth Century Review*); *Fr. 1925*

CLIFFORD, WALTER
Whoso Diggeth a Pit (Gr., Radcliffe, 1/5/16)

CLIFT, E. P. [see also *S. B. VON LEER*]
× Emeralds (Pal., Brighton, 27/4/17; Qns, 30/7/17)
× Dawn in Bethnal Green (D.Y., 5/9/17, *m.*)

CLIFTON, CECIL
× The Gold Thread ('*dramatic pl.*': Court, 7/11/12; Emp., Ardwick Green, 8/10/23, as *The Convicting Thread*; Pallad., 16/10/23, as *The C.T.*)
Those Suburbans ('*family c. for young people*': Court, 16/3/13, Pl. Actors)
× Passion (Guildhall School of Music, 6/1/26, New Pl. Club)

CLIFTON, G. W.
× His Honeymoon (Bury, 21/4/13)

CLIFTON, MYLES
× The Football Club Supper. *Fr. 1929* (printed with '*SEA-MARK*', *The 'Ole in the Road*)

CLINTON, EDITH LEYLAND
× The Second Favourite (Caxton H., 13/11/05)

CLINTON-BADDELEY, V. C.
Behind the Beyond ('*bsq.d.*': St M., 31/12/26) *1932*

CLIVE, COLIN [see *J. DE CASALIS*]

CLIVE, F. WYBERT [see also *L. ELLIS*]
[For earlier plays see *H. E. D.* v, 315]
The Branded Woman (Gai., Burnley, 7/8/05; Stratford, 15/7/07)

CLIVE, GEORGE EDWIN

The Woman from Scotland Yard (K's, Sutton-in-Ashfield, 21/3/07, *cpy.*; Osborne, Manchester, 20/5/07; Stratford, 5/8/07: +*A. C. GRANT*)

The Bonnie Pit Lad. LC, Qns, Farnworth, 16/12/13: title changed later to *The Link that Binds* and *Tangled Threads*

CLIVE, JAMES

Missy Jo ('*m.pl.*', m. H. Fraser-Simson: Pleasure Gdns, Folkestone, 4/7/21; Wimbledon, 29/8/21)

CLOSE, A. H.

× The Lonely Life (K's, Hamm., 25/5/03)

CLOSE, ETTA

The Gates of Paradise (Q, 14/5/28)

CLOUSTON, F. [see *J. S. CLOUSTON*]

CLOUSTON, J. STORER

The Pocket Miss Hercules ('*f.*': Roy., 28/6/07, *m.*; Roy., 22/7/07)

Ways and Means ('*c.*': New, Oxford, 13/1/13; Glo., 18/6/13, as *The Gilded Pill*)

× 2 a.m. LC, Pallad., 27/6/14: +*F. CLOUSTON*)

CLOWES, ALICE ADA

× Susan (Pav., 6/5/14)

CLUNES, ALEC S.

Faerie Castles. LC, '*m.pl.*': New, 24/2/20

CLUTSAM, GEORGE HOWARD

The Queen's Jester; or, Cap and Bells ('*oa.*': Worcester, 22/5/05)

× A Summer Night ('*o.*': H.M., 23/7/10) *1910*

The Damask Rose ('*r.o.*': Golder's Green, 17/6/29)

CLYDE, CONSTANCE

× My Wilkinson's Widow (Lyc., 29/11/12)

CLYDE, DENNIS

Slaves of Vice (Hippo., Mexborough, 28/7/13; Metro., Bootle, 11/8/13)

What Every Woman Wants ('*r.pl.*': Borough, Stratford, 13/4/14)

Anna of the Night Club (E.C., 27/3/15: +*A. HOWARD*)

Temptations of a Lonely Wife (Olympia, W. Bromwich, 23/10/16: +*A. HOWARD*: originally called *Her Japanese Lover*)

Tommy's Best Pal (Wolverhampton, 20/1/19; Stratford, 12/5/19: +*A. HOWARD*)

The White Slave's Wedding (Wolverhampton, 18/8/19: +*A. HOWARD*: called originally *In the Grip of Cocaine*)

Forbidden Love (Wolverhampton, 27/10/19; E.C., 10/11/19): +*A. HOWARD*: called originally *Helpless Children*)

Blind Sight. LC, Gr., Halifax, 2/3/20: +*A. HOWARD*

The Wife who Knew. LC, Wolverhampton, 29/12/20: +*A. HOWARD.*

The Woman from Limehouse. LC, Wolverhampton, 6/1/21: +*A. HOWARD*

The Woman from Gaol. LC, Wolverhampton, 15/3/21: +*A. HOWARD*

Child of a Thief. LC, Wolverhampton, 16/3/21: +*A. HOWARD*

Fear (Stratford, 16/5/21: +*A. HOWARD*)

The Ready-Cash Wife. LC, Barnsley, 25/6/21: +*A. HOWARD*

The Hooded Death (Wolverhampton, 16/9/21: +*A. HOWARD*

The Woman and the Beast (Wolverhampton, 5/12/21: +*A. HOWARD*

The Colbrook Poisoning. LC, Leicester, 10/5/22: +*A. HOWARD*

Don't Tell My Wife. LC, Alh., Morecambe, 17/2/23: +*A. HOWARD*

The Empty Cradle (Metro., Glasgow, 1/10/23: +*A. HOWARD*: called originally *A Sailor's Baby*; title later changed to *Should a Wife Tell?*)

CLYNDES, AIMÉE GRATTAN [see *W. SALTOUN*]

CLYNDES, J. H.

What Women will do for Love (P's, Blackburn, 30/5/12; Stratford, 2/12/12: +*W. SALTOUN*)

COALES, T. R. F. [see *N. DOONE*]

COATES, THOMAS F. G. [see *R. STRAUSS*]

COBBING, J. R.

John Daintry ('*md.*': Castle H., Framlington, 6/10/08)

COCHRAN, HOWARD

×Tempo Furioso (W.G., New Brighton, 24/6/12)

COCHRANE, ROY

Held with Honour (Imp., Bordesley, 14/10/02)

COCKER, W. D.

×The Wooin' o't (Alh., Glasgow, 31/1/12) *1925*

×Graham of Claverhouse. *1929*

×In the Spring of the Year. *1929*

COCKERAN, HENRIETTE [see '*GEORGE PASTON*']

COCKRELL, MAUD

×Golliwog in Fairyland ('*fairy pl.*') *1925*

×Why the Fuchsia Hangs its Head ('*fairy pl.*') *1922*

×The Innkeeper's Shirt ('*fairy pl.*') *1925*

CODY, MAXWELL

×The Long Valley Claim (St John's H., Worthing, 18/9/11)

×The Duchess of Beckley (White Rock H., Hastings, 9/10/13)

[*CODY, S. F.*

[For an earlier play see *H. E. D.* v, 315]

Viva; or, A Woman of War ('*spect.d.*': O.H., Leicester, 21/12/00, *cpy.*)

Nevada ('*m.c.d.*': Carlton, Saltley, 8/1/04, *cpy.*)

COEN, or COHEN, LOUIS

[For earlier plays see *H. E. D.* v, 316]

×Marshal Ney; or, The Soldiers of France (National Sporting Club, 27/4/03; Wynd., 28/7/03)

×The Drummer of the 76th (Cor., 3/7/06, *cpy.*)
×The Widow Capet (Cor., 24/11/06, *cpy.*)
×La Carmencita (Cor., 21/12/06, *cpy.*; Oxf., 13/5/07)
×Nelson (Cor., 2/2/07, *cpy.*; Croydon, 26/8/07; Bed., 24/5/09)
×A Goose from Haarlem (Cor., 17/8/07, *cpy.*)
×Edmund Kean (Stand., 31/1/10)
[Several sketches and playlets produced at music-halls]

[*COHAN, GEORGE MICHAEL*
Broadway Jones (Cohan, N.Y., 23/9/12; Bradford, 22/9/13; P.W., 3/2/14) ***Fr. 1923***
Get-Rich-Quick Wallingford ('*f.c.*': Parson's, Hartford, 5/9/10; Gai., N.Y., 19/9/10; Pleasure Gdns, Folkestone, 6/1/13; Qns, 14/1/13)
Seven Keys to Baldpate (Astor, N.Y., 22/9/13; Apo., 12/9/14) ***Fr. 1914***
What Advertising Brings (Hippo., Derby, 20/12/15: +*L. GRANT*)
Little Nellie Kelly ('*m.pl.*': Tremont, Boston, 31/7/22; Liberty, N.Y., 13/11/22; New Oxf., 2/7/23)
The Baby Cyclone ('*f.*': Apo., Atlantic City, 8/8/27; Henry Miller, N.Y., 13/9/27; Lyr., 10/4/28) ***Fr. 1929***

COHAN, PATRICK
Abie and Peg ('*c.*': Pal., Brighton, 21/5/26)

COHEN, CHARLES
Miriam (T.H., Streatham, 2/5/20, Brixton Jewish Literary Soc.)
The Trupester (T.H., Streatham, 3/4/21, Brixton Jewish Literary Soc.)
Septimus Elopes (T.H., Streatham, 3/4/21, Brixton Jewish Literary Soc.)

COHEN, HARRY C. [=*HARRY C. CARROLL*]
Among those Present (School House, Porchester Road, Bournemouth, 8/12/27, *amat.*; Alex., B'ham, 8/10/28: +*J. GLEITZMAN*)

COHEN, Mrs HERBERT D.
×The Chain (New, Cardiff, 5/9/10; Marlb., Holloway, 7/10/10)
×Mount Pleasant (Com., 26/11/10)
×The Level Crossing (Little, 21/6/14, Pioneer Players)
×The Lonely Festival (Pav., 15/6/16)

COHEN, HILDA
The Benevolent Boor ('*c.*': Little, Leeds, 11/12/25: adapted from C. Goldoni, *Il burbero benefico*, 1771)

COHEN, or COWEN, LAURENCE [see also *H. GINGOLD*]
×Tricked (play refused licence by LC: case at Bow Street for return of manuscript, 8/12/11)
×The Pity of It [see note on preceding play]
×The Daily Tale (D.P., Eastbourne, 21/6/13)
The Joneses ('*pl. of Welsh life*': Str., 1/11/13)
Double Dutch (Apo., 7/4/16)
×Good Gods! LC, St J., 19/12/17

The Hidden Hand (Court, L'pool, 27/5/18; Str., 4/7/18)
Sinners (Fortune, 8/11/24)
Biddy ('*f.c.*': Bristol, 3/8/25; Fortune, 23/12/26) *Fr. 1926*
×An Irish Stew in Three Helpings. *Fr. 1927*
[Several sketches and playlets produced at music-halls]

COHEN, THELMA
×The Priceless Gem. LC, Gai., Hastings, 6/3/14: +*D. M. DELL*
×A Question of Identity (Crippl. Inst., 9/2/17, Warwick Rep. Club)

COKE, DESMOND
One Hour of Life (Kings., 11/10/17)
×The Foiled Fiend; or, The Best Villain in London ('*bsq.*') *Fr. 1921*

[*COLBRON, GRACE ISABEL*
The Guardsman (Gar., N.Y., 13/10/24; St J., 20/6/25: +*H. BARTSCH*: adapted from a play by F. Molnar)

COLE, EDITH
The Fires of Youth (Shak., L'pool, 10/11/19)

COLE, J. PARRY
[For an earlier play see *H. E. D.* v, 316]
Normandelle ('*c.o.*': Bij., 21/6/04)

'*COLEBY, WILFRED T.*' [=*THOMAS PELLATT*]
×The Likes o' Me (Kings., 13/4/08) *Fr. 1912*
The Swayboat (Kings., 9/10/08)
The Truants ('*c.*': Kings., 11/2/09) *Fr. 1913*
×A Bit o' Stuff (Pav., Glasgow, 8/12/11) *Fr. 1912*
×The Young Napoleon (Pallad., 26/2/12: also performed as *The Real Napoleon*) *Fr. 1913*
×Her Point of View (Playh., 6/4/12; Pallad., 6/1/13, as *Their Point of View*) *Fr. 1913* (as *Their Point of View*)
×Aunt Bessie (Playh., 28/9/12) *Fr. 1913*
×The Dusty Path (Playh., 2/11/12) *Fr. 1913*
The Headmaster ('*c.*': Playh., 22/1/13: +*E. KNOBLOCK*) *Fr. 1913*
Yours ('*c.*': Vaud., 31/5/13: +*S. BLOW*)
×The Censor. LC, H., 14/11/13
×The Silver Lining (H., 21/5/14)
Sir Richard's Biography ('*c.*': Crit., 1/10/14)
×The Debt (Col., 19/4/15)
Shortage (Park, Hanwell, 26/5/20; Crit., 26/11/20, *m.*, Once-a-Week Players)
The Top Drawer ('*c.*' *of modern life*': Brighton, 6/12/26; Q, 28/2/27: +*W. W. HILL*)

COLES, ALBERT JOHN [='*JAN STEWER*']

COLIN, ISA
Sisyphus and the Wandering Jew (Little, 7/3/15, Pioneer Players)

COLLARD, AVALON [see also *A. ENGLAND*]
×Her Half-Step Uncle ('*m.f.*', m. P. Bronte: Ass. R., Whitstable, 25/5/12)

COLLARD, LORNA KEELING
The Immortal Rose. LC, '*t.*': Deanesley H., Wincanton, 20/10/26. *1926* (*priv.*)

COLLETT, HENRY HAINES
×Bunney's Blunder. ('*f.*') *1924*

COLLETTE, Mrs CHARLES
×Robert (Qns Gate H., 22/6/00)

COLLIER, CONSTANCE [='*DAVID L'ESTRANGE*', in association with *IVOR NOVELLO*]

COLLIER, H.
×Nurse and Martyr. LC, Recreation H., Wilton, 1/7/16

COLLIER, VINCENT
×My First Patient (New, Ealing, 23/10/05)

COLLIER, WILLIAM [see *V. MAPES*]

COLLINGHAM, GEORGE G. [see *S. B. VON LEER*]

COLLINGWOOD, P. C.
×Unknown. LC, Lecture H., Wimbledon, 17/2/14

COLLINS, ARTHUR [see *H. HAMILTON*]

COLLINS, DALE
Ordeal (New, Cardiff, 20/4/25; Str., 19/5/25)

COLLINS, FRANK
×The Village Fire Brigade (Emp., Crouch End, 22/1/12; Tiv., 29/1/12) *Fr. 1927*

COLLINS, HERBERT
×The Honour of the Joscelyns (All Saints H., St John's Wood, 28/1/09)

COLLINS, HORACE
In the Silence of the Veldt (Court, 21/3/09, Dramatic Debaters)

COLLINS, MABEL [see also *A. CHAPIN*]
Sensa. LC, Court, 20/4/14

COLLINS, NORMAN R.
Overtaken ('*c.*': Cent., 10/6/28, New Players)

[*COLLINS, SEWELL* [see also *O. DAVIS* and *R. STOCK*]
×Are You There? ('*ca.*': Tiv., 6/11/11; Roy., 5/12/11, as *Tuppence, Please*)
×Just like a Woman (Col., 22/4/12) *Fr. 1923*
×The Scrub Lady (Hippo., Manchester, 17/2/13; Col., 3/3/13)
×The Quitter (Kings., 13/5/17, Pioneer Players)
×G.H.Q. Love (Little, 1/9/20)
×Gaspers (Little, 28/3/21) *Fr. 1922*
×Shepherd's Pie (Little, 29/6/21: called originally *Bloomfield & Co.*)
×Haricot Beans (Little, 12/10/21)

Rescuing Anne (P's, Manchester, 31/10/21; Q, 28/3/27, as *Anne One Hundred Per Cent.*; Sav., 23/5/27) *Fr. 1927*
×Broken China. LC, K. G's H., 21/2/22
×To Be Continued (Little, 31/5/22: called originally *Continued in Our Next*)
[Numerous sketches and playlets produced at music-halls]

COLLINS, W. J. TOWNSEND
As a Man Soweth (Lyc., Newport, 2/4/04)
×The Sheriff and the Rosebud (Lyc., Newport, 10/7/05; Hippo., Manchester, 23/6/08; Emp., Shepherd's Bush, 27/7/08)
A Case for Divorce (Y.M.C.A. H., Newport, 11/2/26)

COLLINSON, WILL [see *H. HEWITT*]
[Several sketches and playlets produced at music-halls]

[*COLLISON, WILSON*
Up in Mabel's Room ('*f.*': Eltinge, N.Y., 16/1/19; Playh., 6/4/21: +*O. HARBACH*)

COLLISSON, HOUSTON [see *P. FRENCH*]

COLMAN, ARTHUR T.
A Mouse in the Larder (Gai., Manchester, 11/6/17)

COLMORE, G.
×Entertaining the Dowager ('*c.*': D.P., Eastbourne, 13/6/06)
×Plain Miriam (New, Cambridge, 14/12/11)

COLN, K.
×A Back Number (P.H., Paddington Street, 28/6/23)

COLQUHOUN, DONALD
×Jean (Roy., Glasgow, 16/5/10; Rep., Croydon, 18/3/14) *1914*

COLT-WILLIAMS, E. W. D.
The Octopus (Aldw., 5/10/24, International Players)

COLTON, CHARLES
×A Studio Romance (Bij., 17/5/02)

[*COLTON, JOHN*
Rain (Gar., Philadelphia, 9/10/22; Maxine Elliott, N.Y., 7/11/22; Gar., 12/5/25: +*C. RANDOLPH*) *1923* (New York); *Fr. 1948*
The Shanghai Gesture (N.Y., 2/25; Scala, 12/5/29, Venturers) *1926* (New York)

COLUM, PADRAIC McCORMAC
The Kingdom of the Young (acted 1902, *amat.*) *1902* (in *The United Irishman*)
The Foleys. *1903* (Dublin)
The Saxon Shillin' (? acted 1903, *amat.*)
The Broken Soil (Molesworth H., Dublin, 3/12/03, Irish Nat. Theatre Soc.; Roy., 26/3/04) *1903* (in *The United Irishman*)
The Land (Abbey, Dublin, 9/6/05; St G's H., 28/11/05) *1905* (Dublin)
The Fiddler's House (Large Concert H., Rotunda, Dublin, 21/3/07, Theatre of Ireland; Abbey, Dublin, 19/8/19: a revised version of *The Broken Soil*) *1907* (Dublin)

Thomas Muskerry (Abbey, Dublin, 5/5/10; Court, 10/6/10) *1910* (Dublin)
×The Miracle of the Corn (Abbey, Dublin, 22/5/08; Boudoir, Kensington, 2/5/11, Poetic Drama Soc.) *1921* (in *Theatre Arts Magazine*)
×The Desert. *1912* (Dublin); *1917* (Boston: as *Mogu the Wanderer, or, The Desert*)
×The Betrayal (Manchester, 7/4/13) *1917* (Boston); *1929* (in J. W. Marriott, *One-Act Plays of To-Day*, vol. iv)
The Grasshopper (Abbey, Dublin, 24/10/22: an adaptation from the German of Count Kesserling, but described as a 'peasant play of bygone Irish life': +*F. E. WASHBURN-FREUND*)
×Balloon ('*pl. for dancers*') *1929* (New York)

COLVIN, IAN DUNCAN
×The Three Rogues (H., 22/4/25)
The Leper's Flute ('*o.*', m. E. Bryson: Glasgow, 15/10/26; Hippo., Golder's Green, 7/12/27) *1920*

COLWAYN, J.
×Old China. LC, Ass. R., Tenby, 6/2/18

COMBE, C. RUBY
×The Little Brown Path by Bethlehem ('*Christmas pl.*') *1927* (SPCK)

COMER, GEORGE
[For earlier plays see *H. E. D.* v, 319]
Brave Hearts ('*r.d.*': Middleton, 3/11/1898, *cpy.*; Darwen, 6/3/1899; Stratford, 24/6/01: +*F. BENTON*)

COMFORT, G. C.
×The Return. LC, Christchurch H., Crouch End, 9/10/23. *Fr. 1924*

COMPTON, FRANCIS A.
Gentlemen of the Jury (Arts, 24/7/29)

COMPTON, MONTAGUE [=*Sir EDWARD MONTAGUE COMPTON MACKENZIE*]
The Gentleman in Gray ('*c.*': Lyc., Edin., 22/2/07)

COMPTON-RICKETT, ARTHUR
The Rose Princess ('*fairy m.pl.*', m. S. S. Corry: Scarborough, 23/5/10, *amat.*)
The Sisters (RADA, 22/6/24)
Sovereignty (Q, 31/1/27)

COMPTON-RICKETT, LEONARD ALLEN
Philomela ('*lyrical d.*') *1908*
The Human Touch, with a Fantasy and Poems. *1921*
[*The Human Touch* was presented at a matinée at the Ambassadors' on 14/3/21. The other play in this volume, a one-act fantasy called *The King of Hearts*, was apparently never acted]

[*CONDELL, J. H.*
The Dawn of Freedom ('*Canadian d.*': Goole, 20/4/00; New, Aberdare, 24/2/02; Sur., 28/7/02)

CONDURIER, J. [see *E. BALFOUR* and *Mrs C. PORTER*]

CONLON, T. C.
The Angelus Bell (P.W., Salford, 8/3/15)

CONNELL, M. CHRISTINE
×The Deserted Rivals (Lyc. Club, 14/4/13)
×The Unsophisticated Burglary (St Augustine's H., Fulham, 5/11/13)

CONNELL, F. NORREYS [='*CONAL O'RIORDAN*']

[*CONNELLY, MARC* [see *G. S. KAUFMAN*]

[*CONNERS, BARRY*
The Patsy ('*c.*': K's, Southsea, 10/12/28; Apo., 19/12/28) *Fr. 1928*

CONNOLLY, JOSEPH
The Mine Land ('*c.*': Abbey, Dublin, 2/10/13)

CONNOR, JOHN J.
×Marked Money (Oxf., 13/1/13)

CONNYNGHAME, FREDERICK L.
[For earlier plays see *H. E. D.* v, 320]
A Mother's Love (S. Shields, 13/8/00; Stratford, 18/8/02: +*F. PRICE*)
Is He a Christian? ('*emotional d.*': Rot., L'pool, 10/12/00: +*F. PRICE*)
The Follies of Youth (Court, Warrington, 28/7/02; Terriss, Rotherhithe, 13/7/03; Windsor, 28/11/04, *revised*: +*F. PRICE*)

CONOVER, TOM E.
[A few sketches produced at music-halls]

CONQUEST, ARTHUR [see also *G. B. NICHOLS*]
Tempted to Sin (Sur., 3/11/02: +*H. WHYTE*)
×Something for Nothing. LC, Granville, Walham Green, 6/8/20: +*G. B. DALY*)

CONQUEST, GEORGE [see also *G. B. NICHOLS* and *A. SHIRLEY*]
[For earlier plays see *H. E. D.* v, 320–3, 785]
The Fighting Fifth (Sur., 29/10/00: +*H. LEONARD*)

CONRAD, ANNETTE L.
×The King of Clubs (St G's H., 7/5/01)

CONRAD, JOSEPH
×One Day More (Roy., 26/6/05; Rep., B'ham, 21/9/18, *revised*) *1913* (in *English Review*, Aug. 1913); *1917* (*priv., revised*); *1923* (see below)
The Secret Agent (Ambass., 2/11/22) *1921* (Canterbury, *priv.*); *1923* (*priv.*); *1926*
Laughing Anne. *1923* (printed with *One Day More*)

CONSTABLE, FRED H.

The Tigress. LC, Leicester, 27/3/24

The Tipster ('*c.*': Pal., Neath, 23/9/29)

CONSTABLE, J. MILTON

Hazard and Love ('*r.pl.*': Crippl. Inst., 19/10/27, *m., amat.*)

CONSTANDUROS, MABEL [see also *M. HOGAN*]

×Devoted Elsie. *Fr. 1927*

×The Strutham Amateurs Present. *Fr. 1927*

×Aunt Maria's Wireless. *Fr. 1927*

×The Family Group. *Fr. 1927*

×Cheering Up Maria. *Fr. 1927*

×The Tragedy in Upper Wallop. *Fr. 1927*

×Dick Whittington at Strutham. *Fr. 1929*

CONWAY, LUCIE

×The Meeting (Clavier H., 2/6/12, Arts and Dramatic Club)

×D.H.S. *Fr. 1913*

'*CONWAY, OLIVE*' [=*HAROLD BRIGHOUSE* and *JOHN WALTON*]

Costume Plays. *Fr. 1927*

[This contains four short pieces: 1. *Becky Sharp* (LC, Kennington, 25/5/25); 2. *Mimi*; 3. *Prudence Corner*; and 4. *The King's Waistcoat*. The last of these seems to have appeared first in J. W. Marriott, *One-Act Plays of To-Day*, vol. ii, *1925*]

CONYELL, J. R.

On the Line. LC, P.H., W. Norwood, 12/2/20

COOK, CHARLES HENRY [='*JOHN BICKERDYKE*']

[*COOK, GEORGE CRAM*

Suppressed Desires ('*c.*': Com., N.Y., 23/1/18; Everyman, 4/10/21: +*S. GLASPELL*) *1921* (Cincinnati)

COOK, OSCAR

The Seventh Wave (E.C., 15/11/26)

COOKE, A.

×The Mummy Case. LC, Baths H., Brentford, 15/3/18

COOKE, DAVID

[For an earlier play see *H. E. D.* v, 323]

×Pansies ('*ca.*': Manor, Hackney, 14/11/00)

'Twas Ever Thus (Manor, Hackney, 22/4/01, *cpy.*)

COOKE, EDWARD ALEXANDER

×Oliver Goldsmith. *1924*

COOKE, FREDERICK

[For earlier plays see *H. E. D.* v, 323–4]

Briton and Boer (Star, L'pool, 1/1/00; Morton's, Greenwich, 20/8/00)

[This play is listed under unknown authors in *H. E. D.* v, 653]

On Shannon's Shore; or, The Blackthorn (Garston, 24/11/02; Carlton, Greenwich, 29/6/03)

The Brand of Shame (Lyc., Pentre, 26/2/04, *cpy.*: called originally *Icebound*)

COOKE, GEORGE
×The Golden Rule ('*pl. for children*') *1915*

COOKE, J. G. F.
[For earlier plays see *H. E. D.* v, 324]
×A Happy Little Adventure (Pier, Eastbourne, 28/3/02)
×An Evening at the Detective's (P.W., B'ham, 19/5/08)
×The Private Detective (Stand., 7/2/10)

COOKE, LEONARD
Scotland for Ever ('*military scena*': K's, Southsea, 22/7/12; Pal., Walthamstow, 19/8/12)

COOKE, PERI [see *P. YORKE*]

COOKE, RUPERT CROFT
Banquo's Chair. *1930*

COOKE, STANLEY
Only Half Way ('*f.*': Dunfermline, 7/11/05, *cpy.*)
×His Living Image (Cant., 25/5/08; Cor., 23/11/08)
×The Recompense (Gr., Blackpool, 26/12/10; O.H., Coventry, 2/1/11: +*C. HARCOURT*)
×The Man from Mexico (Gr., B'ham, 3/6/12)
×Sunday Morning (Court, L'pool, 8/4/12; Metropolitan, 6/1/13)
×Pals (Glasgow, 22/3/15) *Fr. 1924*
The Girl from Upstairs ('*f.*': Leamington, 3/4/16; Str., 8/4/16)
Crooked Usage (Lincoln, 12/9/21; Apo., 21/9/21: title later changed to *Crooked Love*)
The Little Lady ('*f.c.*': O.H., Blackpool, 21/3/27)
Paradise Island ('*c. mystery pl.*': D.P., Eastbourne, 12/12/27)
[A few sketches and playlets produced at music-halls]

COOKSON, G. M. [='*JAMES BARTON*']

COOPE, REX
Charlie Goes East ('*m.c.*', m. H. Barnes: Pal., Redditch, 26/7/20; Emp., Edmonton, 25/7/21)

COOPER, A. E.
×Choosing a Husband (Gai., Manchester, 5/10/14)

COOPER, BRYAN RICCO
The Collar of Gold and Other Fantasies. *1920*
[This volume contains seven one-act playlets: 1. *The Collar of Gold* ('*an un-historical discussion*'); 2. *A War Office Jacket* ('*an anachronism*'); 3. *The First Reading* ('*an anachronism*'); 4. *The Chief Secretary*, ('*a statement of ideals*'); 5. *On the Struma Front* ('*a dream*'); 6. *Comrade Thompson* ('*a farcical forecast*'); and 7. *The Assize of Honour* ('*a fantasy*')]

COOPER, EDITH EMMA [see '*MICHAEL FIELD*']

COOPER, EDWARD H.
×Atoms in the French Revolution (D.Y., 7/6/04)

COOPER, ELSIE
An English Flower (B'ham, 23/1/25, *amat.*)

COOPER, ERIC

Victory; or, A Contrast of Families (Drill H., Caterham, 27/1/14, *amat.*)

COOPER, HENRY ST JOHN

The Master of the Mill (Shak., Clapham, 23/5/10: dramatised from his own novel, 1910)

COOPER, JASPER

Nan: A Child of Shame ('*sensational d.*': T.H., Cinderford, 14/3/03)

COOPER, MELICENT

A Perfect Cure, and Other Plays for Girls. *1909*

[This contains, in addition to the title-piece, six playlets: 1. *The Family Relic*; 2. *Sakura, or, The Cherry Trees*; 3. *The Deception of Kitty*; 4. *The Hermit*; 5. *The Day before the Wedding*; 6. *Protection*]

COOPER, WALTER SAVAGE

Wat (Crippl. Inst., 14/3/10, *amat.*)

Love's Enemy (Crippl. Inst., 22/1/12)

The King's Blessing (Crippl. Inst., 10/2/13, *amat.*)

× Jack's Letter. LC, St Andrew's H., Althorne, 30/4/18

× A Supper Party in Suburbia. LC, St Andrew's H., Althorne, 30/4/18

The Magic Key ('*oa.*': Chetwoode-street H., Crewe, 10/12/24, *amat.*)

COOPER-LISSENDEN, W.

Mistress Clare ('*m.c.*', m. F. Schulz: Bij., 25/10/00; St G's H., 18/6/01; Windsor, 7/11/12, as *Beverley's Daughters*: + *R. G. GILLMAN*)

COOPMAN, CECILIE

× The Fairies' Lesson (+ *CONSTANCE COOPMAN*) *Fr. 1910*

COPELAND, FANNY S.

The Liberators (Sur., 27/6/20, People's Theatre Soc.: adapted from a play by Srgjan Tučić) *1918*

Passion's Furnace (St G's H., 8/3/25, Internat. Theatre Soc.: adapted from a play by Josip Kosor) *1917* (in *People of the Universe*, a collection of Kosor's dramas)

COPELAND, GEORGE

At Paradise Farm ('*c.*': W.G., L'pool, 22/10/28: + *M. NESBITT*)

COPPING, BERNARD

[For an earlier play see *H. E. D.* v, 324]

'Twixt Heart and Soul (Vic. H., Newmarket, 8/9/02)

A Black Heart; or, The Hypnotist (Pav., Hastings, 24/11/02; Edmonton, 7/4/03, as *The Hypnotist*)

COQUELICOT, Mdlle

The Song of the River (St G's H., 2/8/00)

Thomas Chatterton (Ladbr. H., 25/7/01)

CORBETT, Mrs GEORGE

[For earlier plays see *H. E. D.* v, 324]

× On the Threshold (*'fairy allegory'*: Bij., 30/4/00)

× Caught (*'ca.'*: St Alban's Parish H., Acton, 25/10/00, *amat.*)

× Today and Yesterday (St Alban's Parish H., Acton, 6/12/00, *amat.*)

× The Shrine of Mammon (St Alban's Parish H., Acton, 6/12/00, *amat.*)

× The Last Recruit (St Alban's Parish H., Acton, 6/12/00, *amat.*)

× A Change of Colour (*'costume ca.'*: T.H., Chiswick, 9/5/01, *amat.*)

× Powder and Shot (St Alban's Parish H., Acton, 6/12/01, *amat.*: + *A. ROSE*)

Lady Featherbrain (Qns Gate H., 23/2/05)

CORBETT, JAMES [see *M. OSMOND*]

CORBETT, THALBERG

The Pride of the Brookes (*'c.'*: Dublin, 25/9/05)

CORELLI, MARIE

The Master Christian (Gr., Leeds, 18/8/00, *cpy.*)

Temporal Power (Roy., Morecambe, 23/8/02, *cpy.*)

CORELLI, VINCENT GORDON

[A few playlets produced at music-halls]

CORENTEZ, LEAH

Less than the Dust (*'morality pl.'*: Vic., Stanley, 3/11/19; Stratford, 7/6/20)

His Temporary Wife (Vic., Stanley, 23/8/20; Pal., Battersea, 5/10/21)

The Much-Married Man (*'c.'*: Wednesbury, 13/9/20; Pal., Battersea, 3/10/21)

When Women Strike (Seaham Harbour, 18/12/20; Pal., Battersea, 7/10/21)

A Broken Butterfly (New, Pontypridd, 3/20; Pal., Battersea, 12/10/21)

CORKERY, DANIEL

The Labour Leader (Abbey, Dublin, 30/9/19) *1920*

× The Yellow Bittern (Abbey, Dublin, 4/5/20) *1920*

× Resurrection. *1924* (*Theatre Arts Monthly*, April, 1924)

CORKHILL, PERCY F.

Cupid and the Consul (*'m.c.'*: Playh., L'pool, 8/12/19, *amat.*)

The Land of Anywhere. LC, Alex. H., Blundellsands, 16/11/22

CORNELIUS, LILIAN

Bongola (Q, 19/4/26: + *C. O. PAYNE*)

CORNILLE-PESCUD, GEORGE E.

In the Land of the Chrysanthemum (*'m.c.'*: Arcadian Pav., Leeds, 12/6/11)

[Numerous sketches and playlets produced at music-halls]

CORNISH, J. F.

The Cruise of H.M.S. Irresponsible (*'m.c.'*, m. G. W. Byng: Roy., Chester, 2/8/00; Broadway, New X, 26/11/00)

CORNWALL, LEWIS

The Marriage of Oberon ('*masque*': Lyr., Hamm., 13/5/18)

The Perfect Woman (T.H., Hunstanton, 7/8/22; Pal., Watford, 14/8/22)

CORNWALLIS-WEST, GEORGE

×Pro Patria (Col., 12/2/17; made into an opera by *A. KALISCH*, m. P. Colson, Lyc., 22/8/19)

The Bill ('*c.*': Roy., Glasgow, 26/3/18; P.W., 25/6/13)

CORNWALLIS-WEST, Mrs GEORGE

His Borrowed Plumes ('*c.*': Hicks', 6/7/09, *m.*; Hicks', 15/7/09)

CORPEL, J.

L'amour (Maskelyne's, 21/3/26, Playmates: +*G. OWEN*: adapted from the play (1924) by H. Kistemaeckers)

A Bird in the Hand (Maskelyne's, 30/5/26, Playmates: +*P. CRESSWELL*)

The Coward (Scala, 26/7/26, Playmates: +*P. CRESSWELL*: adapted from *Le Lâche* (1925) by H. R. Lenormand)

CORRAN, MABEL

×Mum's the Word. LC, Vaud., 19/6/23

CORRIE, JOE

×The Poacher ('*domestic c.*': Lyr., Glasgow, 21/10/26, Scott. Nat. Players) *1927* (in *The Scots Magazine*, vi, 187–96); *1927* (Glasgow)

×The Shillin' a Week Man ('*domestic c.*': Lyr., Glasgow, 22/3/27, Scott. Nat. Players) *1927* (Glasgow)

×Glensheugh ('*c.*': Gothenburg H., Carden, 14/3/28) *1931* (Glasgow)

×The Best Laid Schemes. LC, '*c.*': P.H., Ballantrae, 14/2/29. *1928* (in *The Scots Magazine*, ix, 262–70)

×The Hoose o' the Hill. *1929* (in *The Scots Magazine*, x, 421–31) *Fr. 1932*

×A Near Thing ('*Scots pl.*') *1930* (Glasgow)

CORRIN, HARRY

A Highwayman Bold ('*c.o.*: Hippo., St Helens, 19/1/09, *cpy.*: +*B. HARDING*)

CORSER, E. C.

×A House of Cards ('*c.*': Gai., Manchester, 4/12/16)

CORY, VIVIAN [='*VICTORIA CROSS*']

CORYELL, J. R.

A Western Girl. LC, Sav., 25/6/19

COSAIR, EDGAR

Luke Raeburn, Sinner (O.H., Crouch End, 19/9/02, *cpy.*; Garston, 24/11/02; Carlton, Greenwich, 20/7/03: called originally *The Evil that Men Do*)

COSENS, MONICA [see *B. GIRVIN* and *M. PARR*]

COSHAM, ERNEST
[For an earlier play see *H. E. D.* v, 325]
×His Wife's Picture (Aven., 23/5/00)

COSTELLO, MARY
[For earlier plays see *H. E. D.* v, 325]
×An Heroic Lie (Gai., Dublin, 14/12/00)
×The Gods at Play (Irish Theatrical Club, Dublin, 18/5/10, *amat.*)
×The Coming of Aileen (Irish Theatrical Club, Dublin, 18/5/10, *amat.*; Qns, Dublin, 4/9/11)

COTES, Mrs EVERARD [=*SARA JEANNETTE DUNCAN*]

COTTERILL, HENRY BERNARD
Christopher Sly ('*fant.pl.*': P's, Manchester, 22/8/21; New, 31/8/21: adapted from G. Forzano, *Sly*, 1920)

COTTESMORE, HERBERT [see also *A. D. GRANGE*]
Shadowed Lives (Kennington, 9/2/03: +*A. HARRISON*)
The Geisha Girl ('*m.c.*', m. F. V. Lasque: Emp., Wakefield, 23/10/11)

COTTON, FLORENCE
×Esther Franklin (Kyrle H., B'ham, 11/1/25, Birmingham Jewish Arts Soc.)

COTTON, STEPHANIE
The Legend of Babushka ('*nativity pl.*') *1928* (Village D. Soc.)

COTTON, WILFRED
The Adventures of Moll ('*r.m.c.*': P's, Manchester, 14/6/05)

COURNOS, JOHN
Sport of Gods. *1925*

COURTHOPE, H. [see *M. WOODIFIELD*]

COURTICE, THOMAS
[For an earlier play see *H. E. D.* v, 326]
×Her Brother (H.M., Carlisle, 8/7/01)
Love and Kisses ('*m.fant.*': K's, Hamm., 13/5/18)

COURTLANDT, R. VAN [see *G. FULTON*]

COURTNEIDGE, ROBERT [see also *A. ANDERSON* and *A. M. THOMPSON*]
Petticoat Fair ('*m.c.*', m. A. Wood: Hippo., Newcastle, 23/12/18; Hippo., Golder's Green, 12/5/19)
Fancy Fair ('*m.extravaganza*', m. A. Wood: Hippo., Newcastle, 14/4/19)
Too Many Girls ('*m.c.*', m. A. Wood: Hippo., L'pool, 23/12/19; Hippo., Golder's Green, 26/4/20: +*J. HULBERT* and *H. SIMPSON*)
Gabrielle ('*m.pl.*', m. G. H. Clutsam and A. Joyce: K's, Glasgow, 26/12/21; K's, Hamm., 30/8/23: +*H. WILLIAMS*)
The Little Duchess ('*m.pl.*', m. G. H. Clutsam: K's, Glasgow, 25/12/22; Hippo., Golder's Green, 11/2/24: +*B. DAVIS*)

COURTNEY, WILLIAM LEONARD [see also *G. MURRAY*]
[For earlier plays see *H. E. D.* v, 326]
Undine ('*dream pl.*': Shak., L'pool, 23/9/03; Crit., 23/5/06, first act only) *1902*
Dramas and Diversions. *1908*
[This contains: 1. *Bridals of Blood*; 2. ×*Kit Marlowe's Death*; 3. ×*Gaston Bonnier, or, Time's Revenges;* 4. *Undine* (see above); 5. ×*Father Time and His Children*; 6. ×*Pericles and Aspasia* ('*bsq.*': Roy., 26/6/11); 7. *On the Side of the Angels* (Roy., 16/12/06, Pioneers)]
Le Dedale (Com., 21/9/05: adapted from the play (1902) by P. Hervieu)
×Markheim (Lyr., 14/4/06)
×A Woman's Revolt (Pal., 7/7/09)
×Simætha (Col., 27/8/17)

COUSENS, DOROTHY
×Dicky and John. LC, Parish H., Whitstable, 13/10/22

COUSINS, ALBERT
The Maid of Toledo. LC, St Giles Parish R., Cambridge, 8/1/13

COUSINS, JAMES
×The Sleep of the King (Molesworth H., Dublin, 29/10/02, Irish Nat. Theatre Soc.)
×The Racing Lug (Molesworth H., Dublin, 31/10/02, Irish Nat. Theatre Soc.)

'*COUTTS, FRANCIS*' [=*FRANCIS COUTTS NEVILL, Baron LATYMER*: see also '*G. PASTON*']
The Song of Songs. *1906*
The Romance of Arthur. *1907*
[This volume contains a collection of narrative and dramatic poems]
×Collusion (Apo., 12/4/15)
Enterprising Helen ('*c.*': Brighton, 7/6/15; Vaud., 7/7/15)

COVE, ERNEST GEORGE
×Those Who Wait. LC, Ass. R., Tenby, 27/11/18. *1918* (Cardiff)

'*COVERTSIDE, NAUNTON*' [=*NAUNTON DAVIES*]

COVINGTON, ZELLAH
Three Spoonfuls (Pier, Eastbourne, 5/4/15; Crit., 10/4/15)

COWAN, A. D.
×The New Provost. LC, '*c.*': Victoria United Free Church House, Glasgow, 7/2/29. *1929* (Glasgow)

COWAN, M. A.
×The Sacrifice. LC, Crippl. Inst., 24/2/15: +*A. BYRNE*
×For Sale (Pav., 15/6/16, *m.*: called originally *The Matchmaker*)

COWAN, MAURICE
The Calcutta Sweep ('*m.bsq.*': Pleasure Gdns, Folkestone, 4/2/29: +*A. MARTYN* and *S. MAYO*)

COWARD, NOËL [see also *E. WYNNE*]

[Raymond Mander and Joe Mitchenson have a detailed and comprehensive *Theatrical Companion to Coward* (1957)]

I'll Leave It to You ('*c.*': Gai., Manchester, 3/5/20; New, 21/7/20) *Fr. 1920*

×Bottles and Bones (D.L., 16/5/22, *m.*)

×The Better Half ('*c.*': Little, 31/5/22)

The Young Idea ('*c. of youth*': P's, Bristol, 25/9/22; Sav., 1/2/23) *Fr. 1924*

×Mild Oats. LC, P's, Bristol, 29/9/22. *1931* (in *Collected Sketches*)

×Weatherwise (written 1923: Festival, Malvern, 8/9/32) *1931* (in *Collected Sketches*)

×That Last Resource (written for broadcasting: LC, Shaft., 25/1/23; broadcast 11/12/26)

London Calling ('*revue*': D.Y., 4/9/23: +*R. JEANS*)

The Rat Trap (written 1918: Everyman, 18/10/26) *1924*

The Vortex (Everyman, 25/11/24; Roy., 16/12/24) *1925*

Fallen Angels ('*c.*': Glo., 21/4/25) *1925*

On with the Dance ('*revue*': Pal., Manchester, 17/3/25; Pav., 30/4/25)

Hay Fever ('*c.*': Ambass., 6/8/25) *1925*

The Queen was in the Parlour ('*romance*': St M., 24/8/26) *1926*

Easy Virtue (Broad, Newark, 23/11/26; O.H., Manchester, 31/5/26; D.Y., 9/6/26) *1926*

'This Was a Man' (LC, D.Y., 13/9/26, *licence refused*; Klaw, N.Y., 23/11/26) *1928*

The Marquise ('*c.*': Crit., 16/2/27) *1927*

Home Chat ('*c.*': D.Y., 25/10/27) *1927*

Sirocco (written 1921: Daly's, 24/11/27) *1928*

This Year of Grace! ('*revue*': Pal., Manchester, 28/2/28; Pav., 22/3/28) *1928*

Bitter-Sweet ('*oa.*': Pal., Manchester, 2/7/29; H.M., 18/7/29) *1929*

Private Lives (K's, Edinburgh, 18/8/30; Phoenix, 24/9/30) *1930*

Collected Sketches and Lyrics. *1931*

[This contains selected contributions to various revues]

COWL, RICHARD PAPE

×The Betrothal (Ashburton, 25/2/22, Ashburton Group of the British Drama League: adapted from *Kihlaus* (1872) by A. Kivi) *1928*

COWLES, FREDERICK I.

The Rose of Sharon ('*Epiphany pl.*': Houghton H., Cambridge, 31/12/24, *amat.*)

COWEN, LAURENCE [see *L. COHEN*]

COX, A. B.

Mr Priestley's Adventure (Pal., Brighton, 19/3/28; Roy., 27/3/28, as *Mr Priestley's Night Out*; also called *Mr Priestley's Problem* and *Handcuffs for Two*)

COX, A. NEVILLE [see *H. W. BARBER*]

COX, C. W.
Clementina ('*m.pl.*', m. F. G. Bennett: Pav., Weston, 14/6/20)

COX, CYRIL
Peter's Reputation (Ass. R., Balham, 16/12/13)

COX, EDWARD
Campion; or, A Pearl of Christendom ('*historical and religious pl.*': Corn Exchange, Oxford, 28/11/07, *amat.*)

COX, ERNEST H. G.
×The Other Heir (O.H., Blackpool, 5/11/06)
×The Way Out (Qns, Poplar, 10/4/11)
[A few sketches and playlets produced at music-halls]

COX, FRANK J.
×Here's to the Sailor (Shak., L'pool, 11/11/09, *cpy.*)

COX, HARDING
×The Fatal Dance (Margate, 7/6/09; Com., 23/8/09)

COX, REGINALD KENNEDY
Mary Stuart, Queen of Scots ('*r.pl.*': K's, Hamm., 21/5/06)

COX, WATTY
×The Widow Dempsey's Funeral (Hardwicke Street H., Dublin, 18/12/11, Theatre of Ireland)

COYNE, C. KING
×Cats ('*f.*': Rehearsal, 24/1/13, Black Cat Club)

COYNE, F.
Follow My Leader. LC, Hippo., Aldershot, 21/3/23

COYNE, GARDINER
Willie Reilly; or, The Fair Lady of Boyle (Qns, Dublin, 24/4/05)

CRAIG, EDITH
×Death and the Lady (Kings., 13/5/17, Pioneer Players: +*Mrs C. LOWTHER*)

CRAIGIE, Mrs P. M. T. [='*JOHN OLIVER HOBBES*']

CRAIK, CHARLES H.
×Aeroplane Mad (Manor H., Euston, 30/11/09, *m.*: +*G. S. CRAIK*)
×George Comes to Town ('*c.*': St Simon's Schools, Bristol, 31/5/22)

CRAIK, G. SETON [see *C. H. CRAIK*]

CRAMPTON, ERNEST
Ladies in Power. LC, Pier, Southsea, 28/8/14
Carnival's Call ('*r. revue*': O.H., Bridlington, 25/10/20: +*M. HERBERT*)

CRAN, Mrs GEORGE (MARION)
×The Shell of a Man (Gt. Qn. St., 25/6/07, *m.*)

CRANMER-BYNG, L.
Salma (Midland Inst., B'ham, 2/3/26, *amat.*)

CRANSTON, DOUGLAS

The Girl from the Golden West. LC, '*m.pl.*': Alex., 25/1/21: +*R. ERNEST*

CRAUFORD, J. R. [see also *M. B. SPURR*]

[For earlier plays see *H. E. D.* v, 328]

The Bezsemenovs (Terry's, 23/4/06, Mermaid Soc.: adapted from the play by M. Gorki)

×Who Laughs Last (Hippo., Eastbourne, 29/1/12)

CRAVEN, ARTHUR SCOTT [see also *R. H. BLAND* and *J. E. H. TERRY*]

[For an earlier play see *H. E. D.* v, 329]

×His Eightieth Birthday (Gr., Chatham, 25/3/01)

×The Compleat Angler (Lyc., 11/6/07, *m.*; Hippo., Manchester, 29/6/14; Col., 13/7/14: +*J. D. BERESFORD*) *Fr. 1915*

×A Royal Heart (Empress, 27/4/08; Col., 28/6/09: +*J. D. BERESFORD*)

×The Sirocco (Emp., L'pool, 31/1/10; Vaud., 28/8/13: translated from *Samun* (1890) by A. Strindberg)

The Last of the English (Kings., 21/7/11, *m.*, act II only) *1910*

[*CRAVEN, FRANK*

Too Many Cooks (Brady's, Wilmington, 26/1/14; 39th Street, N.Y., 25/2/14; Sav., 1/9/19) *Fr. 1927*

×A Man of Principle (Hippo., Eastbourne, 2/6/19; Hippo., Willesden, 14/7/19)

The First Year ('*c.t.*': Wood's, Chicago, 6/11/22; Apo., 29/11/26) *Fr. 1921*

CRAVEN, PRISCILLA [*Mrs TEIGNMOUTH SHORE*]

×Jenkins's Widow (Court, 21/3/09, Dramatic Debaters)

×The Painted Nun (K's H., 12/3/13: +*S. RUSKIN*)

CRAVEN, TOM

[For earlier plays see *H. E. D.* v, 329]

The Wife and the Woman (K's, Gateshead, 20/11/05)

When a Lass Loves (Margate, 23/11/08; Dalston, 5/4/09)

The Makings of a Man (Pav., 27/9/09)

×The Mystery of the Cliff (W.L., 25/4/10: +*W. EVANS*)

CRAWFORD, A.

The Man with the Club Foot. LC, Apo., 22/4/18: +*V. WILLIAMS*

[*CRAWFORD, FRANCIS MARION*

[For an earlier play see *H. E. D.* v, 329]

Francesca da Rimini (Shaft., 1/10/01)

The White Sister. LC, Gar., 5/4/09: +*W. HACKETT*. *1937*

The Ideal Wife (Crosby H., Chelsea, 17/5/12; Vaud., 15/7/12: translated from M. Praga, *La moglie ideale*, 1890)

CRAWSHAY-WILLIAMS, ELIOT

Five Grand Guignol Plays. *Fr. 1924*

[This contains: 1. *E. and O.E.* (Little, 12/10/21); 2. *Amends* (Little, 25/1/22); 3. *Rounding the Triangle* (Little, 29/6/21); 4.

The Nutcracker Suite (Little, 3/4/22); and 5. *Cupboard Love* (25/1/22)]
×Spring Cleaning. LC, Little, 27/10/21
The Vicious Quitch. LC, Little, 27/2/24
The Man in the Next Room (Ambass., 13/7/24, Interlude Players)
This Marriage (Com., 7/5/24: called originally *Husbands Can't Help It*)
The Debit Account (New, 4/7/26, Interlude Players)
More Grand Guignol Plays. *Fr. 1927*
[This contains four short plays 1. *The Compleat Lover*; 2. *Grensal Green*; 3. *Teaching Teresa*; and 4. *A Storm in a Breakfast Cup*]
×From Information Received. *1928* (in *The Amateur Stage*, March, 1928)
Out East (Aldershot, 15/4/29)
The Donkey's Nose ('*c.*': P.W., 9/6/29, Sunday Pl. Soc.)

CRAY, OSWALD [see *R. CARLETON*]

CREAGH-HENRY, MAY
×A Bird in the Bush. *Fr. 1903*
×'Liz (Qns Gate H., 17/11/08, *m.*)
×Diogenes and the Damsel (Qns Gate H., 17/11/08, *m.*)
×A Pastoral Postponed (Qns Gate H., 17/11/08, *m.*)
×The Gate of Vision ('*modern mystery pl.*': Church House, Westminster, 21/3/22: +*D. MARTEN*) *1922* (SPCK); *1930* (revised)
×The Unknown Warrior ('*mystical pl.*': +*D. MARTEN*) *1923* (SPCK)
Four Mystical Plays. *1924* (SPCK)
[This contains four short plays: 1. *Outcasts* (Str., 13/1/24); '*Greater Love Hath No Man*'; 3. *The Star* (LC, K. G's H., 21/11/25); 4. *The Gate of Vision* (see above)]
×The Gardener. *Fr. 1924*
×Gold. *Fr. 1925*
×The Way of Atonement. *Fr. 1927*
×The Crib. *Fr. 1929*
×The Victory of the Cross. *Fr. 1929*

CREAGH-HENRY, S.
[For earlier plays see *H. E. D.* v, 418]
The Knave of Diamonds ('*md.*': County, Kingston, 8/4/01)
From the Unseen World ('*md.*': Metro., Gateshead, 17/8/01; Borough, Stratford, 3/7/05)
Dr Janet of Harley Street (Bij., 31/5/04, *cpy.*; C.P., 6/3/05: dramatised from the novel (1893) by Arabella Kenealy)
×Laying the Ghost ('*pl. for boys*') *Fr. 1924*
×Run to Earth ('*pl. for boys*') *Fr. 1924*

CREN, FRED LE
The Stolen Statue. LC, Scala, Seacombe, 3/8/15; title later changed to *She Slipped* and *Models and Muddles*
The Belle of Madrid. LC, Stockport, 25/3/22

CRESSWELL, A. T.
[A few sketches produced at music-halls]

CRESSWELL, PETER [see *J. CORPEL*]

CRESSY, WILL M.
[A few sketches produced at music-halls]

CRITCHETT, RICHARD CLAUDE [='*R. C. CARTON*']

CROCKER, ALFRED
Beatrix ('*historical pl.*': Margate, 13/4/08: dramatised from W. M. Thackeray's novel, *Esmond*)
×Both sides of the Curtain (Emp., Kilburn, 13/2/11)
×The Sacrifice (Little, 18/10/12)
×The Back of Brazil (Court, 15/1/14, Leverton Players)

CROFT, ANNIE
The Lu Lu Girl ('*m.c.*': Lecture H., Hull, 17/1/13)

CROFT, WAL
[A few sketches produced at music-halls]

CROFTON, MARION
×For Her Sake (Ambass., 6/12/20, *m.*)
Rosie in Search of Romance ('*f.c.*': Blfrs., 27/2/28)

CROKER, Mrs BITHIA MARY
Terence ('*c.*': Margate, 18/2/07; Gai., Dublin, 1/3/09; Gr., Fulham, 6/12/09; dramatised from her own novel, 1899)

CROLY, ELIZABETH
Forbidden Revels ('*c.o.*', m. E. Farwell: Gr., Swanage, 20/12/25) *1925* (Swanage)

CROMARTY, COUNTESS of
×The Finding of the Sword (Playh., 30/4/07, *m.*)
×The Tiger of Asshur. LC, Hippo., Aldershot, 19/10/17

CROMO, JACK
Strawberries and Cream ('*m.c.*', m. F. Corri and A. Vernon: King's Lynn, 25/2/18)
Go-As-You-Please ('*m.extravaganza*': Hippo., Richmond, 22/4/18)

CRONE, WILLIAM
×The Bargain (Abbey, Dublin, 5/4/15)

CROPPER, MARGARET BEATRICE
×The Standard Bearers. *1918*
×The Next-Door House. *1920* (SPCK)
×The Map. *1923* (SPCK)
×The Water-Woman. *1926*
×A Farewell. *1927* (Village Drama Soc.)
×The Good Samaritan. *1930* (SPCK)
×The Pearl of Great Price. *1930* (SPCK)
×St Peter is Delivered from Prison. *1930* (SPCK)

CROSS, ALFRED B.
The Monarch of the World (Barry Dock, 29/5/08)

CROSS, A. F. [see also *E. L. SHUTE*]
[For an earlier play see *H. E. D.* v, 330]
×By Still Waters ('*episode in Arcady*': Rugby, 6/11/01)
×Poachers (P.W., Nuneaton, 29/11/01)
Sir Roger de Coverley (P.W., Nuneaton, 28/2/02, *cpy.*)

CROSS, A. W. S.
A Broken Rosary (Ladbr. H., 15/2/10, *cpy.*)

CROSS, DOROTHEA [see also *V. H. HILL*]
×Susan's Mother (Court, 12/3/14)

CROSS, ELSIE
×A Fairy Fantasy. LC, '*wordless pl.*': Barnstaple, 14/5/17

CROSS, FELIX
×A Little Prince. LC, Perth, 18/2/16

CROSS, H. A. A.
Sir Walter Raleigh. *1907*

CROSS, JULIAN
[For earlier plays see *H. E. D.* v, 330]
The Spider's Web (St J., Manchester, 8/9/05)

CROSS, MARGARET BESSIE
Mrs Waterlow, Chaperone (Court, 24/2/11, *amat.*)
×Dandy's Girl. LC, K. G's H., 7/2/24

'*CROSS, SOUTHERN*' [=*F. MARRIOTT-WATSON*]

'*CROSS, VICTORIA*' [=*VIVIAN CORY*]
Five Nights (Gr., Swansea, 1/4/18; Borough, Stratford, 10/6/18: dramatised from her own novel, 1908)
The Greater Law (O.H., Belfast, 1/11/20; Kennington, 15/11/20: dramatised from her own novel, 1914)
×Wit of the East. LC, Harrogate, 16/12/20

CROSSING, WILLIAM [see *F. EATON*]

CROSSLEY, FLORENCE HALTON
The Secret Sin (Qns, Dublin, 20/9/15; Macclesfield, 26/12/16; Stratford, 21/5/17, as *A Daughter of Devon*)
A Thief of Virtue (Darwen, 18/3/11, *cpy.*; title later changed to *A Woman's Honour*)
A Girl of the People. LC, Seaham Harbour, 26/1/16
The Rolling Stone (Emp., Garston, 12/7/17: title later changed to *The Sword of Justice*)

[*CROTHERS, RACHEL*
The Three of Us (Terry's, 10/6/08) *1916* (New York)
Young Wisdom (Playh., 23/9/14)
Let Us Be Gay ('*c.*': Lyr., 18/8/30)

CROWE, Mrs [=*Miss BATEMAN*]

CROWE, CHRISTINE

×The Boss o' the Hoose (broadcast from Aberdeen, 4/11/24) *1925* (in *The Scots Magazine*, iv, 47–55); *1928* (Glasgow)

CROYSDALE, AGNES

The Half-Sister ('*f.*': Guildford, 8/3/15; Apo., 12/4/15)

CROZIER, CHARLES

[For earlier plays see *H. E. D.* v, 331]

[Several sketches and playlets produced at music-halls]

CRUM, E. V.

×Such Stuff as Dreams are Made On. LC, Baillieston, 30/3/20

×A Rum Customer. LC, Baillieston, 30/3/20

CRUM, W. G.

The Spinneys. LC, Ath., Glasgow, 19/10/16

CRUSE, JOHN

The Nineteenth Hole ('*c.*': Lyc. Club, 25/4/26)

CRUTCHLEY, TRISTRAN

The Purple Emperor ('*m.c.*', m. H. Austin: K's, Hamm., 6/12/09: called originally *Emperor Jakes*: +*C. AUSTIN*)

'*CRYPTOS*' [pseudonym of *ADRIAN ROSS, PERCY GREENBANK, IVAN CARYLL* and *LIONEL MONCKTON*, in collaboration]

CUBITT, SYDNEY

[For earlier plays see *H. E. D.* v, 331]

The Maid and the Minstrel ('*m.c.*', m. C. St Amory: Lyr., 19/11/04)

CUBLEY, HAROLD H. S.

The Girl of the Cabaret. LC, Worcester, 27/7/22

[*CULBERTSON, ERNEST HOWARD*

×The End of the Trail (Gate, 30/10/25)

CULLINGFORD, FRED R. [see *J. EDWARDES*]

CULLUM, CHARLES

Uncle Tom's Cabin ('*m.pl.*': Hippo., Coventry, 14/9/25; Richmond, 28/9/25: +*H. MEAR*)

CULLUM, HERBERT H.

[For an earlier play see *H. E. D.* v, 331]

×A Court Romance ('*ca.*': Gr., Douglas, 14/6/01)

CULLUM, RIDGWELL

×Blind Justice (Metropolitan, 3/5/09: +*H. E. GARDEN*)

The Devil's Keg (Borough, Stratford, 27/5/12: +*H. E. GARDEN*)

CULTON, SIDONIE

×The Fair Arabian (Court, 9/7/09, Civic and Dramatic Guild)

CULVERWELL, L. J. [see *R. N. HILL*]

CUMMINS, Miss G. D. [see *S. R. DAY*]

CUMMINS, STEVENSON LYLE
×Haroun el Rashid (Bij., Bedford St., 21/10/22, Regent Dr. Soc.)
×Bluebeard (Bij., Bedford St., 21/10/22, Regent Dr. Soc.)

CUNNINGHAM, Mrs
Christmas Geese ('*f.c.*': Holy Trinity R., Southall, 24/7/11, *amat.*)

[*CUNNINGHAM, ARCHIBALD*
Under the Stars and Stripes (Tyldesley, 3/8/07)

CUNNINGHAM, BEN
×Ivy's Sister. LC, Bradford, 9/11/17
×Circumstance. LC, Gar., 13/12/21

CUNNINGHAM, MARION
×Out of the Storm ('*c.*': Court, 28/4/11, *m.*)
×The Laugh against the Lawyer (Court, 28/4/11, *m.*)
The Hour and the Woman (Cosmopolis, 25/4/13, Advance Players)

CUNNINGHAM-GRAHAM, Mrs
Don Juan's Last Wager (P.W., 27/2/00: adapted from *Don Juan Tenorio* (1877) by J. Zorilla)

CURRIE, CLIVE
×Smike (K's H., 11/12/21, Interlude Players)
Tamaresque (Strand, 11/12/27, Lyc. Club St. Soc.)

CURRYER, CONSTANCE E.
×The Building of the Wall ('*biblical d.*') *1927*

CURTIS, ARTHUR [see *A. ECKERSLEY*]

CURTIS, B. W. [see *A. MacHUGH*]

CURTIS, OSWALD T. [see *A. FAULKNER*]

CURTIS, REGINALD H.
Aunt Maria's Will ('*c.*': Dover, 23/6/04)
Greifenstein (Leicester, 14/12/04, *cpy.*: dramatised from the novel (1889) by F. Marion Crawford)
The Star of Paris (Dover, 2/12/05, *cpy.*: +*G. ANTLEY*)

CURWEN, HARRY (HENRY)
Roulette. LC, '*m.pl.*': Pal., Nelson, 22/10/20
Gay Fleurette ('*m.pl.*': E.C., 18/7/21: title later changed to *Susette*)
The Riviera ('*m.c.*': Pal., Maidstone, 28/10/29)

CURZON, FRANK [see *F. LONSDALE*]

CURZON-HERRICK, Lady KATHLEEN
×In the '45 (H.M., 9/1/17, *m.*)
×It is Expedient (Roy., 14/11/26, Lyc. Club St. Soc.)

[*CUSHING, CATHERINE CHISHOLM*
Kitty Mackay ('*c.*': Shubert, Rochester, 24/11/13; Com., N.Y., 7/1/14; Hippo., Portsmouth, 27/3/16; Qns, 1/4/16) *Fr. 1914*
Pollyanna (Broadway, Philadelphia, 24/1/16; Hudson, N.Y., 18/9/16; P's, Manchester, 20/10/24; St J., 18/12/24: dramatised from the novel by Eleanor H. Porter) *Fr. 1915*

Marjolaine ('*m.pl.*', m. H. Felix: O.H., Blackpool, 28/5/28; Gai., 12/6/28: dramatised from L. N. Parker's *Pomander Walk*, 1912)
Topsy and Eva ('*m.c.*', m. R. and V. Duncan: Hippo., Lewisham, 20/8/28; Gai., 4/10/28)

[*CUSHING, TOM* [*CHARLES C. S. CUSHING*]
Blood and Sand (Emp., N.Y., 20/9/21; P.W., B'ham, 5/12/21; New, 14/12/21: dramatised from the novel by V. Blasco Ibañez).
The Devil in the Cheese ('*fant.*': Charles Hopkins, N.Y., 29/12/26 Com., 4/6/29) *Fr. 1927*

CUSLEY, GIDEON
×The Enchanted Trousers (Abbey, Dublin, 25/11/19)

CUTHBERT, Father O. S. F. S.
The Shepherds (Cathedral H., Westminster, 5/1/15)

CUTHBERTSON, J. C.
The Cardinal's Sin. LC, Leigh, 18/10/22

CUTHBERTSON, J. M.
×The Sentimentalist (Ath., Glasgow, 4/12/08, *amat.*)
×Sickle and Cross (R. Inst., Glasgow, 3/5/12)
×The Cavern (R. Inst., Glasgow, 3/5/12)

CUTLER, JOHN K. C.
×A Brace of Humbugs (Brixton, 1/7/07)
×A Matter-of-fact Husband (Lyc., 14/7/08, *m.*)
×A Narrow Escape (Court, 4/12/13)

CYPRIAN, C.
×Only a Crook. LC, Gr., Old Hill, 7/9/15

DAGNALL, EDWARD
Whose Wife? (D.P., Eastbourne, 29/11/15)
Nearly Divorced ('*f.*': Pal., Brighton, 30/5/27; D.Y., 29/6/27)

DAINOW, DAVID
×Ferdinand (Court, 21/1/12, Play Actors)

DALE, Rev. ARTHUR M.
The Muddler (Brighton, 20/11/16; Qns, 24/4/17, *m.*, as *Muddles*; Gar., 7/3/21: +*E. STANNARD*)

DALE, FREDERICK [see also *L. WORRALL*]
The Bair Legacy. LC, T.H., Chiswick, 12/1/22
The Wanglers. LC, T.H., Chiswick, 2/2/23
Lovey Lock. LC, T.H., Chiswick, 17/3/25
The Stop Gap (K. G's H., 27/5/26, *amat.*)

DALE, H. M.
Lady Hilda, Abbess of Whitby. LC, Spa, Whitby, 20/5/13

DALE, J. C. [see *J. ALFORD*]

DALE, JAMES LITTLEWOOD
×A Conversation at the Styx (Little, 10/7/13, Stage Players)
Honourable Women ('*caricature*': Ambass., 4/11/13, Stage Players)

DALE, LUCY

×Why She Did It (Lyc. Club, 11/5/11, *m.*)
×Seen through a Veil (Lyc. Club, 13/3/21)

DALKEITH, LENA

Little Plays. *1905*
[This contains five short plays for children]

'*DALL, IAN*' [=*CHARLES HIGGINS*]

Noah's Wife. *1925* (Oxford)
[This contains, besides the title-piece, five other short verse plays: 1. *The Bargain;* 2. *Miching Malecho*; 3. *One Sunset*; 4. *The Barnyard*; and 5. *Among Old Instruments*]

DALLAS, W. ALEXANDER

The Great Wilderness ('*md.*': Gr., Fulham, 6/8/06: title changed later to *The World's Great Snare*)

DALLET, JOHN BEDE

John Bunyan's Pilgrim's Progress Dramatised. *1928* (*priv.*)

DALLIBA, Miss K. LYON

Pay Up (Lyr., Ipswich, 17/8/14)

DALMON, CHARLES

×The Picture on the Wall (H.M., Dundee, 18/12/16)

DALRYMPLE, HUGH

East or West ('*c.*': Kings., 21/6/21, *m.*, Playwrights' Theatre)

DALRYMPLE, LEWIS T.

×The Will of Allah (Euston, 18/4/10: called originally *The Evil Eye*)
×A Lesson in Rinking (P.H., Birchington, 13/8/10; Rehearsal, 26/1/11)
×Bouquets for Breakfast (Ladbr. H., 18/10/10, *cpy.*; Rehearsal, 26/1/11, *m.*)

DALTON, C. I. F.

The Masque of Lady Margaret. *1930* (Bedford)

DALTON, MAURICE

Sable and Gold (Abbey, Dublin, 16/9/18) *1922* (Dublin)

DALY, CHARLES M.

[For earlier plays see *H. E. D.* v, 334]
×The Gorilla's Revenge (Aven., Sunderland, 25/6/06)

DALY, F. C.

Who Knows? (Str., 15/6/30, Rep. Players)

DALY, G. BRIAN [see also *A. CONQUEST*, *C. A. EAST*, *J. M. EAST* and '*F. HERBERT*']

[For earlier plays see *H. E. D.* v, 334]
×The Sundowner (Lyr., Hamm., 13/10/00: +*J. M. EAST*)
×An Uninvited Guest (Lyr., Hamm., 18/3/01: +*J. M. EAST*)
Was It Murder? (Sur., 23/6/02: +'*FRANK HERBERT*')
×All Through You (Emp., Shepherd's Bush, 27/3/07)
Happy-go-lucky O'Lynn (Court, Warrington, 5/9/10)

The Texas Ranger, or, The Vanishing Race (P's, Lanport, Portsmouth, 1/7/12; Emp., Holloway, 8/7/12)
×All Crooks (Pal., Hamm., 19/1/20: +*C. A. LEFTWICH* and *JOE HAYMAN*)
For Hearth and Home. LC, P'cess, Portsmouth, 26/5/13

DALY, MARK
[Numerous sketches produced at the Alex. music-hall]

DAM, HENRY J. W.
[For earlier plays see *H. E. D.* v, 334–5, 787]
La Madeleine (Shaft., 27/12/01, *cpy.*)
Skipper and Co., Wall Street ('*c.*': Adel., 28/4/03, *cpy.*)

DAMER, BERTRAM
By Sheer Pluck ('*smuggling d.*': Irving, Seacombe, 14/2/03, *cpy.*; Rot., L'pool, 15/6/03; Sur., 29/6/03)
The Frontier Queen (Alex., Hull, 8/7/11, *m.*; Woolwich, 23/10/11)

DAMERELL, J. [see *R. HARGREAVES*]

DANA, MAY
From Miner to M.P. (Hippo., Ellesmere Port, 25/2/24: title later changed to *That Wonderful Mother of Mine*)
Should a Wife Refuse? LC, Regent, Grimesthorpe, 29/8/25
Only a Shop-Girl. LC, H.M., Barrow-in-Furness, 4/11/25
Auction of Souls. LC, H.M., Barrow-in-Furness, 12/11/25
Wise Parentage. LC, H.M., Barrow-in-Furness, 18/11/25; title later changed to *Ignorance*)

DANCE, Sir GEORGE
[For earlier plays see *H. E. D.* v, 335]
A Chinese Honeymoon ('*m.pl.*', m. H. Talbot: Hanley, 16/10/1899; Str., 5/10/01) *1902*
The Ladies' Paradise ('*m.pl.*', m. I. Caryll: Hanley, 11/3/01)
The West End; or, Doings of the Smart Set ('*m.c.*', m. E. Jones: Norwich, 29/9/02: +*G. ARLISS*)
[A few sketches produced at music-halls]

DANCEY, A. T.
The Master of Clive Chase (O.H., Maidenhead, 13/3/13)
The Harvest of Hate (New, Maidenhead, 15/3/13)
×The Romany Girls (Crippl. Inst., 31/3/16, *amat.*)

DANDOE, ARTHUR [see also *H. ROXBURY*]
×The Wooing of Widder Wiggs. LC, Court, Brighton, 26/5/13

'*DANE, CLEMENCE*' [=*WINIFRED ASHTON*]
A Bill of Divorcement (St M., 14/3/21) *1921*
×The Terror (Playh., L'pool, 10/9/21)
Will Shakespeare ('*invention*': Shaft., 17/11/21) *1921*
×Shivering Shocks; or, The Hiding Place ('*pl. for boys*') *Fr. 1923*
The Way Things Happen ('*story*': Broad St, Newark, 24/12/23; Lyc., N.Y., 28/1/24; Ambass., 2/2/24) *1924*
Naboth's Vineyard ('*stage piece*') *1925*

Granite ('*t.*': Ambass., 15/6/26) *1926*
×A Traveller Returns. *Fr. 1927*
×Mr Fox ('*pl. for boys*') *Fr. 1927*
Adam's Opera ('*m.pl.*', m. R. Addinsell: Old Vic, 3/12/28) *1928*
Mariners ('*t.*': Plymouth, N.Y., 28/3/27; Wynd., 29/4/29) *1927*
Gooseberry Fool (Players, 1/11/29)

[*DANE, ESSEX*
×Heard in Camera. LC, S. Ldn Pal., 1/2/12
×When the Whirlwind Blows (Lyc. Club, 11/11/22) *1926* (Boston)
×Wrong Numbers (Lyc. Club, 13/5/23; Etlinger, 16/7/25) *1938*
×Let It Go at That (Ldn Theatre School, 28/3/28) *1926* (Boston)

DANE, ETHEL
×The Woman who Mattered (Pav., Glasgow, 22/1/12)

DANE, WILFRED
The Blue Girl. LC, '*m.c.*': Hippo., Nuneaton, 29/8/22: title later changed to *Naughty Lady*

DANIEL, FRANCIS
×The Duellist (S. Shields, 1/7/10)
×Hearts versus Diamonds (S. Shields, 20/4/11)
The Other Woman (S. Shields, 15/12/13)
Her Marriage Lines ('*md.*': Crook, 15/5/16; Vic., Walthamstow, 9/10/16)
Drug Lust. LC, S. Shields, 10/2/19: title later changed to *The Dope Woman*

DANIEL, ROLAND
The Princess's Own ('*r.pl.*': Gr., Brighton, 28/4/24; Brixton, 2/6/24: dramatised from his own novel)
The Signal (D.P., Eastbourne, 27/4/25; Str., 4/5/25: dramatised from his own novel)
A Wife or Two (Portsmouth, 21/2/27: +*C. B. POULTNEY*)
Who's Who ('*f.*': Vaud., 2/5/28: +*C. B. POULTNEY*)

DANIELL, DIRK
For the People (Margaret Morris, Chelsea, 26/6/21, Interlude Players)

DANSEY, HERBERT
Ferréol de Meyrac (Roy., 26/2/04: adapted from the play (1875) by V. Sardou)
The Black Devil ('*Sicilian episode*': Rehearsal, 13/11/08, Argonauts: adapted from a play by Carlo Broggi)

DANSON, BERT
The Wrong Miss Gordon ('*f.*': Canterbury, 25/4/04)
Hobbs' Vendetta ('*f.c.*': Worthing, 2/5/04: +*G. ARTHURS*)
×Booster's Billions (Yarmouth, 8/12/13)
[Several sketches produced at music-halls]

DANVERS, C. [see also *G. ARTHURS*]
×The Cinema Girl. LC, '*m.c.*': Hippo., Margate, 13/3/21

DANVERS, FRED
A Chinese Idyll ('*m.f.*', m. E. C. Brierley: Darlington, 17/12/03)

DARBEY, EDWARD
The Shadow of the Guillotine (Stratford, 13/10/13)

DARDY, V.
Sentenced for Life (W. Bromwich, 28/3/00, *cpy.*)

DARE, GEORGE
×Corruption. LC, Picture House, Stonemarket, 1/4/19
×A Little Outcast. LC, Picture House, Stonemarket, 7/4/19
The Egyptian and the Woman (P's, Blackburn, 11/8/24)

'*DARING, GEORGE*' [=*Mme RAOUL DUVAL*]
The Golden Light (Sav., 29/9/04)

DARK, SIDNEY [see also *C. RALEIGH*]
Who's Who? ('*f.*': Sav., 28/5/04: called originally *Poor Uncle Matthew*: adapted from a play by T. Bernard)

DARK, STANLEY
×Mr Smith ('*f.*': Alex., 23/4/00)
×Up in the Air (Emp., Islington, 10/3/13: +*WILLIAM KIRBY*)

DARKE, SILAS
Jack Frost, or, The Re-formation of the Pole ('*m.fant.*': Vic. H., 14/10/11, *cpy.*: +*F. N. PIGGOTT*)

DARLINGTON, WILLIAM AUBREY CECIL
Alf's Button ('*extravaganza*': Portsmouth, 25/8/24; Hippo., Golder's Green, 22/9/24; P's, 24/12/24) *1925*
[Originally presented as a film in 1920]
Magic Slippers ('*fant.f.*': Hastings, 22/7/29; Golder's Green, 29/7/29) *1937* (as *Carpet Slippers*)

DARLISON, JOHN
Foiled by Fate ('*md.*': W.L., 22/10/00)
Three Old Men ('*md.*': Gai., Leith, 20/6/10)
×A Brother of Men (Gai., Leith, 17/3/11)

DARNLEY, JAMES HERBERT [see also *H. B. HILL*]
[For earlier plays see *H. E. D.* v, 336–7]
Facing the Music ('*f.*': P.W., L'pool, 22/5/1899; Brixton, 5/6/1899; Str., 1/2/00; Euston, 25/6/17, as *The Other Mr Smith*) *Fr. 1921*
Her Majesty's Guests ('*m.f.*': P'cess of W., Kennington, 26/3/00: title later changed to *His M.G.*)
Oh! Society ('*f.c.*': P.W., L'pool, 28/5/00)
The Corsican ('*f.c.*': Brighton, 18/6/00; Metro., Camberwell, 25/3/01, as *The Two Mrs Homespuns*: +*H. P. BRUCE*)
Mr Wix of Wickham ('*m.c.*': Borough, Stratford, 21/7/02)
Needles ('*f.c.*': Worthing, 10/12/03)
×Curing the Doctor (Walsingham Club, 26/2/05)
×The Last Hour (Dover, 30/7/06)
A Mother's Sacrifice (Hippo., Mansfield, 9/9/07)

Captain Starlight, of the Kelly Gang (P's, Portsmouth, 21/7/13: +*E. GROSVENOR*)
What a Catch! ('*f.c.*': Brighton, 16/7/17; D.Y., 25/7/17)
Whose Baby? ('*f.*': Gr., Croydon, 2/9/18)
Joan All Alone ('*m.c.*': Hippo., Gloucester, 28/7/24; Metropolitan, 11/8/24: +*W. A. HAINES*)
By Whose Hand? ('*c. thriller*': Q, 12/8/29)
[Several short plays and sketches produced in music-halls]

DARRELL, CHARLES
[For earlier plays see *H. E. D.* v, 337]
×A Ghost of the Past (County H., St Alban's, 1/3/1899; Glasgow, 21/5/00)
The Showman ('*md.*': Gr., Radcliffe, 9/5/04; W.L., 12/6/05, as *The Life of a Showman*: +*G. T. SANTE*)
Her Luck in London (Gr., Blackpool, 16/11/05, *cpy.*; Castleford, 1/1/06; Gr., Islington, 27/8/06)
Sins of Society (Darlington, 26/11/06)
The Idol of Paris (O.H., Middlesbrough, 12/8/07; Dalston, 17/2/08)
×Ladies Only (Pal., Greenwich, 30/11/08)
From Shopgirl to Duchess (Bilston, 25/11/07; Lyr., Hamm., 25/1/09)
The Eyes of the World ('*conflict of sex*': P.W., Grimsby, 21/12/08; Woolwich, 11/1/09; Gr., Fulham, 15/3/09)
What a Man Made Her (Alb., Brighouse, 20/9/09; Stratford, 27/12/09)
I Want to be Loved (P.W., Grimsby, 30/3/10; Brit., 17/10/10, as *Facing the World Alone*)
A Woman of Two Lives ('*mystical d.*': Junction, Manchester, 18/7/10; Stratford, 1/8/10)
Where Angels Fear to Tread ('*md.*': Sheffield, 19/9/10; Woolwich, 10/10/10)
The Girl who Knew a Bit ('*md.*': E.C., 23/10/11)
A Girl's Good Luck (Wolverhampton, 7/10/12)
White as a Lily (E.C., 4/11/12)
In a Man's Grip (Lyr., Hamm., 4/8/13)
When Paris Sleeps ('*md.*': Darlington, 29/12/13)
With Fire and Sword (Darlington, 7/9/14)
The King and the Actress ('*md.*': Darlington, 16/5/16)
The Millionaire and the Woman ('*md.*': Hippo., Batley, 12/6/16; Stratford, 23/4/17; title later changed to *A Woman's Plaything*)
No Man to Defend Her. LC, Crook, 17/5/17
Woman and Her Mate ('*md.*': Stratford, 27/8/17)
Should a Wife Refuse? ('*md.*': E.C., 12/11/17)
Love and the Law ('*md.*': E.C., 4/3/18)
Tommy's French Wife (H.M., Walsall, 5/8/18; Emp., Edmonton, 19/8/18; E.C., 2/12/18)
The Airman's Wife (Alex., B'ham, 28/10/18; Imp., Canning Town, 2/12/18; Stratford, 17/2/19)
Save the Children ('*md.*': Hippo., Maidenhead, 31/3/19; Gr., Brighton, 12/5/19)

A Girl in the Web (New H., Bargoed, 4/8/19; Stratford, 25/10/19)
Money and the Girl (Hippo., Maidenhead, 8/12/19)

DARTON, FREDERICK JOSEPH HARVEY
The Good Fairy. *1922*
[This includes specifications of a simple 'theatre' designed by Albert Rutherston]
The London Review (*'moral pantomine'*) *1923*
[This includes designs by Albert Rutherston]

DARVELL, MAUDE L.
Plays in Rhyme for Little Ones. *1925*
[This contains several short fairy-tale pieces written in collaboration with *GRACE M. TUFFLEY*]

DARWIN, Lady FLORENCE HENRIETTA
Six Plays. *1921* (Cambridge)
[This contains six short plays: 1. *The Lovers' Tasks*; 2. *Bushes and Briars* (LC, Mary Ward Settlement, 5/5/23); 3. *My Man John*; 4. *Princess Royal*; 5. *The Seeds of Love*; and 6. *The New Year*]
Green Boom. *1923* (Cambridge)

DASHFORD, HERBERT
The Sneak. LC, Stratford, 31/1/25

DAVENPORT, ARTHUR [see also *H. C. PÉLISSIER*]
Valentine (*'c.o.'*, m. N. Lambelet: St J., 24/1/18: +*C. WIBROW*)

DAVENPORTE, FREDERICK
Maisie (Gr., Southampton, 4/2/05: +*J. W. BOYLING*: this seems to be connected with *The Compensating of Maisie* (St Barnabas Parish R., Southampton, 6/2/14) ascribed to *FRANK K. DAVENPORTE*)

DAVENTRY, GEORGE
[For earlier plays see *H. E. D.* v, 338]
The Harvest of Sin (Dalston, 25/7/04)
× Monte Carlo (Qns, Poplar, 7/1/07: +*Mrs G. DAVENTRY*)

DAVEY, P. [see *A. CADMAN*]

DAVID, WORTON [see also *G. ARTHURS, H. RODEN*, and *F. THOMPSON*]
The Midnight Sun (*'m.c.'*: Metro., Devonport, 2/4/03, *cpy.*)
× Old China's in China (Olympia, Shoreditch, 19/7/09: +*L. LAKE*)
× King Nobbler (Sur., 3/1/10: +*L .LAKE*)
× Chrysanthemums. LC, K's, Southsea, 25/6/13: +*G. ARTHURS*)
× Watching the People Pop In. LC, K's, Southsea, 27/6/14: +*G. ARTHURS*)
× Stewed Prunes and Prisms. LC, K's, Southsea, 27/6/14: +*G. ARTHURS*)
[Several sketches produced at music-halls]

DAVIDSON, A. W.
× The Toast (Clavier H., 20/4/13)

DAVIDSON, H. E. S.

The Truth Game ('*c.*': Glo., 5/10/28: called originally *Taken by Storm*)

DAVIDSON, JACOB

Gytha ('*fant.*': Mary Ward Settlement, 30/6/22, *amat.*: +*A. M. TROTMAN*)

DAVIDSON, JOHN

[For earlier plays see *H. E. D.* v, 338. His *For the Crown* (1896) provided the libretto for the opera, *The Cross and the Crescent*, music by Colin McAlpine, C.G., 22/9/03]

Self's the Man ('*t.c.*') *1901*

The Knight of the Maypole ('*c.*') *1903*

A Rosary. *1903*

Bohémos (Court, 9/1/04: adapted from a play by M. Zamacois)

A Queen's Romance (Imp., 11/2/04: dramatised from V. Hugo's *Ruy Blas*, 1838) *1904*

The Theatrocrat ('*t.pl.*') *1905*

The Triumph of Mammon. *1907*

Mammon and His Message. *1908*

Where the Heather Grows (L'pool, 11/8/13: this appears to be a posthumously produced adaptation)

DAVIES, A. [see *H. MAJOR*]

DAVIES, Rev. CHARLES BEVERLEY

The Cradle King. LC, '*nativity pl.*': Gr., Flint, 17/12/25. *1930* (SPCK)

DAVIES, DAVID THOMAS

×Ble mà fa? *1913* (Aberystwyth)

×The Committee (Col., Aberystwyth, 15/4/14)

×The Stranger (Col., Aberystwyth, 15/4/14)

×Where is He? (Gai., Manchester, 4/9/16; Court, 8/1/17)

Maesymeillion. LC, Crippl. Inst., 3/6/20

Castell Martin. *1920* (Cardiff)

×Ffrois. *1920* (Cardiff)

Y Pwyllgor. *1920* (Cardiff)

Branwen ferch Llŷr. *1921* (Cardiff)

Pelenni Pitar. *1925* (Abertawe)

The Barber and the Cow (Rep., B'ham, 12/6/26) *1926* (Oxford)

×Troi'r tir. *1926* (Cardiff)

DAVIES, EMILIE [see also *L. DELMER*]

DAVIES, F. NEWNHAM [see *P. RUBENS*]

DAVIES, HUBERT HENRY

The Dream of Love. *1899*

The Weldons ('*d.*': Emp., N.Y., 6/4/1899)

×Fifty Years Ago (Omaha, on tour, 3/1900)

Mrs Gorringe's Necklace (Wynd., 12/5/03) *1910* (in *Plays*, vol. ii); *Fr. 1921*

Cousin Kate ('*c.*': H., 18/6/03) *1910* (in *Plays*, vol. i); *Fr. 1921*

Cynthia ('*c.*': Madison Square, N.Y., 16/3/03; Wynd., 16/5/04)
Captain Drew on Leave (New, 24/10/05)
The Mollusc (Crit., 15/10/07) *1914* (in *Plays*, vol. iv); *Fr. 1922*
Lady Epping's Lawsuit ('*satirical c.*': Crit., 12/10/08) *1914* (in *Plays*, vol. iii)
Bevis ('*c.*': H., 1/4/09)
A Single Man ('*c.*': Playh., 8/11/10) *1914* (in *Plays*, vol. v); *Fr. 1929*
Doormats ('*c.*': Wynd., 3/10/12) *Fr. 1920*
Outcast (Wynd., 1/9/14)

DAVIES, JAMES [see *R. H. ROBERTS*]

DAVIES, MARY FOX [=*MARY FOX-DAVIES*]

DAVIES, NAUNTON [='*NAUNTON COVERTSIDE*']
Foiled (Vic. Drill H., Llandilo, 27/9/00, *amat.*)
The Human Factor (Lyc., Newport, 3/6/12)
Dewin y pentref. *1913* (Cardiff)
×The Village Wizard (Temperance H., Merthyr Tydfil, 5/5/13) *1913* (Cardiff)
The Arrogance of Power. *1920* (Cardiff)
×The Conversion. *1920* (Cardiff)
The Crash. *1920* (Cardiff)
×The Epidemic. *1920* (Cardiff)
The Human Factor. *1920* (Cardiff)
×A Monologue for Me. *1920* (Cardiff)
The Schemer. *1920* (Cardiff)
The Second Son. *1920* (Cardiff)
The Great Experiment. *1924* (Cardiff: +*S. DREWITT*)

DAVIES, RALFE
Professor Tring's Experiment (Ambass., Southend, 27/4/25)
Thomas More (Ambass., Southend, 2/11/25)
×Felicity Goes to Hell (Etlinger, 16/12/26)
The Severed Head (Players, 25/4/30)

DAVIES, WILLIAM HENRY
True Travellers ('*tramp's o.*') *1923*

DAVIES-ADAMS, ALFRED [see also *A. P. HERBERT*]
A Good-for-Nothing Girl (Gr., Halifax, 19/3/20; E.C., 26/4/20)
Qualis ('*o.*': R. College of Music, 24/11/22, *priv.*)

DAVIES-WEBSTER, M.
Carmosina (Alb. H., 13/6/02: adapted from the play (1850) by A. de Musset)

DAVIS, BERTRAND [see also *R. COURTNEIDGE* and *O. HAUERBACH*]
The Pageant and the Plumber ('*m.c.*', m. S. E. Philpot: Portsmouth, 14/10/09, *cpy.*: +*N. D. SLEE*)
[Several sketches produced at music-halls]

DAVIS, C. T.
The Silver Lining (Ambass., 3/3/21)

DAVIS, CHRIS [see also *A. K. MATTHEWS*]
The Variety Girl ('*m.c.*', m. G. W. Byng: O.H., Belfast, 8/9/02)
×The Enemy (Pal., Bedford, 30/11/14)

DAVIS, DENIS
×Keep It Dark. LC, Inverness, 9/9/15
The Clue. LC, Inverness, 11/9/15

DAVIS, GILBERT
×Flies. LC, K. G's H., 8/2/22
×The Love of Pierrot. LC, K. G's H., 8/2/22
Young Shoulders (Inst., Hampstead Garden Suburb, 4/5/28)

DAVIS, JAMES [='*OWEN HALL*']

[*DAVIS, OWEN*
Through the Breakers ('*md.*': Bristol, 12/11/00)
Her Marriage Vow (Blyth, 5/8/07; Pav., 7/12/08)
Nellie, the Beautiful Cloak Model (Kennington, 4/9/16)
Peggy! Behave! (Detroit, 20/4/19; Pier, Brighton, 25/9/22)
9.45 (Playh., N.Y., 28/6/19; Com., 22/12/25: +*S. COLLINS*) *Fr. 1927*
The Nervous Wreck ('*f.*': Majestic, Los Angeles, 5/22; Sam H. Harris, N.Y., 9/10/23; St J., 17/9/24) *1926*
The Interrupted Honeymoon ('*mystery pl.*': Pal., Watford, 28/7/24; Borough, Stratford, 11/8/24)
Easy Come, Easy Go ('*f.*': Broad St, Philadelphia, 9/25, as *Come Easy, Go Easy*; Cohan, N.Y., 26/10/25; Court, L'pool, 6/9/26; Gar., 13/9/26)
The Donovan Affair (Fulton, N.Y., 30/8/26; Hippo., Boscombe, 7/2/27; D.Y., 15/2/27) *1930* (New York)
Icebound (H.M., 29/1/28, Sunday Pl. Soc.) *1923* (New York)

[*DAVIS, RICHARD HARDING* [see also *P. P. SHEEHAN*]
Ransom's Folly (D.Y., 21/7/03, *cpy.*)
The Dictator ('*f.c.*': Com., 3/5/05)
Vera the Medium (Gar., 2/11/08, *cpy.*)
×Blackmail (Alh., Glasgow, 17/6/12; Vic. Pal., 6/1/12)

DAVIS, ROBERT [see *A. ABDULLAH*]

DAVIS, RUTH ELLEN
The Supreme Victory, and Yesterday and Today: Two Plays... with lyrics by Ella Wheeler Wilcox. *1920*

DAVIS, WILFRED
The Belle of Blackpool ('*m.c.*': Goole, 27/11/02)

DAVISON, IAN
The Golden Dawn ('*m.pl.*', m. Leslie Smith: County, Bedford, 1/5/22)

DAVISON, JOHN
Shadows of Strife (Rep., B'ham, 19/10/29; Arts, 8/12/29) *1930*

DAWE, ERNEST
Plays in One Act. *1928*
[This contains: 1. *The Three Games* and 2. *Truth Will Out*]

DAWE, WILLIAM CARLTON
[For an earlier play see *H. E. D.* v, 339]
Dick's Honeymoon ('*f.c.*': Hereford, 19/5/02)
Brother Bill ('*f.c.*': P'cess of W., Kennington, 26/5/02)
The Black Spider (Buxton, 3/3/27; Pal., Chelsea, 20/6/27; Lyr., 26/12/27: originally LC, D.Y., 16/12/10, as *A Splendid Rogue*)

DAWLEY, J. SEARLE
Dreamland's Gateway, or, The Land of Nod (P'cess, 7/10/02, *cpy.*: +*R. DE CORDOVA*)

DAWKINS, C. G. H.
×The Proof (Qns, 29/10/20)

DAWSON, B.
×Somewhere in France. LC, Hibburn, Newcastle, 6/3/18

DAWSON, CATHERINE AMY [see *C. A. DAWSON-SCOTT*]

DAWSON, FORBES [='*F. VAUCROSSAN*': see also *A. SHIRLEY*]
[For earlier plays see *H. E. D.* v, 339]
Her Grace ('*c.*': Gr., Croydon, 11/3/01; Cor., 24/5/06; Vaud., 7/7/15, as *In Old Leicestershire*)
The Blackmailers ('*c.d.*': Court, Wigan, 15/5/01, *cpy.*)
Three of a Suit ('*c.d.*': Bournemouth, 10/6/01; Broadway, New X, 3/2/02)
The Man from Ceylon ('*f.*': Worthing, 28/10/01)
The Triumph of the Blind (W.L., 16/9/12)
On the Rocks ('*f.c.*': Plymouth, 11/10/17)
Three Fairy Plays. *1925*
[This contains: 1. *Columbine in Cricklebury*; 2. *The Fairy Learns the Meaning of Tears*; and 3. *The Poet, the Painter and the Witch Girl*]

DAWSON, HERBERT
The Young Lieutenant ('*c.o.*': Tyne, Newcastle, 28/5/06, *amat.*; R.A., Woolwich, 20/5/07)

DAWSON, MARY [see *F. J. KIRKE*]

DAWSON, O. K.
×Badalia. LC, P.W., 23/6/13

DAWSON, WILLIAM JAMES
Savonarola. *1900*

DAWSON-SCOTT, CATHERINE AMY
×The Holiday Governess (Studio, Victoria-street, 2/7/07)
×Phoca (Studio, Bedford-street, 7/4/11) *1912*
[This also contains *History Repeats Itself*]

DAY, A. L.
×Made in Germany. LC, Worcester, 20/1/14
×The Queen's Revels. LC, Worcester, 21/4/14

DAY, CORYTON [see also *W. THORNELEY*]
The Unknown Philanthropist (Ladbr. H., 7/3/07)

DAY, DAVID

Trixie in Search of a Title ('*m.pl.*': Cavendish R., Mortimer St., 3/5/05)

DAY, GEORGE D. [see *A. REED*]

[For earlier plays see *H. E. D.* v, 339–40]

× Love's Interlude (Bij., 16/12/05)

DAY, JULIUS EDGAR

Grumbletown. LC, Stanley H., S. Norwood, 7/4/14

The Tinker ('*r.m.pl.*', m. A. D. Bullock: St G's H., 30/3/20: called originally *The Tinker's Courtship*)

× The Trap (Emp., Woolwich, 16/5/21: also called *Trapped*)

DAY, SUSANNE ROUVIERE

× Out of Deep Shadows (Kelly's, L'pool, 7/10/12)

Broken Faith (Abbey, Dublin, 24/4/13: +*Miss G. D. CUMMINS*)

Fox and Geese ('*c.*': Abbey, Dublin, 2/2/17; Court, 1/4/18: +*Miss G. D. CUMMINS*) *1917*

Sixes and Sevens ('*c.*': Gai., Manchester, 27/5/18)

DAYLE, GILBERT

× The Game of Love (Str., 8/5/00)

The Man from Australia (P'cess, Llandudno, 2/6/02; Apo., 20/9/02, as *What Would a Gentleman Do?*) *Fr. 1910*

You never Know ('*c.*': Gai., 28/11/1899, *cpy.*; Metro., Birkenhead, 26/9/02; K's, Hamm., 12/5/05)

× Cyrus Q. Blake (Terry's, 28/4/04)

A Princess in Bohemia ('*c.*': Bradford, 29/6/08)

In and Out (of the Inn) ('*f.c.*': Bradford, 27/5/12)

'*DAYLOR, ALFRED M.*' [=*McLEOD LOADER*]

DAYNE, ILMA

× Little Willie. LC, Gem, Gt Yarmouth, 29/11/13: +*E. DUDLEY*

[*DAZEY, FRANK*

Peter Weston (Alcazar, San Francisco, 11/22; Sam H. Harris, N.Y., 18/9/23: Com., 10/6/24)

DE ACOSTA, MERCEDES

Prejudice (Arts, 17/6/28)

DEAKIN, DOROTHEA [see *E. NESBIT*]

DEAN, BASIL [see also *M. KENNEDY*]

× Marriages are Made in Heaven (Gai., Manchester, 7/9/08; Cor., 21/6/09)

× Mother-to-be (Gai., Manchester, 7/2/10)

× Effie (Gai., Manchester, 29/8/10)

Fifinella ('*fairy pl.*': Rep., B'ham, 26/12/12, *m.*; Scala, 20/12/19: +*Sir B. V. JACKSON*) *1912* (Liverpool)

Love Cheats ('*modern pl.*': Cor., 1/6/14)

Come with Me (New, 19/4/28: +*M. KENNEDY*) *1928*

Beau Geste ('*r.d.*': H.M., 30/1/29: +*C. MANN*: dramatised from the novel by P. C. Wren)

DEAN, GODFREY

×The Savage Beneath (Rehearsal, 23/5/08, *amat.*)

DEAN, RONNIE

×Penny's Luck. LC, Reg., Salford, 10/6/19

DEANE, DORA [see also *F. G. BROOKE*]

DEANE, HAMILTON

Dracula (Wimbledon, 9/3/25; Little, 14/2/27: dramatised from the novel by Bram Stoker: +*J. L. BALDERSTON*) *1933* (New York)

DEANS, F. HARRIS

×The Doubt (Emp., 26/11/14: +*P. O'FARRELL*) *Fr. 1928*
Apron Strings ('*c.*': Playh., L'pool, 30/1/22) *1924*
Husbands Are a Problem ('*light c.*': Ambass., 3/8/22) *Fr. 1922*
The Snobs ('*f.c.*': Kings., 22/10/22, Interlude Players)
The Rose and the Ring ('*m.pl.*', m. R. Cox: Wynd., 19/12/23) *Fr. 1928*
The Magic Sword ('*fairy pl.*': Playh., L'pool, 22/12/23)
The Tangled Web (Rusholme, Manchester, 15/3/26)
Aren't Women Wonderful? ('*c.*': Rep., B'ham, 5/11/27; Court, 14/8/28) *Fr. 1929*

DEARDEN, ALBERT J.

×A Barmecide Feast ('*c.*': Ealing, 22/2/04)
×The Dean's Dilemma ('*c.*': Gar., 25/1/06)
×His Satanic Majesty (David Lewis Hostel, L'pool, 30/4/13)

DEARDEN, HAROLD [see also *R. PERTWEE*]

Two White Arms ('*c.*': D.P., Eastbourne, 16/1/28; Ambass., 23/1/28) *Fr. 1928*
The Flaming Sword. *1929*

DEARLOVE, W. H.

[For earlier plays see *H. E. D.* v, 340]
Little Lady Loo ('*m.c.*', m. S. Shaw: O.H., Harrogate, 10/5/00; Gr., Plymouth, 7/3/04)

DEARMER, GEOFFREY

Three Short Plays. *1927*
[This contains: 1. *The Poet Laureate* (Playroom 6, 18/12/27); 2. *The Fall*; and 3. *Three Women* (Playh., L'pool, 15/10/29)]
×The Man with a Cane. *1929*
St Paul. *1929*

DEARMER, JESSIE MABEL WHITE (*Mrs PERCY DEARMER*)

Nan Pilgrim (Court, 8/3/09)
The Soul of the World ('*Christmas mystery pl.*': Imperial Institute, 1/12/11, *m.*, Morality Play Soc.) *1911*
The Dreamer ('*poetic pl.*': K's H., 29/11/12)
×The Playmate ('*mystery pl.*': Little, 3/7/13, Morality Play Soc.) *1910*
×The Cockyolly Bird (Children's Theatre, 1/1/14) *1914*

×Brer Rabbit and Mr Fox (*'m. frolic'*: Little, 11/4/14, *m.*) *1914*
Don Quixote. LC, K. G's H., 6/2/22. *1916* (in *Three Plays*)
[This volume contains *Dox Quixote, The Dreamer* and *The Soul of the World*]

DEARMER, PERCY
×The Christmas Party (*'carol pl.'*) *1926* (SPCK)

DE BARY, ANNA (née *BUNSTON*)
Jephtha's Daughter. *1914*
×The Patriarch. *1931* (SPCK)

DE BEAR, ARCHIBALD
[Numerous short sketches for presentation by 'The Co-Optimists' and in various revues]

DE BEAUVAIS, R. N.
The Giant's Bride (P.H., Ancaster, Grantham, Feb. 1906, *amat.*; T.H., High Wycombe, 10/4/07, *amat., revised*)

DEBENHAM, L.
×A Magic Kiss (*'children's pl.'*) *1900*
×Minstrel or Prince? (*'children's pl.'*) *1901*
×Mistress and Man. *1901*
Ten Dancing Princesses (*'fairy pl.'*: Lyc., 30/3/17, *amat.*)

DEBENHAM, MARY H.
Dialogues, Duologues and Monologues. *1905*
[This contains ten short comic playlets: 1. *Breaking It Gently*; 2. *Exceedingly Correct*; 3. *Woman's Rights*; 4. *A Niece by Marriage*; 5. *Prepared for the Worst*; 6. *Save Us from Our Friends*; 7. *The Secrets of the Stars*; 8. *Josephine*; 9. *First Prize*; and 10. *Profitable Poultry Keeping*]
×The Coming of the Dawn (*'scenes from Anglican Church history'*) *1908*
×The Light-Bearers (*'miracle pl.'*) *1910*
More Dialogues, Duologues and Monologues. *1910*
[This contains eight short comic playlets: 1. *A Needle in a Haystack*; 2. *Spade Work*; 3. *A Suitable Colonist*; 4. *Polly Put the Kettle On*; 5. *Number Ten*; 6. *A Plunge into the World*; 7. *Three Blind Mice*; and 8. *A Defensive Alliance*]
×When the Baby Came (*'Christmas pl.'*) *1911*
St Edmund, King and Martyr (*'miracle pl.'*) *1913*
×Shut Out (*'missionary pl.'*) *1918*
×The Lady with the Lamp (*'missionary pl.'*) *1918*
×A Call from India (*'missionary pl.'*) *1919*
Children of the Dawn (*'overseas pageant'*) *1920*
×The Meeting at the Cross-Roads (*'Christmas mystery'*) *1920*
×Semper Eadem. *1921*
×The Celestials (*'Chinese scene'*) *1922*
×The New Year. *1922*
×The Way of Wonders (*'missionary pageant'*) *1924*
×The Walls of Jerusalem (*'pl. for girls'*) *1926*
×Real Christmas (*'missionary pl.'*) *1927*

×Round the Clock (*'little Christmas pl. for children'*) *1927*
×The Wisdom of the Corner Shop (*'pl. about England and Africa'*) *1928*
×Founders and Builders (*'pl. for boys'*) *1929*
[The majority of these playlets were published under the auspices of church and missionary presses]

DE BERGERAC, BERNICE
Tercentenary Shakespeare Festival: 'In Shakespeare's Garden' (Oxford, September 1916) *1916* (Oxford: *priv.*)
The Oxford Pageant of Victory, 1919. *1919* (Oxford; *priv.*)
The Pageant of Ixworth Abbey (Bury St Edmonds, 1921) *1921* (Thetford; *priv.*)
Glorious England, a Tale of the Crusades. *1922* (Oxford; *priv.*)
By Shakespeare's Fireside (*'pl. of reality'*: T.H., Oxford, 22/2/22)
An Elizabethan Joyance. *1927* (Oxford: *priv.*)

DE BURGH, AIMÉE [see *G. FRANKAU*]

DE BURGH, BEATRICE
×A Loyal Traitor (St J., 10/5/00)
×Bob's Mrs Kenningham (P.W., L'pool, 20/11/02)
×Heart of Gold (*'Russo-Japanese r.'*: Cor., 11/2/05)
×Sal Hawkins (*'episode'*: Crit., 13/7/05, *cpy.*; Pal., Hamm., 25/9/05)
×A Strolling Player (Empress, 10/1/10)
×Lady Betty's Baking (Playh., 25/6/12, *m.*)

DE CANDEY, RAYMOND [see *C. ROWE*]

DE CASALIS, JEANNE
Let's Leave It at That(*'c.'*: P.W., 14/4/29, Sunday Pl. Soc.; Qns, 10/6/29: +*C. CLIVE*)

DE CAUX, H. L. [see *W. GRAHAME*]

DE CORDOVA, RUDOLPH [see *J. S. DAWLEY* and *A. RAMSEY*]

DE COURVILLE, A. P.
Are You There? (*'m.pl.'*, m. R. Leoncavallo: P.W., 1/11/13)
×The Last Laugh (Hippo., 16/12/14)

DE CRESPIGNY, Mrs PHILIP CHAMPION
The Spanish Prisoner (Little, Leeds, 23/2/27)

'DEFFELL, FREDERICK' [=*Sir JOHN POLLOCK*]

[*DE FOREST, MARION*
Little Women (*'character c.'*: Playh., N.Y., 16/10/12; Qns, Manchester, 10/10/19; New, 10/11/19)

DE FRECE, SYBIL [see *C. JUL*]

DEFRIES, AMELIA DOROTHY
Rebirth. *1928* (Oxford)

DE GARNO, VAL
The Scarred Hand (Officers' Club House, Aldershot, 8/11/01, *amat.*; St G's H., 13/1/02: +*L. MONTAGUE*)

DE GRASSAC, P.
The Enchantress (‘*oa.*’: Ladbr. H., 9/10/11, *cpy.*)

DE GRAY, GEORGE A.
[For earlier plays see *H. E. D.* v, 390]
A Traitor Prince (Alex., Widnes, 20/11/02; Smethwick, 3/8/03; Sur., 7/9/03)
A Woman’s Devotion (‘*md.*’: Wallsend, 4/11/03, *cpy.*; Gr., Plymouth, 19/12/04; Gr., Islington, 17/4/05)
The Power of the Cross (‘*md.*’: Roy., Chester, 22/4/05, *cpy.*; Qns, Keighley, 23/12/05; E.C., 14/10/07)
The Angel of His Dreams (Castleford, 26/4/09; Lyr., Hamm., 17/10/10)
The Price of Freedom (Alex., B’ham, 22/4/12)
The Indian Scout (E.C., 5/8/12)
× The People’s King (Pal., Chelsea, 25/11/12)
The Secret Service Spy. LC, Leicester, 27/11/13)
The Gates of Mercy (Osborne, Manchester, 17/5/15; Vic., Walthamstow, 31/1/16)
The Girl from Piccadilly. LC, Castleford, 7/2/19: title later changed to *Modern Morality*
Passion’s Hour (Stratford, 5/5/24)

DE GRÉSAC, FRED [see *T. R. ARKELL*]

DE GREY, ETTA
Girl o’ my Heart. LC, Gr., Wath-upon-Dearne, 23/3/21: later called *Romany Rose*
The Luck o’ the Brierleys. LC, ‘*m.pl.*’: Col., Long Eaton, 31/1/23
× Tinsel and Gold (‘*new-style m. novelty*’: Stratford, 26/3/23)

DE HALSALL, HENRY
The Humbugs (‘*f.*’: Crippl. Inst., 5/4/04, *amat.*)
× Willie’s Medicine (Pal., Camberwell, 9/6/13)

DE HAMEL, HERBERT [see also *CARL ST AMORY*]
× War Mates (Vic. Pal., 15/11/15)
× The Woman and the Apple (D.Y., 12/11/20)
× The Top Floor Back. LC, Minsterworth Court, 11/7/24

DE HAVEN, AUDREY
The Gateway. LC, Ath., Glasgow, 8/12/13

DEHN, RAGNA
× Their Bitter Harvest (Crane H., L’pool, 16/10/18)

DE KEYSER, ALFRED
Stella Maris (Court, L’pool, 15/4/19; K’s, Hamm., 23/5/19)

DE KONINGH, HARRY
Nymphidia (‘*m.pl.*’, m. F. Leeds: St Peter’s H., Brockley, 9/1/09, *amat.*)

DE LA MARE, WALTER JOHN
Crossings (‘*fairy pl.*’: Wick School, Hove, 21/6/19, *amat.*; Lyr., Hamm., 19/11/25, *m.*) *1921* (*priv.*); *1924*

DE LARA, FREDERIC
× The Doctor’s Dream (Steinway H., 19/1/16)

DE LARA, GEORGE

×A Miracle (Brighton, 15/6/08)

×An Eye for an Eye (Sur., 6/6/10)

DE LARA, ISIDORE

×Don Juan. LC, H., 16/12/14

DELAND, MARGARET WADE

The Awakening of Helena Ritchie (P.W., B'ham, 7/10/12: +*C. THOMPSON*: dramatised from the novel by Margaret Deland, 1906)

DE LA PASTURE, Mrs HENRY [ELIZABETH LYDIA ROSABELLE; Lady CLIFFORD]

The Lonely Millionaires ('*c.*': Court, 25/2/05)

Peter's Mother ('*c.*': Wynd., 12/9/06) *Fr. 1910*

×Her Grace the Reformer (H., 12/1/07)

×The Unlucky Family (H.M., 15/7/10, *m.*)

×Luigi's Wife (St J., 31/1/13, taken from her *Lonely Millionaires*)

DELAUNOY, BURFORD

Gabriel Grant, Gambler (Shak., Clapham, 14/2/10)

×The Idol's Eyes (Shak., Clapham, 14/2/10)

×The Silver Lining (Crippl. Inst., 19/4/13, *amat.*)

×A Thief in the Night (Crippl. Inst., 16/2/14)

DELAVAL, FRANCES

Love's Golden Dream (LC, Colne, 23/12/07; Stratford, 10/2/08)

DE LEON, JACK [see *JACK CELESTIN*]

DE LIMA, C. A.

Jumps (Margate, 15/6/14)

DELL, ANTHONY

The Duke of Enghien. *1927*

DELL, D. M. [see *T. COHEN*]

DELL, ETHEL MAY

×The Odds (Emp., Shepherd's Bush, 9/2/20)

The Way of an Eagle (Adel., 20/6/22: based on her own novel, 1912)

The Hundredth Chance (Brixton, 25/7/27: based on her own novel, 1917)

[*DELL, FLOYD*

A Little Accident ('*c.*': Morosco, N.Y., Oct. 1928; Portsmouth, 18/3/29; Hippo., Golder's Green, 25/3/29; Apo., 3/4/29: +*T. MITCHELL*)

DE LLANA, AGNESE

Destruction (Roy., 4/12/22)

DELL, IAN

Noah's Wife. *1915* (Oxford)

DELMER, LEN [see *E. DAVIES*]

A Tangled Skein (Oddfellows' H., Newland, 28/3/21: +*E. DAVIES*)

DELSCHAFT, KATE
The Imp of the Human Heart ('*fairy pl.*': T.H., Gerrard's Cross, 23/4/12)

DE MARNEY, T. [see *P. ROBINSON* and *R. STOCK*]

DE MILLE, WILLIAM C.
Strongheart (Aldw., 8/5/07)
The Warrens of Virginia (Gr., Islington, 14/11/07, *cpy.*)
The Woman (Dalston, 7/4/11, *cpy.*)
× Poor Old Jim. LC, Hippo., Exeter, 17/3/14
× Unearthly ('*spiritualistic sketch*': Col., 31/1/21)
Molly Dear. LC, Pal., Maidstone, 9/8/23

'*DEMOCRITUS*' [=*F. A. LAIDLAW*]
Phryne (translated from the Italian of Riccardo Castelvecchio) *1900*

DE MONTMORENCY, HARVEY
Okutoko; or, The Principality of the Simple Life ('*m.c.*': Market H., Appleby, 19/4/06, *amat.*)
The Millenium ('*m. ext.*': Market H., Appleby, 4/4/07, *amat.*)

DEMPSTER, F. C.
× The Old Violin (T.H., Stratford, 19/1/00)

'*DENBY, EDWARD*' [=*E. G. HEMMERDE*]

DENMAN, CHARLES
[A considerable number of music-hall sketches and musical episodes]

DENMAN-WOOD, F. [see *S. PLANCHÉ*]

DENNY, ANTHONY
× For a Consideration ('*m.pl.*': Crippl. Inst., 21/10/22; Cent., 23/6/26)

DENNY, ERNEST
Cupid and the Scandalmongers ('*c.*': Wynd., 1/2/04, *cpy.* apparently acted in New York, also in 1904, as *Man Proposes*)
All-of-a-Sudden Peggy ('*c.*': D.Y., 27/2/06) *Fr. 1910*
Vanity (Glo., 1/4/13) *Fr. 1925*
Marmaduke ('*c.*': H., 19/6/18). *Fr. 1919* (as *The Irresistible Marmaduke*)
× The Gentle Art of Shopping. *Fr. 1919*
× The Holiday Hump. *Fr. 1920*
Just like Judy ('*light c.*': St M., 11/2/20) *Fr. 1922*
The Mountebank (Stamford, Conn., 23/3/23; Lyc., N.Y., 7/5/23: + *W. J. LOCKE*)
Summer Lightning ('*c.*': Worthing, 18/3/26; Com., 23/3/26) *Fr. 1927*
× Troublesome Wives. *Fr. 1927*
× Lazy-Bones. *Fr. 1929*
The Happy Prodigal. *Fr. 1930*

DENROCHE, PATRICK
× Keep Calm. LC, Aldw., 10/12/21

DENT, CLINTON
×Fruit and Blossom (Playh., 9/4/08, *m.*)

DENT, EDWARD JOSEPH
The Servant of Two Masters (ADC, Cambridge, 5/6/28: adapted from C. Goldoni, *Il servitore di due padroni*) 1922

DENTON, JACK [see also *F. HARRISON*]
The Serpent's Tooth ('*md.*': County, Kingston, 25/4/04; Dalston, 5/12/04, as *Wealth, Women and Wickedness*: also called *A Modern Judas*)
Convict 99 (Crown, Peckham, 22/6/08)
A Queen for a Wife ('*r.d.*': Stratford, 16/12/12)
The Man who Married Beneath Him (Pav., Weston, 25/10/13, '*preliminary pfce*'; Emp., Holloway, 6/4/14, as *Married for Love*)
When a Man's Down (P's, Portsmouth, 4/9/22: originally called *A Real Man's Love*)

DENVILLE, ALFRED [see also *J. MACLAREN*]
The Love Story of Annie Laurie (H.M., Walsall, 22/2/15; Wimbledon, 4/9/16, as *Annie Laurie*: +*J. MACLAREN*)
Reported Missing ('*md.*': Oldham, 27/5/18)
Bills o' Jacks (Oldham, 7/4/19)

DENVILLE, T. C. [see *H. KINGSTON*]

DEPON, CYRIL
The Lady from London ('*f.*': Court, Warrington, 4/12/05)

DERBYSHIRE, Ven. J. RUSSELL
×The Queen's Token. LC, YMCA, Sheffield, 5/1/24

DEREVE, EDGAR
A Gay Girl ('*m.c.*', m. G. Leone; Gr., Maidenhead, 1/5/05)
×The Violin Girl (Richmond Hippo., 6/1/08)
×Shop Hours (Richmond Hippo., 25/5/08)

DERING, CHARLES E.
[For earlier plays see *H. E. D.* v, 343]
The White Ensign (Aston, 2/7/00)
×The Man in the Chair. LC, Scala, Seacombe, 19/3/18: +*B. RIGNOLD*

D'ERLANGER, HENRY [see *J. ROSE*]

DE ROCHES, JEAN
×The Bunkering of Betty (D.L., 11/5/09, *m.*)

DE ROHAN, DAPHNE
×Dawn (St Mark's H., Wimbledon, 8/9/00, *cpy.*)

DE ROHAN, RALPH
×Coffee for Two (Bedford H., Chelsea, 19/11/21, Shakespeare Students' Soc.)

DERRILL, EARL
Sins of Youth (Leicester, 28/6/26)

DERWENT, CLARENCE [see *ELFRIDA DERWENT*]

DERWENT, ELFRIDA

×The Secrecy of the Ballot (Court, 18/12/10, Pl. Actors: +*C. DERWENT*)

×The Vision of the Blind (Cosmopolis, 18/6/14: +*C. DERWENT*)

The Family Failing (Gai., Manchester, 18/9/16: +*C. DERWENT*)

×The Old Miser ('*village playlet*': +*C. DERWENT*) *1920*

DESBOROUGH, PHILIP

×Three Corner Tables. LC, Village H., Cookham, 28/5/14

×The Cathedral. LC, T.H., Maidenhead, 10/11/19

×He, She and It. LC, T.H., Maidenhead, 11/11/19

DE SELINCOURT, HUGH

Loyalty ('*light domestic c.*': Court, 21/6/09, *m.*)

×Life's Importance (Shaft., 20/3/10, St. Soc.: translated from a play by 'Felix Salten' (Sigmund Salzmann))

[This piece was presented together with two others by the same Austrian author, *Count Festenberg* and *The Return*, under the general title of 'Points of View'. Whether all three plays had been translated by De Selincourt is uncertain]

×Getting What You Want; or, Variations on a Matrimonial Theme (Little, 23/6/12, Connoisseurs)

×The Dream of Death (P's, Manchester, 12/8/12)

×Beastie (Little, 15/12/12, Pioneer Players)

×Ninette (K's H., 22/6/13, Playfellows)

DE SMET, R. [see *J. DRINKWATER*]

DESMOND, CLIVE

Honour (Emp., Sunderland, 1/2/26; Wimbledon, 3/5/26)

DESMOND, ROBERT

×The Woman Wins (Hippo., Gateshead, 18/3/18)

×Revelations. LC, Village H., Cobham, 9/5/21

DESMOND, SHAW

My Country. *1921*

D'ESTE-SCOTT, A.

The Daughters of Ishmael (K's H., 1/3/14, Pioneer Players: dramatised from the novel by R. W. Kauffmann)

DE STOURTON, JOHN [see *O. LETHBRIDGE*]

DE SYLVA, B. G. [see *L. SCHWAB* and *R. P. WESTON*]

DE THOREN, OSCAR

×The Spirit of Eleanor (Court, 29/1/14)

DEUCHAR, NORMAN DOUGLAS [see '*N. N. DOUGLAS*']

D'EVELYN, ROSE

×Your Photo while you wait (Imp. H., E. Dulwich, 9/1/05)

×The Tragedy of an Hour (Ass. R., Balham, 25/9/13)

×Proposing to Stella. LC, Alh., Sandgate, 10/11/13

×To Make Her Jealous. LC, Emp., Shoreditch, 21/4/14
×Where There's a Will, There's a Way. LC, Central H., Bolsover, 21/9/14
×Catspaws. LC, Granville, Walham Green, 18/10/22

DEVEREUX, ROY
Like Father, like Son (Playh., L'pool, 19/3/14)

DEVEREUX, WILLIAM [see also *H. HAMILTON*]
Henry of Navarre ('*r.pl.*': Newcastle, 5/11/08; Lyr., 7/1/09) *1908*
Sir Walter Ralegh (B'ham, 4/10/09; Lyr., 13/10/09) *1909*
A Fair Highwayman (Australia, 1913)
The Elton Case (Long Branch, N.Y., 4/7/21; Playh., N.Y., 10/9/21)
Big Business (Hippo., Golder's Green, 5/4/26)
The Wooing of Katherine Parr ('*r.pl.*': Brighton, 2/12/26; Borough, Stratford, 28/2/27)

DEVIZES, STAUNTON
Cuckoo Cottage ('*f.m.d.*': Q, 9/5/27)

DEWER, REX
×Granny (Chalet, Sheffield, 14/9/23)

DEWHURST, GEORGE
×By the Witch Hole (Preston, 12/5/14)

DEWHURST, J.
The Snatcher ('*c. mystery*': Castleford, 17/1/29)

DEXTER, WALTER
Dolly Varden ('*c.*': K's, Hamm., 16/12/07)
Oliver Twist (Broadway, New X, 13/12/09; K's, Hamm., 4/9/22: +*F. T. HARRY*)

DE ZOETE, BERYL [see *FRANK ROS*]

DICK, IVY
×Ambilitis. LC, K's, Edin., 11/2/13

DICKENS, CLAUDE S.
×Sweet Prue (Court, 11/2/01)

DICKENS, STAFFORD
Japhet has his Day (Str., 6/4/30, Rep. Players)

[*DICKEY, PAUL* [see also *C. W. GODDARD*]
×The Lincoln Highwayman (Gr., Douglas, 26/5/19; Col., 21/7/19) *Fr. 1931*
The Broken Wing ('*c.*': Washington, 30/8/20; 48th St., N.Y., 29/11/20; D.Y., 15/8/22: +*C. W. GODDARD*)

DICKIE, J. L.
×A Deal in Mayfair (Court, 24/10/13)

DICKINSON, CHARLES H.
×A Near Thing (P.W., 20/2/11)
×The Pity of It (Court, 22/3/11, *amat.*)

DICKINSON, LIONEL ARTHUR HENRY
'Time Flies' and Other Plays. *1918*
[This contains six one-act plays: 1. '*Birds of a Feather*'; 2. '*Time Flies*'; 3. *A Fantasy* (LC, K. G's H., 6/4/25); 4. *The Love Potion*; 5. '*The Mother of Invention*'; and 6. *Great Historical Pageant of Puddington-on-Slush*]

DICKSON, CHARLES [see also *Mrs R. PACHECO*]
No Account Morgan ('*c.*': Ladbr. H., 23/11/09, *cpy.*)
Bright Eyes ('*m.c.*': Ladbr. H., 23/11/09, *cpy.*)
The Week-End ('*f.*': Ladbr. H., 9/4/12, *cpy.*)

DICKSON, J. BERNARD
×A Dumb Man's Curse (Hippo., Peckham, 27/9/09; Crit. 18/10/09)

DICKSON-KENWIN, W. [see *K. K. ARDASCHIR*]

DIETRICHSTEIN, LEO
[For an earlier play see *H. E. D.* v, 344]
All on Account of Eliza ('*rustic c.*': Shaft., 3/4/02)
Is Matrimony a Failure? ('*c.*': Crit., 4/1/11: adapted from a play by O. Blumenthal and G. Kadelburg)
The Concert ('*c.*': D.Y., 28/8/11: adapted from H. Bahr, *Das Konzert*, 1909)
The Great Lover (Longacre, N.Y., 10/11/15; Shaft., 2/10/20: +*F. L. HATTON*)

DIGNON, EDWARD [see also *C. CAMPION*]
×From Life. LC, Glo., 31/1/24: +*C. CAMPION*

DILKS, NOEL
Modern Technique. LC, YMCA, Nottingham, 21/11/25

DILLON, ARTHUR
The Greek Kalends ('*masque*') *1900* (Buxton, *priv.*); *1906*
King Arthur Pendragon. *1906*
The Bondswoman ('*t.*') *1925*

DINELLI, ADELINA
×The Sculptor's Strad (Passmore Edwards Settlement, 26/4/13)
×An Interrupted Lesson (Ben Greet Academy, 27/1/22)

DISHER, MAURICE WILLSON
Joan of Memories ('*c.*': Shaft., 18/1/20, St. Soc.)
×There Remains a Gesture ('*fant.*': Shaft., 18/1/20, St. Soc.)
Rupert's Revenge. LC, Olympia, 11/4/23

DITTINI, Mme B. M.
All Through Arabella ('*f.*': Londesborough, Scarborough, 25/6/02, *cpy.*; O.H., Blackpool, 8/11/02; C.P., 20/4/03: +*Mrs C. ROUTLEDGE*)

DIX, BEULAH MARIE [see also *E. G. SUTHERLAND*]
Boy O'Carroll; or, The Rapparee Trooper ('*c.*': Newcastle, 27/4/06; Imp., 19/5/06: +*E. G. SUTHERLAND*)
Matt of Merrymount ('*d.*': Newcastle, 11/10/06; New, 20/2/08: +*E. G. SUTHERLAND*)

The Road to Yesterday ('*c.*': Gr., Southampton, 12/4/15: +*E. G. SUTHERLAND*)
Across the Border. *1915*
×Allison's Lad ('*t.*') *1926* (in J. Hampden, *Nine Modern Plays*)
×The Girl Comes Home. *Fr. 1927*
×A Legend of St Nicholas ('*pl. for children*') *Fr. 1928*
×The Princess Dayshine ('*fairy pl.*') *Fr. 1928*
The Weal of Wayland's Well ('*pl. for children*') *Fr. 1928*
×The Captain of the Gate *1930* (in A. E. M. Bayliss, *Junior One-Act Plays of Today*)

DIX, FRANK [see also *E. BARBER* and *R. R. GIBSON*]
The Price of a Girl's Honour (Lyr., Hamm., 5/6/11; Stratford, 3/6/12, as *The Girl from the Jam Factory*; Aston, 7/8/16, as *A Factory Girl's Honour*; E.C., 11/9/16, as *A Factory Girl's Honour*; O.H., Manchester, 16/10/22; Str., 26/10/22, as *The Balance*, revised by *L. M. LION*)
[Numerous sketches produced at music-halls]

DIXON, CAMPBELL
This Way to Paradise ('*c.*': Daly's, 30/1/30: dramatised from Aldous Huxley's novel, *Point Counter-Point*) *1930*
×The Doctor and Mrs Macauley (O.H., Belfast, 18/8/13)
Village Plays. *1920* (Dundalk)

DIXON, W. SCARTH [see *A. HOLMES-GORE*]

DOCKWRAY, CHARLES W.
×The Wisdom Tooth (Lyr., Hamm., 30/3/13: +*H. A. BARWELL*)

[*DODD, LEE WILSON*
The Lien of Life (Court, 31/7/09, *cpy.*)
The Living Dead (Court, 1/2/10, *cpy.*)

DODDS, MADELEINE HOPE
The Golden Apple, LC, Westfield H., Gateshead, 19/2/24

DODDS, RUTH
The Pitman's Pay. LC, '*historical pl.*': People's, Newcastle, 8/12/22. *1923* (Labour Publishing Co.)
The Hilltop. LC, Co-op. H., Dennington, 1/1/25
Hind Horn and Alice Brand ('*two ballad plays for children*') *1925* (Newcastle)
The Battle of Otterburn ('*ballad pl. for children*') (? *1925*: Village Children's Historical Play Soc., Winchelsea)

DODGE, E. THORNELY
×Swiss v. Robinson (Pier, Eastbourne, 27/8/18)
×Nibs (Gr., Peterborough, 30/9/18)

DOE, MARY ELIZABETH
×Cinderella Up-to-date. LC, P.H., Croydon, 4/2/20

DOLAN, WINIFRED
The Melcombe Marriage (Brighton, 15/2/07)
×'Wake Up, John Bull!' ('*political pl.*') *Fr. 1912*

DON, M. J.

×A Broken Holiday (R. Acad. of Music, 25/6/15)

[*DONNELLY, GRATTAN*

The Old Cabin Home; or, Carolina (Darwen, 29/9/06, *cpy.*)

[*DONNELLY, DOROTHY*

Poppy ('*m.pl.*', m. S. Jones and A. Samuels: Apo., N.Y., 3/9/23; Gai., 4/9/24)

The Student Prince ('*light o.*', m. S. Romberg; Apo., Atlantic City, 27/10/24, as *In Heidelburg*; 59th St., N.Y., 2/12/24; H.M., 3/2/26: based on R. Bleichmann's version of W. M. Forster's comedy, *Alt Heidelburg*)

DONOHUE, J. C.

×None but the Brave. LC, K. G's H., 27/1/25

DONOVAN, DESMOND [see *F. FENN*]

DOON, NOEL [see also *J. CELESTIN* and *W. THORNELEY*]

Contraband (Q, 12/3/28: +*W. FAWCETT*)

DOONE, NEVILLE [see also *E. FERRIS*]

[For earlier plays see *H. E. D.* v, 347]

×Sparkle's Little System (Pier, Folkestone, 1/6/1893; Metro., Camberwell, 2/3/03)

×A Woman Tamer; or, How to be Happy though Married (Brompton Hospital, 10/3/1896; C.P., 6/4/03)

Vendetta (Kennington, 28/3/04: dramatised from the novel (1886) by Marie Corelli)

Brooke of Brasenose ('*costume pl.*': Crit., 8/6/05: +*T. R. F. COALES*)

DORANE, WARD

This Year – Next Year ('*light c.*': Everyman, 14/6/27)

DOREMUS, Mrs CHARLES A.

The Duchess of Devonshire ('*c.*': E.C., 1/4/03, *cpy.*)

DORYNNE, JESS

×The Surprise of His Life (K's H., 21/4/12, Pioneer Players)

×The Telegram (Little, 18/10/12)

DOTTRIDGE, ERNEST

My Son Sammy ('*m. absurdity*': Pal., Oldham, 26/2/17; M'sex, 11/6/17: +*A. WHITE*)

DOUGHTY, CHARLES MONTAGU

Adam Cast Forth ('*sacred d.*') *1908*

The Cliffs. *1909*

The Clouds. *1912*

DOUGHTY, HENRY

Oliver Twist (Lyc., Sheffield, 12/5/13)

DOUGLAS, A. I.

×The Tea-Party (R. Inst. H., Glasgow, 19/1/23, Scott. Nat. Theatre Soc.) *1929* (Glasgow)

The Gift. *1927* (in *The Scots Magazine*, viii, 32/43); *1930* (Glasgow)
× The Clock. *1929* (Glasgow)

DOUGLAS, ATHOLL
The Sheik of the Desert (P's, Blackburn, 5/11/23)
The Love Flame (Hippo., Bury, 16/2/25)

DOUGLAS, F. M.
× 'Twixt Cup and Lip (Bij., 2/10/01)
Written in Red (Brighton, 29/5/11; Court, 26/12/12)

DOUGLAS, HARCOURT
The Left Boot ('*crook c.*': Ath., Glasgow, 27/11/28)

[*DOUGLAS, JAMES A.*
× The Outcome of Agitation (Kings., 5/11/10)
A Dream of the Rockies ('*m.pl.*': Hippo., Balham, 18/12/11)
The Duchess's Necklace (Aldw., 7/6/13)
The Pop Corn King (Gai., Hastings, 8/10/14: called originally *An American Alliance*)

DOUGLAS, MADGE
Discharged with Honour (Wolverhampton, 24/2/19; Stratford, 28/4/19)
Her Only Way (Metro., Bootle, 19/7/20; Stratford, 16/8/20)
Little Biddy O'Farrell ('*m.c.*': Bilston, 1/8/21; Stratford, 17/4/22)

DOUGLAS, MALCOLM
A Fight for Millions ('*md.*': Coloss., Oldham, 11/1/04; Carlton, Greenwich, 15/2/04)

DOUGLAS, MARY
The Purple Presence (Little Vic., Brighton, 9/2/25)

DOUGLAS, MAUD ISIDORE
× The Burning Glass. LC, Little, Kensington, 27/4/22

DOUGLAS, MINNIE
Under the Rose ('*c.*': Rehearsal, 4/2/11, English Pl. Soc.)

DOUGLAS, MONA [see *A. P. GRAVES*]

'*DOUGLAS, N. D.*' [=*NORMAN DOUGLAS DEUCHAR*]
× The Syndicalist. *1919* (included in a miscellany, *The Fool Next Door*)

DOUGLAS, NAN
Sauce for the Goose ('*f.*': Pal., Ramsgate, 5/11/23)

DOUGLAS, NORMAN [=*GEORGE NORMAN DOUGLASS*]
South Wind (Kings., 29/4/23, Rep. Players: called originally *Sirocco*: dramatised from his novel, 1917): +*I. C. TIPPETT*)

DOUGLAS, Lady SHOLTO
× A Soldier's Mother (Hippo., Putney, 15/2/14)

DOUGLASS, GEORGE NORMAN [='*NORMAN DOUGLAS*']

DOUGLASS, JOHN THOMAS [see also *F. BATEMAN* and *W. H. BENSON*]

[For earlier plays see *H. E. D.* v, 348–9, 788–9]

The Root of All Evil (Qns, Longton, 11/4/01)

The Prince of Rogues (Worthing, 11/9/02; Stratford, 17/4/05: + *W. H. BENSON*)

Woman Rules the World (Macclesfield, 3/9/03, *cpy.*)

× A Dark Secret (Qns, Poplar, 29/4/07)

× Mary Roper (Cavendish R., Mortimer St., 5/5/08, *amat.*)

× The Married Widow (Foresters, 8/11/09; Sur., 29/11/09)

DOUGLASS, R. H.

Buttercups (Emp., Bristol, 24/9/17; Emp., Croydon, 10/12/17

Puppets of Fate (E.C., 18/4/27)

DOUGLASS, VINCENT R.

The Honourable Deception ('*c.*': W.G., New Brighton, 4/12/16)

The Jeffersons ('*Lancashire c.*': W.G., New Brighton, 25/6/17; Pal., Watford, 27/9/20; Reg., 8/12/24) *Fr. 1926*

The Romance of Punch and Judy (*fairy pl.*': W.G., New Brighton, 26/12/19; W.G., New Brighton, 24/12/21, *revised*, as *Punch and Judy*)

A Christmas Dream ('*m.pl.*': W.G., New Brighton, 26/12/17; W.G., New Brighton, 27/12/20, *revised*)

Princess Posy ('*m.pl.*', m. A. Parker: W.G., New Brighton, 26/12/18, *m.*)

The Partners (W.G., New Brighton, 2/8/20; Pal., Watford, 10/10/21) *Fr. 1926*

The Optimist ('*c.*': W.G., New Brighton, 6/8/23; Gr., Croydon, 25/8/24) *Fr. 1926*

The Perfect Wife ('*c.*': W.G., New Brighton, 29/10/28; Emb., 5/11/28) *Fr. 1929*

× The Tender Passion (W.G., New Brighton, 1/7/29)

DOW, W. GRAHAM

× The Coat Tale ('*f.c.*': Lyr., Glasgow, 16/10/29)

DOWLING, J. J. [see *K. F. RAND*]

DOWN, MESLEY [see also *V. BERINGER*]

The Blue Stockings (Glo., 28/11/13: +'*H. SETON*': adapted from Molière, *Les femmes savantes*) *Fr. 1926*

DOWN, W. OLIPHANT

× The Maker of Dreams ('*fant.*': Pal., 26/11/10; Vaud., **31/8/12**) ***1913***

Three One-Act Plays. *1923*

[This contains: 1. *The Dream Child* (Gai., Manchester, 28/4/13); 2. *Bal Masqué*; and 3. *Tommy-by-the-way* (LC, Alh., 24/6/18)]

× The Pied Piper. LC, Park, Hanwell, 10/2/14

× The Quod Wrangle ('*f.*': Apo., 3/3/14) *Fr. 1914*

× Wealth and Wisdom. *Fr. 1924* (in *One Act Plays for Stage & Study*, vol. i)

× The Idealist. *Fr. 1925* (in *One Act Plays for Stage & Study*, vol. ii)

DOWNES, GWENDOLYN B.

The Finding of the Child ('*Christmas mystery pl.*': Cent., 21/12/26)

DOWNFIELD, STUART

A Daughter of the Synagogue ('*Jewish–Gentile d.*': Birkenhead, 20/1/00, *cpy.*: +*F. E. STEVENS*)

DOWNING, HENRY FRANCIS

The Arabian Lovers, or, The Sacred Jar ('*an Eastern tale*') *1913*
Human Nature, or, The Traduced Wife ('*an original English domestic drama*') *1913*
Lord Eldred's Other Daughter ('*c.*') *1913*
The Shuttlecock, or, Israel in Russia. *1913*
×Placing Paul's Play ('*miniature c.*': +*Mrs H. F. DOWNING*) *1914*

[In 1914 another play by this author, *Voodoo*, was advertised as published, but I have failed to locate a copy]

DOWNING, R. M.

×The Paradise of the Blind (Glo., 27/9/26, Green Room Rag)

DOWNING, RUPERT

The Lady in Command (Gai., Hastings, 28/1/29)

DOWNING, W. F.

Lady Tetley's Divorce (P's, Bristol, 26/8/01: +*Mrs W. F. DOWNING*)
Hearts and Coronets (Worthing, 11/5/03; Gr., Fulham, 18/5/03)
×The Happiest Day of His Life (Brixton, 13/2/05)

DOWNS, HAROLD

The Aylesburys ('*c.*': Little, Bristol, 5/10/25) *1922*

DOWNTON, Rev. H. M.

St Augustine of Canterbury ('*ecclesiastical and historical pl.*') *1902* (Torquay)
St Oswald of Northumbria (Plymouth, Oct. 1909; Crosby H., 20/4/12)
Ruth, a Mother in Israel. LC, Wyndham H., 26/8/15
Mispah. LC, St Peter's H., Plymouth, 29/8/16

DOWSON, ERNEST

×The Pierrot of the Minute ('*d. fantasy*': Bij., 16/12/05) *1897*

DOYLE, Sir ARTHUR CONAN

[For earlier plays see *H. E. D.* v, 350]

Sherlock Holmes (Shak., L'pool, 2/9/01; Lyc., 9/9/01: +*W. GILLETTE*)
Brigadier Gerard ('*r.c.*': Imp., 3/3/06)
The Fires of Fate ('*modern morality*': Lyr., 15/6/09)
The House of Temperley (Adel., 27/12/09)
×A Pot of Caviare (Adel., 19/4/10) *Fr. 1912*
The Speckled Band (Adel., 4/6/10) *Fr. 1912*
×The Crown Diamond (Col., 16/5/21)
×A Duet. *Fr. 1923*

DOYLE, Capt. J. B. H.

The Fool. LC, R. Engineers' Theatre, Brompton Barracks, Chatham, 6/12/22

'DOYLE, LYNN' [=*LESLIE ALEXANDER MONTGOMERY*]

Love and Land ('*c.*': O.H., Belfast, 24/11/13; Little, 13/3/25, as *Persevering Pat*) *1928* (Dublin)

×The Lilac Ribbon (O.H., Belfast, 5/6/19) *1928* (Dublin)

×Turncoats. LC, Playh., L'pool, 2/8/22. *1928* (Dublin)

DRAKE, ANTHONY A.

×Vogi's Bones (Lecture H., Wimbledon, 3/12/13, *amat.*: +*P. C. C. FENWICK*)

×Tryphena & Co. ('*f.*': Lecture H., Wimbledon, 3/12/13, *amat.*: originally licensed as *Cupid and Cupidity*)

×Butterflies. LC, Lecture H., Wimbledon, 19/4/21

DRAKE, DOROTHY

[Several sketches produced at music-halls]

DRAKE, ELLIS

[Several sketches produced at music-halls]

[*DRAKE, WILLIAM A.*

Twelve Thousand (Fest., Cambridge, 27/5/29: adapted from Bruno Frank, *Zwölftausend*, 1926) *1928*

DRAKE, WILLOUGHBY

What Every Girl Can Do (H.M., Walsall, 22/1/17; Pal., Battersea, 1/10/17)

It's Not the Clothes that Make the Man (Stratford, 7/3/21: title later changed to *The Man who Made Good*)

DRAYTON, GODFREY

×Maidenly Manoeuvres ('*f.*': Manor, Hackney, 14/11/00)

DREW, BERNARD

Helen of Troy. *1924*

DREW, EDWIN

[For earlier plays see *H. E. D.* v, 350–1]

×Our Folks (St G's H., 26/7/00)

×Polly's Luck (St G's H., 9/10/00)

DREW, MARGARET

×Pages from our Magazines (A.L.S. Trav. Th., 1925) *1920*

St Valentine's Day and Other Victorian Pieces. *1924*; *Fr. 1926*

[This contains four short plays: 1. *St Valentine's Day*; 2. *Birthdays*; 3. *Sunday Sabbath Day*; and 4. *The Weathercock*]

DREW, PHILIP YALE

The Frozen North (E.C., 31/8/14)

×The Man Hunter. LC, P's, Blackburn, 17/11/24

The Rock of Ages (Roy., Chester, 4/12/24: +*F. LINDO*)

DREW, VIOLET

A Chinese Romance. LC, Pal., Bedford, 14/8/25

DREWITT, S. [see *N. DAVIES*]

DRING, EDWARD

The Lure of the Yellow Man (Vic., Lye, 26/7/20)

DRINKWATER, ALBERT EDWIN

[For earlier plays see *H. E. D.* v, 350–1]

×Afterthoughts (Bij., 12/6/1899; Cor., 22/11/05, *revised*)

×The Red Knave (Cor., 17/3/02)

×Two in a Trap (Wynd., 22/6/09) *Fr. 1921*

×Honours Easy. LC, '*trifle of patches and powder*': P's, Manchester, 21/4/15. *Fr. 1921*

×The Pipe of Peace. *1922* (Birmingham)

DRINKWATER, JOHN

Kendrida (written 1905: +*H. A. SAINTSBURY*: see *Discovery* (1932) p. 115)

The Pursuit of the Polyborns (written *c.* 1906: +*J. E. NEWARK*: see *Discovery* (1932) p. 125)

×An English Medley (m: Rutland Boughton: Cadbury Works Summer Party, 1911: see *Discovery* (1932) p. 195) *1911* (*priv.*); *1925* (in *Collected Plays*)

×Ser Taldo's Bride ('*c.*': Ass. R., B'ham, 21/1/11, Pilgrim Players: +*B. V. JACKSON*)

×Cophetua (Ass. R., Edgbaston, 18/11/11, Pilgrim Players; Rep., B'ham, 27/10/17) *1911*

×The Pied Piper: A Tale of Hamelin City ('*masque*': m. F. W. Sylvester: Cadbury Works Summer Party, 1912, Pilgrim Players) *1912* (*priv.*: B'ham)

Puss in Boots (Ass. R., Edgbaston, 30/12/11, Pilgrim Players; Rep., B'ham, 26/12/16, *revised*; Apollo, 27/11/26, *revised*) *1911* (*priv.*: B'ham); *1913*

×The Only Legend: A Masque of the Scarlet Pierrot (Cadbury Works Summer Party, Bournville, B'ham, 10/7/13) *1913* (*priv.*: B'ham); *1925* (in *Collected Plays*)

Rebellion (Rep., B'ham, 2/5/14) *1914*

×Robin Hood and the Pedlar ('*masque*': m. J. Brier: Cadbury Works Summer Party, Bournville, B'ham, 25/6/14, Pilgrim Players) *1914* (*priv.*); *1925* (in *Collected Plays*)

×The Storm ('*t.*': Rep., B'ham, 8/5/15) *1914* (in *New Numbers*, vol. i, no. 3, August, 1914); *1915* (*priv.*: B'ham); *1917* (in *Pawns: Three Poetic Plays*)

×The God of Quiet ('*lyric d.*': Rep., B'ham, 7/10/16) *1916* (*priv.*: B'ham); *1917* (in *Pawns: Three Poetic Plays*)

×The Wounded (Rep., B'ham, 3/3/17: +*R. DE SMET*)

×$x=0$: A Night in the Trojan War (Rep., B'ham, 14/4/17; New, 8/12/19) *1917* (*priv.*: B'ham); *1917* (in *Pawns: Three Poetic Plays*)

Abraham Lincoln (Rep., B'ham, 12/10/18; Lyr., Hamm., 19/2/19) *1918*

Mary Stuart (Ritz, N.Y., 21/3/21; Everyman, 25/9/22) *1921*; *1922* (*revised*)

Oliver Cromwell (Brighton, 19/2/23; H.M., 29/5/23) *1922*

Robert E. Lee (Reg., 20/6/23) *1923*

Robert Burns. *1925*

The Mayor of Casterbridge (Barnes, 8/9/26: dramatised from the novel (1886) by T. Hardy)

Puss in Boots (*'fairy pl.'*: Apo., 27/12/26)
Bird in Hand (*'c.'*: Rep., B'ham, 3/9/27; Roy., 18/4/28) *1927*
×John Bull Calling (*'political parable'*: Col., 12/11/28) *1928*
×Holiness (Studio, May, 1928)
[The majority of these works are in *Collected Plays*, 2 vols 1925]

DRUMMOND, BARBARA
Guy of Warwick (*'pageant'*: Warwick, 20/7/27)

DRUMMOND, J. H. [see *J. EDWARDS*]

DRUMMOND, Hon. R. C.
×False Colours (Cosmopolis, 17/2/14)

DRURY, WILLIAM PRICE
[For an earlier play see *H. E. D.* v, 351]
A Privy Council (H., 6/9/05: +*R. PRYCE*) *Fr. 1906*
×The Figurehead (Plymouth, 19/10/05)
The Flag Lieutenant (Playh., 16/6/08: +*L. TREVOR*)
×A King's Hard Bargain (Court, 2/11/08, *m.*) *Fr. 1924*
×The Admiral Speaks (Alh., 22/10/10, *m.*) *Fr. 1912*
×Calamity Jane, R.N. (Glo., 8/1/12). *Fr. 1912*
×The Playwright (*'a heresy'*: Pal., 2/9/12) *Fr. 1924*
×His Heritage (Rep., Plymouth, 11/10/16, *m.*)
×The Porter of Hell. LC, Plymouth, 14/1/18

[*DRYDEN, LEO*
The Bowery Girl; or, Beaux and Belles of New York (Avondale H., Clapham, 22/1/02)
Leo Dryden's Songs and Scenas. *1908* (Manchester)

DUCHESNE, P. G.
×The Nursery Governess (*'c.'*: Kennington, 26/10/08)
Judge Not (Qns, 28/5/10)

DUCKWORTH, MADGE
Her Nameless Child (Tonypandy, 18/6/06, *cpy.*; Metro., Devonport, 9/7/06; Shak., Clapham, 9/7/07: +*R. BARRIE*)
The Conscience of a Judge (Qns, L'pool, 10/12/07, *cpy.*; Tonypandy, 23/12/07; E.C., 17/8/08: +*R. BARRIE*)
×Wake Up, England! (Tonypandy, 5/7/09)

DUCKWORTH, Mrs SAM
The Coward (Hippo., Birkenhead, 27/10/10, *cpy.*)

DUDDINGTON, J. NIGHTINGALE
The Bread of Others (*'c.'*: Kings., 22/2/09, St. Soc.)
Reconciliation. *1917* (in *People of the Universe*, a collection of plays by Josip Kosor)

[*DUDLEY, BIDE* [see *O. HARBACH*]

DUDLEY, ERIC [see *I. DAYNE*]

DUDLEY, HOWARD
×Should She? (*'problem sketch'*: Hippo., Putney, 13/7/14)

DUDLEY, MAUDSLEGH
×A False Prophet (*'f.'*: Arts Centre, 28/11/13, Black Cat Club)

DUDLEY, RAYMOND
×The Confession (Stand., Pimlico, 31/1/10)
×The Question (Court, 24/6/13)

DUFF, G. ROYDON [see also *F. MARRIOTT-WATSON*]
A Boy's Best Friend (New, 7/4/08, *cpy.*; Marina, Lowestoft, 10/5/09: + *W. EDWIN*)
Wait till the Clouds Roll By (Qns, Dublin, 26/6/16; P's, Blackburn, 10/7/16)

DUFF, JANET
What Toppety Saw ('*Christmas dream*': Etlinger, 11/12/25: + *S. STRATFORD*)

DUFFY, BERNARD
×The Coiner (O.H., Belfast, 8/12/15; Abbey, Dublin, 8/2/16; Court, 8/4/18) *1916* (Dublin)
×Fraternity ('*satire*': Abbey, Dublin, 4/1/16)
×The Counter-Charm ('*c.*': Abbey, Dublin, 11/12/16; Col., 9/7/23) *1916* (Dublin)
×The Old Lady ('*c.*': O.H., Belfast, 11/12/16) *1916* (Dublin)
×The Piper of Tavran (Abbey, Dublin, 15/11/21)
×The Spell. *1922* (Dublin)
×Special Pleading ('*coincidence*': Col., 27/8/23) *1916* (Dublin)
The Wagon and the Star ('*c.*': Abbey, Dublin, 7/4/29)
Cupboard Love. *1930* (Dublin)

DUFFY, P. J. O'CONNOR
The Treasure of the Mountain, and The Victory of Christ. *1922*
[Both plays are one-acts: peculiarly there is a special title-page for the first in which it is ascribed to 'Shiel MacDara']

DUGDALE, GILES
Owner Gone Abroad (Q, 3/2/30)

DU GUÉ, CECIL
What Men Call Love ('*md.*': Huddersfield, 24/4/03, *cpy.*; Alex., B'ham, 21/3/04; Dalston, 12/6/05, as *Betrayed*)

DUKE, WINIFRED
Madeleine Smith ('*t.c.*') *1928*

DUKES, ASHLEY
Civil War ('*c.*': Aldw., 3/6/10, *cpy.*; Aldw., 5/6/10, St. Soc.) *1911*
×Pride of Life ('*c.*': Aldw., 29/1/11, St. Soc.)
The Parisienne (Roy., 26/6/11: adapted from the play (1885) by Henri Becque) *1943*
The Comedy of the Man who Married a Dumb Wife (H., 15/2/14, St. Soc.; Ambass., 16/3/17: adapted from Anatole France, *La comédie de celui qui épousa une femme muette*, 1912) *1925*
×Au Petit Bonheur (H., 15/2/14, St. Soc.: adapted from the play (1898) by Anatole France)
From Morn to Midnight (Lyr., Hamm., 28/3/20, St. Soc.; Reg., 9/3/26: adapted from G. Kaiser, *Von Morgens bis Mitternachts*, 1916) *1920*
The Machine-Wreckers (Kings., 6/5/23: adapted from E. Toller, *Die Maschinenstürmer*) *1923*
No Man's Land (St M., 2/12/24: adapted from F. de Curel, *La terre inhumaine*, 1922)

The Man with a Load of Mischief ('*c.*': New, 7/12/24, St. Soc.; H., 16/6/25) *1925*
One Can But Try (translated from a play by Anatole France) *1925*
Ulenspiegel (presented in a translation by E. Cammaerts, Théâtre Royal Flamand, Brussels, 1927) *1926* (as *The Song of Drums*)
One More River ('*modern c.*': New, 13/2/27, St. Soc.) *1927*
Such Men Are Dangerous (Majestic, N.Y., 19/1/28, as *The Patriot*; K's, Edin., 6/2/28; D.Y., 19/9/28: adapted from Alfred Neumann, *Der Patriot*) *1928*
The Fountain Head ('*c.*': Arts, 17/10/28) *1928*
× The Dumb Wife of Cheapside. *1929*
Five Plays of Other Times. *1931*
[Besides *The Man with a Load of Mischief*, *Ulenspiegel*, *The Fountain Head* and *The Dumb Wife of Cheapside*, this contains *Matchmakers' Arms* and *Jew Süss* (O.H., Blackpool, 29/7/29; D.Y., 19/9/29: adapted from the novel by Leon Feuchtwanger]

DUMARESQUE, RAY
Oh! Alexander! ('*f.*': Pal., Watford, 2/12/18; Pal., Chelsea, 21/6/20)

DU MAURIER, Sir GERALD [see also '*H. PARSONS*' and '*SAPPER*']
A Royal Rival (Cor., 20/5/01; D.Y., 24/8/01; Lyr., 31/5/10, as *Don Caesar de Bazan*: adapted from P. F. P. Dumanoir and A. D'Ennery, *Don Caesar de Bazan*, 1844)
Charles I and II ('*f.*': Court, 21/10/01: +'*S. O. N. FRERE*', i.e. *GUY DU MAURIER*)
Peter Ibbetson (H.M., 23/7/15, *m.*: +*J. N. RAPHAEL*)

DU MAURIER, GUY LOUIS BOUSSON [='*S. O. N. FRERE*': see also *Sir GERALD DU MAURIER*]
An Englishman's Home (Wynd., 27/1/09)

DUNBAR, JOHN
Two Little Scout Boys (Rotherham, 2/12/12: +*H. LLOYD*)

DUNCAN, MARIE [see *W. T. IVORY*]

DUNCAN, SARA JEANETTE [*Mrs EVERARD COTES*]
His Royal Happiness (P'cess, Toronto, 4/1/15; D.P., Eastbourne, 4/11/18; Emp., Holborn, 24/2/19: +*H. C. M. HARDINGE*)
Beauchamp and Beecham ('*c.*': Lyr., 31/3/16, *m.*)
Julyann (*Irish c.*': Glo., 24/7/17, *m.*)

[*DUNCAN, WILLIAM CAREY* [see also *O. HARBACH*, *L. WYLIE* and *R. J. YOUNG*]
× The Phantom Burglar ('*c.*': Court, 4/4/13: +*E. ELLIS* and *G. JONES*)

DUNKELSBULHER, R. J.
× Just Three Kisses (Little, 26/1/12)
× When We Begin to Think (Little, 26/1/12)

DUNLOP, GEOFFREY
× Juana (Gate, 11/10/26: adapted from the play (1918) by G. Kaiser)
Leonce and Lena (Playroom 6, 15/2/27: adapted from the play (1850) by G. Büchner) *1927*

DUNN, G. A.

The Laws of Justice. LC, P.H., Redbourne, 23/1/22

DUNN, GERALD

×A Dear Little Wife ('*Japanese pl.*': Gai., Manchester, 25/3/12) *Fr. 1916*

×Fancy Dress (Crit., 14/4/13) *Fr. 1913*

[*DUNNING, PHILIP*

Broadway (Broadhurst, N.Y., 16/9/26; Str., 22/12/26: +*G. ABBOTT*) *Fr. 1929*

DUNS, WILLIAM

×Only a Suffragette. LC, The Tower, Portobello, 3/9/13

DUNSANY, Lord (EDWARD JOHN MORETON DRAX PLUNKETT, Baron DUNSANY)

Five Plays. *1914*

[This contains five short plays, the earliest pieces by this author to have been produced: 1. *The Glittering Gate* (Abbey, Dublin, 30/4/09; Court, 6/6/10; Fest., Cambridge, 31/1/27); 2. *King Argimenes and the Unknown Warrior* (Abbey, Dublin, 26/1/11; Court, 26/6/11, as *King Argimenes*); 3. *The Gods of the Mountain* (H., 1/6/11); 4. *The Golden Doom* (H., 19/11/12); and 5. *The Lost Silk Hat* (Gai., Manchester, 4/8/13; Everyman, 15/11/21)]

Plays of Gods and Men. *1917*

[This contains four short plays: 1. *A Night at an Inn* (Neighborhood Playh., N.Y., 23/4/16; Pal., 6/11/17, *m.*; Everyman, 15/11/21); 2. *The Tents of the Arabs* (Playh., L'pool, 19/9/14; Everyman, 15/11/21); 3. *The Queen's Enemies* (Neighborhood Playh., N.Y., 14/11/16); and 4. *The Laughter of the Gods* ('*t.*': Punch and Judy, N.Y., 15/1/19)]

×The Murderers (Shubert Murat, Indianapolis, 14/7/19)

×The Prince of Stamboul (first performance uncertain; probably c. 1919 in U.S.A.)

Plays of Near and Far. *1923*

[This contains: 1. *If* (Ambass., 30/5/21: already published separately in 1921); 2. ×*The Compromise of the King of the Golden Isles*; 3. ×*The Flight of the Queen* (already published separately in 1922); 4. ×*Cheezo* ('*ironic farce*': Everyman, 15/11/21); 5. ×*A Good Bargain*; 6. ×*Fame and the Poet* (Alb. H., Leeds, 8/2/24); and 7. ×*If Shakespeare Lived Today*]

Lord Adrian (P.W., B'ham, 12/11/23)

Alexander and Three Small Plays. *1925*

[This contains a four-act tragedy, *Alexander*, together with three one-act pieces: 1. *The Old King's Tale*; 2. *The Evil Kettle*; and 3. *The Amusements of Khan Kharuda*]

×His Sainted Grandmother. LC, Fortune, 8/12/26. *1928* (see below)

×The Jest of Hahalaba (Playroom 6, 22/3/27) *1928* (see below)

Mr. Faithful (Q, 22/8/27) *Fr. 1939*

Seven Modern Comedies. *1928*

[This contains: 1. ×*Atalanta in Wimbledon*; 2. ×*The Raffle*; 3. ×*The Journey of the Soul*; 4. ×*In Holy Russia*; 5. ×*His Sainted*

Grandmother (see above); 6. ×*The Hopeless Passion of Mr Bunyon*; and 7. ×*The Jest of Hahalaba* (see above)]

DUPRÉE, FRANK
×War in the Air ('*spectacular object lesson*': Pallad., 23/6/13)

DURAND, Sir EDWARD
Lucilla. *1910* (*priv.*)

DURAND, H. L.
Quentin Durward ('*o.*', m. A. McLean: Newcastle, 13/1/20; Lyc., 4/6/20)

DURAND, MAURICE
The New Idol (Roy., 17/3/02, St. Soc.: adapted from F. de Curel, *La nouvelle idole* (1898): +*H. STOKES*)

DURHAM, PHILIP
×The Toll of the Brave (Pembroke H., Earl's Court, 20/1/24, Sunday Players)

DURRANT, J. C. B.
The Romany Maid ('*c.o.*', m. L. Dupère: Bishop's Stortford, 27/11/28, *amat.*)

DURRELL, LEONARD F.
[Numerous sketches produced at music-halls]

DU SOIR, ARTHUR
×Bill's Young Brother (Blfrs, 16/12/29, Quill Club)

DU SOUCHET, H. A.
The Man from Mexico ('*f.c.*': D.P., Eastbourne, 9/11/08; Cor., 23/11/08; Str., 10/9/10)

DUVAL, Mme RAOUL [='*GEORGE DARING*']

DYER, DORIS E.
×The Spy (Rehearsal, 16/3/15)

DYER, EDWARD [see *A. W. ALLEN*]

DYER, ELEANOR N.
Polly Danvers, Heiress (Marina, S. Shields, 25/1/22: called originally *My Lady Caprice*)

DYKE, HENRY VAN
The House of Rimmon (Vic. H., 16/3/08, *cpy.*)

DYMOCK, HENRIETTA
×Getting Her On (Etlinger, 14/3/28: +*J. DYMOCK*)

DYMOCK, J. [see *H. LESLIE*]

DYMOND, ANNIE
The Little Nut Tree ('*fairy pl.*': Playh., 9/4/08, *m.*: +*P. PENLEY*) *Fr. 1909*

[*DYRENFORTH, JAMES*
Sylvia ('*m.c.*', m. C. Gibbons: Abbey, Dublin, 14/5/23; Pier, Eastbourne, 13/8/23; Vaud., 14/12/27: based on *Mary, Mary, Quite Contrary* by St John Ervine)

EAGIN, F. L.
Silvia. LC, '*m.pl.*': School R., Aberford, 30/12/22

EAGLES, J. S.
The Prodigal Crusader ('*c.o.*': H. M. Carlisle, 26/2/24, *amat.*: +*F. W. WADEBY*) *1924* (Carlisle: lyrics only)

EARDLEY, BLANCHE
×Ben (St J., 29/6/05, *cpy.*)

EARL, SYLVIA
The Surplus Man (Court, 21/7/24, *m.*)

EAST, CHARLES A.
What! Another! ('*f.*': W.L., 24/6/01: +*G. B. DALY*: in 1905 title changed to *£1,000 for a Baby*)

EAST, JOHN M. [see also *G. B. DALY*]
[For earlier plays see *H. E. D.* v, 353, 789]
The Kitchen Girl ('*f.*': Ass. R., Taunton, 26/10/1899; Sur. 24/9/00)
×The Flower Girl; or, Life in the East End (Par., Mile End, 2/4/00: +*C. CALVERT*)
×A Wife in Reserve ('*f.sk.*': Lyr., Hamm., 16/12/02; Brit., Hoxton, 16/2/05)
×The Goblin and the Sexton (Lyr., Hamm., 23/11/03: +*C. CALVERT*)
Sexton Blake, Detective (K's, Hamm., 18/1/08, *cpy.*; Crown, Peckham, 24/2/08: +*G. B. DALY*)
Hush Money; or, The Disappearance of Sexton Blake (Shak., Clapham, 3/5/09)

EASTON, JOHN
Chinese Carstead ('*c.*': Lyr., Glasgow, 5/2/29)

EASTWOOD, T. W.
The Test (Court, 3/1/09, Dramatic Productions Club)

EATON, FLORENCE
The Triumph ('*fairy pl.*': Court, 27/11/12: +*W. CROSSING*)

EATON, JACK
Like Father, Like Son (E.C., 9/12/01: +*E. E. NORRIS*)

EATON, WILFRED
The Gentle Shepherd (Glasgow, 3/9/23: adapted from Allan Ramsay's play)

ECCLES, E. M. [see *E. N. FAWCETT*]

ECKERSLEY, ARTHUR
×Squire Dick (T.H., Rugby, 28/1/04)
×Gentlemen Boarders ('*f.*': Pav., Skegness, 26/8/06) *1907*; ***Fr.*** *1914*
×A Boy's Proposal (Emp., B'ham, 15/2/09; Adel., 29/3/09) ***Fr.*** *1909*
×The Trap (W.G., New Brighton, 20/7/09: +*A. CURTIS*)
×Duval Outdone (Gr., Bolton, 21/2/10)
×The Tooth of Necessity (Gai., Hastings, 14/3/10)
×Protecting Mrs Moxon (Gr., Belfast, 24/10/10)
×Our Mutual Wife (Alh., 24/11/10)

×Lady Jane (R.A., Woolwich, 6/3/11)
×The Rescue Boat (Court, 10/6/12: +*A. CURTIS*)
×The Hartleys (P.W., B'ham, 28/9/12) *Fr. 1916*
×Susan's Embellishments (Pal., 23/12/12) *Fr. 1918*
×A Collection will be made ('*f.*': Gar., 15/7/14) *Fr. 1914*
×A Tabloid. *Fr. 1914*
×Edward (Gai., Manchester, 27/3/16)
Odds and Ends of a Learned Clerk. *1922*
[This contains seven short sketches: 1. *Adapted for Amateurs*; 2. *Spoof*; 3. *A Celtic Revue*; 4. *Edward*; 5. *A Collection Will Be Made*; 6. *A Tabloid*; and 7. *Susan's Embellishments*]
[Various other sketches produced at music-halls]

EDDY, CHARLES [see also *B. PAIN*]
×Papers of State (Crit., 30/9/15)
[Several sketches produced at music-halls]

EDEN, GUY
The Mountaineers ('*c.o.*': Sav., 29/9/09; K's, Hamm., 5/9/10, *revised*: +*R. SOMERVILLE*) *1909*
The Love Doctor ('*m.pl.*': Emp., Swansea, 23/2/25; Pal. Chelsea, 4/5/25: +*H. C. SARGENT*)
When the Clock Strikes ('*c.*': Players, 31/3/20: +*ST CLAIR HARNETT*)

EDEN, PAT
The Gold Diggers, or, The Broken Trail (K's, Gateshead, 15/7/12)

EDGAR, HOWARD TRIPP [see also *DUDLEY H. TRIPP*]
John Manger (Little Vic., Brighton, 15/12/24: +*D. H. TRIPP*)

EDGINTON, MAY [see also *R. BESIER*]
×His Lady Friends. LC, K's, Edin., 4/6/18: +*F. MANDEL*
Trust Emily ('*f.c.*': New, Cambridge, 1/10/23; Crit., 10/10/23)
The Fairy Tale (Apo., 6/2/24)
For Better, for Worse (Arts, 5/4/28)
Deadlock (Brighton, 10/9/28; Com., 8/10/28)

EDLIN, HENRY
Lady Lavender ('*m.pl.*', m. C. C. Corri: Manchester, 19/6/11; R.A., Woolwich, 20/11/11)
Sweetheart Mine ('*m.c.*', m. C. C. Corri: Worthing, 5/8/15)
[A few sketches produced at music-halls]

EDMONDS, E. VIVIAN [see also *A. SHIRLEY*]
[For earlier plays see *H. E. D.* v, 354]
×Married Beneath Him (O.H., Workington, 12/10/00)
A Silent Foe (Gr., Stalybridge, 22/9/02)
The King's Romance (P.W., Salford, 28/3/10; K's, Hamm., 15/8/10)
The Maid of the Mill ('*Lancashire pl.*': P's, Blackburn, 22/8/13)
Her Only Son ('*natural pl.*': Barnsley, 27/4/16; Stratford, 3/9/17; E.C., 26/11/17)
The Third Man ('*md.*': Barnsley, 23/4/17; E.C., 29/10/17)

A Hidden Past (Barnsley, 3/9/17)
Called Up (Barnsley, 18/7/18; E.C., 24/3/19, as *Coming Home*)
The Daughter of a Thief (Gr., Halifax, 14/5/20)
Over the Hill (New H., Bargoed, 29/1/23; Emp., Woolwich, 4/6/23)
Broken Homes (St Helens, 14/12/23)
The Price of Coal (O.H., Workington, 4/5/25)
What Parker Did (Hippo., Hulme, 21/6/26: called originally *A Home from Home*: later turned into a m.c. as *June Magic*)

EDMONDS, FRED
Aladdin and Out ('*c.o.*': Frosterley, 21/2/25, *amat.*)

EDMONDS, MILLICENT
× The Reward (Dalston, 6/12/09)

EDMONSTON, C. MAYSIE
The Duke of Christmas Daisies and Other Fairy Plays. *1914*
[In addition to the title-piece, this contains four short playlets: 1. *The Birthday of the Sun and Moon*; 2. *The Little One*; 3. *The Tulips*; and 4. *Mr Weary Discontent*]
The Necklace of Amber ('*fairy fant.*': Ambass., 2/5/16, *m., amat.*)
Plays for Guides and Brownies. *1921*
[Besides the preceding playlet, this contains three pieces by C. M. Edmonston (*Pandora*; *The Brownies of the Wood*; and *The New Recruit*), together with *The Bending of the Twig* by *M. L. FITZWILLIAMS*]

EDMUNDS, JOHN
Jenny Omroyd (O.H., Blackpool, 15/3/15)

EDONI, ENID
True till Death ('*md.*': Castle, Brentford, 12/3/08, *cpy.*)
Victims of Vice ('*md.*': Alh., Openshaw, 1/12/13)

EDOUIN, ROSE
A Spree in Paris, and What Happened ('*m.c.*', m. G. E. Lewis: Belfast, 25/11/07)

EDRIDGE, JOAN
× First Aid ('*unconventional c.*': Rep., Croydon, 5/5/13: +*R. EDRIDGE*) *Fr. 1913*

EDWARDES, E. HENRY [see *E. IRWIN*]

EDWARDES, JOHN
The Mummers ('*c.*': Ladbr. H., 24/5/00, *amat.*: +*F. R. CULLINGFORD*)

EDWARDS, A. HERBAGE
The Burden (Court, 31/3/12, Pl. Actors)

EDWARDS, ANTON
Carletta ('*o.*': T.H., Pontypool, 4/5/27, *amat.*)

EDWARDS, H. SUTHERLAND
[For earlier plays see *H. E. D.* v, 355, 789]
Neighbours ('*m.pl.*', m. V. Leslie: County H., St Albans, 2/9/04)

EDWARDS, JACK

×A Window into Yesterday (K's H., 16/5/06: +*J. H. DRUMMOND*)

×The Call of the Sea (Col., Aberystwyth, 15/4/14)

The Disciple ('*t.*': K's H., 22/6/13, Playfellows)

The Gate in the Wall ('*t.*': Court, 22/6/14)

×A Colour Scheme. LC, Kennington, 3/6/18

×The Two Sons (Etlinger, 27/6/19, Curtain Group)

×Hi! Taxi! (A.L.S. Trav. Th., 1922)

The Odd Trick to Mary (K. G's H., 1/5/22, Pivot Club)

×Mrs Maggs Washes Up. LC, Kennington, 15/2/23

EDWARDS, K.

The Prince and the Gipsy Girl. LC, Emp., Middleton, 20/3/16: +*L. HOLLAND*

EDWARDS, N.

Mischievous Molly. LC, Emp., Swindon, 14/3/15

EDWARDS, OSMAN

The Cloister (Gai., Manchester, 3/10/10: adapted from E. Verhaeren, *Le cloître*, 1900) *1915*

EDWARDS, T. MORGAN

Rhys Lewis (Court, 4/7/08: dramatised from the novel (1888) by Daniel Owen)

EDWARDS, WILLIAM GORDON

The Handful (P.W., 8/3/13)

EDWIN, GRACE [see also *F. MARRIOTT-WATSON*]

The Unknown Woman (Q, 27/6/27: +*F. CARSON*)

'I Pronounce Them—' (Everyman, 3/3/30: dramatised from the novel (1927) by G. A. S. Kennedy)

EDWIN, WALTER [see *G. R. DUFF*]

EGERTON, Lady ALIX

×The Princess and the Stranger ('*interlude*': Stafford House, St James's, 5/7/06)

×The Masque of the Two Strangers (Stafford House, 5/7/07) *1907*

Three Tales by De Maupassant retold by Lady Alix Egerton. *1913*

[A manuscript note by the author in a copy belonging to the present writer states that the first item in the little volume – a short verse play entitled *An Old Story* – was translated for the actor Harcourt Williams, and that the second item – a dramatic poem called *Moonlight* – was translated for Ellen Terry]

×The Were-Wolf ('*mystery pl.*') *1926*

EGERTON, CECIL

×The Silver Tankard (Court, 3/3/09, *amat.*, Players' Association)

'*EGERTON, GEORGE*' [=*Mrs R. GOLDING BRIGHT*]

The Attack (Manchester, 10/11/13; St J., 1/11/14: adapted from H. Bernstein, *L'assaut*, 1912)

Wild Thyme ('*c.*': B'ham, 12/4/15; Com., 19/4/15; P's, 2/5/17, revised as *Good News*)

Camilla States Her Case (Glo., 7/1/25)

ELAND, PETER

The Dragon's Tongue ('*m.f.*', m. R. Illingworth: Roy., Morecambe, 20/4/05)

Treasure Island ('*c.o.*', m. R. Illingworth and V. Exley: Bradford, 7/8/05)

ELDER, B. SCOTT

Smoked Glasses ('*c.*': Embass., 27/5/29: +*W. FOSTER*)

ELDER, G. HARRIS

The Belle of Japan. LC, Emp., Aberdare, 30/1/20

ELDERTON, CHARLES

An Old-time Story (Gr., Douglas, 22/12/02)

The Flower of Japan. LC, '*m.c.*': Seaham Harbour, 12/2/18

ELDRED, ARTHUR [see also *GERTRUDE MOUILLOT*]

×The Coronation March ('*f.*': Gr., B'ham, 19/5/02)

×The Typewriter (Ryde, 6/7/03, *cpy.*)

×Situation Vacant ('*c.*': R.A., Woolwich, 20/3/11)

ELDRIDGE, H. H. M.

Lotusland ('*m.pl.*': Club Theatre, Stratford, 17/3/24, *amat.*, Metropolitan Vickers Amateur Dramatic and Operatic Soc.)

ELEXNER, ANNE CRAWFORD

Miranda of the Balcony (Emp., Huddersfield, 2/9/01, *cpy.*: dramatised from the novel (1899) by A. E. W. Mason)

ELGIN, MAX [see *Mrs L. T. MEADE*]

ELIOT, ARTHUR [see also *B. BAIRNSFATHER*]

[For earlier plays see *H. E. D.* v, 356]

Hidenseek; or, The Romance of a Ring ('*m.pl.*', m. C. Kiefert, C. Scott Gatty and M. Lutz: Glo., 10/12/01: +*E. GRENVILLE*)

ELKINGTON, CARR

[For an earlier play see *H. E. D.* v, 356]

The Guiding Star ('*md.*': P.W., Gt. Grimsby, 17/7/1899; Stratford, 17/6/01)

ELLIOT, DAISY

The Pilgrim's Way (Court, 27/3/05)

ELLIOT, ELLIOT S. [see *L. M. LION*]

ELLIOTT, RICHARD

×A Quiet Honeymoon (Cor., 4/12/11)

ELLIOTT, SARAH BARNWELL

His Majesty's Servant ('*r.pl.*': Imp., 6/10/04: +*M. HOSFORD*)

ELLIS, ALBERT E. [see also *H. S. STEPHENS*]

The Sky Skipper ('*m.c.*': Shak., Clapham, 27/11/11: +*E. W. ROGERS*)

[A few sketches produced at music-halls]

ELLIS, ANTHONY L. [see also *M. BOWER* and *O. SHILLINGFORD*]

Slaves. LC, Kings., 2/6/20: +*H. C. M. HARDINGE*)

ELLIS, ARTHUR

×Journey's End (Court, 30/6/14)

×One Touch of Nature (Court, 30/6/14)

ELLIS, BRANDON

[For earlier plays see *H. E. D.* v, 356–7]

Beneath the Stars (Pal., Newcastle, 21/4/1899; Osborne, Manchester 25/6/00; Sur., 8/10/00)

Through the World; or, A Blind Child's Peril ('*r.d.*': Pav., Mile End, 1/7/01)

A Fatal Crown ('*historical d.*': Pav., Mile End, 22/7/01: +*J. BELL*)

ELLIS, C. K.

The Snow Man (Sav., 22/3/26)

ELLIS, DAVID E. [see also *Mrs G. NORMAN*]

×The Impulse of a Night (Little, 26/12/13: +*Mrs G. NORMAN*)

Payment in Full. LC, Playh., Cardiff, 25/8/24

[*ELLIS, EDITH*

The Moon and Sixpence (New, 24/9/25: dramatised from Somerset Maugham's novel, 1919)

The White Villa (Eltinge, N.Y., February, 1921; Gr., Croydon, 21/2/27)

The Last Chapter (New, 27/5/30, Famous Players' Guild: +*EDWARD ELLIS*)

ELLIS, EDITH [*EDITH MARY OLDHAM, Mrs HAVELOCK ELLIS*: see also *R. O'NEILL*]

×The Subjection of Kezia (Court, 7/1/08) *1908*

Kit's Woman (Court, 27/6/09, Pl. Actors: dramatised from her novel, *Cornish Idyll*, 1907): +*J. BATES*)

ELLIS, FRED A.

The Belle of St Crispin; or, The Lady Cobbler ('*m.c.*', m. P. Knight and B. Harrison: E.C., 25/10/00; Camden, 27/8/06, as *The Lord of the Last*)

The Troubles of Trumble ('*m.c.*', m. P. Knight: Lyc., Stafford, 15/9/04, *cpy.*)

[Several sketches and playlets produced at music-halls]

ELLIS, GEORGE

×Man Proposes but—. LC, Co-op. H., Failsworth, 16/10/13

×A Touch of Memory. LC, Co-op. H., Failsworth, 23/10/13

Back to Nature ('*c.o.*', m. P. N. Parker; K's H., 8/12/26, *amat.*)

ELLIS, HAROLD [see also *F. R. BELL*]

[For earlier plays see *H. E. D.* v, 357]

×A Little Supper (Glo., 6/12/00)

The Blue Moon ('*m.pl.*', m. H. Talbot: O.H., Northampton, 29/2/04; County, Kingston, 14/3/04; Lyr., 28/8/05, revised by *A. M. THOMPSON*: +*P. GREENBANK*) *1905*

ELLIS, Mrs HAVELOCK [see *EDITH M. O. ELLIS*]

ELLIS, JOE

Folly's Fortunes ('*c.d.*': Carlton, B'ham, 20/12/09; Stratford, 11/4/10)

ELLIS, LIONEL

The Folds of the Flag (L'pool, 17/8/14: +*F. W. CLIVE*)

ELLIS, MARCUS [see *J. FLETCHER*]

ELLIS, OLIVER COLIGNY DE CHAMPFLEUR

The Sword of the Lord. *1930* (in *The Manchester Quarterly*, Oct./Dec. 1930) *1930* (Manchester)

ELLIS, T.

×Twelve O'Clock. LC, O.H., Perth, 25/1/18

'*ELLIS, T. E.*' [=*THOMAS EVELYN SCOTT-ELLIS*, **Baron** *HOWARD DE WALDEN*]

Lanval (Playh., 14/5/08, *priv.*; Aldw., 21/5/08) *1908* (*priv.*)

The Children of Don ('*dr. in verse*', adapted as a '*Cymric m. dr.*', Ldn O.H., 15/6/12) *1912* (as a verse play); *1912* (as a 'music drama')

Dylan, Son of the Wave (D.L., 4/7/14) *1918*

The Cauldron of Annwyn. *1922* (*priv.*)

[This is a 'dramatic trilogy', consisting of 1. *The Children of Don* (see above); 2. *Dylan, Son of the Wave* (see above); and 3. *Bronwen* (an 'opera', with music by J. Holbrook, which was printed separately, in a 'private' edition, in 1929)]

Heraclius (Emp., Holborn, 3/11/24, *m.*; Fest., Cambridge, 17/1/27)

Jack and Jill and the Beanstalk. *1926* (*priv.*)

Five Pantomimes. *1930*

[This contains: 1. *The Reluctant Dragon*; 2. *The Beauties and the Beast*; 3. *Bluebeard*; 4. *The Sleeping Beauty*; and 5. *Puss and Brutes*]

ELLIS, WALTER

[For earlier plays see *H. E. D.* v, 357]

Harmless Hypocrites ('*c.*': Brunswick House Dramatic Club, Wandsworth Road, 26/3/01) *1902*

The Two Hearts (Brunswick House Dramatic Club, Wandsworth Road, 4/11/01)

Mrs Garth's Jealousy (Brunswick House Dramatic Club, Wandsworth Road, 8/12/02)

ELLIS, WALTER WILLIAM

[For earlier plays see *H. E. D.* v, 357]

Cupid and the Captain ('*f.c.*': Pier, Brighton, 18/9/11)

×Little Willie (Coll., 22/4/12)

The Beautiful P.G. ('*c.d.*': Pav., Weymouth, 8/6/14)

A Little Bit of Fluff ('*f.*': Pier, Brighton, 11/10/15; Crit., 27/10/15 *Fr. 1922*

×Too Late (Coll., 10/1/16)

Monty's Flapper ('*f.*': Pier, Brighton, 29/1/17)

×The Profiteer (S. Ldn, 9/7/17; Apo., 7/2/17)

A Week-End ('*f.*': York, 26/8/18; Kings., 12/9/18; Hippo., Lewisham, 3/8/25, musical version by *T. WARD*)
Oh, Richard! ('*f.c.*': Granville, 17/2/19: called originally *Miss Cleverdick*)
Hawley's of the High Street ('*eccentric c.*': Brixton, 11/9/22; Apo., 5/12/22) *Fr. 1923*
The Monkey-House (Oxf., 26/1/25)
S.O.S. (St J., 11/2/28) *Fr. 1929*
The Big Idea ('*f.c.*': Q, 13/8/28)
Almost a Honeymoon ('*f.c.*': Gr., Croydon, 20/1/30; Gar., 4/2/30)

ELLWANGER, W. T.
[Several sketches and playlets produced at music-halls]

ELLWOOD, H.
×Did He Really? LC, Railway Mechanics' Inst., Bolton, 23/9/18

ELMER, GEORGE
[For an earlier play see *H. E. D.* v, 359]
Wanted! A King ('*m.c.*': Manor, Hackney, 7/4/00)

ELMWAS, CHRISTOPHER
Reprisals (Gar., 2/3/24, Sunday Players)

ELPINE, CHARLES L.
×Brown's Rooms (O.H., Belfast, 21/10/01)

ELSNER, EDWARD
Under Two Flags (O.H., Cork, 3/3/02; Cor., 1/9/02: dramatised from the novel (1867) by Ouida)

ELSON, ROBERT
×Thirteen (Emp., 24/3/13)
×Alys the Fayre ('*t.*': Little, 10/7/13, Stage Players)
Nobody Loves Me (Playh., L'pool, 11/3/15; Kings., 6/5/15)

ELSTEIN, NOAH
Heredity (Little, Rusholme, 23/8/26)
Israel in the Kitchen (Pav., 6/12/26, Jewish Drama League) *1928*

ELSTOB, CLARE
×Ria's Luck (Emp., Camberwell, 1/8/10; Studio, Victoria-street, 30/1/12)
×Her Kingdom (Studio, Victoria-street, 30/1/12)
×The Whirligig of Time (Studio, Victoria-street, 30/1/12)
×The Borgia (Margaret Morris, 14/6/17: +*M. STORR*)
×The Tragic Muse. LC, Margaret Morris, 3/1/18
Three Months ('*m.f.*': Margaret Morris, 30/3/18: +*M. STORR*)

ELTON, G. W.
The Other Man's Business ('*f.c.*': County, Kingston, 18/6/00; Metro., Camberwell, 24/9/00: +*E. S. PETLEY*)

ELTON, GEORGE
The Other Lady ('*f.*': Pier, Brighton, 13/1/13)
Mother's Brother ('*f.*': Hippo., Margate, 29/11/15) *1929*
×Letting a Flat (Hippo., Balham, 12/3/17)
×Sugar for the Bird. LC, S. Ldn, 20/8/17

×Rule 6 (Little, 27/5/23, Green Room Rag)
×The Confession (P.W., 15/2/25, Green Room Rag)
×The Condemned Cell. LC, P.W., 15/4/25
×The Silver Lining (P.W., 27/9/25, Green Room Rag)
[*Green Room Rags* (1925), a collection of short revue-type pieces by several authors, includes *The Condemned Cell* (see above) as well as three other unimportant sketches by Elton]

ELTON, W. L.
The Widow and the Maid ('*m.c.*', m. S. L. Hampton: Pal., Maidstone, 23/2/20; Emp., Penge, 1/3/20: called originally *The Choice*)

ELVEY, MAURICE [see *L. C. SHAW*]

ELWEN, TOM
Gertie's Boy ('*m.c.*', m. H. Henderson: P.H., Carlisle, 4/10/00, *cpy.*)

ELWES, EVA [see also *K. ALLEN*]
His Sister's Honour ('*md.*': Qns, Fleetwood, 14/1/07)
The Royal Mail (Goddard's, Durham, 11/3/08)
Salome (Emp., Cannock, 6/12/10, *cpy.*)
For Her Son ('*r.pl.*': Col., Saltley, 19/2/12)
The White Slaves of the Streets ('*md.*': P.W., Salford, 12/5/13)
Mary Latimer – Nun ('*md.*': Osborne, Manchester, 15/9/13)
Mother Mine (Osborne, Manchester, 24/8/14; E.C., 7/9/14)
Joy, Sister of Mercy (Hippo., Bilston, 28/12/14; Stratford, 9/8/15)
His Mother's Rosary (Metro., Manchester, 22/2/15; E.C., 27/9/15)
John Raymond's Daughter (Pav., L'pool, 26/7/15; Stratford, 24/1/16: title later changed to *A Soldier's Love Child* and *Somewhere in France*)
The Woman Pays – Back (Emp., Rotherham, 30/8/15)
Pals (Gr., Luton, 27/12/15; Stratford, 10/1/16)
The Sunshine of Paradise Alley (Osborne, Manchester, 28/2/16; E.C., 13/3/16)
Should a Woman Forgive? (Pal., L'pool, 12/6/16)
Heaven at the Helm (Rot., L'pool, 2/8/16; E.C., 13/11/16)
The Cottage Girl (Hippo., Nuneaton, 23/12/16; E.C., 1/10/17)
A Mother's Prayer (Marina, Lowestoft, 26/12/16; Stratford, 8/1/17: title later changed to *The Middy V.C. Comes Home*)
The Fishermaid of Old St Malo (Barnsley, 26/12/16; E.C., 7/5/17)
Honour the Man You Wed (New, Pontypridd, 12/3/17; Stratford, 2/4/17)
The Girl Mother ('*md.*': Hippo., Nuneaton, 3/9/17; E.C., 15/10/17)
Billy's Mother. LC, Hippo., Huddersfield, 7/10/18
His Wife's Good Name ('*md.*': E.C., 18/11/18)
Love's Young Dream (E.C., 2/6/19)
The Child who Stood Between. LC, Pal., Bordesley, 19/7/20
Kitty from Kensington ('*m.c.*': E.C., 8/11/20)
The Scandalmongers (Stratford, 27/1/22)
Not Fit to Marry (Alex., S. Shields, 13/11/22)

Fifty-Fifty. LC, Alex., S. Shields, 16/2/23
Dolly Peel. LC, Alex., S. Shields, 9/8/23
St Joan of Arc. LC, Alex., S. Shields, 27/3/24
Uncle Tom's Cabin. LC, Alex., S. Shields, 11/12/25: also acted later as *Hello Dixie*
Under Red Rule. LC, Alex., S. Shields, 18/11/25: also acted later as *The Tyranny of Freedom*

ELWES, MARY

Temporary Engagements and Other Plays. *1920*
[This contains a two-act play, *Temporary Engagements or Stiggins Entire*, and two one-act pieces, *Two in a Flat* and *In Time of War*]

EMDEN, WALTER

×The Moonchild and the Butterfly ('*fairy fant.*') *1909*
×The Sea-Urchin ('*oa.*', m. B. B. Sayth) *1911*
×Twinkle, Twinkle ('*children's pl.*') *1911*
Bessie, or The Daughter of the Blind Beggar of Bednal Green (Parish H., St Margaret's, Dover, 28/8/12: +*B. S. SMYTH*) *1912*
×Dreamland ('*children's pl.*': Parish H., St Margaret's, Dover, 27/12/12) *1912*
×The Haughty Princess. LC, Parish H., St Margaret's, Dover, 15/10/13
×Toy Life. LC, Parish H., St Margaret's, Dover, 10/11/13

EMERSON, Mrs

×Big Black Bogey. LC, Village H., Esher, 12/1/22

[*EMERSON, JOHN* [see also *A. LOOS*]

The Scarlet Band (Com., 27/8/13: played in N.Y. as *The Conspiracy*: +*R. BAKER*) *1913*

EMERY, C. A.

×The Clown's Mascot (Empress, Brixton, 22/6/08)

EMLYN, CHARLES WILMER

×Moonshine ('*m.pl. for children*') *1911*
×Rip Van Winkle. *1914*
×A Generous Impulse ('*pl. for Scouts*') *1915*
×The Yellow Cap ('*children's pl.*') *1916*

EMM, ANDREW

The Mystery Man (Gr., Brighton, 28/8/22; Emp., Wood Green, 4/9/22; Lyc., 5/3/24, revised as *Under His Protection*)
For England, Home and Beauty ('*md.*': P's, 22/5/15)
The Streets of Brighton (Gr., Brighton, 19/11/28)

ENDERLINE, ERNEST

×Odd Man Out. LC, Rep., Rusholme, 10/5/24
To Be Continued (Rep., Rusholme, 23/11/25)
Skin Deep ('*f.c.*': Portsmouth, 30/4/28; Crit., 22/5/28) *Fr. 1929*

ENGLAND, ALFRED

[For earlier plays see *H. E. D.* v, 358]
The Swineherd and the Princess ('*m.pl.*', m. C. St Amory: Roy., 19/12/01; Court, 18/5/14, *revised*: +*A. COLLARD*)

The Silver Stick ('*Cornish m.pl.*', m. C. St Amory: O.H., Northampton, 17/12/06)

ENGLAND, GEORGE

Night Birds of London ('*md.*': Broadway, New X, 6/8/00: +*M. BODE*)

ENSOR, AUBREY COLLEN

Beggar My Neighbour ('*c.*': Str., 10/9/22, Rep. Players)
×Grab (New, 3/4/25, RADA students)
The Long Lane (Q, 25/1/26)

ENTHOVEN, GABRIELLE [see also *H. M. HARWOOD*]

Ellen Young (Sav., 2/4/16, Pioneer Players: +*E. GOULDING*)
×The Honeysuckle (Lyc., N.Y., 21/3/21, Amer. Acad. of Dram. Art: translated from *Le chèvrefeuille* (1913) by G. D'Annunzio: +*C. SAROTIS*) *1915*

ERARD, MAX

Shepherdland (Emp., Wood Green, 3/2/13)

ERASMUS, S.

Fighting for Honour (P's, Blackburn, 3/8/03)

'*ERICSEN, HUBERT*' [see *G. HILL*]

ERLE, JONATHAN [see *M. BOILEAU*]

ERLE, UNA

×Down in the Mud (Rehearsal, 26/3/09, Curtain Raisers)

ERNE, VINCENT

×The Beauty Spots ('*m.f.*': Coll., 26/8/18)

ERNEST, ROBERT [see *D. CRANSTON*]

ERSKINE, BEATRICE CAROLINE (*Mrs STUART ERSKINE*)

×John Anderson's Chance (K's H., 12/3/13)
Malvaloca (K. G's H., 11/1/25, Sunday Players: adapted from the play, 1912, by S. and J. Álvarez Quintero)

ERSKINE, ELLA

×The Friends (Rehearsal, 28/2/09, Revival Company)
×Fifi (Rehearsal, 28/2/09, Revival Company; Court, 31/7/09, *cpy.*; Marlb., 11/10/09)
×The White Hair ('*c.*': Court, 31/7/09, *cpy.*; Theatre Club, Knightsbridge, 24/4/10)
×The Typist ('*little c.*': Garden Theatre, Olympia, 15/9/09, *m.*)
×The Roman Road (Clavier H., 4/3/12, Drama Soc.)

ERSKINE, HERMANN

The Great Beyond (Court, 28/3/12, *amat.*: +*J. F. NOLAN* and *F. ROBSON*)

ERVINE, ST JOHN GREER [see also *H. G. WELLS*]

Mixed Marriage (Abbey, Dublin, 30/3/11; Court, 7/6/11) *1911* (Dublin); *1914*
×Compensation ('*c.*': Rehearsal, 20/6/11, *m.*, Actresses' Franchise League)
×The Magnanimous Lover (Abbey, Dublin, 17/10/12; Court, 2/6/13) *1912* (Dublin)

×Eight O'Clock. *1913* (Dublin)
Jane Clegg (Gai., Manchester, 21/4/13; Court, 19/5/13) *1914*
×The Orangeman (Pal., Maidstone, 10/10/13) *1914* (Dublin: in *Four Irish Plays*)
×The Critics; or, A New Play at the Abbey Theatre ('*satire*': Abbey, Dublin, 20/11/13) *1914* (Dublin: in *Four Irish Plays*)
John Ferguson (Abbey, Dublin, 30/11/15; Gar., N.Y., 12/5/19; Lyr., Hamm., 17/4/20) *1915* (Dublin); *1919*
×Who Sups with the Devil. LC, Court, 19/3/18
×The Island of Saints, and How to Get Out of It (Abbey, Dublin, 12/10/20)
×Progress (Little, 3/4/22) *1928* (in *Four One-Act Plays*)
The Ship (Playh., L'pool, 24/11/22; Cent., 8/1/25) *1922*
Mary, Mary, Quite Contrary ('*light c.*': Abbey, Dublin, 14/5/23; Pier, Eastbourne, 13/8/23; Brixton, 1/9/24; Sav., 16/6/25) *1923*
The Lady of Belmont (Mary Ward Settlement, 31/5/24; Arts, 6/5/27) *1923*
Anthony and Anna ('*c.*': Playh., L'pool, 9/3/26) *1925*; *1930* (revised)
×Ole George Comes to Tea (Playh., L'pool, 27/5/27) *1928* (in *Four One-Act Plays*)
×She Was No Lady (Playh., L'pool, 8/10/27) *1928* (in *Four One-Act Plays*)
The First Mrs Fraser ('*c.*': H., 2/7/29) *1929*

'*ESMOND, HENRY VERNON*' [=*HENRY VERNON JACK*]
[For earlier plays see *H. E. D.* v, 359, 790]
The Wilderness ('*c.*': St J., 11/4/01) *Fr. 1901*
When We Were Twenty-One (Com., 2/9/01) *Fr. 1921*
The Sentimentalist (D.Y., 26/10/01)
My Lady Virtue (Gar., 27/10/02)
Fools of Nature (D.Y., 11/3/03, *cpy.*)
Billy's Little Love Affair ('*light c.*': Crit., 2/9/03) *Fr. 1920*
Under the Greenwood Tree ('*c.*': Lyr., 10/9/07)
The O'Grindles (Playh., 21/1/08)
×Her Vote (Playh., 18/5/09, *m.*; Court, 24/6/09) *Fr. 1910*
A Young Man's Fancy ('*c.*': O.H., Cheltenham, 12/9/12; Crit., 17/9/12)
Eliza Comes to Stay ('*f.c.*': Pier Brighton, 30/9/12, as *Sandy and His Eliza*; Crit., 12/2/13, *revised*) *Fr. 1913*
The Dear Fool (Lyc., Edin., 4/12/13; Vaud., 5/5/14, as *The Dangerous Age*)
Salad Days ('*r.f.*': Bournemouth, 3/9/17; Pav., 1/10/17, as *A Kiss or Two*)
The Law Divine ('*c.*: Wynd., 29/8/18: called originally *The Amorist*) *Fr. 1922*
×The Terror of Bloomsbury Square (Theatrical Gdn Party, Regent's Park, 30/5/19)
Birds of a Feather ('*c.*': Glo., 9/4/20)
Two Jacks and a Jill ('*f.c.*': Leamington, 17/11/21; Roy., 22/11/21)
×The Woman in Chains (Lyc. Club, 26/2/26) *Fr. 1926*

ESMOND, LOIE

In the Gloaming (Goole, 18/9/08, *cpy.*; Exchange, Wellingborough, 29/9/08)

'ESNOMEL'

Ida Collaborates ('*c.*': New, Cambridge, 17/9/17)

ESPINASSE, BERNARD

×Her Good Name ('*climax*': Imp., 17/4/02)

Ned Kelly, or, The Bushranger (Vaud., 25/9/02, *cpy.*; Gr., Islington, 30/5/04, as *The Bushrangers*: +*H. LEADER*)

Sapho (Junction, Manchester, 13/4/03: dramatised from the novel by A. Daudet)

A Barrier Between (Pal., St Leonards, 9/3/25)

ESPLEN, MACK

In the Dark (Metropolitan, 30/6/19)

ESSON, LOUIS

Dead Timber and Other Plays. *1920*

[This contains four short plays: 1. *Dead Timber* (Melbourne Rep. Theatre, 13/12/11); 2. *The Woman Tamer* (Melbourne, 5/10/10); 3. *The Drovers*; and 4. *The Sacred Place* (Melbourne, 15/5/12)]

ESSORY, PHILIP [see *O. LETHBRIDGE*]

ETTRICK, HAVELOCK

×A Diplomatic Theft ('*c.*': Gar., 17/7/01)

'EUCHAN'

×The Jolly Beggars (Ath., Glasgow, 24/1/22)

EUSTACE, ROBERT [see *Mrs L. T. MEADE*]

EUSTON, LAURENCE

A House of Cards (Little, 18/11/26)

EVANS, A. H.

The Trumpet Major (Corn Exchange, Dorchester, 18/11/08, *amat.*: dramatised from the novel (1880) by Thomas Hardy)

Mellstock Quire (Corn Exchange, Dorchester, 16/11/10, *amat.*: dramatised from Thomas Hardy's novel, *Under the Greenwood Tree*, 1872)

The Woodlanders. LC, (from the novel (1887) by Thomas Hardy) Corn Exchange, Dorchester, 29/10/13

EVANS, B. G.

×Esther. LC, County, Bangor, 21/7/14

EVANS, C. R. T. [see *M. HERBERT*]

EVANS, CARADOC

Taffy ('*pl. of Welsh village life*': P.W., 26/2/23, *m.*; Q, 8/9/25) *1923*

EVANS, DAVID

Boomerang (Lyc. Club, 27/11/27)

EVANS, DOROTHEA

The Call (Yr Alwad) ('*Welsh pl.*': Playh., L'pool, 18/10/15)

EVANS, EDGAR J.

×The Last Joke (T.H., Chiswick, 2/11/25, *amat.*)

EVANS, EVA

Love – and What Then? LC, Stratford, 17/1/13

EVANS, FORD

[Several playlets, many written in collaboration with *J. EVANS*, produced at music-halls]

EVANS, FRANK HOWELL

×The Wrong Side of the Road (Lyr., Hamm., 29/11/05, *cpy.*) *Fr. 1906*
×A Small Holding (Broadway, New Cross, 1/4/09)
×Millie's Mother (Crit., 18/1/10)
×Half-a-Crown (Roy., 31/5/11)

EVANS, FRED

[A few sketches and playlets produced at music-halls]

EVANS, JOE [see *FORD EVANS*]

EVANS, MURIEL

×Albert's Way Out. LC, Central H., Milford Haven, 3/11/20

EVANS, REGINALD

×The Trials of Life (Ambass., 6/12/20, *m.*)

EVANS, WILL [see also *T. CRAVEN*]

×Mother and Daughters. LC, Foresters, 15/4/14
×The Assassin (Crit., 17/5/20)
Tons of Money ('*f.*': O.H., Southport, 20/3/22; Shaft., 13/4/22: +'*VALENTINE*') *Fr. 1927*
The Other Mrs Gibbs ('*f.*': Bournemouth, 2/6/24; Gar., 25/6/24: +*R. GUY-REEVE*)
[Several collaborative sketches produced at music-halls]

EVELYN, CATHERINE

×Exchange and Mart (Rehearsal, 7/11/09)
×The Bookworms (W.L., 1/4/10)

EVELYN, FRANCIS ALVIN

The 'Ion' of Euripides. *1911*
The 'Bacchae' of Euripides. *1913*
×Perpetua ('*an episode in the age of persecution*') *1919*
'The Women of Troy'...by Euripides. *1920*
×The Shield of Pallas ('*lyric pl.*') *1929*
×David and Abigail. *1929*

EVELYN, J. W.

Hands and Hearts (Garston, 21/11/02, *cpy.*)

EVELYN, WALTER FREDERICK

Barnaby Rudge (Broadway, New X, 11/12/11)
David Copperfield (Lyc., 6/6/23)

EVEN, S. M.

It Pays to Advertise (Coll., 21/2/16: +*L. GRANT*)

EVERALL, R. S.
Under the Rose ('*m.c.*': Pier, Brighton, 15/10/28)

EVERSON, NORMAN A.
Celia ('*d. poem*': +*FRANCIS SANDWITH*) *1922*

EVES, HERBERT [see *A. HARE*]

EVETT, ROBERT
The Last Waltz ('*m.pl.*', m. O. Straus: O.H., Manchester, 19/8/22; Gai., 7/10/22: +*T. R. ARKELL*)

EWENS, DOROTHY
×Katharine Audley. *1926* (SPCK)
×Sansovino. *1928* (Oxford)

EWER, MONICA
×My Lady Poverty (Margaret Morris, 23/1/16)
×The Holy Bond (New, 25/2/16, *m.*)
×The Man Who Arrived (Etlinger, 12/7/16)
×Find the Girl (County, Kingston, 28/8/16: called originally *Puzzle – Find the Girl*)
×—and Cruelty (Etlinger, 7/5/19)
×Sweet Adventure (Etlinger, 7/5/20)
×The Queen's Pawn. LC, W.G., 13/5/21
The Best of Both Worlds (Players, 24/1/30) *1925* (Labour Publishing Co.)
Summer Time (Etlinger, 1/3/27)
×Miss Smith, Forward (Etlinger, 7/12/27)

EWING, T.
Jonathan. *1902*

EYRE, ARCHIBALD
Four Plays. *1909*
[This contains four short pieces: 1. *The Leading Lady*; 2. *The Girl in Waiting*; 3. *The Custodian*; and 4. *The Intervention of Miss Watson*]

EYRE, EDITH
Chiquita ('*m.pl.*': C.G., 27/3/24, *m.*, one act only: +*W. EYRE*)

[*EYRE, LAURENCE*
Mis' Nell o' New Orleans ('*fant.c.*': Ford's, Baltimore, 6/1/19, as *Miss Nelly of N' Orleans*; Henry Miller's, N.Y., 4/2/19; D.Y., 14/2/21) *Fr. 1930*
Martinique (Shaft., 14/6/26, Venturers)

EYRE, R.
×Found in a Taxi ('*eccentric f.*': Rehearsal, 30/5/09: +*J. PAIN*)

EYRE, S. J.
Bindle's Luck ('*m.pl.*': Club H., Sevenoaks, 13/4/20)

EYRE, WILFRED [see also *E. EYRE*]
Little Miss Fortune. LC, Scala, 7/4/25
Speed Limit ('*c.*': Everyman, 24/6/29)

FABER, DOROTHY

The House that Jack Built, and Other Plays. *1925*

[Besides the title piece, this contains two other short plays for children – *Pixies' Pitch* and *Wizard Redcap*]

FABER, LESLIE

The Head of the Firm ('*c.*': O.H., Buxton, 13/6/08; Vaud., 4/3/09: adapted from the Danish of H. Bergström)

FAGAN, ELIZABETH [see also *M. WELCHMAN*]

Dear Anne ('*c.*': Aldw., 23/6/25, *m.*)

FAGAN, JAMES BERNARD [see also *G. S. KING*]

[For an earlier play see *H. E. D.* v, 359]

The Prayer of the Sword (Adel., 19/9/04) *1904*

Hawthorne, U.S.A. ('*c.*': Imp., 27/5/05)

Under Which King? (Adel., 5/6/05)

× Shakespeare v. Shaw ('*revue*': H., 18/5/05 *m.*)

The Earth ('*modern pl.*': O.H., Torquay, 8/4/09; Kings., 14/4/09: called originally *The Tyranny*) *1910*

A Merry Devil ('*Florentine f.*': Playh., 3/6/09: called originally *The Joke*)

False Gods (H.M., 14/9/09: adapted from E. Brieux, *La foi*, 1909) *1916*

× The Dressing Room (Hippo., 21/2/10)

Bella Donna (St J., 9/12/11: dramatised from the novel (1909) by Robert Hichens)

The Happy Island (H.M., 24/3/13: adapted from a play by M. Lengyel)

× The Fourth of August (Col., 3/7/16)

× Doctor O'Toole (Col., 5/3/17) *Fr. 1930*

The Wheel (Apo., 1/2/22) *1922*

Treasure Island (Str., 23/12/22: dramatised from the novel (1883) by R. L. Stevenson) *1936*

The Flame (O.H., Leicester, 10/9/23; Wynd., 7/1/24: adapted from C. Mèré, *La flamme*, 1922)

Marlborough Goes to War (Playh., Oxford, 23/2/26: adapted from M. Achard, *Marlborough s'en va-t-en guerre*, 1924)

'And So to Bed' (O.H., Manchester, 30/8/26; Qns, 6/9/26) *1927*

The Greater Love (P's, 23/2/27)

The Ghost Sonata. *1929* (included in a collection of Strindberg's plays: +*E. PALMSTIERNA*)

FAGG, EDWIN H.

Bladud; or, The Swell and the Swineherd ('*c.o.*', m. L. D. C. Thomas and C. Wright: Bath, 11/4/08, *amat.*: +*S. POOLE*)

Dingley Dell; or, A Glimpse of the Immortals ('*c.o.*': Bath, 25/3/09, *amat.*)

FAHEY, ALFRED

× A Poet in Purgatory (Theatre Club, Knightsbridge, 24/4/10)

FAIRFAX, BETTY

Auction of Souls (Gr., Brighton, 16/10/22)

FALKLAND, ARTHUR

[Several sketches and playlets produced at music-halls]

FANE, SYDNEY

×Mixed Addresses. *Fr. 1903*
×Designing People (K's H., 11/5/07, *amat.*)

FARISH, JULIA H.

Jeanne D'Arc. *1924*

FARJEON, ELEANOR [see also *HERBERT FARJEON*]

[For an earlier play see *H. E. D.* v, 361]
×The Registry Office ('*c.o.*', m. H. Farjeon: St G's H., 29/6/00)
×A Gentleman of the Road ('*oa.*', m. H. Farjeon: St G's H., 22/7/02)
×St John's Eve ('*o.*', m. Sir Alexander Mackenzie: Olympia, L'pool, 16/4/24)

FARJEON, HERBERT

The Fan. *1922* (in *Four Comedies by Goldoni*, for which see *CLIFFORD BAX*: +*ELEANOR FARJEON*)
×Friends (Abbey, Dublin, 20/11/17) *Fr. 1923*
Advertising April ('*f.c.*': Rep., B'ham, 9/12/22; Crit., 25/1/23: +*H. HORSNELL*) *1922* (Oxford); *Fr. 1922*; *1923* (revised)
Picnic ('*revue*': Arts, 20/4/27)
Many Happy Returns ('*revue*': Arts, 20/4/28; D.Y., 4/6/28)
[Two sketches from this were published by French's in 1929, as *Happy New Year* and *Your Kind Indulgence*]

FARJEON, JOSEPH JEFFERSON

×Rule of Contrary. LC, Halifax, 30/7/21
No. 17 ('*joyous md.*': W.G., New Brighton, 6/7/25; New, 12/8/25) *1927*
After Dark (Pier, Eastbourne, 6/9/26; Gar., 20/9/26)
Enchantment ('*f. fant.*': Q, 12/12/27; Vaud., 12/3/30)
The Hours Between ('*r.c.*': Q, 12/11/29; Com., 25/11/29, as *The Highwayman*)

FARNOL, JEFFERY

The Honourable Mr Tawnish ('*r.d.*': Manchester, 4/11/20; K's, Hamm., 4/8/24)

FARNSWORTH, HENRY

×Five Minutes Past Four (Mechanics' H., Nottingham, 28/4/15: +*I. SARGENT*)

FARR, FLORENCE

×The Shrine of the Golden Hawk ('*Egyptian pl.*': Bij., 20/1/02: also called *Beloved of Hathor*: +*O. SHAKESPEAR*)
The Mystery of Time ('*masque*') *1905* (Theosophical Publishing Soc.)

FARREN, FRED [see *L. STILES*]

FARREN, J. A.

×The Fairies' Captives ('*fairy pl.*': P.H., W. Norwood, 29/11/13, *amat.*)

FARRINGTON, HERBERT M.
×Mingled Threads (St G's H., 14/2/01)
The Triumph of a Lost Cause ('*r.pl.*': County, Kingston, 26/6/05)

FARROW, HARRY
×The Bargain Hunter. LC, Kennington, 9/2/22

FARSON, NEGLEY [see *D. BRANDON*]

FAULKNER, ALMA
The Bluebird Touch (Apo., 30/9/21, *m.*, Playwrights' Theatre: +*O. T. CURTIS*)

FAULKNER, FRANK
×Help! (Little Vic., Brighton, 1/2/25: +*K. HORNE*: called originally *Miss Mumps' Manoeuvres*)

FAVERSHAM, JULIE OPP
×The House of Pierre (Dublin, 8/11/07; Adel., 14/9/08: +*K. JORDAN*)

FAWCETT, ELIZABETH NOBLE
×The Magic Piper ('*children's pl.*': +*E. M. ECCLES*) *1929*

FAWCETT, MARION [see also *W. THORNELEY*]
East Lynne (Gr., Southampton, 2/2/25; Borough, Stratford, 16/2/25)
The Boy Next Door (Gr., Woking, 16/11/25; adapted from a play by Florence Edna May)

FAWCETT, WARREN [see *N. DOON*]

FAYDON, NITA
×The Great Look ('*c.*': Vic. Pal., 4/12/11) *1912*
×The Clever One (Alb. H., 23/12/17, *priv.*)
×Saving Money (Etlinger, 13/12/18)
The Lonely Wife ('*t. of golf*': Com., 5/7/20, *m.*; D.P., Eastbourne, 9/12/20, as *The Lonely Lady*; D.Y., 24/1/21)

FEARNLY, GEORGE [see *A. BRANSCOMBE*]

FEARON, W. R.
×When Love Came over the Hills (Abbey, Dublin, 22/1/18: +*R. NESBITT*)

FEATHERSTONE, J. L.
[For an earlier play see *H. E. D.* v, 364]
×The Dustman's Find (O.H., Belfast, 13/3/03)

FEENIX, JOHN DALE
×De Mortuis. LC, Works Theatre, Norwich, 22/4/24
The Penge Family Wilkinson. LC, Works Theatre, Norwich, 22/4/24

FEIST, ELLA
×Flyaway Land. LC, Court, 23/1/23

FELIX, PACEY
×A Lesson in Love ('*oa.*': P.H., New Cross, 3/12/03)
The Bonnie Borderland ('*m.pl.*', m. F. W. Courtenay: R.A., Woolwich, 13/5/12)
Leave It to Bertha (St Mary's Parish H., Lewisham, 20/2/25, *amat.*)

FELL, MARIAN

Uncle Vanya (Dublin, 12/2/17)
The Seagull (H., 2/6/19, Art Theatre)
Ivanov (D.Y., 6/12/25, St. Soc.; Barnes, 23/12/25)
[These three translations from the Russian of Anton Chekhov appear in that author's *Plays*, vol. i, *1912*]

FELLOWS, F. [see *F. LITCHFIELD*]

FELTON, FRANK

The Sheriff's Gamble (Stand., 17/1/10)

FELLOWS, FRANK

John Bull ('*Christmas pl.*': Hippo., Cannock, 11/10/17)

FELTON, WILLIAM

× Dad's Mermaid (Brompton Hospital, 20/10/04)
× The Lost Wager (Brompton Hospital, 23/11/05)

FENDALL, PERCY

[For earlier plays see *H. E. D.* v, 364]
Mrs Dering's Divorce ('*c.*': Camden, 14/11/04; Terry's, 18/1/05)
× Mrs Justice Drake (Gd., B'ham, 16/1/11; Hippo., 30/1/11)
[Several sketches and playlets produced at music-halls]

FENN, FREDERICK [see also *W. W. JACOBS* and *B. VEILLER*]

[For an earlier play see *H. E. D.* v, 364]
× Judged by Appearances (Com., 22/3/02) *Fr. 1903*
A Married Woman (H.M., Dundee, 30/10/02; Metro., Camberwell, 24/11/02)
× The Honourable Ghost (Ealing, 29/12/02)
A Scarlet Flower ('*society pl.*': Worthing, 4/6/03: +*R. PRYCE*)
× 'Op-o'-me-Thumb (Court, 14/3/04, *m.*, St. Soc.; St J., 23/4/04: +*R. PRYCE*) *Fr. 1904*
Saturday to Monday ('*irresponsible c.*': St J., 14/4/04: +*R. PRYCE*)
× The Age of Innocence (Roy., 5/12/04, *cpy.*)
× The Convict on the Hearth ('*c.*': Court, 6/2/06) *Fr. 1908*
The Gardeners ('*song pl.*', m. R. H. Walthew: Guildhall School of Music, 12/2/06: +*J. VOGEL*)
× Out of Sight (Roy., 20/5/06, Pioneers: +*R. PRYCE*)
Amasis, an Egyptian Princess ('*c.o.*', m. P. M. Faraday: New, 9/8/06) *1906*
× His Child (Waldorf, 10/9/06: +*R. PRYCE*)
× The Nelson Touch (H., 21/10/07) *Fr. 1908*
× The Conquering Hero (Metropolitan, 14/12/08)
× A Welsh Sunset ('*oa.*', m. P. M. Faraday: Sav., 15/7/08)
Dame Nature (Gar., 20/1/10: adapted from H. Bataille, *La femme nue*, 1908)
The Gay Lady Doctor ('*m.pl.*', m. M. Patrice: Pallad., 22/7/12: +*D. DONOVAN*)
The Girl in the Taxi ('*m.pl.*', m. J. Gilbert: Lyr., 5/9/12: +*A. WIMPERIS*) *1912*
The Olive Branch (Str., 3/10/12: from L. Népoty, *Les petits*, 1912)
× In the Air (New, 23/8/13)

Love and Laughter ('*c.o.*', m. O. Straus: Lyr., 3/9/13: +*A. WIMPERIS*)
A Working Man (Crit., 24/7/14)
×Supper in the Temple (Little, 11/10/14)
An Eye for an Eye. LC, Canteen, Weybridge, 10/9/19

FENN, L. C.
×A Dear Bargain (Court, 8/11/08, Pl. Actors)

FENN, VALENTINE V.
A Tangled Web (Cardiff, 10/4/02, *amat.*)
Billy Banter (Cardiff, 14/12/04, *amat.*)

FENOLLOSA, ERNEST
'Noh', or, Accomplishment: a study of the classical stage of Japan (+*EZRA POUND*) *1916*
[This contains versions of eight Nō dramas, translated by Fenollosa and 'finished' by Pound: 1. *Kagekiyo*, by Motokiyo Seami; 2. *Hagoromo*, by Motokiyo Seami; 3. *Kakitsubata*, by Motokiyo Seami; 4. *Nishikigi*, by Motokiyo Seami; 5. *Aoi No Uye*, by Zenchiku Ujinobu; 6. *Kumasaka*, by Zenchiku Ujinobu; 7. *Kayoi Komachi*, by Kwanami Kiyotsugu; and 8. *Chorio*, by Nobumitsu]

FENTON, F. DE WENDT
The Wounded Bird (Wynd., 1/11/11, *cpy.*: adapted from A. Capus, *L'oiseau blessé*, 1909)

FENTON, FRANK
×The Signing of the Treaty (Shrewsbury, 1/6/14)

FENWICK, E. C.
×Exits and Entrances. LC, Lecture H., Wimbledon, 17/2/14

FENWICK, P. C. COLLINGWOOD [see *A. A. DRAKE*]

[*FERGUSON, FRANK A.*
×Lucky Jim (Gr., B'ham, 16/6/13)

FERGUSON, JOHN ALEXANDER
×The Curate Calls ('*c.*': St Mary's H., Glasgow, 15/2/12 *amat.*)
×Campbell of Kilmohr (Roy., Glasgow, 23/3/14; Col., 26/3/23) *1915*
×The Scarecrow ('*Hallowe'en fant.*': A.L.S. Trav. Th., 1921; Lyr., Glasgow, 13/11/23, Scott. Nat. Th. Soc.) *1922*
×The King of Morven (Lyr., Glasgow, 21/10/26, Scott. Nat. Th. Soc.) *1922*

FERGUSSON, GILBERT [see *O. BERGERE*]

FERNALD, CHESTER BAILEY [see also *R. STOCK*]
[For earlier plays see *H. E. D.* v, 365, 792]
The Married Woman (Aldw., 11/6/11, St. Soc.) *1913*; *Fr. 1927*
98.9 ('*c.*': Crit., 27/2/12; Woolwich, 13/12/12, revised as *The Grace You Admire*: called originally *The Wooer*)
×The Diamond Coronet (Hippo., Manchester, 16/9/12)
The Pursuit of Pamela ('*c.*': Roy., 4/11/13) *Fr. 1914*
×The Two Bold Knights ('*c.*': Emp., N.Y., 5/3/14)

The Day before the Day (St J., 19/5/15)
The Jest (Plymouth, N.Y., 9/4/19; Wimbledon, 9/8/20; Com., 6/9/21, as *The Love Thief*: adapted from S. Benelli, *La cena delle beffe*, 1909)
×Don Carlos (Pallad., 4/7/21)
The Mask and the Face ('*c.*': Everyman, 5/2/24: adapted from L. Chiarelli, *La maschera e il volto*, 1916) *Fr. 1927*
Yvelle (Everyman, 10/2/25)
Three for Diana (Pier, Brighton, 18/1/26)
The Fourteenth of July. LC, OUDS, 14/2/28: adapted from R. Rolland, *Le Quatorze Juillet*, 1901)
To-morrow. *1928*

FERNLEY, DONALD
The Pied Piper ('*children's pl.*') *1912*

FERRABY, HUBERT C. [see also *A. N. MORRIS*]
×The Catastrophe (Rehearsal, 11/3/09, Curtain Raisers; Lyc., 27/9/09, *cpy.*; R.A., Woolwich, 20/2/11)
×The Brothers (Arts Centre, 20/11/13)
×Uncle Dick (Arts Centre, 20/11/13)

FERRAR, H. [see *C. H. E. BROOKFIELD*]

FERRARI, GUSTAVE [see also *T. S. MOORE*]
×An Adventure of Pierrot (Com., 3/4/13)

FERRERS, NEWTON
Yolande and Sylvain ('*legend*': Arts, 30/10/27, New Pilgrims)

FERRIS, EDWARD
[For earlier plays see *H. E. D.* v, 365]
×Dartmoor (Gt. Qn. St., 26/6/00: +*P. HERIOT*)
×Val of the 25th. (Gr., Fulham, 2/7/00; Gr., Margate, 3/9/00, as *The Yellow Peril*; Vaud., 19/9/00: +*P. HERIOT*)
A Silver Wooing ('*c.*': Gr., Fulham, 2/7/00: +*P. HERIOT*)
×Timmins's Ride (H.M., Carlisle, 14/9/00: +*A. STUART*)
×A Royal Betrothal (St J., 3/12/00: +*B. P. MATTHEWS*)
After the Ball ('*f.c.*': Glo., 27/3/01, *cpy.*; Gr., Margate, 29/10/03: +*N. DOONE* and *B. P. MATTHEWS*)
×The Cabinet and Cupid (Sheffield, 12/9/02: +*B. P. MATTHEWS*)
A Beggar on Horseback (County, Kingston, 6/8/06: +*B. P. MATTHEWS*)
The Cheat (Gr., Wolverhampton, 21/9/08; Crown, Peckham, 28/9/08; Lyc., 5/3/10, as *The Fighting Chance*: +*B. P. MATTHEWS*)
×The Reward (Cor., 2/10/11: +*B. P. MATTHEWS*)
The Grand Seigneur (Sav., 4/10/13: +*B. P. MATTHEWS*)

FERRIS, R. [see *C. REAN*]

FERRO, A. H. [see *F. LANGBRIDGE*]

FESTING, GABRIELLE

×St John's Eve ('*fant.*': Alb. H., 7/11/08: +*D. HART*)

×A Castle in Spain (Guildhall School of Music, 19/5/25, Pivot Club)

FIELD, ARTHUR W.

The Pride of Byzantia ('*m.pl.*', m. J. W. McAlister: P's, Bradford, 21/8/11; Dalston, 22/4/12)

×The Star Turn (P's, Bradford, 10/3/13)

The Silver Lining (Alh., Bradford, 26/7/15)

Tipperary Tim (*f.*': Alh., Bradford, 6/8/28: +*G. ARTHURS*)

FIELD, CLAUD HERBERT ALLWYNE

Advent ('*morality*': Vic. H., 12/12/21: translated from the play (1899) by A. Strindberg)

FIELD, LILA

×The Goldfish ('*fairy pl.*': Playh., 3/3/10, *m.*) *1910*

×Plain Fare ('*ca.*': Playh., 3/3/10, *m.*)

×Money and the Girl (Playh., 3/3/10, *m.*)

×The Wallingfords ('*ca.*': Qns, 26/4/10, *m.*)

×The Lily Queen (Qns, 7/6/10, *m.*)

'*FIELD, MICHAEL*' [=*KATHERINE HARRIS BRADLEY* and *EDITH EMMA COOPER*]

[For earlier plays see *H. E. D.* v, 366]

×The Race of Leaves. *1901*

Julia Domna. *1903*

Borgia ('*period pl.*') *1905*

Queen Marianne. *1908*

The Tragedy of Perdon. *1911*

The Accuser. *1911*

[This also includes two short pieces, *Tristran de Léonois* and *A Messiah*]

Deirdre. *1918*

[This also includes two short pieces, *A Question of Memory* and *Ras Byzance*]

In the Name of Time ('*t.*') *1919*

FIELD, R. F.

×The Patchwork Quilt. *1929* (in J. W. Marriott, *One-Act Plays of To-Day*, vol. vi)

FIELD, RACHEL LYMAN

×Cinderella Married. *Fr. 1927*

[*FIELD, SALISBURY*

Be Careful, Baby ('*f.*': Nixon, Pittsburgh, 4/5/14, as *Twin Beds*; Fulton, N.Y., 14/8/14; Plymouth, 30/3/18; Apo., 17/4/18: +*M. MAYO*)

Wedding Bells ('*joyous c.*': Gar., Washington, 26/5/19; Harris, N.Y., 12/11/19; Playh., 31/8/20) *Fr. 1923*

FIELD, TELFOURD S. [see *E. BLYTHE*]

FIELDING, HENRY E.
The Way of the World ('*md.*': W.L., 9/7/00)
A Californian Girl (Tonypandy, 15/8/02, *cpy.*)

[*FIELDS, HERBERT* [see also *R. P. WESTON*]
PeggyAnn ('*m.pl.*', m. R. Rodgers: Philadelphia, 12/26; Vanderbilt, N.Y., 27/12/26; K's, Southsea, 18/7/27; Daly's, 27/7/27)
A Yankee at the Court of King Arthur ('*m.pl.*', m. R. Rodgers: K's, Southsea, 30/9/29; Daly's, 10/10/29)

FIELDS, T. WESTON
×Conce (K's, Edin., 15/7/12)

FIENNES, CARYL [see *Baroness ORCZY*]

FIGGIS, DARRELL
Queen Tara ('*t.*': Gai., Dublin, 25/2/13) *1913*

'*FIGULUS*'
×Three Visitors and Matthews. LC, K. G's H., 6/1/25
×The Sufferers. LC, K. G's H., 6/1/25

FILIPPI, ROSINA [see also *B. PAIN* and *N. PLAYFAIR*]
[For earlier plays see *H. E. D.* v, 366]
×In The Italian Quarter. *1901*
The Bennets (Court, 29/3/01: dramatised from J. Austen's *Pride and Prejudice*)
×The American Widow ('*ca.*': Metro., Camberwell, 24/8/03)
×The Mirror ('*Japanese pl.*': Crit., 15/9/03) *1903*
Belinda (Court, 15/5/05: dramatised from the novel (1883) by Rhoda Broughton)
Beatrice (Court, 29/5/05)
×Gossips (Three Arts Club, 2/7/16)
×Taboo. LC, Lyr., Hamm., 8/6/20
×The Arbuthuot Diamonds. LC, Ass. R., Yeovil, 8/7/20

FINDLAY, JOHN WAINHAN
×The Broached Cargo. *1925* (in *The Scots Magazine*, ii, 319, 360–7)

FINDON, B. W.
[For earlier plays see *H. E. D.* v, 366]
×The Marchioness ('*oa.*': H.M., 23/6/04, *m.*: +*E. JONES*)
×'Melia, 'Enery and It (H.M., 15/6/05, *m.*)
Lady Wychling's Dilemma. *1927*

FINDON, Mrs H. (*EDITH E.*)
×As a Man Sows (Qns, Poplar, 10/4/11)
×A Mare's Nest. LC, Hippo., Aldershot, 9/8/17

FINN, DONALD [see *GEORGE PICKETT*]

FINNEY, ALICE MAY
×Irish Stew (Abbey, Dublin, 12/5/13)
×The Call (Dublin, 30/11/14)

FIRBANK, ARTHUR ANNESLEY RONALD
The Princess Zoubaroff ('*c.*') *1920*

FIRTH, EDWIN
A Fight for Fortune; or, The Village Green (Inverness, 27/10/03, *cpy.*)
×The Thrill. LC, Cant., 16/9/24

FIRTH, IAN
×The Market for Moods (RADA, 23/7/22)

FIRTH, IVAN [see also *K. M. GRANDAGE* and *R. THORNDIKE*]
×That Five-Pound Note (Rehearsal, 14/7/11, *m.*)
×The Flapper and the Hangman (Clavier H., 11/10/12: +*K. M. GRANDAGE*)
×A Verdict of Conscience (Clavier H., 11/10/12)

FISHER, ALFRED HUGH
The Birds of Aristophanes. *1903* (Cambridge)
The Marriage of Ilario (‘*conceited c.*’) *1919*

[*FISHER, BUD*
Mutt and Jeff (‘*m.pl.*’: County, St Albans, 1/9/21; K’s, Hamm., 5/9/21)

FISHER, CECIL
×The Great Day (Little, 18/5/13, Pioneer Players)

FISHER, CHARLES
The Fisher Girl; or, The Flying Dutchman (‘*m.c.d.*’, m. W. T. Gliddon: Paragon, 17/6/07)

FISHER, DAISY
Lavender Ladies (‘*c.*’: Str., 25/2/23, Rep. Players; Com., 29/7/25) *1925*
Simple Simon (‘*f.c.*’: Portsmouth, 10/10/27; Sav., 12/12/27, as *The Cave Man*: +*H. SIMPSON*)

FISHER, H. CECIL
×The Great Day. *1925* (Labour Publishing Co.)

FISHER, REX
The Devil’s Pulpit (Q, 4/11/29)

FISHER, WILSON [see *C. GREGORY*]

[*FISK, MAY ISABEL*
×A Game for Two. LC, Qns, Keighley, 26/6/05
×The Cormorant (Little, 16/6/13)
×Greater Love than This! (Little, 16/6/13: +*M. V. SAMUELS*)
Monologues and Duologues. *Fr. 1914*
[This contains: 1. *A Game for Two* (see above); 2. *The Crossing of the Wires*; 3. *Harmony in A Flat*; and 4. *A Matter of Discretion*]
Little Comedies of Married Life. *1926*
[This contains six short duologues]

FISLI, WALLACE WILFRID BLAIR [=‘*BLAIR*’]

[*FITCH, CLYDE* [see also *C. GORDON-LENNOX*]
[For earlier plays see *H. E. D.* v, 367]
The Masked Ball (‘*f.c.*’: Crit., 6/1/00)
The Last of the Dandies (H.M., 24/10/01)

Sapho (Adel., 1/5/02: dramatised from A. Daudet's novel)
The Climbers (Com., 5/9/03)
Her Own Way (Lyr., 25/4/05)
Toddles ('*f.c.*': D.Y., 3/9/06)
The Truth ('*c.*': Com., 6/4/07)
The Woman in the Case ('*c.*': Gar., 2/6/09)
The City (New, 8/11/09, *cpy.*)
Girls ('*f.c.*': P.W., 10/9/13)
[A collected edition of this author's plays appeared at Boston, in four volumes, in 1915]

FITCH, CYRIL
[A few sketches produced at music-halls]

FITTON, SAM
The Buckleys. LC, Pal., Blackhall Mill, Durham, 8/3/21

FITZGERALD, AUBREY WHITESTONE
[For an earlier play see *H. E. D.* v, 368]
×The Spider and the Fly ('*f.*': Ryde, 25/7/00; Crit., 10/3/10, *cpy.*; Tiv., 18/2/07)
×Springtide ('*oa.*', m. F. Lambert: Coll., 29/7/12)
Eve and the Ogre ('*c.*': Pleasure Gdns, Folkestone, 25/2/24; Q, 10/8/25, as *The Ogre*; called originally *Bachelors*)
[A few sketches produced at music-halls]

FITZGERALD, DESMOND
The Saint ('*miracle pl.*': Abbey, Dublin, 2/9/19)

FITZGERALD, EILEEN
×Pamela's Predicament (Cosmopolis, 20/3/14)

FITZGERALD, F. T.
Rose of My Heart ('*m.c.*': Glo., Deal, 28/7/19: + *Y. RENAUD*)

FITZGERALD, GERALDINE [see also *O. LETHBRIDGE*]
×The Residuary Legatee (Ldn Pav., 5/2/14)

FITZGERALD, IRENE
×A Caprice (Bij., 16/12/05: adapted from the play (1837) by A. de Musset)

FITZGERALD, PERCY
×The Latchkey (Court, 21/11/13, Leverton Players)

FITZGERALD, S. ADAIR [=*S. ADAIR-FITZGERALD*]

FITZJOHN, GULIELMA PENN R.
×A Plume of Feathers (Rehearsal, 4/5/11, English Pl. Soc.)

FITZMAURICE, AUBREY
[A few sketches produced at music-halls]

FITZMAURICE, GEORGE
Five Plays. *1914* (Dublin)
[This contains five one-act plays: 1. *The Country Dressmaker* (Abbey, Dublin, 3/10/07; Court, 28/6/13); 2. *The Pie-Dish* (Abbey, Dublin, 19/3/08; Court, 5/6/11); 3. *The Magic Glasses* (Abbey, Dublin, 24/4/13; Court, 28/6/13); 4. *The Moonlighter*; and 5. *The Dandy Dolls*]

×'Twixt the Giltenans and the Cormodys (Abbey, Dublin, 8/3/23)
×The Green Stone. *1926* (in *The Dublin Magazine*, Jan. 1926)

FITZPATRICK, KATHLEEN
×Rupert the Reckless (*'burlesque md.'*) *Fr. 1900*
×Expiation (Molesworth H., Dublin, 10/2/10, Theatre of Ireland)

FITZROY, YVONNE
×The Farewell Performance. LC, Court, 23/4/14: +*D. ANSTRUTHER*)

FITZWILLIAMS, M. L. [see *C. M. EDMONSTON*]

FLANAGAN, W. P. [see *F. C. MOORE*]

[*FLAVIN, MARTIN*
Children of the Moon (Q, 4/10/26; Roy., 18/10/26) *1924* (New York); *Fr. 1926*

FLECKER, JAMES ELROY
Hassan (H.M., 20/9/23, as adapted for the stage by *BASIL DEAN*, music by Frederick Delius) *1922*
[This play had been written in 1914]
Don Juan (Court, 25/4/26, 300 Club) *1925*
[Although not performed until much later, this drama had been composed three years earlier than *Hassan*, in 1911]
×Joseph and Mary (*'Christmas pl.'*) *1928* (included in R. Moorhouse, *With Pipe and Tabor*)

FLEET, BEN
Before Men's Eyes (Q, 30/8/26: +*C. PEMBER*)

FLEMING, BRANDON [see *B. MERIVALE*]
×The Exchange Hotel (K's, Glasgow, 1/10/15: +*H. M. HAYNES*)
×Lessons. LC, Pal., Hamm., 16/5/16
×The Deceivers (O.H., Leicester, 1/4/18)
The Eleventh Commandment (Playh., Cardiff, 7/11/21; Roy., 16/1/22: originally called *Sinners* when submitted for a licence, LC, 27/5/18)
Down and Out (*'f.'*: Playh., Cardiff, 26/6/22)
In and Out (*'f.'*: Everyman, 26/4/24; Hippo., Golder's Green, 10/8/25, as *Easy Money*; St M., 23/9/25: +*S. W. CARROLL*)
×A Unique Opportunity (Col., 27/10/24: +*B. MERIVALE*)
The Hundredth Night (Gai., Hastings, 7/11/27)
The Lonely House (Gr., Blackpool, 17/6/29: dramatised from the novel (1920) by Mrs Belloc-Lowndes)

FLEMING, CARROLL
Bow Sing (*'Chinese o.'*, m. M. Klein: Ladbr. H., 24/2/11, *cpy.*)

'FLEMING, GEORGE' [=*JULIA CONSTANCE FLETCHER*: see also *M. PEMBERTON*]
[For earlier plays see *H. E. D.* v, 369]
The Fantasticks (*'r.c.'*: Roy., 29/5/00: adapted from E. Rostand's *Les romanesques*, 1894) *1900*

The Light that Failed (Lyr., 7/2/03: adapted from the novel (1890) by Rudyard Kipling)
The Conquest ('*md.*': Lyr., 24/4/09)

FLEMING, NOEL
×Tillie's Note. LC, Ass. R., Tenby, 23/12/18

FLETCHER, CAMPBELL
×Extendency. *1921*
×A Bare Bodkin (K's H., 18/6/22, Interlude Players)
Eugene ('*verse play*': Little, Southend, May 1928) *1929*

FLETCHER, CHARLES [see *G. R. SIMS*]

FLETCHER, J. S.
Hearthstone Corner ('*c.*': Little, Leeds, 20/12/26)

FLETCHER, JOSEPH
Lady Dolly and the Decalogue (Pav., Paignton, 17/9/08: +*M. ELLIS*)

FLETCHER, JULIA CONSTANCE [='*GEORGE FLEMING*']

FLETCHER, LEONARD [see *P. KNIGHT*]

FLETCHER, PHILIP
The Martyrs of Sebaste ('*religious pl.*': Caxton H., 13/10/10, *amat.*)

FLETCHER, R. CAMPBELL
×The Lost Wager (Court, 24/10/13)
×Genius at War ('*masque*') *1914*
×The Wind Wave. *1921*

FLETCHER, RICHARD [see also *Lady TROUBRIDGE*]
×A Bird in a Trap. LC, H.M., 16/11/20

FLEXMORE, F. [see *I. BOWMAN*]

[*FLEXNER, ANNE CRAWFORD* [see *A. H. RICE*]

FLINT, FRANK STEWART
Philip II ('*t.*': Court, 29/9/18, Plough Players: translated from the drama by Émile Verhaeren) *1916* (in *The Plays of Émile Verhaeren*)

FLINT, WALTER R.
The Girl Next Door ('*m.f.*', m. H. Wilkinson and A. Taggart: Aquar., Brighton, 2/7/06; Pier, Brighton, 22/7/07, as *The Blue Monkey*)

FLOOD, ALEC
[Several sketches and playlets produced at music-halls]

FLOWERDEW, FRANK
×Sanctuary (Clavier H., 2/3/13, Arts and Dramatic Club)

FLOYD, JOHN
The Mystery of the Red Tavern ('*md. mystery*': Lyc., Edin., 3/9/28; K's, Hamm., 29/10/28)

FOGERTY, ELSIE

[For an earlier play see *H. E. D.* v, 369]

Scenes from the Great Novelists. *1906*

[This contains four short pieces: 1. *The Changing of the Keys*; 2. *Mrs Pullet's New Bonnet*; 3. *Mrs Poyser Has Her Say Out*; and 4. *The Cratchits' Christmas Dinner*]

Electra (Scala, 16/6/14: from Sophocles' play)

The Queen's Jest, and Two Other Plays. *1915*

[This contains three one-act plays: 1. *The Queen's Jest*; 2. *Love Laughs at Locksmiths*; and 3. *Peint par Francois Boucher*]

The Harrying of the Dove ('*masque*') *1915*

The Miracle of the Rose ('*miracle pl.*': St Paul's Church, Covent Garden, 3/6/20) *1920*

FOLKARD, CHARLES

Teddy Tail. LC, D.Y., 16/12/20

FOMM, LESLIE

[For an earlier play see *H. E. D.* v, 370]

An Offer of Marriage ('*c.*': Glo., 27/4/1899, as *Ambition*; Wynd., 26/6/00)

× Opposites (Qns Gate H., 2/5/02)

× A Modus Vivendi (Bij., 6/12/02)

× Portia Up-to-date (Alb. H., 20/4/04)

FOORD, H. D. G.

The Land of the Christmas Stocking ('*children's pl.*': Rep., Plymouth, 26/12/21, *m.*: +*M. BUCHANAN*)

The Maid of Wokey ('*children's pl.*': Ambass., Southend, 22/12/24: called originally *Rose Red and the Witch of Wokey*)

FOTT, CONSTANCE M.

Moon Children. LC, St Nicholas H., Brighton, 9/5/21: +*D. WOOD*

FORBES, Mrs (of Callendar)

× The Fair Lady. LC, K's, Edin., 13/9/16

FORBES, E. ST CLAIR

The Empty Cradle ('*d.d.*': Bilston, 16/11/08)

× The Brutal Truth (Scala, Seacombe, 30/7/15: +*E. HOGGAN-ARMADALE*)

Daddy's Girl (Hippo., Nuneaton, 30/4/17; Woolwich, 2/7/17)

Our Lost Lass. LC, Glossop, 11/6/18

Shipmates (Woolwich, 20/1/19)

Innocence (Barnsley, 25/8/19)

A Spoiler of Women (E.C., 3/6/21)

FORBES, FRANCES ALICE MONICA

Catholic Plays, founded on Legends of the Saints. *1916, 1918*

[This collection contains four plays: 1. *St Frideswide*; 2. *St Brendan's Quest* ('*an allegory*'); 3. *The White Dove of Erin* ('*scenes from the life of St Brigid*'); and 4. *The Roses of St Dorothy*]

× The Emperor's Royal Robes: An Extravaganza from a Story by Hans Christian Andersen. *1920*

FORBES, JAMES

The Chorus Lady ('*c.*': Vaud., 19/4/09)

The Snow Shop (Hudson, N.Y., 31/12/14; Glo., 18/4/16)

FORBES, NORMAN

[For an earlier play see *H. E. D.* v, 370]

The Man in the Iron Mask (Adel., 11/3/1899; Lyc., 13/5/09, revised, as *The Prisoner of the Bastille*)

FORBES-ROBERTSON, BEATRICE

× Cupid's Throne ('*Arcadian c.*': Regent's Park, 17/6/07)

× The Quest of the Star (Regent's Park, 17/6/07)

[*FORD, HARRIET* [see *H. J. O'HIGGINS* and *E. ROBSON*]

A Gentleman of France (Aven., 4/6/04: from the novel (1893) by Stanley Weyman)

The Argyle Case (Crit., N.Y., 24/12/12; Str., 22/4/15: +*H. J. O'HIGGINS*)

FORD, JANICE

High Tide, Low Tide ('*c.*': Q, 9/12/28)

FORD, JULIAN ELSWORTH

The Mist. LC, Little, 12/11/13

FORD, MARY

The Power of Lies (W. Bromwich, 5/2/01, *cpy.*; Shak., Clapham, 27/7/08: title later changed to *Life's Crossroads*)

Lorna Doone (P'cess, 19/12/01: +*L. RAYNE*; dramatised from the novel (1869) by R. Blackmore)

The Tenderfoot (Barnsley, 9/4/23)

FORD, PERCY

The Yellow Evil. LC, Stratford, 29/8/19

[Numerous sketches and playlets produced at music-halls]

FORDER, WALTER A.

O Nana San ('*m.c.*', m. G. Hart: Agricultural H., Norwich, 10/12/03)

Don Paulo ('*m.pl.*', m. J. T. Gowing: Agricultural H., Norwich, 19/2/06)

FORDWYCH, HERBERT [see also *T. M. WATSON*]

× The Duchess of Silliecrankie (Terry's, 13/4/04)

× A Little Surprise (Rehearsal, 30/5/09)

FOREST, HÉLÈNE

× The Debt (Empress, 10/4/07)

× Sapho (Hippo., Putney, 18/11/12)

FORMAN, JOHN PATRICE

× To Arms! LC, Assembly R., Malvern, 10/9/14

FORREST, CHARLES

× The Shepherd ('*rural pl.*': Rep., L'pool, 11/3/12) *1922*

× The Cobbler's Shop ('*c.*': Rep., B'ham, 18/9/15) *1924*

Runaway Will ('*c.*': Gai., Manchester, 17/5/20: called originally *Runaway Peter*)

The Stolen Horse. *1925*
× The Roadside Farm. *1927*

FORRESTER, ANNE
× Beric ('*c.*') *1927* (Village Drama Soc.)
× Sally Sees It Through ('*ca.*') *1927* (Village Drama Soc.)

FORSHAW, F. F.
Pretty Fanny's Way ('*f.c.*': Kennington, 5/10/06, *cpy.*)

FORSTER, A.
× The Masculine Spinster. LC, Alex., Cowes, 20/12/17

FORSYTH, BERTRAM
× Decidedly Cool (Parochial H., Bennington, 11/1/04)
Hester (Court, 22/3/12)
The Shepherdess without a Heart ('*fairy fant.*': Glo., 19/12/13)
The Crossing (Com., 29/9/20: + *A. BLACKWOOD*)

FORTESQUE, JACK
× The Ruling Vice (Olympia, Shoreditch, 17/3/13)

FORTESCUE, WILLIAM G.
[For an earlier play see *H. E. D.* v, 371; author's name there wrongly cited as 'William S. Fortescue']
The Great Mad City (Birkenhead, 15/7/01; Alex., B'ham, 16/8/15, as *A Motherless Mite*; E.C., 3/7/16: also called *The Heart of London* and *A Mad City*)

FORWOOD, GWEN
× It ('*fairy pl.*': Bendrose Grange, Amersham, 3/2/12)
Iris of the Rainbow ('*fant.*': T.H., Rickmansworth, 15/1/13, *amat.*)

FORWOOD, M. E.
Jane – Errant (Forum Club, 18/11/28)

FOSCROFT, CHARLES T.
× The Bracelet of Diana. LC, YMCA H., Tottenham Court Road, 21/4/21

FOSS, KENELM
The Average Man ('*c.*': Roy., Glasgow, 21/4/13)
× Rahab (Little, 3/2/14)
× The Hem of the Flag. LC, Hippo., Woolwich, 10/9/14
× A Spanish Minx ('*d. surprise*': Metropolitan, 20/5/16)
× Alias Jones (Bath, 28/5/17)
× The Knees of the Gods (Col., 12/11/23)
Second Fiddle (Q, 21/2/27)

FOSTER, A. E. MANNING [see *R. H. BLAND*]

FOSTER, ARDEEN
A Woman's Soul (Kings., 28/7/16, *m.*)

FOSTER, F. D.
Where's Uncle? ('*m.pl.*', C. Locknane: Lyc., Sheffield, 16/5/04; Borough, Stratford, 11/7/04)

FOSTER, G. W. [see *F. W. ALLWOOD*]

FOSTER, LAYTON [see *K. RIDER*]

FOSTER, LUKE [see *W. H. BENSON*]

FOSTER, WILLIAM [see *B. S. ELDER*]

FOTHERGILL, H. S.

×The Circle of the Sword (Midland Inst., B'ham, 12/3/27, *amat.*)

FOTHERINGHAM, E. M.

×The Bad Temper Bureau ('*fairy pl.*') *Fr. 1920*
×A Cash Concern. *Fr. 1920*
×The Christmas Brownies ('*fairy pl.*') *Fr. 1920*
Tiny Plays for Tiny People. *Fr. 1921*

[This, as the title suggests, contains several very short pieces for young children]

×Brummy Crock. *Fr. 1921*
×The Tale of the Tarts ('*fairy pl.*') *Fr. 1922*
×Princess Parsimonia. *Fr. 1922*
×Too Much Monkey. *Fr. 1922*
×Unprofitable Poultry-Keeping. *Fr. 1922*

FOWLER, Mrs [='*G. GERVEX*']

FOWLER, WILLMOTT

A Hunting Morn ('*m.c.*': Pav., Worthing, 21/9/10)

FOX, B. MERVYN

The Price She Paid ('*md.*': Stand., Hatton, 20/1/11, *cpy.*; Gai., Burnley, 17/4/11; Stratford, 12/6/11)
A Woman without a Soul (Lyr., Hamm., 24/3/13)
Napoleon's Divorce. LC, Central, Bolsover, 26/9/13

FOX, FRANK

×The Elopers. LC, Glo., 30/5/14 (duplicated in typescript, 1912)
×Blackmail (duplicated in typescript, 1913)

FOX, IRENE

Sir Herbert ('*f.*': St G's Parochial H., Westminster, 11/5/10, *amat.*)

FOX, J. [see *A. O'CONNELL*]

FOX, MOIREEN

×The Fire-Bringers (Abbey, Dublin, 23/5/20)

FOX, RALPH

Captain Youth ('*r.c. for all Socialist children*') *1922*

FOX, S. MIDDLETON

The Vice-Chancellor ('*f.*': Footlights Club, Cambridge, 26/2/00)
The Waters of Bitterness, a play in three acts, and The Clodhopper, an incredible comedy. *1912*

[The first of these plays, described as a 'tragedy', was presented by the Stage Society at the Imperial Theatre, 8/6/03: the second, a one-act piece, was submitted for licensing, LC, Lake Pav., Keswick, 16/10/11]

This Generation. LC, Lake Pav., Keswick, 16/10/11. *1913*

FOX, TOM
[A few sketches produced at music-halls]

FOX-DAVIES, MARY
Chance (Str., 17/6/28, Rep. Players)

FOXWELL, HARRY
The Outcast of the Family (P.W., Salford, 25/6/08)

FRAEDERSDORFF, EMILY
Good Old Gadesby ('*f.c.*': P.H., Hastings, 24/4/07, *amat.*)

FRANCE, EDWIN S.
×Ring Up 735 East (Hippo., Willesden, 7/12/08)
×An Artful Widow (Empress, 20/6/10; Stand., 25/7/10)

FRANCE, EGERTON
×In the Secret Service (Arcadia, Brighton, 25/9/16)

[*FRANCE, GEORGE*
Marked for Life (Vic., Walthamstow, 29/10/00)

FRANCIS, BEARD
[For an earlier play see *H. E. D.* v, 372]
Twice Removed ('*f.c.*': Colchester, 27/5/12: +*H. LAELAND*)
How Like a Man ('*f.c.*': Pal., Ramsgate, 12/3/23: +*H. LAELAND*)

FRANCIS, EDEN
Fleur-de-Lys. LC, Court, 14/7/16

FRANCIS, JOHN OSWALD
Change ('*Glamorgan pl.*': H., 8/12/13, St. Soc.) *1913* (Cardiff)
×The Bakehouse ('*gossips*' *c.*') *1913*
×The Poacher (Col., Aberystwyth, 15/4/14; Emp., Finsbury Park, 3/5/15) *1924* (Cardiff)
×For France (Hippo., Manchester, 14/9/14; Pallad., 12/10/14)
×The Guns of Victory (Emp., Camberwell, 13/12/15)
×The Dark Little People. LC, P.H., Aberystwyth, 21/4/22. *1922* (Cardiff)
The Crowning of Peace ('*pageant*') *1922* (Cardiff)
Antony Settles Down ('*f.c.*': Shaft., 17/12/22, Rep. Players)
Cross Currents. LC, '*pl. of Welsh politics*': Col., Aberystwyth, 20/11/23. *1922* (Cardiff)
The Beaten Track. LC, '*Welsh pl.*': Pontypool, 17/7/24. *Fr. 1927*
×John Jones. *1927* (Newtown)
×The Perfect Husband. *1927* (Newtown)
×Birds of a Feather ('*Welsh wayside c.*': Col., 11/3/29) *1927* (Newtown)
The Little Village. LC, P.H., Tregaron, 13/12/28. *Fr. 1930*

'*FRANCIS, M. E.*' [=*Mrs FRANCIS BLUNDELL*: see also *S. VALENTINE*]
×The Widow Woos (H., 9/1/04: +*S. VALENTINE*)
×Olf and the Little Maid ('*c.*': H., 8/5/06)
×The Third Time of Asking ('*rustic c.*': Gar., 30/5/06)
×Tom's Second Missus (Playh., 30/4/07, *m.*)
×An Action for Breach (Rehearsal, 13/11/08, *m.*, Argonauts)

FRANK, GRACE

×The Last Visit (Little, 18/5/13, Pioneer Players: adapted from H. Sudermann, *Der letzte Besuch*, 1907)

×Streaks of Light (Arts, 10/7/27: adapted from H. Sudermann, *Lichtbänder*, 1907)

×The Far-away Princess (Etlinger, 21/2/29: adapted from H. Sudermann, *Die ferne Prinzessin*, 1907)

FRANK, JULIAN

The Man Responsible (Q, 13/6/27; Roy., 5/7/27)

[Both *Who's Who in the Theatre* and *The Stage Year Book* record the Q production as a play by *BRIAN MARSH*, but at the Royalty the author's name was given as above]

FRANK, MAUDE MORRISON

Short Plays about Famous Authors. *1916*

[This contains five playlets: 1. *A Mistake at the Manor*; 2. *When Heine was Twenty-One*; 3. *Miss Burney at Court*; 4. *A Christmas Eve with Charles Dickens*; and 5. *The Fairies' Plea*]

FRANKAU, GILBERT

The Heart of a Child (Huddersfield, 6/9/20; Kings., 20/3/21: +*A. DE BURGH*: from the novel (1908) by Frank Danby)

FRANKAU, RONALD

×The Actor. LC, Portsmouth, 14/5/23

×The Bet. LC, Portsmouth, 14/5/23

×The Burglar's Haul. LC, Portsmouth, 14/5/23

FRANKFORT-MOORE, F.

1066 ('*historical d.*': Pal., St Leonards, 14/10/26: adapted from Tennyson's *Harold*)

FRANKLYN, F. E.

It's Lucky. LC, '*m.pl.*': Hippo., Bury, 6/3/23

FRANKLYN, JOHN

×The Unfailing Instinct (Gar., 8/11/24, *m.*: title later changed to *Madame David Garrick*)

FRANKS, FRANK E.

The Gay Lieutenant ('*m.pl.*' m. J. Desormes: Hippo., Newcastle, 20/2/28)

Juno ('*m.pl.*': Emp., Newcastle, 30/7/28)

FRANKS, F. HAWLEY [see *L. REVELL*]

[For earlier plays see *H. E. D.* v, 372]

×An Old Man's Darling (W.L., 24/11/00)

Wanted – a Baby (P.H., Sydenham, 6/3/03)

In Peacock's Feathers. LC, Amersham Common School, 26/10/20

Harmony Corner (Sycamore H., Amersham, 19/11/21, Independent Players)

FRASER, GRACE LOVAT

The Maid Turned Mistress (Lyr., Hamm., 29/1/19: a dramatisation of the libretto of *La Serva Padrona* (1733) used by G. B. Pergolesi for his comic opera)

The Liar (adapted from *Il Bugiardo* (1750) by Carlo Goldoni) *1922*

FRASER, H. [see *C. H. E. BROOKFIELD*]

FRASER, Sir JOHN FOSTER
×The Grousers (Emp., Ardwick, Manchester, 5/11/17)

FRASER, MARY
×The Prize Story (Forum Club, 30/1/21)

FRECKER, C. D.
Pyramids, Limited ('*m.c.*': St G's H., 9/5/02)

'*FREDERICK, CHARLES*' [=*CHARLES WINDERMERE*]

FREDERICK, HELENA
[A few sketches produced at music-halls]

FREEMAN, CHARLES [see also *G. S. KING*]
[For earlier plays see *H. E. D.* v, 372–3]
A White Demon (Stratford, 29/4/07)
The Tiger's Den (Stratford, 6/5/07)
The Martyr (Gr., Lancaster, 22/6/14: +*G. GERALDINE*)

FREEMAN, JAMES
Dick's Dilemma ('*f.c.*': T.H., Ilford, 16/4/03, *amat.*)

FREEMAN, JOHN
Prince Absalom. *1925*

FREER, EDGAR
×Match-making in Mayfair (Court, 24/11/11, *cpy.*)
×Pandora (Court, 24/11/11, *cpy.*)

FREETH, FRANK
A Judge of Character ('*c.*': T.H., W. Hampstead, 18/3/11, *amat.*)

FRENCH, E.
[Numerous musical sketches, chiefly for the Alexandra, Stoke Newington]

FRENCH, F. E.
×Lady Betty (Roy., 14/3/10)

FRENCH, LESLIE
×Russian Tea (A.L.S. Trav. Th., 1926)

FRENCH, PERCY (*WILLIAM PERCY FRENCH*)
Noah's Ark ('*fairy pl.*': Waldorf, 1/1/06: +*B. STEWART*)
×A Frog he would a-wooing ('*m.fant.*', m. J. A. Robertson: Pal., Chelsea, 12/8/12)
An Irish Courtship ('*oa.*': Shorefield Pav., Westcliff, 2/7/19: +*H. COLLISSON*) *1918* (as *The Irish Girl*)

FRERE, Mrs A. HANBURY
×Dame Dumpty's Dilemma (T.H., Walham Green, 23/10/13)

'*FRERE, S. O. N.*' [=*GUY DU MAURIER*; see *Sir GERALD DU MAURIER*]

FREUND, E. WASHBURN [see *P. COLUM*]

FREUND, M. C. WASHBURN
The Vagabond (Court, 29/11/08, Pl. Actors: adapted from a plav by R. Fellinger)

FREWIN, HARRISON

Elijah ('*dramatised version of Mendelssohn's oratorio*': Kelly's, L'pool, 21/2/12; Kennington, 22/7/12) *1912*

×Pan and the Woodnymph (K's H., 29/4/13)

Punch and Judy ('*pantomimical o.*': P's, 11/5/15, '*priv. pfce*')

The Gay Lothario ('*o.*': O.H., Middlesbrough, 4/1/16)

FREY, MILTON

×Lines (Court, 29/1/14: +*P. BUDDEN*)

FRIEND, FAITH

×The Marriage Feast (K. G's H., 8/3/24, Young Age Theatre)

FRITH, JOHN LESLIE

The Years Between (Everyman, 14/6/26: adapted from *Le Printemps des autres* (1924) by J. J. Bernard)

The Sulky Fire (RADA, 20/6/26: +*M. GABAIN*: adapted from J. J. Bernard, *Le Feu qui reprend mal*, 1921) *1939*

Fresh Fruit ('*f.c.*': Court, 24/8/27: adapted from a play by R. Gignoux and J. Théry)

The Unquiet Spirit (Apo., 22/1/28, St. Soc.: adapted from J. J. Bernard, *L'Âme en peine*, 1926) *1939*

Martine (Gate, 4/12/29: adapted from the play (1922) by J. J. Bernard) *1939*

Désiré ('*c.*': New, 2/7/30: adapted from the play (1927) by Sacha Guitry)

FRITH, WALTER

[For earlier plays see *H. E. D.* v, 373–4]

The Man of Forty (Manchester, 27/10/1898; St J., 28/3/00)

×The Iron Duke (Com., 9/10/02)

The Perils of Flirtation ('*c.*': Roy., Glasgow, 16/11/03; Aven., 26/1/04)

The New Governess ('*f.*': Ass. R., Malvern, 19/11/08)

Margaret Catchpole (P.W., B'ham, 30/7/10; Gr., Croydon, 19/10/10; D.Y., 20/5/11)

×The Miniature (St J., 22/9/11) *Fr. 1914*

FROST, H. E.

×Oh, Perkins! LC, K. G's H., 9/10/25

FROST, NORMAN

Nicolette ('*c.o.*', m. P. Barrow: Gai., Dublin, 31/8/25; D.Y., 18/11/25: +*K. LARK*)

'*FRYERS, AUSTIN*' [=*WILLIAM EDWARD CLERY*]

[For earlier plays see *H. E. D.* v, 374]

The Elopement of Elsie (O.H., Harrogate, 22/5/05)

×The Black Pierrot (Hengler's Circus, 2/11/08)

×The Jury Retire (Arts Centre, 22/10/13)

×The Man in the Works (Arts Centre, 22/10/13)

Realities (Court, 18/2/18)

×Todd's Music Pills. LC, Emp., Southend, 3/8/18

FRYTH, WILLIAM

The Bells of Lin-Lan-Lone (Lyc., Newport, 22/5/11)

FULLER, A.

×The Three Outlaws (Worthing, 11/5/03; Gr., Fulham, 18/5/03)

FULLER, HERBERT

The Passion of Life (Merthyr Tydfil, 31/7/1899; Edmonton, 6/8/00; W.L., 4/3/01)

A Triple Vengeance (Fishermen's H., Buckie, 20/1/00: title later changed to *A Noble Mother*)

Fiends of London ('*md.*': Stratford, 22/1/02, *cpy.*; Batley, 3/8/03; Sur., 21/9/03)

×A Burglar's Darling (Gr., Manchester, 26/11/04)

As Your Hair Grows Whiter (O.H., St Helens, 28/5/07, *cpy.*; P's, Blackburn, 23/7/09; Pav., 4/10/09)

The Temptress of Paris (Alex., Sheffield, 17/4/11; Woolwich, 14/8/11)

Motherless (Gr., Lancaster, 12/5/13)

FULLER, LOIE

×A Little Japanese Girl ('*wordless pl.*': D.Y., 26/8/07)

[This seems to be the same as *Otake*, presented at the Hippo., 20/7/08, and attributed to Loie Fuller and W. Shike]

FULLERTON, PERCY

×The Five O'Clock Edition (Hippo., Peckham, 25/7/10)

×The Lamplighter (Kelly's, L'pool, 29/1/12)

In Purple Ink (Shak., L'pool, 16/12/13, *amat.*)

×Drawing a Blank. LC, Scala, Seacombe, 26/1/18

FULTON, ESME

×A Nativity Play. *1927* (SPCK)

FULTON, GEOFFREY

×Her Happiest Birthday. LC, Jarrow, 19/3/13

×Peggy. LC, Grantham, 7/4/14

The Girl who Broke Her Mother's Heart (Pav., L'pool, 7/12/14; E.C., 25/1/15, as *The Law and the Girl*)

A Bad Girl's Wedding (H.M., Walsall, 10/7/16)

FULTON, GRENVILLE [see *R. R. GIBSON*]

×Paid in His Own Coin (Rehearsal, 21/11/12)

×The Hostage (Pav., 11/3/14: +*R. VAN COURTLANDT*)

FULTON, JEFFREY [='*DAVID MUSKERRY*']

FULTON, OLIVE

The Princess and the Vagabond ('*r.pl.*': Gai., Dundee, 9/11/08, *cpy.*; Osborne, Manchester, 1/11/09; Stratford, 1/4/12)

FURBER, DOUGLAS [see also *D. TITHERADGE*]

×Charivari (D.P., Eastbourne, 23/12/16)

Sons of the Sea ('*m.c.*', m. S. Brooke: Olympia, Shoreditch, 17/3/19)

Toni ('*m.f.*', m. H. Hirsch: Hanley, 6/8/23; Shaft., 12/5/24: +*H. GRAHAM*)

Clo-Clo ('*m.pl.*', m. F. Lehar: Emp., L'pool, 26/5/25; Shaft., 9/6/25: +*H. GRAHAM*)

Up with the Lark ('*m.c.*', m. P. Braham: Playh., Cardiff, 25/7/27; Adel.,25/8/27: +*H. CARRICK*)
From London and New York: Revue Sketches. *Fr. 1927*
[This contains nine short pieces]
That's a Good Girl ('*m.pl.*', m. P. Charig and J. Meyer; Emp., Cardiff, 6/2/28; Hippo., Lewisham, 19/3/28; Hippo., 5/6/28)
Lucky Girl ('*m.pl.*': Emp., Newcastle, 17/9/28; Hippo., Golder's Green, 29/10/28; Shaft., 14/11/28: +*R. P. WESTON* and *B. LEE*)

FURNESS, J. R.
[For an earlier play see *H. E. D.* v, 375]
King Henry the Seventh ('*historical d.*': T.H., Conway, 28/11/00, *cpy.*) *1900* (Conway)

FURNISS, A. D.
Miss Angel ('*c.*': K's H., 10/5/06: +*M. D. GIBBS*)

[*FURNISS, GRACE LIVINGSTON*
The Man on the Box ('*c.*': Pav., Eastbourne, 6/8/08; Marlb., Holloway, 31/7/09: from a novel (1904) by Harold McGrath)

FURNISS, HARRY
×The Sheriff's Wife (Castleford, 4/2/13)

FURNISS, PAUL
Between 5 and 7 (Q, 24/3/30)

FURNIVALL, HENRY [see also *C. RIMINGTON*]
[For an earlier play see *H. E. D.* v, 375]
×Our Better Selves (O.H., Wakefield, 6/11/03)

FURNIVALL, OSMER G.
The Conversion of John Lennox ('*c.*': Central H., Priory Schools, Acton, 1/4/13

FURST, E. L. [see *A. CHAPMAN* and *J. H. WOOD*]

FYFE, HENRY HAMILTON
A Modern Aspasia ('*c.*': Aldw., 4/6/09 *cpy.*; Aldw., 6/6/09, St. Soc.)
×The Borstal Boy (H.M., 26/11/11)
×Race Suicide ('*ca.*': K's H., 21/4/12, Pioneer Players)
The Kingdom, the Power and the Glory ('*morality*': Com., 16/1/21, Pl. Actors) *1920*

'*FYFFE, R. E.*' (*Duchess of Sutherland*)
The Conqueror ('*dramatic fant.*': Scala, 23/9/05) *1906* (*priv.*)

FYLEMAN, ROSE
Eight Little Plays for Children. *1924*
[This contains: 1. *Darby and Joan*; 2. *The Fairy Riddle*; 3. *Noughts and Crosses*; 4. *The Weather Clerk*; 5. *The Fairy and the Doll*; 6. *Cabbages and Kings*; 7. *In Arcady*; and 8. *Father Christmas*]
×Christmas Eve ('*fant.*': Old Vic, 19/12/26)
Seven Little Plays for Children. *1928*
[This contains: 1. *The Princess and the Pirate*; 2. '*The Butcher,*

the Baker, the Candlestick-maker'; 3. *The Mermaid*; 4. *Peter Coffin*; 5. *The Armchair*; 6. *Mother Goose's Party*; and 7. *The Coming of Father Christmas*]

FYNES-CLINTON, Rev. H. J.
The Cradle, the Cross and the Altar (Guildhall School of Music, 28/1/22, Catholic Pl. Soc.)

GABAIN, MARJORIE [see *J. L. FRITH*]

GABBOTT, JOHN
×Philippa Comes Back (Steiner H., 17/5/27) *Fr. 1925*

GAIRDNER, WILLIAM HENRY TEMPLE
Saul and Stephen ('*sacred d.*') *1921* (SPCK)
×Passover Night. *1921* (SPCK)
×The Last Passover Night. *1921* (SPCK)
Joseph and His Brothers. *1921* (SPCK)
×The Good Samaritan. *1923* (SPCK)
×King Hezekiah. *1923* (SPCK)

GALBRAITH, G.
Galatea. LC, Bath, 21/3/21

GALLATLY, JAMES M.
×The Dragon (Margate, 9/11/08)

GALLIENNE, RICHARD LE
Orestes ('*t.*': Boudoir, 6/5/12, Drama Soc.) *1910* (New York)

GALLON, TOM [see also *A. CHEVALIER*]
[For earlier plays see *H. E. D.* v, 375]
×The Man who Stole the Castle (Gar., 26/12/00: +*L. M. LION*)
×Aurora's Captive (Ladbr. H., 13/12/04, *cpy.*; Cardiff, 26/10/11; P.W., 18/6/13)
×Lady Jane's Christmas Party (Gar., 21/12/04)
×The Borrowed Uncle (Borough, Stratford, 13/2/05; New, 28/11/07, as *The Fairy Uncle*; Wynd., 7/9/08, as *Filby the Faker*: +*L. M. LION*)
×The Man in Motley (Gd., B'ham, 13/1/08; Col., 20/1/08)
×Law and Order (Pal., 13/1/08)
×The Devil's World (Hippo., Peckham, 19/4/09, as *The Devil's Death*; Pal., Chelsea, 25/7/10; Little, 11/10/14; title later changed to *The Devil Pays*)
The Great Gay Road ('*r.c.*': Torquay, 20/3/11; Court, 21/12/12)
×All's Fair (Tiv., 25/8/13)
Felix Gets a Month ('*c.*': H., 6/2/17: +*L. M. LION*)
×Pistols for Two (Col., 18/6/17: +*L. M. LION*)
×The Heart of a Clown (Hippo., Brighton, 3/8/25; Emp., Holborn, 10/8/25)
[This playlet is attributed to Tom Barry in *The Stage Year Book*, but Gallon seems to have been its author]

GALLSCHALT, KATE [=*KATE GODDARD*]

GALSWORTHY, JOHN

The Silver Box (Court, 25/9/06) *1909*
Joy (Sav., 24/9/07, *m.*) *1909*
Strife (D.Y., 9/3/09, *m.*; H., 20/3/09) *1909*
Justice (D.Y. and Roy., Glasgow, 21/2/10, simultaneous production) *1910*
×The Little Dream (‘*allegory*’: Gai., Manchester, 15/4/11; Court, 29/10/12) *1911*; *1912* (*revised*)
The Pigeon (Roy., 30/1/12) *1912*
The Eldest Son (Kings., 25/11/12) *1912*
The Fugitive (Court, 16/9/13, *m.*; P.W., 25/9/13) *1913*
The Mob (Gai., Manchester, 30/3/14; Cor., 20/4/14) *1914*
The Little Man (‘*farcical morality*’ or ‘*whimsy*’: Rep., B'ham, 15/3/15; Everyman, 21/10/20) *1915*
A Bit o' Love (Kings., 25/5/15: called originally *The Full Moon*) *1915*
The Foundations (‘*extravagant pl.*’: Roy., 26/6/17) *1920*
×The Defeat (Lyr., Hamm., 14/3/20, Curtain Group and People's Theatre Soc.; Everyman, 17/4/22) *1921*
The Skin Game (St M., 21/4/20) *1920*
×The First and the Last (Aldw., 30/5/21, *m.*) *1921*
A Family Man (‘*c.*’: Com., 2/6/21) *1922*
Six Short Plays. *1921*
[This contains, besides *The Little Man*, *The Defeat* and *The First and the Last* (see above), *Hall-marked*, *The Sun* (A.L.S. Trav. Th., 1922; Playh., L'pool, 1/11/22) and *Punch and Go* (Mary Ward Settlement, 15/10/24, Dram. Art Centre; Everyman, 24/5/26)]
Loyalties (St M., 8/3/22) *1922*
Windows (‘*c.*’: Court, 25/4/22) *1922*
The Forest (St M., 6/3/24) *1924*
Old English (H., 21/10/24) *1924*
The Show (St M., 1/7/25) *1925*
Escape (‘*episodic pl.*’: Ambass., 12/8/26) *1926*
Exiled (‘*evolutionary c.*’: Wynd., 19/6/29) *1929*
The Roof (Vaud., 5/11/29) *1929*
The Winter Garden: Four Dramatic Pieces. *1935*
[This includes *The Winter Garden* (written c. 1908) and three fragments – an unused episode for *Escape*, *The Golden Eggs* (written 1925–6) and *Similes* (written 1932)]

GAMBLE, GEORGE

Haji Baba; or, The Star of the East (‘*m.pl.*’, m. W. Robins: St J., 22/1/09, *cpy.*)

GANDY, IDA

×The Gypsy Countess. *1924* (Plays for Villages)
×The Deer Stealers. *1925* (Village Drama Soc.)
×The Fairy Fruit (‘*pl. for children*’) *1925*
×Snowdrop and the Dwarfs (‘*pl. for children*’) *1926*
×A Good Shepherd (Cent., 8/12/26, *amat.*) *1927*

×Lady Cake. *1928*
×The Stranger ('*c.*') *1929* (Village Drama Soc.)

GANTHONY, RICHARD
[For earlier plays see *H. E. D.* v, 376]
The Prophecy ('*r.pl.*': Gr., Fulham, 1/12/02; Aven., 10/3/03)
The Thunderbolt ('*c.*': Dublin, 10/5/06)

GANTHONY, ROBERT
The Ring Mistress ('*f.c.*': D.P., Eastbourne, 17/12/00; Lyr., 20/12/00)
The Meeting ('*duol.*': P.W., 25/6/03) *Fr. 1903*
The British Ambassador ('*c.*': P.W., Richmond, 5/11/03)
Uncle Jack ('*c.*': Castle, Richmond, 30/10/06)
×Garge (Pal., Camberwell, 2/5/10)
×A Thousand Miles a Minute. LC, St G's H., 1/12/13
The Widow's Husband (Lincoln, 27/11/22; Alex., 14/5/23)
The Man who Married Himself (Little, Rusholme, 27/12/26)

GARBETT, M.
×Marigold Immersed. LC, County H., St Albans, 21/12/20

GARDEN, H. E. [see *R. CULLUM*]
[Several sketches produced at music-halls]

GARDINER, H. P.
The Moscow Doctor (Pier, Brighton, 27/4/03: from H. S. Merriman's novel, *The Sowers*, 1896)

GARLAND, ALISON
The Hearthstone Angels ('*c.*': Imp., 14/5/07)
The Better Half (K's H., 6/5/13, Actresses' Franchise League) *1913* (Liverpool)

GARLAND, ELEANOR
×The Piping of the Shi. LC, Steiner H., 15/6/29

GARLAND, PETER
The Heart of Doris (Playh., Cardiff, 9/10/22; Apo., 24/10/22, as *Glamour*)
The Eternal Spring (Playh., Cardiff, 21/1/24; Roy., 29/1/24) *Fr. 1924*

GARMAIN, GERTRUDE
×The Beauty Doctor (Passmore Edwards Inst., 6/5/09)

GARNETT, CONSTANCE CLARA (*Mrs EDWARD GARNETT*)
[For an earlier play see *H. E. D.* v, 376. Mrs Garnett was the outstanding translator of Russian works – notably those of Chekhov, Gogol and Tolstoi – during this period, and many productions were based on her texts either directly or in adaptation. Among these may be specially recorded – *The Cherry Orchard* (Aldw., 28/5/11, St. Soc.; St M., 11/7/20, Art Theatre): *The Bear* (Rep., B'ham, 21/9/18): *The Seagull* (Little, 19/10/25): *The Three Sisters* (Barnes, 16/2/26; Fortune, 23/10/26)]

GARNETT, EDWARD WILLIAM
The Breaking Point (H., 5/4/08, St. Soc.) *1907*

The Feud (Gai., Manchester, 10/4/09; Cor., 11/6/09) *1909*
The Spanish Lovers (Little, 22/5/12: based on F. de Rojas, *La Celestina*
The Trial of Jeanne d'Arc (Ethical Church, Bayswater, 26/10/13) *1912*

GARNETT, RICHARD
William Shakespeare, Pedagogue and Poacher. *1904*

GARR, EDDIE
[Numerous music-hall sketches, chiefly for the Alexandra, Stoke Newington]

GARRETT, W. G. B.
× Midget (Court, 12/2/14)

GARRICK, RAY [probably pseudonym of *P. CHARLES CARRAGHER*]
MacTartan, Millionaire ('*Scottish c.*': St Joseph's H., Dundee, 4/5/21, *priv.*; Arbroath, 25/5/21)

GARROD, W. V.
Murder Will Out (Sunderland, 1/10/09, *cpy.*; Leigh, 16/12/12, as *A Mother's Vengeance*; Pal., Battersea, 5/11/17, as *Love Levels All Ranks*)
A Wife for a Day (Alex., B'ham, 30/7/10, *cpy.*; Emp., Fleetwood, 18/8/10, as *Atonement*; Macclesfield, 6/2/11; Fulham, 17/4/11; Alex., B'ham, 29/7/12, *revised*)
The Love Marriage ('*r.d.*': Pav., Waterhouse, 1/12/15; Emp., Islington, 12/2/17)
The Heart of a Thief (Gr., Halifax, 23/7/17; Emp., Camberwell, 29/10/17)
× What a Wife! (Woolwich, 30/12/18)
One Law for Both (Stratford, 13/1/19)
The Admiral's Daughter (Gr., Plymouth, 12/5/19; Stratford, 23/6/19)
The Right to Live (Gr., Doncaster, 15/9/19; E.C., 1/12/19)
A Respectable Married Woman (Gr., Plymouth, 27/9/20; Pal., Battersea, 11/10/20; also called *A Riddle of the Night*)
Pretending to Be Cinderella ('*c.*': Playh., L'pool, 16/5/21)
Out of Town (Lyr., Sheffield, 29/5/22)
× Quits (Grantham, 14/5/23)
Back from Beyond (Court, Wigan, 19/11/23)
[This play is included by W. V. Garrod in his own list of 'produced' dramas (see below), but in the typescript itself the author's name has been altered in ink to 'B. E. Garrod'. Whether there is any justification for such a change cannot be determined]
Child o' My Heart (Hippo., Mexborough, 17/3/24)
A Stolen Future (Hippo., Burslem, 8/5/24; Coll., 6/9/26: also called *A Man Without a Past*)
The Ragged Millionaire (Hippo., Burslem, 21/8/24; Hippo., Rotherhithe, 26/7/26
Blissful Ignorance ('*c.*': Altrincham, 9/2/25, Garrick Soc.)

Simple Faith (Ashton, 8/2/26: also called *Suspected* and *Double Lives*)
Out of Wedlock (Hippo., Bury, 11/4/27)
The Law Breakers (Hippo., Bury, 18/4/27; Hippo., Rotherhithe, 30/5/27: also called *Fallen Among Thieves*)
The Verdict of the Jury (Pal., Lincoln, 19/7/28)

[A collection of typescripts of plays by this author (see above p. 184), in the possession of the present writer,i ncludes texts of all the pieces listed above, with the exception of *Murder Will Out*, *What a Wife!* and *The Admiral's Daughter*. The collection also includes texts of three one-act pieces broadcast by the B.B.C. – *Cheating the Hangman*, *The Homecoming* and *A Few More Loyalties* – as well as several full-length dramas – *The Law and the Man*, *Happiness* (a comedy), *Dear Sir, Unless* – (a farce), *Dangerous Living*, *Under a Foreign Flag*, *Too Much Marriage* (a farce), *Adam and Evil* (a comedy, originally entitled *Sauce for the Gander*), *The Prince's Bride* (a musical farce), *Years of Discretion* (a comedy originally called *The Prime of Life*), *Give and Take* (a comic sketch), and *The Man from the C.I.D.* Most, if not all, these last-mentioned plays may be of later date: no records concerning them have been found before 1930]

GARROW, DAVID
×What Charity Covers ('*c.*') *Fr. 1911*
×Patty Packs a Bag ('*ca.*': Gr., Southampton, 27/2/11) *Fr. 1911*

GARROW, JAMES
Robert Burns; or, Rantin', Rovin' Robin (Corn Exchange, Kilmarnock, 21/11/02, *cpy.*)

GARRY, CHARLES
×A Daughter of Israel (Cant., 8/2/09)

GARSTANG, W.
The Students' Opera (University, Leeds, 18/12/24, *amat.*)

GARTH, CASWELL [see *ST C. SCOTT*]

GARVICE, CHARLES
Marigold ('*c.*': Roy., Glasgow, 30/3/14: +*A. F. ABBOTT*: revised version by *L. A. HARKER* and *F. R. PRYOR*, D.P., Eastbourne, 8/3/27; Kings., 21/4/27)

GASKELL, Lady KATHERINE MILNES
×An Angel of Grief (Bury St Edmunds, 28/12/12)

GASKELL, W. C.
×Bill's Bounty. LC, P's, Blackburn, 29/5/14

GASKOIN, CATHERINE BELLAIRS
The Lumber Room and Other Plays. *1913*

[This contains eight one-act pieces: 1. *The Lumber Room*; 2. *Fickle Juliet*; 3. *The Fortescues' Dinner Party*; 4. *John Arbery's Dream*; 5. *The P.G.'s*; 6. *Them Banns*; 7. *The Toolip*; and 8. *Wrong Again*]

GATE, G. M.

×Enquire Within. LC, Crippl. Inst., 18/11/19
×To the Sound of the Trumpet. LC, Crippl. Inst., 13/1/25

GATES, ELEANOR [*Mrs FREDERICK FERDINAND MOORE*]

The Poor Little Rich Girl ('*pl. of fact and fancy*': Hudson, N.Y., 21/1/13; New, 30/12/13: dramatised from her own novel, 1913) *1916* (New York)

GATES, S. BARRINGTON

The Mulligatawny Medallion. *1926*

[This contains five one-act pieces: 1. *The Mulligatawny Medallion*; 2. *The Day's Work*; 3. *A Small Hour*; 4. *The Wonderful Son*; and 5. *Time*]

GATHORNE-HARDY, GEOFFREY MALCOLM

The Age of Unreason (Arts, 23/1/29, Guild Players: adapted from a play by Zak Bryn)

GATTIE, A. W.

Sir Jackanapes ('*r. costume pl.*': Court, L'pool, 28/1/24)

GATTY, IVOR [*DAVID IVOR VAUGHAN*]

×Duke or Devil? ('*fant. o.*', m. N. Gatty: Gai., Manchester, 16/12/09; C.P., 21/11/11) *1909* (Hull)

GATTY, NICHOLAS COMYN [afterwards *N. C. SCOTT-GATTY*]

×Prince Ferelon ('*m.ext.*': Etlinger, 26/11/19; Old Vic, 21/5/21)

GATTY, R.

×Greysteel: The Bearsarks Come to Surnadale ('*o.*', m. N. Gatty: Sheffield, 1/3/06; C.P., 24/5/06; Lyr., 6/9/07)

GAWTHORNE, PETER A.

The Island King ('*m.pl.*', m. H. Garstin: Adel., 10/10/22)
The Wishing Well ('*m.c.*', m. H. Garstin: O.H., Southport, 26/1/25)

[A few sketches produced at music-halls]

GAY, JUSTIN

×La tête de canard ('*comédie de salon*', Cosmopolis, 22/6/13: +*H. SYMS*)

GAYE, PAUL [see *A. CHAPIN*]

GEDDES, PATRICK

The Masque of Ancient Learning ('*pageant*', London University, 11/3/13) *1912* (Edinburgh)

GEE, HUGH

Balk and the Big Head. LC, Qns Gate H., 1/1/23

GEERE, FLORENCE

×As a Little Child (Arts Centre, 27/6/14)

GENET, ERNEST

[For earlier plays see *H. E. D.* v, 377]
×Midsummer Eve ('*oa.*', m. T. Mattei: Camden, 11/6/02) *1903*

GENN, EDWARD P.

What's Become of the Fairies? ('*fairy pl.*': David Lewis, L'pool, 26/12/24, *amat.*) *Fr. 1927*

Let's Pretend ('*modern fable*': David Lewis, L'pool, 26/12/25, *amat.*) *Fr. 1927*

× B'loons ('*pl. for children*') *Fr. 1929*

GEORGE, A. D.

The Speyg ('*c.*': Arts, 27/7/29)

GEORGE, BEVERLEY

[For an earlier play see *H. E. D.* v, 377]

The Little Cripple (Runcorn, 22/7/05, *cpy.*)

GEORGE, EDWIN

At the Mercy of the Mormons (Woolwich, 20/1/13)

GEORGE, ERNEST

× Low Tide (Everyman, 12/8/24) *1932*

× All's Fair (New, 3/4/25, *m.*) *Fr. 1925*

Belle; or, What's the Bother? (P.W., 20/10/29, St. Soc.; Vaud., 19/4/30, as *Down Our Street*) *1929*; *1930* (as *Down Our Street*)

GEORGE, NATHANIEL

Her Great Love (K's, Longsight, 7/6/15; Lyr., Hamm., 25/10/15)

GERALDINE, GRACE [see *C. FREEMAN*]

GERANT, JOHN

[For an earlier play see *H. E. D.* v, 377]

The Runaways ('*m.c.*', m. F. Knight Pearce: Jarrow-on-Tyne, 13/12/01; Bridlington, 3/4/02, as *A Runaway Millionaire*); R.A., Woolwich, 28/7/02)

The Father of Her Child (O.H., Buxton, 8/12/09, *cpy.*; Metro., Abertillery, 29/1/12; Cardiff, 19/2/12; Stratford, 25/3/12; also called *The False Witness*)

[A few sketches produced at music-halls]

GERBERDING, ELIZABETH

× In the Patio (Lyc. Club, 23/3/11, *m.*)

GERHARDI, WILLIAM ALEXANDER

Perfectly Scandalous, or The Immorality Lady. *1927*; *1929* (as *Donna Quixote, or Perfectly Scandalous*)

GEROTHWOHL, MAURICE ALFRED

Chatterton (Court, 25/4/09, Dram. Productions Club and Revival Company: from the play (1835) by Alfred de Vigny)

[*GERSTENBERG, ALICE*

× Overtones (Bandbox, N.Y., 8/11/15; Col., 12/11/17)

× Fourteen (Etlinger, 14/3/28)

[Both of these are included in her collection of *Ten One-Act Plays*, no date, New York]

'*GERVEX, GASTON*' [=*Mrs FOWLER*]

× The Accolade (Court, 16/6/10, *m.*)

× The Bishop's Fortune (Court, 8/7/10)

×The Call (Hippo., Golder's Green, 16/3/15)
×The Magnet (Ambass., 26/2/20, *m.*)

GEYL, PIETER

A Beautiful Play of Lancelot of Denmark (St G's H., 22/2/25, International Theatre Soc.) *1924* (The Hague)

GHOSE, S. N.

The Colours of a Great City. *1924*
[This contains two short plays: 1. *The Defaulters*; and 2. '*And Pippa Dances*']

GIBBONS, VIOLET

The Wager ('*m.c.*': Watson H., Tewkesbury, 24/1/12, *amat.*)
×Crooked Nails (Boddington, Cheltenham, 11/4/12)
×Whose Hat? (Boddington, Cheltenham, 11/4/12)
×As Once in May (Boddington, Cheltenham, 11/4/12)
×The Error of His Way (Watson H., Tewkesbury, 27/1/13, *amat.*)

GIBBS, LEONARD ANGAS

Miscellaneous Writings. *1926*
[This contains two full-length plays, *Richard Sheridan* and *Bound Over*, together with three one-act pieces intended for amateurs – 1. *England Expects* (Court, 21/11/13); 2. *The Haunted House*; and 3. *The Chauffeur*]

GIBBS, M. E.

The Moon Maiden. LC, '*m.pl.*': Baths H., Thornton Heath, 16/2/23
Goblin Gold. LC, Baths H., Thornton Heath, 14/2/24

GIBBS, MILDRED D. [see *A. D. FURNISS*]

GIBBS, PHILIP

×The Escape of John Merchant (D.Y., 10/7/06; Court, 31/12/07, as *A Mender of Nets*: +*COSMO HAMILTON*)

GIBSON, Mrs E. H.

×Come and See. LC, Small Qns H., 15/12/15

GIBSON, GEORGE

×The Scarcerow and the Star (Hippo., Putney, 21/11/10)

GIBSON, JAMES

×Six Hundred Chicks! ('*rural c.*') *1930* (Glasgow)

GIBSON, ROLAND R.

Patsy in Willow-Plate Land (Midland, Manchester, 23/12/16: +*G. FULTON*)
The Girl in the Bath ('*m.pl.*': Hippo., Boscombe, 25/3/18; K's, Hamm., 22/4/18: +*G. FULTON* and *F. DIX*)
Mandalay (Q, 4/6/28)

GIBSON, WILFRID WILSON

On the Threshold. *1907* (*priv.*)
[This includes several short dramatic poems]
Stonefolds. *1907* (*priv.*)
[This contains six one-act plays: 1. *Stonefolds*; 2. *The Bridal*; 3. *The Scar*; 4. *Winter Dawn*; 5. *The Ferry*; and 6. *On the Threshold*]

Daily Bread. *1910*

[This contains seventeen one-act plays: 1. *The House of Candles*; 2. *On the Road*; 3. *The Betrothed*; 4. *The Firstborn*; 5. *The Family's Pride*; 6. *The Garret* (Ass. R., Edgbaston, 1911, Pilgrim Players; Etlinger, 27/6/19, Curtain Group Dram. Soc.); 7. *The Shirt*; 8. *The Mother*; 9. *The Furnace*; 10. *Mates* (Ath., Glasgow, 25/10/12); 11. *Agatha Steel*; 12. *The Night Shift*; 13. *The Operation*; 14. *The Call*; 15. *The Wound*; 16. *Summer-Dawn*; and 17. *Holiday*]

×Womenkind (Ass R., Edgbaston, 24/2/12, Pilgrim Players; Alh., Glasgow, 6/1/13) *1912*

Borderlands. *1914*

[This contains three one-act plays: 1. *The Queen's Crags*; 2. *Bloodybush Edge*; and 3. *Hoops* (H.M., 19/5/16, *m.*)]

Krindelsyke. *1922*

Kestrel Edge and other plays. *1924*

[This contains five one-act plays: 1. *Lover's Leap*; 2. *Red Rowan*; 3. *Blackadder*; 4. *Winter's Stob*; and 5. *Kestrel Edge*]

Between Fairs ('*c.*') *1928*

GIBSON-COWAN, W. L.

×Aunt Bertha ('*a trifle*': Blfrs, 30/1/27, I.L.P. Arts Guild) *1929*

GIELGUD, VAL HENRY

Self (Scala, 11/7/26, Playmates)

The Job (Str., 25/3/28, Pl. Actors)

Chinese White (Arts, 13/11/29) 1933 (in *Five Three-Act Plays*)

GIFFARD, E. C.

×Asking Father ('*f.*': Little, Brighton, 2/3/25)

GILBERT, BERNARD

King Lear at Hordle and Other Rural Plays. *1922*

[Besides the title-play (in three acts, LC, Carver Recreation Club, Marple, 19/3/23), this collection includes seven one-act pieces: 1. *A Tanvats Nietsche*; 2. *Eldorado* (LC, Watlington Lecture H., Oxford, 16/11/22); 3. *Gone for Good*; 4. *The Hordle Poacher* (which is probably *The Ruskington Poacher*, LC, Council School, Ballinghay, 15/2/15); 5. *The Old Bull* (LC, Hut, Peaslake, 6/2/23); 6. *Bonfire Night*; and 7. *To Arms!* Several of these plays were also published separately by French: *Eldorado* (*1924*), *The Old Bull* (*1927*), *Gone for Good* and *The Hordle Poacher* (both *1928*)]

×The Prodigal's Return. *Fr. 1928*

×Peers Woodman. *1927* (Oxford)

GILBERT, BERT

[A few sketches produced at music-halls]

GILBERT, ERNEST B.

×Greater Love Hath No Man. LC, Drill H., Bromsgrove, 4/10/13

×Tony's Busy Morning. LC, Drill H., Bromsgrove, 16/10/13

×The Strike. LC, Hippo., Harpenden, 13/1/16

×The Spirits of Salt. LC, Pierrotland, Bognor, 5/10/16
×Morice. LC, Kursaal, Bognor, 16/7/17: later called *The Unwelcome Guest*

GILBERT, FRANCIS [see *M. WALLERTON*]

GILBERT, LEWIS
[For earlier plays see *H. E. D.* v, 378]
×Mistaken Identity (Gloucester, 23/5/00)
The Mysteries of London ('*md.*': Pav., Edin., 22/4/01; Sur., 5/8/01)
A Faithful Friend (Rot., L'pool, 15/12/02; Emp., Balham, 9/11/03; W.L., 18/7/04: +*T. W. RAWSON*)
Delia Dare's Device (Eastbourne, 2/5/03, *cpy.*)
A Daughter of the Sea (Lyr., Hamm., 5/7/09)
A Fair Impostor (Lyr., Hamm., 10/7/11)
A Girl without a Conscience (Woolwich, 20/5/12)

GILBERT, MABEL
An Experiment (Maskelyne's, 11/4/26, Playmates: +*ROBERT GILBERT*)

GILBERT, Sir WILLIAM SCHWENK
[For earlier plays see *H. E. D.* v, 378–81]
The Fairy's Dilemma ('*domestic pantomime*': Gar., 3/5/04) *1911*
Fallen Fairies ('*o.*': Gar., 11/12/09) *1909*
×The Hooligan (Col., 27/2/11) *1911* (in *The Century Illustrated Monthly Magazine*, November 1911, pp. 97–102)

GILCHRIST, ROBERT MURRAY
×The Climax ('*c.*': Manchester, 2/5/13) *1928*
×The Moor Gate (Gai., Manchester, 11/8/13)

GILL, ARTHUR STANLEY
Malinche ('*light o.*': Mechanics' H., Nottingham, 27/10/10, *amat.*)
×The Kiss of Isis (Mechanics' H., Nottingham, 11/5/11, *amat.*; Hippo., Richmond, 5/6/11)
The Ladies of Bagdad ('*c.o.*': Mechanics' H., Nottingham, 26/1/13, *amat.*)
The Dream Princess (Nottingham, 8/12/13, *amat.*)

GILL, DAVID BASIL
Greater Love (Playh., Cardiff, 30/7/23; Pier, Brighton, 14/4/24, as *Handsome Jack*)
Marigold in the Garden ('*r.c.*': Pier, Brighton, 1/10/23; Gr., Putney Bridge, 24/11/24, as *Marigold*) *Fr. 1924*
The Three Musketeers (Hippo., Birkenhead, 13/9/26)
Eve's Flesh (Pier, Brighton, 5/12/27)

[*GILLETTE, WILLIAM* [see also *A. CONAN DOYLE*]
[For earlier plays see *H. E. D.* v, 381, 793]
Clarice ('*c.*': Shak., L'pool, 4/9/05; D.Y., 13/9/05)
×The Robber (Col., 9/8/09)
×Among Thieves (Pal., 6/9/09)

GILLMAN, FREDERICK JOHN

×The Two Pilgrims. *1920*

×The Little Women. *1920*

GILLMAN, R. G. [see *W. COOPER-LISSENDEN*]

GILLPATRICK, WALLACE

The Lowland Wolf (O.H., Leicester, 15/2/11: called originally *The Wolf of the Lowlands*: +*G. MARBURG*: from A. Guimerá, *Terra baixa*, 1896)

GILMER, H.

Marriage. LC, Crook, 13/2/19

GILMER, Mrs W. CHRISTIE

Genius Limited ('*c.*': Byfield H., Barnes, 29/5/07, *amat.*)

One Fair Daughter (Working Men's Inst., Barnes, 9/4/04, *amat.*)

GILSON, ALICIA

Retribution (Pembroke, Kensington, 5/10/18)

GINCOT, ION

×X.Y.Z. LC, 20/7/29. *1926*

GINGOLD, Baroness HÉLÈNE (*Mrs L. COHEN* or *COWEN*)

Abelard and Heloise ('*t.*') *1906*

Looking for Trouble ('*f.*': Pier, Brighton, 4/7/10; Aldw., 13/5/12: called originally *Seeking for Trouble*: +*L. COHEN*) *Fr. 1913*

×Two Men and a Woman (County, Reading, 12/9/10: +*L. COHEN*)

GINNER, RUBY

Love and the Dryad (K's H., 29/4/13)

×Poke Bonnet ('*wordless c.*': Kings., 19/6/17, *m.*: +*Miss MAWER*)

GIRARD, FÉLIX

Mr Willington's Wild Oats (Playh., L'pool, 1/12/20)

GIRVIN, BRENDA

The King's Glove (Lawrie Park Gdns, Sydenham, 3/7/09, *amat.*)

Cautious Campbell ('*modern c.*': Rep., Nottingham, 25/9/22; Q, 15/11/26; Roy., 26/7/27: +*M. COSENS*) *Fr. 1925*

Angel Brown ('*c.*': Rep., Nottingham, 6/11/22; Pier, Eastbourne, 28/6/26, as *The Constant Flirt*: called originally *Fickle 'Earted*: +*M. COSENS*)

The Wee Man ('*m.pl.*', m. R. Boughton: Rep., B'ham, 26/12/23: +*M. COSENS*)

Miss Black's Boy (Q, 20/9/26: +*M. COSENS*: also called *Miss Black's Son*) *1926*

The Red Umbrella ('*fant.*': Q, 24/10/27; Little, 31/10/27: +*M. COSENS*) *Fr. 1928*

Madame Plays Nap ('*c.*': K's, Edin., 2/9/29; New, 17/12/29: +*M. COSENS*)

GLASBY, CONSTANCE

Sinners (Pier, Brighton, 18/11/12)

[*GLASPELL, SUSAN* [see also *G. C. COOK*]
Trifles, and Six Other Short Plays. *1926*
[Of the pieces contained in this collection four were performed in Britain: 1. *Trifles* (K's H., 9/2/19); 2. *The People* (Fellowship H., Glasgow, 8/10/27, Glasgow Clarion Players); 3. *Close the Book* (Etlinger, 14/7/27); and 4. *Woman's Honour* (Etlinger, 6/7/26; Arts, 27/10/27)]
The Verge (Reg., 29/3/25, Pioneer Players) *1924*
Inheritors (Provincetown Playh., N.Y., March, 1921; Playh., L'pool, 25/9/25; Everyman, 28/12/25) *1921* (Boston); *1924*
Bernice (Gate, 30/10/25) *1922*
The Comic Artist (Str., 24/6/28, Pl. Actors: +*NORMAN MATSON*)

[*GLASS, MONTAGUE*
Potash and Perlmutter ('*c.*': Apo., Atlantic City, 4/8/13; Cohan, N.Y., 16/8/13; Qns, 14/4/14: +*C. H. KLEIN*) *Fr. 1925*
Potash and Perlmutter in Society (New Haven, 21/10/15, as *Abe and Mawruss*; Republic, N.Y., 21/10/15; Manchester, 4/9/16; Qns, 12/9/16: *R. C. MEGRUE*)
Business before Pleasure ('*c.*': Apo., Atlantic City, 6/8/17; Eltinge, N.Y., 15/8/17; Sav., 21/4/19: +*J. E. GOODMAN*)
Partners Again ('*c.*': Stamford, 4/22; Selwyn, N.Y., 1/5/22; Gar., 28/2/23: +*J. E. GOODMAN*)
Potash and Perlmutter, Detectives ('*c.*': Plymouth, 12/12/27: +*J. E. GOODMAN*)

GLASSFORD, D. T. [='*MERLIN STRANGE*']

GLAZE, WILL H. [see *A. SKELTON*]

[*GLEASON, JAMES*
The Fall Guy ('*c.*': Davidson, Milwaukee, 14/7/24; Eltinge, N.Y., 10/3/25; Apo., 20/9/26: +*G. ABBOTT*)
Is Zat So? ('*c.*': 39th Street, N.Y., 5/1/25; Apo., 15/2/26: +*R. TABER*) *Fr. 1928*

GLEAVES, E. M.
Moonshine. LC, '*fairy pl.*': Gr., Swansea, 16/8/17

GLEIG, CHARLES
The Misfit Mantle ('*f.c.*': O.H., Cork, 9/2/03)

GLEITZMAN, J. [see *H. C. COHEN*]

GLENISTER, D. J.
Bingle's Luck. LC, '*m.pl.*': Bognor, 25/1/23

GLENN, EDWARD P.
The Witches' Oak ('*fairy pl.*': Crane H., L'pool, 6/5/27, Liverpool Child Repertory Players)

GLENNIE, F. FORBES
Pompilius; or, Rome as it wasn't ('*oa.*': St Nicholas H., Guildford, 7/12/07, *amat.*)

[*GLICK, CARL*
The Devil's Host (Portsmouth, 13/8/28; Com., 22/8/28) *1934* (Boston)

GLIDDON, JOHN
The Pocket-Money Husband ('*c.*': Arts, 4/10/28)

GLIDDON, WILLIAM T.
The Flower Girl ('*m.pl.*': Lincoln, 14/5/08; Gr., Croydon, 30/11/08; Shak., Clapham, 14/12/08; Emp., Swindon, 26/12/10, revised by *G. UNWIN* as *The Missing Maid*; Court, 16/3/12)
×Till Death Do Us Part (Brixton, 18/7/10)

GLORIEL, GEORGE
The House ('*c.*': Court, 31/12/07) *1922* (*priv.*)

GLOVER, EVELYN [see also *F. M. ALEXANDER*]
Mrs Appleyard's Awakening (Rehearsal, 20/6/11, *m.*, Actresses' Franchise League) *1913*
×A Chat with Mrs Chicky (Rehearsal, 20/2/12; Little, 23/6/12, Connoisseurs) *1913*
×Which? (Arts Centre, 24/3/14)
×A Bit of Blighty. LC, Qns, 26/1/17
×Their Mothers (Apo., 4/12/17, *m.*)
×To Let Furnished. LC, Kings., 15/4/18
Time to Wake Up (New, 11/4/19, *m.*; New, 10/5/19)
×Thieves in the Night. LC, W.G., 11/5/21

GLOVER, HALCOTT [see also *H. F. RUBINSTEIN*]
×The Dingle (Little, 1/7/13)
Wat Tyler (Old Vic, 14/11/21) *1920* (*priv.*); *1925*
The King's Jewry. *1921* (*priv.*); *1925*
The Second Round (Everyman, 8/11/23) *1923*
Hail, Caesar! ('*c. of Ireland*': Fest., Cambridge, 9/5/27) *1922* (*priv.*); *1925*
Three Comedies. *1928*
[This contains: 1. *Bellairs*; 2. *God's Amateur*; and 3. *Wills & Ways* (Arts, 1/12/29)]
On the Quota (Arts, 29/1/30)

GLYN, ELINOR
Three Weeks (Adel., 23/7/08, *priv. pfce*: dramatised from her own novel, 1905)

GLYNN, G. FENNIMORE
×Three and a Fool ('*f.c.*': Bed., 20/2/11)
×Dear Old Bean. LC, New, Northampton, 15/5/19

GLYNN, S. L.
Trifle Not with Love (Bedford H., Chelsea, 16/10/21, Pax Robertson Salon: adapted from *On ne badine pas avec l'amour* (1834) by Alfred de Mussset)

GODBOLD, ERNEST HILDER
[For an earlier play see *H. E. D.* v, 382]
×A Political Pair (Rehearsal, 27/6/13, Black Cat Club)

×The Clarion Call (Passmore Edwards Settlement, 26/3/15, Kemble Soc.)
×A Woman's Way (P.H., Redditch, 14/2/01)

[*GODDARD, CHARLES WILLIAM* [see also *P. DICKEY*]
The Misleading Lady (Apo., Atlantic City, 17/11/13; Fulton, N.Y., 25/11/13; Manchester, 28/8/16; Playh., 6/9/16: +*P. DICKEY*) *1913* (New York)

GODDARD, F. W.
A Mystic Romance. LC, Roy., Barrow-in-Furness, 1/4/19

GODDARD, KATE [=*KATE GALLSCHALT*]
×Mistaken Identity. *Fr. 1903*
×The Little Devil Chooses (St John's H., Wembley, 2/12/08; Hippo., Manchester, 27/1/13: +*F. A. STANLEY*)

GODDARD, LESLIE
Earthbound (Q, 10/9/28: +*C. WEIR*)

GODDARD, RICHARD E.
Man's Desire (Rep., Brighton, 21/1/24)
Forward, Young Ladies (K. G's H., 29/5/24)
×Cold Storage. LC, Rep., Brighton, 7/10/25
Bibs and Tuckers ('*c.*': Cent., 23/6/26)

GODEFROI, JOCELYN
The Vultures (Little, 1/7/13: adapted from C. Van Lerberghe, *Les Flaireurs*, 1891)

GODFREY, ARTHUR E.
[Numerous sketches and playlets produced at music-halls]

GODFREY, G. W.
×My Milliner's Bill. *Fr. 1903*
×The Parvenu. *Fr. 1923*

GODFREY, MARCEL
The Oldest Profession (E.C., 18/10/26: dramatised from the novel (1925) by George C. Foster)

GODFREY, PERCY
×Cupid Goes Astray ('*f.*': Pal., Northampton, 22/1/17)
×Escape. LC, Kennington, 20/8/24
Commonplace. LC, Little Vic, Brighton, 21/5/25

GODFREY, PETER
Unseeing ('*modern c.*': The Gables, Surbiton, 16/12/24)
Ten Nights in a Bar Room (adapted from the nineteenth-century melodrama: Gate, 1/1/30)
Long Live Death ('*md.*': Gate, 4/2/30)

GODFREY, Mrs TOM
×A Modern Daughter (Court, 7/7/08)
×The Debt (Aldw., 16/11/09, *m.*, Playwrights' Association: called originally *The Greater Love*)

GOGARTY, OLIVER ST JOHN [see '*A & O*']

GOLDBERG, MAX

[For earlier plays see *H. E. D.* v, 383]

The Rich and Poor of London (Osborne, Manchester, 12/3/00; Stand., 30/4/00)

Nell Gwynne (Croydon, 3/9/00; E.C., 5/11/00)

The Bank of England (Shak., Clapham, 26/11/00)

Secrets (O.H., Northampton, 12/8/01; Lyr., Hamm., 19/8/01: a revised version of *The Secrets of the Harem*, 1896)

The Hand of Justice (Eden, Brighton, 2/12/01; W.L., 9/12/01: revised version of his play originally performed in 1891)

Divorce (Lyr., Hamm., 5/5/02: called originally *Through the Divorce Court*)

Ancestors of the Crown (Gr., Glasgow, 23/6/02; Qns, Manchester, 19/9/04; Junction, Manchester, 6/3/11, as *The Heir to the Throne*)

Rogues of the Turf (Reg., Salford, 1/6/03; Dalston, 4/4/04)

Hard Times In Manchester (Vic., Broughton, 6/7/03: +*E. C. MATTHEWS*)

The Voice of the People (Star, L'pool, 2/5/04; Dalston, 14/11/04)

×Plucky Japan (Metro., Manchester, 8/5/05; Carlton, Greenwich, 7/5/06, as *The Plucky Nipper*)

A Night with the Stars ('*m.c.*': Scala, 11/2/07)

×A Ride to Win (Emp., Croydon, 14/9/08: also called *A Race to Win*)

Won by a Neck (Alex., B'ham, 18/4/21)

×Mademoiselle from Armentières (Alex., S. Shields, 8/8/27)

GOLDIE, JOHN

Business (Aldw., 19/3/11, St. Soc.)

GOLDIN, HORACE

×The Tiger God. LC, K's, Southsea, 1/8/13

GOLDMAN, LIONEL [see *J. G. LEVY*]

GOLDRING, DOUGLAS

The Fight for Freedom. *1919*

GOLDSMID, MURIEL CARMEL [see also *S. GORDON*]

Wasps ('*c.*': Roy., 27/11/06)

×Butterfly Kisses (Pav., Ryde, 30/8/09)

GONZALEZ, MANUEL

The Cleansing Stain (Qns, 4/2/17, Pioneer Players; Rep., B'ham, 21/9/20: adapted from José Echegaray, *Mancha que limpia*, 1895: +*C. SANDEMAN*)

GOODHART, CHARLES [see *CHARLES JAMES*]

[*GOODMAN, JULES ECKERT* [see also *M. GLASS* and *E. KNOBLOCK*]

The Man who Came Back (Stamford, Conn., 10/7/16; Playh., N.Y., 2/9/16; Oxford, 8/4/20)

Morals (Pleasure Gdns, Folkestone, 7/7/24; Wimbledon, 25/8/24)

[*GOODMAN, KENNETH SAWYER*

×A Man can only Do his Best (Gai., Manchester, 6/7/14)

[*GOODRICH, ARTHUR*
So This is London! ('*Anglo-American c.*': Hudson, N.Y., 30/8/22; P.W., 11/4/23)

GOODSALL, ARTHUR
×The Domestic Fowl (Camberley, 1/2/05)

GOODWIN, ERNEST
×The Devil among the Skins ('*f.*': Rep., B'ham, 8/5/15; Crit., 18/6/15) *1925*
Cupid in a Caravan ('*c.*': Emp., Swindon, 9/2/18, *m.*; Kings., 24/6/18)
The Spiritualist (Pal., Ramsgate, 3/5/20)
The Ring of Straw (Church House, Erdington, 2/2/26, *amat.*)
The Duchess of Siona ('*c.*': Church House, Erdington, 19/3/29, *amat.*)

GOODWIN, UNA M.
I Was a Stranger ('*Nativity pl.*') *1923*

GORDON, ALBAN
×Ingratitude. LC, Aquar., Brighton, 23/1/22
Eve Triumphant ('*c.*': K. G's H., 4/10/22)
×Good Men and True (K. G's H., 4/10/22) *1926*
×Peace. *1923*

GORDON, DAHLIA
The Bachelor Benedicts ('*f.c.*': Little, Hove, 25/11/26; Q, 13/2/28, as *Married Bachelors*)

GORDON, DOUGLAS
×Caesar Sups with Caesar ('*f.*': D.P., Eastbourne, 20/4/20)

GORDON, H. KENNETH
Dr Ching Fu. LC, New, Salisbury, 8/5/19
Krishna. LC, Hippo., Stratford-upon-Avon, 10/12/21

'*GORDON, HELEN*' [=*HELEN GORDON LIDDLE*]
The Crowd. *1927* (Village Drama Soc.)

GORDON, HERBERT
×A Rank Outsider (Sur., 10/6/12: +*M. BRADFORD*)

[*GORDON, LEON*
White Cargo (Greenwich Village, N.Y., 5/11/23; Playh., 15/5/24) *1925* (Boston)

GORDON, LESLIE HOWARD [see also *M. H. GORDON*]
×Gold Dust (Court, 24/10/13)

GORDON, MADGE HOWARD
The Borderer ('*r.pl.*': P's, Bristol, 18/11/21; K's, Hamm., 12/3/23: +*L. H. GORDON*)
The House of Unrest ('*mystery pl.*': Q, 23/12/25: +*L. H. GORDON*)

GORDON, SAMUEL
×Daughters of Shem (Roy., 20/5/66, Pioneers: +*M. C. GOLDSMID*)

GORDON-LENNOX, COSMO [=*'COSMO STUART'*: see also *R. HICHENS, A. HOPE* and *C. M. S. McLELLAN*]

The Little French Milliner ('*f.*': Aven., 8/4/02)

The Marriage of Kitty ('*c.*': D.Y., 19/8/02: adapted from Mme Fred de Grésac and F. de Croisset, *La passerelle*, 1902) *Fr. 1909*

How to Win Him ('*c.*': Aven., 17/3/03, *cpy.*; adapted from L. Xanrof and M. Carré, *Pour être aimée*, 1901)

Just Like Callaghan ('*f.*': Crit., 3/6/03: adapted from M. Hennequin and G. Duval, *Le coup de fouet*, 1901)

The Freedom of Suzanne ('*c.*': Crit., 15/11/04)

The Indecision of Mr Kingsbury ('*c.*': H., 6/12/05: from G. Berr, *L'irrésolu*, 1903)

×The Van Dyck (H.M., 16/3/07)

×The Impertinence of the Creature (Marlborough House, 10/6/07) *Fr. 1909*

The Smoke and the Fire ('*c.*': New, 17/9/07, *cpy.*: +*C. FITCH*)

Miquette (D.Y., 26/10/07: from G. A. de Caillavet and R. de Flers, *Miquette et sa mere*, 1906)

The Thief (St J., 12/11/07: from H. Bernstein, *Le voleur*, 1906)

Angela ('*f.c.*': Com., 4/12/07: from G. Duval, *Dix minutes d'arrêt*, 1905)

Rosalie ('*c.*': Shaft., 21/3/08; Com., 18/6/19, as *Wanted a General*, Punch and Judy Players)

×Box B (Roy., 26/6/17)

×Where are those — Matches? (Com., 18/6/19, Punch and Judy Players)

Sylvia's Lovers ('*c.o.*', m. B. Rolt: Portsmouth, 1/12/19; Ambass., 10/12/19: from P. C. Marivaux, *La double inconstance*, 1723) *1921*

GORE, ARTHUR HOLMES

×The Fatal Stockings ('*trifle*': Gr., Blackpool, 18/6/06)

×In the Arena (P's, Bristol, 19/7/06)

GORE, BLANCHE

×A Dangerous Neighbour. LC, Qns Gate H., 30/6/14

GORE, IVAN PATRICK [see also *D. MULLORD*]

×An Actress's Honour (Brit., 21/9/07, *cpy.*; Brit., 16/12/07: +*A. BELL*)

×My Butler (Hippo., Crouch End, 18/4/08)

×The Deputy (Olympia, Shoreditch, 9/11/08)

×The Garden of the Gods ('*m.pl.*', m. H. Weller: Pav., Eastbourne, 6/3/09: +*C. H. WILLIAMS*)

Out of the Darkness (W. Stanley, 12/7/09)

×Miss Smith of Pine Ridge (H.M., Aberdeen, 31/7/09, *cpy.*; Gr., Forest Gate, 15/8/10, as *A Prairie Wooing*)

×The Coming of the King (Sur., 20/9/09)

×Nick Carter (Var., Hoxton, 22/12/09, *cpy.*; S.W., 10/1/10: +*B. MERVYN*)

×Richelieu's Spy (Sur., 28/2/10)

×The Summing Up (Hippo., Woolwich, 20/6/10)

×Sinners Two (Hippo., Rotherhithe, 26/6/11)

×Cupid Intervenes (Clavier H., 23/4/12, Black Cat Club)
×A Lamb among the Wolves (Sur., 13/5/12)
×Pretoria's Love Story (Rehearsal, 16/9/12, Black Cat Club)
The Mormon and the Maid (Gr., Lancaster, 24/10/12)
Her One False Step (Stratford, 9/6/13)
Black Passion (Belfast, 11/8/13)
Les Miserables (Stratford, 10/11/13)
The Devil's Mistress. LC, Qns, Longton, 18/12/13
The White Hope (Hippo., Batley, 1/6/14; E.C., 19/10/14)
Love and the Woman (Metro., Glasgow, 28/7/14; Stratford 12/4/15)
Somewhere a Heart is Breaking (Leigh, 27/3/16; Stratford, 3/4/16)
That which is Forbidden. LC, Bij., Rye, 7/5/19
The Girl and the Drug. LC, County H., St Albans, 23/4/19
Her Honour at Stake (E.C., 5/5/19)
The Price of a Good Time (E.C., 11/8/19)
When Tommy Came Home. LC, New, Pontypridd, 22/4/19
The Law of Nature (E.C., 3/5/20)

GORE, ROBERT
×Counterfeit Coin (Court, Wigan, 4/10/01)

GORE-BOOTH, EVA
×Unseen Kings ('*mythological verse pl.*': Abbey, Dublin, 25/1/12) *1904*
The Triumph of Maeve. *1905*
The Sorrowful Princess. *1907*
×The Sword of Justice. *1918*

GORE-BROWNE, ROBERT F.
Cynara (Playh., 26/6/30: +*H. M. HARWOOD*: from the former's novel, *An Imperfect Lover*, 1929) *1930*

GORING, GRAEME
×His Last Refuge (K's, Edin., 29/4/12)

GORST, Mrs HAROLD (NINA, C. F.)
×Ede's Trouble (Studio Club, 29/5/18)

GOSTLING, Mrs FRANCES M.
×Joan's Kiss (Worthing, 25/1/09, *amat.*)
×Fanny's American (Worthing, 13/7/09, *amat.*)
×The Law of the Zingali (Worthing, 3/5/10; Worthing, 1/5/12, as *The Life of La Santerelli*; Clavier H., 14/7/12, Arts and Dram. Club)
Perkin Warbeck ('*r.d.*': Worthing, 12/2/12, *amat.*: +*W. R. T. STEAD*)
×Tea and Bannocks (Worthing, 13/2/12, *amat.*: +*S. C. MITCHELL*)
×Early One Morning (Worthing, 13/2/12, *amat.*; Clavier H., 14/6/12, Arts and Dram. Club)
×The Third Time (Clavier H., 14/6/12, Arts and Dram. Club)

GOTERE, EUGÈNE
By Whose Hand? (O.H., Harrogate, 2/12/05, *cpy.*; Rot., L'pool, 23/3/06)
The Love of a Life (Rot., L'pool, 24/6/07)

GOULD, Mrs FINLAYSON [see also *J. W. McLAREN*]
A Brass Farthing ('*c.*': Lyc., Edin., 24/5/16, *m.*)

GOULD, NAT
The Chance of a Lifetime (E.C., 27/10/09, *cpy.*; Kennington, 21/8/11)

GOULDING, EDMUND [see also *G. ENTHOVEN* and *E. SELWYN*]
×Out of the Fog (Emp., Camberwell, 21/10/12: called originally *Dawn*; title later to *The Underworld*: +*G. G. BROWN*)
×God Save the King (Pallad., 17/8/14)

GOULDSBURY, CULLEN
The Omelette Maker ('*oa.*': Kings., 17/3/08, *cpy.*: +*T. HOLLAND*)

GOW, ADA [see *R. H. GREY*]

GOW, RONALD
×Breakfast at Eight. *Fr. 1921*
×The Sausage ('*pl. for boys*') *1924*
×Under the Skull and Bones ('*pl. for boys*) *1929*

GOWANS, ADAM LUKE
×Gallant Cassian (Arts, 26/2/28, International Theatre: translated from A. Schnitzler, *Der tapfere Cassian*, 1909) *1914*
×The Intruder (translated from M. Maeterlinck, *L'Intruse*, 1890) *1915*
The Interlude of Youth (rendered into modern English) *1922*

GRACE, G.
×Too Late. LC, RADA, 27/1/25

GRACE, MAURICE
Joan of Arc, The Maid of Orleans ('*historical d.*': Qns, Manchester, 30/7/04)

'*GRAEME, ALASTOR*' [=*Mrs FREDERICK MARRYATT*]
Mummer Mystic Plays. *1900*
[This contains two short pieces: 1. *Cobwebs*; and 2. *What's Gone of Menie?*]

GRAHAM, BERTHA N.
×The Will and the Way (Bij., 21/3/01)
×Their Secret Selves (Studio, Victoria-street, 17/2/05, Amateur Players' Association)
×Our Picnic (Studio, Victoria-street, 7/2/06, Amateur Players' Association)
×A Rose with a Thorn ('*fantastic pl.*': Ladbr. H., 22/11/06)
×Pitch and Toss (Studio, Victoria-street, 6/2/07, Amateur Players' Association; Court, 15/11/11) *1913* (see below)
×Auntie of 'The Finger Post' (Crippl. Inst., 3/4/07)
×An Historical Incident ('*c.*': Studio, Victoria-street, 5/2/08)
×An Alien Star ('*t.*': Studio, Victoria-street, 5/2/08)
×A Lost Chance (Empress, 6/5/08; Rehearsal, 7/11/09)
Oop at Kierstenan's (Court, 20/12/08, Pl. Actors; Q, 15/3/26, as *Young Mrs Greenshaw*) *1929*

×Spoiling the Broth ('*c.*': Court, 3/3/09, Amateur Players' Association) *1913* (in *Spoiling the Broth, and Other Plays*)

[Besides the title play, this contains six other one-act pieces: 1. *Pitch and Toss* (see above); 2. *Oh! the Press* (Women's Inst., Victoria-street, 13/6/10); 3. *Taffy's Wife* (Lyc. Club, 11/5/11, *m.*; Vaud., 21/6/23, *m.*); 4. *The Land of the Free* (Cosmopolis, 27/1/13); 5. *A Rose with a Thorn* (see above); and 6. *The Little Red Box*]

×What the Woman Said (Studio, Victoria-street, 22/3/09)
×The Surprising Sermons (Lyc. Club, 25/2/10, *m.*)
×Securing a Fortune (Lyc. Club, 26/10/11)
×Under Canvass. *1911* (+*F. VERNON*)
×The Blue Bat (Lyc. Club, 4/11/13)
The Royal Way ('*modern Greek romance*': H., 4/5/15)
×Sara (M'sex, 8/11/18)
Rich Martha (Sheffield, 16/12/21)
×The Hero (Court, 15/6/25, *m.*)
×Lolotte (Paddington-street H., 7/12/25, *m.*)
The Corvan Conspiracy (Forum Club, 6/2/27: +*W. E. B. HENDERSON*)
The Manderson Girls (Playroom 6, 22/11/27) *1929*
The Wonderful Week (Cent., 21/3/30)

GRAHAM, DAVID

[See *H. E. D.* v, 386: in addition to *Rizzio*, this author published two other plays before the end of the nineteenth century – *Robert the Bruce* in 1884 and *King James the First* in 1887]

Darnley. *1900*
Pompilia (adapted from Robert Browning's *The Ring and the Book*) *1928*

GRAHAM, GLENDA V. M.

×All in the Day's Work. LC, Ath., Glasgow, 11/11/18
×Uncle Sam's Heiress. LC, Ath., Glasgow, 11/11/18

GRAHAM, HARRY [*HARRY JOCELYN GRAHAM*: see also *D. C. CALTHROP*, *D. FURBER*, *S. HICKS*, *G. E. JENNINGS*, *F. LONSDALE* and *P. A. RUBENS*]

×State Secrets (Crit., 23/2/14) *Fr. 1924*
Sybil ('*c.o.*', m. V. Jacobi: Academy, Baltimore, 3/1/16; Liberty, N.Y., 10/1/16; P's, Manchester, 27/12/20; Daly's, 19/2/21) *1915*
Whirled into Happiness ('*m.f.*', m. R. Stolz: Lyr., 18/5/22)
×The Buried Cable; or, Dirty Work at the Cross-roads (RADA, 13/1/24) *Fr. 1924*
Orange Blossom ('*c.*': Qns, 4/12/24)
The Grand Duchess ('*r.f.c.*': Glo., 20/2/25: adapted from A. Savoir, *La Grande-Duchesse et le garçon d'étage*, 1924)
By Candle Light ('*c.*': K's, Southsea, 10/9/28; P.W., 18/9/28: called originally *Wrong Number*) *Fr. 1930*
Hunter's Moon (P.W., 24/3/29, Sunday Pl. Soc.)
There's No Fool like a Young Fool (Arts, 8/5/29)

GRAHAM, MARTHA [=*HENRY BOWSKILL*]

GRAHAM, MORLAND

×C'est la guerre (Lyr., Glasgow, 21/10/26, Scott. Nat. Players) *1927* (in *The Scots Magazine*, vi, 241–50)

×A Matter o' Money. LC, Pav., Saltcoats, 30/1/28. *1928* (Glasgow)

×The Hoose wi' the Golden Windies (Bearsden, 9/3/28, Scott. Nat. Players) *1931* (Glasgow)

GRAHAM, ROSALIE

×Miss Susan Merridew's Dream. LC, Adult School H., Sutton, 10/11/25

GRAHAME, ARTHUR

×Iron Ann (+*ADELAIDE ST CLARE*) *Fr. 1910*

GRAHAME, RONALD

[For an earlier play see *H. E. D.* v, 387]

The Wicked City (Bristol, 30/9/01; E.C., 21/4/02: +*GUY LOGAN*)

Wanted by the Police (Cardiff, 29/7/07; Woolwich, 11/12/11)

Queen of the Wicked (Edmonton, 27/3/11; Brit., 24/7/11)

The Woman Tempted Me. LC, Gr., Swansea, 12/7/17

×The Tainted Woman. LC, Cinema, Evesham, 22/8/17

The Bolshevik Peril (Temperance H., Tredegar, 22/3/19)

Tainted Lives. LC, Hippo., Langley Moor, 24/9/19

GRAHAME, WILLIAM

×Just in Time (Court, 4/4/13: called originally *A Call in the Night*: +*G. NASH*)

GRAHAME, WINIFRED (*MATILDA WINIFRED MURIEL GRAHAME*, afterwards *CORY*)

Euthanasia. LC, Little, 21/12/21: +*H. L. DE CAUX*

Eve and the Elders (Kasino, Hampton Court, 2/11/24: from her own novel, 1924)

GRANDAGE, K. MALPASS

×The Kid ('*fant.*': Rehearsal, 14/4/12)

×The Passing of Alceste ('*terpsichorean t.*': Clavier H., 11/10/12)

The Woman's Choice (Gr., Halifax, 22/10/23: +*I. FIRTH*)

GRANGE, A. DEMAIN

[For an earlier play see *H. E. D.* v, 388]

×At the Rising of the Moon ('*Irish r.*': Cor., 1/4/01)

The Sweet Girl ('*m.pl.*', m. H. Reichardt: P'cess of W., Kennington, 28/7/02; Nottingham, 27/8/06, revised with *W. CAINE* and *H. COTTESMORE*)

×For a Dream's Sake ('*dream pl.*': Pier, Brighton, 27/11/02)

×Lady Marjorie's Wager (Marlb., Holloway, 26/4/05)

GRANT, ALEXANDER C. [see *G. E. CLIVE*]

GRANT, JACKSON

[A few sketches and playlets produced at music-halls]

GRANT, L. [see *S. M. EVEN* and *G. M. COHAN*]

GRANT, NEIL FORBES [see also *A. STEWART*]

×Policy 1313 (Vic. Pal., 30/1/13)

×A Valuable Rival (Crit., 11/5/14) *1922*

×The Three Sinners (Hippo., Golder's Green, 29/9/24) *1927*

×The Fox of Auchindoune. *1925* (in *The Scots Magazine*, iii, 115–25)

Possessions ('*c.*': Vaud., 23/1/25; Gar., 23/3/25) *Fr. 1925*

Getting Mother Married ('*c.*': Apo., 30/5/26, Pl. Actors; Hippo., Lewisham, 29/7/29)

Thy Name is Woman ('*c.*': Q, 16/8/26; Crit., 23/8/26)

×The Three Sinners. *1927*

×Telling the Tale. *1928*

Petticoat Influence (Str., 2/3/30, Rep. Players; St M., 3/6/30) *Fr. 1932*

GRANVILLE, DOROTHY M. C.

The Better Land (Qns, L'pool, 22/6/08; E.C., 27/7/14: called originally *The Woman with the Child's Mind, or, Married and Mad*)

An Old Man's Darling (P's, Preston, 18/3/09, *cpy.*; Qns, L'pool, 10/4/09)

The Doctor and the Great Problem (Bolton, 24/6/09, *cpy.*)

GRANVILLE, EDWARD

×'Enery Brown (T.H., Chelsea, 20/5/01; New, 23/6/03) *Fr. 1904*

GRANVILLE, FRED

The Woman God Gave Him (Woolwich, 1/12/13)

GRANVILLE-BARKER, HARLEY [=*HARLEY GRANVILLE BARKER*: see also *D. C. CALTHROP, LAURENCE HOUSMAN* and *C. E. WHEELER*]

[In 'The Early Plays of Harley Granville-Barker' (*Modern Language Review*, li, 1956, 334–8) Margery M. Morgan and Frederick May give an interesting account of this author's first contributions to the drama, and their 'List of Writings' printed as an appendix in C. B. Purdom's *Harley Granville-Barker* (1955), pp. 293–309, provides a general bibliography of his theatrical and other works. Between 1895 and 1898 he collaborated with Berte Thomas in the composition of five plays – *A Comedy of Fools, The Family of the Oldroyds, The Weather-Hen, Our Visitor to Work-a-Day* and an unfinished *Henry Esmond*. Typescripts of *The Family of the Oldroyds* and *Our Visitor to Work-a-Day* are in the British Museum, and the original text of *The Weather-Hen* (as performed at a matinée at Terry's Theatre on 29/6/1899) is included in the Lord Chamberlain's collection of plays submitted for licensing: a later revised version of this last piece is in private possession. It should be noted that Granville-Barker frequently made changes in reprintings of his dramas: the most important revisions are recorded in the following list]

Agnes Colander (written in 1901: typescript now preserved in the British Museum)

×A Miracle ('*experiment in verse*', written probably in 1902: Terry's, 23/3/07, Literary Theatre Soc.: typescript submitted for licensing in the British Museum)

The Marrying of Ann Leete (Roy., 26/1/02) *1909*
The Voysey Inheritance (Court, 7/11/05) *1909*; *1913* (revised); *1934* (revised)
Waste (Imp., 24/11/07, *m.*, St. Soc.; Sav., 28/1/08, *cpy.*, with emended text: originally refused licence, but eventually passed 8/12/20: a revised version was produced at the Westminster, 1/12/36) *1909*; *1926* (revised)
[*The Marrying of Ann Leete*, *The Voysey Inheritance* and *Waste* were also published as a collection in 1909 under the general title of *Three Plays*]
The Madras House (D.Y., 9/3/10) *1910*; *1925* (revised)
Anatol. *1911*
[This contains six playlets from Arthur Schnitzler's *Anatol* series, five of which were 'paraphrased' from the originals by Granville-Barker: 1. *Ask No Questions, and You'll Hear No Stories* (Pal., 6/2/11; Little, 11/3/11); 2. *A Farewell Supper* (Bij., 11/3/08, New Stage Club; Pal., 13/2/11; Little, 13/3/11: translated by *EDITH A. BROWNE* and *ALIX GREIN*); 3. *The Wedding Morning* (Pal., 27/2/11; Little, 11/3/11); 4. *A Christmas Present* (Little, 11/3/11); 5. *An Episode* (Little, 11/3/11); and 6. *Keepsakes* (Little, 18/3/11)]
×Rococo ('*c.*': Court, 21/2/11, *m.*) *1917* (published in a collection with *Vote by Ballot* and *Farewell to the Theatre*); *1925*
×The Morris Dance (Little, N.Y., 13/2/13: the original typescript is in the New York Public Library)
The Dynasts (Kings., 25/11/14: a stage version of Thomas Hardy's epic drama)
×Vote by Ballot (Court, 16/12/17, St. Soc.) *1917* (in collection, see above); *1930*
×Farewell to the Theatre. *1917* (in collection, see above); *1925*
The Romantic Young Lady ('*c.*': Roy., 16/9/20: adapted from *El Sueño de una noche de agosto* (1918) by G. Martínez Sierra: +*HELEN GRANVILLE-BARKER*) 1923 (in vol. 2 of the *Collected Plays* of Sierra); *1929*
[The other pieces included in the *Collected Plays* are *The Kingdom of God*, *The Two Shepherds* and *Wife to a Famous Man* – for all of which see below]
Deburau ('*c.*': Belasco, N.Y., 23/12/20; Ambass., 3/11/21: adapted from the play (1918) by Sacha Guitry) *1921*
The Two Shepherds (Rep., B'ham, 29/10/21): adapted from *Los Pastores* (1918) by G. Martínez Sierra: +*HELEN GRANVILLE-BARKER*) *1923* (in collection, see above); *1935*
The Kingdom of God (Abbey, Dublin, 21/10/23; Str., 26/10/27: adapted from *El Reino de Dios* (1916) by G. Martínez Sierra: +*HELEN GRANVILLE-BARKER*) *1923* (in collection, see above); *1927*
The Secret Life. *1923*
Wife to a Famous Man (Aldw., 25/5/24, Pl. Actors: adapted from *La mujer del heroe* (1914) by G. Martínez Sierra: +*HELEN GRANVILLE-BARKER*) *1923* (in collection, see above)

Doctor Knock ('*c.*': D.P., Eastbourne, 19/4/26; Roy., 27/4/26: adapted from the play (1923) by Jules Romains) *1925*

×Six Gentlemen in a Row (Playh., L'pool, 2/10/27: adapted from *Amédée, ou les messieurs en rang* (1923) by Jules Romains) *1927*

His Majesty. LC, Brighton, 26/3/27. *1928*

A Hundred Years Old (Glasgow, 30/4/28; Lyr., Hamm., 21/11/28: adapted from *Papà Juan, centenario* (1909) by S. and J. Álvarez Quintero: +*HELEN GRANVILLE-BARKER*) *1927*

Fortunato ('*t.f.*': Court, 22/10/28: adapted from the play by S. and J. Álvarez Quintero: +*HELEN GRANVILLE-BARKER*) *1927*

The Lady from Alfaqueque ('*c.*': Court, 22/10/28: adapted from *La consulesa* (1914) by S. and J. Álvarez Quintero: +*HELEN GRANVILLE-BARKER*) *1927*

The Women Have Their Way ('*c.*': Playh., Oxford, 26/11/28: adapted from *Pueblo de las mujeres* (1912) by S. and J. Álvarez Quintero: +*HELEN GRANVILLE-BARKER*) *1927*

GRANVILLE-BARKER, HELEN [see *HARLEY GRANVILLE-BARKER*]

GRATTAN, HARRY [*HENRY P. GRATTAN*]

[For earlier plays see *H. E. D.* v, 389, 794]

A Silent Vengeance (Leeds, 16/9/01; Metro., Camberwell, 7/10/01)

The M.I. (Mounted Infantry) (Com., 24/3/03: +*H. CLAYTON*)

×Packing Up. *Fr. 1904*

×The Plumbers (Qns, 29/1/10) *Fr. 1927*

×Buying a Gun (Hippo., Brighton, 16/1/11; Tiv., 30/1/11) *Fr. 1923*

Watch Your Step ('*f.ext.*', m. I. Berlin: Emp., Syracuse, 25/11/14; New Amsterdam, N.Y., 8/11/14; Emp., 4/5/15)

Flora ('*m.c.*', m. H. Darewski and M. Gideon: P.W., 12/3/18)

Jenny Wren ('*m.c.*', m. H. de Rance: Emp., 10/2/22)

×Man, the Brute. *Fr. 1928*

×Emma and 'Erb. *Fr. 1928*

[Several sketches and playlets produced at music-halls]

GRATTAN-CLYNDES, AIMÉE

Her Day of Reckoning (Roy., Chester, 22/1/17; E.C., 23/7/17: +*W. SALTOUN*)

Peg of the Pavement (Pal., Redditch, 4/11/18)

Soiled (Hippo., Maidenhead, 6/1/19; Stratford, 14/4/19, as *The Girl who took Drugs*: title later changed to *A Man's Plaything*)

What is Home without a Mother? LC, Bristol, 11/7/19: title later changed to *The Curse of Marriage* and *A Bad Woman*: +*W. SALTOUN*)

Seven Nights in London (Hippo., Maidenhead, 25/10/20; Stratford, 13/12/20)

A Mormon's Favourite Wife (Alex., B'ham, 16/10/22; Coll., 30/10/22: +*W. SALTOUN*)

She Got What She Wanted (Hippo., Burslem, 10/3/27)

GRAVELEY, GEORGE

The Last Hour and Other Plays. *1928*

[This contains five short plays: 1. *The Fisherman*; 2. *The Last Hour* (Fest., Cambridge, 14/5/28); 3. *The Safer Way*; 4. *The Mercy of Mathilde, A Tale of '93*; and 5. *A Knock in the Night* (St G., 12/10/24)]

×The Axe of Brandomar, or, The Death of the Woodman's Son. *1928*

GRAVELINS, J. E.

The Wundahwatte; or, The Princess's Dream ('*c.o.*', m. E. G. Scott: St Andrew's Parish R., Stoke Newington, 8/2/01)

The Millionairess ('*m.pl.*', m. E. G. Scott: Crippl. Inst., 15/2/04)

GRAVES, ALFRED PERCEVAL

×The Postbag ('*a lesson in Irish*', a '*m.pl.*', m. M. Esposito. LC, St G's H., 6/1/02)

The Progenitors, or, Our First Parents ('*morality*': an old Irish poem translated by A. P. Graves and dramatised by *MONA DOUGLAS*) *1929*

GRAVES, ARNOLD F.

Clytaemnestra. ('*t.*') *1903*

GRAVES, CLOTILDA INEZ MARY

[For earlier plays see *H. E. D.* v, 389, 794]

The Bishop's Eye ('*f.*': Vaud., 22/2/00)

Nurse! ('*f.*': Glo., 17/3/00)

The Lovers' Battle ('*heroical c. in rhyme*') *1902*

St Martin's Summer (Brighton, 7/2/02: +*Lady COLIN CAMPBELL*)

×A Maker of Comedies (Shaft., 9/2/03)

The Mistress of the Robes ('*c.*': Court, L'pool, 3/11/03)

The Bond of Ninon ('*c.*': Sav., 19/4/06)

The Other Side (P's, Manchester, 25/10/07; Gr., Croydon, 26/2/08)

×The General's Past ('*ca.*': Court, 3/1/09, Dram. Productions Club: title later changed to *The General's Glasses*) *1925*

GRAVES, FRANK

×A Scilly Season ('*c.o.*': Perth, 9/1/09, *amat.*)

GRAVES, ROBERT (ROBERT VON RANKE GRAVES)

John Kemp's Wager ('*ballad o.*') *1925* (Oxford)

GRAVES, W. P.

The Absentee ('*m.c.*': Court, 2/7/08, Irish Stage Soc.)

×The Postbag (Court, 3/7/08, Irish Stage Soc.)

GRAY, DELPHINE

×The Conference (Court, 6/2/16, Pioneer Players)

GRAY, DORA

×Oh! What a Day! LC, Bradford, 25/2/14

GRAY, ELEANOR

×Eros and Psyche. *1918*

×The Image Breaker ('*t.*') *1921*

GRAY, ERIC

×Base Coinage (Mem. H., Sanderstead, 18/4/25, *amat.*)

GRAY, Mrs H. J.

×The Test. LC, Cinema H., Penryn, 26/2/24

GRAY, LESLIE C.

×Which? (Pier, Eastbourne, 30/8/17, *m.*)

×Gunpowder Gertie of Gambler's Gulch ('*bsq.*': Pier, Eastbourne, 19/11/17, *amat.*: +*R. C. HICKS*)

GRAY, T. G. [see *R. CROMPTON*]

GRAY, TERENCE

The Life of the King of the South and North Kamaria ('*Egyptian history dramatised*') *1920* (Cambridge)

'And in the Tomb were Found –': Plays and Portraits of Old Egypt. *1923* (Cambridge)

[This contains four short pieces: 1. *The Building of the Pyramid*; 2. *The Nameless*; 3. *A Royal Audience* (Fest., Cambridge, 20/4/23); and 4. '*And in the Tomb were Found –*' (Fest., Cambridge, 30/5/27)]

Cuchulainn: An Epic Drama of the Gaels. *1925* (Cambridge)

Dance-Drama: Experiments in the Art of the Theatre. *1926* (Cambridge)

[This contains six short pieces: 1. *The Eternal Rhythm*; 2. *The Poisoned Kiss*; 3. *The Renaissance*; 4. *The Scorpions of Ysit*; 5. *The Cardinal's Bracelet*; and 6. *The Tremendous Lover*]

GRAY, TOM

×Her Hero. LC, New, Northampton, 3/1/14: +*J. BERNARD*

GREATHEAD, Mrs JOHN

The Master Carver (All Saints Parish R., Southend, 21/11/05)

GREAVES, H. B. [see *I. L. OSBORN*]

GREAVES, MARGARET E.

The Sun and the Wind. LC, St Peter's Church R., Boxhill, 10/5/24

GREEN, Mrs A. W.

Six Characters in Search of an Author (Kings., 26/2/22: translated from *Sei Personaggi in cerca d'autore* (1921) by Luigi Pirandello: another version, apparently, was used for the later performances of this drama at the Arts, 20/5/28, and the Globe, 28/5/28)

GREEN, ANGELA

Anna Morgan (Cent., 24/2/24)

GREEN, FRED

A Scheme that Failed (P's, Accrington, 16/7/08)

GREEN, HENRY GILLIDGE

Snow White (Gai., Manchester, 26/12/11)

GREEN, HERBERT

[For an earlier play see *H. E. D.* v, 392]

The Queen of Diamonds (Empress, Hartlepool, 10/5/01, *cpy.*; Chesterfield, 4/4/02)

[*GREEN, PAUL*
The Field God (Greenwich Village, N.Y., 21/4/27; Etlinger 30/9/27) *1927*

GREENAWAY, Mrs OLIVE C.
×Caprice (Pav., 11/3/14)
×Dawkins (Shaft., 19/4/19, *m.*)
×The Early Bird. LC, Metro., Abertillery, 31/12/20
[A few sketches produced at music-halls]

GREENBANK, PERCY [see also *L. BANTOCK* and *H. ELLIS*]
The Three Kisses ('*m.pl.*', m. H. Talbot: Apo., 21/8/07: +*L. BANTOCK*)
My Nieces ('*m.f.*', m. H. Talbot: Qns, 19/8/21)
Yvonne ('*m.pl.*', m. J. Gilbert and Vernon Duke: P's, Manchester, 24/12/25; Daly's, 22/5/26, *revised*)
×Cupid and the Cutlets ('*bsq. oa.*', m. P. Barrow: Q, 20/5/29)
×The House Agent ('*m.bsq.*', m. P. Barrow: Pav., Bournemouth, 18/11/29)

GREENE, ALICE CLAYTON
×Citizen Morat (Gr., Fulham, 20/4/04; Camden, 20/5/07)
×The Occult Science ('*f.c.*': Camden, 1/5/05)
×The Proof (O.H., Southport, 7/9/08; K's, Hamm., 26/4/09)
Aissé (Court, 13/5/10, *cpy.*)
×Dr Jekyll and Mr Hyde (Bed., 30/5/10)
×For the Sake of Charity (St Alban's Parish H., Acton Green, 30/5/10; New, Cambridge, 27/1/13; Clavier H., 17/4/13)
The Trap ('*c.*': Little, 17/1/11, *m.*, Oncomers' Soc.)

GREENE, RICHARD A.
The Angel of Unrest (Brighton, 4/3/07; Borough, Stratford, 25/3/07; Qns, Manchester, 30/5/10, revised as *The Man of Fate*)

[*GREENSFELDER, ELMER L.*
Six Stokers who Own the Blooming Earth (Gate, 5/7/28)

GREER, T. MacGREGOR
×Cross Purposes (Court, 18/12/13)
×The Compatriots (Court, 15/1/14)

GREEVEN, ALIX [=*Mrs J. T. GREIN*; = '*MICHAEL ORME*']

GREGORY, CHARLES
The Little Postmistress (Terry's, 31/12/02: +*W. FISHER*: from A. Capus, *La Petite fonctionnaire*, 1901)

GREGORY, ELIOT
Under the Old Flag (Glo., 19/4/00, *cpy.*)

GREGORY, ISABELLA AUGUSTA, Lady [see also *W. B. YEATS*]
×Colman and Guaire (written 1901) *1930* (as *My First Play*)
×The Twisting of the Rope (Gai., Dublin, 21/10/01; Boudoir, 2/5/11, Poetic Drama Soc.: adapted from the Gaelic of *DOUGLAS HYDE*) *1901* (in *Samhain*, no. 1, Oct. 1901); *1905*
×A Losing Game. *1902*
Twenty Five (Molesworth H., Dublin, 14/3/03, Irish Nat. Theatre Soc.; Qns Gate H., 2/5/03: revised from *A Losing Game*, above)

×The Lost Saint. *1902* (in *Samhain*, no. 2, Oct. 1902)
×Spreading the News ('*c.*': Abbey, Dublin, 27/12/04; St G's H., 27/11/05) *1904* (Dublin); *1907* (Dublin)
×An Fear Siubail. *1905* (in *Samhain*, no. 5, Oct. 1905)
Kincora (Abbey, Dublin, 25/3/05) *1905* (Dublin); *1912* (revised version, in *Irish Folk-History Plays*)
The White Cockade (Abbey, Dublin, 9/12/05) *1905* (Dublin)
×Hyacinth Halvey (Abbey, Dublin, 19/2/06; Gt. Qn. St., 12/6/07; Cor., 30/5/10) *1905* (Dublin)
The Doctor in Spite of Himself (Abbey, Dublin, 16/4/06: adapted from Molière's *Le Médecin malgré lui*, 1666) *1910* (Dublin: in *The Kiltartan Molière*, see below)
×The Gaol Gate (Abbey, Dublin, 20/10/06; Gt. Qn. St., 12/6/07) *1909* (Dublin: in *Seven Short Plays*)
The Canavans (Abbey, Dublin, 24/11 or 8/12/06; Court, 15/6/14) *1912* (Dublin: in *Irish Folk-History Plays*)
×The Jackdaw (Abbey, Dublin, 23/2/07; Gt. Qn. St., 11/6/07) *1909* (Dublin: in *Seven Short Plays*)
×The Rising of the Moon (Abbey, Dublin, 9/3/07; Gt. Qn. St., 12/6/07) *1904* (in *Samhain*, no. 4, Dec. 1904); *1906* (Dublin)
×The Poorhouse (Passmore Edwards Settlement, 4/6/04; Abbey, Dublin, 3/4/07: +*DOUGLAS HYDE*) *1903* (in *Samhain*, no. 3, Sept. 1903)
×Dervorgilla ('*t.*': Abbey, Dublin, 31/10/07; K's, Glasgow, 4/12/07; Court, 7/6/09) *1908* (in *Samhain*, no. 7, Nov. 1908); *1912* (Dublin: in *Irish Folk-History Plays*)
Teja (Abbey, Dublin, 19/3/08: adapted from the play (1896) by H. Sudermann)
The Rogueries of Scapin (Abbey, Dublin, 4/4/08; Court, 12/6/11: adapted from Molière's *Les Fourberies de Scapin*, 1671) *1910* (Dublin: in *The Kiltartan Molière*)
×The Workhouse Ward (Abbey, Dublin, 20/4/08; Court, 8/6/09) *1909* (Dublin: in *Seven Short Plays*)
The Miser (Abbey, Dublin, 21/1/09; Court, 14/6/13: adapted from Molière's *L'Avare*, 1668) *1910* (Dublin: in *The Kiltartan Molière*)
The Image (Abbey, Dublin, 11/11/09; Court, 1/6/10) *1910* (Dublin)
Mirandolina (Abbey, Dublin, 24/2/10; Everyman, 17/8/25: adapted from *La Locandiera* (1753) by Carlo Goldoni) *1924* (Dublin)
×The Travelling Man ('*miracle pl.*': Abbey, Dublin, 2/3/10; Court, 9/2/12, Morality Play Soc.: +*W. B. YEATS*) *1909* (Dublin: in *Seven Short Plays*)
×The Full Moon (Abbey, Dublin, 10/11/10; Court, 15/6/11) *1913* (Dublin)
×Coats (Abbey, Dublin, 1/12/10; Court, 14/6/11) *1913* (Dublin)
×The Nativity Play (Abbey, Dublin, 5/1/11: translated from the Gaelic of *DOUGLAS HYDE*)
The Deliverer (Abbey, Dublin, 12/1/11) *1912* (Dublin: in *Irish Folk-History Plays*)

×McDonough's Wife (Abbey, Dublin, 11/1/12, as *MacDaragh's Wife*) *1913* (Dublin: in *New Comedies*)
×The Bogie Men (Court, 8/7/12) *1913* (Dublin: in *New Comedies*)
Grania ('*t.*') *1912* (Dublin: in *Irish Folk-History Plays*)
×Damer's Gold (Abbey, Dublin, 21/11/12; Court, 16/6/13) *1913* (Dublin: in *New Comedies*)
×The Marriage (Abbey, Dublin, 25/9/13: translated from the Gaelic of *DOUGLAS HYDE*)
×The Wrens (LC, Court, 30/5/14; Abbey, Dublin, 27/12/21) *1922* (Dublin: in *The Image and Other Plays*)
Shanwalla (Abbey, Dublin, 8/4/15; Little, 17/5/15) *1922* (Dublin: in *The Image and Other Plays*)
The Golden Apple ('*a pl. for Kiltartan children*': Abbey, Dublin, 6/1/20) *1916* (Dublin)
×Hanrahan's Oath (Abbey, Dublin, 29/1/18) *1918* (Dublin)
The Dragon ('*wonder pl.*': Abbey, Dublin, 21/4/19) *1920* (Dublin)
Aristotle's Bellows (Abbey, Dublin, 17/3/21) *1923* (Dublin: in *Three Wonder Plays*)
×The Old Woman Remembers ('*dr. poem*': Abbey, Dublin, 23/12/23)
The Story Brought by Brigit ('*Passion pl.*': Abbey, Dublin, 14/4/24) *1924* (Dublin)
The Jester. *1923* (in *Three Wonder Plays*)
The Would-be Gentleman (Abbey, Dublin, 4/1/26: adapted from Molière's *Le Bourgeois Gentilhomme*, 1670) *1928* (Dublin: in *Three Last Plays*)
×On the Racecourse (a rewritten version of *Twenty Five*) *1926* (Dublin)
Sancho's Master (Abbey, Dublin, 14/3/27) *1928* (Dublin: in *Three Last Plays*)
×Dave (Abbey, Dublin, 9/5/27) *1928* (Dublin: in *Three Last Plays*)

GREGSON, JAMES RICHARD

[There is considerable confusion (and doubt) concerning the dates of this author's plays, and even some of his own statements must be regarded with caution]

T'Marsdens ('*c.*': Stockport, 15/10/17, *amat.*; Everyman, 30/4/23; Everyman, 21/10/27, revised by *M. ROSMER* and *M. MORLEY*) *1924*
The Way of an Angel and Other Plays. (*1928*: Huddersfield)

[This collection contains four one-act pieces: 1. *The Way of an Angel* (Temperance H., Huddersfield, 10/26, Huddersfield Thespians); 2. *Melchisedek* (Unitarian School, Fitzwilliam Street, Huddersfield, 21/11/24, Huddersfield Thespians – but dated 1923 in *Who's Who in the Theatre*); 3. *Liddy* (Carver Recreation Club, Marple, 10/12/19, Marple Literary and Dram. Soc. – but dated 1917 in *Who's Who in the Theatre*); and 4. *Youth Disposes* (Temperance H., Huddersfield, 3/2/21, Huddersfield Thespians)]

Young Imeson ('*c.*': Primitive Methodist School, Compstall, 29/3/19; Everyman, 17/3/24, *revised*: dated 1918 in *Who's Who in the Theatre*) *1924*

[The printed text records the Everyman Theatre production as 18/3/24, but seemingly the correct date is 17/3/24]
Sar' Alice (Alb. H., Leeds, 11/12/25) *1930*
× Morocco Calf (? 1926)
[This 'whimsy', constructed mainly by means of quotations from Shakespeare's plays, is dated 1926 in *Who's Who in the Theatre*, but no certain record of its existence has been found earlier than 1936]
Saint Mary Ellen (? 1928)
[Although dated 1928 in *Who's Who in the Theatre*, the first certain record of this play seems to be its production at the Players Theatre, 25/6/35]
The Devil a Saint ('*c.*': Playh., L'pool, 16/1/28) *1928* (Leeds)

GREIG, F. L. BILLINGTON
× A Meeting o' the Creditors (R. Inst. H., Glasgow, 19/1/23, Scott. Nat. Players)

GREIN, ALIX AUGUSTA [*Mrs J. T. GREIN*, née *GREEVEN*: ='*MICHAEL ORME*': see also *E. A. BROWNE* and *J. T. GREIN*]
[*Who's Who in the Theatre*, under this authoress' pseudonym of 'Michael Orme', gives her name as 'Alice Auguste Greveen', but the British Museum Catalogue, habitually accurate in these matters, records it as Alix Augusta]
A Happy Nook (Court, 25/6/01: translated from *Das Glück im Winkel* (1896) by H. Sudermann: as by *A. GREEVEN* +*J. T. GREIN*)
Renaissance ('*c.*': Shaft., 24/5/05: translated from a play (1897) by F. von Schoenthan and F. Koppel-Ellfeld: as by '*Miss ALIX GREEVEN*')
Those Who Sit in Judgment (St J., 19/9/04: as by '*MICHAEL ORME*')
La Pompadour ('*o.*', m. E. Moor: Sav., 26/1/11)
Wedding Bells ('*o.*', m. E. Moor: Sav., 26/1/11)
× The Widow and the Waiter (Qns, 3/6/15, *m.*; Kings., 26/7/15: as by '*MICHAEL ORME*')
The Eternal Snows (Crit., 28/5/16, Pioneer Players; Q, 6/2/28: as by '*M. ORME*')
× The Hôtel de Waterloo. LC, Court, 29/9/16
× The Woman at the Window-sill (Gr., B'ham, 18/6/17; Col., 31/12/17: this and the following plays were all presented as by '*MICHAEL ORME*')
× Cavalleria Rusticana (Kennington, 3/6/19, Independent Theatre: from the play (1884) by G. Verga)
× Great Aunt Elizabeth (Hippo., Nottingham, 27/10/19; called originally *Crinolines and Khaki*)
The Doctor of Dreams ('*c.*': P.W., 13/7/21, *m.*, from a Dutch play, *Femina*, by Soesman and Van Rossum)
Life'a a Game ('*c.*': Kings., 18/5/22)
× The Greatest Invention of All (Pal., Glasgow, 16/10/22; Vic. Pal., 30/10/22)

×From Information Received (K. G's H., 25/11/22)
×The New Manner (K. G's H., 25/11/22)
Tiger Cats ('*t.c.*': Sav., 25/6/24, *m.*; Gar., 11/8/24: adapted from a play by Karen Bramson)
The Folly of Youth ('*c.*': Gr., Croydon, 10/8/25)
Medusa (Pleasure Gdns, Folkestone, 8/3/26; Gar., 7/4/26, as *The Enchantress*; adapted from a play by Karen Bramson)
The Lady of the Camellias (Gar., 5/7/26, *m.*: adapted from *La Dame aux camélias* (1852) by A. Dumas fils)
Samson and Delilah (Arts, 17/7/27, Internat. Theatre Soc.; Little, 26/6/28, as *Samson and the Philistines*; revised with *KITTY WILLOUGHBY*: later called *A Modern Delilah*: adapted from *Samson og Dalila* (1909) by Sven Lange)
The Lonely Road (Q, 5/9/27)
Out of the Blue (Lyr. Hamm., 1/4/30: adapted from *Das Blaue vom Himmel* by Hans Chlumberg)

GREIN, JACOB THOMAS [see also *ALIX A. GREIN*, *M. LEONARD* and *C. M. ST JOHN*]
The Mouse ('*c.*': Com., 11/12/02: +*H. HOOTON*: adapted from *Le Souris* (1887) by E. Pailleron)
Fiamma (P.W., 9/1/03: +*H. HOOTON*: adapted from *La Fiammina* (1857) by Mario Uchard)
Midsummer Fires (Scala, 13/5/06; Gai., Manchester, 13/9/09, *revised*, +*ALIX A. GREIN*: adapted from *Johannisfeuer* (1900) by H. Sudermann)

GREME, I. T.
Irish Aristocracy ('*m.pl.*': Emp., Chiswick, 2/10/27)

GRENSIDE, DOROTHY
St Bride and the Mantle ('*mystery pl.*': Alb. H., 26/10/17, Players' Guild of the Theosophical Soc.)

GRENVILLE, EDWARD [see *A. ELIOT*]

GRESHAM, R. S.
Thieves of London (LC, Ilkeston, 4/7/04: K's, Hoxton, 28/1/07)

GREVILLE, HENRY
Vilma (Qns, Manchester, 3/10/04; Alex., 17/10/04)

GREVILLE, BEATRICE VIOLET, Baroness
[For earlier plays see *H. E. D.* v, 394]
Luck (Ryde, 19/11/00)
The Moth and the Candle (Wynd., 18/12/01, *cpy.*: +*M. AMBIENT*)
Dear Lady Mary ('*c.*': Vic. H., 21/2/05)
×By Chance (Daly's, 5/5/24, *m.*)

GREW, MARY
John O'Dreams ('*c.*': Little, 27/8/30: adapted from *Jean de la Lune* (1929) by M. Achard)

[*GREW, WILLIAM A.*
The House with the Purple Stairs (P.W., B'ham, 23/4/28)

GREY, ALAN [see also *M. PIREAU*]
[For earlier plays see *H. E. D.* v, 394]
The Battle of Life ('*c.*': Bij., 30/3/01, *cpy.*)

GREY, CLAYTON
× The Call (Philbeach H., 11/3/26, Columbus Soc.)

GREY, CLIFFORD [see also *F. THOMPSON*]
× 100 Years Ago ('*m.pl.*': Emp., Nottingham, 12/3/17: called originally *A Romantic Episode*)
The Smith Family ('*m.pl.*', m. N. D. Ayer: Hippo., L'pool, 28/8/22; Emp., 6/9/22: *S. LOGAN* and *B. PAGE*)
Mister Cinders ('*m.c.*', m. V. Ellis and R. Myers: O.H., Blackpool, 25/9/28; Adel., 11/2/29: +*G. NEWMAN*)

[*GREY, DAVID*
The Best People ('*c.*': Lyc., N.Y., 19/8/24; Gr., Blackpool, 8/3/26; Lyr., 16/3/26: +*A. HOPWOOD*) *Fr. 1928*

GREY, MARCUS
The Lion Tamer (Star, Wolverhampton, 10/7/02, *cpy.*: +*H. B. WILSON*)

GREY, R. HEATON [see also '*CECIL RALEIGH*']
× A 33 to 1 Chance (S.W., 12/7/09)
× Characters (K's H., Dover, 10/8/17, *m.*: +*A. GOW*)
Absent without Leave (Dalston, 15/10/17: +*A. GOW*)
[A few sketches produced at music-halls]

GRIBBLE, GEORGE DUNNING
× The Scene that was to write itself ('*t.c.*': University, L'pool, 21/11/24, *amat.*) *1924*
The Masque of Venice ('*c.*': Mansfield, N.Y., 2/3/26; Sav., 25/1/28) *1924*
The Translation of Nathaniel Bendersnap (Arts, 3/12/27, Interlude Theatre Guild) *1925*
Casanova ('*fant. chronicle*') *1928*
The Artist and the Shadow (Kings., 15/3/30)

GRIBBLE, HARRY WAGSTAFF
[Although he was born in England, this author's career was almost entirely associated with the American stage. During the present period at least, it would seem that only one of his several plays was carried back across the Atlantic]
March Hares ('*fant. satire*': Stamford, Conn., 5/8/21, as *The Temperamentalists*; Bij., N.Y., 11/8/21; Little, 22/6/25, *m.*; Little, Leeds, 8/3/26; Ambass., 12/12/27) *Fr. 1928*

GRIERSON, FLORA
The Tale of the Two Lovers (translated from the Latin *de duobus amantibus historia* by Enea Silvio Piccolomini, Pope Pius II) *1929*

GRIERSON, F. D.
Napoleon of Notting Hill ('*fant.c.*': Pier, Eastbourne, 12/1/20; Reg., 7/3/26, Pl. Actors, revised by *L. F. BERMAN*: +*G. C. W. MILES*: from the novel (1904) by G. K. Chesterton)

GRIFFIN, E. A.
×The Lucky Experiment. LC, Court, 19/5/13

GRIFFIN, W.
×Tod the Tailor (Arts, 29/12/27, Interlude Players)

GRIFFITH, HUBERT
×Two Points of View (K. G's H., 1/5/22, Pivot Club: called originally *A Modern Painter*)
Tunnel Trench (P's, 8/3/25, Rep. Players; Duchess, 25/11/29) *1924*
The Tender Passion. *1926*
The Tragic Muse (Arts, 1/7/28: from the novel (1894) by Henry James) *1927*
Red Sunday (Arts, 27/6/29) *1929*

GRIFFITHS, ETHEL
×Maude Bowen (O.H., Cheltenham, 18/5/09, *cpy.*) *1909* (as *The Black Maying; or, The Legend of Maude's Elm*)

'*GRIM, ANTHONY*' [=*ARTHUR LINECAR*]
×The Deliverer (Court, 24/6/13)

GRISMER, JOSEPH R. [see *L. B. PARKER*]

[*GRISWOLD, GRACE*
×His Japanese Wife (Bij., 15/12/07, Pl. Actors)
×Billie's First Love. LC, Gr., Wolverhampton, 10/6/08. *Fr. 1921*

GROGAN, WALTER E.
[For earlier plays see *H. E. D.* v, 395]
Nell Gwnn (Torquay, 9/5/01)
A Reformed Rake ('*c.*': Lyc., Edin., 14/2/02; Cor., 13/11/08: +*PELHAM HARDWICKE*]
×The Gamester ('*miniature o.*', m. Aiulf Hjovard: Belfast, 4/6/06; Cant., 28/10/07)
Pierrot and Pierrette ('*oa.*', m. J. Holbrooke: H.M., 11/11/09, *m.*, Afternoon Theatre) *1909*
The Blasé Baronet ('*c.*': Huddersfield, 14/1/10)
[A few sketches produced at music-halls]

GROSS, Mrs ALEXANDER
Break the Walls Down (Sav., 16/5/14)
The Forum Club and Her Sections ('*masque*': Forum Club, 1/1/20)

GROSSMITH, GEORGE Jr [see also *H. M. HARWOOD* and *ARTHUR MILLER*]
[For an earlier play see *H. E. D.* v, 395]
The Gay Pretenders ('*c.o.*', m. C. Nugent: Glo., 10/11/00)
Gulliver's Travels ('*m.pl.*', m. A. Barratt: Aven., 23/12/01)
×The Linkman; or, Gaiety Memories (Gai., 21/2/03)
The Love Birds ('*m.c.*', m. R. Roze: Sav., 10/2/04)
The Spring Chicken ('*m.pl.*', m. I. Caryll and L. Monckton: Gai., 30/5/05)
Two Naughty Boys ('*m.pl.*', m. C. Tippett: Gai., 8/1/06)
The Girls of Gottenburg ('*m.c.*', m. I. Caryll and L. Monckton: Gai., 15/5/07: +*L. E. BERMAN*)

Havana ('*m.c.*', m. L. Stuart: Gai., 25/4/08: +*G. HILL*)
×A Night of the Garter (Tiv., 1/8/10)
Peggy ('*m.pl.*', m. L. Stuart: Gai., 4/3/11)
The Guide to Paris ('*m.pl.*': Alh., 27/5/12)
The Bing Boys Are Here ('*picture of London life in seven panels*': Alh., 19/4/16: +*F. THOMPSON*)
×Step in the Office ('*f.*': Hippo., Bristol, 4/12/16; Col., 18/12/16)
The Cabaret Girl ('*m.pl.*', m. J. Kern: W.G., 19/9/22: +*P. G. WODEHOUSE*)
The Beauty Prize ('*m.c.*', m. J. Kern: W.G., 5/9/23: +*P. G. WODEHOUSE*)
Primrose ('*m.pl.*', m. G. Gershwin: W.G., 11/9/24: +*G. BOLTON*)
The Royal Visitor ('*c.*': H.M., 27/9/24: +*J. SOLANO*: from R. de Flers and G. A. de Caillavet, *Le roi*, 1908)
[Numerous sketches contributed to revues]

GROSSMITH, WEEDON [='*ROBERT LASCELLES*']
[For earlier plays see *H. E. D.* v, 395]
The Night of the Party ('*f.c.*': Emp., Southend, 1/4/01; Brixton, 8/4/01; Aven., 1/5/01)
The Cure ('*grim farce*': Gai., Dublin, 18/4/03; K's, Hamm., 8/6/03)
The Duffer ('*c.*': Com., 21/8/05)
Among the Brigands (B'ham, 25/10/07; Cork, 23/3/08, revised as *Billy Rotterford's Descent*; K's, Hamm., 11/5/08; Gar., 23/6/10, as *Billy's Bargain*: as by '*R. LASCELLES*')
The Mystery of Redwood Grange (Portsmouth, 1/3/09; Borough, Stratford, 8/3/09)
×A Ball or a Motor? (K's, Hamm., 14/2/10: as by '*R. LASCELLES*')
×How It's Done (Shaft., 14/7/10, *m.*; Emp., Kilburn, 27/3/11; Glo., 25/2/13; Col., 2/6/13)
[*The London Girl*, apparently not produced, is recorded in his *From Studio to Stage* (1913), pp. 321–2]

GROSVENOR, EDITH [see *J. H. DARNLEY*]

GROSWALD, MARGUERITE
Discontented Peter ('*fairy pl.*': Arts, 15/1/28, Internat. Theatre Soc.: from the Lettish of Anna Brigadere)

GROVE, JESSICA [see *O. RACSTER*]

GROVES, CHARLES [see *E. PHILLPOTTS*]

GROVES, WILLIAM E.
Redeemed (Dalston, 19/2/17)

GRUNDY, SYDNEY
[For earlier plays see *H. E. D.* v, 396–7, 795]
×Sympathetic Souls (P'cess of W., Kennington, 26/2/00) *Fr. 1900*
×The Head of Romulus (St J., 10/5/00) *Fr. 1900*
A Debt of Honour (St J., 1/9/00)

Frocks and Frills ('*c.*': H., 2/1/02: adapted from E. Scribe and E. Legouvé, *Les doigts de fée*, 1858)
The Garden of Lies ('*r.*': St J., 3/9/04)
The Diplomatists ('*f.*': Roy., 11/2/05: adapted from *La Poudre aux Yeux* (1861) by E. Labiche and E. Martin)
Business is Business ('*c.*': H.M., 13/5/05: adapted from O. Mirbeau, *Les Affaires sont les affaires*, 1903)
A Fearful Joy ('*f.c.*': H., 18/4/08: adapted from E. Labiche and E. Gondinet, *Les plus Leureux des trois*, 1870)
×The Right Sort (Gr., B'ham, 12/12/10; Emp., Finsbury Park, 23/1/12)
Mrs Thompson (Lyc., Sheffield, 8/2/15)

GUERNON, CHARLES [see *M. MARCIN*]

GUEST, ENID [='*SHIRLAND QUIN*']

GUGGISBERG, G.
×A Black Mark (Worthing, 9/12/07; Emp., Kilburn, 24/10/10)

GUILBERT, Inspector [see *B. LANDECK*]

GUILLEMAND, MARY E. [see *G. THOMAS*]

GUINAN, JOHN
The Cuckoo's Nest ('*c.*': Abbey, Dublin, 13/3/13) *1933* (Dublin)
The Plough-lifters ('*c.*': Abbey, Dublin, 28/3/16)
×Black Oliver (Abbey, Dublin, 16/5/27) *1927* (Dublin)

GUISE, E. S.
Between the Hills. LC, Midland Inst., B'ham, 11/3/15

GUISE, F. B. [see *P. A. WAYNE*]

GUNDREY, V. GARETH
The Edge of Life (Emb., 21/11/29)

GUNDRY, A. W.
The Cliff. LC, Amersham Common Schools, 21/4/22

GUNN, NEIL MILLER
The Ancient Fire (Lyr., Glasgow, 8/10/29)
×The Hawk's Feather. *1929* (in *The Scots Magazine*, xi, 328–40)

GUNTON, R. T.
×How He Lost His Train (Clavier H., 16/4/13)

GUPTA, KEDAR NATH DAS [*KEDARA NATHA DASA GUPTA*]
×Caliph for a Day: an amusing comedy (LC, Pier, St Leonards, 28/9/15) *1916* (Indian Art and Dram. Soc.)
×The Hero and the Nymph (Grafton Galleries, 27/10/16, Indian Art and Dram. Soc.: translated from Kalidasa, *Vikramorvasiya*)
×Bharata (K. G's H., 24/5/17, Union of East and West: +*MARGARET G. MITCHELL*) *1918* (Union of East and West)
×Malati and Madhara. LC, Lord Leverhulme's Garden, 11/7/17: translated from Bharabhuti, *Malatimadhava*)
×The Pearl Necklace. LC, The Hill, Hampstead, 12/7/19
[In 1918 this was advertised as published with the title *Ratnavali*,

or 'A Necklace', a 'romantic comedy', the original being attributed to King Sri Harsha. No copy, however, has been located]
× Life after Death. LC, K. G's H., 28/4/19
King Harischandra (The Hill, Hampstead, 12/7/19, Union of East and West: P.W., 16/10/19, *m.*, Indian Art and Dram. Soc., as *The Ordeal*: +*K. C. CHUNDER*)
Sakuntala (LC, Coronet, 1/1/14) *1920*
[It is not certain that the LC text is that of the published version]
Divine Vision (Wigmore H., 24/9/24, Union of East and West: adapted from a Bengali play, *Vilwamangal*, by G. C. Ghose)
[About 1918 an advertisement announced the publication of *The Little Clay Cart or 'Mrichchakati'*, adapted from the Sanskrit play attributed to King Sudraka, but no copy of this has been located]

GURNEY, EDMUND [see also *A. NEWMAN*]
× The Great Unknown (Qns, Poplar, 27/12/09)

GURNEY, GERALD G. [see *T. B. THALBERG*]

GURNEY, HAROLD ALFRED
× Get Me a Taxi. LC, Pal., Walthamstow, 26/7/21
The Prodigal Daughter (Aldw., 17/5/22, Playwrights' Theatre)

GURNEY, VAL
A Man of the People. LC, Woolwich, 13/7/14
× Missing (E.C., 14/5/15)
A Sinner in Paradise (New, Oxford, 20/2/19; Brixton, 25/8/19: called originally *All for Him*)
Smouldering Fires (Stratford, 21/3/21)
The Doctor's Temptation. LC, Gr., Woking, 4/4/21
× The Chestnut Tree (*'f. absurdity'*: Emp., Penge, 16/1/22: +*H. LANDECK*)
The Sheik of Araby (Rochdale, 2/7/23)
Suspicion (Darlington, 3/9/28)

GUTHRIE, THOMAS ANSTEY [=*'F. ANSTEY'*]

GUTHRIE, Sir TYRONE
× Victorian Nights (*'charade'*: Lyr., Glasgow, 8/11/27, Scott. Nat. Th. Soc.) *1937* (in J. Belfrage, *Let's Raise the Curtain*)

GUY-REEVE, R. [see also *W. EVANS*]
[Several sketches and playlets produced at music-halls]

GWYNFORD, —
Perthusan. LC, K. G's H., 27/3/24

GWYNN, A. STEPHEN
Fantasio (Oxford, 8/11/27: translated from the play (1866) by A. de Musset)

GWYNNE, VIOLET
A Singer's Love Story. LC, Scala, Newton, 9/9/19

HABERLY, LOYD
× When Cupid Wins, None Lose. *1927* (*priv.*)
Daneway (*'fairy pl.'*) *1929* (*priv.*)

HACKBLOCK, E. M.
×The Price of Leadership (Shaft., 13/7/20, *m.*)

[*HACKETT, WALTER* [see also *G. H. BROADHURST, F. M. CRAWFORD, R. C. MEGRUE* and *F. THURSTON*]
From Nine to Eleven (Wynd., 14/7/14)
Mr and Mrs Ponsonby ('*f.c.*': Com., 14/6/15)
The Barton Mystery (Sav., 22/3/16) *Fr. 1930*
×Wealthy Walter George (Theatrical Gdn Party, Regent's Park, 11/7/16)
Mr Jubilee Drax (H., 30/9/16: +*H. A. VACHELL*)
The Invisible Foe (Sav., 23/8/17)
×The Profiteers (Pav., 3/6/18)
The Freedom of the Seas (H., 1/8/18) *Fr. 1929*
Mr Todd's Experiment ('*f.*': Qns, 30/1/20)
Spanish Treasure (Brighton, 11/7/21; Crit., 19/7/21, as *Ambrose Applejohn's Adventure*) *Fr. 1923*; *1928* (revised)
Pansy's Arabian Night (Qns, 16/8/24)
The Wicked Earl ('*f.*': H.M., 22/2/27)
Other Men's Wives (Brighton, 2/4/28; St M., 9/4/28: called originally *The Maid*) *Fr. 1929*
77, Park Lane ('*adventure*': St M., 25/10/28) *Fr. 1928*
Sorry You've Been Troubled ('*c.*': St M., 24/9/29) *Fr. 1931*
The Way to Treat a Woman (D.Y., 11/6/30)

HADEN-GUEST, Mrs (CARMEL)
×The Proselyte (Portman R., Baker Street, 13/5/12) *1934*
×Mrs Murphy's Bet (Court, 29/1/14)

HADLEY, Mrs W.
The Pilgrim's Progress (Imp., 16/3/07: +*E. V. OULESS*)

HAGGARD, AUDLEY
Little Plays from the Greek Myths. *1929*
[This contains four short pieces: 1. *Pomona*; 2. *Midas*; 3. *Philemon and Baucis*; and 4. *Aurora and Tithonus*]

HAHN, GRETE
×Enchantment (Rehearsal, 2/12/09, *m.*; Pal., Chelsea, 30/5/10)
×Uncle at the Office (Rehearsal, 2/12/09, *m.*)
×The Other Man ('*wordless pl.*') *1913*

HAIG, ROTHWELL
Kynaston's Wife (St J., 10/5/12, *m.*: dramatised from his own novel, 1912)

HAINES, E. S. P.
×A Study in Bereavement (Little, 17/7/14)

HAINES, J., Jr
Nina's Dream ('*fairy story*': Gai., Manchester, 1/4/12)

HAINES, W. A. [see also *J. H. DARNLEY*]
×Joseph's Coat (D.P., Eastbourne, 17/5/15)

HALDANE, BERT
Grand Duchess Aboard ('*nautical oa.*': Star, Barrow, 29/9/02)
The Traitor (Carlton, Greenwich, 27/7/03)

HALE, C. M.
Reprisals. LC, Baths H., Moffat, 2/9/18

HALES, CLAUD
×The Folly of a Fool ('*oa.*', m. W. T. Gliddon: County, Kingston, 20/5/12)

HALFORD, JAMES
×The Secretary's Dilemma (Woodside H., Finchley, 25/4/14, *amat.*)

HALFORD-THOMPSON, EDITH
×Caillette, Jester (Exeter, 16/12/04)

HALIFAX, ROBERT
×The Sleeping Partner (St Peter's Parish H., Stockton, 18/5/11, *amat.*)

HALL, A. E.
Dixon's Divorce ('*f.*': Gai., Hastings, 20/3/11)

HALL, ALLAN [see also *LAURI WYLIE*]
The Third Party ('*f.c.*': Gai., Dublin, 18/3/29; Wimbledon, 5/8/29; Q, 30/9/29)

HALL, ARTHUR [see *H. ROBINSON*]

HALL, ATTE [see *L. WORRALL*]

HALL, CYRIL
×Griselda. LC, Nat. School, Meifod, 15/3/13

HALL, ELSIE M.
The Living Law (Gar., 1/6/30, Anglo-Danish and Lyc. Club Societies: translated from the Danish of Sven Lange and Jakob Knudsen)

HALL, GERTRUDE
×The Way Out. LC, T.H., St Andrews, 18/9/22: +*C. H. LESTER*

['*HALL, HOLWORTHY*' [=*HAROLD EVERETT PORTER*]
×The Valiant ('*t.*': H.M., 10/2/25, *m.*; Glo., 7/2/26: +*R. MIDDLEMASS*) *Fr. 1935*

HALL, HOWARD [see *C. SUMMER*]

HALL, MARSHALL
×Stella ('*o.*': Pallad., 8/6/14)

'*HALL, OWEN*' [=*JAMES DAVIS*]
[For earlier plays see *H. E. D.* v, 399–400]
The Silver Slipper ('*modern ext.*', m. L. Stuart: Lyr., 1/6/01) *1901*
The Girl from Kay's ('*m.c.*', m. C. Cook: Apo., 15/11/02; Adel., 8/6/14, American version as *The Belle of Bond Street*) *1903*
The Medal and the Maid ('*m.f.*', m. S. Jones: Lyr., 25/4/03)
Sergeant Brue ('*m.f.*': Str., 14/6/04: +*L. LEHMANN*) *1904*
The Little Cherub ('*m.pl.*', m. I. Caryll: P.W., 13/1/06; P.W., 5/5/06, as *A Girl on the Stage*)

HALL, S. ELIZABETH
The Revolt of Siena. *1927*

HALL, T. H.

The Government Inspector (D.Y., 13/4/20: translated from N. Gogol, *Revizor*, 1836)

HALL, W. LEMON

The Return of Sybil (Kings., 9/4/22, Pl. Actors)
The Tyranny of Home ('*c.*': Everyman, 16/12/24)

HALL, W. STRANGE [see also *L. M. LION*]

The Stormy Petrel ('*c.*': K's, Glasgow, 25/7/07)
Reconstruction (Aldershot, 11/8/19)

HALL, WILFRED

The Crimson Club ('*md.*': Oldham, 11/5/03; Camden, 15/6/03; Carlton, Saltley, 8/8/10, as *The King of Diamonds*: +*M. JAMES*)

HALL, WILLIAM

× Hushed Up (Gr., Leeds, 4/6/03)
The Vale of Content ('*c.*': O.H., Southport, 19/12/03)

'*HALL-PAGE, M.*' [=*MARIE MENZIES*]

A Rogue's Daughter (Macclesfield, 4/2/03, *cpy.*; Alex., Sheffield, 7/3/04; Carlton, Greenwich, 23/10/05)

HALLIDAY, J., Jr

× A-lad-in, and well out of it (Alb. H., 22/3/09)

HALLING, DAISY [see also *N. TOWERS*]

The Fire Witch ('*mystic d.*': Edmonton, 20/6/04)
Jumbo in Rumboland ('*socialist bsq.*': Parkhurst H., Manchester, 8/1/10, *amat.*)
Pinnacles of the Future (Parkhurst H., Manchester, 12/2/10)
The Forest of Holyoakes ('*pl. for children*') *1927* (Manchester)

HALLIWELL, ALEXANDER L.

Detective Death; or, The Sign of the Scarlet Cross (Pal., New Brighton, 12/11/02, *cpy.*)
× A Woman Fiend ('*t. playlet*': L'pool, 4/2/05, *cpy.*)

HALLWARD, CYRIL R.

[For earlier plays see *H. E. D.* v, 401]
× Two Up and One to Play (Kennington, 24/8/03)
The Sadducee and the Sinner (Manchester, 29/2/04; Kennington, 6/6/04)
The Sister-in-Law (Wynd., 3/8/16)

[*HALMAN, DORIS F.*

× Will-o'-the-Wisp (Etlinger, 14/7/27)

HALSEY, ALICE

× Pam, the Wonder-child. *1926*
× The Fairy Grasshopper. *Fr. 1926*
× An Infant Prodigy. *1929*
× Chris. *1929*
× Bargains and Dilemmas. *1929*
× At a Mannequin Parade. *1929*

HALSEY, FREDERICK [see *L. ARTHUR*]

HALYS, NEVIN

The Hut above the Tarn, and Other Plays. *1930*

[This contains, besides the title-play, eight one-act plays: 1. *Two Shadows*; 2. *The Miser*; 3. *The Echo*; 4. *The Woodcutter's Daughter*; 5. *Gemma*; 6. *Cornelia in Scotland*; 7. *Mrs Witch*; and 8. *Rosemund*, as well as '*a family chronicle in three parts*' entitled *George and David*]

HAMBLING, HORACE S.
×The Owl (City Art Gallery, York, 19/10/02, *amat.*)

HAMILTON, BERYL [see *COSMO HAMILTON*]

HAMILTON, CHRISTINA DALZIEL
Eight Plays for Children. *1925*
[This contains eight short pieces in verse intended for very young children]

HAMILTON, CICELY MARY
×The Serjeant of Hussars (Bij., 23/6/07, Pl. Actors)
×Mrs Vance (Vic. H., 27/10/07, Pl. Actors)
Diana of Dobson's (Kings., 12/2/08) *Fr. 1925*
×How the Vote was won (Caxton H., 15/4/09: +*C. ST JOHN*) *1909*
×The Pot and the Kettle (Scala, 12/11/09: +*C. ST JOHN*)
A Pageant of Great Women. *1910*
Just to Get Married ('*c.*': Little, 8/11/10) *Fr. 1914*
×The Home Coming (Aldw., 18/11/10, *m.*; Cor., 12/3/14, as *After Twenty Years*)
The Cutting of the Knot (Roy., Glasgow, 13/3/11; Little, 9/2/13, Pioneer Players, as *A Matter of Money*)
×Jack and Jill and a Friend (Kings., 8/5/11, *m.*, Pioneer Players; Pav., Glasgow, 15/4/12, as *Jack and Jill*) *Fr. 1911*
×The Constant Husband (Pallad., 19/2/12)
Lady Noggs ('*c.*': Com., 15/2/13)
Phyl (Pier, Brighton, 10/3/13; Gai., Manchester, 13/5/18)
×The Lady Killer. LC, Little, 3/4/14
The Child in Flanders ('*Nativity pl.*': Excelsior H., Bethnal Green, 20/12/19) *Fr. 1922*
×Mrs Armstrong's Admirer. LC, Excelsior H., Bethnal Green, 21/1/20
The Brave and the Fair. LC, Excelsior H., Bethnal Green, 16/2/20
The Human Factor ('*c.*': Rep., B'ham, 8/11/24; Kings., 17/11/25, as *The Old Adam*) *1926*
The Beggar Prince ('*fairy pl.*': Emb., 26/12/29)

HAMILTON, COSMO (see also *R. BARR*, *P. GIBBS*, *S. HICKS*, *B. HOOD* and *A. C. SMEDLEY*)
[For earlier plays see *H. E. D.* v, 401]
×The Policy of the Ostrich (Terry's, 22/1/00)
×The Fortune of War (St J., 2/7/01: title later changed to *Old Crimea*)
The Wisdom of Folly ('*ridiculous piece*': Com., 9/10/02) *Fr. 1902*
×Aubrey Closes the Door (Concert H., Blackheath, 28/1/04) *Fr. 1904*

×The Proud Laird. LC, H., 8/5/05 (+*CHARLES CARTWRIGHT*)
The Mountain Climber ('*f.*': Com., 21/11/05)
A Sense of Humour ('*c.*': Com., 7/1/06; Playh., 31/8/09, revised: +*B. HAMILTON*) *1909*
Castles in Spain ('*c.o.*', m. H. Fragson: Roy., 18/4/06)
×The Traveller Returns (Pier, Brighton, 11/5/06; Wynd., 12/9/06, as *The Sixth Commandment*)
[It should be noted that in *Who's Who in the Theatre* this play is listed both under Cosmo Hamilton and Cicely Hamilton]
×Gran'father Coquesne (Gar., 25/6/06)
Pro Tem. ('*f.c.*': Playh., 29/4/08: adapted from *Le Boût-en-train* (1908) by A. Athis)
×A Soldier's Daughters (Kings., 14/5/08, *m.*) *1911* (see below)
Arsène Lupin (D.Y., 30/8/09: adapted from the play by F. de Croisset and Maurice Leblanc, based on the latter's novel, 1908)
The Merry Peasant ('*oa.*', m. L. Fall: Str., 23/10/09; Str., 20/11/09, *revised*)
×Toller's Wife (T.H., Chiswick, 3/12/09) *1911* (see below)
A Bolt from the Blue (D.Y., 6/9/10: adapted from T. Bernard and A. Athis, *Le costaud des épinettes*, 1910)
Mrs Skeffington (Qns, 21/10/10)
Short Plays for Small Stages. *1911*
[This contains five one-act plays: 1. *In the Haymarket*; 2. *Toller's Wife* (see above); 3. *Why Cupid Came to Earl's Court*; 4. *St Martin's Summer*; and 5. *A Soldier's Daughters* (see above)]
The Blindness of Virtue (Little, 29/1/12: dramatised from his own novel, 1908)
×Marriage (Gr., Croydon, 6/9/15)
Scandal (Washington, D.C., 17/6/18, as *She Burnt Her Fingers*; Str., 7/12/18) *1925* (in *Four Plays*)
The Silver Fox (Woods, Atlantic City, 8/5/21; Maxine Elliott, N.Y., 5/9/21; St M., 2/11/25: adapted from F. Herzceg, *A kék roka*, 1917) *1925* (in *Four Plays*)
His Highness below Stairs ('*c.*': Buffalo, 24/11/23, as *The New Poor*; Playh., N.Y., 7/1/24, with later title of *Guess Again*; New, Oxford, 16/11/25: also called *Who Are They?*) *1925* (in *Four Plays* as *The New Poor*); *Fr. 1929* (as *Who Are They?*)
Mr Pickwick (H., 15/12/28: +*F. C. REILLY*) *1929* (New York: as *Pickwick*)
×Two Women (Sav., 13/1/29, Lyc. Club)
Gentlemen – The King! ('*r.c.*': K's, Southsea, 28/10/29; Gr., Croydon, 4/11/29)
[It should be noted that almost all the plays written by Hamilton after about 1915 were clearly intended for production on the American stage and that the above list includes only those few pieces which were later acted in England. It is also to be observed that no information has been found regarding two early plays included in the relevant entry in *Who's Who in the Theatre* – *The Hoyden* and *The Master Key*]

HAMILTON, GODFREY

×The Aspidistra (Crippl. Inst., 10/4/26, Quill Club Players)

HAMILTON, HAMO

A Perfect Day (Dalston, 27/5/18)
One Hour of Love (Lyr., Hamm., 15/7/18; title later changed to *One Night*)
The Drudge of the Family (Leicester, 10/7/19)
Giovanna of Naples (Leicester, 26/12/19)
When There's Love at Home (Leicester, 5/4/20)

HAMILTON, HENRY [see also *C. RALEIGH*]

[For earlier plays see *H. E. D.* v, 401–2]
The School Girl ('*m.c.*', m. L. Stuart: P.W., 9/5/03: +*P. M. POTTER*) *1903*
The Duchess of Dantzic ('*c.o.*', m. I. Caryll: Lyr., 17/10/03) *1903*
Veronique ('*c.o.*', m. A. Messager: Apo., 18/5/04)
The Little Michus ('*c.o.*', m. A. Messager: Daly's, 29/4/05) *1905*
Robin Hood ('*r.*': Lyr., 17/10/06: +*W. DEVEREUX*)
Moths (K's, Hamm., 14/10/07, *revised*: from the novel (1880) by Ouida)
The Devil (P.W., B'ham, 8/4/08, *cpy.*; Adel., 17/4/09: from *Ar Ördög* (1907) by F. Molnár)
×A Russian Tragedy (H.M., 25/11/09)
Bardelys the Magnificent (B'ham, 29/8/10; Glo., 21/2/11: +*R. SABATINI*)
×Joan of Arc (Col., 3/4/11)
Autumn Manoeuvres ('*m.pl.*', m. E. Kalman: Adel., 25/5/12)
The Crown of India ('*imperial masque*') *1912*
The Best of Luck ('*spect.d.*': D.L., 27/9/16: +*A. COLLINS* and *C. RALEIGH*)

HAMILTON, J. R. C.

Love and the Sword (Hippo., Chesterfield, 7/12/25)
The Black Moth (Gr., Derby, 16/8/26)
The Crimson Crescent ('*mystery pl.*': Darlington, 16/5/27)
The Mist (Darlington, 4/6/28)

HAMILTON, JOHN

×The Magic Sieve. *1908* (Dublin)

HAMILTON, M.

The Dishonour of Frank Scott (Belfast, 7/9/00, *cpy.*: dramatised from his own novel, 1900)

HAMILTON, PATRICK

Rope (Str., 3/3/29, Rep. Players; Ambass., 25/4/29) *1929*
×The Procurator of Judea (Arts, 2/7/30)

HAMILTON, SIDNEY

×The Telegram (Brinsmead Galleries, 27/2/08)
×The Dream Picture (Empress, 19/10/10, *m.*)

HAMILTON-MOORE, EUNICE

×Love and Hate in Corsica (Vic. H., 4/12/06, *cpy.*)
×A Man's Shirt (Vic. H., 4/12/06, *cpy.*; Gai., Manchester, 18/10/09, as *The Dove Uncaged*; Roy., 20/2/12)

HAMLEN, GEORGE J.

Barbara Grows Up ('*c.*': Roy., Glasgow, 6/9/09; Little, 12/11/12) *1911*

×How Cottle Fell from Grace (Roy., Glasgow, 22/8/10) *1911*

The Truth about Dr Courcy ('*c.*': Roy., Glasgow, 26/11/09, *cpy.*; Glasgow, 14/3/10: +*A. WAREING*) *1911*

Colin in Fairyland ('*m.pl.*', m. A. Cazabon: Roy., Glasgow, 22/12/10) *1911*

The Waldies (LC, Roy., Glasgow, 3/5/12; H., 8/12/12, St. Soc.) *1914*

HAMMERSLEIGH, BEVIS

A Sister's Shame (P's, Portsmouth, 4/12/22)

HAMMERSLEY, R. STEVENS

×A Crown of Laurel (T.H., Leek, 19/2/03, *amat.*)

[*HAMMERSTEIN, OSCAR, II* [see also *O. HARBACH*]

The Desert Song ('*m.pl.*', m. S. Romberg: Poli's, Washington, 25/10/26, as *Lady Fair*; Casino, N.Y., 30/11/26; D.L., 7/4/27: +*O. HARBACH* and *F. MANDEL*) *1932*

Show Boat ('*m.pl.*', m. J. Kern: D.L., 3/5/28) *1934*

The New Moon ('*r.m.pl.*', m. S. Romberg: D.L., 4/4/29: +*F. MANDEL* and *L. SCHWAB*) *1935*

HAMMOND, AUGUSTUS

What Became of Totman ('*m.c.*', m. A. Cooke: Glo., Deal, 3/6/01)

HAMMOND, J. A. B. [see *W. CAINE*]

HAMPDEN, JOHN [see *SHEILA KAYE-SMITH*]

HAMPTON, SYDNEY L.

Lolita ('*c.o.*': Hippo., Hulme, 20/11/18)

[A few sketches produced at music-halls]

HAMUND, ST JOHN [see also *O. TREVINE* and *G. SQUIRES*]

×The Ruby Ring ('*m.ca.*': P.H., Sydenham, 9/5/02: +*A. S. BEAUMONT*)

×Making Him Jealous ('*f.*': Scala, 17/7/11)

×Our Grand-daughter ('*ca.*': Scala, 7/8/11)

×What about it? ('*m. trifle*': Scala, 23/3/13)

×Looking Charley Up. LC, Scala, 21/6/13

×Love. LC, Scala, 5/12/13

×Her Perfidy. LC, Scala, 6/1/14

×Milner's Safe. LC, Scala, 9/3/14

×The War Menagerie. LC, Scala, 1/4/15

HANCOCK, Mrs G.

Out of the Mist (Elm H., Leigh, 7/5/23: called originally *Dupes*: title later changed to *His Wife's Secret*)

HANDS, CHARLES E.

Madame Sherry ('*m.pl.*', m. H. Felix: Apo., 23/12/03) *1903*

HANFORD, IAN

The Song of the Torch (Margate, 13/5/07; K's, Hamm., 15/7/07)

HANKIN, ST JOHN (ST JOHN EMILE CLAVERING)

[For an earlier play see *H. E. D.* v, 402]

Mr Punch's Dramatic Sequels. *1901*; *1925* (as *Dramatic Sequels*)

[This contains thirteen amusing, although of course not theatrical, short skits on twelve popular plays and one poem, the *Rubaiyat* of Omar Khayyam: 1. *Hercules Vinctus* (for *Alcestis*); 2. *The New Wing at Elsinore* (for *Hamlet*); 3. *More Ado about Nothing* (for *Much Ado about Nothing*); 4. *The Other Critics* (for *The Critic*); 5. *The Relapse of Lady Teazle* (for *The School for Scandal*); 6. *Still Stooping* (for *She Stoops to Conquer*); 7. *In the Lyons Den* (for *The Lady of Lyons*); 8. *The Vengeance of Caste* (for *Caste*); 9. *Out of Patience, or Bunthorne Avenged* (for *Patience, or, Bunthorne's Bride*); 10. *The Third Mrs Tanqueray* (for *The Second Mrs Tanqueray*); 11. *The Lady on the Sea* (for *The Lady from the Sea*); 12. *Octavian and Cleopatra* (for *Caesar and Cleopatra*). The collection, with the addition of *The Unfortunate Mr Ebbsmith* (for *The Notorious Mrs Ebbsmith*), was later published as *Dramatic Sequels*, 1925]

The Two Mr Wetherbys ('*middle-class c.*': Imp., 15/3/03, St. Soc.) *1912* (in *Dramatic Works*); *Fr. 1921*

The Three Daughters of M. Dupont (K's H., 13/3/05; Ambass., 8/6/17: adapted from E. Brieux, *Les trois filles de M. Dupont*, 1897) *1911* (in *Three Plays by Brieux*)

The Return of the Prodigal ('*c. for fathers*': Court, 26/9/05) *Fr. 1908*

The Charity that Began at Home ('*c. for philanthropists*': Court, 23/10/06) *Fr. 1908*

The Cassilis Engagement ('*c.*': Imp., 10/2/07, St. Soc.) *Fr. 1908*

[The preceding three plays were also published as a collection entitled *Three Plays with Happy Endings*, *1908*]

×The Burglar who Failed (Crit., 27/10/08) *1912*

The Last of the De Mullins ('*c.*': H., 6/12/08, St. Soc.) *1909*

×The Constant Lover ('*c.*': Roy., 30/1/12) *Fr. 1912*

Thompson ('*c.*': Roy., 22/4/13: +*G. CALDERON*) *1913*

HANNAN, CHARLES

[For earlier plays see *H. E. D.* v, 402–3]

Mrs Westerfield –? (Batley, 2/7/00)

A Cigarette-Maker's Romance (Court, 11/2/01: dramatised from the novel (1890) by F. Marion Crawford) *Fr. 1911*

×The Gipsy (Kidderminster, 6/5/01; Court, 21/1/04)

The Clockwork Man ('*f.c.*': Richmond, 12/12/01; K's, Hamm., 4/4/04, as *The Electric Man*; Roy., 10/11/06)

×Richard Wye (Pav., Brighton, 1/3/02)

×The Coachman with Yellow Lace (Gr., Glasgow, 11/9/02, *cpy.*; Lyr., Hamm., 25/3/07)

The World's Way (Pav., 18/5/03; Lyr., Hamm., 8/5/05, as *The Whitechapel King*; Alex., Hull, 8/7/18, as *Vagabond Jo*: called originally *The Way of the World*)

Valentine and Pauline (D.Y., 30/7/03, *cpy.*)

Sweet Olivia (Leamington, 27/3/03; W.L., 29/3/05: from Oliver Goldsmith's novel *The Vicar of Wakefield*)

United States (‘*f.c.*’: O.H., Crouch End, 5/3/06)
Iron Hand and Velvet Glove (Gai., Douglas, 24/6/09)
A White Secret (W. Bromwich, 4/12/11)
×The Lodgers (Pal., Battersea, 9/12/12)
×Men is sich Fules (‘*Scottish c.*’: Empress, Brixton, 29/1/13; Pav., 7/2/13, revised as *The Lost Sheep*)
The Missing Volume (Merthyr Tydfil, 29/9/21)

HANNAN, JACK R.
The Gay Girl (‘*m.c.*’: T.H., Matlock, 23/11/03)

HANNAY, Rev. JAMES OWEN [=‘*GEORGE BIRMINGHAM*’]

HANRAY, LAWRENCE
Autumn Roses (Gai., Hastings, 24/7/11)
×A Roman Holiday (Playh., L'pool, 15/4/12)

HANWORTH, S.
×Mr Gradgrind's System (P's, Llandudno, 3/7/06, *cpy.*)

HAPGOOD, FRANCIS E. C.
False Dawn (Bristol, 8/11/26)

[*HARBACH, OTTO* [see also *W. COLLINSON, O. HAMMERSTEIN, W. A. McGUIRE* and *F. MANDEL*]
The Little Whopper (‘*m.c.*’, m. R. Friml: Ford's, Baltimore, 22/9/19; Casino, N.Y., 13/10/19; Shaft., 20/4/20: +*B. DUDLEY*)
The Blue Kitten (‘*m.c.*’, m. R. Friml: Apo., Atlantic City, 26/12/21; Gai., 23/12/25: +*W. C. DUNCAN*)
Wildflower (‘*m.pl.*’, m. H. Stothart and V. Youmans: Gr., Wilkes-Barre, 26/1/23; Casino, N.Y., 7/2/23; Alh., Bradford, 1/2/26; Shaft., 17/2/26: +*O. HAMMERSTEIN*) *1937*
Rose Marie (‘*m.pl.*’, m. R. Friml and H. Stothart: Imp., N.Y., 2/9/24; D.L., 20/3/25: +*O. HAMMERSTEIN*) *1931*
Sunny (‘*m.c.*’, m. J. Kern: Forrest, Philadelphia, 9/9/25; New Amsterdam, N.Y., 22/9/25; Pal., Manchester, 21/9/26; Hippo., 7/10/26: +*O. HAMMERSTEIN*) *1934*

HARBERTON, CHARLES
Doña Quixote, or, The Mad Proxy. *1926* (Oxford)

HARBURY, CHARLES
The King's Diamond (‘*c.o.*’, m. M. Ball: County, Kingston, 23/5/04)

‘*HARCOURT, CYRIL*’ [?=*CYRIL PERKINS*; see also *S. COOKE*]
The Axis (‘*c.*’: Worthing, 12/9/04; Crit., 5/7/05)
The Reformer (‘*very light c.*’: Court, 8/1/07, *m.*)
A Place in the Sun (‘*c.*’: D.P., Eastbourne, 21/7/13; Com., 3/11/13) *Fr. 1914*
A Pair of Silk Stockings (‘*c.*’: Crit., 23/2/14) *Fr. 1920*
In the Night (Star, Buffalo, 18/9/16, as *Husband, Wife, Man*; Cohan and Harris, N.Y., as *The Intruder*; Kings., 31/12/19)
×Wanted, a Husband (‘*c.*’: P'cess, Montreal, 1/5/16, as *A Lady's Name*; Maxine Elliott, N.Y., 15/5/16; Playh., 9/5/17)

Will you Kiss Me? ('*c.*': Com., 16/11/20: called originally *Too Much Efficiency*)
Just a King ('*c.*': D.P., Eastbourne, 9/2/25; Lyr., 5/5/25)

HARCOURT, ROBERT VERNON
An Angel Unawares ('*light c.*': Bournemouth, 31/7/05; Terry's, 12/9/05)
A Question of Age ('*c.*': Court, 6/2/06)

HARCOURT-WILLIAMS, E.
×The Enchanted Rose (Manchester, 30/4/07, *cpy.*)

HARDIE, JAMES M. [see *W. A. BRABNER*]

HARDING, BERT [see *H. CORRIN*]

HARDING, Mrs D. F. C. [see also *G. B. STERN*]
The Fixed Idea (Court, 15/12/13)
×Signs of the Times (Court, 7/2/18)
×The Safety Valve. LC, Crit., 15/5/18
×According to the Evidence (Ambass., 26/2/20, *m.*, +*B. LEVEAUX*)

HARDING, J. BERTRAM
×The Last Hour of Sosaria (Rehearsal, 7/12/14)

HARDING, NEWMAN [see also *F. HUME*]
×The Flute of Pan ('*dance idyll*', m. G. W. Byng: Playh., 3/3/10, *m.*)

HARDING, THOMAS WALTER
Oliver, an historical play; and Nina Balatka, or, A Maiden of Prague. *1926* (Cambridge)

HARDING-DAVIS, R.
×Miss Civilisation (D.P., Eastbourne, 10/11/14; Col., Glasgow, 26/2/23)

HARDINGE, GEOFFREY
The Flail of Fate (New, Hawick, 13/10/11)
×His Mother (Glasgow, 12/8/12)
×The Broken Vase (Edin., 19/8/12)

HARDINGE, HENRY
Dr Meredith's Experiment (Balfour Inst., L'pool, 23/2/07)
A Woman in Earnest (Balfour Inst., L'pool, 10/1/14)
The Siege (Etlinger, 16/7/25)

HARDINGE, HENRY C. M. [see also *S. J. DUNCAN* and *A. L. ELLIS*]
The Barrier Between (Windsor, 22/7/01; Metro., Camberwell, 2/3/03, as *The Broken Barrier*)
Diane (S. Shields, 11/4/04)
×The Dancer (Court, 20/3/05)
The Little More ('*c.*': Court, 20/3/05)
×Why Not? (New, 2/11/05)
Strangers within the Gates (Court, 7/2/09, Dram. Productions Club)

Carnival (B'ham, 5/5/19; New, 5/2/20: +*M. LANG*: adapted from Pordes-Milo, *Sirocco*) *Fr. 1927*
By-Ways (Glo., 6/4/26)

HARDINGE, MAURICE
The Illustrious Stranger ('*c.o.*', m. H. W. Norman: Dover, 16/7/06)

HARDWICKE, PELHAM [see *W. E. GROGAN*]

HARDY, Mrs
Riding for a Fall ('*c.*': Court, 14/7/19, *m.*)

HARDY, EMIL [see *F. ALFORD*]

HARDY, G. M. [see *G. M. GATHORNE-HARDY*]

HARDY, THOMAS
[For earlier plays see *H. E. D.* v, 404]
The Dynasts. *1903–8*
The Famous Tragedy of the Queen of Cornwall at Tintagel in Lyonesse (Corn Exch., Dorchester, 28/11/23, *amat.*; Glastonbury, 21/8/24, as an o., music by R. Boughton) *1923*
Tess of the D'Urbervilles (Corn Exch., Dorchester, 26/11/24, *amat.*; Barnes, 7/9/25; D.Y., 23/7/29)
[See *Tess in the Theatre*, ed. Marguerite Roberts, 1950, which reproduces two versions]

HARDY, VIOLET
Daphne Decides. LC, Conservative Club, Nuneaton, 17/3/14

HARE, AMORY
Tristam and Iseult. *1930* (*priv.*)

HARE, ARTHUR
The Vengeance of Mrs Vansittart ('*c.*': Gar., 16/7/01: +*H. EVES*)
The Lady and the Lion (P's, Manchester, 14/6/04: +*A. PEARSE*)

HARE, HENRY
× The Better Policy (Cor., 16/7/00)

HARE, IRENE
Our Dear Relations ('*f.c.*': Pier, Eastbourne, 5/12/21; Q, 17/8/25: +*J. R. HARE*)

HARE, J. ROBERTSON [see also *I. HARE*]
× The Silent Witness (Pal., Camberwell, 29/3/20)
The Dark Room (Str., 13/11/27, Rep. Players: +*S. LYNN*)

HARE, KENNETH
The Return to Nature (Lyr., Hamm., 14/3/20, Curtain Group and People's Theatre Soc.)

HARE, TREBOR
The Parish Watchman ('*c.*': Com., 10/7/21, Pl. Actors)
Olwen Comes Home ('*pl. of modern Welsh life*': New, Cardiff, 15/10/23)

HARGREAVES, REGINALD

×A Question of Tactics (Gai., Manchester, 27/5/12)

×Re-adjustment ('*c. of inversion*': K's H., 22/6/13, Playfellows)

Love's Prisoner ('*m.pl.*': Adel., 6/2/25)

HARGREAVES, ROBERT

×Spring Cleaning. LC, K's, Southsea, 5/10/20

×Crêpe de Chine. LC, Emp., Islington, 17/12/20: +*S. J. DAMERELL*

HARINDRANATH CHATTOPADHYAYA

Five Plays. *1929*

[This contains five short dramas: 1. *The Hunter*; 2. *Pundalik*; 3. *Tukaram*; 4. *The Proclamation*; and 5. *Saku Bai*]

HARKER, Mrs LIZZIE ALLEN [see also *CHARLES GARVICE*]

×Spy and Siren. LC, Pav., Glasgow, 26/5/15: +*F. R. PRYOR*

×Her Proper Pride ('*c.*': Rep., B'ham, 18/3/16: +*F. R. PRYOR*) *Fr. 1928*; *1937* (in Jean Belfrage, *Let's Raise the Curtain*)

'Marigold' ('*Arcadian c.*': Kings., 21/4/27: +*F. R. PRYOR*) *Fr. 1928*

[This is evidently a complete rewriting of the *Marigold*, written by Charles Garvice and A. F. Abbott, presented at Glasgow in 1914: for this, see under *CHARLES GARVICE*]

HARNETT, ST CLAIR [see *G. EDEN*]

HARRADEN, BEATRICE

The Dictionary (Bournemouth, 30/6/05, *cpy.*)

×Lady Geraldine's Speech ('*suffragist ca.*': Guildhall School of Music, 15/7/09, *amat.*)

×The Outcast (Scala, 12/11/09: +*B. HATTON*)

×The Traveller and the Temple of Knowledge. *1911* (in Emily Pertwee, *A Second Little Book of Twentieth Century Duologues*)

HARRILD, FRED

×The Interlude. LC, Village H., Orpington, 2/1/14)

HARRIS, BERNARD K.

These Internationals (Gar., 26/2/28, Jewish Drama League)

HARRIS, CLIFFORD

×Somewhere in France (Hippo., Eastbourne, 14/5/17; Col., 28/5/17)

The Lads of the Village ('*m.c.*': Oxf., 11/6/17: +'*VALENTINE*')

The Silver Lining ('*m.f.*': Hippo., Keighley, 19/7/17: +'*VALENTINE*')

HARRIS, E.

Blue Beard ('*bsq.*': Sheffield Garrick Dram. Club, 12/10/12)

HARRIS, FRANK

Mr and Mrs Daventry (Roy., 25/10/00)

Shakespeare and His Love. *1910*

The Bucket Shop (Aldw., 5/4/14, St. Soc.)

Joan la Romée. *1920* (Nice: *priv.*); *1926*

HARRIS, JAMES RENDEL
The Return of the 'Mayflower'. *1918*; *1919* (rewritten)
The Finding of the 'Mayflower'. *1920*
The Last of the 'Mayflower'. *1920*
The Masque of the Apple. *1920*

HARRIS, SYBIL
Daniel (Gai., Manchester, 29/11/20; St J., 15/1/21: adapted from the play (1920) by L. Verneuil and G. Berr)

HARRIS, W. H.
×The Kill (Little, 28/3/21)

HARRIS, WILLIAM
The Skylark ('*m.pl.*', m. F. G. Dossert: Ladbr. H., 10/3/10, *cpy.*)
Pouff, Pouff, Tally-Ho! *1926* (Aberdeen)

HARRISON, ADELINE
×The Devil's Tinsel ('*d.fant.*': Worcester, 19/6/11)
[It is uncertain whether this appeared on 19/6 or 17/7/11]
×Billetted (Imp. Club, Lexham Gdns, 3/7/13)
×Willing to Sleep In. LC, Hippo., Coventry, 28/5/21

HARRISON, ARTHUR [see *H. COTTESMORE*]

HARRISON, CHARLES JAMES [='*CLIVE HOLLAND*']

HARRISON, CYRIL
[A few sketches produced at music-halls]

HARRISON, EDITH
×Stage Struck ('*f.*': Rehearsal, 16/9/12, Black Cat Club)

HARRISON, FORBES
×The Homecoming. LC, Scala, 2/9/22
×Chivalry. LC, Scala, 5/10/22
×The Wisdom of Luxor. LC, Scala, 21/2/23: +*J. DENTON*

HARRISON, FREDERIC
Nicephorus: A Tragedy of New Rome. *1906*

HARRISON, FREDERICK
The Queen of Love ('*c.o.*', m. J. T. Klee: O.H., Leicester, 13/12/00)

HARRISON, L. S.
×Memories. LC, P.W., Rugby, 28/11/22

HARRISON, W. H.
Only Human (Aven., Sunderland, 25/4/06, *cpy.*)

HARRY, F. T. [see *W. DEXTER*]

HART, DOROTHY [see *G. FESTING*]

HART, ERNEST J.
Mrs Swallow ('*f.c.*': Gai., Manchester, 16/3/08)
×What Railing Did (Granville, Walham Green, 24/5/09)

HARTE, BRET [see *T. E. PEMBERTON*]

HARTE, ELIZABETH
Mr. Murphy's Island ('*c.*': Abbey, Dublin, 16/8/26)

HARTFORD, W. S. [see *C. A. CLARKE* and *W. A. TREMAYNE*]

HARTLEY, STEPHEN [see *F. A. R. LEAD*]

HARVEY, ALAN MARTIN
Something Beautiful. *1930*

HARVEY, ARMIGER
A Living Clue (E.C., 9/3/03: +*H. HOKEN*)

HARVEY, FRANK
[For earlier plays see *H. E. D.* v, 408–9]
The Mother (Rochdale, 5/7/00)
The Cotton Spinner (Gr., Fulham, 22/7/01)
The Milestones of Life (Com., Manchester, 3/8/01; Pav., 19/8/01)

HARVEY, FRANK
The Last Enemy (Fortune, 19/12/29) *1930*
Cape Forlorn (Fortune, 31/3/30)

HARVEY, J. M.
×A Woman's Instinct (Saffron's R., Eastbourne, 12/12/13, *amat.*)

HARVEY, K.
Hiawatha. LC, Crippl. Inst., 1/10/13
×Courage. LC, Crippl. Inst., 17/2/14

HARVEY, PRUDENCE
×She'll Do. LC, Portsmouth, 9/6/23

HARVEY, R. M. [see *HAROLD SIMPSON*]

HARVEY-PELLISSIER, W.
What's She Like? ('*m.c.*': County, St Albans, 24/4/16)

HARWOOD, HAROLD MARSH [see also *R. F. GORE-BROWNE* and *F. T. JESSE*]
×Honour Thy Father (Little, 15/12/12, Pioneer Players) *1926*
Interlopers (Roy., 15/9/13: called originally *Paternity* and *Wife or Mother*) *1926* (as *The Supplanters*)
Please Help Emily (Playh., 27/1/16) *1926*
Theodore & Co. ('*m.pl.*', m. Ivor Novello and J. D. Kern: Court, L'pool, 4/9/16; Gai., 19/9/16: +*G. GROSSMITH*) *1915* (lyrics only)
×The Confederates (LC, Wynd., 15/6/17; Ambass., 24/2/30: +*GABRIELLE ENTHOVEN*) *1926*
The Grain of Mustard Seed (Ambass., 20/4/20) *1926*
A Social Convenience (Roy., 22/2/21) *1926*
Eileen ('*light c.*': Glo., 27/5/22)
Excelsior (P's, 13/12/25, St. Soc.; Playh., 5/9/28: adapted from P. Armant and M. Gerbidon, *L'École des cocottes* (1918): called originally *Ginette*)
The Transit of Venus (Ambass., 26/4/27) *1927*
The Golden Calf (Emp., Sheffield, 29/8/27; Glo., 14/9/27)
A Girl's Best Friend ('*c.*': Ambass., 22/10/29) *1929*
The Man in Possession (Ambass., 22/1/30) *1930*

HARWOOD, JOHN

The Pick of Oakham, or, The Girl with the Bad Habit. (+*L. TREVOR*) *Fr. 1910*

×Molly and I and the Baby (Blackburn, 17/6/12)

The Black Torture, or, Spottem from the Yard ('*bsq.*': Theat. Gdn Party, Chelsea, 3/6/13)

×Outwitted (Gai., Manchester, 25/5/14)

×The Ladies' Seminary (Gai., Manchester, 3/4/15)

HASBROUCK, LASCELLES

The Shadow of a Lie (Ladbr. H., 10/1/07, *amat.*)

Life's Golden Key (Little Vic., Brighton, 21/7/24)

HASSELL, MARIE

The Hundredth Woman (P.W., B'ham, 10/5/04, *cpy.*)

HASTINGS, BASIL MACDONALD [see also *B. BAIRNSFATHER, S. LEACOCK* and *E. PHILLPOTTS*]

×Double Dummy (Crippl. Inst., 8/3/10, *amat.*)

The New Sin (Roy., 20/2/12; Crit., 6/5/12) *Fr. 1912*

Love – and What Then? ('*c.*': Playh., 2/5/12) *Fr. 1912*

The Tide ('*emancipated md.*': Qns, 14/12/12; Qns, 30/12/12, *revised*) *1913*

Advertisement (Kings., 15/4/15) *Fr. 1915*

×The Fourth Act (Col., 17/7/16) *Fr. 1916*

A Certain Liveliness ('*revue*': St M., 17/2/19)

Victory (Glo., 26/3/19: from the novel (1915) by Joseph Conrad)

Hanky Panky John ('*c.*': Gai., Manchester, 15/11/20; Playh., 31/1/21)

Any Woman Would. LC, Gai., Manchester, 11/1/21

'If Winter Comes –' (Hippo., Margate, 3/8/22; St J., 31/1/23: +*A. S. M. HUTCHINSON*: from the latter's novel, 1921) *1928*

Faithful Philanderers ('*c.*': Str., 12/6/27, Rep. Players)

HASTINGS, HAROLD

Raleigh (Gr., Lancaster, 30/11/22, *amat.*)

Jeanne d'Arc. *1924*

HASTINGS, Lady KATHLEEN

An Unknown Quantity ('*c.*': Conservative Club, Nuneaton, 9/1/13, *amat.*)

×Zara. LC, Adel., 16/5/14

×Clouds (Court, 30/6/14)

HASTINGS, Sir PATRICK

The River (St J., 2/6/25)

Scotch Mist (St M., 26/1/26) *1926*

HASTINGS-WALTON, GLADYS [see also *O. SILVERSTONE* and *E. WHITTY*]

Honour among Thieves ('*md.*': Pal., L'pool, 24/2/08)

×Texas Jess (Bed., 10/10/10)

×The Pipes of Hamelin. LC, O.H., Coventry, 28/1/14

The Madman ('*md.*': Barnsley, 15/6/14)

×A Pierrot in the Case. LC, Hippo., Peterborough, 24/7/15

A Woman in Khaki. LC, Jarrow, 10/9/15
The Black Sheep of the Family (Stratford, 22/5/16)
If Love Were All (Rot., L'pool, 3/7/16; E.C., 4/12/16)
Somebody Knows, Somebody Cares (E.C., 17/7/16)
Let No Man Put Asunder (Hippo., Altrincham, 26/12/16; Woolwich, 26/11/17; E.C., 3/12/17)
The Light that Leads Me Home (Alh., Stourbridge, 26/12/16; E.C., 4/6/17)
The Heart of a Woman (Gr., Accrington, 8/1/17)
The Roll of Honour ('*md.*': Junction, Manchester, 24/12/17; Stratford, 21/1/18)
A Broken Doll ('*md.*': Barnsley, 31/12/17; Woolwich, 27/5/18; E.C., 3/6/18)
The Woman who Lied (Hippo., Queen's Park, Manchester, 18/11/18; Stratford, 9/6/19)
Betrayed (Metro., Glasgow, 24/3/19: called originally *Brother o' Mine*)
Motherhood (Barnsley, 21/4/19; Stratford, 29/3/20)
×Two Women (Etlinger, 30/10/19)
The Story of Judith (Vic., Stanley, 6/11/19)
Three Women – and a Man (Sunderland, 8/12/19)
The Child Pays. LC, Olympia, Stirling, 18/12/19
Temptation (S. Shields, 27/2/20; Stratford, 23/1/22)
Drifting Apart (Stratford, 14/2/21)
The Way of a Man (Stratford, 25/4/21)
The Wanton (Barnsley, 3/10/21)
King of My Heart (Stratford, 3/4/22: called originally *Give a Dog a Bad Name* and *Kit Come by Chance*)
The Legend of Mab's Cross ('*Lancashire d.*': Court, Wigan, 24/7/22)
A Soul for Sale. LC, O.H., Scarborough, 13/3/23
The House of Red Lanterns. LC, Court, Wigan, 20/11/24

HATCH, BEATRICE

Scenes from Cranford. *Fr. 1902*

[This contains seven short sketches intended for amateur performance]

HATHERLEIGH, J. P.

Affairs at the Shrubbery ('*fant.c.*': Paisley, 9/3/08, *amat.*: +*P. M. ROBERTS*)

HATHERLEY, VIOLET

The Cruise of the Constance ('*m.c.*': Worthing, 10/6/09; Brixton, 10/10/10, as *The Girl on the Boat*: +*C. WINCHCOMB*)

HATTON, BESSIE [see also *B. HARRADEN*]

×The Village of Youth (St J., 18/3/09, *m.*)

[This play had been performed by amateurs in the Rectory Grounds, Radstock, 12/7/1899: see *H. E. D.* v, 409]

×Before Sunrise (Alh., 22/2/10, *m.*; Little, 24/1/11, *m.*) *1911 (priv.)*

[*HATTON, FANNY LOCKE* [see *L. DIETRICHSTEIN* and *FREDERICK HATTON*]

[*HATTON, FREDERICK*
Years of Discretion ('*c.*': LC, Dalston, 22/10/12; Glo., 8/9/13: +*F. L. HATTON*)

HATTON, HILDA
×The School for Snobs (P.H., Dorking, 25/1/09)
For the Land We Love; or, Only a Territorial (Lyc., Stafford, 4/11/10)

[*HATZAN, A. L.*
[A few sketches produced at music-halls]

[*HAUERBACH, OTTO*
Katinka ('*m.pl.*', m. R. Friml: 44th Street, N.Y., 23/12/15; O.H., Leicester, 2/4/23; Shaft., 30/8/23: +*B. DAVIS*) *1948*

HAVELOCK, HENRY
Lights Out (Waldorf, 25/10/05: adapted from F. A. Beyerlein, *Zapfenstreich*, 1903) *1905*

HAVERS, WALTER
[A few sketches produced at music-halls]

HAVILAND, ALEXANDER J.
The Price of Silence ('*md.*': Pal., Ramsgate, 13/1/13)
×Acting Mad (Rehearsal, 7/3/13)

HAWKINS, Sir ANTHONY HOPE [='*ANTHONY HOPE*']

HAWKINS, E. J.
The Seed and the Fruit. LC, '*pageant pl. of the Pilgrim Fathers*': K's H., St Thomas, Exeter, 17/11/20. *1920* (Exeter)

HAWKINS, LANWARNE
[For earlier plays see *H. E. D.* v, 410]
The President's Daughter; or, A Soldier's Sweetheart ('*m.c.*': Morecambe, 17/6/01: +*F. V. LAWTON*)
The Forbidden Thing (Vic. H., Hanley, 21/2/20: called originally *Lying Spirits*)

HAWKINS, LESLIE
Topsy-Turvy Times ('*m.pl.*': Alex., Widnes, 6/12/07; Margate, 22/6/08, as *The Gay Deceivers*, revised with *F. STANMORE* and *M. LESTER*; Alex., Stoke Newington, 9/8/09)
The Right Mr Wrong ('*m.pl.*', m. G. Burton: Gr., Luton, 3/6/12: called originally *Mischief Makers*)
The Swindlers. LC, Hippo., Huddersfield, 12/8/19

HAWKINS, MARJORIE
×A Military Pickle (Crippl. Inst., 25/4/08, *amat.*)

HAWTREY, Sir CHARLES
The Great Name ('*c.*': P.W., 7/9/11: adapted from *Der grosse Name* (1909) by V. Léon and L. Feld)

HAWTREY, GEORGE PROCTER
[For earlier plays see *H. E. D.* v, 410]
Lord of His House ('*c.*': O.H., Coventry, 9/6/02; Com., 12/6/02)
The Gloucestershire Historical Pageant (Cheltenham, 6/7/08) *1908* (Cheltenham)

'*HAY, IAN*' [=*JOHN HAY BEITH*; see also *S. HICKS*]
Getting Together ('*patriotic pl.*': Harmanus Bleecker H., Albany, 11/3/18; Lyr., N.Y., 18/3/18: +*J. HARTLEY MANNERS* and *PERCIVAL KNIGHT*)
Tilly of Bloomsbury ('*c.*': Apo., 10/7/19; musical version as *Tilly* by *H. CLAYTON* and *C. WEST*, m. H. Wood and J. Waller, Emp., Leeds, 21/7/24; Alh., 3/11/24: adapted from his novel, *Happy-Go-Lucky*, 1913) *Fr. 1922*
×The Crimson Cocoanut (K's H., 12/5/20, Pivot Club) *Fr. 1928*
A Safety Match (Str., 13/1/21: from his own novel, 1911) *Fr. 1927*
×Uncle Ga-Ga (Emp., L'pool, 20/10/21; Col., 24/10/21)
The Happy Ending ('*c.*': D.P., Eastbourne, 20/11/22; St J., 30/11/22) *Fr. 1927*
×Archibald's Afternoon (Portsmouth, 27/11/22; Wimbledon, 11/12/22)
The Sport of Kings ('*c.*': Sav., 8/9/24) *Fr. 1926*
False Pretences ('*c.*': Copley, Boston, 22/3/26)
×A Wire Entanglement (Col., 16/8/26)
×A Blank Cartridge. *Fr. 1928*
×Treasure Trove ('*fant.*') *Fr. 1928*
×Personally or By Letter. *Fr. 1928*
A Damsel in Distress ('*c.*': Gr., Blackpool, 6/8/28; New, 13/8/28: +*P. G. WODEHOUSE*) *Fr. 1930*
Baa Baa, Black Sheep ('*clerical error*': K's, Southsea, 1/4/29; Hippo., Golder's Green, 15/4/29; New, 22/4/29: +*P. G. WODEHOUSE*) *Fr. 1930*
The Middle Watch ('*c.*': K's, Southsea, 5/8/29; Shaft., 12/8/29: +*S. KING-HALL*) *1931*
A Song of Sixpence ('*c.*': Daly's 17/3/30: +*G. BOLTON*) *Fr. 1930*

HAY, JULIAN [see *R. HAY*]

HAY, ROBERT
Dicky's Luck ('*c.*': Ladbr. H., 14/6/11, *cpy.*: +*J. HAY*)

HAY-HOWE, Miss E. [see *C. MARSHALL*]

HAY-NEWTON, Mrs F. (*LUCY*)
×Hide and Seek (H.M., 19/11/15, *m.*)

HAYES, ALFRED [see also *W. E. STIRLING*]
Simon de Montfort. *1918*
Boris Godunov (Midland Inst., B'ham, 26/2/25, *amat.*: translated from the play by A. Pushkin) *1918*
Czar Feodor Ioannovitch ('*d. in verse*': translated from the play by A. K. Tolstoi) *1924*

HAYES, ELSIE

The First Stile (‘*c.*’: Kings., 22/4/23, Pl. Actors)
×The Old Nurse. *Fr. 1930*
×Enchantment. *1930* (printed with *Pilgrims* by Rosalind Vallance)

HAYES, M. A.

×The Lost Mermaid. LC, Zion, Hulme, 21/4/22

HAYLOCK, JOHN F.

×Economising (Ashton-under-Lyme, 3/3/13; Kennington, 31/3/13; Hippo., Bury, 1/1/17, revised as *Economic Pressure*)

HAYMAN, JOSEPH [see also *G. B. DALY*]

Jack in the Box (‘*m.ext.*’, m. M. Darewski: Gr., B’ham, 15/4/18; Hippo., Ilford, 24/6/18)
Dardanella (‘*m.pl.*’: Olympia, Shoreditch, 8/11/20)
[Several music-hall sketches and short musical pieces]

[*HAYMER, JOHN B.*

Aloma (Lyr., N.Y., 20/4/25; Adel., 21/5/26: +*LE R. CLEMENS*)

HAYNES, EDMUND SYDNEY POLLOCK

×A Study in Bereavement (‘*c.*’: Little, 27/7/14) *1915*

HAYNES, H. MANNING [see *B. FLEMING*]

HAYNES, LLOYD

Personal (Rehearsal, 21/4/14, Ibsen Club)

HAYTER, FLORA (*Mrs NORTHESK WILSON*)

Becky (Torquay, 22/8/01)
×The Real Morality: A Society Mousmé (Boudoir, 4/2/10; Arts Centre, 26/1/14, as *A Modern Mousmé*)
×The Dream of Annie Brown (Arts Centre, 5/6/14)
×The Soul of a Thief (Arts Centre, 5/6/14)
The Consoler (Unique Centre Club, 28/1/23)

HAYWARD, CHARLES W.

Anthony (the Philosopher). *1910* (Manchester)

HAYWARD, R.

×The Jew’s Fiddle. LC, Playh., L’pool, 2/8/22: +*A. RISH*)

[*HAZELTON, GEORGE*

The Yellow Jacket (D.Y., 27/3/13: +*J. H. BENRIMO*) *1912*
Mistress Nell (K’s, Glasgow, 23/5/18)

HAZELL, RUPERT

Medorah (‘*c.o.*’, m. V. Ennem: Alh., 22/1/20: adapted from the American ‘musical romance’ by Denn Spranklin)

HEAD, F. D.

[For an earlier play see *H. E. D.* v, 415]
A Man from the Mint (‘*f.*’: Worthing, 22/12/02)
The Lotion (‘*f.*’: Court, 21/1/24, *m.*)
The Magic Fishbone (‘*m.pl.*’) *1929*
×250 for Rubber! *1929*

HEANEY, NED JOYCE

×When Women Rule ('*athletic scene*': Pal., Bradford, 15/5/08; Emp., New X, 21/7/13)

HEARN, Mrs T. ELDER (Miss N. WHEELER)

[A few playlets produced at music-halls]

HEARNE, ISABEL

Queen Herzeleid, or, Sorrow-of-Heart' ('*poetic pl.*': Court, 2/4/11, Pl. Actors) *1911*

HEATH, CROSBY

×The Porridge Pot (Lyc. Club, 13/5/23)
×Caroline's Cat (Lyc. Club, 19/4/25)

HEATH, GUYTON

Shakespeare's Dream ('*pageant*': P's, 9/2/12)

HEATH, RUPERT M.

×One Day in June (Surrey Masonic H., 8/12/02, *amat.*)
×A Double Victory (Crippl. Inst., 22/4/11, *amat.*)

HEATHCOTE, ARTHUR M.

[For earlier plays see *H. E. D.* v, 415]
×Cousins Once Removed (Terry's, 10/4/01) *Fr. 1901*
The Chaperon (Bij., 18/12/05) *Fr. 1923*
×His Good Genius (Dorchester, 5/11/06) *Fr. 1907*
The Man who Won (Scala, 24/5/08: from the novel (1905) by Mrs Baillie Reynolds)
×At a Pageant (Court, 18/12/10, Pl. Actors)
×A Junction. *1913* (Actresses' Franchise League)

HEATHER, COLIN F.

×She Ruled as Queen. LC, W. Bromwich, 25/2/13; title later changed to *The Vagabond King*)
In Friendship's Name. W. Bromwich, 23/6/19

HEATLY, U. F.

The Cyclone ('*f.c.*': Ladbr. H., 24/4/00, *amat.*)
×Piccadillettante ('*f.*': Ladbr. H., 24/4/00, *amat.*)

HEATON, HAROLD

×Where There is Smoke (Gr., Croydon, 29/8/03)

HEATON, J. P.

Her Fatal Secret. LC, '*bsq.*': T.H., Annerley, 23/5/18

HEBDEN, HENRY

Maid Marjorie, or, Cavalier and Puritan ('*c.o.*': Halifax, 7/10/12, *amat.*)

HECHT, MAX

×A Scrupulous Man (St J., 23/3/05)

HECTOR, CHARLES [see also *S. C. WEST*]

×My Friend the Thief (Emp., Camberwell, 20/12/09)

HEFFERMAN, TOM

×A Model of Propriety ('*ca.*': Aven., 6/5/05)
A.D. 5005 ('*m.c.*', m. C. W. Nightingale: Ryde, 18/8/05)

HEILBRONN, WILLIAM

×The Straight Game. LC, Sur., 24/1/13

HEILGERS, LOUISE

×The Bridge (Bed., 26/10/14)
Pickings (Plaza, Tynemouth, 13/2/28)

HEINEMANN, WILLIAM

War. *1901*

HEITLAND, BERYL

Original and Progressive Dialogues. [*1920*]
[This contains thirteen very short sketches]

HELMORE, WALTER

×The Parson and the Plumber. LC, Apo., 2/11/20

HEMINGTON, CYRIL [see also *F. KARNO*]

×The Moat. LC, Col., 4/2/16
The Little Fisher Maid ('*m.r.*': O.H., Manchester, 29/9/24

HEMMEN, GEORGE H.

Baron Rottani (St Gabriel's H., Swansea, 11/2/15, *amat.*)

HEMMERDE, EDWARD GEORGE [='*EDWARD DENBY*']

×A Maid of Honour (Qns, 22/9/09: as by '*E. DENBY*') *Fr. 1912*
A Butterfly on the Wheel ('*modern pl.*': Glo., 18/4/11: +*F. NEILSON*) *Fr. 1922*
The Crucible (Com., 7/6/11: +*F. NEILSON*)
Proud Maisie ('*r.pl.*': Aldw., 12/3/12) *1912*
A Cardinal's Romance (Sav., 14/6/13)

HEMSLEY, HENRY MAY

×Through the Picture. LC, St G's H., 13/3/14

HEN-COLLINS, Hon. S. O. [='*RICHARD OGLE*']

HENDER, DAVIDGE

[For an earlier play see *H. E. D.* v, 416]
Our Lot in Life ('*military d.*': Ath., Lancaster, 2/4/00: title later changed to *The Prodigal Son*)

HENDERSON, EDWIN [see *R. PURDELL*]

HENDERSON, G.

The Bully of Berlin. LC, Emp., Camberwell, 15/11/14: title later changed to *The Beast of Berlin*)

HENDERSON, H. F. [see *F. A. STANLEY*]

HENDERSON, ISAAC

[For an earlier play see *H. E. D.* v, 416]
The Mummy and the Humming Bird (Wynd., 10/10/01)

HENDERSON, JOHN

×No Surrender (Qns, Poplar, 28/1/07)
[Several sketches produced at music-halls]

'*HENDERSON, MARY*' [='*JAMES BRIDIE*' = *O. H. MAVOR*]

HENDERSON, W. E. B. [see also *B. N. GRAHAM*]
Polly ('*m.c.*', m. H. Bath: Pal., Chelsea, 31/3/23: +*R. B. SALISBURY*: based on John Gay's ballad opera)

HENDERSON, WILLIAM
×The Last Wish. LC, Crippl. Inst., 31/10/22

HENDRIE, ERNEST
[For earlier plays see *H. E. D.* v, 417]
Dick Hope ('*c.*': Manchester, 20/11/03; Cor., 7/12/03; St J., 16/9/05)
Mistress Wilful ('*c.*': Portsmouth, 23/5/13, as *Peg and the 'Prentice*; Str., 2/1/15)
The Labour Member (Shaft., 4/9/21, Rep. Players)
The Coiners ('*pl. for boys*') *Fr. 1927*

HENDRIES, FREDERIC
Where's Your Wife? ('*m.f.*': Stratford, 23/4/23)

HENGLER, ALBERT
[Numerous spectacular pieces produced at Hengler's, Glasgow]

HENN, JAY
Devonshire Cream ('*m.c.*', m. E. Turner and B. Sedgebeer: Alh., Stourbridge, 11/8/18)

HENNIKER, Hon. Mrs ARTHUR [*FLORENCE ELLEN HUNGERFORD*]
The Courage of Silence (K's, Hamm., 22/5/05)

HENNING, BASIL S.
×The Return. LC, Temperance Inst., Greenock, 3/2/14

HENRY, CHARLES
×Act I (Seaford House, Belgrave Square, 6/10/24, First Studio Theatre)

HENRY, FLORENCE
×Her Niece Louise (Bij., Bedford St., 21/10/22, Regent Dram. Soc.)

HENRY, L.
×Grandpapa (Ath., Glasgow, 12/4/11, *cpy.*)

HENRY, MARTIN
You Never Know, Y'Know ('*f.*': Pier, Brighton, 3/6/18; Crit., 20/6/18: called originally *Who's Which?*: +*H. BENNETT*)
Kiki ('*m.f.*', m. H. Finck: Pal., Ramsgate, 7/3/21; Emp., Chiswick, 1/8/21)

HENRY, PATRICK, J.
×The Home-coming (St Yevesa's H., Dublin, 16/10/24)

HENRY, R. E.
[For earlier plays see *H. E. D.* v, 417]
×Dame Durden's Visit (Steinway H., 8/11/02)

HENSLOW, T. GEOFFREY W.
The Four Seasons Pantomime. *1927*

HENSLOWE, LEONARD
Souls on the Tramp ('*theosophical f.*': Studio, Victoria-street, 12/12/11: adapted from P. N. Loyson, *Les âmes ennemies*, 1907)

[*HEPBURN, THERESA*
Enter The Hero (A.L.S. Trav. Th., 1919)

HEPWORTH-DIXON, ELLA
× The Toy-shop of the Heart (Playh., 26/11/08)

HERBAGE, WALTER
× An Unrecorded Trial (Alb. H., 9/2/04)

HERBERT, Sir ALAN PATRICK
× The Book of Jonah. *1921* (in *The London Mercury*, iii, 601)
× Double Demon ('*absurdity*': Playh., L'pool, 26/3/29) *1923* (in *Four One-Act Plays*)
The Blue Peter ('*c.o.*', m. C. A. Gibbs: R. College of Music, 12/2/24)
King of the Castle ('*pl. for children and their parents*': Playh., L'pool, 20/12/24: + *W. ARMSTRONG*)
At the Same Time (Aldw., 2/7/25, *m.*)
Riverside Nights ('*entertainment*', m. F. Austin and A. Reynolds: Lyr., Hamm., 10/4/26: + *N. PLAYFAIR*) *1926*
The White Witch ('*c.*': H., 29/9/26)
× Two Gentlemen of Soho (Playh., L'pool, 3/9/27; Lyr., Hamm., 24/10/28) *Fr. 1927*
× Plain Jane; or, The Wedding Breakfast ('*bsq. oa.*', m. R. Austin: Greyhound, Croydon, 26/12/27)
× Fat King Melon and Princess Caraway. *1927* (Oxford)
La Vie Parisienne ('*c.o.*', m. J. Offenbach: Lyr., Hamm., 18/4/29: + *A. DAVIES-ADAMS*) *1929*

'*HERBERT, FRANK*' [= *ERNEST LEICESTER*: see also *G. B. NICHOLS* and *H. WADE*]
[For earlier plays see *H. E. D.* v, 418]
Riding to Win (Broadway, New X, 23/7/00: + *W. HOWARD*)
Was It Murder? (Sur., 23/6/02: + *G. B. DALY*)
× The Last Shot (Sur., 21/7/04)
The Mark of a Man (Pier, Eastbourne, 8/9/19)

'*HERBERT, HERBERT HENRY*' [= *H. H. WOODGATE*; see also *G. R. SIMS*]
Toby ('*c.*': Gr., Blackpool, 2/12/18, *amat.*)
Jonathan Kippax (Pier, Brighton, 15/3/20)
Tarzan of the Apes (Brixton, 4/10/20: from the novel (1914) by Edgar Rice Burroughs: + *A. GIBBONS* and *A. CARLTON*)
A Woman's Awakening (E.C., 14/12/25)

HERBERT, JOSEPH W.
[For an earlier play see *H. E. D.* v, 418]
Mademoiselle Napoleon ('*m.c.*', m. G. Luders: Bij., 20/10/03, *cpy.*)
The Rose Shop ('*m.c.*', m. V. Herbert: Ladbr. H., 24/2/11, *cpy.*)

HERBERT, MARTYN [see *E. CRAMPTON*]
Lend Me Your Husband (Pav., Rhyl, 19/2/17; Dalston, 21/5/17)
Wilmot's Wives. LC, United Services, Letchworth, 2/3/23: +*C. R. T. EVANS*

HERBERT, ZOE
[A few playlets and sketches produced at music-halls]

HERBERTSON, AGNES CROZIER
× A Goose's Feather (Lyc. Club, 19/4/25)

HERFORD, MARGARET [see *E. W. MUMFORD*]

HERIOT, PAUL [see *E. FERRIS*]

HERIOT, WALTER
× Jack Tremaine, V.C. (Ath., Lancaster, 3/8/01)

HERIOT, WILTON
[For an earlier play see *H. E. D.* v, 419]
× The Grasshopper (P'cess, 14/1/02)
× Father's Footsteps (Reg., Salford, 22/11/09; Granville, 18/4/10)

HERMANN, CHARLES
[For earlier plays see *H. E. D.* v, 419]
× During the Siege (Gr., Bolton, 5/5/02)

HERNE, HENRY [see also *W. REYNOLDS*]
Counsel for the Defence (Metro., Devonport, 15/7/01)

[*HERNE, JAMES A.*
Shore Acres ('*c.*': Waldorf, 21/5/06)

HERON, GILBERT
In the King's Navy (Alex., Greenock, 23/9/05, *cpy.*)
[A few sketches produced at music-halls]

HERON, TREVOR [see *J. B. TAYLOR*]

HERON-MAXWELL, BEATRICE ETHEL HERNE [see also *M. WOOD*]
× The Long Arms (Tiv., 17/7/09, *m.*)
× The Lie (Gr., Belfast, 17/10/10)
× The Human Note (Court, 4/12/13)
× The Caravanners (Gai., Hastings, 27/2/11)
The Advocate (Crit., 7/6/20, *m.*; D.P., Eastbourne, 28/11/21)
× The Blue Room. LC, Kennington, 2/2/23
Dona Quixota (Worthing, 5/3/23)

HERRING, ELLA C.
× Lady Flora's Namesake. *Fr. 1911*

HERTZ, HENRY
Champions of Morality ('*c.*': Aldw., 22/5/10, St. Soc.: adapted from Ludwig Thoma, *Moral*, 1908)
× The Passing of Talma ('*t.c.*': Aldw., 29/1/11, St. Soc.: adapted from A. Friedmann and A. Polgar, *Thalmas Tod*, 1910)
× Comtesse Mizzi (Aldw., 9/3/13, St. Soc.: adapted from A. Schnitzler, *Komtesse Mizzi*, 1909)

HERVEY, Mrs ARTHUR
×Ilona ('*o.*', m. A. Hervey: Court, 12/5/14)

HERVEY, GEORGE ROWNTREE
×A Poet in the Making (Boudoir, 15/5/14)

HERTZ, FRANK [see *J. LAVER*]

HESLEWOOD, TOM [see *L. IRVING*]

HESLOP, CHARLES, M. G.
The Summer Girl ('*m.c.*': Agricultural H., Norwich, 21/1/04, *amat.*)
The Sunny South ('*bsq.*': Norwich, 30/6/04, open-air performance, *amat.*)
The Princess and the Philosopher ('*m.c.*': Agricultural H., Norwich, 2/2/05, *amat.*)
Priscilla and the President ('*f.r.*': O.H., Wakefield, 24/4/07)
Betty Beguiled (Pav., Weston, 29/9/11)
[A few sketches produced at music-halls]

HEWER, WILLIAM F.
The Custom of the Country (Corn H., Cirencester, 19/4/01)
The Idol of Kano ('*c.o.*', m. T. P. Arkell: Qns, Swindon, 20/4/04)
×The Last Rehearsal. LC, Gr., Wolverhampton, 25/3/13
Sunrise ('*m.pl.*') *1914* (Bath)

HEWITT, ETHEL
×Bina's Fortune ('*c.*') [*1926*]

HEWITT, KATHLEEN D.
Fourth Floor Heaven (Everyman, 7/4/30)

HEWITT, GEORGE
×The Empress Intrudes (Playh., L'pool, May 1925)

HEWITT, HENRY [see also *W. COLLINSON*]
The Major's Daughter; or, A Hopeless Sin ('*military md.*': Inverness, 24/9/02, *cpy.*)

HEWITT, K. D.
African Shadows (Q, 23/9/29)

HEWLETT, DOROTHY
×The Losing Side (Crippl. Inst., 23/4/27, Quill Club Players) *Fr. 1929*

HEWLETT, MAURICE HENRY
×The Youngest of the Angels ('*c.*': Court, 27/2/06)
Pan and the Young Shepherd ('*pastoral pl.*': Court, 27/2/06) *1906*
The Agonists, a Trilogy of God and Man. *1911*
[This consists of three plays – *Minos King of Crete*, *Ariadne in Naxos*, and *The Death of Hippolytus*. The second of these was performed (or read) by the Poets' Club at the Little Theatre, 9/7/11]
×Callisto ('*ballet*', m. A. Hullah: Court, 28/10/12)
×The Ladies' Comedy (Little, 3/2/14)
The Loving History of Peridore and Paravail. *1917*

HEWSON, ARTHUR

×The Widow Mead (The Baths, Thornton Heath, 19/1/01, *amat.*)

HEWSON, J. JAMES

[For earlier plays see *H. E. D.* v, 420, 798]

For the Sake of a Woman ('*m.d.*': Pav., 24/9/00)

A Past Redeemed (Pav., 5/10/03)

Under the Canopy ('*Russo-Jewish d.*': Pav., 2/11/03)

×Fa(u)st and Loose (Hippo., Glasgow, 8/6/08)

×Love, Law and the Lady (Lyr., L'pool, 25/11/12)

The Knight in Silver Armour ('*fant.*': Gr., Blackpool, 13/12/16)

The Coming of Grainger Halkyn (W.G., New Brighton, 9/7/17)

HEYDEMANN, C. H.

×Madam is Served. LC, Crit., 22/9/14)

HEYSE, PAUL

Mary of Magdala. LC, Crit., 26/1/14: +*W. WINTER*

[*HEYWARD, DU BOSE*

Porgy (H.M., 10/4/29: +*DOROTHY HEYWARD*) *1928* (New York)

HEYWOOD, J. HERBERT

The Isle of Indolence ('*light o.*', m. R. Knight: Gr., Oldham, 8/11/09)

×Nancy's Uncle. LC, Gr., Oldham, 23/7/18

×The Burden. LC, Gr., Oldham, 23/7/18

Golden Arrows. LC, Gr., Oldham, 23/7/18

HIBBERT, FRANCIS AIDAN

A Christmas Miracle Play. *1919* (Faith Press)

England's Greatness. *1924* (SPCK)

HIBBERT, WILLIAM

A Soldier of the Czar (Belfast, 26/9/02; Brixton, 21/11/02; Lyr., Hamm., 1/5/05)

When Women Hate (Aston, 8/1/04; Pav., 1/8/04: called also *When Woman Hates*)

The Curse of Her Love (Croydon, 22/5/05; Hyde, 5/4/07, as *The Girl who went Astray*; Stratford, 26/12/07: +*F. BULMER*)

The Hour of Her Triumph (Lyr., Hamm., 26/2/06)

She Stands Alone (Lyr., Hamm., 18/6/06; Rot., L'pool, 14/9/14, as *A Soldier of the King*; Imp., Canning Town, 26/10/14)

HIBBERT-WARE, WILLIAM

A Modern Magdalem (O.H., Southport, 20/1/02; Carlton, Greenwich, 17/2/02, as *The Shadow of the Scaffold*)

HICHENS, ROBERT SMYTHE

[For an earlier play see *H. E. D.* v, 420]

Becky Sharp (P.W., 27/8/01: +*C. GORDON-LENNOX*: dramatised from W. M. Thackeray's *Vanity Fair*)

The Real Woman (Crit., 25/2/09)

The Garden of Allah (Cent., N.Y., 21/10/11; D.L., 24/6/20: +*M. ANDERSON*)

×The Law of the Sands (Ldn O.H., 9/10/16)
×Black Magic. LC, Ambass., 27/3/17
Press the Button! ('*ext.*': Glo., 23/5/18: called originally *Their Own Devices*)
The Voice from the Minaret (Glo., 26/8/19)

HICKEY, D. E.
The Young Lady's Consent (Bedford H., Chelsea, 26/4/24, Pax Robertson Salon: adapted from L. Fernández de Moratín, *El Sí de las niñas*, 1801)
The Marriage School (Bedford H., Chelsea, 1/2/25, Pax Robertson Salon: adapted from M. Bretón de los Herreros, *La escuela del matrimonio*, 1852)

HICKMAN, CHARLES D. [see *H. C. WOODROW*]
[Several sketches produced at music-halls]

HICKS, R. C. [see *L. C. GRAY*]

HICKS, Sir SEYMOUR [see also *B. BAIRNSFATHER*]
[For earlier plays see *H. E. D.* v, 420–1]
For Auld Lang Syne (Lyc., 6/10/00: +*F. G. LATHAM*)
You and I ('*m.f.*', m. W. Slaughter: Vaud., 24/4/01)
Bluebell in Fairyland ('*m. dream pl.*', m. W. Slaughter: Vaud., 18/12/01; Aldw., 23/12/05, revised, as *Bluebell*; condensed version Hippo., Croydon, 17/10/10; Hippo., 31/10/10) *Fr. 1927*
An English Daisy ('*m.pl.*': County, Reading, 11/8/02; Alex., 15/9/02: +*W. SLAUGHTER*) *1903*
The Earl and the Girl ('*m.c.*', m. I. Caryll: Adel., 10/12/03) *1903*
The Cherry Girl ('*m.pl.*', m. I. Caryll: Vaud., 21/12/03) *1903*
The Catch of the Season ('*m.pl.*', m. H. E. Haines and E. Baker: Vaud., 9/9/04: +*C. HAMILTON*)
The Talk of the Town ('*m.c.*', m. H. E. Haines: Lyr., 5/1/05) *1905*
The Beauty of Bath ('*m.pl.*', m. H. E. Haines: Aldw., 19/3/06: +*C. HAMILTON*)
My Darling ('*m.pl.*', m. H. E. Haines: Hicks', 2/3/07) *1907*
The Gay Gordons ('*m.pl.*', m. G. Jones: Aldw., 11/9/07)
×A Dress Rehearsal (Tiv., 2/12/07: +*A. C. ROBATT*)
×My New Cook (Pav., 10/2/08)
The Dashing Little Duke ('*m.pl.*', m. F. E. Tours: Nottingham, 8/2/09; Hicks', 17/2/09) *1909*
×The Hampton Club (Col., 8/11/09)
Captain Kidd ('*m.c.*', m. L. Stuart; Wynd., 12/1/10)
×Cook's Man (Col., 4/4/10)
×The Model and the Man (K's, Southsea, 15/8/10; Hippo., 22/8/10)
×A Lady at Large (K's, Southsea, 10/10/10)
×The Slum Angel (Col., 27/11/11)
×Pebbles on the Beach (Col., 16/12/12: title later changed to *Washed Up*)
×The Bridal Suite (Col., 24/8/14)
England Expects (Ldn O.H., 17/9/14: +*E. KNOBLOCK*)

The Happy Day ('*m.pl.*', m. S. Jones and P. A. Rubens: Daly's, 13/5/16) *1916*
Cash on Delivery ('*m.f.*', m. H. Wood: Gr., Wolverhampton, 1/10/17; Pal., 13/10/17)
Sleeping Partners (St M., 31/12/17)
Jolly Jack Tar ('*m.pl.*', m. H. Darewski: P's, 29/11/18: +*A. SHIRLEY*)
×Peace, Perfect Peace (Empress, Brixton, 23/6/19)
Adam and Eve ('*f.*': O.H., Blackpool, 1/9/19)
×A Perfect Liar. LC, Pav., Glasgow, 28/6/21
A Little Dutch Girl ('*c.o.*', m. E. Kalman: Lyr., 1/12/20: +*H. GRAHAM*)
×The Surprise (Metropolitan, 28/8/21)
The Man in Dress Clothes ('*c.*': Portsmouth, 31/10/21; Gar., 22/3/22)
×A Happy New Year (Little, 31/5/22)
×Waiting for a Lady (Col., 20/11/22)
The Love Habit ('*f.*': Roy., 7/2/23)
Head over Heels ('*m.c.*', m. H. Fraser-Simson: Adel., 8/9/23)
Good Luck ('*d.*': D.L., 27/9/23: +*I. HAY*)
The Price of Silence ('*d.*': Gai., Dublin, 10/8/25)
Mr What's-his-name ('*f.c.*': P.W., B'ham, 7/3/27: Wynd., 25/4/27)
×Mint Sauce (Col., 25/4/27)

HIGGINBOTHOM, ROBERT N.
×The Last Night (York, 3/10/10)
×Kitty (Marlb., 7/8/11; Sav., 23/6/13) *Fr. 1913*
×The First Stone (Rehearsal, 14/4/12)
×As Others See Us (Colchester, 18/4/12; Gai., Manchester, 1/3/15; Little, 3/4/15)
×Clearly and Concisely (St J., 30/1/13) *Fr. 1913*
×Lucky Peter (Gai., Manchester, 7/12/14) *Fr. 1921*
×The Dyspeptics. *Fr. 1921*
A Proper Sport ('*light c.*': Playh., Felixstowe, 22/7/26; R.A., Woolwich, 31/1/27)
[A few other sketches produced at music-halls]

HIGGINBOTTOM, W. HUGH
×The Lay Figure ('*ca.*': R. College of Music, 17/3/10, *amat.*)
A Woman of Westminster; or, Votes for Men ('*c.o.*', m. F. D. Barnes: O.H., Tunbridge Wells, 12/7/10, *amat.*)
×It's Catching. LC, Scala, 4/3/15
The Moon of Carthage ('*c.o.*', m. F. D. Barnes and R. Armand: O.H., Tunbridge Wells, 23/1/12, *amat.*)

HIGGINS, CHARLES [='*IAN DALL*']

HILDYARD, MAUD
The Great Awakening (Scarborough, 17/7/05; Pav., 4/12/05: +*R. VAUN*)
×The Price of a Soul (Hippo., Camden, 16/5/10; Olympia, Shoreditch, 30/5/10; Court, 16/6/11, *m.*, as *Absinthe*)

HILL, ARTHUR [see *C. BROWN*]

HILL, BARTON
Camille (Adel., 8/9/02: adapted from A. Dumas fils, *La Dame aux camélias*)

HILL, CECILIA
The Pageant of Margaret of Scotland. *1912* (Westminster)
The Pageant of Saint Hild, Abbess of Whitby. *1913*

HILL, GRAHAM [see *G. GROSSMITH* and *Mrs LANGTRY*]
×Bridge ('*episode of modern society*': Canterbury, 13/2/06)
Guinevere ('*t.*': Court, 13/10/06, *cpy.*) *1906*
×The Night Rider (Emp., Holb., 12/12/10)
×Between the Nightfall and the Light (Hippo., 6/3/11; Cor., 23/10/11, as '*Twixt N. and the L.*)
The Queen's Champion (Tunbridge Wells, 16/10/11; Broadway, 23/10/11; Aldw., 31/1/14: +'*H. ERICSEN*')
[Several sketches produced at music-halls]

HILL, H. BRINSLEY
The Sailor's Wedding (Marlb., Holloway, 7/9/08)
For Love of His Daughter (Pal., Newcastle, 6/2/11: +*J. H. DARNLEY*)
A Noble Sacrifice ('*md.*': Darlington, 8/4/12: +*J. H. DARNLEY*)
[Several sketches produced at music-halls]

HILL, N. CARLTON
×Dross ('*music d. without words*', m. Paul Corder: R. Academy of Music, 5/5/05)

HILL, R. NOEL
×His Little Trip (Str., 18/6/20, *m.*: +*L. J. CULVERWELL*)

HILL, T.
The Fate of the Fallen (E.C., 19/8/01)
When the Heart is Young (Hippo., Oldham, 24/4/16; S. Ldn, 18/6/17: called originally *When the Sun Sets*)

HILL, V. H. [see also *L. BAGOT*]
×A Tale of Bredon. LC, Chelsea Hospital Grounds, 16/7/21: +*D. CROSS* and *L. BAGOT*)

HILL, WITHERIDGE W. [see *W. T. COLEBY*]

HILL-MITCHENSON, E. [see also *A. SHIRLEY*]
[For earlier plays see *H. E. D.* v, 422]
The French Spy (Morton's, Greenwich, 5/3/00)
The Assassin ('*Russian d.*': Wigan, 23/12/01, *revised*; Stratford, 24/2/02)
The Price of Sin (Carlton, Greenwich, 19/5/02)
When the Lights are Low ('*c.*': Muncaster, Bootle, 11/8/02; R.A., Woolwich, 27/10/02)
The Traitor (Wigan, 27/7/03; Stratford, 23/11/03: called originally *A Judas*)

Who is She? ('*r.pl.*': Hippo., Wigan, 16/12/07; Lyr., Hamm., 15/3/09)
The Blackguard of the Queen's Regiment ('*r.pl.*': Hippo., Wigan, 19/12/10; E.C., 20/3/11)
For Her ('*r.pl.*': Osborne, Manchester, 26/12/11)
Chosen by the People (S. Shields, 27/7/14; Woolwich, 17/5/15)
A Sailor's Wedding-Ring (Middlesbrough, 4/10/15)
The Victim (Middlesbrough, 22/11/15, *revised*: called originally *Dolores*)
The Tramp (Middlesbrough, 22/5/16)
Ruth – Convict 22 (Middlesbrough, 9/10/16)
Ashamed of the Man She Married (Middlesbrough, 6/11/16)
Her Two Husbands. LC, Sunderland, 7/10/18
Somebody's Wife. LC, Oldham, 20/11/18
The Thief and the Woman (Leicester, 1/12/19)
Hands Up (Gr., Halifax, 23/4/20)
A Gentleman from Dartmoor (Leicester, 11/10/20)
Sally in Our Alley (Leicester, 26/12/21)
The Man without a Name. LC, Middlesbrough, 2/9/22
My Man. LC, Leicester, 30/12/22: title later changed to *Eliza*
Forbidden Fruit. LC, Leicester, 13/8/23
A Fallen Woman. LC, Leicester, 31/12/23: title later changed to *The Barrier of Sin*

HILLIARD, ROBERT [see *E. HOLLAND*]

HILLIARD, STAFFORD
×A Storm in a Tea-Shop (Vaud., 9/9/11) *Fr. 1911*

HILLIER, LOUIS
Rapid Promotion ('*f.*': Gai., Hastings, 18/12/16: +*H. F. MALTBY*)

HILLIER, MIRABEL
Peggy Doyle (Rehearsal, 26/6/08, *amat.*)

HILLS, CHARLES E. C.
×The Coming of Arthur (Crippl. Inst., 10/4/26)

HILLS, Miss HAMMOND
[For an earlier play see *H. E. D.* v, 422]
×The Go-ahead Ladies' Club (Bij., 2/10/01)

HILLS, ROSS
Woman and Destiny (Garrick Chambers, Stockport, 14/4/15, Stockport Garrick Soc.)
The Recidivist (People's, Newcastle, 1915)
Letitia Meets the Family ('*c.*': Rep., Rusholme, 20/4/25) *1931* (Norwich)
Undercurrents ('*d.*': Rep., Rusholme, 1/2/26) *1933* (Norwich)

HIME, HENRY WILLIAM LOVETT
Ludvig Holberg...Three Comedies. *1912*
[This contains translations of 1. *Henry and Perilla* (Bedford H., Chelsea, 21/5/22, Pax Robertson Salon); 2. *Captain Bombastes Thunderton*; and 3. *Scatterbrain*]

HINDE, Rev. H. D.
The Lost Dewdrops ('*c.o.*': T.H., Edmonton, 29/2/08, *amat.*)
The Great Yah Boo ('*c.o.*': Village H., Southgate, 13/5/08, *amat.*)
Thorstein Abbey ('*c.o.*': Village H., Southgate, 6/1/09, *amat.*)

HINE, ESMOND
× The Pangs of Jealousy (P.H., Croydon, 22/5/05, *amat.*)
The Petals of a Rose (P.H., Croydon, 22/5/05, *amat.*)

HINE, MURIEL
Her Dancing Partner ('*c.*': Peterborough, 21/5/23)
The Best In Life. LC, Aldw., 12/5/24

HINES, LEONARD JOHN
× Vindication. LC, Little, Leeds, 15/11/29: +*F. KING. 1930*
× Creditors. *1930*
× Fire of Vanity. *Fr. 1930*

HINTON, A. [see *C. BURNETTE*]

HIRD, F.
× The Test. LC, O.H., Tunbridge Wells, 24/2/16

HIRSCHBEIN, PAUL
The Blacksmith's Daughter. LC, Scala, 1/4/24

HIRSTE, GEORGE
[Several sketches and playlets produced at music-halls]

HISCOCK, A. E.
The Playwright (Hull, 26/10/01, *amat.*)

HITCHINGS, ROBERT
× After Many Days (Pav., Eastbourne, 2/12/01)

HOARE, DOUGLAS [see *S. BLOW*]

HOARE, FREDERICK, A.
× A Guard of Honour (H.M., Dundee, 14/7/02)

[*HOBART, GEORGE VERE*
Victoria ('*m.pl.*': Bij., 27/11/08, *cpy.*; title later changed to *When Sweet Sixteen*)
The Girl from Chantilly ('*m.f.*', m. J. Briquest: Ladbr. H., 14/12/10, *cpy.*)
Everywife ('*symbolic symphony*': Ladbr. H., 13/6/11, *cpy.*; Col., 14/4/13)
× Dindlespiel's Christmas. LC, Oxf., 27/5/14

HOBBES, JOHN
A Week's Engagement ('*f.c.*': Pav., St Leonard's, 30/6/13)
War in the Marshall Family ('*f.c.*': Pier, Brighton, 25/2/18)
My Brother Nick. LC, Pav., Torquay, 11/1/18
Uncle Ben's Experiment ('*c.*': New, Salisbury, 17/6/18)
Matilda Goes Abroad. LC, Pier, Herne Bay, 6/9/20
The Mysterious Alexandrovitch. LC, Col., Aberystwyth, 13/7/23

'*HOBBES, JOHN OLIVER*' [=*PEARL MARY TERESA CRAIGIE*]
[For earlier plays see *H. E. D.* v, 422]
Osborne and Ursyne. *1900*

The Wisdom of the Wise ('*c.*': St J., 22/11/00) *1901*
The Bishop's Move ('*c.*': Gar., 7/6/02, *m.*; Gar., 30/7/02: +*M. CARSON*)
The Flute of Pan ('*m.c.*'; Gai., Manchester, 21/4/04; Shaft., 12/11/04) *1904*

[*HOBBLE, JOHN L.*
Daddies ('*c.*': Washington, 10/6/18; Belasco, N.Y., 5/9/18; Hippo., Margate, 25/8/19; H., 3/9/19) *Fr. 1929*

HOBSON, BULMER
Brian of Banba (Cork, c. 1911, *amat.*)

HOBSON, FLORENCE EDGAR (*Mrs J. A. HOBSON*)
Enter the Bishop ('*f.*': South Place Inst., 2/4/09)
A Modern Crusader ('*d. pamphlet*': K's H., 30/4/12) *1912*

HODGES, HORACE
The Little Admiral (Lyr., 9/3/07: +*T. W. PERCYVAL*)
Grumpy (Glasgow, 19/9/13; New, 13/5/14: +*T. W. PERCYVAL*) *Fr. 1914*
May and September (Brighton, 23/4/23; Com., 31/7/23, as *Peace and Quiet*)
[*Who's Who in the Theatre* adds to these another collaboration with T. W. Percyval – *The Little Lady in Blue*]

HODGKINS, Miss MARRIOTT
×Snatched from the Grave (Rehearsal, 28/4/13, Black Cat Club)

HODGSON-BENTLEY, H.
Red Mist (Ambass., Southend, 26/9/27)
Beacham's Wills ('*c.*': Ambass., Southend, 11/6/28)

HODSON, ALICE
×By-and-by ('*social f.*': Lyc. Club, 25/2/10, *m.*)

HODSON, FRANK [see *G. H. CHESTER*]

HODSON, JAMES LANSDALE
×The Back Way. LC, '*c.*': Social Club, Manchester, 25/1/23. *1927*
×The Proof ('*Lancashire pl.*': Rep., Rusholme, 1/9/24) *1927*
The Boom ('*Lancashire c.*': Rep., Rusholme, 12/10/25)
×Harvest (Rep., Rusholme, 4/10/26) *1931*
×George Proposes. *1927*
These Fathers! ('*Lancashire c.*': Rep., Rusholme, 26/3/28; Q, 29/10/28) *1930*
Red Night ('*war pl.*': Qns, 4/3/36) *1930*

HODSON, J. R.
Charles Peace. LC, Com., Rawmarsh, 17/7/19
The Perils of a Miner's Life. LC, Com., Rawmarsh, 18/8/19

HODSON, MILDRED
The Square Peg ('*c.*': Everyman, 18/1/27)

HOFFE, MONCKTON [*REANEY MONCKTON HOFFE-MILES*]
×The Lady who Dwelt in the Dark (Gr., Southampton, 8/6/03; Marlb., Holloway, 8/8/04)
×Father Varien (D.P., Eastbourne, 9/5/07)
The Little Damozel ('*c.*': Wynd., 21/10/09) *Fr. 1912*
×The Missing Hand (Metropolitan, 22/11/09)
Improper Peter ('*c.*': Gar., 19/4/12: title later changed to *Proper Peter*)
Panthea (Ambass., 5/6/13)
Things We'd Like to Know ('*c.*': Apo., 28/3/14)
Poor Little Mookey (Gai., Hastings, 6/12/15)
×Beautiful Mrs Blain (Metropolitan, 21/8/16)
Anthony in Wonderland ('*fant. c.*': P.W., 1/2/17)
Carminetta ('*c.o.*', m. E. Lassailly: Shak., L'pool, 13/8/17; P.W., 22/8/17)
×The Tactical Offensive (Theat. Gdn Party, Regent's Park, 25/6/18)
The Faithful Heart (Com., 16/11/21) *1922*
×The Evening Blast (Pav., Glasgow, 21/11/21)
Pomp and Circumstance ('*c.*': D.Y., 8/6/22)
Cristilinda (Alvin, Pittsburgh, 11/22, as *The Painted Lady*; Broadhurst, N.Y., 25/12/15, as *Lady Cristilinda*; Gar., 21/10/25) *Fr. 1926*
Crooked Friday (New, Cardiff, 11/4/25; Com., 20/5/25) *1927*
The Unnamed Play (Str., 3/10/26, Rep. Players; Ambass., 18/7/28, as *Many Waters*) *1928* (as *Many Waters*)
×The Stolen Rolls. LC, Col., 1/11/26. *Fr. 1927*
The Blue Mazourka ('*m.pl.*', m. F. Lehar: P's, Manchester, 24/12/26; Daly's, 19/2/27)
×On Appro. (Col., 28/2/27)

[*HOFFMAN, AARON* [see also *S. SHIPMAN*]
×The End of the World; or, Toblitsky Says (Hippo., Eastbourne, 21/5/08, *cpy.*; Pal., 9/8/09, as *Toblitsky, or, The End of the World*)
×The Reformation of David; or, The Son of Solomon (Ladbr. H., 2/5/11, *cpy.*)
×Manna Falls for Moses. LC, P's, 10/6/13
Welcome Stranger ('*c.*': Acad., Baltimore, 19/5/19; Cohan and Harris, N.Y., 13/9/20; Lyr., 19/10/21) *Fr. 1927*
×The Unexpected (Com., 18/6/19, Punch and Judy Players)
×The Question ('*psychological crook pl.*': Pal., Chelsea, 4/8/19)
Give and Take ('*f.c.*': Apo., Atlantic City, 4/12/22; 49th St., N.Y., 18/1/23; Glo., 25/1/27)
[A few other sketches produced at music-halls]

HOFFMAN, MAURICE
[Several sketches produced at music-halls]

[*HOFFMAN, PHOEBE*
×Martha's Mourning (Etlinger, 7/12/27)

HOGAN, MICHAEL [=*'LEAHCIM NAGOH'*]
The Idiot (Barnes, 23/8/26; Little, 7/9/26: from the novel by F. M. Dostoievski)
×The Witch Wife (Lyc. Club, 13/3/27: +*M. CONSTANDUROS*)

HOGG, CYRIL WENTWORTH [see also *M. PEMBERTON* and *W. YARDLEY*]
×His Life for Hers (*'r.pl.'*: Spa, Scarborough, 18/7/03, *cpy.*; Arts Centre, 20/3/14) *Fr. 1903*
×The Mirror of Time (Manchester, 9/4/06) *Fr. 1906*
×The Men who Loved Maimie. LC, Castle, Richmond, 3/5/09. *Fr. 1909*
×The Recruit (*'pl. of the moment'*) *Fr. 1914*
×The Story of Corporal Bell (*'pl. for present times'*) *Fr. 1915*

HOGGAN-ARMADALE, E. [see also *E. ST C. FORBES*]
London's Curse (*'md.'*: Darlington, 4/5/00; Star, L'pool, 30/7/00; Sur., 15/7/01)

HOKEN, HEATH [see *A. HARVEY*]

HOLCROFT, GERALD
[For earlier plays see *H. E. D.* v, 424]
Woman's War (*'r.pl.'*: Aldershot, 14/7/02)

HOLDEN, EMILY
×The Shawl (Little, L'pool, 20/10/27, *amat.*)

HOLE, W. G.
Queen Elizabeth (*'historical pl.'*: Everyman, 24/4/28) *1904* (in 4 acts); *1928* (in 2 acts)
The Master. LC, *'poet. pl.'*: Temperance H., Sheffield, 5/10/12. *1913*

HOLLAND, CHRISTOPHER
×The Old Women (Little, 29/6/21)

'HOLLAND, CLIVE' [=*CHARLES JAMES HARRISON*]
The Heart of O Hana San (*'Japanese pl.'*: Pav., Bournemouth, 20/8/02)

HOLLAND, EDWIN
Convicts (New, 24/10/03, *cpy.*: +*R. HILLIARD*)

HOLLAND, GEORGE F.
The Storm (Everyman, 3/12/29: +*MALCOLM MORLEY*: adapted from the play by A. N. Ostrovski) *1930*

HOLLAND, HAROLD
×True Values (Sur., 1/4/18)
Reconstruction (Rep., Rusholme, 28/9/25)
The Big Drum (Q, 17/10/27; Adel., 14/11/27)
×Grey Matter (Adel., 6/5/28, Sunday Pl. Soc.)
Dad. LC, County, St Albans, 26/11/29. *1928*
This Year, Next Year (*'f.c.'*: Pav., Rhyl, 29/4/29)

HOLLAND, L. [see *K. EDWARDS*]

HOLLAND, THEODORE [see *C. GOULDSBURY*]

HOLLANDER, BENOIT

Mietje ('*o.*': Hampstead Conservatoire, 11/5/09)

HOLLES, ALFRED [see also *P. SANDIFORD*]

×The Hag and the Masher (Muncaster, Bootle, 30/12/09)

×The Duchess of Doherty Court. *Fr. 1911*

HOLLES, H. M.

[For an earlier play see *H. E. D.* v, 424]

×David Garrick ('*c.*': County, Kingston, 10/6/01)

HOLLES, JOHN

×Same Lodge (P.W., 26/10/11: +*GUY NEWALL*)

HOLLOWAY, G. H.

×Phrynette. LC, All Saints' H., Clifton, 29/2/16

×The Antidote. LC, Knightstone Pav., Weston, 26/1/20

HOLLOWAY, MARGARET [see *L. IRVING*]

HOLLOWAY, MONA

The White Sheik. LC, P.W., Tamworth, 24/9/25

HOLLOWAY, SYDNEY J.

×On the Brink (Ambass., 27/1/21)

Hitch Your Wagon (Q, 6/12/26)

HOLME, CONSTANCE

×The Home of Vision (K's H., 9/2/19, Pioneer Players) *1932* (Kirby Lonsdale: in *Four One-Act Plays*)

HOLME, H. E.

×High Tea (Court, 14/6/14, Pl. Actors)

HOLMES, PERCY GORDON [see also *ARTHUR BERTRAM*]

The Convict's Daughter (Newcastle, 15/10/03, *cpy.*; Gr., Islington, 7/3/04)

Fascinating Miss Kemp ('*c.*': Margate, 7/11/04; O.H., Crouch End, 5/12/04)

×Domus et placens uxor ('*d.*': Margate, 7/11/04)

A Soldier of Fortune ('*r.pl.*': Londesborough, Scarborough, 9/11/05; O.H., Crouch End, 28/11/05)

The Little Mother (Shak., Clapham, 15/7/07)

The Empire of Ambition ('*r.d.*': W. Bromwich, 5/12/07)

×The Lone Valley Hold-up. LC, Blackburn, 21/8/13

You Made Me Love You (Lyc., 25/2/14)

×A Studio Mystery (Kennington, 20/9/15)

A Night of Temptation (Lyc., 14/4/23)

HOLMES, ROBERT

All Because of Joan. LC, P.H., Streatham, 8/12/13

HOLMES-GORE, ARTHUR

How De Figeac Came to Court (K's, Glasgow, 25/8/05, *cpy.*: +*W. S. DIXON*)

HOLMWOOD, ELEANOR

×The Interval (Hillhead H., Glasgow, 3/12/15)

HOLT, CLAUD

Undercurrents (Crippl. Inst., 22/1/27, *amat.*)

HOLT, S. C.

[Several music-hall sketches presented at the Alexandra, Stoke Newington]

HOLYOAK, W. L.

Dignity and Impudence ('*f.c.*': Wimbledon, 2/9/29)

HOMER, A. N.

Count Tezma ('*r.pl.*': Com., 20/4/01)

HONIG, LEWIS

×Charley's Uncle (Stand., 1/4/07)

HOOD, ARTHUR

×Joanna, from Booker's Flat (Bury St Edmunds, 31/1/10; Lyc. Club, 30/4/12)

×The Rats (Emp., Finsbury Park, 29/4/22, *m.*, Lyc. Club)

HOOD, BASIL [see also *A. WIMPERIS*]

[For earlier plays see *H. E. D.* v, 425, 798]

×Pretty Polly (Colchester, 26/4/00; Sav., 19/5/00)

×Ib and Little Christina ('*picture in three parts*': P.W., 15/5/00; Sav., 14/11/01, with music by F. Leoni) *1901*

×The Great Silence (Cor., 23/7/00)

Sweet and Twenty ('*c.*': Vaud., 24/4/01)

The Emerald Isle, or, The Caves of Carric-Cleena ('*c.o.*', m. Sir Arthur Sullivan and E. German: Sav., 27/4/01)

The Willow Pattern ('*oa.*', m. C. Cook: Sav., 14/11/01) *1901*

Merrie England ('*c.o.*', m. E. German: Sav., 2/4/02) *1902*

My Pretty Maid ('*c.*': Terry's, 5/4/02)

A Princess of Kensington ('*c.o.*', m. E. German: Sav., 22/1/03) *1903*

Little Hans Andersen ('*fairy pl.*', m. W. Slaughter: Adel., 23/12/03)

Love in a Cottage ('*c.*': Terry's, 27/1/04)

The Golden Girl ('*m.c.*', m. H. McCunn: P.W., B'ham, 5/8/05)

The Belle of Mayfair ('*m.c.*', m. L. Stuart: Vaud., 11/4/06: +*C. H. E. BROOKFIELD* and *C. HAMILTON*)

The Merveilleuses ('*c.o.*', m. H. Felix: Daly's, 27/10/06; Daly's, 31/1/07, as *The Lady Dandies*) *1906*

The Dollar Princess ('*c.o.*', m. L. Fall: P's, Manchester, 24/12/08; Daly's, 25/9/09)

The Merry Widow ('*m.pl.*', m. F. Lehar: Daly's, 8/6/07)

[Originally ascribed in the programmes to Edward Morton]

The Count of Luxembourg ('*m.pl.*', m. F. Lehar: Daly's, 20/5/11: originally called *The Castle of Luxembourg*) *1911*

The Five Frankforters ('*c.*': Lyr., 7/5/12: from C. Rössler, *Die fünf Frankfurter*, 1911)

Gipsy Love ('*m.pl.*', m. F. Lehar: Daly's, 1/6/12) *1912*

The Pearl Girl ('*m.c.*', m. H. Felix and H. Talbot: Shaft., 25/9/13) *1913*
Young England ('*light o.*', m. G. H. Clutsam and H. Bath: P.W., B'ham, 20/11/16; Daly's, 23/12/16) *1916*
× Tiddly Winks ('*m.c.*': Bed., 9/12/18)

HOOK, THEO
The Game. LC, New, Pontypridd, 11/11/22

HOOKER, BRIAN [see *W. H. POST*]

HOOPER, R. S. [see *C. WEST*]

HOOTON, HENRY [see *J. T. GREIN*]

HOPE, Mrs ADRIAN C.
Cupid in Arcady ('*fant.*': Regent's R., 21/7/09)

'*HOPE, ANTHONY*' [=*Sir ANTHONY HOPE HAWKINS*; see also *R. MARSHALL*]
[For earlier plays see *H. E. D.* v, 425]
Rupert of Hentzau (Glasgow, 5/10/1899; St J., 1/2/00)
English Nell (P.W., 21/8/00: called originally *Mistress Nell*: dramatised from his novel *Simon Dale* (1898): +*E. ROSE*)
Pilkerton's Peerage ('*c.*': Gar., 18/3/01, *cpy.*; Gar., 28/1/02) *Fr. 1918*
Captain Dieppe ('*light c.*': New, 11/9/03, *cpy.*; D.Y., 15/2/04: +*H. RHODES*)
Helena's Path ('*c.*': D.Y., 3/5/10: +*C. GORDON-LENNOX*)
× Love's Song (Three Arts Club, 2/7/16)

HOPE, BERTHA [see *R. OWEN*]

'*HOPE, ERIC*' [=*The Earl of YARMOUTH*]
The Pigeon House ('*f.*': Bij., 2/7/02; New, Cardiff, 27/6/10, with music; Court, 19/9/10)

HOPE, HELEN A.
Children's Plays of Citizen House, Bath. *1923*
[This contains four short pieces: 1. *Midsummer Eve*; 2. *Piper's Pool*; 3. *The First Christmas Tree*; and 4. *The Soul Maker*]

HOPE, MABEL ELLAMS
The Yellow Streak (Pier, Brighton, 16/5/27; Emb., 11/9/28)
Stephanie ('*t.*': RADA, 23/2/30, Three Arts Club)

HOPE, PRESTON
[For earlier plays see *H. E. D.* v, 426]
× The Gentleman in Khaki ('*m.f.*', m. N. Lambelet: D.L., 15/5/00)

HOPE, R.
× Broken at the Fountain (Parish H., Ladywell, 25/5/05)
The Chivalrous Highwayman (Parish H., Ladywell, 25/5/05)

HOPE, STANLEY
× He Knew It All the Time (O.H., Jersey, 21/4/13)

HOPE-LUMLEY, R.

Marie Sees It Through (Electric, Tiverton, 9/1/17; Pier, Eastbourne, 27/8/17, as *The Enemy Within*; Hippo., Golder's Green, 10/9/17)

[*HOPKINS, ARTHUR*

Burlesque ('*c.*': Portsmouth, 5/11/18; Hippo., Golder's Green, 26/11/28; Qns, 3/12/28: +*GEORGE MANKER WATTERS*)

HOPKINS, GERARD [see *M. SADLEIR*]

HOPKINS, MARK

×Love on Wheels ('*oa.*', m. H. Jenner: Qns Gate H., 30/5/01)

[*HOPWOOD, AVERY* [see also *D. GREY* and *M. R. RINEHART*]

This Woman and This Man (Bij., 18/1/09, *cpy.*)
The Winking Princess ('*m.c.*': Court, 15/9/10, *cpy.*)
Nobody's Widow ('*c.*': Dalston, 20/10/10, *cpy.*; D.P., Eastbourne, 9/9/18, as *Roxana*; Lyr., 18/9/18)
Fair and Warmer ('*f.*': Emp., Syracuse, 25/10/15; Eltinge, N.Y., 6/11/15; P's, Manchester, 6/3/18; P.W., 14/5/18)
The Gold Diggers ('*c.*': Atlantic City, 6/19; Lyc., N.Y., 30/9/19; Gr., Blackpool, 29/11/26; Lyr., 14/12/26)
Bachelor Husbands ('*c.*': Morosco, N.Y., 12/9/22, as *Why Men Leave Home*; D.P., Eastbourne, 25/2/24; Roy., 2/6/24)
Little Miss Bluebeard ('*c.*': Lyr., N.Y., 28/8/23; Wynd., 15/4/25) *1935*
The Garden of Eden (Lyc., Edin., 23/5/27; Lyr., 30/5/27)
The Duchess of Elba ('*c.*': Arts, 2/10/27)
Our Little Wife ('*f.c.*': Pier, Brighton, 30/4/28; Com., 8/5/28)
The Girl in the Limousine (Eltinge, N.Y., 10/19; Pleasure Gdns, Folkestone, 28/10/29)

HOPWOOD, E. R. M.

×Incog. (Court, 26/3/14)

HORAN, JAMES

[Several sketches and playlets produced at music-halls]

HORLER, SYDNEY

Oh! My Aunt! ('*f.*': Alex., B'ham, 17/9/28)

HORLICK, JITTIE

An Indian Summer (P.W., 11/6/14)

HORN, ISABEL

×At Madame Penelope's. LC, Village H., Cowfold, 24/4/22

HORNBLOW, A. [see *J. W. KLEIN*]

HORNE, CHRISTOPHER

×In the Hospital (Court, 28/2/05: adapted from a play by A. Schnitzler)
The Thieves' Comedy (Court, 21/3/05: adapted from a play by G. Hauptmann)

HORNE, I.

The Tall, Tall Castle. LC, Ass. R., Henfield, 5/4/23: +*M. MACNAMARA*

HORNE, KENNETH [see *F. FAULKNER*]

HORNIMAN, ROY

[For an earlier play see *H. E. D.* v, 427]

John Lester, Parson (Lyr., 20/1/02)

[This is listed in *Who's Who in the Theatre* as by Horniman, but elsewhere it appears as the work of *KNIGHT RIDER* and *LAYTON FOSTER*, q.v.]

Lady Flirt ('*c.*': H., 25/5/04)

The Education of Elizabeth (Apo., 19/10/07)

× The Walk (Apo., 27/1/08)

Idols (B'ham, 24/8/08; Gar., 2/9/08)

Bellamy the Magnificent ('*c.*': New, 6/10/08: dramatised from his own novel, 1904)

Billy's Fortune ('*c.*': Crit., 16/1/13)

The Blue Mouse (Brighton, 27/4/14; Crit., 12/5/14)

The Mystery of John Wake (Gai., Hastings, 3/4/16: +*L. WORRALL*)

Three Weeks (Str., 12/7/17: dramatised from the novel (1903) by Elinor Glyn)

The Edge o' Beyond (D.P., Eastbourne, 20/6/21; Gar., 9/8/21: dramatised from the novel (1908) by Gertrude Page: +*RUBY MILLER*)

Love in Pawn (O.H., Southport, 19/2/23; Kings., 31/3/23, *m.*)

Mrs Brown Turns Up ('*f.*': County, Bedford, 13/8/23)

The Money-Lender (Apo., Atlantic City, 17/11/24)

HORNUNG, ERNEST WILLIAM

Raffles, the Amateur Cracksman (Com., 12/5/06: dramatised from his own novel, *The Amateur Cracksman*, 1899: +*E. W. PRESBREY*) *Fr. 1913*

Stingaree, the Bushranger (Qns, 1/2/08)

× A Visit from Raffles (Empress, Brixton, 1/11/09: +*C. SANSOM*)

HORSNELL, H. [see *H. FARJEON*]

HORSPOOL, R.

Rogues and Courtesies (O.H., Bridlington, 19/11/24, Bridlington Augustinian Soc.)

HORTON, EDWARD

× Satisfaction (St Dunstan's H., Acton, 9/6/17, *amat.*)

HOSFORD, MAUDE [see *SARAH B. ELLIOTT*]

HOUGHAM, E. R.

Farther from the East ('*pl. for Scouts and Rovers*') *1928*

Three Plays for Scouts. *1928*

[This contains 1. *The Black Barn*; 2. *The Open Road*; and 3. *The Choice*]

'*HOUGHTON, CLAUDE*' [=*CLAUDE HOUGHTON OLDFIELD*]

Judas ('*t.*') *1922*

× In the House of the High Priest. *1923*

HOUGHTON, STANLEY [see also *F. G. NASMITH*]

[In this author's *Works* (1914) it is stated that he began his career by writing some comedies and farces for amateurs, all of which are now lost, and that he also composed at this time three one-acts, *After Naseby*, *The Last Shot* and *The Blue*, the texts of which also are non-extant]

×The Reckoning (Qns, Manchester, 22/7/07; Crown, Eccles, 30/9/12, as *The Day of Reckoning*: +*FRANK G. NASMITH*)

×The Dear Departed (Gai., Manchester, 2/11/08; Cor., 7/6/09) *Fr. 1910*

[This playlet, together with *Fancy Free*, *The Master of the House*, *Phipps* and *The Fifth Commandment*, was included in a collection called *Five One Act Plays*: see below]

Independent Means (Gai., Manchester, 30/8/09) *Fr. 1911*

×The Master of the House (Gai., Manchester, 26/9/10) *Fr. 1913*; *1913* (in *Five One Act Plays*)

Marriages in the Making (written 1909–10) *1914* (in *The Works*, vol. i)

The Younger Generation ('*c. for parents*': Gai., Manchester, 21/11/10; Cor., 8/5/12; H., 19/11/12) *Fr. 1910*

Ginger ('*sentimental f.*', written in 1910: Halifax, 26/9/13)

×Fancy Free ('*fant. c.*': Gai., Manchester, 10/11/11; Tiv., 17/6/12) *Fr. 1912*; *1913* (in *Five One Act Plays*)

[This provided the basic plot for *Partners*, written towards the end of 1911 but not acted until 1915: see below]

Partners ('*c.*': P's, Manchester, 19/4/15) *1914* (in *The Works*, vol. ii)

[See *Fancy Free*, above]

×The Fifth Commandment (Little, Chicago, 1913; Gai., Manchester, 14/7/14) *Fr. 1913*; *1913* (in *Five One Act Plays*)

[This play was written in 1911, and it also was later turned into a full-length piece, *The Perfect Cure*: see below]

The Perfect Cure ('*c.*': Apo., 17/6/13) *1914* (in *The Works*, vol. ii)

[See *The Fifth Commandment*, above]

Hindle Wakes (Aldw., 16/6/12, St. Soc.; Aldw., 16/7/12) *1912*

[This is also said to have been written in 1911. The London performances were given by Miss Horniman's Manchester company]

×Phipps (Gar., 19/11/12: title changed later to *Ask the Butler*) *Fr. 1913*; *1913* (in *Five One Act Plays*)

×Pearls (Pav., Glasgow, 20/12/12; Col., 6/1/13)

Trust the People (Gar., 6/2/13)

×The Old Testament and the New (Gai., Manchester, 22/6/14) *1914* (in *The Works*, vol. iii)

[This is said, but without any evidence, to have been written in 1905]

The Hillarys ('*c.*': Kelly's, L'pool, 30/4/15; Crit., 2/6/15: +*H. BRIGHOUSE*)

HOULSTON, WILLIAM JACKSON

Louis of Valois ('*r.pl.*': Church House, Erdington, 7/2/28)

HOUSDEN, H. F.

A Woman's Past (Metro., Devonport, 19/1/05; Carlton, Greenwich, 26/3/06)
Bonnie Mary (Sheffield, 26/11/10, *cpy.*; Dewsbury, 5/8/11; Edmonton, 27/11/11)
Midnight London ('*md.*': Star, Swansea, 27/3/11; Edmonton, 6/11/11)
A Blind Girl's Love (Coloss., Oldham, 8/3/12, *cpy.*; E.C., 16/7/12: title later changed to *Swiss Love*)
One Life, One Love ('*md.*': Gr., Halifax, 18/4/12, *cpy.*; Qns, Farnworth, 5/8/12; Metro., Manchester, 12/8/12)
The Mormon and His Wives ('*md.*': Junction, Manchester, 3/6/12; E.C., 24/2/13)
The Pride of the Prairie (E.C., 2/9/12)
Captain Cupid ('*m.c.*': Foresters, 26/5/13: called originally *On His Uppers* and later *Colonel Cupid*: first licensed for Worcester, LC, 27/9/07)
An Amazing Marriage (E.C., 13/10/13)

HOUSE, ROY TEMPLE

Colleague Crampton. LC, St G's H., 30/7/00: adapted from G. Hauptmann, *Kollege Crampton*, 1892)

HOUSMAN, LAURENCE [see also *H. M. PAULL*]

Bethlehem. A Nativity Play performed with music by Joseph Moorat under the stage-direction of Edward Gordon Craig. *1902*
[This was published in connection with an amateur performance at the Imperial Institute. During the same year the play appeared also in *Bethlehem: A Nativity Play. The Pageant of Our Lady & Other Poems*. In a revised version it was set to music by Rutland Boughton and so performed at the Regent Theatre, 19/12/23: the text was printed in 1927. For the bibliography, see *Edward Gordon Craig*, by Ifan Kyrle Fletcher and Arnold Rood (1967), and for the production in 1902 see M. P. Loeffler, *Gordon Craigs frühe Versuche zur Überwindung des Bühnenrealismus* (1969), pp. 90–6]
Prunella, or, Love in a Dutch Garden (Court, 23/12/04: +*H. GRANVILLE-BARKER*) *1906*; *1930* (*revised*)
The Vicar of Wakefield ('*r.o.*', m. L. Lehmann: P's, Manchester, 12/11/06; P.W., 12/12/06) *1906*
The Chinese Lantern ('*fairy pl.*', m. J. Moorat: H., 16/6/08, *m.*) *1908*
×A Likely Story (Court, 27/5/10, *m.*)
×The Lord of the Harvest ('*morality pl.*': Court, 27/5/10, *m.*)
Lysistrata (Little, 11/10/10: adapted from the play by Aristophanes) *1911* (*priv.*)
Alice in Ganderland ('*political skit*': Lyc., 27/10/11, *m.*) *1911* (*priv.*)
Pains and Penalties: the Defence of Queen Caroline (Sav., 26/11/11, Pioneer Players) *1911*
×Nazareth ('*morality pl.*') *Fr. 1916*

×Bird in Hand (*'fairy pl.'*: Vaud., 4/1/18, *m.*) *Fr. 1916*

The Wheel. *1919*

[This contains a 'trilogy', consisting of three short plays: 1. *Apollo in Hades*; 2. *The Death of Alcestis*; and 3. *The Doom of Admetus*]

Angels and Ministers, and Other Victorian Plays. *1921*

[This contains seven short plays, arranged in three sections. The first section, entitled 'Angels and Ministers', has 1. *The Queen: God Bless Her!* (Arts, 8/5/29); 2. *His Favourite Flower*; and 3. *The Comforter* (Lyr., Hamm., 3/10/29, as *Mr Gladstone's Comforter*). The second section, called 'The Everlasting Habitations', is devoted to a single play, *Possession* (*'a peep-show into Paradise'*: LC, Little, Sheffield, 24/4/23). The third section, 'Dethronements', deals with the last days of Parnell, Chamberlain and Woodrow Wilson, in 1. *The King-Maker*; 2. *The Man of Business*; and 3. *The Instrument*]

The Death of Orpheus. *1921*; *1925* (*'adapted for the stage'*)

False Premises: Four One-Act Plays. *1922*

[This contains: 1. *The Christmas Tree*; 2. *The Torch of Time*; 3. *Moonshine*; 4. *A Fool and His Money*; and 5. *The House Fairy* (Glastonbury, 31/8/21, as *The Fairy*)]

Little Plays of St Francis. *1922*

[This contains eighteen short plays: 1. *The Revellers*; 2. *Fellow-Prisoners*; 3. *Brief Life*; 4. *Blind Eyes*; 5. *The Bride Feast*; 6. *Our Lady of Poverty*; 7. *The Builders*; 8. *Brother Wolf*; 9. *Sister Clare*; 10. *The Lepers*; 11. *Sister Gold* (also called *As Good as Gold*); 12. *Brother Sun*; 13. *The Chapter*; 14. *Brother Juniper*; 15. *Brother Elias*; 16. *The Seraphic Vision*; 17. *Brother Sin*; 18. *Sister Death.* The success of these pieces soon led to a number of additions published in subsequent volumes: 1. *Fine Feathers*; 2. *The House of Bondage*; 3. *Naked Truth*; 4. *Blind Heart*; 5. *Sister Agnes*; 6. *The Gate of Death*; 7. *Juniper's First Sermon*; 8. *Bond of Fellowship*; 9. *The Gate of Life*; 10. *Juniper's Miracle*; 11. *The Temptation of Juniper*; 12. *The Odour of Sanctity*; and 13. *Holy Disobedience.* Others were included in separate collections, such as *The Followers of St Francis* (for which, see below). 'Public readings' and performances of many of the plays were given by amateurs at St Peter's Hall, Bournemouth, 20/3/23, and at University College, London, 18/1/27. In addition to these there have been numerous amateur productions of individual pieces selected from this series]

Followers of St Francis. *1923*

[This contains four short plays: 1. *Cure of Souls*; 2. *Lovers' Meeting*; 3. *The Fool's Errand*; and 4. *The Last Disciple*]

×Echo de Paris (*'a study from life'*). *1923*

×The Death of Socrates. *1925*

The Comments of Juniper. *1926*

[This contains six short plays associated with the 'St Francis' series: 1. *The Peace Makers*; 2. *The Mess of Pottage*; 3. *Brother Ass*; 4. *The Makers of Miracles*; 5. *The Order of Release*; and 6.

The Last Comment. It may be noted here that four related plays dealing with St Clare, published in 1934, seem to have been composed before 1930: 1. *Good Beating*; 2. *Kind Comfort*; 3. *Weaker Vessels*; and 4. *Holy Terror.* These were included with the St Francis plays in later editions of the *Little Plays of St Francis*, and most of them, if not all, were also issued separately]

Ways and Means: Five One Act Plays of Village Characters. *1928*

[This contains 1. *The Prize Pigeon*; 2. *The Called and the Chosen*; 3. *A Mint o' Money*; 4. *The Snow Man*; and 5. *A Likely Story*]

Cornered Poets: A Book of Dramatic Dialogues. *1929*

[This collection contains seven short sketches: 1. *The Fire-Lighters*; 2. *The Messengers*; 3. *Charles! Charles!*; 4. *The Cutty-Stool*; 5. *Elegy of a Country Churchyard*; 6. *Sal Volatile*; and 7. *The Mortuary*]

×The New Hangman. *1930*

Palace Plays. *1930*

[This contains two short pieces: 1. *The Revolting Daughter*; and 2. *The Wicked Uncles; or, Victorious Virtue*]

HOUSTON, N. [see *C. E. BLANEY*]

HOWARD, ANNETTE [see *D. CLYDE*]

[*HOWARD, FRANCIS MORTON*

×Money Makes a Difference ('*Cotswold c.*': Col., 2/8/26) *Fr. 1926*

HOWARD, HENRY NEWMAN

Kiartan, the Icelander ('*t.*': Gr., Boscombe, 29/11/01, *cpy.*) *1902*
Savonarola ('*a city's t.*') *1904*
Constantine the Great ('*t.*') *1906*

HOWARD, J. BAKER

Doped Goods. LC, Brynmawr, 30/4/19
A Mormon's Bride (Stratford, 27/11/22)
The Devil's Own (Stratford, 1/12/22)
Why Girls Go Wrong (Stratford, 26/2/23)
His Drunken Wife. LC, Stratford, 27/6/23
Her Egyptian Husband (Stratford, 3/12/23)

HOWARD, Rev. J. G. MORTON

Misunderstood. LC, St Mary's H., Elmsall, 25/11/20
A Goodly Heritage. LC, St Mary's H., Elmsall, 12/1/22
That French Hussy. LC, St Mary's H., Elmsall, 28/11/22
Old South Elmsall. LC, St Mary's H., Elmsall, 4/12/23
The Ring. LC, St Mary's H., Elmsall, 3/2/25

'*HOWARD, KEBLE*' [=*JOHN KEBLE BELL*]

×The Patent Love-Lock ('*c.*': Court, 5/7/01)
×Compromising Martha (Roy., 20/5/06, Pioneers) *Fr. 1906*
×Martha Plays the Fairy (H., 28/5/07) *Fr. 1907*
×Charles, His Friend (Pal., 5/8/07; Shak., Clapham, 14/2/10
The Cheerful Knave ('*c.*': Margate, 11/5/08; Shaft., 10/6/10) *1910*; *Fr. 1913*
×The Dramatist at Home (Vaud., 23/1/09) *Fr. 1909*

×Come Michaelmas (Adel., 26/4/09) *Fr. 1909*
×Old Martha. *Fr. 1909*
×Martha the Soothsayer. *Fr. 1909*
The Girl who Couldn't Lie ('*eccentric c.*': Roy., Glasgow, 29/3/11; Crit., 6/7/11)
×The Embarrassed Butler (Lyr., 28/5/12) *Fr. 1912*
Dropping the Pilot ('*c.*': Gr., Croydon, 12/5/13)
×The New Char (Pal., Chelsea, 13/10/13)
×The Man They Wouldn't Pass. LC, S. Ldn Pal., 11/2/15
Forked Lightning (Lyc., Edin., 15/4/15; Vaud., 11/6/15, as *The Green Flag*) *1918*; *Fr. 1919*
×The Sportsman. LC, Vaud., 22/6/15
×The Test Kiss (Pier, Brighton, 24/6/18; Col., 6/9/20) *Fr. 1922*
Sweet William ('*c.*': Pier, Brighton, 28/3/21; Shaft., 4/5/21) *1922*
The Smiths of Surbiton ('*c.*': New, 19/11/22, Rep. Players: dramatised from his novel, 1906)
×Puss in the Corner (Col., 22/1/23) *Fr. 1923*
×An Order to View (Pallad., 7/5/23)
Lord Babs ('*f.*': K's, Southsea, 29/6/25; Vaud., 26/1/28) *Fr. 1929*
×All in Train. LC, St J., 8/11/23

HOWARD, LOUIS G. REDMOND
An Irishman's Home, or, The Crisis ('*topical pl.*': Emp., Belfast, 18/11/18: +*H. CARSON*)

HOWARD, LESLIE
Collecting Cousins ('*f.*': O.H., Tunbridge Wells, 21/5/28)
Tell Me the Truth ('*f.*': Ambass., 18/6/28) *Fr. 1934*

HOWARD, OLIVE
A Little Child Shall Lead Them (K's, Walton-on-Naze, Jan. 1920; Stratford, 19/7/20)

[*HOWARD, SIDNEY COX*
They Knew What They Wanted ('*c.*': Gar., N.Y., 24/11/24; St M., 18/5/26) *1925*
The Silver Chord (John Golden, N.Y., 20/12/26; St M., 13/9/27) *1927*
Ned McCobb's Daughter. LC, St M., 8/9/27. *1927*

HOWARD, VELMA SWANSEN
Easter (Bedford H., Chelsea, 19/3/22, Pax Robertson Salon; Arts, 10/10/28: adapted from *Påsk* (1901) by A. Strindberg)

HOWARD, WALTER [see also '*F. HERBERT*']
[For earlier plays see *H. E. D.* v, 428]
For the King ('*historical d.*': Gr., Croydon, 27/3/1899; E.C., 26/2/00: title later changed to *Brothers in Heart*: +*S. T. PEASE*)
Man and Wife (Kidderminster, 16/4/00; Star, L'pool, 23/4/00; Stratford, 10/9/00; Gr., Clapham, 30/9/18, as *The Soldier's Bride*)
Why Men Love Women (Stratford, 29/11/00; Osbourne, Manchester, 29/7/01, *revised*)
Two Little Sailor Boys (Plymouth, 15/7/01; Terriss, Rotherhithe, 3/2/02; Stratford, 31/3/02)
Under the Russian Flag ('*r.d.*': Junction, Manchester, 1/9/02)

The Midnight Wedding (Junction, Manchester, 30/10/05; W.L., 25/2/07; Lyc., 15/6/07)
Her Love against the World ('*r.pl.*': Junction, Manchester, 17/9/06; Lyc., 30/3/07)
Second to None (Junction, Manchester, 1/4/07; W.L., 19/8/07: called originally *Midst Shot and Shell*)
The Prince and the Beggar-Maid (Lyc., 6/6/08)
×The Last Hope (Emp., Holloway, 15/2/09)
The Boy King ('*r.pl.*': Junction, Manchester, 3/10/10; M'sex, 15/4/12, condensed version as *The Ragged Prince*)
The Lifesguardsman ('*r.pl.*': Junction, Manchester, 6/9/11; M'sex, 18/3/12, condensed version)
The Soldier Princess ('*r.d.*': Junction, Manchester, 4/9/12; Ealing, 11/11/12)
The Story of the Rosary ('*r.d.*': Junction, Manchester, 17/9/13; P's, 20/12/13)
The Silver Crucifix (Junction, Manchester, 28/8/15; P.W., 26/2/16)
Seven Days' Leave (Lyc., 14/2/17)
The Silent House Mystery (Hippo., Nuneaton, 5/1/20)
The Boy of My Heart (Lyc., 6/3/20)
The Under-dog (York, 17/4/22; Borough, Stratford, 4/8/24)

HOWARD, WILSON
The Kingdom of His Heart (Hebburn, 18/3/09)
To Right His People's Wrongs (W. Stanley, 23/6/13)
The Broken Trail (Gr., Nottingham, 15/10/17; Qns, Poplar, 22/10/17)
Back from Overseas (Dewsbury, 24/5/18)
Let There Be Light (Vic., Lye, Stourbridge, 12/3/19; E.C., 26/8/19, as *Why Blame the Girl?*)

HOWARD DE WALDEN, Lord [see '*T. E. ELLIS*']

HOWARD-TURNER, CECIL
Adrienne Lecouvreur (Cosmopolis, 8/6/13: from the play (1849) by E. Scribe and E. Legouvé)

HOWE, EDNA HAY
×The Dream Woman (Clavier H., 23/6/12)
×The Magic Violin (Passmore Edwards Settlement, 26/4/13)
×The Minuet (Battersea Polytechnic, 12/7/13)
×Cousin Deborah (Passmore Edwards Settlement, 21/11/13)
×O'Flanagan (Passmore Edwards Settlement, 21/11/13)
×The Migration of Birds (Passmore Edwards Settlement, 25/4/14)
The Land of Happiness ('*masque*': Battersea Polytechnic, 17/7/15)
Pierre (Ben Greet Academy, 27/1/22)
The White Lady (O.C., Northampton, 10/9/28)

HOWE, RONALD
×Fowl Play (Broadway, New X, 20/2/11)

HOWE, WALTER
A Victim of Villainy (*md.*': Bij., 26/5/04; Borough, Stratford, 1/8/04)

HOWITT, MARY FORD

Lord Byron (O.H., Harrogate, 18/2/26)

HOWLAND, HARMAN

×Fairy Fay. LC, St G's H., Ealing, 13/12/21: +*L. SPILLER*

Black Magic, and Other Plays. (+*L. SPILLER*) *1923*

[This contains three short plays for children: 1. *Cinderella*; 2. *The Daffodil Fairies*; and 3. *Black Magic*]

The Toy Soldiers, and Other Musical Plays (+*E. STUART MONRO*) *1929*

[Besides the title-piece, this contains two other short plays for children: 1. *Ali Baba*; and 2. *Pepperminto*]

[*HOYT, CHARLES H.*

A Parlour Match ('*f.c.*': Terry's, 4/10/00)

HUBBACK, FRANCIS W.

Alcestis (London University, 15/12/11, Elizabethan St. Soc.; Little, 3/1/12: translated from the play by Euripides)

HUBBARD, PHILIP E. [see also *W. W. JACOBS* and *A. N. LYONS*,

The Barrier (Kelly's, L'pool, 15/7/12; E.C., 18/11/12; Str., 17/7/13: from the novel (1908) by Rex Beach)

East is East ('*c.*': Roy., Glasgow, 23/2/14: title later changed to *Victoria and Albert*)

The Silver Horde (Gr., Blackpool, 22/6/14: from the novel (1909) by Rex Beach)

×The Crumbs that Fall (Gai., Manchester, 20/9/15)

HUBERT, WILLIAM

The Soldier of the Czar (Belfast, 26/9/02; Brixton, 21/11/02)

HUDSON, ERIC V. [see also *C. H. LONGDEN*, *S. ROBERT*, *W. P. SHEEN* and *A. SHIRLEY*]

[For earlier plays see *H. E. D.* v, 429]

Little Heroes (Coloss., Oldham, 29/3/00; Lyr., Hamm., 24/9/00: +*C. H. LONGDEN*)

My Neighbour's Wife (Leamington, 30/11/10: +*C. H. LONGDEN*)

New Wives for Old ('*f.c.*': H.M., Aberdeen, 30/3/22; Hippo., Balham, 21/4/24; Fortune, 16/2/26, as *Do Be Careful*)

Reckless Reggie ('*f.*': Glo., 18/7/23)

The Unfair Sex ('*f.c.*': Playh., Felixstowe, 3/9/25; Sav., 9/9/25) *Fr. 1927*

HUDSON, GILBERT

×In Deadly Earnest. LC, Central H., Pickering, 22/4/19

×The May Moon ('*pl. for children*') *1925* (Berkhamstead, *priv.*)

×The Silver Candlesticks. *1929* (*priv.*)

HUDSPETH, FRANK

×The House Opposite (Pier, Bognor, 8/5/16)

HUEFFER, OLIVER MADOX

The Lord of Latimer Street (Terry's, 26/2/08: dramatised from his own novel (1907) published under the pseudonym of 'Jane Wardle')

The Fifth Queen Crowned (Kings., 19/3/09, *m.*: +'*C. O'RIORDAN*')

Down Stream ('*c.*': Pav., Hastings, 18/9/11)

HUGHES, A. H.

×The Sea ('*fant.*') *Fr. 1919*

×Endymion (Mary Ward Settlement, 23/2/24, Dram. Art Centre Rep. Company)

HUGHES, ANNIE

[For an earlier play see *H. E. D.* v, 430]

Lorna Doone (Aven., 30/6/03: dramatised from the novel (1869) by R. D. Blackmore)

×His First Love (H., 18/5/05)

×After Many Years (Gai., Douglas, 16/9/07)

HUGHES, E. A.

×The Twins Decide. LC, Rep., Plymouth, 6/12/17

HUGHES, H. O.

×The Miller of Monmouth (Lyc., Newport, 12/10/06)

×His Last Stage (Court, 30/1/10, Pl. Actors)

×Coron y Bardd. *1922* (Lerpwl)

×Y Lodger. *1922* (Lerpwl)

[*HUGHES, HATCHER*

Hell-Bent for Heaven (Klaw, N.Y., 30/12/23; Everyman, 6/4/26). *1924* (New York)

HUGHES, LEONARD STANLEY

×A Snake in the Grass (Crippl. Inst., 3/4/07)

HUGHES, P. V.

Molly and the Master (Pav., Worthing, 22/5/09, *cpy.*)

HUGHES, R. J.

×Uncle Barney's Dollars (Emp., Dublin, 25/6/17; Alex., 6/8/17)

Shaun the Post ('*r.o.*', m. H. R. White: Dublin, 15/8/24)

HUGHES, RICHARD ARTHUR WARREN

×The Sisters' Tragedy (Masefield's house, Boar's Hill, Oxford, 24/1/22, *amat.*; Little, 31/5/22) *1922* (Oxford)

The Sisters' Tragedy, and Three Other Plays. *1924*

[Besides the title-piece this contains a one-act play, *The Man Born to Be Hanged* (T.H., Portmadoc, April, 1923; Lyr., Hamm., 26/2/24, Portmadoc Players); *A Comedy of Good and Evil* (Court, 6/7/24, 300 Club; Ambass., 30/3/25); and a play written for broadcasting, *Danger* (B.B.C. broadcast, 15/1/24)]

[*HUGHES, RUPERT*

×A Wooden Wedding ('*c.*': D.P., Eastbourne, 26/5/02; Shaft., 3/6/02)

Excuse Me! ('*Pullman carnival*': Allantown, Pa., 13/1/11; Gai., N.Y., 13/2/11; Gar., 6/3/15) *1912*

HUGHES, TALBOT

[For an earlier play see *H. E. D.* v, 430]

A Bedouin Beauty ('*light o.*', m. F. Rosse and R. King: D.P., Eastbourne, 22/8/10; O.H., Woolwich, 29/8/10)

HULBERT, JACK [see also *M. AMBIENT* and *R. COURTNEIDGE*]
×Acting to Act (New, Cambridge, 3/2/13, *amat.*)
Cheer-oh! Cambridge ('*m.c.*': Qns, 12/6/13, *amat.*)
×The Cambridge Gazette. LC, Chatham, 20/2/14
The Cinema Star ('*m.c.*', m. J. Gilbert: Shaft., 4/6/14)
[A few sketches produced at music-halls]

HUME, FERGUS
[For earlier plays see *H. E. D.* v, 430]
Honours Divided (Gr., Margate, 1/9/02)
×A Scotch Marriage ('*c.*': Crit., 26/12/07)
×The Mystery of the Red Web (Olympia, L'pool, 13/3/08; Cant., 18/5/08: +*N. HARDING*)

HUME, M.
×Barker's Dog. LC, Arcade H., Stirling, 30/4/17

HUME, MARGARET
Marie Antoinette. *1924*

HUME, PHYLLIS [see *W. T. IVORY*]

HUMPHREY, C.
The Smugglers of Beachy Head ('*m.pl.*', m. E. Willoughby: Hippo., Eastbourne, 18/1/26: +*A. W. G. MATTHEWS*)

HUMPHREY, H. E. [see *B. J. McOWEN*]

HUMPHREYS, Mrs DESMOND R. L. [='*RITA*']

HUMPHRY, HUGH MACNAB [='*HUGH MacNAB*']

HUNTER, E. E.
A Fallen Idol. LC, Qns, Farnworth, 28/8/14
Boys of the Bull-dog Breed (Stratford, 6/9/15)

HUNTER, HARRY
The Late Mr. Blackthorne (Pav., Hastings, 15/7/03)

HUNTER, HORACE
×Ex-Corporal Stubbs, Investigator. LC, K's, Southsea, 15/9/15
[Numerous sketches and playlets produced at music-halls]

HUNTER, J. MAURICE
×The Eclectics' Club (Rehearsal, 25/4/11, *m.*)

HUNTER, R. G.
×The Meeting. LC, Glasgow, 10/12/13
The Brain Wave ('*m.c.*', m. R. Letts: Col., 23/5/21)

HUNTER, T. OWEN
×Zingaro (Cant., 11/12/11)

HUNTLEY, G. P.
The Hon'ble Phil ('*m.c.*', m. H. Samuel: Hicks', 3/10/18: +*H. CLAYTON*)

HURGON, AUSTEN A. [see also *P. A. RUBENS*]
×The Impossible Trio (Gr., Croydon, 5/2/06)
×The Eternal Waltz ('*c.o.*', m. L. Fall: Hippo., 22/12/11)
×Arms and the Girl (Hippo., 29/4/12)

The Blue House ('*m.pl.*', m. E. Kalman: Hippo., 28/10/12)
×What Ho! Ragtime! ('*travesty*': Hippo., L'pool, 31/3/13; Emp., Chiswick, 9/6/13)
Suzette ('*m.c.*', m. M. Darewski: Glo., 29/3/17: +*G. ARTHURS*)
Arlette ('*c.o.*', m. J. Vien, G. le Fevre and I. Novello: P's, Manchester, 27/8/17; Shaft., 6/9/17: +*G. ARTHURS*)
Yes, Uncle ('*m.pl.*', m. N. D. Ayer: P.W., 29/12/17: +*G. ARTHURS*)
The Girl for the Boy ('*m.c.*', m. H. Carr and B. Rolt: Qns, Manchester, 23/9/19: +*G. ARTHURS*)
His Girl ('*m.pl.*', m. E. Longstaffe and M. Darewski: Gai., 1/4/22: +*F. W. THOMAS*)

[*HURLBUT, WILLIAM JAMES* [see also *D. BELASCO*]
The Fighting Hope (E.C., 26/8/08, *cpy.*)
The Writing on the Wall (Terry's, 11/1/09, *cpy.*; Wynd., 2/7/23, *m.*)
Trimmed in Scarlet (Nottingham, 25/4/18; Glo., 7/7/19)
Over Sunday ('*f.c.*': Playh., L'pool, 1/9/19; St M., 27/2/20)
Engaged ('*f.*': Portsmouth, 24/5/26; Glo., 1/6/26)

HURN, PHILIP
The Sin Machine (Three Arts Club, 17/11/29)

HURST, CYRIL
[For an earlier play see *H. E. D.* 431]
The Royal Vagrants ('*c.o.*', m. H. W. Warner: Earlham H., Forest Gate, 27/10/1899; Guildhall School of Music, 6/7/00) *1901*
The Officers' Mess ('*m.c.*', m. M. Strong: W.L., 3/4/05; Terry's, 10/4/05)

HUSKINSON, LEONARD
The Widow's Might ('*c.*': H., 15/11/16: +*C. SANDEMAN*)

HUSTON, W. CHAPMAN
×The Ashes of the Past (Passmore Edwards Settlement, 4/6/04)

HUTCHINS, WILL
×Pater Noster (St J., 20/2/08, *m.*) *1915*

HUTCHINSON, A. S. M. [see *B. M. HASTINGS*]

HUTCHINSON, ERNEST
×The Fulfilment (Stafford House, St James's, 11/5/11, *m.*)
×Votes for Children. LC, Little, 18/11/13
×Complaints (Gai., Manchester, 26/10/14)
The Right to Strike (Gar., 28/9/20)

HUTCHINSON, H. E.
×The Home Wind. LC, Bolton, 30/4/17

HUTCHINSON, LANCELOT
The Failure ('*c.*': Court, 9/11/11, *m.*)

HUTCHINSON, M. F.
[Numerous playlets for children, chiefly for girls, printed in 1908 and 1909]

HUTCHINSON, MARY

×The Surrey Zoo. LC, Adel., 21/10/18: +*N. PLAYFAIR*

HUTCHINSON, MURIEL [see *R. WILSON*]

HUTCHINSON, ROBERT

×Reparation. LC, Gr., Lancaster, 19/3/18

HUTTON, CONSTANCE

×The Month of Mary (Little, 18/5/13, Pioneer Players: adapted from the *Mese Mariano* (1898) by S. di Giacomo)

HUTTON, P. D.

Love and the Law (D.P., Eastbourne, 23/2/14)

HUXLEY, ALDOUS LEONARD

The Discovery (RADA, 4/5/24, 300 Club: adapted from the play (1763) by Frances Sheridan) *1924*

HYAMS, HILDA

The Master (Q, 1/3/26)

HYDE, DOUGLAS ARNOLD [see *Lady GREGORY*]

×Casadh-an-tSúgáin (Gai., Dublin, 21/10/01, Irish Literary Theatre) *1902* (Dublin)

×The Marriage (Abbey, Dublin, 30/11/11)

×An tincéar agus an tSídheóg (Abbey, Dublin, 15/1/12)

HYDE, FRANCIS AUSTIN

×Wireless and Sich-like. *1927* (Leeds)

×A Bit of Help. *1928* (Village Drama Soc.)

×Honest Folk. *1928* (Village Drama Soc.)

×First Aid. *1928* (Village Drama Soc.)

×The Ship Comes In. LC, Parish H., Yelverton, 11/12/29. *1929* (Village Drama Soc.)

HYMER, JOHN B. [see *S. SHIPMAN*]

IBBETSON, E. F.

×The Dais. *1930*

IBBOTSON, MACHON

×The Black Dogs. *1929* (Village Drama Soc.)

IDE, LEONARD

These Few Ashes ('*c.*': D.Y., 16/4/29) *Fr. 1937*

ILLINGWORTH, A. E. [see *L. CLIFF*]

INGALL, NORMAN

The Traitress ('*o.*', m. L. Rendle: Arts Centre, 4/3/14)

INGLEBY, FRED G.

The Woman from Russia (Jarrow, 25/7/08, *cpy.*; Alex., Sheffield, 22/9/08)

×Among the Missing (Bed., 22/2/15)

INGLIS, GUY H. [see also *N. YORKE*]

×The Man from Aden (Vic. H., 6/5/05)

×In Search of a Girl (Clavier H., 9/10/12)

INGLIS, W. BERESFORD

Rosette ('*c.o.*', m. G. H. Martin: Glasgow, 29/4/18)

INGRAM, NORMAN C.

×The Cup of Tea. LC, Crippl. Inst., 3/3/15

A Tale of Alsatia ('*o.*', m. V. Thomas: Crane H., L'pool, 14/1/25, *amat.*)

INKSTER, LEONARD

The Emancipation ('*modern pl.*': Temperance H., Sheffield, 9/10/12, *amat.*) *1913*

×The Death of Chopin (LC, Gai., Manchester, 18/8/13)

INNES, MARIE

The Passing of Babel (in English and Esperanto: Dick Inst., Kilmarnock, 4/6/14)

INSTONE, ALFRED

×An Exceptional Case (Ambass., 4/6/20, *m.*)

INSTONE, HARRY

×In Old Virginia (Oldham, 23/9/07)

IRELAND, McNEILL

×A Mirage of Misfortune (Court, 21/11/13)

IRVINE, J. H.

×The Fur Cloak (R.A., Woolwich, 15/2/09)

×A Sense of Humour (Rehearsal, 16/9/12, Black Cat Club)

IRVING, H. B.

Mauricette (Lyr., 31/1/06: adapted from A. Picard, *Jeunesse*, 1905)

IRVING, LAURENCE B. [SYDNEY BROADRIBB IRVING: = 'H. M. CLARK']

[For earlier plays see *H. E. D.* v, 432]

Bonnie Dundee ('*r. historical pl.*': Adel., 10/3/00)

Dante (D.L., 30/4/03: adapted from the play by V. Sardou and É. Moreau)

Richard Lovelace ('*r.pl.*': Worthing, 27/7/03; Kennington, 13/6/04; D.P., Eastbourne, 2/2/25, revised by *M. HOLLOWAY*)

The Lower Depths (Gt. Qn. St., 30/11/03, St. Soc.; Kings., 2/12/11: adapted from *Na dne* (1902) by Maxim Gorki) *1912*

The Incubus (Imp., 24/3/07, St. Soc.; Cor., 24/6/07; Court, 1/10/07: adapted from É. Brieux, *Les Hannetons*, 1906)

×The Phoenix (Cor., 25/6/07; Court, 1/10/07) *Fr. 1907*

×The Lion and the Unicorn (Bolton, 28/8/07: +*T. HESLEWOOD*)

×Peg Woffington (Gr., B'ham, 27/1/08)

×The King and the Vagabond (Col., 7/12/08: adapted from T. de Banville, *Gringoire*, 1866)

The Unwritten Law (Gai., Manchester, 15/8/10; Gr., Croydon, 17/10/10; Gar., 14/11/10: dramatised from F. M. Dostoievsky's *Crime and Punishment*)

×The Terrorist (D.Y., 15/4/11)

The Barber of Seville, or, The Futile Precaution (O.H., Harrogate, 25/7/12: adapted from *La précaution inutile, ou Le barbier de Séville* (1775) by P. A. Caron de Beaumarchais)

Typhoon (Tyne, Newcastle, 3/10/12; H., 2/4/13: adapted from M. Lengyel, *Taifun*) *1913*

IRWIN, Father

× The Irish Attorney (St Mary's H., London, E., 1/6/09, *amat.*)

IRWIN, EDWARD

× When the Cat's Away (Irving, Seacombe, 30/9/07: + *S. LATHBURY*)

His Son (W.G., New Brighton, 10/2/13; D.P., Eastbourne, 30/11/14; Leamington, 3/11/24, as *The Man who Came Home*; Gr., Putney, 8/12/24: + *E. H. EDWARDES*)

IRWIN, MARGARET EDNA FAITH

× The Happy Man ('*children's pl.*') *1921* (Oxford)

ISAACS, SIDNEY C.

Israel (Str., 11/4/26, Jewish Drama League; Everyman, 10/10/27: from the play (1908) by H. Bernstein)

ISAACSON, BEATRICE

The Day of Reckoning (Sur., 10/12/00)

ISHAM, F. S.

× The Toyshop. LC, P's, Manchester, 8/5/15: + *E. WEITZEL*

[This appears to have been a revised version of the 'drama for children', *Fr. 1893*]

IVER, S. D.

× The Outlaw. LC, Crippl. Inst., 15/9/23

IVES, ALICE E.

Starr's Girl ('*r.pl.*': Emp., Southend, 20/11/02)

IVORY, A. W.

A Spanish Romance ('*m.pl.*' : Emp., Edmonton, 21/11/21)

IVORY, WILLIAM T.

The Crimson Butterfly ('*m.c.*', m. E. Coppo: East, Oxford, 31/1/10)

Lucky Miss Chance (Alex., Pontefract, 13/1/13; Gr., Fulham, as a '*c. revue*', *The Revue Girl*, 1/12/13; also called *Happy Go Lucky*: + *K. MORRISON*)

Miss Sauce, of Worcester ('*m.c.*': Playh., Stafford, 24/5/15: + *K. MORRISON*)

Our Miss Cinders ('*m.c.*', m. K. Morrison: Pal., Battersea, 27/3/16)

Joytime ('*m.c.*', m. P. Hume: Pal., Battersea, 4/8/19)

The Girl whom God Forgot (Pal., Battersea, 6/3/22: + *P. HUME*)

The Modern Jezebel. LC, Sunderland, 15/6/24: + *P. HUME*

The Charlady ('*c.*': Pier, Brighton, 23/3/25: + *M. DUNCAN*)

California. LC, Hippo., Wrexham, 8/5/25

JACK, ADOLPHUS ALFRED
The Prince. *1900*
Mathilde. *1908*
The Angry Heart ('*d.d.*') *1928*

JACK, HENRY VERNON [='*H. V. ESMOND*']

JACKSON, Sir BARRY VINCENT [see also *B. DEAN, J. DRINKWATER* and *G. SCHURHOFF*]
Blinkin' Bill ('*f.*': The Grange, B'ham, 1904, *amat.*)
×The Christmas Party ('*children's pl.*': Rep., B'ham, 10/2/14) *1922*
The Marvellous History of St Bernard ('*mystery*': Rep., B'ham, 16/5/25; Kings., 7/4/26: from the play (1924) by H. Ghéon) *1927*
The Marriage of Figaro (Court, 7/11/26, Renaissance Theatre: adapted from Beaumarchais' play)

JACKSON, BLANCHE
Her Little Bit of Heaven (Qns, Dublin, 12/6/16; Vic., Walthamstow, 17/7/16; E.C., 4/9/16: +*J. L. JACKSON*)

JACKSON, FREDERICK
The Naughty Wife ('*c.*': Harris, N.Y., 17/11/17, as *Losing Eloise*; Playh., 11/4/18: +*E. SELWYN*) *Fr. 1925*
The Love Girl ('*m.c.*', m. R. Cox and E. Horan: Pleasure Gdns, Folkestone, 26/7/20: title later changed to *The Purple Lady*)
Stop Flirting ('*m.f.*', m. W. Daly and P. Lannin: Lyc., Edin., 7/5/23; Shaft., 30/5/23: called originally *For Goodness Sake*)
Mercenary Mary ('*m.c.*', m. W. B. Friedlander and C. Conrad: Washington, 30/3/25; Longacre, N.Y., 13/4/25; Alh., Glasgow, 7/9/25; Hippo., 7/10/25)
Beginner's Luck ('*c.*': Glo., 1/9/25)
The Duchess Decides ('*c.*': York, 19/7/26; Alex., 31/1/27)
Just a Kiss ('*m.f.*', m. M. Yvain: P's, Manchester, 31/7/26; Shaft., 8/9/26)
Two Little Girls in Blue ('*m.c.*', m. V. Youmans: Portsmouth, 18/4/27)
The Love-lorn Lady (K's, Southsea, 12/11/28; Gr., Croydon, 26/11/28; Wynd., 26/12/28)
Her Past ('*f.c.*': Hippo., Lewisham, 26/11/28; Shaft., 23/1/29)
Open Your Eyes ('*m.c.*', m. V. Duke and C. Gibbons: Emp., Edin., 26/8/29)
The King's Messenger (Q, 7/7/30)

JACKSON, J. LEICESTER [see also *BLANCHE JACKSON*]
Fourteen Days' Leave (P'cess, Glasgow, 4/11/18)

JACKSON, JOHN
[Numerous sketches and playlets produced at music-halls]

JACKSON, MARGARET NELSON
×The Ending (Court, 7/3/11, Rehearsal Co.)

JACKSON, MYRTLE B. STRODE
The Merry-Thought Plays: six plays for amateur dramatic clubs. *1908*

×Meg, the Match Girl. LC, Court, 26/1/14
×The Play-actress (Pav., Eastbourne, 4/6/17)

JACKSON, PHILIP [see *A. MILTON*]

JACOB, NAOMI
×The Dawn (Ath., Glasgow, 13/11/23, Scott. Nat. Th. Soc.)

JACOBS, BERTRAM
Uriel Acosta (Gar., 11/12/27, Jewish Drama League)

JACOBS, WILLIAM WYMARK [see also *L. N. PARKER*]
×The Grey Parrot (D.P., Eastbourne, 2/11/1899; Str., 6/11/1899: +*C. ROCK*) *Fr. 1908*
Beauty and the Barge (New, 30/8/04: +*L. N. PARKER*) *Fr. 1910*
×The Temptation of Samuel Burge (Imp., 9/11/05: +*F. FENN*)
×The Boatswain's Mate (Wynd., 15/4/07; revised as a c.o., with music by Ethel Smyth, Shaft., 28/1/16: +*H. C. SARGENT*) *Fr. 1907*
×The Ghost of Jerry Bundler (+*C. ROCK*) *Fr. 1908*
×The Changeling (Wynd., 18/3/08: +*H. C. SARGENT*)
×Admiral Peters (Pav., Eastbourne, 3/8/08; Gar., 25/5/09: +*H. MILLS*)
×A Love Passage (Little, 3/2/13: +*P. E. HUBBARD*) *Fr. 1913*
×In the Library (Ldn O.H., 17/2/13: +*H. C. SARGENT*) *Fr. 1913*
×Keeping Up Appearances (Sav., 17/4/15: title later changed to *Departed Spirits*) *Fr. 1919*
×The Castaway (+*H. C. SARGENT*) *Fr. 1924*
×Establishing Relations. *Fr. 1926*
×The Warming Pan. *Fr. 1929*
×Master Mariners. *Fr. 1930*

[*JAFFA, MINNIE Z.*
In Walked Jimmie ('*c.*': Pier, Brighton, 9/3/25; Q, 21/9/25) *Fr. 1920*

JAGGER, ARTHUR
×Arms and the Maid, or Rustic Ribaldry. *Fr. 1929*

JAMES, ADA
[For an earlier play see *H. E. D.* v, 432]
×The Long Road (+*D. JAMES*) *1902*
×The Largesse of the Sea (T.H., W. Hampstead, 1/12/03: +*D. JAMES*)
×Chance the Diplomat (T.H., W. Hampstead, 1/12/03: +*D. JAMES*)
×According to His Lights (Lyc. Club, 26/10/11: +*D. JAMES*)
×The Doctor. LC, Lyc., Dumfries, 18/11/15: +*D. JAMES*

JAMES, BASIL [see also *E. LOCKE*]
×Victims (Cosmopolis, 13/2/13; Bed., 3/10/14: +*W. PEACOCK*)

[*JAMES, BENEDICT*
The Little Brother (Ambass., 6/2/18; Alex., Toronto, 7/10/18; Belmont, N.Y., 25/11/18; Court, 1/6/22, as *The Rabbi and the Priest*)

JAMES, CECIL [see *D. McGEOCH*]

JAMES, CHARLES

[For earlier plays see *H. E. D.* v, 433, 799]

The Value of Being Extinct ('*f.*': County, Kingston, 3/10/04: +*C. GOODHART*)

JAMES, DAVID

Little Nell (Pav., St Leonards, 20/1/02)

The Scottish Bluebells ('*m.c.*', m. O. Carr: Gr., Edin., 31/3/06)

JAMES, DUDLEY [see *A. JAMES*]

JAMES, EDGAR

The Master of the House (Nottingham, 16/6/19)

JAMES, ERIC [see *S. PRINGLE*]

JAMES, FRANK SAMUEL

The Penalty (Q, 10/3/30)

JAMES, GRACE

×The Dancing Shoes. *Fr. 1921*

×The Pork-Pie Hat. LC, Crippl. Inst., 1/11/22. *Fr. 1922*

×The Cucumber Ring ('*Chinese pl.*') *Fr. 1924*

Garden Plays. *Fr. 1926*

[This contains four short plays: 1. *The New Nanny*; 2. *Fancy!*; 3. *The Shepherd's Bundle*; and 4. *The Pierrot's Wedding*]

JAMES, HENRY

[For earlier plays see *H. E. D.* v, 433, 799]

The High Bid ('*c.*': Lyc., Edin., 26/3/08; H.M., 18/2/09, *m.*, Afternoon Theatre: called originally *Covering End*)

×The Saloon (Little, 17/1/11)

The Outcry ('*c.*': Sav., 1/7/17, St. Soc.)

×The Reprobate ('*c.*': Court, 14/12/19, *m.*)

[*The Complete Plays*, edited by Léon Edel, appeared in 1949]

'*JAMES, JAMES*' [=*A. H. ADAMS*]

JAMES, L. CAIRNS

Molly and the Model ('*m.f.*', m. P. Henry: Steinway H., 26/5/02: +*C. AVELING*)

Maud, Chief Justice ('*m.f.*', m. A. Barratt: Steinway H., 21/5/03: +*V. MATHEWS*)

Reforming a Burglar ('*m.f.*', m. P. Henry: Steinway H., 26/5/04: +*V. MATHEWS*)

The Critic; or, An Opera Rehearsal ('*m.f.*', m. Sir C. V. Stanford: Shaft., 14/1/16: adapted from R. B. Sheridan's play)

JAMES, M. [see *WILFRED HALL*]

JAMES, OWEN

The Brand of the Rosary (Metro., Devonport, 21/6/15; Pal., Bow, 6/9/15)

Drug Fiends (Vic., Walthamstow, 14/4/19: title later changed to *The Secret Peril*)

The Wife who Wouldn't. LC, Hippo., Burslem, 4/7/19

The Miners' Agent (Emp., New Tredegar, 23/2/20)

JAMES, SPENCER T.

×The Death Trap (Alex. H., Leeds, 18/3/11, *cpy.*; Arts Centre, 23/7/13)

JAMESON, EDWARD

Myself and the Duchess ('*f.c.*': Peterborough, 17/5/20, *amat.*)

×The Street Musician (Coronation H., Wainfleet, 17/1/24, *amat.*)

JAMESON, R. L.

×Mountain Lovers ('*oa.*', m. H. Baynton-Power: Qns, 29/10/20: +*F. M. FARRER*)

JAMESON, STORM [=*MARGARET STORM JAMESON*]

×Full Circle (Playh., L'pool, 1928) *1928* (Oxford)

JANIS, ELSIE

It's All Wrong ('*m. complaint*', m. H. Finck: Qns, 13/12/20)

JANITSCH, D.

The Raven's Cry ('*r.d.*': Str., 29/3/10)

JANSSEN, Capt.

The Little Match Girl ('*m.pl.*': W.G., Bournemouth, 26/12/17: also performed as *The Dumb Little Match Girl*)

JARMAN, FREDERICK

[For earlier plays see *H. E. D.* v, 434]

The Marriage Market ('*f.c.*': Torquay, 16/1/01)

The Convict (R.A., Woolwich, 29/7/01; Stratford, 18/11/01)

The Spiritualist ('*md.*': Sur., 14/7/02)

In Dark Siberia ('*Anglo-Russian d.*': W.L., 22/2/04)

The 'Varsity Belle ('*m.f.*', m. E. Jones: Dover, 20/2/05)

Lady Lucky ('*m.c.*': O.H., Weymouth, 12/7/06)

A Woman's Shame (Qns, Dublin, 18/1/07)

Under the Iron Heel (Edmonton, 18/10/09)

JAST, LOUIS STANLEY

The Lover and the Dead Woman, and Five Other Plays in Verse. *1923*

[This contains six short plays: 1. *The Lover and the Dead Woman* (Margaret Morris, 25/2/22, Unnamed Soc. of Manchester); 2. *The Geisha's Wedding*; 3. *The Loves of the Elements*; 4. *The Call of the Ninth Wave*; 5. *Venus and the Shepherdess*; and 6. *Harbour* ('*playlet of the soul*': Margaret Morris, 25/2/22, Unnamed Soc. of Manchester)]

×The Pack (Little, Manchester, 17/1/27, Unnamed Soc.)

Shah Jahan ('*historical pl.*': Little, Manchester, 14/1/29, Unnamed Soc.) *1934*

JAY, F.

×The Cobweb (Abbey, Dublin, 13/10/14)

JAY, HARRIET [='*CHARLES MARLOWE*']

JAY, ISABEL

The Inevitable (Gai., Hastings, 26/2/23; St J., 21/3/23)

JAY, J. HERBERT

×Wanted – James Burton (Vic., Ramsgate, 8/7/07)

JAY, THOMAS [see also *W. BRODIE*]
The Man at the Window ('*c.*': Little, Bristol, 29/12/24)
Concerning Mr Conway ('*c.*': Little, Bristol, 2/11/25)

JAZON, E. C.
[Several music-hall sketches and musicals]

JEANS, RONALD [see also *N. COWARD* and *J. TILLER*]
The Cage ('*c.*': Court, 10/6/13, *m.*)
×A Man with a Maid (Gai., Manchester, 10/11/13: called originally *Under Notice* and *The Man and the Maid*)
Two and Two ('*c.*': Playh., L'pool, 26/1/14)
The Kiss Cure ('*c.*': Gai., Manchester, 10/8/14; Kings., 3/5/15)
×Pauline (Kings., 3/5/15)
Hullo, Repertory! ('*bsq. revue*': Playh., L'pool, 24/3/15; Col., 21/6/15)
No Reflection on the Wife ('*c.*': Playh., L'pool, 6/10/15)
Oh! Law! ('*bsq. revue*': K's, Southsea, 8/5/16; Hippo., Balham, 2/10/16, revised as *On and Off*; Emp., Finsbury Park, 15/5/16: also called *Have a Banana*)
Give and Take ('*c.*': Playh., L'pool, 15/11/17)
Wild Geese ('*m.c.*', m. C. Cuvillier: Plymouth, 2/2/20; Com., 12/2/20)
Pot Luck ('*ent.*', m. P. Braham and others: Vaud., 24/12/21: +*D. TITHERADGE*)
Dédé ('*m.c.*', m. H. Christiné: Emp., L'pool, 9/10/22; Gar., 17/10/22)
Rats! ('*revue*': Vaud., 21/2/23)
[From 1918 onwards Jeans collaborated in several revues: the only shows of this kind for which he was solely responsible seem to have been *Rats!*, *Cochran's Revue for 1926* and *One Dam Thing after Another* – for which see below. Numerous sketches contributed to these and to the revues in which he was a collaborator appear in the printed collections listed here]
Vignettes from Vaudeville. *Fr. 1924*
[This contains nine revue sketches]
Sundry Sketches. *Fr. 1924*
[This contains nine revue sketches]
Charlot Revue Sketches. *Fr. 1925*
[This contains ten revue sketches]
Cochran's Revue for 1926 (Pav., 29/4/26)
The Review of Revues. *Fr. 1926*
[This contains nine revue sketches]
Lido Lady ('*m.c.*', m. R. Rodgers: Alh., Bradford, 4/10/26; Gai., 1/12/26)
Bright Intervals. *Fr. 1927*
[This contains nine revue sketches]
One Dam Thing after Another ('*revue*': Pav., 19/5/27)
Odd Numbers. *Fr. 1927*
[This contains nine revue sketches]

One Dam' Sketch after Another. *Fr. 1928*
[This contains nine revue sketches]
The Stage is Waiting. *Fr. 1931*
[This contains nine revue and vaudeville sketches]
[Several sketches and playlets produced at music-halls]

JEFFERSON, ARTHUR
[For earlier plays see *H. E. D.* v, 435]
×Home from the Honeymoon ('*f.c.*': Metro., Glasgow, 7/10/05, *cpy.*; Emp., Hackney, 18/5/08)
×For His Sake (Glasgow, 8/11/07, *cpy.*)
The Perils which Beset Women (Metro., Glasgow, 12/10/12; Broadway, New X, 30/6/13: revised from *The World's Verdict*, 1890)
For the Sake of the Girl He Loved. LC, Broadway, New X, 1/7/13; revised as *Was the Marriage Legal?* (Metro., Glasgow, 9/4/17)
Home from the Trenches (Gr., Nottingham, 20/5/18; Gr., Croydon, 8/7/18)
Back to Wife and Home. LC, Smethwick, 2/12/18
The Price of Her Folly (Metro., Glasgow, 11/10/20)
On Trial for Her Life. LC, Gr., Plymouth, 4/8/21
[Several sketches produced at music-halls]

JEFFERSON, W. GORDON
Carry On (Paisley, 5/8/18: title later changed to *The Secret Aeroplane*: +*R. F. MORRISON*)

JEFFREY, R. E.
The Arm of Li Hung (Glasgow, 8/9/19; Aldw., 30/11/20, revised as *The Dragon*)

JELLEN, B.
Jeannette. LC, '*m.pl.*': K's, Newcastle, 14/5/25: title later changed to *Oh, No, Jeannette*

JELLINGS, LUKE
[Several sketches and playlets produced at music-halls]

JENKINS, BETTY
×The Hat Trick. LC, St Christopher's, Letchworth, 23/12/24
×More Things. LC, St Christopher's, Letchworth, 23/12/24

JENKINS, GEORGE [see *M. STEWART-DYER*]

JENKINS, HERBERT
×With Her Husband's Permission (Bristol, 13/5/14)

JENKINS, R. C. [see *E. O. BROOKS*]

JENKINSON, MARGARET C.
Shadows of the Christ ('*sacred d.*') *1921*

JENNINGS, FREDERICK S. [see also *W. P. SHEEN*]
As Good as Gold (Lyr., Hamm., 14/5/06)
The Girl with a Million (Lyr., Hamm., 20/5/12)
[Several sketches and playlets produced at music-halls]

JENNINGS, GERTRUDE E.

Uncle Robert's Airship ('*f.c.*': Alb. H., 31/5/10)

×Between the Soup and the Savoury (Alb. H., 31/5/10, *cpy.*; Playh., 19/10/10) *Fr. 1911*

×Our Nervous System (Playh., 15/4/11)

The 'Mind the Gates' Girl ('*Futurist Tubist Harlequinade*': +*H. GRAHAM*, *D. C. CALTHROP* and *N. PLAYFAIR*: H.M., 21/5/12, *m.*)

×The Girl behind the Bar (Emp., Finsbury Park, 17/6/12)

×A Woman's Influence. *Fr. 1913*

×Acid Drops (Roy., 23/2/14) *Fr. 1914*

×Ninepence for Fourpence. LC, Empress, 2/3/14

×The Rest Cure (Vaud., 16/3/14) *Fr. 1914*

×The Pros and the Cons. *Fr. 1914*

×The King's Man. LC, Roy., 18/9/14

×In the Fog. LC, Qns, 21/1/15. *Fr. 1915*

×Five Birds in a Cage (H., 19/3/15, *m.*) *Fr. 1915*

×The Bathroom Door (Vic. Pal., 10/1/16) *Fr. 1916*

×Elegant Edward (H., 30/5/16: called originally *Fox and Geese*: +*E. BOULTON*) *Fr. 1919*

×Poached Eggs and Pearls (Apo., 21/11/16) *Fr. 1917*

×No Servants (P's, 17/4/17, *m.*) *Fr. 1919*

×Waiting for the Bus (H., 26/6/17, *m.*) *Fr. 1919*

×The Lady in Red (Col., 23/7/17: also called *The Lady in Black*)

×Allotments. LC, Com., 5/11/17. *Fr. 1918*

After the War ('*f.*': Playh., L'pool, 27/9/18; Little, 6/5/20, as *Husbands for All*)

×At the Ribbon Counter. *Fr. 1919*

The Young Person in Pink ('*c.*': P.W., 10/2/20, *m.*; H., 29/3/20) *Fr. 1921*

×In the Cellar. *Fr. 1920*

×Bobbie Settles Down (Col., 15/3/20) *Fr. 1920*

×I'm Sorry – It's Out! (St J., 30/3/20, *m.*, *amat.*) *Fr. 1920*

×The New Poor. LC, St James H., Worthing, 24/9/20. *Fr. 1920*

Love among the Paint Pots ('*light c.*': Aldw., 2/5/21) *Fr. 1922*

×Mother-of-Pearl (W.G., 30/5/21, *m.*) *Fr. 1921*

×Hearts to Sell. *Fr. 1922*

×'Me and My Diary' (Str., 19/1/22) *Fr. 1922*

×The Secret of the Castle. *Fr. 1922*

Money Doesn't Matter (Aldw., 31/1/22)

×Calais to Dover (RADA, 23/7/22) *Fr. 1922*

Isabel, Edward and Anne ('*c.*': H., 31/3/23) *Fr. 1923*

×Puss in the Corner. *Fr. 1923*

×The Voice Outside (Glo., 28/4/23)

×Cat's Claws (New, 20/1/25, *m.*) *Fr. 1923*

Riquette ('*m.c.*', O. Straus: K's, Glasgow, 21/12/25)

×Oh! These Authors! (New, 3/4/25, *m.*, RADA students) *Fr. 1925*

×Have You Anything to Declare? *Fr. 1926*

×Richmond Park (Col., 12/12/27)

×The Christening. LC, Pal., Luton, 22/2/27. *Fr. 1937*

×Fireworks. *Fr. 1927*
×'Spot'. *Fr. 1927*
These Pretty Things ('*f.c.*': Gar., 14/12/28) *Fr. 1930*
×Scraps (Gar., 31/8/29) *Fr. 1928*
×The Helping Hands. *Fr. 1930*

JENNINGS, HUMPHREY
×The Duke and the Charcoal Burner. *1921* (in *Two Plays from the Perse School*)
[This also includes *The Death of Roland*, by *HUGH RICHMOND*]

JENSEN, J.
The Human Market ('*d.*') *1912*

JENSON, Mrs ASHTON [see *ELLIOTT PAGE*]

JEPSON, EDGAR
×Compromised (Tiv., 19/5/13; Ambass., 7/10/13)
×Les précieuses ridicules (Kennington, 3/6/19, Independent Theatre: adapted from Molière's play)

JEROME, JEROME KLAPKA
[For earlier plays see *H. E. D.* v, 436]
Susan in Search of a Husband ('*f.*': Scala, 16/3/06, *cpy.*)
Tommy ('*c.*': Midland Hotel, Manchester, 27/11/06; Camden, 3/12/06)
Sylvia of the Letters (Playh., 15/10/07, *cpy.*)
The Passing of the Third Floor Back ('*idle fancy*': O.H., Harrogate, 13/8/08; St J., 1/9/08) *Fr. 1910*
Fanny and the Servant Problem ('*c.*': Aldw., 14/10/08) *Fr. 1909*
The Master of Mrs Chilvers ('*c.*': K's, Glasgow, 10/4/11; Roy., 26/4/11) *1911*
Esther Castways (P.W., 21/1/13)
Robina in Search of a Husband ('*f.*': Pier, Brighton, 3/11/13; Vaud., 16/12/13) *Fr. 1914*
The Great Gamble ('*c.*': H., 21/5/14: called originally *The Blessed Folly*)
The Three Patriots (Qns, 27/7/15, *m.*)
Cook ('*f.*': D.P., Eastbourne, 18/6/17; Kings., 18/8/17; Playh., 25/6/28, as *The Celebrity*) *1926* (as *The Celebrity*)
The Soul of Nicholas Snyders ('*mystery play*': Everyman, 13/12/27) *1925*

JERVIS, GEORGE
Back to the Stone Age (Crown, Peckham, 5/8/04, *cpy.*)

JERVIS, HORACE FARNSWORTH
The Learned Professor ('*f.*': Surrey St. H., Sheffield, 3/5/09)

JERVOISE, Lady CLERKE
×The Vow (New, 28/6/04)
×Alfred (New, 28/6/04)

JESSE, FRYNIWYD MARSH TENNYSON
×The Mask (Gar., 9/8/15: +*H. M. HARWOOD*) *1926*

[*Who's Who in the Theatre*, under both Jesse and Harwood, gives the date as 1913]
Billeted (Nixon, Pittsburgh, 17/9/17, as *Lonely Soldiers*; Roy., 21/8/17: +*H. M. HARWOOD*) *Fr. 1920*
The Hotel Mouse ('*f.c.*': Qns, 6/10/21: +*H. M. HARWOOD*: from a play by P. Armont and M. Gerbidon)
Quarantine ('*c.*': Brighton, 29/5/22; Com., 6/6/22)
The Pelican (Ambass., 20/10/24: +*H. M. HARWOOD*) *1926*
Anyhouse (Ambass., 12/3/25) *1925*
How to Be Healthy though Married (Str., 25/5/30, Repertory Players: +*H. M. HARWOOD*) *1930*

JESSOP, GEORGE H.
[For earlier plays see *H. E. D.* v, 437]
My Lady Molly ('*c.o.*', m. S. Jones: Brighton, 11/8/02; Terry's, 14/3/03)
Once Upon a Time ('*fairy cantata*', m. L. Lehmann: Qns H., 22/2/03) *1903*
×Alias Mrs Fairfax (Gai., Manchester, 12/2/12)

JEWEL, JAMES A.
[Several playlets and sketches produced at music-halls]

JEWRY, EDWARD
×A Coster Girl's Romance (Camb., Spennymoor, 27/3/08)

JEWSON, EDITH M.
Rosemary's Garden ('*children's fairy pl.*') *1921*

JOCELYN, L. M. [see *Countess of RODEN*]

JOHN, EVAN
The Dark Path (Lyc. Club, 4/11/28; Sav., 4/11/28)

JOHN, GRAHAM [see also *G. BOLTON*]
My Son John ('*m.pl.*', m. O. Straus: Hippo., Brighton, 1/11/26; Shaft., 17/11/26)

JOHN, GWEN
Plays. *1916*
[This includes six short plays: 1. *Outlaws*; 2. *Corinna, or The Strenuous Life*; 3. *Sealing the Contract*; 4. *Edge o' Dark* (Clavier H., 18/7/12); 5. *The Case of Teresa*; and 6. *In the Rector's Study*]
×Luck of War (Kings., 13/5/17, Pioneer Players) *1922*
×The Only Daughter (Pal., Chelsea, 30/11/20, *m.*)
×The Goblin, the Student and the Huckster (Folk House, Bristol, 20/12/21: title later changed to *The Goblin*)
Plays of Innocence. *1925*
[This contains four short plays: 1. *A Tale that is Told* (Deansgate, Manchester, 23/10/22, Unnamed Soc.); 2. *On the Road* (Forum Club, 2/5/20); 3. *Luck of War* (see above); and 4. *A Peakland Wakes*]
Gloriana (Little, 8/12/25) *1925* (Oxford: as *The Prince*)
×Mr Jardyne ('*mystery*': Playh., L'pool, 15/10/25) *1928*

JOHNS, CECIL STARR

×Cockaine. LC, Whitehall, E. Grinstead. 5/10/21

×Nothing Doing. LC, K. Charles' H., Tunbridge Wells, 26/3/25

JOHNS, W.

×The Cheque. LC, Shak., L'pool, 5/10/17

JOHNSON, FANNY

[Numerous brief plays, mainly of an 'educational' character, printed in *Dramatic Scenes from English Literature* (1909) and *The Little Duke and Other Historical Plays* (1926)]

JOHNSON, HENRY T.

[For earlier plays see *H. E. D.* v, 437]

×A Boer Meisje (Gt. Qn. St., 10/7/00)

×Between the Dances (Aven., 1/10/01)

His Father's Friend (Eden, Brighton, 28/4/02)

×Drifted (Gr., Fulham, 14/9/03)

Alone in China ('*Chinese d.*': Alex., B'ham, 13/6/04; Brixton, 20/6/04)

JOHNSON, JOHN

The Luck of the Brians (Drill H., Hildenborough, 30/1/05, *amat.*: +*D. MAJOR*)

Enemies ('*Georgian d.*': P.H., Hildenborough, 18/2/08, *amat.*: +*D. MAJOR*)

Captain Chris (Drill H., Hildenborough, 21/1/13, *amat.*: +*D. MAJOR*)

JOHNSON, PHILIP

×Legend (David Lewis, L'pool, 11/11/27, *amat.*) *1929* (Oxford)

×Afternoon (Playh., L'pool, 15/3/28) *1929* (Oxford)

×The Lovely Miracle (David Lewis, L'pool, 23/1/29, *amat.*) *Fr. 1930*

×The Good and the Bad (Playh., L'pool, 24/1/29) *1929*

×The Illusionist. LC, Village Inst., Gailsford, 6/9/29. *1929*

×The Spinsters of Lushe. LC, Women's Inst., Bishop's Castle, 23/11/29. *1931* (in J. Hampden, *Four Modern Plays*)

×Derelict (Playh., L'pool, 16/4/30) *1929*

Four Plays. *1929*

[This contains: *Long Shadows* (Everyman, 18/6/30) and three short plays: 1. *The Cage*; 2. *The Lovely Miracle* (see above); and 3. *The Good and the Bad* (see above)]

×Saturday Night. *Fr. 1930*

×The Sister who Walked in Silence. *Fr. 1930*

×World without Men. *Fr. 1930*

×Respectable Facade. *Fr. 1930*

JOHNSON, ROBERT

The Old Land ('*r. Irish d.*': Qns, Dublin, 13/4/03)

JOHNSON, W. BRANCH

The Unchanging Hills. LC, Parkway H., Welwyn, 17/3/25

JOHNSTONE, A. B.

Explorers by Mistake. LC, Grea Wellington St. H., Leith, 11/3/21

JOHNSTONE-DOUGLAS, SYBELL
×The Tatie Bogle (A.L.S. Trav. Th., 1922)

'JONATHAN'
×The Trap (Kings., 27/5/21, *m.*, Playwrights' Theatre)

JONES, CECIL DUNCAN [see also *D. CLEUGH*]
×Peg Woffington's Pearls (Court, 30/1/10, Play Actors: +*D. CLEUGH*)

JONES, D. E.
Uncle Tibbett's Twins. LC, '*c.*': Kings., 17/10/18

JONES, E. BRANDRAM
[For earlier plays see *H. E. D.* v, 439]
Preferment ('*c.*': Wynd., 16/10/02)
Grandfather's Clock ('*c.*': Everyman, 11/7/24)

JONES, EDWARD (see *B. W. FINDON*)

JONES, GRAHAM [see also *W. C. DUNCAN*]
×Towssee Mongalay ('*m.c.*': Court, 2/4/13)

JONES, GREVILLE P.
×A Victim of Circumstances. LC, Parish H., Streatley, 1/4/15

JONES, HENRY ARTHUR
[For earlier plays see *H. E. D.* v, 439–40, 800]
James the Fogey. *1900 (priv.)*
The Lackey's Carnival ('*c.*': D.Y., 26/9/00) *1900 (priv.)*
Mrs Dane's Defence (Wynd., 9/10/00) *1900 (priv.)*; *1905*
The Princess's Nose ('*c.*': D.Y., 11/3/02)
Chance, the Idol (Wynd., 9/9/02) *1902 (priv.)*
Whitewashing Julia ('*c.*': Gar., 2/3/03) *1903 (priv.)*; *Fr. 1905*
Joseph Entangled ('*c.*': H., 19/1/04) *1904 (priv.)*; *Fr. 1906*
The Chevaleer ('*c.*': Gar., 27/8/04) *1904 (priv.)*
Chrysold (written 1904)
Felisha (written 1905)
The Sword of Gideon. *1905 (priv.)*
The Heroic Stubbs ('*c. of a man with an ideal*': Terry's, 24/1/06) *1906 (priv.)*
The Hypocrites (Gr., Hull, 30/8/06, *cpy.*; Hicks', 27/8/07) *Fr. 1908*
The Goal (Chicago, 1907; Pal., 20/5/19, *m.*; H., 12/12/23) *1915* (in *The Theatre of Ideas*, see below)
The Galilean's Victory (Stockport, 25/9/07, *cpy.*: called also *The Evangelist*) *1907 (priv.)*
Dolly Reforming Herself ('*c.*': H., 3/11/08; one-act version as *Dolly's Little Bills*, Hippo., 8/7/12) *1908 (priv.)*; *Fr. 1910*
Dick ('*f.*': written 1908).
×The Knife (Pal., 20/12/09)
×Loo Valance (written 1909)
×Fall In, Rookies! (Alh., 24/10/10) *1910*
We Can't Be as Bad as All That ('*c.*': Nazimova, N.Y., 30/12/10; Hippo., Croydon, 4/9/16) *1910* (New York: *priv.*)
The Ogre) St J., 11/9/11)

×Her Tongue. LC, Gar., 21/2/12. *1915* (in *The Theatre of Ideas*, see below)
Lydia Gilmore (Lyc., N.Y., 1/2/12)
Mary Goes First (Playh., 18/9/13) *1913*; *Fr. 1913*
The Divine Gift. *1913*
The Lie (Harris, N.Y., 24/12/14; New, 13/10/23) *1915*; *Fr. 1925*
The Theatre of Ideas. *1915*
[Besides the title-piece (which is not a play), this contains three one-act plays: 1. *The Goal* (see above); 2. *Her Tongue* (see above); and 3. *Grace Mary* (Playh., L'pool, 10/10/30)]
Cock o' the Walk (*'parable in f.'*: Cohan, N.Y., 27/12/15)
The Pacifists (*'f.'*: O.H., Southport, 27/8/17; St J., 4/9/17) *1917* (*priv.*); *1955*
[In addition to the above, R. A. Cordell, in *Henry Arthur Jones and the Modern Drama* (1932), lists three other plays written in 1916 and 1917: *The Right Man for Sophie, Finding Themselves* and *The Lifted Veil*]

JONES, HOWARD MUMFORD
The Love of the Three Kings (Bedford H., Chelsea, 14/6/24, Pax Robertson Salon: translated from *L'Amore dei tre re* (1910) by S. Benelli)

JONES, J. WILTON
[For earlier plays see *H. E. D.* v, 440–1]
On Her Majesty's Service (Stand., 22/1/00; P's, 26/12/14 (revised as *On His Majesty's Service* by *WALTER MELVILLE*: also called *The Love That Lives*)

JONES, RUSSELL G.
Forbidden Fluids (*'c.'*: Scala, 3/5/25, Interlude Players)

JONES, T. ARTHUR
When Other Lips (Alex., Sheffield, 8/12/06, *cpy.*; East, Oxford, 26/8/07; Terriss, Rotherhithe, 21/10/07)

JONES, TOM
The Law. LC, Guild H., Caernarvon, 24/2/16
×Kindness Repaid. LC, Guild H., Caernarvon, 12/4/16

JONES, TOM S.
×Princess Aurora (*'m.pl.'*, m. R. M. Harvey: Tiv., 22/8/08, *m.*)

JONES, VICTOR
×Of a Clown (O.H., Dudley, 14/12/03)

JONES, WINIFRED ARTHUR [=*'ZERO'*]

JONSON, Mrs G. C. ASHTON
The Hedonists (Wynd., 4/7/02)

JOPLING-ROWE, LOUISE
Mrs Verey's Husband (P.H., Amersham, 21/10/22, Independent Players)
×Too Much Alike (Chiltern Arts Club, Amersham, 16/2/24)

JORDAN, E. HAMILTON
The Island of Desire. LC, Paisley, 20/3/24

JORDAN, JOSHUA
The Dream Kiss ('*c.*': Wimbledon, 28/7/24)

JORDAN, KATE [see *J. O. FAVERSHAM*]

JORDAN, PERCY [see *W. BEVAN*]

JORDAN, ROY
Quicksands of Youth (Scala, 14/7/26, Playmates)
× In the Tunnel. *1930*

JOSEPH, F. A.
For Honour and the Right ('*pageant*': T.H., W. Hampstead, 14/3/18)

JOSEPH, LOUIS
Vision (Kyrle H., B'ham, 11/1/25, B'ham Jewish Arts Soc.)
Discord. LC, Alex., B'ham, 8/12/25

JOSEPH, S. T.
[A few sketches produced at music-halls]

JOY, WARRINGTON
[A few sketches produced at music-halls]

JOYCE, JAMES [*JAMES AUGUSTINE ALOYSIUS*]
Exiles (Neighbourhood Playh., N.Y., 19/2/25; Reg., 14/2/26, St. Soc.) *1918*

JUDD, F. A.
The Rose of India. *1924*

JUDD, JOHN SAVILE
× The Hanging Outlook (Court, 11/7/12, *m.*: +*R. BARR*)
× The Rebel ('*oa.*', m. H. Collisson: Court, 11/7/12, *m.*)

[*JUDGE, JAMES P.*
Square Crooks (P.W., 13/3/28) *Fr. 1928*

JUL, CHRISTEN
First Performance (Str., 23/9/28, Rep. Players: from the Danish of Svend Rindom: +*S. DE FRECE*)

JULIAN, HENRY
Taking a Chance (County, Kingston, 25/9/11)

JUNE, G. MATHERS
× Ayshah. LC, P.H., Croydon, 4/2/20

JURY, CHARLES RISCHBIETH
Love and the Virgins. *1929* (Oxford)

KALISCH, ALFRED [see also *G. CORNWALLIS-WEST*]
[This author was responsible for presenting the English versions of numerous Continental operas – most notably, the following]
The Vagabond and the Princess (+*A. PITT*) *1906*
Iris. *1907*
Loreley. *1907*
Electra. *1908*
Die Fledermaus. *1910*

Ariadne on Naxos. *1912*
The Rose-bearer (Der Rosenkavalier). *1912*
The Three Musketeers ('*r.o.*', m. I. de Lara: Newcastle, 2/5/24; Scala, 17/6/24)

KARNO, FRED

Saturday to Monday ('*m.pl.*', m. D. Powell: P.W., Grimsby, 14/11/03, *cpy.*: +*C. BALDWIN* and *F. KITCHEN*)
Hustle ('*m.pl.*', m. P. Braham: Hippo., Colchester, 22/9/19; Emp., Finsbury Park, 29/9/19: +*W. H. BRIGGS*)
The Love Match ('*m.pl.*': K's, Southsea, 3/3/24; Emp., Stratford, 31/3/24: +*C. HEMINGTON*)
[Numerous music-hall sketches and musical pieces]

[*KATZKIN, W.* [see *H. G. ALSBERG*]

[*KAUFMAN, GEORGE S.*

Dulcy (Cort, Chicago, 20/2/21; Frazee, N.Y., 13/8/21; Gr., Southampton, 24/9/23; K's, Hamm., 6/10/23; Crit., 20/11/23: +*M. CONNELLY*) *Fr. 1923*
Merton of the Movies ('*c.*': Montauk, Brooklyn, 9/10/21; Cort, N.Y., 13/11/21; Shaft., 17/4/23: +*M. CONNELLY*) *Fr. 1925*
Beggar on Horseback (Broadhurst, N.Y., 12/2/24; Qns, 7/5/25: +*M. CONNELLY*) *1925*
The Butter and Egg Man ('*f.*': Belasco, Washington, 5/6/25; Longacre, N.Y., 24/9/25; Playh., Cardiff, 22/8/27; Gar., 30/8/27) *1925*
The Cocoanuts ('*m.pl.*', m. I. Berlin: K's, Southsea, 27/2/28; Gar., 20/3/28)

KAY, FRANCES M.

Lanciotto and Cecilia ('*o.*', m. S. Reeves: Wretham Road Ass. R., B'ham, 8/12/06, *amat.*)
Foiled ('*r.d.*': Harborne Inst., B'ham, 28/1/08, *amat.*)

KAY, T. WYLIE

The End of the Lane (Gr., Blackpool, 14/12/03, *cpy.*)

KAYE, JAY

[Various musical sketches for the Alexandra music-hall]

KAYE-SMITH, SHEILA

Saints in Sussex: Poems and Plays. *1926*
[This includes two religious plays: *The Child Born at the Plough*, and *The Shepherd of Lattenden*]
Mrs Adis...with...The Mockbeggar (+*JOHN HAMPDEN*) *1929*
[Two one-act plays, the first described as a '*tragedy*', the second as a '*comedy*']

KEAN, CHARLES

[Several sketches produced at music-halls]

KEANE, RYDER E.

[A few sketches produced at music-halls]

[*KEARNEY, PATRICK*
An American Tragedy (Longacre, N.Y., 11/10/26; Apo., 26/6/27, Venturers)

KEARY, CHARLES FRANCIS
The Brothers ('*fairy masque*') *1902*

KEATING, JOSEPH
Peggy and Her Husband ('*c.*': Roy., 28/2/14)

KEAY, BARRIE
Moon and Son ('*f.c.*': Ambass., Southend, 4/9/22)

KEENE, URSULA
×The Tramp (Rehearsal, 8/10/09)
×The Final Phase (Qns Gate H., 15/12/09; Rehearsal, 4/2/10)
The Eldest Miss Darrell (Court, 28/10/10, Rehearsal Co.)
A Love Story (Worthing, 31/7/11: +*D. CLEUGH*)
That Affair of Betsy's ('*c.*': Court, 28/9/15)
×The Moon Went Behind a Cloud ('*f.*': Ambass., 4/6/20, *m.*)

KEESING, MAURICE R.
Dramas and Poems. [*1909*] (Auckland)
Dramas and Poems: Second Series. *1914*
[This contains three plays: 1. *The Vagrant King*; 2. *Queen Adelaide*; and 3. *Abu Bakar*]

KEITH, NORAH [see also *S. M. CARSON*]
×After the opera (Emp., 21/6/08; Apo., 9/12/13)
The Builders (Crit., 10/11/08, *m.*)
Babel, LC, Gar., 18/5/14

KEITH, ROYSTON
[For earlier plays see *H. E. D.* v, 442]
Aubrey's Sister ('*f.c.*': Ealing, 22/6/03)

KEITH, SYDNEY
×The Key to the Situation (Bij., 28/4/06)

KELLAND, EVE [see *BEN TRAVERS*]

KELLEHER, DANIEL LAWRENCE
×Stephen Gray (Abbey, Dublin, 11/3/09)

KELLY, CLAUGHTON
A Skeleton in the Cupboard ('*f.c.*': County, Kingston, 18/4/04, a revised version of *Zenobia* (1899))

[*KELLY, GEORGE*
The Torchbearers ('*satirical c.*': 48th St., N.Y., 29/8/22; Ambass., 20/4/25) *Fr. 1924*; *Fr. 1927* (arranged for the English stage by *W. G. BROWNE*)
The Show-off (Apo., Atlantic City, 14/1/24; Playh., N.Y., 5/2/24; Qns, 20/10/24) *Fr. 1924*
Craig's Wife (Buffalo, 28/9/25; Morosco, N.Y., 12/10/25; Nottingham, 5/11/28; Fortune, 31/1/29) *1926* (Boston)

KELLY, JOHN DONALD
×'There is so much good...' *1929*

KELLY, THOMAS
×The Green Field. LC, Rep., Rusholme, 6/3/29. *1929*

KELLY, Mrs TOM
The Master of Kingsgift ('*r.d.*': Aven., 17/10/04)

KELSEY, ENID
The Jade Princess ('*fant.*': Hampstead Gdn Suburb, 20/6/25, *amat.*)

KELSTON, BEATRICE
Love in a Mist ('*c.*': D.P., Eastbourne, 5/11/23)
Harvest (Q, 1/11/26)

KELWAY, VINCENT
×The Follies of a King (Hippo., Greenwich, 25/9/11)

KEMP, GERALDINE
Dynecourt's Venture ('*c.*': Gt. Yarmouth, 9/10/07)

KEMP, THOMAS C.
The Harvest of Faith (Midland Inst., B'ham, 17/3/28)
The Wall (Midland Inst., B'ham, 22/3/29)

KEMPER, SALLIE [see *SIBYL CALDWELL*]

KENDALL, Mrs J. [see *G. SOWERBY*]

KENDALL, JOHN KAYE
Mrs Bill ('*c.*': Court, 9/3/08)
×Laughter in Court (D.L., 11/5/09, *m.*) *Fr. 1910*
Dad (Playh., 4/11/11: from A. de Caillavet and R. de Flers, *Papa*, 1911)
Fond of Peter. *Fr. 1913*
Push. LC, Str., 29/7/20: +*H. A. VACHELL*

KENDALL, LENNOX
×Decree Nisi (Gr., Southampton, 29/4/12)

KENDRICK, J.
[Several sketches produced at music-halls]

KENMORE, OCTAVIA
×To the Death (O.H., Crouch End, 23/10/05)
×The Dust Cloak (Gr., Leeds, 13/11/05)

KENNARD, AUBERON
×The Wanderer ('*pl. for schoolgirls*') *Fr. 1924*

KENNARD, B. [see *V. LANGBRIDGE*]

KENNARD, ELEANOR S.
The Dream Shop. LC, P.H., Croydon, 31/1/22

KENNEDY, Mrs BART
×My Lord (Abbey, Dublin, 16/10/13)

KENNEDY, CHARLES RANN
What Men Dare (Newcastle, 7/8/05: +*M. SHERBROOKE*)
The Winter Feast ('*t.*': Vic. H., 19/6/07, *cpy.*) *1908*
The Servant in the House ('*c.*': Vic. H., 19/6/07, *cpy.*; Adel., 25/10/09) *1908* (New York)
×The Terrible Meek. *1912*
×The Necessary Evil. *1913*

×The Rib of the Man. *1917*
A Repertory of Plays for a Company of Three Players. *1927* (Chicago)
[This includes three short plays performed, or intended to be performed, in England: 1. *The Chastening* (St Paul's Church, C.G., 29/6/24); 2. *The Admiral* (Mary Ward Settlement, 27/5/25); 3. *The Salutation* (St Pancras People's Theatre, 8/7/26)]

KENNEDY, H. ARTHUR
[For earlier plays see *H. E. D.* v, 443]
Tess (Cor., 19/2/00; Com., 14/4/00)
The Devil's House (B'ham, 15/6/00)

KENNEDY, JENNY ORDE
Half-Baked Magic ('*children's pl.*') *Fr. 1930*

KENNEDY, KATHERINE
×Angels at Bethlehem ('*Nativity pl.*') *1923* (SPCK)
×Isaiah, Prince and Prophet. *1924* (SPCK)

KENNEDY, MARGARET [see also *B. DEAN*]
The Constant Nymph (New, 14/9/26: +*B. DEAN*) *1926*; *Fr. 1930*
A Long Week-End. *1927*
Jordan (Str., 22/1/28, Venturers)

KENNEDY, WILLIAM STEWART
The Pied Piper of Hamelin (Balmuto Grounds, Kirkcaldy, 26/6/11)

KENNEDY-COX, Sir REGINALD KENNEDY
The Chetwynde Affair (Roy., 29/8/04)

KENNEDY-FRASER, MARJORY
The Seal Woman ('*o.*', m. Sir G. Bantock: Rep., B'ham, 27/9/24)

KENNEY, HORACE
[Several sketches produced at music-halls]

KENTISH-WRIGHT, DOROTHEA
×Fantasy (Mechanics' H., Nottingham, 28/9/12: an adaptation of a poem of John Drinkwater)

[*KENYON, CHARLES*
By Right of Sword (Bury, 16/12/12: dramatised from the novel (1897) by A. W. Marchmont)

KENYON, KATHARINE
×The Shepherds ('*Christmas pl.*') *1922* (SPCK)
×The Unquenched Fire. LC, K. G's H., 12/2/25

KERR, MOLLY
Requital (Everyman, 23/4/29)

KERRIGAN, T. W.
×Malachi's Daughter. *1918* (Dublin)
×The Visitant (Abbey, Dublin, 28/3/20)

[*KESTER, PAUL*
Sweet Nell of Old Drury ('*c.*': H., 30/8/00) *Fr. 1928*

Mademoiselle Mars (Imp., 25/1/02)
Dorothy o' the Hall (Newcastle, 3/11/04; New, 14/4/06: +*C. MAJOR*)
La Zulma (S. Shields, 5/6/05)
When Knighthood was in Flower (Waldorf, 13/5/07) *Fr. 1931*
Lily, the Bill-Topper (Lyc., Edin., 13/4/11)

KETTERING, RALPH T.
Which Shall I Marry? ('*md.*': Hippo., L'pool, 29/5/16; D.P., Eastbourne, 17/10/21, *revised*)

KEYSER, FRANCES
The Right to Kill (H.M., 4/5/15: +*G. CANNAN*: adapted from P. Frondaie, *L'Homme qui assassina*, 1912)

KIDD, JOHN
×Restitution (Rehearsal, 7/3/11, *m.*)

[*KIDDER, EDWARD E.*
A Jolly American Tramp ('*m.pl.*', m. F. Gagle: Emp., Southend, 21/7/02)

KILBURN-SCOTT, ENID
The Imprisoned Elf ('*fairy pl.*': Christchurch Schoolrooms, Erith, 2/1/14)

KILLBY, STANLEY
×A Holiday Humour ('*r.*': Large H., Guildford, 3/2/04)
×The Vengeance of Jim (King's Lynn, 25/2/09)
×Mr Perkins's Pension (Gai., Manchester, 21/4/13; Court, 15/5/13)

KILLINGWORTH, WARREN
×The Mark of Cain (Court, 15/12/13)

KILMARNOCK, Lord
The Anonymous Letter (Q, 7/3/27)

KILPATRICK, FLORENCE ANTOINETTE
Virginia's Husband ('*f.c.*': Q, 28/6/26; Com., 6/9/26) *Fr. 1931*
Hell Cat Hetty (Portsmouth, 25/4/27; Sav., 20/6/27, as *Wild-cat Hetty*)

KIMBALL, DAVID [see also *H. C. BAILEY*]
×The Black Cottage (Court, 3/3/09, *amat.*; Terry's, 23/5/09)
A Servant of the Public (Margate, 10/4/09; Terry's, 16/5/09, English Pl. Soc.: from the novel (1905) by Anthony Hope)
×An Involuntary Understudy (Terry's, 23/5/09)
×The Worm Turns (Terry's, 23/5/09, Thalia Dram. Soc.)
×The Testimonial (Terry's, 23/5/09, Thalia Dram. Soc.: +*A. W. LOACH*)
The Sowers (K's, Hamm., 8/8/10: +*M. S. WOOLF*: dramatised from the novel (1896) by H. Seton Merriman)
The Duke (Crippl. Inst., 16/4/12, *amat.*: dramatised from the novel (1900) by J. S. Clouston)

KIMBALL, ROSAMUND
×You and I and Joan ('*pl. for girls*') *Fr. 1924*

KIMBERLEY, Mrs F. G. [=*Miss L. ADDISON*]

A Sister's Sin (P's, Accrington, 28/11/00, *cpy.*; E.C., 5/8/01)
Bound to Win (P's, Accrington, 18/12/01, *cpy.*; E.C., 4/8/02)
A Country Rose ('*m.c.d.*', m. S. Jones: Leeds, 1/11/05; K's, Longsight, 2/10/11: title later changed to *The Girl They Couldn't Find*)
A Soldier's Honour (K's, Longsight, 8/8/06, *cpy.*; Junction, Manchester, 25/2/07; E.C., 6/4/08; Hippo., Salford, 12/10/14, *revised*)
The Power of the King (K's, Longsight, 9/10/07, *cpy.*; Junction, Manchester, 2/12/07; Broadway, New X, 30/3/08)
Her Secret Lover (O.H., Dudley, 1/12/08, *cpy.*; Wolverhampton, 8/2/09; Stratford, 27/6/10)
Was She to Blame? (Junction, Manchester, 12/4/09; Woolwich, 7/2/10)
Her Path of Sorrow (Barry Dock, 17/11/09, *cpy.*; P's, Accrington, 27/12/09; Woolwich, 14/3/10)
Why Did She Run Away? (Qns, Longton, 31/8/10, *cpy.*; Wolverhampton, 10/10/10; Woolwich, 17/10/10)
The Heart Bowed Down (Junction, Manchester, 13/2/11; Lyr., Hamm., 27/2/11: title later changed to *His Love for an Actress*)
The Wild Girl of the Forest (Wolverhampton, 14/6/11, *cpy.*; Junction, Manchester, 14/8/11; Woolwich, 4/9/11)
The Pet of the Ranch ('*r. costume d.*': Wolverhampton, 6/4/12; Lyr., Hamm., 22/4/12)
The Prairie Outlaw (K's, Longsight, 16/9/12; Woolwich, 3/3/13)
The Boy Detective (K's, Longsight, 12/5/13)
×That Parson Chap (Gr., Wolverhampton, 24/5/13)
The Collier's Lass (Wolverhampton, 27/5/12; Stratford, 3/2/13)
Australian Nell (Junction, Manchester, 18/8/13)
Miranda of the Wilds (Wolverhampton, 24/12/14: title later changed to *His Canadian Bride*)
The Little Grey Home in the West (Wolverhampton, 2/8/15; Qns, Poplar, 4/10/15)
Brave Women – Who Wait (Wolverhampton, 29/11/15; E.C., 21/2/16)
×Willie's Night Out. LC, Pal., Bordesley, 24/6/16
Just a Little Pair of Shoes (Wolverhampton, 25/9/16; E.C., 9/10/16)
Back Home in Tennessee (Junction, Manchester, 20/11/16; E.C., 9/7/17)
My Home in Kentucky (Pal., Bordesley, 9/4/17; Woolwich, 11/6/17; E.C., 15/6/17)
Pride of the Regiment (Wolverhampton, 10/12/17; Emp., Edmonton, 4/3/18; E.C., 11/3/18)
Ruined Lives (Gr., Brighton, 2/9/18; E.C., 9/9/18)
A Spy in the Ranks (Wolverhampton, 20/5/18; Gr., Croydon, 29/7/18; E.C., 12/8/18)
The Soldier's Divorce (Wolverhampton, 16/9/18; E.C., 11/11/18)
Faithless (E.C., 7/4/19: title later changed to *The Woman Who Didn't Wait*)

Tatters (Gr., Brighton, 28/7/19; E.C., 8/9/19)
Her Life of Pleasure (Gr., Brighton, 6/10/19; E.C., 13/10/19)
That Little Old Mother of Mine (Junction, Manchester, 20/10/19; E.C., 24/11/19)
Her Bridal Night (Wolverhampton, 27/9/20; E.C., 1/11/20)
The Home of the Fairies ('*m.pl.*': Gr., Brighton, 6/9/20; Emp., Edmonton, 4/10/20)
At the Hour of Midnight (E.C., 14/3/21)
Kiddie o' Mine (Gr., Brighton, 25/7/21; Hippo., Rotherhithe, 29/8/21; E.C., 3/10/21)
One Night of Folly (E.C., 31/10/21)
Kid of Arizona (E.C., 3/4/22)
Women of the Night Club (Wolverhampton, 3/7/22)
Peg's Night Out (Wolverhampton, 11/9/22; E.C., 25/10/22)
Granny (Osborne, Manchester, 6/8/23; Stratford, 7/4/24)
Flaming Passion (Stratford, 12/11/23)
×One Night in Paris. LC, Playh., Blackwood, 30/1/25
Foolish Wives. LC, Wolverhampton, 18/6/25

KIMPTON, EDITH M.
×Cousin's Young Man. *1910*

KINDER, MARTIN [see *W. N. MONCK*]

KING, ALLAN
The Philanthropist ('*c.*': Emp., Preston, 28/11/27)
The White Assegai (Rep., B'ham, 9/2/29; Playh., 21/1/30)

KING, CORTON
×Caretaker Within (Margaret Morris, 28/2/16, Woman's Theatre)

KING, FRANK [see *L. J. HINES*]

KING, GEORGE S.
The Most Beautiful Woman in the World (Metro., Hoyland, 25/9/05; Roy., L'pool, 23/12/07, as *A Brand from the Burning*; Lyr., Hamm., 23/3/08)
His Life for Her Love (Metro., Devonport, 24/8/08)
Mother and Home (Metro., Devonport, 21/6/09)
The Mystery of the Fens (Metro., Devonport, 18/7/10)

KING, GEORGE S.
The Beetle (Rep., Plymouth, 30/11/25, +*C. FREEMAN*: revised with *J. B. FAGAN*, Gr., Croydon, 10/9/28; Str. 9/10/28: dramatised from the novel (1897) by Richard Marsh)

KING, I. BOLTON
The Chester Miracle Plays, done into modern English and arranged for acting (+*O. BOLTON KING*) *1930* (SPCK)

KING, JULIAN
×The Misery that Tempts ('*t.*': Rehearsal, 11/5/12)
×L'Entente Cordiale (Rehearsal, 11/5/12)
×The Simple Life (Rehearsal, 11/5/12)

KING, MURRAY [see *C. CLARK*]

KING, OSWALD
Turning the Tables ('*f.c.*': D.P., Eastbourne, 20/6/10)

KING, R. RALEIGH
The Green Lamp (Plymouth, 27/6/27; R.A., Woolwich, 8/8/27)

KING, RACHEL E.
Ann Desmond (Lyc., Ipswich, 13/12/26)
× One Crowded Hour (Lyc., Ipswich, 13/12/26)

KING, RANDOLPH
× Mystery No. 1 (Bed., 15/3/09)

KING, W. GAVAZZI [see *J. BICKERDYKE*]

KING, WILL
The Arctic Cure ('*c.o.*', m. C. T. Loveday: Emp., Southend, 11/3/11, *cpy.*; Emp., Southend, 9/5/11; Gai., Hastings, 4/5/25, revised with *G. BLACKMORE* as *The Polar Bear*)
× The Kalends of Mars (Pal., Southend, 30/9/13)
The Mystery of Edwin Drood. LC, Pal., Westcliffe, 2/2/15
The Ferry Bell. LC, Pal., Westcliffe, 21/4/15
Old Pa Jones ('*c.*': Pal., Westcliffe, 13/12/15)
The Smugglers of Hastings ('*c.o.*', m. A. L. Hall: Gai., Hastings, 26/5/24)
The Strolling Player ('*m.pl.*', m. G. Blackmore: Gai., Hastings, 28/6/26, *amat.*)

KING-HALL, STEPHEN [see also *I. HAY*]
B.J. 1 (Glo., 9/4/30) *Fr. 1930*

KINGSFORD, Rev. H.
The Quest ('*Nativity pl.*': Hampstead Conservatoire, 11/3/20)

KINGSLEY, ELLIS
[For earlier plays see *H. E. D.* v, 444]
× It All Depends on Mary (P's, Manchester, 25/9/03)

KINGSLEY, FRANK
× What We Shall All Come To: Mister Woman in 2013 A.D. (Olympia, Shoreditch, 27/1/13: + *E. C. CARTER*)

KINGSLEY, H.
Margaret of Paris. LC, '*m.pl.*': Emp., Halstead, 7/2/24

KINGSTON, FRANK [see also *V. LEWIS*]
The Websters (Terry's, 11/12/07)

KINGSTON, HARRY
The Shadow Between; or, The Vultures of Kildare ('*md.*': K's, Hoxton, 18/3/07: + *T. C. DENVILLE* and *C. S. SELF*)

[*KINKEAD, CLEVES*
Common Clay (Republic, N.Y., 26/8/15; Rep., Nottingham, 23/1/22; Q, 18/5/25) *Fr. 1920*

KINNISON, ANNA
× Betty versus Dolly (Glo., 2/7/13)
× The Little Peacemaker (Pav., 25/3/14)

KINSEY, M.

×A Double Deception (Rehearsal, 4/5/11, English Pl. Soc.)

KIPLING, RUDYARD

×The Harbour Watch (Roy., 22/4/13, *m.*; Roy., 15/9/13; Seaford House, 5/10/24, First Studio Theatre, revised as *Gow's Watch*)

KIRALFY, BOLOSSY

To-morrow; or, The Story that Never Grows Old (Hippo., 24/12/08: +*F. PARKER*)

KIRBY, ELIZABETH

×The Treasure (Kings., 9/10/08)

KIRBY, W. H.

The Beauty Shop ('*m.c.*', m. G. Ess: Gai., Ayr, 15/11/06)

KIRBY, WILLIAM [see *STANLEY DARK*]

KIRKE, FRED J.

[For an earlier play see *H. E. D.* v, 445]

For the Honour of the Club (Lyr., L'pool, 29/6/01, *cpy.*: +*M. DAWSON*)

A Guilty Inheritance (Alex., Widnes, 21/8/02; Stratford, 14/3/04: +*A. ROUSBY*)

The Naval Detective ('*mc.*', m. O. Dene: Lyr., Eccles, 28/7/04)

KIRKHAM, Mrs [see *E. LANCASTER-WALLIS*]

KIRWAN, PATRICK

×The Fotheringay (Bij., 29/10/03)

×A Dream of Old Versailles (Bij., 31/12/03)

×Asking for Trouble (Steinway H., 19/1/16)

KITCAT, Mrs S. A. P. (MABEL)

The Whip Hand ('*c.*': Village H., Esher, 14/6/05, *amat.*; County, Kingston, 28/10/07; Leeds, 5/12/13: +*K. SNOWDEN*)

KITCHEN, FRED [see also *C. BALDWIN* and *F. KARNO*]

[Many music-hall sketches, mostly in collaboration with *F. LISTER*, *C. BALDWIN*, *E. C. MATTHEWS* and *G. PAYNE*]

KITTS, CHARLES S.

[For an earlier play see *H. E. D.* v, 445]

The Man Fiend (Bilston, 6/4/03)

×The Final Supper (Qns, Poplar, 19/4/09)

×Sadie from Simpson's. LC, Gr., Clapham, 15/1/13

[Various other music-hall sketches]

[*KLEIN, CHARLES H.* [see also *M. GLASS*]

[For earlier plays see *H. E. D.* v, 445 and 801]

The Music Master (E.C., 31/8/04, *cpy.*; Atlantic City, 12/9/04; Belasco, N.Y., 26/9/04; Lyc., Edin., 8/8/27; Apo., 6/9/27) *Fr. 1935*

The Lion and the Mouse (D.Y., 22/5/06) *Fr. 1916*

The Daughters of Men (Margate, 10/6/07) *Fr. 1920*

Find the Woman (Gar., 17/6/12: adapted from Klein's play, *The Third Degree*: +*A. HORNBLOW*) *Fr. 1912*

KLEIN, JOHN W.
The Idealist ('*c.*') *1923*
Pontius Pilate ('*Biblical d.*') *1923*
Shelley. *1924*
Charlotte Corday. *1927*

KNATCHBULL, Mrs [=*DORA BRIGHT*]

KNEEN, ELEANOR G.
Into Unknown Seas, and Other Period Plays. *1913*
[Besides the title-piece, this includes two other short plays: *False Dawn* and *At Sunset*]

KNIGHT, CHARLES
The Proud Princess ('*oa.*', m. C. Courtney: All Saints Church H., Peckham, 6/12/06, *amat.*)

KNIGHT, DOUGLAS [see *J. WRANGHAM*]

KNIGHT, J. S.
× A Traitor. LC, Gr., Manchester, 10/9/14: called also *And the Woman Told* and *The Rotter*

KNIGHT, PERCIVAL [see also *N. BEGBIE* and '*IAN HAY*']
× Nerve. LC, Kennington, 14/11/21: + *L. FLETCHER*
× The Great Belief. LC, Glo., 31/1/24

KNIPE, JOHN
The Dark River (Q, 14/11/27)

KNITTEL, JOHN
The Torch (Brighton, 4/9/22; Apo., 12/9/22)

KNOBLOCK, EDWARD [=*EDWARD KNOBLAUCH*: see also *C. ASKEW, E. A. BENNETT, W. T. COLEBY* and *S. HICKS*]
[For an earlier play see *H. E. D.* v, 445]
× The Pertikler Pet (Brighton, 18/12/05; Waldorf, 17/1/06)
Kismet ('*Oriental spectacular pl.*'): Majestic, Erie, Pa., 9/1/11; Daly's, N.Y., 16/1/11; Gar., 19/4/11) *1911*
Discovering America (LC, Glasgow, 30/8/12; Daly's, N.Y., 7/9/12)
The Faun ('*c.*': P.W., 28/6/13)
My Lady's Dress (Roy., 23/4/14) *1914*; *Fr. 1914*
The Hawk (Albany, N.Y., 26/9/13; Shubert, N.Y., 28/9/14; Roy., 18/9/16: adapted from *L'Épervier* (1914) by F. de Croisset)
Marie-Odile (Belasco, Washington, 19/1/15; Belasco, N.Y., 29/1/15; H.M., 8/6/15) *1915*
× The Night of Nights. LC, Hippo., Newcastle, 1/2/15
× Hajj (Pal., 22/2/15)
× The Way to Win (Col., 14/6/15)
× A War Committee (H., 2/7/15, *m.*) *Fr. 1915*
× How to Get On (Vic. Pal., 12/7/15)
× Long Live England (Theat. Gdn Party, Regent's Park, 20/7/15)
× The Little Silver Ring (Theat. Gdn Party, Regent's Park, 20/7/15) *Fr. 1915*
Mouse (Roy., 5/12/15, Pioneer Players)
The Very Latest, LC, Gai., 1/3/16

Home on Leave ('*c.*': Roy., 18/10/16)
Tiger! Tiger! (Ford's, Baltimore, 4/11/18; Belasco, N.Y., 12/11/18; Pleasure Gdns, Folkestone, 24/5/20; Str., 2/6/20) *1924*
Our Peg ('*m.pl.*', m. H. Fraser-Simson: P's, Manchester, 24/12/19) *Fr. 1929*
Mumsee (Little, 24/2/20)
Cherry ('*m.c.*', m. M. Gideon: Apo., 22/7/20)
Who's Who ('*f.c.*': RADA, 19/11/22)
The Lullaby (Parson's, Hartford, 20/8/23; Knickerbocker, N.Y., 17/9/23; Glo., 6/11/25) *1924*
Simon Called Peter (President, Washington, 10/2/24; Klaw, N.Y., 16/11/24; LC, Edin., 27/2/29: dramatised from the novel (1921) by Robert Keable: +*J. E. GOODMAN*)
Conchita ('*r.d.*': Qns, 19/3/24)
The Mulberry Bush (LC, originally submitted from Wynd., 26/7/27, revised and licensed 1930: Crit., 29/4/30)

KNOLLYS, Lady BEATRICE S.
×My Brother-in-Law ('*c.*': Qns Gate H., Kensington, 14/2/03)
×The Head of the Family (R. College of Music, 29/5/08, *amat.*)

KNOTT, Y.
Alice through the Looking Glass (New, 22/12/03) *1904*

KNOWLES, J. FORBES
×Auld Robin Gray (R.A., Woolwich, 21/3/10)

KNOWLES, JOSEPHINE
Chatterton (Bristol, 2/9/25: originally called *Thomas Chatterton, the Marvellous Boy*)
×His First Money. *1926*

KNOX, DAVID
×Giuliana ('*o.*', m. E. Golixiani: O.H., Cheltenham, 18/11/13)

KOFIE, J. BESSINA
×Her Savage Suitor. LC, P's, Bootle, 4/2/18

KOMISARJEVSKY, THEODORE
The Brass Paper-Weight (Apo., 15/10/28)

KOPESCKY, FRANCIS [see *M. ZLATOGOV*]

KORI, TORAHIKO [see *HESTER SAINSBURY*]

KOTELIANSKY, SAMUEL SOLOMONOVICH
The Green Ring (translated from a play by Z. Hippius) *1920*
The Wood Demon (translated from *Leshii* (1888) by A. Chekhov) *1926* (New York)

KREMER, THEODORE
The Fatal Wedding (P'cess, 25/8/02: title later changed to *The More We Are Together*)
An Actor's Romance (Camden, 8/2/04; Gr., Fulham, 8/8/04, *revised*)
×Page 97 (Lyc., Newport, 23/12/07; Gar., 11/1/08)
For Her Children's Sake (Broadway, New X, 4/8/13)

[*KREYMBORG, ALFRED*
×Monday (A.L.S. Trav. Th., 1925)

[*KUMMER, CLARE*
[For an earlier play see *H. E. D.* v, 446]
×Noah's Ark ('*m.ext.*': Vic. H., 22/4/07, *cpy.*)
Good Gracious, Annabelle! ('*r.f.*': Shubert, New Haven, 25/9/16; Republic, N.Y., 31/10/16; Playh., Cardiff, 29/1/23; D.Y., 14/2/23) *Fr. 1921*

KUSSMANN, LEON
The Way to Liberty (Pav., Mile End, 6/2/13)

KYLE, LESLIE
×Local Colour. LC, County, Kingston, 10/3/17
The Impossible Husband (Pier, Eastbourne, 15/5/22)
Lost, Stolen or Strayed. LC, St Mary's H., Highgate, 22/4/24

L., X.
Society's Verdict (Shaft., 26/3/00)
×The Bird at the Neck (Portsmouth, 9/3/05; K's, Hamm., 22/3/05)

LACE, RICHARD HENRY
A Jugful of Joy ('*c.*': Central H., Hoylake, 21/9/20)

LACKLANDS, JOHN
The Broadway Belles ('*m.c.*': County, Kingston, 5/6/05)

LACY, Mrs DE LACY
×The Enchanted Fountain ('*fairy pl.*': St J., 22/6/00)
My Lord Adam ('*c.*': Roy., 15/1/01)

LACZI, NAGI
×In at the Finish (Pal., Hamm., 13/5/07)

LAELAND, H. [see *B. FRANCIS*]

LAFFAN, Mrs DE COURCY
×Their Experiment (Alb. H., 20/4/04)
×On the Right Road (Court, 2/6/08, *m.*)

LAIDLAW, FREDERICK A. [see '*DEMOCRITUS*']

LAIRD, W.
×The Call (Belfast, 17/4/12, *cpy.*)

LAKE, LEW [see *W. DAVID* and *H. RODEN*]

LALLY, GWEN [*GWENDOLEN*]
×Reggie's Double (H., 14/11/11, *m.*; Court, 25/6/12; Hippo., Golder's Green, 22/11/15, as *The White Feather*)
Jezebel (Com., March 1912, *cpy.*) *1918*
×The Escape (Court, 25/6/12: called originally *An Unfinished Tragedy*)
×Up a Tree (Court, 25/6/12)
×The Temptation of Sir Galahad (Court, 25/6/12)
×Pierrot Philanders ('*modern fant.*': Str., 29/5/17, *m.*)
×The Great Moment (St J., 3/12/18, *m.*)

LAMB, ARTHUR J.
The Fisher Maiden ('*c.o.*', m. H. von Tilzer: Shaft., 11/9/03, *cpy.*)

LAMB, EMILY F. E.
In the Days of Good Queen Bess (All Saints Parish R., Dulwich, 27/1/12, *amat.*)
For the King ('*r.pl.*': S. Place Inst., 13/3/13, *amat.*)

LAMB, RANDAL N.
× Charity (Qns, Dublin, 25/11/17)

LAMB, REGINALD P.
× The Man who Loved His Wife. LC, Worthing, 10/1/13

LAMBE, JOHN LAWRENCE
× The House of the Winds (R. College of Music, 18/7/27)

LAMBERT, CHARLES E.
× Her First Champagne (W.G., New Brighton, 21/6/09)

LAMPREY, SYDNEY
Ramshakel the Great ('*c.o.*', m. H. F. Henniker: Corn Exch., Maidstone, 9/12/02, *amat.*)

LANCASTER-WALLIS, ELLEN
[For earlier plays see *H. E. D.* v, 447]
× Receipted (Cor., 14/4/08, *cpy.*; Empress, Brixton, 21/3/10, as *The Reckoning*: + *Mrs KIRKHAM*)

LAND, JOHN KNOWLES
An Old Reprobate (Saos H., Stretford, 23/4/10, *amat.*)

LANDA, GERTRUDE [= *Mrs M. J. LANDA*]
× Red Ria (Gai., Manchester, 28/3/10; Cor., 22/2/11: + *M. J. LANDA*)
× For all Eternity. LC, Emp., Hackney, 10/4/15: + *M. J. LANDA*)
× The Glazier. LC, T.H., Hove, 12/10/18: + *M. J. LANDA*

LANDA, MYER JACK [see also *R. D. BOYLAN* and *G. LANDA*]
As We Are ('*c.*': Scala, 27/5/26: + *Mrs M. J. LANDA*)

LANDECK, BENJAMIN [see also *M. BLOW*, *A. SHIRLEY* and *T. G. WARREN*]
[For earlier plays see *H. E. D.* v, 447]
The Shadow Dance ('*md.*', m. H. Lambelet: P'cess, 12/11/01)
Dr Nikola (P'cess, 29/3/02: dramatised from the novel (1896) by Guy Boothby: + *O. BRAND*)
The Wedding Ring ('*md.*': County, Reading, 19/3/03, *cpy.*; Dalston, 15/2/04)
Kit Carson, the Blind Detective (Leamington, 26/12/11; Lyr., Hamm., 12/2/12: + *Inspector GUILBERT*)
Women of Paris (Emp., Holloway, 7/12/14: + *G. E. BELLAMY*)
A Woman's Heart ('*r.d.*': Leicester, 6/3/16; Stratford, 13/11/16)
Jess o' the Caravan (Eden, Bishop Auckland, 4/3/18; Stratford, 13/5/18)
The Sealed Door (Stratford, 24/3/19)

An Unemployed King (Hippo., Bury, 4/10/26)
Lost Property ('*c.*': Everyman, 5/1/27; D.Y., 17/1/27)
[Several sketches and playlets produced at music-halls]

LANDECK, HERBERT [see *V. GURNEY*]

[*LANDER, HARRY*
The Night Before (Copley, Boston, Mass., 8/1/16; Lyc., Edin., 7/8/16)

LANDO, BARNETT
[Several sketches produced at music-halls]

LANDON, PERCIVAL
The House Opposite (Qns, 30/11/09)

LANDOR, LUCAS
Bluff! (Pier, Eastbourne, 22/6/16; Gar., 28/6/16)

LANDSTONE, CHARLES
× Reenie. LC, K. G's H., 2/11/25

LANE, FREDERICK [see *C. THOMASON*]

LANE, GERALD M.
× The Monte Carlo Girl ('*m.c.*': Vic. Pal., 7/10/12)
The Lavender Garden (Pier, Brighton, 30/10/22; Barnes, 21/5/25)

LANE, LETTY
× Deceptions. LC, Tyne, Newcastle, 20/2/17

LANE, LUCY [=*Mrs W. K. CLIFFORD*]

LANG, MATHESON [see also *H. C. M. HARDINGE*]
× No Greater Love (Inverness, 9/6/02)
Mehalah (Gr., Croydon, 12/6/05: dramatised from the novel (1880) by S. Baring Gould: +*H. E. ANSON*)
The Purple Mask ('*r.c.*': Plymouth, 22/4/18; Lyr., 10/7/18: from P. Armont and J. Manoussi, *Le chevalier au masque*, 1913) *Fr. 1923*

LANGBRIDGE, Rev. Canon FREDERICK [see also *F. WILLS*]
[For an earlier play see *H. E. D.* v, 448]
The Children of Kings ('*legendary r.*': Dublin, 4/9/02, revised: +*A. H. FERRO*)
The Chevalier of St George: A Tale of the Old Pretender ('*c.*': Pier, Brighton, 1/10/06)

LANGBRIDGE, ROSAMUND
× The Spell: A Tragedy of Truth (Manchester, 2/11/06; Adel., 17/6/07, as *A Tragedy of Truth*)

LANGBRIDGE, VIOLET [see also *C. H. BOURNE*]
Noblesse Dirige. LC, Gai., Manchester, 22/5/15: +*B. KENNARD*
So Early in the Morning ('*c.*': Qns, 23/1/16, St. Soc.)

LANGDON, C. E.
× Kalr-en-Neda ('*fant.*': Lyr., Hamm., 14/3/12, *cpy.*: +*C. SHIRLEY*)
Sally Jones, Actress. LC, Oldham, 26/2/14: title later changed to *The Man who Sold His Daughter*

LANGFORD, SAMUEL

×Bastien and Bastienne (Gai., Manchester, 21/10/12: a new version of Mozart's o.)

LANGLEY, ERIC

The Closed Door. LC, Paisley, 20/3/24

LANGLEY, PERCIVAL

[Several sketches, some written with *S. WALKER*, produced at music-halls]

LANGLOIS, DORA [see *H. A. LANGLOIS*]

LANGLOIS, H. A.

×Loose Tiles (Qns, Poplar, 17/6/07)

The Kiss of Judas (L'pool, 29/9/13: +*D. LANGLOIS*)

LANGTRY, LILY

Virginia (Manchester, 2/10/02; Imp., 8/12/02, as *The Crossways*: +*J. H. MANNERS*)

×A Maid of Many Parts (Court, 13/10/06, *cpy.*: +*G. HILL*)

LANKASON, O. F.

Stunts and Other Plays. *1923*

LARK, KINGSLEY [see also *N. FROST* and *A. SKALSKI*]

×The Impresario. LC, '*oa.*': Glasgow, 13/3/25

LAROCHE, CHARLES

Round the Golden Fleece ('*o. bouffe*', m. J. Rogers: Plymouth, 13/6/02)

'*LASCELLES, ROBERT*' [=*W. GROSSMITH*]

LASH, D. J.

×Timothy's Penny ('*religious pl.*') *1926* (SPCK)

LA SERRE, EDWARD [see *J. M. WATSON*]

LATCHFORD, EDAILE

×The Broken String (Aldw., 4/3/13)

LATHAM, FRED G. [see *S. HICKS*]

LATHBURY, STANLEY [see *E. IRWIN*]

LATHOM, EDWARD WILLIAM BOOTLE-WILBRAHAM, Earl of

The Curtain Goes Up. *1927*

[This contains: 1. *Wet Paint* (P.W., 21/2/26, Venturers); 2. *Tuppence Coloured* (Apo., 19/12/26, Venturers; P.W., 24/1/27); and 3. *The Way You Look at It* (Qns, 27/7/26)]

Second Plays. *1928*

[This contains: 1. *Ostriches* (Com., N.Y., 30/3/25); 2. *Fear* (Str., 27/11/27, Pl. Actors); and 3. *Twenty Houses in a Row* (Str., 1/7/28, Venturers)]

LATHROP, Mrs WAKEMAN

×Jim's Sweetheart (Lyc. Club, 27/4/10, *m.*: +*Mrs H. BENNETT*)

LATYMER, Lord [='*FRANCIS COUTTS*']

LAUDER, A. [see *A. C. ASTOR*]

LAUNDER, FRANK
×There Was No Signpost (Little, Brighton, 29/3/28)

LAURENCE, CLARICE
×Servants of Pan (Margate, 14/10/10; Court, 28/10/10)
×A. E. 24 (Bij., 17/8/15; K's, Southsea, 10/6/17, as *Her Number*)

LAURI, EDWARD [see also *H. C. SARGENT*]
The Maid of the East ('*c.o.*', m. W. Neale: O.H., Harrogate, 20/1/19; Wimbledon, 23/2/20: +*G. D. BURNABY*)

LAVER, JAMES
La Marquise d'Arcis (Str., 13/1/29, Venturers: +*F. HERTZ*: from the play (1919) by Carl Sternheim)
The Circle of Chalk (New, 14/3/29: from Klabund (Alfred Henschke), *Der Kreidekreis*, 1925) *1929*

LAW, ALICE
×A Woman's Day (Lyc. Club, 9/6/15)
Byron (Cent., 30/11/24)

LAW, ARTHUR
[For earlier plays see *H. E. D.* v, 449–50, and 802]
×New Year's Morning (Norwich, 1/1/00)
×Punch and Judy ('*r.m.c.d.*', m. G. Byng and A. Meredyth: Croydon, 25/6/00)
A Country Mouse ('*satirical c.*': Worthing, 24/2/02; P.W., 27/2/02)
The Bride and Bridegroom ('*c.*': New, 5/5/04)
×The Rising Sun (Newcastle, 1/8/04)
My Cousin Marco (Canterbury, 26/1/06)
Three Blind Mice ('*c.*': Margate, 30/7/06; Crit., 14/2/07) *Fr. 1910*
Artful Miss Dearing ('*c.*': D.P., Eastbourne, 3/4/09; Terry's, 10/4/09)
The Strange Case of Mr Begbie ('*f.*': New, Cambridge, 23/4/10)

LAWE, GORDON
Nemonicus Intervenes (Stanley H., S. Norwood, 20/11/22, Neighbourhood Players)

LAWRENCE, ARTHUR
Belowstairs Belinda. LC, Highfield Inst., Southampton, 25/10/19
×Outwitting Arabella. LC, Freemantle Congregational School, Southampton, 14/10/20
Joan. LC, St Barnabas H., Southampton, 28/10/20
The Power Wand. LC, Watt's H., Southampton, 21/4/22
Big-Little-Millie. LC, Watt's H., Southampton, 5/10/22
Belinda from Brixton. LC, Aven. H., Southampton, 31/12/23
The Rebellious One. LC, Freemantle Congregational Schools, 24/10/25: title later changed to *His Second Venture*

LAWRENCE, BOYLE [see also *B. P. BURTON*, *R. McLAUGHLIN* and *L. N. PARKER*]
The Popinjay (Newcastle, 24/10/07; New, 2/2/11)

LAWRENCE, CHARLES EDWARD
×Swift and Stella. *1927*
×The Hour of Prospero. *1927*
×The Year (Q, 22/8/27)
×Spikenard. *1929*

LAWRENCE, DAVID HERBERT
The Widowing of Mrs Holroyd (Unitarian Schools, Altrincham, 9/3/20, Garrick Soc.; Kings., 12/12/26, St. Soc. and 300 Club) *1914*
Touch and Go. *1920*
David (Reg., 22/5/27, St. Soc. and 300 Club) *1926*
A Collier's Friday Night. *1934*

LAWRENCE, E. [see *C. C. WEST*]

LAWRENCE, EWERETTA
[For earlier plays see *H. E. D.* v, 451]
×Her Ladyship's Daughter (Bij., 6/12/02)

LAWRENCE, F.
[For *Matilda, Our Servant Girl* see *H. E. D.* v, 451 and 802]

LAWRENCE, GERALD
The Coping Stone (D.P., Eastbourne, 19/4/07)
Into the Light ('*r.c.*': Bradford, 23/2/08; Court, 30/11/08)

LAWRENCE, GUY
×The Castle of Fate (Court, 29/1/14)

LAWS, GORDON
×Two of Everything. LC, Portsmouth, 14/6/23
×£1000 a Year. LC, Granville, Walham Green, 16/11/22

LAWSON, JOHN
×An Adventure in the Life of Sherlock Holmes (Garston, 8/5/02)

LAWSON, McEWAN
×The Coming ('*Christmas pl.*') *1925* (Congregational Union)

LAWTON, F. VAUGHAN [see *L. HAWKINS*]

LAWTON, V. B.
Ballads for Acting. *1927*
[This contains five short plays: 1. *The Duke of Gordon's Daughter*; 2. *The Heir of Linne*; 3. *Lord Bateman*; 4. *The Undaunted Female*; and 5. *The Barring of the Door*]

LAYARD, GEORGE SOMES
×The Shirt of Nessus. LC, Hamilton H., Felixstowe, 10/12/13

LAYTON, FRANK GEORGE
The Politicians ('*c.*') *1913*
Philip's Wife. *1914*
The Parish Pump ('*c.*': Gai., Manchester, 28/9/14; D.Y., 10/1/16)
×The Painter and the Baby ('*f.*': Rep., B'ham, 8/5/15)
The Ferriport Election (Gai., Manchester, 20/11/16)
×The Invalid (Gai., Manchester, 11/8/17; Kings., 18/8/17)
The Prophet. *1922*

LEA, GORDON

Reconstruction (People's, Newcastle, 4/19; Pav., Newcastle, 30/3/25) *1919* (Cambridge)

× For Russia (Arcade H., Newcastle, 9/6/20, Newcastle Players)

The Sin of Creation ('*allegorical d.*': Arcade H., Newcastle, 9/6/20, Newcastle Players)

A Study in Green ('*c.*': Arcade H., Newcastle, 9/6/20, Newcastle Players)

Dynamite (Socialist H., Newcastle, 30/3/21)

LEA, KATHLEEN

× A Nativity Play. *1922*

LEACOCK, STEPHEN BUTLER

× Q ('*f.*': Col., 29/11/15: +*B. M. HASTINGS*) *Fr. 1915*

LEAD, FREDERICK A. R.

Prince Clodis; or, The Marriage by Proxy ('*c.o.*', m. W. H. Baker: Perth, 4/12/01, *amat.*: +*S. HARTLEY*)

LEADER, HARRY [see also *B. ESPINASSE*]

× An Actor's Honour (Dublin, 20/7/03; O.H., Crouch End, 31/8/03)

LEAHY, EDMUND

Cupid in Kerry ('*c.*': Qns, Dublin, 19/4/06, *cpy.*)

LEAKER, NORMAN

× Before the Dawn (Midland Inst., B'ham, 12/3/27, *amat.*)

LEAPER, MARY

× Content ('*pastoral pl.*') *1928* (included in R. Moorhouse, *With Pipe and Tabor*)

LEASK, GEORGE A.

Queen Mab ('*fairy fant.*') *1924*

LEATHES, AGNES

× On the King's High Way ('*morality pl.*') *1914*

× The Modern Giant Killer ('*Scout pl.*') *1916*

LEAVER, DICK [see *E. B. SKEET*]

LE BRETON, JOHN

× Her Day Off. LC, W.L., 3/6/13

Mrs May Gets (H)in ('*f.c.*': Gr., Brighton, 17/9/23; S. Ldn Pal., 15/10/23)

A Sister to Assist 'Er (originally one-act, County, Kingston, 11/9/11; three acts, Shaft., 10/6/29) *Fr. 1912*

Engaging Bermaline and Five Other Playlets, for Reading and Acting at Home or Abroad. *1921*

[In addition to the title-piece, this contains: 1. *A Lucid Liar*; 2. *Will You Marry Me?*; 3. *The Commercial Instinct*; 4. *The Crystal Gazer*; and 5. *The Invisible Man*]

LECKY, H.

× William the Gardener. LC, K's, Southsea, 26/1/15

LEDGER, WHITMORE

A Nobleman of Nature (Tudor, Ferndale, 4/7/07)

[*LEDOUX, LOUIS*
Yzdra ('*t.*': Wynd., 26/3/08, *cpy.*) *1909*

LEE, ALEXANDER, M.
King Jonathan ('*m.fant.*': Bij., 23/1/06, *amat.*)
×Bulmer's Threat (Bij., 18/6/08, *m.*, *amat.*)

LEE, AURIOL [see *N. SCOTT*]

LEE, BERT [see also *D. FURBER, R. WESTON* and *LAURI WYLIE*]
[Numerous music-hall playlets and sketches, mostly written in collaboration]

LEE, CHARLES JAMES
×Mr Sampson ('*c.*': RADA, 17/12/26) *Fr. 1927*
×The Banns of Marriage (Arts, 1/7/27, *amat.*) *Fr. 1927*

LEE, CYRIL AUSTEN [see *CYRIL AUSTEN-LEE*]

LEE, H. FLETCHER
Robert Burns. *1926*
Second Thoughts (Steiner H., 17/5/27, Prentice Players: +*S. VANSITTART*)

LEE, FRANK
Me and My Girl. LC, Little, Bristol, 9/10/24

LEE, GEORGE
×Gossips. LC, St J., 16/5/16

LEE, JOHN
The Transformers. LC, Crippl. Inst., 22/1/19

LEE, KENNETH [see *H. PAULTON*]

LEE, MACKENZIE
The Rum Runners ('*m.pl.*': King's Lynn, 1/8/27)
For Chaps and Chits. *Fr. 1930*
[This contains ten brief revue sketches]

LEE, NORMAN H. [see also '*RITA*']
Naughty Elizabeth ('*m.f.*': Ass. R., Bromsgrove, 15/2/09, *amat.*)
×Herbert (P's, Bradford, 22/2/15)
The World's Sweetheart ('*m.c.*', m. F. G. Bennett: Guildford, 16/8/20; Sur., 11/10/20)
House Full ('*f.*': Hippo., Putney, 13/11/22)
Oh! Mabel! ('*f.*': Gr., Clapham, 22/1/23)
The Whirl of Paris. LC, Guildford, 26/2/23
A Working Girl. LC, '*m.pl.*': Emp., Kilburn, 27/11/24
Married or Single. LC, '*m.pl.*': Emp., Penge, 3/10/25: title later changed to *Flappers*)
Convicts ('*bsq. md.*': Pal., Camberwell, 7/2/27)
The Strangler ('*mystery pl.*': Hippo., Willesden, 28/2/27)
The Secret Door (Perth, 18/4/28, '*public rehearsal*')
[Numerous sketches, musical pieces and revues produced at music-halls]

LEE, RUBY

His Ignorant Wife (Gr., Nottingham, 10/11/19; Stratford, 6/12/20)
Her Midnight Lover (Gr., Nottingham, 2/8/20: +*E. P. MAY*)
Her Unknown Father. LC, Hippo., Wednesbury, 20/12/20: +*E. P. MAY*)

LEE, SAM

The Belle of Paris ('*m.c.*', m. P. Kurutz: W.L., 29/5/09: +*W. BAILEY*)

LEE, T. HERBERT

Ask Quesbury ('*c.*': Glo., 14/2/13)

'*LEE, VERNON*' [=*VIOLET PAGE*]

Ariadne in Mantua (Gai., 12/5/16, *m.*: dramatised from her own novel, 1903)

LEECH, H. J.

×The King and the Astrologer. LC, New, Manchester, 29/7/13

LEEDS, E. C. MABEL

Lady Selina of 'K' ('*m.c.*', m. C. B. Yearsley: County, Kingston, 4/5/07, *m.*: also called *Miss Selina of 'K'*)

LEER, SARAH B. VON

An Emperor's Legacy (Shak., L'pool, 19/4/05, *cpy.*: +*G. G. COLLINGHAM*)
×Lynch Law (Leeds, 22/5/07, *cpy.*: +*E. P. CLIFT*)

LEES, PHIL MERRY

×Toll for the Brave. LC, Workman's H., Blaengarw, 20/5/20

LEES, W. G. HYDE

×The House Agent's Dilemma (Qns Gate H., 2/5/02)
The Golden Luck (Lyr., Hamm., 7/4/03, *m.*)
×A Japanese Dance (Chiswick, 15/5/06)

LEFFINGWELL, MYRON

When Man Turns to Brute ('*scientific medical problem pl.*': Pav., Weymouth, 6/3/14)

LEFTWICH, CHARLES A. [see also *G. B. DALY*]

×Padlock Domes (Rehearsal, 7/1/13)

LEFUSE, M.

×At 'The Golden Goose'. *Fr. 1910*
×For Lack of Evidence. *Fr. 1910*
×Mistress Runaway. *Fr. 1910*

LEGGE, ROBERT GEORGE

[For an earlier play see *H. E. D.* v, 453]
For Sword or Song ('*poetic m.pl.*', described as 'written by R. G. Legge, made by Louis Calvert, and musick'd by Raymond Roze': Newcastle, 18/9/02; Shaft., 21/1/03) *1902*

LEHMANN, LIZA [see also '*OWEN HALL*']

×The Life of a Rose ('*fant.*': Court, 8/7/10)

LEICESTER, ERNEST [='*FRANK HERBERT*']

LEIGH, ERNEST M. [see also *S. BARING*]
[For an earlier play see *H. E. D.* v, 453]
×Madam or Miss? ('*m.ca.*', m. E. Nicholls: Bij., 14/11/00)

LEIGH, FRANK
Apple Blossoms ('*m.bsq.*', m. D. Powell: Worcester, 20/10/19; E.C., 29/11/20)
Rose Petals ('*m.c.*', m. D. Powell: Hippo., Cannock, 2/8/20)

LEIGH, GERTRUDE
Tasso and Eleonora. *1912*

LEIGH, ROWLAND
The Monkey Talks ('*c.*': Stamford, Conn., 14/12/25; Little, 12/10/25: adapted from *Le singe qui parle*, by René Franchois)
[It seems that the adaptation was by *G. B. UNGER* and that this was further adapted by Leigh for the English production, which later was taken to the U.S.A.]
Oh, Patsy! ('*m.c.*', m. C. Stuart: Pal., Blackpool, 29/3/26; Emp., New X, 16/8/26)
The Might-Have-Beens (P's, 22/5/27, Venturers: adapted from *Les ratés* (1920) by H. R. Lenormand)

LEIGHTNER, FRANCES M.
Queen Elizabeth; or, At the Queen's Command (Vaud., 9/9/01)

LEIGHTON, F. CYRIL
×A Mischievous Missive (Pier, Eastbourne, 10/11/13)

LEITH, ALICIA AMY
Philomir; or, Love's Victory ('*Christmas fant.*': Alb. H., 10/1/06, *amat.*)

LEIVIK, H.
Rags. LC, Scala, 1/4/24

LEJUST, LEON
The Usurers ('*socialist pl.*': Walton College, L'pool, 14/4/12, *amat.*)

LE MARCHANT, PETER
The Turning Point (St J., 1/10/12: adapted from *La flambée* (1911) by H. Kistemaeckers)

LEMIN, EDITH
×Those Fatal Fetters (Polytechnic, Regent St, 8/11/01)

LENA, ROBERTO
The Eve of St Patrick (Qns, Dublin, 12/3/17)
Her Old Kerry Home (Qns, Dublin, 13/8/17)
Sentenced to Death (Qns, Dublin, 12/11/17)

LENNARD, MARY
×Everywhere ('*mystery pl.*') *1922* (SPCK)

LENNOX, COSMO GORDON [see *C. GORDON-LENNOX*]

LENNOX, WILL
×The Burglar's Extra Turn (W.L., 5/6/07)

LEO, FRANK
[A few sketches produced at music-halls]

LEON, H. M.
Domestic Differences ('*f.c.*': Mechanics' H., Nottingham, 19/12/12)

LEONARD, HERBERT [see also *G. CONQUEST*]
[For earlier plays see *H. E. D.* v, 456]
The Gay Lord Mayor ('*m.c.*', m. G. Le Brunn: Metro., Camberwell, 23/9/02)
Lady Tatters ('*r. light o.*', m. W. Slaughter: Marlb., Holloway, 31/8/06, *cpy.*; Shaft., 1/5/07) *1907*
×My Wife's Sweetheart (Metropolitan, 2/12/07)
The Other Woman (Pav., Hastings, 6/1/08)
The Kiss of Judas (Aston, 19/10/08)

LEONARD, MARTIA
Le monde ou l'on s'ennuie ('*c.*': Str., 12/2/01, *m.*; Terry's, 10/4/01, as *The Lion Hunters*; St J., 5/12/12, as *The World of Boredom*: 'faithfully translated' from the play (1881) by E. Pailleron: +*J. T. GREIN*)
Déjanire ('*o.*': translated from Louis Gallet) *1915*
Cleopatra ('*o.*': translated from L. Payen) *1915*
Mârouf ('*o.*': translated from Lucien Nepoty) *1917*
×The Immortal Beloved ('*fantastic impossibility*') *Fr. 1927*

LEONARD, ROBERT
×The Fool (Pal., Bradford, 15/2/15; Metropolitan, 22/2/15)
×Cheap at Half the Price (Qns, 13/4/15, *m.*; Pal., E. Ham, 3/9/17: called originally *Like Father, Like Son*)
×His Wife's Friend (Empress, Brixton, 5/2/17)

LEONARD, VIOLET
×Mrs Markham's Last Flirtation (R. Academy of Music, 17/3/10, *amat.*)

LE QUEUX, WILLIAM
×The Proof (Gr., B'ham, 21/4/24; Vic. Pal., 23/6/24, as *Vendetta*)

LERNER, M.
The Jewess ('*t.*': Pav., 20/9/07)

LERONA, GASTON
×Alsace. LC, Court, 1/4/15: +*L. CAMILLE*

LEROY, BLANCHE [see *E. LEROY*]

LEROY, EDWARD
Only a Half Breed ('*m.pl.*': Stratford, 30/1/22: +*B. LEROY*)

LERTOFF, PAUL P.
Paul among the Jews (P.W., 8/7/28, St. Soc.: adapted from *Paulus unter den Juden* (1926) by F. Werfel)

LESLIE, ARTHUR
×Cupid and a Caravan (Ass. R., Crouch End, 22/4/09, *amat.*)
×Polly Lowe's Lover (Ass. R., Crouch End, 22/4/09, *amat.*)

×The Secretary's Secret (Ass. R., Crouch End, 22/4/09, *amat.*)
×The Widow Budd (Ass. R., Crouch End, 22/4/09, *amat.*)
×Madcap Betty (Freehold Inst., Hornsey, 19/3/10, *cpy.*)
×The Morning After (Freehold Inst., Hornsey, 19/3/10, *cpy.*)
The Purchase Price. LC, Pal., Heywood, 8/10/20
The Yellow Circle ('*mystery pl.*': Hippo., Rotherham, 28/7/24)

LESLIE, ERIC
The Silent Husband ('*c.*': Crippl. Inst., 29/6/20, *m.*)

LESLIE, H. [see *J. LION*]

LESLIE, HENRIETTA [see also *HENRIETTA DYMOCK*]
×Coffee for Two (New, 25/2/16, *m.*) *1936* (in *Ten New One-Acters*)
The Pageant of the Southern Cross (Vic. Pal., 19/10/17, *m.*)
The Loving Heart ('*r.pl.*': New, 12/6/18: +*J. DYMOCK*)
×Yuan Tsan. LC, K. G's H., 1/1/25

LESLIE, SHANE [=*Sir JOHN RANDOLPH SHANE LESLIE*]
The Delightful, Diverting and Devotional Play of Mrs Fitzherbert. *1928*

LESLIE, VERA
×Guinevere (Court, 2/6/08, *m.*: a dramatic version based on Lord Tennyson's poem)

LESLIE, W. H.
A Pageant of Lloyd's ('*fant.pl.*': Savoy Hotel, 25/2/08, *amat.*)

'*LESSER COLUMBUS*'
The World, the Flesh and the Devil (Pav., 1/2/09)

LESTER, ALFRED
×A Restaurant Episode. LC, Shepherd's Bush, 12/3/12. *Fr. 1921*
×The Scene-shifter's Lament. *Fr. 1921*

LESTER, CHARLES HOWARD [see also *G. HALL*]
The Mystery of the Big Black Box. LC, Pal., Gloucester, 15/8/16: +*M. CATLING*
His Passing Fancy. LC, Dalston, 1/7/18: +*M. CATLING*
The Long Lone Trail. LC, Metro., Glasgow, 12/1/22: +*M. CATLING*

LESTER, M. [see *L. HAWKINS*]

LESTOCQ, GEORGE
Just My Luck ('*m.c.*', m. S. Brooke and S. Gordon: Dalston, 10/6/18: +*W. STANFORD*)

'*L'ESTRANGE, DAVID*' [=*CONSTANCE COLLIER* and *IVOR NOVELLO*]
The Rat (Brighton, 14/1/24; R.A., Woolwich, 25/2/24; P.W., 9/6/24)
Down Hill (Pal., Manchester, 14/12/25; Qns, 16/6/26)

LETHBRIDGE, OLIVE
Henry of England ('*r.pl.*': Bij., 4/3/09, *cpy.*: +*J. DE STOURTON*)

×The Blind God (Little, 29/5/11, Oncomers: +*G. FITZGERALD*)
×The Mother (Little, 16/10/11, Oncomers; Lyc. Club, 5/12/20; Glo., 29/11/29, *m.*, expanded into a three-act play)
×The Prime Minister (Little, 27/6/12)
×The Pedestal (Pav., St Leonards, 27/9/12: +*P. ESSORY*)
×'Im (M'sex, 8/11/18, *m.*)
April ('*c.*': Lyc. Club, 21/5/21, Lyc. Club Stage Soc.)
×Liz (Morley College, 22/4/22, Lyc. Club Stage Soc.)
×Honour is Satisfied ('*dream pl.*': Lyc. Club, 11/11/22, Lyc. Club Stage Soc.)
×The Soul of Paris (Lyc. Club, 13/5/23, Lyc. Club Stage Soc.; Aldw., 1/12/24, *m.*, expanded into a three-act play)
The Verdict (Aldw., 22/6/25, *m.*, Lyc. Club Stage Soc.)

LETTS, WINIFRED M.
×The Eyes of the Blind (Abbey, Dublin, 1/4/07)
×The Challenge (Abbey, Dublin, 14/10/09)

LEVEAUX, BIBSIE [see *D. F. C. HARDING*]

LEVEAUX, M. V. [see *C. D. WARD*]

LEVER, BEATRICE, Lady
×The Insurance Act (N. Camberwell Radical Club, 23/12/12)
The Torches of Fate (Vaud., 22/1/15, *m.*)
Brown Sugar ('*light c.*': Gr., Southampton, 28/6/20; D.Y., 7/7/20) *Fr. 1921*

LEVERETT, ARTHUR
×His Lordship ('*oa.*', m. J. Greenhill: Bij., 4/7/01)

LEVERTON, W. J. H.
The Mystery of Marcus, or, Anthony and Cleopatra in a New Light ('*architectural hash*': Guildhall School of Music, 12/2/07, *amat.*)

LEVEY, SIVORI
The King's Messenger ('*oa.*': Caxton H., 19/5/03)
×Parted ('*d. poem*') *1908*
×Burglars! (Bij., 29/4/09)
Carntunderstantinople ('*oa.*': Hampshire House Club, Hamm., 21/5/12)

LEVY, BENN WOLF
This Woman Business ('*c.*': Roy., 18/10/25, Pl. Actors; H., 15/4/26) *1925*
A Man with Red Hair (Little, 27/2/28: dramatised from the novel (1925) by Hugh Walpole) *1928*
Mud and Treacle; or, The Course of True Love ('*shameless tract*': Glo., 9/5/28) *1928*
Mrs Moonlight ('*piece of pastiche*': Kings., 5/12/28) *1929*
Art and Mrs Bottle; or, The Return of the Puritan ('*c.*': Emp., Southampton, 21/10/29; Gr., Croydon, 28/10/29; Crit., 12/11/29) *1929*
The Devil ('*religious c.*': Arts, 12/1/30) *1930*

LEVY, DAVID

×Burglars (T.H., Streatham, 2/5/20, British Jewish Literary Soc.)

LEVY, GEORGE [see *A. ANDERSON*]

LEVY, H. B.

Ginger, the Lonely Soldier ('*m.c.*': Gai., Houghton-le-Spring, 15/8/18: title later changed to *The Love Charm*)

LEVY, JOSÉ GERALD [see also *P. J. BARROW*]

×The Irony of Fate (Bed., 13/4/08; M'sex, 15/3/09)
×The Vampire (Paragon, 27/9/09; Gar., 16/8/15)
×The Human Triangle (Emp., Camberwell, 7/11/10)
×The Veiled Picture (Cant., 5/1/11)
The Glad Eye ('*f.c.*': Pier, Brighton, 4/9/11; Glo., 4/11/11)
×Striking Home (Glasgow, 5/4/12; Gar., 9/5/12)
×Seven Blind Men (Pallad., 2/9/12; Little, 28/3/21)
×The Medium (Pallad., 25/11/12)
×Snore – and you sleep alone (Hippo., Ealing, 3/3/13: +*L. GOLDMAN*)
Who's the Lady? (D.P., Eastbourne, 17/11/13; Gar., 22/11/13)
The Double Mystery (Manchester, 12/6/14; Gar., 14/8/14)
The Nut (Brighton, 15/6/14)
The Girl from Ciro's ('*f.*': Gar., 4/9/16)
Sleeping Partners (St M., 31/12/17)
×How to Be Happy (Little, 1/9/20)
The Risk (Brighton, 26/6/22; Str., 5/7/22: adapted from *Le Caducée* (1921) by A. Pascal)
Zozo ('*f.*': Little, 4/8/22)
The Padre (Lyc., 22/5/26: adapted from *Mon curé chez les riches* (1925) by A. de Lorde, Pierre Chaine and C. Vautel)
Maica (P.W., 14/10/28, Sunday Play Soc.: adapted from a play by L. Verneuil)

LE WARNE, A. [see *A. BEAUMONT*]

LEWES, CEDRIC

Courage (Q, 8/11/26; Wimbledon, 25/3/29, as *The Killing of Anthony Drake*)

LEWIS, ARTHUR [see *ESSEX LEWIS*]

LEWIS, CATHERINE

[For earlier plays see *H. E. D.* v, 459]
×Nell Gwynne, the Player (New, 17/11/08, *m.*)
Fifty Fifty ('*f.*': Bedford H., Chelsea, 4/9/25, Pax Robertson Salon)

LEWIS, CECIL ARTHUR [see also *S. BEHN*]

Jazz Patterns ('*c.*': Everyman, 1/3/27)
The Unknown Soldier (Arts, 5/2/28; Little, 13/2/28, as *The Unknown Warrior*: from P. Raynal, *Le tombeau sous l'Arc de Triomphe*, 1924) *1928*
×His Lordship's Opinion (Steiner H., 23/6/28)

LEWIS, CECIL C.
×The Queen of Spades (T.H., Epson, 4/2/11, *amat.*: +*M. VARCOE*)
×The Outcast (T.H., Epsom, 4/2/11: +*M. VARCOE*)

LEWIS, DOMINIC BEVAN WYNDHAM
×Dilemma (Theat. Gdn Party, Chelsea, 22/6/26)
×Twelve of the Clock (*1927*: in *On Straw and Other Conceits*)

LEWIS, ERIC
×A Lesson in Shakespeare (Playh., 26/11/07)

LEWIS, ESSEX
House Divided (Qns, 8/12/10: called originally *The Sleeper Awakened*: +*A. LEWIS*)

LEWIS, G. EDWIN
×The Founders. *1916* (Labour Publishing Co.)

LEWIS, HAROLD B.
×Paying the Debt (Ashton-under-Lyne, 19/12/08, *cpy.*)

LEWIS, H. H. [see *C. SARKANY*]

LEWIS, J. MORTON
×The Merciful Lie (St John's H., Palmer's Green, 29/4/09, *amat.*: +*F. BENTZ*)
Proxy (Crippl. Inst., 25/11/12, *amat.*)
×The Second Honeymoon (Crippl. Inst., 25/11/12, *amat.*)

LEWIS, J. SAUNDERS
×The Eve of St John. LC, Memorial H., Criccieth, 20/8/24

LEWIS, JOHN D.
×Iolo. *1921* (Cardiff)

LEWIS, M. A.
Yuletide Revels in Merrie England (+*E. M. VERINI*) *1923*

LEWIS, SYD
Righting a Wrong (Pontlottyn, 2/9/25, *amat.*)

LEWIS, VIOLET [*Mrs EDWARD LEWIS*]
×Unavoidable (Ladbr. H., 26/11/05: +*F. KINGSTON*)
×Roses All the Year (Court, 25/3/12: +*A. F. D. CARVALHO*: adapted from Júlio Dantas, *Rosas de todo o ano*, 1907)

LEWIS-RANSOM, SIDNEY
The Hands of Sin (Alex., Widnes, 1/1/06; Vic., Broughton, 12/3/06, as *The Hindoo's Revenge*: title later changed to *Recalled to Life*: +*H. A. SAINTSBURY*)
×The Garter (Shak., Clapham, 18/5/06, *cpy.*; Alh., 25/10/09, as *My Lady's Garter*)
×Your Obedient Servant (C.P., 1/7/09)
×The Malingerer ('*fant. wordless pl.*': P.W., 19/11/12, *m.*)

LEWISOHN, LYDIA
Daniel Deronda (Q, 14/2/27: +*L. TOBIAS*: dramatised from George Eliot's novel)

LEYCESTER, LAURA [see *W. WEAVER*]
×The Power of the Idol (Richmond, 6/4/08)
×Who Was the Woman? (Coll., 22/11/09)
×The Payment (Rehearsal, 13/10/11, *m.*)
×After the Trial (Euston Pal., 14/1/18)
×The Five Wishes (Ambass., 27/1/21, *m.*)
×The Moonshine Laundry (Actors' Club, 29/4/23)
The White Camellia ('*r.m.pl.*', m. P. Theyer: Gr., Blackpool, 27/8/28; Hippo., Lewisham, 4/2/29; Daly's, 26/2/29)

LEYTON, Miss B. M.
The King's Highway (O.H., Jersey, 8/12/03)

LEYTON, F. G.
×The Black Sheep (Rep., B'ham, 29/8/14)

LIDDINGTON, ALVA
×What Happened Afterwards. LC, Ladbr. H., 26/5/13

LIDDLE, HELEN GORDON [='*HELEN GORDON*']

LIEBBRAND, CHARLES HERMANN
Oh! Smiley! ('*m.c.*', m. H. Bayley: P's, 24/5/12, *cpy.*)

LIELL, PATRICIA
Married Love. LC, Aston, 10/1/23

LIGHTNER, FRANCES M.
On Credit (Court, 29/10/09, *cpy.*)

LILLY, MAUD
×A Little Empty Stocking (Cor., 20/9/06, *cpy.*)

LIMB, W. MILLINGTON
When the Heart is Young (Welwyn, 9/2/28)

LIND, FRANK
Come through a Cranford Door (New, 10/7/23, *m.*: +*I. ROSS*)

LIND, STEVEN
×The Trap. LC, D.Y., 16/2/22
Life Goes On (D.Y., 17/3/26)

LINDLEY, GUY
×A Misdeal (Ass. R., Malvern, 19/3/01)

LINDO, FRANK [see also *P. Y. DREW* and *ALFRED MALTBY*]
[For earlier plays see *H. E. D.* v, 460]
Night and Morning (P.W., Salford, 21/1/01; Stratford, 4/2/01; Lyr., Hamm., 18/7/10)
Home Sweet Home (Carlton, Greenwich, 18/5/03; Gr., Islington, 4/7/04; Cant., 22/1/10, as *Cottage or Palace*)
Love, the Conqueror (Pal., Newcastle, 15/12/08; E.C., 4/7/10)
His Child Wife (Brixton, 20/2/11: +*A. SKELTON*)
The Labour Leader ('*md.*': Alh., Openshaw, 9/6/13)
Stolen Goods ('*f.*': Eden, Bishop Auckland, 2/9/27)

LINDON, ALIDA L.
A Son of the People (Vic., Stanley, 15/5/19)

The Other Way (Vic., Stanley, 13/5/20: called originally *The Better Way*)
Things that Money Can't Buy (Vic., Stanley, 30/6/21)
East Lynne. LC, Vic., Stanley, 6/7/22
The Land of My Fathers (Vic., Stanley, 7/9/22)
A Christmas Carol. LC, Vic., Stanley, 8/12/22

LINDSAY, JACK
Helen Comes of Age. *1927*
[This contains three short verse plays: 1. *Helen Comes of Age*; 2. *Ragnhild*; and 3. *Bussy D'Amboise*]
Hereward. *1930*

LINDSAY, MAYNE
The Outsider (Manchester, 15/10/08: +*R. MARSHALL*)

'*LINDSAY, WALTER*' [=*ROBERT BURNS ANNANDALE*]
×Chances ('*an adventure*') *1930* (in Vernon Sylvaine, *The Road of Poplars*)

LINE, CHARLES
Glaucus (Pal., Tottenham, 21/8/12, '*provisional pfce*': from Lord Lytton's novel, *The Last Days of Pompeii*)

LINECAR, ARTHUR [='*ANTHONY GRIM*']

LINFORD, A. HOWARD
Change for a Sovereign ('*m.pl.*': Hampstead Conservatoire, 20/12/13, *amat.*: +*E. M. BATHURST*)

LING, MARJORIE
Peter Piper (K. G's H., 13/5/24, *m.*)
Master (Arts, 14/9/27)

LINTON, MARGARET
×The Little Secret (Rehearsal, 14/3/13)

LION, J.
The Palace of Cards. LC, '*oa.*': Playh., L'pool, 6/12/16: +*H. LESLIE*

LION, KATHLEEN CRIGHTON
×The Wiles of the Widow (Wynd., 11/7/10) *Fr. 1911*
×The Right to Die (Playh., L'pool, 5/2/13)

LION, LEON M. [see also *M. BOWER, F. DIX, T. GALLON, A. PHILLIPS, F. SARGENT* and *H. A. VACHELL*]
×The Fairy Uncle (New, 28/11/07; Wynd., 7/9/08, as *Filby the Faker*)
×The Mobswoman (Playh., 31/8/09: +*W. S. HALL*) *Fr. 1911*
×The Superior Sex (Emp., 13/9/09: +*E. S. ELLIOT*)
×The Touch of the Child (Gr., Blackpool, 4/4/10; Emp., Holborn, 15/8/10: +*T. GALLON*) *Fr. 1913*
Mr Jarvis ('*c.*': Wynd., 16/2/11: +*M. CHERRY*: from the novel, *Madame, Will You Walk?* (1905) by Beth Ellis)
×*C.Q.D.*, or, Called by Wireless (Emp., Glasgow, 20/3/11; Emp., New X, 10/4/11)
×Playing the Game (Glo., 25/11/12: +*A. PHILLIPS*) *Fr. 1913*

×The Creole (Olympic, Littlehampton, 12/5/13; Metropolitan, 30/6/13)
×'Emmer of 'Oxton. LC, Pal., Westcliffe, 23/10/13 (Hippo., Poplar, 17/12/23): +*W. S. HALL*
×The King who had Nothing to Learn (Gai., Manchester, 9/2/14; Hippo., Golder's Green, 27/12/15) *Fr. 1914*
×The Hanging Judge (P.W., Grimsby, 19/4/15)
×The Altar of Liberty (New, 13/5/19, *m.*: +*M. BOWER*)
Jack o' Jingles ('*r.d.*': Gr., Croydon, 18/8/19; New, 4/9/19: +*M. CHERRY*)
In the Snare (Sav., 4/7/24: +*R. SABATINI*: dramatised from the latter's novel *The Snare*, 1917)

[*LIPMAN, CLARA*
Julie Bon-Bon (Waldorf, 26/11/06)

LIPSCOMB, WILLIAM PERCY
Three ('*c.*': Com., 20/3/21, Pl. Actors: adapted from a play by R. Bracco)
×Taking the Liberty (Col., 15/8/21)
Educating Peter (Pier, Eastbourne, 3/10/21: dramatised from his own novel, 1920)

LISLE, MALCOLM
[A few playlets produced at music-halls]

LISSER, H. [see *P. TRIEFUS*]

LISTER, FRANK [see also *F. KITCHEN*]
The Love-Kiss (Sheffield, 27/4/16)

LISTER, RALPH
Her Vow ('*c.*': Gr., Doncaster, 23/12/16)

LISTER, WALTER B. [see *G. S. BROOKS*]

LITCHFIELD, EMMA
A London Actress (Alb., Brighouse, 26/3/02; Terriss, Rotherhithe, 11/1/04)
A Clever Impostor (Muncaster, Bootle, 14/1/07, *cpy.*; Macclesfield, 14/12/07; Stratford, 2/3/08)
His Indian Wife (E.C., 1/8/10)
×The Red-haired Woman (Emp., Camberwell, 30/1/11)
Banished from Home ('*gipsy pl.*': Brit., 29/5/11)
Queen of the Redskins (E.C., 18/9/11)
Allah's Orchard (E.C., 7/10/12)
A Man's Best Pal (Gr., Mansfield, 1/6/14; Stratford, 8/6/14)
The Rival Mothers (E.C., 3/8/14)
×Retribution. LC, Colchester, 21/4/15
Always Welcome (Emp., Tonypandy, 21/5/17; E.C., 28/5/17)
Home Once More ('*md.*': Macclesfield, 26/7/15; E.C., 24/1/16)
The Queen and the Knave (Whitehaven, 29/7/18; E.C., 20/1/19)
Remembrance (Whitehaven, 30/5/21)
Her Chinese Husband (Whitehaven, 4/7/21)

LITCHFIELD, FRANK
A Bedroom Wedding (E.C., 3/11/19: +*F. FELLOWS*)

LITTLE, H.
A Brier Rose ('*c.*': Crippl. Inst., 7/5/07, *amat.*)

LIVESEY, GUS C.
The Battle of Life (W.L., 17/6/04, *cpy.*: +*G. H. TURNER*)

[*LIVINGSTON, ARTHUR*
And That's the Truth (Lyr., Hamm., 17/9/25: adapted from L. Pirandello, *Così è – se vi pare*, 1917) *1923*
Naked (Oxf., 22/6/25; Roy., 18/3/27, *m.*, Forum Club: adapted from L. Pirandello, *Vestire gli ignudi*, 1922) *1925*
×The Man with a Flower in His Mouth (Everyman, 24/5/26: adapted from L. Pirandello, *L'Uomo dal fiore in bocca*, 1923)

LIVINGSTONE, MARY
×The Cat (City Road Hospital, 21/1/14)

LIVINGSTONE, WILLIAM
The Password ('*m.pl.*', m. W. B. Reynolds: Ulster H., Belfast, 8/4/03)
Sir George's Folly (*c.o.*', m. Dr Koeller: Belfast, 27/1/08)

LLEWELLYN, FEWLASS [see also *E. MARTIN* and *E. E. NORRIS*]
[For an earlier play see *H. E. D.* v, 461]
×Only A Quaker Maid (Gr., Fulham, 19/7/1898, *cpy.*; Ass. R., Putney, 26/2/08, *amat.*: dramatised from Sir Walter Besant's novel, *A Fountain Sealed*, 1897)
A Woman's Power; or, More Sinned against than Sinning (Bij., 24/2/02, *cpy.*: +*A. BAWTREE*)
×At Evensong (Gai., Hastings, 27/2/05)
Fighting Her Fate; or, A Maze of Mystery (E.C., 16/10/05: +*E. E. NORRIS*]
Her Wedding Dress ('*oa.*', m. A. Wigley: Ass. R., Putney, 28/2/07, *amat.*; Vic. H., 27/10/07, Pl. Actors)

LLEWELLYN, HENRY
The Re-appearance of Betty ('*f.*': Apo., 27/5/21, *m.*)

LLOYD, ARTHUR
Kokoro ('*modern Japanese problem pl.*': translated from the drama by T. Kitasato) *1905* (in the *Transactions of the Asiatic Society of Japan*, xxxiii, 1905)

LLOYD, ARTHUR
[For earlier plays see *H. E. D.* v, 461]
The Dog Fancier ('*sensational d.*': Lyc., Stafford, 19/5/02: +*M. BRAHM*)

LLOYD, CECIL
A Classical Instance (Kelly's, L'pool, 21/11/11, *cpy.*)

LLOYD, FLORENCE
×Our First Dinner (Roy., Glasgow, 7/3/10)

LLOYD, GLADYS
×Aunts Aren't (Pav., 3/6/14)

×Money for Nothing (Rehearsal, 2/5/18)
×The Latest Craze (Hippo., Derby, 28/4/19; Emp., Holborn, 2/6/19)

LLOYD, HERBERT [see also *J. DUNBAR*]
×The Soul of Private Stephens (*'oa.'*, m. A. Taylor: Drill H., Tettenhall, 13/1/02)

LOACH, ARTHUR W. [see *W. KIMBALL*]

LOADER, A. McLEOD [=*'ALFRED M. DAYLOR'*]
[For an earlier play see *H. E. D.* v, 461]
An Angel on Earth (St Helens, 1/9/02: from C. Dickens' *The Old Curiosity Shop*)
The Greatest Scoundrel Living (*'md.'*: St Helens, 2/3/03; Lyr., Hamm., 2/11/03)
The King of Thieves (Star, L'pool, 19/11/03, *cpy.*; St Helens, 18/4/04; Crown, Peckham, 11/7/04)
For Honour and Revenge (St Helens, 25/10/09)

LOATES, CARR
At the World's Mercy (Stratford, 14/9/08: title later changed to *For a Woman's Love*)
A London Outcast (LC, P.H., Stockbridge, 21/11/10: Pal., Battersea, 29/7/12, in a condensed version)

LOCH, SYDNEY
Forty-Seven (P.W., 2/2/30, St. Soc.)

LOCK, EMIL
×The Test (Little, 22/12/11, Oncomers)
×In War Time (Rehearsal, 24/1/13, Black Cat Club)
×A China Orange (Bed., 31/3/13)
×The Husband of Citoyenne Denise (Forum Club, 30/1/21)

[*LOCKE, EDWARD*
The Inspiration (*'pl. of modern life'*: Bij., 15/2/09, *cpy.*)
The Climax (Com., 26/2/10; D.P., Eastbourne, 20/10/13, revised by *C. M. BRUNE*; Little, 26/8/27)
The Case of Becky (Dalston, 20/10/11, *cpy.*)
The Bubble (*'c.'*: Schenectady, 18/1/15; Booth, N.Y., 5/4/15; Gai., Manchester, 9/9/18; Wimbledon, 28/10/18: +*B. JAMES*)

LOCKE, FRED
[For earlier plays see *H. E. D.* v, 462, 804]
A Trip to the Highlands (*'m.c.'*, m. E. T. de Banzie: Gr., Edin., 3/4/05; Marlb., Holloway, 29/5/05)
Lucky 'Liza (*'m.pl.'*: Paisley, 7/5/06; R.A., Woolwich, 11/4/10)

LOCKE, WILLIAM JOHN
[For earlier plays see *H. E. D.* v, 462]
The Lost Legion (Shak., L'pool, 7/11/98; Brixton, 14/11/98; Gt. Qn. St., 24/5/00)
×Flower o' the Rose (H.M., 23/6/04, *m.*) *1909*
The Morals of Marcus (Gar., 30/8/06: dramatised from his own novel, *The Morals of Marcus Ordeyne*, 1903) *1906* (*priv.*)

The Palace of Puck ('*fant.c.*': H., 2/4/07)
The Beloved Vagabond (Dublin, 10/10/07; H.M., 4/2/08: dramatised from his own novel, 1907)
Butterflies ('*m.c.*', m. J. A. Robertson: Tyne, Newcastle, 20/4/08; Apo., 11/5/08)
[A musical version of his *Palace of Puck*, see above]
× A Blank Cheque (Emp., 16/12/08)
The Man from the Sea (Qns, 20/9/10)
× An Adventure of Aristide Pujol (H., 19/11/12)
The Princess of the Nile. LC, '*c.*': St Mary's H., Hemel Hempstead, 31/12/17
The Mountebank (Stamford, Conn., 23/3/23; Lyc., N.Y., 7/5/23: +*E. DENNY*)
× Under the Terror. LC, Scala, 31/10/22
The Light on the Mountain ('*c.*': Reg., 16/8/26)

[*LOCKEY, JOHN P.*
The Hidden Crime (Sur., 4/5/03)

LOCKWOOD, SCAMMON [see *E. CLARKE*]

LOCKWOOD, T. RENAUD
Families Repaired ('*c.*': Gr., Luton, 26/8/21: dramatised from the novel (1916) by J. S. Fletcher)

[*LOCKWOOD, W. L.* [see *A. ROGERS*]

LODGE, A. E. [see *E. WOODLAND*]

LODGE, MARGARET BEATRICE
Seven Plays of Fairy Days. *1924*
Other Plays of Fairy Days. *1925*
[The various items in these two collections, although not particularly original in theme, have interest in that they are lengthier than the usual fare composed for children's performances: all the plays are in three acts and are designed for a playing time of an hour and a half]

LODGE, Sir OLIVER WILLIAM FOSTER
× The Labyrinth ('*t.*': performed in B'ham, October 1911, by the Pilgrim Players) *1911*

LODGE-PERCY, C. [see also *H. SCHRIER*]
× Nana (City Pal., Leeds, 16/10/11: title changed later to *The Darling of Paris*)
× What Would a Woman Do? (Alex., Pontefract, 4/5/14)

LOFTING, JOHN HENRY
× Faith (Crippl. Inst., 27/2/06, *amat.*)

LOGAN, GUY [see also *R. GRAHAME*]
[For earlier plays see *H. E. D.* v, 462]
When a Man's Married—? ('*m.f.*', m. Colet Dare: Dover, 25/6/00)
The Dream Lady. LC, '*m.pl.*': Vic., Ripley, 13/10/22
Pretty Polly ('*m.pl.*', m. W. St John: O.H., Macclesfield, 18/12/22; Stratford, 17/2/23: title later changed to *Polly the Wonder*)

LOGAN, STANLEY [see also *C. GREY*]
×The New Poor (Kennington, 23/5/21: title later changed to *The Poor Rich*)
×De Mortuis (Little, 25/1/22)
[Several other short plays produced at music-halls]

LOMATH, C.
A Middle-Class Family. LC, Court, Wigan, 8/8/24

LOMATH, STUART
Whom God Hath Joined (E.C., 13/12/09: title later changed to *Wife or Mistress*, *The Wife who Sinned* and *Come Home Daddy*)
The Thief Catcher (R.A., Woolwich, 22/5/11)
×Oh! Phyllis! LC, K's, Longsight, 11/6/15
The Wastrel and the Woman (H.M., Walsall, 23/4/17; Pal., Battersea, 16/7/17: title later changed to *The Unwanted Child*)
The Mill-Girl and the Miner (Pal., Battersea, 29/4/18)

LOMAX, Miss E. L.
×The House of Shadows (R. Acad. of Music, 5/5/05)
×The Demon's Bride ('*o.*', m. B. W. O'Donnell: R. Acad. of Music, 22/5/09)
×The Wolf (R. Acad. of Music, 22/5/09)

LOMAX, H. C. [='*MAX ALLEN*']
Which Loved Him Best? (Alex., Sheffield, 21/10/10, *cpy.*; Junction, Manchester, 10/6/12; M'sex, 14/10/12: title later changed to *For Love and the Navy*)
×Little Mary's Affair. LC, Perth, 30/12/13
Hot Pot ('*c.*': K's, Longsight, 21/3/27)

LOMAX, L. E.
The Brownie and the Piano-Tuner; or, The Piano-Tuner and the Brownie (m. by the author: R. Coll. of Music, 6/5/07, *amat.*)

LOMAX, W. J.
Conscience in Pawn (Q, 22/10/28)

LOMBARD, FRANK ALANSON
An Outline History of the Japanese Drama. *1928*
[This includes translations of seven Japanese plays: 1. *Manju*, by Motokiyo Seami; 2. *Oharo Goko*, by Motokiyo Seami; 3. *Chikuba Shima*, by Zenchiku Ujinobu; 4. *Eguchi*, by Zenchiku Ujinobu; 5. *Fuji*, by Hiyoshi Sa-ami Yasukiyo; 6. *Okina*; and 7. *Shinyu Kamiya-Jihei*]

[*LONG, JOHN LUTHER*[see also *D. BELASCO* and *F. STAYTON*]
Kassa (H., 5/1/09, *cpy.*)
The Dragon Fly (Broadway, New X, 15/9/05: +*E. C. CARPENTER*)

LONG, MARGARET VERA CAMPBELL GABRIELLE [='*MARJORIE BOWEN*']

LONG, PAUL ALARIC MASTERS
×One Better. LC, Village H., Speldhurst, 26/5/22
The Factotum ('*c.*': RADA, 6/5/23)

LONGDEN, CHARLES H. [see also *E. HUDSON* and *F. MOULE*]
[For earlier plays see *H. E. D.* v, 462–3]
Thy Neighbour's Wife (Qns, Leeds, 18/12/05: +*E. HUDSON*)
×Doing Their Bit (Leamington Spa, 7/6/15)

LONGSON, E. H.
While Rome Burns ('*c.*': Rep., B'ham, 10/3/17)

LONNEN, WALTER
Too Many Cooks ('*f.c.*': Emp., Southend, 20/4/03; R.A., Woolwich, 29/6/03)

LONSDALE, FREDERICK [originally *FREDERICK LEONARD*]
Who's Hamilton? (St Helier, Jersey, ? 1906)
The Follies of the Foolish (? 1907, sold to Willie Edouin, but not produced: later re-written as *On Approval*, see below)
The King of Cadonia ('*m.pl.*', m. S. Jones: P.W., 3/9/08)
The Early Worm ('*f.*': Wynd., 7/9/08: originally called *The Worm*)
The Best People ('*c.*': Wynd., 5/8/09)
The Balkan Princess ('*m.pl.*', m. P. A. Rubens: P.W., 19/2/10: +*F. CURZON*)
Betty ('*m.c.*', m. P. A. Rubens: P's, Manchester, 24/12/14; Daly's, 24/4/15, *revised*: +*G. UNGER*)
×The Patriot (Gr., Clapham Junction, 14/5/15)
High Jinks ('*m.c.*': Adel., 24/8/16: title later changed to *By the Seaside*)
×Waiting at the Church (Col., 25/9/16)
The Maid of the Mountains ('*c.o.*', m. H. Fraser-Simson: P's, Manchester, 23/12/16; Daly's, 10/2/17)
Monsieur Beaucaire ('*m.pl.*', m. A. Messager: P.W., B'ham, 7/4/19; P's, 19/4/19)
The Lady of the Rose ('*m.pl.*', m. J. Gilbert: P's, Manchester 26/12/21; Daly's, 21/2/22)
Aren't We All? ('*c.*': Glo., 10/4/23) *1924*; *Fr. 1925*
[This was confessedly a rewritten version of *The Best People*]
Spring Cleaning ('*c.*': Adel., Chicago, 9/9/23; Eltinge, N.Y., 9/11/23; St M., 29/1/25) *1925*
Madame Pompadour ('*m.pl.*', m. L. Fall: Daly's, 20/12/23: +*H. GRAHAM*)
The Street Singer ('*m.pl.*', m. H. Fraser-Simson: P.W., B'ham, 4/2/24; Lyr., 27/6/24) *Fr. 1929*
The Fake (Apo., 13/3/24) *Fr. 1926*
Katja the Dancer ('*m.c.*', m. J. Gilbert: P's, Bradford, 4/8/24; Gai., 21/2/25: +*H. GRAHAM*)
The Last of Mrs Cheyney (St J., 22/9/25) *1925*; *Fr. 1929*
On Approval ('*c.*': Gai., N.Y., 18/10/26; O.H., Southport, 4/4/27; Fortune, 19/4/27) *1927*; *Fr. 1928*
The High Road ('*c.*': Shaft., 7/9/27) *1927*; *Fr. 1928*
Lady Mary ('*m.pl.*', m. A. Sirmay: K's, Southsea, 13/2/28; Daly's, 23/2/28: +*J. H. TURNER*)
Canaries Sometimes Sing ('*c.*': B'ham, 14/10/29; Glo., 21/10/29) *Fr. 1929*

LONSDALE, KEITH
×Her Two Lovers (New, Ealing, 25/5/03)
Who's Hamilton? ('*f.c.*': New, Ealing, 25/5/03)

[*LOOS, ANITA*
The Whole Town's Talking ('*f.c.*', Hempstead, Long Island, 13/11/22; Bij., N.Y., 29/8/23; O.H., Leicester, 23/8/26; Str., 7/9/26: +*J. EMERSON*) *1928*
Gentlemen Prefer Blondes (P.W., 2/4/28: +*J. EMERSON*)

LORD, C. A.
The Lady's Maid ('*m.c.*', m. E. Hastings: New, Cambridge, 21/12/01; Duchess, Balham, 10/2/02)

LORD, RICHARD [see *W. ARMSTRONG*]

LORE, COLDEN
×The Acid Test (Ambass., Southend, 19/6/22: +*W. E. STIRLING*)

LORIMER, ENID
×Honour (Rehearsal, 16/3/15)
×A Question Unanswered (Rehearsal, 16/3/15)

LORIMER, K.
×The Call. LC, Lenzie H., Dumbartonshire, 20/11/14

LORRAINE, PAUL
The Hidden Horror ('*mystery pl.*': Chester, 26/5/27)

LORRAINE, VICTOR
You Never Know Your Luck. LC, Gr., Gravesend, 11/4/23

LOTINGA, ERNEST (ERNIE)
[Several playlets and sketches produced at music-halls]

[*LOUNSBERY, Miss GRACE CONSTANT*
The Picture of Dorian Gray (Vaud., 28/8/13) *1913*

LOVELL, PHYLLIS
Hands Up! LC, '*m.pl.*': Playh., Dorking, 28/6/22

LOVETT, Rev. ERNEST NEVILLE
The Passing of the Bailiff ('*folk pl.*': Church H., Farnham, 9/11/12)

LOVETT, MYRA
John Alden's Choice. *1920* (Southampton)
The Children of Spinalunga ('*pageant pl.*') *1921*
The Road Makers ('*pageant*') *1922*
The Inn of Desire. *1924*
The Other Half ('*fant.*') LC, K. G's H., 16/4/24. *1924*

LOVETT, W. J.
Goin's on at Kelly's ('*c.*': Dufferin Memorial H., Bangor, Co. Down, 4/4/13)
The Pride av the McFetridges ('*c.*': Ward H., Bangor, Co. Down, 12/2/14)

LOWE, SIDNEY
×Jobson's Choice (Aldw., 7/5/09, *m.*)

LOWE, W.

×The Scottish Brigand. LC, Gai., Nethill, 21/5/15

Peace and Plenty. LC, Kursaal, Bognor, 17/3/19

LOWINSKY, XENIA

×Adoption (Ambass., 6/12/20)

Intimate Enemies (Sav., 17/5/26: +*N. McKINNEL*)

LOWNDES, F. S. A.

×Denton (Lab.) (Little, 26/11/10)

×The Last Green (Little, 23/12/12)

LOWNDES, MARIE ADELAIDE [=*MARIE ADELAIDE BELLOC*, afterwards *LOWNDES*]

LOWNDES-YATES, CHRISTABEL

×Wanted – a House (T.H., Amersham, 17/5/20, *amat.*)

×The Water-Hole ('*pastoral c.*': Chesham Bois, 21/8/20, Chiltern Arts Club)

LOWTHER, Mrs CHRISTOPHER [see also *EDITH CRAIG*]

×The Matchmaker (Vaud., 4/1/18, *m.*)

LOWTHER, CLAUDE

The Gordian Knot (H.M., 20/5/03)

LOWTHER, HARRY

[Several playlets and sketches produced at music-halls]

LOYDALL, HENRIETTA A.

A Son of the Sea. LC, Rot., L'pool, 22/9/14: title later changed to *A Woman of Sorrows*

LUCAS, AUDREY

The Peaceful Thief ('*light c.*': Arts, 6/11/27)

LUCAS, EDWARD VERRALL

×The Visit of the King (Pal., 2/12/12)

The Same Star ('*c.*': Art, Leeds, 20/4/25) *1924*

LUCEY, AGATHA

×Smugglers All (Cent., 8/12/26, *amat.*)

LUDLOW, W. H. [see *T. W. WALKER*]

LUDOVIC, FREDERIC [see *F. C. SOMERFIELD*]

LUMLEY, RALPH R.

[For earlier plays see *H. E. D.* v, 464–5]

In the Soup ('*f.c.*': O.H., Northampton, 16/8/00; Str., 28/8/00)

LUNT, H. [='*MILTON ROSMER*']

LUNT, W. J. [='*ARTHUR MILTON*']

LUPINO, STANLEY

So This is Love ('*m.c.*', m. H. Brody: O.H., Blackpool, 26/3/28; W.G., 25/4/28: +*A. RIGBY*)

Oh! Letty! ('*m.f.*', m. B. Mayerl: Hippo., Lewisham, 18/2/29)

Love Lies ('*m.pl.*', m. H. Brody: K's, Southsea, 4/3/29: Gai., 20/3/29: +*A. RIGBY*)
The Love Race ('*m.pl.*', m. J. Clarke: Gai., 25/6/30)

LUTTRELL, Mrs MOIRA
The Awakening of the Woodland. LC, '*m.pl.*': Vic. H., Sheldon, 14/9/21

'*LYALL, EDNA*' [=*ADA ELLEN BAYLY*]
In Spite of All ('*r.pl.*': D.P., Eastbourne, 4/1/00; Com., 5/2/00)

LYALL, ERIC
Two Pierrot Plays. *1918*
[This includes two short plays: 1. *The Dream Stone* (LC, Lyc., Edin., 15/6/14); and 2. *The Dream Gate* (LC, Picture House, N. Berwick, 12/10/18)]
×The Sin-Eater (K's, Glasgow, 22/2/26, Scott. Nat. Players: dramatised from a story by Fiona MacLeod: +*J. McKENZIE*)
×The Skirlin' o' the Pipes (Lyr., Glasgow, 8/11/27)

LYND, LESLIE
×The Summons (O.H., Belfast, 25/3/18)

LYNDALL, FLORENCE
Girls will be Girls ('*m.c.*', m. A. Gatburn and H. Sydney: Roy., Llanelly, 19/3/00)

LYNDON, PEARL
Paris Gay ('*m.c.*': Worthing, 24/2/19)

LYNN, J. WELLESLEY
The Doctor's Experiment (Scala, 10/3/08; Lyc., Stafford, 6/3/11; Fulham, 24/4/11)

LYNN, NEVILLE
[For earlier plays see *H. E. D.* v, 465]
×Joining the Company (Bij., 19/12/03, *cpy.*)
Geoffrey Stirling (Gr., Fulham, 3/7/05: from the novel (1885) by Mrs De Courcy Laffan)

LYNN, SYDNEY [see *V. SYLVAINE*]

LYNTON, FORD
×The Open Window (St G's H., 16/2/05)

LYON, KATE
×The Rose (Qns, 26/7/10)
×Peace (Qns, 26/7/10)

LYON, M. D.
×The Warmth that Kills. LC, New, Cambridge, 31/5/22: +*E. MASCHWITZ* and *H. ROTTENBURG*

LYON, HASTINGS, G.
Fate Plays a Hand (Worthing, 4/12/22)
The Quiet Season ('*f.*': Worthing, 30/4/23)

LYONS, ALBERT NEIL [see also *G. UNGER*]
×Three Common People (Court, 8/2/12; Vaud., 31/10/12, as

Penny a Bunch: +'*HENRY SETON*') *Fr. 1920* (as *A Penny Bunch*)
×The Gentleman who was Sorry (Little, 18/10/12: +*P. E. HUBBARD*)
×Getting at Facts (People's, Newcastle, 4/14, *amat.*)
×A Bit of a Lad (St J., 2/3/17, *m.*)
The Ring o' Bells ('*c.*': P's, Manchester, 1/6/25; Com., 24/11/25)

LYSCEA, HARRY
The Purple Disk. LC, T.H., Chiswick, 20/3/24

LYTTLETON, Hon. Mrs ALFRED (EDITH) [=*Dame EDITH SOPHY LYTTLETON*]
Warp and Woof (Camden, 6/6/04; Vaud., 27/6/04: called originally *Theodosia Hemming*) *1908*
The Macleans of Bairness (Crit., 19/6/06)
×A Christmas Morality Play. *1908*
St Ursula's Pilgrimage ('*miracle pl.*': Court, 29/11/09) *1909*
Peter's Chance (Roy., 17/5/12) *1912*
×The Thumbscrew (Little, 15/12/12, Pioneer Players)
Two Pierrots (Little, 7/3/15, Pioneer Players: adapted from E. Rostand, *Les deux Pierrots*, 1892)
×Dame Julian's Window ('*morality*': Little, 3/7/13, Morality Pl. Soc.)
×Home from the Ball (St G's House, Regent-Street, 18/11/13, Theatre in Eyre)

LYTTLETON, GEORGE
[For an earlier play see *H. E. D.* v, 466]
At War with the World (Carlton, Greenwich, 9/5/04)

M., P. D.
×The Starling (Alh., Glasgow, 10/6/12; Playh., 25/6/12, *m.*; Pav., 8/7/12)

'*MAARTENS, MAARTEN*' [*JOUST MARIUS WILLEM VAN DER POORTEN-SCHWARTS*]
×The Jailbird (Wynd., 9/2/04)

MAC, T. C.
Miss Lamb – of Canterbury ('*m.c.*': Woolwich, 25/5/14: +*H. L. OSMOND*: attributed in LC to *F. C. MAGUIRE* at Pal., Northampton, 26/8/15)

McARDLE, DOROTHY
Asthara (Little, Dublin, 24/5/18)
Atonement (Abbey, Dublin, 17/12/18)
Ann Kavanagh (Abbey, Dublin, 6/4/22) *1937*
The Old Man (Abbey, Dublin, 24/2/25)

MACARTHUR, BESSIE B. J.
×The Clan of Lochlinn, and Silis: Two Celtic Plays. *1928* (Edinburgh)

McARTHUR, JAMES [see *M. PEMBERTON* and *A. THOMAS*]

MACBETH, ALLAN [see *A. STEPHENSON*]

McBRIDE, ANGUS
×Sauce for the Goose. LC, P.H., Streatham, 18/11/13

MacBRIDE, MELCHIOR
A Message from the Gods. LC, '*mystery pl.*': Wellington H., St John's Wood, 14/11/10. *1910*

McBRIDE, Mrs PHYLLIS
The Brown Velvet Skirt (Sheffield, 16/12/21, *amat.*)

MacCABE, J. W.
The Major's Double ('*f.c.*': Belfast, 4/6/06)

McCALLUM, FRANCES A.
×At Aphrodite's Temple ('*Greek idyll*': P.H., W. Norwood, 19/4/12, *amat.*; Ambass., 14/11/13, Stage Players, as *At the Temple of Aphrodite*)
×A Perfect Day (Arts Centre, 11/2/14)

McCARTHY, EUGENE [see *A. O'CONNELL*]

MacCARTHY, JOHN BERNARD
×Kinship (Abbey, Dublin, 2/4/14)
The Supplanter (Court, 4/6/14)
The Crusaders (Abbey, Dublin, 19/1/17) *1918* (Dublin)
×The Men in Possession (Emp., Dublin, 11/3/18) *1922* (Dublin)
The Romantic Lover ('*c.*': Emp., Dublin, 26/8/18) *1922* (Dublin)
×The Duplicity of David (Abbey, Dublin, 4/4/20)
The Rising Generation ('*c.*': Qns, Dublin, 20/2/22, *amat.*)
×Wrecked ('*t.*') *1922* (Dublin)
×Cough Water ('*f.*') *1922* (Dublin)
×The Long Road to Garranbraher (Abbey, Dublin, 9/1/23) *1928* (Dublin)
×The Down Express. LC, '*f.c.*': Argyle, Birkenhead, 2/8/24. *1928* (Dublin)
The Able Dealer ('*f.c.*') *1928* (Dublin)
×Fine Feathers. *1928* (Dublin)
Old Acquaintance ('*f.c.*') *1928* (Dublin)
×Poachers. *1928* (Dublin)
Who Will Kiss Cinderella? ('*r.c.*') *1929* (Dublin)

McCARTHY, JUSTIN HUNTLY [see also *R. C. CARTON*]
[For earlier plays see *H. E. D.* v, 467, 804]
If I Were King (St J., 30/8/02: dramatised from his own novel, 1901) *1922*
A Proud Prince: A Story of Robert, King of Sicily (Vaud., 11/9/03, *cpy.*; Lyc., 4/9/09)
The Lady of Loyalty House (Gr., Margate, 21/9/04, *cpy.*: dramatised from his own novel, 1904)
The Dryad (Gr., Margate, 15/3/05, *cpy.*) *1905*
Needles and Pins (Hippo., Margate, 23/4/07, *cpy.*)
Caesar Borgia (Edin., 21/11/07)
Don Quixote (Hippo., Margate, 17/2/08, *cpy.*)

The Duke's Motto ('*md.*': B'ham, 31/8/08; Lyr., 8/9/08: adapted from *Le bossu* (1862) by P. Féval)
The O'Flynn (H.M., 1/2/10)
× The Highwayman. *Fr. 1910*
Sir Roger de Coverley ('*c.*': H.M., Aberdeen, 28/11/14)
Stand and Deliver ('*r.d.*': H.M., 30/3/16)

McCARTHY, MARION
× Paulina (Court, 7/2/18, prologue to a three-act pl.)

MacCATHMHAOIL, SEOSAMB [=*JOSEPH CAMPBELL*]
The Little Cowherd of Slainge (Clarence Place H., Belfast, 4/5/05, Ulster Literary Theatre)

McCLELLAND, W. T.
[For an earlier play see *H. E. D.* v, 467]
A Woman Adrift (Emp., Oldham, 18/2/01; Stand., 15/7/01)
Laughter Land ('*m. mystical, pantomimical c.*': R.A., Woolwich, 9/2/03)

MacCLURE, VICTOR [see also *V. WOODHOUSE*]
× Two Up, Right. LC, Ath., Glasgow, 4/4/13
× Latitude 15°S (Little, 29/6/21: called originally *On the Fringe*)

McCLYMONT, MURRAY
The Mannock Family (Rep., B'ham, 26/2/27)
The Good Die Young ('*postprandial c.*': Playh., L'pool, 5/3/29)

[*McCORMICK, ARTHUR LANGDON*
Hearts Adrift (Gr., B'ham, 20/2/05; Gr., Fulham, 27/2/05)
× Train 44 (Emp., Wood Green, 16/6/13)
× A Mile a Minute. LC, Hippo., L'pool, 5/9/13
× The Forest Fire (Olympia, L'pool, 23/2/14; Pallad., 27/4/14: title later changed to *The Burning Forest*)
× How Could She Do It? (Hippo., Balham, 25/5/14)
The Storm (National, Washington, 5/9/10; 48th St., N.Y., 2/10/19; Str., 23/11/20)

McCRIE, LILIAS
'Let There Be Light!' ('*pl. for the people*') *1922*

McCULLOUGH, BRIAN
× The Wrong Letter ('*f. absurdity*': Metropolitan, 8/4/07)
× Jack (Sur., 10/6/07)
× 1920 (Sur., 28/6/09)

MACDERMOTT, NORMAN
× Jealous Barbouillé (Everyman, 15/6/21: adapted from Molière, *La jalousie de Barbouillé*)
Home Affairs ('*c.*': Everyman, 20/1/25: called originally *Margaret of Navarre*)
The Hell Within ('*c.*': Arts, 13/7/29: adapted from a translation by *NOEL DE VIC BEAMISH* of a play by Guido Stacchini)

MACDONA, C. L. [see *M. TERRY*]

MacDONAGH, JOHN
× Author, Author! ('*c.*': Irish, Dublin, 27/12/15)

Weeds (Irish, Dublin, 6/1/19)
The Irish Jew ('*c.*': Emp., Dublin, 12/12/21)
The Pride of Petravore ('*c.*': Emp., Dublin, 20/3/22)
The Remains (Abbey, Dublin, 21/5/28)

MacDONAGH, THOMAS
When the Dawn is Come ('*t.*': Abbey, Dublin, 15/10/08) *1908* (Dublin)
×Metempsychosis; or, A Mad World (Hardwicke St. H., Dublin, 18/4/12, Theatre of Ireland)
Pagans ('*modern pl. in two conversations*': Dublin, 19/4/15, Theatre of Ireland) *1920* (Dublin)

MacDONALD, ALLAN
[A few playlets produced at music-halls]

MacDONALD, B.
×The Most Important. LC, Qns College, Harley St., 6/12/17

MacDONALD, LAURA
×Paint. *1925*

MacDONALD, MARGARET
The Bushranger's Daughter ('*md.*': Metro., Glasgow, 12/5/19: called originally *The Girl from Down Under*)

MacDONALD, NEIL
×The Beautiful White Devil (Glo., 27/9/26, Green Room Rag)

MacDONALD, R. H.
The Opal Queen ('*m.pl.*': P.H., Pitlochry, 19/11/24)

MacDONALD, RONALD
[For earlier plays see *H. E. D.* v, 468]
The Sword of the King ('*r.pl.*': Wynd., 9/4/04)
The Sea Maid ('*c.*': Qns, Manchester, 16/1/06, *cpy.*)
×Jocelyn the Jester ('*c.*': C.P., 4/3/07; Gr., Croydon, 17/2/08)
The Chief-of-Staff (Lyr., 2/2/09)
×The Frame (Court, 20/3/10, Pl. Actors; Empress, 2/5/10)
The Red Herring (Court, 1/5/10, Pl. Actors)
The Carcase (K's, Greenock, 2/2/15)

McDONALD, ROSALIN
×Nae Bourne o' Mine. LC, T.H., Uttoxeter, 16/2/14

MacDONALD, WILLIAM [='*CORMAC SIMPSON*']

MACDONELL, AMICE
The Story of the Armada. *1908*
Historical Plays for Children. *1909–1913*
[This collection of short plays appeared in nine 'series', with variant titles *Historical Plays for Young People* and *Historical and Other Plays*]
×The Sacred Fire ('*morality pl.*') *1924*

McDONNELL, LILY
Vingt-et-un ('*fairy oa.*': Court, 2/5/14)

[*MacDONOUGH, GLEN*
[For earlier plays see *H. E. D.* v, 469]
Jones's Jaunt ('*f.c.*': H.M., Aberdeen, 12/9/04; called originally *The Prodigal Father*: title later changed to *Ananias the Second*)

McDOWALL, H. M.
× Jezebel ('*t.*') *1924* (Oxford)

McEVOY, CHARLES ALFRED
David Ballard (Imp., 9/6/07, St. Soc.) *1907*
× His Helpmate (Midland Hotel, Manchester, 23/9/07) *1907*
× Lucifer (Midland Hotel, Manchester, 9/11/07; Little, 6/12/10) *1907*
When the Devil was Ill ('*c.*': H.M., Carlisle, 29/8/08; Cor., 14/6/09) *1908*
The Three Barrows (Gai., Manchester, 22/3/09; Cor., 10/6/09) *1924*
× Gentlemen of the Road (Gai., Manchester, 5/10/08; H., 12/10/09) *1907*
The Village Wedding (Village Theatre, Aldbourne, 26/2/10; Cor., 23/5/10)
All that Matters (H., 8/2/11) *1911*
The Situation at Newbury (Playh., L'pool, 18/3/12; Rep., Croydon, 28/4/13)
× The Red Hen (Tiv., Manchester, 8/4/12) *1914*
Her Ladyship (Abbey, Dublin, 24/6/18; Portsmouth, 20/2/22)
× The Dew Necklace ('*pl. for Brownies*') *Fr. 1922*
The Likes of Her (T.H., Battersea, 30/1/23; St M., 15/8/23) *Fr. 1923*

McFARLANE, A. D. [see *R. J. McLENNAN*]

MacFARLANE, W. W. [see *G. A. PEACOCK*]

McGEOCH, DAISY
× Collaborators (Clavier H., 10/6/12) *Fr. 1904*
× Nobby, V.C. (Oxf., 22/9/13)
× The Best Man (Pav., 21/6/15, *m.*: + *C. JAMES*)
Concert Cameos. LC, Crippl. Inst., 1/11/22. *Fr. 1922*

MacGILL, PATRICK
Moleskin Joe (Ambass., 7/2/21, *m.*, Playwrights' Theatre)
Suspense (D.Y., 8/4/30)

MACGILLIVRAY, INA
× Pan. LC, Lauriston H., Edin., 23/3/14

McGOWAN, JOHN [see also *R. P. WESTON*]
Heads Up ('*m.c.*', m. R. Rodgers: Pal., 1/5/30: + *P. G. SMITH*)

McGOWAN, M. SLIEVE
× Trimmings (Rehearsal, 25/4/11, *m.*)

McGOWRAN, W. K.
Wolves of the Night (Gr., Derby, 29/8/27)

McGREGOR, REGINALD JONES
A Daughter of the Philistines ('*c.*': Little, Bristol, 23/2/28)

[*McGUIRE, WILLIAM ANTHONY*
Kid Boots ('*m.c.*', m. H. Tierney: Earl Carroll, N.Y., 31/12/23; K's, Southsea, 25/1/26; W.G., 2/2/26: +*O. HARBACH*)
Six-Cylinder Love. LC, Brighton, 9/10/24
Twelve Miles Out (Ford's, Baltimore, 26/10/26, as *Somewhere East of Gotham*; Playh., N.Y., 16/11/26; Str., 26/1/27)
The Three Musketeers ('*r.m.pl.*', m. R. Friml: D.L., 28/3/30)

[*MacHUGH, AUGUSTIN*
Officer 666 ('*f.*': Glo., 30/10/12: +*B. W. CURTIS*) *1912*

McHUGH, MARTIN J.
×A Minute's Wait (Abbey, Dublin, 27/8/14) *1944* (Dublin)
×The Philosopher (Abbey, Dublin, 5/4/15)
×Tommy-Tom-Tom (Abbey, Dublin, 8/1/17)

McINTYRE, ALAN
[A few playlets produced at music-halls]

MacINTYRE, JOHN [='*JOHN BRANDANE*']

McIVER, N. E.
×Another Chance, and Age Limited. *1929*
[This contains two one-act plays]

MACK, H. N.
×What Do *You* Think? LC, Albion H., Horsham, 23/11/22. *1922*
×Nowhere in Henfield. LC, Ass. R., Henfield, 26/2/24
×A W.I. Charade. *1926*
×In Aid of— (London Theatre School, 28/3/28)

MACK, MARGARET M.
The Gates of the Morning (Shaft., 1/3/08, St. Soc.)
×Emily (H.M., 8/12/08, *m.*, Afternoon Theatre)
×Unemployed (Aldw., 3/5/09, St. Soc.; Gai., Manchester, 30/8/09)

[*MACK, WILLARD*
Kick In (Proctor's, N.Y., 10/3/13; Vaud., 28/8/15: title later changed to *Once a Thief*) *Fr. 1925*
Tiger Rose (Playh., Wilmington, 30/4/17; Lyc., N.Y., 3/10/17; Bournemouth, 6/10/19; Sav., 16/10/19)

MACKAIL, DENIS
Patricia ('*m.c.*', m. G. Gwyther: Pal., Manchester, 29/9/24; H.M., 31/10/24)

MACKAY, A. B.
How Nihilists Are Made (Roy., Llanelly, 21/9/06, *cpy.*; Roy., Llanelly, 24/9/06; Stratford, 28/10/07, as *A Woman Worth Winning*)
The Greater Sin; or, The Beginning and the End (Gr., Aberaman, 19/2/10; Stratford, 16/5/10)

MACKAY, R. FENTON
[For earlier plays see *H. E. D.* v, 470]
Why Brown went to Brighton ('*f.c.*': P'cess of W., Kennington, 5/5/02; Aven., 20/12/02, as *Brown at Brighton*: +*W. STEPHENS*)

×Cutting Out a Prize (Gr., Margate, 18/7/04)
×Richelieu (Pallad., 27/2/11: condensed version of Lord Lytton's pl.)
My Uncle the J.P. (Emp., Southend, 8/10/17: musical version of *The J.P.*, O.C., 16/3/1897)

MACKAY, W. GAYER [see also '*R. ORD*']
[For earlier plays see *H. E. D.* v, 470]
×Just a Man's Fancy (Court, 2/5/01)
The Two Miss Pettifers ('*c.*': Newcastle, 3/3/04: +'*R. ORD*')
Dr Wake's Patient ('*c.*': Shak., L'pool, 5/9/04; Adel., 5/9/05: +'*R. ORD*') *Fr. 1921*
Barry Doyle's Rest Cure ('*c.*': Court, 25/9/07: +'*R. ORD*')
×The Port Arms (Pier, Brighton, 4/10/09: +'*R. ORD*')
×The Prize (M'sex, 24/5/15: +'*R. ORD*')
Paddy the Next Best Thing ('*c.*': Shubert, N.Y., 25/8/20; Qns, Manchester, 24/2/20; Sav., 5/4/20: +'*R. ORD*': from the novel (1908) by Gertrude Page) *Fr. 1927*

[*MACKAYE, PERCY*
The Canterbury Pilgrims. LC, Gar., 6/4/03. *1903* (New York)
Jeanne d'Arc (Waldorf, 24/4/07) *1906* (New York)
Sappho and Phao ('*t.*': Manchester, 30/4/07) *1907* (New York)
Mater ('*c.*': Van Ness, San Francisco, 3/8/08; Playh., 4/6/15, *m.*) *1908* (New York)
The Scarecrow. LC, Bristol, 14/11/14. *1907* (New York)

McKELVIN, H. C.
Sold by Auction. LC, Little, 16/11/23

MacKENNA, ROSE
×Aliens (Abbey, Dublin, 12/3/18)

MacKENZIE, A. LORD
She Feared Divorce. LC, Crook, 13/10/19

MACKENZIE, COMPTON [*Sir EDWARD MONTAGUE COMPTON*: see also under *MONTAGUE COMPTON*]
Columbine (Alex., Toronto, 18/11/12, as *The Carnival*; Rep., Nottingham, 4/10/20; Kennington, 18/10/20; P's, 3/11/20: dramatised from his own novel, *Carnival*, 1912)

McKENZIE, ERSKINE
Our Kid ('*f.c.*': Gr., Chorley, 22/9/13)

McKENZIE, J. [see *E. LYALL*]

McKENZIE, JACK
The Belle of Barcelona ('*m.c.*': K's, Sutton-in-Ashfield, 3/4/11: title later changed to *Pretty Darlings*: +*H. L. OSMOND*)

MACKENZIE, MARGARET [see also *Mrs G. NORMAN*]
×The Child who Had Never Heard of Christmas. LC, Hippo., Richmond, 7/11/22. *1922*

MACKEOWN, M. J. J.
×The Pension. 1929 (Dublin)
The Real McCoy ('*c.*': T.H., Dundalk, 9/12/25; Olympia, Dublin, 25/6/28; K's, Hamm., 20/8/28) *1930* (Dublin); *Fr. 1931*

McKEOWN, NORMAN

Stephen Maquoid M.P. (of Lambeth Road) ('*c.*': Bury, 5/10/11)
Margery Marries (Brighton, 3/3/13; Cor., 2/6/13)
× A Flash of Lightning (Playh., L'pool, 24/3/15)

MACKEY, CHALMERS

Rollicking Rory ('*r. Irish pl.*': Preston, 3/8/07)
The Soggarth Aroon (Kelly's, L'pool, 16/8/15; Gr., Croydon 18/10/15: +*J. McLAREN*)

MACKIE, JOHN

× Wanted – A Wife. LC, Crippl. Inst., 30/11/25
[This seems to be the same as *The Wooing of Widow Wallington*, printed in *Dialect Poems, and a Play, 1925*]

McKINNEL, NORMAN [see also *X. LOWINSKY*]

× The Bishop's Candlesticks (D.Y., 24/8/01) *Fr. 1908*
× Dick's Sister (Dalston, 5/10/05; Tiv., 31/8/08) *Fr. 1911*

MACKINNON, DAVID

Ahasuerus ('*Persian pl.*') *1920*

MACKINNON, EWART

× Expert Opinion (T.H., Maidenhead, 16/11/11; St J., 21/11/11, *m.*)
× Columbine (Oxf., 20/11/11, *m.*; Tiv., 11/12/11)
× One Afternoon (Pier, Eastbourne, 16/12/12)

MACKINNON, MINA

Should a Husband Forgive? (Gr., Aberaman, 23/8/20; Stratford, 1/11/20)
Ashes of Love. LC, New, Ystradgynlais, 21/1/21

MACKINTOSH, R. D.

The Playactress (Castle Ass. R., Richmond, 26/4/05)

'*MACLAGAN, BRIDGET*' [=*MARY BORDEN-TURNER*]

Collision (Vaud., 1/10/13: dramatised from her own novel, 1913)

[*MacLAREN, DONALD*

The Last of His Race ('*r.d.*': originally acted in America as *The Redskins*; Glasgow, 8/4/07; D.L., 18/5/07)

MACLAREN, DONALD R.

It Looks Like a Change ('*c.*': Lyr., Glasgow, 5/3/29, Scott. Nat. Players)

McLAREN, J. A.

× The Chaperones ('*oa.*': St Gabriel's H., Swansea, 28/12/03)

McLAREN, J. WILSON

Weir of Hermiston (Edin., 12/3/21: +*Mrs F. GOULD*)

MACLAREN, Rev. JOHN [see also *M. AUSTIN, A. DENVILLE, C. MACKEY* and *L. ZILLWOOD*]

The Miracle (Metro., Gateshead, 26/4/12, *cpy.*; Hippo., Stoke, 9/9/12: +*A. DENVILLE*)
The Story of a Jewess (H.M., Walsall, 3/1/16: +*A. DENVILLE*)
Maria Martin, or, The Red Barn (K's, Colne, 4/3/18; Stratford, 5/8/18: +*M. AUSTIN*)

McLAREN, WILSON

Over the Sea to Skye (Edin., 2/5/25)

McLAUGHLIN, ROBERT

Decameron Nights (m. H. Finck: D.L., 20/4/22: +*B. LAWRENCE*)

MACLAURIN, H. G.

Hong Kong ('*c.o.*', m. C. Jessop: Sheffield, 10/3/25, *amat.*) *1925*

[*McLAURIN, KATE L.*

Whispering Wires ('*mystery pl.*': Apo., Atlantic City, 17/4/22; 49th St., N.Y., 7/8/22; Portsmouth, 7/11/27; Apo., 19/12/27)

MACLEAN, ALEXANDER

The Grey Mask (Margate, 27/5/12: +*D. MOORE*)
By the King's Leave (Margate, 30/5/12: +*D. MOORE*)
×At the Sign of the 'Two Crows' (D.P., Eastbourne, 10/6/12)

MACLEAN, HUGH

'Light of the World': A Flower from the Garden of History. *1922* (*priv.*)

[There is no clue as to the intended purpose of this peculiar piece – a kind of scenario (without dialogue) set in the period 1569–1627, concentrating mainly on the Moghul court but including Shakespeare among its many characters]

McLELLAN, C. M. S. [='*HUGH MORTON*']

Leah Kleschna (New, 2/5/05; Bed., 6/4/14, condensed version) *Fr. 1920*
On the Love Path ('*c.*': H., 6/9/05)
The Jury of Fate (Shaft., 2/1/06)
Nelly Neil ('*m.c.*', m. I. Caryll: Aldw., 10/1/07)
The Pickpockets (Gar., 14/12/08, *cpy.*)
The Strong People (Lyr., 31/1/10)
The Pink Lady ('*m.c.*': New Amsterdam, N.Y., 13/3/11; Glo., 11/4/12) *1912*
The Little Café ('*m.c.*': Playh., 28/9/12) *1913*
Oh! Oh! Delphine! ('*m.c.*', m. I. Caryll: Shaft., 18/2/13) *1912* (as *The Gay Delphine* and as *Oh! Oh! Delphine!*)
Round the Map ('*m.pl.*', m. H. Finck: Alh., 19/7/17: revised by *C. GORDON-LENNOX*)

McLELLAN, HUGH

×The Old Story ('*c.*': Little, 12/10/21)

MACLENNAN, R. J.

×Elders' Hours (K's, Southsea, 6/1/13; Emp., Holborn, 14/7/13)
×A Button for Luck (Pav., Glasgow, 20/3/16)
×Silent Advertising. LC, Vic. Pal., 25/2/18
A (K)night in Venice ('*m.c.*': K's, Greenock, 23/8/20: +*A. D. McFARLANE*)

McLEOD, ADDISON

×The Enchanted Hour (Cent., 19/1/26, *m.*: adapted from a play by J. Benavente)

Love's Unfortunate (Bedford H., Chelsea, 25/2/23, Pax Robertson Salon: adapted from G. Giacosa, *Tristi amori*, 1887)
The Summer Holidays (Cent., 19/1/26, *m.*: adapted from a play by J. Benavente)
Christmas Eve (Cent., 19/1/26, *m.*: adapted from a play by E. Zamacois)

'*MacLEOD, FIONA*' [=*WILLIAM SHARP*: see also *E. LYALL*]
The House of Usna (Glo., 29/4/00, St. Soc.) *1900* (in *The Fortnightly Review*, July 1900); *1903* (Portland, Maine); *1910* (in *Poems and Dramas*)
The Immortal Hour (Glastonbury, 26/8/14; Reg., 13/10/22, as a 'music drama' with music by Rutland Boughton) *1900* (in *The Fortnightly Review*, Nov. 1900); *1907* (Portland, Maine); *1908* (Edinburgh); *1910* in (*Poems and Dramas*); *1928* (as a music drama)
[This and *The House of Usna* were originally planned to be parts of a series, 'The Theatre of the Soul' or 'Psychic Drama']
Vistas. *1906*
[This contains several very short sketches, hardly plays: 1. *Finis*; 2. *The Passion of Père Hilarion*; 3. *The Birth of a Soul*; 4. *A Northern Night*; 5. *The Black Madonna*; 6. *The Fallen God*; 7. *The Coming of the Prince*; 8. *The Passing of Lilith*; and 9. *The Whisperer*]

McLOREN, JOHN
Phil the Fiddler. LC, League of the Cross H., Glasgow, 6/2/23
The Jackets Green. LC, League of the Cross H., Glasgow, 6/2/23

McLOUGHLIN, A.
×The Fugitive (Abbey, Dublin, 31/5/10)

McLOUGHLIN, D.
×Maggie McFadden's Breach of Promise Case (Emp., Belfast, 10/12/17)

McMANUS, J. E.
In Her White Innocence (Hippo., Croydon, 11/10/15: +*L. STORMONT*)
[Several playlets and sketches produced in music-halls]

MacMANUS, SEUMAS
×The Townland of Tamney (Molesworth H., Dublin, 14/1/04, Irish Nat. Th. Soc.)

'*MacNAB, HUGH*' [=*HUGH MACNAB HUMPHRY*]
Atahualpa, the Last of the Incas. *1923*

MACNAB, JAMES STUART
A Modern Miracle (Ath., Glasgow, 9/10/02)

McNAB, R. DUNCAN
My Lady's Garden ('*c.*': Court, 22/6/13, Pl. Actors)

MACNAGHTEN, HUGH VIBART
×The Children of Sparta. *1897* (Eton)
Antigone (a version of Sophocles' play) *1926*

Virgil's Secret, and Other Plays. *1927*
[This contains five 'literary' plays: 1. *Clodia*; 2. *Caesar and Catallus*; 3. *Virgil and Augustus*; 4. *Horace and Augustus*; and 5. *Virgil's Secret*. Of these the second piece had already appeared in the *National Review*, Oct. 1925]

McNALLY, JOHN
The Paper Chase ('*c.*': Harrogate, 22/2/26; Little, 25/3/26) *Fr. 1926*

McNALLY, M.
× The Siege of Berlin (Little, 11/10/14: +*P. CARR*)

'*MACNAMARA, BRINSLEY*' [=*A. E. WELDON*]
The Rebellion in Ballycullen ('*c.*': Abbey, Dublin, 11/3/19)
The Land for the People (Abbey, Dublin, 30/11/20)
The Glorious Uncertainty ('*c.*': Abbey, Dublin, 27/11/23)
Look at the Heffernans ('*c.*': Abbey, Dublin, 19/4/26)
The Master (Abbey, Dublin, 6/3/28)

MACNAMARA, FRANCIS
× The Schemers (Crosby H., Chelsea, 17/5/12)

'*MACNAMARA, GERALD*' [=*HARRY C. MORROW*]
× The Mist that does be on the Bog (O.H., Belfast, 7/3/10: LC, Playh., L'pool, 2/8/22)
× Thompson in Tir-na-n-og (O.H., Belfast, 9/12/12; Scala, 29/6/23) *1918* (Dublin)
The Throwbacks (O.H., Belfast, 3/12/17)
× Sincerity (Gai., Dublin, 31/5/18)
× Fee Faw Fum. LC, Playh., L'pool, 31/8/23
Who Fears to Speak ('*t.f.*': O.H., Belfast, 23/1/29)

MACNAMARA, MARGARET [see also *I. HORNE*]
Our Little Fancies (Gai., Manchester, 13/11/11)
A Masque of Fashion ('*pageant*': Court, 15/5/12)
George and Jenny ('*kitchen c.*': Etlinger, 1/6/17)
× The Baby in the Ring. LC, Ass. R., Henfield, 12/9/18) *1918*
× Love-Fibs ('*rustic c.*') *1920*
× The Witch (Etlinger, 18/7/28) *1920*
× Light Gray or Dark? *1920*
× Mrs Hodges. *1920*
× The Miss Dodsons that were ('*costume playlet*') *1922*
× In Safety. LC, Mission H., Newcastle, 26/4/24. *1924*
× By the Wayside ('*pastoral c.*') *1924*
× St George and the Turkish Knight. LC, K. G's H., 16/12/24
× Mrs Jupp Obliges. *1925*
× Enjoying the Business. LC, Ass. R., Enfield, 5/2/25. *1924*
Yesterday ('*historical c.*') *1926*
× The Tall, Tall Castle ('*burlesque mime*') *1927*
× A Penny for the Guy! *1928* (Oxford)

MACNAMARA, WALTER
[A few playlets produced at music-halls]

McNEIL, DANE
×Glendarnel. *1929* (in *The Scots Magazine*, xii, 177–87)

MacNEILE, HERMAN CYRIL [='*SAPPER*']

McNEILL, WILLIAM S.
In the Long Run ('*md.*': Colosseum, Oldham, 11/3/12)

McNULTY, EDWARD
The Lord Mayor ('*c.*': Abbey, Dublin, 13/3/14) *1917* (Dublin)
×Food Shortage (Emp., Dublin, 18/6/17)
The King of Dublin ('*m.pl.*': Qns, Dublin, 15/4/18: +*T. MADDEN*)
Mrs Mulligan's Millions ('*c.*': Emp., Dublin, 24/6/18) *1918* (Dublin)
The Gay Clerkette ('*c.o.*': Emp., Dublin, 5/5/19)
The Courting of Mary Doyle (Abbey, Dublin, 8/11/21) *1922* (Dublin)

MACOWAN, NORMAN [see also *F. WARE*]
The Travellers (P's, 4/2/12, St. Soc.)
The Demagogue ('*c.*': Court, 10/3/12, Pl. Actors)
The Blue Lagoon (P.W., 28/8/20: +*C. MANN*: dramatised from the novel (1915) by H. de Vere Stacpoole) *1920*
Lord o' Creation ('*c.*': O.H., Blackpool, 21/1/24; Sav., 12/2/24)
The Infinite Shoe-Black (Arts, 12/4/29; Com., 29/4/29) *1924*
Jacob's Ladder (Roy., 13/5/25) *1935*
The New Tenant (Str., 18/3/28, Rep. Players) *1935*

[*McOWEN, B. J.*
The Skull (Shaft., 6/8/28: +*H. E. HUMPHREY*)

MACPHERSON, JEAN
×The Sin Eater (Lyr., 17/3/08, *cpy.*)

McQUILLAND, LOUIS J. [see *F. WILLIAMS*]

McQUIRE, T. C.
Eugene Aram ('*r.pl.*': Margate, 4/7/01)
×A Wandering Minstrel ('*m.c.*': Eastbourne, 8/2/04)
[Several playlets produced at music-halls]

MACRAE, FRANK
×Annette (Rehearsal, 21/12/12, Black Cat Club; Clavier H., 29/1/13)
×Merely Players (Rehearsal, 24/2/13, Black Cat Club)

MacROBERT, J. S.
The Children of the Year, and Other Plays. *1921*
[Besides the title-piece, this contains two other short plays by MacRobert – 1. *Where Fields Are Gold*, and 2. *Pan and the Pine-tree* – as well as *The Magic Mirror*, by *BEATRICE CLAY* and *CLARIBEL SPURLING*]

MacSWINEY, TERENCE J.
The Revolutionist (Abbey, Dublin, 24/2/21) *1914* (Dublin)

MADDEN, CECIL

×Little Angel, or Angelita. *1925* (Bristol)
×Parted ('*t.*': Abbey, Dublin, 5/4/27)
The Equator (RADA, 26/2/28: adapted from a play by H. R. Lenormand)
The Hero (Q, 21/5/28)
Through the Veil ('*psychic d.*': Emb., 13/1/30; Duchess, 27/1/30: +*GILBERT STONE* – also cited as *X. Y. STONE*)

MADDEN, TOM [see also *E. McNULTY*]

Acushla ('*m.c.*': Emp., Dublin, 6/4/17)

MADDISON, ADELA

The Song (Court, 3/5/26, *m.*)
Ippolita in the Hills ('*o.*': Pal., Chelsea, 22/11/26)

MAGIAN, A. C.

×A Family Affair (Nottingham, 28/7/13: +*Countess MAX*)

MAGNUS, EUGÉNIE

×The Willow Pattern Plate ('*m.pl.*': Emp., Camberwell, 16/9/08; Terry's, 10/4/09)
×The Decoy (Stand., 9/8/09)
×The Black Angel (Qns, Poplar, 10/1/10; Bed., 13/2/11)
×The Mermaid's Arms. LC, S. Ldn Pal., 23/10/14

MAGNUS, LEONARD ARTHUR

A. V. Lunacharski, Three Plays (+*H. WALTER*) *1923*
[This contains three translations: *Faust and the City*; *Vasilisa the Wise*; and *The Magi*]

[*MAGUIRE, W. A.*

The Divorce Question (Whitney O.H., Chicago, 20/4/12; Playh., Llanhilleth, 29/3/20; E.C., 17/5/20)

MAHER, DANIEL CONCEPTA

×Partition (Abbey, Dublin, 15/11/16; Col., 13/8/17) *1918* (Dublin)
×Patsy Cann (Qns, Dublin, 16/7/17)

MAHOMED, DUSE

The Lily of Bermuda ('*m.c.*', m. M. Strong and H. M. Wellman: Manchester, 8/11/09: +*E. TRIMINGHAM*)

MAHONEY, RICHARD

Eileen Alannah; or, The Outlaws of the Glen ('*Irish d.*': Myddelton H., Islington, 5/9/03)

MAINWARING, Mrs HENRY GERMAINE

Caged (Arts, 21/12/27, *m.*)

MAITLAND, Viscountess

The Key of Life ('*fant.*': Scala, 28/5/08, *amat.*)

MAITLAND, FRED

[Several sketches and short musicals produced at music-halls]

MAITLAND, LAUDERDALE

×A New Year's Lesson ('*dream pl.*': Cor., 24/5/06)

×The Black Devil (Pal., Hamm., 31/8/08)
×The (K)night in Queer Street. LC, Hippo., Bristol, 11/12/15

MAITRA, H. N.
Ayesha (Whitney, 6/6/12: +*N. PAL*)

'*MAJOR*' [=*JAMES SABBEN*]
The Lure (Str., 25/3/23, Rep. Players)

MAJOR, CHARLES [see *P. KESTER*]

MAJOR, DAGNEY [see also *J. JOHNSON*]
The Pilgrim's Rest (Drill H., Hildenborough, 5/2/06)

MAJOR, HARRY
The Bogus Prince ('*m.pl.*': Emp., Holborn, 19/12/27: +*A. DAVIES*)

MAJOR, TALFOURD
×A Stage Mask (Brompton Hospital, 25/11/02)

MALCOLM, CHARLES HORACE
Bachelors' Brides ('*c.*': Q, 6/5/29)

MALCOLM, E. J.
×The Cure (O.H., Coventry, 9/10/22)

MALCOLM, N. [see *C. YOUNG*]

MALCOLM, MAX
The Scarlet Highwayman (Lyr., Hamm., 28/5/08, *cpy.*)

MALDEN, K. S.
Kamil, and Baber the Lion. LC, K. G's H., 7/4/23. *1922* (S.P.G.)
×Missionary Pennies. LC, K. G's H., 9/4/23: +*M. S. SMITH*
×The Hut in the Jungle ('*a Chota Nagpur pl.*') *1924* (S.P.G.)

MALEWYN-DAVIES, Rev. D.
A Pageant of Wales. LC, Barry, 15/2/18

MALLAHEN, AUBREY [see *J. R. BROWN*]

MALLESON, Lady CONSTANCE MARY
The Way (Arts, 25/3/28)

MALLESON, MILES [see also *A. BROSNAN*]
A Man of Ideas (Court, 16/11/13: also played later in a one-act 'condensed' form) *1918* (in *Young Heaven and Three Other Plays*)
The Threshold (Roy., Glasgow, 9/3/14)
×Hide and Seek (Crit., 12/5/14)
×'D' Company (written 1914: New, Oxford, 10/2/17) *1916*; *1924*
[By Government order the copies of the 1916 printing (which also contained *Black 'Ell*, see below) were destroyed]
×Black 'Ell (Gate, 21/6/26) *1916*; *1924*
[See preceding item]
×The Little White Thought ('*fantastic scrap*': Wynd., 30/3/15, *amat.*) *1916*
Youth (Court, 26/3/16, St. Soc.) *1916*
×Paddly Pools ('*little fairy pl.*': New, 11/4/16, *m.*, *amat.*) *1916*; *Fr. 1934*

Young Heaven and Three Other Plays. *1918*
[This contains: 1. *A Man of Ideas* (see above); 2. *Michael* (adapted from Leo Tolstoi's *What Men Live By*: St J., 3/4/17, *m., amat.*); 3. *The Artist* (K's H., 9/2/19, Pioneer Players); and 4. *Young Heaven* (+*JEAN CAVENDISH*)]
×Maurice's Own Idea (Wynd., 26/3/18, *amat.*)
×The Young Ladies Get Their Medals (Glo., 22/3/21, *m.*, RADA students)
Conflict ('*c.*': Q, 30/11/25; Qns, 7/4/26) *1925*
The Bargain (Pier, Eastbourne, 14/6/26: dramatised from a novel, *The Daughter Pays* (1915), by Mrs Baillie Reynolds)
Merrileon Wise (Str., 28/11/26, Pl. Actors) *1926*
A Night in Montmartre (Q, 20/12/26: +*W. PEACOCK*)
The Fanatics ('*c.*': Ambass., 15/3/27) *1924*
Love at Second Sight ('*c.*': Shak., L'pool, 15/8/27; Roy., 22/8/27: dramatised from a novel, *Safety First* (1924), by Margot Neville) *Fr. 1929*
Four People ('*c.*': St M., 10/5/28) *1928*

MALLETT, WALTER HOWARD
×Another Man's Money (Bij., 27/11/01, *amat.*)
The Music Master ('*m.f.*', m. H. Smith: Bij., 22/4/03, *amat.*)

MALLOCH, GEORGE RESTON
×The Cracksman's Mate (M'sex, 26/6/09)
×A Nicht wi' Burns (Lyc., Edin., 25/7/10)
The Career of Henry Jones (Court, 30/10/10, Pl. Actors)
Arabella ('*modern c.*': Court, 8/10/12) *1912*
×Thomas the Rhymer (Ath., Glasgow, 2/12/24, Scott. Nat. Players)
Soutarness Water (Ath., Glasgow, 19/1/26, Scott. Nat. Players) *1927*
×The House of the Queen (Ath., Glasgow, 19/1/26, Scott. Nat. Players) *1923* (Montrose)
×Memory (Fellowship H., Glasgow, 8/10/27, Glasgow Clarion Players)
The Coasts of India (Lyr., Glasgow, 23/10/28, Scott. Nat. Players)
×The Broken Field. *1928* (in *The Scots Magazine*, x, 15–23)

MALLOCK, J. E.
×Crisis (Bij., Teddington, 13/7/03: +*H. N. BRAILSFORD*)

MALONE, HENRY L'ESTRANGE
The Prince who Woke Up (K. G's H., 22/11/23)
The Children's King (Crippl. Inst., 20/12/24)

MALTBY, ALFRED
A Silver Spoon ('*f.c.*': Pav., Buxton, 22/6/00: +*F. LINDO*)

MALTBY, HENRY FRANCIS [see also *L. HILLIER* and *F. THOMPSON*]
The Youngest of Three ('*costume pl.*': O.H., Jersey, 28/7/05; Worthing, 8/3/06; C.P., 18/3/07)
×Hounslow Heath (Plymouth, 7/5/06)

×Fannikin (*'m.c.'*, m. K. Barry: Pav., Hastings, 24/5/06: called originally *When Her Hair was Down*)

Sir George of Almack's (*'c.'*: Dover, 28/2/07; County, Kingston, 11/12/07)

×The Miser's Legacy (Llanelly, 20/5/07; Gr., Derby, 10/4/11, as *Haunted*)

Ernestine: the Romance of a Typist (Exeter, 4/5/08; St Albans, 5/2/20, as *Eve*)

The Laughter of Fools (*'c.'*: H.M., Carlisle, 21/5/09; Little, 9/3/11, *m.*, Oncomers; P.W., 29/5/15) *Fr. 1932*

×What Some Men Don't Know (W.G., Blackpool, 1/5/11; Little, 29/5/11, Oncomers)

The Profit – and the Loss (Playh., L'pool, 23/4/14)

The Rotters (*'tale of a respectable family'*: W.G., New Brighton, 10/7/16; Gar., 29/7/16) *1925*

Petticoats (Gar., 10/3/17)

A Temporary Gentleman (*'c.'*: Pier, Brighton, 17/3/19; R.A., Woolwich, 31/3/19; Oxf., 9/6/19)

×The Wangler. LC, Guildford, 7/4/19

Such a Nice Young Man (Pal., Westcliffe, 17/5/20; R.A., Woolwich, 24/5/20; Apo., 17/6/20)

×What Did Her Husband Say? (*'c.'*: Little, 27/9/20)

×A Person Unknown (Little, 17/1/21: called originally *Her Promise*)

×Take Me Out to Dinner (Kennington, 18/4/21)

×Amelia's Suitors, or, Colonel Chutney's First Defeat (Little, 3/4/22)

Mr Budd, of Kennington, S.E. (*'travesty'*: Pier, Brighton, 28/8/22; Roy., 3/10/22) *1927*

Three Birds (*'f.c.'*: Pier, Brighton, 5/9/23; Crit., 1/11/23) *1924*

The Cheerful Liar (O.H., Leicester, 2/6/24)

The Oyster (Pier, Herne Bay, 18/8/23; Pier, Eastbourne, 6/4/25: +*C. WINDERMERE*)

The Two Roses (Rep., Rusholme, 12/1/25)

The Right Age to Marry (*'c.'*: Rochdale, 23/3/25; Brixton, 13/4/25; Playh., 18/5/25) *Fr. 1933*

On Change. LC, P's, Manchester, 8/5/25

×Pick-Me-Up (Vic. Pal., 8/11/25)

The New Religion (Rep., Rusholme, 26/4/26)

What Might Happen (*'piece of extravagance'*: Ambass., Southend, 23/2/26; Sav., 10/6/26) *1927*

The Shingled Honeymoon (*'f.c.'*: Pier, Brighton, 26/4/26; Hippo., Golder's Green, 31/5/26)

Our Countess (Str., 5/2/28, Rep. Players)

×Something More Important (Little, 14/5/28)

The Age of Youth (Gr., Croydon, 5/11/28: +*F. WYNN*) *Fr. 1935*

Bees and Honey (*'f.'*: Str., 12/5/29, Rep. Players; New, 30/7/29) *Fr. 1936*

Azaïs (*'c.'*: Str., 29/9/29, Rep. Players: from the play (1925) by G. Beer and L. Verneuil)

MALYON, E. J.

[For earlier plays see *H. E. D.* v, 473 and 805]

My Wife's Intended ('*f.*': Worthing, 16/1/02: called also *My Wife's Fiancé*)

MALYON-HESFORD, H.

Willie's Mrs ('*f.c.*': Str., 20/3/00)

[*MANDEL, FRANK* [see also *M. EDGINTON*, *O. HAMMERSTEIN* and *E. NYITRAY*]

Mary ('*m.pl.*', m. L. Hirsch: Gar., Philadelphia, 5/4/20; Knickerbocker, N.Y., 18/10/20; Qns, 27/4/21: +*O. HARBACH*)

No, No, Nanette ('*m.pl.*': Chicago, 5/4/24; Glo., N.Y., 16/9/25; Alh., Glasgow, 23/2/25; Pal., 11/3/25: +*O. HARBACH* and *I. CAESAR*)

MANDEL, S.

A Month in the Country (Roy., 5/7/26: translated from I. S. Turgenev, *Mesiats v derevne*)

MANDER, MILES

Common People ('*c.*': Everyman, 12/4/27)

It's a Pity about Humanity (Arts, 8/4/30)

MANLEY, ALICK [see *V. MATHEWS*]

MANN, CHARLTON [see also *B. DEAN* and *N. MACOWAN*]

The Knave of Diamonds (Gai., Manchester, 24/1/21; Glo., 23/4/21: dramatised from the novel (1913) by Ethel M. Dell)

MANN, F. C. T.

× Life's Irony (P.H., Woking, 21/4/04)

MANN, KATHERINE

× The Scottish Emigrant (Ath., Glasgow, 25/10/12)

× The Panel Doctor (Pav., Glasgow, 5/5/13; Alex., 9/2/14)

× The Pewter Pot (Paisley, 21/6/15)

MANN, MARDEN

× Viola. LC, T.H., Pontypridd, 28/1/18

MANNERS, JOHN HARTLEY [see also *IAN HAY* and *LILY LANGTRY*]

[For an earlier play see *H. E. D.* v, 474. It should be noted that after 1903 this author identified himself with the American stage: the following list includes only those among his plays which received productions in England]

× As Once in May ('*modern c.*': Shaft., 23/1/02) *Fr. 1903*

× Just as Well ('*modern r.c.*': Shaft., 8/7/02) *Fr. 1903*

The Great John Ganton (Academy of Music, Baltimore, 8/2/09, as *Ganton and Co.*; Aldw., 14/9/12)

Barbaraza (Playh., 22/8/10, *cpy.*)

× The Woman Intervenes (Tiv., 12/8/12)

Peg o' My Heart ('*c.*': Shubert, Rochester, N.Y., 25/11/12; Cort, N.Y., 20/12/12; D.P., Eastbourne, 5/10/14; Com., 10/10/14; musical version, as *Peg o' Mine*, Emp., Sunderland, 31/10/27) *1913*

The Panorama of Youth (Bournemouth 5/4/15; St J., 14/4/15)

×Happiness (Cort, N.Y., 6/3/14; D.L., 27/4/15, *m.*) *1914*; ***Fr.*** *1920* (in 4 acts)
×The Passing of Fanny and Joseph (Theatrical Gdn Party, Regent's Park, 20/7/15)
One Night in Rome (Mayflower, Providence, 24/11/19; Crit., N.Y., 2/12/19; Pal., Ramsgate, 26/4/20; Gar., 3/5/20)
×God's Outcast (Little, 18/3/23, *m.*, Green Room Rag) *1920* (New York: in *Three Plays*)

MANNING, A. S.
The Governor's Bride ('*c.o.*', m. R. A. Smith: Tyne, Newcastle, 16/3/08, *amat.*)

MANNING, WILLIAM
[For earlier plays see *H. E. D.* v, 474]
A Hot Night ('*m.c.*', m. H. Louther: Preston, 3/8/01)

MANNIX, J. J.
[A few playlets produced at music-halls]

MANSFIELD, A. F.
David Copperfield. LC, Canterbury, 19/5/25

MANSFIELD, HERBERT
The Heir to the Throne (O.H., Wakefield, 5/7/20: +*A. W. MARCHMONT*)

MANTELL, FREDERICK
×Spinks and Co. (Curzon H., B'ham, 27/2/11)

[*MAPES, VICTOR* [see also *W. SMITH*]
The Hottentot ('*f.*': Apo., Atlantic City, 11/1/20; Geo. M. Cohan, N.Y., 1/3/20; Gr., Blackpool, 25/1/26; Qns, 3/2/26: +*W. COLLIER*) *Fr. 1923*

MARBURG, GUIDO [see *W. GILLPATRICK*]

MARCH, CHARLES
[For an earlier play see *H. E. D.* v, 475]
The Silent House (Carlton, Greenwich, 1/7/01)
The Priest of the Temple (Lyr., L'pool, 21/7/02)
The Saint and the Woman (Cambridge, Spennymoor, 10/6/07)
Flight (Stanley, 25/4/10)
Tilly Takes the Tiller. LC, Glo., Walmer, 24/5/22

MARCHMONT, ARTHUR WILLIAM [see also *H. MANSFIELD*]
A Courier of Fortune ('*r.d.*': Bath, 30/3/05, *cpy.*: dramatised from his own novel (1905): +*R. STUART*)
Aunt Martha. LC, Shak., L'pool, 22/6/20

MARCHMONT, GEOFFREY
×The Decree Absolute. LC, Gar., 14/12/21

[*MARCIN, MAX* [see also *S. SHIPMAN*]
Cheating Cheaters (Sav., Ashbury Park, N.J., 19/6/16; Eltinge, N.Y., 9/8/16; Str., 4/2/18)
The Eyes of Youth (Stamford, Conn., 12/5/17; Maxine Elliot, N.Y., 22/8/17; St J., 2/9/18: +*C. GUERNON*)

Three Live Ghosts (Greenwich Village, N.Y., 29/9/20; Hippo., Margate, 11/5/25: +*G. BOLTON*)
The Nightcap (Lyc., Baltimore, 28/3/21; 39th St., N.Y., 15/8/21; D.Y., 23/1/22: +*G. BOLTON*)
Silence ('*md.*': Gr., Chicago, 2/3/24; National, N.Y., 12/11/24; 28/1/25)
The House of Glass (Apo., Atlantic City, 21/6/15; Chandler, N.Y., 1/9/15; B'ham, 17/12/25; P.W., 27/1/26)

MARCUS, M. C.
The Pine Tree (adapted from *Matsu* by Takeda Izumo) *1916*
[This also has 'an introductory causerie on the Japanese Theatre']

'MARENAS, VASCO' [see *O. ASCHE*]

MARGRIE, WILLIAM
Moses ('*cosmic d.*') [*1922*]

MARILLIER, CHRISTABEL
The Rose and the Ring ('*light o.*': D.P., Eastbourne, 12/11/28; Apo., 20/11/28) *1928*

MARINETTE, F. T.
×A Moonbeam (Lyr., Hamm., 8/12/18, Plough Players)

'MARIUS' [see *'SEAMARK'*]

MARKHAM, A. G.
In Luck ('*m. vaudeville*': Eton Mission H., Hackney Wick, 26/3/00)

MARKIEVICZ, Count CASIMIR DUNIN
The Memory of the Dead (Abbey, Dublin, 14/4/10)
Mary ('*c.*': Abbey, Dublin, 15/4/10)
Rival Stars (Gai., Dublin, 12/12/11)

MARKS, GODFREY [=*'J. F. SWIFT'*]

MARKS, Mrs LIONEL S. [=*JOSEPHINE P. PEABODY*]

MARKS, MONTAGUE
Compromised ('*c.*': Gr., Fulham, 27/9/00, *cpy.*)
The Man Trap (Roy., 3/4/03, *cpy.*: from the novel (1900) by Sir William Magnay)

[*MARLOW, B.* [see *B. MERIVALE*]

MARLOW, HARRY
The Love of Sin (Emp., Southend, 17/7/05: +*F. MORGAN*)

'MARLOWE, CHARLES' [=*HARRIET JAY*; see also *ROBERT BUCHANAN*]
[For earlier plays see *H. E. D.* v, 435 and 799)
When Knights Were Bold ('*f.*': Nottingham, 17/9/06; Wynd., 29/1/07)

MARLOWE, FRANCIS
×Where was He? LC, Vaud., 10/7/17

[*MARQUIS, DON*

Out of the Sea (Eltinge, N.Y., 5/12/27; K's, Glasgow, 8/10/28; Str., 23/11/28) *1927*

MARRIOTT-WATSON, FLORENCE [=*'SOUTHERN CROSS'*]

[For earlier plays see *H. E. D.* v, 616]

The Black Mask (St J., Manchester, 31/7/1899; Stratford, 29/12/02)

What a Woman Did (*'r.m.pl.'*: R.A., Woolwich, 5/10/03; W.L., 4/7/04)

A False Wife (Ass. R., Pontefract, 2/3/05; W.L., 10/7/05: called originally *The Death Warrant*)

The Man Tempted Me (*'md.'*: Brit., 2/9/12)

Two Daughters of One Father (Gr., Plymouth, 8/3/15; Vic., Walthamstow, 21/2/16: title later changed to *What Happened at Midnight*

The Voice in the Dark (*'r.d.'*: Pal., L'pool, 9/7/17: +*G. R. DUFF*)

Beyond the Veil (*'Lancashire pl.'*: Ripley, 6/5/21; Stratford, 20/2/22; Sav., 28/6/22, *m.*, revised with *G. EDWIN*, as *Concerning Mary Dewhirst*)

For the Third Time. LC, Ass. R., Berwick, 16/11/22

MARRIOTT-WATSON, H. B.

[For an earlier play see *H. E. D.* v, 616]

×At Bay (Court, 27/2/12, *amat.*: +*G. W. R. BINGHAM*)

×Babes in the Wood (T.H., Anerley, 11/11/09, *m.*: +*G. W. R. BINGHAM*)

MARRIOTT-WATSON, NAN [see also *E. CARTER*]

Before Sunset (Pier, Brighton, 9/7/23; Aldw., 20/5/24, *m.*)

MARRIS, EDWARD

[In *H. E. D.*, v, 477 a double error requires correction. Hildyard Marris is the author of *Sunny Florida* and *An Armenian Girl*: these have nothing to do with *Somebody's Sweetheart*, a musical play presented at W. Hartlepool, 17/7/1899 and later at Stratford, 22/6/03: this was an early work by Edward Marris]

The Dandy Doctor (*'m.f.c.'*, m. D. Powell: Aven., Sunderland, 26/3/00; Duchess, Balham, 16/7/00)

As Midnight Chimes (Alex., Hull, 11/7/04; Dalston, 31/10/04)

The Double Event (*'f.c.'*: Qns, Swindon, 13/5/05, *cpy.*; O.H., Torquay, 29/5/05, as *The Unrelated Twins*: also called *Tranter's Double*)

The Gentleman Jockey (*'m.c.'*: St Julian's, Jersey, 18/10/07; C.P., 10/4/09)

×Dingle's Double (O.H., Jersey, 18/5/08)

×First Stop, London (S.W., 30/11/08)

×A Medical Muddle (Cant., 28/2/10)

A Criminal's Bride (Gr., Brighton, 25/7/10; Pav., Mile End, 1/8/10)

That Chauffeur Chap (*'m.pl.'*, m. A. Roby: O.H., Belfast, 24/4/11; Broadway, New X, 14/8/11; Pal., Maidstone, 17/2/13, as *Mum's the Word*)

×Her Madcap Majesty (Coll., 20/11/11)

×Faking the Film, or, Skinnymacolour (Hippo., Margate, 30/9/12; Empress, 14/10/12)
×An Emperor's Sword. LC, Hippo., Colchester, 25/3/13
×The Dandy Band (O.H., Dudley, 18/9/13; Emp., Finsbury Park, 7/11/13)
×The Lady Commercial. LC, Pal., Watford, 10/12/15
×Rehearsing a Revue (Pal., Tottenham, 3/4/16)
Scotch and Polly ('*m.c.*', m. Haidée de Rance: Hippo., Birkenhead, 17/3/24; Pal., E. Ham, 14/4/24)

MARRYATT, Mrs FREDERICK [='*ALASTOR GRAEME*']

MARS, ANTONY [see *H. RAYMOND*]

MARSH, AVON
Sarenna ('*o.*', m. H. Löhr: Lyr., 6/9/07) *1907* (as '*an episode at the cross-roads*')

MARSH, BRIAN [see *JULIAN FRANK*]

MARSH, RICHARD
Peggy's Little Flutter ('*c.*': O.H., Buxton, 17/2/19)

MARSHALL, Major
The Islander ('*m.c.*', m. P. M. Faraday: Apo., 23/4/10)

MARSHALL, ABIGAIL
[A few playlets produced at music-halls]

MARSHALL, CECIL
×A Wee Drappie (Rehearsal, 7/5/14: +*E. HAY-HOWE*)

MARSHALL, Rev. E. G.
The Prodigal's Return (Parish H., Leyland, 29/1/06, *amat.*)

MARSHALL, F. W.
[For an earlier play see *H. E. D.* v, 478]
Subalterns ('*f.c.*': Aldershot, 29/4/01)

MARSHALL, HAZEL MAY
The Morals of Vanda ('*c.*': Gr., Croydon, 1/4/18; Everyman, 29/11/23)
×A Busy Morning. *1930*

MARSHALL, ROBERT [see also *M. LINDSAY*]
[For earlier plays see *H. E. D.* v, 478]
The Noble Lord ('*c.*': Crit., 18/10/00)
The Second in Command ('*c.*': H., 27/11/00) *Fr. 1910*
There's Many a Slip ('*c.*': H., 23/8/02)
The Unforeseen (H., 2/12/02) *Fr. 1930*
The Duke of Killiecrankie ('*f.r.*': Crit., 20/1/04) *Fr. 1910*
×The Track of Blood ('*bsq.*': Theatrical Gdn Party, Regent's Park, 8/7/04)
The Lady of Leeds ('*f.r.*': Wynd., 9/2/05)
Everybody's Secret ('*c.*': H., 14/3/05: +*L. N. PARKER*: adapted from P. Wolff, *Le secret de Polichinelle*, 1903)
The Alabaster Staircase ('*c.*': Com., 21/2/06)
×Gruesome Grange; or, The Banished Earl ('*bsq.*': Theatrical Gdn Party, Regent's Park, 6/7/06: +*A. HOPE* and *J. W. C. CARR*)

×A Wire Entanglement (Com., 22/9/06) *Fr. 1908*
×The Desperate Duke, or, The Culpable Countess ('*bsq.*': Theatrical Gdn Party, Chelsea, 5/7/07: +*A. SUTRO*)

MARSHALL-HOLE, MOLLY
Water (Q, 8/10/28; Little, 25/6/29)

MARSLAND, Miss H.
In Old New York (P.H., Forest Gate, 19/9/03, *cpy.*)

MARSON, Rev. CHARLES
×Just like Nettie (Clavier H., 23/5/12)

MARSON, GERALD FRANCIS
Jerusalem and Bethany ('*Passion pl.*') *1928* (SPCK)
St Christopher ('*miracle pl.*') *1928* (SPCK)

MARSTON, FREDERICK A.
The Wrongs of Woman (Leicester, 24/6/10: +*M. SCOTT*)

MARTEN, D. [see *M. CREAGH-HENRY*]

MARTEYN, LEOPOLD
×The Crystal Gazer (Alb. H., 14/11/06)

MARTIN, C.
×A Sister's Revenge (Rehearsal, 29/1/09, *cpy.*)

MARTIN, DAVID
×The Bailie's Nominee (R. Inst. H., Glasgow, 13/4/21, Scott. Nat. Players) *1926* (Ardrossan)

MARTIN, ERNEST [see also *C. ROSS*]
The Coal King (E.C., 24/10/04: +*F. LLEWELLYN*)
Love at First Sight (Bij., 26/7/06: +*F. LLEWELLYN*)
×Matrimony Ltd. ('*ca.*': Ass. R., Putney, 28/2/07, *amat.*; Studio, Bedford St., 3/12/09)
×The Professor's Dilemma. *1907*

MARTIN, HAROLD
Ruth (Glo., 18/5/30, Venturers)

MARTIN, HUGH
×The Darling Devil ('*c.*': Rehearsal, 28/5/13)
×Futurist Love (Rehearsal, 28/5/13)
×£100 and 'A' (Rehearsal, 28/5/13)

MARTIN, JAMES SACKVILLE
×A study in 'A' Flat (Ass. R., Leigh, 16/3/09, *cpy.*; K's, Hamm., 8/6/03)
×A Question of Property (Margate, 13/1/08; Cor., 7/5/12)
×Woman's Rights (Rochdale, 23/3/08; Cor., 14/6/09)
Cupid and the Styx ('*c.*': Gai., Manchester, 8/2/09; Cor., 14/5/12) *Fr. 1912*
×The Purse of Gold (Court, 9/5/09, Pl. Actors; Gai., Manchester, 28/2/10)
Nellie Lambert (K's H., 5/5/12, Pioneer Players)
×The Wife Tamer. LC, Apo., 8/9/13
Cupid in Hospital ('*c.*': Pal., Watford, 23/5/21)
The Locum Tenens. LC, Social Guild H., Fulwood, 13/2/25

MARTIN, M. MACDONALD
Dalma. LC, P.H., Croydon, 6/2/19

MARTIN, N. RADCLIFFE
The Weak Point (Gai., Manchester, 1/11/15)
×Love's Young Dream (Gai., Manchester, 18/9/16)
×Congratulations (Gai., Manchester, 2/10/16)

MARTIN, O. PERCY
Teddy Travers ('*c.*': Ladbr. H., 16/4/07, *amat.*)
×The Best Policy. LC, Apo., 14/11/12

MARTINDALE, MAY
Sporting Simpson ('*f.*': Roy., Glasgow, 22/9/02; Roy., 4/10/02)
Gamblers All ('*c.*': Wynd., 9/6/15)

MARTYN, ARTHUR [see *MAURICE COWAN*]

MARTYN, EDWARD
[For an earlier play see *H. E. D.* v, 479]
Maeve ('*psychological d.*': Gai., Dublin, 20/2/00) *1899* (Dublin)
The Place Hunters. *1902* (Dublin)
The Tale of a Town, and An Enchanted Sea. *1902* (Dublin)
×Romulus and Remus. *1907* (Dublin)
Grangecolman (Abbey, Dublin, 25/1/12) *1912* (Dublin)
The Dream Physician (Upper O'Connell Street, Dublin, 2/11/14, Irish Theatre) *1918* (Dublin)
Privilege of Place (Hardwick Street H., Dublin, 8/11/15)
Regina Eyre ('*symbolical d.*': Irish Theatre, Dublin, 28/4/19)

MARTYN, MARTYN C.
The Tale of a Telegram ('*f.c.*': Cleveland H., Barnes, 21/2/03)
Milord's Dilemma ('*c.*': Vic. H., 20/5/05)

[*MARVIN, JEAN*
The Cowpuncher (E.C., 31/5/12, *cpy.*; O.H., Northampton, 2/9/12; Brit., 30/9/12: acted also under the title of *The Sheriff of Lonesome Pine*)
Mexican Hearts Aflame (Belfast, 26/4/13; Lyr., Hamm., 9/6/13: title later changed to *The Gambler's Sweetheart*)

MARZETTI, EDGAR
The Peckham Pretender ('*f.c.*': Pav., Herne Bay, 12/6/11)

MASCHWITZ, E. [see *M. D. LYON*]

MASEFIELD, JOHN
×The Campden Wonder (Court, 8/1/07) *1909*
The Tragedy of Nan (Roy., 24/5/08, Pioneers; H., 2/6/08) *1909*
×Mrs Harrison. *1909*
The Witch (Roy., Glasgow, 10/10/10; Court, 31/1/11: called originally *Anne Pedersdotter*: adapted from the play by H. Wiers-Jenssen) *1917* (as *Anne Pedersdotter*)
The Tragedy of Pompey the Great ('*t.*': Aldw., 4/12/10, St. Soc.; revised version given by Manchester University Dram. Soc. in 1915; Fest., Cambridge, 24/10/27) *1910*; *1914* (*revised*)

×Philip the King (Bristol, 26/10/14; C.G., 5/11/14, *m.*) *1914*
The Faithful (*'Japanese t.'*: Rep., B'ham, 4/12/15; K's H., 13/4/19, St. Soc.) *1915*
×The Sweeps of '98 (Rep., B'ham, 7/10/16) *1916* (*priv.*); *1918*
×Good Friday (Gar., 25/2/17, St. Soc.) *1916* (*priv.*); *1917*
×The Locked Chest (St M., 28/4/20, *m., amat.*) *1916* (*priv.*); *1918*
Esther (translated from Racine's play) *1921*
Berenice (translated from Racine's play) *1921*
A King's Daughter (*'t.'*: Playh., Oxford, 25/5/23, *amat.*; Steiner H., 25/3/28, Dram. Pl. Soc.; RADA, 6/5/28) *1923*
Melloney Holtspur; or, The Pangs of Love (*'fant.'*: St M., 10/7/23, *m.*) *1922*
×Easter (*'pl. for singers'*) *1922*
The Trial of Jesus (RADA, 28/3/26) *1925*
Tristan and Isolt (Cent., 21/2/27) *1927*
×The Coming of Christ (*'pl. for singers'*) LC, Boar's Hill, Oxford, 27/8/28. *1928*

MASKELYNE, J. NEVIL [see also *D. C. MURRAY*]
[Author of several plays designed to exhibit 'magical' effects: the following seem to be the most interesting]
×Daylight Ghosts (*'c. of terrors'*: St G's H., 3/9/06)
×Spectres of the Sanctum (St G's H., 1/5/07)
×The Philosopher's Diamond (St G's H., 4/8/08)
×The Balisham Buddhists (St G's H., 2/8/09)
×The Scarab (St G's H., 26/5/10)
×In Quest of a Mahatma. LC, St G's H., 15/10/15

MASON, A. K.
×The Human Way. LC, Qns, Poplar, 31/5/13

MASON, ALFRED EDWARD WOODLEY [see also *G. P. BANCROFT*]
[For earlier plays see *H. E. D.* v, 480]
Marjory Strode (*'c.'*: Playh., 19/3/08)
Colonel Smith (*'c.'*: St J., 23/4/09)
The Witness for the Defence (St J., 1/2/11) *Fr. 1913*
Open Windows (St J., 11/3/13)
Green Stockings (*'c.'*) *Fr. 1914*
At the Villa Rose (Str., 10/7/20: dramatised from his own novel, 1910) *1928*
Running Water (Wynd., 5/4/22)
The House of the Arrow (Hippo., Golder's Green, 23/4/28; Vaud., 11/5/28: dramatised from his own novel, 1924)
No Other Tiger (O.H., Leicester, 8/10/28; Hippo., Golder's Green, 3/12/28; St J., 26/12/28: dramatised from his own novel, 1927)

MASON, J. R.
Oh! Frenchy! LC, Gai., B'ham, 1/4/19

MASON, M. H.
×The Scapegrace. LC, Castle Campbell, Dollar, 31/1/24

MASON, SYDNEY

[Several short plays produced at music-halls]

MASSE, CHARLES

× Moll (Scarborough, 24/6/10, *cpy.*)
× The Page (Emp., Oldham, 28/1/11, *cpy.*)

MASSINGHAM, DOROTHY

× Glass Houses (Rep., B'ham, 9/3/18)
× The Goat (Kings., 27/5/21, *m.*, Playwrights' Theatre) *Fr. 1921*
× Washed Ashore (Kings., 2/4/22, Playwrights' Theatre) *Fr. 1921*
Not in Our Stars (Wynd., 4/2/24: dramatised from the novel (1923) by Michael Maurice)

MASSON, ROSALINE

× A New Departure (St Cuthbert's H., Edin., 19/3/15)

MASTERS, BERNARD

The Duchess of Europe ('*f.c.*': Brixton, 6/4/03)

MATHERS, GILBERT, Jr

× Dawn. LC, P.H., Croydon, 6/2/19
× Leonorita. LC, P.H., Croydon, 9/5/19
The White Star. LC, P.H., Croydon, 31/1/21

MATHESON, ELIZABETH FOX

× Robin Hood and His Merry Men. *1914*
× The Shoemaker and the Elves, and Dick Whittington. *1928*

MATHEWS, GEORGE [see *MAY MATHEWS*]

MATHEWS, MAY

The Legend of Buhl (Ass. R., Erdington, 1/2/27, *amat.*: +*G. MATHEWS*)

MATHEWS, VIVIAN [see also *L. C. JAMES*]

Little Red Robin Hood; or, The Dey and the Knight ('*bsq. ext.*': Bedford Park Club, 8/1/01: +*A. MANLEY*)

MATSON, NORMAN [see *S. GLASPELL*]

MATTHEWS, A. KENWARD

[For earlier plays see *H. E. D.* v, 480]
× The Double-Shuffle (York, 25/10/00)
× The Bachelors' Club (Pal., Chelsea, 15/6/14: +*C. DAVIS*)
The Royal Chef (Ambass., 3/4/14)
Courting ('*c.*': Gar., 20/4/25) *Fr. 1926*
The Fifty-Shilling Suit ('*c.*': Pier, Folkestone, 14/1/29)

MATTHEWS, A. W. G. [see also *C. HUMPHREY*]

The Inca Love Call ('*m.r.*', m. E. Willoughby: Hippo., Eastbourne, 21/1/29)

MATTHEWS, ADELAIDE [see also *M. M. STANLEY*]

Just Married ('*f.c.*': Portsmouth, 1/12/24; Com., 15/12/24: +*A. NICHOLS*) *Fr. 1929*
Much Married Mary (R.A., Woolwich, 12/5/30: +*MARTHA M. STANLEY*)

MATTHEWS, BERTRAM P. [see also *E. FERRIS*]
Beau Brummel ('*r. costume pl.*': B'ham, 5/11/28)

MATTHEWS, E. CAMERON [see also *M. GOLDBERG* and *F. KITCHEN*]
[For earlier plays see *H. E. D.* v, 481]
×My Retribution (Great H., Tunbridge Wells, 19/9/02; Cor., 22/9/02)
×No Other Way (Shrewsbury, 18/3/07)
×The Honeymoon Baby (Emp., Camberwell, 26/3/07)
×The Thin Red Line (Pal., Walthamstow, 12/7/07)
×Salvation Jack (Pal., Walthamstow, 23/9/07: +*C. S. SELF*)
×Bustown by the Sea (Empress, Brixton, 21/10/07: +*WAL PINK*)
×When Two Play One Game (Hippo., Richmond, 3/2/08: +*J. WEAVER*)
×Coward or Hero? (Emp., Camberwell, 21/9/08)
×Mr and Mrs John Bull (Reg., Hackney, 15/7/09, *cpy.*)
Cloudland ('*m.pl.*': Reg., Hackney, 27/8/09)
Court Cards ('*m.pl.*', m. S. Gordon: Rehearsal, 26/10/09)
The Black Horror (Emp., Edmonton, 23/9/12)
×I've Bought a Pub (Emp., Shoreditch, 7/4/13)
×Chasing Chickweed. LC, Alh., Glasgow, 9/4/13
×The Son of His Father (Cant., 27/1/13)
×A Tale of Geraniums (Empress, Brixton, 16/6/13)
×The Dunmow Flitch. LC, Sur., 12/6/14
×A Small Special (Gr., Rawtenstall, 8/2/15: +*J. H. PRICE*)
×The Rank Outsider. LC, Hippo., Maidenhead, 30/4/15
×When the Clock Went Wrong. LC, Alex., Stoke Newington, 4/1/17
×The Last Instalment. LC, Hippo., Nottingham, 20/8/17
×Oh! What a Wife! LC, Loughborough, 24/6/19
×His Affinity (Granville, 15/9/19)
×Photo Fix. LC, Pal., E. Ham, 13/5/20
×A Star Tip. LC, Gr., Walsall, 23/2/21

MATTHEWS, ROSE
The Parasites (Bij., 23/6/07, one scene presented by Pl. Actors; Scala, 23/6/07)
×The Smack (Court, 27/5/10, *m.*)

MATTHEWS, WALTER R.
×The Price of Fame. *Fr. 1913*
×The Pictures (Gai., Manchester, 13/9/15; D.Y., 24/1/16)
×The East Window (Unitarian Schools, Altrincham, 17/11/15, Garrick Soc.)
×The Magic Circle (Unitarian Schools, Altrincham, 17/11/15, Garrick Soc.)
Hymen and Co. ('*c.*': Gai., Manchester, 27/3/16)
The Will and the Way ('*c.*': Unitarian Schools, Altrincham, 15/1/20, Garrick Soc.)

Lazybones ('*c.*': Ambass., 13/2/21, St. Players)
Hey Presto! ('*quaint adventure*': Kings., 13/5/23, Interlude Players)

MATTOS, ALEXANDER TEXEIRA DE MATTOS
[For earlier plays see *H. E. D.* v, 481 and 806. The following list includes only those among his many translations from Maurice Maeterlinck which were presented on the stage]
The Blue Bird (H., 8/12/09) *1909*
Mary Magdalene (Rehearsal, 17/3/12; Old Vic, 25/3/29) *1910*
Joyzelle (Greek Studio, Chelsea, 16/3/17) *1906*
The Burgomaster of Stilemonde (Lyc., Edin., 4/10/18; Scala, 10/1/19, *m.*; Lyc., 26/10/21, *m.*) *1918*
The Betrothal (Shubert, N.Y., 18/11/18, as *The Betrothed*; Gai., 8/1/21) *1918*
×The Miracle of St Anthony (Fest., Cambridge, 6/12/26) *1918*

MAUD, CONSTANCE ELIZABETH
A Daughter of France (Ambass., 21/10/13: +*P. BERTON*)

MAUDE, AYLMER [see *LOUISE MAUDE*]

MAUDE, CHARLES [see *M. CHOLMODELY*]

MAUDE, LOUISE
Leo Tolstoy: Plays (translated in collaboration with *AYLMER MAUDE*) *1914*
[This contains: 1. *The Power of Darkness* (Roy., 18/12/04, St. Soc.); 2. *The First Distiller* (Rep., B'ham, 26/10/16; Grafton Galleries, 1/5/17); 3. *Fruits of Culture* (Arts, 2/11/28, as *The Fruits of Enlightenment*); 4. *The Live Corpse* (Gr., Leeds, 18/8/19, as *Reparation*; St J., 26/9/19); 5. *The Cause of It All* (Little, 28/4/12, Adelphi Pl. Soc.); and 6. *The Light that Shines in Darkness*]

MAUGHAM, WILLIAM SOMERSET
[The majority of the plays listed below are included in the *Collected Works*, and the order in which many of the earlier dramas were written is outlined in *The Summing Up* (1938). 'A pictorial record of the first performances' is usefully presented in the *Theatrical Companion to Maugham* (1955) by Raymond Mander and Joe Mitchenson]
×Marriages Are Made in Heaven (written in 1898; printed in *The Venture*, vol. i, 1903; translated into German by Maugham himself under the title, *Schiffbrüchig*. This was presented in Berlin at the small intimate theatre called Schall und Rauch: Mander and Mitchenson give the date of the première as 3/1/02: in *The Era Annual* it appears as 28/12/01)
×Mademoiselle Zampa (written between 1896 and 1897: Aven., 18/2/04)
A Man of Honour ('*new modern pl.*': written in 1898: Imp., 22/2/03, St. Soc.; re-written in 1902; Aven., 18/2/04, with further revisions) *1903* (*priv.*); *1903* (supplement to the *Fortnightly Review*, March 1903)
Lady Frederick ('*c.*': written in 1903: Court, 26/10/07) *1912*

Jack Straw ('*c.*': written in 1905: Vaud., 26/3/08) *1911*
Mrs Dot ('*light c.*': written in 1904 or 1905: Com., 27/4/08: originally called *Worthley's Entire*) *1912*
The Explorer (written in 1899: Lyr., 13/6/08; Lyr., 19/5/09, *revised*) *1912*
Penelope ('*c.*': written in 1908: Com., 9/1/09: originally called *Man and Wife*) *1912*
The Noble Spaniard ('*Victorian f.*': written in 1908: Roy., 20/3/09: adapted from *Les gaîtés du veuvage* by Ernest Grenet-Dancourt) *1953*
Smith ('*c.*': Com., 30/9/09) *1913*
The Tenth Man (Glo., 24/2/10) *1913*
Grace (D.Y., 15/10/10: originally called *Landed Gentry*) *1913* (as *Landed Gentry*)
Loaves and Fishes ('*satire*': written in 1903: D.Y., 24/2/11) *1924*
×A Trip to Brighton (New, 29/5/11, *m.*: adapted from a play by Abel Tarride)

[This piece appears not to be listed by Mander and Mitchenson or referred to by Maugham himself in *The Summing Up*]

The Perfect Gentleman (H.M., 27/5/13)

[The extraordinary story of this version of Molière's *Le Bourgeois Gentilhomme*, which brings into conjunction six of the most famous theatre-men of the period (Maugham, Beerbohm Tree, Thomas Beecham, Reinhardt, von Hofmannsthal and Richard Strauss), has been told by C. P. Gruber on the basis of documents found by him in the Enthoven Collection (*Theatre Notebook*, xxvi, 1972, 151–8). Two texts exist: 1. Maugham's full translation, with his own dramatic 'prologue', rehearsed in 1912 but never produced; and 2. some mutilated scenes disastrously attached to the London presentation of *Ariadne auf Naxos*, in 1913]

The Land of Promise (Hyperion, New Haven, Conn., 26/11/13; Lyc., N.Y., 25/12/13; D.Y., 26/2/14) *1913* (*priv.*); *1922*
Caroline ('*light c.*': New, 8/2/16: originally called *The Unattainable*) *1923* (as *The Unattainable*)
Our Betters (written in 1915: Nixon, Atlantic City, 8/3/17; Hudson, N.Y., 12/3/17; Glo., 12/9/23) *1923*
Love in a Cottage (Glo., 26/1/18)
Caesar's Wife (Roy., 27/3/19) *1922*
Home and Beauty ('*f.*': Glo., Atlantic City, 4/8/19, as *Too Many Husbands*; Booth, N.Y., 8/10/19, under the same title; Playh., 30/8/19) *1923*
The Unknown (Aldw., 9/8/20) *1920*
The Circle ('*modern c.*': H., 3/3/21) *1921*
East of Suez (Woods, Atlantic City, 28/8/22; Eltinge, N.Y., 21/9/22; H.M., 2/9/22) *1922*
The Camel's Back ('*f.*': Worcester, Mass., 5/11/23; Vanderbilt, N.Y., 13/11/23; Playh., 31/1/24)

[Mander and Mitchenson give 29/10/23 as the date of the première at Worcester, Mass.]

The Road Uphill (never produced: manuscript text discovered by

Mander and Mitchenson, dateable about 1924: see *Theatrical Companion to Maugham*, pp. 195–9)
The Constant Wife ('*c.*': Ohio, Cleveland, Ohio, 1/11/26; Maxine Elliott, N.Y., 29/11/26; Str., 6/4/27) *1926* (New York); *1927*
The Letter (Playh., 24/2/27) *1927*
The Sacred Flame (Belasco, Washington, 12/11/28; Henry Miller, N.Y., 19/11/28; Playh., 8/2/29) *1928* (New York); *1929*
The Breadwinner ('*c.*': Vaud., 30/9/30) *1930*

MAULE, DONOVAN
Found Guilty (Leicester, 5/12/21)
The Waster, M.P. (Vic., W. Stanley, 18/12/22)
× The Ivory Box (Rep., Plymouth, 29/6/25)

MAURICE, EDMUND [see also *H. CARRICK*]
× Blind (Emp., New X, 27/4/08; Col., 10/10/10)

MAURICE, IVY
Back to Blighty ('*md.*': Pal., Barnoldswick, 16/9/18: title later changed to *Her Kingdom of Love*)
× Only a Broken Toy (Pal., Battersea, 10/2/22)

MAURICE, RICHARD
× The Origin of Species (Rehearsal, 28/4/13, Black Cat Club)
× The Lady Doctor (Rehearsal, 27/6/13, Black Cat Club)

MAVOR, OSBORNE HENRY [='*JAMES BRIDIE*' and '*MARY HENDERSON*']

MAWER, Miss [see *R. GINNER*]

MAX, Countess [see *A. C. MAGIAN*]

MAXWELL, FREDERICK
[For an earlier play see *H. E. D.* v, 482]
The Heathen and the Christian ('*oriental d.*': Edmonton, 31/3/02, in one act; St J., Manchester, 8/7/07, as a four-act play Greenwich, 25/1/09)
× A Prodigal Wife (Pal., Cardiff, 18/11/07)
× Hawksley's Luck (Bed., 9/3/08)
× The Last Command (Bed., 30/3/08)
× Give a Man a Chance (Pav., Leicester, 9/11/08)
× Territorials (Bed., 11/1/09; Empress, Brixton, 22/2/09)
× The Bride Elect (Emp., Shepherd's Bush, 25/10/09)
× The Revolution (Emp., Camberwell, 6/12/09; Pal., Hamm., 17/10/10)
× The Russian Princess (Emp., Camberwell, 3/1/10)
Lord Harkaway; or, The Sporting Detective (Gr., Nelson, 18/3/12)
× Should He Forgive Her? LC, Emp., Shoreditch, 6/1/14
× A Man's Sacrifice. LC, Emp., Edmonton, 17/2/14

MAXWELL, H.
× The Futurists ('*c.*': K's, Southsea, 7/11/21; Col., 14/11/21)

MAXWELL, H. B.
[For earlier plays see *H. E. D.* v, 482]
Too Soon ('*c.o.*', m. W. Neale: Shak., L'pool, 28/4/04, *cpy.*)

MAXWELL, J. H.
Joan of Arc ('*bsq.*': Aquar., Brighton, 27/8/00)

MAXWELL, M.
The King's Dancer ('*c.*': O.H., Jersey, 17/11/11: +*A. F. MORTIMER*)

MAXWELL, Major General PATRICK
Minna von Barnhelm, or A Soldier's Luck (translated from the play (1767) by G. E. Lessing) *1900*

MAXWELL, WILLIAM BABINGTON [see also '*GEORGE PASTON*']
[For an earlier play see *H. E. D.* v, 482]
The Ragged Messenger (Broadway, New X, 15/9/05, *cpy.*: dramatised from his own novel (1904): +'*G. PASTON*')
× The Last Man In (Roy., Glasgow, 14/3/10; Everyman, 21/2/28) *1910*
The Unknown Factor (Playh., L'pool, 26/9/21)

MAXWELL, WALTER [see *F. VERNON*]

MAY, C. EDGAR
× Reggie's Ruse (Spear's H., Highgate, 8/10/10, *amat.*)
× Man Proposes, Woman Disposes (St Peter's H., Hornsey, 24/1/11, *amat.*)
× The Inheritance (Iron R., Stroud Green, 9/2/11, *amat.*)
× Deceivers Three (Freehold Social Inst., New Southgate, 14/2/11, *amat.*)
× A Husband's Device (Spear's H., Highgate, 25/3/11, *amat.*)

MAY, ERIC PAUL [see also *R. LEE*]
Her Secret Husband. LC, Sunderland, 12/5/19
The Devil's Own. LC, Vic., W. Stanley, 19/8/21

[*MAY, FLORENCE EDNA*
Unloved (New, Cardiff, 10/3/24: called originally *The Unloved Wife*)

MAY, JANE
× Wanted, a French Maid (P'cess of W., Kennington, 22/4/01)

MAY, MOLLY ERNLE
× In Queen Anne's Orangery. LC, K. G's H., 24/6/24

[*MAYER, EDWIN JUSTUS*
The Firebrand ('*c.*': Morosco, N.Y., 15/10/24; Wynd., 8/2/26) *1926*

MAYER (or *MEYER*), *GASTON*
× French as He is Spoke (Playh., 15/8/07: adapted from *L'Anglais tel qu'on le parle* (1899) by Tristan Bernard) *Fr. 1909*
× The Chauffeur (Playh., 3/6/09: adapted from the play (1908) by Max Maurey)

In the Clouds ('*c.*': Bournemouth, 17/7/11: adapted from *Château historique* (1900) by J. Berr de Turique and A. Bisson)

MAYHEW, ATHOL
The Scilly Girl (*m.c.*', m. W. Neale: Gr., Woolwich, 12/12/04)

MAYNARD, Mrs THEODORE
Brady ('*c.*': Abbey, Dublin, 4/8/19)

MAYNE, DENIS
Sinister House (Aldershot, 4/3/29)

MAYNE, ERIC
East Lynne (Lyc., 13/11/09)

MAYNE, KATHLEEN [see *A. BECKETT*]

MAYNE, N. THORPE
Mary of England ('*t.*') *1909*
×The Love of Leslie Heseltine (County, Kingston, 27/11/09)
×Thou Shalt Not (Bed., 1/4/12; Vic. Pier, Folkestone, 22/7/12)

MAYNE, RUTHERFORD
The Drone ('*c.*': Garrick Chambers, Stockport, 11/1/11, *amat.*; Roy., 6/2/12) *1909* (Dublin)
×The Troth. *1909* (Dublin)
Captain of the Hosts (Gr., Belfast, 8/3/10)
×The Turn of the Road (c. 1910, Cork Dr. Soc.: LC, Kelly's, L'pool, 2/5/11) *1912* (in *The Drone and Other Plays*)
×Red Turf (O.H., Belfast, 5/12/11; Abbey, Dublin, 7/12/11) *1912* (in *The Drone and Other Plays*)
If! ('*f.*': O.H., Belfast, 25/11/13)
×Evening (O.H., Belfast, 2/3/14)
×The Gomeril (O.H., Belfast, 1/5/16)
Neil Gallina (O.H., Belfast, 13/12/16)
Industry (O.H., Belfast, 6/12/17)

MAYNE, W. M. [see *M. B. SPURR*]

[*MAYO, MARGARET* [see also *S. FIELD* and *Mrs H. WARD*]
Divorçons ('*c.*': D.Y., 12/6/07: adapted from V. Sardou's play, 1880)
Baby Mine ('*c.*': Fort Wayne, 6/6/10; Chicago, 8/6/10; Daly's, N.Y., 23/8/10; Crit., 22/2/11)
×Being Fitted (Vic. Pal., 10/2/19)

MAYO, SAM [see *M. COWAN*]

MAYO, WINIFRED
La Gioconda (Bij., 8/12/07: adapted from G. D'Annunzio's play, 1899)

MAYOR, BEATRICE
×The Girl and the City ('*fant.*': Kings., 2/4/22, Playwrights' Theatre)
×Thirty Minutes in a Street (Kings., 2/4/22, Playwrights' Theatre) *1923*
The Pleasure Garden (Reg., 29/6/24, St. Soc.; Fest., Cambridge, 24/1/27; Everyman, 8/3/29) *1925*

Four Plays for Children. *1926* (Oxford)
[This contains four one-act plays: 1. *In a Street*; 2. *The Old Home*; 3. *In a Shop* (LC, K. G's H., 15/1/23; and 4. *The Musical Box*]
Christine (Ldn Theatre School, 28/3/28)

MEAD, CHARLES [see *H. H. MUNRO*]

MEADE, Mrs L. T.
The Brotherhood of the Seven Kings (S. Shields, 30/4/00, *amat.*: +*R. EUSTACE* and *M. ELGIN*)

MEADE, WALTER
×A Bargain from Basra (Everyman, 17/4/22: also called *The Bargain*)

[*MEADER, CLARENCE LINTON*
The Sabine Women (Everyman, 3/4/28: adapted from N. Andreev, *Prekrasnie Sabiniaki*, 1912: +*F. N. SCOTT*) *1915*

MEADOWS, CONNIE
A Woman's Silence ('*r.m.d.*': Leigh, 26/11/04, *cpy.*)

MEADS, FREDERICK
×The Crime of Poverty (Gr., Manchester, 20/2/12)

MEAR, HARRY [see *C. CULLUM*]

MEARS, FRANK C. [see *Lady MARGARET SACKVILLE*]

MEARS, STANNARD [see *S. STANGE*]

[*MEDCRAFT, RUSSELL G.*
The Swordsman ('*m.pl.*', m. L. E. Gensler: Nottingham, 24/12/27: +*NORMA MITCHELL*)
Sauce for the Gander ('*f.c.*': K's, Southsea, 23/1/28; Lyr., 30/1/28: called originally *The Cradle Snatchers*: +*NORMA MITCHELL*) *Fr. 1931*

MEDHURST, W. C.
The Dream Jewel. LC, '*children's pl.*': Lyr., Hamm., 10/12/18

MEEK, E. WARREN
Snow-White. LC, Torquay, 5/5/25

MEEKIN, ANNETTE
Polyeucte. *1929* (translated from the play by P. Corneille)

[*MEGRUE, ROI COOPER* [see also *M. GLASS*]
×An Unlucky Star (Pal., 27/6/10)
It Pays to Advertise ('*f.*': Apo., Atlantic City, 27/4/14; Cohan, N.Y., 8/9/14; Gai., Hastings, 21/1/24; Aldw., 1/2/24: +*W. HACKETT*) *Fr. 1928*
Under Cover (Cort, N.Y., 26/8/14; Gr., Blackpool, 8/1/17; Str., 17/1/17) *1914*
Tea for Three ('*c.*': Belasco, Washington, 3/6/18; Maxine Elliott, N.Y., 19/9/18; H., 3/2/20) *1924* (Boston)

MEIKLEJOHN, A. L.
×At the Boar's Head ('*oa.*', m. G. Holst: O.H., Manchester, 3/4/25: based on scenes from Shakespeare's *Henry IV*)

MELFORD, AUSTIN [see also *E. BLORE* and *S. BRIGHTMAN*]
Yes, Papa! ('*m.f.*', m. P. Braham: Col., Cheltenham, 21/2/21; Emp., Finsbury Park, 28/2/21: +*ERIC BLORE*)
French Beans ('*m.f.*', m. L. Alleyn: Jubilee H., Weymouth, 25/4/21; Emp., Stratford, 5/9/21: +*E. BLORE* and *FENTON MACKAY*)
×Tact (K's H., 18/6/22, Interlude Players)
The Dare-Devil ('*f.*': Pier, Brighton, 21/1/24; Str., 28/1/24; musical version, Bed., 21/7/24)
×The Pride of the Yard (Theatrical Gdn Party, Chelsea, 24/6/24)
Austin Melford's Revue Sketches. *Fr. 1928*
[This contains nine short playlets]
Austin Melford's Nonsense. *Fr. 1930*
[This contains seven short playlets]
×Kit Marlowe (Qns, 2/4/29) *Fr. 1930*

MELFORD, MARK
[For earlier plays see *H. E. D.* v, 484]
The Humbug ('*f.c.*': Ladbr. H., 31/10/01)
Like No Other Love (Gr., Croydon, 11/12/05)
Mark Melford's Music Hall Sketches. *Fr. 1910*
×The Tale of a Tigress (Gr., Clapham, 22/4/07)
×Non-Suited. LC, Sur., 9/8/23
Who's My Father? ('*m.f.*': Gr., Swansea, 27/10/24, adapted by *A. RIGBY*)

MELLOR, E. K.
×Goldenheart and Silverstar. LC, P.H., Croydon, 7/2/19
×The Zephyr and the Dewdrop. LC, P.H., Croydon, 9/5/19

MELLOR, FRANK R.
×Sparrows (Boudoir, 15/5/14, Black Cat Club)

MELLOR, H. CHRISTIAN
Aboudahur. *1919*

MELROSE, MATT
Camouflage ('*m.c.*', m. Bertram Knowldon: Pal., St Leonards, 21/6/20)
Molly o' Mine. LC, '*m.pl.*': Cradley Heath, Worcester, 6/7/21

MELTZER, CHARLES HENRY
The Duchess of Marlborough ('*historical pl.*': Canterbury, 22/2/06)
The Sunken Bell (Waldorf, 22/4/07: adapted from G. Hauptmann, *Die versunkene Glocke*, 1896) *1900*

MELVILL, HARRY
The Man of the Moment (St J., 13/6/05: called originally *The Victim*: adapted from A. Capus and E. Arène, *L'adversaire*, 1903)
The Whirlwind (B'ham, 9/4/06; Crit., 23/5/06: adapted from H. Bernstein, *La Rafale*, 1905)

'*MELVILL, RUTH*' [=*Miss MORTLOCK-BROWN*]
The Call of Conscience (Margaret Morris, 22/7/16, *amat.*)

MELVILLE, ANDREW

Robespierre (Gr., Brighton, 17/10/27)

MELVILLE, FREDERICK [see also *W. MELVILLE*]

In a Woman's Grip (Stand., 7/10/01)
Between Two Women (Terriss, Rotherhithe, 27/10/02)
Her Forbidden Marriage (Terriss, Rotherhithe, 4/4/04)
The Ugliest Woman on Earth (Terriss, Rotherhithe, 14/11/04)
The Beast and the Beauty (Stand., 9/10/05)
Her Road to Ruin (Terriss, Rotherhithe, 20/5/07)
Married to the Wrong Man (E.C., 3/8/08)
The Bad Girl of the Family (E.C., 4/10/09; Aldw., 27/12/09)
The Monk and the Woman (Lyc., 28/2/12)
× One Way of War (Brixton, 9/11/14)

MELVILLE, LEWIS

His Grace ('*c.*': K. G's H., 22/2/23, Warwick Rep. Co.)

MELVILLE, WALTER

[For earlier plays see *H. E. D.* v, 485]
The World of Sin (Stand., 5/11/00; Stand., 4/8/02, as *When a Woman is Married*)
That Wretch of a Woman (Stand., 4/11/01)
Her Second Time on Earth (Stand., 9/10/02)
A Girl's Cross Roads (Stand., 5/10/03)
The Female Swindler (Terriss, Rotherhithe, 12/10/03)
A Disgrace to Her Sex (Terriss, Rotherhithe, 23/5/04)
The Girl who Lost Her Character (Stand., 10/10/04)
× The Wheel of Fortune (Terriss, Rotherhithe, 1/9/05)
The Girl who Took the Wrong Turning (Stand., 1/10/06)
A Soldier's Wedding (Terriss, Rotherhithe, 8/10/06)
The Girl who Wrecked His Home (Stand., 30/9/07)
The Beggar-Girl's Wedding (E.C., 19/10/08)
The Sins of London (Lyc., 14/9/10)
The Shop-Soiled Girl (E.C., 3/10/10)
The Adventures of the Count of Monte Cristo (P's, 9/10/12: +*F. MELVILLE*)
The Female Hun (Lyc., 2/10/18)

MELVYN, WILLIAM

Shattered Vengeance (Vic., Broughton, 1/5/11)
The New Jack Sheppard (Vic., Broughton, 8/5/11)
Women of Shame (Vic., Broughton, 12/8/12: title later changed to *A Lad's Love*)
Hypocrisy (Stratford, 21/2/21)
Gossip. LC, Alex., S. Shields, 2/3/23

MENCE, HERBERT

× Per Pro Simon (Court, 12/3/14)

[*MENCKEN, H. L.*

× The Artist ('*satire*': Little, Manchester, 28/3/27, Unnamed Soc.) *1917*

MENDEL, VERA

Masses and Man (translated from E. Toller, *Masse-Mensch*, 1921) *1924*

Brokenbrow (translated from *Hinkemann* (1923) by Ernst Toller) *1926*

MENNION, W. J.

The Bounder ('*c.*': T.H., Wandsworth, 24/2/10, *amat.*)

×Love and the Press Gang (Ass. R., Balham, 21/5/13)

MENZIES, MARIE [='*M. HALL-PAGE*']

MEREDITH, GEORGE

×The Sentimentalists ('*scenes from an unfinished c.*': D.Y., 1/3/10, Rep. Th.)

MEREDITH, H. O.

The Forerunners ('*t. of the abstract past*': Lyr., Hamm., 19/12/20, St. Soc.)

MEREDYTH, CONSTANCE

×The Turquoise Necklace (Crit., 14/7/10, *m.*)

MEREFIELD, BERNARD [see *D. NEWTON*]

MERIVALE, BERNARD [see also *B. FLEMING*, *A. RIDLEY* and *L. WORRALL*]

×Fancy Dress (Playh., L'pool, 7/9/18) *Fr. 1913*

Matrimonial Secrets (Playh., L'pool, 18/6/19)

Marriage by Instalments (Gr., Southampton, 16/5/21; Ambass., 29/3/23: +*R. BIRD*)

The Bull Pup ('*f.md.*': O.H., Southport, 19/10/25; Q, 19/7/26, as *None But the Brave*; Gar., 30/7/26: +*B. FLEMING*) *Fr. 1931*

×Are You Insured? (Col., 8/2/26: +*B. FLEMING*)

A House Divided (Gr., Croydon, 23/6/26)

The Horror (Gr., Fulham, 27/8/28)

The Command to Love (Arts, 5/2/30; Daly's, 10/6/30: adapted from a comedy by *H. BERNSTEIN* and *B. MARLOW* (Stamford, Conn., 2/9/27; Longacre, N.Y., 20/9/27), itself taken from a Viennese play by Rudolph Lothar and Fritz Gottwald)

MERRICK, HOPE (*Mrs LEONARD MERRICK*)

×Jimmy's Mother (Pav., Eastbourne, 19/1/04, *cpy.*; Scala, 26/11/05, St. Soc.)

×The Odd Girl (K's, Hamm., 4/4/04: called originally *Mattie – A Kitchen Courtship*)

Mary-Girl (Vaud., 13/1/14)

MERRICK, LEONARD [see also *G. R. SIMS*]

The Impostor (Roy., Glasgow, 16/4/12; Q, 9/2/15, as *The Fraud*: +*M. MORTON*)

×The Tragedy of a Comic Song (Roy., Glasgow, 16/4/12: +*A. WAREING*)

×Poor Dear George ('*f.*': Church House, Erdington, 1/10/25)

×The Suicides in the Rue Sombre (Midland Inst., B'ham, 22/3/29)

'MERRICK, MICHAEL'
×Maraquita (Court, 8/11/08, Pl. Actors)

MERRIMAN, HENRY
A Human Terror (Pav., 9/3/03)
The Master Criminal (Gr., Margate, 16/5/04; E.C., 23/5/04)

MERRIMORE, L. M.
×The Permanent Lodger (Court, 12/2/14)

MERRITT, GEORGE
The Dance of Death (St G's H., 23/11/24, part 1; 21/12/24, part 2, Sunday Players; Apo., 16/1/28: translated from A. Strindberg, *Dodsdansen*, 1901)
The Brothers Karamazov (Gate, 7/6/26: dramatised from the novel by F. M. Dostoievski)
Nju (Gate, 19/7/26: from the play by O. Dymov, 1908)
Oktobertag (Gate, 24/4/30: translated from the play (1928) by G. Kaiser)

MERRYMAN, KATHERINE
×Persephone ('*pl. for schools*') *1917*

MERVYN, ANTHONY
The Dreamers (Q, 12/11/28)

MERVYN, BERNARD [see also *I. P. GORE*]

MERVYN, EDWARD
[For an earlier play see *H. E. D.* v, 488]
The New Commander ('*naval m.c.*': Gai., Hastings, 22/2/04; C.P., 7/3/04)
The King of Mystonia ('*m.c.*': Gr., Chorley, 28/3/10; Emp., Fleetwood, 18/4/10)
×The Sandow Girl. LC, Cant., 23/7/13

METCALFE, JOHN
Bunderley Boggard, and Other Plays. *1919*
[Besides the title-play, this contains three one-act pieces: 1. *T'Roadmen*; 2. *A Rum an' Tea Doo*; and 3. *T' Kal 'Oil*]
Mrs Clarke's Garden Party. LC, Moravian School, Baildon, 8/7/20

METCALFE, M. G.
×Where There's a Will, There's a Way. *1930*

METCALFE, WILLIAM
×The Seven Princesses (translated from *Les Sept Princesses* (1891) by Maurice Maeterlinck) *1909*

METHLEY, VIOLET MARY
Sauce for the Gander, and Other Plays. *1910*
×Cousin Chrissie. *Fr. 1919*
×Footprints. *Fr. 1919*
×Buster. *Fr. 1920*
×Clever Kid! *Fr. 1921*
×Freckles. *Fr. 1924*
×The Injured. *Fr. 1924*

×The Magic Stockings. *Fr. 1924*
The Mulberry Bush, and Other Plays. *1927*
×Remember, Remember. *Fr. 1927*

MEYER, GASTON [see *GASTON MAYER*]

MEYNELL, ROBERT
×Defiance (St Luke's School, Stroud Green, 13/12/13)

MIALL, AGNES M.
×Love's Young Dream. LC, Crippl. Inst., 1/11/22. *Fr. 1922*
×The Understudy. LC, Crippl. Inst., 1/11/22. *Fr. 1922*
×No Followers Permitted. *Fr. 1923*
×A Prince in Chains. *Fr. 1925*

MIALL, BERNARD
The Arm of the Law (Gar., 16/2/04: called originally *The Red Robe*: adapted from E. Brieux, *La robe rouge*, 1900) *1916*
Sister Beatrice (Court, 28/3/09, Pl. Actors: translated from M. Maeterlinck, *Sœur Béatrice*, 1899) *1902*
Ariadne and Barbe Bleue (Etlinger, 18/7/28: translated from M. Maeterlinck, *Ariane et Barbe-Bleue*, 1901) *1901*

MICHELSON, MIRIAM
The Duchess of Suds (Brighton, 8/6/14)

MIDDLEMASS, ROBERT [see *H. HALL*]

MIDDLETON, EDGAR CHARLES
Potiphar's Wife (Glo., 17/8/27)
Tin Gods (Gar., 1/2/28)
Banned by the Censor. *1929*
[This contains ten short playlets]

[*MIDDLETON, GEORGE* [see also *S. OLIVER*]
Polly with a Past ('*c.*': Belasco, N.Y., 6/9/17; St J., 2/3/21: +*G. BOLTON*)
Adam and Eva ('*c.*': Gar., Detroit, 17/2/19; Longacre, N.Y., 13/9/19; Byfield H., Barnes, 1/5/24; Little, 13/4/25: +*G. BOLTON*)
×The Reason (P.W., 15/2/25, Green Room Rag)
×Collusion (Arts, 10/11/27)

MIDDLETON, RICHARD
×The District Visitor ('*bsq.*': Court, 5/3/14)

MIDGLEY, TOM
The Reward of Sin (T.H., Todmorden, 18/11/05, *amat.*)

MIGNON, SARA [see *R. BALMAIN*]

MILBURN, HARTLEY [see *HENRY BAGGE*]

MILES, G. C. W. [see *F. D. GRIERSON*]

MILES, P. NAPIER
×Westward Ho! LC, Lyc., 19/11/13
×Markheim ('*o.*': Vic. R., Clifton, Bristol, 13/10/24)
×Music Comes ('*o.*': Vic. R., Clifton, Bristol, 13/10/24)

MILL, C. WATSON [see *C. WATSON-MILL*]

MILL, JOHN

[For earlier plays see *H. E. D.* v, 488]

Hearts of Erin ('*m.pl.*', m. J. Bruske: Pal., Newcastle, 10/2/02)

MILLANE, JOSEPH [see also *W. P. SHEEN*]

Women and War (Osborne, Manchester, 29/3/15: +*C. SHIRLEY*)

Somewhere a Voice is Calling (Emp., Rotherham, 29/5/15; E.C., 15/11/15: +*ROYCE CARLETON*)

The Confessions of a Wife (Leeds, 29/11/15; E.C., 20/3/16: +*ROYCE CARLETON*)

MILLAR, ROBINS [see also *P. WILSON*]

× Getting Rid of Her (Pal., Chelsea, 15/4/18)

Let Greytown Flourish. (Ath., Glasgow, 20/12/21, Scott. Nat. Players)

The Shawlie. *1924*

Thunder in the Air (D.Y., 5/4/28) *Fr. 1928*

× Colossus (Ath., Glasgow, 4/6/28) *1935* (in J. M. Reid, *Scottish One-Act Plays*); *1938* (Edinburgh)

Dream Island (Glasgow, 4/11/29, Masque Theatre)

MILLARD, ALFRED

Raselle, the Boy Musician (Qns, Manchester, 19/4/09)

MILLARD, F. J.

× When Shadows Fall. LC, W. Bromwich, 17/11/16

MILLBANK, EDITH

Tancred (Kings., 16/7/23: dramatised from Benjamin Disraeli's novel)

MILLER, ALAN

× Ninepence for Fourpence. LC, B'ham, 20/2/13

× The Pilgrim's Progress. LC, Medical Theatre, B'ham, 19/11/13

× Cut That Nerve. LC, B'ham, 17/2/14

× The Ray. LC, Hippo., Birkenhead, 13/5/24

× Vallingdale Hall. LC, Hippo., Birkenhead, 19/5/24

A Lace Handkerchief. LC, Tapestry Works H., Birkenhead, 13/11/24

MILLER, ALICE DUER

The Charm School ('*c.*': Auditorium, Baltimore, 19/4/20; Bij., N.Y., 2/8/20; Com., 23/12/20: +*R. MILTON*) *1919* (New York)

× Happy Dreams. LC, Emp., Peterborough, 1/12/20. *Fr. 1923*

MILLER, ARTHUR [see also *G. ARTHURS*]

A Night Out ('*m.pl.*', m. W. Redstone: W.G., 18/9/20: +*G. GROSSMITH*)

The Gipsy Princess ('*oa.*', m. E. Kalman: P.W., 26/5/21)

The Rose Garden ('*m.pl.*', m. A. Wood: Hippo., Boscombe, 1/5/22; Emp., Penge, 8/5/22: +*E. BAYNES*)

The Early Girl ('*m.pl.*', m. C. Webb-Johnson: O.H., Southport, 23/4/23)

MILLER, Dr ARTHUR

Has a Wife the Right? (Hippo., Stockport, 26/11/23; Pal., E. Ham, 17/12/23; Hippo., Putney, 25/2/24, as *Three Wives*: called originally *Motherhood*)

MILLER, ELISABETH YORKE

×Breakfast at Mrs Morgan's (Qns, 27/7/15, *m.*)
×Matchboxes (Col., 17/1/16)

MILLER, IRENE

×In a Russian Village (K's H., 2/4/22, Interlude Players)

MILLER, RUBY [see *R. HORNIMAN*]

MILLER, ST AUBYN

[For earlier plays see *H. E. D.* v, 488]
The Guilty Man (Brit., 23/7/00)
A Sister's Sacrifice (Rot., L'pool, 30/7/00; Sur., 3/6/01: +*M. TURNER*)
Fatal Fortune (Carlton, Saltley, 28/3/03; Metro., Camberwell, 2/5/04)
Her Great Revenge (Qns, Dublin, 8/10/23)

MILLER, WILLIAM J.

The Throne of Terror (Carlton, Greenwich, 26/6/05)
×A Daughter of Belgium (Hippo., Balham, 29/3/15)
×Dante and Beatrice ('*oa.*': Shaft., 7/6/18)

MILLER, WYNN F.

[For earlier plays see *H. E. D.* v, 489]
The Star of Hope (St J., Manchester, 14/1/01: +*C. A. CLARKE*)
×The Picture (Bradford, 27/5/12)

MILLIGAN, ALICE

×The Last Feast of the Fianna ('*dramatic legend*': Gai., Dublin, 19/2/00, Irish Lit. Theatre) *1900*

MILLINGTON, C. S.

The Uplifting of Eugene Demayne (Abbey, Dublin, 8/9/16)

MILLS, A. V.

Do Let's Be Serious ('*c.*': Q, 3/12/28)

MILLS, Mrs CLIFFORD

×One of These Little Ones (Alb. H., 2/7/09)
Where the Rainbow Ends ('*fairy pl.*', m. R. Quilter: Sav., 21/12/11: +*R. OWEN*) *1912*
The Basker ('*c.*': St J., 6/1/16)
The Luck of the Navy (Bournemouth, 1/8/18; Qns, 5/8/18)
×Virginia (Pal., 15/11/21, *m.*, Lyc. Club)
In Nelson's Days ('*pl. of adventure*': York, 23/1/22; Shaft., 11/3/22)
The Man from Hong Kong (Qns, 3/8/25)

MILLS, F. B.

Beauty and the Beetle. LC, Crippl. Inst., 5/12/25

MILLS, HORACE [see *W. W. JACOBS*]

MILLS, OSCAR

×Brothers and Chums (Tudor H., Ferndale, 6/8/00)

MILLS, PHILIP

Wanted – a Spy ('*f.*': Polytechnic, Holloway, 25/5/18)

MILLWARD, FLORENCE M.

Four Short Plays. *1922*

[This contains: 1. *Irene Obliges* (LC, O.H., Dudley, 11/9/17); 2. *The Alternative*; 3. *Henry Wakes Up*; and 4. *This Room is Engaged*]

Three More Plays. *1924*

[This contains three one-act plays: 1. *Re-enter Mrs Roylance*; 2. *When the Post Has Been*; and 3. *Her Chance*]

MILNE, ALAN ALEXANDER

First Plays. *1919*

[This contains: 1. *Wurzel Flummery* ('*c.*': New, 7/4/17, in two acts: originally written in three acts, and in this edition reduced to one act: the two-act form is in *Fr. 1922*); 2. *The Lucky One* ('*t.c.*': Gar., N.Y., 20/11/22; A.D.C., Cambridge, 6/6/23; RADA, 1/6/24); 3. ×*The Boy Comes Home* (Vic. Pal., 9/9/18); 4. *Belinda* ('*an April folly*', New, 8/4/18); and 5. ×*The Red Feathers* ('*oa.*': LC, Emanuel Inst., Leeds, 4/2/20; Everyman, 26/5/21)]

Second Plays. *1923*

[This contains: 1. *Make Believe* ('*children's pl.*': Lyr., Hamm., 24/12/18); 2. *Mr Pim Passes By* ('*c.*': Gai., Manchester, 1/12/19; New, 5/1/20); 3. ×*The Camberley Triangle* ('*c.*': Col., 8/9/19); 4. *The Romantic Age* ('*c.*': Com., 18/10/20); and 5. ×*The Stepmother* (Alh., 16/11/20). Of these plays, no. 2 had been printed separately in *1921*, no. 4 in *1922*, and no. 5 in *1921*]

Three Plays. *1923*

[This contains: 1. *The Great Broxopp* ('*c.*': Punch and Judy, N.Y., 14/11/21; St M., 6/3/23); 2. *The Dover Road* ('*c.*': Bij., N.Y., 23/12/21; H., 7/6/22); and 3. *The Truth about Blayds* (Glo., 20/12/21)]

×The Artist. *Fr. 1923*

Four Plays. *1926*

[This contains: 1. *To Have the Honour* ('*c.*': Wynd., 22/4/24); 2. *Ariadne, or, Business First* (Gar., N.Y., 23/2/25; H., 22/4/25); 3. ×*Portrait of a Gentleman in Slippers* (Playh., L'pool, 4/9/26; RADA, 19/6/27); and 4. *Success* (H., 21/6/23). Of these plays nos. 1 and 2 had been printed separately in *1925*, and no. 4 in *1923*]

×Berlud, Unlimited (Theatrical Gdn Party, Chelsea, 23/6/22)

×The Man in the Bowler Hat ('*bsq.*': P.W., 27/9/25, Green Room Rag) *Fr. 1923*

×The Princess and the Woodcutter. *1927* (in J. Hampden, *Eight Modern Plays for Juniors*)

×Miss Marlow at Play (Col., 11/4/27)

The Fourth Wall ('*detective story*': H., 29/2/28) *Fr. 1929*

Let's All Talk about Gerald ('*c.*': Arts, 11/5/28)

The Ivory Door (*'legend'*: H., 17/4/29) *Fr. 1930*
Toad of Toad Hall (*'children's pl.'*, m. H. Fraser-Simson: Playh., L'pool, 21/12/29) *1929*
Michael and Mary (N.Y., 13/12/29; St J., 1/2/30) *1930*

MILNE, BETTY LUMSDEN
The Crickleham Mystery (Blackfriars, 27/11/26, Quill Club Players)

MILNER, FRANK G.
Pretty Babetta (*'m.pl.'*, m. U. Joyce: King's Lynn, 22/11/20)

MILTON, ALLAN
The Class-Leader (O.H., Buxton, 24/11/15: +*P. JACKSON*)
Spingle's Silver (*'c.'*: O.H., Buxton, 5/5/19: title later changed to *Cousin Wilfred*)
All in Good Time (*'f.c.'*: Pal., Ramsgate, 9/5/21; Rep., Brighton, 2/2/24, as *Oh! Colin!*)

'MILTON, ARTHUR' [=*W. J. LUNT*: see *P. MILTON*]

MILTON, DEBORAH
×Getting Uncompromised (Arts Centre, 1/5/14)

MILTON, ERNEST
Christopher Marlowe. *1924*

MILTON, PERCY
[For earlier plays see *H. E. D.* v, 490 and 807]
The Cruise of the Calabar (*'m.c.'*: Court, Warrington, 3/8/03: +*A. MILTON*)

MILTON, ROBERT [see *A. D. MILLER*]

MILTON, ROY
×A Woman of Paris (Tiv., Manchester, 4/7/07; Cant., 17/8/08)
×Varina (Ath., Lancaster, 7/8/07, *cpy.*)

MILWARD, DAWSON [see also *E. H. CLARK*]
×An Unexpected Visit (St G's H., 3/2/00)
×Parents. LC, Roy., 8/10/17. *Fr. 1919*
×Cornered (Court, 9/5/19, *m.*: title later changed to *History Repeats Itself*) *Fr. 1919*
×Jealousy (St J., 23/5/19, *m.*) *Fr. 1919*
×The Diamond Star. LC, Glo., 15/12/19

MILWARD, JOHN S. [see *M. ROBSON*]

MINCE, H. W.
×Cold Mutton (Brixton, 28/9/08)

MINGARD, H. DE VERE
×A Rehearsal. LC, Park, Hanwell, 14/3/18

MINLORE, DAVID
×Number 24 (Playh., Cardiff, 24/11/24; St J., 6/1/25)
Family Pride (D.P., Eastbourne, 8/3/26)
Flotsam (Everyman, 16/3/27)
We Hamiltons (*'f.c.'*: Pier, Eastbourne, 10/10/27)
Compromise (Sav., 25/3/28, Lyc. Club)

MIST, WILLIAM F. R.

×Sweet Mignonette (Canterbury, 29/5/13)

A Bigamy of Convenience ('*f.*': Arcadia, Redcar, 15/3/23: +*M. ROMER*)

MITCHELL, ALEXANDER GORDON

Jephtha (translated from the Latin drama by George Buchanan) *1903* (Paisley)

MITCHELL, BASIL

×A Real Man (O.H., Wakefield, 27/1/11)

MITCHELL, CHALMERS

The Girl and the Puppet (P's, 17/2/18, Pioneer Players: adapted from a play by P. Louys and P. Frondaie)

MITCHELL, DAVID M.

Sir Tristram ('*t.*') *1927*

MITCHELL, E.

×In a Waiting Room. LC, Gar., 25/7/16

MITCHELL, H.

The Curse of the Black Pearl. LC, S. Shields, 12/5/19

[*MITCHELL, LANGDON ELWYN*

[For earlier plays see *H. E. D.* v, 490]

The Adventures of François (Gr., Halifax, 25/10/00, *cpy.*)

The New York Idea ('*c.*': Apo., 27/11/07)

MITCHELL, NORMA [see *R. MEDCRAFT*]

MITCHELL, SYBIL C. [see also *F. M. GOSTLING* and *P. B. SYMONDS*]

A Daughter of Doyle's ('*c.*': Worthing, 7/4/10)

×A Morning's Work (Worthing, 14/2/12)

MITCHELL, T. [see *F. DELL*]

MITCHELSON, E. HILL [see *E. HILL-MITCHELSON*]

MOAR, MARTIN J.

×Compulsion. LC, Glasgow, 29/8/13

MOCKRIDGE, R. W.

×Remember Louvain (Court, 13/7/15, *m.*)

[*MOELLER, PHILIP* [see *J. L. A. BURRELL*]

Madame Sand ('*c.*': Academy, Baltimore, 20/10/17; Crit., N.Y., 19/11/17; D.Y., 3/6/20) *1920*

Caprice (St J., 4/6/29) *1929*

MOFFATT, GRAHAM

×Annie Laurie (Ath., Glasgow, 26/3/08)

Till the Bells Ring ('*c.*': Ath., Glasgow, 26/3/08; Playh., 6/6/11: originally called *Causey Saints*)

×The Concealed Bed in the Parlour (Ath., Glasgow, 23/4/09; Pav., 10/4/11)

A Scrape o' the Pen ('*c.*': Ath., Glasgow, 23/4/09; Com., 4/9/12) *Fr. 1912*

×Football Results (Pal., 25/9/11)
Bunty Pulls the Strings ('*c.*': Playh., 4/7/11, *m.*; H., 18/7/11) *Fr. 1932*
×The Maid and the Magistrate. *Fr. 1919*
Don't Tell ('*c.*': Alh., Glasgow, 29/3/20)
Susie Knots the Strings ('*c.*': Gar., 2/4/24, *m.*)
Granny ('*c.*': Alh., Glasgow, 22/3/26; Roy., 6/12/26) *Fr. 1932*
Susie Tangles the Strings. LC, '*c.*': Drill H., Camberley, 21/8/29. *Fr. 1932*

[*MOFFETT, CLEVELAND*
For Better, for Worse (New, 12/11/09, *cpy.*)

MONCK, WALTER NUGENT
×The Angel Boy (R. Academy of Music, 28/3/00; St G's H., 29/6/00)
×The Man in Rags (St G's H., 12/7/01, ADA students)
×The Adversity of Advertisement ('*triviality*': O.H., Yeovil, 26/1/03)
×The Domestic Fowl (O.H., Yeovil, 26/1/03)
×The Primrose Way ('*serious interlude*': O.H., Yeovil, 26/1/03; Emp., Balham, 21/9/03)
×Life's Measure ('*morality pl.*': Vic. H., 8/6/05, English Drama Soc.) *1906*
The Hour ('*c.*': Vic. H., 6/5/07, English Drama Soc.)
×The Song of Songs (Qns Gate H., 8/3/08, English Drama Soc.)
The Mill (Scala, 23/6/08, English Drama Soc.)
The Mancroft Pageant (Norwich, 26/6/12) *1912* (Norwich)
×Aucassin and Nicolette. LC, Norwich, 24/10/13: +*M. KINDER*)
The Masque of Anne Boleyn (Blickling H., Norfolk, 6/8/25)
×The Magic Casement. LC, Maddermarket, Norwich, 19/11/25
Robert, King of Sicily ('*miracle pl.*': Kirkstall Abbey, Leeds, 4/7/27)

MONCKTON, FRED
The Devil's Decoy (Gr., Aberavon, 2/8/09, *cpy.*)

MONCKTON, NOEL
×The Grey Lady. LC, St Andrew's H., Westminster, 31/1/24

MONCRIEFF, C. K. SCOTT [see *C. K. SCOTT-MONCRIEFF*]

MONCRIEFFE, EDWARD
[For an earlier play see *H. E. D.* v, 491]
My Runaway Daughter ('*f.*': T.H., Ilford, 12/9/02, *amat.*)
×The Girl from Where? ('*m.f.*': T.H., Ilford, 25/9/03, *amat.*)

MONK, JOHN O.
The Romance of a King (Qns, Manchester, 23/5/10)

MONKHOUSE, ALLAN NOBLE
×Reaping the Whirlwind ('*t.*': Gai., Manchester, 28/9/08) *1913* (in *Four Tragedies*)
×The Choice ('*problem pl.*': Gai., Manchester, 6/6/10) *1916* (in *War Plays*)

Mary Broome ('*c.*': Gai., Manchester, 9/10/11; Cor., 24/5/12) *1912*

×Resentment (Temperance H., Sheffield, 8/10/12) *1913* (in *Four Tragedies*)

The Education of Mr Surrage ('*c.*': Playh., L'pool, 4/11/12; Cent., 26/10/25) *1913*

The Stricklands. *1913* (in *Four Tragedies*)

×Nothing Like Leather (Gai., Manchester, 29/9/13)

Shamed Life. *1916* (in *War Plays*)

Night Watches. *1916* (in *War Plays*)

×The Grand Cham's Diamond (Rep., B'ham, 21/9/18) *1924*

The Conquering Hero (Alb. H., Leeds, 23/2/24; Aldw., 23/3/24, Pl. Actors; Qns, 3/4/24) *1923*

The Hayling Family (Aldw., 26/10/24, Pl. Actors) *1913* (in *Four Tragedies*)

First Blood (Stockport Garrick Soc., 1925; Little, Leeds, 11/1/26; Gate, 6/12/26) *1924*

Sons and Fathers (RADA, 24/1/26) *1925*

×The King of Barvender ('*md.*': A.L.S. Trav. Th., 1930) *1927*

×O Death, Where is Thy Sting? (LC, Arcadia, Scarborough, 13/3/28: A.L.S. Trav. Th., 1928) *1926*

The Rag. *1928*

×The Wiley One (A.L.S. Trav. Th., 1929)

×Nothing Like Leather ('*an indiscretion*') *1930* (*revised*)

Paul Felice. *1930*

MONRO, ERIC STUART [see also *H. HOWLAND*]

×The King's Riddle. LC, Longfield H., Ealing, 21/12/20

The Bankside Pantomime Book. *1930*

[This contains four short plays for children: 1. *Ali Baba*; 2. *Cinderella*; 3. *Dick Whittington*; and 4. *Aladdin*]

MONSON, W. J.

×Much Ado about Nothing. *1908* (*priv.*)

MONTAGUE, F. C.

Mother Eve (Ambass., 25/4/21, *m.*, Playwrights' Theatre)

Yetta Polowski (Kings., 12/11/22, Pl. Actors; Fortune, 2/4/25)

MONTAGUE, HAROLD

×First Aid to the Wounded. *Fr. 1905*

×Only Amateurs (Balfour Inst., L'pool, 17/4/09, *amat.*) *Fr. 1916*

×The Dud of the Family, or, The Worst Woman in the Profession ('*bsq.*': Crit. Restaurant, 27/2/10)

MONTAGUE, LEOPOLD [see *V. DE GARNO*]

[For earlier plays see *H. E. D.* v, 491]

×The Enemy's Country (T.H., Crediton, 7/11/00, *cpy.*)

×Love among the Roses ('*fant.oa.*', m. T. H. Bairnsfather: P.H., Bideford, 17/12/02, *amat.*)

×The Question of the Day (T.H., Crediton, 14/1/03, *amat.*)

The Lady Dentist ('*f.*': Broadway, New Cross, 10/4/05: +*A. ATWOOD*)

×The Three Fishers (T.H., Crediton, 15/11/05, *cpy.*)

The Sword of Honour ('*c.*': Balfour Inst., L'pool, 19/1/07)
The Dark Lady ('*f.c.*': T.H., Crediton, 4/1/11, *amat.*)
Something Must Be Done ('*c.*': T.H., Crediton, 30/10/23, *amat.*)

MONTAGUE, NELL ST JOHN
×Room 7 (Ambass., 22/4/20, *m.*)

MONTAGUE, PAUL
The Regimental Kiddy (Newcastle, 25/5/03; Gr., Fulham, 14/9/03)

MONTESOLE, MAX
×A Thing of Rags and Patches (Gr., Swansea, 9/11/07: +*C. REX*)

MONTGOMERY, HUGH
[For an earlier play see *H. E. D.* v, 491]
The Life Beyond (Gai., Leith, 30/5/04)
Wolves of London ('*r.d.*': Greenock, 13/8/04, *cpy.*)

[*MONTGOMERY, JAMES*
The Aviator ('*c.*': Lyc., Sheffield, 28/9/11, *cpy.*)
Ready Money ('*c.*': New, 12/8/12) *Fr. 1920*
Nothing But the Truth ('*f.*': Shubert, Newark, 13/3/16; Longacre, N.Y., 14/9/16; D.P., Eastbourne, 28/1/18; Sav., 5/2/18) *Fr. 1920*
Irene ('*m.c.*', m. H. Tierney: Maxine Elliott, N.Y., 15/8/16, as *Broadway and Buttermilk*; Poli's, Washington, 9/11/19; Vanderbilt, N.Y., 18/11/19; Emp., 7/4/20)

MONTGOMERY, LESLIE ALEXANDER [='*LYNN DOYLE*']

MONTRESOR, F. F.
Kathaeryn the Quene ('*historical d.*': Rep., Nottingham, 14/3/21)

[*MOODY, WILLIAM VAUGHN*
The Great Divide (Crit., 4/9/06; Adel., 15/9/09) *1909* (New York)

MOORE, AUGUSTUS [see also *F. CARRÉ*]
The Giddy Goat ('*f.c.*': O.H., Weymouth, 12/8/01; Terry's, 22/8/01)

MOORE, BERTHA
×Miss or Mrs? (Qns Gate H., 14/6/01) *Fr. 1903* (as *Mrs or Miss?*)
×A Happy Ending (Qns Gate H., 14/6/01; Court, 24/6/09, *m.*) *Fr. 1901*
×Neuchar's Junction (Qns Gate H., 14/6/01) *Fr. 1901*
×Aunt Jane's Flat (Qns Gate H., 14/6/01) *Fr. 1901*
×The Hermit (Roy., 6/6/05)
×The Kipper (Roy., 6/6/05)
×Prudence Foster ('*mezzotint*': Roy., 6/6/05)
×Just a Little Change (Alb. H., 28/6/07)
×Which is it? (Alb. H., 28/6/07)
×The Terror (Alb. H., 28/6/07)
×The Angel (Court, 24/6/09, *m.*)
×Bunkered. *Fr. 1922*

[*MOORE, CARLYLE*
Stop Thief! (Gai., N.Y., 25/12/12; York, 14/10/15; New, 21/10/15)

MOORE, DOROTHEA [see also *A. MACLEAN*]
My Lady Bellamy (Margate, 11/4/10; Woolwich, 20/6/10)
Lilies and Lavender ('*r.pl.*': Forum Club, 16/6/29; Nottingham, 15/7/29)

MOORE, DUGALD [see also *L. CLARANCE*]
×The Red Cross (Consett, 16/12/01)

MOORE, Miss E. HAMILTON
Ygraine ('*t.*': Qns, Manchester, 14/5/04)
×A Dove Uncaged (Gai., Manchester, 18/10/09) *Fr. 1912*
×The Blood Flower (Gai., Manchester, 13/11/11)
×A Little Christmas Miracle (Abbey, Dublin, 26/12/12)

MOORE, F. C.
×By Word of Mouth (Abbey, Dublin, 27/1/15: +*W. P. FLANAGAN*)

MOORE, FRANK FRANKFORT
[For earlier plays see *H. E. D.* v, 492]
×An Impudent Comedian (Cor., 16/11/09, *m.*)
×Houp-la! (New, Oxford, 3/5/15)
Kitty Clive and Other Plays in One Act. *Fr. 1929*
[This contains: 1. *Kitty Clive*; 2. *The Jessamy Bride*; 3. *A Poor Actress*; and 4. *The Sword of Damocles*]

MOORE, GEORGE
[For his earlier plays see *H. E. D.* v, 492]
The Bending of the Bough ('*c.*': Gai., Dublin, 21/2/00, Irish Lit. Theatre) *1900*
Diarmuid and Grania (Gai., Dublin, 21/10/01, Irish Lit. Theatre: +*W. B. YEATS*)
The Apostle. *1911* (Dublin); *1923*
Esther Waters (Apo., 10/12/11, St. Soc.: dramatised from his own novel, 1894) *1913*
Elizabeth Cooper ('*c.*': H., 22/6/13, St. Soc.; St J., 17/7/23, *m.*, revised as *The Coming of Gabrielle*) *1913*; *1920* (as *The Coming of Gabrielle*)
×The Making of an Immortal (Arts, 1/4/28) *1927* (New York)
The Passing of the Essenes (Arts, 1/10/30) *1930*

MOORE, G. HAMILTON
×Aunty Bligh (Gt. Qn. St., 24/4/05, Mermaid Rep. Theatre Soc.)

MOORE, J. CHARLES
Secrets of State (Court, 1/6/11, *amat.*)

MOORE, JOSEPH
The Girl from Granada ('*oa.*': Delecta H., Watford, 28/1/19)

MOORE, MARSHALL
The Girl from over the Border ('*m.ext.*', m. C. Locknane and A. J. Lawrence: K's, Hamm., 18/5/08)
×Two Toreadors (Empress, 2/8/09)

MOORE, SPENCER
Aurelian ('*d. of the later Empire*') *1905*

MOORE, THOMAS STURGE

Absalom ('*chronicle pl.*') *1903* (*priv.*)

×Aphrodite against Artemis ('*t.*': K's H., 1/4/06, Literary Theatre Club) *1901* (*priv.*)

Mariamne. *1911* (*priv.*)

×The Wilderness ('*Greek ballad dance*': Emp., 19/4/15: +*GUSTAVE FERRARI*)

×Judith (Qns, 23/1/16, St. Soc.)

Tragic Mothers. *1920*

[This contains three short plays: 1. *Medea* (LC, Hill Crest, Boar's Hill, Oxford, 30/12/24); 2. *Niobe*; and 3. *Tyrfing*]

MOORMAN, FREDERIC WILLIAM

The May King. *1914*

Plays of the Ridings. *1919*

[This contains three short plays: 1. *An All Souls' Night's Dream*; 2. *Potter Thompson*; and 3. *The Ewe Lamb*]

MOORWOOD, ROLAND

Jill the Reckless ('*c.*': YMCA H., Sheffield, 21/10/26, *amat.*: dramatised from the novel (1921) by P. G. Wodehouse)

MORAUD, M. R.

×A Foggy Day (Belfast, 23/7/00)

MORGAN, CHARLES D.

×Search Me! LC, Ambass., 7/12/16

MORGAN, FRED [see *H. MARLOW*]

MORGAN, H. E. [see *J. WELLS*]

MORGAN, J. DUDLEY

The End of a Story (Wynd., 12/4/02)

'*MORGAN, STEPHEN*'

The Serf (Abbey, Dublin, 5/10/20)

MORIN, CATHERINE A.

Pedlar's Pack...Philippine: Plays. *1924*

[This contains two plays written in collaboration with *MAUD MORIN* – 1. *Pedlar's Pack*, and 2. *Philippine, or The Quest in the Greenwood*]

Pocket-Sleeve. *1927*

[This contains two short plays for children, also written in collaboration with *MAUD MORIN* – 1. *Pocket-Sleeve*, and 2. *Puppets*]

MORIN, MAUD [see also *CATHERINE A. MORIN*]

×The Patient Elizabeth. LC, Edin., 23/10/24

MORISON, MARY

Lonely Lives (Str., 1/4/01; Court, 8/11/12: translated from *Einsame Menschen* (1891) by G. Hauptmann) *1898*

The Weavers (C.P., 1/4/01; Scala, 10/12/07: translated from *Die Weber* (1893) by G. Hauptmann) *1899*

The Jensen Family (Crit., 23/4/01: translated from a play by E. Höyer)

MORLAND, FRANK H.
[For earlier plays see *H. E. D.* v, 493]
A Pair of Parrots ('*f.c.*': O.H., Belfast, 21/10/01)

MORLEY, CUTHBERT
×A Midnight Meeting (Glo., 21/5/10)

MORLEY, R. MALCOLM [see also *A. ARGYLL* and '*H. SETON*']
×How to Be a Hero (Rehearsal, 2/12/09, *m.*)

MOROV, ANTON
×The Receipt (Crit., 16/6/14)

MORPETH, WILLIAM
Above Suspicion (H., 28/6/11)

MORRELL, BEATRICE M.
Pageants of the Christian Year. *1923* (Faith Press)
[This contains three religious pageants]

MORRELL, CHARLES
Mother of Pearl (Little, 8/5/27)
Dracula (Court, Warrington, 5/11/27: from the novel (1897) by Bram Stoker)

MORRELL, FRANCES
Venture and Vengeance (Alh., Openshaw, 8/12/11)

MORRIS, A. NEILSON
×As Man Sows (Myddleton H., Islington, 12/12/07, *amat.*; Passmore Edwards Settlement, 20/3/15, The Players)
×The Chosen One (Alb. H., 21/2/08, *amat.*; Rehearsal, 7/5/14)
×The End of the Story (Court, 3/3/09, *amat.*)
×My Lady's Glove (Rehearsal, 11/3/09, Curtain Raisers: +*H. C. FERRABY*)
×The River of Light (K's H., 6/4/10, *cpy.*) *Fr. 1917*
×A Daughter of Poland (Marlb., Holloway, 23/4/10)
×The Verdict of the Majority (Court, 18/12/10, Pl. Actors)
×The Honour of the Braccios (Clavier H., 29/4/12, Twelfth Night Players)
×Trapped (Clavier H., 29/4/12, Twelfth Night Players)
×The Panther (Passmore Edwards Settlement, 20/3/15, The Players)
Rosalyn Plays a Part (Crippl. Inst., 1/11/21)
Enter Elizabeth. LC, Hampstead Conservatoire, 9/4/23
×The Heart's Desire. LC, Crippl. Inst., 17/3/24

MORRIS, ALFRED J.
Princess Lolah; or, The Love of the Rajah of Tittipompom ('*c.o.*', m. W. Tilbury: Pav., 18/2/01; Court, 21/10/01)

MORRIS, ARTHUR
×'Shop!' (P.H., Harrow, 13/4/04). *Fr. 1904*
×'Tilda 'elps a Bit. *Fr. 1916*

MORRIS, Mrs CLAYTON
×The Dupe. LC, Parish R., Boldmere, B'ham, 1/11/23

MORRIS, FRED J.

×The Deserter (Qns, Manchester, 21/8/16)

×The Girl from Lancashire (Alex., 12/3/17)

×The Carry On. LC, Scala, Saltcoats, 12/3/18: title later changed to *Peter*

×The Stroke of Ten (Rehearsal, 4/4/18, *m.*)

×The Lamp that Failed (Granville, Walham Green, 7/6/20: +*C. LANGHAM*)

×The Garden of Anna (Coloss., Oldham, 4/4/21; Hippo., Putney, 6/6/21)

Cecelia ('*m.c.*': Parish H., Hessle, 10/4/23, *amat.*)

×Rush Tactics. LC, Gr., Woking, 14/9/23.

MORRIS, G.

×While There's Life –. LC, Norwich, 22/1/18

MORRIS, JOSEPHINE A. M.

Kenilworth. LC, '*masque*': Worcester, 21/4/14

MORRIS, NOEL [see *E. BLYTHE*]

MORRIS, PAUL [see *A. F. ROBBINS*]

MORRIS, PHYLLIS

The Rescue Party ('*c.*': Reg., 28/3/26, Rep. Players; Com., 26/4/26)

Made in Heaven (Everyman, 5/10/26: called also *The False Claim*)

Tinker, Tailor – ('*c.*': Roy., 8/3/28)

MORRIS, WILLIAM [see *F. WYATT*]

MORRISON, ARTHUR

×That Brute Simmons (New, 30/8/04: +*H. C. SARGENT*) *Fr. 1904*

×The Dumb-Cake (Hicks', 19/6/07: +*R. PRYCE*) *Fr. 1907*

×A Stroke of Business (Kings., 18/11/07: +*H. W. C. NEWTE*)

MORRISON, GEORGE E.

Alonzo Quixano, otherwise Don Quixote (Memorial, Stratford-upon-Avon, 3/5/07; Cor., 2/3/08: +*R. P. STEWART*) *1895*

×The Shortest Story of All (Little, 17/1/21)

MORRISON, KENNETH [see *W. T. IVORY*]

MORRISON, R. F. [see *W. G. JEFFERSON*]

[Several playlets produced at music-halls]

MORROW, HARRY C. [='*GERALD MACNAMARA*']

MORSHIEL, GEORGE S. [see *GEORGE SHIELS*]

MORTIMER, ARTHUR FERRIS [see *M. MAXWELL*]

MORTIMER, Mrs ARTHUR

×A Pot of Caviare (O.H., Jersey, 13/11/08, *amat.*)

MORTIMER, CHARLES

×Evidence (Bij., 2/4/27, Soho Players)

MORTIMER, JAMES

[For earlier plays see *H. E. D.* v, 494 and 807]

My Bachelor Past ('*c.*': Wynd., 1/8/01: adapted from *Célimar, le bien-aimé* (1863) by E. Labiche and A. Delacour)

MORTIMER, LEONARD

[For earlier plays see *H. E. D.* v, 494]

×Dutton's Dilemma (Gr., Rawtenstall, 28/9/06)
×The Passing of Paul (S.W., 30/12/07)
×The Mischief-Makers (Pal., Camberwell, 28/9/08)
×The Golden Ace, or, Bubbles (Bed., 4/1/09)
×A State Secret (Pal., Tottenham, 30/8/09)
×Wild Woodbine (Emp., Edmonton, 5/12/10)
×Billy Boy (Pal., Bow, 13/3/11)
×Dwellers in Darkness (Pal., E. Ham, 27/3/11)
The Glorious Day ('*m.pl.*': Playh., Llanhilleth, 26/12/14; E.C., 15/2/15, altered into a revue; Emp., Camberwell, 16/8/15, revised as *Don't Be Silly*)
When Love Creeps in Your Heart ('*md.*': E.C., 17/1/16)
Mother Machree (E.C., 2/10/16)
The Lane without a Turning (Imp., Canning Town, 30/7/17; Col., Burslem, 3/9/17, as *Damaged Lives*)
Deliver the Goods (Stratford, 3/12/17)
The Black Book (Gr., Croydon, 15/7/18)
The Soul of Motherhood. LC, Playh., Faversham, 5/9/18
All a Girl Can Give. LC, Emp., Alexandria, 19/1/20: title later changed to *Just Call Me Bill*
The House that John Built. LC, Playh., Dorking, 25/2/21
×Tony's Drum ('*supernatural playlet*': Kennington, 28/3/21)
Me and My Boy (Pal., Battersea, 18/9/22)

MORTLOCK-BROWN, Miss [='*RUTH MELVILL*']

MORTON, EDWARD

The Machine (Rep., Bushey, 18/2/14)

MORTON, GUY MAINWARING [='*PETER TRAILL*']

['*MORTON, HUGH*' [=*C. M. S. McLELLAN*]

[For earlier plays see *H. E. D.* v, 495]

An American Beauty ('*m.c.*', m. G. Kerker: Shaft., 25/4/00)
The Girl from Up There ('*m.c.*', m. G. Kerker: D.Y., 23/4/01) *1901*
The Whirl of the Town ('*m. absurdity*', m. G. Kerker: Cent., 11/9/01)
Glittering Gloria ('*f.*': Wynd., 21/7/03)

[*MORTON, MARTHA*

[For earlier plays see *H. E. D.* v, 497]

A Four-Leaf Clover ('*c.*': Sav., 30/9/05, *cpy.*)

MORTON, MICHAEL [see also *L. MERRICK*]

[For earlier plays see *H. E. D.* v, 497]

Colonel Newcome (Terry's, 25/4/01, *cpy.*; H.M., 29/5/06)
Resurrection (H.M., 17/2/03: adapted from the play, *Résurrection* (1905), by Henry Bataille, based on Leo Tolstoi's novel)

Marguerite (Cor., 5/9/04: adapted from *Le montansier* (1904) by G. A. de Caillavet, R. de Flers and H. G. Jeoffrin-Ibels)
The Little Stranger ('*f.*': Gr., Middlesbrough, 9/10/05, *cpy.*; Canterbury, 8/2/06; Crit., 14/2/06; called originally *Home Sweet Home*)
My Wife ('*c.*': H., 28/5/07: adapted from P. Gavault and R. de Charvay, *Mlle Josette, ma femme*, 1906) *Fr. 1912*
×Charlie, the Sport (H., 25/7/07)
Her Father (H., 28/1/08: adapted from A. Guinon and A. Bouchinet, *Son père*, 1907)
×The Heart of the City (B'ham, 8/3/09: +*J. WELLESLEY*)
Detective Sparks. LC, '*c.*': Com., 17/8/09
Tantalising Tommy ('*c.*': Playh., 15/2/10: adapted from P. Gavault, *La petite chocolatière*, 1908)
The Runaway ('*c.*': Lyc., N.Y., 9/10/11)
×I Dine with My Mother (Pal., 21/2/10; Sav., 26/5/13)
×What a Game! (Pal., 31/3/13)
The Yellow Ticket (Eltinge, N.Y., 20/1/14; Playh., 12/9/17)
Jeff (Emp., Syracuse, 2/10/16)
×My Superior Officer (Emp., Chiswick, 27/11/16)
Remnant (Roy., 3/3/17)
On with the Dance (Nat., Washington, 22/10/17; Republic, N.Y., 29/10/17)
In the Night Watch (Oxf., 2/12/18: adapted from C. Farrère and L. Népoty, *La veillée d'armes*, 1917)
Woman to Woman (Hudson, Schenectady, 2/3/21; Glo., 8/9/21)
The Talking Shop (Apo., Atlantic City, 11/4/21)
The Guilty One (Apo., Atlantic City, 6/8/22: +*P. TRAILL*)
×After the Theatre (Goldsmid H., Sudeley, 29/8/24: +'*P. TRAILL*') *1924*
Fallen Angels (P.H., Sutton, 13/10/24; Cent., 23/10/24: +'*P. TRAILL*')
Five Minutes Fast (Cent., 19/2/25)
By Right of Conquest (Scala, 10/5/25, Pl. Actors: +'*P. TRAILL*')
Salvage (Q, 22/11/26; Wynd., 4/4/28, as *The Stranger in the House*: +'*P. TRAILL*')
Riceyman Steps (Ambass., 25/11/26, *m.*: dramatised from the novel (1923) by Arnold Bennett)
Alibi (P.W., 15/5/28: from a novel by Agatha Christie) *Fr. 1929*
Because of Irene (D.P., Eastbourne, 18/3/29; Little, 6/6/29: +'*P. TRAILL*')
Beauty ('*c.*': Str., 16/7/29)

MOSLEY, HERBERT
Soul Mates ('*f.*': Pier, Brighton, 10/5/26)

MOSS, GEOFFREY McNEILL
Sweet Pepper (Everyman, 1/12/25: from his own novel, 1923)

MOSS, J. FARRIES
×A Jolly Good Sort (Parish Church H., Ladywell, 17/5/05)

MOSS, MABEL J.

×Johnny Explains (Rehearsal, 5/2/14)
×A Legend of Myona. LC, '*fairy pl.*': Holy Trinity Parish H., Stroud Green, 6/5/18
×The Charm. *1920*

MOUILLOT, FREDERICK [see *E. A. PARRY*]

MOUILLOT, GERTRUDE

×A Divided Duty (Lyc. Club, 30/3/09)
×Master (Scala, 12/11/09)
×Collaborators (Gai., 26/12/10: +*A. ELDRED*)

MOULE, FRED

[For earlier plays see *H. E. D.* v, 498]
A Little Vagrant (Alex., Cleethorpes, 8/7/1897; Gr., Boscombe, 19/3/00; Morton's, Greenwich, 16/7/00: +*E. W. AVERY*)
The Life that Kills ('*pl. of passion*': Smethwick, 21/6/01; Dewsbury, 16/12/01; Sur., 9/6/02)
A Heart of Stone (Edmonton, 11/8/02: +*C. H. LONGDEN*)
Bigamy (Croydon, 8/2/04; S.W., 28/11/10, revised with *F. BAUGH*: title later changed to *The Worst Girl of All*)
×What Women Do (M'sex, 9/12/07)
×Doreen (Emp., Ardwick, 8/3/09)
×The Annexers (S.W., 22/3/09)
×A Broken Butterfly (Pal., Battersea, 5/4/09)
×Adventures of the Black Hand (S.W., 28/3/10)
×Dare-Devil Dripping (Sur., 4/4/10; Pal., Battersea, 26/12/10, revised as *Admiral Daredevil*: +*E. D. NICHOLS*)
×Gretna Green (S.W., 11/7/10)
×The Yellow Bird (Pal., Bow, 22/8/10: +*E. D. NICHOLLS*)
Rogues of the Ring (Foresters, 30/10/11: expanded from *Gretna Green*, see above)
The Black Hand ('*detective d.*': Foresters, 26/12/11; Foresters, 15/3/15, revised as *A Belgian Princess*; Woolwich, 2/8/15)
The Mormon Danger (Foresters, 24/6/12)
Would You Hang Him? ('*problem pl.*': Pal., Bow, 16/12/12: title later changed to *Should the Man Speak?*)
The Great Murder Mystery. LC, Pal., Bow, 11/9/15
×Jim Jam Jim (Reg., Gt Yarmouth, 26/10/16)
×Woman Power (Pal., Battersea, 4/12/16: +*F. BROUGH*)

MOUNTFORD, HARRY

[For earlier plays see *H. E. D.* v, 498]
Tess (Gr., Blackpool, 5/1/00, *cpy.*: dramatised from Thomas Hardy's novel)

MOWBRAY, ALAN

Dinner is Served ('*f.c.*': Players, 7/2/30)

MOYLAN, THOMAS KING

Paid in His Own Coin (Abbey, Dublin, 22/4/09)
×The Naboclish (Abbey, Dublin, 31/5/10)
×Oh! Lawsy-Me! (Emp., Dublin, 7/5/17)

× Tactics (Irish Club, 9/8/17; Court, 1/4/18)
× The Movies (Emp., Dublin, 4/3/18)
× Flat-Iron Flynn (Emp., Dublin, 28/4/19)
The Curse of the Country (Abbey, Dublin, 14/12/19, Leinster Players) *1917* (Dublin, as *The Curse of the Countryside*)

MOYSTON, G. [see *L. BELLINGER*]

MUGGERIDGE, MARIE
× The Rest Cure. *Fr. 1906*
× After Seven Years (Belfast, 26/4/07)
× A Long Journey (Birkenhead, 5/10/08)
× Roma (Empress, 6/12/09)

MUIR, JESSIE
Beyond Human Power (Roy., 7/11/01: adapted from *Over ævne* (1883) by B. Björnson)

MUIR, WILLA
Two Anglo-Saxon Plays: The Oil Islands (and) Warren Hastings, by Lion Feuchtwanger. *1929*

MUKERJI, DHAN GOPAL
× Kunala. LC, Lord Leverhulme's house, 1/9/21

MULDOON, J. MALACHI
× A Hospital Ward (Qns, Dublin, 4/9/11, *m.*)
A Trinity Student ('*c.*') *1913* (Dublin)
Children of the Lost Provinces. *1930* (Dublin)

MULGAN, ALAN E.
Three Plays of New Zealand. *1923*
[This contains: 1. *For Love of Appin* (Auckland, 16/8/20); 2. *The Daughter*; and 3. *The Voice of the People*]

MULLALLY, DON
Conscience (Little, 24/10/29)

MULLORD, DOROTHY
× Dicky's Mother (Foresters, 24/10/10)
In the Hands of the Huns (Hippo., Willesden, 12/4/15; Hippo., Croydon, 8/11/15, as *The Princess and the Soldier*)
The Story of the Angelus (Hippo., Willesden, 7/2/16)
The Man with Three Wives (Hippo., Willesden, 28/8/16)
Across the Sands of Time (Pal., Battersea, 11/3/18)
Married on Leave (Woolwich, 15/4/18; E.C., 22/4/18; Emp., Penge, 22/9/19, revised as *The King of the Air*)
For Services Rendered (Hippo., Willesden, 3/3/19)
A Mother Should Tell (E.C., 18/8/19: +*I. P. GORE*)
The Priest and the Sinner (Hippo., Willesden, 8/12/19: +*I. P. GORE*)
Her Night of Sacrifice (E.C., 24/1/21)
His Chinese Bride (E.C., 25/7/21: +*I. P. GORE*)
Traffic in Souls (Emp., Woolwich, 4/9/22: +*I. P. GORE*)
The Wife who Came Back. LC, Coll., 1/6/23
Mademoiselle from Armentières (Coll., 22/8/27: +*CLIFFORD REAN*)

[*MUMFORD, ETHEL WATTS*
Maw; or, The Squab Lady ('*c.*': Terry's, 6/10/10, *m.*: +*M. HERFORD*)
Goodnight, Nurse ('*f.*': Gai., N.Y., 25/2/18; Pier, Brighton, 24/2/19)

MUNK, EDMUND
Lilac Land ('*m.c.*', m. B. Page: Mechanics' H., Nottingham, 8/5/11, *amat.*)

'*MUNRO, C. K.*'
The Wanderers (Qns, 21/3/15, St. Soc.)
At Mrs Beam's ('*c.*': Kings., 27/2/21, St. Soc.; Roy., 2/4/23) *1923*; *Fr. 1925*
The Rumour (Glo., 3/12/22, St. Soc.; Fest., Cambridge, 14/2/27; Court, 21/2/29) *1923*
Progress (New, 20/1/24, St. Soc.; Fest., Cambridge, 17/10/27) *1924*
Storm; or, The Battle of Tinderley Down ('*c.*': Ambass., 13/8/24) *1924*
The Mountain; or, The Story of Captain Yevan ('*symbolic d.*': Shaft., 30/5/26, St. Soc.) *1926*
Cocks and Hens (Roy., 3/3/27)
Veronica ('*c.*': Arts, 18/9/29)

MUNRO, H. H. [='*SAKI*']

MUNRO, NEIL
Macpherson ('*c.*': Roy., Glasgow, 20/11/09)

MUNRO, NOEL
×An Evening on Dartmoor. *1930*

MURE, Miss B. G.
×A Counter Reformation (Ben Greet Academy, 7/4/11)

MURPHY, IMOGEN
Seven Plays for Little Players. *1925*
[This contains seven short plays: 1. *Truants*; 2. *The Little Stranger*; 3. *Petronilla's Visitors*; 4. *The Portal, or The Grave and Gate*; 5. *Let's Pretend*; 6. *The Three Bears*; and 7. *Snow-White*]

MURRAY, ALFRED [see *J. T. TANNER*]

MURRAY, DAVID CHRISTIE
[For earlier plays see *H. E. D.* v, 500]
George Garth (Gr., Fulham, 28/7/02: +*H. MURRAY* and *J. L. SHINE*)
The Coming Race (St G's H., 2/1/05: dramatised from the novel (1871) by Lord Lytton: +*J. N. MASKELYNE*)

[*MURRAY, DOUGLAS*
×A Sentimental Cuss (Vaud., 31/10/07)
The Great Mrs Alloway (Glo., 8/11/09)
Kit (Newcastle, 20/11/11)
The New Duke ('*f.*': Manchester, 25/8/13; Com., 30/9/13)
×A Fine Bit o' Work (Pal., Hamm., 6/11/16)

×Burgess Decides (Hippo., Leeds, 17/9/17; Pallad., 3/12/17)
The Man from Toronto ('*c.*': Roy., 30/5/18) *Fr. 1919*
Uncle Ned ('*c.*': Lyc., Sheffield, 24/3/19; St J., 27/3/20) *Fr. 1920*
Blink. LC, '*c.*': Aldw., 8/10/20
Sarah of Soho ('*c.*': Sav., 23/2/22)
Time and the Hour (Arts, 2/10/29; Hippo., Golder's Green, 14/10/29, as *What Fools We Are*)

MURRAY, Sir GILBERT (GEORGE GILBERT AIMÉE MURRAY)
[For an earlier play see *H. E. D.* v, 500. In the following list are cited only those dramas for which there is evidence of performance: it should, however, be remembered that Murray's printed translations were of wide influence on numerous playwrights of this period and that many were presented by amateurs]
Andromache (Gar., 25/2/01) *1900*; *1914* (revised)
[It should be noted that this is an original play, not a translation]
Hippolytus (Lyr., 26/5/04: translated from the play by Euripides) *1902*
The Trojan Women (Court, 11/4/05: translated from the play by Euripides) *1905*
Electra (Court, 16/1/06: translated from the play by Euripides) *1905*
Medea (Sav., 22/10/07, *m.*: translated from the play by Euripides) *1906*
The Bacchae (Court, 10/11/08: translated from the play by Euripides) *1904*
Œdipus Rex (C.G., 15/1/12: translated from the play by Sophocles, adapted by *W. L. COURTNEY*) *1911*
Iphigenia in Tauris (Kings., 19/3/12: translated from the play by Euripides) *1910*
Alcestis (Glastonbury, 26/8/22, m. by R. Boughton; C.G., 11/1/24: translated from the play by Euripides) *1915*

MURRAY, HENRY [see *D. C. MURRAY*]

MURRAY, KEITH
Some Bird ('*c.*': New, Salisbury, 25/9/16)

MURRAY, PATRICIA [see *Mrs L. MYERS*]

MURRAY, THOMAS CORNELIUS
×The Wheel of Fortune (Cork, 2/12/09; Abbey, Dublin, 11/9/13, revised as *Sovereign Love*; Court, 8/6/14)
Birthright (Abbey, Dublin, 27/10/10; Court, 8/6/11) *1911* (Dublin); *1928*
Maurice Harte (Court, 20/6/12) *1912*
×A Stag at Bay. *1912*
Spring and Other Plays. *1917* (Dublin)
[This contains three short plays: 1. *Spring* ('*t.*': Abbey, Dublin, 7/1/18); 2. *Sovereign Love* ('*c.*': Abbey, Dublin, 11/9/13; Court, 8/6/14); and 3. *The Briery Gap* ('*t.*')]
Aftermath (Abbey, Dublin, 10/1/22) *1922* (Dublin)
Autumn Fire (Abbey, Dublin, 8/9/24; Q, 22/3/26; Little, 13/4/26) *1925*

×The Pipe in the Fields (Abbey, Dublin, 3/10/27; Playh., L'pool, 1/6/28) *1911* (Dublin); *1928*
The Blind Wolf (Abbey, Dublin, 30/4/28)

MURRAY, TOM E.
The Harem Doctor ('*m.pl.*': Hippo., Manchester, 4/9/11: +*E. BAYNES*)

MURRAY, V. T.
×Bringing It Home (Ashburton R., Red Lion Square, 17/7/26, *amat.*)

MURREY, BERTHA
The Godless. LC, Wynd., 5/11/25: translated from a play by Karen Bramson.
The Lady-in-Law ('*c.*': Wynd., 29/9/27: translated from *Maître Balbec et son mari* (1926) by G. Berr and L. Verneuil)
The Man They Buried ('*c. of fear*': Ambass., 6/6/28: translated from a play by Karen Bramson) *1929*

MURRY, JOHN MIDDLETON
Cinnamon and Angelica. *1920*

'*MUSKERRY, DAVID*' [=*J. FULTON*]
The Poor Must Live (Qns, Longton, 23/1/05, Carlton, Greenwich, 13/2/05)
The Dear Old Homeland ('*md.*': Sunderland, 27/8/06)
A Girl Redeemed from Sin (S. Shields, 15/7/07; Aston, 19/8/07; Stratford, 24/2/08)
A Collier's Daughter (Alex., B'ham, 18/6/09)

MUSKERRY, WILLIAM [see *E. C RACKSTRAW* and *A. SHIRLEY*]
[For earlier plays see *H. E. D.* v, 500–1]

MYDDLETON, FAY
×Dewy Dear. LC, Crippl. Inst., 26/5/23

MYDDLETON-MYLES, A.
The White Slave Traffic (S.W., 24/3/13: title later changed to *Should the Preacher Tell?*)
The Worst Girl of All ('*society d.*': E.C., 24/11/13)
The Great White Silence, or, Heroes of the Antarctic (S.W., 13/4/14)
War, Red War (Brixton, 31/5/15; E.C., 2/8/15, as *The Girl Who Waits at Home*)
×The Real Lady Raffles (Hippo., Rotherhithe, 11/9/16)
Beware Germans (Pal., Battersea, 11/11/18)
×What a Birthday! (Hippo., Putney, 2/12/18)
Silver Threads among the Gold (Pal., Battersea, 1/11/20)

MYERS, Mrs LEO (MARTHA)
×Kitty's Catch (Margaret Morris, 28/2/16, *m.*: +*P. MURRAY*)
×Take Cover (Shakespeare Hut, Gower St., 1/3/19)
×A Scrap of Silk (Forum Club, 2/5/20)
×Wolf! Wolf! (Pal., 15/11/21, *m.*, Lyc. Club)
Notoriety ('*c.*': Gar., 12/5/29, Lyc. Club: +*E. PAGE*)

MYLES, A. MYDDLETON [see *A. MYDDLETON-MYLES*]

MYLO, JULIETTE
×Yvette's Dilemma (Cosmopolis, 7/3/13)

MYTTON, HUGH
×The First Locust. *Fr. 1911*
The Masque of Time (Crane H., L'pool, 20/12/24, *amat.*) *1911* (Surbiton)
Violets ('*r.d.*': Ass. R., Surbiton, 13/1/12)
×Tanks (D.P., Eastbourne, 28/2/18)
The Masque of Empire. *1921*
×Christ-Love: The Angel of the Star. *1926*

'*NAGOH, LEAHCIM*' [=*MICHAEL HOGAN*]

NAGRA, NELLA
Educating Anne ('*light c.*': Q, 27/2/28)

NALLY, T. H.
The Spancel of Death (announced at the Abbey, Dublin, for performance on 25/4/16, but apparently not produced)
Finn Varra Maa: The Irish Santa Klaus (Dublin, 26/12/17) *1917* (Dublin)

NANCE, FREDERIC H.
Where's Your Wife? ('*m.c.*': Pav., New Brighton, 7/3/10)

NANKIVELL, AMY [see *E. RYND*]

NAPIER, LEOPOLD [see *W. E. BRANDON*]

NAPPEL, A.
A Tragic Comedy. LC, Drill H., Northwich, 2/5/13

NASH, GEORGE [see *W. GRAHAME*]

NASH, PERCY
The Suffrage Girl ('*m.c.*', m. F. Armstrong: Court, 3/3/11, *amat.*)

NASMITH, FRANK G. [see also *S. HOUGHTON*]
The Intriguers (Ath., Manchester, 19/10/06, *amat.*: +*S. HOUGHTON*)

NATHAN, WILFRID A.
×Hamlet; or, The Little Glass Slipper. LC, St Gabriel's H., Cricklewood, 4/4/21
×One Good Turn. LC, St Gabriel's H., Cricklewood, 6/4/21

NATION, WILLIAM HAMILTON CODRINGTON
[For an earlier play see *H. E. D.* v, 808]
×Weighed in the Balance (Terry's, 6/2/07)
×A Wolf in Sheep's Clothing (Roy., 21/11/08)
×The Land of Nonlocia (Roy., 4/3/11)

NEAL, R. G. [see *E. A. SYKES*]

NEALE, A.
Soap v. Society. LC, T.H., Arundel, 16/4/14

NEALE, RALPH [see also *ADA CHESTERTON*]
The Watcher (Everyman, 20/1/30)

'NEAN'
Oine, or, The Oreole and the Wondrous Gem. *1911*

NEAVE, ADAM
Woman and Superwoman (*'a c. of 1963'*) *1914*

NEEDHAM, RAYMOND
×Anna Michaelovna (Rehearsal, 4/7/09)
The Celibate (Court, 3/12/11, Pl. Actors)
×Yacht 'Grasshopper' (Clavier H., 10/3/12, Arts and Dram. Club)
×The Novice (Clavier H., 10/3/12, Arts and Dram. Club)

NEILL, A. S.
×The Piper Passes. LC, Inst., Hampstead Gdn Suburb, 13/5/21
×Casting Out Fear. LC, Inst., Hampstead Gdn Suburb, 13/5/21

NEILSON, FRANCIS [see also *E. G. HEMMERDE*]
The Desire for Change (*'c.'*: Playh., 26/10/25)

NEILSON, MARIE
×When the Tide Comes In (*'m.pl.'*, m. H. Matthews: Pav., Eastbourne, 8/10/13)

NELLEMOSE, W.
×Television (Glo., 27/9/26, Green Room Rag)

NELSON, ERNEST K.
[Various sketches and playlets produced at music-halls]

[*NELSON, GEORGE M.*
Strings (*'c.'*: P's, Manchester, 21/5/17: +*M. VELSOR-SMITH*)

NELSON, JOSEPH
The Golden Age (*'m.fant.'*: Southsea, 11/7/25, *amat.*: +*J. ARMSTRONG*)

NELSON, LARS P.
Gurli (*'c.'*: Gr., Croydon, 21/5/00: +*A. CANTAM*) translated from a play by H. Christiernson)

NELSON, THOMAS
Dickson Dalwood, R.N. (O.H., Southport, 17/10/27: +*R. THORNDIKE*)

NERREY, TERENCE
The Armourer's Daughter (Lyc., Eccles, 14/10/01)
The Goddess of Destruction (*'r.d.'*: Qns, L'pool, 6/3/08, *cpy.*; New, Oswestry, 12/2/12, *revised cpy.*)
[This author's name is cited both as Nerrey and as Norrey: the former appears to be correct]

NESBIT, E.
×The King's Highway (Freemasons' H., Woolwich, 11/5/05, *amat.*)
×The Philandrist; or, The Lady Fortune-Teller (Freemasons' H., Woolwich, 11/5/05, *amat.*: +*D. DEAKIN*)
×The Magician's Heart (*'fairy pl.'*: St G's H., 14/1/07)

NESBIT, W. D.

The Girl of My Dreams ('*m.pl.*', m. K. Hoschna: Ladbr. H., 22/7/10, *cpy.*)

NESBITT, C. M.

A Demshur Man, or, The Devil looks after his own ('*rural c.*': Inst., Hampstead, 12/4/23) *Fr. 1924*

×The Net. *1926* (in *The Marble God, and Other One-Act Plays*, Oxford)

NESBITT, FRANK

The Magic Whistle, and Other Fairy Tale Plays. *1906*

[This contains six plays: 1. *The Magic Whistle*; 2. *The Mole King's Daughter*; 3. *Rumpelstiltskin*; 4. *The Golden Goose*; 5. *Beauty and the Beast*; and 6. *The Goose Girl*]

NESBITT, MARGARET [see *G. COPELAND*]

NESBITT, ROY [see *W. R. FEARON*]

NETTLEFOLD, ARCHIBALD

×The Dong with a Luminous Nose. LC, Kings., 5/10/21

NEVILL, JOHN CRANSTOUN

Two and Two ('*c.*': Str., 27/3/27, Pl. Actors)

NEVINSON, MARGARET WYNNE

×In the Workhouse (Kings., 8/5/11, *m.*, Pioneer Players)

NEVITT, MARY ROSS

×The Rostof Pearls. *Fr. 1912*

NEW, J. C.

Aunt Gabrielle ('*c.*': Strathblaine H., St John's Hill, 5/6/08, *cpy.*)

NEWALL, GUY P. [see also *J. HOLLES*]

×Take It to Heart (County, Kingston, 13/12/09)

Husband Love ('*c.*': Pleasure Gdns, Folkestone, 3/11/24; Gr., Putney Bridge, 10/11/24)

×Curing a Selfish Husband (D.P., Eastbourne, 4/4/10)

[Other playlets produced at music-halls)

NEWARK, J. E. [see *J. DRINKWATER*]

NEWBOLT, Sir HENRY JOHN

The Travelling Companion ('*o.*', m. Sir Charles V. Stanford: David Lewis, L'pool, 30/4/25)

NEWBOULT, F. J.

×The Upstroke (Leeds, 8/12/13) *Fr. 1914*

×The Devil's Star (Gai., Manchester, 19/10/14) *Fr. 1916*

NEWCOMBE, Rev. R.

The Coward. LC, P's H., Plymouth, 8/4/14

NEWING, DE WITT

The Rose of Picardy (Pier, Brighton, 28/10/29)

NEWLANDSMITH, ERNEST (*Brother ERNEST*)

The Heavenly Vision ('*wordless mystery pl.*': Rehearsal, 13/6/10)

NEWMAN, A.
Three Little Britons (Torquay, 30/7/00: +*E. GURNEY*)

NEWMAN, GREATREX [see *R. H. BURNSIDE* and *C. GREY*]

NEWMARCH, ROSA
The Tale of a Soldier (m. I. Stravinsky: Arts, 10/7/27: translated from the text of C. F. Ramuz) *1924*

NEWTE, HORACE W. C. [see also *C. BURNETTE* and *A. MORRISON*]
[For earlier plays see *H. E. D.* v, 503]
×The Triumph (Pleasure Gdns, Folkestone, 26/3/00)
×In a Distant Land (Emp., Southend, 25/6/00)
Lorna Doone (O.H., Crouch End, 4/2/02: dramatised from the novel (1869) by R. D. Blackmore)
×Gentleman Jack (Aven., 26/5/02)
×An Ideal (Bij., 9/2/04)

NEWTON, ALEXANDER
×Espionage. LC, Lyr., L'pool, 31/10/14

NEWTON, DOUGLAS
×When East Gets West ('*m.pl.*: St Mary's Guildhall, Clapham, 9/1/22: +*B. MEREFIELD*)

NEWTON, HENRY CHANCE [see also *W. STEPHENS*]
[For earlier plays see *H. E. D.* v, 503 and 808]
The Up-River Girl ('*m.c.*', m. R. Coverley: H., 8/2/04, *cpy.*)
Mr Gull's Fortune ('*f.c.*': Terry's, 6/2/07)
×Wellington ('*m. hist. scena*': Oxf., 22/1/12)
×The Celestial Bride (Hippo., Balham, 9/12/18)

NEWTON, ROBERT
Uneven Temperature (Cent., 23/7/26)
The Madonna of the Golden Heart (Players, 7/7/30)

'*NIB, A. J.*' [=*CHARLES WINDERMERE*]

NICHOLL, THEODORE
Sung before the Bridal. *1930*

NICHOLLS, E. D. [see *F. MOULE*]

NICHOLLS, HARRY [see also *H. SHELLEY* and *J. T. TANNER*]
[For earlier plays see *H. E. D.* v, 504 and 808: the name should, it seems, be spelt *NICHOLLS*]
Another Girl ('*m.c.*', m. C. Cook: Bedford Park Club, 13/1/04)
If We Only Knew ('*r.pl.*', m. J. Crook: Gr., Fulham, 28/9/08: +*C. ROSS*)

[*NICHOLS, ANNE*
Abie's Irish Rose ('*c.*': Stamford, Conn., 6/3/22; Fulton, N.Y., 23/5/22; P's, Manchester, 28/3/27; Apo., 11/4/27) *1923* (Ottawa)

NICHOLS, BEVERLEY
The Stag (Glo., 2/4/29) *1933* (in *Failures*)
Cochran's 1930 Revue (Pav., 27/3/30)

NICHOLS, G. B.

[For earlier plays see *H. E. D.* v, 504]

Under the Red Cross (Ass. R., Taunton, 16/4/00; Stratford, 30/7/00)

The Way Women Love (Ass. R., Yeovil, 2/1/01; Sur., 5/5/02)

Peerless and Peerlot ('*c.o.*', m. H. A. Jeboult: Ass. R., Taunton, 7/2/01, *amat.*)

Lady Templemore's Future ('*society pl.*': Ass. R., Taunton, 8/4/01, *cpy.*)

One Husband for One Wife (Brit., 10/11/02)

The Man She Loves (Sur., 24/11/02: +*F. HERBERT*)

×Eve the Temptress (Sur., 24/2/03: +*A. CONQUEST*)

×The Old Old Story (Sur., 25/5/03)

Her Partner in Sin (Sur., 2/11/03: *G. CONQUEST*)

NICHOLS, ROBERT MALISE BOWYER

Guilty Souls (RADA, 16/11/24, 300 Club) *1922*

Twenty Below (Gate, 15/5/28: +*J. TULLY*) *1927*

Wings over Europe (Martin Beck, N.Y., 10/12/28: +*M. BROWNE*. *1932*

[Apparently this was not publicly produced in England until its performance at the Glo., 27/4/32]

NICHOLS, WALLACE BERTRAM [see also *E. PERCY*]

Earl Simon: A Trilogy. *1922*

[This consists of a one-act piece, *Runnymede*, the main play of *Earl Simon*, and a concluding one-act, *Viterbo*. The last was given at the Bij., 2/4/27, by the Soho Players]

×The Glory of the World. LC, Polytechnic, Regent St., 11/12/24. *1924*

NICHOLSON, CLARK

×Between Dances (Roy., Glasgow, 22/11/10)

NICHOLSON, Mrs HAROLD [see *Mrs F. R. BENSON* and *E. POUNDS*]

[*NICHOLSON, KENYON*

The Barker (Emp., Cardiff, 9/4/28; Playh., 7/5/28) *Fr. 1927*

NICHOLSON, R. T.

The Marble Pallas; or, The Mannikins ('*c.o.*': Lopping H., Loughton, 3/11/08, *cpy.*: +*A. WIMPERIS*)

Tarara; or, The Brigand's Trust ('*c.o.*': Lopping H., Loughton, 28/11/07)

Athene ('*f.o.*': King's Lynn, 6/2/11)

Robert X. LC, Lopping H., Loughton, 20/1/13

NICHOLSON, SUSANNAH

The Nipper (Reg., 4/11/27)

NICHOLSON, Sir SYDNEY HUGO

×The Boy Bishop ('*o. for boys*') *1926* (Faith Press)

NIGON, J. G.

When My Ship Comes Home (Pier, Brighton, 14/7/24: title later changed to *The Happy Mariner*)

NIMMO, M. PRENTICE
Buffins. LC, Lyc., Edin., 23/11/21

NIRDLINGER, CHARLES FREDERICK
Slander (B'ham, 9/12/08; Adel., 15/6/09, *m.*, as *The World and His Wife*: adapted from J. Echegaray, *El gran Galeoto*, 1881)

NIXEY, WALTER
A Sower Went Forth (Roy., Llanelly, 27/4/08, *cpy.*)
The Bond of Marriage (Roy., Llanelly, 7/1/09, *cpy.*; Roy., Llanelly, 5/5/09; Star, L'pool, 14/6/09, as *The Derelict*)

NOBLE, SYBIL
×Sawney (Court, 14/3/09, Pl. Actors)
×Nancy's Manoeuvre (Alb. H., 14/4/10)
×An Old-World Romance (Alb. H., 14/4/10)
×Podger's Predicament (Alb. H., 14/4/10)
×The Surrender of Juan (Roy., Glasgow, 18/3/13: title later changed to *How She Caught Him*)

NOEL, EDGAR L.
In the Land of the Czar (Brixton, 19/4/06, *cpy.*)
×The Candle ('*Cornish t.*': Bed., 20/6/10)
×Wife or Woman (Emp., Camberwell, 14/7/13)

NOLAN, J. F. [see also *H. ERSKINE*]
×Maysie (Crippl. Inst., 13/4/04: +*F. ROLISON*)
The Other Mrs Hudson ('*f.c.*': Crippl. Inst., 8/4/05, *cpy.*) +*F. ROLISON*)
×The Impressions of Stella (Crippl. Inst., 6/12/05: +*F. ROLISON*)
Where Were You Last Night? LC, Club H., Sevenoaks, 12/3/20

NORDEN, A.
The Belle of the Ball ('*m.c.*', m. E. T. De Banzie and M. Dwyer: O.H., Southport, 27/7/08; Macclesfield, 1/8/08: Crown, Peckham, 19/10/08)

[*NORDSTROM, FRANCES*
×All Wrong (Pav., Glasgow, 17/6/18; Emp., Holborn, 7/10/18)
Her Market Price (Lyc., 17/4/24)
The Ruined Lady ('*c.*': Poughkeepsie, N.Y., 28/4/19; Playh., N.Y., 19/1/20; Worthing, 21/6/20; Com., 25/6/20)

NORIN, JANE
Tiger-Lily. LC, '*m.c.*': Crippl. Inst., 17/2/13

NORMAN, E. B.
×Goggles (Shak., L'pool, 28/1/13, '*provisional pfce.*')
×Watson, Sherlock's, Holmes ('*bsq.*': Gai., Manchester, 15/3/18)

NORMAN, Mrs GEORGE [see also *D. E. ELLIS*]
The Love of Woman (Court, 9/5/09, Pl. Actors)
×Stalls for Two (Rehearsal, 17/6/10: +*D. E. ELLIS*)
The Call of the Road (Playh., L'pool, 4/12/18; Gr., Croydon, 13/5/22: +*D. E. ELLIS*: dramatised from the novel, *The Great Gay Road* (1910), by T. Gallon)

The Young Visiters (Pal., Ramsgate, 16/2/20; Court, 24/2/20: +*M. MACKENZIE*: from the book (1919) by Daisy Ashford)

NORMAN, HUBERT
The Medium (Vic. Pal., 29/4/26, *m.*)

NORRIE, RUSSELL
Her King of Men (Emp., Swindon, 17/3/10, *cpy.*; Alex., Widnes, 3/10/10)
A Soldier's Oath (Eden, Bishop Auckland, 23/7/14)

NORRIS, ERNEST E. [see also *J. EATON* and *F. LLEWELLYN*]
[For an earlier play see *H. E. D.* v, 505]
The Three Musketeers (O.H., Crouch End, 31/3/02)
A Gentleman of England ('*r.pl.*': E.C., 2/12/04: +*F. LLEWELLYN*)
× A Brother's Portrait (E.C., 3/4/05: +*F. LLEWELLYN*)

'NORTH, FELIX'
The Price (Terry's, 4/7/09, English Pl. Soc.)
Compensation (Court, 9/6/14)

NORTH, OLIVER
Dangers of a Great City (Colosseum, Oldham, 18/9/05)

NORTHCOTE, A.
× The Choice (W.G., New Brighton, 15/11/12)
× Behind the Curtain. LC, O.H., Harrogate, 31/3/13
The Bargain. LC, Hippo., Margate, 10/3/14
× William Sykes, Esq. LC, Pal., Westcliff-on-Sea, 18/9/14

NORTON, CHARLES
Adam's Eve. LC, '*c.*': Torquay, 20/2/25

NORTON, Mrs EDWARD (ELEANOR)
× A Woman Triumphant. *Fr. 1903*
The Vision of Purity ('*morality*': H.M., 21/4/04, *cpy.*; K's H., 11/3/06, as *The Vision*)
× The Azure Lily (St. J., 7/5/15, *m.*)
× The Triumph of Pierrot (Alex., B'ham, 26/4/17, *m.*)
× Camilla's Christmas Eve. LC, Court, 5/1/20
× The Poet and the Dryad. LC, Court, 5/1/20
× The Hussy. LC, Bingham H., Cirencester, 4/5/20

NORTON, FLORENCE [see *H. STOREY*]

NORTON, FREDERIC [see *A. NOYES* and *A. WIMPERIS*]

NORTON, GEORGE ROSE
Facile; or, Love the Conqueror (Wellington H., St John's Wood, 18/12/05, *amat.*: +*F. CHAMIER*)

NORWOOD, EILLE [see also *A. F. OWEN-LEWIS* and *M. PEMBERTON*]
[For earlier plays see *H. E. D.* v, 505]

The Talk of the Town ('*f.*': Str., 10/8/01: revised version of *The Noble Art*, 1892)
The Favours of Fortune (O.H., York, 28/2/02)

NOT-BOWER, W. G.
×Changing Guard ('*fant.*': Little, 25/1/22)

NOTREVEL, E.
×A Writer of Plays (Court, 12/3/14)

NOVELLO, IVOR [*DAVID IVOR DAVIES NOVELLO*: in association with *C. COLLIER*='*DAVID L'ESTRANGE*']
The Truth Game ('*light c.*': Glo., 5/10/28) *Fr. 1929*
Symphony in Two Flats ('*c.*': Emp., Edin., 23/9/29; New, 4/10/29)

NOYES, ALFRED
Orpheus in the Underground ('*o.*': H.M., 20/12/11: +*F. NORTON* and *Sir H. TREE*)
×A Belgian Christmas Eve. *1915*
Robin Hood (Cent., 27/12/26) *1926*

NUTTALL, S.
×A Bolt from the Blue ('*oa.*', m. F. Blunt: County H., St Albans, 20/5/03, *amat.*: +*R. RAYNE*)

'*NYDIA*'
On Jhelum River ('*m.pl.*', m. A. Woodforde-Finden: Aldw., 22/6/09)

[*NYITRAY, EMILE*
His Lady Friends ('*c.*': Gr., Akron, 16/9/19, as *My Lady Friends*; Com., N.Y., 3/12/19; Brighton, 2/8/20; St. J., 17/8/20: +*F. MANDEL*)

OBERMER, SEYMOUR
The House of Bondage (H.M., 16/3/09, *m.*, Afternoon Theatre)
×When the Clock Strikes Nine (Hippo., Portsmouth, 26/3/17; Vic. Pal., 25/6/17)

O'BRENNAN, KATHLEEN M.
Full Measure (Abbey, Dublin, 27/8/28)

O'BRIEN, KATE
Distinguished Villa (Aldw., 2/5/26, Rep. Players; Little, 12/7/26) *1927*

O'BRIEN, SEUMAS
×Duty (Abbey, Dublin, 16/12/13; Col., 28/6/15)

O'CASEY, SEAN
[Before *The Shadow of a Gunman* was presented at the Abbey, Dublin, O'Casey had written at least four short plays: *The Robe of Rosheen* (c. 1918), *The Frost in the Flower* (c. 1919), *The Harvest Festival* (c. 1920) and *Crimson in the Tri-colour* (c. 1921)]
The Shadow of a Gunman (Abbey, Dublin, 9/4/23; Court, 27/5/27) *1925*
×Cathleen Listens In (Abbey, Dublin, 1/10/23)

Juno and the Paycock ('*t.*': Abbey, Dublin, 3/3/24; Roy., 16/11/25) *1925*
×Nannie's Night Out ('*f. of Dublin love life*': Abbey, Dublin, 29/9/24)
The Plough and the Stars ('*t.*': Abbey, Dublin, 8/2/26; Fortune, 12/5/26) *1926*
The Silver Tassie ('*t.c.*': Apo., 11/10/29) *1928*

O'CONNELL, ADRIAN
A Royal Revenge (Windsor, 26/9/04; Stratford, 21/7/05; called originally *A Romance of Spain*: also called *To Thy Cross I Cling*: +*J. FOX* and *E. McCARTHY*]

O'CONNOR, E. NOLAN
×The Agent (Coloss., Oldham, 6/1/02: +*F. WARDEN-REED*)
×The Princess of Pain (Pier, Brighton, 18/6/06)
×Lucifer and His Angel ('*present-day playlet*': Tiv., 2/9/12)

O'CONNOR, Mrs T. P. (ELIZABETH)
A Lady from Texas ('*c.*': Gt. Qn. St., 1/6/01)
The Temptation (Shak., L'pool, 1/6/05)
×A Royal Blackmail (Emp., Holloway, 9/12/07)
The Blackmailers (County, Kingston, 19/10/08: +*R. H. BLAND*)

O'CUISIN, SEUMAS
×The Sleep of the King (Antient Concert R., Dublin, 29/10/02)
×The Racing Lug (Antient Concert R., Dublin, 31/10/02)

ODDIE, ARTHUR C.
Kipling, Detective (Ass. R., Horsham, 8/3/12, *cpy.*; 24/6/12, *amat.*)
Modern Slavery. LC, Ass. R., Horsham, 5/2/13
Milord. LC, Ass. R., Horsham, 20/3/13
The Atonement. LC, Ass. R., Horsham, 18/3/14

ODDY, NORMAN
×Enthusiasm. LC, Midland, Manchester, 20/1/14

O'DEMPSEY, F.
Judas (Little, Leeds, 6/2/28: adapted from F. V. Ratti, *Giuda*, 1923)

ODLE, EDWIN V.
First Love ('*c.*': Rehearsal, 7/10/11)

O'DONNELL, FRANK J. HUGH
The Dawn-Mist. *1919* (Dublin)
The Drifters (Abbey, Dublin, 7/9/20)
Anti-Christ ('*commentary*': Abbey, Dublin, 17/3/25; Q, 21/11/27)
O'Flaherty's Star (Q, 16/4/28)

O'DUFFY, EIMAR ULTAN
The Phoenix on the Roof (Hardwick-st. H., Dublin, 4/1/15, Irish Theatre)

O'FARRELL, PHILIP [see *F. H. DEANS*]

O'FLAHERTY, LIAM
Darkness ('*t.*') *1926*

OGAIN, SEAN O. B.
The Farm (Abbey, Dublin, 6/12/26)

OGILVIE, GLENCAIRN STUART
[For earlier plays see *H. E. D.* v, 506 and 808]
Cyrano de Bergerac (Gr., Blackpool, 5/3/00; Wynd., 19/4/00: +*L. N. PARKER*: from the play (1897) by Edmond Rostand)
John Durnford, M.P. (Court, 5/9/01)

OGILVY, DRAYTON
×1588 (New, 5/11/07)

'*OGLE, RICHARD*' [=*Hon. S. O. HEN-COLLINS*]
The Maid of Memphis; or, The Queen's Portrait ('*c.o.*', m. O. Eve: K's, Hamm., 28/4/13, *amat.*; O.H., Woolwich, 9/12/14, as *The Queen's Portrait*)
×Twenty Guineas in the Rue de la Paix. LC, Cent., 9/2/25
×The Front Door (Paddington-st. H., 7/12/25, *m.*)
×Pressure (Paddington-st. H., 7/12/25, *m.*)

OGLESBY, ROBERT P. [see also *C. H. PIERSON*]
Two Hearts of Gold ('*md.*': P's, Bradford, 11/2/03, *cpy.*; P's, Bradford, 30/3/03: +*C. H. PIERSON*)

O'GRADY, FAND
×Apartments (Abbey, Dublin, 3/9/23)

O'HANLON, HENRY B.
Speculations (Hardwick-st. H., Dublin, 19/11/17)
All Alone (Hardwick-st. H., Dublin, 17/6/18) *1918* (Dublin)

O'HARE, F. J.
The Renegade (Qns, Dublin, 4/6/06)

[*O'HIGGINS, HARVEY J.* [see also *H. FORD*]
The Dummy ('*c.*': Hudson, N.Y., 13/4/14: P.W., 21/9/15; Emp., 16/7/21, as '*Some*' *Detective*: +*H. FORD*)
Mr Lazarus ('*c.*': Shubert, New Haven, 8/6/16; Shubert, N.Y., 5/9/16; Leamington, 3/10/21: +*H. FORD*)
The Wrong Number ('*f.*': D.Y., 16/6/21: +*H. FORD*) *Fr. 1923*
×The Dicky Bird (Col., 30/1/22)

O'KELLY, SEUMAS
×The Matchmakers (Abbey, Dublin, 13/12/07, Theatre of Ireland) *1907* (Dublin)
×The Flame on the Hearth (Abbey, Dublin, 24/11/08, Theatre of Ireland: later called *The Stranger*)
The Shuiler's Child ('*t.*': Abbey, Dublin, 29/4/09, Theatre of Ireland; Abbey, Dublin, 24/11/10) *1909* (Dublin)
The Bribe (Abbey, Dublin, 18/12/13) *1914* (Dublin)
×Driftwood (Gai., Manchester, 11/10/15; D.Y., 10/1/16)
The Parnellite (Abbey, Dublin, 24/9/17)
×Meadowsweet (Abbey, Dublin, 7/10/19) *1925* (Dublin)

OLDFIELD, CLAUDE HOUGHTON [='*CLAUDE HOUGHTON*']

OLDFIELD, Lady
The Child (Lyc. Club, 12/10/24)
The Specialist (Cent., 24/5/25, Lyc. Club)

OLDMEADOW, CECILIA
×Caecilia (St Jude's H., Hampstead Gdn Suburb, 20/11/26, Roswitha Soc.) *1927* (*priv.*)
×The Robe Celestial. *1930* (*priv.*)

O'LEARY, CON
×The Crossing (Abbey, Dublin, 23/9/14)
×The Queer Ones (Abbey, Dublin, 14/10/19)

OLIPHANT, LANCELOT
×Fantasy and Flame (Court, 19/9/13)

OLIVER, ARTHUR ROLAND
The Night Hawk (Gr., Blackpool, 15/10/28; Gr., Croydon, 22/10/28)

OLIVER, HERBERT
The Vauxhall Belles ('*c.o.*': Scala, 24/3/27, *amat.*)

OLIVER, J. H.
×Tangled Wedlock (Clavier H., 11/10/12)

OLIVER, LAURENCE
Fast and Loose ('*f.c.*': K's, Hamm., 25/11/29)

OLIVER, NORMAN
×December 13 (Court, 31/3/12, Pl. Actors: +*C. F. BROOKES*)

OLIVER, ROLAND
Wife or Widow? (Sur., 9/4/03, *cpy.*)
The Girl from Bond Street ('*m.c.*', m. L. La Rondelle: Central, Northwich, 5/9/04)
×Her Last Dance (Pal., Chelsea, 7/1/07)
×His Shop-Girl Bride (Pal., Camberwell, 13/1/08)

[*OLIVIER, STUART*
The Bride ('*c.*': Gar., Washington, 18/2/24; 39th St., N.Y., 5/5/24; Gai., Hastings, 13/7/25: +*G. MIDDLETON*)

OLIVIER, Sir SYDNEY
Eyvind of the Mountains (Court, 13/6/15, St. Soc.: translated from the play by Jóhann Sigurjónsson)

O'MAHONY, MICHAEL
×The Corner Shop (Playh., L'pool, 20/5/18: +*J. SEXTON*)

O'MALLEY, PATRICK
Come What May (Worthing, 18/2/18; Gr., Croydon, 4/3/18)
The Third Eye. LC, Pier, Brighton, 18/7/18

OMMANNEY, CHARLES
The New Clown ('*m.c.*', m. T. Wood: Pal., Rugby, 26/12/11)

O'NEAL, JOHN D. [see *M. BOYNE*]

[*O'NEIL, PEGGY*
×The Line of No Resistance. LC, St M., 8/7/24

O'NEILL, BARRY

Essex (P.H., Croydon, 3/1/25, *amat.*)

O'NEILL, CLEMENT

×Wanted, a Housekeeper (Ladbr. H., 14/6/11, *cpy.*)

[*O'NEILL, EUGENE*

×Ile (Greenwich Village Players, N.Y., 18/4/18; Everyman, 17/4/22) *1929*

Diff'rent (Provincetown Playh., N.Y., 26/12/20; Everyman, 4/10/21) *1922*

×In the Zone (Everyman, 15/6/21) *1929*

Anna Christie (New Amsterdam, N.Y., 2/11/21; Str., 10/4/23) *1922*

×Bound East for Cardiff (Playh., L'pool, 23/4/24) *1929*

×The Long Voyage Home (Everyman, 12/6/25) *1929*

The Emperor Jones (Provincetown Playh., N.Y., 1/11/20; Ambass., 10/9/25) *1921*

Beyond the Horizon (Morosco, N.Y., 3/2/20; Reg., 31/1/26, Rep. Players; Everyman, 22/3/26) *1920*

All God's Chillun Got Wings (Provincetown Playhouse, N.Y., 15/5/24; Gate, 8/11/26; Court, 17/6/29) *1925*

Gold (Frazee, N.Y., 2/6/26; Playh., L'pool, 9/11/26) *1924*

The Great God Brown (Greenwich Village Players, N.Y., 23/1/26; Str., 19/6/27, St. Soc.) *1926*

The Hairy Ape (Provincetown Playh., N.Y., 6/3/22; Little, Manchester, 28/3/27, Unnamed Soc.; Gate, 26/1/28) *1922*

×Before Breakfast (Etlinger, 14/7/27) *1926*

×Where the Cross is Made (Arts, 27/10/27) *1929*

×Welded (Playroom 6, 16/2/28; Gate, 5/6/29) *1925*

×The Dreamy Kid (Fest., Cambridge, 14/5/28) *1926*

O'NEILL, MARY

×Coming Home (Roy., Glasgow, 19/1/10)

O'NEILL, ROSE

×Travelling Abroad. LC, Bij., 23/7/13

The Wonder Tales of Nathaniel Hawthorne ('*children's pl.*': Ambass., 22/12/17: +*E. WELTCH*)

Dick Wyatt's Wager ('*f.c.*': Edin., 28/11/21: +*E. ELLIS*)

[A revised version, under the title of *Make Your Fortune*, was presented at Barnes, 6/6/25, when the authorship was given to *ELIZABETH RAE*]

O'NEILL, SEOSAMH

The Kingdom-Maker. *1917* (Dublin)

O'NEILL-FOLEY, ANASTASIA

Father O'Flynn (Qns, Dublin, 15/10/17)

ONGLEY, BYRON [see *WINCHELL SMITH*]

O'NOLAN, FERGUS

×A Royal Alliance (Abbey, Dublin, 21/9/20)

ONSLOW, ARTHUR

A Devil's Bargain (W.L., 23/3/08: from the novel (1908) by Florence Warden)

OPENSHAW, CHARLES ELTON [see also *J. E. AGATE* and *H. WOODWARD*]
Three Days (Court, 27/1/24, Rep. Players)
All the King's Horses ('*light c.*': Glo., 25/1/26) *Fr. 1927*
Payment ('*c.*': Pier, Eastbourne, 3/9/28; Arts, 12/9/28)

OPENSHAW, MARY
×My First Client. *Fr. 1903*

OPPENHEIM, E. PHILLIPS [see also *H. D. BRADLEY* and *F. THOMPSON*]
×The Money-Spider (Col., 20/7/08; Scala, 13/11/11)
×The Gilded Key (Hippo., Blackpool, 26/9/10; Hippo., Woolwich, 16/1/11)

ORAM, E. WERGE
The Golden Myth (People's, 7/6/26)

ORCZY, EMMUSEA, Baroness
The Scarlet Pimpernel ('*r.c.*': Nottingham, 15/10/03; New, 5/1/05: +*M. BARSTOW*)
The Sin of William Jackson (Lyr., 28/8/06: +*M. BARSTOW*)
The Tangled Skein (Cor., 30/3/08, *cpy.*: dramatised from her own novel (1907): +*M. BARSTOW*)
Beau Brocade ('*r.d.*': D.P., Eastbourne, 4/5/08; Cor., 1/6/08; dramatised from her own novel (1907): +*M. BARSTOW*)
Petticoat Government ('*c.*': Wynd., 12/8/09, *cpy.*: dramatised from her own novel (1910) +*M. BARSTOW*)
A True Woman (Wynd., 21/4/11, *cpy.*: dramatised from her own novel, 1911)
×The Duke's Wager (Dalston, 3/11/11, *cpy.*; P's, Manchester, 8/11/11)
The Legion of Honour ('*r.pl.*': Bradford, 27/5/18; Aldw., 24/8/21: dramatised from her own novel, *A Sheaf of Bluebells*, 1917)
Leatherface ('*r.d.*': Portsmouth, 25/9/22; Hippo., Golder's Green, 2/10/22: dramatised from her own novel (1916): +*C. FIENNES*)

'*ORD, ROBERT*' [=*EDITH OSTLERS* (*Mrs W. GAYER MACKAY*)]
×A Midnight Visitor (Alh., Brighton, 22/10/10, *m.*: +*W. G. MACKAY*)
×A Thief (Metropolitan, 24/8/14)

O'REILLY, P. J.
[Several sketches produced at music-halls]

O'REILLY, W. H.
The Myrtle Maiden; or, The Girl of Granada ('*c.o.*', m. E. Jakobowski: Ladbr. H., 13/7/12)

O'RELL, Mrs MAX
×For Peace and Quietness ('*c.*': Boudoir, 24/10/11)

O'RIORDAN, CONAL HOLMES O'CONNELL [=*'F. NORREYS CONNELL'*: see also *O. M. HUEFFER*]

×Time: A Passing Phantasy (Bloomsbury H., 1/12/06, New Stage Club; Abbey, Dublin, 1/4/09; Court, 21/6/09)

×The Piper (Abbey, Dublin, 13/2/08; County, Manchester, 18/2/09) *1912* (see below)

Count Hannibal (*'r.pl.'*: P's, Bristol, 18/3/09; New, 20/10/10: +*O. ASCHE*: from the novel (1901) by Stanley Weyman)

Thalia's Teacup; or, The Delights of Deceit (*'light c.'*: Court, 24/7/09)

×An Imaginary Conversation (Abbey, Dublin, 13/5/09; Court, 9/6/09; P.W., 19/11/12) *1912*

Shakespeare's End and Other Irish Plays. *1912*

[Besides the title-play, this includes *The Piper*, described as 'an unended argument', and *An Imaginary Conversation*]

Rope Enough. 1914 (Dublin)

×The King's Wooing (Little, 30/11/13, Pioneer Players) *1929*

Thank Your Ladyship (*'c.'*: Playh., 13/2/14)

The Patience of the Sea. LC, Ambass., 20/4/14

His Majesty's Pleasure (*'r.c.'*: Rep., B'ham, 30/10/15) *1925* (originally printed in *The Irish Review*, 1912)

Napoleon's Josephine (Fortune, 24/9/28)

ORM, W.

×Liquid Magic. LC, W.L., 9/10/13

'ORME, MICHAEL' [=*Mrs J. T. GREIN*]

ORME, ROWAN

The Scandalmongers (*'c.'*: Court, 3/7/05)

Mrs Ellison's Answer (*'serious c.'*: New, 5/11/07)

×The Anarchists (Court, 7/7/08, *m.*)

×The Sentence (Court, 7/7/08, *m.*)

ORNA, D. L.

Three Plays: The Dream Doctor, Man and His Phantoms, The Coward, translated from H. R. Lenormand. *1925*

[Of these, the first was presented at the Gate, 5/11/29, as *The Eater of Dreams*]

OSBORN, INNES L.

The Seventh Guest (Pier, Southsea, 27/8/28; Emb., 10/10/28: +*A. J. AUBREY*)

×Red Fire (D.P., Eastbourne, 19/11/28: +*H. B. GREAVES*)

OSBORNE, F. W.

×Borrowed Plumes. LC, Garrison, Tidworth, 2/7/21

OSBOURNE, LLOYD

The Exile (Roy., 9/5/03: +*A. STRONG*)

×The Little Father of the Wilderness (Com., 21/11/05: +*A. STRONG*)

OSGOOD, IRENE

×Lady Marguerite's Hobby. LC, O.H., Northampton, 15/5/13

×The Woman who had Everything. LC, O.H., Northampton, 23/5/13
The Spanish Slave. LC, O.H., Northampton, 2/8/13
Cortes the Conqueror. LC, O.H., Northampton, 20/9/13
The Menace. LC, O.H., Northampton, 14/12/14

OSMASTON, FRANCIS P. B.
Cromwell. *1906*

OSMOND, HENRY L. [see *T. C. MAC*, *J. McKENZIE* and *H. WARDROPER*]

OSMOND, MARION
The Chinese Bungalow ('*md.*': Gr., Hull, 2/10/25: K's, Hamm., 23/11/25; D.Y., 9/1/29: +*J. CORBET*: dramatised from her own novel, 1923)

OSTLERS, EDITH [*Mrs W. GAYER MACKAY*: ='*R. ORD*']

O'SULLIVAN, PATRICK
The Lure of—. LC, W. Bromwich, 27/5/19

O'SULLIVAN, VINCENT
The Hartley Family (Court, 5/11/11, Pl. Actors) *1910*

OSWALD, ROBERT
×The Royalist (Gr., Swansea, 5/9/07)

OULD, HERMON LEONARD
Between Sunset and Dawn (Vaud., 23/10/13) *1914*; *Fr. 1914*
×What Fools These Mortals Be! *1916* (Nat. Labour Press)
Christmas Eve ('*folk m.pl.*': Etlinger, 27/6/19, Curtain Group Dram. Soc.)
The Black Virgin. *1922*
The Dance of Life (Little, York, 3/12/24; K's, Hamm., 3/6/25) *1924*
New Plays from Old Stories. *1924*
[This, the first volume of a series to which were later added two further parts, contains: 1. *Peter the Pied Piper*; 2. *The Princess in the Sleeping Wood*; and 3. *Rip Van Winkle*]
×Joan the Maid. *1924*
Plays of Pioneers. *Fr. 1925*
[This contains three short plays: 1. *Joan the Maid* (see above); 2. *The Discovery*; and 3. *The Pathfinder*]
The Piper Laughs. *1927*
The Moon Rides High (Wynd., 12/4/29) *1927*
The Light Comedian ('*c.*': RADA, 11/5/30) *1928*
Hoppla! (Fest., Cambridge, 25/2/29; Gate, 19/2/29: adapted from the play (1927) by E. Toller) *1928*
Pierrot before the Seven Doors (translated from a play by A. J. Cantillon) *1930*
×The Peacemaker. *1930*

OULESS, Miss E. U. [see also *Mrs W. HADLEY*]
×Our Pageant. *1926* (in *Three Plays*, Village Drama Soc.)
[Between about 1929 and 1934 this authoress published translations of a number of plays by Hans Sachs and other authors:

these appeared separately, and some of them were also issued as a collection in *Seven Shrovetide Plays*. The titles are as follows: *A Charm for the Devil*, *The Children of Eve*, *Dame Truth*, *Death in the Tree*, *Five Poor Travellers*, *Happy as a King*, *The Horse Thief*, *The Old Game*, *The Wandering Scholar* and *A Way with Surly Husbands*]

The Way of Honour (translated from Lessing's *Minna von Barnhelm*) *1929*

OURSLER, CHARLES FULTON

The Spider ('*mystery md.*': W.G., 1/3/28: +*L. BRENTANO*, adapted by *R. PERTWEE*)

OUSLEY, GIDEON

×A Serious Thing (Abbey, Dublin, 19/8/19)

The Enchanted Trousers (Abbey, Dublin, 25/11/19)

OUVRY, Rev. J. DELAHAIZE

The Match-girl's Dream of Fairyland ('*children's pl.*': Pav. H., Greasley, 9/1/12)

OVERTON, ROBERT

[For earlier plays see *H. E. D.* v, 509]

No Quarter ('*military c.*': Drill H., Brentwood, 3/3/00, *cpy.*)

×Fortune Favours Fools (Hippo., Manchester, 3/5/15)

OWEN, GEORGE [see also *J. CORPEL* and *R. L. SCOTT*]

×A Question of Propriety (Cosmopolis, 11/7/13)

OWEN, HARRY COLLINSON

×An Object Lesson. *1929*

OWEN, HAROLD [see also *H. M. VERNON*]

×A Little Fowl Play (Pal., Manchester, 21/10/12; Col., 28/10/12) *Fr. 1913*

×The Angels at Mons. LC, Col., 2/3/16: +*A. TURNER*

Such is Life ('*c.*': Princess', New York, 25/11/16)

Loyalty (St J., 21/11/17) *1918*

Fatherhood (Barnes, 2/5/25)

×Still Engaged! LC, National School, Todmorden, 18/11/25. *1924*

A Man Unknown (Cardiff, 24/5/26; Com., 17/6/26)

His Wife's Children (Worthing, 30/1/28; Gr., Clapham, 7/5/28)

The Man who Missed It (Playh., Cardiff, 28/10/29; Str., 27/11/29)

OWEN, HARRISON

The Gentleman in Waiting ('*c.*': Pleasure Gdns, Folkestone, 8/6/25; Com., 2/7/25)

The Happy Husband ('*light c.*': Portsmouth, 23/5/27; Crit., 15/6/27)

OWEN, JACKSON

A (K)night of the Garter ('*m.c.*': Gr., Mansfield, 2/8/20; Emp., Edmonton, 11/10/20; title later changed to *Oh Yes*: +*A. SHAW*)

OWEN, REGINALD [='*JOHN RAMSEY*': see also *Mrs CLIFFORD MILLS*]

The Jolly Family ('*c.*': Q, 28/11/27: +*B. HOPE*)

OWEN, W. ARMITAGE

Sarah Ann Holds Fast ('*Lancashire pl.*': Gr., Oldham, 10/12/28)

OWEN-LEWIS, A. F.

×A Point of Honour (R. Hospital, Dublin, 27/2/02, *amat.*; Adel., 22/5/03: +*E. NORWOOD*)

×Colonel Cleveland, V.C. (Col., 20/10/13: +*E. NORWOOD*)

OXENHAM, JOHN

Darkness and Light ('*pageant*': R. Agricultural H., 4/6/08)

P., M.

Love – without License (E.C., 7/7/19)

The Woman who Saw (E.C., 15/3/20)

[*PACHECO, Mrs R.*

The Three Twins ('*f.c.*': Vic. H., 3/3/08, *cpy.*: +*C. DICKSON*)

PACKER, HARRIET

The Spinsters' Club (Raleigh H., Brixton, 16/2/05, *amat.*)

×The Treasure (Raleigh H., Brixton, 15/12/11, *amat.*)

PAGE, AUSTIN

By Pigeon Post (Gar., 30/3/18)

The Beating on the Door (St J., 6/11/22)

The Devil in Bronze (Str., 11/9/29)

PAGE, BERNARD [see also *C. GREY* and *N. PAGE*]

Jedediah the Scarecrow ('*oa.*', m. G. G. Vincent: Crippl. Inst., 28/5/05)

[This had originally been published in 1895]

Robin Hood ('*m.ext.*'; Rep., Nottingham, 8/10/21)

PAGE, DUDLEY STUART

The Usurpers ('*c.o.*', m. H. S. Brooke: King's Lynn, 28/10/12, *amat.*)

PAGE, EDMUND

×The Newsboy's Dream ('*m.fant.*': K's, Edin., 21/10/16, *m.*)

PAGE, ELLIOTT [see also *M. MYERS* and *D. WYLLARD*]

The Wheat King (Apo., 16/4/04: +*Mrs A. JENSON*: from Frank Norris' novel, *The Pit*, 1903)

The Lesser Evil (Court, 21/11/09, Pl. Actors: +*N. VYNNE*)

×Preparing Croary (Lyc. Club, 25/1/12)

PAGE, GERTRUDE

Pathfinders, or, Builders of Empire (Miners, Ashington, 5/8/12)

PAGE, NORMAN

The Black Prince ('*m.pl.*': Mechanics' H., Nottingham, 29/6/03: +*B. PAGE*)

Nero and Co. ('*c.o.*': m. B. Page: Mechanics' H., Nottingham, 11/5/08)

PAGE, PHOEBE FENWICK

The Land of Funny Features. LC, Margaret Morris, 20/12/21

PAGE, VIOLET [='*VERNON LEE*']

PAIN, Mrs BARRY (AMELIA)

[This authoress produced a very large number of plays for children. Typical collections are *Short Plays for Amateur Acting* (1906), *More Short Plays for Amateurs* (1908) and *The Nine of Diamonds, and Other Plays* (1913)]

PAIN, BARRY

×The White Elephant (Emp., Stratford, 2/3/14; +*C. EDDY*)
×Eliza. LC, Lyr., Hamm., 6/4/21: +*R. FILIPPI*

PAIN, J. [see *R. EYRE*]

PAINTER, GERTRUDE

The Snow Storm (Q, 12/4/26)

PAKENHAM-WALSH, W. S.

Anne Boleyn, or, The Queen of May. *1921*

PAKINGTON, Hon. MARY AUGUSTA

×A Doctor's Engagements. *Fr. 1903*
×Ready! ('*pl. for boys*') *1910*
×The Patriot (Worcester, 7/12/14)
×Shakespeare for Merry England. LC, Worcester, 17/4/15
Plays for Scout Entertainments. *1920* (Glasgow)

[This contains five one-act plays: 1. *One Good Turn Deserves Another*; 2. *Jane, or The Scout's Nightmare*; 3. *The Laurel Crown*; 4. *Mixed Pickles*; and 5. *The N'th Scout Law*]

×The Polar Post (Ambass., 22/4/20, *m.*) *Fr. 1929*
×Rosalind of the Farmyard (Shaft., 13/7/20, *m.*)
Two Christmas Plays. *1923*

[This contains her short play '*Nowell!*', together with *Seeing and Believing* by Constance E. Britton]

The Queen of Hearts ('*pageant*') *1926*

[This was originally presented at Hartlebury Castle: it appears in LC, dated 12/10/26, for performance at the Institute of Hampstead Garden Suburb]

×The House with the Twisty Windows (Cent., 12/4/26) *Fr. 1928*
The True Likeness ('*fant.*') *1928*
×The Scarlet Mantle. LC, Blackfriars, 30/4/28. *Fr. 1928*
The Tower (Everyman, 15/7/29; Players, 23/6/30)
×The Black Horseman. *1929* (Oxford)

PAL, NIRANJAN [see also *H. N. MAITRA*]

The Goddess (D.Y., 6/6/22, *m.*, Indian Players; Ambass., 19/6/22)
What a Change! ('*f.c.*': Gr., Swansea, 19/5/24; Scala, 7/7/24, as *The Magic Crystal*: called also *The Blue Bottle*)

PALLING, ARTHUR

×Flirting. LC, K's, Hamm., 5/2/13

PALMER, DAMPIER

To Reach the Stars (Apo., 11/12/21, Rep. Players)

PALMER, FREDERICK C.

×The Poet and the Purse. LC, T.H., Cheltenham, 4/4/21.
Pilate ('*t.*') *1923* (Cheltenham & London)
The Dream Pedlar ('*oa.*', m. P. D'Auvergne: Reg., 1/5/25)

PALMER, HERBERT EDWARD
The Judgment of Francois Villon (‘*pageant-episode pl.*’) *1927*

PALMER, JOHN LESLIE
×Over the Hills (H.M., 10/11/12) *1914*

PALMER, WILLIAM
Ivanhoe (Qns, Manchester, 10/9/06: dramatised from Sir Walter Scott's novel)

PALMSTIERNA, E. [see *J. B. FAGAN*]

PALROW, T. W.
A Whitechapel Girl (Norwich, 29/10/00)

PARDOE, MAY
Margot (Windsor, 18/5/03; Metro., Camberwell, 25/5/03; Court, 12/12/04)

PARES, Sir BERNARD
The Mischief of Being Clever (translated from *Gore ot uma* by A. S. Griboiedov) *1925*

PARGETER, E. W.
×The Trinket (St John's R., Stockton-on-Tees, 23/2/11, *amat.*)

PARK, J. K.
Rob Roy (T.H., Wishaw, 6/9/05: from Sir Walter Scott's novel)

PARK, V.
×The Kingdom of Kennaquhair (‘*m.pl.*’: Roy., 26/12/08)

PARKE, WALTER [see also *F. C. PHILIPS* and *A. SHIRLEY*]
[For earlier plays see *H. E. D.* v, 512 and 809]
Bobadil; or, Sultan for a Day (‘*c.o.*’, m. L. Searelle: Bij., Teddington, 5/1/03, *cpy.*)
Brer Rabbit and Uncle Remus (‘*c.o.*’, m. F. Pascal: Ladbr. H., 17/12/03, *cpy.*) *1905*
×Wooing a Widow (‘*c.o.*’, m. F. Pascal: Ladbr. H., 17/12/03, *cpy.*) *1905*
×Goliah Quagg (Ladbr. H., 15/2/10, *cpy.*)
×The Understudy (Court, 9/12/10, *m.*, Rehearsal Co.)

PARKER, ALFRED
Camouflage (‘*m.f.*’, m. L. Wright: K's, Portsmouth, 4/3/18; M'sex, 11/3/18: title later changed to *Khaki and Blue*)
Gay Bohemia (‘*m.pl.*’, m. H. Stafford, L. Wright and H. Carr: Shak., L'pool, 5/5/19; Wimbledon, 8/12/19)

PARKER, FRANK [see *B. KIRALFY*]

PARKER, Sir GILBERT
At Point o' Bugles (Clavier H., 17/10/12)

PARKER, JAMES
I Love You (‘*c.*’: Ambass., 20/9/13: from a play by R. Bracco)

[*PARKER, LEM B.*
The Life of Dora Thorne (Lincoln, 17/11/05, *cpy.*)

[*PARKER, LOTTIE BLAIR*
[For an earlier play see *H. E. D.* v, 513]
Way Down East (Aldw., 23/4/08, revised by *J. R. GRISMER*)

PARKER, LOUIS NAPOLEON [see also *H. CAINE, W. W. JACOBS, R. MARSHALL, S. OGILVIE* and *Mrs H. WARD*]
[For earlier plays see *H. E. D.* v, 513]
The Sacrament of Judas (P.W., 9/10/1899, as a one-act play; Com., 22/5/01, expanded to three acts; H.M., 18/2/09, *m.*, as *A Soul's Flight*, in one act)
The Swashbuckler ('*r.c.*': D.Y., 1/1/00)
The Cardinal (Montreal, 21/11/01; St J., 31/8/03) *Fr. 1923*
The Twin Sister ('*c.*': D.Y., 1/1/02: adapted from *Zwillingschwester* by Ludwig Fulda)
The Heel of Achilles (Glo., 6/2/02: +*B. LAWRENCE*)
The Optimist (Philadelphia, 1903)
Burnside & Co.: A House of Cards (Dublin, 1/10/03; Terry's, 28/4/04, as *The House of Burnside*)
The Sorceress (Washington, D.C., 1904)
The Monkey's Paw (H., 6/10/03, *m.*, *benefit pfce.*; H., 4/3/05: +*W. W. JACOBS*) *Fr. 1910*
×The Creole (H., 6/5/05, *m.*)
The Harlequin King ('*masquerade*': Imp., 3/1/06: +*S. BRINTON*)
The Sherborne Pageant. *1905* (Sherborne)
The Warwick Pageant (Warwick Castle, 2/7/06) *1906* (Warwick)
The Duel (Gar., 23/4/07: adapted from a play (1905) by Henri Lavedan)
Mr George ('*c.*': Vaud., 25/4/07)
×Jemmy (Vaud., 25/4/07)
The Bury St Edmund's Pageant (Bury St Edmund's, 8/7/07) *1907* (Bury St Edmund's)
A Masque of Life (Claremont, 9/3/07)
The Dover Pageant (Dover, 1908)
The Colchester Pageant (Colchester, 21/6/09) *1909* (Norwich)
The York Pageant (York, 1909)
Beethoven (H.M., 25/11/09: adapted from the play (1909) by René Fauchois)
Pomander Walk ('*c.*': Toronto, 12/12/10; Playh., 29/6/11) *Fr. 1921*
Disraeli (P'cess, Montreal, 23/1/11; Wallack's, N.Y., 18/9/11; Roy., 4/4/16) *1911* (New York); *1916*
Chantecler (Knickerbocker, N.Y., 23/1/11: adapted from the play (1910) by E. Rostand)
Sire ('*c.*': Crit., N.Y., 24/1/11)
The Lady of Coventry (Montreal, 30/10/11; Daly's, N.Y., 20/11/11)
The Redemption of Evelyn Vaudray (Richmond, Va., 1911)
The Woman and the Sheriff (N.Y., 1911)
Drake ('*pageant pl.*': H.M., 3/9/12) *1913*
The Paper Chase ('*c.*': Wallack's, N.Y., 25/11/12)

Joseph and His Brethren (Cent., N.Y., 11/1/13; H.M., 2/9/13: called originally *The Deliverer*) *1913*
Bluff King Hal (Gar., 4/9/14)
David Copperfield (Wallack's, N.Y., 26/10/14, as *The Highway of Life*; H.M., 24/12/14) *Fr. 1914*
A Masque of War and Peace (D.L., 27/4/15, *m.*) *1915*
Mavourneen (H.M., 23/10/15)
Through Toil to Victory ('*pageant*': D.L., 14/4/16, *m.*)
The Women's Tribute ('*pageant*': C.G., 8/7/16)
The Aristocrat (St J., 25/1/17) *1917*
Wonderful James ('*c.*': Gar., 26/3/17, revised version of *Gudgeons* (1893): +*S. M. CARSON*)
A Pageant of Fair Women. LC, Qns H., 5/5/17
×Moonshine. LC, St J., 18/10/17
The Treasures of Britain ('*masque*': Shaft., 19/4/18, *m.*)
The Pageant of Freedom (Qns H., 7/5/18)
The Pageant of Drury Lane Theatre (D.L., 27/9/18) *1918*
L'Aiglon (Glo., 19/11/18: adapted from the play (1900) by E. Rostand: an early version had been acted at New York in 1900) *1902*
Lourdes (K's H., 1/4/19, Strolling Players) *1935* (Boston)
The Great Day (D.L., 12/9/19: +*G. R. SIMS*)
×Summertime ('*c.*': Roy., 30/10/19, as *Summer is a-comin' in*) *Fr. 1922*
Pageant of the Girls' Friendly Society. LC, Qns H., 1/7/20. *1925* (as *The Quest*)
×Typho (P.W., 13/7/21, *m.*)
Mr Garrick (Brighton, 15/5/22; Wimbledon, 22/5/22; Court, 29/9/22)
×A Minuet (RADA, 19/11/22) *Fr. 1922*
Arlequin ('*c.fant.*': Emp., 21/12/22: adapted from a play by M. Magre)
Angelo (Apo., N.Y., 23/12/22, as *Johannes Kreisler*; D.L., 28/3/23: adapted from a play by C. Meinhard and R. Bernauer)
The Lord of Death (Plymouth, 28/5/23; New, 6/4/24, Catholic Pl. Soc.: adapted from *Le maître de la mort* (1920) by Marguerite Allotte de la Fuye) *1923*
×Monsieur D'Artagnan (Pal., Chelsea, 14/12/23, *m.*)
The Right Hand of the Prince ('*r.c.*': Church House, Erdington, 29/2/24, *amat.*; K's, Hamm., 7/4/24, Stock Exchange Operatic and Dramatic Soc.)
Our Nell ('*m.pl.*', m. H. Fraser-Simson and I. Novello: Gai., 16/4/24: +*T. R. ARKELL*)
The Lost Duchess ('*modern c.*': Church House, Erdington, 2/10/24; Adel., 12/6/25, *m.*)
×Their Business in Great Waters. LC, Lyc., 26/11/28

PARKER, MARGARET

×Her Twenty-first Birthday (Euston, 23/7/10)
×The End of the Season (Euston, 26/5/13)

PARKER, OSCAR
The New Harem ('*c.o.*': Little, 12/1/11, *m.*)

PARKER, Mrs STEPHENS
×Their Infinite Variety. LC, Church of England School, Snaith, 10/3/13

PARKER, W. M.
Witching Willow (Ath., Glasgow, 30/1/22)

PARKES, JAMES WILLIAM
The Pageant of English Literature. *1922* (Birkenhead)

PARKES, W. KINETON
×Sugarine. LC, Vaud., 20/12/17

PARKHILL, DAVID
Barly Reforms. LC, Roy., 14/10/25

PARR, E. F.
×Escape? *Fr. 1921*
×The Woman Juror. LC, Crippl. Inst., 1/11/22 *Fr. 1922*
×The Nurse in Charge of the Case. *Fr. 1927*

PARR, MAUDE
Pam and Billy ('*children's pl.*': T.H., Annerley, 30/1/12, *amat.*: +*M. COSENS*)

PARRISH, GLADYS
Barton's Folly (Court, 14/12/24)

PARRY, BERNARD
Where There's a Will— ('*c.*': Crit., 26/11/12)
×Navy Blue (Emp., New X, 29/9/13)
The Purse-Strings ('*c.*': Gar., 28/1/19) *Fr. 1919*

PARRY, Sir EDWARD ABBOTT
England's Elizabeth (*hist.pl.*': Manchester, 29/4/01: +*L. CALVERT*)
Katawampus, ('*m.pl. for children of all ages*': P.W., 23/12/01: +*L. CALVERT*) *1901*
When the Wife's Away ('*f.c.*': Dublin, 6/3/05; Gr., Southampton, 28/6/05, as *The Absence of Mrs Barrington*; Wynd., 2/8/05, as *What the Butler Saw*: +*F. MOUILLOT*)
×Charlotte on Bigamy (Kings., 19/5/08)
×The Tallyman (Gai., Manchester, 28/2/10; Cor., 20/2/11)
The Captain of the School (Gai., Manchester, 14/11/10; Gai., 10/12/10: +*F. MOUILLOT*)
×Napoleon's Victory (Gai., Dublin, 3/7/11)
×Disraeli (Gai., Manchester, 9/10/16)
Robert Byron. LC, Rusholme, 28/2/25

PARRY, HUGH
The Historical Pageant of Nonconformity (R. Agricultural H., 12/2/12) *1912*
The Historical Pageant of the Mayflower. LC, Drill H., Plymouth, 6/8/20. *1920*

Oliver Cromwell. LC, Crippl. Inst., 12/1/22. *1922* (*priv.*)
The Historical Pageant of Faith and Freedom. *1926*

PARRY, Mrs MARIE
An Ideal Thief (T.H., High Wycombe, 11/11/11, *amat.*; Pal., Watford, 6/12/19, *amat.*)
The Girl of Lone Island ('*c.*': Ricksmansworth, 6/12/20, *amat.*)

PARRY, PERCY F.
[For an earlier play see *H. E. D.* v, 514]
The Burglar ('*m.f.*': St Peter's H., Brockley, 11/4/01)

PARRY, RAY
The Eleventh Hour (Alex., B'ham, 2/12/21)
Spring Cleaning ('*f.c.*': Perth, 1/5/22)
×Diana Goes Dancing (Bournemouth, 19/5/24)

PARRY-COLE, J.
The Flower Girl ('*c.o.*': Bij., 20/6/01)

'*PARSONS, HUBERT*' [=*Sir GERALD DU MAURIER* and *VIOLA TREE*]
The Dancers (Wynd., 15/2/23)

PARSONS, R. E. (see *E. SCUDAMORE*)

'*PASTON, GEORGE*' [=*EMILY MORSE SYMONDS*: see also *W. B. MAXWELL*]
The Pharisee's Wife (D.Y., 12/7/04)
Clothes and the Woman ('*c.*': Imp., 26/5/07, Pioneers; St J., 30/6/19, *m.*) *Fr. 1922*
×The Picture of the Year (K's H., 22/3/08, Pl. Actors: +*H. COCKERAN*)
×Feed the Brute ('*uninstructive conversation*': Roy., 24/5/08, Pioneers; Roy., 20/3/09) *Fr. 1909*
×Tilda's New Hat (Court, 8/11/08, Pl. Actors; Wynd., 21/10/09) *Fr. 1909*
×The Parent's Progress (P.W., 25/1/10) *Fr. 1910*
The Naked Truth ('*f.c.*': Wynd., 14/4/10: +*W. B. MAXWELL*) *Fr. 1910*
Nobody's Daughter (Wynd., 3/9/10) *1924*
×Stuffing (Aldw., 18/11/10, *m.*) *Fr. 1912*
×The Kiss (H., 24/11/10, *m.*) *Fr. 1912*
×Colleagues (Emp., Kilburn, 30/1/11)
The Conynghams (Playh., L'pool, 14/4/13)
In and Out (Shaft., 16/12/13: called originally *A Knight of the Chisel*: adapted from L. Bénière, *Papillon, dit Lyonnais le Juste*, 1909)
×Divorce While You Wait (Hippo., Manchester, 15/2/15; Col., 22/2/15: +*F. COUTTS*)
A Great Experiment ('*c.*': Lyc., N.Y., 7/1/16)
×Double or Quits. LC, Hippo., Hyde, 26/4/16. *Fr. 1919*
Gold Fields (Gar., 21/6/20, *m.*: adapted from M. Gerbidon, *Une affaire d'or*, 1912)
×Stars. *Fr. 1925*

When Adam Delved ('*c.*': Q, 18/7/27)
The Theatre of Life (Arts, 5/4/29: translated from N. Evreinov and F. Nozière, *Teatr kak takovoi*, 1929)

PASTON, GUY
Joan of Arc (St Helen's, 22/5/24)

'*PATCH, PURPLE*'
The Rise and Fall of Architecture ('*f.*': K's H., 24/3/09, *amat.*)

PATERNOSTER, G. SIDNEY
The Dean of St Patrick's (Abbey, Dublin, 23/1/13)
×Jonathan Swift (Vaud., 13/12/23, *m.*)

PATMORE, W. J.
[For earlier plays see *H. E. D.* v, 515]
Life's Handicap (Pav., 10/9/00)
×How Nick Carter Solved the Mystery of the Living and the Dead (Pal., Bow, 20/6/10)

PARTREIDGE, NORMAN
Charlie on the Spree. LC, Gr., Halifax, 11/11/15: +*B. SEYMOUR*

PATRICK, H. FORBES
Twenty One. LC, Market H., Redhill, 27/6/25

PATTERSON, ARTHUR
Colonel Cromwell (Glo., 11/9/00: +*C. CARTWRIGHT*)

PATTERSON, FREDERICK C.
×Jeanette (Aldw., 14/2/22, *m.*)

PATTERSON, MARJORIE
×Pan in Ambush (Court, 6/2/16, Pioneer Players)

PATTISON, FRED
[Several sketches and playlets produced at music-halls]

PAUL, Mrs CLIFFORD
The Fugitive King, or The Adventure of Charles II in Dorset. *1926*

PAUL, WILLIAM
The Jerry Builders (O.H., Belfast, 5/12/11)
Sweeping the Country ('*c.*': O.H., Belfast, 10/12/12)
The Tumilty Case ('*c.*': O.H., Belfast, 13/12/16)

PAULE, T. M.
A Play without a Name ('*society d.*': Oxford, 20/7/08)
×Nina (Hippo., Willesden, 10/10/10)

PAULETTE, F.
At Piney Ridge. LC, Cambridge, Spennymoor, 22/1/19

PAULL, HARRY MAJOR
[For earlier plays see *H. E. D.*, v, 516]
The New Clown ('*f.*': Gr., Margate, 3/2/02; Terry's, 8/2/02)
My Lord from Town ('*past. pl.*': Worcester College, Oxford, 18/6/04) *Fr. 1913*

The Duchess of Bermondsey ('*f.c.*': Lyc., Edin., 20/4/08; Crown, Peckham, 25/5/08, as *The Fortunes of Fan*)
×A Game of Bluff (Court, L'pool, 11/5/08)
The Painter and the Millionaire ('*modern morality pl.*': Court, 21/1/12, Pl. Actors)
×The Lady Cashier (Cor., 5/2/12)
×The Unknown Star ('*Christmas Mystery*': +*L. HOUSMAN*) *1919* (in *The Nineteenth Century*, Dec. 1919)

[*PAULTON, EDWARD A.* [see also *H. PAULTON* and *A. PHILIPP*]
Miss Walker of Wooloomooloo ('*m.c.*', m. E. Jakobowski: Glo., 5/10/00, *cpy.*)
An Eye-Opener ('*f.c.*: Pier, Brighton, 11/11/01: +*C. BRADLEY*)
All at Sea ('*m.c.*', m. W. Arthur: County, Kingston, 15/6/03; Crown, Peckham, 7/9/03)
×The Naked Truth (Col., 17/5/09)
Her Temporary Husband ('*f.c.*': Stamford, Conn., 9/5/22; Frazee, N.Y., 31/8/22; D.P., Eastbourne, 2/4/23; D.Y., 8/5/23) *Fr. 1927*

[*PAULTON, HARRY*
[For earlier plays see *H. E. D.* v, 516–17 and 809]
×The Magic Beans (Pier, Brighton, 15/4/01: +*E. PAULTON*)
A Man with a Past ('*f.c.*': Worthing, 9/5/01: +*E. PAULTON*)
Smith, Brown, Jones and Robinson ('*f.c.*': O.H., Coventry, 29/7/01; Shak., Clapham, 5/8/01; Brixton, 9/11/03: +*E. PAULTON* and *K. LEE*)
Miles Carew, Highwayman (O.H., Cheltenham, 3/9/06: +*E. PAULTON*)
×The Chalice (Daly's, 25/5/08, *m.*, Catholic Actors' Guild: +*E. PAULTON*)
The Old Firm ('*eccentric c.*': Newcastle, 17/8/08; Qns, 4/9/08: +*E. PAULTON*)
A Double Woman ('*c.*': D.P., Eastbourne, 11/3/12: +*E. PAULTON*)

PAULUS, JAN
The Birthright (Little, 25/2/12, Adel. Pl. Soc.)

PAUMIER, ALFRED
Our Friend the Jew (Merthyr Tydfil, 12/8/04, *cpy.*)
Pat in Africa ('*c.*': Abergavenny, 16/9/26)

PAWLE, LENNOX [see *P. J. WODEHOUSE*]

PAXTON, GUY
×Pestilence. LC, Chalet, Sheffield, 18/9/22
The Chance (Pal., Watford, 10/3/24: called originally *A Hero's Chance*)

PAXTON, M. E.
The Spider and the Fly. LC, Arcadia, Scarborough, 5/5/25

PAYNE, B. IDEN
×The Postern Gate (P.W., B'ham, 13/8/08)

PAYNE, C. OWEN [see *L. CORNELIUS*]

PAYNE, EDMUND [see *E. T. REED*]

PAYNE, GILBERT [see also *C. BALDWIN*]
A Cruise to Carnoustie ('*m.f.c.*', m. J. de Gabriel: Emp., Dundee, 24/7/05: +*FRANK PERCIVAL*)
The Honeymoon ('*m. absurdity*': Emp., Dundee, 17/9/06; Hippo., Rotherham, 20/3/16, as *Wedding Bell(e)s*)
The Marriage Mart ('*m.pl.*': H.M., Carlisle, 11/4/10)
×The Trainer's Daughter, LC, Ward's, Salisbury, 2/10/16
×Bingle's Bungle (Euston, 3/12/17)
×His Best Pal. LC, Woolwich, 16/6/19

PAYNE, W. M.
Sigurd Slembe (Bedford H., Chelsea, 29/7/23, Pax Robertson Salon: revised version of a rendering of the play (1862) by B. Björnson)

[*PEABODY, JOSEPHINE PEABODY* (*Mrs LIONEL S. MARKS*)
Marlowe. *1901* (Boston and New York); *1911*
The Piper (Shakespeare Memorial, Stratford-upon-Avon, 26/7/10; St J., 21/12/10) *1909* (Boston)
The Wolf of Gubbio ('*c.*') *1913*
Portrait of Mrs W. *1922* (Boston and New York)

PEACEY, HOWARD
×A Case of Arson (Roy., 11/2/05; Shaft., 13/11/05, as *The Factory Fire*)
Links (Scala, 31/5/08, St. Soc.; Playh., L'pool, 23/9/26: +*W. R. BRANDT*: translated from a play by H. Heijermans)
The Fifth of November. *1924*
The Nature of the Evidence (RADA, 19/4/25)
El Dorado. *1925* (Oxford)
Magic Hours (Q, 27/4/25) *1925*
Warren Hastings (Wynd., 23/4/29) *1928*
Hazard (RADA, 17/2/29)

PEACH, LAWRENCE DU GARDE
×Twin Souls. LC, Wynd., 31/7/00
×Wind o' the Moors ('*t.*': Gai., Manchester, 1/9/13) *1925* (in *Three One-Act Plays*)
×The Parting. LC, Bury St Edmunds, 7/4/14
×Sale by Auction (P's, Manchester, 14/4/15) *Fr. 1926*
Ever Ready Plays. *Fr. 1926*
[This contains five pieces originally intended for broadcasting]
Five Country Plays. *Fr. 1926*
[This contains five short plays: 1. *The Criminal*; 2. *The World Beyond*; 3. *Oak Chests*; 4. *The Marrying of William*; and 5. *The Man and the Moon*]
More Ever Ready Plays. *Fr. 1926*
[This contains five pieces originally intended for broadcasting]
×Numbered Chickens. *Fr. 1926*

Broadcast Sketches. *Fr. 1928*

[This contains six brief sketches originally intended for broadcasting]

The Proposals of Peggy. *Fr. 1928*

[This contains five duologues: 1. *The Wild Oat*; 2. *The Power of the Press*; 3. *The Stamp of Truth*; 4. *Twin Souls*; and 5. *The He-Man*]

× Motoring without Tears (*'revue sketch'*) *Fr. 1929*

PEACOCK, G. A.

× The Insect Seller of Fushiyama (*'Japanese idyll'*: Lyc., Edin., 11/5/00: + *W. W. MacFARLANE*)

PEACOCK, LESLIE

The Gay Young Bride (*'f.'*: Pal., Ramsgate, 31/12/23: Emp. Edmonton, 25/2/24)

PEACOCK, WADHAM

Bonita (*'c.o.'*, m. H. Fraser-Simson: Qns, 22/9/11)

PEACOCK, WALTER [see *B. JAMES* and *M. MALLESON*]

PEAKE, BLADEN

× The Romantics (Council H., B'ham, 17/3/25, *amat.*)

× The Veil (Council H., B'ham, 16/3/26, *amat.*)

× Pity the Blind (Midland Inst., B'ham, 12/3/27, *amat.*)

PEAKE, CHARLOTTE M. A.

A Masque of Day and Night (Boxford Rectory, 31/7/12) *1915* (Newbury)

The Crowning of the Year. *1915* (Newbury)

The Rivers (*'pastoral masque'*) *1916* (Newbury)

The Well in the Wood (*'pastoral masque'*) *1923* (Newbury)

× Women Will Gossip. *1927*

PEARN, VIOLET A. [see also *A. BLACKWOOD*]

× White Witch. LC, Worthing, 10/12/12. *1924* (Village Dr. Soc.)

Hush! (*'c.'*: Playh., L'pool, 30/3/16; Court, 7/5/17)

× A Prisoner Escaped. *1924* (Village Dr. Soc.)

The Otways (Little, Bristol, 11/1/26)

Their Angels (*'Christmas pl. for children'*) *Fr. 1927*

Wild Birds (Bristol, 19/5/14; Blackfriars, 22/2/28)

The Invisible Playmate. *Fr. 1930*

PEARSE, ASHTON [see also *A. HARE*]

× Her Proper Mate (Playh., 9/2/09, *m.*)

× A Month Come Sunday (Pier, Brighton, 16/6/16)

PEARSE, PADRAIC HENRY

The Singer and Other Plays. [*1921*? (Dublin)]

[This contains four short plays: 1. *The Singer* (Foresters, Dublin, 13/12/17); 2. *The King*; 3. *The Master*; and 4. *Iosagan*)

PEARSON, E. A. [see *F. SOBIENOWSKY*]

PEASE, HOWARD

The Tragedy of Holyrood (*'fourteen essential scenes from the life of Mary Queen of Scots'*) *1920*

PEASE, SIDNEY T. (see also *W. HOWARD*)
×The Man from Down There ('*m.bsq. ext.*': Emp., Oxford, 3/3/02)

PECHEY, ARCHIBALD THOMAS [='*VALENTINE*']

PECHEY, E. P.
×The Twin Brethren ('*mystery pl.*') *1918* (*priv.*)
Two Masques. *1922* (Village Dr. Soc.)
[This contains: 1. *The Crock of Gold*; and 2. *John o' the Field*]
Harry Vane the Younger ('*pageant pl.*': Fairlawne, Tonbridge, 28/5/23)

PECK, RAYMOND W.
Castles in the Air ('*m.c.*', m. P. Wenrich: Olympic, Chicago, 22/11/25; Selwyn, N.Y., 6/9/26; O.H., Blackpool, 7/3/27; Shaft., 29/6/27)

PEDLER, MARGARET
Who Pays? (Com., 26/6/21, Rep. Players)

PEILE, FREDERICK KINSEY [see also '*F. ANSTEY*']
[For earlier plays see *H. E. D.* v, 518]
×In a Fog (P.W., 15/1/01)
Bébé ('*m.c.*': Emp., Southend, 21/10/01; Metro., Camberwell, 28/10/01)
×The Man who Was (H.M., 8/6/03, *m.*; H.M., 18/1/06)
×Tubby and Gawks (Aven., 31/12/03) *Fr. 1913*
Mrs L'Estrange ('*c.*': Shaft., 22/5/05)
The Adventurer ('*r. costume pl.*': Gai., Hastings, 10/7/05; O.H., Tunbridge Wells, 2/8/06; Shak., Clapham, 13/8/06)
×The Stratagem (Gr., Croydon, 12/2/06; Court, 2/7/07; Pav., 18/3/12, as *The Shooting Star*)
×The Mummer's Wife (O.H., Tunbridge Wells, 2/8/06; Shak., Clapham, 13/8/06: adapted from *La femme de Tabarin* (1887) by Catulle Mendès)
×The Door upon the Latch (H.M., 14/6/07)
×Money and the Girl (Shak., L'pool, 10/4/09)
×Twelve O'Clock (Emp., Finsbury Park, 15/1/12)
×Biff (Pal., Chelsea, 2/12/12)
×The Pink Nightgown (Tiv., 22/9/13: originally called *Feminine Attire*)
The Sybarite (Daly's, 4/5/24, *m.*; Everyman, 14/9/25)
×Max Hensig (Gate, 18/9/29: +*A. BLACKWOOD*)

PELLATT, THOMAS [see '*W. T. COLEBY*']

PÉLLISSIER, H. C.
×Love's Garden (Apo., 1/12/08: +*A. DAVENPORT*)

PELTON, MARY OLLIS
The Gladding Light ('*Nativity pl.*') *1930*

'*PEM*'
×The Royal Flower (Cor., 29/8/06)

PEMBER, CLIFFORD [see *B. FLEET*]

PEMBERTON, FRED
A Strange Sequel (Qns H., Seaford, 15/7/03)

PEMBERTON, LEIGH
The Hole in the Roof. LC, Drill H., Sittingbourne, 15/1/14

PEMBERTON, Sir MAX [see also *A. M. THOMPSON* and *A. WIMPERIS*]
The Huguenot Lover ('*r.c.*': Glo., 24/5/01: +*J. McARTHUR*)
The Finishing School (Wynd., 16/6/04)
×The Prima Donna. *Fr. 1906*
×Lights Out! *Fr. 1906*
×The House of Nightingales. *Fr. 1907*
A Woman of Kronstadt (Gar., 8/2/08: +'*G. FLEMING*': dramatised from Pemberton's novel, *Krondstadt*, 1898)
The Lady of the Pageant ('*f.c.*': D.P., Eastbourne, 20/7/08: +*C. W. HOGG*)
×The Grey Room (York, 23/11/11: +*E. NORWOOD*) *Fr. 1912*
×Diane's Diamonds (Coll., 12/8/12)
Garrick (Col., 14/7/13)
×The Bells of St Valoir (Col., 30/11/14)
×The Haunted Husband (Col., 5/7/15)
Oh! Don't, Dolly! ('*m.f.*', m. G. Dorlay: Pleasure Gdns, Folkestone, 16/1/19; Crit., 3/3/19: +*E. PONSONBY*)

PEMBERTON, MAY
Christmas Plays for Children. *1914*
[This contains three short playlets: 1. *Lost Toys*; 2. *Mistletoe and Holly*; and 3. *Christmas in Rhyme-Land*]

PEMBERTON, THOMAS EDGAR
[For earlier plays see *H. E. D.* v, 519 and 810]
Mothering Sunday (O.H., Belfast, 10/10/01)
Held Up (Worcester, 24/8/03: +*B. HARTE*)

PEMBERTON-BILLING, N.
High Treason (Str., 7/11/28)

PEMBURY, G. [see *J. L. BARRY*]

PENDER, CHARLES
×The Ghost (Abbey, Dublin, 1/5/13)

PENDERED, MARY L.
William Penn. LC, Trinity Congregational H., Leeds, 26/2/24. *1922* (*priv.*)

PENLEY, BLANCHE [see *A. DYMOND*]

PENN, RACHEL
[For earlier plays see *H. E. D.* v, 623]
John Malone's Love Story (Court, 10/1/09, Pl. Actors)

PENSON, L. CYRIL
The Anomaly (Roy., 12/12/03, *cpy.*)

[*PEPLE, EDWARD HENRY*
The Prince Chap (Crit., 16/7/06)
×The Man. LC, Apo., 15/10/13
×The Girl (Vic. Pal., 19/1/14) *1926* (in *Five Plays from the Other Side*)
A Pair of Sixes ('*f.*': New Haven, Conn., 16/2/14; Longacre, N.Y., 20/3/14; P.W., B'ham, 30/8/20; Qns, 15/9/20) *1914* (New York)

PEPPLEWELL, OLIVE
×Tyranny and Tea Cakes. LC, O.H., Harrogate, 2/5/29

PERCIVAL, FRANK [see *G. PAYNE*]

PERCIVAL, R. M.
×The Lute Player (All Saints H., St John's Wood, 28/1/09)

'*PERCY, EDWARD*' [=*EDWARD PERCY SMITH*: see also '*M. ROSMER*']
Coloman (Str., 21/1/23, Rep. Players: +*W. B. NICHOLS*) *1916*
Joseph of Arimathea ('*r. morality*') *1920*
If Four Walls Told ('*village tale*': Unitarian Schools, Altrincham, 24/9/20, Garrick Soc.; Com., 12/3/22, Rep. Players; Roy., 13/4/22) *1922*
Trespasses (Brighton, 5/3/23; Ambass., 16/4/23) *1923*
Ancient Lights ('*c.*': Playh., Cardiff, 17/9/23; Everyman, 1/10/23)
×Merry Widow Welcome; or, the Treasure Hunters. *Fr. 1924*
×The Peer and the Paper Girl. *Fr. 1924*
The Rigordans (YMCA, Coventry, 6/12/27, *amat.*) *1924*
Slaves All (Bij., N.Y., 6/12/26)
Sadie Dupont (Str., 18/12/27, Rep. Players)
Electra (translated from the play by Sophocles) *1928*
The Misdoings of Charley Peace (Ambass., 12/9/29)
×A Perfect Little Fool. *Fr. 1930*
The Fiddler Play'd It Wrong (Str., 2/2/30, Rep. Players)

PERCYVAL, T. WIGNEY [see *H. HODGES*]

PEREIRA, JOAN
×La grisette étourdi ('*wordless t.*': Actors' Association, Strand, 7/4/08)
×Mademoiselle Fifi (Rehearsal, 13/12/08, Cercle Artistique; Ambass., 20/9/13, *revised*)
×A Queen's Honour (Coll., 17/10/10)

PERINI, EDWARD
×The Flame (Stedman's Academy, 9/3/12)
×The Drum (Stedman's Academy, 9/3/12)

PERKINS, CYRIL [='*CYRIL HARCOURT*']

PERKINS, Rev. F. L.
Disinherited. LC, '*pageant pl.*': Festival Concert R., York, 14/2/14

PERRIN, G. H., Jr
The Typewriter Girl ('*m.c.*': Ass. R., Portishead, 27/4/05)

PERRETTE, W. H.

×State Insurance; or, The Doctor's Minimum Wage (Gr., Manchester, 16/12/12)

PERRY, L. [=*'LADDIE CLIFF'*]

PERRY, T. GILBERT

[For an earlier play see *H. E. D.* v, 520]

The Isle of Champagne ('*m.c.*', m. A. Sugden: Alh., Stourbridge, 4/8/02; Duchess, Balham, 19/1/03)

[There is a puzzle concerning this play. It is recorded in *The Era Annual*, 1904, as above, at the Duchess, Balham, in 1903, with a statement that originally it had been presented at Stourbridge the year before: in *The Era Annual*, 1903, however, *The Isle of Champagne* performed at Stourbridge is described as a domestic drama written by J. F. Stanfield. In all probability the second statement is in error]

The Sporting Girl ('*m.pl.*', m. A. Sugden: Carlton, Greenwich, 30/5/04: title later changed to *The Girl from New York*)

'PERSONNE'

The Bachelor. LC, Industrial, Leeds, 6/2/22

PERTWEE, ROLAND [see also *D.C.CALTHROP* and *F. OURSLER*]

×Seein' Reason (Court, 21/11/13)

×Falling Upstairs (Court, 26/6/14)

×Swank (Court, 26/6/14)

×'Vantage Out (Court, 26/6/14)

×The Return of Imray (Court, 26/6/14)

×Told the Soldier. LC, Pav., Weston-super-Mare, 2/7/14

×Test Me. LC, P's, Bristol, 28/8/15

×Early Birds (Sav., 30/5/16, *m.*) *Fr. 1927*

×Postal Orders (H., 15/11/16) *Fr. 1919*

×Ten Minutes Tension (Theatrical Gdn Party, Chelsea, 10/7/17)

×Man to Man; or, A Post-War Reckoning (Theatrical Gdn Party, Chelsea, 22/6/20)

×The Odd Streak. *Fr. 1920*

The Eagle and the Wren. LC, Pier, Brighton, 16/12/20

×Honours Easy. *Fr. 1921*

×The Bitter Truth (Theatrical Gdn Party, Chelsea, 26/6/21)

I Serve (Ambass., Southend, 21/8/22; Kings., 14/9/22)

×Packing Up (Theatrical Gdn Party, Chelsea, 26/6/23; Col., 14/2/27

×The Chap Upstairs (Col., 28/4/24)

×Evening Dress Indispensable. LC, Col., 12/5/24. *Fr. 1925*

Slipping on the Peel (RADA, 18/1/25)

×The Loveliest Thing. *Fr. 1927*

Interference (St J., 29/1/27: dramatised from his own novel (1927): +*H. DEARDEN*) *Fr. 1929*

×A Voice Said 'Good Night'. *Fr. 1928*

Heat Wave (New, Cardiff, 7/10/29; St J., 15/10/29) *1933* (in *Five Three-Act Plays*)

Honours Easy (St M., 7/2/30) *Fr. 1932*

PERUGINI, MARK EDWARD

×The Flame (*'wordless pl.'*: Broadway, New X, 12/12/07, *cpy.*) *1908*

PERUGINI, STELLA

×Peggy (Broadway, New X, 12/12/07, *cpy.*)

×In the Good Old Days (P's, 6/7/15, *m.*)

PESCUD, G. E. CORNILLE [see *G. E. CORNILLE-PESCUD*]

PETERMAN, JOE

×The Station-Master (K's, Southsea, 20/1/12, *cpy.*; Pal., Walthamstow, 11/3/12)

The Girl with the Auburn Hair (*'operatic sensation'*: Pal., Chelsea, 28/2/16)

The Far East (*'m.c.d.'*: Emp., Wolverhampton, 5/1/20)

×The Unemployed V.C. (Qns, Leeds, 26/11/23)

[Several sketches and playlets produced at music-halls]

PETERS, GEORGE

Peter the Pensmith (*'c.'*: Portsmouth, 7/6/26)

PETERSON, JOHN

Mary of Scots. *1922*

Her Daughter (*'c.'*: Everyman, 24/6/24) *1917* (Calcutta)

PETERSON, MARGARET

The Summons (Q, 4/4/27)

PETHERICK, MAURICE

Where Am I? (*'f.c.'*: D.P., Eastbourne, 12/5/24: adapted by *A. STEWART*: based on a play by L. Barzini and A. Fraccaroli)

PETLEY, E. S. [see *G. W. ELTON*]

PETRIE, Sir CHARLES ALEXANDER

The White Rose. LC, Little, 11/6/23. *1923*

PETRIE, WALTER WADHAM

The Gold Diggers (*'c.o.'*: Duchess, Balham, 9/6/02; Bath, 16/4/06, revised with *C. AVELING*)

PETTINGELL, FRANK

×A Cowboy's Honour. LC, Qns, Longton, 10/9/13

PETTITT, D. H.

The Pranks of Julia (Amersham Common, 7/4/23, *amat.*)

PETTITT, HENRY

The Scarlet Hand (*'md.'*: Shak., Clapham, 5/12/10)

The Edge of the Storm (County H., St Albans, 2/12/12, *cpy.*)

'PHARAMOND'

Save the Mark (*'f.'*: Arts, 10/11/27)

PHELPS, CHARLES H.

[For an earlier play see *H. E. D.* v, 522]

The Blind Foundling (Birkenhead, 18/12/1899; Carlton, Greenwich, 15/4/01)

Man's Inhumanity (Gai., Burnley, 7/7/02: +*F. SERARD*)

One Woman's Wickedness (Smethwick, 15/12/02)

Man or Beast? (*'r.d.'*: Star, Swansea, 27/7/08; Stratford, 30/11/08)

[*PHELPS, PAULINE*
Shavings (Hartford, Conn., 29/12/19; Knickerbocker, N.Y., 16/2/20; Portsmouth, 25/10/26; Apo., 1/11/26: +*MARION SHORT*) *Fr. 1930*

PHIBBS, Mrs HARLOW
× The Rack (Rehearsal, 20/2/12, *m.*)

PHILIPP, ADOLF
Adèle ('*m.pl.*', m. J. Briquet: Gai., 30/5/14: +*E. A. PAULTON*)

'*PHILIPPA*'
× Oh! What a Surprise! (Clavier H., 22/4/12, Black Cat Club)

PHILIPS, ALFRED [see *BEATRICE WEBB*]

PHILIPS, F. C.
Lady Paddington ('*f.c.*': Pav., Hastings, 26/7/02: +*W. PARKE*)
Breaking It Off ('*f.c.*': Pav., Hastings, 4/5/03: +*W. PARKE*)

PHILLIP, W.
× William. LC, Crippl. Inst., 17/2/22

PHILLIPS, ARTHUR K.
× A Love Episode ('*wordless pl.*': Playh., L'pool, 17/9/13; Kings., 17/5/15)

PHILLIPS, AUSTIN [see also *L. M. LION*]
× The Fourth Man (Gai., Manchester, 10/4/16: +*EDWARD CECIL*)
× Promotion (Col., 24/3/24: +*L. M. LION*)

PHILLIPS, BEN
× The Renewal (Rehearsal, 13/11/08, *m.*, Argonauts)
× Colonel and Mrs Henderson (Playh., 27/11/10)

PHILLIPS, B. MANDEVILLE
× Doubtful Engagements (Pav., Eastbourne, 26/5/13)

PHILLIPS, CATHERINE ALISON
Don Juan (translated from a play by Azorin) *1923*

PHILLIPS, CECIL
Drink; or, Saved by a Child's Prayer (T.H., Cley-next-the-Sea, 14/6/07)

PHILLIPS, HERBERT G.
Lady Exmore's Embarrassment ('*c.*': Concert H., St Leonard's, 20/2/09, *amat.*)

PHILLIPS, STEPHEN
Herod (H.M., 31/10/00) *1900*
Ulysses (H.M., 1/2/02) *1902*
Paolo and Francesca ('*t.*': St J., 6/3/02) *1900*
The Sin of David (Sav., 9/7/14) *1904*
× Aylmer's Secret (Adel., 4/7/05)
Nero (H.M., 25/1/06) *1906*
The Bride of Lammermoor (K's, Glasgow, 23/3/08; Adel., 5/10/08, as *The Last Heir*: dramatised from Sir Walter Scott's novel)

Faust (H.M., 5/9/08: +*J. W. COMYNS CARR*: adapted from Goethe's drama) *1908*
Pietro of Siena (Studio, Victoria St., 10/10/11, Drama Soc.) *1910*
The King ('*t.*') *1912*
Everywoman: Her Pilgrimage in Quest of Love ('*modern morality pl.*': D.L., 11/9/12: originally written by *W. BROWNE* and produced in America, adapted for the English stage by Phillips) *1912*
×Iole ('*t.*': Cosmopolis, 11/7/13)
Lyrics and Dramas. *1913*
[In addition to *The King* (see above), this contains two short plays: *Nero's Mother* and *The Adversary*]
Armageddon ('*modern epic d.*': New, 1/6/15) *1915* (New York)
Harold ('*chronicle pl.*') *1927*

PHILLIPS, W. E. [see *S. PRINGLE*]

PHILLIPS, Rev. W. FORBES
For Church or Stage ('*society d.*': Aquar., Yarmouth, 8/6/03; Sav., 12/11/04)
Lord Danby's Love Affair ('*society r.*': Leamington, 24/4/05; Cor., 22/5/05)
A Maid of France ('*c.*': Yarmouth, 10/7/05)
When It Was Dark (County, Kingston, 12/2/06: dramatised from the novel (1903) by Guy Thorne)
The Puritans. LC, Ass. R., Tenby. 5/2/15
×The Call (Ass. R., Tenby, March 1916)
×The Lost Legacy (Playh., L'pool, 5/12/17)

PHILLIPSON, A.
Rhoda Fleming (Ambass., 21/3/21, *m.*, Playwrights' Theatre: from George Meredith's novel, 1865)

PHILLPOTTS, EDEN
[For earlier plays see *H. E. D.* v, 524]
×For Love of Prim (Court, 24/1/1899; D.Y., 19/8/02)
×A Golden Wedding (Playh., 22/2/08: +*C. GROVES*)
The Secret Woman (Kings., 22/2/12, '*private pfce.*': Rep., B'ham, 14/10/22) *1912*
Curtain Raisers. *1912*
[This contains three short plays: 1. *The Point of View* (St G's House, Regent Street, 18/11/13, Theatre in Eyre; Hippo., Bristol, 21/12/25; Col., 28/12/25); 2. *Hiatus* (Gai., Manchester, 22/9/13; Court, 20/10/13); and 3. *The Carrier Pigeon* (Roy., Glasgow, 7/4/13)]
The Shadow (Gai., Manchester, 6/10/13; Court, 20/10/13) *1913*
The Mother (Playh., L'pool, 22/10/13; Q, 15/2/26) *1913*
The Angel in the House ('*c.*': Sav., 3/6/15: +*B. M. HASTINGS*) *Fr. 1915*
Bedrock ('*c.*': Gai., Manchester, 16/10/16; Crippl. Inst., 18/11/24, Illyrian Dram. Soc.: +*B. M. HASTINGS*) *1924*
The Farmer's Wife ('*c.*': Rep., B'ham, 11/11/16; Court, 11/3/24: +*M. A. E. PHILLPOTTS*) *1916* (New York); *1917*

St George and the Dragons ('*c.*': Rep., B'ham, 30/3/18; Kings., 11/6/19: title later changed to *The Bishop's Night Out*) *1919*
×The Market-Money (Playh., L'pool, 5/6/29) *1923*
Devonshire Cream ('*c.*': Rep., B'ham, 6/12/24; R.A., Woolwich, 13/9/26; Playh., 13/2/30: +*M. A. E. PHILLPOTTS*) *1925*; *Fr. 1930*
A Comedy Royal. *1925* (*priv.*)
Jane's Legacy ('*c.*': Rep., B'ham, 24/10/25) *1931* (described as '*a folk pl.*')
The Blue Comet ('*c.*': Rep., B'ham, 11/9/26; Court, 23/2/27) *1927*
Yellow Sands ('*c.*': H., 3/11/26): +*M. A. E. PHILLIPOTTS*) *1926*
Three Short Plays. *1928*
[This contains: 1. *The Market-Money* (see above); 2. *Something to Talk About* (Col., 17/1/27); and 3. *The Purple Bedroom* (Court, 3/5/26, *m.*; Col., 27/12/26)]
My Lady's Mill ('*c.*': Lyr., 2/7/28: +*M. A. E. PHILLPOTTS*)
The Runaways ('*c.*': Rep., B'ham, 1/9/28; Gar., 14/11/28) *1928*
Buy a Broom ('*c.*') *1929*

PHILLPOTTS, MARY ADELAIDE EDEN [see also *EDEN PHILLPOTTS*]
Arachne. *1920*
×Camillus and the Schoolmaster. *1923*
×Savitri the Faithful. *1923*
Akhnaton. *1926*
The Mayor ('*c.*': Rep., B'ham, 28/1/29; Roy., 11/3/29)

PIAGGIO, G. VESIAN
×At the Play. *1913*

PIC, G. VESIAN
The Foreign Woman ('*hist. pl.*': P.W., Wolverhampton, 25/10/02; Qns, Manchester, 31/8/03) *1902*

PICKETT, GEORGE [see also *J. G. BRANDON*]
The Scorpion (K's, Hamm., 4/8/30: +*DONALD FINN*)

PIERCE, LUCIE FRANCE
Love o' Life (Court, 17/6/10, *cpy.*)

PIERSON, C. HARVARD [see also *R. P. OGLESBY*]
×The Night Mail (Qns, Keighley, 8/6/03)
The Blanchard Diamonds (Aven., Sunderland, 8/11/04; Gr., Hull, 13/2/05: +*R. P. OGLESBY*)

PIGGOTT, F. NEVILLE [see *S. DARKE*]

PIGOTT, Sir FRANCIS
×London Voices (H.M., 7/12/15, *m.*)

PIGOTT, J. SMYTH
Kitty Grey ('*f.*': Vaud., 25/4/00: P's, Bristol, 27/8/00, as a 'm.pl.'; Apo., 7/9/01: adapted from *Les fêtards* (1897) by A. Mars and M. Henniquin)
The Old Love ('*c.*': Glo., 31/5/00)

PIGOTT, MOSTYN

[For an earlier play by this author see *H. E. D.* v, 524: it seems uncertain whether his name should be spelt Piggott or Pigott – but probably the latter]

All Fletcher's Fault (Aven., 19/12/03)

PIGOTT, Sir FRANCIS

× London Voices (H.M., 7/12/15, *m.*)

PILCHER, VELONA

The Searcher. *1929*

[*PILLOT, EUGENE*

My Lady Dreams (Guildhall School of Music, 6/1/26, New Play Club)

'*PIMPLE*'

Mademoiselle from Armentiers ('*bsq.*': Gr., Luton, 19/9/27)

PINCHBECK, W. H.

× Lydia's Sacrifice (Gai., Manchester, 24/3/13)

[The production date is that given in Rex Pogson's *Miss Horniman and the Gaiety Theatre Manchester*: elsewhere it is cited as 22/3/13]

PINERO, Sir ARTHUR WING

[For earlier plays see *H. E. D.* v 524–5 and 810]

Iris (Gar., 21/9/01) *1901* (*priv.*); *1902*

Letty (D.Y., 8/10/03) *1903* (*priv.*): *1904*

A Wife without a Smile ('*c.*': Wynd., 12/10/04) *1904* (*priv.*); *1905*

His House in Order ('*c.*': St J., 1/2/06) *1905* (*priv.*); *1906*

The Thunderbolt ('*episode in the history of a provincial family*': St J., 9/5/08) *1908* (*priv.*); *1909*

Mid-Channel (St J., 2/9/09) *1909* (*priv.*); *1911*

Preserving Mr Panmure ('*c.*': Com., 19/1/11) *1910* (*priv.*); *1912*

The 'Mind the Paint' Girl ('*c.*': D.Y., 17/2/12) *1912* (*priv.*); *1913*

× The Widow of Wasdale Head ('*fant.*': D.Y., 14/10/12) *1912* (*priv.*)

× Playgoers ('*domestic edpisode*': St J., 31/3/13) *Fr. 1913*

The Big Drum (St J., 1/9/15) *1915* (*priv.*); *1915*

× Mr Livermore's Dream (Col., 15/1/17)

The Freaks ('*idyll of suburbia*': New, 14/2/18) *1917* (*priv.*); *1922*

× Monica's Blue Boy ('*wordless pl.*', m. Sir Frederic Cowen: New, 8/4/18)

Quick Work (Springfield, Mass., 17/11/19)

× A Seat in the Park (W.G., 21/2/22, *m.*) *Fr. 1922*

The Enchanted Cottage ('*fable*': D.Y., 1/3/22) *1922*

× A Private Room (Little, 14/5/28) *Fr. 1928*

Two Plays. *1930*

[This contains *Dr Harmer's Holidays* ('*a contrast*') and *Child Man* ('a sedate farce')]

PINK, WAL [see also *E. C. MATTHEWS*]
A Father of Ninety ('*m.f.*', m. H. Darnley: Eden, Brighton, 29/9/02; E.C., 1/12/02; Leamington, 10/9/17, as *Mr Mayfair*; Hippo., Willesden, 15/10/17: called also *The Merry Mormon*)
[Numerous sketches and playlets produced at music-halls]

PINKERTON, PERCY
[For an earlier play see *H. E. D.* v, 525 and 810]
At the Harbour Side ('*o.*', m. N. Spinelli: Brighton, 17/3/00; Cor., 14/11/00)
The Cricket on the Hearth ('*o.*', m. C. Goldmark: Brixton, 23/11/00)
Nigel ('*r.o.*', m. S. E. Philpot: Gr., B'ham, 25/1/07; Shak., Clapham, 8/2/07)

PINKERTON, PERCY E.
Nerina ('*lyrical d.*') *1927* (Cambridge)

PIREAU, MAX
[For an earlier play see *H. E. D.* v, 525]
Savonarola (Central, Northwich, 22/3/01, *cpy.*: +*A. GREY*)
×For King Monmouth ('*costume pl.*': Pier, Brighton, 27/11/02; Ass. R., Balham, 28/10/03, *cpy.*)
The Waters of Strife ('*costume c. past.*': Bedford Park, 15/9/06)

PITT, A. [see *A. KALISCH*]

[*PIXLEY, FRANK*
The Prince of Pilsen ('*m.c.*', m. G. Luders: St G's H., 5/5/02, *cpy.*; Shaft., 14/5/04)
The Grand Mogul ('*c.o.*', m. G. Luders: Bij., 1/11/06)

PLANCHÉ, S.
[For earlier plays see *H. E. D.* v, 528]
A Voice from the Grave (Gr., Walsall, 21/7/02; Sur., 30/3/03: +*F. DENMAN-WOOD*)

PLATT, AGNES [see also *N. S. PUGH*]
My Pretty Little Coz (St G's H., 5/2/00)
The Good King (Glasgow, 21/5/28)

PLAYFAIR, GILES
×The K.C.'s Comedy (Arts, 8/5/29)

PLAYFAIR, Sir NIGEL [see also *P. CARR*, *A. P. HERBERT*, *G. E. JENNINGS*, *M. HUTCHINSON* and *P. SELVER*]
×Amelia (Gar., 22/1/03)
×Alice (Court, 29/5/05: +*R. FILIPPI*)
×The Bridegroom (Playh., 4/5/08, ADA students)
The Insect Play (Jolson, N.Y., 31/10/22, as *The World We Live In*; Reg., 5/5/23: also called *And So ad infinitum*: +*C. BAX* and *P. SELVER*: adapted from the play (1921) by Karel Čapek) *1923*
When Crummles Played (Lyr., Hamm., 2/6/27) *1927*
The Lady of the Camelias (translated from the play by A. Dumas: +*E. REYNOLDS*) *1930*

PLEON, HARRY

[For earlier plays see *H. E. D.* v, 528]

The Boy from Down There (‘*f.*’: Marina, Ramsgate, 23/5/01, *cpy.*)

× A Club Raid (‘*realistic d. episode*’: Aston, 20/4/03)

‘*PLEYDELL, GEORGE*’ [= *G. P. BANCROFT*]

PLINGE, WALTER

The Wooing of Wundle. LC, K. G’s H., 6/2/22

PLOWMAN, MARY

× Daphne Writes a Novel (Court, 15/1/14)

PLUMMER, WILLIAM BRETT

× Cupid in Mischief (Ass. R., Balham, 29/4/01)

PLUMPSTEAD, H. P.

× The Admiralty Regrets...(‘*t.*’: Gate, 18/9/29)

PLUNKETT, IRENE ARTHUR LIFFORD

Chin Chin. LC, ‘*c.*’: K. G’s H., 24/11/22. *1921* (Milford-on-Sea)

POCOCK, ARCHIBALD HENRY

Love in Autumn (‘*c.*’: Bij., 12/7/04, *amat.*)

The Defence of Lady Rosa (‘*c.*’: Bij., 18/5/05)

Love and a Shadow (‘*c.*’: Hampstead Conservatoire, 30/5/07, *amat.*)

× The Third Way (Crippl. Inst., 18/12/09, *amat.*)

× Lydia and the Parson (Alh., Brighton, 4/7/10; Emp., Camberwell, 17/10/10)

× In Male Attire (Empress, 30/11/10)

The Blunderers (‘*c.*’: Kursaal, Bognor, 2/5/12)

POCOCK, ROGER [see *LENA ASHWELL*]

PODGSON, N. A.

Bushido (Everyman, 15/6/21: adapted from a Japanese play, *Sugawara*)

× Sayonara (Kings., 21/6/21, *m.*, Playwrights’ Theatre)

PODMORE, C. T.

The Real Jeff Carbury (Crown, Eccles, 23/8/26)

POEL, WILLIAM

[For earlier plays see *H. E. D.* v, 529 and 811]

The First Franciscans (St G’s H., 6/4/05, Eliz. Stage Soc.)

Lilies that Fester (and) Love’s Constancy. *1906*

[Two one-act plays based on scenes taken from the Elizabethan dramas, *Arden of Feversham* and *Edward III*]

The Redemption of Agnes (‘*Italian medieval religious pl.*’: Vic. H., 14/2/07, *cpy.*; Cor., 30/3/07) *1908* (as *The Temptation of Agnes*)

Life in Camp (New, Oxford, 11/8/11: adapted from scenes in Schiller’s *Wallenstein*)

POINTING, H. B.

The White Lady. LC, T.H., Dunstable, 6/1/25. [? *1925* (Lechmere) *priv.*]

POLE, Mrs RICHARD
[A few playlets produced at music-halls]

POLINI, G. M.
A Lady's Maid's Honour (Bournemouth, 20/11/09)

POLLEY, SYDNEY ARTHUR
× Where Truth Lies. LC, Sanderstead H., 12/3/24
× A Spark upon the Air (Sanderstead H., 4/10/24, *amat.*)
× Not Forgetting the Gate Post (St James' H., Kenley, 19/1/25, *amat.*) *1925*
× The Half of Wisdom (Sanderstead H., 3/10/25, *amat.*)
Firelight ('*c.*': Sanderstead H., 6/2/26, *amat.*)
Bridle-way ('*c.*': Greyhound, Croydon, 11/10/27; Q, 3/3/30)
Portrait of a Lady (Q, 26/8/29) *1933*

[*POLLOCK, CHANNING*
In the Bishop's Carriage (Waldorf, 24/6/07: from the novel (1904) by Miriam Michelson)
The Red Widow ('*m.c.*', m. C. J. Gebest: Ladbr. H., 31/8/11: *R. WOLF*)
The Sign on the Door (Glo., Atlantic City, 15/12/19, as *A Room at the Ritz*; Republic, N.Y., 19/12/19; Playh., 1/9/21) *Fr. 1924*
The Fool (Times Square, N.Y., 23/10/22; Apo., 18/9/24) *1922* (New York)
The Enemy (Parson's, Hartford, 5/10/25; Times Square, N.Y., 20/10/25; K's, Edin., 4/6/28; Hippo., Golder's Green, 2/7/28; Str., 23/7/28) *1925* (New York)

POLLOCK, FRED [see *NANCY POLLOCK*]

POLLOCK, GUY [see *W. H. POLLOCK*]

POLLOCK, Sir JOHN, Bt [='*FREDERICK DEFELL*': see also *Prince BARIATINSKY* and *Z. VENGEROVA*]
Twelve One-Acters. *1926*
[This contains a dozen short plays, dating from the start of the author's dramatic career on to a time shortly before publication: 1. *Rosamond* (Little, 8/12/10, *m.*; Roy., 28/2/11); 2. *The Invention of Dr Metzler* (Scala, 17/6/06, Stage Soc.); 3. *Mademoiselle Diana* (K's H., 14/7/12); 4. *The Love of Mrs Pleasance* (Kings., 13/5/11, as *Mrs Pleasance*, and credited to '*FREDERICK DEFFELL*'); 5. *On the Frontier*; 6. *Lolotte* (Col., 10/3/13); 7. *Conchita*; 8. *A King in England*; 9. *For Russia!* (Col., 4/1/15); 10. *In the Forests of the Night* (Col., 5/7/20, as *In the Darkness of the Night*); 11. *The Luck King* (Ambass., 16/10/21, Rep. Players); and 12. *The Dream of a Winter Evening* (Ambass., 3/3/21, *m.*)]
The Parisienne (Roy., 26/6/11: adapted from the play (1885) by Henri Becque)
Anna Karenina (Ambass., 1/12/13: dramatised from Tolstoi's novel)
Damaged Goods (Little, 16/2/14, Authors' Producing Soc.;

St M., 17/3/17: adapted from *Les Avariés* (1902) by E. Brieux *1911* (in *Three Plays of Brieux*)
[This volume also includes Pollock's translation of *Maternité*]
× The King's Favourite (Ambass., 3/3/21, *m.*)

POLLOCK, LEON
[Several sketches and playlets produced at music-halls]

POLLOCK, NANCY
Who's Who. LC, Pearce Inst. H., Govan, 15/12/21: +*F. POLLOCK*

POLLOCK, WALTER HARRIES [see also *E. CASTLE*]
[For earlier plays see *H. E. D.* v, 529]
Hay Fever ('*f.c.*': P'cess, 27/2/02, *cpy.*: +*G. POLLOCK*)
The Very Man ('*f.c.*': P'cess, 27/2/02, *cpy.*: +*G. POLLOCK*)
× Love's Magnet (P's, Manchester, 9/10/03; Alex., 23/11/03)

POLLOCK, WILLIAM
Kimono (Q, 26/7/26: from the novel (1921) by John Paris)

POLMWOOD, MARION
× A Nicht's Wark. LC, Union H., Selkirk, 10/3/22: +*NORMAN POLMWOOD*

PONSONBY, CLAUDE
Percy the Altruist (County, Bedford, 12/12/12, *amat.*)

PONSONBY, EUSTACE [see also *M. PEMBERTON* and *W. T. SAWARD*]
[For an earlier play see *H. E. D.*, v, 529]
Ladyland ('*m.c.*', m. F. Lambert: Aven., 12/12/04) *1905*
× The Magic Table ('*m.fant.*': P.W., 30/6/16, *m.*)

PONSONBY, MAGDALEN
× Idle Women (Little, 21/6/14, Pioneer Players) *1914*

POOLE, S. [see *E. H. FAGG*]

PORTER, ADRIAN
× Vive l'Empereur! (County H., Guildford, 6/1/11, English Play Soc.; Little, 12/6/11, *m.*, English Play Soc., as *After Jena*)

PORTER, Mrs CALEB [see also *Mrs F. WRIGHT*]
× A 24-H.P. Elopement (New, 1/7/04: +*J. CONDURIER*)
× The Marauder (Adel., 21/3/10)

PORTER, HAROLD E. [='*HOLWORTHY HALL*']

PORTER, Mrs JESSIE
Betty at Bay (Court, 11/3/18; Str., 9/4/18)
Restitution (Lyc. Club, 5/12/20)
Lady Larcombe's Lapse ('*c.*': Kings., 5/2/22, Pl. Actors)

PORTER, JOHN
× A Bit of Old Worcester (Parish R., Friern Barnet, 24/4/00)

PORTER, MARY [see *I. K. CLARK*]

POST, LEVI ARNOLD
Three Plays by Menander: The Girl from Samos, The Arbitration, The Shearing of Glycera. *1929*

POST, VAN ZO

So Like Me ('*f.*': Q, 5/7/26)

POST, W. H.

[For an earlier play see *H. E. D.* v, 529]

×Christmas Eve (Court, Wigan, 2/2/00)

×Conscription (Pal., Battersea, 21/11/10)

×Never Say Die ('*c.*': Apo., 13/9/13)

The Vagabond King ('*m.pl.*', m. R. Friml: Casino, N.Y., 21/9/25; O.H., Manchester, 4/4/27; W.G., 19/4/27: +*B. HOOKER*) *Fr. 1929*

Winona ('*m.pl.*', m. R. Friml: Emp., Southampton, 22/12/28: +*B. HOOKER*)

POTAPENKO, MARIE

×The Theatre of the Soul (Little, 7/3/15, Pioneer Players: translated from N. Evreinov, *V kulisakh dushi*, 1912: +*CHRISTOPHER ST JOHN*) *1915*

POTTER, FRANK ERNEST

×La Marseillaise (Worcester, 6/9/06)

×The Knave of Hearts (Ladbr. H., 22/11/06, *amat.*)

×Proteus in Petticoats (Gr., Wolverhampton, 11/1/09; Dalston, 7/6/09)

×The Password (Aven., Sunderland, 17/2/13: called originally *The Comrade of the Blues*: title later changed to *The French Spy*)

POTTER, GEORGE

The Tiger's Cub (Gr., Southampton, 6/12/15; Gar., 29/1/16)

POTTER, PAUL M. [see *H. HAMILTON*]

[For earlier plays see *H. E. D.* v, 530]

Twenty Days in the Shade ('*f.c.*': Margate, 29/3/09)

Parasites (Glo., 5/10/10: adapted from E. Fabre, *La rabouilleuse*, 1903)

POULTNEY, CLIFFORD B. [see *R. DANIEL*]

POULTON, J. A.

The Governor-General ('*m.c.*': Gr., Gainsborough, 23/1/11)

POUND, EZRA [see *ERNEST FENOLLOSA*]

POUNDS, E.

The Banquet ('*masque*': H.M., 9/1/17, *m.*: +*Mrs H. NICHOLSON*)

POWELL, Mrs MORTON

How Girls are brought to Ruin (Qns, L'pool, 25/1/09; Shak., Clapham, 12/7/09)

A Girl's Temptation (Star, L'pool, 12/7/09; Shak., Clapham, 1/11/09)

Driving a Girl to Destruction (Belfast, 7/2/10; Edmonton, 23/5/10)

From Mill Girl to Millionairess (Pav., 22/8/10)

The Ruin of Her Life (Leicester, 31/10/10; Marlb., Holloway, 13/2/11)

A Girl without a Home (E.C., 24/7/11)

POWELL, RICHARD HENRY
×The White Dove (Roy., Glasgow, 21/4/09)
The Wynmartens ('*c.*': Playh., 30/5/14)
×The King's Counterfeit (Qns, 29/10/20)

POWELL, T. MORTON [see also *C. A. CLARKE*]
The Covered Wagon. LC, Qns, Farnworth, 16/10/24

POWELL-ANDERSON, CONSTANCE
×The Heart of a Clown ('*autumn fant.*') *1920*
×The Courting of the Widow Malone ('*c.*') *1922*
×The Greatest Gift ('*vision*') *1926*
×When Love Grows Up ('*fant.*') *1926*
×Barren ('*modern everyday t.*') *1928*

POWER, ARTHUR
×The Drapier Letters (Abbey, Dublin, 22/8/27)

POWER, VICTOR O'D.
The Ordeal of David (Hardwick-st. H., Dublin, 1/7/12, Theatre of Ireland)
David Mahony (Abbey, Dublin, 29/1/14)
The Peril of Sheila (Coatbridge, 19/11/17)
×When the Cat's Away the Mice Can Play (and) Dinny Donoghue's Damsel: Two Farces. *1927* (Dublin)

POYSER, ARTHUR
×The King's Arms ('*oa.*': St J., 28/11/12, *m.*)
×Captain Scarlet ('*oa.*': St J., 28/11/12, *m.*)
×Burnham Beeches ('*oa.*': St J., 28/11/12, *m.*)

'*PREEDY, GEORGE R.*' [=*GABRIELLE MARGARET VERE CAMPBELL*]
Captain Banner (Arts, 25/4/29; Little, 29/4/29) *1930*

[*PRESBREY, EUGENE WYLEY* [see *E. W. HORNUNG*]

PRESCOTT, NORMAN
[For an earlier play see *H. E. D.* v, 530]
The Gay Cadets ('*m.c.*', m. B. Davies: P.W., B'ham, 24/6/01; Metro., Camberwell, 16/6/02: +*J. THOMSON*)

'*PRESLAND, JOHN*' [=*GLADYS SKELTON*]
The Marionettes ('*puppet show in two parts*') *1907*
Joan of Arc ('*hist. d.*') *1909*
Mary Queen of Scots ('*hist. d.*') *1910*
King Monmouth. LC, T.H., W. Hampstead, 10/10/10; Maddermarket, Norwich, 14/3/22. *1916*
Marcus Aurelius. *1912*
Belisarius, General of the East. *1913*
Satni ('*t.*') *1929*

PRESNALL, ROBERT R. [see also *R. BACON*]
Rust (Q, 12/1/26)

PRESTON, JOHN F.
[For earlier plays see *H. E. D.* v, 530]
Constantinople 1915 (Rot., L'pool, 19/4/15)
Youth will be Youth (Leicester, 7/7/19)

'PREVOST, FRANCIS' [=*H. F. PREVOST BATTERSBY*]

PRICE, ADDISON

Elaine. LC, Pav., Llandrindod, 5/9/14

×Branwen. LC, Pav., Llandrindod, 5/9/14

×The Nuns of Ardbor (Shak., L'pool, 3/5/18)

'PRICE, EVADNE' [=*HELEN ZENNA SMITH*]

The Haunted Light (*'mystery'*: Emp., Penge, 10/9/28: +*J. ROY-BYFORD*) *Fr. 1929*

PRICE, FRANK [see also *F. L. CONNYNGHAME*]

[For earlier plays see *H. E. D.* v, 530]

A Country Girl in London (Macclesfield, 1/8/08; Edmonton, 15/3/09; Gr., Fulham, 19/4/09: called originally *A Woman of Shame*)

Are You the Man? (County, Reading, 13/3/09, *cpy.*; O.H., Burton, 13/5/09)

A Child of the Streets (Gr., Walsall, 20/9/09; Stratford, 3/1/10)

A Bad Woman's Vengeance (Oldham, 19/1/14)

A Pitman's Daughters (O.H., Workington, 3/8/14; Stratford, 2/11/14)

Mother's Sailor Boy (Hippo., Salford, 11/9/16)

If Those Lips Could Only Speak. LC, Gr., Halifax, 25/3/18

The Girl from Canada (Pal., Newcastle, 24/6/18; Stratford, 23/9/18)

Dope (*'md.'*: Darlington, 21/3/19; Stratford, 1/5/22)

The Fortunes of Eileen (Stratford, 5/5/22)

Should They Marry? (Stratford, 8/5/22)

Our Mary (Stratford, 12/5/22; Darlington, 27/11/22, as *Sunshine Sally*)

[Numerous sketches and playlets produced at music-halls]

PRICE, GRAHAM

×The Absolution of Bruce. *1911*

×The Capture of Wallace. *1911*

×The Song of the Seal (Ath., Glasgow, 25/10/12) *1912*

×Marriages Are Made in Heaven – and Elsewhere. *1914*

×The Perfect Housekeeper (Ben Greet's Academy, 15/4/15) *1922*

×The Coming of Fair Annie (*'ballad p.'*) *1916*

×The Magic Rose-bush (*'fairy pastoral'*: York House, Twickenham, 29/7/16)

PRICE, J. H.

[A few sketches and playlets produced at music-halls]

PRICE, NANCY [see *R. THURNAM*]

PRICHARD, H. HESKETH

Don Q (Pal., Ramsgate, 14/3/21; Apo., 24/3/21)

PRICHARD, STANGER

×The Reaper (T.H., Chiswick, 15/4/02)

The Crystal Ring (*'fairy pl.'*; Ass. R., Norwich, 24/10/03; K. Edward's H., Finchley, 27/4/22)

PRIESTLEY, W. J.

×Ashes (People's, Newcastle, 3/14)

PRINGLE, ARTHUR E.

Other People's Money (P's, Bradford, 21/3/01, *cpy.*; Garston, 14/10/01: title later changed to *A Miserable Marriage* and *A Secret Marriage*)

×The Phantom Earl (Reg., Salford, 19/3/07)

PRINGLE, STUART

×After Business Hours. LC, K's, Walton, 2/6/21: +*W. E. PHILLIPS*

Oh! Richard! ('*f.*': O.H., Bridlington, 19/7/20; Gr., Luton, 19/3/23, as *Richard, How Could You?*: also called *Friends of the Master's*: +*E. JAMES*)

PRITCHARD, E. W.

Dick —? ('*c.o.*': Surrey Masonic H., 30/4/07, *amat.*: +*H. J. BODEN*)

'*PRITCHARD, LAURENCE*' [=*Mrs CECIL CAMPBELL*]

Talleyrand ('*spectacular pl.*') *1924* (Bristol: *priv.*)

'*PRITCHETT, RALPH*' [see *V. H. SUTTON-VANE*]

PRITT, STEPHEN

[For earlier plays see *H. E. D.* v, 531]

Lady Folly (Preston, 18/11/01; Gr., Fulham, 25/8/02: title later changed to *A Woman's Passion*)

His Wife No Longer (Preston, 21/9/08)

Almost His Bride (Preston, 13/9/09; Lyr., Hamm., 4/4/10)

PROCTOR, C. VERNON

The Real Mr Jonathan ('*f.c.*': Pav., Paignton, 15/6/08; Brighton, 6/12/09)

The Good Samaritan ('*md.*': Edmonton, 20/11/11)

The Unmarried Mother (E.C., 19/7/15)

The Unwanted Daughter (Ilfracombe, 2/8/15; Vic., Walthamstow, 23/8/15: originally called *Patty*)

The Wife with Two Husbands (E.C., 24/7/16: also called *Back to Wife and Blighty*)

×Kissing Belinda. LC, Pier, Brighton, 9/2/17

The Man who Made Good (Metro., Glasgow, 21/1/18; E.C., 15/4/18: title later changed to *Redeemed by Love*)

The Profiteer ('*md.*': New H., Bargoed, 1/4/18; E.C., 6/5/18)

The Plaything of an Hour ('*md.*': Metro., Glasgow, 30/12/18; E.C., 3/3/19)

Childless Wives (P's, Portsmouth, 3/6/19; Stratford, 16/6/19: title later changed to *The Call of a Little Child*)

Her Market Value (P's, Portsmouth, 14/6/20; Stratford, 27/6/21)

The Other Man's Child (P's, Portsmouth, 21/6/20; Stratford, 8/11/20)

Stand by Your Pals (P's, Portsmouth, 28/6/20; Stratford, 30/8/20)
Her Jungle Man (Pal., Gloucester, 1/8/21; E.C., 8/8/21: title later changed to *Savage Love*)
The Right to Motherhood (Stratford, 5/6/22)
Love and Laughter ('*r.m.pl.*', m. G. Seymour: Qns, Leeds, 2/4/23)
All the Nice Girls Love a Sailor (P's, Portsmouth, 24/12/23: called originally *Her Night of Love*)
If the Dead Could Speak (P's, Portsmouth, 7/1/24: title later changed to *The Silent Answer*)
The Girl in the Park (Coll., 27/6/27)

PROSPER, JOHN
See a Fine Lady ('*c.*': Q, 18/3/29)

PROTHEROE, JOHN
The Wolves (Portsmouth, 15/8/27; New, 31/8/27; adapted from a play by G. G. Toudouze)
Dancing Shadows (Arts, 16/10/29: adapted from M. Pagnol, *Jazz*, 1926)

PROVO, ROBERT
From Portland to Liberty (Lyr., Hamm., 10/3/13)

PROWSE, R. O.
Ina (Court, 15/5/04, St. Soc.)

PRYCE, RICHARD [see also *W. P. DRURY, F. FENN* and *A. MORRISON*]
×Liz's Baby (Metro., Camberwell, 22/4/01; Little, 28/3/21, as *The Love Child*: +*F. FENN*)
×The Visit (Playh., 1/12/09) *Fr. 1910*
Little Mrs Cummin ('*c.*': Playh., 1/12/09) *Fr. 1910*
Helen with the High Hand (Vaud., 17/2/14: dramatised from the novel (1910) by Arnold Bennett) *Fr. 1914*
The Old House (Court, 23/6/20)
Thunder on the Left (Arts, 26/7/28; Kings., 3/10/28: dramatised from the novel (1915) by Christopher Morley) *1934*

PRYCE-JENKINS, J. T.
[For an earlier play see *H. E. D.* v, 531]
The Sands of Time (Shak., Clapham, 23/2/03)

PRYNNE, A. L.
Columbine's Legacy. LC, St Faith's Inst., Gosport, 21/4/23

PRYOR, F. R. [see also *C. GARVICE* and *L. A. HARKER*]
The Autocrat (Kings., 16/5/29: +*C. H. PRYOR*)

PUGH, NORMAN S.
Helping Hands ('*f.*': Playh., Cardiff, 24/11/24; St J., 6/1/25, as *The Meddlers*: +*A. PLATT*)

PULLEY, HONOR M.
×Oranges and Lemons ('*children's pl.*') *1924* (*priv.*)
×Pat-a-Cake (and) Elsie Marley. *1925* (*priv.*)
×Tipperary ('*fant.*': Kings., 27/5/21, *m.*, Playwrights' Theatre)

PUNSHUN, E. R.
Learning Business ('*c.*': Q, 28/5/28)

PURCELL, R. J.
×The Spoiling of Wilson (Abbey, Dublin, 13/11/17)

PURDELL, REGINALD
I'll Tell the World ('*c.*': Everyman, 28/8/25: +*E. HENDERSON*)

PURDON, KATHLEEN FRANCES
×Candle and Crib ('*nativity pl.*': Abbey, Dublin, 27/12/20) *1914*

PURDON, LILLIAN FRANCES
×Persephone ('*pl. for girls*') *1905*
×Psyche ('*pl. for girls*') *1906*
×An Egyptian Cinderella; or, The Shoes of Rhodopis ('*pl. for girls*': LC, Passmore Edwards Settlement, 9/1/15) *1907*
×The Nut-Brown Maid ('*masque for morris-dancers*') *1909*
The Talisman of Saladin. LC, T.H., Bedford, 19/12/18
Undine ('*fant.*': LC, Pembroke H., Kensington, 1/11/21) *1921*

PYM, PAUL
×The Ne'er-do-weel ('*m.pl.*': Cranford H., Maidenhead, 29/6/11, *amat.*)

PYNE, ELLERSLIE
×The Veteran (Shotton, 6/11/05)

'*Q*' [=*Sir ARTHUR QUILLER-COUCH*]
The Mayor of Troy ('*c.*': H., 22/4/16)

'*Q., L.*'
×What's in a Name? (Ass. R., Surbiton, 21/5/13)

QUARITCH, A. H.
The Golden Land of Fairy Tales (Aldw., 14/12/11: +*M. RAYE*)
The Little Midshipman ('*oa.*', adapted to the English stage) *1911*
The King of Sharpers ('*oa.*', adapted to the English stage) *1912*

'*QUERY*'
Beyond the Moonbeams; or, Sylvia and the Three Bears (Playh., Newcastle, 23/12/25: called originally *Puck and Sylvia*)

QUEST, SOMERS
Gossip (Emp., Newcastle, 20/2/28; Hippo., Lewisham, 5/3/28)

QUIN, HOLMAN
×The Siren, or, The Actress's Triumph (Rehearsal, 17/11/10, *m.*)

'*QUIN, SHIRLAND*' [=*ENID GUEST*]
That Which Counts (D.Y., 4/10/25, Rep. Players) *1927*
The Blue Ray (D.P., Eastbourne, 28/11/27)
Before Midnight (Little, 8/4/29)

'*RACEWARD, THOMAS*'
When the Devil Drives ('*md.*': Qns, Manchester, 24/6/01)
A Bloodhound of the Law ('*md.*': Crown, Peckham, 24/3/02)
Sunday (D.P., Eastbourne, 11/1/04; Com., 2/4/04)

RACKOW, W.
Back to the Faith, LC, Pav., Mile End, 19/11/18

RACKSTRAW, E. C.
×'Make Believe' (Margate, 16/5/10: +*W. MUSKERRY*) *Fr. 1910*

RACSTER, OLGA
Dr James Barry. LC, St J., 7/7/19: +*J. GROVE*
Poor 'Em ('*c.*': Pier, Brighton, 27/3/22: title later changed to *The Londoners*: + *J. GROVE*)

RADCLIFFE, CLAUDE
×Holed Out in One. *Fr. 1919*
×Borgia. *Fr. 1927*
Will o' the Wisp. *Fr. 1930* ('*r.pl.*' or children)

RADFORD, Mrs ERNEST
The Ransom (Little, 9/6/12, *amat.*)

RADLOWE, EDWARD
Who Killed This Woman? LC, Sur., 8/10/20.

RAE, ELIZABETH [see also *ROSE O'NEILL*]
Blindfold ('*c.*': Church House, Erdington, 30/9/26)

RAE, KATHARINE T.
×The Ambition of Annabella Stordie ('*problem pl.*') *1927*

RAE, NITA
Mixed Pickles ('*m.c.*': Gr., Rawtenstall, 25/1/01, *cpy.*: also called *Gone Wrong*)
The Way of Transgressors (Lyc., Glasgow, 15/11/01, *cpy.*)
The Sins of a City (O.H., Morriston, 1/5/02; Terriss, Rotherhithe, 14/12/03)
We are But Human (Marina, Lowestoft, 28/1/03, *cpy.*; W.L., 15/2/04, as *Her Fatal Past*)
The Lunatics ('*m.c.*': R.A., Woolwich, 8/6/03)
The Queen of Spades (P's, Blackburn, 14/2/05, *cpy.*; P's, Portsmouth, 18/12/05, as *Her Lost Self*; Stratford, 30/4/06: title later changed to *The Queen of Crime*)
The Shadow of a Crime (County, Reading, 17/8/05, *cpy.*; Pav., Hastings, 28/5/06; Dalston, 18/3/07: title later changed to *At the Price of His Life*)
Geoffrey Langdon's Wife (Qns, L'pool, 18/12/05: title later changed to *A Beautiful Criminal*)
×When the Cat's Away (Tiv., Manchester, 19/4/07, *m.*)
Who Was the Woman? (L'pool, 28/10/07: title later changed to *One False Step*)
A Mother's Salvation (Wednesbury, 27/4/08; Stratford, 18/5/08; Leamington, 13/9/15, as *His Mother's Boy*: also called *Only a White Slave*)
A Woman's Love (Muncaster, Bootle, 22/6/08)
For Love of a Woman (Lyc., Stafford, 27/7/08; Tyldesley, 10/8/08; Stratford, 7/12/08)

No Mother to Guide Her (Gai., Musselburgh, 26/1/10; Stratford, 2/1/11)
Married to the Wrong Woman (Gai., Dundee, 1/8/10; Stratford, 11/1/15, as *Margaret, Red Cross Nurse*)
A Daughter of Israel (Lyc., Stafford, 20/5/12: title later changed to *A Fallen Idol* and *Reaping the Whirlwind*)
Only an Artist's Model (Alex., Hull, 24/3/13; Woolwich, 1/9/13)
The Little Fortune-Teller (P's, Portsmouth, 23/2/14: called originally *The White Witch*)
As a Man Sows (Pav., Pontnewynydd, 20/5/15: title later changed to *A Man and Two Women*)

RAE-BROWN, CAMPBELL
[For earlier plays see *H. E. D.* v, 533]
× The Show Girl (M'sex, 19/4/09)
× Coming a Cropper. *1912*
× Algy and the Actress. LC, Pier, Portsmouth, 23/3/14. *1912*
× Daddy Joyce. *1912*
× Percival's Twins. *1912*
× In the Conservatory. *1912*
× 'The Love Germ'. *1912*
× Poor Mamma's Secret. *1912*
× Too Handsome by Half. *1912*

RAIKES, CHARLES S. M.
Omar Khayyam (Stanley H., S. Norwood, 5/10/20; Court, 21/8/23)

RAINGER, HERBERT T.
The Bitter Sea (*'r.pl.'*: Vic. R., Cheltenham, 21/4/04, *amat.*)
× The Cap-Maker's Daughter (Vic. R., Cheltenham, 3/2/05, *amat.*)
The Rose of Dawn (Vic. R., Cheltenham, 22/2/07, *amat.*)
× Love's Honour (O.H., Cheltenham, 23/12/10)
× For France (Emp., Camberwell, 13/3/11)
The Secret Agent (*'m.c.'*, m. H. Nicholls: O.H., Cheltenham, 9/5/11)
The Vicar of Wakefield (W.G., Cheltenham, 24/4/12, *amat.*: dramatised from Oliver Goldsmith's novel)
The Masquerade (*'r.c.o.'*, m. S. J. Grove: O.H., Cheltenham, 12/12/22, *amat.*)

RALEIGH, ALICE
The Bartered Bride (*'c.o.'*, m. B. Smetana: Oxford University Opera Club, 26/11/29: translated from the libretto of K. Sabina) *1929*

'RALEIGH, CECIL' [=*CECIL ROWLANDS*: see also *H. HAMILTON* and *P. A. RUBENS*]
[For earlier plays see *H. E. D.* v, 533–4]
The Price of Peace (D.L., 20/9/00: condensed version, Sur., 12/9/10: +*R. H. GREY*)
The Great Millionaire (D.L., 19/9/01: condensed version, Olympia, Shoreditch, 14/11/10)

The Best of Friends ('*d. of modern life*': D.L., 18/9/02)
The Flood Tide ('*melo-farce*': D.L., 17/9/03; condensed version, Sur., 24/1/10: + *R. H. GREY*)
×The Doom of Delilah (Pal., Hamm., 11/3/07)
The Sins of Society (D.L., 12/9/07: +*H. HAMILTON*) *1909*
The Marquis ('*sentimental f.*': Scala, 9/2/08, Pl. Actors: +*S. DARK*)
×Nance Arden; or, The Woman who did (Empress, Brixton, 30/3/08; Varieties, Euston, 29/7/12, *revised*)
×The Police Trap (Tiv., 15/6/08)
The Marriages of Mayfair ('*d. of modern life*': D.L. 21/9/08: +*H. HAMILTON*) *1909*
The Whip (D.L., 9/9/09: + *H. HAMILTON*)
Behind the Veil (Cor., 1/11/10)
×The Winner (Hippo., 27/3/11)
×The Prime Minister (Emp., Camberwell, 17/4/11)
The Hope (D.L., 14/9/11: +*H. HAMILTON*)
Sealed Orders (D.L., 11/9/13: +*H. HAMILTON*)
×A King's Minister. LC, Sur., 18/11/15

RALEIGH, FRANK
The World and the Widow. LC, Col., Long Eaton, 29/7/21: +*KITTY RALEIGH*

RA-LESLIE, ETHEL
×Pharaoh's Daughter ('*o.*', m. J. Tabrar: Vic. H., 2/9/07, Pl. Actors; Emp., Camberwell, 16/9/07)

RAMSBOTTOM, HERWALD
The Labour Member ('*f.*': Bij., 8/5/06)

RAMSDALE, FREDERICK [see also *J. BOND*]
Betty-fra-Lancashire ('*m.pl.*': Vic, Lye, 9/8/20)
The Ruby Pendant ('*m.c.*', L. K. Lennard: Bury St Edmunds, 23/5/21; Sur., 13/6/21: +*J. BOND*)

RAMSDEN, E. A.
×Only Betsy ('*pl. for villages*') *1923*

RAMSEY, ALICIA
[For earlier plays see *H. E. D.* v, 534. The name of this authoress should be spelt 'Ramsey', not 'Ramsay']
The Mandarin ('*md.*': Gr., 15/4/01: +*R. DE CORDOVA*: title later changed to *The Shadow Behind the Throne*)
Honor ('*pl. of modern life*': Kennington, 23/11/03: +*R. DE CORDOVA*)
The Typhoon ('*d. spectacle*': Hippo., 1/4/07: +*R. DE CORDOVA*)
×The Password (Imp., 7/7/04: +*R. DE CORDOVA*)
×Edmund Kean (Emp., Hackney, 29/7/07: +*R. DE CORDOVA*)
×The Price of a Hat (Emp., Shepherd's Bush, 26/8/07: +*R. DE CORDOVA*)
Bridge (Gar., 14/10/07, *cpy.*)

×The Volcano (Hippo., 20/4/08: +*R. DE CORDOVA*)
×The Organ Grinder (Emp., New X, 24/8/08: +*R. DE CORDOVA*)
×The Sands o' Dee (Hippo., 31/8/08: +*R. DE CORDOVA*)
×Her Guardian Angel (Empress, Brixton, 15/8/10)
×Her Wedding Night (Col., 27/10/13)
×The Mannikin (Pal., Chelsea, 23/8/15; Metropolitan, 9/7/17, as *Trying On*)
Byron (Portsmouth, 14/1/29; Lyr., 22/1/29)

'*RAMSEY, JOHN*' [=*REGINALD OWEN*: see *E. SCHOFIELD*]

[*RAND, KATHERINE F.*
A Forlorn Hope ('*md.*': Reg., Salford, 8/4/01; Pav. 29/7/01, revised by *J. J. DOWLING* and *J. O. STEWART*, as *The Golden Prospect*)

RANDALL, J. [see *W. H. SQUIRE*]

RANDALL, WOOTON
He Walked in Her Sleep ('*c.*': D.P., Eastbourne, 8/11/26)

RANDOLPH, CHARLES [see *M. BELLOC-LOWNDES*]

RANDOLPH, CLEMENCE [see *J. COLTON*]

RANKEN, FREDERICK
The Chaperones ('*m.c.*' m. I. Witmark: St G's H., 23/4/01, *cpy.*)

RANKIN, Miss F. M.
×The Rights of the Soul (Kings., 22/2/09, St. Soc.; Bedford H., Chelsea, 5/2/22, Pax Robertson Salon: adapted from G. Giacosa, *Diritti dell' anima*, 1894)
The Apostle (H.M., Carlisle, 11/9/13)
Romanticismo (Com., 19/3/18: adapted from the play (1903) by G. Rovetta)
×The Bracelet (Bedford H., Chelsea, 1/4/22, Shakespeare Students' Soc.)
Mirandolina (Bedford H., Chelsea, 26/7/24, Pax Robertson Salon: adapted from C. Goldoni, *La locandiera*, 1753)

RANKINE, IAN
Love and Let Love (Playh., L'pool, 12/5/20)
Pure and Simple ('*c.*': RADA, 15/11/25)
A Place in the Shade (Reg., 28/2/26, Rep. Players) *1925* (Labour Publishing Co.)

[*RANSLEY, H. GERALD*
The Risin' o' the Moon ('*md.*': St Francis Xavier College H., L'pool, 18/4/07, *amat.*)
In Washington's Days ('*c.*': St Francis Xavier College H., L'pool, 25/9/07, *amat.*)
Bunkered, or, Too Many Cooks Spoil the Broth (Balfour Inst., L'pool, 11/4/08, *amat.*)
The Earl of Iona ('*m.c.*': Balfour Inst., L'pool, 24/11/08, *cpy.*; Florence Inst., L'pool, 28/11/08)
Cupid's Isle ('*m.c.*': David Lewis, L'pool, 3/4/09)

RANSOM, SIDNEY LEWIS [see *S. LEWIS-RANSOM*]

RAPHAEL, JOHN NATHANIEL [see also *G. DU MAURIER*]

×Ma Gosse (Pal., 18/10/09)
×At Savoy Mansions (Emp., Shepherd's Bush, 24/1/10)
×Just a Minute (Pal., 27/2/11)
The Uninvited Guest ('*c.*': P.W., 26/10/11: adapted from *Le Danseur inconnu* (1909) by T. Bernard)
×Between Five and Seven (Tiv., 25/11/12)
×Between Twelve and Three (Marlb., 12/3/17)
×The Infernal Machine (Tiv., Dublin, 9/4/17)

RAPHAELSON, SAMSON

Young Love ('*c.*': Arts, 3/7/29)

RASHDALL, CONSTANCE HASTINGS

×St Frideswide of Oxford. *1911* (Oxford)

RATCLIFFE, DOROTHY UNA

Dale Dramas. *1923*
[This contains nine one-act Yorkshire plays: 1. *The Courting of Margaret Ruth*; 2. *Desormais*; 3. *The Return of Mr Wiggleswick*; 4. *Time*; 5. *The Price*; 6. *Mary of Scotland in Wensleydale*; 7. *Robinetta*; 8. *Thieves' Gill*; and 9. *Alison Elizabeth*]
×Nathaniel Baddeley, Bookman, *1924* (Leeds)
×The Blind Man of Hiltune. *1929*
×A Spanish Lady. *1929*

RATCLIFFE, ELEANOR

Fairyland ('*children's pl.*': D.P., Eastbourne, 16/1/17)

RAVENSWOOD, CECIL [see *A. ROGERS*]

RAWSON, GRAHAM

×Down Stream (Shaft., 13/7/20, *m.*) *1919*
The Measure. *1919*
×Reconstruction (Ambass., 6/12/20).
The Race with the Shadow (Court, 22/5/21, St. Soc.; Everyman, 31/10/21: +*T. RAWSON*: adapted from W. von Scholtz, *Der Wettlauf mit dem Schatten*, 1920
×Shoeing the Mare (Apo., 30/9/21, Playwrights' Theatre)
The Mental Athletes ('*c.*': Lyr., Hamm., 18/2/23, St. Soc.: +*T. RAWSON*: adapted from G. Duhamel, *L'œuvre des athlètes*, 1920)
Faust. LC, Vic. H., 23/1/24: +*T. RAWSON*. *1933*
His Little Hour ('*c.*': Cent., 4/10/25, Lyc. Club)
Der Weibstüfel (Str., 10/4/27, St. Soc.: +*T. RAWSON*: translated from the play (1915) by K. Schönherr)
The Golden Hind. *1928*
The Family Tree (Q, 26/3/28)
The Dictator (Gar., 1/4/28, St. Soc.: +*T. RAWSON*: adapted from the play by J. Romains, 1926)
The Princess (Apo., 17/2/29, St. Soc.: +*T. RAWSON*: adapted from a play by J. Benavente)

Douaumont; or, The Return of the Soldier Ulysses (P.W., 1/12/29, St. Soc.: +*T. RAWSON*: adapted from the play (1924) by E. W. Moeller). *1930*
Scandal at Court. *1930*

RAWSON, M. S.
Something to Declare. LC, Parish H., Goring, 6/2/23

RAWSON, Mrs STEPNEY (MAUD)
×After Worcester (Qns Gate H., 19/12/12)

RAWSON, T. W. [see *L. GILBERT*]

RAWSON, TRISTAN [see *G. RAWSON*]

'*RAY, CONSTANCE*' [=*DOT ALLEN*]
×Snowdrifts (Alh., Glasgow, 17/11/13)
×Yellow Fever (Roy., Glasgow, 9/2/14)

RAY, HARRY
The Bluff Boys ('*m.f.c.*': Pal., Gloucester, 3/12/17; Pal., Chelsea, 22/4/18: +*H. CALDEN*)

RAY, ILETT
The Yellow Dread ('*modern Chinese d.*': Irving, Seacombe, 29/2/04)

RAY, L. WILLIAM [see *H. SETON*]

RAY, R. J.
The White Feather (Abbey, Dublin, 16/9/09)
The Casting Out of Martin Whelan (Abbey, Dublin, 29/9/10; Court, 14/6/11, *m.*)
The Gombeen Man (Court, 30/6/13, Irish Nat. Theatre)
×The Strong Hand (Abbey, Dublin, 25/4/17)
×The Moral Law (Abbey, Dublin, 29/8/22)

RAY, WATSON
The Morning After ('*f.*': Lyc., Newport, 14/3/27; Gr., Fulham, 13/6/27)

RAYE, MAURICE [see *A. H. QUARITCH*]

RAYMOND, ERNEST
The Berg (Q, 4/3/29; H.M., 12/3/29). *1929*

RAYMOND, H.
Nuts in May ('*f.*': D.Y., 9/5/22: +*V. ROGER* and *A. MARS*)

RAYMOND, WALTER
Two Men o' Mendip. *1923* (Somerset Folk Press)
[Dramatised from his novel (1899)]

RAYNE, Mrs K. DONALD
Her Last Card (Lincoln, 18/3/04, *cpy.*)

RAYNE, LEONARD [see *M. FORD*]

RAYNE, R. [see *S. NUTTALL*]

RAYNER, ALBERT
The Girl from Dunnowhere. LC, Glo., Wilmer, 21/10/15

RAYNOR, JOHN
×The Deadbeat (S.W., 9/2/10)

REA, MARGUERITE
Fledglings (St M., 1/11/23, *m.*, Playbox: adapted from P. Géraldy, *Les noces d'argent*, 1917)

REED, CLARA
Dethroned (W. Central H., Alfred Place, 11/4/24)

READ, JOHN
×Dober Zoyman's Oderclap. LC, Ass. R., Burton, 14/5/25
Conjurer Lintern. LC, Birkbeck College, 9/1/25

READ, JONATHAN
Rustic Loyalty ('*m.d.*': Emp., Swindon, 25/4/14)

READ, T. H.
×A Matter of Business. LC, Gr., Bolton, 31/7/14
×Birds of a Feather. LC, O.H., Leicester, 25/2/16

READY, STUART
×The Knave (T.H., Anerley, 12/2/27, *amat.*)
×The Matrimonial Expert (T.H., Anerley, 12/2/27, *amat.*)
×Sunset at Kilhowan (T.H., Anerley, 12/2/27, *amat.*)
×Captain Cook and the Widow (Hippo., Rotherhithe, 12/2/27, *amat.*)
×Cain (T.H., Anerley, 12/2/27, *amat.*)
×The Old Man of the Sea. *1930*

REAN, CLIFFORD [see also *D. MULLORD*]
A Son of Satan (Smethwick, 9/10/02; Aston, 27/7/03)
A Tempter of Women (Aston, 25/7/04; Stratford, 12/9/04)
Robin Hood (Star, L'pool, 24/12/06)
A Sportsman and a Gentleman (W. Stanley, 20/6/10)
The Queen and the Man ('*modern r. military d.*': Emp., Southend, 8/2/12)
Westward Ho! (Qns, Longton, 1/9/13: dramatised from Charles Kingsley's novel)
Napoleon and His Washerwoman. LC, O.H., Blackpool, 29/10/13
The Last Days of Pompeii (Qns, Longton, 13/4/14: dramatised from Lord Lytton's novel)
The Girl who Stayed at Home (Osborne, Manchester, 3/12/15: title later changed to *The Girl He Left Behind Him*)
×My Wife's Baby (Hippo., Putney, 6/3/16)
His Last Leave ('*md.*': Middlesbrough, 17/5/17; E.C., 8/10/17)
The Light in His Darkness (Middlesbrough, 21/5/17)
For Those in Peril on the Sea (Gr., Plymouth, 9/7/17; Woolwich, 21/1/18, as *A Son of the Sea*; E.C., 4/2/18)
Tainted Goods (Stratford, 18/3/18)
When the Joy-Bells are Ringing ('*md.*': Woolwich, 1/4/18; E.C., 8/4/18)
The Girl who Changed Her Mind ('*md.*': L'pool, 22/4/18; Stratford, 21/10/18)

On Leave for His Wedding (W. Bromwich, 10/6/18; E.C., 19/8/18)
Duty! And the Girl (Stratford, 22/7/18)
Ignorance (K's, Gainsborough, 28/10/18; Stratford, 18/11/18)
Lest We Forget (E.C., 17/2/19)
The World of Dreams. LC, Winchester, 4/2/19: title later changed to *The Forbidden Pleasure*
Safe Home Again. LC, L'pool, 7/4/19
The Sailor Lad (Worthing, 28/4/19; Dalston, 5/5/19)
Should a Doctor Tell? LC, Gr., Pentre, 7/5/19
Wireless (Hippo., Maidenhead, 19/5/19; E.C., 26/5/19)
Forgotten (W. Bromwich, 26/5/19; Stratford, 2/6/19)
Has England Forgotten? LC, Hippo., Burslem, 24/6/19
The Unjust Law (Metro., Abertillery, 11/8/19; Stratford, 10/11/19)
The Great Barrier (W. Bromwich, 2/2/20; Stratford, 15/3/20; title later changed to *A White Man's Way*)
The Danger Line of Love ('*m.c.*', m. T. Sutton: E.C., 23/2/20: title later changed to *A Spanish Romance*)
Moderation (Stratford, 19/3/20)
Kidnapped. LC, Vic., Lye, 3/5/20
Guilty Husbands and Wives (Metro., Glasgow, 17/1/21)
The Other Woman's Husband. LC, O.H., Cheltenham, 25/7/21
The Treasure Seekers (P's, Portsmouth, 12/11/23)
×No. 9, Brook Street. LC, P's, Portsmouth, 18/3/24: +*R. FERRIS*
Cinders (Coll., 17/4/25)
The Vendetta. LC, Coll., 27/10/25
For Husbands Only (Coll., 1/3/26)
The Beauty Shop (Coll., 30/5/27)
The Star of Burmah (Hippo., Rotherhithe, 8/8/27)

RECHT, CHARLES

At the Chasm ('*dream*': Bedford H., Chelsea, 13/1/24, Pax Robertson Salon: from J. Vrchlický, *Nad propastí*, 1924)

REDDIN, KENNETH SHEILS [='*KENNETH SARR*']

REDDING, JOSEPH D.

Natoma ('*o.*', m. V. Herbert: Ladbr. H., 25/2/11, *cpy.*) *1911*

REDFORD, G. A.

×Contrasts (Clavier H., 29/10/12, Drama Soc.)
×A Snug Retreat (Rehearsal, 21/4/14)

REDGRAVE, ROY

[For earlier plays see *H. E. D.* v, 537]
A Man of Mystery ('*md.*': Vic., Broughton, 29/7/01; Gr., 12/8/01: +*A. BELL*)
×The King of Terrors (Pal., Battersea, 1/3/09: +*HARRY ROXBURY*)
×Sweet Mistress Dorothy (Foresters, 18/5/08)
×Wrinkles on the Rink ('*m.c.*': Hippo., Paisley, 20/2/09, *cpy.*; Pal., Reading, 7/3/10: +*HARRY ROXBURY*)

×The Thrust of Navarre (Sur., 29/3/09)
Merry Widow Twankey ('*m.f.*': Wolverhampton, 28/4/09, *cpy.*: title later changed to *The Gay Countess*)

REDMOND, JOHANNA
×Leap Year in the West (Court, 2/7/08, Irish Stage Soc.)
×Falsely True (Pal., 6/3/11) *1918* (Dublin)
×Honor's Choice (Qns, Dublin, 26/6/11)
×Pro Patria (Qns, Dublin, 4/9/11, *m.*)
×The Best of a Bad Bargain (Gai., Dublin, 26/7/11)

REDPATH, HELEN L.
×Wisdom's Foolishness ('*moral pl.*') *1913*

REDWOOD, ETHEL
A Legend of Spring (T.H., W. Hampstead, 4/1/06, *amat.*)

REECE, FRANK M.
×A Maiden Widow (P.W., Salford, 27/1/06, *cpy.*)

REED, ALLAN
Old Flames ('*f.c.*': Gr., Fulham, 8/12/02: +*G. D. DAY*)

REED, CLARA
The Two Crowns ('*historical d.*': W. Central H., 20/10/22, Poetic Players) *1923*
The Beloved Countess (W. Central H., 8/12/22, Poetic Players)
×The Soul of Japan. LC, Royal H., Harrogate, 6/3/24
Thomas à Becket ('*t.*': W. Central H., 29/5/25)

REED, E. T.
A Pre-historic Lord Mayor's Show (D.L., 7/3/07, *m.*: +*E. PAYNE*)

REED, EDWARD C.
O-Kai ('*fant. of now and then*') *1921*

REED, F. WARDEN [see *F. WARDEN-REED*]

REED, LANGFORD
A Daughter of France (Kennington, 18/4/08, *cpy.*)
×The Awakening (Empress, 19/9/10)

REED, MURIEL
×The Feminologist (Rehearsal, 24/2/13, Black Cat Club)

REES, ROSEMARY
×Her Dearest Friend (Cor., 4/2/07) *Fr. 1910*
A Desperate Marriage (Gr., Brighton, 2/3/08; Lyr., Hamm., 16/3/08: called originally *A Beggar Bride*)
×The New Gun (Emp., Camberwell, 23/12/12)
×Uncle Bill (Gr., Clapham Junct., 26/5/13; Glo., 18/6/13)
×Will You Walk into My Parlour? (R.A., Woolwich, 18/10/15; Emp., Chiswick, 24/1/16)

REEVE, FRANCIS
The One-Day Millionaire ('*c.o.*', m. B. Rideau: Surrey Masonic H., 3/1/08, *amat.*)

REEVE, R. GUY
[Several sketches produced at music-halls]

[*REID, HAL (JAMES HALLOCK REID)*
At Cripple Creek ('*md.*': Dover, 5/1/05; Bor., Stratford, 13/3/05)
Human Hearts (Kennington, 5/6/05)
The Night Before Christmas (O.H., Coventry, 1/3/09; Greenwich, 15/3/09)
To Serve the Cross (Dalston, 3/2/11)
A Homespun Heart (Gr., Swansea, 17/7/11)

REILLY, FRANK C. [see *C. HAMILTON*]

[*REITZENSTEIN, ELMER L.*
On Trial (Stamford, Conn., 14/8/14; Candler, N.Y., 19/8/14 Lyr., 29/4/15)

RENAUD, Y. [see *F. T. FITZGERALD*]

RENNEF, SIDNEY
×His Prairie Bride (K's, Gateshead, 22/5/12)

RENNISON, A. V.
×The Magic Spell ('*o.*': Craiglands Hydro, 14/11/13)

RENSON, WILFRED [see *J. STILLWELL*]

REVELL, LILIAN
From Shadow to Sunshine (E.C., 22/7/01: +*F. H. FRANCKS*)

REX, CORVUS [see *M. MONTESOLE*]

REYNOLDS, E. [see *NIGEL PLAYFAIR*]

REYNOLDS, JOHN
×Pauline (Playh., L'pool, 16/5/13)

REYNOLDS, MARY
×The Waxen Man. LC, Green R., Manchester, 29/4/29. *1934* (in C. M. Martin, *Fifty One-Act Plays*)

REYNOLDS, WALTER
[For earlier plays see *H. E. D.* v, 541]
The Sin of a Life (P'cess, 30/9/01; O.H., Middlesbrough, 1/11/09, revised as *An Unpardonable Sin*: dramatised from a novel, *Wanda*, (1883) by Ouida)
For the Defence: or, Victims of the Law (Leeds, 4/8/02; Terriss, Rotherhithe, 15/9/02: +*H. HERNE*)
Flatland ('*c.*': Bristol, 11/6/04, *cpy.*)
Mr Smith (Nottingham, 27/2/05; Campden, 6/3/05)

REYNOR, ARNOLD
×The Man who Stayed at an Hotel (H.M., Carlisle, 14/4/15)
The Nik-Nak Millionaire ('*f.c.*': Gr., Woking, 18/1/23; Bor., Stratford, 26/2/23)

RHIND, ROY
Till Kingdom Come ('*r.d.*': Leicester, 6/7/14)

[*RHODES, BENRIMO*
The Willow Tree ('*Japanese fant.*': Cohan & Harris, N.Y., 6/3/17; Glo., 22/10/17: +*H. RHODES*)

RHODES, BERT

×The House on the Cliff (O.H., Tunbridge Wells, 27/11/16: +*BLANCHE RHODES*)

RHODES, BLANCHE [see *BERT RHODES*]

[*RHODES, HARRISON* (see '*A. HOPE*' and *BENRIMO RHODES*)

RHODES, KATHLYN

×A Man's Wife (Little, 27/6/12, Oncomers)

RHODES, RAYMOND CROMPTON

×Black Sheep. *1927*

RHYS, ERNEST

Gwenevere ('*Celtic m.d.*' or '*lyrical pl.*', m. V. Thomas: Cor., 13/11/05) *1905*

×The Quest of the Holy Grail ('*masque*', m. V. Thomas: Court, 3/7/08, Irish Stage Soc.; Hampstead Conservatoire, 9/1/14) *1908* (as *The Masque of the Grail*)

Enid ('*o.*', m. V. Thomas: Court, 24/11/08) *1908*

RHYS, Mrs GRACE

The Sons of Jacob (Scala, 22/5/25, *m.*, Internat. Play Soc.: translated from a play by J. Raïnis) *1924*

'*RIADA*' [=*FRANK ADAIR*]

The Painted Woman (Shak., Clapham, 21/7/02; revised as *Held Apart*, 27/8/06)

It's Always the Woman ('*md.*': Shak., Clapham, 20/6/10)

Married by Force (L'pool, 22/7/12)

A Mill Girl's Secret; or, A Lad and His Lass ('*md.*': Junction, Manchester, 23/2/14: +*C. A. CLARKE*)

RICCIARDI, WILLIAM

Mr Malatesta (Court, 30/6/21)

[*RICE, ALICE HEGAN*

Mrs Wiggs of the Cabbage Patch ('*c.*': Terry's, 27/4/07: +*A. C. FLEXNER*

[*RICE, ELMER L.*

The Adding Machine (Str., 16/3/24, St. Soc.; Fest., Cambridge, 2/5/27; Court, 9/1/28) *1923*

The Subway (Fest., Cambridge, 5/11/28; Gar., 14/7/29, Lyc. Club) *Fr. 1929*

Street Scene. LC, Shaft., 18/7/29. *Fr. 1929*

RICE, F. A. BESANT

×Forty Shillings (Brixton, 9/4/06)

Major Jennings ('*f.*': Camden, 11/2/07)

RICE, F. ANDREW

Folly ('*m.pl.*': Str., 15/6/23, *amat.*)

The Canon in Residence ('*c.*': Civic Playh., Leeds, 1/10/28)

RICHARDS, JOHN

The Charm of Life (D.Y., 14/7/11, *m.*)

RICHARDS, S.

×My King (Stand., 22/11/09)

RICHARDSON, ANTHONY

Through a Window (Arts, 1/11/29)

RICHARDSON, Mrs BENJAMIN

×A Comedy of Resolution. LC, Richardson H., Worsley, 4/3/13
×Caravaning. LC, Richardson H., Worsley, 10/3/13
×A Woodland Rehearsal. LC, Richardson H., Worsley, 17/11/14
×Friendship. LC, Richardson H., Worsley, 3/3/15

RICHARDSON, FRANK

×Bonnie Dundee. *Fr. 1910*

RICHARDSON, GRACE

Puck in Petticoats and Other Fairy Plays. *1914*

[This contains five short plays: 1. *Puck in Petticoats* (St John's H., Palmer's Green, 3/7/14); 2. *The Wishing Well* (St John's H., Palmer's Green, 3/7/14); 3. *The Ring of Salt* (St John's H., Palmer's Green, 3/7/14); 4. *The Moon Dream*; and 5. *Hansel and Gretel*]

×Burglars, Beware. LC, Emp., Chiswick, 15/9/20: title later changed to *White Rabbits*.

A Kitchen Prima Donna (St Paul's Inst., Winchmore Hill, 23/2/22)

RICHARDSON, H. M.

×The Few and the Many (Gai., Manchester, 4/5/08; Cor., 9/6/09)
×Bringing It Home (Gai., Manchester, 5/10/08)
×Going on Parade (Gai., Manchester, 15/3/09)
Gentlemen of the Press (Gai., Manchester, 12/9/10)
The Awakening Woman (Gai., Manchester, 28/11/13)

RICHARDSON, IAN

×The Virtues of Mrs McTodd (Emp., Camberwell, 24/2/13)
×A Legend of the Desert (Cosmopolis, 22/7/13)
×The Absent Mr Johnston (Cosmopolis, 22/7/13)

RICHARDSON, PEARL

Nifwy the Proud. *Fr. 1924*

RICHINS, CHARLES

×Our Suburb (Park H., Hanwell, 12/3/02)

[*RICHMAN, ARTHUR*

Ambush (Gar., N.Y., 10/10/21; Gar., 1/9/23)
The Awful Truth ('*c.*': Columbia, San Francisco, 15/5/22; Henry Miller, N.Y., 18/9/22; Roy., 26/7/26)

RICHMOND, HUGH [see *H. JENNINGS*]

RICHMOND, SUSAN

×At the Gate (Cent., 18/3/25, Foundlings) *1930*
×The Conquest of Humility (A.L.S. Trav. Th., 1925)

RICK, ALF

The Happy Man ('*m.c.*': Seaham Harbour, 2/8/20)

RICKETT, ARTHUR COMPTON

The Charmer ('*pl. of modern life*': Londesborough, Scarborough, 28/11/02; K's H., 13/10/07, Pl. Actors; Ass. R., Rotherham, 2/10/13, *revised*)

RIDDALL, WALTER

The Prodigal (Abbey, Dublin, 30/9/14)

RIDER, KNIGHT

John Lester, Parson (Lyr., 20/1/02: +*L. FOSTER*)

RIDGE, WILLIAM PETT

[For an earlier play see *H. E. D.* v, 543]

London, Please. *1925*

[This contains four short plays: 1. *Some Showers* (Tyne, Newcastle, 16/3/10; Playh., 6/7/11); 2. *Damages for Breach*; 3. *Early Closing*; and 4. *Happy Returns*]

RIDGWELL, CHARLES [see also *C. AUSTIN*]

×The Labour Exchange (Empress, 8/5/11: +*G. A. STEVENS*)

RIDGEWELL, GEORGE

Casting Stones (Q, 3/6/29)

RIDLEY, ARNOLD

The Ghost Train (Brighton, 22/6/25; Hippo., Golders Green, 6/7/25; St M., 23/11/25) *Fr. 1930*

The God o' Mud (Playh., Oxford, 29/11/26; Blackfriars, 4/3/27, Interlude Theatre Guild)

The Wrecker (Brighton, 24/10/27; New, 6/12/27: +*B. MERIVALE*) *1930*

Keepers of Youth (D.Y., 22/5/29) *1929*

The Flying Fool (Alh., Glasgow, 12/8/29; Golders Green, 26/8/29; P's, 14/9/29: +*B. MERIVALE*: called originally *Paris by Air*)

Unholy Orders ('*f.c.*': Bath, 9/9/29; Ambass., 19/11/29) *1929* (as *Third Time Lucky*); *Fr. 1930*

RIECROFT, CHARLES

×The Alternative (Ambass., 6/12/20)

RIETTI, VITTORIO

Three Lovers (Rudolf Steiner H., 3/7/30: translated from *I Tre Amanti* (1920) by Guglielmo Zorzi)

RIGBY, ARTHUR [see also *L. LUPINO* and *M. MELFORD*]

Turned Up ('*m.f.c.*', m. J. Tunbridge: Gr., Blackpool, 11/1/26 Oxf., 28/1/26)

RIGBY, EDWARD

×The Thirteenth (Com., 3/11/13: +*P. AUSTIN*)

RIGHTON, EDWARD

[For earlier plays see *H. E. D.* v, 543 and 813]

Sally ('*m.pl.*': Torquay, 5/11/03: +*A. SMITH*)

×Only a Woman (Lyr., Hamm., 26/5/11, *m.*)

RIGHTON, MARY

[For earlier plays see *H. E. D.* v, 543]

×The King's Oath (Lyr., Hamm., 26/5/11, *m.*)

RIGNOLD, B. [see *C. E. DERING*]

RIGNOLD, H. H.
[For an earlier play see *H. E. D.* v, 543]
×Fido. LC, P's, Bristol, 19/2/14

RILEY, GEORGE A.
The University Prig (Gr., Blackpool, 21/3/03, *cpy.*: +*S. S. WATERHOUSE* and *H. BROOKES*)

RILEY, KATE E.
Dorothy Davenport (Stockport, 29/6/25)

RIMINTON, CHARLES
[For earlier plays see under 'Rimington' in *H. E. D.* v, 543]
Through Dark to Dawn, or, A Wife's Honour (Alb., Brighouse, 30/11/05: +*H. FURNIVAL*)
The Play Actor ('*f.c.*': Preston, 12/9/07)
Hetty's Violin (Pav., Southend, 7/10/07)

RIND, E. E.
×Mrs Riggles Makes a Match (Pembroke H., Croydon, 17/10/07)

[*RINEHART, MARY ROBERTS*
Seven Days ('*c.*': Trenton, 1/11/09; Astor, N.Y., 10/11/09; O.H., Harrogate, 20/2/13; New, 15/3/15: +*A. HOPWOOD*) *Fr. 1931*
The Bat (Morosco, N.Y., 23/8/20; St J., 23/1/22: +*A. HOPWOOD*) *Fr. 1931*

RISH, A. [see *R. HAYWARD*]

RISK, R. K.
The Excelsior Dawsons ('*c.*': Roy., Glasgow, 14/2/10)
×Macallister's Dream ('*fant*'.: Roy., Glasgow, 20/3/11)

RISQUE, W. H. [see also *J. T. TANNER*]
[For earlier plays see *H. E. D.* v, 544, 813]
The Thirty Thieves ('*m. ext.*', m. E. Jones: Terry's, 1/1/01: also called *Miss Mariana*)
Miss Wingrove ('*m.pl.*', m. H. Talbot: Str., 4/5/05) *1905*
×A Lucky Miss ('*m.c. incident*', m. H. Talbot: Pav., 13/7/14)

'*RITA*' [=*Mrs* (*ELIZA MARGARET*) *DESMOND R. L. HUMPHREYS*]
Daughters of Eve (P's, Manchester, 14/6/20; St J., 13/7/20, *m.*)
The Devil to Pay (Bath, 18/5/25: +*R. WHITEHOUSE*)
Naughty Mrs Gordon (Pal., Brighton, 15/8/27; R.A., Woolwich, 22/8/27: +*N. LEE*)

RITA, A. [see *W. BENGE*]

RITCHIE, F. BARCLAY
The Whirlwind Girl. LC, '*m.pl.*': Alex., 10/8/22

RITTENBERG, MAX
×Axes to Grind (Rehearsal, 21/7/12)

RIVETT-CARNAC, E. H.

The Shaming of the Two, and The Borrowed Clothes of Princess Rose. *1910*

[Two short plays intended 'for schools or parish entertainment']

RIX, ALICE

× The Mermaid of Margate (Qns, Poplar, 1/7/07)

ROBATT, A. C. [see *S. HICKS*]

ROBBINS, Sir ALFRED FARTHING

[For earlier plays see *H. E. D.* v, 544]

Old Scores (Metro., Camberwell, 25/2/01; O.H., Crouch End, 17/2/02, as *An Eye for an Eye; or Paying off Old Scores*: + *P. MORRIS*)

ROBBINS, WAL

× Caroline Brown (W.L., 10/11/13)

ROBERT, STEPHEN

Ye Gods! ('*f.*': Kings., 20/5/16: + *ERIC HUDSON*]

ROBERTON, Sir HUGH S.

Kirsteen (and) Christ in the Kirkyard: Two Plays. *1922*

[Two short plays, of which the second was presented at the Ath., Glasgow, 31/10/21, by the Scottish National Players]

ROBERTON, MARION

× Afterwards. *1911*

ROBERTS, ARTHUR O.

× Cloudbreak (T.H., Portmadoc, April 1923; Lyr., Hamm., 26/2/24, *m.*; A.L.S. Trav. Th., 1926) *1925* (in *Three One-Act Plays*)

× Midsummer morning. LC, Memorial H., Criccieth, 20/8/24

ROBERTS, BERTIE

× All for the Want of a Baby. LC, Worthing, 3/2/14

ROBERTS, CECIL

A Tale of Young Lovers ('*t.*': Rep., Nottingham, 26/11/21)

The Right to Kiss (Nottingham, 31/5/26)

ROBERTS, CYRIL

The Eternal Lover (New, Cardiff, 28/6/26)

× So Good. *Fr. 1927*

× Village Industries. *Fr. 1928*

× Genuine Antique. *Fr. 1928*

Young Love. *Fr. 1928*

ROBERTS, GEORGE

× The Pride of the Regiment (Vic. H., 20/2/09)

ROBERTS, K. E.

× The Kingdom of Queen Mab ('*pastoral pl. for children*') *1913*

ROBERTS, MAUDE

× The Magic Wood ('*fairy fant.*': P's, 2/11/15, *amat.*)

× Doris and Her Friends. LC, Ambass., 11/1/16

× The Dream Castle (Boudoir, 21/12/16)

ROBERTS, MORLEY [see also *A. P. WHARTON*]

×Mrs Simpson? (Metropolitan, 15/11/09: +*H. SETON*)
False Dawn (Court, 20/11/10, Play Actors: +'*H. SETON*')
Four Plays. *1911*

[This contains four short plays: 1. *The Hour of Greatness* (LC, Emp., Holborn, 29/9/24); 2. *The Lamp of God* (LC, Emp., Holborn, 29/9/24); 3. *The Lay Figure* (LC, Emp., Holborn, 29/9/24); and 4. *The White Horse*]

ROBERTS, P. M. [see *J. P. HATHERLEIGH*]

ROBERTS, R. A.

Straight from the Shoulder (Gr., Brighton, 3/8/07; Broadway, New X, 10/8/08)
×Cruel Coppinger (Bury, 25/8/09; Hippo, 11/10/09)
×£20,000, or, Who's the Lucky Man? (Gr., Gravesend, 17/3/13)
[Several playlets produced at music-halls]

ROBERTS, R. ELLIS

Peer Gynt (translated from Ibsen's drama) *1912*

ROBERTS, R. H.

The Garden Citizens (T.H., Ilford, 19/10/12, *amat.*: +*J. DAVIES*)

ROBERTS, RALPH

×The Woman's Heritage (Margate, 7/7/02)
×Buffo: The Story of a Broken Heart (H.M., Dundee, 5/9/04)
×In the Trenches. LC, Emp., Chiswick, 4/8/16

ROBERTS, RANDAL [see '*H. SETON*']

ROBERTS, W. H.

Dwellers in Glass Houses ('*c.*': D.P., Eastbourne, 30/11/11)
Out of Evil. LC, Cambridge, Spennymoor, 20/5/19

ROBERTS, WILLIAM J.

×Father Christmas Comes to Town (Emp., Chiswick, 28/12/21)

ROBERTS, WILLIAM L.

For Her Sake (O.H., Cheltenham, 18/4/07; Gr., Fulham, 5/8/07: title later changed to *From Slave to Princess*)

ROBERTSON, ATHOLE

Peggy ('*c.*': Pier, Brighton, 25/6/06; Woodside H., N. Finchley, 26/4/21, *amat.*, as *My Peggy*)

ROBERTSON, Mrs B.

×Behind the Footlights (Ass. R., Andover, 13/11/12, *amat.*)

ROBERTSON, F. [see *G. W. BOYLE*]

ROBERTSON, IAN

[For earlier plays see *H. E. D.* v, 545]
×The Golden Rose, or, The Scarlet Woman ('*bas-relief*': Imp., 8/6/03, St. Soc.)
×A Play in Little (P.W., B'ham, 26/4/09)

ROBERTSON, JANE W.

Poverty is No Crime ('*c.*': Bedford H., Chelsea, 14/1/23, Pax Robertson Salon: translated from the play (1854) by A. N. Ostrovski)

ROBERTSON, Miss LEFANU

A Daughter of Erin ('*Irish c.*': Dublin, 19/8/01)

ROBERTSON, MARION [see also *K. RORKE*]

×An Episode (Guildhall School of Music, 25/2/08)
×Afterwards (D.P., Eastbourne, 24/1/11; St J., 19/5/11, *m.*)
×Salvation Sal (Alb. H., 28/3/11, *m.*)

ROBERTSON, NORA

×On the Road to Cork (Court, 30/3/14, Pl. Actors)

ROBERTSON, PAX

Lew Yuen Wac (Margaret Morris, 3/4/21, Pax Robertson Salon: adapted from an early Chinese play) *1923* (*priv.*)

ROBERTSON, WALFORD GRAHAM

[For an earlier play see *H. E. D.* v, 547]

Gold, Frankincense and Myrrh, and Other Pageants for a Baby Girl. *1907*

[This contains three one-act pieces: 1. *Gold, Frankincense and Myrrh*; 2. *The Wishing-Well*; and 3. *A Masque of Midsummer Eve*]

Pinkie and the Fairies ('*fairy pl.*': H.M., 19/12/08) *1909*
A Masque of May Morning (Gr., Croydon, 3/6/19)
Old Chiddingfold. LC, '*pageant pl.*': Chiddingfold, 27/5/21. *1921* (Chiddingfold)
×The Slippers of Cinderella and Other Plays. *Fr. 1919*
×Alexander the Great, or, Romps and Romance (London Theatre School, 28/3/28) *Fr. 1923*
×Archibald. *Fr. 1924*
The Town of the Ford ('*pageant pl.*': Guildford, 18/5/25)

[*ROBERTSON, WILLARD*

Black Velvet (Arts, 9/2/29)

ROBERTSON, WILLIAM

Cardinal Beaton (Rep., Edin., 24/11/24)

ROBEY, M. P.

×The Guest. LC, St Peter's Parish H., Plymouth, 29/10/17

ROBINS, ELIZABETH

Votes for Women ('*dramatic tract*': Court, 9/4/07, *m.*) *1909*

ROBINS, GERTRUDE L.

Makeshifts, and Other Short Plays. *1909*

[This contains five short plays: 1. *Makeshifts* ('*middle-class c.*': Gai., Manchester, 5/10/08; Cor., 8/6/09; Playh., 16/7/12); 2. *The Exit*; 3. *Lancelot and the Leading Lady*; 4. *Old Jan* (Gai., Manchester, 18/3/12); and 5. *The Point of View* (Gai., Manchester, 17/10/10)]

×Pot Luck (Schoolroom, Naphill, 19/11/10; Pal., 7/8/11) *Fr. 1911*

×A Debt of Honour (Rehearsal, 4/5/11, English Play Soc.)
×Realities ('*middle-class c.*': Gai., Manchester, 23/10/11) *1912*
×The Home-Coming (Abbey, Dublin, 10/4/13)
Loving as We Do, and Other Plays. *1912*
[This contains four short plays: 1. *Loving as We Do* (Gai., Manchester, 2/2/14; Cor., 11/5/14); 2. *The Return*; 3. *After the Case*; and 4. *'Ilda's Honourable*]
×The Plaything (Gai., Manchester, 9/11/14)

ROBINSON, Mrs CAYLEY
Castles in the Air ('*oa.*', m. P. Lincke: Scala, 11/4/11)

ROBINSON, GEORGE
Mistaken Identities (B'ham, 23/1/25, *amat.*)

ROBINSON, GERALD
By Gum! ('*f.*': Pal., St Leonards, 26/1/20: title later changed to *In Possession*: +*C. CLAIRE*)
[Several sketches and playlets produced at music-halls]

ROBINSON, H. JUDGE
Fifty-Fifty (Gr., Woking, 28/1/24; Qns, Poplar, 14/4/24)

ROBINSON, HUGH
The Girl with the Cash; or, How He Collared It ('*bsq.*': Kings., 20/9/11, The Sorries: +*A. HALL*)

ROBINSON, LENNOX (ESMÉ STUART LENNOX ROBINSON)
×The Clancy Name (Abbey, Dublin, 8/10/08; Court, 19/6/11) *1908* (Dublin)
The Cross-Roads (Abbey, Dublin, 1/4/09; Court, 20/6/10) *1909* (Dublin)
×The Lesson of His Life (Cork, 2/12/09)
Harvest (Abbey, Dublin, 19/5/10; Court, 7/6/10) *1911* (Dublin)
Patriots (Abbey, Dublin, 11/4/12; Court, 10/6/12) *1912* (Dublin)
The Dreamers (Abbey, Dublin, 10/2/15) *1915* (Dublin)
The White-headed Boy ('*c.*': Abbey, Dublin, 13/12/16; Gai., Manchester, 13/9/20; Ambass., 27/9/20) *1920*
The Lost Leader (Abbey, Dublin, 19/2/18; Court, 10/6/19) *1918* (Dublin)
The Round Table ('*comic t.*': Abbey, Dublin, 31/1/22; Q, 16/3/25; Wynd., 11/5/25) *1924*; *1928* (*revised*)
×Crabbed Youth and Age ('*c.*': Abbey, Dublin, 14/11/22; Mary Ward Settlement, 15/10/24, Dram. Art Centre) *1924*
×Never the Time and the Place (Abbey, Dublin, 8/4/24) *1924*
×Portrait (Abbey, Dublin, 31/3/25; University of Liverpool, 11/11/26, *amat.*) *1926*
The White Blackbird (Abbey, Dublin, 12/10/25; Playh., Oxford, 30/11/25) *1925* (Dublin); *1926*
The Big House (Abbey, Dublin, 6/9/26) *1928*
The Far-off Hills (Abbey, Dublin, 22/10/28; Q, 30/3/29) *1931*
Give a Dog – (Str. 20/1/29) *1928*
Ever the Twain ('*c.*': Abbey, Dublin, 8/10/29) *1930*

ROBINSON, M. J.

Blarney; or, The Love Cure ('*c.o.*', m. J. Barnardo: Sav., 7/1/10, *cpy.*)

ROBINSON, PERCY

×The Last Rose of Summer (Margate, 11/5/08)
×Con o' the Hills. LC, P.W., Grimsby, 28/8/14
×In the Flat Below (S. Ldn Pal., 5/9/21)
For None Can Tell (Q, 7/6/26; Wynd., 30/10/28, as *To What Red Hell*) *1928*
The Whispering Gallery (Q, 5/3/28: +*T. DE MARNEY*) *Fr. 1930*
In the Duchess's Arms ('*f.*': Gr., Croydon, 16/8/29)

ROBINSON, W. BEVAN

×For Love of a Lady (Vic. H., 11/2/01)
Bells across the Snow ('*md.*': Carlton, Greenwich, 2/1/05)

ROBINSON, W. SNELL [see *H. B. CLAIR*]

ROBL, KARL [see '*C. SCHWARTZ*']

'*ROBOT*'

'The Secret' and Other Plays. *1926*
[This contains one full-length play, *The Whirlpool*, and five one-act pieces: 1. *The Secret*; 2. *The Traitor*; 3. *The House of Exchange*; 4. *The Sword*; and 5. *The Darkness*]

ROBSON, ELEANOR

In the Next Room (O.H., Providence, 1/10/23; Vanderbilt, N.Y., 27/11/23; St M., 6/6/24: +*H. FORD*) *Fr. 1925*

ROBSON, FRANK [see *H. ERSKINE*]

ROBSON, LEONARD

×The Girl from Biarritz (H.M., Aberdeen, 29/10/06)

ROBSON, MASIE

Betty Wakes Up ('*m.c.*', m. K. Shortland: Pal., Rugeley, 2/9/18; Hippo., Maidenhead, 9/9/18: +*J. S. MILWARD*)

ROBSON, E. M.

×Their Mutual Friend (Gai., Manchester, 7/8/16)

ROBY, B. SOANE [see *B. SOANE-ROBY*]

'*ROCHE, DRUMMOND*'

×Cupid's Ally (Gai., Dublin, 7/6/05)

ROCHEFORT, JULIAN

Vultures of London; or, In the Toils of Terror (Sur., 9/11/03)
The Curse of Crime (Sur., 21/3/04)
×Music Hath Charms. LC, Pal., Battersea, 30/5/13

ROCHESTER, A.

×The Cradle (Court, 11/3/13, *m.*)

ROCK, CHARLES [see *W. W. JACOBS*]

RODEN, Countess of

Dorinda (Tullymore Park, 24/8/12)
The Other John. LC, Court, 1/4/14: + *L. M. JOCELYN*

RODEN, HARRY

The Adventures of Nobbler and Jerry (Stratford, 29/6/10, *cpy.*: +*W. DAVID* and *L. LAKE*)

ROE, NORMAN

×England: A Play without a Plot (Vic., Ramsgate, 4/7/07)

ROGER, VICTOR [see *H. RAYMOND*]

[*ROGERS, ALBERT*

Alaska; or, Life in the Frozen North (Stockton, 6/8/06, adapted by *W. L. LOCKWOOD*)

Sloper's Day Out ('*m.ext.*': Hippo., Hulme, 21/3/27: +*C. RAVENSWOOD*)

ROGERS, CHARLES

[For earlier plays see *H. E. D.* v, 548]

In the King's Name ('*r.pl.*': K's, Hamm., 27/3/05)

ROGERS, E. W. [see *A. E. ELLIS*]

ROGERS, KENNETH

King James III of Scotland ('*t.*') *1923* (Paisley)

Two Dukes of Milan. *1924* (Paisley)

[This contains: 1. *Duke Galeazzo-Maria Sforza*, and 2. *Lodovico Sforza*]

ROGERS, MERRILL

Her First Affair (Hippo., Lewisham, 4/8/30)

ROGERSON, HARRY

[For an earlier play see *H. E. D.* v, 549]

Herne the Hunter ('*historical bsq.*': N. Shields, 28/7/02)

Mrs Finch's Flat ('*bsq.*': Empress, 20/12/15: +*F. SPENCER*)

ROGERSON, S. BUCHANAN [see *C. A. CLARKE*]

When It Was Dark (Qns, Farnworth, 25/1/06, *cpy.*; Emp., Cradley Heath, 9/2/06; Manchester, 12/3/06, as *Darkness*; W.L., 8/4/07, *revised*: dramatised from the novel (1903) by Guy Thorne)

The Woman who Gambles (Colosseum, Oldham, 29/1/06; P's, Poplar, 2/7/06)

'*ROHMER, SAX*' [=*ARTHUR SARSFIELD WADE*]

Round in 50 ('*m.pl.*', m. H. Finck and J. Tate: Emp., Cardiff, 6/3/22; Hippo., 16/3/22: +*J.* and *L. WYLIE*)

The Eye of Siva ('*mystery pl.*': New, 8/8/23)

Secret Egypt (Q, 4/8/28)

ROLISON, FRANK [see *J. F. NOLAN*]

ROLLIT, GEORGE

The Money Makers ('*f.c.*': Roy., 13/5/04; P's, Bradford, 6/5/18, as *Money for Nothing*)

×My Friend the Devil ('*fant.*': Pal., 27/4/07, *m.*)

×Robbed (Euston, 30/7/17)

×Switch No. 7 (Vic. Pal., 1/4/18)

ROLLS, ERNEST C.

[Several sketches and playlets produced at music-halls]

ROMANES, N. H.
The Medium. LC, Guildhall School of Music, 10/8/25

ROME, FRED [see also *T. R. ARKELL*]
The Silent Prompter, and Other Sketches. *Fr. 1928*
[This contains nine revue sketches]
[Numerous sketches and playlets produced at music-halls]

ROMER, M. [see *W. F. R. MIST*]

RONALD, LANDON
×Recognition of the Union (People's, Newcastle, 3/14)

ROONEY, HUBERT
Slumberland ('*m. fairy pl.*': Gai., Dublin, 7/3/12) *1912*

ROPES, ARTHUR REED [='*ADRIAN ROSS*']

RORKE, KATE
×The Price (Rehearsal, 19/10/09: +*M. ROBERTSON*)

ROS, FRANK
The Bias of the World (P's, 6/5/12, St. Soc.; Everyman, 15/9/20, as *The Bonds of Interest*: +*B. DE ZOETE*: adapted from J. Benavente, *Los intereses creados*, 1907)
The Open Sea (Manchester, 5/4/09; Marlb., Holloway, 10/5/09: +*G. AMES*: adapted from A. Guimera, *Mar y cielo*, 1888)

ROSE, ADA M.
×A Man of Ideas. *Fr. 1901*
×At Cross Purposes (Steinway H., 8/11/02) *Fr. 1920*
×Two Naughty Old Ladies. *Fr. 1902*

ROSE, AGATHA [see *Mrs GEORGE CORBETT*]

'*ROSE, ARTHUR*' [=*CLARKSON ROSE*: see also *P. A. RUBENS* and *J. E. TERRY*]
For the Love of a Child (Middlesbrough, 21/7/04)
×The Key (Qns, Poplar, 13/12/09)
Pretty Peggy ('*m.c.*', m. A. E. Adams: Emp., Kilburn, 25/8/19; P's, 3/2/20: +*C. AUSTIN*)
The Dark Horse ('*f.*': Col., Ilkeston, 1/10/23: +*E. BARBER*)
The Last Warning (Com., 24/10/23: adapted from the play by *T. F. FALLON*, originally presented at Stamford, Conn., 22/9/22)
[Numerous sketches produced at music-halls]

ROSE, CECIL
×The Atonement (Steiner H., 12/3/29, Benefit Players: +*H. TIGHE*) *1929* (Village Drama Soc.)

ROSE, COLIN NEIL
×Pierette's Birthday (New, 24/6/08)

ROSE, CUTHBERT
Katreeno; or, Brokers Ahead ('*o.bsq.*': Pagoda, Littlehampton, 17/5/11)

ROSE, EDWARD [see also '*A. HOPE*' and *R. THORNDIKE*]
[For earlier plays see *H. E. D.* v, 549–550]
Queen o' Scots ('*poetical d.*': P'cess of W., Kennington, 5/10/00: +*J. TODHUNTER*)
Grandmamma ('*c.*': Bij., 22/3/04, *cpy.*)

[*ROSE, EDWARD EVERETT*
The Rosary (E.C., 30/6/13) *Fr. 1926*
The Little Lost Sister (Dalston, 7/10/18)
The Daughter of Mother Machree (D.P., Eastbourne, 24/3/19)

ROSE, FRANK HORACE
The Whispering Well (Gai., Manchester, 24/3/13; Court, 15/5/13)
×The Second Mrs Banks (Playh., L'pool, 15/10/13)
×The Hanging of Hey-go-mad Jack (Gai., Manchester, 13/4/14; Cor., 20/4/14)
×The Young Guv'nor (Playh., L'pool, 30/4/14)
Trouble in the House ('*c.*': H.M., Carlisle, 19/5/22)
Just a Darling (Steiner H., 19/5/27)
Madame Kurenda (O.H., Leicester, 29/8/27)

ROSE, JULIAN
Peggy, Be Careful ('*modern c.*': Brighton, 10/12/23)
Bandits ('*md. c.*': Hippo., Lewisham, 31/3/30: +*HENRY D'ERLANGER*)

ROSE, L. ARTHUR
Fire (Everyman, 30/6/27)

ROSE, OSCAR W.
×By the Light of a Candle (Ladbr. H., 12/4/02)

ROSEBERRY, ARTHUR
The Master Man (Plymouth, 18/4/10; Pav., Mile End, 25/4/10; Borough, Stratford, 6/8/17, as *For Sweethearts and Wives*)
Three Little Britons. LC, Stratford, 24/12/14
Real Sports ('*m.pl.*', m. E. Vousden: Borough, Stratford, 5/8/18)
The Silent Watch (Gr., Halifax, 22/8/19: E.C., 2/2/20)
Crossing the Line ('*m.pl.*': Gr., Halifax, 10/9/20; County, Shrewsbury, 20/12/20, as *Merry King Neptune*)
The Queen's Rival. LC, Wimbledon, 13/8/21
Playthings. LC, Pal., Battersea, 13/2/22
Derby Day (Gr., Fulham, 16/3/25)

ROSENBERG, ISAAC
×Moses (written 1916: in *Collected Poems*, 1947)

ROSENFELD, SYDNEY
[For earlier plays see *H. E. D.* v, 550]
The Purple Lady ('*f.c.*': Shak., L'pool, 8/11/01)

ROSENTHAL, Rev. G. D.
Duty (Balsall Heath Inst., B'ham, 27/9/09, *amat.*: +*J. J. BLOOD*)

ROSKRUGE, ETHEL
×Them Buns. *1929* (Village Drama Soc.)

ROSKRUGE, FRANCIS

×The Tale of a Royal Vest (‘*bsq. mime*’) *1930* (Village Drama Soc.)

‘*ROSMER, MILTON*’ [=*L. HUNT*]

A Magalen’s Husband (St M., 1/1/24, *m.*: + *E. PERCY*)

ROSS, A. M.

×Flying Kites. LC, Temperance H., Sheffield, 25/1/15

‘*ROSS, ADRIAN*’ [=*ARTHUR REED ROPES*: see also *C. ALDIN* and *F. F. SHEPHARD*)

[For earlier plays see *H. E. D.* v, 551 and 814]

×Ordered South: A Sketch in Khaki (St G’s Lawn Tennis Club, Forest Hill, 28/7/00)

The Antelope (‘*m.pl.*’: m. H. Félix: Waldorf, 28/11/08)

Our Miss Gibbs (‘*m.pl.*’, m. I. Caryll and L. Monckton: announced as by ‘*CRYPTOS*’ (i.e. ‘*ADRIAN ROSS*’, *PERCY GREENBANK*, *IVAN CARYLL* and *LIONEL MONCKTON* in collaboration) and ‘constructed’ by *J. T. TANNER*: Gai., 23/1/09)

×The Wedding Morning (Tiv., 30/9/12)

Lilac Time (‘*m.pl.*’, m. F. Schubert: Glo., Atlantic City, 22/3/21, as *Blossom Time*; Ambass., N.Y., 29/9/21; Lyr., 22/12/22)

Love’s Awakening (‘*light o.*’, m. E. Kunneke: Emp., 19/4/22)

The Beloved Vagabond (‘*m.pl.*’, m. D. Glass: D.Y., 1/9/27: dramatised from the novel (1906) by W. J. Locke) *1930*

ROSS, Mrs ADRIAN

×An Awful Shock (Forum Club, 2/5/20)

ROSS, CHARLES [see also *H. NICHOLLS*]

My Fairy Fanciful (County, Kingston, 15/4/04, *cpy.*: +*E. MARTIN*)

ROSS, GEORGE

×Modesty Forbids. LC, Lyr., L’pool, 19/5/13

ROSS, IRENE [see *F. LIND*]

ROSS, JANE [see *WALTON TREVOR*]

ROSS, LESLIE

×Puppets Limited. LC, Alex., 7/1/21

×Who’s the Girl? LC., Alex., 14/1/21

ROSS, Sir RONALD

×Evil (Music R., Boar’s Hill, Oxford, 19/11/25)

ROSS, W. A.

The Worship of Mammon. LC, P.H., Bolton, 5/1/18

The Wooing of Carmen. LC, P.H., Bolton, 31/12/19

The Will of Allah. LC, Inst., Bolton, 2/1/25

ROSS-SCOTT, T.

×The Flying Scotsman. LC, Coatbridge, 23/9/16

The Tartan Peril (D.Y., 25/5/21)

ROSSOMER, ROSALINE

The Fires Divine (Scala, 15/9/25)

ROTHERY, W. G.
[For earlier plays see *H. E. D.* v, 551 and 814]
×A Lucky Star ('*c.*': Scala, 18/12/07)

ROTTENBURG, HENRY [see also *M. D. LYON*]
The Honorary Degree ('*m.f.*', m. J. W. Ivimey: New, Cambridge, 7/6/07, *amat.*)
The Socialist ('*m.pl.*', m. J. W. Ivimey: New, Cambridge, 17/11/10, *amat.*; Court, 12/12/10, *amat.*)
The Vegetarians ('*m.pl.*', m. J. W. Ivimey: Court, 13/6/12, *amat.*)
Was It the Lobster? ('*m.f.*': Qns, 19/6/14, *amat.*)
What a Picnic! ('*m.f.*': Shaft., 20/6/21, *m.*)
×The Living Dead. LC, New, Cambridge, 1/6/22
The Soap Bubble (New, Cambridge, 12/2/23)

ROUND, DORA
Adam the Creator (Fest., Cambridge, 28/5/28: translated from J. and K. Čapek, *Adam stvořitel*, 1927) *1929*

ROUSBY, ALFRED [see *F. J. KIRKE*]

ROUTLEDGE, Mrs CALVERT [see *Mme. B. M. DITTINI*]

ROWAN, HARRY D.
The Lady Mayoress ('*c.*': All Saints Parish H., E. Finchley, 19/5/08, *amat.*)
×Miss March is Engaged. LC, St Andrew's Church H., London, N.10, 2/11/21

ROWE, CARLOTTA
×The Bacillus Amoris (Court, 19/9/13: +*R. DE CANDEY*)

ROWE, G. C.
×The Light of Day. LC, Exeter, 20/1/12

ROWE, REGINALD
The Worst of Being William ('*c.*': Q, 11/2/29)

ROWELL, ROBERT H.
×The Wheels of Time. LC, Ass. H., Benton, 17/12/12)

ROWLAND, DOROTHY A.
×A Bit o' Laikin. *1929* (Village Drama Soc.)

ROWLANDS, CECIL [='*CECIL RALEIGH*']

ROWLANDS, EFFIE ADELAIDE
×Home Truths (Cor., 28/9/10)

ROWLANDS, GEORGE [see also *J. SALTER*]
[A few music-hall sketches, mostly written in collaboration]

'*ROWLEY, ANTHONY*'
A Weaver's Shuttle ('*c.*': Roy., Glasgow, 21/11/10) *1911*
The Probationer (Roy., Glasgow, 13/11/11) *1911*

ROWLEY, J. DELAMARE
×The Prince of Tartary ('*oa.*': Stanley H., S. Norwood, 28/5/10, *amat.*)

'*ROWLEY, RICHARD*' [=*RICHARD VALENTINE WILLIAMS*]
×Apollo in Mourne. *1926*

ROXBOROUGH, CATHERINE
×The Convenient Lover (Roy., Glasgow, 29/4/09)

ROXBURGH, R. A.
Tukeson's Thumb ('*c.*': Rep., Edin., 27/11/24)

ROXBURY, HARRY [see also *ROY REDGRAVE*]
×On the Track (Emp., Leeds, 24/1/10)
Mary Had a Little Lamb ('*m.c.*': Hippo., Eastbourne, 16/6/19; Emp., Edmonton, 1/9/19: +*ARTHUR DANDOE*)
[A few sketches, mostly written in collaboration, produced at music-halls]

ROY-BYFORD, JOAN [see '*EVADNE PRICE*']

ROYD, LYNN
[For an earlier play see *H. E. D.* v, 552]
A Waiting Maid ('*oa.*', m. P. A. Henry: Manor, Hackney, 20/2/00)

ROYDAN, J. KINGSLEY
A Little Heroine ('*m.pl.*': T.H., Sutton-in-Ashfield, 30/10/02)

ROYDE-SMITH, NAOMI
A Balcony (Everyman, 25/8/26) *1927*
Mafro, Darling ('*c.*': Qns, 25/2/29) *1929*

ROYDON-DUFF, G.
Joan and Son ('*c.*': Rep., Plymouth, 31/5/20)

[*ROYLE, EDWIN MILTON*
A White Man (Lyr., 11/1/08)
These Are My People (Gar., 1/10/09, *cpy.*)

ROZANT, INA
×A Stage Name (Rehearsal, 4/4/09)

RUBENS, PAUL A.
[For earlier plays see *H. E. D.* v, 553]
×The Nineteenth Century (St J., 3/12/01)
Three Little Maids ('*m.c.*': Apo., 10/5/02)
Lady Madcap ('*m.c.*': P.W., 17/12/04: +*F. N. DAVIES*)
Mr Popple, of Ippleton ('*c.*': Apo., 14/11/05)
Miss Hook of Holland ('*m.c.*': P.W., 31/1/07: +*A. A. HURGON*) *1907*
Skittles ('*c.*': Ass. R., Bath. 14/2/08, *amat.*; Pal., Westcliff, 26/5/19, revised by *L. WORRALL* and *A. ROSE*; R.A., Woolwich, 11/7/21; Apo., 30/7/21)
My Mimosa Maid ('*m.pl.*': P.W., 21/4/08: +*A. A. HURGON*) *1908*
×The Fly-by-Night (Pal., 14/12/08)
×The Queen of Sheba (Sur., 3/5/09)
Dear Little Denmark ('*m.pl.*': P.W., 1/9/09)
Lovely Woman ('*f.*': Canterbury, 1/8/10, Old Stagers: +*H. WHITAKER*)
×Selfrich's Bargain Day (Sav., 22/10/10)
The Sunshine Girl ('*m.pl.*': Gai., 24/2/12: +*C. RALEIGH*)
After the Girl ('*revusical c.*': Gai., 7/2/14)

Striking ('*c.*': Apo. 5/5/15: +*G. UNGER*)
Tina ('*m.pl.*': Adel., 2/11/15: +*H. GRAHAM*)
The Miller's Daughters ('*m.pl.*': P's, Manchester, 24/12/15; Ldn. O.H., 15/5/16)

RUBINSTEIN, HAROLD FREDERICK
×Her Wild Oats (Rehearsal, 7/3/11, *m.*)
Consequences ('*c.*': Gai., Manchester, 9/2/14; Cor., 4/5/14)
Over the Wall (Gai., Manchester, 21/11/14)
The Earlier Works of Sir Roderick Athelstane (K's H., 2/6/18, Pioneer Players)
The Spirit of Parsifal Robinson ('*c.*': K's H., 11/3/19, St. Soc.)
×Old Boyhood (Lyr., Hamm., 14/12/19, Curtain Group)
Shakespeare (+*C. BAX*) *1921*
What's Wrong with the Drama? *1923*
[This contains five one-act plays: 1. *The Theatre* (LC, Kings., 16/6/24); 2. *A Specimen*; 3. *Repertory*; 4. *Arms and the Drama*; and 5. *Grand Guignol*]
Peter and Paul (Scala, 1/2/25, Pl. Actors) *1924*
Exodus (Circus, Glasgow, 30/3/25: +*H. GLOVER*) *1923*
Churchill ('*chronicle c.*': Little, Leeds, 8/11/26: + *A. J. TALBOT*) *1925*
×Insomnia ('*modern morality play*': Etlinger, 31/3/27) *1927*
The House (Blackfriars, 13/6/27, Interlude Theatre Guild) *1926*
Isabel's Eleven ('*c.*') *1927*
Plays Out of Time. *1930*
[This contains three plays: 1. *Hippodrome Hill* ('*a pl. of conscience in five prospects*'); 2. *Britannia Calling* ('*an adventure*'); and 3. *Stephen into Dickens*]

RUBINSTEIN, RONALD
×Boodle (Gai., Manchester, 11/9/16)
×Silhouettes. LC, K. G's H., 3/3/23

RUDD, H. A. L.
×A Lucky Spill (New, 8/6/08)

RUDD, STEELE
On Our Selection ('*c.*': Pal., Ramsgate, 16/8/20; Lyr., 24/8/20)

RUDDERHAM, FRED
Cymru and Byth. LC, Workmen's H., Glamorgan, 3/2/22

RUDERT, GEORGE
The Princess and the Doll; or, The Golden Comb (Alb. H., 11/1/10, *m.*, *amat.*: +*DICKSON RUDERT*)

RUDSTONE, CARNABY
Darby and Joan ('*d.d.*': Stratford, 30/5/21)

RUEGG, Judge
John Clutterbuck (Q, 10/2/30)

RUSHBROOKE, E.
×In Johannesburg (Cosmopolis, 17/2/14)

RUSKIN, SYBIL [see also *P. CRAVEN*]
The Monk of St Marco (Bij., Bedford-St, 29/9/07, third act only; Court, 19/12/09)
× Lucie (Lyc. Club, 23/3/11, *m.*)
× Little Satan (P's, Bristol, 3/5/11)
The Three Musketeers. LC, Brixton, 4/12/14

RUSSELL, E. HASLINGDEN
[For an earlier play see *H. E. D.* v, 553]
× His Lucky Star (Studio, Victoria Street, 29/1/08)

RUSSELL, EMERSON
× Antiques. *Fr. 1926*

RUSSELL, FRANK A.
Harwood Blood (Kings., 9/9/23, Rep. Players)

RUSSELL, GEORGE WILLIAM ('*A. E.*')
Deirdre (St Theresa's H., Dublin, 2/4/02, Irish Literary Theatre) *1907*

RUSSELL, HERBERT
On Watch (Gr., Plymouth, 27/6/04)

RUSSELL, MARION, Countess
× The Matchmakers. *1929* (Village Drama Soc.)

RUSSELL, MARJORY RISIEN
× The Tango-Queen (Etlinger, 28/6/16)
× The Cabaret Queen (Guildhall School of Music, 11/7/28)

RUSSELL-YOUNG, J. FRITZ
The Sacrifice (Vic. H., 31/1/07, *amat.*)

'*RUTHERFORD, JOHN*'
The Breed of the Treshams ('*r.d.*': Newcastle, 28/9/03; Kennington, 7/12/03; Lyr., 3/6/05)

RYAN, FRED
The Laying of the Foundations (Antient Concert R., Dublin, 29/10/02, Irish National Theatre Soc.; Qns Gate H., 2/5/03)

RYAN, HUBERT S.
× Feet of Clay (Crippl. Inst., 28/3/03, *amat.*)

RYAN, P. F. W.
The Marlboroughs (P's, Bristol, 16/11/23; Wimbledon, 23/3/25)

RYAN, REX
The Mandarin Wong Koo (Pal., Nottingham, 1/8/29)

RYAN, W. P.
× The Jug of Sorrow (Abbey, Dublin, 20/10/14)

RYAN, WILLIAM
A Knight of the Road. LC, Pier, Brighton, 7/1/13: +*ELIZABETH RYAN*

RYDE, THOMAS

The Angel of the Blue Canyon. LC, Gr., Glasgow, 26/2/14
×The Fatal Card. LC, Gr., Glasgow, 14/3/14
The Girl He Left Behind. LC, Gr., Glasgow, 28/3/14

RYECROFT, BLANCHE

The Wonder Garden (*'oa.'*: Crippl. Inst., 16/2/17, *amat.*)

RYLAND, CLARA

×The Yellow Dwarf (*'pl. for children'*) *1930*

[*RYLEY, Mrs MADELEINE LUCETTE*

[For earlier plays see *H. E. D.* v, 554]
The Mysterious Mr Bugle (*'f.'*: Stockton, 29/1/97, *cpy.*, as *The Vanishing Husband*; Str., 29/5/00)
My Lady Dainty (*'c.'*: Brighton, 2/7/00)
×Realism (Gar., 4/10/00)
Mice and Men (*'r.c.'*: Manchester, 27/11/01; Lyr., 27/1/02) *1903*
The Grass Widow (*'f.'*: D.P., Eastbourne, 26/5/02; Shaft., 3/6/02)
The Altar of Friendship (*'c.'*: Crit., 24/3/03)
Mrs Grundy (Scala, 16/11/05) *1924*
The Great Conspiracy (D.Y., 4/3/07: adapted from P. Berton, *La belle Marseillaise*, 1905)
The Sugar Bowl (*'c.'*: Qns, 8/10/07)

RYND, E.

×Mr Riggles Joins the Choir (Alb. H., 7/11/08, *amat.*: +*A. NANKIVELL*)

SABATINI, RAFAEL [see also *S. BARING*, *H. HAMILTON* *L. M. LION* and *J. E. H. TERRY*]

×Fugitives (Emp., Kilburn, 26/6/11)
The Tyrant (B'ham, 9/3/25; New, 18/3/25) *1925*
Scaramouche (*'r.d.'*: K's, Glasgow, 4/4/27; Gar., 18/4/27)

SABBEN, JAMES

It Doesn't Matter Which (*'f.c.'*: Str., 21/9/24, Rep. Players)

SABINE, LILLIAN KEAL

The Rise of Silas Lapham (*'c.'*: Gar., N.Y., 25/11/19; Lyr., 20/2/22, *m.*) *Fr. 1927*

SACKVILLE, Lady MARGARET

×Hildris the Queen. *1908*
Bertrud and Other Dramatic Pieces. *1911*
Three Plays for Pacifists. *1919*
[This contains three one-act pieces: 1. *The Sewing Party*; 2. *The Man Who Came Back*; and 3. *The V.C.*]
Madriala. LC, *'m.pl.'*: Gar., 26/5/23
A Masque of Edinburgh (Music Hall, Edin., 23/11/23: +*F. C. MEARS*)
Elva of the Faery Folk (Gr., Putney Bridge, 15/12/24)
Three Fairy Plays. *1925*

[The plays included in this collection, although published under the name of Lady Margaret Sackville, were written by Forbes Dawson on fairy-tale themes composed by her: 1. *Columbine in Cricklebury*; 2. *The Fairy Learns the Meaning of Tears*; and 3. *The Poet, the Painter and the Witch-Girl*]
×Alicia and the Twilight. *1929*

SADLEIR, MICHAEL
The Warden ('*c.*': Roy., 12/6/27, Lyc. Club Stage Soc.: +*G. HOPKINS*: dramatised from Anthony Trollope's novel)

SADLER, DOROTHY
×Miss Brown's Brother (Court, 18/12/13)

SAFFERY, G. [see *L. STACK*]

SAINSBURY, HESTER
The Toils of Yoshitomo ('*t.*': Little, 3/10/22: +*T. KORI*: adapted from an early Japanese play)
×May Day (LC, K. G's H., 12/12/24; A.L.S. Trav. Th., 1921)

ST ALBANS, BLANCHE
Come Back to Erin (Qns, Dublin, 28/5/17)

ST ALBANS, KHYVA
The Painted Laugh (Gar., 16/11/21, *m.*: translated from *Krasnii smekh* by L. N. Andreev)

ST AMORY, CARL
×A Swan Song. LC, Little, 21/6/13: +*H. DE HAMEL*

ST AUBYN, J.
×The Domestic Agency (Etlinger, 15/11/18)

ST CLAIR, WINIFRED
×Two of the Odd Boys (Caxton H., 3/7/12)
×Heartless Mr Jones (Unitarian Church, Brixton, 20/1/13, *amat.*)
×The Voice Within (Rehearsal, 4/7/13)
×More Immediate Interest (Arts Centre, 18/3/14)
×The Snubbing of Fanny. *1914*
×The Death Certificate (Bij. 6/2/19)

ST CLAIR-FORBES, E.
The Crown of Motherhood. LC, Glossop, 31/7/14

ST CYR, DIRCE [see also *G. CANNAN*]
The Hidden Spring (Bedford H., Chelsea, 24/9/22, Pax Robertson Salon: adapted from R. Bracco, *La piccola fonte*, 1905)

ST EON, BARON
The Rose-scented Handkerchief ('*c.*': Bij., 28/4/06, *amat.*)

ST GEORGE, JOHN
×Perkie Nutts, 'Tec. LC, Playh., Faversham, 3/4/19

ST JOHN, ARTHUR
[For earlier plays see *H. E. D.* v, 554]
Dishonoured (W.L., 20/6/04, revised from the play of 1896)

ST JOHN, CHRISTOPHER MARIE [see also *C. HAMILTON, M. POTAPENKO* and *M. V. SALVAGE*]
The Good Hope (Imp., 27/4/03, St. Soc.; K's, Hamm., 27/4/04: +*J. T. GREIN*: adapted from *Op Hoop van Zegen* (1900) by H. Heijermans)
×Eriksson's Wife (Roy., 3/9/04)
Du Barri (Sav., 18/3/05)
×On the East Side ('*t.*': Court, 7/7/08, *m.*; K's H., 9/2/19, as *Nell 'Est*, Pioneer Players)
×The Wilson Trial (Court, 14/12/09)
×The First Actress (Kings., 8/5/11, *m.*, Pioneer Players) *1911* (*priv.*)
×The Coronation (Sav., 28/1/12, Pioneer Players: +*C. THURSBY*. *1912*
×Macrena ('*t.*': K's H., 21/4/12, Pioneer Players)
The Brothers Karamazov (Aldw., 16/2/13, St. Soc.: adapted from *Les Frères Karamozov* (1911) by J. Copeau and J. Croué)
×Paphnutius (Sav. 11/1/14, Pioneer Players)
[See *The Plays of Roswitha*, below]
×Her Will. LC, Concert H., Olympia, 14/4/14
The Hired Girl (St M., 25/2/17, *m.*, St. Soc.: from *De Meid* (1900) by H. Heijermans)
Just a Wife or Two ('*c.*': Pier, Brighton, 24/11/19: called originally *In Clover*)
The Children's Carnival (Kings., 20/6/20, Pioneer Players: adapted from *Carnaval des enfants* (1910) by St Georges de Bouhelier)
×The Dream of a Spring Morning (Rep., B'ham, 29/10/21: adapted from *Sogno d'una mattina di primavera* (1897) by G. D'Annunzio)
Spanish Lovers (Kings., 21/6/22: adapted from *Aux jardins de Murcie* (1923), by C. de Battle and A. Lavergne, itself based on a play by J. Feliu y Codina)
The Plays of Roswitha. *1923*
[This contains translations of six of Roswitha's plays: 1. *Gallicanus*; 2. *Dulcitius*; 3. *Callimachus*; 4. *Abraham*; 5. *Paphnutius*; and 6. *Sapientia*]

ST JOHN-LOE, GLADYS
×Death Sentence (Lyc. Club, 26/2/26)
Life (K's, Southsea, 2/9/29; Apo., 11/9/29, as *Yesterday's Harvest*)

ST MICHAEL, W.
×The Day of Reckoning (Darwen, 6/3/16)

SAINTSBURY, H. A. [see also *J. DRINKWATER* and *S. LEWIS-RANSOM*)
[For earlier plays see *H. E. D.* v, 554]
Benvenuto Cellini (Cor. 9/7/00)
The King of the Huguenots (Gr., Croydon, 21/1/01)
Jim: A Romance of Cockayne (County, Kingston, 6/7/03)
×Almost a Queen (Shak., L'pool, 11/9/05)

Anna of the Plains (Worthing, 28/1/07; C.P., 4/3/07: from the novel (1906) by Alice and Claude Askew)
×The Angel of the Swamp (Lincoln, 9/9/07: +*GENE STRATTON-PORTER*)
The Friend of the People (Plymouth, 10/3/24; Brixton, 21/4/24)
×The Cardinal's Collation (Glo., 7/2/26, Green Room Rag: adapted from *A Ceia dos cardeis* (1909) by J. Dantas) *1926*

SAKER, ANNIE
×A Passing Cloud (H.M., Carlisle, 5/6/03)

'*SAKI*' [=*H. H. MUNRO*]
The Watched Pot ('*Edwardian c. of manners*': ADC, Cambridge, 29/11/24) *1924* (in *The Square Egg and other sketches, with three plays*)
[Besides *The Watched Pot*, this also includes two one-acts: 1. *The Death Trap*, and 2. *Karl-Ludwig's Window*)
×A Baker's Dozen. LC, W.G., 16/12/24

SAKURAI, JOJI [see *M. C. STOPES*]

SALISBURY, A.
Toodee-oo ('*m.f.*': P.H., Runcorn, 3/4/19)

SALISBURY, R. B. [see *W. E. B. HENDERSON*]

SALTER, JAMES
Boy Wanted ('*m.c.*', m. G. Shaw: Hippo., Margate, 18/11/18: +*G. ROWLANDS*)

SALTOUN, WALTER [see *A. GRATTAN-CLYNDES*]
The Abode of Love (E.C., 23/8/15)
The Girl who Wouldn't Marry (Emp., Rotherham, 29/5/16; Vic., Walthamstow, 5/6/16)
Her Forbidden Sacrifice (Gr., Halifax, 30/10/16; E.C., 11/6/17)
The Man She Bought (Stratford, 11/2/18)
The Serpent in the Garden (Dewsbury, 28/6/18; Woolwich, 30/9/18, as *A Married Man's Sweetheart*: called originally *A Man and His Money*)
Married Sinners (W. Bromwich, 28/11/19; Stratford, 22/12/19)
Too Many Bits of Fluff. LC, Hippo., Maidenhead, 9/6/20
A Fight for a Wife (Bristol, 14/11/21; E.C., 24/4/21: +*A. GRATTAN-CLYNDES*: called originally *Have You Seen Parker?*)

SALVAGE, M. V.
The Rising Sun (Lyr., Hamm., 1/6/19, Pioneer Players: Playh. L'pool, 26/5/26; Kings., 9/10/29: +*C. ST JOHN*: adapted from *De opgaande Zon* (1908) by H. Heijermans

SAMPSON, S. SARSFIELD
The Compromise ('*c.*'; Irish, Dublin, 24/2/19)

SAMUEL, HORACE B.
The Green Cockatoo and Other Plays by Arthur Schnitzler. *1913*
[This contains translations of three one-act plays: 1. *The Green*

Cockatoo, from *Der grüne Kakadu*; 2. *The Mate*, from *Der Gefärtin*; and 3. *Paracelsus*]

×Simoon (Arts, 28/1/28: translated from *Samun* (1900) by A. Strindberg) *1914*

Comrades (Everyman, 21/2/28: translated from *Kamraterna* (1888) by A. Strindberg) *1914*

SAMUEL, MONTAGUE

×It's Never Too Late to Wed (Brondesbury Synagogue, 22/2/09, *amat.*)

×Ten and Sixpence (Brondesbury Synagogue, 27/2/10, *amat.*)

SAMUELS, MAURICE V. [see *M. I. FISK*]

SANDBY, ALFHILD FINCH MYHR

The Life of Hans Anderson ('*r.pl.*': Scala, 7/2/27)

SANDEMAN, CHRISTOPHER [see *M. GONZALEZ, L. HUSKISON* and *D. WELBY*]

The Match-breaker ('*c.*': Little, 13/6/12, Oncomers)

×Midsummer Madness (Little, 30/5/13, Oncomers)

Blind Fate (Little, 30/5/13, Oncomers)

The River (Rep., B'ham, 20/11/13: adapted from *Der Strom* (1904) by M. Halbe)

The Self-Starter ('*light c.*': St J., 6/5/27, *m.*)

SANDERS, M. F.

×The Rival (Rehearsal, 4/5/11, English Pl. Soc.)

SANFORD-TERRY, G.

×Coffee and Cupid (Leeds, 25/9/25: a version of Bach's *Coffee Cantata*)

SANDIFORD, PERCY

A Woman's Folly (Carlton, Greenwich, 21/3/04: +*A. HOLLES*: title later changed to *John Durnford, Bachelor*)

SANDWITH, FRANCIS [see *N. A. EVERSON*]

SANSOM, CHARLES [see *E. W. HORNUNG*]

SANSOME, FLETCHER

Jack's Sweetheart ('*m.c.*', m. A. Leopold: Workington, 2/2/03; R.A., Woolwich, 15/6/03)

'*SANSOVINO*' [=*E. BLYTHE* and *N. MORRIS*]

SANTE, GEORGE TESTO [see *C. DARRELL*]

SANTLEY, KATE

[For an earlier play see *H. E. D.* v, 555]

Mixed Relations ('*c.*': Roy., 4/2/02: adapted from V. Sardou and E. de Najac, *Divorçons*, 1880)

SAPIO, ROMUALDO

The Dance of Death ('*m.pl.*', m. W. Kienzel: Kelly's, L'pool, 23/1/14; P.W., 13/7/14)

'*SAPPER*' [=*HERMAN CYRIL McNEILE*]

Bulldog Drummond (Wynd. 29/3/21: +*Sir GERALD DU MAURIER*) *Fr. 1925*

The Way Out (Com., 23/1/30)

SAPTE, W., Jr.

[For earlier plays see *H. E. D.* v, 555–6]

The Crammers; or, A Short Vacation ('*light c.*': Str. 2/7/03)

Curtain Raisers and Sketches. 4 vols. *1914*

[Each of the volumes contains four sketches, making sixteen in all: 1. *A Lesson in Proposing*; 2. *A Mesalliance*; 3. *Daddy*; 4. *His Girl and His Guv'nor*; 5. *The Photograph*; 6. *James and the Telephone*; 7. *Waiting for the Truth*; 8. *The Rightful Heir;* 9. *The Actor;* 10. *Leasehold Marriage*; 11. *Harmony*; 12. *Mortara, or the Poisoned Chalice*; 13. *Conway-Chauffeur*; 14. *After Many Years*; 15. *An Afternoon Call*; and 16. *The Lioness*]

SARGENT, FREDERICK

×Love's Comedy (O.H., Leicester, 8/2/04; Rehearsal, 4/2/10: +*L. M. LION*)

×Expiation (Rehearsal, 14/7/11)

×An Object Lesson (H., 19/3/12) *Fr. 1912*

An Interrupted Divorce ('*f.*': K's, Hamm., 9/9/12)

×Mrs Bunce's Bet (Pal., Hamm., 30/6/19)

SARGENT, HERBERT C. (see also *R. L. CASSON, G. EDEN, W. W. JACOBS* and *A. MORRISON*]

The Lust of Gold ('*md.*': Edmonton, 23/6/02)

The Ring that Binds (P.W., Wolverhampton, 25/3/03; P.W., Southampton, 27/7/03; Alex., 7/9/03; Lyr., Hamm., 30/11/03)

×Ancient Britons (Emp., L'pool, 13/5/07)

×Pyjamas (Ldn Pav., 12/7/07)

×The Lady Bandits ('*oa.*': County, Kingston, 15/4/08: +*E. LAURI*)

×The Governor's Nephew (Emp., Holb., 3/8/08)

Water Birds ('*musical water absurdity*': M'sex, 20/11/16: later called *Sporting Times*)

Sonny Jim ('*m.pl.*', m. W. Neale: Emp., Kingston, 23/2/20)

×The Wasp. LC, Pal., 19/7/20

Pierrot Playlets. *Fr. 1920*

[This contains ten brief pieces as '*cackle for concert parties*']

Pierrotechnics. *Fr. 1923*

[A collection similar to the above]

Bits and Pieces. *Fr. 1924*

[A collection of revue sketches]

Auntie. LC, County H., St Alban's, 26/2/24; title later changed to *A Mix Up*

The Police Force ('*c.bsq.*': Pal., Camberwell, 6/9/26: +*C. WEST*)

August 1914 ('*c.*': Gr., Clapham Junction, 12/9/27: +*C. WEST*)

Mrs Hamblett Again. *Fr. 1930*

[A collection of revue sketches]

SARGENT, IDA [see *H. FARNSWORTH*]

SARGENT, JOHN

[For earlier plays see *H. E. D.* v, 556]

The Master of the Chain (Plymouth, 21/2/00, *cpy.*; Plymouth,

11/6/00; Carlton, Greenwich, 17/12/00; Duchess, Balham, 25/8/02, as *The Nihilist Queen*: +*J. W. CARSON*)
×A Sculptor's Dream. LC, Lyr., Hamm., 5/2/13

SARGUSOUR, JOHN
The Last Act. LC, Com., 2/7/20: +*ELLA SARGUSOUR*

SARKANY, CHARLES
×The Latest New York Sensation; or, The Twenty Four Hours' Millionaire (E.C., 13/11/12, '*preliminary pfce.*': +*H. H. LEWIS*)

SAROTIS, CECILE [see *G. ENTHOVEN*]

'*SARR, KENNETH*' [=*KENNETH SHEILS REDDIN*]
×The Changeling ('*allegory*': Abbey, Dublin, 28/11/20, *m.*)
×The Passing ('*t.*': Abbey, Dublin, 9/12/24) *1924* (Dublin)
×Old Mag ('*Christmas pl.*': Abbey, Dublin, 22/12/24) *1924* (Dublin)

SASOULIN, G. G.
Paying the Penalty ('*Russian f.*': Cosmopolis, 19/4/13)

SAUNDERS, FRANK HEATH
×Francesco the Monk (Emp., Preston, 19/2/17; Bed., 12/11/17)

SAUNDERS, GERTRUDE M.
×Diana Disappears (Ldn Pav., 6/11/13)
×John The Stoic (M'sex, 8/11/18, *m.*)
×Co-opportunists. LC, Algernon Road School, Hendon, 16/3/25

SAUNDERS, LOUISE
×The Woodland Princess ('*fairy pl. for children*') *Fr. 1918*
×The Knave of Hearts. *1925* (New York)

SAUNDERSON, EVA
×Camouflage. LC, Memorial, Stratford-on-Avon, 25/11/18

SAVAGE, COURTENAY
I'm Wise ('*f.c.*': K's, Southsea, 14/10/29; Hippo., Golder's Green, 21/10/29)

SAVI, Mrs ANGELO (DORA)
×Love is Passing (Rehearsal, 23/5/10)
Where Ambition Leads. LC, '*allegorical pl.*': Park, Hanwell, 10/12/17

SAVILLE, FRED S.
Aphrodite (Rep., B'ham, 8/5/27, *amat.*) *1934* (Birmingham)

SAVILLE, JESSIE FAUCIT
Love in a Maze (Circus-St. H., Nottingham, 12/11/24, *amat.*)

SAVILLE, T. G.
Absorbing Perdita ('*chimerical f.*': Fest., Cambridge, 14/11/27; O.H., Southampton, 11/2/29, as *Perdita Comes to Town*)

SAWARD, Rev. W. T.
Orestes. *1903*
Glastonbury ('*historical d.*': Corn Exchange, Bedford, 6/2/12) *1911*

The Dragon (County, Bedford, 9/12/12: +*E. PONSONBY*)
The Casuists. LC, Bath, 10/4/13

SAWYER, AMY

×The Brown Pot (D.P., Eastbourne, 2/4/25, *amat.*; Cent., 8/12/26, *amat.*)
×At the Sign of the Bow-legged Blackbird (D.P., Eastbourne, 2/4/25, *amat.*)
[*Sussex Village Plays and Others* (1934) includes both of the above plays, together with twenty-two others]

SAWYER, LYDELL

×That Impious Piano (Scala, 17/12/06, *amat.*)
×The Awakening (Terry's, 16/5/09, English Pl. Soc.)
A Matter of Agreement (County H., Guildford, 6/1/11, English Pl. Soc.)
×MacGregor's Mixture (Little, 12/6/11, *m.*, English Pl. Soc.)
×The Art of Timmins (Little, 12/6/11, *m.*, English Pl. Soc.)

SAXE-WYNDHAM, H.

×The Transformation of Bacchus ('*dance scena*', m. Grace Hawkins: Guildhall School of Music, 2/7/12; Kennington, 22/7/12)

'*SCARAMEL*'

×Reuben's Wife. LC, Bristol, 6/5/14

SCATCHERD, HARRY

×A Christmas Storm (Smethwick, 4/5/07, *cpy.*)

[*SCHEFFAUER, HERMANN GEORGE*

The New Shylock ('*c.*': Gai., Manchester, 5/10/14; Lyr., 29/10/14)
Gas (Rep., B'ham, 24/11/23: adapted from G. Kaiser, *Gas*, 1918) *1924*
Melodrama ('*c.*': Gate, 17/1/27: translated from a play by G. Kaiser)

SCHLESINGER, E. G. [see *H. W. BARBER*]

SCHLEUSSNER, ELLIE

Creditors (P's, 11/3/12, St. Soc.: translated from A. Strindberg, *Fordringsagare*, 1888)

SCHLITZER, D.

×The Workhouse (Beaumont H., Mile End, 14/6/09, *amat.*)
×The Registrar (Beaumont H., Mile End, 14/6/09, *amat.*)

SCHLOESSER, F. [='*FRANK CASTLES*']

SCHOFIELD, ERNEST

The Joker ('*f.*': New, 17/4/15: +*J. RAMSEY*)

SCHOFIELD, STEPHEN

×Men at War. *1920*
×The Bruiser's Election. *1925* (Labour Publishing Co.)
×On the Moor. *Fr. 1926*
×The Marble God (Gate, 21/6/26) *1926* (in *The Marble God and Other One-Act Plays*)
×Saving Lady Jane. *Fr. 1927*
×Sir George and the Dragon. *1927* (Labour Publishing Co.)

×The Judge of All the Earth. *1927* (Labour Publishing Co.)
×Good Old Uncle Amos. *Fr. 1927*
×The Odour of Sanctity ('*an anacronism*') *1927* (Labour Publishing Co.)
×The Paths of Glory. *Fr. 1930*

SCHOMER, A. S.
Devil Dick (Apo., 16/11/22)

SCHRIER, HENRIETTA (*Mrs C. LODGE-PERCY*)
[All but the last of the following plays were written in collaboration with *C. LODGE-PERCY*]
The Woman He Wanted (Stratford, 23/12/12; Dalston, 18/3/18, as *For His Lady's Honour*)
The Crackswoman (Rochdale, 23/6/13)
The Custody of the Child (Hippo., Huddersfield, 13/4/14; Stratford, 12/10/14)
It's a Long Way to Tipperary (Castleford, 21/12/14; Woolwich, 11/1/15)
Mary from Tipperary (Chatham, 28/6/15; Woolwich, 16/8/15: title later changed to *Her Sister's Secret*)
The Devil's Rosary (Kelly's, L'pool, 31/7/15; E.C., 20/12/15, as *The Blind Girl's Rosary*)
When the Angelus is Ringing (Stratford, 1/11/15)
The Slacker (Gr., Nottingham, 27/3/16, with title changed during run to *My Heart is Calling You*; Stratford, 8/4/18, as *Her Second Chance*: also called *The Man who Came Back*)
The Girl who Went Straight (P's, Blackburn, 17/4/16; Stratford, 11/9/16)
The Heart of a Shop-girl (K's, Longsight, 11/9/16; Stratford, 30/10/16)
For Love of Peg (Lincoln, 18/1/17; Stratford, 12/2/17)
Why She Got Married (Hippo., Mexborough, 8/2/17; Stratford, 9/4/17)
His Good Angel (Yarmouth, 21/1/18; Dalston, 25/3/18)
Mother or Mistress? (Stratford, 12/8/18)
It's a Long Way – No Longer (Yarmouth, 28/2/19; Stratford, 7/7/19)
Shame (Metro., Glasgow, 25/12/19; Stratford, 26/1/20)
Love Holds the Key (Playh., Llanhilleth, 27/2/20; Stratford, 11/7/21)
The Little Mother (W. Bromwich, 31/5/20; Stratford, 5/7/20)
A Sister's Secret (Stratford, 12/7/20)
A Prodigal Wife (Metro., Glasgow, 20/12/20; Stratford, 10/1/21)
Nana's Daughter (Stratford, 4/7/21)
The Sheik (Hippo., Chesterfield, 29/1/23; S. Ldn. Pal., 2/4/23)

SCHURHOFF, GERTRUDE
He Who Gets Slapped (Rep., B'ham, 20/2/26; Everyman, 8/11/27: +*B. V. JACKSON*: adapted from N. Andreev, *To, to poluchaet poshchetschini*, 1915)

[*SCHWAB, LAURENCE* [see also *O. HAMMERSTEIN*)

Queen High ('*m.c.*', m. L. E. Gensler: Providence, 4/26; Ambass., N.Y., 8/9/26; Emp., Sunderland, 25/10/26; Qns, 2/11/26: +*B. G. DE SYLVA*)

Good News ('*m.c.*', m. R. Henderson: Pal., Manchester, 6/8/28; Carlton, 15/8/28: +*B. G. DE SYLVA*)

Follow Through ('*m.c.*': Emp., Southampton, 16/9/29: Dominion, 3/10/29: +*B. G. DE SYLVA*)

'*SCHWARTZ, CAMILLO*' [=*KARL ROBL* and his father]

×The Broken Mirror (Worthing, 7/7/11, *cpy.*; Hippo., 23/10/11)

SCHWARTZ, JACOB

The Golden Calf. LC, St J., 11/10/09. *1922*

SCHWARTZ, M. W. POORTEN [='*M. MAARTENS*']

'*SCOT, ALARIC*'

Black St Anthony (Str., 7/4/29, Rep. Players)

SCOTT, AFFLECK

×Breaking It Gently (K's H., 22/3/08, Pl. Actors; Vaud., 20/5/08; Tiv., 13/6/10, as *The Odd Man Out*)

×Amina (K's H., 22/3/08, Pl. Actors)

×Olivia's Elopement (K's, Hamm., 17/12/08)

×Darracott's Wife (Court, 14/3/09, Pl. Actors: +*A. CARMICHAEL*)

×Henry (Court, 18/12/10, Pl. Actors)

×The Stranger at the Inn (Court, 24/6/13)

SCOTT, Lady AIMÉE BYNG

The Iron Law (Court, 10/3/29, Lyc. Club)

SCOTT, AUDREY

The Wallflower ('*c.*': Arts, 28/12/28; Str., 31/5/29, as *Why Drag in Marriage?*)

SCOTT, Rev. CLEMENT VICTOR ROUGH

Children in Fiction. LC, '*pageant*': Bury, 12/3/17. *1916* (Bury)

SCOTT, EDITH HOPE

×The Pocket Knife. *1927*

SCOTT, ERIC

×We Three (Ladbr. H., 24/6/02)

SCOTT, FRED NEWTON [see *C. L. MEADER*]

SCOTT, G. G. DAWSON

Green Stones (Playroom 6, 1/3/27: +*L. VOLLMER*)

SCOTT, H. A.

×Pearls Before Swine. LC, W.G., 5/5/21

SCOTT, HADDON

Dabchick, M.P. (Metro., Glasgow, 3/7/18)

SCOTT, HELEN McLEOD

The Heid o' th' Hoose (Tiv., Aberdeen, 7/10/12; Emp., Finsbury Park, 23/12/12)

SCOTT, HERBERT
The Rival Poets ('*oa.*', m. E. German: St G's H., 7/3/01)
×The Minstrel and the Maid (Vic. H., 4/11/09)
×Rich Miss Rustle (Vic. H., 4/11/09)

SCOTT, M. A.
The Gay Widow ('*m.c.*': Pier, Brighton, 9/10/11)

SCOTT, M. CLEMENT [see *C. H. BOURNE*]

SCOTT, Miss M. F.
×Charity (O.H., Belfast, 4/12/11, Ulster Literary Theatre)
×Family Rights (O.H., Belfast, 9/12/12, Ulster Literary Theatre)

SCOTT, MAURICE [see *F. A. MARSTON*]

SCOTT, NOEL
×Desperation (Court, 18/12/13)
The Fairway ('*c.*': New, 4/1/25, Rep. Players: adapted from J. Deval, *Une faible femme*, 1920: +*AURIOL LEE*)
The Broken Thread (Aldw., 8/2/25, Rep. Players)
Half a Loaf ('*c.*': Gr., Croydon, 4/10/26; Com., 9/11/26: adapted from C. R. Marx, *La pensionnaire*)
The Joker (Roy., 19/1/27) *Fr. 1929*
Dawn (Portsmouth, 31/1/27; Hippo., Golder's Green, 13/6/27)

SCOTT, R. L.
The Golden Key (Q, 9/1/28: +*G. OWEN*)

SCOTT, ROBERT H. [see *E. R. WARD*]

SCOTT, ST CLAIR
The Odd Man ('*c.*': Q, 24/8/25: +*C. GARTH*)

SCOTT, T. ROSS
The Hookin' o' Sandy ('*c.*': Paisley, 22/1/14)
Muriel Comes In ('*anti-tuberculosis propaganda pl.*': Lyr., Glasgow, 24/2/21)

SCOTT, WILL
The Limping Man (Gr., Croydon, 28/4/30)

SCOTT-GATTY, A. S.
The Three Bears ('*m.pl.*': Vaud., 20/6/27)

SCOTT-GATTY, CHARLES
The Military Girl ('*m.pl.*': Sav., 16/4/12, *amat.*: +*MURIEL SCOTT-GATTY*)
Claude Abroad ('*m.pl.*', m. author and Sir Alfred Scott-Gatty: Aldw., 27/5/13, *amat.*: +*MURIEL SCOTT-GATTY*)

SCOTT-GATTY, NICHOLAS COMYN [see *NICHOLAS COMYN GATTY*]

SCOTT-MAXWELL, Mrs FLORIDA
The Flash-Point. *1914*

SCOTT-MONCRIEFF, C. K.
The Game as He Played It (Y.M.C.A., Sheffield, 24/2/27, *amat.*: adapted from *Ciascuno a suo modo* by L. Pirandello)
Lazarus (Huddersfield, 8/7/29: adapted from *Lazzaro* (1929) by L. Pirandello)

SCUDAMORE, E.

In the Mormon's Clutches (Star, Finedon, 20/8/27: +*R. E. PARSONS*)

SCUDAMORE, F. A.

A Bad Character (Gr., Fulham, 8/4/01)
Because I Love You ('*m.d.*': Gr., Fulham, 4/8/02)
A World of Women ('*c.*': Gr., Fulham, 13/4/03)
The Biggest Scamp on Earth ('*md.*': Sur., 3/8/03)
The Beautiful Avenger (Stratford, 4/4/04)
The Vengeance of Women (W.L., 24/7/05; Clarence, Pontypridd, 5/12/10, as *Her Ruined Life*; Woolwich, 15/5/11)

SCUDAMORE, LIONEL

His Brother's Keeper (Cambridge, Spennymoor, 24/12/00; Terriss, Rotherhithe, 15/7/01: +*P. BARRY*)
× Grandfather's Clock (Empress, Brixton, 20/4/08)
× Moving In (Emp., Cambridge, 26/2/15)
× All's Well (Barnard's, Chatham, 1/3/15)
The Man Who Lived Again (Stratford, 26/2/12; Alh., Stourbridge, 3/4/13, as *A Wife's Devotion*)
Married to a Rotter (Stratford, 22/11/20)

SCUDDER, EVARTS SEELVE

The Crusaders. *1925*

'*SEAMARK*' [=*AUSTIN J. SMALL*]

When the Blue Hills Laughed ('*c.*': Huddersfield, 13/6/27; Crit., 20/9/27: +'*MARIUS*')
× The 'Ole in the Road. *Fr. 1929*

SEARS, DAVID

Juggernaut (Gate, Dublin, 19/3/29)

SEATON, MORRICE

× Better Late than Never (P.W., L'pool, 7/5/00)
× Frenchy (Clavier H., 18/12/12, Arts and Dram. Club)
Enter Eilah McDonald ('*c.*': Little, 15/12/22, *m.*)

SECCOMBE, CHARLES EDWARD

× Round the Manger ('*scenes representing the nativity of Our Lord*') *1917*
× The Torch Bearers. *1919* (Brixton: Missionary Literature Supply)
× Spirit of Man and Another. *1923* (Faith Press)

SEDGWICK, Rev. SIDNEY NEWMAN

× The Policeman's Lot (Leatherhead, 18/1/05)
× The Irrelevant Hobby ('*one-act melodrama*') *1927* (S.P.G.)
× At the Main Gate. *1929* (Parish Plays)
A Reel of Time. *1929*

SELBIT, P. T.

[Numerous sketches and playlets produced at music-halls]

SELF, CHARLES STANLEY [see also *H. KINGSTON* and *E. C. MATTHEWS*]
The Ghosts of Spectre Grange ('*mystery m.c.*': Pal., E. Ham, 6/5/12)
× Visions of a Night (Emp., Camberwell, 21/4/13)

SELVER, PERCY PAUL [see also *N. PLAYFAIR*]
The Woman (translated from a play by Josip Kosor) *1917* (in *People of the Universe: Four Serbo-Croatian Plays*)
The Invincible Ship (translated from a play by Josip Kosor) *1917* (in *People of the Universe: Four Serbo-Croatian Plays*)
R.U.R. ('*fant. md.*': Gar., N.Y., 9/10/22; St M., 24/4/23: translated from the play (1921) by K. Čapek, and adapted by *N. PLAYFAIR*) *1923*
× June (99 Lancaster Gate, 4/3/23, Unique Centre Club: translated from *Červen* (1905) by F. Šrámek)
The Land of Many Names (Gate, 29/3/26; translated from *Země mnoha jhen* (1925) by J. Čapek) *1926*
The Makropoulos Secret (Arts, 8/7/30; Embassy, 6/9/31: originally submitted for licensing to LC by the Repertory, Hull, 1/11/29: translated from *Več Makropulos* (1922) by K. Čapek) *1927*

[*SELWYN, EDGAR* (see also *F. JACKSON*)
× A Friend in Need (Adel., 17/2/02)
× When Denny Comes Marching Home (P'cess, 28/4/02)
The Adoption of Archibald ('*f.c.*': Worthing, 2/2/03; Aven., 6/2/03)
× High Life in Jail (S. Ldn Pal., 6/1/17)
Dancing Mothers (Washington, 5/5/24; Booth, N.Y., 11/8/24; Qns, 17/3/25: +*E. GOULDING*)

SENIOR, WILLIAM
× The Laggard (Bij., Bedford-st., 10/11/07, Pl. Actors)

SENNETT, HENRY ARNCLIFFE
× An Englishwoman's Home. *1911*
× Pillars of State (Court, 19/5/13, Pl. Actors)

SEPTANT, HOPE
Ten Thousand a Year (P's, Portsmouth, 21/8/22)

SERARD, FLORENCE [see *C. H. PHELPS*]

'*SETON, HENRY*' [=*VERA BERINGER*: see also *M. DOWN*, *A. N. LYONS* and *M. ROBERTS*]
The Boys ('*f.c.*': Gr., Croydon, 11/5/08; Court, 9/7/08, *m.*)
× Pierrot's Little Joke (Court, 8/2/12)
× The Morning Post (Court, 11/3/13, *m.*: +*M. ROBERTS*)
× The Absent-minded Husband (Court, 11/3/13, *m.*; Pal., Chelsea, 13/3/18)
× Set a Thief ('*miniature md.*': Pal., Chelsea, 24/5/13)
Lucky Jim ('*f.c.*': Plymouth, 19/7/15; St J., 19/10/16)
× Darling (Pav., Glasgow, 15/10/16; Emp., Shepherd's Bush, 5/11/16)
× A Pair (Ambass., 15/5/17, *m.*: +*R. ROBERTS*)

× The Honourable Gertrude (Empress, Brixton, 17/6/18)
× There Was a Door. LC, Court, 28/4/19
× Honours Even. LC, Pav., Glasgow, 26/5/19: +*L. W. RAY*
Biffy ('*f.c.*': Plymouth, 24/5/20; Kennington, 13/9/20; Gar., 28/11/22: +*L. W. RAY*)
× Noblesse Oblige. *Fr. 1921*
Beltane Night (Aldw., 23/3/23, *m.*; Q, 20/4/25)
The Painted Lady ('*f.c.*': New, Cardiff, 27/8/23; Everyman, 12/1/24)
× The Perfect Pair (Lyc. Club, 13/3/27) *Fr. 1924*
× South-East and South-West. *Fr. 1925*
The Call of the Legion ('*r.m.pl.*', m. V. Ellis: Emp., Finsbury Park, 7/11/27: from P. C. Wren's novel, *The Wages of Virtue*, 1916)
The Ugly Duchess (Arts, 15/5/30)

SEWARD, WALTER
× Susan and the Nine. LC, '*m.pl.*': Christ Church H., Crouch End, 26/11/23
× On a Mantelpiece. LC, Crippl. Inst., 31/1/22. *Fr. 1923*

SEWELL, REGINALD M.
After the Harlequinade. LC, K. G's H., 21/1/21

SEWELL, WILLIAM A.
× The Yawn (University, Leeds, 14/2/24, *amat.*)

SEXTON, JAMES [see also *M. O'MAHONY*]
The Riot Act (Playh., L'pool, 3/2/14)
× Boys of the Old Brigade (Lyr., L'pool, 20/3/16)

SEYLER, CLIFFORD
× Squibs (Brighton, 3/8/10, *cpy.*; Col., 28/6/15)
The Will and the Way ('*f.c.*': Brighton, 3/8/10, *cpy.*)
× A Priceless Pair. LC, Emp., Croydon, 4/7/19

SEYMOUR, ARTHUR
[Several sketches and playlets, mostly written in collaboration, produced at music-halls]

SEYMOUR, BILLIE [see *N. PARTREIDGE*]

SEYMOUR, EDWARD MARTIN
[For earlier plays see *H. E. D.* v, 561]
× The Bridge of Sighs ('*d. study*': Lyric Club, 2/6/01)
In Letters of Fire (K's, Walthamstow, 11/8/02)
Cupid in a Convent ('*c.o.*', m. M. di Capri: Gr., Fulham, 18/7/03, *cpy.*)

SEYMOUR, HAMILTON
× The Curate's Dilemma (Rehearsal, 6/2/13)

SEYMOUR, MARJORIE F.
× Sanoya ('*Japanese idyll*': Lyr., Hamm., 26/6/12)
× A Lesson in Harmony ('*fairy pl.*': Crippl. Inst., 13/2/22, *amat.*)
× Three Fish on a Hook (K's H., 18/6/22, Interlude Players)

SEYMOUR, TOM
[A few playlets produced at music-halls]

SHAIRP, ALEXANDER MORDAUNT
The Offence (Barnes, 20/7/25; Wynd., 26/8/25) *1925*
The Bend in the Road (Apo., 30/1/27, Pl. Actors)
The Crime at Blossoms (Rep., Hull, 11/2/29) *1932*

SHAKERLEY, IRENE
× The Rescue. LC, Somerford Park, Congleton, 15/9/13

SHAKERLEY, MABEL
The Top o' the Hill. LC, P.H., Adderley Edge, 28/4/20

SHAKERLEY, WALTER
The Dividing Line. LC, Somerford Park, Congleton, 12/12/13

SHAKESPEARE, O. [see *F. FARR*]

SHAMMON, NOEL
The Biters Bitten ('*c.*': Str., 11/6/22, Rep. Players)
What Money Can Buy. LC, St J., 7/11/22
The Tropic Line. LC, Everyman, 20/5/24
Frenzied Finance ('*f.*': Arts, 15/10/27)
The Snare of the Fowler (Sav., 28/2/28)
Out of the Blue ('*c.*': St M., 28/5/28)

SHAND, MORETON [see *G. V. WILLIAMS*]

SHANKAR, PUNDIT
× The Dreamer Awakened ('*m.pl.*': Little, 24/7/22)
× The Queen of Chittore (Little, 24/7/22)

SHANKS, EDWARD [see *ETHEL SMYTH*]

SHARMAN, H. G.
× His Lordship's Wooing. LC, Association H., Leicester, 13/4/28

SHARP, EVELYN
[For an earlier play see *H. E. D.* v, 561]
× The Loafer and the Loaf (K. G's H., 13/5/25, Half Circle Players) *1926*

SHARP, ROBERT FARQUHARSON
[For an earlier play see *H. E. D.* v, 816]
A Gauntlet (Court, 16/2/13, Pl. Actors: translated from B. Björnson, *En hanske*, 1883) *1912*
The Newly-married Couple (Court, 19/5/13, Pl. Actors: translated from B. Björnson, *De nygifte*, 1865) *1912*
The King. LC, Court, 10/2/14: translated from B. Björnson, *Kong Sverre*, 1861) *1914*
Rosmersholm (Kings., 30/9/26: translated from the play (1886) by H. Ibsen) *1913*
The Bankrupt (Q, 22/1/28, Sunday Players: translated from B. Björnson, *En fallit*, 1874) *1914*

SHARP, WILLIAM [=*FIONA MACLEOD*]

SHARPE, A. C.

The Best of the Bargain. LC, St Mary's H., Westerham, 23/11/22
Somewhere Else. LC, Parish H., Horsell, 16/12/24
Rose Alone. LC, Parish H., Horsell, 8/12/25

SHAW, OF DUNFERMLINE, Lord

Darnley – A Historie. *1925* (*priv.*)

SHAW, ALF [see also *J. OWEN*]

Arabian Love ('*m.pl.*': Norwich, 30/10/22; Stratford, 5/2/23)

SHAW, GEORGE BERNARD

[Since few of Shaw's plays written before 1900 became known to playgoers until after that year, the following short list of his dramatic writings includes both his earlier and his later dramas. Further information concerning the performances of these dramas is conveniently summarised in the comprehensive *Theatrical Companion to Shaw* (1954) compiled by Raymond Mander and Joe Mitchenson. It is well known that many of Shaw's plays were first printed in 'proof' copies used in the theatre during rehearsals: these are not cited here: information concerning them is obtainable in F. E. Loewenstein's *The Rehearsal Copies of Bernard Shaw's Plays* (1950)]

Widowers' Houses ('*didactic realistic pl.*': Roy., 9/12/1892, Independent Theatre Soc.; Midland, Manchester, 7/10/07; Cor., 7/6/09) *1893*

Arms and the Man ('*r.c.*': Aven., 21/4/94; Sav., 30/12/07) *1898*

Candida (S. Shields, 30/3/1895, *cpy.*; H.M., Aberdeen, 30/7/1897, Independent Theatre Soc.; Str., 1/7/00, St. Soc.; Court, 26/4/04, *m.*) *1898*

The Devil's Disciple ('*md.*': Bij., 17/4/1897, *cpy.*; Hermanus Bleeker H., Albany, N.Y., 1/10/1897; Fifth Avenue, N.Y., 4/10/1897; P'cess of Wales, Kennington, 26/9/1899; Sav., 14/10/07) *1901*

×The Man of Destiny ('*trifle*': Gr., Croydon, 1/7/1897; Com., 29/3/01, *m.* (J. T. Grein's 'Sunday Special' matinée); Court, 4/6/07) *1898*

You Never Can Tell (Bij., 23/3/1898, *cpy.*; Roy., 26/11/1899, St. Soc.; Str., 2/5/00) *1898*

The Gadfly, or, The Son of the Cardinal (Bij., 23 or 31/3/1898, *cpy.*)

[This hurriedly written piece has no particular significance but it is an excellent testimony to Shaw's generosity. According to F. E. Loewenstein, Shaw's own records showed that the performance took place on March 31; according to Mander and Mitchenson the date was March 23]

The Philanderer ('*topical c.*': Bij., 30/3/1898, *cpy.*; Crippl. Inst., 20/2/05, New Stage Club; Court, 5/2/07) *1898*

Mrs Warren's Profession (New Lyric Club, 5/1/02, St. Soc.; Hyperion, New Haven, Conn., 27/10/05; Gar., N.Y., 30/10/05; P.W., B'ham, 27/7/25; Reg., 28/9/25) *1898*

Caesar and Cleopatra ('*history*': Newcastle, 15/3/1899, *cpy.*;

Fine Arts Building, Chicago, 1/5/01, 'costume recital' by students; Neues Theater, Berlin, 31/3/06, in a German version by Siegfried Trebitsch; New Amsterdam, N.Y., 30/10/06; Gr., Leeds, 16/9/07; Sav., 25/11/07) *1901*

Captain Brassbound's Conversion ('*adventure*': Court, L'pool, 10/10/1899, *cpy.*; Str., 16/12/00, St. Soc.; Qns, Manchester, 12/5/02; Court, 20/3/06, *m.*) *1901*

The Admirable Bashville, or, Constancy Unrewarded (Bij., c. 1901, *cpy.*; Pharos Club, C.G., 14/12/02, *amat.*; Imp., 7/6/03, St. Soc.; Manchester, 22/9/05; H.M., 26/1/09, *m.*, 'Matinée Theatre' pfce.) *1909*

Man and Superman ('*a c. and a philosophy*': Bij., 29/6/03, *cpy.*; Court, 21/5/05, St. Soc.; Court, 23/5/05) *1903*

[*Don Juan in Hell*, 'a dream, from *Man and Superman*', was presented at the Court, 4/6/07. In its entirety the play first appeared at the Lyc., Edin., 11/6/15, and had its London première at the Reg., 23/10/25]

×How He Lied to Her Husband (Berkeley Lyc., N.Y., 26/9/04; Court, 28/2/05, *m.*) *1909*

John Bull's Other Island (Court, 1/11/04, *m.*) *1909*

×Passion, Poison and Petrifaction, or The Fatal Gazogene ('*brief t. for barns and booths*': Theatrical Garden Party, Regent's Park, 14/7/05) *1905* (in *Harry Furniss's Christmas Annual*); *1926*

Major Barbara ('*a discussion*': Court, 28/11/05, *m.*) *1909*

The Doctor's Dilemma ('*t.*': Court, 20/11/06, *m.*) *1911*

×The Interlude at the Playhouse (Playh., 28/1/07) *1907* (in *The Daily Mail*, January 29, 1907); *1927* (in Cyril Maude's *Behind the Scenes with Cyril Maude*, pp. 163–73)

Getting Married ('*disquisitory pl.*' or '*conversation*': H., 12/5/08, *m.*; H., 1/6/08) *1911*

×Press Cuttings ('*topical sketch*': Court, 9/7/09, *m.*, Civic and Dram. Guild; Gai., Manchester, 27/9/09; Kings., 21/6/10, *m.*, Actresses' Franchise League) *1909*

×The Shewing-up of Blanco Posnet ('*sermon in crude md.*': Abbey, Dublin, 25/8/09; Aldw., 5/12/09, St. Soc.; Playh., L'pool, 10/4/16, Abbey company; Everyman, 14/3/21; Qns, 20/7/21) *1911*

×The Fascinating Foundling ('*a disgrace to the author*': said to have been performed by amateurs in 1909 or 1910; Arts, 28/1/28) *1926*

Misalliance ('*debate in one sitting*': D.Y., 23/2/10) *1914*

×The Dark Lady of the Sonnets ('*interlude*': H., 24/11/10, *m.*; Everyman, 14/3/21; Qns, 20/7/21) *1914*

Fanny's First Play ('*easy pl. for a little theatre*': Little, 19/4/11: originally billed as by 'Xxxxxxx Xxxx') *1914*

×Overruled (D.Y., 14/10/12) *1912* (*priv.*, as *Trespassers Will Be Prosecuted*); *1916*

Androcles and the Lion ('*fable pl.*': Kleines Theater, Berlin, 25/11/12, in a German version by Siegfried Trebitsch; St J., 1/9/13) *1916*

×Great Catherine (*'thumbnail sketch of Russian court life in the XVIII century'*: Vaud., 18/11/13) *1919*
×The Music Cure (*'a piece of utter nonsense'*: Little, 28/1/14) *1926*
Pygmalion (*'romance'*: Hofburg, Vienna, 16/10/13, in a German version by Siegfried Trebitsch; H.M., 11/4/14) *1914* (in *Nash's Magazine*, November and December, 1914); *1916*
×The Inca of Perusalem (*'almost historical ca.'*: Rep., B'ham, 9/10/16; Crit., 16/12/17, Pioneer Players; Bed., 30/5/49) *1919*
[Mander and Mitchenson give the date of the première as 7/10/16; the theatre's records give 9/10/16 – which seems correct, since October 7 was a Saturday]
×Augustus Does His Bit (*'unofficial dramatic tract on war saving and cognate subjects'* and *'a true-to-life farce'*: Court, 21/1/17, St. Soc.; Polio's, Washington, 10/12/17, Drama League Players, *amat.*; Com., N.Y., 12/3/19) *1919*
×O'Flaherty, V.C. (*'reminiscence of 1915'*: amateur performance, by officers of the Royal Flying Corps, in Belgium, 17/2/17; 39th St., N.Y., 21/6/20; Lyr., Hamm., 19/12/20, St. Soc.) *1919*
×Annajanska, the Wild Grand Duchess (*'revolutionary romancelet'*: Col., 21/1/18) *1919* (as *Annajanska, the Bolshevik Empress*)
Heartbreak House (*'fantasia in the Russian manner'*: Gar., N.Y., 10/11/20; Court, 18/10/21) *1919*
Back to Methuselah (*'metabiological pentateuch'*: Gar., N.Y., 27/2/22 (parts I and II) 6/3/22 (parts III and IV), 13/3/22 (part V); Rep., B'ham, 9/10/23 to 12/10/23 (all five parts); Court, 18/2/24 to 22/2/24 (all five parts) *1921*
Jitta's Atonement (*'t.c.'*: Shubert, Washington, 8/1/23; Com., N.Y., 17/1/23; Gr., Putney Bridge, 26/1/25, Partnership Players; Arts, 30/4/30: adapted from *Frau Gittas Sühne* (1920) by Siegfried Trebitsch) *1926*
Saint Joan (*'chronicle pl.'*: Gar., N.Y., 28/12/23; New, 26/3/24) *1924*
×The Glimpse of Reality (*'tragedietta'*: Fellowship H., Glasgow, 8/10/27, Glasgow Clarion Players; Arts, 20/11/27) *1926*
The Apple Cart (*'political extravaganza'*: Teatr Polski, Warsaw, in a Polish translation, *Wielki Kram*, by Floryan Sobienowski, 14/6/29; Malvern Festival, 19/8/29; Qns, 17/9/29) *1930*

SHAW, Mrs GEORGE BERNARD (CHARLOTTE FRANCES)
Maternity (K's H., 8/4/06: translated from *Maternité* (1903) by Eugène Brieux) *1907*
Woman on Her Own (Cor., 8/12/13, Woman's Theatre: translated from *La Femme Seule* (1912) by Eugène Brieux) *1916*

SHAW, GLENN WILLIAM
The Priest and His Disciples (translated from the Japanese of Hyakuzo Kurata) *1927* (Tokyo)

SHAW, LEONARD
Cinder-Ellaline (*'fairy pl.'*: St Peter's Mission, Friern Barnet, 22/4/09, *amat.*)

SHAW, LUCY CARR

Miss Julia (Little, 28/4/12, Adel. Pl. Soc.: translated from *Fröken Julie* (1888) by A. Strindberg: +*M. ELVEY*)

SHEARIM, ADA

The Challenge (K's H., Ilkley, 11/9/13; Pav., Hastings, 1/10/13, as *The Dilemmas of Daphne*)

Brains Will Tell. LC, Parish H., Prescot, 20/2/25

SHEEHAN, P. P.

×Efficiency. LC, Adel., 2/7/17: +*R. H. DAVIS*

SHEEN, WILLIAM P.

[For earlier plays see *H. E. D.* v, 562]

Why Woman Sins (Leeds, 30/9/1899, *cpy.*, as *O'er Land and Sea*; Wigan, 10/5/00; Terriss, Rotherhithe, 28/1/01: +*F. S. JENNINGS*)

The Temptress ('*md.*': Vic., Broughton, 23/6/02; Pav., 29/2/04)

In the Jaws of Death (Gr., Fulham, 25/5/03: revised from *Braving the Storm* (1890))

Man, Woman and Fate (Vic., Broughton, 26/2/04, *cpy.*)

For Better or Worse (Hyde 23/10/05)

×Luke Sharpe, of London ('*m.c.sk.*': Sur., 29/4/07)

×The Luck (Sur., 2/6/13: +*ERIC HUDSON*)

×Uncle's in Time (Gr., Clapham, 11/8/13)

×The Swankers. LC, Granville, Walham Green, 29/10/17

Hushed Up ('*mystery pl.*': Pal., Redditch, 2/6/19; E.C., 9/6/19: title later changed to *The Silent Wife*)

The Judgement. LC, New, Pontypridd, 20/7/20

The Woman Hunter. LC, Hippo., Cleator Moor, 11/3/21: +*J. MILLANE*

[*SHELDON, EDWARD* [see also *M. A. BARNES*]

The Boss (St J., 2/1/11, *cpy.*) *1913* (New York)

Romance (Maxine Elliott, N.Y., 10/2/13; D.P., Eastbourne, 30/9/15; D.Y., 4/10/15) *1912* (Ottawa)

The Song of Songs. LC, Qns, 25/5/15. *1914* (Ottawa)

SHELDON, Mrs M. FRENCH

Pilate ('*classical d.*': Bij., 30/7/00, private reading: +*A. BOND*)

SHELDON, GEORGE

×A King for a Day ('*m. absurdity*': Emp., Ardwick, 15/4/07)

×The Queen of the Adriatic ('*m.c.*': Hippo., Hulme, 25/11/07)

The Rose of Sicily ('*c.o.*': Emp., Camberwell, 4/4/10)

×Before the Dawn (Scala, 29/5/11)

×An Ocean Maid (Sur., 2/9/12)

The New Creation (Tiv., Nelson, 23/5/27)

SHELDON, H. SOPHUS

The Havoc (Gar., 19/11/12)

SHELLEY, HERBERT

[For earlier plays see *H. E. D.* v, 562]

The Handy Man ('*m.c.*', m. author and J. Neat: County, Kingston, 4/6/00)

Claude Melnotte ('*c.o.*', m. F. E. Tours: Bij., 22/8/00, *cpy.*; Cor., 30/9/01, as *Melnotte*; also called *The Gardener's Bride*)
Bill Adams ('*m.pl.*', m. S. R. Philpot: D.P., Eastbourne, 26/2/03; Alex., 30/3/08; Hippo., Crouch End, 22/4/12, as *Bill Adams, the Hero of Waterloo*: +*R. BACCHUS*)
In Gay Algiers ('*m.c.*', m. S. R. Philpot: Bij., 16/5/03, *cpy.*; Kennington, 5/6/11, as *The Algerian Girl*: +*R. BACCHUS*)
The Echo of a Crime (County, Reading, 12/6/1899, as *The Mighty Hand*; P.W., L'pool, 12/10/03)
×The Golden Kite ('*m.pl.*', m. S. R. Philpot: Bij., 8/3/05, *cpy.*)
Dan the Outlaw (LC, Bradford, 29/5/06, in one act; Hippo., Willesden, 17/2/13, as a melodrama in 4 acts)
×The Manoeuvres of Sam (Pal., Hamm., 26/5/08: +*H. NICHOLLS*)
×Apples and Pairs (Hippo., Crouch End., 29/3/09)
The Marriage of Mignon (Gr., Fulham, 31/7/09)
×A Green Room Match (Pal., Chelsea, 15/8/10)
Uncle Sam ('*f.*': Nottingham, 19/8/12; K's, Hamm., 30/9/12)
A Mill Girl's Wedding (Gai., Burnley, 26/11/13; Stratford, 16/2/14)
The Lass of Dingley Moor (Inverness, 10/9/15)
A Woman's Victory (Hippo., Maidenhead, 23/7/17; Stratford, 30/7/17; title later changed to *The King's Vale Mystery*)
My Aunt from New York ('*f.c.*': Edin., 10/10/18; Hippo., Putney, 26/7/20)
×The Heart of Inverary. LC, County, Reading, 28/7/19
The Romance of the Rosary. LC, New H., Bargoed, 4/2/20

SHEPPARD, F. FIRTH
×The Window Cleaner (M'sex, 10/4/16)
Oh, Julie! ('*m.c.*', m. H. S. Brooke and H. Darewski: Shaft., 22/6/20: +*L. H. BRANSON*)
Faust on Toast ('*m.bsq.*', m. W. Redstone and M. Gideon: Gai., 19/4/21: +*A. ROSS*)
Dear Little Billie ('*m.c.*', m. B. Hedley and J. Strachey: Lyc., Sheffield, 18/5/25; Shaft., 25/8/25)
Lady Luck ('*m.pl.*', m. H. B. Hedley and J. Strachey: O.H., Blackpool, 14/3/27; Carlton, 27/4/27)

SHEPPARD, Sir JOHN TRESIDDER
Œdipus Tyrannus. LC, ADC, Cambridge, 13/12/22: translated from Sophocles' play. *1920*
Helen. LC, ADC, Cambridge, 24/3/25: translated from Euripides' play. *1925*
The Cyclops. LC, ADC, Cambridge, 24/3/25: translated from Euripides' play. *1923*

SHEPPERD, IVY
×A Sacrifice to Kali (Rehearsal, 27/3/11, *amat.*)

SHEPPHERD, MAY
×A Matrimonial Error (Ruskin Manor Recreation H., 26/12/12)
×A Fairy Sketch. LC, Crippl. Inst., 3/6/14
×The Masque of Peace (Guildhall School of Music, 13/7/16)

SHERBROOKE, MICHAEL [see *C. R. KENNEDY*]

SHERIDAN, H. BRINSLEY

Pango-Pango ('*m. burletta*', m. H. S. Pepper: Court, 26/3/14)

SHERMAN, JOSEPH

The Child of Warsaw. LC, Pav., Mile End, 24/12/14

A Wife by Instalments (Emp., Holborn, 19/4/17: title later changed to *The Unwanted Child*)

SHERRATT, TOM [see *T. M. CARTWRIGHT*]

SHERRIFF, ROBERT CEDRIC

Profit and Loss (Gables, Surbiton, 10/1/23, *amat.*)

Cornlow-in-the-Downs (Gables, Surbiton, 10/12/23, *amat.*)

The Feudal System. LC, Ass. R., Surbiton, 20/2/25

Mr Birdie's Finger ('*c.*': Ass. R., Surbiton, 26/2/26, *amat.*)

Journey's End (Apo., 9/12/28, St. Soc.; Sav., 21/1/29) *1929*

Badger's Green ('*c.*': P.W., 12/6/30) *1930*

[This play was largely based on *Mr Birdie's Finger*, above]

SHERRY, GORDON

[A few sketches produced at music-halls]

[*SHERWOOD, ROBERT EMMET*

The Road to Rome (Str., 16/5/28) *1927* (New York)

The Queen's Husband ('*c.*': Crane H., L'pool, 12/3/29, *amat.*) *1928*; *Fr. 1932*

SHIELS, GEORGE [='*GEORGE S. MORSHIEL*']

[It has been said that 'George Shiels' is itself a pseudonym used by *LYNN BOYLE*; this statement, however, I have been unable positively to confirm]

Away from the Moss (O.H., Belfast, 25/11/18: advertised as by 'George Morshiel')

Felix Reid and Bob (O.H., Belfast, 12/11/19: advertised as by 'George Morshiel')

×Bedmates ('*doss-house allegory*': Abbey, Dublin, 6/1/21) *1922* (Dublin)

Insurance Money ('*c.*': Abbey, Dublin, 13/12/21)

Paul Twyning ('*f.*': Abbey, Dublin, 3/10/22) *1927*

×First Aid (Abbey, Dublin, 26/12/23)

×The Retrievers (Abbey, Dublin, 12/5/24)

Professor Tim ('*c.*': Abbey, Dublin, 14/9/25; Vaud., 22/3/27) *1927*

Cartney and Kevney ('*c.*': Abbey, Dublin, 29/11/27) *1930*

Mountain Dew (Abbey, Dublin, 5/3/29) *1930*

SHIELS, HARRY

[A few sketches produced at music-halls]

SHILLINGFORD, OSMOND

The Nun and the Barbarian (Margate, 26/11/06: translated from *La loca de la casa* (1893) by B. Pérez Galdós)

The Daisy (Kings., 14/9/20; K's, Southsea, revised as *Liliom*; D.Y., 23/12/26: +*A. L. ELLIS*; adapted from *Liliom* (1909), by F. Molnár).

SHINE, JOHN L. [see also *D. C. MURRAY*]
[For earlier plays see *H. E. D.* v, 563]
×An Actor's Art (Emp., Camberwell, 7/1/07)
×Invasion; or, Wake Up, England! (Cant., 29/3/09)

[*SHIPMAN, LOUIS EVAN*
John Ermine (Com., 30/7/03, *cpy.*)
D'Arcy of the Guards ('*c.*': St J., 27/9/10)

[*SHIPMAN, SAMUEL*
The Woman of Today (Court, 5/9/10, *cpy.*)
Uncle Sam ('*c.*': Apo., Atlantic City, 28/2/18, as *Friendly Enemies*; Hudson, N.Y., 22/7/18; H., 12/2/19: +*A. HOFFMAN*)
East is West ('*c.*': Academy, Baltimore, 9/12/18; Astor, N.Y., 25/12/18; Lyr., 9/6/20: +*J. B. HYMER*)
Lawful Larceny ('*md. c.*': Republic, N.Y., 2/1/22; Sav., 26/8/22)
Crime (Walnut St., Philadelphia, 7/2/27; Eltinge, N.Y., 23/2/27; K's, Southsea, 10/10/27; Qns, 18/10/27: +*J. B. HYMER*)
The Woman in Room 13 (Gar., 4/11/29: +*M. MARCIN*)

SHIPP, JESSE A.
In Dahomey ('*m.pl.*', m. W. M. Cook: Shaft., 16/5/03)

SHIPTON, HELEN
Elsa and the Trolls, and Other Plays for Little People. *1903*
[This includes three medium-length plays: 1. *Elsa and the Trolls*; 2. *The Babes in the Wood*; and 3. *Dick Whittington*]

SHIRLEY, ARTHUR [see also *J. BUONAPARTE, S. HICKS* and *G. R. SIMS*]
[For earlier plays see *H. E. D.* v, 563–5]
The Better Life (Adel., 5/2/00: +*SUTTON VANE*)
Midnight Paris (Pav., 14/5/00)
A Criminal Judge; or, The Light of Truth (Pav., 5/11/00: +*B. LANDECK*)
×The Little Corporal (Richmond, 4/3/01)
The World, the Flesh and the Devil ('*md.*': Sur., 10/6/10: +*F. DAWSON*)
Carmita ('*m.c.*', m. J. Williams: Vic., Broughton, 7/10/01; P'cess of W., Kennington, 28/10/01: +*W. PARKE*)
The Boom of Big Ben (Pav., 18/11/01; P'cess, 16/12/01)
The Sinful City (Qns, Leeds, 4/4/02: +*W. MUSKERRY*: later performed as *A City of Sin*)
Little Jim ('*md.*': Dalston, 28/4/02: +*B. LANDECK*)
The London Fireman (Sur., 13/10/02: +*G. CONQUEST*)
The Midnight Mail (Lyr., Hamm., 20/10/02)
Her Secret Sin (Dalston, 27/10/02: +*B. LANDECK*)
The Devil Worshippers (Leigh, 29/1/03, *cpy.*: +*E. HUDSON*)
The Father of Her Child (W.L., 9/2/03: +*F. DAWSON*)
His Fatal Beauty ('*m.f.c.*', m. J. Crook: Metro., Camberwell, 27/4/03)
I Defy the World (Wigan, 20/7/03; Carlton, Greenwich, 22/2/04: +*E. HILL-MITCHELSON*)
The Lightning's Flash ('*musical md.*': Carlton, Saltley, 3/8/03,

revised from *A Lightning Flash* (Sur., 17/12/1891); Carlton, Greenwich, 4/4/04)
A Great Sensation (Pav., 31/8/03: +*B. LANDECK*)
A Path of Thorns (Camden, 31/8/03: +*SUTTON VANE*: title later changed to *Two Lancashire Lasses in London*)
The White Slaves of London (Lyr., Hamm., 21/9/03: title later changed to *Tricked by a Woman*)
The Woman from Nowhere ('*md.*': Gr., Islington, 16/5/04)
×Ben (Croydon, 10/12/04)
The Admiral's Lady ('*r.c.*': Brixton, 22/2/05)
The Gayest of the Gay, or, The Life of a Woman (Birkenhead, 18/4/05; Borough, Stratford, 11/11/07: +*E. V. HUDSON*)
The Curse of the Country (E.C., 22/5/05)
The See-Saw of Life (Worcester, 3/7/05; W.L., 30/10/05: +*H. L. BEDFORD*: called originally *Riches and Rags*)
×A Happy Medium (New, 2/11/05)
The Troubles of Tuffin ('*m.pl.*', m. W. Slaughter: Col., 12/3/06)
The Spider and the Fly (Gr., Brighton, 16/4/06; Kennington, 6/8/06; S.W., 12/5/13, as *Two Big Vagabonds*: +*SUTTON VANE*: title later changed to *Weary Willie and Tired Tim, Two Big Vagabonds*)
A Queen without a Crown ('*r.d.*': Nottingham 23/4/06: +*B. LANDECK*: called originally *The Secret of the King*)
×Two Pictures (Pal., Chelsea, 7/1/07)
The Step-mother (Emp., Camberwell, 18/3/07; Crown, Peckham, 27/5/07)
×My Lady (Emp., Holborn, 24/2/08)
Salvation (Smethwick, 5/3/08, *cpy.*)
He's a Jolly Good Fellow (W.L., 28/5/08, *cpy.*; Dalston, 15/6/08: +*E. V. EDMONDS*)
London with the Lid Off (Stratford, 3/8/08)
×The Silver Crucifix (M'sex, 31/8/08)
×The Love of an Ape (Hippo., Colchester, 31/5/09)
The Artfulness of Ada ('*f.c.*': Pleasure Gdns., Folkestone, 28/2/10; R.A., Woolwich, 21/3/10)
×The Bottom Dog (Hippo., Peckham, 20/6/10)
×The Home of the Hero (Qns, Keighley, 25/11/10, *cpy.*; Metro., 14/10/12, as *Forgotten*)
For Mother's Sake (Dalston, 22/5/11: +*B. LANDECK*)
The Three Musketeers (Lyc., 8/11/11: *B. LANDECK*)
In a Man's Power (E.C., 19/2/12: +*B. LANDECK*)
The Women of France ('*r.d.*': Lyc., 12/6/12: +*B. LANDECK*)
×The Circus Girl (Emp., Camberwell, 1/7/12: +*B. LANDECK*)
The Open Door (Lyc., 2/10/12: +*B. LANDECK*: called originally *A Light in the Dark* and *The Messenger of Peace*)
Nell Gwynne, the King's Favourite (Lyc., 19/2/13: +*B. LANDECK*)
Under Two Flags (Lyc., 29/10/13)
A Heritage of Hate (Junction, Manchester, 6/1/14; Aldw., 27/6/14)
×Allies (Ardwick Emp., Manchester, 7/9/14)

Fallen by the Way (Emp., Holloway, 13/4/14)
A Fight to a Finish (K's, Hamm., 31/8/14)
The Days of England's Danger (L'pool, 14/9/14)
My Old Dutch ('*m.pl.*', m. A. H. West: Gai., Hastings, 5/6/16; Brixton, 5/5/19; Lyc., 14/7/20: +*A. CHEVALIER*)
British to the Backbone (Hippo., Richmond, 19/11/17)
×Auld Robin Grey (P'cess, Glasgow, 30/11/17)
Khaki and Clogs ('*md.*': Gr., Oldham, 1/7/18: called originally *Daddy*)
Do Be Careful ('*f.*': O.H., Belfast, 24/3/19: called originally *Dashing Dunbar*: title later changed to *The Compleat Wangler*)
Edmund Kean ('*r.pl.*': P's, Manchester, 24/6/19; Kennington, 5/4/20, as *Ned Kean of Old Drury*; D.L., 9/5/23)
The Wild Widow (Lyc., 6/9/19: +*B. LANDECK*)
The Savage and the Woman ('*r.d.*': Lyc., 3/3/21: +*B. LANDECK*)
×Trouble for Three. LC, Metropolitan, 11/8/21
A Fallen Star (O.H., Northampton, 7/10/21; Brixton, 2/10/22: +*A. CHEVALIER*)
Here Comes the Bride ('*f.*': Brixton, 23/10/22)
What Money Can Buy (Lyc., 26/9/23: +*B. LANDECK*)
The Blind Bride ('*md.*': Osborne, Manchester, 19/5/24)
The Sheik of Shepherd's Bush ('*m.f.c.*', m. A. Wood: Brixton, 24/11/24: title later changed, first to *Jasmine*, and afterwards to *Tit for Tat*)

SHIRLEY, CLARE [see also *C. E. LANGDON* and *J. MILLANE*]
×The Motor Man (Cleveland H., Brotton, 9/4/08)
×At Silver Creek (Empress, Buxton, 1/4/12)
×The Hand of Fate (Emp., Camberwell, 3/6/12)

SHIRLEY, GEORGE WILLIAM
Prince Charlie and the '45 (Lyc., Dumfries, 23/11/25, *amat.*)
×The Mairtyr's Crown. *1926* (in *The Scots Magazine*, iv, 431–9)

SHIRLEY, MAUDE
The Twelfth Hour ('*mystery pl.*': Q, 16/12/29)

SHORE, Mrs TEIGNMOUTH [=*PRISCILLA CRAVEN*: see also *F. D. BONE*]
×A Painted Nun (Etlinger, 11/12/25)

SHORE, WILLIAM
Dot, or, The Cricket on the Hearth (Crippl. Inst., 22/12/08, *amat.*: dramatised from Charles Dickens' novel)

SHUTE, E. L.
×Jappy Chappy ('*ext.*': Stafford House, St James's, 11/5/11, *m.*; Little 28/11/13)
Romola. LC, Hippo., Nuneaton, 6/10/23: +*A. F. CROSS*: dramatised from the novel by George Eliot)
The Price (Q, 6/6/27)

SIBBALD, DAVID
×Tapsalteerie. LC, T.H., St Andrews, 28/6/29. *1929* (Edinburgh)

SICHEL, CATHERINE

×Puck. LC, T.H., Ilford, 12/1/23

SICHEL, QUEENIE

×Won by Waiting (Bij. 6/12/02)

SIDDONS, ROBERT H.

Fan Tan (Pier, Aberystwyth, 19/7/20)

SIDGWICK, B. J.

×Father (Court, 19/9/13)

SIDGWICK, ETHEL

Four Plays for Children. *1913*

[This contains four several-scened fairy-tale dramas: 1. *The Rose and the Ring*; 2. *The Goody-Witch*; 3. *The Goose Girl*; and 4. *Boots and the North Wind*]

Two Plays for Schools. *1922*

[The two plays included here, similar in style to the above, are *The Three Golden Hairs* and *The Robber Bridegroom*]

Fairy Tale Plays. *1926*

[This contains *The Elves and the Shoemaker* and *Riquet with the Tuft*]

SIDNEY, HERBERT

[Numerous sketches and playlets produced at music-halls]

[*SIDNEY, SIDNEY*

The Muddle-Up ('*m.c.*', m. H. Vernon: Colosseum, Oldham, 10/9/00)

SIEDLE, A. EDWARD

[For an earlier play see *H. E. D.* v, 566]

The Marauders; or, The Power of Love ('*c.o.*', m. D. W. Lott: Gr., Swansea, 28/4/03, *amat.*)

Your Only Sarah ('*f.*': Gr., Swansea, 21/9/04, *cpy.*)

The Gay Musician ('*c.o.*', m. J. Edwards: Bij., 3/4/08, *cpy.*)

SILAS, ADRIAN

The Diplomacy of Sue (Studio, Victoria St., 18/3/07)

SILBURN, GEORGE B. [see also *B. CLIFFORD*]

Meddlesome Matty ('*m.pl.*', m. U. Joyce: Glo., Deal, 3/10/21)

SILL, LOUISE MORGAN

The Tidings Brought to Mary ('*mystical d.*': Str., 10/6/17, Pioneer Players: translated from *L'annonce faite à Marie* (1912) by P. Claudel)

SILVA, H. R. [see *C. A. CLARKE*]

SILVER, W. E.

Adventure (Rep., Rusholme, 19/4/26)

SILVERSTONE, OSWALD

The Power of Hate (Court, Warrington, 14/2/01)

Good Luck ('*md.*': P's, Horwich, 10/2/02)

The Ruin of a Countess ('*md.*': Sheffield, 31/7/11; Woolwich, 24/2/13: +*G. HASTINGS-WALTON*)

SIM, Mrs CHARLES

×A Soldier's Daughter (Com., 5/2/00)

×Love and Be Silent (Gar., 17/5/01)

SIMMS, A.

Otherland Plays. *1922*

[This contains six short plays for children, all set in different foreign countries: 1. *In the Desert*; 2. *The Dutch*; 3. *'Neath Italy's Blue Skies*; 4. *Indian Village Life*; 5. *The Plantation*; and 6. *The Red Indians*]

'*SIMPSON, CORMAC*' [= *WILLIAM MacDONALD*]

×The Last Move (Thankerton, 25/1/26, Scott. Nat. Players) *1935* (in J. M. Reid, *Scottish One-Act Plays*)

Ayont the Hill (Lyr., Glasgow, 22/3/27, Scott. Nat. Players) *1934*

The Flower in the Vase (Lyr., Glasgow, 25/12/28, Scott. Nat. Players) *1934*

SIMPSON, HAROLD [see also *L. BANTOCK*, *Mrs C. BRAUN*, *R. COURTNEIDGE*, *D. FISHER* and *H. A. VACHELL*)

×A Cup of Coffee (Emp., Kilburn, 6/2/11)

×The Submarine F. 7 (Pal., Tottenham, 25/3/12)

The Lion and the Lamb ('*m.c.*', m. C. Moore: Lyc., Sheffield, 8/4/12)

×Sixty Miles an Hour (Emp., Kilburn, 22/9/13)

×A Cabinet Secret ('*m.f.*': H., 29/2/16, *m.*)

The Girl of the Future ('*m. fant.*', m. A. Klein: K's, Southsea, 23/10/16; Emp., Finsbury Park, 30/10/16)

×Anthony's Dilemma (Gr., B'ham, 22/1/17; Pal., Chelsea, 26/3/17: title later changed to *A Musical Incident in Two Flats and One Key*)

The Rose of Araby ('*c.o.*', m. M. Morgan: Wimbledon, 9/2/20: called originally *A Desert Rose*) *Fr. 1930*

×Adam's Apple. *Fr. 1921*

×A Tooth for a Tooth. LC, Kemble, Hereford, 4/3/21

The Little Girl in Red ('*m.pl.*': Gai., 10/12/21: +*A. STANLEY*)

×Kippers and Kings (Hippo., Boscombe, 24/4/22; Col., 1/5/22: +*B. DAVIS*]

Seeing Life ('*m.bsq.*': Emp., Wood Green, 10/9/23)

Revue Sketches. *Fr. 1924*

[This contains eight brief sketches]

The 'Nine O'Clock Revue' Book (+*R. M. HARVEY*) *Fr. 1924*

[This contains ten sketches]

Straws on the Wind. *Fr. 1925*

[This contains nine revue sketches]

The Fiddle Maker (K's, Edin., 16/8/26: +*C. MARQUAND*)

Oh – By the Way. *Fr. 1926*

[This contains nine revue sketches]

×In Port (Glo., 3/4/27)

Airy Nothings. *Fr. 1927*

[This contains twelve sketches written for broadcasting]

Nine to Eleven. *Fr. 1927*

[This contains nine revue sketches]

SIMPSON, HELEN DE GUERRY

A Man of His Time. *1923* (Sydney, Australia)

The Cautious Lovers (Lyc. Club, 1/6/24)

The School for Wives. LC, Pal., Chelsea, 8/10/25; adapted from Molière, *L'école des femmes*)

SIMPSON, HERBERT

Nana ('*m. stage society pl.*', m. J. Crook and H. May: Gr., B'ham, 1/5/02)

SIMPSON, KATE A.

[For earlier plays see *H. E. D.* v, 568]

Lovelornia; or, The Witch versus Cupid ('*fairy oa.*', m. W. M. Wood: Tyne, Newcastle, 17/6/01)

SIMPSON, LILIAN E.

Pierrot at Play ('*fant.*': Bij., 4/7/19, Ben Greet's students)

SIMPSON, VIOLET A.

The Bonnet Conspirators ('*r.c.*': Court, 13/7/09)

×What No One Knew (Forum Club, 31/10/26)

×The Other Man (Forum Club, 31/10/26)

SIMS, G. R. [see also *L. N. PARKER*]

[For earlier plays see *H. E. D.* v, 568–70]

The City of Pleasure (P.W., B'ham, 22/4/1895; Gr., Islington, 31/8/03)

The Scarlet Sin (Shak., L'pool, 3/9/00; Crown, Peckham, 17/9/00: +*A. SHIRLEY*)

Molly of the Duke's ('*costume d.*': Court, 11/3/01: +*A. SHIRLEY*)

A Woman in the Case ('*c.*': Court, 2/5/01: +*L. MERRICK*)

Hagar (Cor., 24/2/02: +*A. SHIRLEY*)

The Woman from Gaol (Pav., 7/9/03; County, Reading, 16/4/06, revised as *For Life – and After*)

The Dancing Girls of Spain ('*m.pl.*', m. C. C. Corri: Hull, 24/6/07)

[This is a revised version of *Miss Chiquita* (1899)]

×The Beggars' Hotel (S.W., 15/6/08)

The Belle of Andalusia ('*m. show*', m. H. Finck: W.G., Blackpool, 6/7/08: +*CHARLES FLETCHER*)

×The White Hand of a Woman (S.W., 28/9/08)

Amsterdam; or, By the Side of the Zuyder Zee ('*ballet*', m. Herman Finck: W.G., Blackpool, 12/7/09: +*CHARLES FLETCHER*)

×Buonaparte's Boy; or, Two New Year's Days (Olympia, L'pool, 18/10/09; Gr., Clapham, 22/11/09)

×Nanon Lafarge (Metropolitan, 14/8/10)

×The Viperess's Vengeance; or, The Fingermarks of Fate ('*bsq.*': Theatrical Gdn Party, Regent's Park, 2/7/12)

The Ever-Open Door (Aldw., 6/9/13: +*H. H. HERBERT*)

×Jenny o' Mine. LC, Aldw., 4/8/14

The Staircase of Fortune ('*md.*': Hippo., Croydon, 31/8/14)

×The Golden God. LC, Alex., Stoke Newington, 27/3/17

×Punch and Judy (Emp., Finsbury Park, 29/10/17)

SIMS, SIDNEY H.

Prince Charlie, Prince of Highland Hearts (Gt. Qn St., 23/3/05, *amat.*: also called *Prince Charlie, or King of the Highland Hearts*)

SIMS, VIOLET

The Brand of Cain ('*md.*': Windsor, 4/7/04; Carlton, Greenwich, 5/9/04)

[*SINCLAIR, UPTON*

Singing Jailbirds (Apo., 9/2/30) *1924* (*priv.*, California)

SINNETT, A. P.

Married by Degrees ('*c.*': Court, 5/3/11, Pl. Actors; Court, 16/9/11)

SITWELL, Sir OSBERT, Bart.

For First-Class Passengers Only (Arts, 27/11/27: +*SACHEVERELL SITWELL*) *1927* (as *All At Sea, A Social Tragedy*)

SITWELL, P. G.

The Call of the Sea. LC, Leamington, 27/11/19

SITWELL, SACHEVERELL [see *O. SITWELL*]

SKALSKI, ANDRÉ [see also *MERVYN BOND*]

The Apothecary ('*oa.*': m. Haydn: K's, Hamm., 3/9/25: +*K. LARK*)

SKARDON, HERBERT [see also *H. WAGNER*]

Send Him Victorious (P's, Horwich, 30/12/07; Stratford, 25/5/08)

SKEA, JAMES

×The Captain of the 'Sarah Jane' (Sur., 19/3/12, *cpy.*)
×A Rough Reception (Sur., 19/3/12, *cpy.*)

SKEET, EDGAR B.

×A Terrible Teaser (Coll., 18/10/09)
×Raising the Rent. LC, Hippo., Putney, 11/6/14
×The Snake and the Mormon. LC, Emp., Mile End, 27/8/17 title later changed to *Unmasked.*
The Little Companion ('*c.*': Q, 27/7/25: +*D. LEAVER*)

SKELTON, ARTHUR [see also *F. LINDO*]

[For an earlier play see *H. E. D.* v, 570]

Children of the Night ('*md.*': Pav., Ventnor, 3/8/00, *cpy.*; Gr., Stalybridge, 10/9/00)
×Flash Adelaide (Emp., Shoreditch, 6/12/09)
Breaking a Woman's Heart (Lyr., Hamm., 27/11/11: +*W. H. GLAZE*)

SKELTON, GLADYS [='*JOHN PRESLAND*']

SKEMP, A. R.

Guenevere. LC, Bristol, 27/10/14

SKINNER, A. G.

×Taffy. LC, Parish H., Bude, 9/5/23

SLADE, F. COURTNEY

The Query Mystery Play. LC, Ralli H., Hove, 4/2/25

SLADEN-SMITH, FRANCIS

×St Simeon Stylites (Margaret Morris, 25/2/22, Unnamed Soc. of Manchester; Mary Ward Settlement, 15/10/24, Dram. Art Centre) *1923* (in *Four One-Act Plays*, Oxford)

×The Invisible Duke ('*Gothic f.*': Deansgate, Manchester, 23/10/22, Unnamed Soc.; Fest., Cambridge, 7/3/27) *1927*

Solomon and Sheba (Deansgate, Manchester, 23/3/25, Unnamed Soc.)

×Edward About to Marry ('*f.*') *1926*

×The Saint's Comedy. *1927*

×The Crown of St Felice. *1928*

×The Sacred Cat ('*diversion*': A.L.S. Trav. Th., 1928) *1928*

×The Man who wouldn't go to Heaven. *1929*

×Wonderful Zoo. *1930*

SLAUGHTER, TOD

Spring-Heeled Jack ('*md.*': Pal., Clapham, 9/7/28: +*G. L. CARLILE*)

SLAUGHTER, W. [see *S. HICKS*]

SLAYTON, P. E.

×The Passing of the Ironside (Rehearsal, 7/3/10)

SLEE, NORMAN D. [see also *B. DAVIS*]

The King of Celaria ('*c.o.*', m. J. Ansell: H.M., Walsall, 2/5/01)

A Tangerine Tangle ('*c.o.*', m. W. and M. Slaughter: Vaud., 2/7/09, *cpy.*)

The King's Bride ('*c.o.*', m. J. Ansell: Kennington, 19/6/11; Lyr., 13/5/18, as *Violette*)

[Several sketches and 'operettas' produced at music-halls]

SMALE, EDITH C.

×A Baffled Spinster. *Fr. 1902*

SMALL, AUSTIN J. [='*SEAMARK*']

SMALL, LOTHIAN

×The Lure of the Lurid (K. G's H., 13/5/25, Half Circle Players)

SMART, KITTY

×Her Next Novel (Ladbr. H., 22/11/06, *amat.*)

SMEDLEY, ANNE CONSTANCE (*Mrs ARMFIELD*)

×Mrs Jordan; or, On the Road to Inglefield (Roy., 19/2/00)

×The Honour of a Rogue (Roy., 31/1/03: +*COSMO HAMILTON*)

×The Listeners (Portsmouth, 17/3/04)

×The Eleventh Hour (Vic. H., 15/4/13)

×Mother's Rights. LC, Vic., Dursley, 28/10/13

×Pierrot's Welcome (LC, Vic., Dursley, 28/10/13: Pal., 15/11/21, *m.*) *Fr. 1930* (as '*a moonlight past.*')

×The Ghost. LC, Vic, Dursley, 28/10/13

×The Hundredth Year. LC, Holloway Inst., Stroud, 11/4/14

×The Woman-Haters. LC, Holloway Inst., Stroud, 11/4/14

Greenleaf Rhythmic Plays. *1922–5*

[This series includes five short plays by Constance Smedley and three by her husband: 1. *The Curious Herbal* (LC, Red Triangle Hut, Woodchester, 2/9/22; A.L.S. Trav. Th., 1925); 2. *The Gilded Wreath* (LC, Red Triangle Hut, Woodchester, 2/9/22); 3. *Belle and Beau*; 4. *Red Riding Hood's Wood*; 5. *The Fortunate Shepherds* (LC, Greenleaf, Mockbeggar, Hants., 5/9/25), and, by M. Armitage, 1. *The Minstrel*; 2. *The Grassblade* ('Chinese fable'); and 3. *Lost Silver*.]

×Eve – Bird and Beast (Kings., 21/10/27, *m.*, Greenleaf Theatre: +*M. ARMFIELD*)

×The King Decrees (Kings., 21/10/27, *m.*, Greenleaf Theatre: +*M. ARMITAGE*)

×The Seventh Devil (Kings., 21/10/27, *m.*, Greenleaf Theatre: +*M. ARMITAGE*)

×Oranges and Beans ('*Californian rhapsody*') *Fr. 1930*

SMITH, ADAM [see *E. RIGHTON*]

[*SMITH, EDGAR*

×The Collegettes ('*m.pl.*', m. M. Levi: Aldw., 27/2/09)

Philopoena ('*farrago of fun, fancy and foolishness*', m. M. Levi: Aldw., 27/2/09)

SMITH, FRANK STANLEY

[For an earlier play see *H. E. D.*, v, 572]

×Dust. LC, T.H. Lancaster, 10/11/13

SMITH, GORDON

Napoleon and Josephine, A Royal Romance (Emp., Holloway, 26/10/14)

SMITH, HAROLD

The March Hare ('*f.c.*': Birkenhead, 26/4/09, *cpy.*, *amat.*; Ambass., 10/7/13)

×The Old Puritan (Qns, 27/7/15, *m.*)

[*SMITH, HARRY BACHE*

The Casino Girl ('*m.f.*', m. L. Englander: Shaft., 11/7/00)

The Belle of Bohemia ('*m.c.*', m. L. Englander: St G's H., 17/9/00, *cpy.*; Apo., 21/2/01)

The Fortune-Teller ('*c.o.*', m. V. Herbert: Shaft., 9/4/01)

Dolly Dollars ('*m.c.*': Vic. H., 26/8/05, *cpy.*)

The Belle of the West ('*m.pl.*', m. K. L. Hoschna: Vic. H., 28/8/05, *cpy.*)

The Tattooed Man ('*c.o.*', m. V. Herbert: Vic. H., 11/2/07, *cpy.*)

The Lilac Domino ('*oa.*', m. C. Cuvillier: 44th St., N.Y., 28/10/14; Emp., 21/2/18: +*R. B. SMITH*)

Angel Face ('*m.f.*', m. V. Herbert: Colonial, Chicago, 8/6/19; Knickerbocker, N.Y., 30/12/19; O.H., Blackpool, 8/9/22; Str., 11/10/22)

SMITH, HELEN ZENNA [='*EVADNE PRICE*']

SMITH, HENRY CLAPP

×A Sprig of Rosemary. *Fr. 1930*

SMITH, J. M.

×The Intrusion of Nancy (R. Inst. H., Glasgow, 26/4/23, Scott. Nat. Players)

A House in the West End (and) Puir Man's Pride. *1926* (Arbroath)

[These two one-acts are described as 'Scots plays': the second appears in LC, Pav., Carnoustie, 3/11/25]

SMITH, LITA

[For earlier plays see *H. E. D.* v, 573 and 817]

×Wrangles (Corn Exch., Cheltenham, 26/3/00)

SMITH, MARY ELLIS

×That Frenchwoman (Ladbr. H., 7/1/03)

SMITH, MARY STAFFORD [see also *K. S. MALDEN*]

×The Shadow on the Blind (Stand., Pimlico, 6/7/08)

Her Love for Him (Lyr., Hamm., 27/8/06; Fulham, 8/5/11, as *A Freak of Fate*)

×Simple Silas (Pal., Battersea, 13/11/11: title changed later to *Cornered*)

×The Conversion (Manchester, 20/9/11; Marlb., Holloway, 23/11/11)

×The Passing of Claude (Gr., Leeds, 2/9/12; Borough, Stratford, 7/10/12)

×A Man, a Woman and a Mangle. LC, Hippo., Putney, 19/12/13

×My Pardner. LC, Pal., Southampton, 22/1/14

Dying to Live ('*f.c.*': K's H., Ilkley, 13/7/14; Gai., Manchester, 10/4/16; P.W., 26/5/17, as *Penny Wise*)

SMITH, NAOMI ROYDE [see *NAOMI ROYDE-SMITH*]

SMITH, PAUL GERARD [see also *R. P. WESTON*]

[A few sketches produced at music-halls]

[*SMITH, R. B.* [see *H. B. SMITH*]

SMITH, RITA CREIGHTON

×The Rescue (Guildhall School of Music, 19/5/25, Pivot Club)

SMITH, ROSE

Idene. LC, Ath., Glasgow, 16/1/20

SMITH, SHEILA KAYE [see *SHEILA KAYE-SMITH*]

SMITH, VERE

The Dandy Duke; or, The Man Who Wasn't ('*m.bsq.*': Brighton, 17/12/06)

SMITH, WELLESLEY

×Off to Gretna Green ('*c.o.*', m. G. Ess and J. Rutt: Qns, Poplar, 8/4/07)

[*SMITH, WINCHELL* [see also '*M. ARLEN*' and *P. ARMSTRONG*]

Brewster's Millions ('*c.*': Hicks', 1/5/07: +*B. ONGLEY*) *Fr. 1925*

The Fortune Hunter ('*c.*': Qns, 17/12/13) *Fr. 1929*

The Boomerang ('*c.*': Playh., Wilmington, 5/4/15; Belasco, N.Y., 10/8/15; D.P., Eastbourne, 8/5/16; Qns, 11/5/16: +*V. MAPES*) *Fr. 1915*

Lightnin' (National, Washington, 28/1/18; Gai., N.Y., 26/8/18; D.P., Eastbourne, 19/1/25; Shaft., 27/1/25: +*F. BACON*) *Fr. 1918*

SMITH-DAMPIER, ELEANOR MARY
The Queen's Minister, *1922*

SMITH-WRIGHT, J.
Mr Studley Revokes ('*f.c.*': K's H., 2/4/22, Interlude Players)
×Dear John (K's H., 14/5/22, Interlude Players)

SMYTH, BASIL S. [see *W. EMDEN*]

SMYTH, Dame ETHEL MARY
The Wreckers ('*Cornish d.*', translated from *Les Naufrageurs* (by Henry B. Brewster) and with music by Ethel Smyth) *1909* (*priv.*, Woking)
×Fête Galante ('*dance dr.*': Rep., B'ham, 4/6/23; C.G., 11/6/23: +*E. SHANKS*) *1923*

SNAITH, J. C. [see *H. A. VACHELL*]
Araminta Arrives ('*c.*': W.G., New Brighton, 3/10/21; Com., 11/10/21: +*D. BRANDON*)

SNELSON, J. T.
Magnolia. LC, '*m.pl.*': School, Old Bletchley, 21/1/22

SNOW, MICHAEL
×The Dancing Faun. LC, '*m.pl.*': D.P., Eastbourne, 19/3/20

SNOWDEN, KEIGHLEY [see *Mrs S. A. P. KITCAT*]

SNOWE, LUCY
Two Stage Plays: Danzill Herbert's Atonement; Bondage. *1900*
×Croesus ('*classical pl.*' '*for boys*') *1903*

SOANE-ROBY, B.
[For an earlier play see *H. E. D.* v, 573]
[Several sketches, on episodes from novels by Charles Dickens, produced at music-halls]

SOBIENIOWSKY, FLORIAN
Peace, War and Revolution (Roy., 17/2/29, International Theatre: +*E. A. PEARSON*: from the Polish of W. Grubinski)

SODEN, JOHN
[For earlier plays see *H. E. D.*, 573 and 817]
For Wife and Home (Qns, Manchester, 3/8/06; Emp., Cradley Heath, 21/5/09, as *Her Soul's Awakening*)

SOLANO, J. [see also *G. GROSSMITH*]
×Salvage (Qns, 5/7/18, *m.*)

SOLOMON, JESSICA
Born to be Loved ('*f.*': Alb. H., 19/1/09, *amat.*)
×The Contest (Lyc. Club, 26/1/11, *m.*)
×Below Street Level ('*basement c.*': Rehearsal, 2/5/18)

SOMERFIELD, FRED C.

The Tyrant (‘*r.d.*’: Osborne, Manchester, 17/12/06; Dalston, 24/8/08: +*F. LUDOVIC*)

Geoffrey Langdon's Wife (Rot., L'pool, 22/6/08; Stratford, 17/1/10)

SOMERS, A. C. C.

Compensation (Qns, Manchester, 23/5/10)

× Mrs Bradshaw's Neighbours (Tiv., Manchester, 30/9/10)

SOMERS, DENE

× The Experiment (P.W., Grimsby, 6/4/25, *m.*)

× Intolerance (‘*t.*’: P.W., Grimsby, 6/4/25, *m.*) *1925* (Grimsby)

× The Extremists (P.W., Grimsby, 6/4/25, *m.*)

× The Paragon (‘*t.c.*’: P.W., Grimsby, 6/4/25, *m.*)

× The Choice (P.W., Grimsby, 6/4/25, *m.*) *1924* (Grimsby)

× The Stranger. *1924* (Grimsby)

The Sacrifice. (‘*fant.*’: P.W., Grimsby, 6/4/25, *m.*)

Goodness Gracious! What Next? LC, P.W., Grimsby, 11/9/25. *1925* (Grimsby)

Windmills (‘*fant.*’) *1926*

SOMERSET, C. W.

[For earlier plays see *H. E. D.* v, 574 and 817]

The Woman in White (Kennington, 11/9/05: dramatised from the novel by Wilkie Collins)

× My Friend Mr White (Hippo., 25/10/09)

The Little Grey Home in the West (D.P., Eastbourne, 23/11/14)

A Little Flutter (Pier, Brighton, 28/7/24; R.A., Woolwich, 18/8/24)

SOMERVILLE, PETER F.

The Local Rag (‘*c.*’: Q, 7/1/29) *1947* (Manchester)

SOMERVILLE, REGINALD [see also *G. EDEN*]

× A Pair of Two's (‘*m.f.c.*’: Hippo., Putney, 29/3/15: title later changed to *Family Frays*)

Antoine (‘*o.*’, m. by author: Lyc., 23/7/19)

David Garrick (‘*c.o.*’: C.G., 9/12/20)

SOREL, HENRY

Foolish Wives. LC, County, Chelmsford, 3/3/23

SORENSEN, REGINALD WILLIAM

Tolpuddle; or, ‘Who's Afeared?’ LC, ‘*democratic episode*’: St Pancras H., 25/11/26. *1929*

SORROW, GLORIA

× In Love (St J., 26/7/11, *cpy*)

SOTHERN, E. H.

[For an earlier play see *H. E. D.* v, 574]

The Light that Lies in a Woman's Eyes (‘*c.*’: Crit., 11/9/03, *cpy.*)

× The Last Appeal. LC, Vaud., 3/1/13

SOUTAR, ANDREW

If We But Knew (Com., 7/6/28)

SOUTAR, FARREN

Almond Eye ('*m.pl.*', m. F. Rosse: Scala, 26/12/23: +*A. C. T. VEASEY*)

SOUTH, ROBERT

The Divine Aretino, and Other Plays. *1903*

[In addition to the title-play, a comedy, this contains three other full-length dramas: 1. *The White Rose, A Study of a Lost Cause*; 2. *Savonarola*; and 3. *Sabado*]

Sir Walter Raleigh. *1904*

The Smithy. *1905*

SOUTHWART, ELIZABETH

Ishmael (Textile H., Bradford, 10/26, *amat.*; Str., 15/5/27, Pl. Actors) *Fr. 1931*

SOUTHWELL, MARTIN G.

×You Don't Know Doris. LC, K. G's H., 20/11/24

SOWERBY, KATHERINE GITHA (*Mrs JOHN KENDALL*)

Little Plays for School and Home. *1910*

[This collection, issued in two 'books', contains four short pieces: 1. *The Magic Wand, or, Civility Costs Nothing*; 2. *King Cophetua and the Beggar Maid*; 3. *Bearskin*; and 4. *Fortunatus and Cassandra*]

Rutherford and Son (Court, 31/1/12, *m.*; Little, 18/3/12) *1912*

×Before Breakfast (Playh., 2/5/12) *Fr. 1913*

×Jinny (Emp., N.Y., 5/3/14)

A Man and Some Women (Gai., Manchester, 26/10/14)

Sheila (St J., 7/6/17)

The Stepmother (New, 13/1/24, Pl. Actors)

SPARKES, J. LESLIE [see also *S. BENEDICT*]

×The Lie (Arts Centre, 8/4/14)

×A Holiday Title (Passmore Edwards Settlement, 25/4/14)

×Rotter Footer (Rehearsal, 7/12/14)

First Love ('*f.c.*': Kings., 7/4/20)

Bluff. LC, Corn Exch., Spalding, 1/3/22: +*S. BENEDICT*

The Springbok ('*f.c.*': Pier, Brighton, 2/2/25)

SPARKES, RICHARD

×Tango Teas. LC, Qns, 29/9/13

'*SPARROWDROP*'

×A Matrimonial Bureau (Qns, Dublin, 11/2/07)

SPAULL, HEBE

Fighting Death, and Other Plays. *1922* (League of Nations Union)

[This contains three short pieces designed as propaganda for the League of Nations: 1. *Fighting Death*; 2. *An Averted Tragedy*; and 3. *Mill Girls, East and West*]

SPE, F. F.

×Giving Her Socks (Extra Special). LC, Kings., 6/11/16

SPEARS, H. H.

The Mayor of Ecksville. LC, Congregational Inst., W. Bromwich, 22/10/25

SPEED, H. A.

Past and Future; or, Three Times on Earth ('*serio-comic o.*': Douglas H., London N. 10/12/08, *amat.*)

SPENCE, J. C.

×The Dreamer (Playh., L'pool, 11/10/28)

SPENCE, LEWIS

×The Provost's Predicament (Glasgow, 31/3/15)

[*SPENCE, RALPH*

The Gorilla ('*mystery pl.*': Belasco, Washington, 13/4/25; Selwyn, N.Y., 28/4/25; Court, L'pool, 22/6/25; Oxf., 30/6/25) *Fr. 1950*

SPENCER, A. M.

Circumstances. LC, Kings., 5/2/23: +*D. AINSLIE*

SPENCER, ALICE

The Vale of Content (Cor., 8/6/09: translated from *Das Glück im Winkel* (1896) by H. Sudermann)

SPENCER, CHARLES N.

The Lion Tamer (Gate, 4/3/30: adapted from *Le Dompteur* (1925) by Alfred Savoir)

SPENCER, DENTON

[Numerous sketches and playlets produced at music-halls]

SPENCER, FRED [see *H. ROGERSON*]

SPENDER, S.

Reality. LC, Glossop, 22/1/19

SPENCER, SYDNEY

[For an earlier play see *H. E. D.* v, 576]

The Hero of the Flag ('*naval d.*': R.A., Woolwich, 2/3/03)

A Destroyer of Men ('*Russian d.*': Edmonton, 2/10/05: +*C. BURNETTE*)

A Wonderful Woman ('*costume c.*': Pav., St Leonards, 15/6/08: a revised version of a play (1849) by G. Dance)

SPENCER, T. H.

×A Sea of Troubles (Surrey Masonic H., 6/3/11, *amat.*)

SPICER, A.

×Absent-minded George. LC, New, Cambridge, 4/2/18

SPIERS, H. F. [see *C. A. CLARKE*]

SPIERS, K. O.

If Youth but Knew! *1924* (*priv.*)

SPILLER, LEONARD [see also *H. HOWLAND*]

×Things that Matter. LC, Park, Hanwell, 3/2/19

×Mixed Pickles. LC, Park, Hanwell, 3/2/19

The Trial. LC, '*m.pl.*': Park, Hanwell, 27/5/20

×The Lost Diamond. LC, Park, Hanwell, 24/4/22. *1923* (in H. Howland, *Black Magic and Other Plays*)
×Zippity Zoppit. LC, Park, Hanwell, 24/4/23. *1923* (in H. Howland, *Black Magic and Other Plays*)

SPLATT, Miss M. G.
×The Dream Made Absolute (Lyc. Club, 29/11/12)

SPOONER, CECIL
One Day. LC, E.C., 24/4/20

SPOTTISWOODE, SYBIL [see *R. BESIER*]

SPRANGE, W. E. [see *F. BOWYER*]

SPRINGSON, SAM
[A few sketches and playlets produced at music-halls]

SPROSTON, S.
×The Fairy Transformed ('*fairy pl. for children*') *Fr. 1913*
×Midsummer Fairies ('*fant. sketch*') *1914*
×The Pudding made of Plum ('*t.c. for children*') *1914*

SPURLING, C. [see *B. E. CLAY* and *J. S. MacROBERT*]

SPURR, HARRY A.
The Woman Pays (Hull, 20/5/04, *cpy.*)

SPURR, MEL B.
[For earlier plays see *H. E. D.* v, 577]
The Twiddleton Twins ('*m.f.*', m. G. Lardelli: Crippl. Inst., 3/3/00: +*J. R. CRAUFORD*)
×His Other Eyes (Pier, Brighton, 4/3/01: +*W. M. MAYNE*)

SQUIRE, Sir JOHN COLLINGS [see also *J. L. BALDERSTON*]
Pride and Prejudice (Pal., 24/3/22, *m.*: +*H. A. EILEEN SQUIRE*: adapted from the novel by Jane Austen) *1929*
Robin Hood ('*farcical romantic pastoral*': +*JOAN R. YOUNG*) *1928*

SQUIRE, W. H.
×An Interrupted Rehearsal (Gr., Croydon, 20/7/00; St G's H., 12/4/02, *amat.*: +*J. RANDALL*)

SQUIRES, GRAHAM
The Belle of the Skies ('*m.pl.*', m. Guy Jones: B'ham, 22/5/11, *amat.*)
The Democrats. ('*m.pl.*', m. Guy Jones: B'ham, 13/5/12, *amat.*: +*ST J. HAMUND*)

SQUIRES, S. R.
A Midnight Mystery (Stratford, 29/6/14)

STACE, HENRY
The Member for Turrington (Players, 21/2/30)

STACEY, CYRIL
The Golden Bell ('*m.c.*': Watson Memorial H., Tewkesbury, 27/1/13, *amat.*)

STACK, KINGSTON
Kitty Breaks Loose (Wynd., 14/5/18)

STACK, LILY
×His Coming of Age (Brixton, 1/3/20: +*G. SAFERY*)

STAFFORD, ALFRED
[For earlier plays see *H. E. D.* v, 578]
Conscience and Crime ('*r.d.*': Qns, Fleetwood, 12/3/06)

STAFFORDS, W. J.
Playmates ('*m.pl.*': K's, Southsea, 21/10/29)

'*STAG, W.*'
×Avunculitis (Arts Centre, 28/11/13, Black Cat Club)
×Her Dreadful Past (Arts Centre, 23/1/14)

STAKE, T. [see *L. AMBLER*]

STALLARD, Mrs ARTHUR (*CONSTANCE L.*)
The Ladies of Llangollen (Mary Ward Settlement, 22/11/24, Dram. Art Centre)
Small Plays of St Cuthbert. *1930*
[This contains five one-act pieces: 1. *The Miracle*; 2. *The Call*; 3. *The Feast*; 4. *The Hermit*; and 5. *The Gate of Heaven*]

STAMM, IDA
The Brownies ('*c.o.*': Broomwood-road School, Clapham, 9/6/10, *amat.*)

STANFIELD, JOHN F.
For Love and Money ('*md.*': Vic., Broughton, 5/3/02, *cpy.*; Com., Manchester, 4/8/02; Pav., 15/6/03)
×Ashes (Paisley, 20/3/06: +*M. E. WARD*)

STANFORD, WYBERT [see *G. LESTOCQ*]

[*STANGE, HUGH STANISLAUS*
[For an earlier play see *H. E. D.* v, 578]
Quo Vadis? (Adel., 5/5/00)
Dolly Varden ('*m.c.*', m. J. Edwards: Aven., 1/10/03)
The School for Husbands ('*c.*': Scala, 10/3/06)
The Chocolate Soldier ('*c.o.*', m. O. Straus: Lyr., 10/9/10)
Growing Pains (Ambass., 20/10/25: +*S. MEARS*: dramatised from Booth Tarkington's novel, *Seventeen* (1916)) *1924*

STANGER, HUGH
The Little Innocents ('*c.o.*', m. L. Varney: Gr., Islington, 28/10/01)

STANHOPE, HESTER
The Money-Grabber ('*society satire*': Kings., 27/2/08)

STANLAWS, PENRHYN
Instinct (Playh., L'pool, 14/10/12; D.Y., 6/11/12: from *L'Instinct* (1905) by H. Kistemaeckers)

STANLEY, ARTHUR [see also *H. SIMPSON*]
×Cock-a-Doodle-Doo! ('*m.pl.*': County, Kingston, 21/3/10)
Jolly Japan ('*m.pl.*': County, Kingston, 18/7/10)

×Phrenology (B'ham, 1/5/14)
The Man who Knew the Future ('*fant.*': Pier, Brighton, 17/11/19)
The Pater ('*c.*': Playh., Jesmond, 12/4/26)

STANLEY, CLARE
×Saved by the British (Aquar., Yarmouth, 12/10/14; S. Ldn. Pal., 30/11/14)

STANLEY, ERIC
×The Amorous Colonel (Selwyn H., Wisbech, 27/1/04)

STANLEY, FLO
The Cruise of H.M.S. Victory ('*m.c.*': Edmonton, 15/9/06, *cpy.*)
×The Prince of the Dandies ('*m.c.*': Emp., Camberwell, 11/10/09: title later changed to *Sprouts*)

STANLEY, FREDERIC A. [see also *K. GODDARD*]
A Sailor's Sweetheart ('*nautical d.*': Gr., Fulham, 29/9/02: +*H. F. HENDERSON*)

STANLEY, GERALD [see *L. ALAN*]

STANLEY, HORACE
[For an earlier play see *H. E. D.* v, 579]
The 10-30 Down Express ('*md.*': Muncaster, Bootle, 19/6/1899; Stratford, 26/3/00)
Guilty Gold (Alex., B'ham, 3/6/07; R.A., Woolwich, 10/7/11)
The Female Detective ('*md.*': Osborne, Manchester, 30/5/10; Stratford, 27/2/11)
Goodbye, Sweetheart, Goodbye (Stratford, 12/1/14)
The Son of a Soldier (Macclesfield, 22/3/15; Brixton, 27/3/16)
A Child of Charity. LC, Hippo., Bilston, 28/2/17
Parted at the Church (Pal., Rugeley, 25/2/18; W. Bromwich, 4/3/18: called originally *The Cross Roads of Life*)
Ashamed of Her Mother. LC, Emp., Aberdare, 4/11/18
Jim Mason, Minesweeper (Sunderland, 16/12/18)
Faith, Hope and Charity. LC, Gr., Halifax, 15/4/19
Her Mad Marriage. LC, Pal., Rugeley, 7/2/20

STANLEY, LEEDHAM
[A few sketches produced at music-halls]

[*STANLEY, MARTHA M.*
Innocent Anne ('*c.*': P's, Bradford, 22/3/26: +*A. MATTHEWS*) *Fr. 1929* (as *Where Innocence is Bliss*)
Nightie Night ('*f.*': Wilmington, 14/4/19; P'cess, N.Y., 15/9/19; Manchester, 7/3/21; Qns, 22/3/21: +*A. MATTHEWS*) *Fr. 1929*

STANLEY, VICTOR
×The Padded C(s)ell (H.M., Carlisle, 23/9/12)
×The Right Stuff (New, Cardiff, 14/6/15)

STANMORE, FRANK [see also *LESLIE HAWKINS*]
×A Successful Failure (Qns Gate H., 2/5/02)
Such a Nice Girl ('*m. absurdity*', m. E. Paschall: Worthing, 1/7/07; County, Kingston, 8/7/07; W.G., Bootle, 3/10/10, as *Chasing Cynthia*)
[A few sketches produced at music-halls]

STANNARD, ANNA

×A Command Performance (Col., 26/1/20)

STANNARD, ELLIOT [see also *A. M. DALE*]

The Last Straw ('*f.c.*': D.P., Eastbourne, 10/12/17)
The Man-eater ('*f.*': Pier, Brighton, 2/3/25)

STANTON, MARY [see *HESTER WHITE*]

STANWAY, E. L.

Easy Payments (Playh., L'pool, 12/2/30)

STAPLETON, J. [see *P. G. WODEHOUSE*]

[*STARLING, LYNN*

Meet the Wife ('*c.*': Gr., Llandudno, 18/4/27; St M., 1/7/27) *Fr. 1928*

STARR, HARRY

[For earlier plays see *H. E. D.* v, 579]
Schwenk, the Dreamer ('*r.c.o.*': Gloucester, 23/11/00)
×Napoleon the Man (P's, Preston, 7/4/05)
The Unseen Power ('*m.pl.*': Ath., Lancaster, 10/9/06)

STATON, E. W. A. B.

×John Bull at Market (E. Oxford, 3/8/07, *cpy.*)

STAYTON, FRANK

[For an earlier play see *H. E. D.* v, 579]
The Despatch Bearer (Richmond, 25/2/01; Emp., Islington, 14/11/10)
Mrs Willoughby's Kiss (Brighton, 2/5/01; Aven., 18/10/02)
×Rash Promises. LC, Lyc., Eccles, 30/9/01
The President ('*f.m.d.*': P.W., 30/4/02)
×Angelina's Lover (Wynd., 24/9/03) *Fr. 1903*
A Maid from School ('*c.*': Pleasure Gdns, Folkestone, 30/11/03; Terry's, 31/3/04)
×The Five-Guinea Hat. LC, P.H., Hartley Wintney, 4/5/08
The Two Pins ('*c.*': Newcastle, 2/4/08; Aldw., 8/6/08)
×Love in a Railway Train (Jubilee H., Hartley Wintney, 5/10/08; Brixton, 31/7/12) *Fr. 1909*
Tantrums ('*c.*': Crit., 22/10/12)
The Inferior Sex ('*c.*': Com., 3/4/13)
Lady Betty Martingale (Buffalo, 19/9/14; Nixon, Pittsburgh, 21/9/14: +*J. L. LONG*)
The Joan Danvers (Gai., Manchester, 8/11/15; D.Y., 7/2/16) *Fr. 1923*
×Room 314 (Hippo., Manchester, 28/8/16; Metropolitan, 25/9/16)
Enter Thompson (Portsmouth, 6/10/19)
The Other Fellow ('*adventure*': D.P., Eastbourne, 14/2/21)
Threads ('*c.*': St J., 23/8/21)
×The Double Cross. LC, Crippl. Inst., 1/11/22. *Fr. 1921*
Special Licence ('*f.r.*': New, Cardiff, 3/3/24: dramatised from his own novel, 1923)
The Hour and the Man ('*d. of today*': O.H., Manchester, 2/8/24; New, 28/10/24: called originally *Noblesse Oblige*)

The Passionate Adventure (Aldw., 26/4/25, Interlude Players)
The Jazz Marriage ('*f.c.*': Gr., Hull, 4/5/25; Crit., 9/6/25, as *Mixed Doubles*: called originally *Does It Matter?*) *Fr. 1927*
Love's a Terrible Thing ('*f.c.*': Sav., 4/10/26: a completely revised version of *Special Licence*, above) *1934*
The Intriguing Ladies (Q, 15/8/27)
Their Wife ('*f.*': Ambass., Southend, 12/9/27; Little, 3/10/27)

STAYTON, MARIANNE
×The Flame (Shaft., 30/6/10, *m.*)
×In Saramede ('*c. past.*') *Fr. 1912*
×A Question of Division. *Fr. 1912*
×Mollie and the Milliner. LC, Crippl. Inst., 1/11/22. *Fr. 1922*

STEAD, W. R. TROTTER [='*DEAN BALLYN*': see *F. M. GOSTLING*]

STEDMAN, PHILIP B. KIRK
×A Love-crowned King (St Mary's Church R., Primrose Hill, 17/4/09, *amat.*) *1911* (Stoke-on-Trent)
×Hope (St Mary's Church R., Primrose Hill, 17/4/09, *amat.*)

STEED, Rev. A. J.
Lords or Colonels ('*c.*': T.H., Aylsham, 28/4/03, *amat.*)

STEEL, ROBERT
Night Air (Roy., 24/9/04, *cpy.*)

STEELE, CHARLES D.
×The Awakening of 'Erb (St Peter's H., Brockley, 2/12/15)

STEELE, CHRISTOPHER
The Scarlet Garter ('*f.*': Hippo., Richmond, 28/1/21, *m.*)
×The Lamp-post (Kings., 27/5/21, *m.*, Playwrights' Theatre)

STEER, JANETTE [='*JAN VAN WETHERHELT*']
[For earlier plays see *H. E. D.* v, 580]
All Sorts and Conditions of Men (Metro., Camberwell, 1/12/02: from the novel (1882) by Sir Walter Besant)
Geraldine Wants to Know ('*c.*': York, 14/8/11)
The Sphinx (Court, 3/10/14)

STEINER, LESLIE HOWARD
×Deception (Stanley H., S. Norwood, 20/12/13, *amat.*)

STEPHENS, H. C. C.
×Reprieved (P.W., 15/2/25)

STEPHENS, H. S.
The Soldier Girl ('*c.o.*': Emp., Penge, 20/1/19: +*ALBERT E. ELLIS* and *C. BALDWIN*)

STEPHENS, JAMES
×The Marriage of Julia Elizabeth (Hardwicke-st. H., Dublin, 17/11/11, Theatre of Ireland) *1929* (New York: as *Julia Elizabeth*)

STEPHENS, RICARDO
×The Right to Die (Little, 27/6/12, Oncomers)

STEPHENS, ROBERT NEILSON

Miss Elizabeth's Prisoner ('*r.c.*': Imp., 16/4/04: +*E. L. SWETE*) *Fr. 1921*

STEPHENS, W. THWAITES

×The Way Out (Studio Theatre, Victoria-street, 10/5/11, One-Act Play Soc.)

STEPHENS, WALTER [see also *R. F. MACKAY*]

[For earlier plays see *H. E. D.* v, 581 and 817]

Are You a Smoker? or, A Nicotine Nightmare (Waldorf, 27/12/06: +*H. C. NEWTON*)

Paradise Lost (adapted from Milton's poem) *1906*

The Pilgrim's Progress (dramatised from Bunyan's work, and described as a '*sacred drama*') (*1914*)

Charley's Uncle ('*f.c.*') *1914*

STEPHENS, WILFRED (see also *B. CHALLONER*)

[For earlier plays see *H. E. D.* v, 581]

×As Dreams Are Made Of (Rehearsal, 24/2/13, Black Cat Club)

×Keeping Sunday (Rehearsal, 18/3/13)

×On Tour (Rehearsal, 3/4/13)

×The Sunlight Way (Rehearsal, 28/4/13, Black Cat Club)

×Contracts (10/11/13, Black Cat Club)

×Ringing Him Up (10/11/13, Black Cat Club)

STEPHENS, WILFRED T.

Please Be Good ('*f.c.*': Brighton, 3/5/26)

STEPHENSON, ANN

Oh! My Aunt! (Emp., Shepherd's Bush, 31/3/24)

It Happened in Ardoran ('*Scottish c.*': Court, 19/10/24, Rep. Players; Everyman, 24/2/25: +*A. MACBETH*)

×Nerves (Court, 15/6/25, *m.*) *Fr. 1925*

Life's Little Sideshows (+*A. MACBETH*) *Fr. 1925*

[This contains the following sketches: 1. *Gaffer Halfpenny and the District Visitor*; 2. *Giggles*; 3. *A Glimpse of Home Life*; 4. *At the Hospital*; 5. *Blood and Pastry*; 6. *Buying a Haddock*; 7. *A Drop of Irish*; 8. *Lost Property*; 9. *Music and Memories*; 10. *A Scottish Courting*; 11. *The Marriage Makers*; and 12. *Seeing the First Godson*]

STEPHENSON, B. C. [see *W. YARDLEY*]

[For earlier plays see *H. E. D.* v, 582 and 818]

STEPHENSON, CECIL [see *G. BLUMBERG*]

STEPHENSON, CHARLES A.

The Sunny South. LC, '*m.pl.*': Gr., Luton, 22/11/23

STEPHENSON, MARY

×The Tenant (St J., 7/5/15, *m.*)

STEPNEY-RAWSON, Mrs MAUDE

×A Love Tangle ('*pastoral duologue*', m. G. H. Clutsam: Wynd., 17/6/01)

STERLING, C. DAVID

×Compromised (Granville, Walham Green, 7/4/19)
The Golden Ballot ('*c.*': RADA, 28/6/25)

STERLING, MAX

×The Inquisition (Hippo., B'ham, 4/4/11; Sur., 8/5/11)

STERN, GLADYS BRONWYN

×A Dance at Dawn (Marlb., Holloway, 31/7/09)
×For One Night Only (Little, 29/5/11, *m.*, Oncomers)
×For Husbands Only (Ambass., 4/6/20, *m.*: +*Mrs D. C. F. HARDING*)
The Matriarch (Roy., 8/5/29: from her novel, *The Tents of Israel,* 1924) *Fr. 1931*
Debonair ('*c.*': Lyr., 23/4/30: dramatised from her own novel (1928): +*F. VOSPER*)

STERNDALE, JAMES

Kind Heart and Coronet (Lyr., Hamm., 14/3/20, *m.*, Curtain Group and People's Theatre Soc.; Everyman, 20/12/20)

STERNDALE-BENNETT, J. B.

×The Morden Luck. LC, Aldw., 13/2/22

STERNER, LAWRENCE

[For an earlier play see *H. E. D.* v, 583]
×The Water Cure (Brixton, 14/3/04; Com., 14/2/05; title later changed to *Love and Laudanum*)
Off the Rank ('*f.c.*': Gai., Douglas, 16/6/04; Str., 11/3/05)
[Several sketches and playlets produced at music-halls]

STEVENS, F. ERIC [see *S. DOWNFIELD*]

STEVENS, G. A. [see also *C. RIDGWELL*]

[A few sketches produced at music-halls]

STEVENS, HAROLD CHARLES GILBARD

×In the Light of Day (Little, 4/9/18)
×Walking Out (Glo., 7/2/26)
×Out of Order (Gate, 18/9/29)
To Meet the King!...Release...The House on the Hill...The Captain (four one-act plays published together) *1930*

STEVENS, THOMAS WOOD

Camille in Roaring Camp (Str., 16/2/30, Venturers Soc.)

STEVENS, VAL

×The Reformation of Mat. LC, Merthyr Tydfil, 4/4/24

STEVENS, VICTOR

[For earlier plays see *H. E. D.* v, 581]
The Gay Cavalier ('*m.c.*', m. by author: Plymouth, 5/11/02, *cpy.*)
×Playlets Limited; or, Percy's Proposal (Rehearsal, 4/11/08, *m.*)

STEVENSON, JAMES Jr

Run to Earth; or, Justice at Last ('*md.*': Croydon, 8/3/05, *cpy.*)
A Modern Martyr (Nuneaton, 31/8/05)

STEWARD, B. D.
×The Almighty Waiter. *Fr. 1930*

STEWART, ATHOLE [see also *M. PETHERICK*]
×Through the Post (Apo., 9/1/13)
×His Duty (Court, 30/6/14: +*N. F. GRANT*)
Life – Palpitating Life ('*f.c.*': Q, 5/12/27)
Leave Well Alone ('*f.c.*': Pav., Colwyn Bay, 29/9/29)

STEWART, BRENDEN [see *P. FRENCH*]

STEWART, COLIN McDOUGALL
×Dark Horses (Gai., Manchester, 31/7/15)

STEWART, HAL DOUGLAS
×More Things. *1929*
×Rizzio's Boots ('*historical impertinence*': Ath., Glasgow, 17/1/30) *1930*

STEWART, HUBERT
The Widow ('*f.c.*': Rehearsal, 29/10/12) *1901* (Perth, Western Australia; printed with *Home from Abroad*)
×A Gipsy's Daughter (Rehearsal, 27/6/13, Black Cat Club)
×Marion's Crime (Pav., 25/3/14)

STEWART, J.
[A few sketches produced at music-halls]

STEWART, J. BARRETT
×All the Comforts of a Home. LC, Emp., Holloway, 25/4/13
The Soul's Awakening (Kennington, 21/10/18: +*E. CARLTON*)

STEWART, J. O. [see *KATHERINE F. RAND*]

STEWART, R. P. [see *G. E. MORRISON*]

STEWART, REX
Gay Pierrette ('*m.ext.*': Bury St Edmunds, 2/4/23)

STEWART, ROBERT
Tattercoats ('*m.pl.*': m. A. Scott-Gatty and N. Scott-Gatty: Sav., 22/2/00; Sav., 5/5/02, *revised*)

STEWART-DYER, M.
The Eye of Wang ('*m.pl.*': Corn Exch., Wallingford, 30/4/12, *amat.*: +*G. JENKINS*)

'*STEWER, JAN*' [=*A. J. COLES*]
Revel Day ('*m.pl.*': Torquay, 23/4/12, *amat.*)

STEYNOR, MORLEY
Lancelot and Guenevere. *1909*
Lancelot and Elaine. *1909*

STIGANT, ARTHUR
The Time Machine ('*m.fant.*', m. M. Strong: Bradford, 13/11/03)

STILES, LESLIE
×Only a Model (T.H., Chelsea, 10/4/02)
×A Burmese Idol (County, Kingston, 20/5/07)
The Love Mills ('*c.o.*', m. A. Van Oost: Glo., 3/10/11)

×The Contemptible Little Army (Sur., 14/12/14)
×Stage Struck ('*bsq.*': Vic. Pal., 11/1/15; Emp., 1/3/15: +*F. FARREN*)
Be My Friend ('*f.*': Gr., Blackpool, 18/6/23)
Riki-Tiki ('*m.pl.*', m. E. Hunneke: Gai., 16/4/26)
Lumber Love ('*m.pl.*', m. B. and E. Adams: P.W., B'ham, 23/1/28; Lyc., 15/3/28)
[Numerous sketches and playlets produced at music-halls]

STILLWELL, JAMES
Bleak House (Margate, 26/11/03: +*W. RENSON*: dramatised from Charles Dickens' novel)

STIRLING, W. EDWARD [see also *D. K. BROSTER, C. LORE* and *F. B. YOUNG*]
The Mayflower (Rep., Plymouth, 30/8/20; Sur., 20/9/20; +*A. HAYES*) *1920*
Smiling Madame Beudet (Ambass., 16/10/21, Rep. Players: from *La souriante Madame Beudet* (1921) by D. Amiel and A. Obey)

STOBART, Mrs ST CLAIR (MABEL ANNIE)
×The Bushwife (St J., 4/6/09, *m.*)
×Meringues. *Fr. 1909*
×The Blessings of Balaam (St J., 4/6/09, *m.*)
When Eyes Are Opened (Kings., 24/3/22, Playwrights' Theatre)
The Dean's Dilemma ('*psychic pl.*': Steiner H., 26/10/26)

STOCK, RALPH
South of the Line (Q, 12/6/25)
Habit (Q, 25/10/26; Rep., B'ham, 30/3/29, rewritten as *Out of the Frying Pan*)
Chinook (Str., 20/2/27, Rep. Players: +*S. COLLINS*)
The Quest ('*c.*': Hippo., Margate, 15/12/27; Crit., 20/12/27)
Always Afternoon (Portsmouth, 12/11/28; Lyr., 5/2/29, revised with *C. B. FERNALD*)
Love in a Muddle ('*f.c.*': Brighton, 16/12/29: +*T. DE MARNEY*)
Search (Gar., 6/7/30, Venturers Soc.: +*T. DE MARNEY*)

STOCKS, MARY DANVERS
×Everyman of Everystreet ('*nativity pl.*') *1929*

STOKER, BRAM
The Mystery of the Sea (Lyc., 17/3/02, *cpy.*: dramatised from his novel, 1902)

STOKES, ELLA
×Marriage by Arrangement (Chiltern Arts Club, Amersham, 16/2/24)

STOKES, HUGH [see *M. DURAND*]

STOKES, JOHN
[A few sketches produced at music-halls]

STONE, GILBERT [see *C. MADDEN*]

STONE, SUZANNE

Mime Plays. *1930*

[This contains six short pieces: 1. *The Photograph*; 2. *Pandora's Box*; 3. *Pluto and Persephone*; 4. *The Princes in the Tower*; 5. *Lord Nithdale's Escape*; and 6. *Cinderella*]

STONEHILL, CHARLES

× Indictment. *1929*

STOPES, MARIE CHARLOTTE CARMICHAEL

Plays of Old Japan: The Nō. *1913*

[This contains translations, written in collaboration with Joji Sakurai, of three plays: 1. *The Maiden's Tomb*, by Kwanami Kiyotsugu; 2. *Kagekiyo*, by Seami Motokiyo; and 3. *The Sumida River*, by Motomasa. The last of these, with music composed by C. Raybould and described as an 'opera', was performed at the Rep., B'ham, 9/12/16]

Conquest; or, A Piece of Jade. *Fr. 1917*

'Gold in the Wood' and 'The Race' (*'plays of life'*) *1918*

Our Ostriches (Court, 14/11/23) *1923*

Vectia (*'banned pl.'*) *1926*

STORER, EDWARD

Three Plays of Luigi Pirandello. *1925*

[This contains: 1. *Right You Are (If You Think So)*; 2. *Six Characters in Search of an Author*; and 3. *Henry IV*. Of these, the third was presented at the Everyman, 15/7/25, and later at the Qns (as *The Mock Emperor*), 29/1/29]

STOREY, HAROLD

The Bargain (*'c.'*: W.G., New Brighton, 16/7/17: +*F. NORTON*)

STORM, CECIL

The Kommandatur (*'c.'*: Shak., L'pool, 8/3/15: +*I. CAMARSON*)

STORMONT, LEO [see *J. E. McMANUS*]

STORR, MARGUERITE [see *C. ELSTOB*]

STOUT, ETHEL ALMAR

Inheritance (K's H., 4/3/23, Interlude Players)

STRACHEY, GILES LYTTON

The Son of Heaven (*'t.md.'*: Scala, 12/7/25, Civic and Dram. Guild)

STRAIN, J. B.

× Finnigan's Fortune (Gai., Belfast, 29/6/25)

STRANGE, J. E.

Married midst Shot and Shell. LC, Pal., Stroud, 19/4/15: title later changed to *The Bride of the Battlefield* and *The War Bride*: +*J. WRIGHT*

The Unexpected Wife (Gr., Wath-on-Dearne, 27/3/16: title later changed to *The Unwilling Mother*)

Three Mothers. LC, Crook, 12/7/17
In the Grip of a Fiend. LC, Gr., Stalybridge, 1/7/18
A Mill Girl's Sacrifice. LC, Hippo., Bolton, 12/9/18

'STRANGE, MERLIN' [=*D. T. GLASSFORD*]
The Guinea-Pig ('*f.c.*': Rep., Nottingham, 20/10/21)
Raymond Lull, the Crusader ('*r.d.*': Rep., Nottingham, 2/6/24)

STRANGEWAYS, MARK
Socks ('*f.c.*': Pier, Brighton, 26/6/20, *m.*: title later changed to *Sally Darns the Socks*)

STRATFORD, SUSAN [see *J. DUFF*]

STRATTON, SIDNEY PEARSON
The Deadlock (Court, 18/1/10, *cpy.*)

STRATTON-PORTER, GENE [see *H. A. SAINTSBURY*]

STRAUSS, RITA
× In Bells and Motley ('*m.fant.*': m. W. Slaughter: Col., 18/12/05: +*T. F. G. COATES*) *1911* (in C. Bullivant, *Home Plays*)
× The Wooden Shoe (Crit., 15/3/07, *m.*)

STREATFIELD, Mrs ERIC [=*KITTY BARNE*]

STREATFIELD, NOEL
When Daydreams End ('*fant.*': D.P., Eastbourne, 13/1/16)

STREATFIELD, RUTH
× Toadstools ('*children's fairy pl.*': Drill H., Eastbourne, 22/12/13)

STREET, GEORGE SLYTHE
× Miss Brumshott's Engagement (P.W., 30/4/02)
Great Friends ('*c.*': Court, 30/1/05, St. Soc.)
× The Anonymous Letter (Vaud., 18/6/07: title later changed to *Enterprising Helen*)
The Bad Man (Imp. Pal., 9/2/14)
[A few sketches produced in music-halls]

STRODE, ELIZABETH [see *E. BALFOUR*]

[*STRONG, AUSTIN* [see also *LLOYD OSBOURNE*]
× The Drums of Oude ('*miniature md.*': Com., 6/4/06: called originally *Devil's Wind*) *Fr. 1923*
The Toymaker of Nuremberg ('*r.c.*': Playh., 15/3/10, *m.*) *1926* (in *The Drums of Oude and Other One-Act Plays*)
[This collection includes, besides the above-listed playlet and *The Drums of Oude*, *Popo* (a '*morality play in pantomime*') and *The Little Father of the Wilderness* (written in collaboration with *L. OSBOURNE*)]
The Mysterious Murder in the Mill; or Would You If You Could? (Theatrical Gdn Party, Regent's Park, 11/7/11: +*D. C. CALTHROP*)
Rip Van Winkle (Playh., 21/9/11)
Three Wise Fools ('*c.*': Parson's, Hartford, 13/10/18, as *Three Wise Men*; Crit., N.Y., 31/10/18; Worthing, 7/7/19; Com., 12/7/19) *Fr. 1919*

A Good Little Devil ('*fairy pl.*': Dalston, 2/12/12, '*preliminary pfce.*')
Seventh Heaven (Apo., Atlantic City, 16/5/22; Booth, N.Y., 30/10/22; Str., 2/9/27) *1922*

STUART, AIMÉE
The Life Line ('*c.*': Q, 28/9/25; Crit., 8/4/26, as *The Cat's Cradle*: +*P. STUART*) *1929* (as *The Cat's Cradle*)
No Gentleman ('*c.*': St M., 8/3/27: +*P. STUART*)
Clara Gibbings ('*c.*': Vaud., 19/11/28: +*P. STUART*) *1929*
Her Shop ('*c.*': Crit., 7/2/29: +*P. STUART*) *1929*
Nine till Six (Arts, 22/1/30; Apo., 29/1/30 +*P. STUART*) *1930*

STUART, ALEC
Love and Sport. LC, Workman's H., Ferndale, 14/2/20: title later changed to *Why Pay Tax?*)

STUART, ARTHUR [see *E. FERRIS*]

STUART, CHARLES
The Bargain (Constitutional Club, Sevenoaks, 25/8/27, *amat.*)
×A Fair Sale (Constitutional Club, Sevenoaks, 25/8/27, *amat.*)

STUART, CONSTANCE
Comin' through the Rye (Cheltenham, 18/9/22; K's, Hamm., 30/10/22: dramatised from the novel (1875) by Helen Mathers)

'*STUART, COSMO*' [=*COSMO GORDON-LENNOX*]

STUART, DONALD
The Shadow (O.H., Manchester, 7/5/28; Emb., 20/11/28)

STUART, FRANK
Her Great Mistake (E. Oxford, 9/9/07)

STUART, GERALD VILLIERS [=*GERALD VILLIERS-STUART*]

STUART, M. B.
The Wolf. LC, Pal., Arbroath, 27/4/15

STUART, MURIEL
The Bond (Everyman, 19/8/30)

STUART, PHILIP [see *AIMÉE STUART*]

STUART, RALPH [see also *A. W. MARCHMONT*]
A Dollar Did It (Dalston, 11/10/12, '*provisional pfce.*')

STUART, ROBERT LOUIS
Orpheus ('*o.*', m. Monteverdi: Scala, 30/12/29) *1925*

STUDD, FREDERICK J.
Violette ('*m.c.*': Rock Picture House, Mansfield, 3/7/22)

STURGESS, ARTHUR
[For earlier plays see *H. E. D.* v, 586 and 818]
Lolo ('*c.o.*', m. J. M. Glover: P's, Manchester, 8/9/00; Bradford, 13/5/01, revised as *Loloh*; or, *The False Oracle*); Crown, Peckham, 3/3/02)
Les Saltimbanques; or, The Bohemians ('*c.o.*', m. L. Ganne; Northampton, 24/3/02)

×A General Joke (*'operatic comedyish skit'*: Kursaal, Bexhill, 29/3/02)
Jasper Bright, By Special Appointment (*'c.'*: Pleasure Gdns, Folkestone, 1/5/05; Aven., 6/5/05)
The Gay Lord Vergy (*'c.o.'*, m. C. Terrasse: Apo., 30/9/05)
Yellow Fog Island (*'m.pl.'*, m. W. H. C. Nation and N. Lambelet: Terry's, 29/9/06)
Lovely Lucerne, or, The Adventures of a Blue Diamond (*'ballet ext.'*: W.G., Blackpool, 11/7/10)

STURGIS, JULIAN RUSSELL
[For earlier plays see *H. E. D.* v, 586]
Much Ado about Nothing (*'o.'*, m. V. Stanford: C.G., 30/5/01) *1901*
The Cricket on the Hearth (*'o.'*, m. Sir A. Mackenzie: Royal Academy of Music, 6/6/13; Glasgow, 13/8/23)
×Fire Flies (*'o.'*, m. P. N. Miles: Vic R., Clifton, 13/10/24)

SUGDEN, CHARLES [='*MARY LE BONE*']
×A Limit of the Law (Gai., Manchester, 4/3/12)

SUGDEN, Mrs CHARLES
The Woman who was Bored (*'c.'*: W.G., Bournemouth, 21/11/05)

SULLIVAN, B. M.
×One Bad Little Quarter of an Hour. LC, T.H., Cheltenham, 21/3/21

SULLIVAN, JOHN J.
×The King of the Golden Mountains (*'children's pl.'*: New, Manchester, 29/12/13)

SULLIVAN, VERE
The Sign in the Sun (Reg., 3/5/25, Catholic Pl. Soc.)
The Twin (Everyman, 29/6/26: +*G. BRENCHLEY*)
The Village (*'c.'*: Q, 11/4/27; Glo., 18/7/27)

SULMAN, DOROTHY LLOYD
Bob-over-the-Wall (*'fairy pl.'*: Court, 10/7/15, *m.*) *Fr. 1920*

[*SUMMER, CHARLES*
The Natural Law (Parson's, Hartford, 15/5/15; Republic, N.Y. 3/4/15; Rochdale, 19/5/19: +*HOWARD HALL*)

SUMMERS, JOHN
Oliver Cromwell (*'historical d.'*) *1906*
Cupid's Carnival, or, What is Love? (*'c.o.'*) *1924*

SUMMERS, WALTER
[For earlier plays see *H. E. D.* v, 587]
×Oberine; or The Nymph of the Adriatic (*'ext.'*: Court, L'pool, 21/12/01)
×The Sultan of Ranogoo (*'m.pl.'*: Hippo., L'pool, 6/7/03)

SURFIELD, G. C. [see *H. K. CAMPBELL*]

SURRAGE, LYDDON
The Paying Guest (*'f.c.'*: Lecture H., Faversham, 8/10/23)
×Birds of Prey (Gar., 2/3/24, Sunday Players)
The Singer in the Street (Pier, Herne Bay, 23/6/24)

SUTCLIFFE, J. J. SPENCER
[A few sketches produced at music-halls]

SUTHERLAND, Duchess of [=*R. E. FYFFE*]

SUTHERLAND, EVELYN GREENLEAF [see *B. M. DIX* and *B. TARKINGTON*]
Stigmata ('*miracle pl.*': Court, 31/7/09, *cpy.*; Brighton, 21/1/24; Hippo., Golder's Green, 12/5/24: +*B. M. DIX* and *E. UNSELL*)
Young Fernald ('*c.*': New, 28/9/10: +*B. M. DIX*)
×His Own (Cent., 22/2/26)

SUTRO, ALFRED [see also *R. MARSHALL*]
[For an earlier play see *H. E. D.* v, 588]
×Carrots (Dublin, 18/10/00; P'cess of W., Kennington, 21/11/00; Gar., 22/4/02) *Fr. 1904*
The Cave of Illusion. *1900.*
×A Marriage Has Been Arranged (H., 6/5/02) *Fr. 1904*
The Death of Tintagiles ('*t.*': St G's H., 22/7/02: translated from the play (1894 by M. Maeterlinck) *1907*
Arethusa ('*f.c.*': K's, Hamm., 25/5/03)
The Walls of Jericho (Gar., 31/10/04) *Fr. 1904*
Aglavaine and Selysette (Court, 15/11/04: translated from the play (1896) by M. Maeterlinck) *Fr. 1904* (acting version)
×A Maker of Men (St J., 27/1/05). *Fr. 1905*
Mollentrave on Women ('*c.*': St J., 13/2/05) *Fr. 1905*
×The Correct Thing (D.L., 29/6/05, *m.*; Shaft., 4/11/05: originally licensed for the Metro., Camberwell, 19/9/01) *Fr. 1905*
×The Salt of Life. *Fr. 1905*
×A Game of Chess. *Fr. 1905*
The Perfect Lover (Imp., 14/10/05) *1905* (priv.); *Fr. 1905*
The Fascinating Mr Vanderveldt ('*c.*': Com., 4/1/06, *cpy.*; Gar., 26/4/06) *Fr. 1906*
×The Open Door. *Fr. 1906*
×Ella's Apology (Bloomsbury H., 8/11/06) *Fr. 1905*
John Glayde's Honour (St J., 8/3/07) *Fr. 1907*
×Mr Steinmann's Corner (H.M., 4/6/07, *m.*: originally licensed for Qns Gate H., 27/2/05) *Fr. 1905*
×A Lonely Life (Qns, Manchester, 22/7/07) *1903 (priv.)*
The Barrier (Com., 10/10/07) *Fr. 1908*
×The Romantic Barber (Dublin, 2/3/08: Gr., Fulham, 23/3/08)
×The Man on the Kerb (Aldw., 24/3/08, *m.*) *Fr. 1908*
×The Gutter of Time (Pav., Eastbourne, 3/8/08) *Fr. 1905*
The Builder of Bridges (St J., 11/11/08) *1908 (priv.)*; *Fr. 1921*
Making a Gentleman ('*c.*': Gar., 11/9/09)
×Alladine and Palomides (translated from the play (1894) by M. Maeterlinck) *1909*
Monna Vanna (Court, 1/6/11, *m.*, Women's Aerial League; Qns, 21/7/14: from the play (1902) by M. Maeterlinck) *1904*
The Perplexed Husband ('*c.*': Wynd., 12/9/11) *Fr. 1913*
×The Man in the Stalls (Pal., 2/10/11) *Fr. 1911*
The Firescreen ('*c.*': Gar., 7/2/12) *Fr. 1912*

×The Bracelet (Rep., L'pool, 26/2/12) *Fr. 1912*
The Two Virtues ('*c.*': St J., 5/3/14) *Fr. 1914*
The Clever Ones ('*c.*': Wynd., 23/4/14)
Rude Min and Christine ('*c.*') *1915* (*priv.*)
[This was called later *The Two Miss Farndons* and *Uncle Anyhow*: see below]
Freedom. *1916*
[Apparently this play had been written in 1914]
×The Great Redding Street Burglary (Col., 31/7/16)
The Two Miss Farndons ('*c.*': Gai., Manchester, 21/5/17; H., 1/5/18, as *Uncle Anyhow*) *Fr. 1919* (as *Uncle Anyhow*)
[This play was called originally *Rude Min and Christine*: as such, it was printed in 1915]
×The Marriage...will not take place (Col., 13/8/17) *Fr. 1917*
×The Trap (Col., 11/3/18)
The Choice (Wynd., 8/9/19) *1920*
The Laughing Lady ('*c.*': Glo., 17/11/22) *1922*
The Great Well (New, 19/12/22) *1922*
Far Above Rubies ('*c.*': Com., 27/3/24) *1924*
The Man with a Heart (Wynd., 14/3/25) *1925*
The Desperate Lovers ('*frivolous c.*': Com., 28/1/27) *1927*
Living Together ('*c.*': K's, Southsea, 14/1/29; Wynd., 29/1/29) *1928* (*priv.*); *1929*
×The Blackmailing Lady. *Fr. 1929*

SUTTON, E. GRAHAM
×Pierrotesque. LC, Bristol, 10/9/14

SUTTON, HAROLD
×The Recoil (Woodside H., N. Finchley, 10/1/14, *amat.*)

SUTTON-VANE, — [see *SUTTON VANE*]
[*Who's Who in the Theatre* describes *VANE SUTTON-VANE* as the 'son of the late Sutton-Vane', but it would appear that the latter's first name was, in fact, 'Sutton' and that he never indulged in any hyphenation]

SUTTON-VANE, VANE HUNT
[There are several uncertainties concerning the first five plays in the following list. The entry concerning this dramatist in *Who's Who in the Theatre* gives *His Heart in Japan* as his first dramatic work, but it seems certain that he was responsible for *The Persian Cat* (credited to 'V. H. Sutton Vane') and *The Girl Who Grew Younger* (credited to 'Vane Sutton-Vane'). The other three appeared as by 'Sutton Vane' but the fact that there is a gap of several years between the last playlet which can indubitably be given to Sutton Vane the elder and *The Lost Chord* may suggest that his son started his career with that play]
×The Lost Chord (Worcester, 23/11/06, *cpy.*: +*A. R. CARLTON*)
The Blossom of Brittany ('*c.o.*', m. E. Jones: Brighton, 25/6/07, *cpy.*)

The Lady of Kensington ('*c.*': Lyr., Hamm., 3/4/08, *cpy.*)
The Persian Cat ('*c.o.*', m. H. Bailey: Hippo., Brighton, 26/1/09, *cpy.*)
The Girl Who Grew Younger ('*farcical absurdity*': Chatham, 5/6/11)
His Heart in Japan ('*spectacular d.*': Smethwick, 3/7/11; Woolwich, 17/7/11; Lyr., Hamm., 24/7/11)
Very Much Married (Little, 20/6/12)
The Blow (Little, 3/4/15)
By All Means, Darling ('*light c.*': Hippo., Margate, 20/9/20; Com., 29/7/21)
[At the production in Margate this play seems to have been credited to '*RALPH PRITCHETT*', possibly a pseudonym used on that particular occasion by Sutton-Vane]
×A Case of Diamonds ('*detective pl.*': Pal., Ramsgate, 7/11/21; Wimbledon, 13/11/22)
Outward Bound ('*fant.*': Everyman, 17/9/23; Gar., 15/10/23: originally called *The Tide*) *1924*
Falling Leaves ('*c.*': Pleasure Gdns, Folkestone, 2/6/24; Little, 25/11/24) *1924*
Overture ('*fant.*': Everyman, 11/4/25) *1925*
I'll Tell You a Story ('*fant. c.*': Worthing, 13/7/25)
Regatta (O.H., Blackpool, 5/12/27; P.W., 17/1/28)
The Key to Happiness ('*c.*': Newcastle, 21/10/29)

SWAIN, C. R.
×With a View to Matrimony (P.H., Stevenage, 4/12/07, *amat.*)

SWAN, ANNIE S.
Aldersyde. LC, St Andrew's H., Glasgow, 11/2/20
[It is not certain whether this dramatisation of Annie S. Swan's novel of 1883 was or was not made by her]

SWAN, MARK E. [see also *G. BROADHURST*]
Whose Baby Are You? (Leamington, 2/4/14; Pal., Chelsea, 13/7/14, as *Whose Is It?*)

SWAN, SIDNEY H.
×The Last Chapter (Passmore Edwards Settlement, 4/3/05, *amat.*)

SWEARS, HERBERT [see also *E. BURNEY*]
[For earlier plays see *H. E. D.* v, 589]
×Such is Fame (Guildhall School of Music, 23/3/01; St G's H., 1/3/02) *Fr. 1899*
×Too Many Cooks. *Fr. 1902*
×The Mere Man. *Fr. 1904*
×Two on a Bus. *Fr. 1905*
A Tight Corner ('*c.*': Portsmouth, 9/5/06; Cor., 29/4/07) *Fr. 1910*
×Hero and Heroine ('*melodramatic absurdity*': Scala, 13/12/05; Pal., 22/1/09) *Fr. 1911*
×The Nonsensor (Emp., 2/12/07)
×Pansy: That's for Thoughts ('*impression*': Playh., 6/6/07, *m.*) *Fr. 1903*

The Whirlpool (New, Cardiff, 22/2/08; Marlb., Holloway, 21/9/08)
The House of Clay (H.M., Blackpool, 24/4/08; Cor., 2/10/08: adapted from *La maison d'argile* (1907) by E. E. Fabre)
×Granny's Juliet (47 Brook St., 23/5/11) *Fr. 1911*
The Unknown Quantity (Pier, Brighton, 6/12/15) *Fr. 1916*
×Dog Days. *Fr. 1915*
Captain X ('*f.*': Rep., Plymouth, 12/4/20; K's H., 29/1/21, Bancroft Dramatic Club) *Fr. 1920*
×Who Laughs Last. LC, Emp., 7/6/20
×Cupboard Love. LC, Crippl. Inst., 1/11/22. *Fr. 1922*
×Tit-Bits. LC, Crippl. Inst., 1/11/22. *Fr. 1922*
×Widows. LC, Crippl. Inst., 1/11/22. *Fr. 1922*
×The Young Idea. LC, Crippl. Inst., 1/11/22. *Fr. 1922*
A Disturber of Traffic ('*c.*': New, 25/5/23, *m.*)
×Woman's Crowning Glory. *Fr. 1926*
×Things Are Seldom What They Seem. *Fr. 1927*
×The Anniversary. *Fr. 1930*
×Dumb Jewels. *Fr. 1930*
×Interlude. *Fr. 1930*

SWEENEY, AUSTIN GILLOW
First-Fiddle Forshaw ('*c.*': Park, Hanwell, 26/11/19)

SWETE, E. LYALL [see *R. N. STEPHENS*]
Pitch and – Soap ('*c.*': H., 16/4/12)
The Philatelist (Kings., 24/9/22, Interlude Players)

'*SWIFT, J. F.*' [=*GODFREY MARKS*]
×The Lady Councillor: or, Urban Urbanity ('*oa.*': Concert H., Liscard, 2/4/00)

SWINLEY, ION
×The Aspirations of Archibald (D.P., Eastbourne, 28/6/09; Clavier H., 3/7/12)
×The Lady of the Shadowed Hill (Kings., 21/7/11, *m.*)
Keepers of the Garden ('*c.*': K's H., 10/11/12, Playfellows; Rep., B'ham, 9/10/15)
The Lifting of the Dark (Lyr., Hamm., 14/12/19, Curtain Group)
×The Man in the Chair (Sav., 11/2/21, *m.*; Col., 24/4/22)
The Lonely Piper (Kings., 28/9/24, *amat.*)

SYDENHAM, AIMÉE
The Course of True Love ('*f.*': St Peter's H., Bournemouth, 13/3/24, *amat.*)
×The Specialist (St Peter's H., Bournemouth, 13/3/24, *amat.*)
×Yesterday and Today. LC, Alex. Lodge, Bournemouth, 6/6/25

SYDNEY, FRED W.
Colonel Clay ('*c.*': P's, Manchester, 25/5/03)

SYDNEY, HERBERT
The Vicar's Wife (Junction, Manchester, 29/11/15; Woolwich, 24/4/16; E.C., 26/6/16)
[A few sketches produced at music-halls]

SYDNEY, SYDNEY

Miss Lancashire, Ltd. ('*f.*': Gr., Croydon, 4/9/05: title later changed to *Jane the Duchess*)

[A few sketches produced at music-halls]

SYKES, ARTHUR A. [=*W. SCOTT*]

The Inspector-General ('*c.*': Scala, 17/6/06, St. Soc.: translated from N. V. Gogol, *Revizor*) *1892*

×The Bear (Kings., 13/5/11: translated from A. Chekhov, *Medved* (1888))

SYKES, CLAUDE

Magda (D.P., Eastbourne, 12/12/07: translated from *Die Heimat* (1893) by H. Sudermann)

SYKES, ERNEST A.

The Lady's Maid ('*m.c.*': St Michael's H., Northampton, 16/11/05: +*R. G. NEAL*)

Cinderella ('*m.ext.*': Guildhall, Northampton, 24/4/16)

SYKES, J. A. C.

The Disarranger ('*f.*': H.M., Carlisle, 28/5/09)

SYKES, PERCIVAL H. T.

[For earlier plays see *H. E. D.* v, 589]

[Numerous playlets produced at music-halls]

SYLVAINE, VERNON

The Phantom Fear (H.M., 31/7/28: +*S. LYNN*)

×The Road of Poplars (Playh., L'pool, 3/5/30) *1930*

SYLVESTER, PAUL

×Anthony Dean's Double (H., 11/6/06)

SYMON, DUDLEY J.

The Tragedy of Guido Fawkes (St James' Church H., Britannia Row, 15/1/10, *amat.*)

The Curse of Carados ('*m.c.*', m. F. J. Bodilly: St James' Church H., Britannia Row, 9/1/11, *amat.*)

SYMONDS, EMILY MORSE [='*GEORGE PASTON*']

SYMONDS, P. BIDDULPH

Four to One ('*f.c.*': Helne Church R., Worthing, 17/5/12, *amat.*: +*S. C. MITCHELL*)

×The Keeper of the Keys (Emp., Littlehampton, 4/11/13)

SYMONDS, VERNON

The Legend of Abd-el-Krim. *1930* (*priv.*)

SYMONS, ARTHUR

[For an earlier play see *H. E. D.* v, 589]

The Dead City ('*t.*': Court, 25/2/18, St. Soc.: translated from *La Citta morta* (1898) by G. D'Annunzio) *1900*

Gioconda (translated from the play (1899) by G. D'Annunzio) *1901*

Francesca da Rimini (translated from the play (1901) by G. D'Annunzio) *1902*

×The Fool of the World ('*morality*': Bij., 7/4/06, New Stage Club) *1906*
×Cleopatra in Judea (Bij., 6/5/07, English Drama Soc.) *1916*
×Electra ('*t.*': New, 27/11/08, *m.*: translated from the play (1903) by H. von Hofmannsthal)
The Dawn ('*t.*': translated from *Les Aubes* (1898) by E. Verhaeren) *1915*
Tragedies. *1916*
[This contains three verse plays: 1. *The Harvesters*; 2. *The Death of Agrippina*; and 3. *Cleopatra in Judea*. For the last of these, see above]
The Toy Cart (Qns, 9/7/16, St. Soc.: adapted from *Mrichchakati* by Sudraka) *1919* (Dublin)
Tristan and Iseult. *1917*

SYMS, H. [see *J. GAY*]

SYNGE, JOHN MILLINGTON
×In the Shadow of the Glen (Molesworth H., Dublin, 8/10/03; Roy., 26/3/04, Irish Nat. Theatre Soc.) *1904* (in *Samhain*, no. 4, Dec. 1904); *1905* (Dublin); *1910*
[This play has also been printed and acted as *The Shadow of the Glen*]
×Riders to the Sea (Molesworth H., Dublin, 25/1/04; Roy., 26/3/04, Irish Nat. Theatre Soc.) *1903* (in *Samhain*, no. 3, Sept. 1903; *1905* (Dublin)
The Well of the Saints (Abbey, Dublin, 4/2/05; St G's H., 27/11/05, Abbey Theatre company) *1905* (Dublin)
The Playboy of the Western World ('*c.*': Abbey, Dublin, 26/1/07; Gt. Qn St., 10/6/07, Irish Nat. Theatre Soc.) *1907* (Dublin)
The Tinker's Wedding ('*c.*': H.M., 11/11/09, *m.*, Afternoon Theatre) *1907* (Dublin)
Deirdre of the Sorrows ('*t.*': Abbey, Dublin, 13/1/10; Court, 30/5/10) *1910* (Churchtown, *priv.*); *1910* (Dublin)

SYRETT, NETTA
The Finding of Nancy (St J., 8/5/02)
Six Fairy Plays for Children. *1904*
[This contains: 1. *The Dream-Lady* ('*pastoral*': Hermitage, Barnes, 13/7/12, *amat.*); 2. *Little Bridget*; 3. *White Magic* (St J., 10/1/05); 4. *The Wonderful Rose*; 5. *The Gift of the Fairies* (LC, Alb. H., 26/1/04); and 6. *In Arcady*]
×The Younger Generation (Terry's, 3/2/06)
The Fairy Doll and Other Plays for Children. *1906*
[This contains five one-act plays: 1. *The Fairy Doll* (Court, 29/12/13, Children's Theatre); 2. *Christmas in the Forest*; 3. *The Christening of Rosalys*; 4. *The Enchanted Garden* (Court, 29/12/13, Children's Theatre); and 5. *The Strange Boy* (Court, 29/12/13, Children's Theatre)
×Might is Right (H., 13/11/09)
Robin Goodfellow, and Other Fairy Plays for Children. *1918*
[This contains two three-act plays and four shorter pieces:

1. *Robin Goodfellow*; 2. *Princess Fragoletta*; 3. *The Old Toys* (LC, K. G's H., 11/12/24); 4. *Venus and Cupid*; 5. *The Dryad's Awakening*; and 6. *Queen Flora's Court* (a '*masque of flowers*')]
×The Two Domestics. LC, Cripp. Inst., 1/11/22. *Fr. 1922*
×The Two Elizabeths (Sanderstead, 8/11/24, *amat.*) *1924*

TABER, R. [see *J. GLEASON*]

TABRAR, JOSEPH
[A few sketches produced at music-halls]

TAGORE, Sir RABINDRANATH
×The Post Office (Abbey, Dublin, 17/5/13; Court, 10/7/13: translated by *DEVABRATA MUKERJEE*) *1916* (Churchtown, *priv.*)
The King of the Dark Chamber. *1914*
The Cycle of Spring. *1917*
Sacrifice, and Other Plays. *1917*
[This contains four short plays: 1. *Sanyasi, or, The Ascetic*; 2. *Malini* (Grafton Galleries, 8/6/15, Indian Dramatic Soc.); 3. *Sacrifice* (K. G's H., 9/2/18, Indian Dramatic Soc.); and 4. *The King and the Queen* (Com., 12/2/19, Indian Dramatic Soc.)]
×Autumn Festival (Wigmore H., 6/3/20, Union of East and West)
×Chitra. (LC, P.W., 28/4/20.) *1913* (in *The Royal India and Pakistan Society Papers*, iii); *1914*
×The Mother's Prayer (Wigmore H., 28/7/20, Union of East and West) *1919* (in *The Modern Review*, June, 1919); *1919* (Calcutta)
×The Farewell Curse (Wigmore H., 28/7/20, Union of East and West Indian Dram. Soc.)
×The Deserted Mother (Wigmore H., 28/7/20, Union of East and West Indian Dram. Soc.)
×The Sinner (Wigmore H., 28/7/20, Union of East and West Indian Dram. Soc.)
×Suttee (Wigmore H., 28/7/20, Union of East and West Indian Dram. Soc.)
Trial by Luck. LC, Wigmore H., 17/10/21
×The Farewell (D.P., Eastbourne, 4/9/24)
[His *Collected Poems and Plays* appeared in 1936]

TALBOT, ALFRED JULIAN [see also *H. F. RUBINSTEIN*]
×In the Outer Darkness (Mary Ward Settlement, 23/2/24, Dramatic Art Centre) *Fr. 1930*
×Emily's Excuse (LC, K. G's H., 23/10/24: A.L.S. Travelling Theatre, 1924) *1926*
×Red Oleanders. *1925*
×Incorrigible. *1926* (in *The Marble God and Other One-Act Plays*)
The Iron Duke ('*chronicle pl.*') *1926*
×The Mannequin Doll; or, The Wax Peach ('*oa.*', m. C. Wallace: St Pancras People's Theatre, 12/5/27)

×The Old Firm's Awakening (A.L.S. Travelling Theatre, 1926; Little, 14/5/28) *1927*
×Daniel in the Lionesses' Den (A.L.S. Travelling Theatre, 1927) *Fr. 1929*
×A Social Evening. *Fr. 1928*
×The White Hope's Quandary. *Fr. 1928*
×November the Tenth. *Fr. 1928*
×The Fur Coat. *Fr. 1928*
×In a Dentist's Waiting-Room. *Fr. 1928*
×White Jasmine. *Fr. 1929*
×The Casket Scene Up-to-date. *Fr. 1929*
×At the Pit Door (Playh., L'pool, 25/11/30) *Fr. 1930*
×The Betrothal of the Princess. *Fr. 1930*
×The Duke of Cul-de-sac. *Fr. 1930*
×The Passing of Galatea. *Fr. 1930*
×A Quarter of an Hour. *Fr. 1930*
×The Ray of Reason. *Fr. 1930*
×The Spartan Girl. *Fr. 1930*

TALBOT, F. A.
The Miser's Daughter (Great H., Tunbridge Wells, 16/10/00: +*J. WARNER*)

TALBOT, GEORGE
×Annerly's Bride (T.H., W. Hampstead, 18/3/11, *amat.*)
×A Singer of Songs (Rehearsal, 7/5/14)

TALBOT, HARRY
×For a Child's Sake (Castle Pav., Littlehampton, 19/6/11)
×At Willow Creek (Castle Pav., Littlehampton, 19/6/11)
[Several sketches produced at music-halls]

TALFOURD, M.
×The Heart of a Songbird (Eastbourne, 26/1/01)

TAMWORTH, JOAN
The Lover from Japan ('*c.o.*': m. A. Standford: Royal Academy of Music, 14/3/18)

TANNER, BERYL
×A Well-Matched Pair. *Fr. 1911*

TANNER, GEORGE S.
Mrs Duncombe's Past (Borough H., Godalming, 22/4/05, *amat.*)
The Old Lady (County H., Guildford, 15/10/07, *amat.*)
×Li 'Iggs (Vic. H., 23/1/08)
Let Furnished ('*f.c.*': County H., Guildford, 27/11/08, *amat.*)

TANNER, JAMES T. [see also '*CRYPTOS*']
[For earlier plays see *H. E. D.* v, 590–1]
The Messenger Boy ('*m.c.*', m. I. Caryll and L. Monckton: Gai., 3/2/00: +*A. MURRAY*)
The Toreador ('*m.c.*', m. I. Caryll and L. Monckton: Gai., 17/6/01: +*H. NICHOLLS*)
A Country Girl: or Town and Country ('*m.pl.*', m. L. Monckton: Daly's, 18/1/02)

The Orchid (‘*m.c.*’, m. I. Caryll and L. Monckton: Gai., 26/10/03,
The Cingalee; or, Sunny Ceylon (‘*m.pl.*’, m. L. Monckton: Daly’s, 5/3/04)
The New Aladdin (‘*m.ext.*’, m. I. Caryll and L. Monckton: Gai., 29/9/06: +*W. H. RISQUE*)
The Quaker Girl (‘*m.pl.*’, m. L. Monckton: Adel., 5/11/10)
The Dancing Mistress (‘*m.pl.*’, m. L. Monckton: Adel., 19/10/12)
The Girl on the Film (‘*m.pl.*’, m. W. Kollo: Gai., 5/4/13)
The Girl from Utah (‘*m.pl.*’, m. S. Jones and P. A. Rubens: Adel., 18/10/13)

TANNER, L. E.
×Bubble and Squeak. LC, ‘*oa.*’: P.H., Clevedon, 18/12/25

[*TARKINGTON, BOOTH*
Monsieur Beaucaire (‘*r.c.*’: Shak., L’pool, 6/10/02; Com. 25/10/02: adapted by *E. G. SUTHERLAND*)

TARPEY, W. KINGSLEY
Windmills (‘*eccentric c.*’: Com., 17/6/01, St. Soc.; Crit., 13/10/06, as *The Amateur Socialist*)
×The Collaborators (Crit., 5/11/06)

TATE, HARRY
[Several sketches produced at music-halls]

TATE, J. W.
[Several sketches produced at music-halls]

TAUNTON, WINFRIDE TRAFFORD
The Chichester Case (T.H., Hunstanton, 13/9/22)

TAYLER, ALISTAIR N. [see also *C. BROOKING*]
×As Played before His Highness (P’s, Manchester, 4/5/04)
×The Use of Poets (Com., 18/7/01, *m.*)

TAYLOR, BEN
[A few sketches and playlets produced at music-halls]

TAYLOR, CECIL H. [see *W. A. BRABNER*]
×The Reptile’s Devotion (Qns, Leeds, 9/7/08, *cpy.*; Emp., Gainsborough, 19/10/08)

TAYLOR, EMILY
Kitty of Ours (O.H., Harrogate, 30/10/12)
×Liza (Vic. Pal., 18/8/18)

TAYLOR, FRANK
The Carthaginian (‘*t.*’: Little, Sheffield, 12/11/23) *1916*
×The Last Name (St Pancras People’s Theatre, 12/5/27)

TAYLOR, GERTRUDE WINIFRED
The Real Marlborough (‘*character study*’) *1927*
×Pilate (‘*Passion pl.*’) *1928*
Joseph of Arimathea (‘*Passion pl.*’) *1930*

TAYLOR, HELEN
×Two of Us (Stedman’s Academy, 25/4/11, *amat.*)

TAYLOR, J. BELL
Hold Baby ('*f.*': O.H., Southport, 18/6/28; Hippo., Golder's Green, 23/7/28: + *T. HERON*)

[*TAYLOR, LEILA MANNING*
Echo (Rep., B'ham, 14/9/29)

TAYLOR, LOUIS
[A few playlets produced at music-halls]

TAYLOR, RICA BROMLEY [see *R. BROMLEY-TAYLOR*]

TAYLOR, T. W.
A Colonel's Heroic Sin ('*m.d.*': O.H., Blackpool, 8/3/05, *cpy.*)

TCHERNINE, ODETTE
Michael Makes Good. LC, Sav., 28/7/17
Back Windows. LC, Sav., 4/1/18
× The Kaiser, the Dream and the Devil. LC, Sav., 19/7/18
The Return. LC, Sav., 19/7/18
The Storm (Ambass., 5/6/19, British and International Theatre Association)
The Test. LC, Sav., 22/10/18

TEARLE, GODFREY
× A Waiting Game (D.Y., 3/6/11, *cpy.*; Pav., 4/9/11)

TEBB, BEATRICE HAYDEN
Man's Heritage (Rehearsal, 28/4/10)
× The Machinations of Maria (Rehearsal, 28/4/10)
Betty (Rehearsal, 28/4/10)

TEMPLE, FLORENCE [see *S. WHYTE*]

TEMPLE, FORTUNIO
The Tale of Sir Launfal ('*pageant*': Hampstead Gdn Suburb, 19/6/26)

TEMPLE, JOAN [see *Baroness VON HUTTEN*]
The Plunge (RADA, 12/2/22: dramatised from the novel (1921) by St John Welles Lucas)
× The Lesson (RADA, 5/10/24)
The Widow's Cruise ('*c.*': Ambass., 3/3/26) *1926*
Aspidistras (Str., 5/12/26, Rep. Players; Sav., 22/7/27, as *The Cage*)
A Hen upon a Steeple ('*c.*': Glo., 23/3/27)
Charles and Mary (Everyman, 4/2/30; Glo., 28/2/30) *1930*

TEMPLE, V.
Some Day (P.W., Salford, 1/2/07)

TERRISS, TOM
× In Gay Paree (Gai., 6/2/01, *cpy.*)
× The Agony Column (Gai., 6/2/01, *cpy.*)
A Woman of the World (Lyr., 13/6/03, *cpy.*)

TERRY, HERBERT E.
[A few sketches produced at music-halls]

TERRY, J. E. HAROLD [see also *L. WORRALL*]
×A King's Ransom (Pallad., 12/6/11)
×The Knight of the Garter (Tiv., 3/3/13)
×April Fools (Vaud., 11/6/15)
General Post ('*c.*': D.P., Eastbourne, 26/2/17; H., 14/3/17) *1917*
×Master Wayfarer ('*happening of long ago*': Apo., 4/12/17, *m.*; Qns, 20/4/18: +*A. S. CRAVEN*) *Fr. 1921*
The Fulfilling of the Law (Pal., Ramsgate, 11/2/21; Gar., 23/2/21)
The Rattlesnake ('*r.pl.*': York, 4/11/21; Shaft., 10/1/22: +*R. SABATINI*)
The Return of Sherlock Holmes (Playh., Cardiff., 1/10/23; P's, 9/10/23: +*A. ROSE*)
Collusion (Bournemouth, 18/2/24; Ambass., 1/4/24) *1930*
The Carolinian (Bonstelle, Detroit, 5/10/25; Sam H. Harris, N.Y., 2/11/25: +*R. SABATINI*) *1925*
Insult (Little, 15/4/30: +*H. TIGHE*: adapted from *Dolle Hans* (1916) by Jan Fabricius) *1930*
[*Who's Who in the Theatre* cites as his first play *Old Rowley the King* (1908) but this has not been located]

TERRY, MURIEL
The Artist, the Jester and the Girl. LC, '*oa.*': Col., 31/12/20
The Knave of Hearts and Arts. LC, Kings., 30/6/24: +*C. L. MACDONA*

TERRY, WILLIAM HENRY
The Insurrection ('*historical pl.*') *1927* (*priv.*)
The Interregnum ('*historical d.*') *1928*
[This is a lengthy trilogy, the three parts being called *The Great Crime*, *The Power of the Sword*, and *The Return of the Gown*]

THACKWELL, A. J.
Birds of a Feather ('*c.*': Pal., Redditch, 21/9/16, *amat.*)

THANE, EDWARD [see also *W. BAILEY*]
The Slave of Sin ('*md.*': Gr., Chorley, 30/1/01, *cpy.*; Halifax, 29/7/01; W.L., 5/6/06, as *The Worst of All Women*: also called *A Daughter of the Devil* and *The Love that Lasts for Ever*)
The Mockery of Marriage (Gr., Chorley, 31/1/01, *cpy.*; W.L., 10/3/02; Emp., Camberwell, 12/8/12, condensed into one act)
Every Inch a Man (K's, Hoxton, 12/2/06)
Lured to London; or, Natty the Hoxton Boy (K's, Hoxton, 1/10/06)
Dark Deeds of the Night (Stratford, 17/8/08)
×At England's Command (Qns, Poplar, 24/8/08)
×Bitter Enemies (Qns, Poplar, 29/3/09)
×Aunt Sally (Muncaster, Bootle, 25/11/09
×Bella Runs Away (Gr., Clapham, 20/3/11)
×A Case for Divorce (Emp., Camberwell, 10/7/11: +'*F. L. S.*')
A White Slave (Star, Swansea, 9/12/12; Lyr., Hamm., 3/3/13)
The Man who Came Between ('*md.*': Qns, Poplar, 28/7/13)
The Queen of the Air ('*md.*': Alex., B'ham, 8/12/13; Stratford, 22/12/13)

THARP, R. C.

The Queen of the Fair ('*c.o.*', m. B. Horsfall: Emp., Camberwell, 7/3/10)

THERVAL, LAURENCE [see also *J. J. BELL*]

The Cardinal's Guard (Leamington, 12/3/15)

THIRKELL, ANGELA

Uplifted (Sheffield, 23/3/23; Brixton, 28/9/23: adapted from *L'élévation* (1917) by H. Bernstein)

THOMAS, Mrs

A Romance of Chalvedune (Chaldon, 19/6/20, *m.*, *amat.*)

[*THOMAS, ALBERT ELLSWORTH*

Her Husband's Wife ('*light c.*': Broad St., Philadelphia, 14/2/10; Glo., 14/2/10, *cpy.*; New, 5/9/16) *Fr. 1921*

The Rainbow (D.Y., 26/2/12, *cpy.*)

Come Out of the Kitchen ('*c.*': Columbia, San Francisco, 14/8/16; Cohan, N.Y., 23/10/16; New, Oxford, 16/2/20; Str., 15/3/20) *Fr. 1921*

[*THOMAS, AUGUSTUS*

Arizona (Adel., 3/2/02)

Beside the Bonnie Brier Bush (Shak., L'pool, 3/4/05; St J., 27/12/06: +*J. McARTHUR*)

De Lancy (Vaud., 4/9/05, *cpy.*)

×A Man of the World (Cardiff, 18/9/05; Com., 27/9/05)

On the Quiet (Cardiff, 18/9/05; Com., 27/9/05)

The Earl of Pawtucket ('*c.*': Playh., 25/6/07)

THOMAS, BERTE W.

[For earlier plays see *H. E. D.* v, 595]

Anna (Bij., 30/10/03, *cpy.*)

A Little Brown Branch ('*c.*': Court, 14/12/04)

×Planchette (Court, 21/11/13)

×For My Country (Emp., Shoreditch, 28/5/17)

THOMAS, BERTHA

×The Lucky Sister ('*fairy pl.*') *1904*

THOMAS, BRANDON

[For earlier plays see *H. E. D.* v, 595–6]

Women Are So Serious ('*c.*': Court, 31/5/01)

×Fourchette and Company (O.H., Northampton, 21/11/04; Com., 5/12/04)

A Judge's Memory (Terry's, 13/3/06)

×Thespis Cottage (O.H., Cheltenham, 6/5/11)

×Marusa (Marlb., Holloway, 7/3/12, *cpy.*: B'ham, 31/5/12; P.W., 20/12/13)

THOMAS, EVELYN

Roses of Picardy ('*m.pl.*': Hippo., Cannock, 5/8/18; Stratford, 3/3/19)

Friend o' Mine (Glo., Deal, 19/1/20; Stratford, 26/2/20)

Sands of the Desert ('*m.pl.*': Pal., Weston, 22/3/20)

THOMAS, F. C.
×A Knotty Question (*'f.c.'*: P.H., Woking, 26/11/04)

THOMAS, F. W. [see *A. A. HURGON*]

THOMAS, G. BRUCE
×A Rose of Chinatown (Crane H., L'pool, 11/11/19, *amat.*)

THOMAS, GLADYS
Cyrano de Bergerac (*'r.c.'*: K's, Edin., 3/3/19; Gar., 28/3/19: +*M. E. GUILLEMAND*: adapted from the play (1897) by E. Rostand)

THOMAS, Mrs HAIG
×A Decadent Duologue (Lyc. Club, 30/3/09)

THOMAS, HERBERT
Lady Emma's Romance (*'light c.'*: Bournemouth, 4/2/18; St J., 16/5/21, as *Emma*; Col. 8/4/18, condensed into one act under the title of *Stopping the Breach*)
Out of Hell (Parson's, N.Y., 6/5/18, as *My Boy*; Eltinge, N.Y., 20/8/18, as *Under Orders*; Ambass., 5/1/18)
Sinners Both (Gr., Croydon, 19/9/18; Kings., 16/3/20)
My Son (D.P., Eastbourne, 12/12/21; Ambass., 2/2/22)
The Law of Moses (Pleasure Gdns, Folkestone, 12/2/23)

THOMAS, LEOPOLD
The Medium (Everyman, 10/1/23)

THOMAS, LESLIE
×Bertha Brent (Rehearsal, 11/3/09, Curtain Raisers)

THOMAS, S. JENKYN
The Fairy Changeling. LC, K. Edward H., Finchley, 17/8/23

THOMAS, VAUGHAN
Daily Bread (Everyman, 17/4/22: adapted from *Le pain de ménage* (1898) by J. Renard)

THOMAS, VINCENT
Eos and Gwevril (*'Celtic o.'*: St G's H., 18/4/02)
×He, She and Another. LC, Crippl. Inst., 3/3/15
×A May-night Idyll (*'m.pl.'*: H., 29/2/16, *m.*, London Welsh Stage Soc.)

THOMASON, CHARLES
×Kimono San (*'oa.'*: Col., Aberystwyth, 28/6/09: +*F. LANE*)

THOMPSON, ALEXANDER M. [see also *M. AMBIENT* and *H. ELLIS*]
[For earlier plays see *H. E. D.* v, 597]
Chilperic (*'c.o.'*: Cor., 9/3/03)
[This seems to have been a new version of the libretto composed in 1870 by R. Reece, F. A. Marshall and R. Mansell]
The Dairy Maids (*'m.c.'*, m. P. A. Rubens and E. Tours: Apo., 14/4/06: +*R. COURTNEIDGE*) *1906*
Tom Jones (*'o.'*, m. E. German: P's, Manchester, 30/3/07; Apo., 17/4/07: +*R. COURTNEIDGE*) *1909*

The Mousmé ('*m.pl.*', m. L. Monckton and H. Talbot: Shaft., 9/9/11: +*R. COURTNEIDGE*) *1911*
Princess Caprice ('*m.pl.*', m. L. Fall: Shaft., 11/5/12) *1913*
Oh Caesar! ('*m.f.*': Lyc., Edin., 23/12/16: +*M. PEMBERTON*)
The Rebel Maid ('*c.o.*', m. M. Philips: Emp., 12/3/21) *1921*
The Maid of the Sea. LC, '*m.pl.*': Worthing, 24/4/23
The Bohemians (P.W., B'ham, 18/2/24: +*R. COURTNEIDGE*)
Le Sexe Fort ('*c.*': Sav., 19/2/26, *m.*: described as 'une comédie ...par Eric Hudson, traduite par Alex. M. Thompson')

THOMPSON, BERTIE
Schnapp of Rotterdam ('*m.c.*', m. G. Le Brunn: Hippo., Eastbourne, 29/7/11: called originally *An Irish Honeymoon*)

THOMPSON, CHARLOTTE [see *M. W. DELAND* and *K. D. WIGGIN*]

THOMPSON, EDITH HALFORD [see *E. HALFORD-THOMPSON*]

THOMPSON, EDWARD JOHN
The Enchanted Lady ('*c.*') *1910*
Krishna Kumari ('*historical d.*') *1924*
Atonement ('*pl. of modern India*') *1924*
Three Eastern Plays. *1927*
[This contains three short plays: of these, *The Queen of Ruin* and *The Clouded Mirror* are by E. J. Thompson, and *Easter Evening* by *THEODOSIA THOMPSON*]

THOMPSON, FRED [see also *W. BLOSSOM, G. BOLTON* and *G. GROSSMITH*]
Tonight's the Night ('*m.f.*', m. P. A. Rubens: Gai., 28/4/15)
Mr Manhattan ('*m.pl.*', m. H. Talbot: Gr., Blackpool, 20/3/16; P.W., 30/3/16: +*C. H. BOVILL*)
Houp-La! ('*c. with music*', m. N. D. Ayer and H. Talbot: St M., 23/11/16)
The Boy ('*m.c.*', m. L. Monckton and H. Talbot: Adel., 14/9/17)
Who's Hooper? ('*m.c.*', m. H. Talbot and I. Novello: Adel., 13/9/19)
Baby Bunting ('*m.f.*', m. N. D. Ayer: P's, Manchester, 15/9/19; Shaft., 25/9/19: +*W. DAVID*)
Afgar ('*m.ext.*', m. C. Cuvillier: Pav., 17/9/19: + *W. DAVID*)
The Kiss Call ('*m.c.*', m. I. Caryll: Gai., 8/10/19)
Maggie ('*m.c.*': Oxf., 22/10/19: +*H. F. MALTBY*)
The Eclipse ('*m.c.*', m. H. Darewski and M. Gideon: Gar., 12/11/19: +*E. P. OPPENHEIM*)
The Golden Moth ('*m.pl.*', m. I. Novello: Adel., 5/10/21: +*P. G. WODEHOUSE*)
Phi-Phi ('*m.ent.*', m. 'Christine': Hippo., Portsmouth, 7/8/22; Pav., 16/8/22: +*C. GREY*)
The Cousin from Nowhere ('*m.c.*', m. E. Kunneke: P.W., B'ham, 26/12/22; P's, 24/2/23)

Tell Me More ('*m.pl.*', m. G. Gershwin: Gai., N.Y., 13/4/25; W.G., 26/5/25: +*W. K. WELLS*)

Funny Face ('*m.c.*', m. G. Gershwin: Emp., L'pool, 24/9/28; P's, 8/11/28: +*P. G. SMITH*)

Sons o' Guns ('*m.c.*', m. B. Swanstrom, B. Davis and F. Coots: Hippo., 26/6/30: +*J. DONOHUE* and *BOBBY CONNOLLY*)

THOMPSON, G. COWRIE

The Patchwork Princess. LC, Gr., Blackpool, 5/12/17

THOMPSON, GEORGE H.

The Pride of Takahara ('*o.*': Terminus H., Littlehampton, 19/2/08, *amat.*)

THOMPSON, MAUDE

×Ye Playhouse Plot (Pav., St Leonard's, 5/4/06, *cpy.*)

×Old Maids' Corner (Plymouth, 16/11/08; Marlb., Holloway, 15/2/09)

×In Lilac Time (Lyc., Crewe, 27/9/09)

×Trapped (Pal., St Leonards, 28/12/11, *cpy.*)

THOMPSON, THEODOSIA [see *EDWARD J. THOMPSON*]

THOMSON, ARTHUR

A Demshur Maid's Dream ('*fairy tale of the Devon moors*': Ass. R., Teignmouth, 12/2/20, *amat.*)

THOMSON, BASIL

×The Elixir. LC, Vaud., 14/10/17

THOMSON, DAVID CLEGHORNE

×No Room at the Inn ('*Christmas morality*') *1928*

×The War Memorial. LC, Philosophic Inst., Edin., 12/10/29

Five One-Act Plays for a Scots Theatre. *1930*

[This contains: 1. *No Room at the Inn* (see above); 2. *The Kipper* ('*charade of clay feet*'); 3. *The Mainlander*; 4. *The War Memorial* (see above); and 5. *The Cateran's Heir*]

THOMSON, HERBERT

×Paving the Way (Shrewsbury, 8/4/01)

The Power of the Eye ('*m.d.*': Gai., Hastings, 16/12/01; Alex., 6/1/02)

THOMSON, HILDA TREVELYAN

All Through Eliza. LC, St Michael's H., Middlesbrough, 8/4/13

×The Link. LC, Hippo., Brighton, 26/1/22

×The Sewing Room (Forum Club, 18/10/25)

×The Man who Arrived (Forum Club, 21/3/27)

×Le Château (Forum Club, 21/3/27)

×My Son, the Candidate (Forum Club, 9/2/30)

THOMSON, J. [see *N. PRESCOTT*]

THOMSON, J. A. S. [see *C. B. ATTENBURY*]

THORN, GEOFFREY

[For earlier plays see *H. E. D.* v, 598–9]

His Father's Will (Gr., Islington, 22/3/04, *cpy.*)

THORNDIKE, ARTHUR RUSSELL [see also *T. R. ARKELL* and *T. NELSON*]

Saul ('*historical t.*') *1906*

×A Christmas Carol. LC, Vic H., 1/1/17

Oliver Twist. LC, Vic. H., 22/5/17: +*E. ROSE*

×Here We Go. LC, New, 11/11/20

Dr Syn (Wynd., 11/10/25, Interlude Players; Str., 7/12/27: dramatised from his own novel (1915): +*I. FIRTH*)

THORNE, ANTHONY

×Hers to Command (P.W., 27/9/25, Greenroom Club Rag)

Thirteen O'Clock. *1929*

THORNE, FRANK M. [see also *G. V. WYBROW*]

Her One Great Sin (Vic., Broughton, 21/10/01; Terriss, Rotherhithe, 29/6/03; called originally *A Blind Mother*: title later changed to *The Heavenly Twins*)

That Woman from France (K's, Nottingham, 27/3/02, *cpy.*; Metro., Manchester, 25/8/02; Sur., 15/9/02)

Napoleon the Great (P's, Blackburn, 15/4/03, *cpy.*; P.W., Preston, 29/8/04; W.L., 20/8/06)

The Woman Pays (Metro., Gateshead, 18/7/07; O.H., Wakefield, 2/9/07)

THORNELEY, WILFRED

×The Humourist (Inst., Winchmore Hill, 15/11/05)

The Blue Geranium ('*c.*': Inst., Winchmore Hill, 15/11/05: +*C. DAY*)

The Angelus ('*o.*', m. E. W. Naylor: C.G., 27/1/09)

The Other Mr Baverstock ('*f.*': Q, 17/9/28: +*N. DOON* and *M. FAWCETT*)

THORNEYCROFT, E. E.

×Partners. LC, Ass. R., Dolgarrog, 26/3/19

THORNLEY-DODGE, E.

×The Red Blind (Hippo., Rotherhithe, 1/11/15)

×Lady Cantelope. LC, Gai., Manchester, 19/5/16

×The Voice in the Street (Ambass., 27/1/21, *m.*)

THORNTON, A. G.

A Divorce Has Been Arranged ('*c.*': Embassy, 20/5/29)

THORNTON, CHARLES E. C.

The Sensible Costanza ('*serious c.*': Kings., 11/5/08)

The Goose ('*f.c.*': Margate, 17/5/09: +*U. VALENTINE*)

Madame Marguerite ('*c.*': Glo., 13/2/20, *m.*)

THORP, JOSEPH

Broken Bridges, or, The Bolshevist ('*industrial pl.*') *1920*

THORPE, E. M.

Lady Venborough's Vow (Little, 16/10/11, Oncomers)

×A Bit of Blue Ribbon (Little, 13/6/12, Oncomers)

×An Unorthodox Bishop (Little, 27/6/12, Oncomers)

THORPE, FOLLETT [see *H. WESTON*]

THORPE-MAYNE, GERTRUDE
×Curing Eliza (O.H., Scarborough, 1/5/11)

THORPE-TRACEY, F.
A Prince of the People (Gai., Dundee, 5/7/09)

THURLOW, Miss E. A.
×The Anderson Heirlooms (D.Y., 7/6/04)

THURLSTONE, WALTER
Violet the Dancer ('*r.m.d.*': Goole, 1/2/06)

THURNAM, ROWLAND
Ginevra ('*c.*': Everyman, 17/9/29: +*N. PRICE*: adapted from *Ginevra degli Almieri* (1928) by G. Forzano)
The Exchange (Little, 2/5/15, Pioneer Players: from *Échange* (1900) by P. Claudel)

THURSBY, CHARLES [see also *CHRISTOPHER ST JOHN*]
[For earlier plays see *H. E. D.* v, 600]
×A Broken Halo (Glo., 17/3/00)
×The Passion Flower (Duchess, Balham, 22/5/00; Wynd., 15/6/00: +*A. APPLIN*)
×A Pinch o' Snuff (Pal., Chelsea, 11/10/09)

THURSTON, ERNEST TEMPLE
John Chilcote, M.P. (St J., 1/5/05)
Sally Bishop (K's, Glasgow, 15/5/11; P.W., 25/7/11)
The Greatest Wish ('*c.*': Gar., 20/3/13: dramatised from his novel, *The Greatest Wish in the World*, 1910)
×Always Tell Your Wife (Col., 22/12/13)
×The Eleventh Hour (Col., 2/2/14)
Driven (H., 17/6/14) *Fr. 1914*
The Cost ('*pl. of the moment*': Vaud., 13/10/14) *1914*
×Ollaya (D.L., 9/5/16, *m.*)
The Wandering Jew (Manchester, 23/8/20; New, 9/9/20) *1920*
A Roof and Four Walls ('*c.*': Apo., 16/1/23) *1923*; *Fr. 1925*
The Phantom Ship ('*r.pl.*': Lyc., Sheffield, 7/12/23)
×Snobs (Hippo., Nottingham, 21/7/24) *Fr. 1925*
The Blue Peter (Pier, Eastbourne, 1/9/24; P's, 11/10/24) *1924*
Judas Iscariot (Scala, 23/21/24, Rep. Players) *1923*
Emma Hamilton (K's, Southsea, 9/9/29; New, 17/9/29)

THURSTON, F.
The Fisher Girl ('*m.bsq.*': Hippo., Hyde, 7/10/18: +*W. HACKETT*)

TIDMARSH, VIVIAN
×Landing the Shark (Col., 21/2/27)
Fetters (Q, 1/10/28)

TIERNEY, LOUIS A.
The Demon's Paw ('*c.o.*', m. E. J. Taylor: Qns, Dublin, 11/11/18)

TIGHE, HARRY [see *C. ROSE* and *J. E. H. TERRY*]
Open Spaces (Q, 3/1/27)
Old Mrs Wylie (Q, 26/9/27)

TILBURY, HARRY
His Dishonoured Wife (Stratford, 30/3/08)

TILLARD, IRENE
×Passions in Little Puddicombe (Court, 24/6/13)

TILLER, JOHN
Monte Carlo and Tokio. LC, '*m.ent.*': Hippo., Balham, 11/3/15
Sparks of Wit and Flashes of Humour ('*spectacle*', m. H. Darewski and J. H. Wilson: W.G., Blackpool, 26/6/20: +*R. JEANS*)

TILLEY, T. H.
The Return of the Native. LC, Corn Exch., Dorchester, 8/10/20 dramatised from Thomas Hardy's novel (1878)
A Desperate Remedy (Corn Exch., Dorchester, 15/11/22, *amat.* K's H., 21/11/22, *amat.*: dramatised from Thomas Hardy's *Desperate Remedies*, 1871)

TILLYARD, HENRY JULIUS WETTENHALL
The Plays of Roswitha. *1923*

TILSON, W. MUSKERRY
The Ironfounder (D.P., Eastbourne, 6/12/07)

TINDALL, TOM
[Several playlets produced at music-halls]

TINSLEY, LOUIE
[Several playlets produced at music-halls]

TIPPETT, ISABEL C. [see also *N. DOUGLAS*]
×Such Stuff as 'Eroes Are Made Of (T.H., Chelsea, 15/11/12)

TIPTAFT, NORMAN
Cowards (People's, Newcastle, 19/10/12)

TITHERADGE, DION [see also *T. R. ARKELL* and *R. JEANS*]
×Jim the Rat (Tiv., 29/5/11)
×The Watchman's Wife (Hippo., Balham, 23/6/13)
×Peg for Short. LC, Hippo., Margate, 8/9/17
The K.C. ('*c.*': Playh., L'pool, 29/4/18; Kings., 17/6/23, Interlude Players)
Kate a' Whimsies (K's H., 12/5/20, Pivot Club)
×The Lion Tamer. LC, Oxf., 19/7/21
×The Unwritten Law. LC, P.W., 27/10/21
×Sacrifices (Pier, Eastbourne, 26/6/22)
From the Prompt Corner. *1925*
[This contains nine brief revue sketches]
Out of the Box. *1925*
[This contains nine brief revue sketches]
The Apache ('*m.pl.*': B'ham, 20/9/26; Pallad., 15/2/27)
Behind the Curtain. *1926*
[This contains eight brief revue sketches]
Ups and Downs from Revue. *1926*
[This contains nine brief revue sketches]
The Crooked Billet (Roy., 13/10/27) *Fr. 1930*
×The End (Adel., 6/5/28, Sunday Play Soc.)

The Tiger in Men (Brighton, 22/7/29; Adel., 31/7/29)
Dear Love ('*m.c.*', m. H. Wood: B'ham, 21/10/29; Pal., 14/11/29: *L. WYLIE* and *H. CLAYTON*)
Silver Wings ('*m.c.*', m. J. Waller and J. Tunbridge: Emp., L'pool, 10/12/29; Dominion, 14/2/30: +*D. FURBER*)

TOBIAS, LILY [see *L. LEWISOHN*]

TOBIN, SEAN
Clan Falvey (City H., Cork, 5/8/19)

TODD, CAMPBELL
'Gentlemen, the King!' (Hippo., Putney, 30/8/09) *Fr. 1913*

TODHUNTER, JOHN [see also *E. ROSE*]
[For earlier plays see *H. E. D.* v, 600]
Isolt of Ireland ('*legendary d.*') *1927*
The Poison Flower. *1927* (printed with the above)

TOLKIEN, FREDERICK
[For an earlier play see *H. E. D.* v, 600]
Lola Descartes ('*o.*': Leeds, 24/11/22)

TOMLINSON, JOHN E.
×Dick Goodman's Redemption (Goole, 26/12/05)

TOMS, KIT
The Dollar Baby. LC, Alex., Pontefract, 3/9/18

TONKS, S. W.
×The Upper Hand. LC, Ass. R., Edgbaston, 13/12/13, *amat.*)
×John Dent, Dramatist (Ass. R., Edgbaston, 14/2/14)

TONSLEY, CHARLES J.
The Lord Protector ('*c.o.*': Temperance H., Leicester, 1/12/10, *amat.*)
Sir Francis Drake ('*c.o.*': Temperance H., Leicester, 7/5/12, *amat.*)

TOOMBS, J. S. M.
×Emily (Rep., L'pool, 16/5/13)

TOOSE, ALFRED
[A few playlets produced at music-halls]

TOOTELL, GEORGE
The Crusader ('*o. for juveniles*': Pier, Lytham, 6/11/06)

TORAHIKO, KORI
×Kanawa: The Incantation ('*pl. for marionettes*') *1918*
Saul and David ('*epic d.*') *1918*
Absalom. *1920*

TORR, A. C.
×A Comfortable Situation (Yeadon, 5/2/13, '*preliminary pfce.*')
×Sammywell Smith's Visit to London (Yeadon, 5/2/13, '*preliminary pfce.*')
×The Morning After. LC, Empress, 7/1/20: title later changed to *A Naughty Night*)

TORRENCE, ERNEST

×The Revellers ('*m.p.*': Cor., 10/1/10)

TORRY, E. NORMAN

[Several sketches and playlets produced at music-halls]

TOVEY, DUNCAN

×Brown of B. Company (Crippl. Inst., 26/10/01)

TOWER, A. F. ALLEN

The Hindustanee; or, Jones at Jonesipore ('*m.c.bsq.*': Emp., Oxford, 5/3/06: +*L. WOOD*)

The Great Gamgee ('*m.pl.*', m. W. McConnell-Wood: Newcastle, 13/12/09)

TOWERS, NORMAN

The Fire Witch ('*mystic d.*': Stratford, 20/4/08: title later changed to *The Woman from Hades*)

[There is a puzzle about this play, since a drama with an identical title and similarly described, acted at Edmonton in 1904, was credited to *DAISY HALLING*]

The Robe of Righteousness (Ilkeston, 13/3/07)

TOWNROW, DOROTHY LLOYD

Within Our Gates (K's, Longsight, 1/5/16: title later changed to *For Motherland*)

Fame or the Woman ('*md.*': O.H., Wakefield, 25/2/18)

TOWNROE, B. S.

A Nation in Arms (Court, Warrington, 20/9/09; Sav., 25/7/12, *m.*)

[*TOWNSEND, CHARLES*

What Became of Mrs Racket ('*f.c.*': Margate, 17/6/01; R.A., Woolwich, 22/6/03)

TOWNSEND, ERIC

Shadows of the Underworld. *1921* (Amersham, *priv.*)

TOWNSEND, Mrs R. S.

Uncle Vanya (Aldw., 10/5/14, St. Soc.: translated from the play (1899) by A. Chekhov)

TOWNSHEND, Marchioness (GLADYS ETHEL GWENDOLINE EUGENIA)

The Novice (T.H., Maidenhead, 22/2/09, *amat.*)

×John and the Couturière (Court, 4/5/12: title later changed to *The Little Dressmaker*)

×All Souls' Eve (St G's H., 6/5/12)

×The Monk and the King's Daughter (St J., 7/5/15, *m.*)

×A Midnight Meeting (Qns, 9/7/15, *m.*)

The Fold (Gai., Manchester, 1/3/20; Qns, 30/3/20)

×Nemesis (LC, Reg., Lowestoft, 13/5/21)

Shares ('*c.*': Kings., 17/12/22, Interlude Players: called originally *Business is Pleasure*)

TOWYN, —

The New Police; or, Girls from the Amazon Club ('*m.c.*', m. O. Trevine and J. Armstrong: Nottingham, 22/5/05)

TOYE, E. GEOFFREY

×The Fairy Cap ('*mime pl.*': H.M., 16/11/11, *m.*, students of Royal College of Music)

TOYE, FRANCIS

The Extra Shilling ('*c.*': Roy., 10/6/07, *m.*)

TOYNBEE, WILLIAM

×When the Devil Drives ('*c. satire*') *1902*
Necessity Knows No Law (Court, 30/6/04)
×Dolly's Ordeal (Court, 30/6/04)
The Firefly (Scala, 17/12/05, Pioneers)

TRACY, MARGUERITE [see *CLIFFORD BAX*]

'*TRAILL, PETER*' [=*GUY MAINWARING MORTON*: see *MICHAEL MORTON*]

TRANT, WILLIAM

×Gentle Rain (Roy., 9/2/04)
×The Rose Garden (Roy., 9/2/04)
×The Vital Spark (Roy., 9/2/04)

TRAVERS, BEN

The Dippers ('*f.c.*': Court, L'pool, 10/4/22; Crit., 22/8/22, *revised*)
The Three Graces ('*m.pl.*', m. F. Lehar: Emp., 26/1/24; K's, Southsea, 29/1/26, revised by *E. KELLAND*; Emp., Stratford, 5/4/26)
A Cuckoo in the Nest ('*f.*': Court, L'pool, 13/7/25; Aldw., 22/7/25) *1938*
Rookery Nook ('*f.*': K's, Southsea, 21/6/26; Aldw., 30/6/26) *1930*
Thark ('*f.*': K's, Southsea, 27/6/27; Aldw., 4/7/27) *1932*
Plunder ('*f.*': K's, Southsea, 18/6/28; Aldw., 26/6/28) *1931*
Mischief ('*c.*': K's, Southsea, 9/7/28; Fortune, 17/7/28)
A Cup of Kindness ('*f.*': K's, Southsea, 29/4/29; Aldw., 7/5/29)
A Night Like This ('*f.*': Aldw., 18/2/30)

TRAVERS-BORGSTROEM, ARTHUR

The Language of the Birds ('*c.*': Rep., B'ham, 31/3/23; Playroom 6, 21/3/28: adapted from *Die Sprache der Vögel* (1911) by A. Paul) *1922*

TRAVIS, A. C.

×A Sprig of Jasmine (Vic. H., Ripon, 5/10/06: +*F. BENTZ*)

TRAYNOR, JOHN F.

[Several sketches and playlets produced at music-halls]

TREE, Sir HERBERT BEERBOHM [see *A. NOYES*]

×Six and Eightpence. *Fr. 1900*

TREE, VIOLA [see also '*HUBERT PARSONS*']

The Swallow (Everyman, 6/5/25)

TREHANE, BRINSLEY

×The Daughter of Herodias ('*m.pl.*', m. Granville Bantock: Com., 25/2/07, *cpy.*; Roy. 10/6/07, *m.*: at a later revival attributed to the Hon. *ELANOUR NORTON*)

TREMAYNE, W. A.

A Free Lance (Brit., 20/10/02; Blackburn, 21/8/11, as *The Swordsman of Wolfsberg*)
×Blind Love (M'sex, 28/6/09: +*W. S. HARTFORD*)
The Alien (H.M., Montreal, 3/6/18; Court, Warrington, 11/11/18: +*W. S. HARTFORD*)
×The McTaggart (Little, 13/9/18)
The Black Feather (Scala, 1/5/19)

TRENCH, FREDERIC HERBERT

Napoleon (Qns, 19/10/19, St. Soc.) *1919* (Oxford)

TRENT, DENNIS

The Cynic (Arcadia, Colwyn Bay, 12/3/28)

'*TRESSALL, ROBERT*' [=*ROBERT NORMAN*]

The Ragged-trousered Philanthropists. LC, T.H., Edmonton, 13/3/28: dramatised from his own novel (1914). *1928* (Labour Publishing Co.)

TREVELYAN, CLAUDE

[For earlier plays see *H. E. D.* v, 603]
×The Passing of Paul Dombey (Borough, Stratford, 22/4/09, *m.*)

TREVELYAN, H. B.

The Dark Angel. *1928*

TREVELYAN, ROBERT CALVERLEY

Cecilia Gonzaga. *1903*
The Birth of Parsival. *1905*
Sisyphus ('*operatic fable*') *1908*
The New Parsifal ('*operatic fable*') *1914*
The Bride of Dionysus ('*music d.*') *1912*
Cheiron. *1917*
Ajax (translated from Sophocles' play) *1919*
Antigone (translated from Sophocles' play) *1924*
The Oresteia (Fest., Cambridge, 22/11/26: translated from Aeschylus' trilogy) *1920*
Meleager. LC, Masefield's house, Boar's Hill, Oxford, 6/11/29. *1927*

TREVILIAN, M. F. CELY

Defendamus. A Pageant of Taunton (Taunton, 12/6/28) (*1928*: Taunton)

TREVINE, OWEN

Uncle Ned ('*m.f.*': P.W., L'pool, 11/5/03)
The Scarlet Patrol ('*m.c.*': County, Kingston, 26/8/07; Fulham, 16/9/07: +*ST J. HAMOND*)

TREVOR, CHARLES

The Vagabond King (W. Bromwich, 3/3/13)

TREVOR, GEORGE

×A Game of Bridge (Alb. H., 6/7/03)

TREVOR, LEO [see also *W. P. DRURY*]
[For earlier plays see *H. E. D.* v, 604]
× In the Cause of Charity (St G's H., 3/2/00)
Our Little Cinderella ('*m.pl.*', m. H. Löhr: Playh., 20/12/10, *m.*)

TREVOR, P.
× Limited Liability. LC, Court, 23/6/14
× Silence is Golden. LC, Court, 23/6/14
× Wild Oats. LC, Court, 23/6/14

TREVOR, PHILIP
The Strugglers (Scala, 18/7/26, Playmates)

TREVOR, WALTON
Happy Families (Q, 2/4/28: Gar., 1/10/29, where attributed to *AUDREY* and *WAVENEY CARTEN* and *JANE ROSS*)
[It seems probable that *WALTON TREVOR* was a pen-name used by the three authors]

TREVOSPER, MARGUERITE (see also *W. BURNOT*)
[For an earlier play see *H. E. D.* v, 604]
Just a Girl ('*m.pl.*': Lyc., Stafford, 2/10/11: title later changed to *Capt. Bligh, V.C.*)

TREVOSSO, ALMUND
The Headless Horses (Q, 25/7/27)

TRIEFUS, PAUL
× Polly Archie sur mer. LC, '*m.pl.*': RADA, 11/11/22: +*H. LISSER*
× MacHamlet (P.W., 15/2/25, Green Room Rag)

TRIMINGHAM, ERNEST [see *D. MAHOMED*]

TRIPP, DUDLEY HOWARD [see also *H. T. EDGAR*]
× The Chords of Memory (Alex., Stoke Newington, 6/11/16)
The Passion of John Manger. LC, Little Vic., Brighton, 25/11/24: +*H. TRIPP EDGAR*

TROODE, CHARLES [see *W. WALLER*]

TROTMAN, ANNIE M. [see *J. DAVIDSON*]

TROTMAN, GEORGE HENRY
Lady Kinton's Necklace; or, The Hypnotist (Ilkeston, 15/10/06)

TROUBRIDGE, Lady LAURA
Mrs Oakleigh (New, 3/12/03)
× The Goldfish (Tiv., 15/12/13: +*R. FLETCHER*)

TROWBRIDGE, E.
× The Oracle. LC, '*oa.*': David Lewis, L'pool, 31/1/24

TROWBRIDGE, W. R. H.
× The Patriot (Passmore Edwards Settlement, 12/11/02; Gr., Fulham, 6/4/03)

TRUMAN, NEVIL P.
The Star ('*Nativity pl.*': Meadows H., Nottingham, 5/1/24, *amat.*)

TUCKER, BERYL

The Equality of Carberry ('*f.c.*': O.H., Jersey, 19/2/09)
The Murder of Adolphus (T.H., Maidenhead, 14/12/09: +*R. H. BLAND*)

TUCKER, C. M.

×Art and Indigestion (Cosmopolis, 20/3/14)
Beyond His Power ('*an indictment*': Arts Centre, 1/5/14, Play Producers)

TUCKER, R. CAREY

In Cyderland ('*m.pl.*', m. E. Sherwood: Crippl. Inst., 10/5/09)

TUCKER, STANLEY PATTERSON

Pomponette ('*light o.*', m. R. Cleveland: P.W., B'ham, 3/12/17)

TUDOR, CATHERINE

×Aunt Minerva (Guildhall School of Music, 15/3/02) *Fr. 1899*
×King Christmas ('*masquerade*') *Fr. 1899*
×The Message of Peace ('*Christmas pl.*') *1920*

TUFFLEY, GRACE M. [see *M. L. DARVELL*]

TUITE, HUGH

×A Tangled Skein (Roy., Glasgow, 24/2/05, *cpy.*)

TULLOCK, AUGUSTA

[For an earlier play see *H. E. D.* v, 604]
The Web of Fate (Lecture H., Braintree, 9/10/1899; E.C., 9/7/00)
The Convent Bell (Sur., 30/5/04)
Sinner's Point (St J., Manchester, 22/1/03, *cpy.*; Sunderland, 6/4/03)
The End Crowns All (Ilkeston, 22/4/07)
×Christine (Pal., Manchester, 2/10/07, *m.*)
Judith (Central, Altrincham, 15/6/08, in one act; Pal., Boston, 7/12/08, in four acts, as *The Woman who Sinned*; Edmonton, 10/5/09, in four acts, as *Judith, the Woman who Sinned*; Woolwich, 8/7/12, in two acts, as *The Woman who Atoned*)
From Mill to Mansion (Woolwich, 19/6/11)
The Mormon's Wife (Woolwich, 16/12/12)
John Barnett's Millions (Gr., Halifax, 13/9/15)
The Fortunate Mill Girl ('*md.*': Hippo., Bolton, 3/4/18)

TULLOCK, OLIVE

Fate and the Footman ('*m.pl.*': Terminus H., Littlehampton, 17/9/08, *amat.*)

TULLY, JIM [see *R. NICHOLS*]

TULLY, MAY

Mary's Ankle ('*f.*': Pleasure Gdns, Folkestone, 23/1/28)

[*TULLY, R. W.*

The Bird of Paradise (Rochester, USA, 25/12/11; Daly's, N.Y., 8/1/12; Lyr., 11/9/19)

TURNBULL, J. P. [see *W. CAINE*]

TURNER, A. STANLEY

×Nemesis. LC, Macclesfield, 5/5/14

TURNER, ALFRED [see also *H. OWEN*]

The Waterspout ('*c.*': Aldw., 21/8/16)
×Missing the Tide (O.H., Leicester, 6/8/17)

TURNER, CECIL HOWARD

[A few playlets produced at music-halls]

TURNER, EARDLEY

[For earlier plays see *H. E. D.* v, 604]
Next Door ('*t.f.*': Newcastle, 7/9/08)

TURNER, FREDERICK G.

The Land of Cherry Blossom ('*m.pl.*': Library H., Stoke Newington, 25/2/09, *amat.*)

TURNER, G. H. [see *G. C. LIVESEY*]

TURNER, JOHN HASTINGS [see also *F. LONSDALE*]

×Account Rendered (Gai., Manchester, 22/9/13)
Havoc (Pier, Eastbourne, 3/11/13)
Iris Intervenes (Kings., 16/10/15)
Bubbly ('*m.ent.*', m. P. Braham: Com., 5/5/17, *m.*)
×A Breath of Fresh Air (Pal., 7/12/17, *m.*)
Tails Up ('*m.ent.*', m. P. Braham: Com., 1/6/18)
×The Curious Tale of the Charm that Worked. LC, Com., 9/12/18
×A Strange Tale of 500 Years after the War. LC, Com., 10/12/18
×Ladies and Gentlemen (Empress, 10/2/19)
Back Again ('*song show*': Ambass., 28/8/19)
×The Reformers; or, The Pathetic Story of the Unfortunately Good Young Man; or, Nothing Succeeds like Satan (Theatrical Gdn Party, Chelsea, 22/6/20)
Every Woman's Privilege ('*c.*': Glo., 28/9/20: called originally *My Lady Superior*)
The Naughty Princess ('*c.o.*', m. C. Cuvillier: Adel., 7/10/20)
×The House of Uncommons (Alh., 16/11/20, *m.*: +*H. CARRICK*)
Jumble Sale ('*revue*': Vaud., 16/12/20)
The House Next Door (Theatrical Gdn Party, Chelsea, 28/6/21)
Now and Then ('*m.ext.*', m. P. Braham: Vaud., 17/9/21)
The Fun of the Fayre ('*revue*': Pav., 17/10/21)
Mayfair and Montmartre ('*revue*': Oxf., 9/3/22)
×Arnold (Theatrical Gdn Party, Chelsea, 23/6/22)
The Lilies of the Field ('*c.*': Ambass., 5/6/23) *1923*; *Fr. 1927*
Rescued from Revues. *Fr. 1923*
[This contains nine brief revue sketches]
×Devastatin'. LC, Pallad., 16/10/23
Yoicks! ('*revue*': Kings., 11/6/24)
×Our Little Baby (Theatrical Gdn Party, Chelsea, 24/6/24)
×Sisters under Their Skins. LC, St M., 7/7/24
The Sea Urchin ('*c.*': New, Oxford, 26/1/25; Str., 31/3/25) *Fr. 1928*

His Queen (Belasco, Washington, 27/4/25, as *Queen Mab*; Hudson, N.Y., 11/5/25)
Cleopatra ('*m.c.*', m. O. Straus: O.H., Manchester, 11/5/25; Daly's, 2/6/25)
Betty in Mayfair ('*m.c.*', m. H. Fraser-Simson: Emp., Sunderland, 26/10/25; Adel., 11/11/25) *Fr. 1929*
Evenings at Eight. *Fr. 1925*
[This contains nine brief revue sketches]
Merely Molly ('*m.c.*', m. H. Finck and J. Meyer: B'ham, 13/9/26; Adel., 22/9/26)
The Scarlet Lady ('*c.*': Crit., 30/9/26) *1927*
The Spot on the Sun ('*c.*': Ambass., 28/6/27) *Fr. 1928*
The Lord of the Manor ('*c.*': Apo., 20/9/28) *Fr. 1929*
Wake Up and Dream! ('*revue*', m. Cole Porter: Pal., Manchester, 5/3/29; Pav., 27/3/29)

TURNER, MARGARET STORRS
×The Extra Special (H., 1/6/15, *m.*)

TURNER, MONTAGUE [see also *ST A. MILLER*]
[For earlier plays see *H. E. D.* v, 605]
Petronella; or, A Royal Romance ('*c.o.*', m. W. T. Gliddon: Gt. Qn. St., 26/5/06)
×The Park-Keeper (Chesterfield, 3/6/12; Emp., Edmonton, 8/7/12)
×The Confession (Hippo., Putney, 14/4/13)

TURNER, S. [see *F. ALDWORTH*]

TURNER, WALTER JAMES
The Man who Ate the Popomack ('*t.c. of love*': Sav., 12/6/23, *m.*; Fest., Cambridge, 29/11/26, *revised*) *1922*; *1929* (*revised*)
Smaragda's Lover ('*dramatic phantasmagoria*': Court, 22/2/25, 300 Club)

[*TURRELL, CHARLES ALFRED*
×The Claws (Bedford H., Chelsea, 17/12/22, Pax Robertson Salon: from M. Linares Rivas, *La garra*, 1914) *1919* (Boston)
×The Passing of the Magi (Bedford H., Chelsea, 15/12/23, Pax Robertson Salon: from *Los Reyes pasan* by E. Zamacois) *1919* (Boston)

TWEEDALE, BERNARD
×Promise or Strategy ('*m.c.*': P.H., Sydenham, 12/1/01)
×When Trust is All (P.H., Sydenham, 12/1/01)
×A Woman's Judgment (P.H., Sydenham, 1/2/02)
×The Main Chance (Norbreck H., Blackpool, 31/3/02, *cpy.*)

TWISS, J. OLIVER
Magnificent Mac ('*c.*': County, Kingston, 30/10/16)
The French Dancer (Gai., Hastings, 13/2/22: title later changed to *Beauty and the Burglar*)
The Red Dog ('*f.*': Streatham Hill, 25/8/30)

TWYFORD, CYRIL
×Kiddie (Gar., 19/1/09, *cpy.*; Hippo., 6/12/09)
×Thin Ice (Gar., 19/1/09, *cpy.*)

×009 West (Gar., 19/1/09, *cpy.*; Hippo., Putney, 7/7/19)
Joanna Godden (Gr., Southampton, 11/1/26; Borough, Stratford, 22/2/26: dramatised from the novel (1921) by Sheila KayeSmith)
[Several sketches and playlets produced at music-halls]

TWYFORD, J. HENRY
×Ex-BEF ('*t.*': Little Vic., Brighton, 30/6/24)

TYLER, FROOM
×The Living and the Dead (Little, Bristol, 8/3/28)
×The Woman who was Enchanted. *1929* (Bath)

TYLER, M. G.
Hospital Blue. LC, Gai., Hastings, 31/1/19

TYRWHITT-DRAKE, E. H.
Sir Francis Drake (Emp., Kingston, 13/7/12)

[*UNDERHILL, JOHN GARRETT*
The Evil Doers of Good ('*c.*': Bedford H., Chelsea, 26/11/22, Pax Robertson Salon: translated from J. Benavente y Martínez, *Los malhechores del bien*, 1905)
The Cradle Song (Bedford H., Chelsea, 2/2/24, Pax Robertson Salon; Fortune, 2/11/26: from G. Martínez Sierra, *Canción de cuna*, 1911)
The Passion Flower (Everyman, 11/3/26: translated from J. Benavente y Martínez, *La malquerida*, 1913)
×The Lover (Fortune, 2/11/26: translated from G. Martínez Sierra, *El enamorado*, 1912)
Madame Pepita (Fest., Cambridge, 21/5/28: translated from a play by G. Martínez Sierra)
[All these texts were taken from *The Plays of Benavente* (1920–1923, New York) and *The Plays of Sierra* (1923, New York)]

UNDERWOOD, MARIANNE
God Keep You Safe (Lyr., Hamm., 29/5/16: title later changed to *The Worst Marriage in the World*)

[*UNGER, GLADYS B.* [see also *R. LEIGH*, *F. LONSDALE* and *P. A. RUBENS*]
×Edmund Kean (Vaud., 10/1/03)
Mr Sheridan ('*c.*': Brighton, 29/8/04; Gar., 6/3/07)
×The Lemonade Boy (Crit., 13/10/06)
The Knave of Hearts; or, The Man who Won Back ('*md.*': Roy., Glasgow, 16/9/07; Gr., Croydon, 4/11/07)
L'éventail ('*c.*': New, 27/12/07, *cpy.*: adapted from the play (1903) by R. de Flers and A. Caillavet)
Henry of Lancaster ('*r.d.*': Nottingham, 28/2/08; Borough, Stratford, 27/4/08)
Love Watches ('*c.*': Lyc., N.Y., 27/8/08; H., 11/5/09: adapted from *L'amour veille* (1907) by R. de Flers and A. Caillavet)
×In an Arab Garden (Vaud., 12/11/08: also called *The Arab Gardener*)
Inconstant George ('*c.*': P.W., 1/10/10: adapted from *L'âne de Buridan* (1909) by R. de Flers and A. Caillavet)

Decorating Clementine ('*c.*': Glo., 28/11/10: adapted from *Le bois sacré* (1910) by R. de Flers and A. Caillavet)
Better Not Enquire ('*c.*': P.W., 20/4/11: adapted from *Les deux écoles* (1902) by A. Capus)
The Marionettes ('*c.*': Com., 23/9/11: adapted from *Les Marionnettes* (1910) by P. Wolff)
The Night-Birds ('*m.c.*', m. J. Strauss: Lyr., 30/12/11)
The Son and Heir ('*modern c.*': D.P., Eastbourne, 27/1/13; Str., 1/2/13) *Fr. 1913*
The Marriage Market ('*m.c.*', m. V. Jacobi: Daly's, 17/5/13)
Toto ('*m.pl.*', m. A. Joyce and M. Morgan: Plymouth, 10/4/16; D.Y., 19/4/16)
London Pride (Wynd., 6/12/16, *m.*: +*A. N. LYONS*)
Our Mr Hepplewhite ('*c.*': Crit., 4/10/19) *Fr. 1919*
The Sunshine of the World ('*m.pl.*', m. C. Cuvillier: Brighton, 19/1/20; Emp., 18/2/20: +*K. K. ARDASCHIR*)
×A Man in Mary's Room (Little, 15/12/20)
[For several plays performed in the USA after this date see *Who's Who in the Theatre*]

UNSELL, EVE [see *E. G. SUTHERLAND*]

UNWIN, GEORGE [see also *W. T. GLIDDON*]
×The Last Post (Lyc., Stafford, 26/9/02; Marlb., Holloway, 12/6/05)
×The Way Out (Newcastle, 3/8/08)
×The Home-coming (W.L., 28/3/08, *cpy.*; Qns, L'pool, 22/4/08: title later changed to *After Twenty Years*)

UPJOHN, DORA
Fortune's Wheel. LC, T.H., Fulham, 12/4/21

UPTON, SWEYN
×A Thief to Catch a Thief (Gai., Hastings, 28/3/12) *Fr. 1912*

URCH, Mrs M. C.
×At the Sign of the Lamb (Guildhall School of Music, 10/6/25)

URICH, JOHN
×The Cicada ('*m.pl.*': Sav., 25/6/12)

URQUHART, J. HAMILTON
×Oh, That Major! (T.H., Leven, 10/9/06)

URWICK, GABRIELLE
×The First of April. LC, Crippl. Inst., 22/6/20

USHER, LANCELOT [see also *M. WALLERTON*]
A Woman of the World (Gr., Boscombe, 1/3/00, *cpy.*)

V., T.
×The Dancer (K's H., 12/3/13)

VACHELL, HORACE ANNESLEY [see also *W. HACKETT* and *J. KENDALL*]
The Nightingale (Imp., 25/4/02: +*H. WYNDHAM*)
Her Son ('*c.*': Glasgow, 15/11/06; Playh., 12/3/07; New, 2/9/07, *revised*: dramatised from his novel, 1907)

Jelf's ('*c.*': Wynd., 10/4/12) *1912*; *Fr. 1920*
×Sunny Bushes (Emp., Shepherd's Bush, 9/12/12)
Searchlights (Sav., 11/2/15) *1915*
Quinney's ('*c.*': H., 20/4/15) *1915*
The Case of Lady Camber (Sav., 16/10/15) *1916*; *Fr. 1920*
Who is He? ('*c.*': H., 9/12/15)
Pen ('*c.*': St J., 3/5/16: dramatised from Morley Roberts' novel, *Lady Penelope*, 1905)
Fishpingle ('*c.*': H., 30/5/16)
Mrs Pomeroy's Reputation ('*c.*': Bradford, 13/10/16; K's, Hamm., 9/4/17; Qns, 4/7/17: +*THOMAS COBB*)
Humpty-Dumpty (Sav., 14/6/17)
×The Mirror (H., 26/6/17, *m.*)
The House of Peril (Qns, 8/3/19: from the novel, *The Chink in the Armour* (1912) by Mrs Belloc-Lowndes)
The Hour and the Man (Glo., 11/2/21: +*J. C. SNAITH*: called originally *The Minotaur*)
Back to Earth ('*c.*': D.P., Eastbourne, 11/4/21; Gar., 26/4/21, as *Count X*)
Her Destiny (Portsmouth, 4/7/21: called originally *A Disconcerting Guest*: adapted from *L'inconnu* (1920) by L. Verneuil)
Plus Fours ('*c.*': H., 17/1/23: +*H. SIMPSON*: called originally *Miss Marionette*) *Fr. 1930*
Blinkers ('*c.*': Shak., L'pool, 20/8/23; Sav., 21/3/24: +*L. M. LION*)

'*VALENTINE*' [=*ARCHIBALD THOMAS PECHEY*: see also *W. EVANS* and *C. HARRIS*]
The Night Before ('*m.f.*', m. H. Lonsdale; Metropolitan, 15/9/13)
Naughty Poppette ('*m.c.*', m. G. Blackmore: Hippo., Darlington, 30/8/26)
Compromising Daphne (Shak., L'pool, 29/8/27; P's, 28/9/27)
[Several sketches and playlets produced at music-halls]

VALENTINE, JOHN
The Stronger Sex (Apo., 22/1/07)

VALENTINE, SIDNEY [see also '*M. E. FRANCIS*']
Fiander's Widow ('*c.*': Gar., 28/8/07: +'*M. E. FRANCIS*')

VALENTINE, UFFINGTON [see *C. THORNTON*]

VALLINGS, HAROLD
Hattie Off the Rails (P.H., Altrincham, 13/10/24, Altrincham Garrick Rep. Co.)

VANDERBILT, CORNELIUS
The Sousa Girl ('*m.c.*': Bij., 17/12/02)

VAN DRUTEN, JOHN
The Return Half ('*c.*': RADA, 5/10/24)
Chance Acquaintance ('*c.*': Str., 11/9/27, Rep. Players; Crit., 2/11/27)
Young Woodley (New, 12/2/28, 300 Club; Sav., 5/3/28) *1928*
The Return of the Soldier (Playh., 12/6/28: from the novel (1918) by Rebecca West) *1928*

Diversion (Arts, 26/9/28; Little, 1/10/28) *1928*
After All ('*c.*': Apo., 5/5/29, St. Soc. and 300 Club; Arts, 30/3/30, *revised*; Crit., 2/2/31) *1929*

VANE, CHARLES
×Nell (Edin., 13/11/05)
[A few sketches produced at music-halls]

VANE, SUTTON [see also *VANE HUNT SUTTON-VANE*]
[For earlier plays see *H. E. D.* v, 606–7]
×The Betting Book (Pav., 14/4/02)
×Jack and Jill (Pier, Brighton, 9/8/02, *cpy.*)

VAN NOORDEN, W. [see *S. J. ADAIR-FITZGERALD*]

VANSITTART, ROBERT GILBERT, Baron VANSITTART
Les Pariahs (Théâtre Molière, Paris, 1905)
The Cap and Bells ('*c.*': Little, 17/4/13) *Fr. 1913*
People Like Ourselves (Glo., 16/10/13)
×Dusk (Little, 24/4/14) *1914*
×Foolery (Little, 25/5/15, *m.*) *1912*
×Romance (Little, 25/5/15, *m.*; Ambass., 16/3/17, as *Class*)

VANSITTART, SIBELL [see *H. F. LEE*]

VANTINI, MARIE
×Robespierre (Rehearsal, 28/4/13, Black Cat Club)

VARCOE, MITFORD [see *C. C. LEWIS*]

VARESI, GILDA
Enter Madame ('*c.*': Gar., N.Y., 16/8/20; Roy., 15/2/22: +*D. BYRNE*) *1921*

VASEY, GRACE
Those who Dwell on the Threshold (Metro., Gateshead, 4/2/11)
The Love that Forgave (Lyr., Hamm., 28/7/13)
The Man who Did His Bit. LC, Pal., Newton, Alfreton, 28/11/17
Two Eyes of Grey. LC, Pal., Watford, 24/3/21

VASSIDY, NOEL
Fancy Dress ('*c.*': Century, 13/7/25, Trial Players)

'*VAUCROSSAN, F.*' [=*F. DAWSON*]

VAUGHAN, DAVID IVOR [see *IVOR GATTY*]

VAUN, RUSSELL [see also *M. AMBIENT*, *A. ATWOOD*, *M. HILDYARD* and *A. YORKE*]
[For earlier plays see *H. E. D.* v, 607]
×What Might Have Been (O.H., Llandudno, 14/5/1896; Bij., 19/12/1896; Wynd., 13/12/00)
Nicandra ('*mystic f.*': New, Cambridge, 2/6/1898; Parkhurst, Holloway, 3/10/1898; Aven., 6/4/01)
The Green Goddess (Metro., Camberwell, 16/12/01)
A Daughter's Crime (Crown, Peckham, 1/8/04; Lyr., Hamm., 21/6/09, as *Temptation*)
Is Marriage a Failure? ('*f.c.*': Worthing, 10/10/07; Terry's, 23/12/07: +*A. ATWOOD*)

×The Moreton Pearls (Pal., Hamm., 20/7/08)
×A Good Sort (Court, 16/6/11, *m.*)
×Only a Woman (Court, 16/6/11, *m.*)

VEASEY, ARTHUR C. T. [see *F. SOUTAR*]

VEDRENNE, L. W.
Collapse (P.W., 11/3/28, Sunday Play Soc.)

[*VEILLER, BAYARD*
Within the Law (P'cess, Chicago, 6/4/12; Eltinge, N.Y., 11/9/12; H., 24/5/13: adapted by *A. WIMPERIS* and *F. FENN*)
The Thirteenth Chair (Van Curler, Schenectady, 16/10/16; 48th St., N.Y., 20/11/16; D.Y., 16/10/17) *Fr. 1922*
The Trial of Mary Dugan (Hippo., Golder's Green, 27/2/28; Qns, 6/3/28) *Fr. 1928*

VEITCH, EDITH [see also *N. VEITCH*]
×Proserpine (Socialist H., Newcastle, 10/12/13)

VEITCH, NORMAN [see also *P. BEEK*]
The Nightingale (People's, Newcastle, 1917: +*E. VEITCH*)
×Colonel Bogey (D.P., Eastbourne, 17/3/24)
King Midas (People's, Newcastle, 1927: +*E. VEITCH*)

VELSOR-SMITH, — [see *G. NELSON*]

VELY, A.
×An English School. LC, Ambass., 24/7/16

VENGEROVA, ZINAIDA
The Man who was Dead (Court, 6/12/12, Literary Theatre Soc.: +*J. POLLOCK*: adapted from *Zhivoi trup* (1911) by L. Tolstoi)

VENNER, NORMAN
Who's Who ('*f.*': Q, 14/3/27)

VERINI, E. M. [see *M. A. LEWIS*]

VERNER, GERALDINE
A Boy Wanted ('*m.c.*, m. W. Pringle: P.W., Southampton, 9/6/02)

VERNON, FRANK [see also *B. N. GRAHAM* and *V. VERNON*]
When It Was Dark (O.H., Cheltenham, 9/11/05, *cpy.*: +*W. MAXWELL*: from the novel (1903) by Guy Thorne)
×The Chance (Terry's, 30/12/07) *Fr. 1913*
His Majesty's Pleasure (Sav., 11/2/21, *m.*)

[*VERNON, HARRY MAURICE* [see also *A. WIMPERIS*]
×The Deputy Sheriff (Gar., 21/7/09, *m.*)
×My Lady's Visit (New, 8/11/09, *cpy.*; Brixton, 5/8/16)
×Inspector Wise C.I.D. (Qns, 1/4/11)
×All Men Are Fools (Com., 19/9/12)
Mr Wu (New, 27/10/13; Str., 27/11/13: +*H. OWEN*)
×A Steal (New, 13/7/17, *m.*)
The Bamboula ('*m.pl.*', m. A. Sirmay and H. Rosenthal: H.M., 24/3/25: +*G. BOLTON*)

Happy Go Lucky ('*m.pl.*', m. T. Johnstone: Walnut St., Philadelphia, 1/6/25, as *When You Smile*; National, N.Y., 5/10/25; B'ham, 6/12/26; P.W., 21/12/26)

[Numerous sketches and playlets produced at music-halls]

VERNON, MAUD VENABLES

×Pan's Meadow (Manchester, 15/9/15)

×Through the Green Door ('*children's fairy pl.*': Gai., Manchester, 20/12/19)

VERNON, VIRGINIA

×The Bronze Lady and the Crystal Gentleman (translated from the play by Henri Duvernois: LC, Little, 10/5/22) *1933* (in *Modern One-Act Plays from the French*)

Maya (Gate, 22/11/27: +*F. VERNON*: adapted from the play (1924) by S. Gantillon) *1930*

×After Death (Little, 15/5/28: +*F. VERNON*)

Red Rust (Little, 28/2/29: +*F. VERNON*: adapted from a play by V. M. Kirshon and A. V. Ouspenski)

The Shadow of the East (Str., 26/4/29: +*F. VERNON*: adapted from *Dans l'ombre du harem* (1927) by L. Besnard)

VICKERS, GERTRUDE

Prince Romance. LC, K's, Leeds, 21/2/23

Saint Martha of the Mill. LC, K's, Leeds, 27/2/23

Granny, You're My Mammy's Mammy. LC, Vic. H., Pudsey, 3/5/23

A Daughter of Lucifer (Gosport, 3/12/23)

×Three Blind Mice ('*c.*': Gosport, 17/12/23)

Desire of the Desert. LC, Leicester, 14/2/24

A Warning to Them. LC, Hippo., Burslem, 27/3/24

The Redemption of Sapho (Qns, Farnworth, 10/8/25)

The Gipsy's Warning (T.H., Nantwich, 24/2/26)

The Angel Mother (Hippo., Burslem, 5/5/27)

The Shilling Shocker (Hippo., Burslem, 1/8/27)

VICTOR, FREDERICK

In the Midst of Life (Belfast, 15/7/01; W.L., 21/4/02)

VIGO, THERESA

×A Business Deal (Forum Club, 29/2/20)

Creation ('*c.*': Pal., Chelsea, 30/11/20, *m.*)

×Lozenges (Pav., Eastbourne, 17/4/22)

VILLIERS-STUART, GERALD

×The Drums of Doom ('*impressionistic d.*': Scala, 23/6/08, English Drama Soc.)

VINCENT, C. VICTOR H.

The Rose of the Border ('*c.o.*', m. H. E. Smith: Emp., Sunderland, 8/12/24, *amat.*)

The Northumbrians ('*historical pl.*': Aven., Sunderland, 3/10/27, *amat.*)

'Shelley in the Shop' and Other Plays. *1927*

[This contains five one-act plays: 1. '*Shelley in the Shop*';

2. *Here's to Our Enterprise, or, Henry Irving's Debut*; 3. *He Who Stood Mute*; 4. *George, You're Wonderful*; and 5. *Getting Rid of Richard*]

VIVIAN-EDMONDS, E.

×The Wedding Morn (Reg., Salford, 25/8/03)

The Ways of Men (Gr., W. Hartlepool, 11/3/09, *cpy.*; Rochdale, 19/4/09: title later changed to *The Man and the Parson*)

[There is uncertainty concerning the authorship of this play: at Hartlepool it was credited to Albert Ward]

VOGEL, HARRY B.

Love in a Tangle ('*c.*': Aldw., 16/11/09, *m.*)

VOGEL, JETTA [see *F. FENN*]

VOLK, CONRAD

The Intruder (Q, 7/5/28)

[*VOLLMER, LULA* [see also *G. G. D. SCOTT*]

Sun-Up (Provincetown Playh., N.Y., 25/5/23; Vaud., 4/5/25) *1924*

The Shame Woman (Greenwich Village, N.Y., 15/10/23; E.C., 23/11/25)

VON HERDER, ALEXANDRA

×The Little Mermaid. *1906*

The Tenth of August (New, 16/12/07, *m.*)

Montezuma; or, The Blessed Virgin of the Roses ('*miracle d.*') *1911* (*priv.*)

×Jesus of Nazareth ('*poetic d.*') *1913*

×Damages (Rehearsal, 8/2/14)

Dido and Aeneas ('*t.*': Ambass., 26/5/14, Drama Soc.)

×The Wisdom of Akhnaton. *1920*

×The Twilight Hour of Young Kuei Fei ('*dram. poem*') *1923* (Shanghai)

VON HUTTEN, BETTINA, Baroness

The Halo ('*c.*': Gr., Southampton, 27/7/25: dramatised from her own novel (1907): +*JOAN TEMPLE*)

VON LEER, S. B. [see *E. S. CLIFT* and *G. G. COLLINGHAM*]

VOSPER, FRANK [see also *G. B. STERN*]

The Combined Maze (Str., 13/3/27, Rep. Players; Roy., 30/5/27: from the novel (1913) by May Sinclair)

Murder on the Second Floor (Lyr., 21/6/29) *1929*

People Like Us ('*symbolic pl.*': Str., 3/11/29, Rep. Players; Arts, 10/12/29) *1929* (serialised by *The Evening Standard*)

Lucky Dip ('*light c.*': Com., 23/10/30) *Fr. 1931*

VOSS-BARK, C. H.

The Lone Man ('*c.*': Gr., Bridlington, 14/3/07, *amat.*)

VOTIERI, ADELINE

[For earlier plays see *H. E. D.* v, 609]

The Court Dressmaker, Coralie & Co. ('*f.c.*': Bij., 24/2/00, *cpy.*; Gr., 7/4/02, as *The Dressmaker*)

Eneda, or, The Mad Princess ('*c.o.*', m. D. Harrison: P'cess, 15/5/02, *cpy.*)

VROOM, EDWARD
Marsac of Gascony ('*r.c.*': P.W., B'ham, 11/11/1899; D.L., 21/4/00)

VULLIAMY, BLANCHE G.
Give Heed ('*modern morality*': Court, 29/6/09, *m.*) *1910*

VYNNE, NORA (see *E. PAGE*)

W., H. S.
× A Dream of Dresden China ('*wordless pl.*': Guildhall School of Music, 2/7/12)

WADDELL, HELEN JANE
The Spoiled Buddha. *1919* (Dublin)

WADDELL, WILLIAM FREELAND
World Power or Downfall. (*1919*)

WADE, ARTHUR SARSFIELD [see '*SAX ROHMER*']

WADE, HELEN
The Rake's Wife (County, Kingston, 8/7/01; Crown, Peckham, 16/5/04: +'*F. HERBERT*')

WADE, WILLIAM
× A Rosy Dawn (Com., Manchester, 13/12/02)
Old Manchester; or, When James I was King (Qns, Manchester, 26/5/04)
× Tracked (Brit., 16/8/12)

WADEBY, F. W. [see *J. S. EAGLES*]

WADHAM, MILL
The Hill of Vision ('*morality*': Rep., Nottingham, 26/3/23)

WADMORE, MABEL FLORENCE
The Moving Finger. *1929*
[This contains fifteen very short plays intended for performance by school-children. All deal with historical episodes extending from the time of Hereward the Wake to the Jameson Raid]

WAGNER, HAROLD [see *NELLIE WHITBREAD*]
Other Men's Wives (Jarrow, 17/5/20: +*H. SKARDON*)

WAGNER, LEOPOLD
× An Old Musician (Earlham H., Forest Gate, 12/4/02, *amat.*)

WAIGHT, JAMES F.
William the Conqueror. *1905*
Henry III. *1920*
Richard II. *1920*
Edward I. *1922*
[The last three historical plays formed a 'Trilogy of Freedom']

WAILES, Mrs
× The Return of Columbine (Crippl. Inst., 16/2/17, *amat.*)

WAINWRIGHT, ALBERT
Michael Gabriel (Little, Leeds, 5/2/26)
× No Room at the Inn. *1928* (Leeds: *priv.*)

WAINWRIGHT, W.

×Pettipher's Baby (T.H., Richmond, 1/4/01)

WAKEFIELD, GILBERT EDWARD

A Marriage of Inconvenience ('*f.c.*': Aldw., 11/5/24, Rep. Players)

[This was billed originally as by Henry Lussac]

The Yorick Hotel Case (Q, 17/1/27; Court, 24/4/29, revised as *The Garey Divorce Case*)

×The Coach (Scala, 7/11/27, Central School of Speech Training)

La Prisonniere (Arts, 14/12/27: from the play (1926) by E. Bourdet)

WAKELING, T. G.

×For Valour (Court, 19/9/13)

WALBROOK, BARBARA [see *MARTIN WALKER*]

WALBROOK, HENRY MACKINNON

Sunshine and Rain ('*fanciful c.*': Pier, Brighton, 22/4/01; Dover, 25/6/06, as *John Drayton, Millionaire*; Cent., 23/9/25)

×The Touch of Truth (St. J., 27/5/11, *m.*) *1911*

×The Jug of Wine (H.M., 26/11/11, *m.*)

×The Visitor ('*fant.*': Playh., L'pool, 30/5/24; K's, Hamm., 11/7/25, Playaday Players)

×The Knock on the Door (David Lewis, L'pool, 11/11/26, *amat.*)

WALDEN, Lord HOWARD DE [='*T. E. ELLIS*']

WALDRON, Rev. A. J.

×Should a Woman Tell? (Vic., Pal., 27/10/13)

The Carpenter ('*morality*': Empress, 30/3/14)

×What Would You Do? (Emp., L'pool, 14/9/14)

Should They Marry? (Osborne, Manchester, 6/9/15; Lyr., Hamm., 18/10/15: title later changed to *His Unmarried Wife*)

The Wages of Hell (Emp., Camberwell, 8/5/16: title later changed to *Once a German, Always a German*)

×Is It Immoral? (Woolwich, 24/2/19)

×With This Ring – (Vic. Pal., 23/2/20)

WALDRON, W. R.

[For earlier plays see *H. E. D.* v, 610–11]

The Three Graces ('*c.*': Thespian, Norton, 31/5/04, *amat.*)

WALEY, ARTHUR DAVID

×Callimachus (H., 7/2/19, m., Art Theatre: translated from the play by Hrotswitha)

The Nō Plays of Japan. *1921*

[This contains twenty plays by seven different authors. From the work of Seami Motokiyo eight plays are selected: 1. *Atsumori*; 2. *Tsunemasa*; 3. *Kagekiyo*; 4. *Hachi No Ki*; 5. *Aya No Tsuzumi*; 6. *Kantan*; 7. *Hagoromo*; 8. *Ikenije*; and 9. *Haku Rakuten*. Two plays are by Komparu Zembo Motoyasu: 1. *Ikuta* and 2. *Hatsuyuki*. Zenchiku Ujinobu is represented by: 1. *Kumasaka*; 2. *Aoi No Uye*; 3. *Hōkasō*; and 4. *Tanikō*. The other authors are represented by single plays each: Miyamasu (*Eboshi-Ori*), Hiyoshi Sa-ami Yasukiyo (*Benkei on the Bridge*), Kwanami Kiyotsugu (*Sobota Komachi*), and Enami Nō Sayemon (*Ukai*). One 'Kyogen' comedy, *Esashi Juo*, is also included in the collection]

WALKER, BLANCHE

×The Cap of Dreams ('*fantasy mime pl.*': Pier, Eastbourne, 11/5/25)

'*WALKER, HOLMES*' [=*GEORGE WALKLEY*]

The Death Trap (Middlesbrough, 5/3/28)

WALKER, MARTIN

Cut Grass ('*c.*': Lyc. Club, 23/5/30: +*BARBARA WALBROOK*)

WALKER, ROGER

×The Baths of Borcovicus ('*c.*') *1930*

[*WALKER, STUART*

Six Who Pass By While the Lentils Boil (Acad. of Music, Baltimore, 2/3/26; R. Acad. of Music, 18/6/26, *amat.*)

WALKER, SYD [see *P. LANGLEY*]

WALKER, T. WARBURTON

Ye Goldin Dolphins: A Tale of Old Tetbury ('*c.o.*': Inst. H., Tetbury, 6/11/12, *amat.*)

WALKER, YEOMAN

The Anti-Big Wigs. LC, '*m.pl.*': David Lewis, L'pool, 26/10/21

WALKERLY, OWEN

Little Miss Joliquet. LC, P.H., Croydon, 4/11/15

WALKLEY, GEORGE [='*HOLMES WALKER*']

WALL, HARRY

×The Good Fairy (Tyne, Newcastle, 4/4/13)
Ruts ('*c.*': Court, 19/2/17)
The Chin of Elizabeth ('*f.c.*': Pav., Torquay, 16/8/20; Playh., 26/1/21, *m.*, as *A Lady Calls on Peter*)
Renovating Eve ('*f.c.*': Rep., Nottingham, 21/2/21; Gr., Croydon, 20/3/22; Gai., Hastings, 24/3/24, as *Painting the Lily*)
Mrs Winterbotham's Woes ('*f.c.*': P's, Bradford, 12/6/22; Emp., Croydon, 10/7/22)
Bloggs ('*f.c.*': Rep., Nottingham, 23/10/22)
×The Night Porter (Col., 26/12/22) *Fr. 1925*
Havoc (Reg., 4/11/23, Rep. Players; H., 16/1/24)
The Puppet Show (Aldw., 30/3/24, Rep. Players)
Southernwood ('*c.*': Aldw., 3/5/25, Rep. Players)
×The Colonel (Court, 15/6/25, *m.*)
Stop Press ('*revue in 22 editions*', m. Noel Gay: K's, Southsea, 16/11/25)
Minetta ('*c.*': Str., 5/9/26, Rep. Players)
Sunday Island ('*f.c.*': Str., 24/4/27, Rep. Players)

WALLACE, A. C.

×Chrysanthemums. *Fr. 1903*

WALLACE, AGATHA WILLOUGHBY

Pastoral Plays. *Fr. 1921*

[This contains three one-act pieces: 1. *The Haymakers*; 2. *Under the Stars*; and 3. *A Daughter of Erin*]

WALLACE, EDGAR [RICHARD HORATIO EDGAR WALLACE: see also *R. J. YOUNG*]

×The Forest of Happy Dreams ('*African fant.*': Hippo., Camden, 6/6/10; Qns, 15/4/11)

×Dolly Cutting Herself (Hippo., 2/1/11)

×Hello, Exchange! (Pav., 7/4/13)

×The Manager's Dream (Pal., Chelsea, 14/4/13)

M'Lady (Playh., 18/7/21)

The Ringer (Wynd., 1/5/26) *1929*

[Apparently Gerald du Maurier aided Wallace in the writing of this play]

×The Mystery of Room 45 (Theatrical Gdn Party, Chelsea, 22/6/26)

The Terror (W.G., New Brighton, 21/2/27; Brixton, 7/3/27) *1929*

Double Dan (O.H., Blackpool, 4/4/27: Sav., 7/5/27)

×A Perfect Gentleman (New, 26/4/27, *m.*)

The Yellow Mask ('*m.pl.*', m. V. Duke: B'ham, 5/11/27; Carlton, 8/2/28)

The Flying Squad (New, Oxford, 5/3/28; Hippo., Golder's Green, 2/4/28; Lyc., 7/6/28)

The Man who Changed His Name (Apo., 14/3/28) *1929*

The Squeaker (Apo., 29/5/28) *1929*

The Lad (Wimbledon, 3/9/28; Shaft., 24/12/28)

Persons Unknown (Shaft., 8/5/29)

The Calendar (Pal., Manchester, 5/8/29; Hippo., Golder's Green, 2/9/29; Wynd., 18/9/29) *Fr. 1932*

On the Spot (Wynd., 2/4/30)

WALLACE, G. CARLTON

The Village Blacksmith (Qns, Leeds, 8/1/03, *cpy.*; Bury, 20/2/03; Stratford, 1/8/04)

The Love that Women Desire (Qns, Leeds, 28/4/05, *cpy.*; Leigh, 24/7/05; Gr., Islington, 23/7/06)

The Lancashire Lad (Vic., Broughton, 16/9/07; Lyr., Hamm., 27/4/08)

×The Holy War (Woolwich, 22/6/08)

A Thief in the Night (E.C., 2/8/09)

The Apple of Eden ('*r.pl.*': E.C., 22/8/10; P's, 17/4/12)

The Woman Conquers ('*r.d.*': Kennington, 19/3/13, '*preliminary pfce.*'; E.C., 4/8/13)

×The Mystery Gun (Sur., 10/5/15)

The Amazing Marriage (Castleford, 4/9/15)

The Enemy in Our Midst (Dalston, 13/9/15)

Joan of the Sword (Norwich, 16/6/19; E.C., 2/8/20)

Spirits under Proof. LC, Marine, Lowestoft, 23/4/20
Simple Simon's Baby (O.H., Northampton, 7/8/22; Emp., Edmonton, 19/2/23)

WALLACE, WILLIAM
Muguette ('*c.o.*', m. E. Missa: H.M., 25/5/10) *1910*

WALLER, JACK [see *H. CLAYTON*]

WALLER, WALLETT
×The Chaperone (Vaud., 8/2/09, *cpy.*: +*C. TROODE*)

WALLERSTEIN, G. A.
The Gamblers ('*f.*': Keble College, Oxford, 20/6/26, *amat.*: translated from a play by N. Gogol)

WALLERTON, MYLES
[For earlier plays see *H. E. D.* v, 612]
Under False Colours (W.L., 18/3/01; Emp., Edmonton, 6/9/15, as *How Far a Girl Can Go*: +*F. GILBERT*)
The Curse of Kivah (Edmonton, 9/6/02: +*F. GILBERT*)
The Best Must Win (Shak., Clapham, 15/12/02: +*F. GILBERT*)
For the Woman He Loves (Bristol, 23/2/03; Dalston, 17/8/03; Aven., Sunderland, 4/6/06, as *The Marriage Trap*: +*F. GILBERT*)
Dan the Rake ('*m.d.*': Exeter, 5/6/03: +*F. GILBERT* and *L. USHER*)
The Price of Pleasure (Macclesfield, 17/8/03; Metro., Camberwell, 16/5/04: +*F. GILBERT*)
Her First False Step (Shak., Clapham, 30/1/05, *cpy.*; Qns, L'pool, 8/2/09, as *Another Man's Wife*; Pav., 11/10/09: +*F. GILBERT*)
An Abandoned Woman (Pal., Newcastle, 6/3/05; W.L., 9/4/06; +*F. GILBERT*)

WALLIS, Mrs A.
×A Midnight Muddle (Central H., Acton, 2/5/00)
×Any Orders? (Central H., Acton, 2/5/00)

WALLIS, H. H.
×The Sportsman. LC, Monastery, Rye, 16/2/25
×Outposts. LC, Monastery, Rye, 16/2/25

WALPOLE, Sir HUGH SEYMOUR [see *R. BESIER*]

WALSH, DOUGLAS [see *P. V. BRADSHAW*]

WALSH, PERCY
Trust O'Brien (Q, 6/9/26)
×Chin-Chin-Chinaman ('*tabloid thriller*': Col., 26/8/29) *Fr. 1929*

WALSH, SHEILA
Mother (O.H., Coventry, 15/1/09)
Only a Mill Girl (Junction, Manchester, 16/1/11)
The Gambler (Junction, Manchester, 19/8/12)
The Pride o' the Mill (Junction, Manchester, 5/11/13)
Up, Boys, and at 'Em (Metro., Manchester, 5/4/15; E.C., 5/6/16)
Keep the Home Fires Burning (Barnsley, 7/2/16; E.C., 28/2/16)

The Young Minister (S. Shields, 30/7/17; E.C., 17/9/17)
When Our Lads Come Marching Home (S. Shields, 18/2/18; Junction, Manchester, 8/4/18; E.C., 10/6/18)
The Wife and the Other Woman (Junction, Manchester, 24/2/19)
The Old Times Back Again (S. Shields, 30/6/19; Stratford, 11/8/19)

[*WALTER, EUGENE*
Paid in Full (Aldw., 8/9/08)
× The Flag Station (Aldw., 29/10/08)
The Easiest Way (Stuyvesant, N.Y., 19/1/09; Pier, Eastbourne, 5/2/12; Glo., 10/2/12)
The Knife (Harmanus Bleecker H., Albany, 20/2/17; Bij., N.Y., 12/4/17; Com., 10/4/18)
Jealousy (Fortune, 5/12/28) *1932*

WALTER, FRANZ WILFRID
Happy and Glorious (Gate, 9/12/20) *1945*

WALTER, H. [see *L. A. MAGNUS*]

WALTERS, CUMING
The Golden Bank (P's, Manchester, 1/6/22: +*B. WILLIAMS*)

WALTERS, GEORGE
Joseph in Canaan. LC, Glasgow, 12/9/13

WALTERS, J. B.
× Of Two Opinions (Rehearsal, 20/6/11, *m.*, Actresses' Franchise League)

WALTHER, C. HERBERT
[A few playlets produced at music-halls]

WALTHER, T. HENRY
Shades of the Mighty. LC, New, Cardiff, 26/5/23

WALTON, GLADYS HASTINGS [see *G. HASTINGS-WALTON*]

WALTON, JOHN [see also '*OLIVE CONWAY*']
The Old Order and the New. LC, Culcheth Sunday School, 2/3/15
× Green Pastures and Piccadilly (Ambass., 7/8/19)
Clogs to Clogs ('*Lancashire c.*': Everyman, 10/11/24)
I'm Master Here (Rusholme, 7/9/25)

WALTON, WILLIAM
The Great Unknown. LC, P.H., Irlams o' th' Height, 8/2/13

WANTON, H. O.
The Pearl and the Girl ('*bsq.*': H.M.S. Bulwark at Chatham, 13/11/07)

WARD, ALBERT [see also *E. VIVIAN-EDMONDS*]
If Men Were Honest (Pav., 11/11/03, *cpy.*)
× A Noble Revenge (Gr., Croydon, 10/12/04)
× Living in a Flat (Gr., W. Hartlepool, 11/3/09, *cpy.*)
The Ways of Men (Gr., W. Hartlepool, 11/3/09, *cpy.*; Rochdale, 19/4/09)

East Lynne LC, Kennington, 29/4/14
×Evidence for Divorce. LC, Lyr., 17/3/24
The Man and the Parson (E.C., 8/8/27)

WARD, ARTHUR H.
[For earlier plays see *H. E. D.* v, 613]
The Shadow of the Cross; or, Anno Domini 670 ('*historical d.*': Stratford, 26/9/04)

WARD, C. DUDLEY
×Nell Gwyn (Pal., Chelsea, 26/12/10: +*M. V. LEVEAUX*)
Flies and Treacle (Arts, 4/3/28)
Down Wind (Arts, 15/7/28)

WARD, CLEMENTINA
The Spirit of the Wood ('*fairy pl.*': Court, 7/11/14)
Pearl, the Fishermaiden. LC, '*o.*': School H., Longnor, 10/3/22
Princess Ju-Ju ('*oa.*': Temperance H., Chester, 21/2/26, *amat.*)

WARD, CHARLES
One People (Court, L'pool, 19/3/03; Cor., 1/5/03)

WARD, EDWARD
The Man who Took a Chance (Blackburn, 11/4/27)

WARD, ERIC R.
×Let In (Lecture H., Wimbledon, 3/12/13, *amat.*: +*R. H. SCOTT*)

WARD, FREDERICK
×The Legacy (Little, 23/6/12, Connoisseurs)
The Bigamist (Clavier H., 3/10/12, Arts and Dramatic Club)

WARD, Mrs HUMPHRY (MARY AUGUSTA)
Eleanor (Court, 30/10/02; Court, 29/6/05, *revised*: dramatised from her own novel, 1900) *1903*
Agatha (St J., 7/3/05: +*L. N. PARKER*) *1904*
The Marriage of William Ashe (Terry's, 22/4/08: from her own novel (1905): +*M. MAYO*)

WARD, JAMES
The Showman ('*m.c.*': Hyde, 31/1/01, *cpy.*)

WARD, Mrs JAMES
×Man and Woman ('*folk pl.*': Brondesbury H., 14/1/09, *m.*)

WARD, Miss M. E. [see *J. F. STANFIELD*]

WARD, MARY R.
Agatha. *1904* (*priv.*)
Eleanor. *1905* (*priv.*)

WARD, T. [see *W. W. ELLIS*]

'*WARDEN, FLORENCE*' [=*FLORENCE ALICE PRICE*]
[For earlier plays see *H. E. D.* v, 613]
×A Patched-up Affair (St J., 10/5/00)
Parlez-vous français? ('*c.*': Gt. Qn St., 6/3/06)
The Case for the Lady ('*c.*': Kings., 7/3/09)
×Dolly's Week-End (Ladbr. H., 14/6/11, *cpy.*)
The Verekers (Worthing, 5/2/23)

WARDEN, GERTRUDE
[For earlier plays see *H. E. D.* v, 613]
× Miss Cinderella (Str., 29/5/00)

WARDEN-REED, F. [see *E. N. O'CONNOR*]

WARDROP, Mrs C. CAMPBELL
The Indiscretion of Elizabeth (Balfour Inst., L'pool, 17/4/09, *amat.*)
The House Divided (Balfour Inst., L'pool, 23/4/10, *amat.*)
Ambition and the Woman (Balfour Inst., L'pool, 31/3/11, *amat.*)

WARDROPER, HENRY
[For an earlier play see *H. E. D.* v, 614]
Miss Plaster of Paris ('*m.f.*': Pier, New Brighton, 14/3/10: +*H. L. OSMOND*: title later changed to *Biff Bang* and *Miss U.S.A.*

WARE, FABIAN
The Chalk Line (Qns, 2/3/12: +*N. MACOWAN*)

WAREING, ALFRED [see *G. J. HAMLEN* and *L. MERRICK*]

WARMINGTON, S. J.
× The Darkest Hour (P.W., 15/2/25, Green Room Rag)

[*WARNER, ANNE*
The Rejuvenation of Aunt Mary (Margate, 5/10/07, *cpy.*; Terry's, 22/8/10)

WARNER, JESSIE [see *F. A. TALBOT*]

WARNOCK, E.S.
[A few sketches produced at music-halls]

WARR, JOHN
All Clear ('*m.f.*': Pleasure Gdns, Folkestone, 12/11/17)
Buckshee. LC, '*m.c.*': Pal., Ramsgate, 13/3/19: title later changed to *The Lily of the Valley*)
× The Char and the Star (Hippo., Rotherhithe, 6/12/20)

WARRANT, MARC
A Wise Child ('*c.*': Gar., 12/2/28, Play Actors)

WARREN, B. J.
The Elopement of Mary Ellen. LC, Worthing, 29/3/15

WARREN, F. BROOKE
[For earlier plays see *H. E. D.* v, 615]
Mysteries of the Thames (Gr., Stalybridge, 20/7/01; W.L., 26/9/04)
An Evil Life (Smethwick, 19/9/1898; Middlesbrough, 20/7/03, *revised*)
The Coiner's Wife (Colchester, 20/2/11)
The Spendthrift ('*md.*': Scarborough, 30/9/18)

WARREN, GEOFFREY
Jim Quixote ('*c.*': Halifax, 3/8/25; Gr., Croydon, 17/8/25)
Loose Ends (D.Y., 19/4/26)

WARREN, GEORGE

The Four Just Men (Colchester, 31/8/06, *cpy.*; K's, Hamm., 8/10/06: dramatised from the novel (1905) by Edgar Wallace)

WARREN, LOW

×Revenge (Broughton T.H., Manchester, 23/5/09, *amat.*)

WARREN, RICHARD

×Breaking It Gently (River Parish R., Dover, 9/5/06)

WARREN, T. GIDEON

[For earlier plays see *H. E. D.* v, 615]

×Punctured (Str., 28/8/00) *Fr. 1904*

Em'ly (Adel., 1/8/03: +*B. LANDECK*)

WASHBURN-FREUND, Mrs F. E. [see also *P. M. COLUM*]

×The Fool and the Wise Man (P's, 11/3/12, St. Soc.)

WATERHOUSE, S. SHARPE [see *G. A. RILEY*]

WATERS, BERNARD

×Not Exactly (Midland Inst., B'ham, 17/3/28)

WATKIN, G. HAROLD

Money in Dreamland. LC, Co-op. H., Colchester, 31/1/13

WATKIN-WYNNE, W.

Light in the Darkness (Qns, B'ham, 25/6/02, *cpy.*; Lyr., Hamm., 10/8/08; Gr., Brighton, 28/7/17, revised as *Until We Meet Again*; Stratford, 17/9/17)

WATKINS, A. R. D.

×War in Wittenberg (ADC, Cambridge, 2/12/25)

WATSON, A. CAMPBELL

×Reverie (Ath., Glasgow, 13/11/23, Scott. Nat. Players)

WATSON, CLORINDA SCOTT

Jacob's Ladder (Gr., Derby, 27/8/02, *cpy.*; Emp., Maidenhead, 16/3/03, with subtitle, *The Scarlet Woman*, and described as by *C. S. BEAULIEU*)

WATSON, F. MARRIOTT [see *F. MARRIOTT-WATSON*]

WATSON, GWENDOLEN JOHNSTON

Sneewittchen ('*fairy c.*': Cavendish R., Mortimer St., 27/6/01)

WATSON, HELEN H.

×Enter – Honoria! *1930*

WATSON, HILDA SPENCER

The Princess and the Swineherd ('*fairy pl.*': Margaret Morris, 21/12/18; Studio, Kensington, 14/11/27)

WATSON, MACDONALD

×The Prizewinner ('*c.*': Coll., 7/6/15) *1928*

Lass o' Mine ('*c.*': Pav., Torquay, 14/8/19; H.M., Aberdeen, 20/9/20, as *What Fools Men Are*; Kings., 12/5/21, as *Hunky Dory*) *Fr. 1926* (as *Hunky Dory*)

×A Masterful Man ('*c.*') *1928*

×The Blarney Stone. *1929*

×The Suit of Serge. *1929*

WATSON, NAN MARRIOTT [see *N. MARRIOTT-WATSON*]

WATSON, T. MALCOLM

[For earlier plays see *H. E. D.* v, 616]

×Church and Stage (Crit., 13/12/00)

×Sheerluck Jones ('*dramatic criticism in four burlesque paragraphs*': Terry's, 29/10/01: +*E. LA SERRE*)

Captain Kettle (Adel., 23/10/02: +*S. M. CARSON*)

Winnie Brooke, Widow ('*c.*': Gr., Boscombe, 2/4/04; Crit., 1/9/04; Leicester, 13/3/16, revised as *A Modern Eve*: +*H. FORDWYCH*)

×The Conversion of Nat Sturge (H.M., 23/6/04, *m.*; Gar., 9/7/04) *Fr. 1904*

Two Men and a Maid ('*c.*': O.H., Northampton, 1/3/05, *cpy.*: also called *Molly*)

An Exile from Home ('*m.f.*': m. P. E. Fletcher and E. Hess: Sav., 12/6/06)

Handsome Jim (Margate, 16/7/06)

×Sanctuary (Emp., 15/12/09)

×A Change of Front (Emp., 25/1/10)

×A Loose End (Pal., 7/11/10)

The Double Event (Oxf., 27/10/13)

×A Court of Enquiry (Col., 28/8/16)

×The Tale of a Ring. LC., Hippo., Portsmouth, 28/9/17

WATSON, WILLIAM G.

×Memories (Freemasons' H., Woolwich, 16/2/12, *amat.*)

×The Heart of a Fool (Shooter's H., Bowling Club., Woolwich, 18/7/12, *amat.*)

Fine Feathers (T.H., Woolwich, 29/3/13, *amat.*)

WATSON-MILL, C. [see also *F. BATEMAN*]

The Seal of Silence (Gr., Croydon, 10/2/02; Stratford, 14/7/02)

A Wrecker of Men (Carlton, Saltley, 10/12/03; Carlton, Greenwich, 18/4/04)

A Warning to Women ('*r.d.*': Lyc., Eccles, 28/5/06; Stratford, 23/7/06)

×A Society Woman (Ldn. Music Hall, 14/1/07)

The Eve of Her Wedding (Miners', Ashington, 13/5/07; Sunderland, 27/5/07; Woolwich, 18/9/11)

The Love of the Princess (Gr., Nelson, 13/4/08; E.C., 14/9/08)

For Love and the King (P.W., Mexborough, 13/4/08; E.C., 20/7/08)

The Sinner (Sunderland, 26/7/09; E.C., 18/4/10)

Can a Woman Be Good? (Chatham, 6/9/09; Pav., 18/10/09: title later changed to *The Night Side of London*)

For Old Times' Sake (Carlton, Saltley, 21/3/10)

A Prince of Pleasure (O.H., Kidderminster, 20/2/11)

Mid Pleasures and Palaces (Gr., Mansfield, 23/9/12)

The Pirate Ship (Sunderland, 1/9/13)

All Ye that Pass By (Stanley, 3/8/14; Stratford, 14/12/14: title later changed to *The Unseen Hand*)

In Time of War (S. Shields, 14/9/14; Lyc., 22/5/15)
The Man with the Silver Badge (Leamington, 6/10/19; E.C., 14/7/19)
The Eternal Flame (Leamington, 1/10/28; Court, 7/1/29)

[*WATTERS, GEORGE MANKER* [see *A. HOPKINS*]

WATTS, Mrs M. F.
The Claimant ('*c.*': Qns, 11/9/24)

WATTS, W. H.
×The Horoscope. *1927*

WAUD, W. O.
×Blind Jealousy (Ladbr. H., 21/1/04)

WAUGH, CONSTANCE E.
Holiday Plays for Girls. *1909*
[This contains three short pieces: 1. *Under Distinguished Patronage*; 2. *Aunt Penelope*; and 3. *Wanted – A Governess*]

WAUGH, JOSEPH LAING
×Cute McCheyne ('*c.*': R. Inst. H., Glasgow, 13/1/21, Scott. Nat. Players: +*A. P. WILSON*)
×Luiffy (Ath., Glasgow, 20/12/21, Scott. Nat. Players; Col., 2/12/23: +*A. P. WILSON*)
×A Sprig o' Appleringie (R. Inst., H., Glasgow, 26/4/23, Scott. Nat. Players: +*A. P. WILSON*)

WAY, ARTHUR SANDERS
[As is well known, this scholar was a prolific translator of classical dramas, responsible for producing verse renderings of Aeschylus, Sophocles, Euripides and Aristophanes]

WAYNE, P. A.
×Two Women. LC, B'ham University, 13/2/14: +*F. B. GUISE*

WEARMOUTH, C. H. V.
×Here's to Our Enterprise (Aven., Sunderland, 31/10/27, *amat.*)

WEAVER, J. [see *E. C. MATTHEWS*]

WEAVER, WYN
In Holy Orders ('*md.*': Dover, 18/6/06: title later changed to *A Parson and a Man*)
×Golf Clubs (Hippo., L'pool, 22/11/20) *Fr. 1925*
The Rising Generation ('*c.*': O.H., Southport, 1/10/23; Shaft., 3/12/23: +*L. LEYCESTER*) *1924*

WEBB, BEATRICE
Uncle's Courtship (Emp., Islington, 7/10/07: +*ALFRED PHILIPS*)

WEBB, N. F.
×Passed Unanimously (O.H., Belfast, 23/1/28)

WEBB, SIDNEY H.
Sam. LC, Crippl. Inst., 31/3/14

WEBLING, PEGGY
Westward Ho! (Gai., Manchester, 1/2/13; Pallad., 24/2/13: dramatised from Charles Kingsley's novel)
Frankenstein (Emp., Preston, 7/12/27)

[*'WEBSTER, JEAN'* [=*ALICE JANE CHANDLER WEBSTER*]
Daddy Long Legs (Atlantic City, 20/2/14; Gai., N.Y., 28/9/14; D.Y., 29/5/16) *Fr. 1922*

WEBSTER, ROBERT G.
×The Conversion of Aunt Sarah (Court, 12/2/14)

WEEKS, KENNETH
Esau and the Beacon. Five Plays. *1912*
Five Unpractical Plays. *1913*
Dramatic Inventions. Five Pieces. *1913*

WEIMAN, RITA
The Acquittal (*'modern pl.'*: Portsmouth, 25/1/28; Gr., Croydon, 6/2/28)

WEINER, BLANCHE
×The Chemist (Little, 28/3/21)

WEIR, CECIL [see *L. GODDARD*]

WEITZEL, E. [see *F. S. ISHAM*]

WELBY, DÉSIRÉE
The Temptation of Eve (Q, 30/1/28: +*C. SANDEMAN*)

WELCH, ERNEST F.
The Gent. from Lenton's (*'m.f.'*: Colosseum, Dudley Port, 7/1/03, *cpy.*)

WELCH, RUBEN G.
[Several sketches produced at music-halls]

WELCHMAN, MABEL
Hannah Learns How (*'m. fant.'*: Scala, 2/11/26, *m.*: +*E. FAGAN*)

WELD-BLUNDELL, C. J.
Mrs Fitzherbert. *1912* (Newcastle: *priv.*)

WELDON, A. E. [=*'BRINSLEY MACNAMARA'*]

WELLARD, TOM
×The Way of Bethlehem (*'nativity pl. for young people'*) *1929* (SPCK)

WELLESLEY, JULIAN [see *M. MORTON*]

[*WELLS, CHARLOTTE ELIZABETH*
Love and the Law (Vic., H., 16/3/08, *cpy.*)

WELLS, GEORGE
×The King of Palestine (Olympia, Shoreditch, 1/8/10)

WELLS, HERBERT GEORGE
Kipps (Vaud., 6/3/12: dramatised from his own novel (1905): +*R. BESIER*)

The Wonderful Visit (St M., 10/2/21: dramatised from his own novel (1895): +*ST J. ERVINE*)

WELLS, H. WESTON

Wee Willie Winkie ('*children's pl.*': St Peter's H., Brockley, 6/4/07, *amat.*)

WELLS, JANE

×The Origin of Alf (Apo., 12/6/13)

×The Flag Day (Three Arts Club, 2/7/16: +*H. E. MORGAN*)

WELLS, NANNIE KATHARIN

×Skaith. *1929* (in *The Scots Magazine*, x, 345–50)

WELLS, WILLIAM K. [see *F. THOMPSON*]

WELSFORD, E. H. [see *S. G. CARPENTER*]

WELTCH, ETHEL [see *R. O'NEIL*]

WELTON, WILFRED

×At the Court of Xerxes (Little, 6/4/11)

WENSLEY, SHAPCOTT

Little Snow White. LC, '*oa.*': Sav., 21/6/20

WENTWORTH, VERA

×An Allegory (Rehearsal, 25/4/11, *m.*) *1913*

WERTH, A.

Mozart and Salieri. LC, Alb. H., 28/9/27: adapted from the dramatic poem by A. S. Pushkin. *1925* (in *The Glasgow Book of Prose and Verse, 1923–1924*)

WESSEX, JOHN

A Masque of the Seasons. *1911* (Sturminster-Newton, *priv.*)

WEST, ARTHUR

Captain Billy (Redditch, 29/2/12)

WEST, CON C. [*PERCIVAL C. WEST*: see also *S. G. ANDERSON*, *H. CLAYTON*, '*IAN HAY*' and *H. C. SARGENT*]

The Flour Girl ('*m. millodrama*', m. Cecil Goodall: Gr., Clapham, 15/12/13)

×Dinner Together (Vic. Pal., 26/3/14: +*STUART G. ANDERSON*)

Cross Talk. *Fr. 1919*

[This contains ten short duologues, written in collaboration with *S. G. ANDERSON*]

×Seasoned to Taste (Metropolitan, 1/12/19)

Ideas ('*revue*': Emp., Bristol, 22/12/23)

Love and Laughter ('*m.pl.*', m. R. Eckersley: New, Northampton, 24/3/24; Emp., New X, 31/3/24: +*R. S. HOOPER* and *E. LAWRENCE*)

Pages ('*revue*': Emp., Penge, 17/11/24)

Tilly ('*m.c.*', m. Haydn Wood and Jack Waller: Emp., Leeds, 21/7/24; Alh., 3/11/24: based on Ian Hay's comedy, *Tilly of Bloomsbury*: +*H. CLAYTON*)

Cupid Whispers ('*revue*': Hippo., Willesden, 10/8/25)

My 'Erb ('*revue*': Hippo., Ilford: 31/8/25)

High Life (*'revue'*: Hippo., Lewisham, 18/1/26)
Tangles (*'m.f.'*, m. P. Manton: Playh., Walton-on-Thames, 22/2/26, *amat.*: +*H. SARGENT*)
Pontoon (*'revue'*: Hippo., St Helen's, 21/2/27)
Sunshine Sal (*'m.pl.'*: Emp., Nottingham, 12/3/28)
All Right on the Western Front (*'m.bsq.'*: Gr., B'ham, 9/12/29)

WEST, GEORGE

A Trip to Wembley. LC, *'m.pl.'*: Seaham Harbour, 18/9/24

WEST, JULIUS

×The Dear Departing (Court, 6/2/16, Pioneer Players: translated from *Linbov k bliksneli* by L. Andreev) *1916*
×The Proposal (Rep., B'ham, 18/3/16; St J., 3/12/18, *m.*: translated from *Predlozhenie* (1889) by A. Chekhov) *1916*
×The Wedding (Grafton Galleries, 14/5/17; St M., 25/1/20, *m.*, Pioneer Players: translated from *Svadba* (1890) by A. Chekhov) *1916*
×On the High Road (St M., 25/1/20, *m.*, Pioneer Players: translated from *Na bolshoi doroge* (1884) by A. Chekhov) *1916*
×The Anniversary (Kings., 8/5/21, Rep. Players: translated from *Zhubilei* (1892) by A. Chekhov) *1916*

WEST, STANLEY C.

Phillida. LC, Pier, Brighton, 28/3/14: +*C. HECTOR*
×Settled Out of Court. LC, Crippl. Inst., 1/11/22. *Fr. 1922*
[A few sketches and playlets produced at music-halls]

WESTBROOK, HERBERT

Brother Alfred (*'c.'*: D.P., Eastbourne, 3/3/13; Sav., 8/4/13: +*P. G. WODEHOUSE*)

WESTCOTT, ARTHUR

×The Dream Goddess (Rehearsal, 23/5/09)

WESTLAKE, ANNIE L.

×Boasts – and a Bruise. *Fr. 1922*

WESTON, F. G.

Kate; or, Love Will Find Out the Way (*'fant. ballad o.'*: Kings., 25/2/24)

WESTON, HAROLD

The Heiress (B'ham, 13/6/10: +*F. THORPE*)
[A few sketches produced at music-halls]

WESTON, ROBERT P. [see also *D. FURBER* and *L. WYLIE*]

Mr. Tickle, M.P. (*'m.pl.'*: Gr., Blackpool, 29/9/24; Emp., Finsbury Park, 26/1/25: +*B. LEE*)
King Rags (*'m.c.'*, m. H. Weston: Emp., Leeds, 23/8/26; Emp., Finsbury Park, 27/9/26: +*B. LEE*)
The Girl Friend (*'m.c.'*, m. C. Conrad: Emp., L'pool, 15/8/27; Pal., 8/9/27: +*B. LEE*)
Hit the Deck (*'m.c.'*, m. V. Youmans: adapted to the English stage by *R. P. WESTON* and *B. LEE* from the musical by *H. FIELDS*: Alh., Glasgow, 10/10/27; Hippo., 3/11/27)

Merry Merry ('*m.c.*': Emp., Southampton, 11/2/29; Carlton, 28/2/28: +*B. LEE*)
Hold Everything ('*m.c.*': adapted to the English stage by *R. P. WESTON* and *B. LEE* from a musical by *B. G. DE SYLVA* and *J. McGOWAN*: Alh., Glasgow, 27/5/29; Pal., 12/6/29)
Here Comes the Bride ('*m.c.*', m. A. Schwartz: adapted to the English stage by *R. P. WESTON* and *B. LEE* from a musical by *E. MacGREGOR* and *O. HARBACH*: O.H., Blackpool, 7/10/29; Piccadilly, 20/2/30)
[For an account of this author's various contributions to the stage see *Who's Who in the Theatre*]

WESTROM, F.
Bobby ('*f.*': St G's H., 26/10/24, Sunday Players)

'*WETHERHELT, JAN VAN*' [=*J. STEER*]

WETTON, MILDRED
Dido, Queen of Carthage. LC, Aubrey House, Campden Hill, 30/6/16

WHAITE, HERBERT HOYLE
×Fame. LC, Ass. H., Erdington, 4/4/13
The Way Back ('*md.*': Alex., B'ham, 25/4/21)
The Supercrank ('*c.*': Alex., B'ham, 27/4/21)
The Devil's Half Holiday. LC, Ass. H., Erdington, 15/4/14: title later changed to *Peradventure*
The Incompatibles. LC, Church House H., Erdington, 15/12/22
The Hunchback of Whittington. LC, Church House H., Erdington, 15/12/22
×Fidelitas ('*t.*') *Fr. 1922*

WHARNCLIFF, PATRICK
Burglars ('*f.*': T.H., Wandsworth, 19/1/03, *cpy.*)

WHARNCLIFFE, JOSEPH M.
Foiled by a Woman ('*md.*': Junction, Manchester, 4/12/11; Stratford, 20/5/12: called originally *Playing for Love*)
The White Slave Girl ('*md.*': Gai., Methill, 12/12/12; Stratford, 17/2/13)
The Woman of Death (Rot., L'pool, 25/8/13; Stratford, 18/5/14)
The Great Conspiracy (L'pool, 13/10/13; Stratford, 15/2/15, as *When There Was War*)
The Bishop's Emeralds (H.M., Carlisle, 18/3/16)
The Right Way. LC, Oldham, 22/4/19
Luck o' Love (Gr., Aberaman, 14/3/21; Stratford, 18/7/21)
[Several playlets produced at music-halls]

'*WHARTON, ANTHONY P.*' [=*ALISTER McALLISTER*, who also used the pseudonym of '*LYNN BROCK*']
Irene Wycherley (Kings., 9/10/07)
×A Nocturne (Kings., 19/5/08) *Fr. 1913*
At the Barn ('*c.*': P.W., 11/4/12) *Fr. 1912*
Sylvia Greer ('*c.*': Qns, 16/11/12)

13 Simon Street (Vaud., 1/5/13; Col., 13/10/13, as *The House in Simon Street*) Fr. *1913*
A Guardian Angel. LC, Emp., Penge, 28/5/15
The Riddle (New, 17/6/16: +*M. ROBERTS*)
Needles and Pins ('*f.*': Str., 16/6/29, Rep. Players)
[*Who's Who in the Theatre* records another play, *Benvenuto Cellini* (1915) but concerning this no particulars have been found]

WHARTON, EDITH NEWBOLD
The Joy of Living (New, 24/6/03: translated from *Es lebe das Leben* (1902) by H. Sudermann) *1903*

WHEATLEY, F. G.
Spanish Bits. LC, '*m.pl.*': Ass. R., Pontefract, 16/2/24

WHEELER, C. E. (see also *JANET ACHURCH* and *SYBIL AMHERST*)
×Das Märchen (Little, 28/1/12, Adel. Play Soc.: +*H. GRANVILLE-BARKER*: translated from the play (1893) by A. Schnitzler)
The Golden Fleece (H., 14/6/14, St. Soc.)

WHEELER, D. W. [see *M. C. BARNE*]

WHEELER, EDITH
×A Nice Little Supper. *1905*
×A Woman's Way (Wellington Minor H., Belfast, 4/12/03) *1906*
×A Bouquet. *1907*
×A Discord. *1907*
×In Wonderland ('*fairy operetta for children*') *1908*
×The Sentence. *1908*

WHEELER, MONROE
Orphée (Gate, 11/4/28: translated from the play (1926) by J. Cocteau)

WHEELER, PENELOPE
×The Green Cockatoo (Aldw., 9/3/13, *m.*, St. Soc; Vaud., 23/10/13: adapted from *Der grüne Kakadu* (1898) by A. Schnitzler)

WHEELER, WORLAND S.
[A few playlets produced at music-halls]

WHELDON, F. W.
The Red King. LC, Maddermarket, Norwich, 3/11/24

WHELEN, FREDERICK
×The Lethal Hotel ('*grotesque*': H.M., 7/12/09: adapted from a play by A. M. Willner)

WHELPTON, Miss C. M.
The Plum Cake ('*fant.*': St Saviour's Church R., Eastbourne, 13/1/03) *1900*

WHINYATES, AMY
×Sir Rupert and Cecily; or, The Young Cavalier (Court, 8/12/14, as *The Young Cavalier*) *1890*
×A Royal Rose of Merry England (Court, 10/7/15, *m.*) *1902*

Ali Baba and the Forty Thieves. *1904*
The Yellow Dwarf. *1905*
Princess O Ione San. *1909*
Bluebeard, or, The Fatal Effects of Curiosity. *1910*
× Jack Frost ('*fairy fant.*': Court, 8/12/14)

WHITAKER, HAROLD [see also *P. A. RUBENS*]
× Cold Poison (Emp., Kilburn, 22/5/11) *Fr. 1913*

WHITAKER, S. F. G.
L'Avocat Pathelin (translated from the play (1706) by D. A. de Brueys) *1905*

WHITBREAD, E. A. J.
× A Lesson in Love (Park, Hanwell, 4/10/16)

WHITBREAD, HAROLD W.
Plays of Myth and History. *1929*
[This contains four plays designed for performance by children: 1. *Beowulf and Grendel*; 2. *Anlaf, the Sea-King*; 3. *Harold the Saxon*; and 4. *1066*]

WHITBREAD, J. W.
[For earlier plays see *H. E. D.* v, 620]
Rory O'More (Qns, Dublin, 16/4/00)
The Insurgent Chief, Michael Dwyer (Qns, Dublin, 31/3/02)
The Ulster Hero, Henry Joy McCracken (Qns, Dublin, 12/1/03)
The Sham Squire (Qns, Dublin, 26/12/03)
Sarsfield: a Story of the Siege of Limerick (Qns, Dublin, 26/12/04)
The Irish Dragoon (Qns, Dublin, 26/12/05)
The French Hussar (Qns, Dublin, 24/12/06)
Robert Emmett (Castlebar, 6/12/12)
The Soldier Priest (Wolverhampton, 31/1/16)

WHITBREAD, NELLIE
The Blackmailer ('*Irish-American d.*': Qns, Dublin, 9/1/05)
An Irishman's Home (O.H., Cork, 27/3/15; Paisley, 25/9/16, as *The Pride of the O'Grady's*)
× The Spider (Granville, 28/4/19)
Disgraced (Stratford, 8/9/19: +*H. WAGNER*)

WHITBY, CHARLES
Ambition (Little, Bristol, 19/1/25)

WHITBY, HOLT
The Master of Iron (Tyne, Newcastle, 4/5/14: adapted from *Le Maître de forges* (1883) by G. Ohnet)

WHITE, ARTHUR [see also *E. DOTTRIDGE*]
× The New Detective (Tiv., Manchester, 4/11/12)
Sammy in Society ('*m.c.*': Pal., Oldham, 26/12/21, *m.*)

WHITE, BARTON
[For earlier plays see *H. E. D.* v, 620]
Mostly Fools (Gr., Fulham, 1/4/01)
Amorelle ('*m.c.*', m. G. Serpette: Kennington, 8/6/03; Com., 18/2/04) *1904*

Jack and Jill ('*m.f.*', m. A. Banes: Gai., Manchester, 29/10/06)
×The Second Mrs Grundy (Roy., 23/7/07)
The Pin and the Pudding (Margate, 7/6/09; Com., 23/8/09)
×Sir 'Erbert (County, Kingston, 2/5/10)
×The Last Drop (Nottingham, 16/5/10)
The Remedy ('*f.*': Court, 5/5/11, *m.*)
×Off the Map (Windsor, 30/9/12)

WHITE, C.
The Man-of-All Work. LC, Stanley, Durham, 17/7/17

WHITE, Mrs DERING
×Of Gloucester-Place (Brompton Hospital, 15/3/04)

WHITE, Miss E.
[For an earlier play see *H. E. D.* v, 620]
×In Face of the Enemy (Wynd., 16/10/02) *1912* (Amersham, *priv.*)
×A Snapt Gold Ring (Ladbr. H., 7/1/03: +*E. WOLSTENHOLME*)
×Patriotism (Pav., Herne Bay, 2/10/03)

WHITE, E. L.
The Port of Yesterday (Str., 29/4/28, Rep. Players)

WHITE, HELEN
×The Powder Puff (Little Vic., Brighton, 7/12/24)
×Love in the Larder (Little Vic., Brighton, 4/1/25)

WHITE, HESTER
×A Fugitive (+*MARY STANTON*) *1928* (Village Drama Soc.)
×Harmony Hall (+*MARY STANTON*) *1928* (Village Drama Soc.)

WHITE, JACK
[A few sketches and playlets produced at music-halls]

WHITE, LEONARD CHARLES
The Squire of Little Clodbury ('*c.*': Stanley H., S. Norwood, 7/5/04)
×The Fairy Godfather ('*f.c.*': Bij., 31/1/06, *amat.*)
×A Slight Misunderstanding (Bij., 31/1/06, *amat.*)
×Amy's Burglar (P.H., Croydon, 11/6/07, *amat.*)
×The Greater Law (RADA, 13/1/24) *1924*
×The Perfect Marriage (Col., 7/1/29)

WHITE, MADELINE
×The Right to Buy (K's H., 17/6/22, Interlude Players)

WHITE, WALTER
Just a Story ('*fant.*': Lyr., Hamm., 16/12/21, *m.*, Lancelyn Players)

WHITEHEAD, CECIL M.
A Dear Little Devil ('*f.c.*': Pier, Brighton, 24/11/19; St M., 1/12/19, as *A Dear Little Lady*)

WHITEHEAD, GORDON (see also *S. BLOW*)
Wrongs and Rights ('*c.*': Str., 9/12/28)

WHITEHOUSE, MARY

×The Enchanted Hour. LC, Church House H., Erdington, 11/3/25

WHITEHOUSE, ROBERT [see *A. BUCHANAN* and '*RITA*']

WHITELEY, ARNOLDINE

×Margaretta (Court, 26/3/14)

WHITESTONE, HENRY

The Londoners ('*f.c.*': Apo., 26/3/03: from the novel (1898) by Robert Hichens)
'Tally Ho!' ('*c.*': Bradford, 28/11/07, *m.*)

WHITLEY, Rev. ARTHUR

Mehalah (Com., Manchester, 14/11/00: from the novel (1880) by S. Baring-Gould)

WHITLOCK, CHARLES

[For earlier plays see *H. E. D.* v, 621]
The Missionary ('*md.*': Ilkeston, 19/5/00, *cpy.*; Court, Warrington, 23/7/00)
Guy Fawkes, the Traitor (N. Shields, 15/7/01)
The King's Secret (Aquar., Yarmouth, 5/4/06)
The Sporting King (Metro., Gateshead, 27/5/07)
The Old Wife and the New (Osborne, Manchester, 20/4/14: +*G. WHITLOCK*)
The War Baby (H.M., Walsall, 19/7/15: +*G. WHITLOCK*)

WHITLOCK, GEORGINA [see *C. WHITLOCK*]

WHITMARSH, F. J.

A Narrow Squeak ('*c.o.*': Hippo., Manchester, 26/5/13; Col., 16/6/13)
Midnight ('*m.f.*': Vic. Pal., 13/9/15)

WHITMES, ERNEST A.

×Dumbstruck. LC, Corn Exchange, Maidstone, 30/9/13

[*WHITTAKER, CHARLES*

Apron Strings (Str., 1/4/28, Venturers; Q, 23/4/28)

WHITTAKER, ROBERT R.

The Immortal Memory ('*c.*': Court, 26/2/17)
The Third Finger (Art, Leeds, 16/11/25; Rep., B'ham, 9/2/27, with revised third act; Everyman, 6/2/28)
The Sphinx ('*c.*': Alb. H., Leeds, 1/11/26)
As Dreams Are Made On (Little, Leeds, 11/2/29)

WHITTY, EDWARD

The Hand of Destiny (Stratford, 25/11/12: +*G. HASTINGS-WALTON*)

WHITWORTH, GEOFFREY ARUNDEL

×Father Noah ('*Mystery of the Ark*': Margaret Morris, 25/2/22, Unnamed Soc. of Manchester; Sav., 12/6/23, *m.*) *1918*
×Miss de Crespigny's Moment. LC, Red Triangle Hut, Woodchester, 2/9/22
Not Yet (Kings., 7/10/23, Rep. Players)

WHYTE, CEDRIC [see *S. WHYTE*]

WHYTE, HAROLD [see also *A. CONQUEST*]

[For earlier plays see *H. E. D.* v, 621]

The Red Terror ('*md.*': O.H., Londonderry, 6/8/00; Edmonton, 10/8/03)

The Pleasures of London (P.H., Sydenham, 11/11/01: originally licensed in 1897 as *London Chimes*)

True to the Queen ('*military pl.*': Crown, Peckham, 26/11/00; Gr., 29/7/01, *revised*; Gr., Fulham, 3/5/09, as *An Englishman's Honour*)

Women of London ('*md.*': Crown, Peckham, 1/4/01)

A Girl's False Step (K's, Hoxton, 30/1/05)

Oliver Twist (K's, Walthamstow, 2/10/05: +*R. BALMAIN*)

Her King ('*r.pl.*': Crown, Peckham, 9/9/08, *cpy.*)

WHYTE, MARJORY

Brodling (St Pancras People's Theatre, 5/5/27)

Disillusion (Etlinger, 14/7/27)

WHYTE, SYLVIA

×Madame Amalie, Milliner (Arts Centre, 20/3/14)

×The Whirlwind (Bij., 10/12/21: +*F. TEMPLE*)

The Waiting Game ('*c.*': Pier, Eastbourne, 18/4/29: +*C. WHYTE*)

WIATT, HAROLD COMBER

Money and Man ('*modern pl.*': Bradford, 5/4/09; E.C., 19/4/09: from the novel, *Whoever Shall Offend* (1904) by F. Marion Crawford)

Holiday Home (Corona H., Hamm., 14/12/09, *amat.*)

The Fool (Bristol, 13/8/23; called originally *The Realms of Eternity*: title later changed to *The Great Ambassador* and *The Gateway of the East*)

The Wish Tower (Gai., Ayr, 28/1/24: title later changed to *Would You Believe It?*: +*J. SMITH WRIGHT*)

The Third Person. LC, Pal., Hinderwell, 5/5/24

The Moral Gamblers. LC, Pal., Hinderwell, 3/6/24

Doubting Castle ('*c.*': Little, Hove, 9/6/27)

The Social Butterfly ('*c.*': Little, Hove, 13/1/28)

Our Idols (Little, 5/2/28)

WIBROW, C. [see *A. DAVENPORT*]

WICKENS, JOHN

×Charley's Uncle (Ambass., 4/6/20, *m.*)

WICKHAM, JOHN J.

×The Question (Gai., Manchester, 19/8/12)

WICKS, ANDREW

×Back to the Land (Sav., 30/10/05)

WIDNELL, VICTOR

A Woman of Impulse (Court, L'pool, 24/3/02; P'cess of W., Kennington, 7/4/02; Com., 16/9/02, as *Secret and Confidential*)

The Orange Blossom ('*c.*': Str., 18/1/04, *cpy.*; Terry's, 23/1/08)

[*WIGGIN, KATE DOUGLAS*
Rebecca of Sunnybrook Farm (Glo., 2/9/12: +*C. THOMPSON*)

[*WILBUR, CRANE*
The Monster (New, Cardiff, 23/1/28; Pal., Chelsea, 5/3/28; Str., 17/3/28)
The Stranger Within (Gar., 20/6/29)

WILBY, THOMAS
Seven O'clock (Kings., 31/5/27, *m.*)

WILCOX, ELLA WHEELER
×A Poem in Pantomime (Little, 17/1/11, *m.*, Oncomers Soc.)

WILD, J. J.
[Numerous sketches and playlets produced at music-halls]

WILDE, NORA
The Test ('*c.*': Little Vic., Brighton, 26/1/25)

[*WILDE, PERCIVAL L.*
×The Traitor (S. Ldn. Pal., 17/5/09) *Fr. 1915*
×The Toy-Shop. LC, Pal., Doncaster, 21/7/15. *1915*
×Confessional (LC, Crippl. Inst., 1/11/22; A.L.S. Trav. Th., 1922) *Fr. 1923*
×The Dyspeptic Ogre. LC, Crippl. Inst., 1/11/22. *Fr. 1922*
×The Sequel. LC, Crippl. Inst., 1/11/22. *Fr. 1922*
×Reverie. *1924*

WILDIG, LAURA
Once upon a Time (St M., 22/12/19, *m.*)
Priscilla and the Profligate (Portsmouth, 4/10/20; D.Y., 13/10/20)
Punchinello (Court, 22/6/24, Interlude Players)

WILFORD, EDGAR
Widow's Weeds ('*c.*': Kings., 10/12/22, Pl. Actors) *1940*
×She Never Could Housekeep (Blackfriars, 21/4/29, Guild Players)

WILFORD, ROBERT
The Marshal ('*historical pl.*': Court, L'pool, 8/5/02, *cpy.*)
The Dissemblers (Sunderland, 21/5/02, *cpy.*)
The Jester ('*historical pl.*': Sunderland, 22/5/02, *cpy.*)
Captain Dare ('*c.*': St J., Manchester, 22/1/03, *cpy.*)
The Crown (O.H., Leicester, 5/9/04, *cpy.*)
Count Morata (Roy., Barrow-in-Furness, 10/9/04, *cpy.*)
The Cynics ('*c.*': Roy., Barrow-in-Furness, 10/9/04, *cpy.*)
×Hallowe'en (Ath., Lancaster, 7/8/07, *cpy.*)
×Summer Roses (Ath., Lancaster, 7/8/07, *cpy.*)
×The Red Flag (Hippo., Balham, 3/7/11)
×The Plain Sort (Bournemouth, 2/3/14)

WILKES, ALLENE TUPPER
The Man in the Wheel Chair ('*mystery pl.*': Bognor, 19/4/24; Com., 22/7/24, as *The Creaking Chair*) *Fr. 1927*

WILKINSON, GEOFFREY
The New Tenants ('*c.*': Rehearsal, 30/7/08)

×On the Latch (Rehearsal, 7/2/11)
×A Cure for Indifference. *Fr. 1916*
×The Empty House. LC, Emp., Southend, 15/9/17
×Releasing a Man (St J., 23/5/19, *m.*)
Lady Dearmer's Difficulties ('*c.*': Philbeach H., Earl's Court, 10/3/21)

WILKINSON, HARRY
Love Dreams ('*m.c.*': Hippo., Mexborough, 27/8/28)

WILKINSON, K. E. T.
Killibeg; or, The Peer of the Pacific ('*c.o.*', m. T. T. Noble: York, 27/11/11)

WILKINSON, L. G.
×Goloshins. LC, Margaret Morris, 6/3/16
×Father Has the Fantods. LC, Margaret Morris, 6/3/16
×The Magic Stick. LC, Margaret Morris, 6/3/16
×The Puppet in the Soup-Pot. LC, Margaret Morris, 6/3/16
×Shut the Door. LC, Margaret Morris, 6/3/16

WILKINSON, MATT
[For earlier plays see *H. E. D.* v, 623]
Saturday Night in London (Bristol, 12/6/1899; Carlton, Greenwich, 29/4/01)
A Touch of Nature (Bristol, 19/5/02)
Is Law Justice? (Gr., Walsall, 21/12/03; S.W., 11/3/12)
Fortunes of the Turf. LC, Foresters, 27/2/14
Wireless on the Brain ('*f.c.*': Gr., Abingdon, 30/4/23)
Sweeney Todd (E.C., 6/2/28)
Jack Sheppard (E.C., 30/4/28)

WILKINSON, W.
×Lord Dryasdust. LC, Margaret Morris, 6/3/16
×The Witch Bewitched. LC, Margaret Morris, 6/3/16

WILLARD, JAMES
A Woman of Pleasure (P.W., Southampton, 22/11/00, *cpy.*; P'cess of W., Kennington, 8/7/01)
The Crimson Horseshoe (Crown, Peckham, 1/6/03; title later changed to *A Woman's Pluck*)
The Girl with the Angel Face ('*mystery d.*': Shak., Clapham Junction, 3/8/08)
Paying the Price (Alex., Hull, 13/6/10; Brixton, 26/9/10)
There's Millions in It ('*m.pl.*': Pal., Oldham, 30/7/23)
[Several playlets produced at music-halls]

[*WILLARD, JOHN*
The Cat and the Canary (National, N.Y., 7/2/22; Portsmouth, 9/10/22; Shaft., 31/10/22) *Fr. 1927*
The Green Beetle ('*md.*': Main-street, Asbury Park, U.S.A., 14/7/24; Klaw, N.Y., 2/9/24; Gr., Fulham, 23/9/29)

WILLCOCK, S. [see *G. CHANDOS*]

WILLETT, ERNEST

A White Passion Flower ('*pl. of modern life*': Kennington, 9/11/03)

WILLIAM, ISIDORE

Stepchild of the World. LC, Scala, 6/7/21

WILLIAMS, Mrs ANTONIA R.

The Heart of the Machine (Roy., 27/6/07, *m.*) *1910* (see below)

The Street (Midland, Manchester, 5/11/07; Little, 30/11/13, Pioneer Players) *1908* (in *Three New Plays*)

[Besides *The Street*, the volume of *Three New Plays* includes two short pieces, 1. *Fame and the Artist*, and 2. *Jack Hamlin, Gambler*]

The Bread of Life, and Other Plays. *1910*

[This contains, besides the title-play, 1. *The Heart of the Machine* (see above), and 2. a short piece, *Before the King*]

Fairy Plays for Fairy People. *1912*

[This contains five short plays for children: 1. *What Happened to Sylvia*; 2. *Princess Charming*; 3. *Sylvia's King*; 4. *The Gift of Gold*; and 5. *Rainbow Children*]

Isolt: A New Telling. *1915* (*priv.*)

WILLIAMS, BARRY

[For earlier plays see *H. E. D.* v, 624]

The Red Coat ('*costume d.*': W.L., 21/6/00)

A Bid for Fortune (Croydon, 21/6/01; Rot., L'pool, 8/12/02; Carlton, Greenwich, 14/9/03)

The World's Desire (R.A., Woolwich, 14/4/02)

× A Fighting Chance (Euston, 7/9/08)

WILLIAMS, BRANSBY [see *C. WALTERS*]

WILLIAMS, BROCK

The Guv'nors ('*f.c.*: Gai., Hastings, 12/11/28: + *A. BLACKMAN* and *G. CARNEY*)

Sparring Partners ('*f.c.*: Q, 25/2/29: + *A. BLACKMAN* and *G. CARNEY*)

Nerves ('*f.*': K's, Edin., 22/4/29)

The Burglar ('*c. thriller*': Gr., Swansea, 29/4/29)

WILLIAMS, CHARLES H. [see *I. P. GORE*]

WILLIAMS, E. B.

A Troubled Conscience. LC, Qns College, Harley St., 6/12/17

WILLIAMS, Mrs E. BAUMER

Historical Dramatic Sketches. *1910*

[This contains a number of very short playlets of an 'educational' kind]

WILLIAMS, ELIOT CRAWSHAY [see *E. CRAWSHAY-WILLIAMS*]

WILLIAMS, E. G. HARCOURT

The Philosopher in the Apple Orchard ('*past.*': Gar., 22/4/02)

Four Fairy Plays. *Fr. 1920*

[This contains: 1. *Snow-White and Rose-Red*; 2. *Little Tuk's Dream*; 3. *The Three Bears* (LC, Margaret Morris, 10/12/17); and 4. *Puss-in-Boots*. All of these had been acted 'at Jean Sterling Mackinley Children's Seasons']

×The Mouth Organ. LC, Pav., Blackpool, 26/7/21

Three Fairy Plays. *1925*

[This contains: 1. *The Emperor's New Clothes*; 2. *Beauty and the Beast* (LC, Scala, 14/11/21); and 3. *The Wooden Bowl*]

×Alice Becomes a Queen. LC, Everyman, 24/11/22

×The Rubber Nose. LC, Pav., Blackpool, 31/8/23

×The Tailor of Gloucester. LC, Kings., 3/12/23

×Ginger and Pickles. *1930*

WILLIAMS, ELLEN

A Christmas Eve Adventure. LC, Parish H. Ealing, 1/1/15

WILLIAMS, EMLYN (GEORGE EMLYN WILLIAMS)

The Full Moon (Playh., Oxford, 28/2/27; Arts, 30/1/29)

Glamour (Aldershot, 3/12/28; Emb., 10/12/28)

A Murder Has Been Arranged ('*ghost story*': Str., 9/11/30, Rep. Players; St J., 26/11/30) *1930*

WILLIAMS, F. EIRENE

Palamon and Arcite. *1925*

WILLIAMS, FRANK

×A Tragedian's Supper (Ward H., Belfast, 24/7/05: +*L. J. McQUILLAND*)

WILLIAMS, G. VALENTINE

Light o' Love (H.M., 14/5/09, *m.*, Afternoon Theatre; Kings., 7/12/25, revised by *M. SHAND*: adapted from *Liebelei* (1895) by A. Schnitzler)

WILLIAMS, HAROLD

×The Rich Relation (Gai., Manchester, 11/12/16)

WILLIAMS, HELEN [see *R. COURTNEIDGE*]

WILLIAMS, JACK

One Hour. LC, H.M., Barrow-in-Furness, 3/11/25

One Night of Love. LC, H.M., Barrow-in-Furness, 3/12/25

[*WILLIAMS, JESSE LYNCH*

Why Marry? ('*c.*': Cohan's, Chicago, 5/11/17; Astor, N.Y., 25/12/17; Com., 12/5/20)

WILLIAMS, LLOYD

×In Search of a Sweetheart. LC, Coll., 10/11/13

Gaffer's Tonic ('*c. oa.*', m. L. Guest: P.H., Carshalton, 11/12/24

WILLIAMS, RICHARD VALENTINE [='*RICHARD ROWLEY*']

WILLIAMS, V. [see *A. CRAWFORD*]

WILLIAMSON, HEDWORTH

×A Perfect Treasure (Darlington, 26/1/00)

The Teraph ('*classical d.*': Darlington, 26/1/00; Court, 29/5/00)

WILLIAMSON, MARJORIE

× Slaves of the Drug (Court, 24/11/11, *cpy.*)
× The Opium Den (Court, 22/6/14)
× The Boss of the Gang (Court, 22/6/14)

WILLIAMSON, MAUD

[Several playlets produced at music-halls]

WILLIAMSON, SIDNEY

× The Reaping. LC, All Saints Parish H., Battersea, 21/5/20

WILLIAMSON, T.

× The Ballet of Time. LC, '*fant.*': O.H., Harrogate, 19/4/17

WILLIAMSON, W. H.

The Dash for the Dowry ('*f.c.*': Rep., Plymouth, 18/6/23)

WILLIS, GEORGE ANTHONY ARMSTRONG [='*ANTHONY ARMSTRONG*']

WILLIS, Miss H. G.

× After Good Night (Pav., Shanklin, 2/8/12, *amat.*; K's H. 15/2/13)

WILLMORE, EDWARD

× The Church Undermined ('*mystery pl.*') *1921*
Cromwell, the Protector. *1923*

WILLMOTT, J. E.

× On the Border (Kyrle H., B'ham, 28/2/03, *amat.*)

WILLOUGHBY, F.

× The Decent Thing (Court, 30/1/10, Play Actors)

WILLOUGHBY, H. V.

His Happy Home ('*f.*': Com., 5/1/20, *m.*)

WILLOUGHBY, KITTY [see *ALIX A. GREIN*]

WILLOUGHBY, LEWIS

Paula, a Dead Love (Irving, Seacombe, 28/11/02: +*A. CHAPIN*)

WILLS, FREEMAN

[For earlier plays see *H. E. D.* v, 627]
After All (Dublin, 7/10/01; Aven., 15/1/02: +*F. LANGBRIDGE*: dramatised from Lord Lytton's novel, *Eugene Aram*)
Count Hannibal ('*r.pl.*': Alex., 11/4/06: +*F. LANGBRIDGE*: dramatised from the novel (1901) by Stanley Weyman)
Griffith Gaunt; or, Jealousy (Margate, 19/10/08: +*F. LANGBRIDGE*: dramatised from the novel (1866) by Charles Reade)

WILLS-CHANDLER, BLANCHE

× The Inspiration of Nance (Court, 9/5/09, Play Actors)

WILMOT, J. R.

× A Heart Attack (David Lewis, L'pool, 10/1/25, *m.*)

WILSON, ALAN

× The Child of Kwasind (Hippo., Rotherhithe, 19/7/15)
× Esmeralda. LC, Pier Pav., Worthing, 3/4/17
× Sir Jasper's Vow. Pier Pav., Worthing, 6/7/17
× Sea Dogs. LC, Pier Pav., Worthing, 25/7/17

WILSON, ANDREW PATRICK [see also *J. L. WAUGH*]
×The Herd's Wife (Ath., Glasgow, 12/5/13; Pal., Chelsea, 23/6/13)
×The Washing Day. LC, Emp., Motherwell, 14/2/14
×The Cobbler (Abbey, Dublin, 13/4/14; Court, 15/6/14)
The Slough ('*d. of Dublin slum life*': Abbey, Dublin, 3/11/14)
Bauldy ('*Scottish c.*': Pal., Arbroath, 11/10/15; Dalston, 12/3/17)
The Lovers' Arms ('*c.*': Kelly's, L'pool, 14/8/16)
×Sonnie (Glasgow, 2/10/16)
My Bonnie Jean (W.G., New Brighton, 1/10/17)
×McCrae, the Stoker. LC, Pav., Glasgow, 17/10/17
×A Joint Engagement (Alex., Stoke Newington, 19/11/17)
×John Smith. LC, Alex., Stoke Newington, 13/3/18
×Old Down and Out (Alex., Stoke Newington, 27/5/18)
×His Dearest Wish (Alex., Stoke Newington, 30/5/18)
Puggles ('*c.*': Pal., Clacton, 6/10/19: title changed later to *Puggles Grows Up*)
The Green Thumb Paint. LC, '*c.*': T.H., High Wycombe, 5/5/20
×Our Liz (Alex., Stoke Newington, 5/7/20)
×The Jolly Beggars (Ath., Glasgow, 24/1/22, Scott. Nat. Players)
Sentimental Sandy ('*c.*': P's, Bradford, 20/8/23)
×Bang Goes Saxpence! (Alh., 11/2/14)
Simple Sandy ('*f.c.*': Morton Parish H., Thornhill, 30/8/26; Q, 13/12/26, as *Sandy*: apparently a revised version of *Sentimental Sandy*, see above)
A Crony o' Mine ('*c.*': Perth, 25/8/27)
The Bogey Man. LC, '*c.*': P.H., Blairgowrie, 21/8/29
×The Gundy Shop ('*Scots pl.*') *1930*

WILSON, EDWARD A.
Old King Coal (RADA, 27/10/29; Everyman, 19/5/30)

WILSON, G. P.
The Treadmill of Society (Brighton, 19/6/05)

WILSON, H. BONHATE [see *M. GREY*]

WILSON, JANE
Conscience (O.H., Leicester, 9/5/02, title changed later to *Mrs Hamilton's Silence*; Gr., Fulham, 2/6/02)

WILSON, JOHN
The Pagans (Q, 4/7/27)

WILSON, JOHN P.
Nobody's Boy ('*m.c.*', m. E. A. Horan: Gar., 2/7/19)

WILSON, LUCY
The Alternative (Everyman, 12/3/23: +*A. ALLINGTON*)

WILSON, Mrs NORTHESK [=*FLORA HAYTER*]

WILSON, PAT
The Centre Forward. LC, Vale Emp., Alexandria, 4/4/22: +*R. MILLAR*

WILSON, RATHMELL

×Fortune's Fool (Rehearsal, 28/2/09, Revival Co.)

×The House of the Traitor (Court, 21/3/09, Dramatic Debaters)

×The Snake Woman (Clavier H., 22/4/12, Black Cat Club)

The Experimentalists ('*unusual c.*': Clavier H., 29/10/12, Drama Soc.: +*M. HUTCHINSON*) *1912*

×The Passer-by (Cosmopolis, 26/5/13, Drama Soc.: translated from F. Coppée, *Le Passant* (1869)) *1913* (in *Another Book of the Sirens*)

×Open or Shut (Cosmopolis, 2/12/13, Drama Soc.: translated from *Il faut qu'une porte soit ouverte ou fermée* by A. de Musset)

×The Little Abbé (Rehearsal, 31/3/14: translated from *Le petit abbé* by H. Bocage and A. Levrat)

×Jean Marie (Rehearsal, 31/1/14: translated from the play (1871) by A. Theuriet)

×A Caprice (Rehearsal, 31/3/14: translated from *Un Caprice* by A. de Musset)

WILSON, THEODORA WILSON

A Pig in a Poke ('*c.*': Emb., 29/4/29)

WILSON, VERNON

×The Honour of the Gualdranas. LC, Streatham H., Streatham, 18/11/13

WILSON, W. CRONIN

×Mr Sparrow Gets Leave (Glo., 11/6/26, Green Room Rag)

[A few sketches and playlets produced at music-halls]

WILSON, WILLIAM

Brand (Court, 11/11/12; translated from the play by H. Ibsen)

[*WILSTACH, PAUL*

[For an earlier play see *H. E. D.* v, 629]

Thais (Court Square, Springfield, Mass., 9/2/11; Crit., N.Y., 14/3/11; Ladbr. H., 7/2/11, *cpy.*)

WILTON, ROBB

[Numerous sketches and playlets produced at music-halls]

WIMBURY, HAROLD

×Broken Bridges. *1930*

WIMPERIS, ARTHUR [see also *F. FENN*, *R. T. NICHOLSON* and *B. VEILLER*]

The Laughing Husband ('*m.c.*', m. E. Eysler: New, 2/10/13; Lyr., 18/12/13, revised as *The Girl Who Didn't*)

Mam'selle Tralala ('*m.c.*', m. J. Gilbert: Lyr., 16/4/14; Gar., 19/6/15, as *Oh! Be Careful!*: +*H. CARRICK*)

The Passing Show ('*revue*': Pal., 20/4/14)

The Little Lamb ('*f.*'; Apo., 27/5/14: +*H. CARRICK*)

×The Rajah's Ruby (Pal., 21/9/14: *H. CARRICK*)

Bric-a-Brac ('*m. piece*', m. L. Monckton and H. Finck: Pal., 18/9/15: +*B. HOOD*)

Vivien ('*c.o.*', m. H. Talbot and H. Finck: P.W., B'ham, 27/12/15; Shaft., 1/3/16, as *My Lady Frayle*: +*M. PEMBERTON*)

Follow the Crowd ('*m.pl.*', m. I. Berlin: Emp., 19/2/16: from the American musical *Stop! Look! Listen!* (Forest, Philadelphia, 1/12/15; Glo., N.Y., 25/12/15): +*H. CARRICK*)
Vanity Fair ('*revue*': Pal., 6/11/16)
A Perfect Fit (Emp., Syracuse, 19/1/17; Cohan and Harris, N.Y., 27/8/17; Shaft., 10/4/24: +*H. M. VERNON*)
Pamela ('*m.c.*': Pal., 10/12/17: +*F. NORTON*)
As You Were ('*fant. revue*': Pav., 3/8/18)
The Shop Girl ('*m.c.*'; Gai., 25/3/20: rewritten from a musical composed by H. J. W. Dam in 1894)
Just Fancy! ('*revue*': Vaud., 26/3/20)
London, Paris and New York ('*revue*': Pav., 4/9/20)
The Trump Card ('*f.*': Str., 10/8/21)
The Curate's Egg ('*revue*': Ambass., 22/3/22)
Bluebeard's Eighth Wife ('*c.*': Qns, 26/8/22: adapted from *La huitième femme de Barbe-bleue* (1921) by A. Savoir)
The Return ('*c.*': B'ham, 28/8/22; Glo., 5/9/22)
The Elopement ('*c.*': Com., 28/8/23)
Louis the Fourteenth ('*m.pl.*', m. S. Romberg: Ford's, Baltimore, 17/2/25; Cosmopolitan, N.Y., 2/3/25)
Princess Charming ('*m.r.*', m. A. Szirmai: Alh., Glasgow, 20/9/26; Pal., 21/10/26: +*L. WYLIE*)
Who's Pickles? ('*f.c.*': Portsmouth, 16/5/27; K's, Hamm., 30/5/27, as *A Warm Corner*: +*L. WYLIE*)
Sexes and Sevens ('*c.*': Glo., 15/1/28, *priv.*: *licence refused*)
The Song of the Sea ('*m.pl.*', m. E. Kunneke: Emp., L'pool, 6/8/28; H.M., 6/9/28: +*L. WYLIE*)
He's Mine ('*c.*': B'ham, 30/9/29; Lyr., 29/10/29)

WIN, JACK

[A few sketches produced at music-halls]

WINCHCOMB, CHARLES [see *V. HATHERLEY*]

WINCKWORTH, W. F.

×Desperate Remedies. *Fr. 1901*

WINDERMERE, CHARLES [='*CHARLES FREDERICK*' and '*A. J. NIB*': see also *H. F. MALTBY*]

[For an earlier play see *H. E. D.* v, 629]
The Publisher ('*c.*': O.H., Cork, 18/6/00)
×By Mutual Consent (Greenock, 15/4/01; Aven., 6/2/03)
×Twixt Love and Duty (Dublin, 11/5/01)
The Shadow Between (Gr., Margate, 16/7/01, *cpy.*: +*L. ARTHUR*)
×The Pantry Bell (Roy., Barrow-in-Furness, 3/10/02)
×Clause No. 6 (Duchess, Balham, 29/12/02)
The New Housemaid (Margate, 19/10/03; Crown, Peckham, 9/5/04: also performed as *Our Housemaid*)
Where is William? ('*f.*': Worthing, 21/6/06; Castle, Richmond, 9/9/09; Gr., Fulham, 11/4/10; Court, 13/2/12)
×How He Rose to the Occasion (Bury St Edmunds 8/4/12)

Just the Thing ('*c.*': Margate, 14/6/12; Little, 22/10/12; Aldw., 4/9/16, as *Sally Sleeps Out*: also called *As Others See Us*)
How Jerry Got Off ('*f.*': Lyc., Ipswich, 13/12/15; Gr., Croydon, 7/2/16; D.Y., 2/3/16, as *Jerry*)
×The Bookworm. LC, Pav., Weymouth, 31/5/17
×The Winning Way (Emp., Wood Green, 30/12/18)
×Double Harness ('*c.*': O.H., Buxton, 17/5/20; Granville, 12/11/23)
×Just Like Jim. LC, Yarmouth, 31/10/22
The Oyster ('*c.*': Pier, Herne Bay, 18/8/24; Pier Pav., Eastbourne, 6/4/25, revised with *H. F. MALTBY*)
Square Rigged ('*c.*': Gr., Blackpool, 5/12/27)

WINSTON, BRUCE
Angel Grayce (Emp., Holborn, 17/11/24, *m.*)

WINTER, JOHN STRANGE [see also *B. B. ASHFORD*]
Trixie ('*c.*': Scala, 10/7/08)

WINTER, WILLIAM [see *P. HEYSE*]

WINTHROP, CHARLES
A Petticoat Prince ('*o.*', m. B. Johnson: O.H., Bridlington, 28/1/13, *amat.*)

WINTLE, LUCY
Twenty-One ('*fairy oa.*': Bij., 22/6/05)

WINTOUR, JAMES
The Match of the Season. LC, Qns, Glasgow, 9/7/20

WITNEY, FREDERICK C.
Bed and Breakfast ('*f.*': Kings., 26/11/22, Interlude Players)
Idle Hands ('*c.*': RADA, 11/2/23; Q, 25/5/25)
All's Fair in Love? ('*c.*': Gr., Putney Bridge, 20/10/24, Partnership Players) *1924*
The Adventurous Age ('*f.c.*': Gr., Swansea, 21/5/25; Gr., Fulham, 3/6/25)
×Coals of Fire (Arts, 10/11/27)
×The Wedding Day (Little, 14/5/28)

WODEHOUSE, PELHAM GRANVILLE [see also *G. BOLTON*, *G. GROSSMITH*, *I. HAY*, *F. THOMPSON*, *H. WESTBROOK* and *V. WYNGATE*]
×The Dumb (?) Waiter (Tiv., 24/10/10: +*LENNOX PAWLE*)
A Gentleman of Leisure ('*c.*': Hyperion, New Haven, Conn., 18/4/11; Playh., N.Y., 24/8/11: +*J. STAPLETON*)
A Thief for a Night (McVicker's, Chicago, 31/3/13: +*J. STAPLETON*)
Have a Heart ('*m.c.*', m. Jerome Kern: Liberty, N.Y., 11/1/17: +*GUY BOLTON*)
Leave It to Jane ('*m.c.*', m. Jerome Kern: Atlantic City, N.J., 30/7/17; Longacre, N.Y., 28/8/17: +*GUY BOLTON*)
The Riviera Girl ('*m.c.*', m. E. Kalman: Forrest, Philadelphia, 10/9/17; New Amsterdam, N.Y., 24/9/17: +*GUY BOLTON*)

Oh! Lady, Lady! ('*m.c.*', m. Jerome Kern: Albany, N.Y., 7/1/18; P'cess, N.Y., 31/1/18: +*GUY BOLTON*)

See You Later ('*m.c.*', m. J. Szulc: Academy, Baltimore, 15/11/18: +*GUY BOLTON*)

Ask Dad ('*m.c.*', m. L. A. Hirsch: Alexandra, Toronto, 5/11/18; P'cess, N.Y., 26/11/18, as *Oh, My Dear!*: +*GUY BOLTON*)

Sitting Pretty ('*m.pl.*', m. Jerome Kern: Buffalo, 31/3/24; Fulton, N.Y., 8/4/24: +*GUY BOLTON*)

Hearts and Diamonds ('*m.pl.*', m. B. Granichstadten: Str., 1/6/26: +*L. WYLIE*)

The Nightingale ('*m.pl.*', m. Armand Vecsey: New Haven, Conn., 22/11/26; Jolson, N.Y., 4/1/27: +*GUY BOLTON*)

Good Morning, Bill ('*c.*': D.P., Eastbourne, 7/11/27; D.Y., 28/11/27) *1928*; *Fr. 1928*

The Play's the Thing ('*c.*': Civic Playh., Leeds, 12/11/28; St J., 4/12/28)

'*WODEN, GEORGE*' [=*GEORGE WILSON SLANEY*]

The Money's the Thing (Ath., Glasgow, 1/11/21, Scott. Nat. Players) *1921* (Glasgow)

Thistledown ('*r.pl.*': Court, 25/11/23, Play Actors)

WOGAN, JUDITH

×Home Rule (Gai., Dublin, 11/4/13, *amat.*; Gai., Manchester, 2/6/15)

WOLF, RENNOLD [see *C. POLLOCK*]

WOLFGANG, HAROLD

[Several sketches and playlets produced at music-halls]

WOLFIT, DONALD

The Worm ('*c.*': Rep., Sheffield, 22/10/28)

WOLLETT, Mrs L. B.

Marye the Queen. LC, K. G's H., 20/8/24

WOLSTENHOLME, EDWARD [see *E. WHITE*]

WOOD, A.

That Terrible Tomboy ('*m.c.*', m. C. Legrand: Windsor, 9/3/03)

WOOD, A. C. FRASER

[For earlier plays see *H. E. D.* v, 630]

The Afterglow ('*c.*': Gr., Llandudno, 11/9/03)

The Higher Court (Masonic H., Sutton Coldfield, 11/12/05, *amat.*)

WOOD, CLAUDIA L.

×I Tell'd Yer So. *1927* (Leeds)

×The Prodigal Husband. *1927*

WOOD, DOROTHY [see also *C. M. FOOT*]

The Dream Children ('*fant.*': Court, 20/7/23, *m.*)

WOOD, FANNY MORRIS

×The Eve of the Wedding (Rehearsal, 20/2/10)

×Courtship – Ancient and Modern (Qns, 3/6/15, *m.*)

WOOD, H. F. WIBER

Lady Hamilton; or, The Last Signal (Gr., Islington, 22/11/04)

WOOD, JANE [see *R. BACON*]

WOOD, J. HICKORY [see also *F. CARRÉ* and *F. KARNO*]

[For earlier plays see *H. E. D.* v, 824]

×A Doubtful Proposal ('*m. trifle*': Gt. Qn St., 26/6/00)

×Where's Baby? (Bij., 21/4/03: +*E. L. FURST*)

Percy, the Lady-Killer ('*m.f.*', m. F. Leo: O.H., Tunbridge Wells, 25/5/03; Kennington, 22/6/03, as *The Lady Killer*)

The Maid and the Motor Man ('*m.c.*', m. A. Romilli: New, Cardiff, 27/5/07)

[Several sketches and playlets produced at music-halls]

WOOD, JOHN

×A Glimpse of Reality ('*pl. for boys*') *1930*

WOOD, KINCHEN

Strange. LC, Little Vic., Brighton, 5/5/25

Salvage (Gr., Brighton, 12/12/25)

WOOD, LEON [see *A. F. A. TOWER*]

WOOD, M. PAIGE

×Good Riders. *1930* (Village Drama Soc.)

WOOD, METCALFE

[For earlier plays see *H. E. D.* v, 631]

The Housekeeper ('*f.*': P.W., B'ham, 29/11/04; Camden, 5/12/04; St J., 12/10/05: +*B. HERON-MAXWELL*)

Dombey and Son (Sav., 14/6/11)

×Two Peeps at Pickwick (Sav., 8/7/11)

×Wilkins Micawber (Emp., 27/11/11)

Aschile of Chenepeurde. LC, Knebworth Park, 26/4/24

Watch My Wife (Pier, Brighton, 26/10/25)

WOODGATE, HENRY HERBERT [='*HERBERT HENRY HERBERT*']

WOODHEAD, ERNEST

The Sam-Sings (the Warriors); or, The Maiden and the Mandarin ('*Chinese o.*', m. F. Vaughan Lawton: Huddersfield, 27/5/01, *amat.*; Pal., Chelsea, 29/9/20)

[When presented at the Chelsea Palace, the 'book' was said to have been written by H. Ting Ucey]

The Golden Rook ('*c.o.*', m. F. V. Lawton: Huddersfield, 18/11/07, *amat.*)

WOODHILL, H.

×First on the Roll. LC, Rep., Plymouth, 28/9/21

WOODHOUSE, BRUCE

Today and Yesterday. LC, Philbeach H., 17/2/22

WOODHOUSE, SIDNEY CHAWNER

Four Plays for Young Performers. *1919*

[This contains four short pieces: 1. *Auntie*; 2. *Raising the Wind*; 3. *A Marriage of Convenience*; and 4. *The Incubus*]

WOODHOUSE, VERNON

×Affinities ('*tragical f.*') *Fr. 1919*

×How They Kept Her ('*seasonable satire*': Pier, Brighton, 2/6/19) *Fr. 1919*

The Limpet ('*f.c.*': Pier, Eastbourne, 10/7/22; Kings., 7/8/22: +*V. MacCLURE*) *1924*

Following Ann ('*f.*': Hippo., Margate, 10/1/27: +*K. R. G. BROWNE*)

WOODHULL, ZULA MAUD

Affinities ('*occult pl.*': P.W., 26/7/21, Union of East and West)

[It is a peculiar coincidence that a play called *Affinities* appears immediately above under the name of *VERNON WOODHOUSE*. Presumably there is no connection between the two pieces: the first was in one act, the second in four acts. Zula Maud Woodhull had been responsible for a duologue, *Proposals*, printed in 1889]

WOODIFIELD, MARY

Young England (St Andrew's H., W. Kensington, 27/6/03; +*H. COURTHORPE*)

Foil and Counterfoil (St G's H., 28/6/06, *amat.*)

WOODLAND, E.

The Pink Elephant ('*o.*': Huddersfield, 15/10/15: +*A. E. LODGE*)

WOODROW, H. CORY

[For an earlier play see *H. E. D.* v, 631]

×Life's Reverie ('*oa.*', m. L. Basset and H. French: E.C., 20/8/00: +*C. D. HICKMAN*)

WOODVILLE, H.

×Confederates (P.W., Grimsby, 6/2/12, *amat.*) *Fr. 1899*

WOODWARD, HUBERT

Bold Robin Hood and His Merry Men. LC, Chatham, 4/6/24: +*C. E. OPENSHAW*

WOODWARD, J. WILLOUGHBY

×Going to the Ball (New, Oxford, 6/6/10)

WOODWARD, WILLIAM HARRISON

La Figlia di Iorio: An English Transcript (translated from the play (1923) by G. D'Annunzio) *1926* (*priv.*)

WOOLF, ARNOLD

The Priest and the Woman (Gr., Plymouth, 9/21; Stratford, 20/3/22)

[*WOOLF, EDGAR ALLAN*

[Numerous sketches and playlets produced at music-halls]

WOOLF, FRANK J.

×Don't Forget to Vote (J.A.T. Headquarters, Cabin Restaurant, Strand, 26/3/22)

WOOLF, HERMAN IRWELL

Three Tibetan Mysteries...translated from the French version by Jacques Bacot. *1914*

WOOLF, MONTAGUE S. [see *D. KIMBALL*]

WOOLF, S.

The Best Way. LC, Pav., Mile End, 12/11/25

WOOLFE, H. GEOFFREY

Come to Meet the Bride ('*c.*': Str., 22/5/27, Jewish Drama League)

A Gambler in Brides ('*c.*': Emb., 21/10/29)

WOOLNOTH, MARJORIE H.

×Alcides (Court, 26/11/13)

WORDEN, J. COWPER

Eulalie, the Lodestar ('*m.c.*', m. J. C. Higgin: O.H., Blackpool, 1/12/02)

WORDSWORTH, A. E. V.

The Crusade ('*mystery pl.*': Pembroke H., 30/4/17, *amat.*)

WORKMAN, AGNES

×What Others Have to Say (Rep., Plymouth, 14/11/27: +*A. ADAMS*)

WORRALL, LECHMERE [see also *R. HORNIMAN* and *P. RUBENS*]

×A Domestic Problem (Vic. H., Newquay, 30/5/05; Court, 12/11/07) *Fr. 1913*

The Husbands of Elizabeth (Vic. H., Newquay, 30/5/05)

×Chips (Piccadilly Hotel, 23/2/09; H., 8/6/09)

Daddy Dufard (Montreal, 28/11/10; Hackett's, N.Y., 6/12/10: +*A. CHEVALIER*)

Ann ('*modern c.*': Crit., 18/6/12) *Fr. 1912*

Her Side of the House (Gai., Hastings, 24/2/13; Aldw., 4/3/13: +*A. HALL*)

Other People's Babies ('*c.*': Gai., Manchester, 11/8/13)

The Night Hawk (Pier, Eastbourne, 1/12/13; Glo., 6/12/13: +*B. MERIVALE*)

×The Man who Stayed at Home (Roy., 10/12/14: +*J. E. H. TERRY*) *Fr. 1916*

×The New Moon. LC, Emp., Chiswick, 10/5/15

High Spirits ('*f.*': Kursaal, Bexhill, 19/8/15; W.G., Hoylake, 25/10/23, as *The £100 Ghost*: +*F. DALE*)

The Man who Went Abroad (Glo., 1/3/17: +*J. E. H. TERRY*)

Reprisals. LC, '*c.*': P.H., Cleveden, 17/4/19

Skittles ('*c.*': Pal., Westcliffe-on-Sea, 26/5/19; R.A., Woolwich, 11/7/21; Apo., 30/7/21: +*A. ROSE*)

Mr Peter (Playh., L'pool, 15/3/20: +*B. MERIVALE*)

A Piccadilly Puritan ('*c.*': Pier, Brighton, 10/1/21; Ambass., 14/5/23)

The Man who Stayed in Bed (Rochdale, 26/8/21: +*F. DALE*)

The Resurrection of David Grant (Roy., 11/11/21, *m.*)

False Values ('*c.*': Everyman, 11/9/24)

WORRALL-THOMPSON, HENRY
The Ordeal (Rep., Nottingham, 26/2/23)

WORTHINGTON, FRANK
×The Dancing Poisoner. LC, Kings., 5/2/23
Mavana ('*African d.*': Sav., 22/11/27, *m.*)
I.D.B. (Aldw., 31/5/28, *m.*, Student Players)

WRAIGHT, H. S.
In Every Port. LC, Plymouth, 23/11/22

WRANGHAM, JOHN
Joy Cometh; or, An Innocent Sinner (Gr., Douglas, 5/9/03, *cpy.*: +*D. KNIGHT*)

WRAY, VINCENT [see *L. CLARANCE*]

WRAY-MILNES, T.
The Widow of Ephesus. *1925* (Leeds: *priv.*)

WRIGHT, Mrs FRANK
A Bridge Tangle ('*society c.*': Court, 12/11/08, *m.*: +*Mrs C. PORTER*)

WRIGHT, FRED, Jr [see also *H. WRIGHT*]
[For earlier plays see *H. E. D.* v, 633]
The Wicked Uncle (Gai., 6/12/00)
×The War Special (Canterbury, 26/12/00; Crit., 9/4/01)
×Toff Jim (Apo., 11/5/01)
[A few sketches and playlets produced at music-halls]

WRIGHT, HAIDÉE
The Little Mother (Brixton, 3/4/02: +*F. WRIGHT*)
×Companions of the Road (D.L., 11/5/09, *m.*; Col., 12/7/09)

WRIGHT, HUGH E.
×Punch and Judy Introduce Their Players (Com., 18/6/19, Punch and Judy Players)
×Ha! Ha! (Little, 27/5/23, Green Room Club Rag)
×Laughter (P.W., 27/9/25, Green Room Club Rag)
[A few playlets produced at music-halls]

WRIGHT, HUNTLEY
Dashing Prince Hal ('*m.ext.*', m. C. C. Corn and A. Vernon: Lyr., Ealing, 16/6/02)

WRIGHT, J. [see *J. E. STRANGE*]

WRIGHT, J. SMITH [see *H. C. WIATT*]

WRIGHT, MAY IRENE
[For an earlier play see *H. E. D.* v, 633]
The Light of the World (Darlington, 1/7/07)
The Faith of Our Fathers (W. Stanley, 13/7/10)
At the Mercy of Tiberius (Qns, Longton, 8/6/14: from the novel (1887) by Augusta J. Evans Wilson)

WRIGHT, PAUL H.
×The Word of God: A Miracle Play founded on the Mediaeval York Cycle. *1926* (York)

[From an advertisement on the cover of this booklet, it appears that at least nine other adaptations from plays included in the York cycle were published: I have not been able to locate any of these, and only *The Word of God* is in the British Museum]

WRIGHT-AITKIN, J.
The Vicar's Sin (Woolwich, 29/5/16)

WRIGHTON, NORMAN
×Britain's Awakening (W.L., 8/2/08: also acted as *Wake Up, England!*)

WROUGHTON, CICELY
A Northern Romance (Creaton, 20/4/06, *amat.*; Com., 5/2/07, *amat.*)
The Fenton Pearls (Court, 16/5/12)
×Deborah's Lover ('*domestic t.*': Sav., 11/7/12)

WYATT, FRANK
[For earlier plays see *H. E. D.* v, 633]
A Naked Truth ('*c.*': Aven., Sunderland, 13/5/01; P'cess of W., Kennington, 15/9/02)
×Pierrot and Pierrette ('*pl. without words*': Alb. H., 7/5/02)
Mrs Temple's Telegram ('*f.*': Waldorf, 10/9/06: +*W. MORRIS*)

[*WYBORG, MARY HOYT*
Voodoo (Sam H. Harris, N.Y., 4/4/22, as *Taboo*; O.H., Blackpool, 20/7/22)

WYBROW, GEORGE V.
A Beautiful Fiend; or, In Cruel Russia ('*md.*': Hyde, 22/12/00; Crown, Peckham, 12/8/01: +*F. M. THORNE*)
One of the Right Sort (Rochdale, 6/3/02, *cpy.*; Reg., Salford, 29/9/02)

WYBURD, ELLIS
×His Leading Lady (Rehearsal, 14/4/12)

WYKE, E. BYAM [see also *C. BALDWIN*]
Topsy's Baby. LC, Hippo., Aldershot, 28/2/21
Eastern Love ('*m.c.*': Gai., Houghton-le-Spring, 14/11/21)
[A few sketches produced at music-halls]

WYLIE, IDA ALEXA ROSS
×The Enemy (New, Cambridge, 2/4/17; Alex., 16/4/17)
×The Rendezvous (Apo., 20/11/21, Rep. Players)
Jungle Law (Playh., Cardiff, 12/1/25; Barnes, 18/6/25)

WYLIE, JULIAN [see *S. ROHMER*]

'*WYLIE, LAURI*' [=*MORRIS LAWRENCE SAMUELSON*: see also *S. ROHMER, D. TITHERADGE, J. H. TURNER, A. WIMPERIS* and *P. G. WODEHOUSE*]
Shanghai ('*oa.*', m. I. Witmark: D.L., 28/8/18: +*W. C. DUNCAN*)
The Virgin Queen ('*m. fant.*': Gr., Blackpool, 17/7/22: +*R. P. WESTON* and *B. LEE*)

The Grass Widow ('*m.c.*', m. V. Ellis: Emp., Bristol, 8/8/27; Emp., Stratford, 7/11/27)
The Other Girl ('*m.c.*', m. V. Ellis: Emp., Bristol, 17/10/27)
Making a Man (Hippo., Lewisham, 28/4/30: +*ALLAN HALL*)
[Numerous sketches produced at music-halls: also largely responsible for the books of many revues]

WYLLARD, DOLF
His Lordship's Cure ('*c.*': Apo., 12/7/10, *m.*: +*E. PAGE*)
×Old Furniture (Lyc. Club, 12/3/22)

WYMAN, RITA
×The Watch-Dog. LC, Roy., 11/6/15

WYNDHAM, ALBERT
[A few sketches and playlets produced at music-halls]

WYNDHAM, HORACE [see *H. A. VACHELL*]

WYNGATE, VALERIE
×Marigold ('*pl. for children*') *1919*
×On 'Er Honour (Brixton, 12/7/20: called originally *The Little Things*)
×Patchwork (Forum Club, 24/5/23)
×Old Man (Forum Club, 18/10/25; Col., 20/6/27)
Her Cardboard Lover (Leeds, 6/8/28; Lyr., 21/8/28: +*P. G. WODEHOUSE*)
×After Midnight. *Fr. 1929*
×Pyjamas. *Fr. 1930*

WYNN, FREDI [see *H. F. MALTBY*]
[This dramatist is cited variously as Fredi Wynn, Fred Wynne and Freda Wayne. In French's edition (1935) of *The Age of Youth* (Gr., Croydon, 1928) the collaborators are given as *H. F. MALTBY* and *FREDI WYNN*]

WYNN-PARRY, H.
×The Sin (Steiner H., 25/6/28)

WYNNE, C. PRESTON
×Honesty (New, Oxford, 7/12/00)

'*WYNNE, CHARLES WHITWORTH*' [=*CHARLES WILLIAM CAYZER*]
David and Bathshua. *1903*.
Donna Marina (Gt. Qn. St., 5/10/05, *cpy.*)
Poems and Plays. *1906*
Undine ('*t.*') *1909*

WYNNE, ESME
×Woman and Whiskey (Wimbledon, 21/1/18: +*N. COWARD*)

WYNNE, FRED [see *FREDI WYNN*]

WYNNE, FRED E.
Subsidence (Gai., Manchester, 11/4/10)

WYNNE, VASHTI
[A few playlets produced at music-halls]

WYNNE-BOWER, BETTY

Slings and Arrows (Kings., 24/3/22, Playwrights' Theatre)
The Aftermath (Gai., Hastings, 12/7/26)
Hostility (Q, 11/10/26)
Holding Out the Apple ('*c.*': O.H., Southport, 7/5/28; Glo., 16/6/28)

WYNNE-TYSON, ESMÉ

Little Lovers ('*c.*': Aldw., 22/10/22, Rep. Players)

WYNTOUR, ST BERNARD

The Scarlet Clue (Windsor, 30/3/05; Gr., Islington, 28/5/06)

WYON, ERNEST

× Tried for Her Life ('*free trade pl.*': Nat. Liberal Club, 10/6/09)

'*X*'

× Bianca (Clavier H., 23/4/12, Black Cat Club)
× The Division of Labour (Theatrical Gdn. Party, Regent's Park, 11/7/16)

'*X. Y. Z.*'

Jephtha's Daughter (Garrick Chambers, Stockport, 27/1/13, *amat.*)

'*YAFFLE*'

Foiling the Reds or the Heart of a Labourer. *1926*

YARDLEY, W.

[For earlier plays see *H. E. D.* v, 634–5 and 825]
× Passports, Please (Little, 24/6/13: +*B. C. STEPHENSON*: arranged by *C. W. HOGG*)

YARMOUTH, Earl of [='*ERIC HOPE*']

YATES, BARTON SHEPHERD

The Crowning of the King (Qns, Manchester, 29/5/11)

YATES, CHRISTABEL LOWNDES

× What is a Gentleman? LC, Railway Inst., Eastleigh, 7/1/20
Marrying Mark ('*c.*': T.H., Amersham, 12/2/20)
× No Change (T.H., Amersham, 17/5/20)
× Coming Home. LC, T.H., Amersham, 31/3/21
× If Three Believe (Pav., Amersham, 7/12/22)

YEATS, WILLIAM BUTLER [see also *Lady GREGORY* and *G. MOORE*]

[For earlier plays see *H. E. D.* v, 635. For the printings of the plays reference should be made to Allan Wade's *A Bibliography of the Writings of W. B. Yeats*, 3rd. edition, 1968]
× Cathleen Ni Hoolihan (St Theresa's H., Dublin, 2/4/02, Irish Literary Theatre; Qns Gate H., 2/5/03: the spelling of the title was altered later to *Kathleen Ni Houlihan*) *1902* (in *Samhain*, Oct. 1902); *1902* (Chiswick, *priv.*); *1904* (in *Plays for an Irish Theatre*, ii); *1906* (Dublin)
× The Pot of Broth (Antient Concert R., Dublin, 30/10/02, Irish Nat. Theatre Soc.; Qns Gate H., 2/5/03) *1903* (in *The Gael*,

New York, Sept. 1903); *1904* (in *Plays for an Irish Theatre*, ii); *1905* (Dublin)

×The Hour Glass ('*morality*': Molesworth H., Dublin, 14/3/03, Irish Nat. Theatre Soc.; Qns Gate H., 2/5/03; Court, 9/2/12; Abbey, Dublin, 21/11/12, second version) *1903* (in *The North American Review*, Sept. 1903); *1904* (in *Plays for an Irish Theatre*, ii); *1907* (Dublin); *1913* (in *The Mask*, April 1913, second version)

×The King's Threshold (Molesworth H., Dublin, 14/3/03, Irish Nat. Theatre Soc.; Roy., 26/3/04; Abbey, Dublin, 13/10/13, second version) *1904* (New York, *priv.*); *1904* (in *Plays for an Irish Theatre*, iii); *1905* (Dublin); *1906* (second version in *Poems*, Dublin)

×The Shadowy Waters (Molesworth H., Dublin, 14/1/04, Irish Nat. Theatre Soc.; Gt. Qn Street., 11/6/07) *1900* (in *The North American Review*, May 1900); *1900*; *1906* (second version, in *Poems*, Dublin); *1907* ('acting version')

Where There is Nothing (Court, 26/6/04) *1902* (as supplement to *The United Irishman*, November 1, 1902); *1903* (in *Plays for an Irish Theatre*, i); *1903*

×On Baile's Strand (Abbey, Dublin, 27/12/04; St G's H., 27/11/05; Fest., Cambridge, 31/1/27) *1903* (in *The Seven Woods*, Dundrum); *1904* (in *Plays for an Irish Theatre*, iii); *1905* (Dublin); *1906* (new version, in *Poems*, Dublin)

The Unicorn from the Stars (Abbey, Dublin, 21/11/07: +*Lady GREGORY*: a revised version of *Where There is Nothing*) *1908*

×The Golden Helmet (Abbey, Dublin, 19/3/08, prose version) *1908* (New York); *1908* (in *Collected Works*)

×Deirdre (Abbey, Dublin, 24/11/06; New, 27/11/08) *1907* (in *Plays for an Irish Theatre*, v); *1908* (in *Samhain*, Nov. 1908); *1913*

×The Green Helmet (Abbey, Dublin, 10/2/10; Court, 22/6/10: verse reworking of *The Green Helmet*) *1910* (Dundrum); *1911*

×At the Hawk's Well or Waters of Immortality (privately performed in London, 2/4/16) *1917* (in *Harper's Bazaar*, March 1917); *1917* (in *To-Day*, June 1917); *1917* (in *The Wild Swans at Coole*, Dundrum); *1923* (in *Plays and Controversies*)

Two Plays for Dancers. *1919* (Dundrum, *priv.*)

[This contains: 1. *The Dreaming of the Bones* (Abbey, Dublin, 6/12/31: also printed in *The Little Review*, June 1919); and 2. *The Only Jealousy of Emer* (also printed in *Poetry* (Chicago), January 1919 and in *Plays and Controversies*, 1923)]

×The Player Queen (K's H., 25/5/19, St. Soc.; Fest., Cambridge, 16/5/27) *1922* (in *Plays in Prose and Verse*)

Four Plays for Dancers. *1921*

[This contains: 1. *At the Hawk's Well* (see above); 2. *The Only Jealousy of Emer* (see above); 3. *The Dreaming of the Bones* (see above); and 4. *Calvary*]

Oedipus the King (Abbey, Dublin, 7/12/26) *1928* (as *King Oedipus*)

×The Resurrection (Abbey, Dublin, 30/7/34) *1927*
Oedipus at Colonus (Abbey, Dublin, 12/9/27) *1934* (in *Collected Plays*)
×Fighting the Waves (‘*ballet pl.*’: Abbey, Dublin, 13/8/29) *1934* (in *Wheels and Butterflies*)

YORK, ISAAC
×The Philosopher's Stone (Roy., 1/3/08, Play Actors)

YORKE, ALEXANDER
...Love My Dog (‘*f.c.*’: H., 9/7/03: +*R. VAUN*)

YORKE, E. F.
×The Home Accessory (C.P., 1/7/09)

YORKE, E. N.
×The Lady Doctor (Pier, Brighton, 12/10/03)

YORKE, NANCY
Soap at Home (‘*f.*’: Bij., 6/5/05: +*G. H. INGLIS*)

[*YORKE, PHILIP*
The Musical Martians (Aldw., 4/10/09: +*P. COOKE*)

YORKE, ROLAND
The Old Home (P.W., Salford, 11/5/08; Stratford, 21/3/10)

YOUNG, BASIL
×What True Love Can Do (P.H., Croydon, 25/10/06, *amat.*)
×Two to One. LC, P.H., Croydon, 16/1/14
×With or Without Bread. LC, P.H., Croydon, 27/10/14

YOUNG, C.
A House to Let. LC, County, St Albans, 28/11/22: +*N. MALCOLM*

YOUNG, CATHERINE CHILVERD
The Crimson Rambler (Crippl. Inst., 28/4/06, *amat.*)
His Birthright (Crippl. Inst., 30/11/07, *amat.*)
The House in Green Street (K's H., 18/5/08, *amat.*)

YOUNG, DONALD ROY
×The Lady of the Road (K's H., 6/2/21, Revival Players)
×The Scarlet Cloak (K's H., 6/2/21, Revival Players)
×Youth and Its Betters (Str., 11/6/22, Rep. Players)

YOUNG, ETHEL
Married to a Mormon. LC, Pal., Cresswell, 30/5/22

YOUNG, FRANCIS BRETT
The Third Sex (Rep., Plymouth, 12/5/19: +*W. E. STIRLING*)
Crepe-de-Chine (‘*c.*’: Rep., Plymouth, 19/5/19; Kings., 8/5/21, Rep. Players: +*W. E. STIRLING*)
Captain Swing (‘*r.d.*’: Rep., Plymouth, 26/5/19: +*W. E. STIRLING*) *1919*
The Crescent Moon (Rep., Plymouth, 5/4/20: +*W. E. STIRLING*)

The Powder Puff ('*c.*': Apo., 20/11/21, Rep. Players: +*W. E. STIRLING*)
The Furnace (Kings., 18/12/21, Play Actors: +*W. ARMSTRONG*) *1928*

YOUNG, Sir FRANK POPHAM
A Dog's Chance (Q, 21/6/26)
Queer Fish (W.G., New Brighton, 13/9/26; Gr., Croydon, 20/9/26; Wynd., 25/8/27, as *The One-Eyed Herring*)

YOUNG, GEORGE S.
Miffins in a Muddle ('*m.c.*': Gar., Edin., 24/2/19)

YOUNG, G. H. R.
'Just as you say, dear' ('*f.*': Q, 23/1/28)

YOUNG, H. HILLIER
×A Man's Treachery (Carlton, Greenwich, 17/12/01)

YOUNG, HOWARD IRVING
Afraid of the Dark ('*c.*': Brighton, 18/2/29; Hippo., Golder's Green, 18/3/29; Roy., 28/3/29)

YOUNG, JOAN R. [see *J. C. SQUIRE*]

YOUNG, MARGARET E. M.
[For earlier plays see *H. E. D.* v, 636]
×Matches – Made in England (Steinway H., 10/3/02)
The Edge of the Storm (D.Y., 1/6/04)
The Wreathed Dagger (St J., 23/10/08, *cpy.*)
×At a Junction (Caxton H., 15/4/09; Playh., 18/5/09)
×Self Supporting. *Fr. 1914*
×From Louvain (Ambass., 17/10/14)
The Higher Court (Str., 11/4/20, Pioneer Players; Playgoers, Kensington, 18/4/27)
×An Alabaster Box. *1927*

[*YOUNG, RIDA JOHNSON*
Naughty Marietta ('*m.c.*', m. V. Herbert: Ladbr. H., 24/10/10, *cpy.*)
The Soldier Boy ('*m.c.*', m. S. Rombeau and F. Chappelle: Shubert, Newark, 3/4/16; Astor, N.Y., 6/12/16; P's, Manchester, 10/6/18; Apo., 26/6/18: +*E. WALLACE*)
Lot 79 ('*f.*': Apo., Atlantic City, 19/6/16, as *Buried Treasure*; N.Y., 13/11/16, as *Captain Kidd, Jun.*; Pier, Eastbourne, 30/4/17; Qns., 20/4/18)
His Little Widows ('*m.f.*', m. W. Schroeder: Johnstown, Pa., 24/3/17; Astor, N.Y., 30/4/17; Hippo., Leeds, 5/5/19; Wynd., 16/6/19: +*W. C. DUNCAN*)
Sometime ('*m.c.*', m. R. Friml: Atlantic City, 26/8/18; Shubert, N.Y., 4/10/18; Vaud., 5/2/25)
Cock o' the Roost ('*c.*': Belasco, Washington, 22/9/24; Liberty, N.Y., 13/10/24; O.H., Southport, 2/1/26; Gar., 2/7/26)

YOUNG, RUTH
×The Iron Law (Arts Centre, 8/17/13, Actresses' Franchise League)

[*YOUNG, STARK*
The Colonnade (Aldw., 5/4/25, St. Soc.) *1920*

YOUNG, Sir W. LAWRENCE
×A Society Saint (Canterbury, 5/8/01, Old Stagers)

[*YOUNG, WILLIAM*
Ben Hur (D.L., 3/4/02)
×Woman's Wiles (Brighton, 26/11/06)

YOUNGHUSBAND, Sir FRANCIS
The Reign of God. *1930*

YUILL, A. W. [see also *J. BRANDANE*]
[For an earlier play see *H. E. D.* v, 637]
Birds of Passage (Glasgow, 19/4/15)
Weir of Hermiston (Ath., Glasgow, 21/3/22, Scottish Nat. Players)

ZANGWILL, ISRAEL
[For earlier plays see *H. E. D.* v, 637]
The Revolted Daughter ('*c.*': Com., 22/3/01)
Merely Mary Ann ('*c.*': Corn Exch., Wallingford, 22/10/03, *cpy.*; D.Y., 8/9/04) *1921*
Nurse Marjorie ('*c.*': Crit., 14/9/06, *cpy.*)
The Melting-Pot (Terminus H., Littlehampton, 21/8/08, *cpy.*; Yiddish People's Theatre, 5/6/12; Court, 26/1/14, Play Actors; Qns, 7/2/14) *1909*
The War God ('*t.*': H.M., 8/11/11, *m.*) *1911*
The Next Religion (Ldn. Pav., 18/4/12, New Players: *refused licence*) *1912*
Plaster Saints ('*high c.*': Com., 23/5/14)
×The Moment Before ('*psychical md.*': Pal., Plymouth, 18/9/16; Pallad., 25/9/16)
Too Much Money ('*f.*': Glasgow, 18/2/18; Ambass., 9/4/18) *1924*
The Cockpit ('*r.d.*') *1921*
We Moderns ('*c.*': Wilmington, U.S.A., 23/12/22; Gai., N.Y., 11/3/23: O.H., Southport, 4/5/25; New, 7/7/25) *1926*
The King of Schnorrers ('*f.*': Scala, 1/11/25, Jewish Drama League)
The Forcing House; or, The Cockpit Continued ('*t.c.*': Little, 9/2/26) *1922*

ZELLAR, B. [see *P. T. SELBIT*]

'*ZERO*' [=*WINIFRED ARTHUR JONES*]
It is Foretold (Worthing, 27/9/26)

ZILBOORG, GREGORY
He Who Gets Slapped (translated from the play (1915) by N. Andreev) *1922*

ZILLWOOD, LEILA
The Broken Rosary (Stratford, 2/8/15)
The Great Sacrifice (Stratford, 7/8/16)
A Boy's Best Friend (Aston, 18/12/16; Pal., Battersea, 19/3/17; E.C., 2/4/17)

His Australian Wife (Metro., Glasgow, 29/7/18; Stratford, 19/8/18)
A Warning to Mothers (Stratford, 5/5/19: +*J. MACLAREN*)
Suspected (Metro., Glasgow, 19/6/20)

ZILLWOOD, RUTH A.
Her Favourite Son (P's, Bradford, 25/9/16; E.C., 20/11/16)
His Wife's Husband (Dalston, 6/8/17)

ZLATOGOV, MAXIM
×For Serbia (Lyr., 16/3/15, *m.*: +*F. KOPESCKY*)

ZORN, D. FRITZ L.
The Designers ('*f.c.*': Amersham H., New Cross, 21/4/04, *amat.*; O.H., Torquay, 6/2/05; Brixton, 13/2/05; Q, 5/10/25)

ADDENDA

[The following supplementary additions and notes include a few items inadvertently omitted in the typing and printing, together with some others which came to my attention after the Hand-List had been completed. The arrangement of this supplementary material follows the pattern adopted in the *History of English Drama, 1660–1900*, a + sign being employed to indicate authors and plays not recorded in the main catalogue.]

p. 484] *ARTHURS, GEORGE*
+Odd Numbers ('*f.*': Com., 6/3/30: +*A. MILLER*)

p. 487] *AVELING, CLAUDE*
+[This author was responsible for the preparation of English versions of numerous opera libretti – *Armida* (by Philippe Quinault) *1906*; *Germania* (by Luigi Illica) *1907*; *Tess* (by Luigi Illica) *1909*; *Lakmé* (by E. Gondinet and P. H. Gille) *1910*; *Susanne's Secret* (by Enrico Golisciani) *1911*; *The Jewels of the Madonna* (by E. Wolf-Ferrari) *1911*; *Don Quixote* (by Jacques Le Lorrain) *1911*; *Doctor Cupid* (by Enrico Golisciani) *1914*; and *Colonel Clabert* (by H. W. von Waltershausen) *1915*]

p. 494] *BARING, Hon. MAURICE*
+ ×Palamon and Arcite ('*pl. for puppets*') *1913* (Oxford)

p. 497] *BARRIE, Sir JAMES MATTHEW*
+ ×When Wendy Grew Up ('*an afterthought*': D.Y., 22/2/08) *1957* (Edinburgh)
[This playlet was performed just once in a single, and 'secret', production on the last night of the 1907–1908 run of *Peter Pan*. The text was edited, with a prefatory note, in 1957 by Sydney Blow, the husband of Hilda Trevelyan (who took the part of Wendy)]

p. 510] *BERKELEY, REGINALD CHEYNE*
+The Man I Killed (Streatham Hill, 7/4/30; Apo., 2/3/32: adapted from *L'Homme que j'ai tué* (1921) by Maurice Rostand)

p. 513] *BLACK, CHARLES STUART*
+[*The Guinea's Stamp*, which had been performed in 1923 and which later was published separately in 1927, was first printed in *The Scots Magazine* (1924, ii, 10–22)]

p. 514] '*BLAIR*' [=*WALLACE WILFRID BLAIR FUSLI*]
+ ×The Death of Shakespeare ('*chronicle pl. in two scenes*') *1922* (in *Youth*, i, 2, March 1922)

p. 523] +*BOYD, ERNEST*
Illusion (Everyman, 8/1/30)

p. 523] *BOYD, THOMAS JAMIESON LAYCOCK STIRLING*
+ ×The Key (Lyc., Edin., 2/7/15)

p. 525] *BRADLEY, LILIAN TRIMBLE*
+Virtue for Sale (Streatham Hill, 13/1/30)

p. 528] +*BRIDGE, FREDERICK MAYNARD*
×The Happy Farm ('*c.oa.*') *1913*
×The Bey of Bamra ('*f.c.*') *1913*
Daffodil Grange ('*Elizabethan c.*') *1919*

p. 531] *BRIGHTMAN, STANLEY*
Darling, I Love You ('*m.c.*', m. H. Hedley and Harry Acres: Gai., 22/1/30: +*ARTHUR RIGBY*)

p. 546] *CAMPION, CYRIL*
+[*Green Room Rags* (*Fr. 1925*) includes two short sketches by this author – *Disgrace* and *The Pact*]

p. 551] +*CARTER, JOHN L.*
Every Mother's Son (Players', 10/3/30; Str. 29/5/30, with title altered to *Moloch* and described as an '*anti-war pl.*': +*WINIFRED CARTER*)

p. 557] +*CHARLTON, BASIL*
[*Green Room Rags* (*Fr. 1925*) includes three short sketches by this author – *Wow Wow*, *It Is So Simple* and *Mustard*]

p. 565] *CLUTSAM, GEORGE HOWARD*
+[*The Damask Rose*, after its first presentation at Golder's Green in 1929, was performed at the Savoy, 26/3/30: on that occasion *ROBERT COURTNEIDGE* was credited as part-author]

.609] *DILLON, ARTHUR*
+Pelops ('*a tetralogy*') *1912*

p. 610] +*DOBBS, MARGARET E.*
×The Doctor and Mrs Macauley (O.H., Belfast, 18/8/13)
Village Plays. *1920* (Dundalk)
[This contains four short playlets in the dialect of County Antrim]

p. 631] +[*EMERY, GILBERT*
Tarnish (Main Street, Asbury Park, U.S.A., 30/7/23; Belmont, N.Y., 1/10/23; Vaud., 30/3/25)

p. 632] +*ENTWHISTLE, HAROLD*
The Dowry (Pal., Chelsea, 12/3/17)

p. 633] +*ESDAILE, KATHARINE ADA*
×The Shepherd's Children ('*Nativity pl.*') *1928* (SPCK)

p. 640] *FENDALL, PERCY*
×Arrival of a Rival (Col., 3/4/16: +*F. EMNEY*) *Fr. 1918*

p. 651] +*FORSTER-BOVILL, W. B.*
×Nature's Call ('*problem pl.*': Vic. Pal., 22/1/17: +*A. J. WALDRON*)
×The White Card (Emp., Middlesbrough, 28/5/17: +*A. J. WALDRON*)

p. 665] +*GERALD, EDWARD*
The Inquest of Truth. *1921* (Manchester, *priv.*)

p. 670] +*GLAZER, BENJAMIN FLOYER*
Plays of Molnar (*1927*)

p. 685] +*GREENWOOD, W. H.*
The Philosophy of Patience ('*domestic d.*') (*1918*, Chorley)

p. 685] *GREGORY, ISABELLA AUGUSTA, Lady*
[Attention may be called here to the recently-published *Collected Plays*, edited by Anne Saddlemyer, 5 volumes, *1971*]

p. 708] +*HARVEY, NORMAN*
×The Price of Sin (Barnard's, Greenwich, 7/2/07)

p. 715] +*HENDERSON, LOUIS COSSART*
The Call. *1927*

p. 728] +*HOLE, MOLLY MARSHALL*
When God Stopped (Cent., 30/5/30, 1930 Players)

p. 732] *HORLER, SYDNEY*
+The House of Secrets ('*detective pl.*': Q, 10/1/27)

p. 740] +*HUEFFER, FORD MADOX*
×A House ('*modern morality pl.*') *1921* (issued as *Monthly Chapbook*, no. 21)

p. 749] *JAMES, EDGAR*
[This author was American. His *The Master of the House* was copyrighted in the U.S.A. in 1911, and copyright was secured in 1912 for a revised version: in 1913 the play was printed as 'adapted' by Edward Marshall. It is uncertain which text was used for the English production in 1919]

p. 751] *JEANS, RONALD*
+[His *The Kiss Cure* was published by *French* in *1915*]

p. 762] +*KENCHINGTON, FRANK*
×Dick Whittington ('*performed by members of the 85th Field Ambulance, Christmas 1915*') *1916* (*priv.*)
×Aladdin ('*a pantomime by members of the 85th Field Ambulance*') *1917* (*priv.*)

p. 777] *LE BRANDT, JOSEPH*
On the Stroke of Twelve (Gr., Nottingham, 12/5/02; Carlton, Greenwich, 23/3/03)
Over Niagara Falls (Gr., Islington, 27/4/03)
Through Death Valley; or, The Mormon Peril (Shak., Clapham, 11/12/11)

p. 777] *LE BRETON, JOHN*
['John Le Breton' is a pseudonymn used by two authors, M. Harte Potts and T. Murray Ford, writing in collaboration]

p. 808] +*MACQUEEN-POPE, W. JAMES*
[For four plays, apparently never performed in England, see *Who's Who in the Theatre*, vi, 1930, 673]

p. 811] *MALLOCH, GEORGE RESTON*
+ ×The Grenadier. *1930* (Stirling)

p. 819] +*MARTINDALE, CYRIL CHARLES*
The Marriage of St Francis (adapted from *La Vie profonde de St François*, 1926, by Henri Ghéon) *1927*

p. 860] *O'BRIEN, KATE*
+The Bridge (Arts, 31/5/27)

p. 878] *PEACEY, HOWARD*
+[*Links*, as performed in 1926, was published in *Poet Lore*, spring 1927]

p. 882] +*PERCIVAL, B. M.*
×The Voice of Isis (All Saints' H., St John's Wood, 28/1/09)

p. 898] +*PURCELL, LEWIS*
×The Reformers (Cork, *c.* 1912, *amat.*)
×The Pagan ('*c. in two scenes*') *1907* (Dublin)

p. 905] +*REA, HOPE*
[The following dramas were issued, separately, under the general title of *Garden City Plays*, 'by the Theosophical Publishing Society...in connection with the Stratford-on-Avon Folk-Drama Association':
The Dweller in the Body ('*mystery pl.*') *1911*
The Passing of Baldur ('*a winter's mystery*', in two parts called *Odin the Watcher* and *Forlorn Gods*) *1911*
Dawn ('*folk miracle pl.*') *1911*]

p. 907] +*REES, HAMILTON*
×Jacob Carter at the Singing Competition ('*f.*') *1928* (Village Play Series)
×The Night-Watchman (*1930*)

p. 935] *SCOTT, AFFLECK*
+ ×The Gulf (Court, 20/3/10, Pl. Actors)

p. 938] +*SELLON, Rev. Father ST J.*
The Sealed Island (St Alban's H., Finchley, 24/11/10, *amat.*)
Bad Dreams and Good Fairies (St Alban's H., Finchley, 15/11/12, *amat.*)
The Runaways ('*m.f.fairy fant.*': St Alban's H., Finchley, 30/12/13, *amat.*)
×The Hidden Gem (St Paul's H., Finchley, 26/4/21, *amat.*)

p. 990] *THURSTON, ERNEST C.*
+Red and White Earth (O.H., Cork, 20/10/02)

p. 995] *TREVELYAN, H. B.*

The Dark Angel. *1928*

[This play presents a peculiar problem. The 1928 text appeared as vol. lxi in the 'Contemporary British Dramatists' series under the name of H. B. Trevelyan. In *The Stage Year Book, 1926* there are records of its performance at Philadelphia on 23/1/1925 and at the Longacre Theatre, New York, on 10/2/25: for both these records the author's name is cited as H. B. Trevelyan, but in the same volume reference to a performance at the Everyman Theatre on 3/11/25 credits the play to *GUY BOLTON*. The sixth edition of *Who's Who in the Theatre* not only gives the name of Guy Bolton as the author in the 'London Playbills' section but also lists *The Dark Angel* among Bolton's dramatic writings – and the same information appears in all later editions of this standard work.]

p. 1001] *VACHELL, HORACE ANNESLEY*

+ ×The Yellow Girl ('*c.*') *1909* (printed in the *Souvenir of the Drury Lane Matinee for the Queen Alexandra Sanatorium, Davos, May 11, 1909*)

p. 1006] +'*VIRENS, VIRENS H.*'

×The Man in the Case ('*problem*': Pal., 18/12/11)

p. 1017] *WEBB, N. F.*

+The Blue Coast (Everyman, 30/5/30)

p. 1020] *WEST, JULIUS*

+The Seagull (translated from *Chaika* by Anton Chekhov) *1915*

[*Note.* Among the printed plays only two have remained bafflingly anonymous. Not only were they both published without any indications of authorship, all attempts to determine the playwrights responsible for their composition have proved futile. The titles are:

In Old Japan: a Play in Verse, touching on the History of Japan in the Tenth Century of our Christian Era. *1929*

and

Lancelot & Guinevere: A Study in Three Scenes. *1919*

It seems probable that each of these was published in a strictly limited number of copies.]

INDEX

[Since the main Handlist is arranged alphabetically, the names of the authors whose plays are catalogued there have been omitted in the index. References to authors have, however, been included when these appear in the comments or in the 'Addenda'.]